D1432271

The Oxford Italian Minidictionary

Second Edition
with new phrasefinder

ITALIAN–ENGLISH
ENGLISH–ITALIAN

ITALIANO–INGLESE
INGLESE–ITALIANO

OXFORD
UNIVERSITY PRESS

OXFORD
UNIVERSITY PRESS

Great Clarendon Street, Oxford OX2 6DP

Oxford University Press is a department of the University of Oxford.
It furthers the University's objective of excellence in research, scholarship,
and education by publishing worldwide in

Oxford New York

Athens Auckland Bangkok Bogotá Buenos Aires Calcutta
Cape Town Chennai Dar es Salaam Delhi Florence Hong Kong Istanbul
Karachi Kuala Lumpur Madrid Melbourne Mexico City Mumbai
Nairobi Paris São Paulo Singapore Taipei Tokyo Toronto Warsaw

with associated companies in Berlin Ibadan

Oxford is a registered trade mark of Oxford University Press
in the UK and in certain other countries

Published in the United States
by Oxford University Press Inc., New York

British Library Cataloguing in Publication Data

Data available

Library of Congress Cataloging in Publication Data

Data available

ISBN 0-19-860253-7
ISBN 0-19-860291-X (Italian cover edition only)

10 9 8 7 6 5 4 3 2 1

Printed in Great Britain by
Charles Letts (Scotland) Ltd
Dalkeith, Scotland

Contents/Indice

First Edition/Prima edizione
Editor/Redazione
Joyce Andrews

Second Edition/Seconda edizione
Editors/Redazione
Debora Mazza, Donatella Boi, Sonia Tinagli-Baxter
Peter Terrell, Jane Goldie, Francesca Logi, Carla Zipoli

Copy Editors/Segreteria di redazione
Jacqueline Gregan, Daphne Trotter

Project management by/A cura di
LEXUS

Phrasefinder/Trovafrasi
Loredana Riu, Neil and Roswitha Morris

....

Preface/Prefazione

This new edition of the *Oxford Italian-English Minidictionary* is an updated and expanded version of the dictionary edited by Joyce Andrews. Colloquial words and phrases figure largely, as do neologisms. Noteworthy additions include terms from special areas such as computing and business that have become a familiar feature of current language. The dictionary also includes a unique **Phrasefinder**, which groups together all the essential phrases you will need for everyday conversation. The section is thematically arranged and covers 8 key topics: *going places, keeping in touch, food and drink, places to stay, shopping and money, sports and leisure, good timing* and *conversion charts*.

Questa nuova edizione del *mini dizionario Oxford Italiano-Inglese* è il risultato di un lavoro di ampliamento e aggiornamento della precedente edizione curata da Joyce Andrews. Un'attenzione particolare è stata rivolta a vocaboli ed espressioni colloquiali di coniazione recente e a termini relativi a settori specifici, quali l'informatica e il commercio, divenuti ricorrenti nella lingua di tutti i giorni. Il dizionario comprende anche un prezioso **"Trovafrasi"** che contiene tutte le espressioni essenziali per l'uso quotidiano della lingua. La sezione è ordinata per temi e copre 8 argomenti fondamentali: *in viaggio, comunicazioni, mangiare e bere, dove alloggiare, spese e soldi, sport e tempo libero, l'ora giusta* e *tabelle di conversione*.

Proprietary terms/Marchi registrati

This dictionary includes some words which are, or are asserted to be, proprietary names or trade marks. Their inclusion does not imply that they have acquired for legal purposes a non-proprietary or general significance, nor is any other judgement implied concerning their legal status. In cases where the editor has some evidence that a word is used as proprietary name or trade mark this is indicated by the symbol ®, but no judgement concerning the legal status of such words is made or implied thereby.

Questo dizionario include alcune parole che sono o vengono considerate marchi registrati. La loro presenza non implica che abbiano acquisito legalmente un significato generale, né si suggerisce alcun altro giudizio riguardo il loro stato giuridico. Qualora il redattore abbia trovato testimonianza dell'uso di una parola come marchio registrato, quest'ultima è stata contrassegnata dal simbolo ®, ma nessun giudizio riguardo lo stato giuridico di tale parola viene espresso o suggerito in tal modo.

Introduction

In order to give the maximum information about English and Italian in the space available, this new dictionary uses certain space-saving conventions.

A swung dash ~ is used to replace the headword within the entry.

Where the headword contains a vertical bar | the swung dash replaces only the part of the headword that comes in front of the |. For example: **efficien|te** *a* efficient. **~za** *nf* efficiency (the second bold word reads **efficienza**).

Indicators are provided to guide the user to the best translation for a specific sense of a word. Types of indicator are:

field labels (see the list on pp ix–x), which indicate a general area of usage (commercial, computing, photography etc);

sense indicators, eg: **bore** *n* (*of gun*) calibro *m*; (*person*) seccatore, -trice *mf*;

typical subjects of verbs, eg: **bond** *vt* (*glue:*) attaccare;

typical objects of verbs, placed after the translation of the verb, eg: **boost** *vt* stimolare (*sales*); sollevare (*morale*);

nouns that typically go together with certain adjectives, eg: **rich** *a* ricco; (*food*) pesante.

A solid black circle means that the same word is being translated as a different part of speech, eg. **partition** *n* ... ● *vt* ...

English pronunciation is given for the Italian user in the International Phonetic Alphabet (see p viii).

Italian stress is shown by a ' placed in front of the stressed syllable in a word.

Square brackets are used around parts of an expression which can be omitted without altering the sense.

Introduzione

Allo scopo di fornire il maggior numero possibile di informazioni in inglese e in italiano, questo nuovo dizionario ricorre ad alcune convenzioni per sfruttare al massimo lo spazio disponibile.

Un trattino ondulato ~ è utilizzato al posto del lemma all'interno della voce.

Qualora il lemma contenga una barra verticale |, il trattino ondulato sostituisce solo la parte del lemma che precede |. Ad esempio: **dark|en** *vt* oscurare. **~ness** *n* buio *m* (la seconda parola in neretto va letta **darkness**).

Degli indicatori vengono forniti per indirizzare l'utente verso la traduzione corrispondente al senso voluto di una parola. I tipi di indicatori sono:

etichette semantiche (vedi la lista a pp ix-x), indicanti l'ambito specifico in cui la parola viene generalmente usata in quel senso (commercio, informatica, fotografia ecc);

indicatori di significato, es.: **redazione** *nf* (*ufficio*) editorial office; (*di testi*) editing;

soggetti tipici di verbi, es.: **trovarsi** *vr* ⟨*luogo:*⟩ be;

complementi oggetti tipici di verbi, collocati dopo la traduzione dello stesso verbo, es: **superare** *vt* overtake ⟨*veicolo*⟩; pass ⟨*esame*⟩;

sostantivi che ricorrono tipicamente con certi aggettivi, es.: **solare** *a* ⟨*energia, raggi*⟩ solar; ⟨*crema*⟩ sun.

Un pallino nero indica che la stessa parola viene tradotta come una diversa parte del discorso, es. **calcolatore** *a* ... ● *nm* ...

La pronuncia inglese è data usando l'Alfabetico Fonetico Internazionale (vedi p viii).

L'accento tonico nelle parole italiane è indicato dal segno ' collocato davanti alla sillaba accentata.

Delle parentesi quadre racchiudono parti di espressioni che possono essere omesse senza alterazioni di senso.

Pronunciation of Italian

Vowels:

a	is broad like *a* in *father*: **casa**.
e	has two sounds: closed like *ey* in *they*: **sera**; open like *e* in *egg*: **sette**.
i	is like *ee* in *feet*: **venire**.
o	has two sounds: closed like *o* in *show*: **bocca**; open like *o* in *dog*: **croma**.
u	is like *oo* in *moon*: **luna**.

When two or more vowels come together each vowel is pronounced separately: **buono**; **baia**.

Consonants:

b, d, f, l, m, n, p, t, v are pronounced as in English. When these are double they are sounded distinctly: **bello**.

c	before **a, o** or **u** and before consonants is like *k* in *king*: **cane**.
	before **e** or **i** is like *ch* in *church*: **cena**.
ch	is also like *k* in *king*: **chiesa**.
g	before **a, o,** or **u** is hard like *g* in *got*: **gufo**.
	before **e** or **i** is like *j* in *jelly*: **gentile**.
gh	is like *g* in *gun*: **ghiaccio**.
gl	when followed by **a, e, o, u** is like *gl* in *glass*: **gloria**.
gli	is like *lli* in *million*: **figlio**.
gn	is like *ni* in *onion*: **bagno**.
h	is silent.
ng	is like *ng* in *finger* (not *singer*): **ringraziare**.
r	is pronounced distinctly.
s	between two vowels is like *s* in *rose*: **riso**.
	at the beginning of a word it is like *s* in *soap*: **sapone**.
sc	before **e** or **i** is like *sh* in *shell*: **scienza**.
z	sounds like *ts* within a word: **fazione**; like *dz* at the beginning: **zoo**.

The stress is shown by the sign ' printed before the stressed syllable.

Pronuncia inglese

SIMBOLI FONETICI

Vocali e dittonghi

æ *bad*	ʊ *put*	aʊ *now*
ɑː *ah*	uː *too*	aʊə *flour*
e *wet*	ə *ago*	ɔɪ *coin*
ɪ *sit*	ɜː *work*	ɪə *here*
iː *see*	eɪ *made*	eə *hair*
ɒ *got*	əʊ *home*	ʊə *poor*
ɔː *door*	aɪ *five*	
ʌ *cup*	aɪə *fire*	

Consonanti

b *boy*	l *leg*	t *ten*
d *day*	m *man*	tʃ *chip*
dʒ *page*	n *new*	θ *three*
f *foot*	ŋ *sing*	ð *this*
g *go*	p *pen*	v *verb*
h *he*	r *run*	w *wet*
j *yes*	s *speak*	z *his*
k *coat*	ʃ *ship*	ʒ *pleasure*

Note: ' precede la sillaba accentata.
La vocale nasale in parole quali *nuance* è indicata nella
trascrizione fonetica come ɒ̃: njuːɒ̃s.

Abbreviations/Abbreviazioni

adjective	*a*	aggettivo
abbreviation	*abbr*	abbreviazione
administration	*Admin*	amministrazione
adverb	*adv*	avverbio
aeronautics	*Aeron*	aeronautica
American	*Am*	americano
anatomy	*Anat*	anatomia
archaeology	*Archaeol*	archeologia
architecture	*Archit*	architettura
astrology	*Astr*	astrologia
attributive	*attrib*	attributo
automobiles	*Auto*	automobile
auxiliary	*aux*	ausiliario
biology	*Biol*	biologia
botany	*Bot*	botanica
British English	*Br*	inglese britannico
Chemistry	*Chem*	chimica
commerce	*Comm*	commercio
computers	*Comput*	informatica
conjunction	*conj*	congiunzione
cooking	*Culin*	cucina
definite article	*def art*	articolo determinativo
	ecc	eccetera
electricity	*Electr*	elettricità
et cetera	*etc*	
feminine	*f*	femminile
familiar	*fam*	familiare
figurative	*fig*	figurato
formal	*fml*	formale
geography	*Geog*	geografia
geology	*Geol*	geologia
grammar	*Gram*	grammatica
humorous	*hum*	umoristico
indefinite article	*indef art*	articolo indeterminativo
interjection	*int*	interiezione
interrogative	*inter*	interrogativo
invariable	*inv*	invariabile
(no plural form)		
law	*Jur*	legge/giuridico
literary	*liter*	letterario
masculine	*m*	maschile
mathematics	*Math*	matematica
mechanics	*Mech*	meccanica
medicine	*Med*	medicina

masculine or feminine	*mf*	maschile o femminile
military	*Mil*	militare
music	*Mus*	musica
noun	*n*	sostantivo
nautical	*Naut*	nautica
pejorative	*pej*	peggiorativo
personal	*pers*	personale
photography	*Phot*	fotografia
physics	*Phys*	fisica
plural	*pl*	plurale
politics	*Pol*	politica
possessive	*poss*	possessivo
past participle	*pp*	participio passato
prefix	*pref*	prefisso
preposition	*prep*	preposizione
present tense	*pres*	presente
pronoun	*pron*	pronome
psychology	*Psych*	psicologia
past tense	*pt*	tempo passato
	qcno	qualcuno
	qcsa	qualcosa
proprietary term	®	marchio registrato
rail	*Rail*	ferrovia
reflexive	*refl*	riflessivo
religion	*Relig*	religione
relative pronoun	*rel pron*	pronome relativo
somebody	*sb*	
school	*Sch*	scuola
singular	*sg*	singolare
slang	*sl*	gergo
something	*sth*	
technical	*Techn*	tecnico
telephone	*Teleph*	telefono
theatrical	*Theat*	teatrale
television	*TV*	televisione
typography	*Typ*	tipografia
university	*Univ*	università
auxiliary verb	*v aux*	verbo ausiliare
intransitive verb	*vi*	verbo intransitivo
reflexive verb	*vr*	verbo riflessivo
transitive verb	*vt*	verbo transitivo
transitive and intransitive	*vt/i*	verbo transitivo e intransitivo
vulgar	*vulg*	volgare
cultural equivalent	≈	equivalenza culturale

Aa

a (**ad** before vowel) prep to; (stato in luogo, tempo, età) at; (con mese, città) in; (mezzo, modo) by; **dire qcsa a qcno** tell sb sth; **alle tre** at three o'clock; **a vent'anni** at the age of twenty; **a Natale** at Christmas; **a dicembre** in December; **ero al cinema** I was at the cinema; **vivo a Londra** I live in London; **a due a due** two by two; **a piedi** on o by foot; **maglia a maniche lunghe** long-sleeved sweater; **casa a tre piani** house with three floors; **giocare a tennis** play tennis; **50 km all'ora** 50 km an hour; **2 000 lire al chilo** 2,000 lire a kilo; **al mattino/alla sera** in the morning/evening; **a venti chilometri/due ore da qui** twenty kilometres/two hours away

a'bate nm abbot

abbacchi'ato a downhearted

ab'bacchio nm [young] lamb

abbagli'ante a dazzling ● nm headlight, high beam

abbagli'are vt dazzle. **ab'baglio** nm blunder; **prendere un ~** make a blunder

abbai'are vi bark

abba'ino nm dormer window

abbando'na|re vt abandon; leave (luogo); give up (piani ecc). **~rsi** vr let oneself go; **~rsi a** give oneself up to (ricordi ecc). **~to** a abandoned. **abban'dono** nm abandoning; fig abandon; (stato) neglect

abbassa'mento nm (di temperatura, acqua, prezzi) drop

abbas'sar|e vt lower; turn down (radio, TV); **~e i fari** dip the headlights. **~si** vr stoop; (sole ecc:) sink; fig demean oneself

ab'basso adv below ● int down with

abba'stanza adv enough; (alquanto) quite

ab'batter|e vt demolish; shoot down (aereo); put down (animale); topple (regime); (fig: demoralizzare) dishearten. **~si** vr (cadere) fall; fig be discouraged

abbatti'mento nm (morale) despondency

abbat'tuto a despondent, down-in-the-mouth

abba'zia nf abbey

abbel'lir|e vt embellish. **~si** vr adorn oneself

abbeve'ra|re vt water. **~'toio** nm drinking trough

abbi'ente a well-to-do

abbiglia'mento nm clothes pl; (industria) clothing industry, rag trade

abbigli'ar|e vt dress. **~si** vr dress up

abbina'mento nm combining

abbi'nare vt combine; match (colori)

abbindo'lare vt cheat

abbocca'mento nm interview; (conversazione) talk

abboc'care vi bite; (tubi:) join; fig swallow the bait

abboc'cato a (vino) fairly sweet

abbof'farsi vr stuff oneself

abbona'mento nm subscription; (ferroviario ecc) season-ticket; **fare l'~** take out a subscription

abbo'na|re vt make a subscriber. **~rsi** vr subscribe (**a** to); take out a season-ticket (**a** for) (teatro, stadio). **~to, -a** nmf subscriber

abbon'dan|te a abundant; (quantità) copious; (nevicata) heavy; (vestiario) roomy. **~te di** abounding in. ~te'mente *adv* ⟨*mangiare*⟩ copiously. ~za *nf* abundance

abbon'dare *vi* abound

abbor'da|bile *a* ⟨*persona*⟩ approachable; ⟨*prezzo*⟩ reasonable. ~ggio *nm* Mil boarding. ~re *vt* board ⟨*nave*⟩; approach ⟨*persona*⟩; ⟨*fam: attaccar bottone a*⟩ chat up; tackle ⟨*compito ecc*⟩

abbotto'na|re *vt* button up. ~'tura *nf* ⟨*row of*⟩ buttons. ~to *a fig* tight-lipped

abboz'zare *vt* sketch [out]; ~ un sorriso give a hint of a smile. ab'bozzo *nm* sketch

abbracci'a|re *vt* embrace; hug, embrace ⟨*persona*⟩; take up ⟨*professione*⟩; *fig* include. ab'braccio *nm* hug

abbrevi'a|re *vt* shorten; ⟨*ridurre*⟩ curtail; abbreviate ⟨*parola*⟩. ~zi'one *nf* abbreviation

abbron'zante *nm* sun-tan lotion

abbron'za|re *vt* bronze; tan ⟨*pelle*⟩. ~rsi *vr* get a tan. ~to *a* tanned. ~'tura *nf* [sun-]tan

abbrusto'lire *vt* toast; roast ⟨*caffè ecc*⟩

abbruti'mento *nm* brutalization. abbru'tire *vt* brutalize. abbru'tirsi *vr* become brutalized

abbuf'fa|rsi *vr fam* stuff oneself. ~ta *nf* blowout

abbuo'nare *vt* reduce

abbu'ono *nm* allowance; *Sport* handicap

abdi'ca|re *vi* abdicate. ~zi'one *nf* abdication

aber'rante *a* aberrant

aberrazi'one *nf* aberration

a'bete *nm* fir

abi'etto *a* despicable

'abil|e *a* able; ⟨*idoneo*⟩ fit; ⟨*astuto*⟩ clever. ~ità *nf inv* ability; ⟨*idoneità*⟩ fitness; ⟨*astuzia*⟩ cleverness. ~'mente *adv* ably; ⟨*con astuzia*⟩ cleverly

abili'ta|re *vt* qualify. ~to *a* qualified. ~zi'one *nf* qualification; ⟨*titolo*⟩ diploma

abis'sale *a* abysmal. a'bisso *nm* abyss

abi'tabile *a* inhabitable

abi'tacolo *nm* Auto passenger compartment

abi'tante *nmf* inhabitant

abi'ta|re *vi* live. ~to *a* inhabited ●*nm* built-up area. ~zi'one *nf* house

'abito *nm* ⟨*da donna*⟩ dress; ⟨*da uomo*⟩ suit. ~ da cerimonia/da sera formal/evening dress

abitu'al|e *a* usual, habitual. ~'mente *adv* usually

abitu'ar|e *vt* accustom. ~si a *vr* get used to

abitu'dinario, -a *a* of fixed habits ●*nmf* person of fixed habits

abi'tudine *nf* habit; d~ usually; per ~ out of habit; avere l'~ di fare qcsa be in the habit of doing sth

abnegazi'one *nf* self-sacrifice

ab'norme *a* abnormal

abo'li|re *vt* abolish; repeal ⟨*legge*⟩. ~zi'one *nf* abolition; repeal

abomi'nevole *a* abominable

abo'rigeno, -a *a & nmf* aboriginal

abor'rire *vt* abhor

abor'ti|re *vi* miscarry; ⟨*volontariamente*⟩ have an abortion; *fig* fail. ~vo *a* abortive. a'borto *nm* miscarriage; ⟨*volontario*⟩ abortion. ~sta *a* pro-choice

abrasi'one *nf* abrasion. abra'sivo *a & nm* abrasive

abro'ga|re *vt* repeal. ~zi'one *nf* repeal

'abside *nf* apse

abu'lia *nf* apathy. a'bulico *a* apathetic

abu's|are *vi* ~ di abuse; over-indulge in ⟨*alcol*⟩; ⟨*approfittare di*⟩ take advantage of; ⟨*violentare*⟩ rape. ~ivo *a* illegal

a'buso *nm* abuse. ~ di confidenza breach of confidence

a.C. *abbr* (avanti Cristo) BC

'acca *nf fam* non ho capito un'~ I understood damn all

acca'demi|a *nf* academy. A~a di

Belle Arti Academy of Fine Arts. **~co, -a** *a* academic ● *nmf* academician

acca'd|ere *vi* happen; **accada quel che accada** come what may. **~uto** *nm* event

accalappi'are *vt* catch; *fig* allure

accal'carsi *vr* crowd

accal'da|rsi *vr* get overheated; *fig* get excited. **~to** *a* overheated

accalo'rarsi *vr* get excited

accampa'mento *nm* camp. **ac-cam'pare** *vt fig* put forth. **ac-cam'parsi** *vr* camp

accani'mento *nm* tenacity; (*odio*) rage

acca'ni|rsi *vr* persist; (*infierire*) rage. **~to** *a* persistent; (*odio*) fierce; *fig* inveterate

ac'canto *adv* near; **~ a** *prep* next to

accanto'nare *vt* set aside; *Mil* billet

accaparra'mento *nm* hoarding; *Comm* cornering

accapar'ra|re *vt* hoard. **~rsi** *vr* grab; corner (*mercato*). **~'tore, ~'trice** *nmf* hoarder

accapigli'arsi *vr* scuffle; (*litigare*) squabble

accappa'toio *nm* bathrobe; (*per spiaggia*) beachrobe

accappo'nare *vt* **fare ~ la pelle a qcno** make sb's flesh creep

accarez'zare *vt* caress, stroke; *fig* cherish

accartocci'ar|e *vt* scrunch up. **~si** *vr* curl up

acca'sarsi *vr* get married

accasci'arsi *vr* flop down; *fig* lose heart

accata'stare *vt* pile up

accatti'vante *a* beguiling

accatti'varsi *vr* **~ le simpatie/la stima/l'affetto di qcno** gain sb's sympathy/respect/affection

accatto'naggio *nm* begging. **ac-cat'tone, -a** *nmf* beggar

accaval'la|re *vt* cross (*gambe*). **~si** *vr* pile up; *fig* overlap

acce'cante *a* (*luce*) blinding

acce'care *vt* blind ● *vi* go blind

ac'cedere *vi* enter; (*acconsentire*) comply with

accele'rare *vi* accelerate ● *vt* speed up, accelerate; **~re il passo** quicken one's pace. **~to** *a* rapid. **~'tore** *nm* accelerator. **~zi'one** *nf* acceleration

ac'cender|e *vt* light; turn on (*luce, TV ecc*); *fig* inflame; **ha da ~e?** have you got a light?. **~si** *vr* catch fire; (*illuminarsi*) light up; (*TV ecc*) turn on; *fig* become inflamed

accendi'gas *nm inv* gas lighter; (*su cucina*) automatic ignition

accen'dino *nm* lighter

accendi'sigari *nm* cigar-lighter

accen'nare *vt* indicate; (*melodia*) ● *vi* **~ a** a beckon to; *fig* hint at; (*far l'atto di*) make as if to; **accenna a piovere** it looks like rain. **ac'cenno** *nm* gesture; (*con il capo*) nod; *fig* hint

accensi'one *nf* lighting; (*di motore*) ignition

accen'tare *vt* accent; (*con accento tonico*) stress. **~zi'one** *nf* accentuation. **ac'cento** *nm* accent; (*tonico*) stress

accentra'mento *nm* centralizing

accen'trare *vt* centralize

accentu'a|re *vt* accentuate. **~rsi** *vr* become more noticeable. **~to** *a* marked

accerchia'mento *nm* surrounding

accerchi'are *vt* surround

accerta'mento *nm* check

accer'tare *vt* ascertain; (*controllare*) check; assess (*reddito*)

ac'ceso *a* lighted; (*radio, TV ecc*) on; (*colore*) bright

acces'sibile *a* accessible; (*persona*) approachable; (*spesa*) reasonable

ac'cesso *nm* access; (*Med: di rabbia*) fit; **vietato l'~** no entry

acces'sorio *a* accessory; (*secondario*) of secondary importance ● *nm* accessory; **accessori** *pl* (*rifiniture*) fittings

ac'cetta *nf* hatchet

accet'tabile *a* acceptable

accet'tare *vt* accept; (*aderire a*) agree to

accettazi'one *nf* acceptance; (*luogo*) reception. ~ **[bagagli]** check-in. **[banco]** ~ check-in [desk]

ac'cetto *a* agreeable; **essere bene** ~ be very welcome

accezi'one *nf* meaning

acchiap'pare *vt* catch

acchito *nm* **di primo** ~ at first

acciac'care *vt* crush; *fig* prostrate. ~**to, -a** *a* crush all over. **acci'acco** *nm* infirmity; **acciacchi** *pl* aches and pains

acciaie'ria *nf* steelworks

acci'aio *nm* steel; ~ **inossidabile** stainless steel

acciden'tale *a* accidental. ~**l'mente** *adv* accidentally. ~**to a** (*terreno*) uneven

acci'dente *nm* accident; *Med* stroke; **non capisce/non vede un** ~ *fam* he doesn't understand/can't see a damn thing. **acci'denti!** *int* damn!

accigli'a|rsi *vr* frown. ~**to** *a* frowning

ac'cingersi *vr* ~ **a** be about to

acci'picchia *int* good Lord!

acciuf'fare *vt* catch

acci'uga *nf* anchovy

accla'ma|re *vt* applaud; (*eleggere*) acclaim. ~**zi'one** *nf* applause

acclima'tar|e *vt* acclimatize. ~**si** *vr* get acclimatized

ac'clu|dere *vt* enclose. ~**so** *a* enclosed

accocco'larsi *vr* squat

accogli'en|te *a* welcoming; (*confortevole*) cosy. ~**za** *nf* welcome

ac'cogliere *vt* receive; (*compiacere*) welcome; (*contenere*) hold

accol'larsi *vt* take on (*responsabilità, debiti, doveri*). **accol'lato** *a* high-necked

accoltel'lare *vt* knife

accomia'tar|e *vt* dismiss. ~**si** *vr* take one's leave (**da** *of*)

accomo'dante *a* accommodating

accomo'dar|e *vt* (*riparare*) mend; (*disporre*) arrange. ~**si** *vr* make oneself at home; **si accomodi!** come in!; (*si sieda*) take a seat!

accompagna'mento *nm* accompaniment; (*seguito*) retinue

accompa'gna|re *vt* accompany; ~**re qcno a casa** see sb home; ~**re qcno alla porta** show sb out. ~**'tore, -'trice** *nmf* companion; (*di comitiva*) escort; *Mus* accompanist

accomu'nare *vt* pool

acconci'a|re *vt* arrange. ~**tura** *nf* hair-style; (*ornamento*) headdress

accondiscen'den|te *a* too obliging. ~**za** *nf* excessive desire to please

accondi'scendere *vi* ~ **a** condescend; comply with (*desiderio*); (*acconsentire*) consent to

acconsen'tire *vi* consent

acconten'tar|e *vt* satisfy. ~**si** *vr* be content (**di** with)

ac'conto *nm* deposit; **in** ~ on account; **lasciare un** ~ leave a deposit

accop'pare *vt fam* bump off

accoppia'mento *nm* coupling; (*di animali*) mating

accoppi'a|re *vt* couple; mate (*animali*). ~**rsi** *vr* pair off; mate. ~**ta** *nf* (*scommessa*) bet placed on two horses for first and second place

acco'rato *a* sorrowful

accorci'ar|e *vt* shorten. ~**si** *vr* get shorter

accor'dar|e *vt* concede; match (*colori ecc*); *Mus* tune. ~**si** *vr* agree

ac'cordo *nm* agreement; *Mus* chord; (*armonia*) harmony; **andare d'~** get on well; **d'~!** agreed!; **essere d'~** agree; **prendere accordi con qcno** make arrangements with sb

ac'corgersi *vr* ~ **di** notice; (*capire*) realize

accorgi'mento *nm* shrewdness; (*espediente*) device

ac'correre *vi* hasten

accor'tezza *nf* ⟨*previdenza*⟩ forethought

ac'corto *a* shrewd; **mal ~** incautious

accosta'mento *nm* ⟨*di colori*⟩ combination

acco'star|e *vt* draw close to; approach ⟨*persona*⟩; set ajar ⟨*porta ecc*.⟩. **~si** *vr* **~si a** come near to

accovacci'arsi *vr* crouch, squat down. **~to** *a* squatting

accoz'zaglia *nf* jumble; ⟨*di persone*⟩ mob

accoz'zare *vt* **~ colori** mix colours that clash

accredita'mento *nm* credit; **~ tramite bancogiro** Bank Giro Credit

accredi'tare *vt* confirm ⟨*notizia*⟩; *Comm* credit

ac'cresc|ere *vt* increase. **~ersi** *vr* grow larger. **~i'tivo** *a* augmentative

accucci'arsi *vr* ⟨*cane*:⟩ lie down; ⟨*persona*:⟩ crouch

accu'dire *vi* **~ a** attend to

accumu'la|re *vt* accumulate. **~rsi** *vr* pile up, accumulate. **~'tore** *nm* accumulator; *Auto* battery. **~zi'one** *nf* accumulation. **ac'cumulo** *nm* ⟨*di merce*⟩ build-up

accura'tezza *nf* care

accu'rato *a* careful

ac'cusa *nf* accusation; *Jur* charge; **essere in stato di ~** *Jur* have been charged; **la Pubblica A~** *Jur* the public prosecutor

accu'sa|re *vt* accuse; *Jur* charge; complain of ⟨*dolore*⟩; **~re ricevuta di** *Comm* acknowledge receipt of. **~to**, **-a** *nmf* accused. **~'tore** *nm* *Jur* prosecutor

a'cerbo *a* sharp; ⟨*immaturo*⟩ unripe

'acero *nm* maple

a'cerrimo *a* implacable

ace'tone *nm* nail polish remover

a'ceto *nm* vinegar

A.C.I. *abbr* (**Automobile Club d'Italia**) Italian Automobile Association

acidità *nf* acidity. **~ di stomaco** acid stomach

'acido *a* acid; ⟨*persona*⟩ sour ● *nm* acid

a'cidulo *a* slightly sour

'acino *nm* berry; ⟨*chicco*⟩ grape

'acne *nf* acne

'acqua *nf* water; **fare ~** *Naut* leak; **~ in bocca!** *fig* mum's the word!. **~ di Colonia** eau de Cologne. **~ corrente** running water. **~ dolce** fresh water. **~ minerale** mineral water. **~ minerale** mineral water. **~ minerale gassata** fizzy mineral water. **~ naturale** still mineral water. **~ potabile** drinking water. **~ salata** salt water. **~ tonica** tonic water

acqua'forte *nf* etching

ac'quaio *nm* sink

acquama'rina *a* aquamarine

acqua'rello *nm* = **acquerello**

ac'quario *nm* aquarium; *Astr* Aquarius

acqua'santa *nf* holy water

acqua'scooter *nm* *inv* waterscooter

ac'quatico *a* aquatic

acquat'tarsi *vr* crouch

acqua'vite *nf* brandy

acquaz'zone *nm* downpour

acque'dotto *nm* aqueduct

'acqueo a vapore **~** water vapour

acque'rello *nm* water-colour

acqui'rente *nmf* purchaser

acqui'si|re *vt* acquire. **~to a** acquired. **~zi'one** *nf* attainment

acqui'st|are *vt* purchase; ⟨*ottenere*⟩ acquire. **ac'quisto** *nm* purchase; **uscire per ~i** go shopping; **fare ~i** shop

acqui'trino *nm* marsh

acquo'lina *nf* **far venire l'~ in bocca a qcno** make sb's mouth water

ac'quoso *a* watery

'acre *a* acrid; ⟨*al gusto*⟩ sour; *fig* harsh

a'crilico *nm* acrylic

a'croba|ta *nmf* acrobat. **~'zia** *nf* acrobatics *pl*

a'cronimo *nm* acronym

acu'ir|e vt sharpen. **~si** vr become more intense

a'culeo nm sting; Bot prickle

a'cume nm acumen

acumi'nato a pointed

a'custic|a nf acoustics pl. **~o** a acoustic

acu'tezza nf acuteness

acutiz'zarsi vr become worse

a'cuto a sharp; (suono) shrill; (freddo, odore) intense; Gram, Math, Med acute ● nm Mus high note

adagi'ar|e vt lay down. **~si** vr lie down

a'dagio adv slowly ● nm Mus adagio; (proverbio) adage

adattabi'lità nf adaptability

adatta'mento nm adaptation; **avere spirito di ~** be adaptable

adat'ta|re vt adapt; (aggiustare) fit. **~rsi** vr adapt. **~'tore** nm adaptor. **a'datto** a suitable (**a** for); (giusto) right

addebita'mento nm debit. **~ diretto** direct debit

addebi'tare vt debit; ascribe (colpa)

ad'debito nm charge

addensa'mento nm thickening; (di persone) gathering

adden'sar|e vt thicken. **~si** vr thicken; (affollarsi) gather

adden'tare vt bite

adden'trarsi vr penetrate

ad'dentro adv deeply; **essere ~ in** be in on

addestra'mento nm training

adde'strar|e vt train. **~si** vr train

ad'detto, -a a assigned ● nmf employee; (diplomatico) attaché; **addetti** pl **ai lavori** persons involved in the work. **~ stampa** information officer, press officer

addiaccio nm **dormire all'~** sleep in the open

addi'etro adv (indietro) back; (nel passato) before

ad'dio nm & int goodbye. **~ al celibato** stag night, stag party

addirit'tura adv (perfino) even;

(assolutamente) absolutely; **~!** really!

ad'dirsi vr **~ a** suit

addi'tare vt point at; (in mezzo a un gruppo) point out; fig point to

addi'tivo a & nm additive

addizio'nal|e a additional. **~'mente** adv additionally

addizio'nare vt add [up]. **addizi-'one** nf addition

addob'bare vt decorate. **ad'dobbo** nm decoration

addol'cir|e vt sweeten; tone down (colore); fig soften. **~si** vr fig mellow

addolo'rar|e vt grieve. **~rsi** vr be upset (**per** by). **~to** a pained, distressed

ad'dome nm abdomen. **~i'nale** a abdominal; [muscoli] **addominali** pl abdominals

addomesti'ca|re vt tame. **~'tore** nm tamer

addormen'ta|re vt put to sleep. **~rsi** vr go to sleep. **~to** a asleep; fig slow

addos'sar|e vt **~e a** (appoggiare) lean against; (attribuire) lay on. **~si** vr (ammassarsi) crowd; shoulder (responsabilità ecc)

ad'dosso adv on; **~ a** prep on; (molto vicino) right next to; **mettere gli occhi ~ a** qcno/qcsa hanker after sb/sth; **non mettermi le mani ~!** keep your hands off me!; **stare ~ a** qcno fig be on sb's back

ad'durre vt produce (prova, documento); give (pretesto, esempio)

adegua'mento nm adjustment

adegu'a|re vt adjust. **~rsi** vr conform. **~to** a adequate; (conforme) consistent

a'dempi|ere vt fulfil. **~'mento** nm fulfilment

ade'noidi nfpl adenoids

ade'ren|te a adhesive; (vestito) tight ● nmf follower. **~za** nf adhesion. **~ze** npl connections

ade'rire vi **~ a** stick to, adhere

to; support ⟨sciopero, petizione⟩; agree to ⟨richiesta⟩

adesca'mento nm soliciting

ade'scare vt bait; fig entice

adesi'one nf adhesion; fig agreement

ade'sivo a adhesive ● nm sticker; Auto bumper sticker

a'desso adv now; ⟨poco fa⟩ just now; ⟨tra poco⟩ any moment now; **da ~ in poi** from now on; **per ~** for the moment

adia'cente a adjacent; **~ a** next to

adi'bire vt **~ a** put to use as

'adipe nm adipose tissue

adi'ra|rsi vr get irate. **~to a** irate

a'dire vt resort to; **le vie legali** take legal proceedings

'adito nm **dare ~** a give rise to

adoc'chiare vt eye; ⟨con desiderio⟩ covet

adole'scen|te a & nmf adolescent. **~za** nf adolescence. **~zi'ale** a adolescent

adom'brar|e vt darken; fig veil. **~si** vr ⟨offendersi⟩ take offence

adope'rar|e vt use. **~si** vr take trouble

ado'rabile a adorable

ado'ra|re vt adore. **~zi'one** nf adoration

ador'nare vt adorn

adot't|are vt adopt. **~ivo** a adoptive. **adozi'one** nf adoption

ad prep = **a** ⟨davanti a vocale⟩

adrena'lina nf adrenalin

adri'atico a Adriatic ● nm **l'A~** the Adriatic

adu'la|re vt flatter. **~tore**, **~trice** nmf flatterer. **~zi'one** nf flattery

adulte'ra|re vt adulterate. **~to a** adulterated

adul'terio nm adultery. **a'dultero, -a** a adulterous ● nm adulterer ● nf adulteress

a'dulto, -a a & nmf adult; ⟨maturo⟩ mature

adu'nanza nf assembly

adu'na|re vt gather. **~ta** nf Mil parade

a'dunco a hooked

ae'rare vt air ⟨stanza⟩

a'ereo a aerial; ⟨dell'aviazione⟩ air attrib ● nm aeroplane, plane

ae'robic|a nf aerobics. **~o** a aerobic

aerodi'namic|a nf aerodynamics sg. **~o** a aerodynamic

aero'nautic|a nf aeronautics sg; Mil Air Force. **~o** a aeronautical

aero'plano nm aeroplane

aero'porto nm airport

aero'scalo nm cargo and servicing area

aero'sol nm inv aerosol

'afa nf sultriness

affa'bil|e a affable. **~ità** nf affability

affacen'da|rsi vr busy oneself ⟨a with⟩. **~to a** busy

affacci'arsi vr show oneself; **~ alla finestra** appear at the window

affa'ma|re vt starve [out]. **~to a** starving

affan'na|re vt leave breathless. **~rsi** vr busy oneself; ⟨agitarsi⟩ get worked up. **~to a** breathless; **dal respiro ~to** wheezy. **af'fanno** nm breathlessness; fig worry

af'fare nm matter; Comm transaction, deal; ⟨occasione⟩ bargain; **affari** pl business; **non sono affari tuoi** fam it's none of your business. **affa'rista** nmf wheeler-dealer

affasci'nante a fascinating; ⟨persona, sorriso⟩ bewitching

affasci'nare vt bewitch; fig charm

affati'camento nm fatigue

affati'car|e vt tire; ⟨sfinire⟩ exhaust. **~si** vr tire oneself out; ⟨affannarsi⟩ strive

af'fatto adv completely; **non... ~** not... at all; **niente ~!** not at all!

affer'ma|re vt affirm; ⟨sostenere⟩ assert. **~rsi** vr establish oneself

affermativa'mente adv in the affirmative

afferma'tivo a affirmative

affermazi'one nf assertion; ⟨successo⟩ achievement

affer'rar|e vt seize; catch ⟨oggetto⟩; ⟨capire⟩ grasp; **~e al volo** fig be quick on the uptake. **~si** vr **~si a** grasp at

affet'ta|re vt slice; ⟨ostentare⟩ affect. **~to** a sliced; ⟨sorriso, maniere⟩ affected ●**nm** cold meat, sliced meat. **~zi'one** nf affectation

affet'tivo a affective; **rapporto ~** emotional tie

af'fetto[1] nm affection; **con ~** affectionately

af'fetto[2] a **~ da** suffering from

affettuosità nf inv ⟨gesto⟩ affectionate gesture

affettu'oso a affectionate

affezio'na|rsi vr **~rsi a** grow fond of. **~to** a devoted ⟨a to⟩

affian'car|e vt put side by side; Mil flank; fig support. **~si** vr come side by side; fig stand together; **~si a qcno** fig help sb out

affiata'mento nm harmony

affia'ta|rsi vr get on well together. **~to** a close-knit; **una coppia ~ta** a very close couple

affibbi'are vt **~qcsa a qcno** saddle sb with sth; **~ un pugno a qcno** let fly at sb

affi'dabil|e a dependable. **~ità** nf dependability

affida'mento nm ⟨Jur: dei minori⟩ custody; **fare ~ su qcno** rely on sb; **non dare ~** not inspire confidence

affi'dar|e vt entrust. **~si** vr **~si a** rely on

affievo'lirsi vr grow weak

af'figgere vt affix

affi'lare vt sharpen

affili'ar|e vt affiliate. **~si** vr become affiliated

affi'nare vt sharpen; ⟨perfezionare⟩ refine

affin'ché conj so that, in order that

affin|e a similar. **~ità** nf affinity

affiora'mento nm emergence; Naut surfacing

affio'rare vi emerge; fig come to light

af'fisso nm bill; Gram affix

affitta'camere nm inv landlord ● nf inv landlady

affit'tare vt ⟨dare in affitto⟩ let; ⟨prendere in affitto⟩ rent; **'af'fittasi'** 'to let', 'for rent'

af'fitto nm rent; **contratto d'~** lease; **dare in ~** let; **prendere in ~** rent. **~u'ario, -a** nmf Jur lessee

af'fligger|e vt torment. **~si** vr distress oneself

af'fli|tto a distressed. **~zi'one** nf distress; fig affliction

afflosci'arsi vr become floppy; ⟨accasciarsi⟩ flop down; ⟨morale:⟩ decline

afflu'en|te a & nm tributary. **~za** nf flow; ⟨di gente⟩ crowd

afflu'ire vi flow; fig pour in

af'flusso nm influx

affo'ga|re vt/i drown; Culin poach; **~re in fig** be swamped with. **~to** a ⟨persona⟩ drowned; ⟨uova⟩ poached. **~to al caffè** nm ice cream with hot espresso poured over it

affol'la|re vt, **~rsi** vr crowd. **~to** a crowded

affonda'mento nm sinking

affon'dare vt/i sink

affossa'mento nm pothole

affran'car|e vt redeem ⟨bene⟩; stamp ⟨lettera⟩; free ⟨schiavo⟩. **~rsi** vr free oneself. **~'trice** nf franking machine. **~'tura** nf stamping; ⟨di spedizione⟩ postage

af'franto a prostrated; ⟨esausto⟩ worn out

af'fresco nm fresco

affret'ta|re vt speed up. **~rsi** vr hurry. **~ta'mente** adv hastily. **~to** a hasty

affron'tar|e vt face; confront ⟨il nemico⟩; meet ⟨le spese⟩. **~si** vr clash

af'fronto nm affront, insult; **fare un ~ a qcno** insult sb

affumi'ca|re vt fill with smoke; Culin smoke. **~to** a ⟨prosciutto, formaggio⟩ smoked

affuso'la|re vt taper [off]. **~to** a tapering

afo'risma nm aphorism

a'foso a sultry

'**Africa** nf Africa. **afri'cano, -a** a & nmf African

afrodi'siaco a & nm aphrodisiac

a'genda nf diary

agen'dina nf pocket-diary

a'gente nm agent; **agenti** pl **atmosferici** atmospheric agents. **~ di cambio** stockbroker. **~ di polizia** policeman

agen'zia nf agency; (filiale) branch office; (di banca) branch. **~ di viaggi** travel agency. **~ immobiliare** estate agency

agevo'lare vt facilitate. **~zi'one** nf facilitation

a'gevole a easy; (strada) smooth. **~'mente** adv easily

agganci'are vt hook up; Rail couple. **~si** vr (vestito:) hook up

ag'geggio nm gadget

agget'tivo nm adjective

agghiacci'ante a terrifying

agghiacci'are vt fig **~** qcno make sb's blood run cold. **~si** vr freeze

agghin'dare vt fam dress up. **~rsi** vr (fam:) doll oneself up. **~to** a dressed up

aggiorna'mento nm up-date

aggior'nare vt (rinviare) postpone; (mettere a giorno) bring up to date. **~rsi** vr get up to date. **~to** a up-to-date; (versione) updated

aggi'rare vt surround; (fig: ingannare) trick. **~si** vr hang about; **~si su** (discorso ecc:) be about; (somma:) be around

aggiudi'carle vt award; (all'asta) knock down. **~si** vr win

aggi'un|gere vt add. **~ta** nf addition. **~'tivo** a supplementary. **~to** a added ● a & nm (assistente) assistant

aggiu'stare vt mend; (sistemare) settle; (fam: mettere a posto) fix. **~si** vr adapt; (mettersi in ordine) tidy oneself up; (decidere) sort things out; (tempo:) clear up

agglomera'mento nm conglomeration

agglome'rato nm built-up area

aggrap'par|e vt grasp. **~si** vr **~si a** cling to

aggra'vante Jur nf aggravation ● a aggravating

aggra'var|e vt (peggiorare) make worse; increase (pena); (appesantire) weigh down. **~si** vr worsen

aggrazi'ato a graceful

aggre'dire vt attack

aggre'ga|re vt add; (associare a un gruppo ecc) admit. **~rsi** vr **~rsi a** join. **~to a** associated ● nm aggregate; (di case) block

aggressi'one nf aggression; (atto) attack

aggres'si|vo a aggressive. **~ività** nf aggressiveness. **~ore** nm aggressor

aggrin'zare, aggrin'zire vt wrinkle

aggrot'tare vt **~ le ciglia/la fronte** frown

aggrovigli'a|re vt tangle. **~rsi** vr get entangled; fig get complicated. **~to** a entangled; fig confused

agguan'tare vt catch

aggu'ato nm ambush; (tranello) trap; **stare in ~** lie in wait

agguer'rito a fierce

agia'tezza nf comfort

agi'ato a (persona) well off; (vita) comfortable

a'gibille a (palazzo) fit for human habitation. **~ità** nf fitness for human habitation

'agille a agile. **~ità** nf agility

'agio nm ease; **mettersi a proprio ~** make oneself at home

a'gire vi act; (comportarsi) behave; (funzionare) work; **~ su** affect

agi'tar|e vt shake; wave (mano); (fig: turbare) trouble. **~rsi** vr toss about; (essere inquieto) be restless; (mare:) get rough. **~to** a restless; (mare) rough. **~'tore, ~'trice** nmf (persona) agitator. **~zi'one** nf agitation; **mettere in ~zione** qcno make sb worried

'**agli** = a + gli

'**aglio** nm garlic

a'**gnello** nm lamb

agno'**lotti** nmpl ravioli sg

a'**gnostico, -a** a & nmf agnostic

'**ago** nm needle

ago'**ni|a** nf agony. **~z'zare** vi be on one's deathbed

ago'**nistic|a** nf competition. **~o** a competitive

agopun'**tura** nf acupuncture

a'**gosto** nm August

a'**grari|a** nf agriculture. **~o** a agricultural ●nm landowner

a'**gricol|o** a agricultural. **~'tore** nm farmer. **~'tura** nf agriculture

agri'**foglio** nm holly

agritu'**rismo** nm farm holidays, agro-tourism

'**agro** a sour

agroalimen'**tare** a food attrib

agro'**dolce** a bitter-sweet; Culin sweet-and-sour; **in ~** sweet and sour

agrono'**mia** nf agronomy

a'**grume** nm citrus fruit; (pianta) citrus tree

aguz'**zare** vt sharpen; **~ le orecchie** prick up one's ears; **~ la vista** look hard

aguz'**zino** nm slave-driver; (carceriere) jailer

ahimè int alas

'**ai** = a + I

'**Aia** nf L'**~** The Hague

'**aia** nf threshing-floor

Aids nmf Aids

ai'**rone** nm heron

ai'**tante** a sturdy

aiu'**ola** nf flower-bed

aiu'**tante** nmf assistant ●nm Mil adjutant. **~ di campo** aide-de-camp

aiu'**tare** vt help

ai'**uto** nm help, aid; (assistente) assistant

aiz'**zare** vt incite; **~ contro** set on

'**al** = a + il

'**ala** nf wing; **fare ~** make way

ala'**bastro** nm alabaster

'**alacre** a brisk

a'**lano** nm Great Dane

'**alba** nf dawn

Alba'**n|ia** nf Albania. **a~ese** a & nmf Albanian

albeggi'**are** vi dawn

albe'**ra|to** a wooded; (viale) tree-lined. **~'tura** nf Naut masts pl.

albe'**rello** nm sapling

al'**bergo** nm hotel. **~o diurno** hotel where rooms are rented during the daytime. **~'tore, ~'trice** nmf hotel-keeper. **~hi'ero** a hotel attrib

'**albero** nm tree; Naut mast; Mech shaft. **~ genealogico** family tree. **~ maestro** Naut mainmast. **~ di Natale** Christmas tree

albi'**cocc|a** nf apricot. **~o** nm apricot-tree

al'**bino** nm albino

'**albo** nm register; (libro ecc) album; (per avvisi) notice board

'**album** nm album. **~ da disegno** sketch-book

al'**bume** nm albumen

'**alce** nm elk

'**alcol** nm alcohol; Med spirit; (liquori forti) spirits pl; **darsi all'~** take to drink. **al'colici** nmpl alcoholic drinks. **al'colico** a alcoholic. **alco'lismo** nm alcoholism. **~iz'zato, -a** a & nmf alcoholic

alco'**test** nm inv Breathalyser®

al'**cova** nf alcove

al'**cun, al'cuno** a & pron any; **non ha ~ amico** he hasn't any friends, he has no friends. **alcuni** pl some, a few; **~i suoi amici** some of his friends

alea'**torio** a unpredictable

a'**letta** nf Mech fin

alfa'**betico** a alphabetical

alfabetizzazi'**one** nf **~ della popolazione** teaching people to read and write

alfa'**beto** nm alphabet

alfi'**ere** nm (negli scacchi) bishop

al'**fine** adv eventually, in the end

'**alga** nf seaweed

'**algebra** nf algebra

Alge'ri|a *nf* Algeria. **a~no, -a** *a & nmf* Algerian

ali'ante *nm* glider

'alibi *nm inv* alibi

aliena|re *vt* alienate. **~rsi** *vr* become estranged; **~rsi le simpatie di qcno** lose sb's good will. **~to, -a** *a* alienated ● *nmf* lunatic

a'lieno, -a *nmf* alien ● *a* **è ~ da invidia** envy is foreign to him

alimen'ta|re *vt* feed; *fig* foment ● *a* food *attrib*; *(abitudine)* dietary ● *nm* **~ri** *pl* food-stuffs. **~'tore** *nm* power unit. **~zi'one** *nf* feeding

ali'mento *nm* food; **alimenti** *pl* food; *Jur* alimony

a'liquota *nf* share; *(di imposta)* rate

ali'scafo *nm* hydrofoil

'alito *nm* breath

'alla = a + la

allaccia'mento *nm* connection

allacci'ar|e *vt* fasten *(cintura)*; lace up *(scarpe)*; do up *(vestito)*; *(collegare)* connect; form *(amicizia)*. **~si** *vr* do up, fasten *(vestito, cintura)*

allaga'mento *nm* flooding

alla'gar|e *vt* flood. **~si** *vr* become flooded

allampa'nato *a* lanky

allarga'mento *nm* *(di strada, ricerche)* widening

allar'gar|e *vt* widen; open *(braccia, gambe)*; let out *(vestito ecc)*; *fig* extend. **~si** *vr* widen

allar'mante *a* alarming

allar'ma|re *vt* alarm. **~to a** panicky

al'larme *nm* alarm; **dare l'~** raise the alarm; **falso ~** *fig* false alarm. **~ aereo** air raid warning

allar'mis|mo *nm* alarmism. **~ta** *nmf* alarmist

allatta'mento *nm* *(di animale)* suckling; *(di neonco)* feeding

allat'tare *vt* suckle *(animale)*; feed *(neonato)*

'alle = a + le

alle'a|nza *nf* alliance. **~to, -a** *a* allied ● *nmf* ally

alle'ar|e *vt* unite. **~si** *vr* form an alliance

alle'gare[1] *vt Jur* allege

alle'gare[2] *vt* *(accludere)* enclose; set on edge *(denti)*. **~to a** enclosed ● *nm* enclosure; **in ~to** attached, appended. **~zi'one** *nf Jur* allegation

allegge'rir|e *vt* lighten; *fig* alleviate. **~si** *vr* become lighter; *(vestirsi leggero)* put on lighter clothes

allego'ria *nf* allegory. **alle'gorico** *a* allegorical

allegra'mente *adv* breezily

alle'gria *nf* gaiety

al'legro *a* cheerful; *(colore)* bright; *(brillo)* tipsy ● *nm Mus* allegro

alle'luia *int* hallelujah!

allena'mento *nm* training

alle'na|re *vt*, **~rsi** *vr* train. **~'tore, ~'trice** *nmf* trainer, coach

allen'tar|e *vt* loosen; *fig* relax. **~si** *vr* become loose; *Mech* work loose

aller'gia *nf* allergy. **al'lergico** *a* allergic

al'lerta *nf* **stare ~** be alert, be on the alert

allesti'mento *nm* preparation. **~ scenico** *Theat* set

alle'stire *vt* prepare; stage *(spettacolo)*; *Naut* fit out

allet'tante *a* alluring

allet'tare *vt* entice

alleva'mento *nm* breeding; *(processo)* bringing up; *(luogo)* farm; *(per piante)* nursery; **pollo di ~** battery chicken

alle'vare *vt* bring up *(bambini)*; breed *(animali)*; grow *(piante)*

allevi'are *vt* alleviate; *fig* lighten

alli'bito *a* astounded

alli'bra'tore *nm* bookmaker

allie'tar|e *vt* gladden. **~si** *vr* rejoice

alli'evo, -a *nmf* pupil ● *nm Mil* cadet

alliga'tore *nm* alligator

alline'a'mento *nm* alignment

alline'ar|e *vt* line up; *Typ* align; *Fin* adjust. **~si** *vr* fall into line

'allo = a + lo

al'locco nm Zool tawny owl

al'lodola nf [sky]lark

alloggi'are vt (persona:) put up; (casa:) provide accommodation for; Mil billet ● vi put up, stay; Mil be billeted. **al'loggio** nm (appartamento) flat; Mil billet

allontana'mento nm removal

allonta'nar|e vt move away; (licenziare) dismiss; avert (pericolo). **~si** vr go away

al'lora adv then; (in quel tempo) at that time; (in tal caso) in that case; **d'~ in poi** from then on; **e ~?** what now?; **(e con ciò?)** so what?; **fino ~** until then

al'loro nm laurel; Culin bay

'alluce nm big toe

alluci'na|nte a fam incredible; **sostanza ~nte** hallucinogen. **~to, -a** nmf fam space cadet. **~zi'one** nf hallucination

allucino'geno a (sostanza) hallucinatory

al'ludere vi ~ a allude to

allu'minio nm aluminium

allun'gar|e vt lengthen; stretch [out] (gamba); extend (tavolo); (diluire) dilute; **~e il collo** crane one's neck. **~e le mani su** qcno touch sb up. **~e il passo** quicken one's step. **~si** vr grow longer; (crescere) grow taller; (sdraiarsi) lie down

allusi'one nf allusion

allu'sivo a allusive

alluvi'onale a alluvial

alluvi'one nf flood

al'meno adv at least; **[se] venisse il sole!** if only the sun would come out!

a'logeno nm halogen ● a **lampada alogena** halogen lamp

a'lone nm halo

'Alpi nfpl le ~ the Alps

alpi'nismo nm mountaineering. **~ta** nmf mountaineer

al'pino a Alpine ● nm Mil **gli alpini** the Alpine troops

al'quanto a a certain amount of
● adv rather

alt int stop

alta'lena nf swing; (tavola in bilico) see-saw

altale'nare vi fig vacillate

alta'mente adv highly

al'tare nm altar

alta'rino nm **scoprire gli altarini di** qcno reveal sb's guilty secrets

alte'ra|re vt alter; adulterate (vino). **(falsificare)** falsify; **~rsi** vr be altered; (cibo:) go bad; (merci:) deteriorate; (arrabbiarsi) get angry. **~to** a (vino) adulterated. **~zi'one** nf alteration; (di vino) adulteration

al'terco nm altercation

alter'nanza nf alternation

alter'na|re vt, **~rsi** vr alternate. **~'tiva** nf alternative. **~'tivo** a alternate. **~to** a alternating. **~'tore** nm Electr alternator

al'terno a alternate; **a giorni ~i** every other day

al'tero a haughty

al'tezza nf height; (profondità) depth; (suono) pitch; (di tessuto) width; (titolo) Highness; **essere all'~ di** be on a level with; fig be up to

altezzo'sa|mente adv haughtily. **~ità** nf haughtiness

altez'zoso a haughty

al'ticcio a tipsy, merry

altipi'ano nm plateau

alti'tudine nf altitude

'alto a high; (di statura) tall; (profondo) deep; (suono) high-pitched; (tessuto) wide; Geog northern; **a notte alta** in the middle of the night; **avere degli alti e bassi** have some ups and downs; **ad alta fedeltà** high-fidelity; **a voce alta, ad alta voce** in a loud voice; (leggere) aloud; **essere in ~ mare** be on the high seas. **alta finanza** nf high finance. **alta moda** nf high fashion. **alta tensione** nf high voltage ● adv high; **in ~** at the top; (guardare:) up; **mani in ~!** hands up!

alto'forno nm blast-furnace

altolà int halt there!

altolo'cato a highly placed

altopar'lante nm loudspeaker

altopi'ano nm plateau

altret'tanto a & pron as much; (pl) as many ●adv likewise; **buona fortuna! – grazie, ~ good luck!** – thank you, the same to you

altri'menti adv otherwise

'**altro** a other; **un ~, un'altra** another; **l'altr'anno** last year; **domani l'~** the day after tomorrow; **l'ho visto l'~ giorno** I saw him the other day ●pron other [one]; **un ~, un'altra** another [one]; **ne vuoi dell'~?** would you like some more?; **l'un l'~** one another; **nessun ~** nobody else; **gli altri** (la gente) other people ●nm something else; **non fa ~ che lavorare** he does nothing but work; **desidera ~?** (in negozio) anything else?; **più che ~, sono stanco** I'm tired more than anything; **se non ~** at least; **senz'~** certainly; **tra l'~** what's more; **~ che!** and how!

altroi'eri nm **l'~** the day before yesterday

al'tronde adv **d'~** on the other hand

al'trove adv elsewhere

al'trui a other people's ●nm other people's belongings pl

altru'is|mo nm altruism. **~ta** nmf altruist

al'tura nf high ground; Naut deep sea

a'lunno, -a nmf pupil

alve'are nm hive

al'za|re vt lift, raise; (costruire) build; Naut hoist; **~re le spalle** shrug one's shoulders; **~re i tacchi** fig take to one's heels. **~rsi** vr rise; (in piedi) stand up; (da letto) get up; **~rsi in piedi** get to one's feet. **~ta** nf lifting; (aumento) rise; (da letto) getting up; Archit elevation. **~to a** up

a'mabile a lovable; (vino) sweet

a'maca nf hammock

amalga'mar|e vt, **~si** vr amalgamate

a'mante a **~ di** fond of ●nm lover ●nf mistress, lover

ama'rena nf sour black cherry

ama'retto nm macaroon

a'ma|re vt love; be fond of, like (musica, sport ecc). **~to, -a** a loved ●nmf beloved

ama'rezza nf bitterness; (dolore) sorrow

a'maro a bitter ●nm bitterness; (liquore) bitters pl

ama'rognolo a rather bitter

ama'tore, -'trice nmf lover

ambasci'a|ta nf embassy; (messaggio) message. **~'tore, ~'trice** nm ambassador ●nf ambassadress

ambe'due a & pron both

ambien'ta|le a environmental. **~lista** a & nmf environmentalist

ambien'tar|e vt acclimatize; set (personaggio, film ecc). **~si** vr get acclimatized

ambi'ente nm environment; (stanza) room; fig milieu

ambiguità nf inv ambiguity; (di persona) shadiness

am'biguo a ambiguous; (persona) shady

am'bire vi **~ a** aspire to

'**ambito** nm sphere

ambiva'len|te a ambivalent. **~za** nf ambivalence

ambizi'o|ne nf ambition. **~so** a ambitious

'**ambra** nf amber. **am'brato** a amber

ambu'lante a wandering; **venditore ~** hawker

ambu'lanza nf ambulance

ambula'torio nm (di medico) surgery; (di ospedale) out-patients' [department]

a'meba nf amoeba

'**amen** int amen

a'meno a pleasant

A'merica nf America. **~ del Sud** South America. **ameri'cano, -a** a & nmf American

ame'tista *nf* amethyst

ami'anto *nm* asbestos

ami'chevole *a* friendly

ami'cizia *nf* friendship; **fare ~ con qcno** make friends with sb; **amicizie** *pl* (*amici*) friends

a'mico, -a *nmf* friend; **~ del cuore** bosom friend

'amido *nm* starch

ammac'ca|re *vt* dent; bruise (*frutto*). **~rsi** *vr* (*metallo*:) get dented; (*frutto*:) bruise. **~to** *a* dented; (*frutto*) bruised. **~tura** *nf* dent; (*livido*) bruise

ammae'stra|re *vt* (*istruire*) teach; train (*animale*). **~to** *a* trained

ammai'nare *vt* lower (*bandiera*); furl (*vele*)

amma'la|rsi *vr* fall ill. **~to, -a** *a* ill ● *nmf* sick person; (*paziente*) patient

ammali'are *vt* bewitch

am'manco *nm* deficit

ammanet'tare *vt* handcuff

ammani'cato *a* **essere ~** have connections

amma'raggio *nm* splashdown

amma'rare *vi* put down on the sea; (*nave spaziale*:) splash down

ammas'sar|e *vt* amass. **~si** *vr* crowd together. **am'masso** *nm* mass; (*mucchio*) pile

ammat'tire *vi* go mad

ammaz'zar|e *vt* kill. **~si** *vr* (*suicidarsi*) kill oneself; (*rimanere ucciso*) be killed

am'menda *nf* amends *pl*; (*multa*) fine; **fare ~ di qcsa** make amends for sth

am'messo *pp di* **ammettere** ● *conj* **~ che** supposing that

am'mettere *vt* admit; (*riconoscere*) acknowledge; (*supporre*) suppose

ammic'care *vi* wink

ammini'stra|re *vt* administer; (*gestire*) run. **~'tivo** *a* administrative. **~'tore, ~'trice** *nmf* administrator; (*di azienda*) manager; (*di società*) director. **~tore delegato** managing director. **~zi'one** *nf* ad-

ministration; **fatti di ordinaria ~zione** *fig* routine matters

ammi'raglio *nm* admiral. **~'ato** *nm* admiralty

ammi'ra|re *vt* admire. **~to a re-stare/essere ~to** be full of admiration. **~'tore, ~'trice** *nmf* admirer. **~zi'one** *nf* admiration. **ammi'revole** *a* admirable

ammis'sibile *a* admissible

ammissi'one *nf* admission; (*approvazione*) acknowledgement

ammobili'a|re *vt* furnish. **~to** *a* furnished

am'modo *a* proper ● *adv* properly

am'mollo *nm* **in ~** soaking

ammo'niaca *nf* ammonia

ammoni'mento *nm* warning; (*di rimprovero*) admonishment

ammo'ni|re *vt* warn; (*rimproverare*) admonish. **~'tore** *a* admonishing. **~zi'one** *nf Sport* warning

ammon'tare *vi* **~ a** amount to ● *nm* amount

ammonticchi'are *vt* heap up

ammorbi'dente *nm* (*per panni*) softener

ammorbi'dir|e *vt*, **~si** *vr* soften

ammorta'mento *nm Comm* amortization

ammor'tare *vt* pay off (*spesa*); *Comm* amortize (*debito*)

ammortiz'za|re *vt Comm* = **ammortare**; *Mech* damp. **~'tore** *nm* shock-absorber

ammosci'ar|e *vt* make flabby. **~si** *vi* get flabby

ammucchi'a|re *vt*, **~rsi** *vr* pile up. **~ta** *nf* (*sl: orgia*) orgy

ammuf'fi|re *vi* go mouldy. **~to** *a* mouldy

ammuti'namento *nm* mutiny

ammuti'narsi *vr* mutiny

ammuto'lire *vi* be struck dumb

am'nesia *nf* amnesia

amne'stia *nf* amnesty

'amo *nm* hook; *fig* bait

amo'rale *a* amoral

a'more *nm* love; **fare l'~** make love; **per l'amor di Dio/del cielo!** for heaven's sake!; **andare d'~ e**

d'accordo get on like a house on fire; ~ **proprio** self-respect; **è un** ~ ⟨persona⟩ he/she is a darling; **per** ~ **di** for the sake of; **amori** pl love affairs. **~ggi'are** vi flirt. **amo'revole** a loving

a'morfo a shapeless; ⟨persona⟩ colourless, grey

amo'roso a loving; ⟨sguardo ecc⟩ amorous; ⟨lettera, relazione⟩ love

ampi'ezza nf ⟨di esperienza⟩ breadth; ⟨di stanza⟩ spaciousness; ⟨di gonna⟩ fullness; ⟨importanza⟩ scale

'ampio a ample; ⟨esperienza⟩ wide; ⟨stanza⟩ spacious; ⟨vestito⟩ loose; ⟨gonna⟩ full; ⟨pantaloni⟩ baggy

am'plesso nm embrace

amplia'mento nm ⟨di casa, porto⟩ enlargement; ⟨di strada⟩ widening

ampli'are vt broaden ⟨conoscenze⟩

amplifi'ca|re vt amplify; fig magnify. **~'tore** nm amplifier. **~zi'one** nf amplification

am'polla nf cruet

ampol'loso a pompous

ampu'ta|re vt amputate. **~zi'one** nf amputation

amu'leto nm amulet

anabbagli'ante a Auto dipped ● nmpl **anabbaglianti** dipped headlights

anacro'nis|mo nm anachronism. **~tico** a **essere** ~ be an anachronism

a'nagrafe nf ⟨ufficio⟩ registry office; ⟨registro⟩ register of births, marriages and deaths

ana'grafico a dati nmpl **anagrafici** personal data

ana'gramma nm anagram

anal'colico a non-alcoholic ● nm soft drink, non-alcoholic drink

a'nale a anal

analfa'be|ta a & nmf illiterate. **~tismo** nm illiteracy

anal'gesico nm painkiller

a'nalisi nf inv analysis; Med test. ~ **grammaticale/del periodo/logica** parsing. ~ **del sangue** blood test

ana'li|sta nmf analyst. **~tico** a analytical. **~z'zare** vt analyse; Med test

anal'lergico a hypoallergenic

analo'gia nf analogy. **a'nalogo** a analogous

'ananas nm inv pineapple

anar'chi|a nf anarchy. **a'narchico, -a** a anarchic ● nmf anarchist. **~smo** nm anarchism

A.N.A.S. nf abbr ⟨Azienda Nazionale Autonoma delle Strade⟩ national road maintenance authority

anato'mia nf anatomy. **ana-'tomico** a anatomical; ⟨sedia⟩ contoured, ergonomic

'anatra nf duck

ana'troccolo nm duckling

'anca nf hip; ⟨di animale⟩ flank

ance'strale a ancestral

'anche conj also, too; ⟨persino⟩ even; ~ **se** even if; ~ **domani** tomorrow also o too, also tomorrow

anchilo'sato a fig stiff

an'cora adv still, yet; ⟨di nuovo⟩ again; ⟨di più⟩ some more; ~ **una volta** once more

'anco|ra nf anchor; **gettare l'~ra** drop anchor. **~'raggio** nm anchorage. **~'rare** vt anchor

anda'mento nm ⟨del mercato, degli affari⟩ trend

an'dante a ⟨corrente⟩ current; ⟨di poco valore⟩ cheap ● nm Mus andante

an'da|re vi go; ⟨funzionare⟩ work; ~ **via** ⟨partire⟩ leave; ⟨macchia⟩ come out; ~ **bene** ⟨confarsi⟩ suit; ⟨taglia⟩: **ti ti va bene alle tre?** does three o'clock suit you?; **non mi va di mangiare** I don't feel like eating; ~ **di fretta** be in a hurry; ~ **fiero di** be proud of; ~ **di moda** be in fashion; **va per i 20 anni** he's nearly 20; **ma va' [là]!** come on!; **come va?** how are things?; ~ **a male** go off; ~ **a fuoco** go up in flames; **va spedito [entro] stamattina** it must be sent this morning; **ne va del mio lavoro** my job is at stake; **come è andata**

a finire? how did it turn out?;
cosa vai dicendo? what are you
talking about?; **~rsene** go away;
(*morire*) pass away ●*nm* going; **a
lungo** ~re eventually

'andito *nm* passage

an'drone *nm* entrance

a'neddoto *nm* anecdote

ane'lare *vt* ~ a long for. **a'nelito**
nm longing

a'nello *nm* ring; (*di catena*) link

ane'mia *nf* anaemia. **~nemico** *a*
anaemic

a'nemone *nm* anemone

aneste'si|a *nf* anaesthesia; (*so-
stanza*) anaesthetic. **~sta** *nmf*
anaesthetist. **ane'stetico** *a & nm*
anaesthetic

an'fibi *nmpl* (*stivali*) army boots

an'fibio *nm* (*animale*) amphibian
●*a* amphibious

anfite'atro *nm* amphitheatre

'anfora *nf* amphora

an'fratto *nm* ravine

an'gelico *a* angelic

'angelo *nm* angel. **~ custode**
guardian angel

angli'c|ano *a* Anglican. **~ismo**
nm Anglicism

an'glofilo, -a *a & nmf* Anglophile

an'glofono, -a *nmf* English-
speaker

anglo'sassone *a & nmf* Anglo-
Saxon

ango'la|re *a* angular. **~zi'one** *nf*
angle shot

'angolo *nm* corner; *Math* angle. **~
[di] cottura** kitchenette

ango'loso *a* angular

an'gosci|a *nf* anguish. **~'are** *vt*
torment. **~'ato** *a* agonized. **~'oso**
a (*disperato*) anguished; (*che dà
angoscia*) distressing

angu'illa *nf* eel

an'guria *nf* water-melon

an'gusti|a *nf* (*ansia*) anxiety; (*pe-
nuria*) poverty. **~'are** *vt* distress.
~'arsi *vr* be very worried (**per**
about)

an'gusto *a* narrow

'anice *nm* anise; *Culin* aniseed;
(*liquore*) anisette

ani'dride *nf* ~ **carbonica** carbon
dioxide

'anima *nf* soul; **non c'era ~ viva**
there was not a soul about; **all'~!**
good grief!; **un'~ in pena** a soul in
torment. **~ gemella** soul mate

ani'ma|le *a & nm* animal; **~li
domestici** *pl* pets. **~'lesco** *a* animal

ani'ma|re *vt* give life to; (*ravviva-
re*) enliven; (*incoraggiare*) encourage. **~rsi** *vr* come to life; (*acca-
lorarsi*) become animated. **~to** *a*
animate; (*discussione*) animated;
(*paese*) lively. **~'tore, ~'trice** *nmf*
leading spirit; *Cinema* animator.
~zi'one *nf* animation

'animo *nm* (*mente*) mind; (*indole*)
disposition; (*cuore*) heart; **perdersi d'~** lose heart; **farsi ~** take
heart. **~sità** *nf* animosity

ani'moso *a* brave; (*ostile*) hostile

'anitra *nf* = **anatra**

annac'qua|re *vt anche fig* water
down. **~to** *a* watered down

annaffia|re *vt* water. **~'toio** *nm*
watering-can

an'nali *nmpl* annals

anna'spare *vi* flounder

an'nata *nf* year; (*importo annuale*)
annual amount; (*di vino*) vintage

annebbia'mento *nm* fog build-up;
fig clouding

annebbi'ar|e *vt* cloud (*vista, men-
te*). **~si** *vr* become foggy; (*vista,
mente:*) grow dim

annega'mento *nm* drowning

anne'ga|re *vt/i* drown

anne'rir|e *vt/i* blacken. **~si** *vr* be-
come black

annessi'one *nf* (*di nazione*) an-
nexation

an'nesso *pp di* **annettere** ●*a* attached; (*stato*) annexed

an'nettere *vt* add; (*accludere*) enclose; annex (*stato*)

annichi'lire *vt* annihilate

anni'darsi *vr* nest

annienta'mento *nm* annihilation

annien'tar|e *vt* annihilate. **~si** *vr* abase oneself

anniver'sario *a* & *nm* anniversary. **~ di matrimonio** wedding anniversary

'anno *nm* year; **Buon A~!** Happy New Year!; **quanti anni ha?** how old are you?; **Tommaso ha dieci anni** Thomas is ten [years old]. **~ bisestile** leap year

anno'dar|e *vt* knot; do up *(cintura)*; *fig* form. **~si** *vr* become knotted

annoi'a|re *vt* bore; *(recare fastidio)* annoy. **~rsi** *vr* get bored; *(condizione)* be bored. **~to a** bored

anno'ta|re *vt* note down; annotate *(testo)*. **~zi'one** *nf* note

annove'rare *vt* number

annu'a|le *a* annual, yearly. **~rio** *nm* year-book

annu'ire *vi* nod; *(acconsentire)* agree

annulla'mento *nm* annulment; *(di appuntamento)* cancellation

annul'lar|e *vt* annul; cancel *(appuntamento)*; *(togliere efficacia a)* undo; disallow *(gol)*; *(distruggere)* destroy. **~si** *vr* cancel each other out

annunci'a|re *vt* announce; *(preannunciare)* foretell. **~'tore, ~'trice** *nmf* announcer. **~zi'one** *nf* Annunciation

an'nuncio *nm* announcement; *(pubblicitario)* advertisement; *(notizia)* news. **annunci** *pl* **economici** classified advertisements

'annuo *a* annual, yearly

annu'sare *vt* sniff

annuvo'lar|e *vt* cloud. **~si** *vr* cloud over

'ano *nm* anus

anoma'lia *nf* anomaly

a'nomalo a anomalous

anoni'mato *nm* **mantenere l'~** remain anonymous

a'nonimo, -a *a* anonymous ● *nmf* *(pittore, scrittore)* anonymous painter/writer

anores'sia *nf* Med anorexia

ano'ressico, -a *nmf* anorexic

anor'mal|e *a* abnormal ● *nmf* deviant, abnormal person. **~ità** *nf inv* abnormality

'ansa *nf* handle; *(di fiume)* bend

an'sare *vi* pant

'ansia, ansi'età *nf* anxiety; **stare/essere in ~ per** be anxious about

ansi'oso *a* anxious

antago'nis|mo *nm* antagonism. **~ta** *nmf* antagonist

an'tartico *a* & *nm* Antarctic

antece'dente *a* preceding ● *nm* precedent

ante'fatto *nm* prior event

ante'guerra *a* pre-war ● *nm* pre-war period

ante'nato, -a *nmf* ancestor

an'tenna *nf* Radio, TV aerial; *(di animale)* antenna; Naut yard. **~ parabolica** satellite dish

ante'porre *vt* put before

ante'prima *nf* preview; **vedere qcsa in ~** have a sneak preview of sth

anteri'ore *a* front *attrib*; *(nel tempo)* previous

antiade'rente *a* *(padella)* non-stick

anti'aereo *a* anti-aircraft *attrib*

antial'lergico *a* hypoallergenic

antia'tomico *a* **rifugio ~** fallout shelter

antibi'otico *a* & *nm* antibiotic

anti'caglia *nf* *(oggetto)* piece of old junk

antica'mente *adv* in ancient times, long ago

anti'camera *nf* ante-room; **far ~** be kept waiting

antichità *nf inv* antiquity; *(oggetto)* antique

antici'clone *nm* anticyclone

antici'pa|re *vt* advance; Comm pay in advance; *(prevedere)* anticipate; *(prevenire)* forestall ● *vi* be early. **~ta'mente** *adv* in advance. **~zi'one** *nf* anticipation; *(notizia)* advance news

an'ticipo *nm* advance; *(caparra)*

deposit; **in ~** early; *(nel lavoro)* ahead of schedule

an'tico *a* ancient; *(mobile ecc)* antique; *(vecchio)* old; **all'antica** old-fashioned ● *nmpl* **gli antichi** the ancients

anticoncezio'nale *a & nm* contraceptive

anticonfor'mis|mo *nm* unconventionality. **~ta** *nmf* nonconformist. **~tico** *a* unconventional, nonconformist

anticonge'lante *a & nm* antifreeze

anti'corpo *nm* antibody

anticostituzio'nale *a* unconstitutional

anti'crimine *a inv* ⟨squadra⟩ crime *attrib*

antidemo'cratico *a* undemocratic

antidolo'rifico *nm* painkiller

an'tidoto *nm* antidote

anti'droga *a inv* ⟨campagna⟩ anti-drugs; ⟨squadra⟩ drug *attrib*

antie'stetico *a* ugly

antifa'scismo *nm* anti-fascism

antifa'scista *a & nmf* anti-fascist

anti'forfora *a inv* dandruff *attrib*

anti'furto *nm* anti-theft device; *(allarme)* alarm ● *a inv* ⟨sistema⟩ anti-theft

anti'gelo *nm* antifreeze; *(parabrezza)* defroster

antigi'enico *a* unhygienic

An'tille *nfpl* **le ~** the West Indies

an'tilope *nf* antelope

antin'cendio *a inv* **allarme ~** fire alarm; **porta ~** fire door

anti'nebbia *nm inv* Auto [faro] ~ foglamp, foglight

antinfiamma'torio *a & nm* anti-inflammatory

antinucle'are *a* anti-nuclear

antio'rario *a* anti-clockwise

anti'pasto *nm* hors d'oeuvre, starter

antipa'tia *nf* antipathy. **anti'patico** *a* unpleasant

an'tipodi *nmpl* antipodes; **essere agli ~** *fig* be poles apart

antiquari'ato *nm* antique trade

anti'quario, -a *nmf* antique dealer

anti'quato *a* antiquated

anti'ruggine *nm inv* rust-inhibitor

anti'rughe *a inv* anti-wrinkle *attrib*

anti'scippo *a inv* theft-proof

antise'mita *a* anti-Semitic

anti'settico *a & nm* antiseptic

antisoci'ale *a* anti-social

antista'minico *nm* antihistamine

an'stante *a prep* in front of

anti'tarlo *nm inv* woodworm treatment

antiterro'ristico *a* antiterrorist *attrib*

an'titesi *nf inv* antithesis

antolo'gia *nf* anthology

'antro *nm* cavern

antropolo'gia *nf* anthropology. **antro'pologo, -a** *nmf* anthropologist

anu'lare *nm* ring-finger

'anzi *conj* in fact; *(o meglio)* or better still; *(al contrario)* on the contrary

anzianità *nf* old age; *(di servizio)* seniority

anzi'ano, -a *a* old, elderly; *(di grado ecc)* senior ● *nmf* elderly person

anziché *conj* rather than

anzi'tempo *adv* prematurely

anzi'tutto *adv* first of all

a'orta *nf* aorta

apar'titico *a* unaligned

apa'tia *nf* apathy. **a'patico** *a* apathetic

'ape *nf* bee; **nido** *nm* **di api** honeycomb

aperi'tivo *nm* aperitif

aperta'mente *adv* openly

a'perto *a* open; **all'aria aperta** in the open air; **all'~** open-air

aper'tura *nf* opening; *(inizio)* beginning; *(ampiezza)* spread; *(di arco)* span; Pol overtures *pl*; Phot aperture; **~ mentale** openness

'apice *nm* apex

apicol'tura *nf* beekeeping

ap'nea *nf* immersione in ~ free diving

a'polide *a* stateless ● *nmf* stateless person

a'postolo *nm* apostle

apostro'fare *vt* (*mettere un apostrofo a*) write with an apostrophe; reprimand ⟨*persona*⟩

a'postrofo *nm* apostrophe

appaga'mento *nm* fulfilment

appa'ga|re *vt* satisfy. **~rsi** *vr* **~rsi di** be satisfied with

appai'are *vt* pair; mate ⟨*animali*⟩

appallotto'lare *vt* roll into a ball

appalta'tore *nm* contractor

ap'palto *nm* contract; **dare in ~** contract out

appan'naggio *nm* (*in denaro*) annuity; *fig* prerogative

appan'nar|e *vt* mist ⟨*vetro*⟩; dim ⟨*vista*⟩. **~si** *vr* mist over; ⟨*vista*⟩ grow dim

appa'rato *nm* apparatus; (*pompa*) display

apparecchi'a|re *vt* prepare ● *vi* lay the table. **~'tura** *nf* (*impianti*) equipment

appa'recchio *nm* apparatus; (*congegno*) device; (*radio, tv ecc*) set; (*aeroplano*) aircraft. **~ acustico** hearing aid

appa'ren|te *a* apparent. **~te'mente** *adv* apparently. **~za** *nf* appearance; **in ~za** apparently

appa'ri|re *vi* appear; (*sembrare*) look. **~'scente** *a* striking; *pej* gaudy. **~zi'one** *nf* apparition

apparta'mento *nm* flat, apartment *Am*

appar'ta|rsi *vr* withdraw. **~to** *a* secluded

apparte'nenza *nf* membership

apparte'nere *vi* belong

appassio'nante *a* ⟨*storia, argomento*⟩ exciting

appassio'na|re *vt* excite; (*commuovere*) move. **~rsi** *vr* **~rsi a** become excited by. **~to** *a* passionate; **~to di** (*entusiastico*) fond of

appas'sir|e *vi* wither. **~si** *vr* fade

appel'larsi *vr* **~ a** appeal to

ap'pello *nm* appeal; (*chiamata per nome*) rollcall; (*esami*) exam session; **fare l'~** call the roll

ap'pena *adv* just; (*a fatica*) hardly ● *conj* [**non**] **~** as soon as, no sooner... than

ap'pendere *vt* hang [up]

appendi'abiti *nm inv* hat-stand, hallstand

appen'dice *nf* appendix. **appendi'cite** *nf* appendicitis

Appen'nini *nmpl* **gli ~** the Apennines

appesan'tir|e *vt* weigh down. **~si** *vr* become heavy

ap'peso *pp di* **appendere** ● *a* hanging; (*impiccato*) hanged

appe'ti|to *nm* appetite; **aver ~to** be hungry; **buon ~to!** enjoy your meal!. **~'toso** *a* appetizing; *fig* tempting

appezza'mento *nm* plot of land

appia'nar|e *vt* level; *fig* smooth over. **~si** *vr* improve

appiat'tir|e *vt* flatten. **~si** *vr* flatten oneself

appic'care *vt* **~ il fuoco a** set fire to

appicci'car|e *vt* stick; **~e a** (*fig: appioppare*) palm off on ● *vi* be sticky. **~si** *vr* stick; (*cose:*) stick together; **~si a qcno** *fig* stick to sb like glue

appiccia'ticcio *a* sticky; *fig* clingy

appicci'coso *a* sticky; *fig* clingy

appie'dato *a* **sono ~** I don't have the car; **sono rimasto ~** I was stranded

appi'eno *adv* fully

appigli'arsi *vr* **~ a** get hold of; *fig* stick to. **ap'piglio** *nm* fingerhold; (*per piedi*) foothold; *fig* pretext

appiop'pare *vt* **~ a** palm off on; (*fam: dare*) give

appiso'larsi *vr* doze off

applau'di|re *vt/i* applaud. **ap'plauso** *nm* applause

appli'cabile *a* applicable

appli'ca|re *vt* apply; enforce ⟨*legge ecc*⟩. **~rsi** *vr* apply oneself. **~'tore**

nm applicator. **~zi'one** *nf* application; (*di legge*) enforcement

appoggi'ar|e *vt* lean (**a** against); (*mettere*) put; (*sostenere*) back. **~si** *vr* **~si a** lean against; *fig* rely on.

ap'poggio *nm* support

appollai'arsi *vr fig* perch

ap'porre *vt* affix

appor'tare *vt* bring; (*causare*) cause. **ap'porto** *nm* contribution

apposita'mente *adv* especially

ap'posito *a* proper

ap'posta *adv* on purpose; (*espressamente*) specially

apposta'mento *nm* ambush; (*caccia*) lying in wait

appo'star|e *vt* post (*soldati*). **~si** *vr* lie in wait

ap'prend|ere *vt* understand; (*imparare*) learn. **~i'mento** *nm* learning

appren'di|sta *nmf* apprentice. **~'stato** *nm* apprenticeship

apprensi'one *nf* apprehension; **essere in ~ per** be anxious about. **appren'sivo** *a* apprehensive

ap'presso *adv & prep* (*vicino*) near; (*dietro*) behind; **come ~ as** follows

appre'star|e *vt* prepare. **~si** *vr* get ready

apprez'za|bile *a* appreciable. **~'mento** *nm* appreciation; (*giudizio*) opinion

apprez'za|re *vt* appreciate. **~to** *a* appreciated

ap'proccio *nm* approach

appro'dare *vi* land; **~ a fig** come to; **non ~ a nulla** come to nothing. **ap'prodo** *nm* landing; (*luogo*) landing-stage

approfit'ta|re *vi* take advantage (**di** of), profit (**di** by). **~'tore**, **~'trice** *nmf* chancer

approfondi'mento *nm* deepening; **di ~** (*fig: esame*) further

approfon'dire *vt* deepen. **~to a** (*studio, ricerca*) in-depth

appropri'ar|si *vr* (*essere adatto a*) suit; **~rsi di** take possession of.

~to a appropriate. **~zi'one** *nf Jur* appropriation. **~zione indebita** *Jur* embezzlement

approssi'ma|re *vt* **~re per eccesso/difetto** round up/down. **~rsi** *vr* draw near. **~tiva'mente** *adv* approximately. **~'tivo a** approximate. **~zi'one** *nf* approximation

appro'va|re *vt* approve of; approve (*legge*). **~zi'one** *nf* approval

approvvigiona'mento *nm* supplying; **approvvigionamenti** *pl* provisions

approvvigio'nar|e *vt* supply. **~si** *vr* stock up

appunta'mento *nm* appointment, date *fam*; **fissare un ~** make an appointment; **darsi ~** decide to meet

appun'tar|e *vt* (*annotare*) take notes; (*fissare*) fix; (*con spillo*) pin; (*appuntire*) sharpen. **~si** *vr* **~si su** (*teoria:*) be based on

appun'ti|re *vt* sharpen. **~to a** (*mento*) pointed

ap'punto[1] *nm* note; (*piccola critica*) niggle

ap'punto[2] *adv* exactly; **per l'~!** exactly!; **stavo ~ dicendo...** I was just saying...

appu'rare *vt* verify

a'pribile *a* that can be opened

aribot'tiglie *nm inv* bottle-opener

a'prile *nm* April; **il primo d'~** April Fools' Day

a'prir|e *vt* open; turn on (*luce, acqua ecc*); (*con chiave*) unlock; open up (*ferita ecc*). **~si** *vr* open; (*spaccarsi*) split; (*confidarsi*) confide (**con** in)

apri'scatole *nf inv* tin-opener

aqua'planing *nm* **andare in ~** aquaplane

'aquila *nf* eagle; **non è un'~a!** he is no genius!. **~lino a** aquiline

aqui'lone *nm* (*giocattolo*) kite

ara'besco *nm* arabesque; *hum* scribble

A'rabia Sau'dita *nf* **l'~** Saudi Arabia

'arabo, -a *a* Arab; ⟨*lingua*⟩ Arabic
● *nmf* Arab ● *nm* ⟨*lingua*⟩ Arabic

a'rachide *nf* peanut

ara'gosta *nf* lobster

a'rancia *nf* orange. **~'ata** *nf* orangeade. **~o** *nm* orange-tree; ⟨*colore*⟩ orange. **~'one** *a & nm* orange

a'rare *vt* plough. **~tro** *nm* plough

ara'tura *nf* ploughing

a'razzo *nm* tapestry

arbi'trare *vt* arbitrate in; *Sport* referee. **~ietà** *nf* arbitrariness. **~io** *a* arbitrary

ar'bitrio *nm* will; **è un ~** it's very high-handed

'arbitro *nm* arbiter; *Sport* referee; ⟨*nel baseball*⟩ umpire

ar'busto *nm* shrub

'arca *nf* ark; ⟨*cassa*⟩ chest

ar'caico *a* archaic. **~'ismo** *nm* archaism

ar'cangelo *nm* archangel

ar'cata *nf* arch; ⟨*serie di archi*⟩ arcade

archeolo'gia *nf* archaeology. **~o'logico** *a* archaeological. **~'ologo, -a** *nmf* archaeologist

ar'chetto *nm* Mus bow

architet'tare *vt fig* devise; **cosa state architettando?** *fig* what are you plotting?

archi'tet|to *nm* architect. **~'tonico** *a* architectural. **~'tura** *nf* architecture

archivi'are *vt* file; *Jur* close

ar'chivio *nm* archives *pl*; *Comput* file

archi'vista *nmf* filing clerk

ar'cigno *a* grim

arci'pelago *nm* archipelago

arci'vescovo *nm* archbishop

'arco *nm* arch; *Math* arc; ⟨*arma, Mus*⟩ bow; **nell'~ di una giornata/due mesi** in the space of a day/two months

arcoba'leno *nm* rainbow

arcu'a|re *vt* bend. **~rsi** *vr* bend. **~to** *a* bent, curved; ⟨*schiena di gatto*⟩ arched

ar'dente *a* burning; *fig* ardent. **~'mente** *adv* ardently

ar'dere *vt/i* burn

ar'desia *nf* slate

ar'di|re *vi* dare. **~to** *a* daring; ⟨*coraggioso*⟩ bold; ⟨*sfacciato*⟩ impudent

ar'dore *nm* ⟨*calore*⟩ heat; *fig* ardour

'arduo *a* arduous; ⟨*ripido*⟩ steep

'area *nf* area. **~ di rigore** ⟨*in calcio*⟩ penalty area. **~ di servizio** service area

a'rena *nf* arena

are'nar|si *vr* run aground; ⟨*fig: trattative*⟩ reach deadlock; **mi sono arenato** I'm stuck

'argano *nm* winch

argen'tato *a* silver-plated

argente'ria *nf* silver[ware]

ar'gento *nm* silver

ar'gil|la *nf* clay. **~'loso** *a* ⟨*terreno*⟩ clayey

argi'nare *vt* embank; *fig* hold in check, contain

'argine *nm* embankment; ⟨*diga*⟩ dike

argomen'tare *vi* argue

argo'mento *nm* argument; ⟨*motivo*⟩ reason; ⟨*soggetto*⟩ subject

argu'ire *vt* deduce

ar'gu|to *a* witty. **~zia** *nf* wit; ⟨*battuta*⟩ witticism

'aria *nf* air; ⟨*aspetto*⟩ appearance; *Mus* tune; **andare all'~** *fig* come to nothing; **avere l'~...** look...; **corrente d'~** draught; **mandare all'~** qcsa *fig* ruin sth

aridità *nf* aridity, dryness

'arido *a* arid

arieggi'are *vt* air. **~to** *a* airy

ari'ete *nm* ram. **A~** *Astr* Aries

ari'etta *nf* ⟨*brezza*⟩ breeze

a'ringa *nf* herring

ari'oso *a* ⟨*locale*⟩ light and airy

aristo'cra|tico, -a *a* aristocratic ● *nmf* aristocrat. **~'zia** *nf* aristocracy

arit'metica *nf* arithmetic

arlec'chino *nm* Harlequin; *fig* buffoon

'arma *nf* weapon; **armi** *pl* arms; ⟨*forze armate*⟩ [armed] forces;

chiamare alle armi call up; **sotto le armi** in the army; **alle prime armi** *fig* inexperienced, fledg[e]-ling. **~ da fuoco** firearm. **~ impropria** makeshift weapon. **~ a doppio taglio** *fig* double-edged sword

armadi'etto *nm* locker, cupboard

ar'madio *nm* cupboard; (*guardaroba*) wardrobe

armamen'tario *nm* tools *pl*; *fig* paraphernalia

arma'mento *nm* armament; *Naut* fitting out

ar'mare *vt* arm; (*equipaggiare*) fit out; *Archit* reinforce. **~rsi** *vr* arm oneself (**di** with). **~ta** *nf* army; (*flotta*) fleet. **~'tore** *nm* shipowner. **~'tura** *nf* framework; (*impalcatura*) scaffolding; (*di guerriero*) armour

armeggi'are *vi fig* manoeuvre

armi'stizio *nm* armistice

armo'ni|a *nf* harmony. **ar'monica** *nf* **~** [**a bocca**] mouth organ. **ar'monico** *a* harmonic. **~'oso** *a* harmonious

armoniz'zar|e *vt* harmonize • *vi* match. **~si** *vr* (*colori:*) go together, match

ar'nese *nm* tool; (*oggetto*) thing; (*congegno*) gadget; **male in ~** in bad condition

'arnia *nf* beehive

a'roma *nm* aroma; **aromi** *pl* herbs. **~tera'pia** *nf* aromatherapy

aro'matico *a* aromatic

aromatiz'zare *vt* flavour

'arpa *nf* harp

ar'peggio *nm* arpeggio

ar'pia *nf* harpy

arpi'one *nm* hook; (*pesca*) harpoon

arrabat'tarsi *vr* do all one can

arrabbi'a|rsi *vr* get angry. **~to** *a* angry. **~tura** *nf* rage; **prendersi un'~tura** fly into a rage

arraf'fare *vt* grab

arrampi'ca|rsi *vr* climb [up]. **~ta** *nf* climb. **~'tore**, **~'trice** *nmf*

climber. **~'tore sociale** social climber

arran'care *vi* limp, hobble; *fig* struggle, limp along

arrangia'mento *nm* arrangement

arrangi'ar|e *vt* arrange. **~si** *vr* manage; **~si alla meglio** get by; **ar'rangiati!** get on with it!

arra'parsi *vr fam* get randy

arre'care *vt* bring; (*causare*) cause

arreda'mento *nm* interior decoration; (*l'arredare*) furnishing; (*mobili ecc*) furnishings *pl*

arre'da|re *vt* furnish. **~tore**, **~trice** *nmf* interior designer. **ar'redo** *nm* furnishings *pl*

ar'rendersi *vr* surrender

arren'devo|le *a* (*persona*) yielding. **~'lezza** *nf* softness

arre'star|e *vt* arrest; (*fermare*) stop. **~si** *vr* halt. **ar'resto** *nm* stop; *Med*, *Jur* arrest; **la dichiaro in [stato d']arresto** you are under arrest; **mandato di arresto** warrant. **arresti pl domiciliari** *Jur* house arrest

arre'tra|re *vt/i* withdraw; pull back (*giocatore*). **~to** *a* (*paese ecc*) backward; (*Mil: posizione*) rear; **numero ~** *nm* (*di rivista*) back number; **del lavoro ~** a backlog of work • *nm* (*di stipendio*) back pay

arre'trati *nmpl* arrears

arricchi'mento *nm* enrichment

arric'chi|re *vt* enrich. **~rsi** *vr* get rich. **~to**, **-a** *nmf* nouveau riche

arricci'are *vt* curl; **~ il naso** turn up one's nose

ar'ringa *nf* harangue; *Jur* closing address

arrischi'a|rsi *vr* dare. **~to** *a* risky; (*imprudente*) rash

arri'va|re *vi* arrive; **~re a** (*raggiungere*) reach; (*ridursi*) be reduced to. **~to**, **-a** *a* successful; **ben ~to!** welcome! • *nmf* successful person

arrive'derci *int* goodbye; **~ a domani** see you tomorrow

arri'vismo *nm* social climbing;

(*nel lavoro*) careerism. **~ta** *nmf* social climber; (*nel lavoro*) careerist

ar'**rivo** *nm* arrival; *Sport* finish

arro'**gan|te** *a* arrogant. **~za** *nf* arrogance

arro'**garsi** *vr* ~ **il diritto di fare qcsa** take it upon oneself to do sth

arros'**samento** *nm* reddening

arros'**sar|e** *vt* make red, redden (*occhi*). **~si** *vr* go red

arros'**sire** *vi* blush, go red

arro'**stire** *vt* roast; toast (*pane*); (*al ferri*) grill. **ar'rosto** *a* & *nm* roast

arroto'**lare** *vt* roll up

arroton'**dar|e** *vt* round; *Math ecc* round off. **~si** *vr* become round; (*persona*) get plump

arrovel'**larsi** *vr* ~ **il cervello** rack one's brains

arroven'**ta|re** *vt* make red-hot. **~rsi** *vr* become red-hot. **~to** *a* red-hot

arruf'**fa|re** *vt* ruffle; *fig* confuse. **~to** *a* (*capelli*) ruffled

arruffianarsi *vr* ~ **qcno** *fig* butter sb up

arruggi'**ni|re** *vi* rust. **~rsi** *vr* go rusty; *fig* (*fisicamente*) stiffen up; (*conoscenze*) go rusty. **~to** *a* rusty

arruola'**mento** *nm* enlistment

arruo'**lar|e** *vt/i*, **~si** *vr* enlist

arse'**nale** *nm* arsenal; (*cantiere*) [naval] dockyard

ar'**senico** *nm* arsenic

'**arso** *pp di* **ardere** ●*a* burnt; (*arido*) dry. **ar'sura** *nf* burning heat; (*sete*) parching thirst

'**arte** *nf* art; (*abilità*) craftsmanship; **le belle arti** the fine arts. **arti figurative** figurative arts

arte'**fa|re** *vt* adulterate (*vino*); disguise (*voce*). **~tto** *a* fake; (*vino*) adulterated

ar'**tefice** *nmf* craftsman; craftswoman; *fig* author

ar'**teria** *nf* artery. ~ (*stradale*) arterial road

arteriosc**le'rosi** *nf* arteriosclerosis, hardening of the arteries

'**artico** *a* & *nm* Arctic

artico'**la|re** *a* articular ●*vt* articulate; (*suddividere*) divide. **~rsi** *vr fig* ~**si in** consist of. **~to** *a Auto* articulated; *fig* well-constructed. **~zi'one** *nf Anat* articulation

ar'**ticolo** *nm* article. ~ **di fondo** leader

artifici'**ale** *a* artificial

ar'**tifi|cio** *nm* artifice; (*affettazione*) affectation. **~'oso** *a* artful; (*affettato*) affected

artigia'**na|lle** *a* made by hand; *hum* amateurish. **~'mente** *adv* with craftsmanship; *hum* amateurishly

artigia'**nato** *nm* craftsmanship; (*ceto*) craftsmen *pl*. **~'ano, -a** *nm* craftsman ● *nf* craftswoman

artigli'**ere** *nm* artilleryman. **~e'ria** *nf* artillery

ar'**tiglio** *nm* claw; *fig* clutch

ar'**tist|a** *nmf* artist. **~ica'mente** *adv* artistically. **~ico** *a* artistic

'**arto** *nm* limb

ar'**trite** *nf* arthritis

ar'**trosi** *nf* rheumatism

arzigogo'**lato** *a* fantastic, bizarre

ar'**zillo** *a* sprightly

a'**scella** *nf* armpit

ascen'**den|te** *a* ascending ●*nm* (*antenato*) ancestor; (*influenza*) ascendancy; *Astr* ascendant

ascensi'**one** *nf* ascent; **l'A~** the Ascension

ascen'**sore** *nm* lift, elevator *Am*

a'**scesa** *nf* ascent; (*al trono*) accession; (*al potere*) rise

a'**scesso** *nm* abscess

a'**sceta** *nmf* ascetic

'**ascia** *nf* axe

asciugabianche'**ria** *nm inv* (*stenditoio*) clothes horse

asciugaca'**pelli** *nm inv* hair dryer, hairdrier

asciuga'**mano** *nm* towel

asciu'**gar|e** *vt* dry. **~si** *vr* dry oneself; (*diventare asciutto*) dry up

asci'**utto** *a* dry; (*magro*) thin; (*risposta*) curt; **essere all'~** *fig* be hard up

ascol'ta|re vt listen to ● vi listen. ~'**tore**, ~'**trice** nmf listener

a'scolto nm listening; **dare ~ a** listen to; **mettersi in ~** Radio tune in

asfal'tare vt asphalt

a'sfalto nm asphalt

asfis'si|a nf asphyxia. ~'**ante** a (caldo) oppressive; (fig: persona) annoying. ~'**are** vt asphyxiate; fig annoy

'Asia nf Asia. **asi'atico, -a** a & nmf Asian

a'silo nm shelter; (d'infanzia) nursery school. ~ **nido** day nursery. ~ **politico** political asylum

asim'metrico a asymmetrical

'asino nm donkey; (fig: persona stupida) ass

'asma nf asthma. **a'smatico** a asthmatic

asoci'ale a asocial

'asola nf buttonhole

a'sparagi nmpl asparagus sg

a'sparago nm asparagus spear

asperità nf inv harshness; (di terreno) roughness

aspet'ta|re vt wait for; (prevedere) expect; ~**re un bambino** be expecting [a baby]; **fare ~re qcno** keep sb waiting ● vi wait. ~**rsi** vr expect. ~'**tiva** nf expectation

a'spetto[1] nm appearance; (di problema) aspect; **di bell'~** good-looking

a'spetto[2] nm **sala d'~** waiting room

aspi'rante a aspiring; (pompa) suction attrib ● nmf (a un posto) applicant; (al trono) aspirant; **gli aspiranti al titolo** the contenders for the title

aspira'polvere nm inv vacuum cleaner

aspi'ra|re vt inhale; Mech suck in ● vi ~**re a** aspire to. ~'**tore** nm extractor fan. ~**zi'one** nf inhalation; Mech suction; (ambizione) ambition

aspi'rina nf aspirin

aspor'tare vt take away

aspra'mente adv (duramente) severely

a'sprezza nf (al gusto) sourness; (di clima) severity; (di suono) harshness; (di odore) pungency

'aspro a (al gusto) sour; (clima) severe; (suono, parole) harsh; (odore) pungent; (litigio) bitter

assag'gi|are vt taste. ~'**gini** nmpl Culin samples. **as'saggio** nm tasting; (piccola quantità) taste

as'sai adv very; (moltissimo) very much; (abbastanza) enough

assa'li|re vt attack. ~'**tore**, ~'**trice** nmf assailant

as'salto nm attack; **prendere d'~** storm (città); fig mob (persona); hold up (banca)

assapo'rare vt savour

assassi'nare vt murder, assassinate; fig murder

assas'sin|io nm murder, assassination. ~**o, -a** a murderous ● nm murderer; nmf murderess

'asse nf board ● nm Techn axle; Math axis. ~ **da stiro** ironing board

assecon'dare vt satisfy; (favorire) support

assedi'are vt besiege. **as'sedio** nm siege

asse'gna|mento nm allotment; **fare ~ su** rely on

asse'gna|re vt allot; award (premio). ~'**tario** nmf recipient. ~**zi'one** nf (di alloggio, borsa di studio) allocation; (di premio) award

as'segno nm allowance; (bancario) cheque; **contro ~** cash on delivery. ~ **circolare** bank draft. **assegni** pl familiari family allowance. ~ **non trasferibile** cheque made out to 'account payee only'

assem'blea nf assembly; (adunanza) gathering

assembra'mento nm gathering

assen'nato a sensible

as'senso nm assent

assen'tarsi *vr* go away; *(da stanza)* leave the room

as'sen|te *a* absent; *(distratto)* absent-minded ● *nmf* absentee. **~te'ismo** *nm* absenteeism. **~te'ista** *nmf* frequent absentee. **~za** *nf* absence; *(mancanza)* lack

asse'r|ire *vt* assert. **~'tivo** *a* assertive. **~zi'one** *nf* assertion

assesso'rato *nm* department

asses'sore *nm* councillor

assesta'mento *nm* settlement

asse'star|e *vt* arrange; **~e un colpo** deal a blow. **~si** *vr* settle oneself

asse'tato *a* parched

as'setto *nm* order; *Naut, Aeron* trim

assicu'ra|re *vt* assure; *Comm* insure; register *(posta)*; *(fissare)* secure; *(accertare)* ensure. **~rsi** *vr* *(con contratto)* insure oneself; *(legarsi)* fasten oneself; **~rsi che** make sure that. **~'tivo** *a* insurance *attrib*. **~'tore**, **~'trice** *nmf* insurance agent ● *a* insurance *attrib*. **~zi'one** *nf* assurance; *(contratto)* insurance

assidera'mento *nm* exposure. **asside'rato** *a Med* suffering from exposure; *fam* frozen

assidu|a'mente *adv* assiduously. **~ità** *nf* assiduity

as'siduo *a* assiduous; *(cliente)* regular

assil'lante *a (persona, pensiero)* nagging

assil'lare *vt* pester

as'sillo *nm* worry

assimi'la|re *vt* assimilate. **~zi'one** *nf* assimilation

as'sise *nfpl* assizes; **Corte d'A~** Court of Assize[s]

assi'sten|te *nmf* assistant. **~te sociale** social worker. **~te di volo** flight attendant. **~za** *nf* assistance; *(presenza)* presence. **~za sociale** social work

assistenzi'al|e *a* welfare *attrib*. **~'lismo** *nm* welfare

as'sistere *vt* assist; *(curare)* nurse

● *vi* **~ a** *(essere presente)* be present at; watch *(spettacolo ecc)*

'asso *nm* ace; **piantare in ~** leave in the lurch

associ'a|re *vt* join; *(collegare)* associate. **~rsi** *vr* join forces; *Comm* enter into partnership. **~rsi a** join; subscribe to *(giornale ecc)*. **~zi'one** *nf* association

assogget'tar|e *vt* subject. **~si** *vr* submit

asso'lato *a* sunny

assol'dare *vt* recruit

as'solo *nm* Mus solo

as'solto *pp di* assolvere

assoluta'mente *adv* absolutely

assolu'tismo *nm* absolutism

asso'lu|to *a* absolute. **~zi'one** *nf* acquittal; *Relig* absolution

as'solvere *vt* perform *(compito)*; *Jur* acquit; *Relig* absolve

assomigli'a|re *vi* **~e a** be like, resemble. **~si** *vr* resemble each other

assom'marsi *vr* combine; **~ a qcsa** add to sth

asso'nanza *nf* assonance

asson'nato *a* drowsy

asso'pirsi *vr* doze off

assor'bente *a & nm* absorbent. **~ igienico** sanitary towel

assor'bire *vt* absorb

assor'da|re *vt* deafen. **~nte** *a* deafening

assorti'mento *nm* assortment

assor'ti|re *vt* match *(colori)*. **~to** *a* assorted; *(colori, persone)* matched

as'sorto *a* engrossed

assottigli'ar|e *vt* make thin; *(aguzzare)* sharpen; *(ridurre)* reduce. **~si** *vr* grow thin; *(finanze:)* be whittled away

assue'fa|re *vt* accustom. **~rsi a** get used to. **~tto** *a (a caffè, aspirina)* immune to the effects; *(a droga)* addicted. **~zi'one** *nf (a caffè, aspirina)* immunity to the effects; *(a droga)* addiction

as'sumere *vt* assume; take on *(im-*

piegato); ~ **informazioni** make inquiries

as'sunto *pp di* **assumere** ● *nm* task. **assunzi'one** *nf (di impiegato)* employment

assurdità *nf inv* absurdity; ~ *pl* nonsense

as'surdo *a* absurd

'asta *nf pole; Mech* bar; *Comm* auction; **a mezz'~** at half-mast

a'stemio *a* abstemious

aste'nersi *vr* abstain (**da** from). **~si'one** *nf* abstention

aste'nuto, -a *nmf* abstainer

aste'risco *nm* asterisk

astig'ma|tico *a* astigmatic. **~'tismo** *nm* astigmatism

asti'nenza *nf* abstinence; **crisi di ~** cold turkey

'asti|o *nm* rancour; **avere ~ contro** qcno bear sb a grudge. **~'oso** *a* resentful

a'stratto *a* abstract

astrin'gente *a & nm* astringent

'astro *nm* star

astrolo'gia *nf* astrology. **a'strologo, -a** *nmf* astrologer

astro'nauta *nmf* astronaut

astro'nave *nf* spaceship

astrono'mia *nf* astronomy. **~o'nomico** *a* astronomical. **a'stronomo** *nm* astronomer

astrusità *nf* abstruseness

a'stuccio *nm* case

a'stu|to *a* shrewd; *(furbo)* cunning. **~zia** *nf* shrewdness; *(azione)* trick

ate'ismo *nm* atheism

A'tene *nf* Athens

'ateo, -a *a & nmf* atheist

a'tipico *a* atypical

at'lant|e *nm* atlas. **~ico** *a* Atlantic; **l'[Oceano] A~ico** the Atlantic [Ocean]

at'let|a *nmf* athlete. **~ica** *nf* athletics *sg.* **~ica leggera** track and field events. **~ica pesante** weight-lifting, boxing, wrestling, *etc.* **~ico** *a* athletic

atmo'sfer|a *nf* atmosphere. **~o** *a* atmospheric

a'tomic|a *nf* atom bomb. **~o** *a* atomic

'atomo *nm* atom

'atrio *nm* entrance hall

a'troc|e *a* atrocious; *(terrible)* dreadful. **~ità** *nf inv* atrocity

atrofiz'zarsi *vr Med, fig* atrophy

attaccabot'toni *nmf inv* [crashing] bore

attacca'brighe *nmf inv* troublemaker

attacca'mento *nm* attachment

attacca'panni *nm inv* [coathanger; *(a muro)* clothes hook

attac'car|e *vt* attach; *(legare)* tie; *(appendere)* hang; *(cucire)* sew on; *(contagiare)* pass on; *(assalire)* attack; *(iniziare)* start ● *vi* stick; *(diffondersi)* catch on. **~si** *vr* cling; *(affezionarsi)* become attached; *(litigare)* quarrel

attac'ciccio *a* sticky

at'tacco *nm* attack; *(punto d'unione)* junction

attar'darsi *vr* stay late; *(indugiare)* linger

attec'chire *vi* take; *(moda ecc.)* catch on

atteggia'mento *nm* attitude

atteggi'ar|e *vt* assume. **~si** *vr* **~si a pose as**

attem'pato *a* elderly

at'tender|e *vt* wait for ● *vi* **~e a** attend to. **~si** *vr* expect

atten'dibil|e *a* reliable. **~ità** *nf* reliability

at'tenersi *vr* **~ a stick to**

atten'ta *adv* attentively

atten'ta|re *vi* **~re a** make an attempt on. **~to** *nm* act of violence; *(contro politico ecc)* assassination attempt. **~tore, ~'trice** *nmf (a scopo politico)* terrorist

at'tento *a* attentive; *(accurato)* careful; **~!** look out!; **stare ~** pay attention

attenu'ante *nf* extenuating circumstance

attenu'a|re *vt* attenuate; *(minimizzare)* minimize; subdue *(colori*

ecc); calm ⟨dolore⟩; soften ⟨colpo⟩.
~**rsi** vr diminish. ~**zi'one** nf
lessening

attenzi'one nf attention; ~**!** watch
out!

atter'ra|ggio nm landing. ~**re** vt
knock down ● vi land

atter'rir|e vt terrorize. ~**si** vr be
terrified

at'tesa nf waiting; ⟨aspettativa⟩
expectation; **in** ~ **a di** waiting for.
~**o** pp di **attendere**

atte'sta|re vt state; ⟨certificare⟩
certify. ~**to** nm certificate. ~**zi-
'one** nf certificate; ⟨dichiarazione⟩
declaration

'**attico** nm attic

at'tiguo a adjacent

attil'lato a ⟨vestito⟩ close-fitting

'**attimo** nm moment

atti'nente a ~ **a** pertaining to

at'tingere vt draw; fig obtain

atti'rare vt attract

atti'tudine nf ⟨disposizione⟩ aptitude; ⟨atteggiamento⟩ attitude

atti'v|are vt activate. ~**ismo** nm
activism. ~**ista** nmf activist.
attività nf inv activity; Comm assets pl. ~**o** a active; Comm productive ● nm assets pl

attiz'za|re vt poke; fig stir up.
~**toio** nm poker

'**atto** nm act; ⟨azione⟩ action;
Comm, Jur deed; ⟨certificato⟩ certificate; **atti** pl ⟨di società ecc⟩ proceedings; **mettere in** ~ put into
effect

at'tonito a astonished

attorcigli'ar|e vt twist. ~**si** vr get
twisted

at'tore nm actor

attorni'ar|e vt surround. ~**si** vr
~**si** di surround oneself with

at'torno adv around, about ● prep
~ **a** around, about

attrac'care vt/i dock

attra'ente a attractive

attra'rre vt attract. ~**rsi** vr be at-
tracted to each other. ~**t'tiva** nf
charm. ~**zi'one** nf attraction.

~**zioni** pl **turistiche** tourist at-
tractions

attraversa'mento nm ⟨di strada⟩
crossing. ~ **pedonale** pedestrian
crossing, crosswalk Am

attraver'sare vt cross; ⟨passare⟩
go through

attra'verso prep through; ⟨obli-
quamente⟩ across

attrezza|re vt equip; Naut rig.
~**rsi** vr kit oneself out; ~**tura** nf
equipment; Naut rigging

at'trezzo nm tool; **attrezzi** pl
equipment; Sport appliances pl;
Theat props pl

attribu'ir|e vt attribute. ~**si** vr as-
cribe to oneself; ~**si il merito di**
claim credit for

attri'buto nm attribute. ~**zi'one**
nf attribution

at'trice nf actress

at'trito nm friction

attu'abile a feasible

attu'al|e a present; ⟨di attualità⟩
topical; ⟨effettivo⟩ actual. ~**ità** nf
topicality; ⟨avvenimento⟩ news;
programma di ~**ità** current affairs programme. ~**iz'zare** vt up-
date. ~**mente** adv at present

attu'a|re vt carry out. ~**rsi** vr be
realized. ~**zi'one** nf carrying out

attu'tire vt deaden; ~ **il colpo** soften the blow

au'dac|e a daring, bold; ⟨insolente⟩
audacious;. ~**ia** nf daring, boldness; ⟨insolenza⟩ audacity

'audience nf inv ⟨telespettatori⟩
audience

'**audio** nm audio

audiovi'sivo a audiovisual

audi'torio nm auditorium

audizi'one nf audition; Jur hearing

'**auge** nm height; **essere in** ~ be
popular

augu'rar|e vt wish. ~**si** vr hope.
au'gurio nm wish; ⟨presagio⟩
omen; **auguri!** all the best!; ⟨a
Natale⟩ Happy Christmas!; **tanti
auguri** best wishes

'**aula** nf classroom; ⟨università⟩

lecture-hall; (*sala*) hall. **~ magna** (*in università*) great hall. **~ dei tribunale** courtroom

aumen'tare *vt/i* increase. **au'mento** *nm* increase; (*di stipendio*) [pay] rise

au'reola *nf* halo

au'rora *nf* dawn

auscul'tare *vt Med* auscultate

ausili'are *a* & *nmf* auxiliary

auspicabile *a* è ~ **che...** it is to be hoped that...

auspi'care *vt* hope for

au'spicio *nm* omen; **auspici** (*pl: protezione*) auspices

austerità *nf* austerity

au'stero *a* austere

Au'strali|a *nf* Australia. **a~'ano, -a** *a* & *nmf* Australian

'Austria *nf* Austria. **au'striaco, -a** *a* & *nmf* Austrian

autar'chia *nf* autarchy. **au'tarchico** *a* autarchic

autenti'c|are *vt* authenticate. **~ità** *nf* authenticity

au'tentico *a* authentic; (*vero*) true

au'tista *nm* driver

'auto *nf inv* car

'auto+ *pref* self+

autoabbron'zante *nm* self-tan ● *a* self-tanning

autoambu'lanza *nf* ambulance

autoartico'lato *nm* articulated lorry

autobio|gra'fia *nf* autobiography. **~'grafico** *a* autobiographical

auto'botte *nf* tanker

'autobus *nm inv* bus

auto'carro *nm* lorry

autocommiserazi'one *nf* self-pity

autoconcessio'nario *nm* car dealer

auto'critica *nf* self-criticism

autodi'datta *nmf* self-educated person, autodidact

autodi'fesa *nf* self-defence

auto'gol *nm inv* own goal

au'tografo *a* & *nm* autograph

autolesio'nis|mo *nm fig* self-destruction. **~tico** *a* self-destructive

auto'linea *nf* bus line

au'toma *nm* robot

automatica'mente *adv* automatically

auto'matico *a* automatic ● *nm* (*bottone*) press-stud; (*fucile*) automatic

automatiz'za|re *vt* automate. **~zi'one** *nf* automation

auto'mezzo *nm* motor vehicle

auto'mobi|le *nf* [motor] car. **~'lismo** *nm* motoring. **~'lista** *nmf* motorist. **~'listico** *a* (*industria*) automobile *attrib*

autonoma'mente *adv* autonomously

autono'mia *nf* autonomy; *Auto* range; (*di laptop, cellulare*) battery life. **au'tonomo** *a* autonomous

autop'sia *nf* autopsy

auto'radio *nf inv* car radio; (*veicolo*) radio car

au'tore, -'trice *nmf* author; (*di pitture*) painter; (*di furto ecc*) perpetrator; **quadro d'~** genuine master

auto'revo|le *a* authoritative; (*che ha influenza*) influential. **~'lezza** *nf* authority

autori'messa *nf* garage

autori|tà *nf inv* authority. **~'tario** *a* autocratic. **~ta'rismo** *nm* authoritarianism

autori'tratto *nm* self-portrait

autoriz'za|re *vt* authorize. **~zi'one** *nf* authorization

auto'scontro *nm inv* bumper car, dodgem

autoscu'ola *nf* driving school

auto'stop *nm* hitch-hiking; **fare l'~** hitch-hike. **~'pista** *nmf* hitch-hiker

auto'strada *nf* motorway

autostra'dale *a* motorway *attrib*

autosuffici'en|te *a* self-sufficient. **~za** *nf* self-sufficiency

autotraspor'ta|tore, ~'trice *nmf* haulier, carrier

auto'treno *nm* articulated lorry, roadtrain

autove'icolo *nm* motor vehicle

auto've lox *nm inv* speed camera

autovet'tura *nf* motor vehicle

autun'nale *a* autumn[al]

au'tunno *nm* autumn

aval'lare *vt* endorse, back (*cambiale*); *fig* endorse

a'vallo *nm* endorsement

avam'braccio *nm* forearm

avangu'ardia *nf* vanguard; *fig* avant-garde; **essere all'~** be in the forefront; *Techn* be at the leading edge

a'vanti *adv* (*in avanti*) forward; (*davanti*) in front; (*prima*) before; **~!** (*entrate*) come in!; (*suvvia*) come on!; (*su semaforo*) cross now, walk *Am*; **va' ~!** go ahead!; **andare ~** (*precedere*) go ahead; (*orologio:*) be fast; **~ e indietro** backwards and forwards **● a** (*precedente*) before **● prep ~ a** before; (*in presenza di*) in the presence of

avanti'eri *adv* the day before yesterday

avanza'mento *nm* progress; (*promozione*) promotion

avan'za|re *vi* advance; (*progredire*) progress; (*essere d'avanzo*) be left [over] **● vt** advance; (*superare*) surpass; (*promuovere*) promote. **~rsi** *vr* advance; (*avvicinarsi*) approach. **~ta** *nf* advance. **~to a** advanced; (*nella notte*) late; **~ta** elderly. **a'vanzo** *nm* remainder; *Comm* surplus; **avanzi** *pl* (*rovine*) remains; (*di cibo*) left-overs

ava'ri|a *nf* (*di motore*) engine failure. **~'ato** *a* (*frutta, verdura*) rotten; (*carne*) tainted

ava'rizia *nf* avarice. **a'varo, -a** *a* stingy **●** *nmf* miser

a'vena *nf* oats *pl*

a'vere *vt* have; (*ottenere*) get; (*indossare*) wear; (*provare*) feel; **ho trent'anni** I'm thirty; **ha avuto il posto** he got the job; **~ fame/freddo** be hungry/cold; **ho mal di denti** I've got toothache; **cos'ha a che fare con lui?** what has it got to do

with him?; **~ da fare** be busy; **che hai?** what's the matter with you?; **nei hai per molto?** will you be long?; **quanti ne abbiamo oggi?** what date is it today?; **avercela con qcno** have it in for sb **● v aux** have; **non l'ho visto** I haven't seen him; **lo hai visto?** have you seen him?; **l'ho visto ieri** I saw him yesterday **●** *nm* **averi** *pl* wealth *sg*

avia'tore *nm* flyer, aviator. **~zi'one** *nf* aviation; *Mil* Air Force

avidità *nf* avidness. **'avido** *a* avid

avio'getto *nm* jet

'avo, -a *nmf* ancestor

avo'cado *nm inv* avocado

a'vorio *nm* ivory

Avv. *abbr* avvocato

avva'lersi *vr* avail oneself (**of** di)

avvalla'mento *nm* depression

avvalo'rare *vt* bear out (*tesi*); endorse (*documento*); (*accrescere*) enhance

avvam'pare *vi* flare up; (*arrossire*) blush

avvantaggi'ar|e *vt* favour. **~si** *vr* **~si di** benefit from; (*approfittare*) take advantage of

avve'd|ersi *vr* (*accorgersi*) notice; (*capire*) realize. **~uto** *a* shrewd

avvele'na'mento *nm* poisoning

avvele'na|re *vt* poison. **~rsi** *vr* poison oneself. **~to a** poisoned

avve'nente *a* attractive

avveni'mento *nm* event

avve'nire¹ *vi* happen; (*aver luogo*) take place

avve'ni|re² *nm* future. **~'ristico** *a* futuristic

avven'ta|rsi *vr* fling oneself. **~to a** (*decisione*) rash

av'vento *nm* advent; *Relig* Advent

avven'tore *nm* regular customer

avven'tu|ra *nf* adventure; (*amorosa*) affair; **d'~** (*film*) adventure *attrib*. **~'rarsi** *vr* venture. **~'ri'ero, -a** *nm* adventurer **●** *nf* adventuress. **~'roso a** adventurous

avve'rabile *a* (*previsione*) that may come true. **~rsi** *vr* come true

av'verbio nm adverb

avver'sar|e vt oppose. **~io, -a** a opposing ● nmf opponent

aversi|'one nf aversion. **~tà** nf inv adversity

av'verso a (sfavorevole) adverse; (contrario) averse

avver'tenza nf (cura) care; (avvertimento) warning; (avviso) notice; (premessa) foreword; **avvertenze** pl (istruzioni) instructions

avverti'mento nm warning

avver'tire vt warn; (informare) inform; (sentire) feel

avvez'zar|e vt accustom. **~si** vr accustom oneself. **av'vezzo** a **avvezzo a** used to

avvia'mento nm starting; Comm goodwill

avvi'a|re vt start. **~rsi** vr set out. **~to** a under way; **bene ~to** thriving

avvicenda'mento nm (in agricoltura) rotation; (nel lavoro) replacement

avvicen'darsi vr take turns, alternate

avvicina'mento nm approach

avvici'nar|e vt bring near; approach (persona). **~si** vr come nearer, approach; **~si a** come nearer to, approach

avvi'lente a demoralizing; (umiliante) humiliating

avvili'mento nm despondency; (degradazione) degradation

avvi'li|re vt dishearten; (degradare) degrade. **~rsi** vr lose heart; (degradarsi) degrade oneself. **~to** a disheartened; (degradato) degraded

avvilup'par|e vt envelop. **~si** vr wrap oneself up; (aggrovigliarsi) get entangled

avvinaz'zato a drunk

avvin'cente a (libro ecc) enthralling. **av'vincere** vt enthral

avvinghi'ar|e vt clutch. **~si** vr cling

av'vio nm start-up; **dare l'~ a qcsa** get sth under way; **prendere l'~** get under way

avvi'sare vt inform; (mettere in guardia) warn

av'viso nm notice; (annuncio) announcement; (avvertimento) warning; (pubblicitario) advertisement; **a mio ~** in my opinion. **~ di garanzia** Jur notification that one is to be the subject of a legal enquiry

avvi'stare vt catch sight of

avvi'tare vt screw in; screw down (coperchio)

avviz'zire vi wither

avvo'ca|to nm lawyer; fig advocate. **~tura** nf legal profession

av'volger|e vt wrap [up]. **~si** vr wrap oneself up

avvol'gibile nm roller. blind

avvol'toio nm vulture

aza'lea nf azalea

azi'en|da nf business, firm. **~ agricola** farm. **~ di soggiorno** tourist bureau. **~'dale** a (politica, dirigente) company attrib; (giornale) in-house

aziona'mento nm operation

azio'nare vt operate

azio'nario a share attrib

azi'one nf action; Fin share; **d'~** (romanzo, film) action[-packed]. **azio'nista** nmf shareholder

a'zoto nm nitrogen

azzan'nare vt seize with its teeth; sink its teeth into (gamba)

azzar'd|are vt risk. **~arsi** vr dare. **~ato** a risky; (precipitoso) rash. **az'zardo** nm hazard; **gioco d'azzardo** game of chance

azzec'care vt hit; (fig: indovinare) guess

azzuf'farsi vr come to blows

az'zur|ro a & nm blue; **il principe ~** Prince Charming. **~'rognolo** a bluish

Bb

bab'beo *a* foolish ● *nm* idiot

'babbo *nm fam* dad, daddy. **B~ Natale** Father Christmas

bab'buccia *nf* slipper

babbu'ino *nm* baboon

ba'bordo *nm Naut* port side

baby'sitter *nmf inv* baby-sitter; **fare la ~** babysit

ba'cato *a* wormeaten

'bacca *nf* berry

baccalà *nm inv* dried salted cod

bac'cano *nm* din

bac'cello *nm* pod

bac'chetta *nf* rod; *(magica)* wand; *(di direttore d'orchestra)* baton; *(di tamburo)* drumstick

ba'checa *nf* showcase; *(in ufficio)* notice board. **~ elettronica** *Comput* bulletin board

bacia'mano *nm* kiss on the hand; **fare il ~ a qcno** kiss sb's hand

baci'ar|e *vt* kiss. **~si** *vr* kiss [each other]

ba'cillo *nm* bacillus

baci'nella *nf* basin

ba'cino *nm* basin; *Anat* pelvis; *(di porto)* dock; *(di minerali)* deposit

'bacio *nm* kiss

'baco *nm* worm. **~ da seta** silkworm

ba'cucco *a* **un vecchio ~** a senile old man

'bada *nf* **tenere qcno a ~** keep sb at bay

ba'dare *vi* take care (**a** of); *(fare attenzione)* look out; **bada ai fatti tuoi!** mind your own business!

ba'dia *nf* abbey

ba'dile *nm* shovel

'badminton *nm* badminton

'baffi *nmpl* moustache *sg*; *(di animale)* whiskers; **mi fa un baffo** I don't give a damn; **ridere sotto i ~** laugh up one's sleeve

baf'futo *a* moustached

ba'gagli *nmpl* luggage, baggage. **~'aio** *nm Rail* luggage van; *Auto* boot

ba'gaglio *nm* luggage; **un ~** a piece of luggage. **~ a mano** hand luggage, hand baggage

baggia'nata *nf* **non dire baggianate** don't talk nonsense

bagli'ore *nm* glare; *(improvviso)* flash; *(fig: di speranza)* glimmer

ba'gnante *nmf* bather

ba'gna|re *vt* wet; *(inzuppare)* soak; *(immergere)* dip; *(innaffiare)* water; *(mare, lago:)* wash; *(fiume:)* flow through. **~rsi** *vr* get wet; *(al mare ecc)* swim

bagnasci'uga *nm inv* edge of the water, waterline

ba'gnato *a* wet

ba'gnino, -a *nmf* life guard

'bagno *nm* bath; *(stanza)* bathroom; *(gabinetto)* toilet; *(in casa)* toilet, bathroom; *(al mare)* swim, bathe; **bagni** *pl* *(stabilimento)* lido; **fare il ~** have a bath; *(nel mare ecc)* [have a] swim or bathe; **andare in ~** go to the bathroom or toilet; **mettere a ~** soak. **~ turco** Turkish bath

bagnoma'ria *nm* **cuocere a ~** cook in a double saucepan

bagnoschi'uma *nm inv* bubble bath

'baia *nf* bay

baio'netta *nf* bayonet

'baita *nf* mountain chalet

bala'ustra, balaus'trata *nf* balustrade

balbet't|are *vt/i* stammer; *(bambino:)* babble. **~io** *nm* stammering; babble

bal'buzi|e *nf* stutter. **~'ente** *a* stuttering ● *nmf* stutterer

Bal'cani *nmpl* Balkans. **b~ico** *a* Balkan

balco'nata *nf Theat* balcony, dress circle

balcon'cino *nm* **reggiseno a ~** underwired bra

bal'cone *nm* balcony

baldac'chino *nm* canopy; **letto a ~** four-poster bed

bal'dan|za *nf* boldness. **~'zoso** *a* bold

bal'doria *nf* revelry; **far ~** have a riotous time

Bale'ari *nfpl* **le [isole] ~** the Balearics, the Balearic Islands

ba'lena *nf* whale

bale'nare *vi* lighten; *fig* flash; **mi è balenata un'idea** I've just had an idea

bale'niera *nf* whaler

ba'leno *nm* **in un ~** in a flash

ba'lera *nf* dance hall

'balia *nf* wetnurse

ba'lia *nf* **in ~ di** at the mercy of

ba'listico *a* ballistic; **perito ~** ballistics expert

'balla *nf* bale; (*fam: frottola*) tall story

bal'labile *a* good for dancing to

bal'la|re *vi* dance. **~ta** *nf* ballad

balla'toio *nm* (*nelle scale*) landing

balle'rino, -a *nmf* dancer; (*classico*) ballet dancer; **ballerina** (*classica*) ballet dancer, ballerina

bal'letto *nm* ballet

bal'lista *nmf fam* bull-shitter

'ballo *nm* dance; (*il ballare*) dancing; **sala da ~** ballroom; **essere in ~** (*lavoro, vita:*) be at stake; (*persona:*) be committed; **tirare qcno in ~** involve sb

ballonzo'lare *vi* skip about

ballot'taggio *nm* second count (*of votes*)

balne'a|re *a* bathing *attrib.* **stagione ~** swimming season. **stazione ~** seaside resort. **~zi'one** *nf* **è vietata la ~zione** no swimming

ba'lordo *a* foolish; (*stordito*) stunned; **tempo ~** nasty weather

'balsamo *nm* balsam; (*per capelli*) conditioner; (*lenimento*) remedy

'baltico *a* Baltic. **il [mar] B~** the Baltic [Sea]

balu'ardo *nm* bulwark

'balza *nf* crag; (*di abito*) flounce

bal'zano *a* (*idea*) weird

bal'zare *vi* bounce; (*saltare*) jump; **~ in piedi** leap to one's feet.

'balzo *nm* bounce; (*salto*) jump;

prendere la palla al balzo seize an opportunity

bam'bagia *nf* cotton wool; **vivere nella ~** *fig* be in clover

bambi'nata *nf* childish thing to do/say

bam'bi|no, -a *nmf* child; (*appena nato*) baby; **avere un ~no** have a baby. **~'none, -a** *nmf pej* big or overgrown infant

bam'boccio *nm* chubby child; (*sciocco*) simpleton; (*fantoccio*) rag doll

'bambo|la *nf* doll. **~'lotto** *nm* male doll

bambù *nm* bamboo

ba'nal|e *a* banal; **~ità** *nf inv* banality; **~iz'zare** *vt* trivialize

ba'nan|a *nf* banana. **~o** *nm* banana-tree

'banca *nf* bank. **~ [di] dati** data-bank

banca'rella *nf* stall

ban'cario, -a *a* banking *attrib*; **trasferimento ~** bank transfer ● *nmf* bank employee

banca'rotta *nf* bankruptcy; **fare ~** go bankrupt

banchet'tare *vi* banquet. **ban'chetto** *nm* banquet

banchi'ere *nm* banker

ban'china *nf Naut* quay; (*in stazione*) platform; (*di strada*) path; **~ non transitabile** soft verge

ban'chisa *nf* floe

'banco *nm* (*di scuola*) desk; (*di negozio*) counter; (*di officina*) bench; (*di gioco, banca*) bank; (*di mercato*) stall; (*degli imputati*) dock; **sotto ~** under the counter; **medicinale da ~** over the counter medicines. **~ informazioni** information desk. **~ di nebbia** fog bank

'bancomat® *nm inv* autobank, cashpoint; (*carta*) bank card, cash card

ban'cone *nm* counter; (*in bar*) bar

banco'nota *nf* banknote, bill *Am*; **banco'note** *pl* paper currency

'**banda** *nf* band; (*di delinquenti*) gang. ~ **d'atterraggio** landing strip. ~ **rumorosa** rumble strip
banderu'ola *nf* weathercock; *Naut* pennant
bandi'e|ra *nf* flag; **cambiare** ~**ra** change sides, switch allegiances. ~**rina** *nf* (*nel calcio*) corner flag. ~**rine** *pl* bunting *sg*
ban'di|re *vt* banish; (*pubblicare*) publish; *fig* dispense with (*formalità, complimenti*). ~**to** *nm* bandit. ~**tore** *nm* (*di aste*) auctioneer
'**bando** *nm* proclamation; ~ **di concorso** job advertisement (*published in an official gazette for a job for which a competitive examination has to be taken*)
bar *nm inv* bar
'**bara** *nf* coffin
ba'rac|ca *nf* hut; (*catapecchia*) hovel; **mandare avanti la** ~**ca** keep the ship afloat. **vivere in una** ~**ca** *person living in a makeshift shelter*. ~**chino** *nm* (*di gelati, giornali*) kiosk; *Radio* CB radio. ~**cone** *nm* (*roulotte*) circus caravan; (*in luna park*) booth. ~**copoli** *nf inv* shanty town
bara'onda *nf* chaos; **non fare** ~ don't make a mess
ba'rare *vi* cheat
'**baratro** *nm* chasm
barat'tare *vt* barter. **ba'ratto** *nm* barter
ba'rattolo *nm* jar; (*di latta*) tin
'**barba** *nf* beard; (*fam: noia*) bore; **farsi la** ~ shave; **è una** ~ (*noia*) it's boring
barbabi'etola *nf* beetroot. ~ **da zucchero** sugar-beet
bar'barico *a* barbaric. **bar'barie** *nf* barbarity. '**barbaro** *a* barbarous ● *nm* barbarian
'**barbecue** *nm inv* barbecue
barbi'ere *nm* barber; (*negozio*) barber's
barbi'turico *nm* barbiturate
bar'bone *nm* (*vagabondo*) vagrant; (*cane*) poodle

bar'boso *a fam* boring
barbu'gliare *vi* mumble
bar'buto *a* bearded
'**barca** *nf* boat; **una** ~ **di** *fig* a lot of. ~ **a motore** motorboat. ~ **da pesca** fishing boat. ~ **a remi** rowing boat, rowboat *Am*. ~ **di salvataggio** lifeboat. ~ **a vela** sailing boat, sailboat *Am*. ~**l'olo** *nm* boatman
barcame'narsi *vr* manage
barcol'lare *vi* stagger
bar'cone *nm* barge; (*di ponte*) pontoon
bar'dar|e *vt* harness. ~**si** *vr hum* dress up
ba'rel|la *nf* stretcher. ~**li'ere** *nm* stretcher-bearer
'**Barents: il mare di** ~ the Barents Sea
bari'centro *nm* centre of gravity
ba'ri|le *nm* barrel. ~**lotto** *nm fig* tub of lard
ba'rista *nm* barman ● *nf* barmaid
ba'ritono *nm* baritone
bar'lume *nm* glimmer; **un** ~ **di speranza** a glimmer of hope
'**barman** *nm inv* barman
'**baro** *nm* cardsharper
ba'rocco *a* & *nm* baroque
ba'rometro *nm* barometer
ba'rone *nm* baron; **i baroni** *fig* the top brass. **baro'nessa** *nf* baroness
'**barra** *nf* bar; (*lineetta*) oblique; *Naut* tiller. ~ **spazio** *Comput* space bar. ~ **strumenti** *Comput* tool bar
bar'rare *vt* block off (*strada*)
barri'ca|re *vt* barricade. ~**ta** *nf* barricade
barri'era *nf* barrier; (*stradale*) road-block; *Geol* reef. ~ **razziale** colour bar
bar'ri|re *vi* trumpet. ~**to** *nm* trumpeting
barzel'letta *nf* joke; ~ **sporca** *o* **spinta** dirty joke
basa'mento *nm* base
ba'sar|e *vt* base. ~**si** *vr* ~**si su** be based on; **mi baso su ciò che ho visto** I'm going on [the basis of] what I saw

'basco, -a *nmf* & *a* Basque ●*nm* (*copricapo*) beret

'base *nf* basis; (*fondamento*) foundation; *Mil* base; *Pol* rank and file; **a ~ di** containing; **in ~ a** on the basis of. **~ dati** database

'baseball *nm* baseball

ba'setta *nf* sideburn

basi'lare *a* basic

ba'silica *nf* basilica

ba'silico *nm* basil

ba'sista *nm* grass roots politician; (*di un crimine*) mastermind

'basket *nm* basketball

bas'sezza *nf* lowness; (*di statura*) shortness; (*viltà*) vileness

bas'sista *nmf* bassist

'basso, -a *a* low; (*di statura*) short; (*acqua*) shallow; (*televisione*) quiet; (*vile*) despicable; **parlare a bassa voce** speak quietly, speak in a low voice; **la bassa Italia** southern Italy ●*nm* lower part; *Mus* bass. **guardare in ~** look down

basso'fondo *nm* (*pl* **bassifondi**) shallows *pl*; **bassifondi** *pl* (*quartieri poveri*) slums

bassorili'evo *nm* bas-relief

bas'sotto *nm* dachshund

ba'stardo, -a *a* bastard; (*di animale*) mongrel ●*nmf* bastard; (*animale*) mongrel

ba'stare *vi* be enough; (*durare*) last; **basta!** that's enough!; **that'll do!**; **basta che** (*purchè*) provided that; **basta così** that's enough; **basta così?** is that enough?, will that do?; (*in negozio*) will there be anything else?; **basta andare alla posta** you only have to go to the post office

Basti'an con'trario *nm* contrary old so-and-so

basti'one *nm* bastion

basto'nare *vt* beat

baston'cino *nm* (*da sci*) ski pole. **~ di pesce** fish finger, fish stick *Am*

ba'stone *nm* stick; (*da golf*) club; (*da passeggio*) walking stick

ba'tosta *nf* blow

bat'taglia *nf* battle; (*lotta*) fight. **~'are** *vi* battle; *fig* fight

bat'taglio *nm* (*di campana*) clapper; (*di porta*) knocker

battagli'one *nm* battalion

bat'tello *nm* boat; (*motonave*) steamer

bat'tente *nm* (*di porta*) wing; (*di finestra*) shutter; (*battaglio*) knocker

'battere *vt* beat; (*percorrere*) scour; thresh (*grano*); break (*record*) ●*vi* (*bussare, urtare*) knock; (*cuore*) beat; (*ali ecc*) flap; *Tennis* serve; **~e a macchina** type; **~e gli occhi** blink; **~e le mani** clap [one's hands]; **~e le ore** strike the hours. **~si** *vr* fight

bat'teri *nmpl* bacteria

batte'ria *nf* battery; *Mus* drums *pl*

bat'terio *nm* bacterium. **~'logico** *a* bacteriological

batte'rista *nmf* drummer

bat'tesimo *nm* baptism, christening

battez'zare *vt* baptize, christen

battiba'leno *nm* **in un ~** in a flash

batti'becco *nm* squabble

batticu'ore *nm* palpitation; **mi venne il ~** I was scared

bat'tigia *nf* water's edge

batti'mano *nm* applause

batti'panni *nm inv* carpetbeater

batti'stero *nm* baptistery

batti'strada *nm inv* outrider; (*di pneumatico*) tread; *Sport* pacesetter

battitap'peto *nm inv* carpet sweeper

'battito *nm* (*del cuore*) [heart]beat; (*alle tempie*) throbbing; (*di orologio*) ticking; (*della pioggia*) beating

bat'tuta *nf* beat; (*colpo*) knock; (*spiritosaggine*) wisecrack; (*osservazione*) remark; *Mus* bar; *Tennis* service; *Theat* cue; (*dattilografia*) stroke

ba'tuffolo *nm* flock

ba'ule *nm* trunk

'**bava** *nf* dribble; (*di cane ecc*) slobber; **aver la ~ alla bocca** foam at the mouth

bava'glino *nm* bib

ba'vaglio *nm* gag

'**bavero** *nm* collar

ba'zar *nm inv* bazaar

baz'zecola *nf* trifle

bazzi'care *vt/i* haunt

be'arsi *vr* delight (**di** in)

beati'tudine *nf* bliss. **be'ato** *a* blissful; *Relig* blessed; **beato te!** lucky you!

beauty-'case *nm inv* toilet bag

bebè *nm inv* baby

bec'caccia *nf* woodcock

bec'care *vt* peck; *fig* catch. **~rsi** *vr* (*litigare*) quarrel. **~ta** *nf* peck

beccheggi'are *vi* pitch

bec'chino *nm* grave-digger

'**bec|co** *nm* beak; (*di caffettiera ecc*) spout. **~'cuccio** *nm* spout

be'fana *nf* Epiphany; (*donna brutta*) old witch

'**beffa** *nf* hoax; **farsi beffe di qcno** mock sb. **bef'fardo** *a* derisory; (*persona*) mocking

beffar|e *vt* mock. **~si** *vr* **~si di** make fun of

'**bega** *nf* quarrel; **è una bella ~** it's really annoying

be'gonia *nf* begonia

'**beige** *a & nm* beige

be'la|re *vi* bleat. **~to** *nm* bleating

'**belga** *a & nmf* Belgian

'**Belgio** *nm* Belgium

'**bella** *nf* (*in carte, Sport*) decider

bel'lezza *nf* beauty; **che ~!** how lovely!; **chiudere/finire in ~** end on a high note

'**bellico** *a* war *attrib*. **~'coso** *a* warlike. **~ge'rante** *a & nmf* belligerent

'**bello** *a* nice; (*di aspetto*) beautiful; (*uomo*) handsome; (*moralmente*) good; **cosa fai di ~ stasera?** what are you up to tonight?; **oggi fa ~** it's a nice day; **una bella cifra** a lot; **nel bel piatto di pasta** a big plate of pasta; **nel bel mezzo** right in the middle; **un bel niente**

absolutely nothing; **bell'e fatto** over and done with; **bell'amico!** [a] fine friend he is/you are!; **questa è bella!** that's a good one!; **scamparla bella** have a narrow escape ● *nm* (*bellezza*) beauty; (*innamorato*) sweetheart; **sul più ~** at the crucial moment; **il ~ è che…** the funny thing is that…

'**belva** *nf* wild beast

be'molle *nm* Mus flat

ben *vedi* **bene**

benché *conj* though, although

'**benda** *nf* bandage; (*per occhi*) blindfold. **ben'dare** *vt* bandage; blindfold (*occhi*)

'**bene** *adv* well; **ben ~** thoroughly; **~! good!; star ~** (*di salute*) be well; (*vestito, stile:*) suit; (*finanziariamente*) be well off; **non sta ~** (*non è educato*) it's not nice; **sta/va ~!** all right!; **ti sta ~!** [it] serves you right!; **ti auguro ~** I wish you well; **di ~ in meglio** better and better; **fare ~** (*aver ragione*) do the right thing; **fare ~ a** (*cibo:*) be good for; **una persona per ~** a good person; **per ~** (*fare*) properly; **è ben difficile** it's very difficult; **come tu ben sai** as you well know; **lo credo ~!** I can well believe it! ● *nm* good; **per il tuo ~** for your own good. **beni** *nmpl* (*averi*) property *sg*; **un ~ di famiglia** a family heirloom

bene'detto *a* blessed

bene'di|re *vt* bless. **~zi'one** *nf* blessing

benedu'cato *a* well-mannered

benefat|'tore, -'trice *nm* benefactor ● *nf* benefactress

benefi'care *vt* help

benefi'cenza *nf* charity

benefici'ar|e *vi* **~e di** profit by. **~io, -a** *a & nmf* beneficiary. **bene'ficio** *nm* benefit. **be'nefico** *a* beneficial; (*di beneficenza*) charitable

bene'placito *nm* consent, approval

be'nessere *nm* well-being

bene'stante _a_ well-off ● _nmf_ well-off person

bene'stare _nm_ consent

benevo'lenza _nf_ benevolence. **be'nevolo** _a_ benevolent

ben'fatto _a_ well-made

'beni _nmpl_ property _sg_; _Fin_ assets; ~ **di consumo** consumer goods

benia'mino _nm_ favourite

be'nigno _a_ kindly; _Med_ benign

beninfor'mato _a_ well-informed

benintenzio'nato, -a _a_ well-meaning ● _nmf_ well-meaning person

benin'teso _adv_ needless to say, of course

benpen'sante _a_ & _nmf_ self-righteous

benser'vito _nm_ **dare il ~ a** qcno give sb the sack

bensì _conj_ but rather

benve'nuto _a_ & _nm_ welcome

ben'visto _a_ **essere ~** go down well (**da** with)

benvo'lere _vt_ **farsi ~ da** qcno win sb's affection; **prendere** qcno **in ~** take a liking to sb; **essere benvoluto da tutti** to be well-liked by everyone

ben'zina _nf_ petrol, gas _Am_; **far ~** get petrol. **~ verde** unleaded petrol. **benzi'naio, -a** _nmf_ petrol station attendant

'bere _vt_ drink; (_assorbire_) absorb; _fig_ swallow ● _nm_ drinking; (_bevande_) drinks _pl_

berga'motto _nm_ bergamot

ber'lina _nf_ _Auto_ saloon

Ber'lino _nm_ Berlin

ber'muda _nfpl_ (_pantaloni_) Bermuda shorts

ber'noccolo _nm_ bump; (_disposizione_) flair

ber'retto _nm_ beret, cap

bersagli'are _vt_ _fig_ bombard. **ber'saglio** _nm_ target

be'stemmia _nf_ swear-word; (_maledizione_) oath; (_sproposito_) blasphemy. **~'are** _vi_ swear

'bestia _nf_ animal; (_persona brutale_) beast; (_persona sciocca_) fool;

andare in ~a _fam_ blow one's top. **~'ale** _a_ bestial; (_espressione, violenza_) brutal; (_fam: freddo, fame_) terrible. **~alità** _nf inv_ bestiality; _fig_ nonsense. **~'ame** _nm_ livestock

'bettola _nf_ _fig_ dive

be'tulla _nf_ birch

be'vanda _nf_ drink

bevi'tore, -'trice _nmf_ drinker

be'vut|a _nf_ drink. **~o** _pp di_ **bere**

bi'ada _nf_ fodder

bianche'ria _nf_ linen. **~ intima** underwear

bi'anco _a_ white; (_foglio, pagina ecc_) blank ● _nm_ white; **mangiare in ~** not eat any fried or heavy foods; **andare in ~** _fam_ not score; **in ~ e nero** (_film, fotografia_) black and white, monochrome; **passare una notte in ~** have a sleepless night

bian'core _nm_ (_bianchezza_) whiteness

bianco'spino _nm_ hawthorn

biasci'care _vt_ (_mangiare_) eat noisily; (_parlare_) mumble

biasi'mare _vt_ blame. **bi'asimo** _nm_ blame

'Bibbia _nf_ Bible

bibe'ron _nm inv_ [baby's] bottle

bi'bita _nf_ [soft] drink

'biblico _a_ biblical

bibliogra'fia _nf_ bibliography

biblio'te|ca _nf_ library; (_mobile_) bookcase. **~'cario, -a** _nmf_ librarian

bicarbo'nato _nm_ bicarbonate. **~ di sodio** bicarbonate of soda

bicchi'ere _nm_ glass

bicchie'rino _nm fam_ tipple

bici'cletta _nf_ bicycle; **andare in ~** ride a bicycle

bico'lore _a_ two-coloured

bidè _nm inv_ bidet

bi'dello, -a _nmf_ janitor, [school] caretaker

bido'nata _nf fam_ swindle

bi'done _nm_ bin; (_fam: truffa_) swindle; **fare un ~ a** qcno _fam_ stand sb up

bien'nale *a* biennial

bi'ennio *nm* two-year period

bi'etola *nf* beet

bifo'cale *a* bifocal

bi'folco, -a *nmf fig* boor

bifor'c|arsi *vr* fork. **~azi'one** *nf* fork. **~uto** *a* forked

biga'mia *nf* bigamy. **'bigamo, -a** *a* bigamous ● *nmf* bigamist

bighello'nare *vi* loaf around. **bighel'lone** *nm* loafer

bigiotte'ria *nf* costume jewellery; (*negozio*) jeweller's

bigliet't|aio *nm* booking clerk; (*sui treni*) ticket-collector. **~e'ria** *nf* ticket-office; *Theat* box-office

bigli'et|to *nm* ticket; (*lettera breve*) note; (*cartoncino*) card; (*di banca*) banknote. **~to da visita** business card. **~'tone** *nm* (*fam: soldi*) big one

bignè *nm inv* cream puff

bigo'dino *nm* roller

bi'gotto *nm* bigot

bi'kini *nm inv* bikini

bi'lanc|ia *nf* scales *pl*; (*di orologio, Comm*) balance; **B~a** *Astr* Libra. **~'are** *vt* balance; *fig* weigh. **~o** *nm* budget; *Comm* balance sheet; **fare il ~o** balance the books; *fig* take stock

'bil|e *nf* bile; *fig* rage

bili'ardo *nm* billiards *sg*

'bilico *nm* equilibrium; **in ~** in the balance

bi'lingue *a* bilingual

bili'one *nm* billion

bilo'cale *a* two-room

'bimbo, -a *nmf* child

bimen'sile *a* fortnightly

bime'strale *a* bimonthly

bi'nario *nm* track; (*piattaforma*) platform

bi'nocolo *nm* binoculars *pl*

bio'chimica *nf* biochemistry

biodegra'dabile *a* biodegradable

bio'etica *nf* bioethics

bio'fisica *nf* biophysics

biogra'fia *nf* biography. **bio'grafico** *a* biographical. **bi'ografo, -a** *a* *nmf* biographer

biolo'gia *nf* biology. **bio'logico** *a* biological. **bi'ologo, -a** *nmf* biologist

bi'ond|a *nf* blonde. **~o** *a* blond ● *nm* fair colour; (*uomo*) fair-haired man

bio'sfera *nf* biosphere

bi'ossido *nm* **~ di carbonio** carbon dioxide

biparti'tismo *nm* two-party system

'birba *nf*, **bir'bante** *nm* rascal, rogue. **bir'bone** *a* wicked

biri'chino, -a *a* naughty ● *nmf* little devil

bi'rillo *nm* skittle

'birr|a *nf* beer; **a tutta ~a** *fig* flat out. **~a chiara** lager. **~a scura** brown ale. **~e'ria** *nf* beer-house; (*fabbrica*) brewery

bis *nm inv* encore

bi'saccia *nf* haversack

bi'sbetic|a *nf* shrew. **~o** *a* bad-tempered

bisbigli'are *vt/i* whisper. **bi'sbiglio** *nm* whisper

'bisca *nf* gambling-house

'biscia *nf* snake

bi'scotto *nm* biscuit

bisessu'ale *a* & *nmf* bisexual

bise'stile *a* **anno ~** leap year

bisetti'manale *a* fortnightly

bi'slacco *a* peculiar

bis'nonno, -a *nmf* great-grandfather; great-grandmother

biso'gn|are *vi* **~a agire subito** we must act at once; **~a farlo** it is necessary to do it; **non ~a venire** you don't have to come. **~o** *nm* need; (*povertà*) poverty; **aver ~o di** need. **~oso** *a* needy; (*povero*) poor; **~oso di** in need of

bi'sonte *nm* bison

bi'stecca *nf* steak

bisticci'are *vi* quarrel. **bi'sticcio** *nm* quarrel; (*gioco di parole*) pun

bistrat'tare *vt* mistreat

'bisturi *nm inv* scalpel

bi'torzolo *nm* lump

'bitter nm inv (bitter) aperitif

bi'vacco nm bivouac

'bivio nm crossroads; (di strada) fork

bizan'tino a Byzantine

'bizza nf tantrum; fare le bizze ⟨bambini:⟩ play up

biz'zarro a bizarre

biz'zeffe adv a ~ galore

blan'dire vt soothe; (allettare) flatter. 'blando a mild

bla'sone nm coat of arms

blate'rare vi blether, blather

'blatta nf cockroach

blin'da|re vt armour-plate. ~to a armoured

blitz nm inv blitz

bloc'car|e vt block; (isolare) cut off; Mil blockade; Comm freeze. ~si vr Mech jam

blocca'sterzo nm steering lock

'blocco nm block; Mil blockade; (dei fitti) restriction; (di carta) pad; (unione) coalition; in ~ Comm in bulk. ~ stradale road-block

bloc-'notes nm inv writing pad

blu a & nm blue

blue-'jeans nmpl jeans

bluff nm inv (carte, fig) bluff. bluf'fare vi (carte, fig) bluff

'blusa nf blouse

'boa nm boa {constrictor}; (sciarpa) {feather} boa ● nf Naut buoy

bo'ato nm rumbling

bo'bina nf spool; (di film) reel; Electr coil

'bocca nf mouth; a ~ aperta dumbfounded; in ~ al lupo! fam break a leg!; fare la respirazione ~ a ~ a qcno give sb mouth to mouth resuscitation or the kiss of life

boc'caccia nf grimace; far boccacce make faces

boc'caglio nm mouthpiece

boc'cale nm jug; (da birra) tankard

bocca'porto nm Naut hatch

boc'cata nf (di fumo) puff; prendere una ~ d'aria get a breath of fresh air

boc'cetta nf small bottle

bocchegg'iare vi gasp

boc'chino nm cigarette holder; (di pipa, Mus) mouthpiece

'bocc|ia nf (palla) bowl; ~e pl (gioco) bowls sg

bocci'a|re vt (agli esami) fail; (respingere) reject; (alle bocce) hit; essere ~to fail; (ripetere) repeat a year. ~tura nf failure

bocci'olo nm bud

boccon'cino nm morsel

boc'cone nm mouthful; (piccolo pasto) snack

boc'coni adv face downwards

'boia nm executioner

boi'ata nf fam rubbish

boicot'tare vt boycott

bo'lero nm bolero

'bolgia nf (caos) bedlam

'bolide nm meteor; passare come un ~ shoot past [like a rocket]

Bo'livi|a nf Bolivia. b~'ano, -a a & nmf Bolivian

'bolla nf bubble; (pustola) blister

bol'la|re vt stamp; fig brand. ~to a fig branded; carta ~ta paper with stamp showing payment of duty

bol'lente a boiling [hot]

bol'let|ta nf bill; essere in ~ta be hard up. ~tino nm bulletin; Comm list

bol'lino nm coupon

bol'li|re vt/i boil. ~to nm boiled meat. ~tore nm boiler; (per l'acqua) kettle. ~tura nf boiling

'bollo nm stamp

bol'lore nm boil; (caldo) intense heat; (fig) ardour

'bomba nf bomb; a prova di ~ bomb-proof

bombarda'mento nm shelling; (con aerei) bombing; fig bombardment. ~ aereo air raid

bombar'd|are vt shell; (con aerei) bomb; fig bombard. ~i'ere nm bomber

bom'betta nf bowler [hat]

'bombola nf cylinder. ~ di gas gas bottle, gas cylinder

bombo'lone *nm* doughnut
bomboni'era *nf* wedding keepsake
bo'naccia *nf Naut* calm
bonacci'one, -a *nmf* good-natured person ● *a* good-natured
bo'nario *a* kindly
bo'nifica *nf* land reclamation. **bonifi'care** *vt* reclaim
bo'nifico *nm Comm* discount; (bancario) [credit] transfer
bontà *nf* goodness; (gentilezza) kindness
'**bora** *nf* bora (cold north-east wind in the upper Adriatic)
borbot'ta|re *vi* mumble; (stomaco:) rumble. **~io** *nm* mumbling; (di stomaco) rumbling
'**borchia** *nf* stud. **~'ato** *a* studded
bor'da|re *vt* border. **~'tura** *nf* border
bor'deaux *a inv* (colore) claret
bor'dello *nm* brothel; *fig* bedlam; (disordine) mess
'**bordo** *nm* border; (estremità) edge; **a ~** *Naut, Aeron* on board
bor'gata *nf* hamlet
bor'ghese *a* bourgeois; (abito) civilian; **in ~** in civilian dress; (poliziotto) in plain clothes
borghe'sia *nf* middle classes *pl*
'**borgo** *nm* village; (quartiere) district
'**bori|a** *nf* conceit. **~'oso** *a* conceited
bor'lotto [**fagiolo**] **~** borlotto bean
boro'talco *nm* talcum powder
bor'raccia *nf* flask
'**bors|a** *nf* bag; (borsetta) handbag; (valori) Stock Exchange. **~a dell'acqua calda** hot-water bottle. **~a frigo** cool-box. **~a della spesa** shopping bag. **~a di studio** scholarship. **~al'olo** *nm* pickpocket. **~el'lino** *nm* purse. **~'sista** *nmf Fin* speculator; *Sch* scholarship holder
bor'se|llo *nm* (portamonete) purse; (borsetto) man's handbag.

~tta *nf* handbag. **~tto** *nm* man's handbag
bo'scaglia *nf* woodlands *pl*
boscai'olo *nm* woodman; (guardaboschi) forester
'**bosco** *nm* wood. **bo'scoso** *a* wooded
bossolo *nm* cartridge case
bo'tanic|a *nf* botany. **~o** *a* botanical ● *nm* botanist
botola *nf* trapdoor
'**botta** *nf* blow; (rumore) bang; **fare a botte** come to blows. **~ e risposta** *fig* thrust and counterthrust
'**botte** *nf* barrel
bot'te|ga *nf* shop; (di artigiano) workshop. **~'gaio, -a** *nmf* shopkeeper. **~'ghino** *nm Theatr* box-office; (del lotto) lottery-shop
bot'tiglia *nf* bottle; **in ~a** bottled. **~e'ria** *nf* wine shop
bot'tino *nm* loot; *Mil* booty
'**botto** *nm* bang; **di ~** all of a sudden
bot'tone *nm* button; *Bot* bud
box *nm inv* (per cavalli) loosebox; (recinto per bambini) play-pen
'**boxe** *nf* boxing
'**bozza** *nf* draft; *Typ* proof; (bernoccolo) bump. **boz'zetto** *nm* sketch
'**bozzolo** *nm* cocoon
brac'care *vt* hunt
brac'cetto *nm* **a ~** arm in arm
bracci'a|le *nm* bracelet; (fascia) armband. **~'letto** *nm* bracelet; (di orologio) watch-strap
bracci'ante *nm* day labourer
bracci'ata *nf* (nel nuoto) stroke
'**bracci|o** *nm* (pl *nf* **braccia**) arm; (di fiume, pl **bracci**) arm. **~'olo** *nm* (di sedia) arm[rest]; (da nuoto) armband
'**bracco** *nm* hound
bracconi'ere *nm* poacher
braci|e *nf* embers *pl*; **alla ~e** chargrilled. **~i'ere** *nm* brazier. **~'ola** *nf* chop
'**brado** *a* **allo stato ~** in the wild

'**brama** nf longing. **bra'mare** vt long for. **bramo'sia** nf yearning
'**branca** nf branch
'**branchia** nf gill
'**branco** nm (di cani) pack; (pej: di persone) gang
branco'lare vi grope
'**branda** nf camp-bed
bran'dello nm scrap; **a brandelli** in tatters
bran'dire vt brandish
'**brano** nm piece; (di libro) passage
Bra'sile nm Brazil. **b~i'ano, -a** a & nmf Brazilian
bra'vata nf bragging
'**bravo** a good; (abile) clever; (coraggioso) brave; **~!** well done!. **bra'vura** nf skill
'**breccia** nf breach; **sulla ~** fig very successful, at the top
bre'saola nf dried, salted beef sliced thinly and eaten cold
bre'tella nf shoulder-strap; **bretelle** pl (di calzoni) braces
'**breve** a brief, short; **in ~** briefly; **tra ~** shortly
brevet'tare vt patent. **bre'vetto** nm patent; (attestato) licence
brevità nf shortness
'**brezza** nf breeze
'**bricco** nm jug
bric'cone nm blackguard; hum rascal
briciol|a nf crumb; fig grain. **~o** nm fragment
'**briga** nf (fastidio) trouble; (lite) quarrel; **attaccar ~** pick a quarrel; **prendersi la ~ di fare qcsa** go to the trouble of doing sth
brigadi'ere nm (dei carabinieri) sergeant
bri'gante nm bandit; hum rogue
bri'gare vi intrigue
bri'gata nf brigade; (gruppo) group
briga'tista nmf Pol member of the Red Brigades
'**briglia** nf rein; **a ~ sciolta** at breakneck speed
bril'lante a brilliant; (scintillante) sparkling ●nm diamond

bril'lare vi shine; (metallo:) glitter; (scintillare) sparkle
'**brillo** a tipsy
'**brina** nf hoar-frost
brin'dare vi toast; **~ a qcno** drink a toast to sb
'**brindisi** nm inv toast
bri'tannico a British
'**brivido** nm shiver; (di paura ecc) shudder; (di emozione) thrill
brizzo'lato a greying
'**brocca** nf jug
broc'cato nm brocade
'**broccoli** nmpl broccoli sg
bro'daglia nf pej dishwater
'**brodo** nm broth; (per cucinare) stock. **~ ristretto** consommé
broglio nm **~ elettorale** gerrymandering
bron'chite nf bronchitis
'**broncio** nm sulk; **fare il ~** sulk
bronto'l|are vi grumble; (tuono ecc:) rumble. **~io** nm grumbling; (di tuono) rumbling. **~one, -a** nmf grumbler
'**bronzo** nm bronze
bros'sura nf **edizione in ~** paperback
bru'care vt (pecora:) graze
bruciacchi'are vt scorch
brucia'pelo adv **a ~** point-blank
bruci'a|re vt burn; (scottare) scald; (incendiare) set fire to ●vi burn; (scottare) scald. **~rsi** vr burn oneself. **~to a** fig burnt-out. **~tore** nm burner. **~tura** nf burn. **bruci'ore** nm burning sensation
'**bruco** nm grub
bru'folo nm spot
brughi'era nf heath
bruli'c|are vi swarm. **~hio** nm swarming
'**brullo** a bare
'**bruma** nf mist
'**bruno** a brown; (occhi, capelli) dark
brusca'mente adv (di colpo) suddenly
bru'schetta nf toasted bread rubbed with garlic and sprinkled with olive oil

'**brusco** *a* sharp; (*persona*) brusque, abrupt; (*improvviso*) sudden

bru'sio *nm* buzzing

bru'tal|e *a* brutal. **~ità** *nf inv* brutality. **~iz'zare** *vt* brutalize. '**bruto** *a & nm* brute

brut'tezza *nf* ugliness

'**brut|to** *a* ugly; (*tempo, tipo, situazione, affare*) nasty; (*cattivo*) bad; **~ta copia** rough copy; **~to tiro** dirty trick. **~'tura** *nf* ugly thing

'**buca** *nf* hole; (*avvallamento*) hollow. **~ delle lettere** (*a casa*) letter-box

buca'neve *nm inv* snowdrop

bu'car|e *vt* make a hole in; (*pungere*) prick; punch (*biglietti*) ● *vi* have a puncture. **~si** *vr* prick oneself; (*con droga*) shoot up

bu'cato *nm* washing

'**buccia** *nf* peel, skin

bucherel'lare *vt* riddle

'**buco** *nm* hole

bu'dello *nm* (*pl f* **budella**) bowel

bu'dino *nm* pudding

'**bue** *nm* (*pl* **buoi**) ox; **carne di ~** beef

'**bufalo** *nm* buffalo

bu'fera *nf* storm; (*di neve*) blizzard

buf'fetto *nm* cuff

'**buffo** *a* funny; *Theat* comic ● *nm* funny thing. **~'nata** *nf* (*scherzo*) joke. **buf'fone** *nm* buffoon; **fare il buffone** play the fool

bu'gi|a *nf* lie; **~a pietosa** white lie. **~'ardo, -a** *a* lying ● *nmf* liar

bugi'gattolo *nm* cubby-hole

'**buio** *a* dark ● *nm* darkness; **al ~** in the dark; **~ pesto** pitch dark

'**bulbo** *nm* bulb; (*dell'occhio*) eyeball

Bulga'ria *nf* Bulgaria. **'bulgaro, -a** *a & nmf* Bulgarian

buli'mia *nf* bulimia. **bu'limico** *a* bulimic

'**bullo** *nm* bully

bul'lone *nm* bolt

'**bunker** *nm inv* bunker

buona'fede *nf* good faith

buona'notte *int* good night

buona'sera *int* good evening

buon'giorno *int* good morning; (*di pomeriggio*) good afternoon

buon'grado: di ~ *adv* willingly

buongu'staio, -a *nm* gourmet. **buon'gusto** *nm* good taste

bu'ono *a* good; (*momento*) right; **dar ~** (*convalidare*) accept; **alla buona** easy-going; (*cena*) informal; **buona notte/sera** good night/evening; **buon compleanno/Natale!** happy birthday/merry Christmas!; **~ senso** common sense; **di buon'ora** early; **una buona volta** once and for all; **buona parte di** the best part of; **tre ore buone** three good hours ● *nm* good; (*in film*) goody; (*tagliando*) voucher; (*titolo*) bond; **con le buone** gently; **~ sconto** money-off coupon ● *nmf* **buono, a a nulla** dead loss

buontem'pone, -a *nmf* happy-go-lucky person

buonu'more *nm* good temper

buonu'scita *nf* retirement bonus; (*di dirigente*) golden handshake

burat'tino *nm* puppet

'**burbero** *a* surly; (*nei modi*) rough

buro'cra|te *nm* bureaucrat. **buro'cratico** *a* bureaucratic. **~'zia** *nf* bureaucracy

bur'ra|sca *nf* storm. **~'scoso** *a* stormy

'**burro** *nm* butter

bur'rone *nm* ravine

bus'car|e *vt*, **~si** *vr* catch; **~le** *fam* get a hiding

bus'sare *vi* knock

'**bussola** *nf* compass; **perdere la ~** lose one's bearings

'**busta** *nf* envelope; (*astuccio*) case. **~ paga** pay packet. **~ per medicine**) sachet

busta'rella *nf* bribe. **bu'stina** *nf* (*di tè*) tea bag; (*per medicine*) sachet

'**busto** *nm* bust; (*indumento*) girdle

but'tar|e *vt* throw; **~e giù** (*demolire*) knock down; (*inghiottire*) gulp down; scribble down (*scritto*); *fam* put on (*pasta*); (*scoraggiare*) dishearten; **~e via** throw away.

~**si** *vr* throw oneself; *(saltare)* jump

butte'rato *a* pock-marked

buz'zurro *nm fam* yokel

....

Cc

....

caba'ret *nm inv* cabaret

ca'bina *nf Naut, Aeron* cabin; *(balneare)* beach hut. ~ **elettorale** polling booth. ~ **di pilotaggio** cockpit. ~ **telefonica** telephone box. **cabi'nato** *nm* cabin cruiser

ca'cao *nm* cocoa

'cacca *nf fam* pooh

'caccia *nf* hunt; *(con fucile)* shooting; *(inseguimento)* chase; *(selvaggina)* game ● *nm inv Aeron* fighter; *Naut* destroyer

cacciabombardi'ere *nm* fighter-bomber

cacciagi'one *nf* game

cacci'a|re *vt* hunt; *(mandar via)* chase away; *(scacciare)* drive out; *(ficcare)* shove ● *vi* go hunting. ~**rsi** *vr* hide; *(nascondersi)* hide; ~**rsi nei guai** get into trouble; **alla** ~**'tora** *a Culin* chasseur. ~**'tore, -'trice** *nmf* hunter. ~**tore di frodo** poacher

caccia'vite *nm inv* screwdriver

ca'chet *nm inv Med* capsule; *(colorante)* colour rinse; *(stile)* cachet

'cachi *nm inv (albero, frutta)* persimmon

'cacio *nm (formaggio)* cheese

'caco *nm fam (frutto)* persimmon

'cactus *nm inv* cactus

ca'da|vere *nm* corpse. ~**'verico** *a fig* deathly pale

ca'dente *a* falling; *(casa)* crumbling

ca'denza *nf* cadence; *(ritmo)* rhythm; *Mus* cadenza

ca'de|re *vi* fall; *(capelli ecc:)* fall out; *(capitombolare)* tumble; *(vestito ecc:)* hang; **far** ~ *(di mano)*

drop; ~ **dal sonno** feel very sleepy; **lasciar** ~ drop; ~ **dalle nuvole** *fig* be taken aback

ca'detto *nm* cadet

ca'duta *nf* fall; *(di capelli)* loss; *fig* downfall

caffè *nm inv* coffee; *(locale)* café. ~ **corretto** espresso coffee with a dash of liqueur. ~ **lungo** weak black coffee. ~ **macchiato** coffee with a dash of milk. ~ **ristretto** extra-strong espresso coffee. ~ **solubile** instant coffee. ~**'ina** *nf* caffeine. ~**'latte** *nm inv* white coffee.

caffetti'era *nf* coffee-pot

cafo'naggine *nf* boorishness

cafo'nata *nf* boorishness

ca'fone, -a *nmf* boor

ca'gare *vi fam* crap

cagio'nare *vt* cause

cagio'nevole *a* delicate

cagli'ar|e *vi,* ~**si** *vr* curdle

'cagna *nf* bitch

ca'gnara *nf fam* din

ca'gnesco *a* **guardare qcno in** ~ scowl at sb

'cala *nf* creek

cala'brone *nm* hornet

cala'maio *nm* inkpot

cala'mari *nmpl* squid *sg*

cala'mita *nf* magnet

calamità *nf inv* calamity

ca'lar|e *vi* come down; *(vento:)* drop; *(diminuire)* fall; *(tramontare)* set ● *vt (abbassare)* lower; *(nei lavori a maglia)* decrease ● *nm (di luna)* waning. ~**si** *vr* lower oneself

'calca *nf* throng

cal'cagno *nm* heel

cal'care¹ *nm* limestone

cal'care² *vt* tread; *(premere)* press [down]; ~ **la mano** *fig* exaggerate; ~ **le orme di qcno** *fig* follow in sb's footsteps

'calce¹ *nf* lime

'calce² *nm* **in** ~ at the foot of the page

calce'struzzo *nm* concrete

cal'cetto *nm* *Sport* five-a-side [football]

calci'a|re *vt* kick. **~'tore** *nm* footballer

cal'cina *nf* mortar

calci'naccio *nm* (*pezzo di intonaco*) flake of plaster

'calcio¹ *nm* kick; *Sport* football; (*di arma da fuoco*) butt; **dare un ~ a** kick. **~ d'angolo** corner [kick]

'calcio² *nm* (*chimica*) calcium

'calco *nm* (*su carta*) tracing; (*arte*) cast

calco'la|re *vt* calculate; (*considerare*) consider. **~'tore** *a* calculating ● *nm* calculator; (*macchina elettronica*) computer

'calcolo *nm* calculation; *Med* stone

cal'daia *nf* boiler

caldar'rosta *nf* roast chestnut

caldeggi'are *vt* support

'caldo *a* warm; (*molto caldo*) hot ● *nm* heat; **avere ~** be warm/hot; **fa ~** it is warm/hot

calen'dario *nm* calendar

'calibro *nm* calibre; (*strumento*) callipers *pl*; **di grosso ~** (*persona*) top *attrib*

'calice *nm* goblet; *Relig* chalice

ca'ligine *nm* fog; (*industriale*) smog

calligra'fia *nf* handwriting; (*cinese*) calligraphy

cal'lista *nmf* chiropodist. **'callo** *nm* corn; **fare il callo a** become hardened to. **cal'loso** *a* callous

'calma *nf* calm. **cal'mante** *a* calming ● *nm* sedative. **cal'mare** *vt* calm [down]; (*lenire*) soothe. **cal'marsi** *vr* calm down; (*vento:*) drop; (*dolore:*) die down. **calmo** *a* calm

'calo *nm* *Comm* fall; (*di volume*) shrinkage; (*di peso*) loss

calorosa'mente *adv* (*cordialmente*) warmly

ca'lore *nm* heat; (*moderato*) warmth; **in ~** (*animale:*) on heat. **calo'roso** *a* warm

calo'ria *nf* calorie

ca'lorico *a* calorific

calo'rifero *nm* radiator

calpe'stare *vt* trample [down]; *fig* trample on (*diritti, sentimenti*); **vietato ~ l'erba** keep off the grass

calpe'stio *nm* (*passi*) footsteps

ca'lunnia *nf* slander. **~'are** *vt* slander. **~'oso** *a* slanderous

ca'lura *nf* heat

cal'vario *nm* Calvary; *fig* trial

cal'vizie *nf* baldness. **'calvo** *a* bald

'calza *nf* (*da donna*) stocking; (*da uomo*) sock. **~a'maglia** *nf* tights *pl*; (*per danza*) leotard

cal'zante *a* *fig* fitting

cal'za|re *vt* (*indossare*) wear; (*mettersi*) put on ● *vi* fit

calza'scarpe *nm inv* shoehorn

calza'tura *nf* footwear

calzatu'rificio *nm* shoe factory

cal'zetta *nf* è **una mezza ~** *fig* he's no use

calzet'tone *nm* knee-length woollen sock. **cal'zino** *nm* sock

calzo'l|aio *nm* shoemaker. **~e'ria** *nf* (*negozio*) shoe shop

calzon'cini *nmpl* shorts. **~ da bagno** swimming trunks

cal'zone *nm* *Culin* folded pizza with tomato and mozzarella or ricotta inside

cal'zoni *nmpl* trousers, pants *Am*

camale'onte *nm* chameleon

cambi'ale *nf* bill of exchange

cambia'mento *nm* change

cambi'ar|e *vt/i* change; move (*casa*); (*fare cambio di*) exchange; **~e rotta** *Naut* alter course. **~si** *vr* change. **'cambio** *nm* change; (*Comm, scambio*) exchange; *Mech* gear; **dare il cambio a** qcno relieve sb; **in cambio di** in exchange for

'camera *nf* room; (*mobili*) [bedroom] suite; *Phot* camera; **C~** *Pol, Comm* Chamber. **~ ardente** funeral parlour. **~ d'aria** inner tube. **C~ di Commercio** Chamber of Commerce. **C~ dei Deputati** *Pol* ≈ House of Commons. **~ doppia**

double room. ~ **da letto** bedroom. ~ **matrimoniale** double room. ~ **oscura** darkroom. ~ **singola** single room

came'ra|ta¹ *nf* (*dormitorio*) dormitory; *Mil* barrack room

came'ra|ta² *nmf* (*amico*) mate; *Pol* comrade. **~'tismo** *nm* comradeship

cameri'era *nf* maid; (*di ristorante*) waitress; (*in albergo*) chambermaid; (*di bordo*) stewardess

cameri'ere *nm* manservant; (*di ristorante*) waiter; (*di bordo*) steward

came'rino *nm* dressing-room

'camice *nm* overall. **cami'cetta** *nf* blouse. **ca'micia** *nf* shirt; **uovo in camicia** poached egg. **camicia di notte** nightdress

cami'netto *nm* fireplace

ca'mino *nm* chimney; (*focolare*) fireplace

'camion *nm inv* lorry *Br*, truck

camion'cino *nm* van

camio'netta *nf* jeep

camio'nista *nmf* lorry driver *Br*, truck driver

cam'mello *nm* camel; (*tessuto*) camel-hair ● *a inv* (*colore*) camel

cam'meo *nm* cameo

cammi'na|re *vi* walk; ⟨*auto, orologio*⟩ go. **~ta** *nf* walk; **fare una ~ta** go for a walk. **cam'mino** *nm* way; **essere in cammino** be on the way; **mettersi in cammino** set out

camo'milla *nf* camomile; (*bevanda*) camomile tea

ca'morra *nf* local mafia

ca'moscio *nm* chamois; (*pelle*) suede

cam'pagna *nf* country; (*paesaggio*) countryside; *Comm, Mil* campaign; **in ~** in the country. **~ elettorale** election campaign. **~ pubblicitaria** marketing campaign. **campa'gnolo, -a** *a* rustic ● *nm* countryman ● *nf* countrywoman

cam'pale *a* field *attrib*; **giornata ~** *fig* strenuous day

cam'pa|na *nf* bell; (*di vetro*) belljar. **~'nella** *nf* (*di tenda*) curtain ring. **~'nello** *nm* door-bell; (*cicalino*) buzzer

campa'nile *nm* belfry

campani'lismo *nm* parochialism

campani'lista *nmf* person with a parochial outlook

cam'panula *nf Bot* campanula

cam'pare *vi* live; (*a stento*) get by

cam'pato *a* ~ **in aria** unfounded

campeggi'a|re *vi* camp; (*spiccare*) stand out. **~tore**, **~'trice** *nmf* camper. **cam'peggio** *nm* camping; (*terreno*) campsite

cam'pestre *a* rural

'camping *nm inv* campsite

campio'nari|o *nm* [set of] samples ● *a* samples; **fiera ~a** trade fair

campio'nato *nm* championship

campiona'tura *nf* (*di merce*) range of samples

campi'on|e *nm* champion; *Comm* sample; (*esemplare*) specimen. **~'essa** *nf* ladies' champion

'campo *nm* field; (*accampamento*) camp. **~ da calcio** football pitch. **~ di concentramento** concentration camp. **~ da golf** golf course. **~ da tennis** tennis court

campo'santo *nm* cemetery

camuf'far|e *vt* disguise. **~si** *vr* disguise oneself

'Cana|da *nm* Canada. **~'dese** *a & nmf* Canadian

ca'naglia *nf* scoundrel; (*plebaglia*) rabble

ca'nal|e *nm* channel; (*artificiale*) canal. **~iz'zare** *vt* channel ⟨*acque*⟩. **~izzazi'one** *nf* channelling; (*rete*) pipes *pl*

'canapa *nf* hemp

cana'rino *nm* canary

cancel'la|re *vt* cross out; (*con la gomma*) rub out; *fig* wipe out; (*annullare*) cancel; *Comput* delete, erase. **~'tura** *nf* erasure. **~zi'one** *nf* cancellation; *Comput* deletion

cancelle'ria *nf* chancellery; *(articoli per scrivere)* stationery

cancelli'ere *nm* chancellor; *(di tribunale)* clerk

can'cello *nm* gate

cance'ro|geno *nm* carcinogen ●*a* carcinogenic. ~'**roso** *a* cancerous

can'crena *nf* gangrene

'**cancro** *nm* cancer. **C~** *Astr* Cancer

candeg'gi|na *nf* bleach. ~'**are** *vt* bleach. **can'deggio** *nm* bleaching

can'de|la *nf* candle; *Auto* spark plug; ~'**labro** *nm* candelabra. ~**li'ere** *nm* candlestick

candida'mente *adv* candidly

candi'da|rsi *vr* stand as a candidate. ~**to, -a** *nmf* candidate. ~'**tura** *nf Pol* candidacy; *(per lavoro)* application

'**candido** *a* snow-white; *(sincero)* candid; *(puro)* pure

can'dito *a* candied

can'dore *nm* whiteness; *fig* innocence

'**cane** *nm* dog; *(di arma da fuoco)* cock; **un tempo da cani** foul weather. ~ **da caccia** hunting dog

ca'nestro *nm* basket

cangi'ante *a* iridescent; **seta ~** shot silk

can'guro *nm* kangaroo

ca'ni|le *nm* kennel; *(di allevamento)* kennels *pl.* ~ **municipale** dog pound

ca'nino *a & nm* canine

'**canna** *nf* reed; *(da zucchero)* cane; *(di fucile)* barrel; *(bastone)* stick; *(di bicicletta)* crossbar; *(asta)* rod; *(fam: hascisch)* joint; **povero in ~** destitute. ~ **da pesca** fishing-rod

can'nella *nf* cinnamon

can'neto *nm* bed of reeds

canni'ba|le *nm* cannibal. ~'**lismo** *nm* cannibalism

cannocchi'ale *nm* telescope

canno'nata *nf* cannon shot; **è una ~** *fig* it's brilliant

cannon'cino *nm* *(dolce)* cream horn

can'none *nm* cannon; *fig* ace

can'nuccia *nf* [drinking] straw; *(di pipa)* stem

ca'noa *nf* canoe

'**canone** *nm* canon; *(affitto)* rent; **equo ~** fair rents act

canoniz'za|re *vt* canonize. ~**z'zare** *vt* canonize. ~**zzazi'one** *nf* canonization

ca'noro *a* melodious

ca'notta *nf* *(estiva)* vest top

canot'taggio *nm* canoeing; *(voga)* rowing

canotti'era *nf* singlet

canotti'ere *nm* oarsman

ca'notto *nm* [rubber] dinghy

cano'vaccio *nm* *(trama)* plot; *(straccio)* duster

can'tante *nmf* singer

can't|are *vt/i* sing. ~**au'tore, ~a'trice** *nmf* singer-songwriter. ~**icchi'are** *vt* sing softly; *(a bocca chiusa)* hum

canti'ere *nm* yard; *Naut* shipyard; *(di edificio)* construction site. ~ **navale** naval dockyard

canti'lena *nf* singsong; *(ninna-nanna)* lullaby

can'tina *nf* cellar; *(osteria)* wine shop

'**canto¹** *nm* singing; *(canzone)* song; *Relig* chant; *(poesia)* poem

'**canto²** *nm* *(angolo)* corner; *(lato)* side; **dal ~ mio** for my part; **d'altro ~** on the other hand

canto'nata *nf* **prendere una ~** *fig* be sadly mistaken

can'tone *nm* canton; *(angolo)* corner

can'tuccio *nm* nook

canzo'na|re *vt* tease. ~'**torio** *a* teasing. ~'**tura** *nf* teasing

can'zo|ne *nf* song. ~'**netta** *nf fam* pop song. ~**ni'ere** *nm* songbook

'**caos** *nm* chaos. **ca'otico** *a* chaotic

C.A.P. *nm abbr* (**Codice di Avviamento Postale**) post code, zip code *Am*

ca'pac|e *a* able; *(esperto)* skilled;

⟨*stadio, contenitore*⟩ big; **~e di** (*disposto a*) capable of. **~ità** *nf inv* ability; (*attitudine*) skill; (*capienza*) capacity

capaci'tarsi *vr* **~ di** (*rendersi conto*) understand; (*accorgersi*) realize

ca'panna *nf* hut

capan'nello *nm* **fare ~ intorno a qcno/qcsa** gather round sb/sth

capan'none *nm* shed; *Aeron* hangar

ca'parbio *a* obstinate

ca'parra *nf* deposit

capa'tina *nf* short visit; **fare una ~ in città/da qcno** pop into town/ in on sb

ca'pel|lo *nm* hair; **~li** *pl* (*capigliatura*) hair *sg*. **~lone** *nm* hippie. **~luto** *a* hairy

capez'zale *nm* bolster; *fig* bedside

ca'pezzolo *nm* nipple

capi'en|te *a* capacious. **~za** *nf* capacity

capiglia'tura *nf* hair

ca'pire *vt* understand; **~ male** misunderstand; **si capisce!** naturally!; **si, ho capito** yes, I see

capi'ta|le *a Jur* capital; (*principale*) main ● *nf* (*città*) capital ● *nm* *Comm* capital. **~lismo** *nm* capitalism. **~lista** *nmf* capitalist. **~listico** *a* capitalist

capitane'ria *nf* **~ di porto** port authorities *pl*

capi'tano *nm* captain

capi'tare *vi* (*giungere per caso*) come; (*accadere*) happen

capi'tello *nm Archit* capital

capito'la|re *vi* capitulate. **~zi'one** *nf* capitulation

ca'pitolo *nm* chapter

capi'tombolo *nm* headlong fall; **fare un ~** tumble down

'capo *nm* head; (*chi comanda*) boss *fam*; (*di vestiario*) item; *Geog* cape; (*in tribù*) chief; (*parte estrema*) top; **a ~** (*in dettato*) new paragraph; **da ~** over again; **in ~ a un mese** within a month; **giramento di ~** dizziness; **mal di ~** head-

ache; **~ d'abbigliamento** item of clothing. **~ d'accusa** *Jur* charge, count. **~ di bestiame** head of cattle

capo'banda *nm Mus* bandmaster; (*di delinquenti*) ringleader

ca'poccia *nm* (*fam: testa*) nut

capocci'one, -a *nmf fam* brainbox

capo'danno *nm* New Year's Day

capofa'miglia *nm* head of the family

capo'fitto *nm* **a ~** headlong

capo'giro *nm* giddiness

capola'voro *nm* masterpiece

capo'linea *nm* terminus

capo'lino *nm* **fare ~** peep in

capoluogo *nm* main town

capo'rale *nm* lance-corporal

capo'squadra *nmf Sport* team captain

capo'stipite *nmf* (*di famiglia*) progenitor

capo'tavola *nmf* head of the table

capo'treno *nm* guard

capouf'ficio *nmf* head clerk

capo'verso *nm* first line

capo'vol|gere *vt* overturn; *fig* reverse. **~gersi** *vr* overturn; (*barca:*) capsize; *fig* be reversed. **~to** *pp di* **capovolgere** *a* upside-down

'cappa *nf* cloak; (*di camino*) cowl; (*di cucina*) hood

cap'pel|la *nf* chapel. **~lano** *nm* chaplain

cap'pello *nm* hat. **~ a cilindro** top hat

'cappero *nm* caper

'cappio *nm* noose

cap'pone *nm* capon

cap'potto *nm* [over]coat

cappuc'cino (*frate*) Capuchin; (*bevanda*) white coffee

cap'puccio *nm* hood; (*di penna stilografica*) cap

'capra *nf* goat. **ca'pretto** *nm* kid

ca'priccio *nm* whim; (*bizzarria*) freak; **fare i capricci** have tantrums. **~'oso** *a* capricious; (*bambino*) naughty

Capri'corno *nm Astr* Capricorn
capri'ola *nf* somersault
capri'olo *nm* roe-deer
'**capro** *nm* [billy-]goat. ~ **espiatorio** scapegoat. **ca'prone** *nm* [billy] goat
'**capsula** *nf* capsule; *(di proiettile)* cap; *(di dente)* crown
cap'tare *vt Radio, TV* pick up; catch *(attenzione)*
cara'bina *nf* carbine
carabini'ere *nm* carabiniere; **carabini'eri** *pl* Italian police force (which is a branch of the army)
ca'raffa *nf* carafe
Ca'raibi *nmpl (zona)* Caribbean *sg; (isole)* Caribbean Islands; **il mar dei ~** the Caribbean [Sea]
cara'mella *nf* sweet
cara'mello *nm* caramel
ca'rato *nm* carat
caratte|re *nm* character; *(caratteristica)* characteristic; *Typ* type; **di buon ~re** good-natured. **~'ristico, -a** *a* characteristic; *(pittoresco)* quaint ● *nf* characteristic. **~riz'zare** *vt* characterize
carbon'cino *nm (per disegno)* charcoal
car'bone *nm* coal
carboniz'zare *vt* burn to a cinder
carbu'rante *nm* fuel
carbura'tore *nm* carburettor
car'cassa *nf* carcass; *fig* old wreck
carce'ra|rio *a* prison *attrib*. **~to, -a** *nmf* prisoner. **~zi'one** *nf* imprisonment. **~zione preventiva** preventive detention
'**carcer|e** *nm* prison; *(punizione)* imprisonment. **~i'ere, -a** *nmf* gaoler
carci'ofo *nm* artichoke
car'diaco *a* cardiac
cardi'nale *a & nm* cardinal
'**cardine** *nm* hinge
cardio|chi'rurgo *nm* heart surgeon. **~lo'gia** *nf* cardiology. **cardi'ologo** *nm* heart specialist. **~'tonico** *nm* heart stimulant
'**cardo** *nm* thistle
ca'rena *nf Naut* bottom

ca'ren|te *a* **~te di** lacking in. **~za** *nf* lack; *(scarsità)* scarcity
care'stia *nf* famine; *(mancanza)* dearth
ca'rezza *nf* caress; **fare una ~ a** caress
cari'a|rsi *vi* decay. **~to** *a* decayed
'**carica** *nf* office; *Mil, Electr* charge; *fig* drive. **cari'care** *vt* load; *Mil, Electr* charge; wind up *(orologio)*. **~'tore** *nm (per proiettile)* magazine
carica'tu|ra *nf* caricature. **~'rale** *a* grotesque. **~'rista** *nmf* caricaturist
'**carico** *a* loaded **(di** with); *(colore)* strong; *(orologio)* wound [up]; *(batteria)* charged ● *nm* load; *(di nave)* cargo; *(il caricare)* loading; **a ~ di** *Comm* to be charged to; *(persona)* dependent on
'**carie** *nf* [tooth] decay
ca'rino *a* pretty; *(piacevole)* agreeable
ca'risma *nm* charisma. **cari'smatico** *a* charismatic
carit|à *nf* charity; **per ~à!** *(come rifiuto)* God forbid!. **~a'tevole** *a* charitable
carnagi'one *nf* complexion
car'naio *nm fig* shambles
car'nale *a* carnal; **cugino ~** first cousin
'**carne** *nf* flesh; *(alimento)* meat; **~ di manzo/maiale/vitello** beef/pork/veal
car'nefi|ce *nm* executioner. **~'cina** *nf* slaughter
carne'va|le *nm* carnival. **~'lesco** *a* carnival
car'nivoro *nm* carnivore ● *a* carnivorous
car'noso *a* fleshy
'**caro, -a** *a* dear; **cari saluti** kind regards ● *nm fam* darling, dear; **i miei cari** my nearest and dearest
ca'rogna *nf* carcass; *fig* bastard
caro'sello *nm* merry-go-round
ca'rota *nf* carrot
caro'vana *nf* caravan; *(di veicoli)* convoy

caro'vita *nm* high cost of living

'**carpa** *nf* carp

carpenti'ere *nm* carpenter

car'pire *vt* seize; (*con difficoltà*) extort

car'pone, car'poni *adv* on all fours

car'rabile *a* suitable for vehicles; **passo** ~ *vedi* **carraio**

car'raio *a* **passo** ~ entrance to driveway, garage etc where parking is forbidden

carreggi'ata *nf* roadway; **doppia** ~ dual carriageway, divided highway *Am*

carrel'lata *nf TV* pan

car'rello *nm* trolley; (*di macchina da scrivere*) carriage; *Aeron* undercarriage; *Cinema, TV* dolly. ~ **d'atterraggio** *Aeron* landing gear

car'retto *nm* cart

carri'e|ra *nf* career; **di gran ~ra** at full speed; **fare ~ra** get on. **~'rismo** *nm* careerism

carri'ola *nf* wheelbarrow

'**carro** *nm* cart. ~ **armato** tank. ~ **attrezzi** breakdown vehicle, wrecker *Am*. ~ **funebre** hearse. ~ **merci** truck

car'rozza *nf* carriage; *Rail* car, coach. ~ **cuccette** sleeping car. ~ **ristorante** restaurant car

carroz'zella *nf* (*per bambini*) pram; (*per invalidi*) wheelchair

carrozze'ria *nf* bodywork; (*officina*) bodyshop

carroz'zina *nf* pram; (*pieghevole*) push-chair, stroller *Am*

carroz'zone *nm* (*di circo*) caravan

'**carta** *nf* paper; (*da gioco*) card; (*statuto*) charter; *Geog* map. ~ **d'argento** ≈ senior citizens' railcard. ~ **assorbente** blotting-paper. ~ **di credito** credit card. ~ **geografica** map. ~ **d'identità** identity card. ~ **igienica** toilet-paper. ~ **di imbarco** boarding card *or* pass. ~ **da lettere** writing-paper. ~ **da parati** wallpaper. ~ **stagnola** silver paper; *Culin* aluminium foil. ~ **straccia** waste

paper. ~ **stradale** road map. ~ **velina** tissue-paper. ~ **verde** *Auto* green card. ~ **vetrata** sandpaper

cartac'bone *nm* carbon paper

car'taccia *nf* waste paper

carta'modello *nm* pattern

cartamo'neta *nf* paper money

carta'pesta *nf* papier mâché

carta'straccia *nf* waste paper

cartave'trare *vt* sand [down]

car'tel|la *nf* (*per documenti ecc*) briefcase; (*di cartone*) folder; (*di scolaro*) satchel. **~la clinica** medical record. **~'lina** *nf* document wallet, folder

cartel'lino *nm* (*etichetta*) label; (*dei prezzi*) price-tag; (*di presenza*) time-card; **timbrare il ~** clock in; (*all'uscita*) clock out

car'tel|lo *nm* sign; (*pubblicitario*) poster; (*stradale*) road sign; (*di protesta*) placard; *Comm* cartel. **~'lone** *nm* poster; *Theat* bill

carti'era *nf* paper-mill

carti'lagine *nf* cartilage

car'tina *nf* map

car'toccio *nm* paper bag; **al ~** *Culin* baked in foil

carto'|laio, -a *nmf* stationer. **~le'ria** *nf* stationer's. **~libre'ria** *nf* stationer's and book shop

carto'lina *nf* postcard. ~ **postale** postcard

carto'mante *nmf* fortune-teller

carton'cino *nm* (*materiale*) card

car'tone *nm* cardboard; (*arte*) cartoon. ~ **animato** [animated] cartoon

car'tuccia *nf* cartridge

'**casa** *nf* house; (*abitazione propria*) home; (*ditta*) firm; **amico di** ~ family friend; **andare a** ~ go home; **essere di** ~ be like one of the family; **fatto in** ~ homemade; **padrone di** ~ (*di pensione ecc*) landlord; (*proprietario*) house owner. ~ **di cura** nursing home. ~ **popolare** council house. ~ **dello studente** hall of residence

ca'sacca *nf* military coat; (*giacca*) jacket

ca'saccio *adv* a ~ at random

casa'lin|ga *nf* housewife. ~o *a* domestic; *(fatto in casa)* home-made; *(amante della casa)* home-loving; *(semplice)* homely

ca'scante *a* falling; *(floscio)* flabby

ca'sca|re *vi* fall [down]. ~ta *nf (di acqua)* waterfall

ca'schetto *nm* [capelli a] ~ bob

ca'scina *nf* farm building

'casco *nm* crash-helmet; *(asciugacapelli)* [hair-]drier; ~ **di banane** bunch of bananas

caseggi'ato *nm* block of flats *Br*, apartment block

casei'ficio *nm* dairy

ca'sella *nf* pigeon-hole. ~ **postale** post office box; *Comput* mailbox

casel'lante *nmf (per treni)* signalman

casel'lario *nm* ~ **giudiziario** record of convictions; **avere il ~ giudiziario vergine** have no criminal record

ca'sello [autostra'dale] *nm* [motorway] toll booth

case'reccio *a* home-made

ca'serma *nf* barracks *pl*; *(dei carabinieri)* [police] station

casi'nista *nmf fam* muddler.
ca'sino *nm fam (bordello)* brothel; *(fig: confusione)* racket; *(disordine)* mess; **un casino di** loads of

casinò *nm inv* casino

ca'sistica *nf (classificazione)* case records *pl*

'caso *nm (fortuito; fatto, circostanza, Med, Gram)* case; **a ~** at random; ~ **mai** if need be; **far ~ a** pay attention to; **non far ~** take no account of; **per ~** by chance. ~ [giudiziario] [legal] case

caso'lare *nm* farmhouse

'caspita *int* good gracious!

'cassa *nf* till; *Comm* cash; *(luogo di pagamento)* cash desk; *(mobile)* chest; *(istituto bancario)* bank. ~ **automatica prelievi** cash dispenser, automatic teller. ~ **da**

morto coffin. ~ **toracica** *Anat* ribcage

cassa'forte *nf* safe

cassa'panca *nf* linen chest

casseru'ola *nf* saucepan

cas'setta *nf* case; *(per registratore)* cassette. ~ **delle lettere** postbox, letterbox. ~ **di sicurezza** strong-box

cas'set|to *nm* drawer. ~'tone *nm* chest of drawers

cassi'ere, -a *nmf* cashier; *(di supermercato)* checkout assistant, checkout operator; *(di banca)* teller

'casta *nf* caste

ca'stagn|a *nf* chestnut. casta-'gneto *nm* chestnut grove. ~o *nm* chestnut[-tree]

ca'stano *a* chestnut

ca'stello *nm* castle; *(impalcatura)* scaffold

casti'gare *vt* punish

casti'gato *a (casto)* chaste

ca'stigo *nm* punishment

castità *nf* chastity. 'casto *a* chaste

ca'storo *nm* beaver

ca'strare *vt* castrate

casu'al|e *a* chance *attrib.* ~'mente *adv* by chance

ca'supola *nf* little house

cata'clisma *nm fig* upheaval

cata'comba *nf* catacomb

cata'fascio *nm* andare a ~ go to rack and ruin

cata'litico *a* marmitta catalitica *Auto* catalytic converter

cataliz'za|re *vt fig* heighten. ~'tore *nm Auto* catalytic converter

catalo'gare *vt* catalogue. ca'talo-go *nm* catalogue

catama'rano *nm (da diporto)* catamaran

cata'pecchia *nf* hovel; *fam* dump

catapul'tar|e *vt (scaraventare fuori)* eject. ~**si** *vr (precipitarsi)* dive

catarifran'gente *nm* reflector

ca'tarro *nm* catarrh

ca'tasta *nf* pile

ca'tasto *nm* land register

ca'tastrofe *nf* catastrophe. **cata-'strofico** *a* catastrophic
cate'chismo *nm* catechism
catego'ria *nf* category. **~'gorico** *a* categorical
ca'tena *nf* chain. **~ montuosa** mountain range. **catene** *pl* **da neve** tyre-chains. **cate'naccio** *nm* bolt
cate'nella *nf* (*collana*) chain. **~'nina** *nf* chain
cate'ratta *nf* cataract
ca'terva *nf* **una ~ di** heaps of
cati'nella *nf* basin; **piovere a ~e** bucket down
ca'tino *nm* basin
ca'torcio *nm fam* old wreck
ca'trame *nm* tar
'cattedra *nf* (*tavolo di insegnante*) desk; (*di università*) chair
catte'drale *nf* cathedral
catti'veria *nf* wickedness; (*azione*) wicked action
cattività *nf* captivity
cat'tivo *a* bad; (*bambino*) naughty
cattoli'cesimo *nm* Catholicism
cat'tolico, **-a** *a* & *nmf* [Roman] Catholic
cat'tu**ra** *nf* capture. **~'rare** *vt* capture
cauc'ciù *nm* rubber
'causa *nf* cause; *Jur* lawsuit; **far ~ a** qcno sue sb. **cau'sare** *vt* cause
'caustico *a* caustic
cauta'mente *adv* cautiously
cau'tela *nf* caution
caute'la**re** *vt* protect. **~si** *vr* take precautions
cauteriz'z|are *vt* cauterize. **~io-ne** *nf* cauterization
'cauto *a* cautious
cauzi'one *nf* security; (*per libertà provvisoria*) bail
'cava *nf* quarry; *fig* mine
caval'ca**re** *vt* ride; (*stare a caval-cioni*) sit astride. **~ta** *nf* ride; (*corteo*) cavalcade. **~'via** *nm* flyover
cavalci'oni: **a ~** *adv* astride
caval'iere *nm* rider; (*titolo*) knight; (*accompagnatore*) escort; (*al ballo*) partner
cavalle|'resco *a* chivalrous. **~'ria**

nf chivalry; *Mil* cavalry. **~'rizzo, -a** *nm* horseman ● *nf* horsewoman
caval'letta *nf* grasshopper
caval'letto *nm* trestle; (*di macchi-na fotografica*) tripod; (*di pittore*) easel
caval'lina *nf* (*ginnastica*) horse
ca'vallo *nm* horse; (*misura di po-tenza*) horsepower; (*scacchi*) knight; (*dei pantaloni*) crotch; **a ~** on horseback; **andare a ~** go horse-riding. **~ a dondolo** rocking-horse
caval'lone *nm* (*ondata*) roller horse
caval'luccio ma'rino *nm* sea horse
ca'var|e *vt* take out; (*di dosso*) take off; **~sela** get away with it; **se la cava bene** he's doing all right
cava'tappi *nm inv* corkscrew
ca'ver|na *nf* cave. **~'noso** *a* (*voce*) deep
'cavia *nf* guinea-pig
cavi'ale *nm* caviar
ca'viglia *nf* ankle
cavil'l|are *vi* quibble. **ca'villo** *nm* quibble
cavità *nf inv* cavity
'cavo *a* hollow ● *nm* cavity; (*di metallo*) cable; *Naut* rope
cavo'lata *nf fam* rubbish
cavo'letto *nm* **~ di Bruxelles** Brussels sprout
cavolfi'ore *nm* cauliflower
'cavolo *nm* cabbage; **~!** *fam* sugar!
caz'zo *int vulg* fuck!
caz'zott|o *nm* punch; **prendere qcno a ~i** beat sb up
caz'zu'ola *nf* trowel
c/c *abbr* (**conto corrente**) c/a
CD-Rom *nm inv* CD-Rom
ce *pers pron* (*a noi*) (to) us ● *adv* there; **~ ne sono molti** there are many
'cece *nm* chick-pea
cecità *nf* blindness
ceco, **-a** *a* & *nmf* Czech; **la Repub-blica Ceca** the Czech Republic
Cecoslo'vacc|hia *nf* Czechoslo-vakia. **c~o, -a** *a* & *nmf* Czechoslo-vak

'cedere vi (arrendersi) surrender; (concedere) yield; (sprofondare) subside ● vt give up; make over ⟨proprietà ecc⟩. **ce'devole** a ⟨terreno ecc⟩ soft; fig yielding. **cedi'mento** nm ⟨di terreno⟩ subsidence

'cedola nf coupon

'cedro nm ⟨albero⟩ cedar; ⟨frutto⟩ citron

C.E.E. nf abbr (Comunità Economica Europea) E[E]C

'ceffo nm ⟨muso⟩ snout; ⟨pej: persona⟩ mug

cef'fone nm slap

ce'lare vt conceal. **~si** vr hide

cele'bra|re vt celebrate. **~zi'one** nf celebration

'celebre a famous. **~ità** nf inv celebrity

'celere a swift

ce'leste a ⟨divino⟩ heavenly ● a & nm ⟨colore⟩ sky-blue

celi'bato nm celibacy

'celibe a single ● nm bachelor

'cella nf cell

'cellofan nm inv cellophane; Culin cling film

'cellula nf cell. **~ fotoelettrica** electronic eye

cellu'lare nm ⟨telefono⟩ cellular phone ● nm ⟨furgone⟩ ~ nm police van. **[telefono] ~** nm cellular phone

cellu'lite nf cellulite

cellu'loide a celluloid

cellu'losa nf cellulose

celt|a nm Celt. **~ico** a Celtic

cemen'tare vt cement. **ce'mento** nm cement. **cemento armato** reinforced concrete

'cena nf dinner; ⟨leggera⟩ supper

ce'nacolo nm circle

ce'nare vi have dinner

cenci|o nm rag; ⟨per spolverare⟩ duster. **~'oso** a in rags

'cenere nf ash; ⟨di carbone ecc⟩ cinders

ce'netta nf ⟨cena semplice⟩ informal dinner

'cenno nm sign; ⟨col capo⟩ nod; ⟨con la mano⟩ wave; ⟨allusione⟩ hint; ⟨breve resoconto⟩ mention

ce'none nm il **~ di Capodanno/ Natale** special New Year's Eve/ Christmas Eve dinner

censi'mento nm census

cen's|ore nm censor. **~ura** nf censorship. **~u'rare** vt censor

centelli'nare vt sip

cente'n|ario, -a a & nmf centenarian ● nm ⟨commemorazione⟩ centenary. **~'nale** a centennial

cen'tesimo a hundredth ● nm ⟨di dollaro⟩ cent; **non avere un ~** be penniless

cen'ti|grado a centigrade. **~metro** nm centimetre

centi'naio nm hundred

'cento a & nm a or one hundred; **per ~** per cent

cento'metrista nmf Sport one hundred metres runner

cento'mila a or one hundred thousand

cen'trale a central ● nf ⟨di società ecc⟩ head office. **~ atomica** atomic power station. **~ elettrica** electrical power station. **~ nucleare** nuclear power station. **~ telefonica** [telephone] exchange

centra'li|na nf Teleph switchboard. **~'nista** nmf operator

centra'lino nm Teleph exchange; ⟨di albergo ecc⟩ switchboard

centra'li|smo nm centralism. **~z'zare** vt centralize

cen'trare vt ~ qcsa hit sth in the centre; ⟨fissare nel centro⟩ centre; fig hit on the head ⟨idea⟩

centri'fu|ga nf spin-drier. **~ [asciugaverdure]** shaker. **~'gare** vt Techn centrifuge; ⟨lavatrice:⟩ spin

cen'trino nm doily

'centro nm centre. **~ [città]** city centre. **~ commerciale** shopping centre, mall. **~ sociale** community centre

'ceppo nm ⟨di albero⟩ stump; ⟨da ardere⟩ log; ⟨fig: gruppo⟩ stock

'cera nf wax; (aspetto) look. **~ per il pavimento** floor-polish

ce'ramica nf (arte) ceramics; (materia) pottery; (oggetto) piece of pottery

ce'rato a (tela) waxed

cerbi'atto nm fawn

'cerca nf **andare in ~ di** look for

cercaper'sone nm inv beeper

cer'care vt look for ● vi **~ di** try to

cerchi|a nf circle. **~'are** vt circle (parola). **~'ato** a (occhi) black-ringed. **~'etto** nm (per capelli) hairband

'cerchi|o nm circle; (giocattolo) hoop. **~'one** nm alloy wheel

cere'ale nm cereal

cere'brale a cerebral

'cereo a waxen

ce'retta nf depilatory wax

ceri'moni|a nf ceremony. **~'ale** nm ceremonial. **~'oso** a ceremonious

ce'rino nm (wax) match

cerni'era nf hinge; (di borsa) clasp. **~ lampo** zip[-fastener], zipper Am

'cernita nf selection

'cero nm candle

ce'rone nm grease-paint

ce'rotto nm [sticking] plaster

certa'mente adv certainly

cer'tezza nf certainty

certifi'ca|re vt certify. **~to** nm certificate

'certo a certain; (notizia) definite; (indeterminativo) some; **sono ~ di riuscire** I am certain to succeed; **a una certa età** at a certain age; **certi giorni** some days; **un ~ signor Giardini** a Mr Giardini; **una certa Anna** somebody called Anna; **certa gente** pej some people; **ho certi dolori** I'm in such pain!. **certi** pron pl some; (alcune persone) some people ● adv of course; **sapere per ~** know for certain, know for sure; **di ~** surely; **~ che sì!** of course!

cer'vel|lo nm brain. **~'lone, -a** nmf hum genius. **~'lotico** a (macchinoso) over-elaborate

'cervo nm deer

ce'sareo a Med Caesarean

cesel'la|re vt chisel. **~to** a chiselled. **ce'sello** nm chisel

ce'soie nfpl shears

ce'spuglio nm bush. **~'oso** a (terreno) bushy

ces'sa|re vi stop, cease ● vt stop. **~re il fuoco** ceasefire. **~zi'one** nf cessation

cessi'one nf handover

'cesso nm sl (gabinetto) bog, john Am; (fig: locale, luogo) dump

'cesta nf [large] basket. **ce'stello** nm (per lavatrice) drum

cesti'nare vt throw away. **ce'stino** nm [small] basket; (per la carta straccia) waste-paper basket. **'cesto** nm basket

'ceto nm [social] class

'cetra nf lyre

cetri'olino nm gherkin. **cetri'olo** nm cucumber

cfr abbr (**confronta**) cf.

che pron rel (persona: soggetto) who; (persona: oggetto) that, who, whom fml; (cosa, animale) that, which; **questa è la casa [che] ~ ho comprato** this is the house [that] I've bought; **il ~ mi sorprende** which surprises me; **dal ~ deduco che...** from which I gather that...; **avere di ~ vivere** have enough to live on; **grazie! – non c'è di ~** thank you! – don't mention it!; **il giorno ~ ti ho visto** fam the day I saw you ● a inter what; (esclamativo: con aggettivo) how; (con nome) what a; **~ macchina prendiamo, la tua o la mia?** which car are we taking, yours or mine?; **~ bello!** how nice!; **~ idea!** what an idea!; **~ bella giornata!** what a lovely day! ● pron inter what; **a ~ pensi?** what are you thinking about? ● conj that; (con comparazioni) than; **credo ~ abbia ragione** I think [that] he is right; **era così commosso ~ non riusciva a parlare** he was so moved [that] he couldn't speak; **aspetto ~ telefoni** I'm waiting for him to phone; **è da**

un po' ~ non lo vedo it's been a while since I saw him; **mi piace più Roma ~ Milano** I like Rome better than Milan; **~ ti piaccia o no** whether you like it or not; **~ lo sappia** as far as I know

checché *indef pron* whatever

chemiotera'pia *nf* chemotherapy

chero'sene *nm* paraffin

cheru'bino *nm* cherub

cheti'chella: alla ~ *adv* silently

'cheto *a* quiet

chi *rel pron* whoever; (*coloro che*) people who; **ho trovato ~ ti può aiutare** I found somebody who can help you; **c'è ~ dice che…** some people say that…; **senti ~ parla!** listen to who's talking! ● *pron inter* (*soggetto*) who; (*oggetto*, *con preposizione*) who, whom *fml*; (*possessivo*) **di ~** whose; **~ sei?** who are you?; **~ hai incontrato?** who did you meet?; **di ~ sono questi libri?** whose books are these?; **con ~ parli?** who are you talking to?; **a ~ lo dici!** tell me about it!

chi'acchie|ra *nf* chat; (*pettegolezzo*) gossip. **~rare** *vi* chat; (*far pettegolezzi*) gossip. **~rata** *a* essere **~rato** (*persona*): be the subject of gossip; **~re** *pl* chitchat; **far quattro ~re** have a chat. **~'rone, -a** *a* talkative ● *nmf* chatterer

chia'ma|re *vt* call; (*far venire*) send for; **come ti chiami?** what's your name?; **mi chiamo Roberto** my name is Robert; **~re alle armi** call up. **~re ~ be called. **~ta** *nf* call; *Mil* call-up

chi'appa *nf fam* cheek

chiara'mente *adv* clearly

chia'rezza *nf* clarity; (*limpidezza*) clearness

chiarifi'ca|re *vt* clarify. **~'tore** *a* clarificatory. **~zi'one** *nf* clarification

chiari'mento *nm* clarification

chia'ri|re *vt* make clear; (*spiegare*) clear up. **~si** *vr* become clear

chi'aro *a* clear; (*luminoso*) bright;

(*colore*) light. **chia'rore** *nm* glimmer

chiaroveg'gente *a* clear-sighted ● *nmf* clairvoyant

chi'as|so *nm* din. **~'soso** *a* rowdy

chi'av|e *nf* key; **chiudere a ~e** lock. **~e inglese** monkey-wrench. **~i'stello** *nm* latch

chiaz|za *nf* stain. **~'zare** *vt* stain

chic *a inv* chic

chicches'sia *pron* anybody

'chicco *nm* grain; (*di caffè*) bean; (*d'uva*) grape

chi'eder|e *vt* ask; (*per avere*) ask for; (*esigere*) demand. **~si** *vr* wonder

chi'esa *nf* church

chi'esto *pp di* **chiedere**

'chiglia *nf* keel

'chilo *nm* kilo

chilo'grammo *nm* kilogram[me]

chilome'traggio *nm Auto* mileage

chilo'metrico *a* in kilometres

chi'lometro *nm* kilometre

chi'mera *nf fig* illusion

'chimic|a *nf* chemistry. **~o, -a** *a* chemical ● *nmf* chemist

'china *nf* (*declivio*) slope; **inchiostro di ~** Indian ink

chi'nar|e *vt* lower. **~si** *vr* stoop

chincaglie'rie *nfpl* knick-knacks

chinesitera'pia *nf* physiotherapy

chi'nino *nm* quinine

'chino *a* bent

chi'notto *nm* sparkling soft drink

chi'occia *nf* sitting hen

chi'occiola *nf* snail; **scala a ~** spiral staircase

chi'odo *nm* nail; (*idea fissa*) obsession. **~ di garofano** clove

chi'oma *nf* head of hair; (*fogliame*) foliage

chi'osco *nm* kiosk; (*per giornali*) news-stand

chi'ostro *nm* cloister

chiro'man|te *nmf* palmist. **~'zia** *nf* palmistry

chirur'gia *nf* surgery. **chi'rurgico** *a* surgical. **chi'rurgo** *nm* surgeon

chissà *adv* who knows; **~ quando**

arriverà I wonder when he will arrive

chi'tar|ra nf guitar. **~rista** nmf guitarist

chi'uder|e vt shut, close; (con la chiave) lock; turn off (luce, acqua ecc); (per sempre) close down (negozio, fabbrica ecc); (recingere) enclose ● vi shut, close. **~si** vr shut; (tempo:) cloud over; (ferita:) heal over; fig withdraw into oneself

chi'unque pron anyone, anybody ● rel pron whoever

chi'usa nf enclosure; (di canale) lock; (conclusione) close

chi'u|so pp di chiudere ● a shut; (tempo) overcast; (persona) reserved. **~'sura** nf closing; (allacciatura) fastener. **~sura lampo** zip, zipper Am

ci pron (personale) us; (riflessivo) ourselves; (reciproco) each other; (a ciò, di ciò ecc) about it; **non ci disturbare** don't disturb us; **aspettateci** wait for us; **ci ha detto tutto** he told us everything; **ce lo manderanno** they'll send it to us; **ci consideriamo...** we consider ourselves...; **ci laviamo le mani** we wash our hands; **ci odiamo** we hate each other; **non ci penso mai** I never think about it; **pensaci!** think about it! ● adv (qui) here; (lì) there; (moto per luogo) through it; **ci siamo** we are here; **ci siete?** are you there?; **ci siamo passati tutti** we all went through it; **c'è** there is; **ce ne sono molti** there are many; **ci vuole pazienza** it takes patience; **non ci vedo/sento** I can't see/hear

cia'bat|ta nf slipper. **~'tare** vi shuffle

ciabat'tino nm cobbler

ci'alda nf wafer

cial'trone nm (mascalzone) scoundrel

ciam'bella nf Culin ring-shaped cake; (salvagente) lifebelt; (gonfiabile) rubber ring

cianci'are vi gossip

cianfru'saglie nfpl knick-knacks

cia'notico a (colorito) puce

ci'ao int fam (all' arrivo) hello!, hi!; (alla partenza) bye-bye!, cheerio!

ciar'la|re vi chat. **~'tano** nm charlatan

cias'cuno a each ● pron everyone, everybody; (distributivo) each [one]; **per ~** each

ci'bar|e vt feed; **~ie** nfpl provisions. **~si** vr eat; **~si di** live on

ciber'netico a cybernetic

'cibo nm food

ci'cala nf cicada

cica'lino nm buzzer

cica'tri|ce nf scar. **~z'zante** nm ointment

cicatriz'zarsi vr heal [up].

cicatrizzazi'one nf healing

'cicca nf cigarette end; (fam: sigaretta) fag; (fam: gomma) [chewing] gum

cic'chetto nm fam (bicchierino) nip; (rimprovero) telling-off

ci'cci|a nf fam fat, flab. **~'one, -a** nmf fam fatty, fatso

cice'rone nm guide

cicla'mino nm cyclamen

ci'clis|mo nm cycling. **~ta** nmf cyclist

'ciclo nm cycle; (di malattia) course

ciclomo'tore nm moped

ci'clone nm cyclone

ci'cogna nf stork

cico'ria nf chicory

ci'eco, -a a blind ● nm blind man ● nf blind woman

ci'elo nm sky; Relig heaven; **santo ~!** good heavens!

'cifra nf figure; (somma) sum; (monogramma) monogram; (codice) code

ci'fra|re vt embroider with a monogram; (codificare) code. **~to** a monogrammed; coded

'ciglio nm (bordo) edge; (pl nf ci'glia: delle palpebre) eyelash

'cigno nm swan

cigo'l|are vt squeak. **~io** nm squeak

'Cile nm Chile

ci'lecca nf far ~ miss

ci'leno, -a a & nmf Chilean

cili'egi|a nf cherry. **~o** nm cherry [tree]

cilin'drata nf cubic capacity, c.c.; **macchina di alta ~** highpowered car

ci'lindro nm cylinder; (cappello) top hat

'cima nf top; (fig: persona) genius; **da ~ a fondo** from top to bottom

ci'melio nm relic

cimen'tar|e vt put to the test. **~si** vr (provare) try one's hand

'cimice nf bug; (puntina) drawing pin, thumbtack Am

cimini'era nf chimney; Naut funnel

cimi'tero nm cemetery

ci'murro nm distemper

'Cina nf China

cin cin! int cheers!

cincischi'are vi fiddle

'cine nm fam cinema

cine'asta nmf film maker

'cinema nm inv cinema. **cine'presa** nf cine-camera

ci'nese a & nmf Chinese

cine'teca nf (raccolta) film collection

ci'netico a kinetic

'cingere vt (circondare) surround

cinghia nf strap; (cintura) belt

cinghi'ale nm wild boar; **pelle di ~** pigskin

cinguet't|are vi twitter. **~io** nm twittering

'cinico a cynical

ci'niglia nf (tessuto) chenille

ci'nismo nm cynicism

ci'nofilo a (unità) dog-loving

cin'quanta a & nm fifty. **cinquan'tenne** a & nmf fifty-year-old. **cinquan'tesimo** a a fiftieth. **cinquan'tina** nf una cinquantina di about fifty

'cinque a & nm five

cinquecen'tesco a sixteenth-century

cinque'cento a five hundred ● nm il C~ the sixteenth century

cinque'mila a & nm five thousand

'cinta nf (di pantaloni) belt; **muro di ~** [boundary] wall. **cin'tare** vt enclose

'cintola nf (di pantaloni) belt

cin'tura nf belt. **~ di salvataggio** lifebelt. **~ di sicurezza** Aeron, Auto seat-belt

cintu'rino nm **~ dell'orologio** watch-strap

ciò pron this; that; **~ che** what; **~ nondimeno** nevertheless

ci'occa nf lock

ciocco'la|ta nf chocolate; (bevanda) [hot] chocolate. **~'tino** nm chocolate. **~o** nm chocolate. **~to al latte/fondente** milk/plain chocolate

cioè adv that is

ciondo'l|are vi dangle. **ci'ondolo** nm pendant. **~oni** adv fig hanging about

cionono'stante adv nonetheless

ci'otola nf bowl

ci'ottolo nm pebble

ci'polla nf onion; (bulbo) bulb

ci'presso nm cypress

'cipria nf [face] powder

'Cipro nm Cyprus. **cipri'ota** a & nmf Cypriot

'circa adv & prep about

'circo nm circus

circo'la|re a circular ● nf circular; (di metropolitana) circle line ● vi circulate. **~'torio** a Med circulatory. **~zi'one** nf circulation; (traffico) traffic

'circolo nm circle; (società) club

circon'ci|dere vt circumcise. **~si'one** nf circumcision

circon'dar|e vt surround. **~io** nm (amministrativo) administrative district. **~si di** vr surround oneself with

circonfe'renza nf circumference. **~ dei fianchi** hip measurement

circonvallazi'one nf ring road

circo'scritto a limited

circoscrizi'one nf area. **~ eletto'rale** constituency

circo'spetto a wary

circospezi'one nf con **~** warily

circo'stante a surrounding

circo'stanza nf circumstance; (occasione) occasion

circu'ire vt (ingannare) trick

cir'cuito nm circuit

circumnavi'gare vt circumnavigate. **~zi'one** nf circumnavigation

'ciste nf inv cyst

ci'sterna nf cistern; (serbatoio) tank

'cisti nf inv cyst

ci'tare vt (riportare brani ecc) quote; (come esempio) cite; Jur summons. **~zi'one** nf quotation; Jur summons sg

citofo'nare vt buzz. **ci'tofono** nm entry phone; (in ufficio, su aereo ecc) intercom

ci'trullo nm fam dimwit

città nf inv town; (grande) city

citta'della nf citadel

citta|di'nanza nf citizenship; (popolazione) citizens pl. **~'dino, -a** nmf citizen; (abitante di città) city dweller

ciucci'are vt fam suck. **ci'uccio** nm fam dummy

ci'uco nm ass

ci'uffo nm tuft

ci'urma nf Naut crew

ci'vet|ta nf owl; (fig: donna) flirt; [auto] **~** unmarked police car. **~'tare** vi flirt. **~te'ria** nf coquettishness

'civico a civic

ci'vil|e a civil. **~iz'zare** vt civilize. **~iz'zato** a (paese) civilized. **~izzazi'one** nf civilization. **~'mente** adv civilly

civiltà nf inv civilization; (cortesia) civility

clacson nm inv horn. **clacso'nare** vi beep the horn, hoot

cla'mo|re nm clamour; fig cause a sensation. **~rosa'mente** adv (sbagliare) sensationally.

~'roso a noisy; (sbaglio) sensational

clan nm inv clan; fig clique

clandestin|a'mente adv secretly. **~ità** nf secrecy

clande'stino a clandestine; **movimento ~** underground movement; **passeggero ~** stowaway

clari'netto nm clarinet

'classe nf class. **~ turistica** tourist class

classi'cis|mo nm classicism. **~ta** nmf classicist

'classico a classical; (tipico) classic ● nm classic

clas'sifi|ca nf classification; Sport results pl. **~'care** vt classify. **~'carsi** vr be placed. **~ca'tore** nm (cartella) folder. **~cazi'one** nf classification

clas'sista nmf class-conscious person

'clausola nf clause

claustro|fo'bia nf claustrophobia. **~'fobico** a claustrophobic

clau'sura nf Relig enclosed order

clavi'cembalo nm harpsichord

cla'vicola nf collar-bone

cle'men|te a merciful; (tempo) mild. **~za** nf mercy

cleri'cale a clerical. **'clero** nm clergy

clic nm Comput click; **fare ~ su** click on

cli'en|te nmf client; (di negozio) customer. **~'tela** nf customers pl

'clima nm climate. **cli'matico** a climatic; **stazione climatica** health resort

'clinica nf clinic. **clinico** a clinical ● nm clinician

clo'aca nf sewer

'cloro nm chlorine. **~'formio** nm chloroform

clou a inv **i momenti ~** the highlights

coabi'ta|re vi live together. **~zi'one** nf cohabitation

coagu'la|re vt, **~rsi** vr coagulate. **~zi'one** nf coagulation

coaliz|i'one *nf* coalition. **~'zarsi** *vr* unite

co'atto *a* Jur compulsory

'cobra *nm inv* cobra

coca'ina *nf* cocaine. **cocai'noma-ne** *nmf* cocaine addict

cocci'nella *nf* ladybird

'coccio *nm* earthenware; *(frammento)* fragment

cocciu'taggine *nf* stubbornness. **~'uto** *a* stubborn

'cocco *nm* coconut palm; *fam* love; **noce di ~** coconut

cocco'drillo *nm* crocodile

cocco'lare *vt* cuddle

co'cente *a (sole)* burning

'cocktail *nm inv (ricevimento)* cocktail party

co'comero *nm* watermelon

co'cuzzolo *nm* top; *(di testa, cappello)* crown

'coda *nf (di abito)* train; *(fila)* queue; **fare la ~** queue [up], stand in line *Am.* **~ di cavallo** *(acconciatura)* ponytail. **~ dell'occhio** corner of one's eye **~ di paglia** guilty conscience

co'dardo, -a *a* cowardly ● *nmf* coward

'codice *nm* code. **~ di avviamento postale** postal code, zip code *Am.* **~ a barre** bar-code. **~ fiscale** tax code. **~ della strada** highway code.

codifi'care *vt* codify

coe'ren|te *a* consistent. **~za** *nf* consistency

coesi'one *nf* cohesion

coe'sistere *vi* coexist

coe'taneo, -a *a & nmf* contemporary

cofa'netto *nm* casket. **'cofano** *nm (forziere)* chest; *Auto* bonnet, hood *Am*

'cogliere *vt* pick; *(sorprendere)* catch; *(afferrare)* seize; *(colpire)* hit

co'gnato, -a *nmf* brother-in-law; sister-in-law

cogni'zione *nf* knowledge

co'gnome *nm* surname

'coi = con + i

coinci'denza *nf* coincidence; *(di treno ecc)* connection

coin'cidere *vi* coincide

coinqui'lino *nm* flatmate

coin'vol|gere *vt* involve. **~gi-'mento** *nm* involvement. **~to** *a* involved

'coito *nm* coitus

col = con + il

colà *adv* there

cola'brodo *nm inv* strainer; **ridotto a un ~brodo** *fam* full of holes. **~'pasta** *nm inv* colander

co'la|re *vt* strain; *(versare lentamente)* drip ● *vi (gocciolare)* drip; *(perdere)* leak; **~re a picco** Naut sink. **~ta** *nf (di metallo)* casting; *(di lava)* flow

colazi'one *nf (del mattino)* breakfast; *(di mezzogiorno)* lunch; **prima ~** breakfast; **far ~** have breakfast/lunch. **~ al sacco** packed lunch

co'lei *pron f* the one

co'lera *nm* cholera

coleste'rolo *nm* cholesterol

colf *nf abbr* (**collaboratrice familiare**) home help

'colica *nf* colic

co'lino *nm* [tea] strainer

'colla *nf* glue; *(di farina)* paste. **~ di pesce** gelatine

collabo'ra|re *vi* collaborate. **~'tore, ~'trice** *nmf* collaborator. **~zi'one** *nf* collaboration

col'lana *nf* necklace; *(serie)* series

col'lant *nm* tights *pl*

col'lare *nm* collar

col'lasso *nm* collapse

collau'dare *vt* test. **col'laudo** *nm* test

'colle *nm* hill

col'lega *nmf* colleague

collega'mento *nm* connection; *Mil* liaison; *Radio ecc* link. **colle'gar|e** *vt* connect. **~si** *vr* TV, *Radio* link up

collegi'ale *nmf* boarder ● *a (responsabilità, decisione)* collective

col'legio nm ⟨convitto⟩ boarding-school. **~ elettorale** constituency

col'lera nf anger; **andare in ~** get angry. **col'lerico** a irascible

col'letta nf collection

collet|tività nf inv community. **~tivo** a collective; ⟨interesse⟩ general; **biglietto ~tivo** group ticket

col'letto nm collar

collezio|'nare vt collect. **~'one** nf collection. **~o'nista** nmf collector

colli'mare vi coincide

col'li|na nf hill. **~'noso** a ⟨terreno⟩ hilly

col'lirio nm eyewash

collisi'one nf collision

'collo nm neck; ⟨pacco⟩ package; **a ~** high-necked. **~ del piede** instep

colloca'mento nm placing; ⟨impiego⟩ employment

collo'ca|re vt place. **~rsi** vr take one's place. **~zi'one** nf placing

colloqui'ale a ⟨termine⟩ colloquial. **col'loquio** nm conversation; ⟨udienza ecc⟩ interview; ⟨esame⟩ oral ⟨exam⟩

collusi'one nf collusion

colluttazi'one nf scuffle

col'mare vt fill [to the brim]; bridge ⟨divario⟩; **~ qcno di gentilezze** overwhelm sb with kindness. **'colmo** a full ● nm top; fig height; **al colmo della disperazione** in the depths of despair; **questo è il colmo!** ⟨con indignazione⟩ this is the last straw!; ⟨con stupore⟩ I don't believe it!

co'lomb|a nf dove. **~o** nm pigeon

co'loni|a¹ nf colony; **~a** ⟨estiva⟩ ⟨per bambini⟩ holiday camp. **~'ale** a colonial

co'lonia² nf ⟨acqua di⟩ = [eau de] Cologne

co'lonico a ⟨terreno, casa⟩ farm

coloniz'za|re vt colonize. **~'tore**, **~'trice** nmf colonizer

co'lon|na nf column. **~ sonora** sound-track. **~ vertebrale** spine. **~'nato** nm colonnade

colon'nello nm colonel

co'lono nm tenant farmer

colo'rante nm colouring

colo'rare vt colour; colour in ⟨disegno⟩

co'lore nm colour; **a colori** in colour; **di ~** coloured. **colo'rito** a coloured; ⟨viso⟩ rosy; ⟨racconto⟩ colourful ● nm complexion

co'loro pron pl the ones

colos'sale a colossal. **co'losso** nm colossus

'colpa nf fault; ⟨biasimo⟩ blame; ⟨colpevolezza⟩ guilt; ⟨peccato⟩ sin; **dare la ~ a** blame; **essere in ~** be at fault; **per ~ di** because of. **col'pevole** a guilty ● nmf culprit

col'pire vt hit, strike; **~ nel segno** hit the nail on the head

'colpo nm blow; ⟨di arma da fuoco⟩ shot; ⟨urto⟩ knock; ⟨emozione⟩ shock; Med, Sport stroke; ⟨furto⟩ raid; **di ~** suddenly; **far ~** make a strong impression; **a ~ venire un ~ a qcno** fig give sb a fright; **perdere colpi** ⟨motore⟩ keep missing; **a ~ d'occhio** at a glance; **a ~ sicuro** for certain. **~ d'aria** chill. **~ basso** blow below the belt. **~ di scena** coup de théâtre. **~ di sole** sunstroke; **colpi pl di sole** ⟨su capelli⟩ highlights. **~ di stato** coup [d'état]. **~ di telefono** ring; **dare un ~ di telefono a qn** give sb a ring. **~ di testa** [sudden] impulse. **~ di vento** gust of wind **col'poso** a **omicidio ~** manslaughter

coltel'lata nf stab. **col'tello** nm knife

colti'va|re vt cultivate. **~'tore**, **~'trice** nmf farmer. **~zi'one** nf farming; ⟨di piante⟩ growing

'colto pp di **cogliere** ● a cultured

'coltre nf blanket

col'tura nf cultivation

co'lui pron inv m the one

'coma nm inv coma; **in ~** in a coma

comanda'mento nm commandment

coman'dante nm commander; Naut, Aeron captain

coman'dare *vt* command; *Mech* control ● *vi* be in charge. **co'mando** *nm* command; *(di macchina)* control

co'mare *nf (madrina)* godmother

combaci'are *vi* fit together; *(testimonianze:)* concur·

combat'tente *a* fighting ● *nm* combatant. **ex ~** ex-serviceman

com'bat|tere *vt/i* fight. **~ti'mento** *nm* fight; *Mil* battle; **fuori ~timento** *(pugilato)* knocked out. **~'tuto** *a (gara)* hard fought

combi'na|re *vt/i* arrange; *(mettere insieme)* combine; *(fam: fare)* do; **cosa stai ~ndo?** what are you doing?. **~rsi** *vr* combine; *(mettersi d'accordo)* come to an agreement. **~zi'one** *nf* combination; *(caso)* coincidence; **per ~zione** by chance

com'briccola *nf* gang

combu'sti|bile *a* combustible ● *nm* fuel. **~'one** *nf* combustion

com'butta *nf* gang; **in ~** in league

'come *adv* like; *(in qualità di)* as; *(interrogativo, esclamativo)* how; **questo vestito è ~ il tuo** this dress is like yours; **~ stai?** how are you?; **~ va?** how are things?; **~ mai?** how come?; **~?** what?; **non sa ~ fare** he doesn't know what to do; **~ sta bene!** how well he looks!; **~ no!** that will be right!; **~ tu sai** you know; **fa ~ vuoi** do as you like; **~ se** as if ● *conj (non appena)* as soon as

co'meta *nf* comet

'comico, -a *a* comic[al]; *(teatro)* comic ● *nm* funny side ● *nmf (attore)* comedian, comic actor ● *nf (a torte in faccia)* slapstick sketch

co'mignolo *nm* chimney-pot

cominci'are *vt/i* begin, start; **a ~ da oggi** from today; **per ~** to begin with

comi'tato *nm* committee

comi'tiva *nf* party, group

co'mizio *nm* meeting

com'mando *nm inv* commando

com'medi|a *nf* comedy; *(opera teatrale)* play; *fig* sham. **~a musicale** musical. **~'ante** *nmf* comedian; *fig pej* phoney. **~'ografo, a** *nmf* playwright

commemo'ra|re *vt* commemorate. **~zi'one** *nf* commemoration

commen'sale *nmf* fellow diner

commen't|are *vt* comment on; *(annotare)* annotate. **~'ario** *nm* commentary. **~a'tore, ~a'trice** *nmf* commentator. **com'mento** *nm* comment

commerci'a|le *a* commercial; *(relazioni, trattative)* trade; *(attività)* business. **centro ~le** shopping centre. **~'lista** *nmf* business consultant; *(contabile)* accountant. **~liz'zare** *vt* market. **~lizzazi'one** *nf* marketing

commerci'ante *nmf* trader, merchant; *(negoziante)* shopkeeper. **~ all'ingrosso** wholesaler

commerci'are *vi* **~ in** deal in

com'mercio *nm* commerce; *(internazionale)* trade; *(affari)* business; **in ~** *(prodotto)* on sale. **~ all'ingrosso** wholesale trade. **~ al minuto** retail trade

com'messo, -a *pp di* **commettere** ● *nmf* shop assistant. **~ viaggiatore** commercial traveller ● *nf (ordine)* order

comme'stibile *a* edible. **commestibili** *nmpl* groceries

com'mettere *vt* commit; make *(sbaglio)*

commi'ato *nm* leave; **prendere ~ da** take leave of

commise'rare *vt* commiserate. **~si** *vr* feel sorry for oneself

commissa'ri'ato *nm (di polizia)* police station

commis'sario *nm* [police] superintendent; *(membro di commissione)* commissioner; *Sport* steward; *Comm* commission agent. **~'ario d'esame** examiner. **~'one** *nf (incarico)* errand; *(comitato ecc)* commission; *(Comm: di merce)* order; **~ioni** *pl (acquisti)* **fare ~ioni** go shopping. **~ione d'esa-**

me board of examiners. **C~ione Europea** European Commission

commit'tente *nmf* purchaser

com'mo|sso *pp di* **commuovere** ● *a* moved. **~'vente** *a* moving

commozi'one *nf* emotion. **~ cerebrale** concussion

commu'over|e *vt* touch, move. **~si** *vr* to be touched

commu'tare *vt* change; *Jur* commute

comò *nm inv* chest of drawers

comoda'mente *adv* comfortably

como'dino *nm* bedside table

comodità *nf inv* comfort; (*convenienza*) convenience

'comodo *a* comfortable; (*conveniente*) convenient; (*spazioso*) roomy; (*facile*) easy; **stia ~l** I don't get up!; **far ~** be useful ● *nm* comfort; **fare il proprio ~** do as one pleases

compae'sano, -a *nmf* fellow countryman

com'pagine *nf* (*squadra*) team

compa'gnia *nf* company; (*gruppo*) party; **fare ~ a qcno** keep sb company; **essere di ~** be sociable. **~ aerea** airline

com'pagno, -a *nmf* companion; (*Comm, Sport, in coppia*) partner; *Pol* comrade. **~ di scuola** schoolmate

compa'rabile *a* comparable

compa'ra|re *vt* compare. **~'tivo** *a* & *nm* comparative. **~zi'one** *nf* comparison

com'pare *nm* (*padrino*) godfather; (*testimone di matrimonio*) witness

compa'rire *vi* appear; (*spiccare*) stand out; **~ in giudizio** appear in court

com'parso, -a *pp di* **comparire** ● *nf* appearance; *Cinema* extra; *Theat* walk-on

compartecipazi'one *nf* sharing; (*quota*) share

comparti'mento *nm* compartment; (*amministrativo*) department

compas'sato *a* calm and collected

compassi'one *nf* compassion;

aver ~ per feel pity for; **far ~** arouse pity. **~'nevole** *a* compassionate

com'passo *nm* [pair of] compasses *pl*

compa'tibil|e *a* (*conciliabile*) compatible; (*scusabile*) excusable. **~ità** *nf* compatibility. **~'mente** *adv* **~mente con i miei impegni** if my commitments allow

compa'tire *vt* pity; (*scusare*) make allowances for

compatri'ota *nmf* compatriot

compat'tezza *nf* (*di materia*) compactness. **com'patto** *a* compact; (*denso*) dense; (*solido*) solid; *fig* united

compene'trare *vt* pervade

compen'sar|e *vt* compensate; (*supplire*) make up for. **~si** *vr* balance each other out

compen'sato *nm* (*legno*) plywood

compensazi'one *nf* compensation

com'penso *nm* compensation; (*retribuzione*) remuneration; **in ~** (*in cambio*) in return; (*d'altra parte*) on the other hand; (*invece*) instead

'comper|a *nf* purchase; **far ~e** do some shopping

compe'rare *vt* buy

compe'ten|te *a* competent. **~za** *nf* competence; (*responsabilità*) responsibility

compe'tere *vi* compete; **~ a** (*compito:*) be the responsibility of

competi|ti'vità *nf* competitiveness. **~'tivo** *a* (*prezzo, carattere*) competitive. **~'tore, ~'trice** *nmf* competitor. **~zi'one** *nf* competition

compia'cen|te *a* obliging. **~za** *nf* obligingness

compia'c|ere *vt/i* please. **~ersi** *vr* (*congratularsi*) congratulate. **~ersi di** (*degnarsi*) condescend. **~i'mento** *nm* satisfaction; *pej* smugness. **~i'uto** *a* satisfied; (*aria, sorriso*) smug

compi'an|gere *vt* pity; (*per lutto*

ecc) sympathize with. **~to** *a* lamented ● *nm* grief

'**compier|e** *vt* (*concludere*) complete; commit (*delitto*); **~e gli anni** have one's birthday; **~si** *vr* end; (*avverarsi*) come true

compi'la|re *vt* compile; fill in (*modulo*). **~zi'one** *nf* compilation

compi'mento *nm* **portare a ~ qcsa** conclude sth

com'pire *vt* = **compiere**

compi'tare *vt* spell

com'pito² *a* polite

'**compito²** *nm* task; *Sch* homework

compi'ut|o *a* **a avere 30 anni ~i** be over 30

comple'anno *nm* birthday

complemen'tare *a* complementary; (*secondario*) subsidiary

comple'mento *nm* complement; *Mil* draft. **~ oggetto** direct object

comples|sità *nf* complexity. **~siva'mente** *adv* on the whole. **~'sivo** *a* comprehensive; (*totale*) total. **com'plesso** *a* complex; (*difficile*) complicated ● *nm* complex; (*di cantanti ecc*) group; (*di circostanze, fattori*) combination; **in ~so** on the whole

completa'mente *adv* completely

comple'tare *vt* complete

com'pleto *a* complete; (*pieno*) full [up]; **essere al ~** (*teatro:*) be sold out; **la famiglia al ~** the whole family ● *nm* (*vestito*) suit; (*insieme di cose*) set

compli'ca|re *vt* complicate. **~rsi** *vr* become complicated. **~to** *a* complicated. **~zi'one** *nf* complication; **salvo ~zioni** all being well

'**complic|e** *nmf* accomplice ● *a* (*sguardo*) knowing. **~ità** *nf* complicity

complimen'tar|e *vt* compliment. **~si** *vr* **~si con** congratulate

compli'menti *nmpl* (*ossequi*) regards; (*congratulazioni*) congratulations; **far ~** stand on ceremony

compli'mento *nm* compliment

complot'tare *vi* plot. **com'plotto** *nm* plot

compo'nente *a* & *nm* component ● *nmf* member

compo'nibile *a* (*cucina*) fitted; (*mobili*) modular

componi'mento *nm* composition; (*letterario*) work

com'por|re *vt* compose; (*ordinare*) put in order; *Typ* set. **~si** *vr* **~si di** be made up of

comporta'mento *nm* behaviour

compor'tar|e *vt* involve; (*consentire*) allow. **~si** *vr* behave

composi|'tore, -'trice *nmf* composer; *Typ* compositor. **~zi'one** *nf* composition

com'posta *nf* stewed fruit; (*concime*) compost

compo'stezza *nf* composure

com'posto *pp di* **comporre** ● *a* composed; (*costituito*) comprising; **stai ~!** sit properly! ● *nm* *Chem* compound

com'pra|re *vt* buy. **~tore, ~'trice** *nmf* buyer

compra'vendita *nf* buying and selling

com'pren|dere *vt* understand; (*includere*) comprise. **~'sibile** *a* understandable. **~sibil'mente** *adv* understandably. **~si'one** *nf* understanding. **~'sivo** *a* understanding; (*che include*) inclusive.

com'preso *pp di* **comprendere** ● *a* included; **tutto compreso** (*prezzo*) all-in

com'pressa *nf* compress; (*pastiglia*) tablet

compressi'one *nf* compression. **com'presso** *pp di* **comprimere** ● *a* compressed

com'primere *vt* press; (*reprimere*) repress

compro'me|sso *pp di* **compromettere** ● *nm* compromise. **~t'tente** *a* compromising. **~ttere** *vt* compromise

comproprietà *nf* multiple ownership

compro'vare *vt* prove

com'punto a contrite

compu'tare vt calculate

com'puter nm computer. **~iz'zare** vt computerize. **~iz'zato** a computerized

computiste'ria nf book-keeping. **'computo** nm calculation

comu'nale a municipal

co'mune a common; (condiviso) mutual; (ordinario) ordinary ●nm borough, council; (amministrativo) commune; **fuori del ~** out of the ordinary. **~'mente** adv commonly

comuni'ca|re vt communicate; pass on (malattia); Relig administer Communion to. **~rsi** vr receive Communion. **~'tiva** nf communicativeness. **~'tivo** a communicative. **~to** nm communiqué. **~to stampa** press release. **~zi'one** nf communication; Teleph [phone] call; **avere la ~zione** get through; **dare la ~zione a qcno** put sb through

comuni'one nf communion; Relig [Holy] Communion

comu'nis|mo nm communism. **~ta** a & nmf communist

comunità nf inv community. **C~ [Economica] Europea** European [Economic] Community

co'munque conj however ●adv anyhow

con prep with; (mezzo) by; **~ facilità** easily; **~ mia grande gioia** to my great delight; **è gentile ~ tutti** he is kind to everyone; **col treno** by train; **~ questo tempo** in this weather

co'nato nm **~ di vomito** retching

'conca nf basin; (valle) dell

concate'na|re vt link together. **~zi'one** nf connection

'concavo a concave

con'ceder|e vt grant; award (premio); (ammettere) admit. **~si** vr allow oneself (pausa)

concentra'mento nm concentration

concen'tra|re vt, **~rsi** vr concen-

trate. **~to** a concentrated ●nm. **~to di pomodoro** tomato purée. **~zi'one** nf concentration

concepi'mento nm conception

conce'pire vt conceive (bambino); (capire) understand; (figurare) conceive of; devise (piano ecc)

con'cernere vt concern

concer'tar|e vt Mus harmonize; (organizzare) arrange. **~si** vr agree

concer'tista nmf concert performer. **con'certo** nm concert; (composizione) concerto

concessio'nario nm agent

concessi'one nf concession

con'cesso pp di **concedere**

con'cetto nm concept; (opinione) opinion

concezi'one nf conception; (idea) concept

con'chiglia nf [sea] shell

'concia nf tanning; (di tabacco) curing

conci'a|re vt tan; cure (tabacco); **~re qcno per le feste** give sb a good hiding. **~rsi** vr (sporcarsi) get dirty; (vestirsi male) dress badly. **~to** a (pelle, cuoio) tanned

concili'abile a compatible

concili'ante a conciliatory

concili'a|re vt reconcile; settle (contravvenzione); (favorire) induce. **~rsi** vr go together; (mettersi d'accordo) become reconciled. **~zi'one** nf reconciliation; Jur settlement

con'cilio nm Relig council; (riunione) assembly

conci'mare vt feed (pianta). **con'cime** nm manure; (chimico) fertilizer

concisi'one nf conciseness. **con'ciso** a concise

conci'tato a excited

concitta'dino, -a nmf fellow citizen

con'clud|ere vt conclude; (finire con successo) achieve. **~dersi** vr come to an end. **~si'one** nf conclusion; **in ~sione** (insomma) in short. **~'sivo** a conclusive. **~so** pp di **concludere**

concomi'tanza nf (di circostanze, fatti) combination

concor'da|nza nf agreement. **~re** vt agree; Gram make agree. **~to** nm agreement; Jur, Comm arrangement

con'cord|e a in agreement; (unanime) unanimous

concor'ren|te a concurrent; (rivale) competing ● nmf Comm, Sport competitor; (candidato) candidate. **~za** nf competition. **~zi'ale** a competitive

con'correre vi (contribuire) concur; (andare insieme) go together; (competere) compete. **~so** pp di **concorrere** ● nm competition. **fuori ~so** not in the official competition. **~so di bellezza** beauty contest

concreta'mente adv concretely

concre|'tare vt (concludere) achieve. **~tiz'zare** vt put into concrete form (idea, progetto)

con'creto a concrete; **in ~** in concrete terms

concussi'one nf extortion

con'danna nf sentence; **pronunziare una ~** pass a sentence. **condan'nare** vt condemn; Jur sentence. **condan'nato, -a** nmf convict

conden'sa|re vt, **~rsi** vr condense. **~zi'one** nf condensation

condi'mento nm seasoning; (salsa) dressing. **con'dire** vt flavour; dress (insalata)

condiscen'den|te a indulgent; pej condescending. **~za** nf indulgence; pej condescension

condi'videre vt share

condizio'na|le a & nm conditional ● nf Jur suspended sentence. **~'mento** nm Psych conditioning

condizio'na|re vt condition. **~to** a conditional. **~tore** nm air conditioner

condizi'one nf condition; **a ~ che** on condition that

condogli'anze nfpl condolences; **fare le ~** a offer condolences to

condomini'ale a (spese) common. **con'dominio** nm joint ownership; (edificio) condominium

condo'nare vt remit. **con'dono** nm remission

con'dotta nf conduct, (circoscrizione di medico) district; (di azienda ecc) management; (tubazione) piping

con'dotto pp di **condurre** ● a **medico ~** district doctor ● nm pipe; Anat duct

condu'cente nm driver

con'du|rre vt lead; drive (veicoli); (accompagnare) take; conduct (gas, elettricità ecc); (gestire) run. **~rsi** vr behave. **~'tore, ~'trice** nmf TV presenter; (di veicolo) driver ● nm Electr conductor. **~'ttura** nf duct

confabu'lare vi have a confab

confa'cente a suitable. **con'farsi** vr confarsi a suit

confedera'zione nf confederation

confe'renz|a nf (discorso) lecture; (congresso) conference. **~a stampa** news conference. **~'iere, -a** nmf lecturer

confe'rire vt (donare) give ● vi confer

con'ferma nf confirmation. **confer'mare** vt confirm

confes'sa|re vt, **~rsi** vr confess. **~io'nale** a & nm confessional. **~i'one** nf confession. **~ore** nm confessor

con'fetto nm sugared almond

confet'tura nf jam

confezio'na|re vt manufacture; make (abiti); package (merci). **~to** a (vestiti) off-the-peg; (gelato) wrapped

confezi'one nf manufacture; (di abiti) tailoring; (di pacchi) packaging; **confezioni** pl clothes. **~ regalo** gift pack

confic'car|e vt thrust. **~si** vr run into

confi'd|are vi **~are in** trust ● vt

confide. **~arsi** vr **~arsi con** confide in. **~ente** a confident ● nmf confidant

confi'denz|a nf confidence; (familiarità) familiarity; **prendersi delle ~e** take liberties. **~'iale** a confidential; (rapporto, tono) familiar

configu'rare vt Comput configure. **~zi'one** nf configuration

confi'nante a neighbouring

confi'na|re vi (relegare) confine ● vi **~re con** border on. **~rsi** vr withdraw. **~to** a confined

con'fine nm border; (tra terreni) boundary. **~o** nm political exile

con'fisca nf (di proprietà) forfeiture. **~'scare** vt confiscate

con'flitt|o nm conflict. **~u'ale** a adversarial

conflu'enza nf confluence; (di strade) junction

conflu'ire vi (fiumi:) flow together; (strade:) meet

con'fonder|e vt confuse; (turbare) confound; (imbarazzare) embarrass. **~si** vr (mescolarsi) mingle; (turbarsi) become confused; vr (sbagliarsi) be mistaken

confor'ma|re vt, **~rsi** vr conform. **~zi'one** nf conformity (a with); (del terreno) composition

con'forme a according. **~'mente** adv accordingly

confor'mi|smo nm conformity. **~sta** nmf conformist. **~tà** nf (a norma) conformity

confor'tante a comforting

confor't|are vt comfort. **~evole** a (comodo) comfortable. **con'forto** nm comfort

confron'tare vt compare

con'fronto nm comparison; **in ~ a** by comparison with; **nei tuoi confronti** towards you; **senza ~** far and away

confusi|o'nario a (persona) muddle-headed. **~'one** nf confusion; (baccano) racket; (disordine) mess; (imbarazzo) embarrassment. **con'fuso** pp di **confondere**

● a confused; (indistinto) indistinct; (imbarazzato) embarrassed

confu'tare vt confute

conge'dar|e vt dismiss; Mil discharge. **~si** vr take one's leave

con'gedo nm leave; **essere in ~** be on leave. **~ malattia** sick leave. **~ maternità** maternity leave

conge'gnare vt devise; (mettere insieme) assemble. **con'gegno** nm device

congela'mento nm freezing; Med frost-bite

conge'la|re vt freeze. **~to** a (cibo) deep-frozen. **~'tore** nm freezer

congeni'ale a congenial

con'genito a congenital

congestio'na|re vt congest. **~to** a (traffico) congested; (viso) flushed. **congesti'one** nf congestion

conget'tura nf conjecture

congi'unger|e vt join; combine (sforzi). **~si** vr join

congiunti'vite nf conjunctivitis

congiun'tivo nm subjunctive

congi'unto pp di **congiungere** ● a joined ● nm relative

congiun'tu|ra nf joint; (circostanza) juncture; (situazione) situation. **~'rale** a economic

congiunzi'one nf Gram conjunction

congi'u|ra nf conspiracy. **~'rare** vi conspire

conglome'rato nm conglomerate; fig conglomeration; (da costruzione) concrete

congratu'la|rsi vr **~rsi con per** congratulate sb on. **~zi'oni** nfpl congratulations

con'grega nf band

congre'ga|re vt, **~rsi** vr congregate. **~zi'one** nf congregation

con'gresso nm congress

'congruo a proper; (giusto) fair

congu'aglio nm balance. **congu'agliare** vt balance.

coni'are vt coin

'conico a conical

co'nifera nf conifer

co'niglio nm rabbit

coniu'gale a marital; ⟨vita⟩ married

coniu'ga|re vt conjugate. ~rsi vr get married. ~zi'one nf conjugation

'coniuge nmf spouse

connazio'nale nmf compatriot

connessi'one nf connection. con'nesso pp di connettere

con'nettere vt connect ● vi think rationally

conni'vente a conniving

conno'ta|re vt connote. ~to ñm distinguishing feature; ~ti pl description

con'nubio nm fig union

'cono nm cone

cono'scen|te nmf acquaintance. ~za nf knowledge; ⟨persona⟩ acquaintance; ⟨sensi⟩ consciousness; perdere ~za lose consciousness; riprendere ~za regain consciousness, come to

co'nosc|ere vt know; ⟨essere a conoscenza di⟩ be acquainted with; ⟨fare la conoscenza di⟩ meet. ~i'tore, ~i'trice nmf connoisseur. ~i'uto pp di conoscere ● a well-known

con'quist|a nf conquest. conqui'stare vt conquer; fig win

consa'cra|re vt consecrate; ordain ⟨sacerdote⟩; ⟨dedicare⟩ dedicate. ~rsi vr devote oneself. ~zi'one nf consecration

consangu'ineo, -a nmf blood-relation

consa'pevo|le a conscious. ~'lezza nf consciousness. ~l'mente adv consciously

'con•cio a conscious

conse'cutivo a consecutive; ⟨seguente⟩ next

con'segna nf delivery; ⟨merce⟩ consignment; ⟨custodia⟩ care; ⟨di prigioniero⟩ handover; ⟨Mil: ordine⟩ orders pl; ⟨Mil: punizione⟩ confinement; pagamento alla ~ cash on delivery

conse'gnare vt deliver; ⟨affidare⟩

give in charge; Mil confine to barracks

consegu'en|te a consequent. ~za nf consequence; di ~za ⟨perciò⟩ consequently

consegui'mento nm achievement

consegu'ire vt achieve ● vi follow

con'senso nm consent

consensu'ale a consensus-based

consen'tire vi consent ● vt allow

con'serto a a braccia conserte with one's arms folded

con'serva nf preserve; ⟨di frutta⟩ jam; ⟨di agrumi⟩ marmalade. ~ di pomodoro tomato sauce

conser'var|e vt preserve; ⟨mantenere⟩ keep. ~si vr keep; ~si in salute keep well

conserva'|tore, -'trice nmf Pol conservative

conserva'torio nm conservatory

conservazi'one nf preservation; a lunga ~ long-life

conside'ra|re vt consider; ⟨stimare⟩ regard. ~to a ⟨stimato⟩ esteemed. ~zi'one nf consideration; ⟨osservazione, riflessione⟩ remark

conside'revole a considerable

consigli'abile a advisable

consigli|'are vt advise; ⟨raccomandare⟩ recommend. ~'arsi vr ~arsi con qcno ask sb's advice. ~'ere, -a nmf adviser; ⟨membro di consiglio⟩ councillor

con'siglio nm advice; ⟨ente⟩ council. ~ d'amministrazione board of directors. C~ dei Ministri Cabinet

consi'sten|te a substantial; ⟨spesso⟩ thick; ⟨fig: argomento⟩ valid. ~za nf consistency; ⟨spessore⟩ thickness

con'sistere vi ~ in consist of

consoci'ata nf ⟨azienda⟩ associate company

conso'lar|e¹ vt console; ⟨rallegrare⟩ cheer. ~si vr console oneself

conso'la|re² a consular. ~to nm consulate

consolazi'one nf consolation; ⟨gioia⟩ joy

con'sole nf inv (tastiera) console

'console nm consul

consoli'dar|e vt, **~si** vr consolidate

conso'nante nf consonant

'consono a consistent

con'sorte nmf consort

con'sorzio nm consortium

con'stare vi **~ di** consist of; (risultare) appear; **a quanto mi consta** as far as I know; **mi consta che** it appears that

consta'ta|re vt ascertain. **~zi'one** nf observation

consu'e|to a & nm usual. **~tudi-'nario** a (diritto) common; (persona) set in one's ways. **~'tudine** nf habit; (usanza) custom

consu'len|te nmf consultant. **~za** nf consultancy

consul'ta|re vt consult. **~rsi con** consult with. **~zi'one** nf consultation

consul'tivo a consultative. **~orio** nm clinic

consu'ma|re vt (usare) consume; wear out (abito, scarpe); consummate (matrimonio); commit (delitto). **~rsi** vr consume; (abito, scarpe:) wear out; (struggersi) pine

consu'mato a (politico) seasoned; (scarpe, tappeto) worn

consuma'|tore, -'trice nmf consumer. **~zi'one** nf (bibita) drink; (spuntino) snack

consu'mis|mo nm consumerism. **~ta** nmf consumerist

con'sumo nm consumption; (di abito, scarpe) wear; (uso) use; **generi di ~** consumer goods or items. **~ [di carburante]** [fuel] consumption

consun'tivo nm [bilancio] **~** final statement

conta'balle nmf fam storyteller

con'tabil|e a book-keeping ● nmf accountant. **~ità** nf accounting; **tenere la ~ità** keep the accounts

contachi'lometri nm inv mileometer, odometer Am

conta'dino, -a nmf farm-worker; (medievale) peasant

contagi'|are vt infect. **con'tagio** nm infection. **~'oso** a infectious

conta'gocce nm inv dropper

contami'na|re vt contaminate. **~zi'one** nf contamination

con'tante nm cash; **pagare in contanti** pay cash

con'tare vt/i count; (tenere conto di) take into account; (proporsi) intend

conta'scatti nm inv Teleph time-unit counter

conta'tore nm meter

contat'tare vt contact. **con'tatto** nm contact

'conte nm count

conteggi'are vt put on the bill ● vi calculate. **con'teggio** nm calculation. **conteggio alla rovescia** countdown

con'te|gno nm behaviour; (atteggiamento) attitude. **~'gnoso** a dignified

contem'pla|re vt contemplate; (fissare) gaze at. **~zi'one** nf contemplation

con'tempo nm **nel ~** in the meantime

contempo|ranea'mente adv at once. **~'raneo, -a** a & nmf contemporary

con'tendente nmf competitor. **con'tendere** vi compete; (litigare) quarrel ● vt contend

conte'n|ere vt contain; (reprimere) repress. **~ersi** vr contain oneself. **~i'tore** nm container

conten'tarsi vr **~ di** be content with

conten'tezza nf joy

conten'tino nm placebo

con'tento a glad; (soddisfatto) contented

conte'nuto nm contents pl; (soggetto) content

contenzi'oso nm legal department

con'tes|a nf disagreement; Sport

contest. **~o** *pp di* **contendere** ● *a* contested

con'tessa *nf* countess

conte'sta|re *vt* contest; *Jur* notify. **~tario** *a* anti-establishment. **~tore**, **~'trice** *nmf* protester. **~zi'one** *nf (disputa)* dispute

con'testo *nm* context

con'tiguo *a* adjacent

continen'tale *a* continental. **conti'nente** *nm* continent

conti'nenza *nf* continence

contin'gen|te *nm* contingent; *(quota)* quota. **~za** *nf* contingency

continua'mente *adv (senza interruzione)* continuously; *(frequentemente)* continually

continu'are *vt/i* continue; *(riprendere)* resume. **~a'tivo** *a* permanent. **~azi'one** *nf* continuation. **~ità** *nf* continuity

con'tinu|o *a* continuous; *(molto frequente)* continual. **corrente ~a** direct current; **di ~o** continually **'conto** *nm* calculation; *(in banca, negozio)* account; *(di ristorante ecc)* bill; *(stima)* consideration; **a conti fatti** all things considered; **far ~ di** *(supporre)* suppose; *(proporsi)* intend; **far ~ su** rely on; **in fin dei conti** when all is said and done; **per ~ di** on behalf of; **per ~ mio** *(a mio parere)* in my opinion; *(da solo)* on my own; **starsene per ~ proprio** be on one's own; **rendersi ~ di qcsa** realize sth; **sul ~ di qcno** *(voci, informazioni)* about sb; **tener ~ di qcsa** take sth into account; **tenere da ~ qcsa** look after sth; **fare i conti con qcno** *fig* sort sb out. **~ corrente** current account, checking account *Am.* **~ alla rovescia** countdown

con'torcer|e *vt* twist. **~si** *vr* twist about

contor'nare *vt* surround

con'torno *nm* contour; *Culin* vegetables *pl*

contorsi'one *nf* contortion. **con'torto** *pp di* **contorcere** ● *a* twisted

contrabban|'dare *vt* smuggle. **~di'ere**, **-a** *nmf* smuggler. **contrab'bando** *nm* contraband

contrab'basso *nm* double bass

contraccambi'are *vt* return. **contrac'cambio** *nm* return

contracce|t'tivo *nm* contraceptive. **~zi'one** *nf* contraception

contrac'col|po *nm* rebound; *(di arma da fuoco)* recoil; *fig* repercussion

con'trada *nf (rione)* district

contrad'detto *pp di* **contraddire**

contrad'dir|e *vt* contradict. **~'torio** *a* contradictory. **~zi'one** *nf* contradiction

contraddi'stin|guere *vt* differentiate. **~to** *a* distinct

contra'ente *nmf* contracting party

contra'ereo *a* anti-aircraft

contraf'fa|re *vt* disguise; *(imitare)* imitate; *(falsificare)* forge. **~tto** *a* forged. **~zi'one** *nf* disguising; *(imitazione)* imitation; *(falsificazione)* forgery

con'tralto *nm* countertenor ● *nf* contralto

contrap'peso *nm* counterbalance

contrap'por|re *vt* counter; *(confrontare)* compare. **~si** *vr* contrast; **~si a** be opposed to

contraria'mente *adv* contrary (a to)

contrari'a|re *vt* oppose; *(infastidire)* annoy. **~'arsi** *vr* get annoyed. **~età** *nf inv* adversity; *(ostacolo)* set-back

con'trario *a* contrary, opposite; *(direzione)* opposite; *(sfavorevole)* unfavourable ● *nm* contrary, opposite; **al ~** on the contrary

con'trarre *vt* contract

contras|se'gnare *vt* mark. **~'segno** *nm* mark; **[in] ~segno** *(spedizione)* cash on delivery, COD

contra'stante *a* contrasting

contra'stare *vt* oppose; *(contestare)* contest ● *vi* clash. **con'trasto** *nm* contrast; *(litigio)* dispute

contrattac'care *vt* counter-attack. **contrat'tacco** nm counter-attack

contrat'ta|re vt/i negotiate; (mercanteggiare) bargain. **~zi'one** nf (salariale) bargaining

contrat'tempo nm hitch

con'tratt|o pp di **contrarre** ● nm contract. **~o a termine** fixed-term contract. **~u'ale** a contractual

contravve'n|ire vi contravene. **~zi'one** nf contravention; (multa) fine

contrazi'one nf contraction; (di prezzi) reduction

contribu'ente nmf contributor; (del fisco) taxpayer

contribu'ire vi contribute. **contri'buto** nm contribution

'**contro** prep against; **~ di me** against me ● nm **il pro e il ~** the pros and cons pl

contro'battere vt counter

controbilanci'are vt counterbalance

controcor'rente a (idee, persona) non-conformist ● adv upriver; fig upstream

controffen'siva nf counter-offensive

controfi'gura nf stand-in

controfir'mare vt countersign

controindicazi'one nf Med contraindication

control'la|re vt control; (verificare) check; (collaudare) test. **~rsi** vr have self-control. **~to** a controlled

con'trol|lo nm control; (verifica) check; Med check-up. **~lo delle nascite** birth control. **~'lore** nm controller; (sui treni ecc) [ticket] inspector. **~lore di volo** air-traffic controller

contro'luce nf **in ~** against the light

contro'mano adv in the wrong direction

contromi'sura nf countermeasure

contropi'ede nm **prendere in ~** catch off guard

controprodu'cente a self-defeating

con'trordin|e nm counter order; **salvo ~i** unless I/you hear to the contrary

contro'senso nm contradiction in terms

controspio'naggio nm counter-espionage

contro'vento adv against the wind

contro'vers|ia nf controversy; Jur dispute. **~o** a controversial

contro'voglia adv unwillingly

contu'macia nf default; **in ~** in one's absence

contun'dente a (corpo, arma) blunt

contur'ba|nte a perturbing

contusi'one nf bruise

convale'scen|te a convalescent. **~za** nf convalescence; **essere in ~za** be convalescing

con'vali|da nf validation. **~'dare** vt confirm; validate (atto, biglietto)

con'vegno nm meeting; (congresso) congress

conve'nevol|e a suitable; **~i** pl pleasantries

conveni'en|te a convenient; (prezzo) attractive; (vantaggioso) advantageous. **~za** nf convenience; (interesse) advantage; (di prezzo) attractiveness

conve'nire vi (riunirsi) gather; (concordare) agree; (ammettere) admit; (essere opportuno) be convenient ● vt agree on; **ci conviene andare** it is better to go; **non mi conviene stancarmi** I'd better not tire myself out

con'vento nm (di suore) convent; (di frati) monastery

conve'nuto a fixed

convenzi|o'nale a conventional. **~'one** nf convention

conver'gen|te a converging. **~za** nf fig confluence

con'vergere *vi* converge
conver'sa|re *vi* converse. **~zi'one** *nf* conversation
conversi'one *nf* conversion
con'verso *pp di* **convergere**
conver'tibile *nf Auto* convertible
conver'ti|re *vt* convert. **~rsi** *vr* be converted. **~to, -a** *mf* convert
con'vesso *a* convex
convin'cente *a* convincing
con'vin|cere *vt* convince. **~to a** convinced. **~zi'one** *nf* conviction
con'vitto *nm* boarding school
convi'ven|te *nm* common-law husband ●*nf* common-law wife. **~za** *nf* cohabitation. **con'vivere** *vi* live together
convivi'ale *a* convivial
convo'ca|re *vt* convene. **~zi'one** *nf* convening
convogli'are *vt* convey; ⟨*navi*⟩ convoy. **con'voglio** *nm* convoy; ⟨*ferroviario*⟩ train
convulsi'one *nf* convulsion. **con-'vulso** *a* convulsive; ⟨*febbrile*⟩ feverish
coope'ra|re *vi* co-operate. **~'tiva** *nf* co-operative. **~zi'one** *nf* co-operation
coordina'mento *nm* co-ordination
coordi'na|re *vt* co-ordinate. **~ta** *nf Math* coordinate. **~zi'one** *nf* co-ordination
co'perchio *nm* lid; ⟨*copertura*⟩ cover
co'perta *nf* blanket; ⟨*copertura*⟩ cover; *Naut* deck
coper'tina *nf* cover; ⟨*di libro*⟩ dustjacket
co'perto *pp di* **coprire** ● *a* covered; ⟨*cielo*⟩ overcast ●*nm* ⟨*a tavola*⟩ place; ⟨*prezzo del coperto*⟩ cover charge; **al ~** under cover
coper'tone *nm* tarpaulin; ⟨*gomma*⟩ tyre
coper'tura *nf* covering; *Comm, Fin* cover
'copia *nf* copy; **bella/brutta ~** fair/rough copy. **~ su carta** hardcopy. **copi'are** *vt* copy

copi'one *nm* script
copi'oso *a* plentiful
'coppa *nf* ⟨*calice*⟩ goblet; ⟨*per gelato ecc*⟩ dish; *Sport* cup. **~ [di] gelato** ice-cream ⟨*carica*⟩. **~** ⟨*carica*⟩ gelato ice-cream ⟨*served in a dish*⟩
cop'petta *nf* ⟨*di ceramica, vetro*⟩ bowl; ⟨*di gelato*⟩ small tub
'coppia *nf* couple; ⟨*in carte*⟩ pair
co'prente *a* ⟨*cipria, vernice*⟩ covering
copri'capo *nm* headgear
copri'fu'oco *nm* curfew
copri'letto *nm* bedspread
copripiu'mino *nm* duvet cover
co'pri|re *vt* cover; drown ⟨*suono*⟩; hold ⟨*carica*⟩. **~si** *vr* ⟨*vestirsi*⟩ cover up; *fig* cover oneself; ⟨*cielo:*⟩ become overcast
coque *sf* **alla ~** ⟨*uovo*⟩ soft-boiled
co'raggi|o *nm* courage; ⟨*sfacciataggine*⟩ nerve; **~o!** come on. **~'oso** *a* courageous
co'rale *a* choral
co'rallo *nm* coral
co'rano *nm* Koran
co'raz|za *nf* armour; ⟨*di animali*⟩ shell. **~'zata** *nf* battleship. **~'zato** *a* ⟨*nave*⟩ armour-clad
corbelle'ria *nf* nonsense; ⟨*sproposito*⟩ blunder
'corda *nf* ⟨*spago, Mus*⟩ string; ⟨*fune*⟩ rope; ⟨*cavo*⟩ cable; **essere giù di ~** be depressed; **dare ~ a** qcno encourage sb. **corde** *pl vocali* vocal cords
cor'data *nf* roped party
cordi'al|e *a* cordial ● *nm* ⟨*bevanda*⟩ cordial; **saluti ~i** best wishes. **~ità** *nf* cordiality
cor'doglio *nm* grief; ⟨*lutto*⟩ mourning
cor'done *nm* cord; ⟨*schieramento*⟩ cordon. **~ ombelicale** umbilical cord
core|ogra'fia *nf* choreography. **~'ografo, -a** *nmf* choreographer
cori'andoli *nmpl* confetti *sg*
cori'andolo *nm* ⟨*spezia*⟩ coriander
cori'ca|re *vt* put to bed. **~si** *vr* go to bed
co'rista *nmf* choir member

cor'nacchia nf crow

corna vedi **corno**

corna'musa nf bagpipes pl

'**cornea** nf cornea

cor'nett|a nf Mus cornet; (del telefono) receiver. ~o nm (brioche) croissant

cor'ni|ce nf frame. ~ci'one nm cornice

'**corno** nm (pl nf **corna**) horn; **fare le corna a qcno** be unfaithful to sb; **fare le corna** (per scongiuro) touch wood. **cor'nuto** a horned ● nm (fam: marito tradito) cuckold; (insulto) bastard

'**coro** nm chorus; Relig choir

co'**rolla** nf corolla

co'**rona** nf crown; (di fiori) wreath; (rosario) rosary. ~'**mento** nm (di impresa) crowning. **coro'nare** vt crown; (sogno) fulfil

cor'**petto** nm bodice

'**corpo** nm body; (Mil, diplomatico) corps inv; **a ~ a ~** man to man; **andare di ~** move one's bowels. **~ di ballo** corps de ballet. **~ insegnante** teaching staff. **~ del reato** incriminating item

corpo'**rale** a corporal

corporati'**vismo** nm corporatism

corpora'**tura** nf build

corporazi'**one** nf corporation

cor'**poreo** a bodily

cor'**poso** a full-bodied

corpu'**lento** a stout

cor'**puscolo** nm corpuscle

corre'**dare** vt equip

corre'**dino** nm (per neonato) layette

cor'**redo** nm (nuziale) trousseau

cor'**reggere** vt correct; lace (bevanda)

corre'**lare** vt correlate

cor'**rente** a running; (in vigore) current; (frequente) everyday; (inglese ecc) fluent ● nf current; (d'aria) draught; **essere al ~** be up to date. **~'mente** adv (parlare) fluently

'**correre** vi run; (affrettarsi) hurry; Sport race; (notizie:) circulate; ~

dietro a run after ● vt run; ~ **un pericolo** run a risk; **lascia ~!** don't bother!

corre|tta'**mente** adv correctly.

cor'**retto** pp di **correggere** ● a correct; (caffè) with a drop of alcohol. **~zi'one** nf correction. **~zione di bozze** proof-reading

cor'**rida** nf bullfight

cor'**ridoio** nm corridor; Aeron aisle

corri'**dore** -'**trice** nmf racer; (a piedi) runner

corri'**era** nf coach, bus

corri'**ere** nm courier; (posta) mail; (spedizioniere) carrier

corri'**mano** nm bannister

corri'**spettivo** nm amount due

corrispon'**den|te** a corresponding ● nmf correspondent. **~za** nf correspondence; **scuola/corsi per ~za** correspondence course; **vendite per ~za** mail-order [shopping]. **corri'spondere** vi correspond; (stanza:) communicate; **corrispondere a** (contraccambiare) return

corri'**sposto** a (amore) reciprocated

corrobo'**rare** vt strengthen; fig corroborate

cor'**roder|e** vt, **~si** vr corrode

cor'**rompere** vt corrupt; (con denaro) bribe

corrosi'**one** nf corrosion. **corro'sivo** a corrosive

cor'**roso** pp di **corrodere**

cor'**rotto** pp di **corrompere** ● a corrupt

corrucci'**ar|si** vr be vexed. **~to** a upset

corru'**gare** vt wrinkle; ~ **la fronte** knit one's brows

corruzi'**one** nf corruption; (con denaro) bribery

'**corsa** nf running; (rapida) dash; Sport race; (di treno ecc) journey; **di ~** at a run; **fare una ~** run

cor'**sia** nf gangway; (di ospedale) ward; Auto lane; (di supermercato) aisle

cor'sivo *nm* italics *pl*

'**corso** *pp di* **correre ●** *nm* course; (*strada*) main street; *Comm* circulation; **lavori ~ in** work in progress; **nel ~ di** during. **~ d'acqua** watercourse

'**corte** *nf* [court]yard; (*Jur, regale*) court; **fare la ~ a qcno** court sb. **~ d'appello** court of appeal

cor'teccia *nf* bark

corteggia'mento *nm* courtship

coreggia'a|re *vt* court. **~'tore** *nm* admirer

cor'teo *nm* procession

cor'te|se *a* courteous. **~'sia** *nf* courtesy; **per ~sia** please

cortigi'ano, -a *nmf* courtier **●** *nf* courtesan

cor'tile *nm* courtyard

cor'tina *nf* curtain; (*schermo*) screen

'**corto** *a* short; **per faria corta in** short; **essere a ~** be short of. **~ circuito** *nm* short [circuit]

cortome'traggio *nm* Cinema short

cor'vino *a* jet-black

'**corvo** *nm* raven

'**cosa** *nf* thing; (*faccenda*) matter; *inter, rel* what; [**che**] **~** what; **nessuna ~** nothing; **ogni ~** everything; **per prima ~** first of all; **tante cose** so many things; (*augurio*) all the best

'**cosca** *nf* clan

'**coscia** *nf* thigh; *Culin* leg

cosci'en|te *a* conscious. **~za** *nf* conscience; (*consapevolezza*) consciousness

co'scri|tto *nm* conscript. **~zi'one** *nf* conscription

così *adv* so; (*in questo modo*) like this, like that; (*perciò*) therefore; **le cose stanno ~** that's how things stand; **fermo ~!** hold it; **proprio ~!** exactly!; **basta ~!** that will do!; **ah, è ~?** it's like that, is it?; **~ ~** so-so; **e ~ via** and so on; **per ~ dire** so to speak; **più di ~** any more; **una ~ cara ragazza!** such a nice girl!; **è stato ~**

generoso da aiutarti he was kind enough to help you **●** *conj* (*allora*) so **●** *a inv* (*tale*) like that, such; **una ragazza ~** a girl like that, such a girl

cosicché *conj* and so

cosid'detto *a* so-called

co'smesi *nf* cosmetics

co'smetico *a & nm* cosmetic

'**cosmico** *a* cosmic

'**cosmo** *nm* cosmos

cosmopo'lita *a* cosmopolitan

co'spargere *vt* sprinkle; (*disseminare*) scatter

co'spetto *nm* **al ~ di** in the presence of

co'spicuo *a* conspicuous; (*somma ecc*) considerable

cospi'ra|re *vi* conspire. **~'tore**, **~'trice** *nmf* conspirator. **~zi'one** *nf* conspiracy

'**costa** *nf* coast, coastline; *Anat* rib

costà *adv* there

co'stan|te *a & nf* constant. **~za** *nf* constancy

co'stare *vi* cost; **quanto costa? how much is it?**

co'stata *nf* chop

costeggi'are *vt* (*per mare*) coast; (*per terra*) skirt

co'stei *pers pron vedi* **costui**

costellazi'one *nf* constellation

coster'na|to *a* dismayed. **~zi'one** *nf* consternation

costi'er|a *nf* stretch of coast. **~o a** coastal

costi'pa|to *a* constipated. **~zi'one** *nf* constipation; (*raffreddore*) bad cold

costitu'ir|e *vt* constitute; (*formare*) form; (*nominare*) appoint. **~si** *vr Jur* give oneself up

costituzio'nale *a* constitutional.

costituzi'one *nf* constitution; (*fondazione*) setting up

'**costo** *nm* cost; **ad ogni ~** at all costs; **a nessun ~** on no account

'**costola** *nf* rib; (*di libro*) spine

costo'letta *nf* cutlet

co'storo *pron vedi* **costui**

co'stoso *a* costly

co'stretto *pp di* **costringere**

co'strin|gere *vt* compel; (*stringere*) constrict. ~**t'tivo** *a* coercive. ~**zi'one** *nf* constraint

costru|'ire *vt* build, construct. ~**t'tivo** *a* constructive. ~**zi'one** *nf* building, construction

co'stui, co'stei, *pl* co'storo *prons* (*soggetto*) he, she, *pl* they; (*complemento*) him, her, *pl* them

co'stume *nm* (*usanza*) custom; (*condotta*) morals *pl*; (*indumento*) costume. ~ **da bagno** swim-suit; (*da uomo*) swimming trunks

co'tenna *nf* pigskin; (*della pancetta*) rind

coto'letta *nf* cutlet

co'tone *nm* cotton. ~ **idrofilo** cotton wool, absorbent cotton *Am*

'cotta *nf* (*fam: innamoramento*) crush

'cottimo *nm* **lavorare a** ~ do piece-work

'cotto *pp di* **cuocere** ● *a* done; (*fam: infatuato*) in love; (*fam: sbronzo*) drunk; **ben** ~ (*carne*) well done

'cotton fi'oc® *nm inv* cotton bud

cot'tura *nf* cooking

co'vare *vt* hatch; sicken for (*malattia*); harbour (*odio*) ● *vi* smoulder

'covo *nm* den

co'vone *nm* sheaf

'cozza *nf* mussel

coz'zare *vi* ~ **contro** bump into. 'cozzo *nm fig* clash

C.P. *abbr* (**Casella Postale**) PO Box

'crampo *nm* cramp

'cranio *nm* skull

cra'tere *nm* crater

cra'vatta *nf* tie; (*a farfalla*) bow-tie

cre'anza *nf* politeness; **mala** ~ bad manners

cre|'are *vt* create; (*causare*) cause. ~**tività** *nf* creativity. ~**'tivo** *a* creative. ~**'ione** *nm* creation. ~**'tore, ~'trice** *nmf* creator. ~**zi'one** *nf* creation

crea'tura *nf* creature; (*bambino*) baby; **povera ~!** poor thing!

cre'den|te *nmf* believer. ~**za** *nf* belief; *Comm* credit; (*mobile*) sideboard. ~**zi'ali** *nfpl* credentials

'creder|e *vt* believe; (*pensare*) think ● *vi* ~**e in** believe in; **credo di sì** I think so; **non ti credo** I don't believe you. ~**si** *vr* think oneself to be; **si crede uno scrittore** he flatters himself he is a writer. **cre'dibile** *a* credible.

credibilità *nf* credibility

'credi|to *nm* credit; (*stima*) esteem; **comprare a ~to** buy on credit. ~**'tore, ~'trice** *nmf* creditor

'credo *nm inv* credo

credulità *nf* credulity

'credu|lo *a* credulous. ~**'lone, -a** *nmf* simpleton

'crema *nf* cream; (*di uova e latte*) custard. ~ **idratante** moisturizer. ~ **pasticciera** egg custard. ~ **solare** suntan lotion

cre'ma|re *vt* cremate. ~**'torio** *nm* crematorium. ~**zi'one** *nf* cremation

crème cara'mel *nf* crème caramel

creme'ria *nf* dairy (*also selling ice cream and cakes*)

Crem'lino *nm* Kremlin

'crepa *nf* crack

cre'paccio *nm* cleft; (*di ghiacciaio*) crevasse

crepacu'ore *nm* heart-break

crepa'pelle: **a ~** *adv* fit to burst; **ridere a ~** split one's sides with laughter

cre'pare *vi* crack; (*fam: morire*) kick the bucket; ~ **dal ridere** laugh fit to burst

crepa'tura *nf* crevice

crêpe *nf inv* pancake

crepi'tare *vi* crackle

cre'puscolo *nm* twilight

cre'scendo *nm* crescendo

'cresc|ere *vi* grow; (*aumentare*) increase ● *vt* (*allevare*) bring up; (*aumentare*) increase. ~**ita** *nf* growth; (*aumento*) increase. ~**i'uto** *pp di* **crescere** 'cresi|ma *nf* confirmation. ~**'mare** *vt* confirm

'crespo *a* ⟨*capelli*⟩ frizzy ● *nm* crêpe

'cresta *nf* crest; ⟨*cima*⟩ peak

'creta *nf* clay

'Creta *nf* Crete

cre'tino *a* & *nmf* idiot

'cric *nm* jack

'cricca *nf* gang

cri'ceto *nm* hamster

crimi'nal|e *a* & *nmf* criminal. ~**ità** *nf* crime. '**crimine** *nm* crime

crimi'noso *a* criminal

'crin|e *nm* horsehair. ~**i'era** *nf* mane

'cripta *nf* crypt

crisan'temo *nm* chrysanthemum

'crisi *nf inv* crisis; *Med* fit

cristal'lino *a* crystal

cristalliz'zar|e *vt*, ~**si** *vr* crystallize; ⟨*fig: parola, espressione:*⟩ become part of the language

cri'stallo *nm* crystal

Cristia'nesimo *nm* Christianity

cristi'ano, -a *a* & *nmf* Christian

'Cristo *nm* Christ; **un povero c~** a poor beggar

cri'terio *nm* criterion; ⟨*buon senso*⟩ [common] sense

'criti|ca *nf* criticism; ⟨*recensione*⟩ review. **criti'care** *vt* criticize. ~**co** *a* critical ● *nm* critic. ~**cone, -a** *nmf* faultfinder

crivel'lare *vt* riddle (**di** with)

cri'vello *nm* sieve

croc'cante *a* crisp ● *nm* type of crunchy nut biscuit

croc'chetta *nf* croquette

'croce *nf* cross; **a occhio e c~** roughly; **fare testa e ~** spin a coin. **C~ Rossa** Red Cross

croce'via *nm inv* crossroads *sg*

croci'ata *nf* crusade

cro'cicchio *nm* crossroads *sg*

croci'era *nf* cruise; *Archit* crossing

croci'fig|gere *vt* crucify. ~**ssi'one** *nf* crucifixion. ~**sso** *pp di* **crocifiggere** ● *a* crucified ● *nm* crucifix

crogio'larsi *vr* bask

crogi[u]'olo *nm* crucible; *fig* melting pot

crol'lare *vi* collapse; ⟨*prezzi:*⟩ slump. '**crollo** *nm* collapse; ⟨*dei prezzi*⟩ slump

cro'mato *a* chromium-plated. '**cromo** *nm* chrome. **cromo'soma** *nm* chromosome

'cronaca *nf* chronicle; ⟨*di giornale*⟩ news; *TV, Radio* commentary; **fatto di ~** news item. **~ nera** crime news

'cronico *a* chronic

cro'nista *nmf* reporter

crono'logico *a* chronological

crono'traggio *nm* timing

crono'metrare *vt* time

cro'nometro *nm* chronometer

'crosta *nf* crust; ⟨*di formaggio*⟩ rind; ⟨*di ferita*⟩ scab; ⟨*quadro*⟩ daub

cro'staceo *nm* shellfish

cro'stata *nf* tart

cro'stino *nm* croûton

crucci'arsi *vr* worry. '**cruccio** *nm* worry

cruci'ale *a* crucial

cruci'verba *nm inv* crossword [puzzle]

cru'del|e *a* cruel. ~**tà** *nf inv* cruelty

'crudo *a* raw; ⟨*rigido*⟩ harsh

cru'ento *a* bloody

cru'miro *nm* blackleg, scab

'crusca *nf* bran

cru'scotto *nm* dashboard

'Cuba *nf* Cuba

cu'betto *nm* — **di ghiaccio** ice cube

'cubico *a* cubic

cubi'tal|e *a* **a caratteri ~i** in enormous letters

'cubo *nm* cube

cuc'cagna *nf* abundance; ⟨*baldoria*⟩ merry-making; **paese della ~** land of plenty

cuc'cetta *nf* ⟨*su un treno*⟩ couchette; *Naut* berth

cucchia'ino *nm* teaspoon

cucchi'a|io nm spoon; **al ~io** ⟨dolce⟩ creamy. **~i'ata** nf spoonful

'cuccia nf dog's bed; **fa la ~!** lie down!

cuccio'lata nf litter

'cucciolo nm puppy

cu'cina nf kitchen; ⟨il cucinare⟩ cooking; ⟨cibo⟩ food; ⟨apparecchio⟩ cooker; **far da ~** cook; **libro di ~** cook[ery] book. **~ a gas** gas cooker

cuci'n|are vt cook. **~ino** nm kitchenette

cuci'|re vt sew; **macchina per ~re** sewing-machine. **~to** nm sewing. **~'tura** nf seam

cucù nm inv cuckoo

'cuculo nm cuckoo

'cuffia nf bonnet; ⟨da bagno⟩ bathing-cap; ⟨ricevitore⟩ headphones pl

cu'gino, -a nmf cousin

'cui pron rel ⟨persona: con prep⟩ who, whom fml; ⟨cose, animali: con prep⟩ which; ⟨tra articolo e nome⟩ whose; **la persona con ~ ho parlato** the person [who] I spoke to; **la ditta per ~ lavoro** the company I work for, the company for which I work; **l'amico ~ libro è stato pubblicato** the friend whose book was published; **in ~** ⟨dove⟩ where; ⟨quando⟩ that; **per ~** ⟨perciò⟩ so; **la città in ~ vivo** the city I live in, the city where I live; **il giorno in ~ l'ho visto** the day [that] I saw him

culi'nari|a nf cookery. **~o a** culinary

'culla nf cradle. **cul'lare** vt rock

culmi'na|nte a culminating. **~re** vi culminate. **~to** nm peak

'culo nm vulg arse; ⟨fortuna⟩ luck

'culto nm cult; Relig religion; ⟨adorazione⟩ worship

cul'tu|ra nf culture. **~ra generale** general knowledge. **~'rale** a cultural

cultu'ris|mo nm body-building. **~ta** nmf body-builder

cumula'tivo a cumulative; **biglietto ~** group ticket

'cumulo nm pile; ⟨mucchio⟩ heap; ⟨nuvola⟩ cumulus

'cuneo nm wedge

cu'netta nf gutter

cu'ocere vt/i cook; fire ⟨ceramica⟩

cu'oco, -a nmf cook

cu'oio nm leather. **~ capelluto** scalp

cu'ore nm heart; **cuori** pl ⟨carte⟩ hearts; **nel profondo del ~** in one's heart of hearts; **di [buon] ~** ⟨persona⟩ kind-hearted; **nel ~ della notte** in the middle of the night; **stare a ~ a qcno** be very important to sb

cupi'digia nf greed

'cupo a gloomy; ⟨suono⟩ deep

'cupola nf dome

'cura nf care; ⟨amministrazione⟩ management; Med treatment; **a ~ di** edited by; **in ~** under treatment. **~ dimagrante** [slimming] diet. **cu'rante** a **medico curante** GP, doctor

cu'rar|e vt take care of; Med treat; ⟨guarire⟩ cure; edit ⟨testo⟩. **~si** vr take care of oneself; Med follow a treatment; **~si di** ⟨badare a⟩ mind

cu'rato nm parish priest

cura'tore, -'trice nmf trustee; ⟨di testo⟩ editor

'curia nf curia

curio'sare vi be curious; ⟨mettere il naso⟩ pry ⟨in into⟩; ⟨nei negozi⟩ look around. **~ità** nf inv curiosity. **curi'oso** a curious; ⟨strano⟩ odd

cur'sore nm Comput cursor

'curva nf curve; ⟨stradale⟩ bend. **~ a gomito** U-bend. **cur'vare** vt curve; ⟨strada:⟩ bend. **cur'varsi** vr bend. **'curvo** a curved; ⟨piegato⟩ bent

cusci'netto nm pad; Mech bearing

cu'scino nm cushion; ⟨guanciale⟩ pillow. **~ d'aria** air cushion

'cuspide nf spire

cu'stod|e nm caretaker. **~e giudiziario** official receiver. **~ia**

nf care; *Jur* custody; *(astuccio)* case. **~la cautelare** remand. **custo'dire** *vt* keep; *(badare)* look after

cu'taneo *a* skin *attrib*
'cute *nf* skin
cu'ticola *nf* cuticle

•••••••••••••••••••••••••••••••••

Dd

•••••••••••••••••••••••••••••••••

da *prep* from; *(con verbo passivo)* by; *(moto a luogo)* to; *(moto per luogo)* through; *(stato in luogo)* at; *(temporale)* since; *(continuativo)* for; *(causale)* with; *(in qualità di)* as; *(con caratteristica)* with; *(come)* like; **da Roma a Milano** from Rome to Milan; **staccare un quadro dalla parete** take a picture off the wall; **i bambini dai 5 al 10 anni** children between 5 and 10; **vedere qcsa da vicino/lontano** see sth from up close/from a distance; **scritto da** written by; **andare dal panettiere** go to the baker's; **passo da te più tardi** I'll come over to your place later; **passiamo da qui** let's go this way; **un appuntamento dal dentista** an appointment at the dentist's; **il treno passa da Venezia** the train goes through Venice; **dall'anno scorso** since last year; **vivo qui da due anni** I've been living here for two years; **da domani** from tomorrow; **piangere dal dolore** cry with pain; **ho molto da fare** I have a lot to do; **occhiali da sole** sunglasses; **qualcosa da mangiare** something to eat; **un uomo dai capelli scuri** a man with dark hair; **è un oggetto da poco** it's not worth much; **l'ho fatto da solo** I did it by myself; **si è fatto da sé** he is a self-made man; **non è da lui** it's not like him

dac'capo *adv* again; *(dall'inizio)* from the beginning
dacché *conj* since
'dado *nm* dice; *Culin* stock cube; *Techn* nut
daf'fare *nm* work
'dagli = da + gli. 'dai = da + i
'dai *int* come on!
'daino *nm* deer; *(pelle)* buckskin
dal = da + il. 'dalla = da + la. 'dalle = da + le. 'dallo = da + lo
'dalia *nf* dahlia
dal'tonico *a* colour-blind
'dama *nf* lady; *(nei balli)* partner; *(gioco)* draughts *sg*
dami'gella *nf* *(di sposa)* bridesmaid
damigi'ana *nf* demijohn
da'naro *nm* = **denaro**
dana'roso *a (fam: ricco)* loaded
da'nese *a* Danish ●*nmf* Dane ●*nm (lingua)* Danish
Dani'marca *nf* Denmark
dan'na|re *vt* damn; **far ~re qcno** drive sb mad. **~to** *a* damned. **~zi'one** *nf* damnation
danneggia'mento *nm* damage. **~'are** *vt* damage; *(nuocere)* harm
'danno *nm* damage; *(a persona)* harm. **dan'noso** *a* harmful
Da'nubio *nm* Danube
'danza *nf* dance; *(il danzare)* dancing. **dan'zare** *vi* dance
dapper'tutto *adv* everywhere
dap'poco *a* worthless
dap'prima *adv* at first
'dardo *nm* dart
'dar|e *vt* give; sit *(esame)*; have *(festa)*; **~ qcsa a qcno** give sb sth; **~ da mangiare a qcno** give sb something to eat; **~ la buonanotte a qcno** say good night to sb; **~ del tu/del lei a qcno** address sb as "tu"/"lei"; **~ del cretino a qcno** call sb an idiot; **~ qcsa per scontato** take sth for granted; **cosa danno alla TV stasera?** what's on TV tonight? ●*vi* ~ nel-

l'occhio be conspicuous; ~ alla testa go to one's head; ~ su (finestra, casa) look on to; ~ sui o ai nervi a qcno get on sb's nerves ●nm Comm debit. ~si vr (scambiarsi) give each other; ~si da fare get down to it; si è dato tanto da fare! he worked so hard!; ~si a (cominciare) take up; ~si al bere take to drink; ~si per (malato, assente) pretend to be; ~si per vinto give up; può ~si maybe

'darsena nf dock

'data nf date. ~ di emissione date of issue. ~ di nascita date of birth. ~ di scadenza cut-off date

da'ta|re vt date; a ~re da as from. ~to a dated

'dato a given; (dedito) addicted; ~ che seeing that; given that ●nm datum. ~ di fatto well-established fact; dati pl data. da'tore nm giver. datore, datrice nmf di lavoro employer

'dattero nm date

dattilogra'f|are vt type. ~ia nf typing. datti'lografo, -a nmf typist

dattilo'scritto a (copia) typewritten

dat'torno adv togliersi ~ clear off

da'vanti adv before; (dirimpetto) opposite; (di fronte) in front ●a inv front ●nm front; ~ a prep before, in front of

davan'zale nm window sill

da'vanzo adv more than enough

dav'vero adv really; per ~ in earnest; dici ~? honestly?

'dazio nm duty; (ufficio) customs pl

d.C. abbr (dopo Cristo) AD

'dea nf goddess

debel'lare vt defeat

debili'ta|nte a weakening. ~re vt weaken. ~rsi vr become debilitated. ~zi'one nf debilitation

debita'mente adv duly

'debi|to a due; a tempo ~ in due course ●nm debt. ~'tore, ~'trice nmf debtor

'debo|le a weak; (luce) dim; (suono) faint ●nm weak point; (preferenza) weakness. ~'lezza nf weakness

debor'dare vi overflow

debosci'ato a debauched

debut'ta|nte nm (attore) actor making his début ●nf actress making her début. ~re vi make one's début. de'butto nm début

deca'den|te a decadent. ~'tismo nm decadence. ~za nf decline; Jur loss. deca'dere vi lapse. deca-di'mento nm (delle arti) decline

decaffei'nato a decaffeinated ●nm decaffeinated coffee, decaf fam

decan'tare vt (lodare) praise

decapi'ta|re vt decapitate; behead (condannato). ~zi'one nf decapitation; beheading

decap'pot'tabile a convertible

de'ce|dere vi (morire) die. ~'duto a deceased

dece'lerare vt decelerate, slow down

decen'nale a ten-yearly. de'cen-nio nm decade

de'cen|te a decent. ~te'mente adv decently. ~za nf decency

decentra'mento nm decentralization

de'cesso nm death; atto di ~ death certificate

de'cider|e vt decide; settle (questione). ~si vr make up one's mind

deci'frare vt decipher; (documenti cifrati) decode

deci'male a decimal

deci'mare vt decimate

'decimo a tenth

de'cina ·nf Math ten; una ~ di (circa dieci) about ten

decisa'mente adv definitely, decidedly

decisio'nale a decision-making

deci'si|one nf decision. ~'sivo a decisive. de'ciso pp di decidere ●a decided

decla'ma|re *vt/i* declaim. **~'torio** *a* (*stile*) declamatory

declas'sare *vt* downgrade

decli'na|re *vt* decline. **~re ogni responsabilità** disclaim all responsibility ●*vi* go down; (*tramontare*) set. **~zi'one** *nf* Gram declension. **de'clino** *nm* decline; **in declino** (*popolarità:*) on the decline

decodificazi'one *nf* decoding

decol'lare *vi* take off

décolle'té *nm inv* décolleté, low neckline

de'collo *nm* take-off

decolo'ra|re *vt* bleach. **~re** *vt* bleach

decolorazi'one *nf* bleaching

decom'po|rre *vt*, **~rsi** *vr* decompose. **~sizi'one** *nf* decomposition

deconcen'trarsi *vr* become distracted

deconge'lare *vt* defrost

decongestio'nare *vt* Med, fig relieve congestion in

deco'ra|re *vt* decorate. **~'tivo** *a* decorative. **~to** *a* (*ornato*) decorated. **~'tore, ~'trice** *nmf* decorator. **~zi'one** *nf* decoration

de'coro *nm* decorum

decorosa'mente *adv* decorously. **decoroso** *a* dignified

decor'renza *nf* **~ dal...** starting from...

de'correre *vi* pass; **a ~ da** with effect from. **de'corso** *pp di* decorrere ●*nm* passing; Med course

de'crepito *a* decrepit

decre'scente *a* decreasing. **de'crescere** *vi* decrease; (*prezzi:*) go down; (*acque:*) subside

decre'tare *vt* decree. **de'creto** *nm* decree. **decreto legge** *decree which has the force of law*

'dedalo *nm* maze

'dedica *nf* dedication

dedi'ca|re *vt* dedicate. **~si** *vr* dedicate oneself

'dedi|to *a* **~ a** given to; (*assorto*) engrossed in; addicted to (*vizi*). **~zi'one** *nf* dedication

de'dotto *pp di* dedurre

dedu'cibile *a* (*tassa*) allowable

de'du|rre *vt* deduce; (*sottrarre*) deduct. **~t'tivo** *a* deductive. **~zi'one** *nf* deduction

defal'care *vt* deduct

defe'rire *vt* Jur remit

defezi|o'nare *vi* (*abbandonare*) defect. **~'one** *nf* defection

defici'en|te *a* (*mancante*) deficient; Med mentally deficient ●*nmf* mental defective; *pej* halfwit. **~za** *nf* deficiency; (*lacuna*) gap; Med mental deficiency

'deficit *nm inv* deficit. **~'tario** *a* (*bilancio*) deficit *attrib*

defi'larsi *vr* (*scomparire*) slip away

défilé *nm inv* fashion show

defi'ni|re *vt* define; (*risolvere*) settle. **~tiva'mente** *adv* for good. **~'tivo** *a* definitive. **~to** *a* definite. **~zi'one** *nf* definition; (*soluzione*) settlement

deflazi'one *nf* deflation

deflet'tore *nm* Auto quarterlight

deflu'ire *vi* (*liquidi:*) flow away; (*persone:*) stream out

de'flusso *nm* (*di marea*) ebb

defor'ma|re *vt* deform (*arto*); *fig* distort. **~si** *vr* lose its shape. **de'forme** *a* deformed. **~ità** *nf* deformity

defor'ma|to *a* warped. **~zi'one** *nf* (*di fatti*) distortion; **è una ~zione professionale** put it down to the job

defrau'dare *vt* defraud

de'funto, -a *a* & *nmf* deceased

degene'ra|re *vi* degenerate. **~to** *a* degenerate. **~zi'one** *nf* degeneration. **de'genere** *a* degenerate

de'gen|te *a* bedridden ●*nmf* patient. **~za** *nf* confinement

'degli = di + gli

deglu'tire *vt* swallow

de'gna|re *vt* **~e qcno di uno sguardo** deign to look at sb. **~si** *vr* deign, condescend

'degno *a* worthy; (*meritevole*) deserving

degrada'mento *nm* degradation

degra'dante *a* demeaning

degra'dare *vt* degrade. **~rsi** *vr* lower oneself; *(città:)* fall into a state of disrepair. **~zi'one** *nf* degradation

de'grado *nm* damage; **~ ambientale** *nm* environmental damage

degu'stare *vt* taste. **~zi'one** *nf* tasting

'dei = di + i. **'del** = di + il

dela'tore, -'trice *nmf* [police] informer. **~zi'one** *nf* informing

'delega *nf* proxy

dele'gare *vt* delegate. **~to** *nm* delegate. **~zi'one** *nf* delegation

dele'terio *a* harmful

del'fino *nm* dolphin; *(stile di nuoto)* butterfly [stroke]

de'libera *nf* bylaw

delibe'rare *vt/i* deliberate; **~ su/in** rule on/in. **~to** *a* deliberate

delicata'mente *adv* delicately

delica'tezza *nf* delicacy; *(fragilità)* frailty; *(tatto)* tact

deli'cato *a* delicate; *(salute)* frail; *(suono, colore)* soft

delimi'tare *vt* delimit

deline'are *vt* outline. **~rsi** *vr* be outlined; *fig* take shape. **~to** *a* defined

delin'quen|te *nmf* delinquent. **~za** *nf* delinquency

deli'rante *a Med* delirious; *(assurdo)* insane

deli'rare *vi* be delirious. **de'lirio** *nm* delirium; *fig* frenzy

de'litto *nm* crime. **~u'oso** *a* criminal

de'lizi|a *nf* delight. **~'are** *vt* delight. **~'oso** *a* delightful; *(cibo)* delicious

'della = di + la. **'delle** = di + le. **'dello** = di + lo

'delta *nm inv* delta

delta'plano *nm* hang-glider; **fare ~** go hang-gliding

delucidazi'one *nf* clarification

delu'dente *a* disappointing

de'lu|dere *vt* disappoint. **~si'one** *nf* disappointment. **de'luso** *a* disappointed

dema'gogico *a* popularity-seeking, demagogic

demar'ca|re *vt* demarcate. **~zi'one** *nf* demarcation

de'men|te *a* demented. **~za** *nf* dementia. **~zi'ale** *a (assurdo)* zany

demilitariz'za|re *vt* demilitarize. **~zi'one** *nf* demilitarization

demistificazi'one *nf* debunking

demo'cra|tico *a* democratic. **~zia** *nf* democracy

democristi'ano, -a *a & nmf* Christian Democrat

demogra'fia *nf* demography. **demo'grafico** *a* demographic

demo'li|re *vt* demolish. **~zi'one** *nf* demolition

'demone *nm* demon. **de'monio** *nm* demon

demoraliz'za|re *vt* demoralize. **~si** *vr* become demoralized

de'mordere *vi* give up

demoti'vato *a* demotivated

de'nari *nmpl (nelle carte)* diamonds

de'naro *nm* money

deni'gra|re *vt* denigrate. **~'torio** *a* denigratory

denomi'na|re *vt* name. **~'tore** *nm* denominator. **~zi'one** *nf* denomination; **~zione di origine controllata** mark guaranteeing the quality of a wine

deno'tare *vt* denote

densità *nf inv* density. **'denso** *a* thick, dense

den'ta|le *a* dental. **~rio** *a* dental. **~ta** *nf* bite. **~'tura** *nf* teeth *pl*

'dente *nm* tooth; *(di forchetta)* prong; **al ~** *Culin* just slightly firm. **~ del giudizio** wisdom tooth. **~ di latte** milk tooth. **denti'era** *nf* dentures *pl*, false teeth *pl*

denti'fricio *nm* toothpaste

den'tista *nmf* dentist

'dentro *adv* in, inside; *(in casa)* indoors; **da ~** from within; **qui ~** in here ● *prep* in, inside; *(di tempo)* within, by ● *nm* inside

denuclearizzazi'one *nf* denuclearization

denu'dar|e *vt* bare. **~si** *vr* strip

de'nuncia, de'nunzia *nf* denunciation; *(alla polizia)* reporting; *(dei redditi)* [income] tax return. **~'are** *vt* denounce; *(accusare)* report

denu'tri|to *a* underfed. **~zi'one** *nf* malnutrition

deodo'rante *a & nm* deodorant

dépendance *nf inv* outbuilding

depe'ri|bile *a* perishable. **~'mento** *nm* wasting away; *(di merci)* deterioration. **~re** *vi* waste away

depi'la|re *vt* depilate. **~rsi** *vr* shave *(gambe)*; pluck *(sopracciglia)*. **~'torio** *nm* depilatory

deplo'rabile *a* deplorable

deplo'r|are *vt* deplore; *(dolersi di)* grieve over. **~evole** *a* deplorable

de'porre *vt* put down; lay down *(armi)*; lay *(uova)*; *(togliere da una carica)* depose; *(testimoniare)* testify

depor'ta|re *vt* deport. **~to, -a** *nmf* deportee. **~zi'one** *nf* deportation

deposi'tar|e *vt* deposit; *(lasciare in custodia)* leave; *(in magazzino)* store. **~io, -a** *nmf* *(di segreto)* repository. **~si** *vr* settle

de'posi|to *nm* deposit; *(luogo)* warehouse; *Mil* depot. **~to bagagli** left-luggage office. **~zi'one** *nf* deposition; *(da una carica)* removal

depra'va|re *vt* deprave. **~to** *a* depraved. **~zi'one** *nf* depravity

depre'ca|bile *a* appalling. **~re** *vt* deprecate

depre'dare *vt* plunder

depressi'one *nf* depression. **de'presso** *pp di* **deprimere** ● *a* depressed

deprez'zar|e *vt* depreciate. **~si** *vr* depreciate

depri'mente *a* depressing

de'primer|e *vt* depress. **~si** *vr* become depressed

depu'ra|re *vt* purify. **~'tore** *nm* purifier

depu'ta|re *vt* delegate. **~to, -a** *nmf* Member of Parliament, MP

deraglia'mento *nm* derailment

deragli'are *vi* go off the lines; **far ~** derail

'derby *nm inv* *Sport* local Derby

deregolamentazi'one *nf* deregulation

dere'litto *a* derelict

dere'tano *nm* backside, bottom

de'ri|dere *vt* deride. **~si'one** *nf* derision. **~'sorio** *a* derisory

de'riva *nf* drift; **andare alla ~** drift

deri'va|re *vi* **~re da** *(provenire)* derive from ● *vt* derive; *(sviare)* divert. **~zi'one** *nf* derivation; *(di fiume)* diversion

dermato|lo'gia *nf* dermatology. **~'logico** *a* dermatological. **derma'tologo, -a** *nmf* dermatologist

'deroga *nf* dispensation. **dero'gare** *vi* **derogare a** depart from

der'ra|ta *nf* merchandise. **~e alimentari** foodstuffs

deru'bare *vt* rob

descrit'tivo *a* descriptive. **des'critto** *pp di* **descrivere**

des'crivere *vt* describe. **~'vibile** *a* describable. **~zi'one** *nf* description

de'serto *a* uninhabited ● *nm* desert

deside'rabile *a* desirable

deside'rare *vt* wish; *(volere)* want; *(intensamente)* long for; *(bramare)* desire; **desidera?** what would you like?, can I help you?; **lasciare a ~** leave a lot to be desired

desi'de|rio *nm* wish; *(brama)* desire; *(intenso)* longing. **~'roso** *a* desirous; *(bramoso)* longing

desi'gnare *vt* designate; *(fissare)* fix

desi'nenza *nf* ending

de'sistere *vi* **~ da** desist from

'desktop 'publishing *nm inv* desktop publishing

deso'lante *a* distressing

deso'la|re *vt* distress. **~to** *a* desolate; *(spiacente)* sorry. **~zi'one** *nf* desolation

'despota nm despot

de'star|e vt waken; fig awaken. ~si vr waken; fig awaken

desti'na|re vt destine; (nominare) appoint; (assegnare) assign; (indirizzare) address. ~'tario nm (di lettera, pacco) addressee. ~zi'one nf destination; fig purpose

de'stino nm destiny; (fato) fate

destitu'ire vt dismiss. ~zi'one nf dismissal

'desto a liter awake

'destra nf (parte) right; (mano) right hand; prendere a ~ turn right

destreggi'ar|e vi, ~si vr manoeuvre

de'strezza nf dexterity; (abilità) skill

'destro a right; (abile) skilful

detei'nato a tannin-free

dete'ne|re vt hold; (polizia:) detain. ~uto, -a nmf prisoner. ~zi'one nf detention

deter'gente a cleaning; (latte, crema) cleansing ● nm detergent; (per la pelle) cleanser

deteriora'mento nm deterioration

deterio'rar|e vt cause to deteriorate. ~si vr deteriorate

determi'nante a decisive

determi'na|re vt determine. ~rsi vr ~rsi a resolve to. ~'tezza nf determination. ~'tivo a Gram definite. ~to a (risoluto) determined; (particolare) specific. ~zi'one nf determination; (decisione) decision

deter'rente a & nm deterrent

deter'sivo nm detergent. ~ per i piatti washing-up liquid

dete'stare vt detest, hate

deto'nare vi detonate

de'tra|rre vt deduct (da from). ~zi'one nf deduction

detri'mento nm detriment; a ~ di to the detriment of

de'trito nm debris

'detta nf a ~ di according to

dettagli'ante nmf Comm retailer

dettagli'a|re vt detail. ~ta'mente adv in detail

det'taglio nm detail; al ~ Comm retail

det'ta|re vt dictate; ~re legge fig lay down the law. ~to nm, ~'tura nf dictation

'detto a said; (chiamato) called; (soprannominato) nicknamed; ~ fatto no sooner said than done ● nm saying

detur'pare vt disfigure

deva'sta|re vt devastate. ~to a devastated. ~zi'one nf devastation; fig ravages pl

devi'a|re vi deviate ● vt divert. ~zi'one nf deviation; (stradale) diversion

devitaliz'zare vt deaden (dente)

devo'lu|to pp di devolvere ● a devolved. ~zi'one nf devolution

de'volvere vt devolve

de'vo|to a devout; (affezionato) devoted. ~zi'one nf devotion.

di prep of; (partitivo) some; (scritto da) by; (parlare, pensare ecc) about; (con causa, mezzo) with; (con provenienza) from; (in comparazioni) than; (con infinito) to; la casa di mio padre/dei miei genitori my father's house/my parents' house; compra del pane buy some bread; hai del pane? do you have any bread?; un film di guerra a war film; piangere di dolore cry with pain; coperto di neve covered with snow; sono di Genova I'm from Genoa; uscire di casa leave one's house; più alto di te taller than you; è ora di partire it's time to go; crede di aver ragione he thinks he's right; dire di sì say yes; di domenica on Sundays; di sera in the evening; una pausa di un'ora an hour's break; un corso di due mesi a two-month course

dia'bet|e nm diabetes. ~ico, -a a & nmf diabetic

dia'bolico a diabolical

dia'dema *nm* diadem; (*di donna*) tiara

di'afano *a* diaphanous

dia'framma *nm* diaphragm; (*divisione*) screen

dia'gnosi *nf inv* diagnosis. **~ti'care** *vt* diagnose

diago'nale *a* & *nf* diagonal

dia'gramma *nm* diagram

dia'lettale *a* dialect. **dia'letto** *nm* dialect

dialo'gante a unità ~ *Comput* interactive terminal

di'alogo *nm* dialogue

dia'mante *nm* diamond

di'ametro *nm* diameter

di'amine *int* **che ~...** what on earth...

diaposi'tiva *nf* slide

di'ario *nm* diary

diar'rea *nf* diarrhoea

di'avolo *nm* devil; **va al ~** go to hell!; **che ~ fai?** what the hell are you doing?

di'battere *vt* debate. **~ersi** *vr* struggle. **~ito** *nm* debate; (*meno formale*) discussion

dica'stero *nm* office

di'cembre *nm* December

dice'ria *nf* rumour

dichia'rare *vt* state; (*ufficialmente*) declare. **~rsi** *vr* **si dichiara innocente** he says he's innocent. **~zi'one** *nf* statement; (*documento, di guerra*) declaration

dician'nove *a* & *nm* nineteen

dicias'sette *a* & *nm* seventeen

dici'otto *a* & *nm* eighteen

dici'tura *nf* wording

didasca'lia *nf* (*di film*) subtitle; (*di illustrazione*) caption

di'dattica *nf* didactics. **~o** *a* didactic; (*televisione*) educational

di'dentro *adv* inside

didi'etro *adv* behind ● *nm hum* hindquarters *pl*

di'eci *a* & *nm* ten

die'cina = **decina**

'diesel *a* & *nf inv* diesel

di'esis *nm inv* sharp

di'eta *nf* diet; **essere a ~** be on a diet. **die'tetico** *a* diet. **die'tista** *nmf* dietician. **die'tologo** *nmf* dietician

di'etro *adv* behind ● *prep* behind; (*dopo*) after ● *a* back; (*di zampe*) hind ● *nm* back; **le stanze di ~** the back rooms; **le zampe di ~** the hind legs

dietro'front *nm inv* about-turn; *fig* U-turn

di'fatti *adv* in fact

di'fendere *vt* defend. **~dersi** *vr* defend oneself. **~'siva** *nf* **stare sulla ~siva** be on the defensive. **~'sivo** *a* defensive. **~'sore** *nm* defender; **avvocato ~sore** defence counsel

di'fesa *nf* defence; **prendere le ~ di qcno** come to sb's defence. **~o** *pp di* **difendere**

difet'tare *vi* be defective; **~are di** lack. **~ivo** *a* defective

di'fetto *nm* defect; (*morale*) fault, flaw; (*mancanza*) lack; (*in tessuto, abito*) flaw; **essere in ~to** be at fault; **far ~to** be lacking. **~'toso** *a* defective; 〈abito〉 flawed

diffa'mare *vt* (*con parole*) slander; (*per iscritto*) libel. **~'torio** *a* slanderous; (*per iscritto*) libellous. **~zi'one** *nf* slander; (*scritta*) libel

diffe'rente *a* different. **~za** *nf* difference; **a ~za di** unlike; **non fare ~za** make no distinction (*fra* between). **~zi'ale** *a* & *nm* differential

differenzi'are *vt* differentiate. **~si** *vr* **~si da** differ from

diffe'rire *vt* postpone ● *vi* be different. **~ta** *nf* **in ~ta** *TV* prerecorded

diffi'cile *a* difficult; (*duro*) hard; (*improbabile*) unlikely ● *nm* difficulty. **~'mente** *adv* with difficulty

diffi'coltà *nf inv* difficulty

dif'fida *nf* warning

diffi'dare *vi* **~are di** distrust ● *vt* warn. **~ente** *a* mistrustful. **~enza** *nf* mistrust

dif'fondere *vt* spread; diffuse 〈*calore, luce ecc*〉. **~si** *vr* spread.

diffusi'one nf diffusion; (di giornale) circulation
dif'fu|so pp di **diffondere** ● a common; (malattia) widespread; (luce) diffuse. ~'**sore** nm (per asciugacapelli) diffuser
difi'lato adv straight; (subito) straightaway
dige'ribile a digestible
dige'rire vt digest; fam stomach. ~**sti'one** nf digestion. ~'**stivo** a digestive ● nm digestive; (dopo cena) liqueur
digi'tale a digital; (delle dita) finger attrib ● nf (fiore) foxglove
digi'tare vt key in
digiu'nare vi fast
digi'uno a essere ~ have an empty stomach ● nm fast; a ~ (bere ecc) on an empty stomach
digni'tà nf inv dignity. ~'**tario** nm dignitary. ~'**toso** a dignified
digressi'one nf digression
digri'gnare vi ~ **i denti** grind one's teeth
dila'gare vi flood; fig spread
dilani'are vt tear to pieces
dilapi'dare vt squander
dila'ta|re vt, ~**rsi** vr dilate; (metallo, gas) expand. ~**zi'one** nf dilation
dilazio'nabile a postponable
dilazi|o'nare vt delay. ~'**one** nf delay
dilegu'ar|e vt disperse. ~**si** vr disappear
di'lemma nm dilemma
dilet'tan|te nmf amateur. ~'**tistico** a amateurish
dilet'tare vt delight
di'letto, -a a beloved ● nm (piacere) delight ● nmf (persona) beloved
dili'gen|te a diligent; (lavoro) accurate. ~**za** nf diligence
dilu'ire vt dilute
dilun'gar|e vt prolong. ~**si** vr su dwell on (argomento)
diluvi'are vi pour [down]. **di'luvio** nm downpour; fig flood

dima'gr|ante a slimming, diet. ~**i'mento** nm loss of weight. ~**ire** vi slim
dime'nar|e vt wave; wag (coda). ~**si** vr be agitated
dimensi'one nf dimension; (misura) size
dimenti'canza nf forgetfulness; (svista) oversight
dimenti'car|e vt, ~**si** vr ~ [di] forget. **dimentico** a **dimentico di** (che non ricorda) forgetful of
di'messo pp di **dimettere** ● a humble; (trasandato) shabby; (voce) low
dimesti'chezza nf familiarity
di'metter|e vt dismiss; (da ospedale ecc) discharge. ~**si** vr resign
dimez'zare vt halve
diminu'i|re vt/i diminish; (in maglia) decrease. ~'**tivo** a & nm diminutive. ~**zi'one** nf decrease; (riduzione) reduction
dimissi'oni nfpl resignation sg; **dare le** ~ resign
di'mo|ra nf residence. ~'**rare** vi reside
dimo'strante nmf demonstrator
dimo'stra|re vt demonstrate; (provare) prove; (mostrare) show. ~**rsi** vr prove [to be]. ~'**tivo** a demonstrative. ~**zi'one** nf demonstration; Math proof
di'namico, -a a dynamic ● nf dynamics sg. **dina'mismo** nm dynamism
dinami'tardo a **attentato** ~ bomb attack
dina'mite nf dynamite
di'namo nf inv dynamo
di'nanzi adv in front ● prep ~ **a** in front of
dina'stia nf dynasty
di'niego nm denial
dinocco'lato a lanky
dino'sauro nm dinosaur
din'torn|i nmpl outskirts; **nei** ~**i di** in the vicinity of. ~**o** adv around
'dio nm (pl **'dei**) god; **D**~ God
di'ocesi nf inv diocese

dipa'nare *vt* wind into a ball; *fig* unravel

diparti'mento *nm* department

dipen'den|te *a* depending ● *nmf* employee. **~za** *nf* dependence; *(edificio)* annexe

di'pendere *vi* **~ da** depend on; *(provenire)* derive from; **dipende** it depends

di'pinger|e *vt* paint; *(descrivere)* describe. **~si** *vr* *(truccarsi)* make up. **di'pinto** *pp* di **dipingere** ● *a* painted ● *nm* painting

di'plo|ma *nm* diploma. **~'marsi** *vr* graduate

diplo'matico *a* diplomatic ● *nm* diplomat; *(pasticcino)* millefeuille *(with alcohol)*

diplo'mato *nmf* person with school qualification ● *a* qualified

diplo'mazia *nf* diplomacy

di'porto *nm* imbarcazione da ~ pleasure craft

dira'dar|e *vt* thin out; make less frequent *(visite)*. **~si** *vr* thin out; *(nebbia:)* clear

dira'ma|re *vt* issue ● *vi*, **~rsi** *vr* branch out; *(diffondersi)* spread. **~zi'one** *nf* *(di strada)* fork

'dire *vt* say; *(raccontare, riferire)* tell; **~ quello che si pensa** speak one's mind; **voler ~** mean; **volevo ben ~!** I wondered!; **~ di sì/no** say yes/no; **si dice che...** rumour has it that...; **come si dice "casa" in inglese?** what's the English for "casa"?; **questo nome mi dice qualcosa** the name rings a bell; **che ne dici di...?** how about...?; **non c'è che ~** there's no disputing that; **e ~ che...** to think that...; **a dir poco/tanto** at least/most ● *vi* ~ **bene/male** di speak highly/ill of sb; **dica pure** *(in negozio)* how can I help you?; **dici sul serio?** are you serious?; **per modo di ~** in a manner of speaking

diretta'mente *adv* directly

diret'tissima *nf* **per ~** *Jur* without

going through the normal procedures

diret'tissimo *nm* fast train

diret'tiva *nf* directive

di'retto *pp* di **dirigere** ● *a* direct. **~ a** *(inteso)* meant for. **essere ~ a** be heading for. **in diretta** *(trasmissione)* live ● *nm* *(treno)* through train

diret'tore, -'trice *nmf* manager; manageress; *(di scuola)* headmaster; headmistress. **~tore d'orchestra** conductor

direzi'one *nf* direction; *(di società)* management; *Sch* headmaster's/ headmistress's office *(primary school)*

diri'gen|te *a* ruling ● *nmf* executive; *Pol* leader. **~za** *nf* management. **~zi'ale** *a* management *attrib*, managerial

di'riger|e *vt* direct; conduct *(orchestra)*; run *(impresa)*. **~si** *vr* **~si verso** head for

dirim'petto *adv* opposite ● *prep* ~ **a** facing

di'ritto[1] *a* straight; *(destro)* right ● *adv* straight; **andare ~** go straight on ● *nm* right side; *Tennis* forehand; **fare un ~** *(a maglia)* knit one

di'ritto[2] *nm* right; *Jur* law. **~i** *pl* **d'autore** royalties

dirit'tura *nf* straight line; *fig* honesty. **~ d'arrivo** *Sport* home straight

diroc'cato *a* tumbledown

dirom'pente *a* *fig* explosive

dirot'ta|re *vt* reroute *(treno, aereo)*; *(illegalmente)* hijack; divert *(traffico)* ● *vi* alter course. **~'tore, -'trice** *nmf* hijacker

di'rotto *a* *(pioggia)* pouring; *(pianto)* uncontrollable; **piovere a ~** rain heavily

di'rupo *nm* precipice

dis'abile *nmf* disabled person

disabi'tato *a* uninhabited

disabitu'arsi *vr* **~ a** get out of the habit of

disac'cordo *nm* disagreement

disadat'tato, -a *a* maladjusted ● *nmf* misfit

disa'dorno *a* unadorned

disa'gevole *a* (*scomodo*) uncomfortable

disagi'ato *a* poor; (*vita*) hard

di'sagio *nm* discomfort; (*difficoltà*) inconvenience; (*imbarazzo*) embarrassment; **sentirsi a ~** feel uncomfortable; **disagi** *pl* (*privazioni*) hardships

disappro'vare *vt* disapprove of. **~zi'one** *nf* disapproval

disap'punto *nm* disappointment

disar'mante *a* *fig* disarming

disar'mare *vt/i* disarm. **di'sarmo** *nm* disarmament

disa'strato, -a *a* devastated ● *nmf* disaster victim

di'sastro *nm* disaster; (*fam: grande confusione*) mess; (*fam: persona*) disaster area. **disa'stroso** *a* disastrous

disat'tento *a* inattentive. **~zi'one** *nf* inattention; (*svista*) oversight

disatti'vare *vt* de-activate

disa'vanzo *nm* deficit

disavven'tura *nf* misadventure

dis'brigo *nm* dispatch

dis'capito *nm* **a ~ di** to the detriment of

dis'carica *nf* scrap-yard

discen'den|te *a* descending ● *nmf* descendant. **~za** *nf* descent; (*discendenti*) descendants *pl*

di'scendere *vt/i* descend; (*dal treno*) get off; (*da cavallo*) dismount; (*sbarcare*) land. **~ da** (*trarre origine da*) be a descendant of

di'scepolo, -a *nmf* disciple

di'scernere *vt* discern

di'sces|a *nf* descent; (*pendìo*) slope; **~a in picchiata** (*di aereo*) nosedive; **essere in ~a** (*strada:*) go downhill. **~a libera** (*in sci*) downhill race. **disce'sista** *nmf* (*sciatore*) downhill skier. **~o** *pp di* **discendere**

dis'chetto *nm* Comput diskette

dischi'uder|e *vt* open; (*svelare*) disclose. **~si** *vr* open up

disci'oglier|e *vt*, **~si** *vr* dissolve; (*neve:*) thaw; (*fondersi*) melt. **disci'olto** *pp di* **disciogliere**

disci'pli|na *nf* discipline. **~'nare** *a* disciplinary ● *vt* discipline. **~'nato** *a* disciplined

'disco *nm* disc; Comput disk; Sport discus; Mus record; **ernia del ~** slipped disc. **~ fisso** Comput hard disc. **~ volante** flying saucer

discogra'fia *nf* (*insieme di incisioni*) discography. **disco'grafico** *a* (*industria*) record *attrib*, recording; **casa discografica** record company, recording company

'discolo *nmf* rascal ● *a* unruly

discol'par|e *vt* clear. **~si** *vr* clear oneself

disco'noscere *vt* disown (*figlio*)

discontinuità *nf* (*nel lavoro*) irregularity. **discon'tinuo** *a* intermittent; (*fig: impegno, rendimento*) uneven

discor'dan|te *a* discordant. **~za** *nf* mismatch

discor'dare *vi* (*opinioni:*) conflict. **dis'corde** *a* clashing. **dis'cordia** *nf* discord; (*dissenso*) dissension

discor'rere *vi* talk (**di** about). **~'sivo** *a* colloquial. **dis'corso** *pp di* **discorrere** ● *nm* speech; (*conversazione*) talk

dis'costo *a* distant ● *adv* far away; **stare ~** stand apart

disco'te|ca *nf* disco; (*raccolta*) record library. **~'caro** *nmf* pej disco freak

discre'pan|te *a* contradictory. **~za** *nf* discrepancy

dis'creto *a* discreet; (*moderato*) moderate; (*abbastanza buono*) fairly good. **~zi'one** *nf* discretion; (*giudizio*) judgement; **a ~zione di** at the discretion of

discrimi'nante *a* extenuating

discrimi'na|re *vt* discriminate. **~'torio** *a* (*atteggiamento*) discriminatory. **~zi'one** *nf* discrimination

discussi'one *nf* discussion; (*alter-*

co) argument. **dis'cusso** *pp di* **discutere** ● *a* controversial

dis'cutere *vt* discuss; (*formale*) debate; (*litigare*) argue; ~ **sul prezzo** bargain. **discu'tibile** *a* debatable; (*gusto*) questionable

disde'gnare *vt* disdain. **dis'degno** *nm* disdain

dis'dett|a *nf* retraction; (*sfortuna*) bad luck; *Comm* cancellation. **~o** *pp di* disdire

disdi'cevole *a* unbecoming

dis'dire *vt* retract; (*annullare*) cancel

diseduca'tivo *a* boorish, uncouth

dise'gna|re *vt* draw; (*progettare*) design. **~'tore**, **~'trice** *nmf* designer. **di'segno** *nm* drawing; (*progetto, linea*) design

diser'bante *nm* herbicide, weedkiller ● *a* herbicidal, weed-killing

disere'da|re *vt* disinherit. **~to** *a* dispossessed ● *nmf* **i ~ti** the dispossessed

diser'tare *vt/i* desert; **~tare la scuola** stay away from school. **~'tore** *nm* deserter. **~zi'one** *nf* desertion

disfaci'mento *nm* decay

dis'fa|re *vt* undo; strip (*letto*); (*smantellare*) take down; (*annientare*) defeat; **~re le valigie** unpack [one's bags]. **~rsi** *vr* fall to pieces; (*sciogliersi*) melt; **~rsi di** (*liberarsi di*) get rid of; **~rsi in lacrime** dissolve into tears. **~tta** *nf* defeat. **~tto** *a fig* worn out

disfat'tis|mo *nm* defeatism. **~ta** *a & nmf* defeatist

disfunzi'one *nf* disorder

dis'gelo *nm* thaw

dis'grazi|a *nf* misfortune; (*incidente*) accident; (*sfavore*) disgrace. **~ata'mente** *adv* unfortunately. **~'ato, -a** *a* unfortunate ● *nmf* wretch

disgre'gar|e *vt* break up. **~si** *vr* disintegrate

disgui'do *nm* **~ postale** mistake in delivery

disgu'st|are *vt* disgust. **~arsi** *vr*

~arsi di be disgusted by. **dis'gusto** *nm* disgust. **~oso** *a* disgusting

disidra'ta|re *vt* dehydrate. **~to** *a* dehydrated

disil'lu|dere *vt* disenchant. **~si'one** *nf* disenchantment. **~so** *a* disillusioned

disimbal'lare *vt* unpack

disimpa'rare *vt* forget

disimpe'gnar|e *vt* release; (*compiere*) fulfem; redeem (*oggetto dato in pegno*). **~si** *vr* disengage oneself; (*cavarsela*) manage. **disim'pegno** *nm* (*locale*) vestibule

disincan'tato *a* (*disilluso*) disillusioned

disinfe'sta|re *vt* disinfest. **~zi'one** *nf* disinfestation

disinfet'tante *a & nm* disinfectant

disinfet'ta|re *vt* disinfect. **~zi'one** *nf* disinfection

disinfor'mato *a* uninformed

disini'bito *a* uninhibited

disinne'scare *vt* defuse ⟨*mina*⟩. **disin'nesco** *nm* (*di bomba*) bomb disposal

disinse'rire *vt* disconnect

disinte'gra|re *vt*, **~rsi** *vr* disintegrate. **~zi'one** *nf* disintegration

disinteres'sarsi *vr* **~ di** take no interest in. **disinte'resse** *nm* indifference; (*oggettività*) disinterestedness

disintossi'ca|re *vt* detoxify. **~rsi** *vr* come off drugs. **~zi'one** *nf* giving up alcohol/drugs

disin'volto *a* natural. **disinvol'tura** *nf* confidence

disles'sia *nf* dyslexia. **dis'lessico** *a* dyslexic

disli'vello *nm* difference in height; *fig* inequality

dislo'care *vt Mil* post

dismenor'rea *nf* dysmenorrhoea

dismi'sura *nf* excess; **a ~** excessively

disobbedi'ente *a* disobedient

disobbe'dire *vt* disobey

disoccu'pa|to, -a *a* unemployed

● *nmf* unemployed person. **~zi'one** *nf* unemployment

disone'stà *nf* dishonesty. **diso'nesto** *a* dishonest

disono'rare *vt* dishonour. **diso'nore** *nm* dishonour

di'sopra *adv* above ● *a* upper ● *nm* top

disordi'na|re *vt* disarrange. **~ta'mente** *adv* untidily. **~to** *a* untidy; (*sregolato*) immoderate. **di'sordine** *nm* disorder, untidiness; (*sregolatezza*) debauchery

disorganiz'za|re *vt* disorganize. **~to** *a* disorganized. **~zi'one** *nf* disorganization

disorienta'mento *nm* disorientation

disorien'ta|re *vt* disorientate. **~rsi** *vr* lose one's bearings. **~to** *a* *fig* bewildered

di'sotto *adv* below ● *a* lower ● *nm* bottom

dis'paccio *nm* dispatch

dispa'rato *a* disparate

'dispari *a* odd, uneven. **~tà** *nf inv* disparity

dis'parte *adv* in **~** apart; **stare in ~** stand aside

dis'pendi|o *nm* (*spreco*) waste. **~'oso** *a* expensive

dis'pen|sa *nf* pantry; (*distribuzione*) distribution; (*mobile*) cupboard; *Jur* exemption; *Relig* dispensation; (*pubblicazione periodica*) number. **~'sare** *vt* distribute; (*esentare*) exonerate

dispe'ra|re *vi* despair (**di** of). **~rsi** *vr* despair. **~ta'mente** (*piangere*) desperately. **~to** *a* desperate. **~zi'one** *nf* despair

dis'per|dere *vt*, **~dersi** *vr* scatter, disperse. **~si'one** *nf* dispersion; (*di truppe*) dispersal. **~'sivo** *a* disorganized. **~so** *pp* di **disperdere** ● *a* scattered; (*smarrito*) lost ● *nm* missing soldier

dis'pet|to *nm* spite. **~to di** in spite of; **fare un ~to a qcno** spite sb. **~'toso** *a* spiteful

dispia'c|ere *nm* upset; (*rammari*

co) regret; (*dolore*) sorrow; (*preoccupazione*) worry ● *vi* **mi dispiace** I'm sorry; **non mi dispiace** I don't dislike it; **se non ti dispiace** if you don't mind. **~i'uto** *a* upset; (*dolente*) sorry

dispo'nibil|e *a* available; (*gentile*) helpful. **~ità** *nf* availability; (*gentilezza*) helpfulness

dis'por|re *vt* arrange ● *vi* dispose; (*stabilire*) order; (*avere* **re di** have at one's disposal. **~si** *vr* (*in fila*) line up

disposi'tivo *nm* device

disposizi'one *nf* disposition; (*ordine*) order; (*libera disponibilità*) disposal. **dis'posto** *pp* di **disporre** ● *a* ready; (*incline*) disposed; **essere ben disposto verso** be favourably disposed towards

di'spotico *a* despotic. **dispo'tismo** *nm* despotism

dispregia'tivo *a* disparaging

disprez'zare *vt* despise. **dis'prezzo** *nm* contempt

'disputa *nf* dispute

dispu'ta|re *vi* dispute; (*gareggiare*) compete. **~si** *vr* **~si qcsa** contend for sth

dissacra'torio *a* debunking

dissangua'mento *nm* loss of blood

dissangua'|re *vt*, **~rsi** *vr* bleed. **~rsi** *vr fig* become impoverished. **~to** *a* bloodless; *fig* impoverished

dissa'pore *nm* disagreement

dissec'car|e *vt*, **~si** *vr* dry up

dissemi'nare *vt* disseminate; (*notizie*) spread

dis'senso *nm* dissent; (*disaccordo*) disagreement

dissente'ria *nf* dysentery

dissen'tire *vi* disagree (**da** with)

dissertazi'one *nf* dissertation

disser'vizio *nm* poor service

disse'sta|re *vt* upset; *Comm* damage. **~to** *a* (*strada*) uneven. **dis'sesto** *nm* ruin

disse'tante *a* thirst-quenching

disse'ta|re vt **~re qcno** quench sb's thirst

dissi'dente a & nmf dissident

dis'sidio nm disagreement

dis'simile a unlike, dissimilar

dissimu'lare vt conceal; (fingere) dissimulate

dissi'pa|re vt dissipate; (sperperare) squander. **~rsi** vr (nebbia:) clear; (dubbio:) disappear. **~to** a dissipated. **~zi'one** nf squandering

dissoci'ar|e vt, **~si** vr dissociate

disso'dare vt till

dis'solto pp di **dissolvere**

disso'luto a dissolute

dis'solver|e vt, **~si** vr dissolve; (disperdere) dispel

disso'nanza nf dissonance

dissua'|dere vt dissuade. **~si'one** nf dissuasion. **~'sivo** a dissuasive

distac'car|e vt detach; Sport leave behind. **~si** vr be detached. **di'stacco** nm detachment; (separazione) separation; Sport lead

di'stan|te a far away; (fig: person) detached ● adv far away. **~za** nf distance. **~zi'are** vt space out; Sport outdistance

di'stare vi be distant; **quanto dista?** how far is it?

di'sten|dere vt stretch out (p rte del corpo); (spiegare) spr.ad; (deporre) lay. **~dersi** vr stretch; (sdraiarsi) lie down; (rilassarsi) relax. **~si'one** nf stretching; (rilassamento) relaxation; Pol détente. **~'sivo** a relaxing

di'steso, -a pp di **distendere** ● nf expanse

distil'l|are vt/i distil. **~azi'one** nf distillation. **~e'ria** nf distillery

distingu|ere vt distinguish. **~rsi** vr distinguish oneself. **distin'guibile** a distinguishable

di'stinta nf Comm list. **~ di pagamento** receipt. **~ di versamento** paying-in slip

distinta'mente adv (separatamente) individually, separately; (chiaramente) clearly

distin'tivo a distinctive ● nm badge

di'stin|to, -a pp di **distinguere** ● a distinct; (signorile) distinguished; **~ti saluti** Yours faithfully. **~zi'one** nf distinction

di'stogliere vt **~ da** (allontanare) remove from; (dissuadere) dissuade from. **di'stolto** pp di **distogliere**

di'storcere vt twist

distorsi'one nf Med sprain; (alterazione) distortion

di'stra|rre vt distract; (divertire) amuse. **~rsi** vr get distracted; (svagarsi) amuse oneself; non ti **distrarre!** pay attention!. **~rsi** vr (deconcentrarsi) be distracted. **~tta'mente** adv absently. **~tto** pp di **distrarre** ● a absent-minded; (disattento) inattentive. **~zi'one** nf absent-mindedness; (errore) inattention; (svago) amusement

di'stretto nm district

distribu'|ire vt distribute; (disporre) arrange; deal (carte). **~'tore** nm distributor; (di benzina) petrol pump; (automatico) slot-machine. **~zi'one** nf distribution

distri'car|e vt disentangle. **~si** vr fig get out of it

di'strug|gere vt destroy. **~t'tivo** a destructive; (critica) negative. **~tto** pp di **distruggere** ● a destroyed; **un uomo ~tto** a broken man. **~zi'one** nf destruction

distur'bar|e vt disturb; (sconvolgere) upset. **~si** vr trouble oneself. **di'sturbo** nm bother; (indisposizione) trouble; Med problem; Radio, TV interference; **disturbi** pl Radio, TV static. **disturbi di stomaco** stomach trouble

disubbidi'en|te a disobedient. **~za** nf disobedience

disubbi'dire vi **~ a** disobey

disugu|agli'anza nf disparity. **~'ale** a unequal; (irregolare) irregular

disu'mano a inhuman

di'suso *nm* **cadere in ~** fall into disuse

di'tale *nm* thimble

di'tata *nf* poke; *(impronta)* finger-mark

'**dito** *nm* (*pl nf* **dita**) finger; *(di vino, acqua)* finger. ~ **del piede** toe

'**ditta** *nf* firm

dit'tafono *nm* dictaphone

ditta'tor|e *nm* dictator. ~**i'ale** *a* dictatorial. **ditta'tura** *nf* dictatorship

dit'tongo *nm* diphthong

di'urno *a* daytime; **spettacolo ~** matinée

'**diva** *nf* diva

diva'ga|re *vi* digress. ~**zi'one** *nf* digression

divam'pare *vi* burst into flames; *fig* spread like wildfire

di'vano *nm* settee, sofa. ~ **letto** sofa bed

divari'care *vt* open

di'vario *nm* discrepancy; **un ~ di opinioni** a difference of opinion

dive'n|ire *vi* = **diventare**. ~**uto** *pp di* **divenire**

diven'tare *vi* become; *(lentamente)* grow; *(rapidamente)* turn

di'verbio *nm* squabble

diver'gen|te *a* divergent. ~**za** *nf* divergence; ~**za di opinioni** difference of opinion. **di'vergere** *vi* diverge

diversa'mente *adv* *(altrimenti)* otherwise; *(in modo diverso)* differently

diversifi'ca|re *vt* diversify. ~**rsi** *vr* differ, be different. ~**zi'one** *nf* diversification

diver|si'one *nf* diversion. ~**sità** *nf inv* difference. ~**'sivo** *nm* diversion. **di'verso** *a* different; **diversi** *pl (parecchi)* several ● *pron* several [people]

diver'tente *a* amusing. **diverti'mento** *nm* amusement

diver'tir|e *vt* amuse. ~**si** *vr* enjoy oneself

divi'dendo *nm* dividend

di'vider|e *vt* divide; *(condividere)* share. ~**si** *vr* *(separarsi)* separate

divi'eto *nm* prohibition; ~ **di sosta** no parking

divinco'larsi *vr* wriggle

divinità *nf inv* divinity. **di'vino** *a* divine

di'visa *nf* uniform; *Comm* currency

divisi'one *nf* division

di'vismo *nm* worship; *(atteggiamento)* superstar mentality

di'vi|so *pp di* **dividere**. ~**'sore** *nm* divisor. ~**'sorio** *a* dividing; **muro** ~**sorio** partition wall

'**divo, -a** *nmf* star

divo'rar|e *vt* devour. ~**si** *vr* ~**si da** be consumed with

divorzi'a|re *vi* divorce. ~**to, -a** *nmf* divorcee. **di'vorzio** *nm* divorce

divul'ga|re *vt* divulge; *(rendere popolare)* popularize. ~**rsi** *vr* spread. ~**'tivo** *a* popular. ~**zi'one** *nf* popularization

dizio'nario *nm* dictionary

dizi'one *nf* diction

do *nm* *Mus (chiave, nota)* C

'doccia *nf* shower; *(grondaia)* gutter; **fare la ~** have a shower

do'cen|te *a* teaching ● *nmf* teacher; *(di università)* lecturer. ~**za** *nf* university teacher's qualification

docile *a* docile

documen'tar|e *vt* document. ~**si** *vr* gather information (**su** about)

documen'tario *a* & *nm* documentary

documen'ta|to *a* well-documented; *(persona)* well-informed. ~**zi'one** *nf* documentation

docu'mento *nm* document

dodi'cesimo *a* & *nm* twelfth.

'**dodici** *a* & *nm* twelve

do'gan|a *nf* customs *pl; (dazio)* duty. **doga'nale** *a* customs. ~**i'ere** *nm* customs officer

doglie *nfpl* labour pains

'**dogma** *nm* dogma. **dog'matico** *a* dogmatic. ~**'tismo** *nm* dogmatism

'dolce *a* sweet; (*clima*) mild; (*voce, consonante*) soft; (*acqua*) fresh ● nm (*portata*) dessert; (*torta*) cake; **non mangio dolci** I don't eat sweet things. ~'mente *adv* sweetly. dol'cezza *nf* sweetness; (*di clima*) mildness

dolce'vita *a inv* (*maglione*) roll-neck

dolci'ario *a* confectionery

dolci'astro *a* sweetish

dolcifi'cante *nm* sweetener ● *a* sweetening

dolci'umi *nmpl* sweets

do'lente *a* painful; (*spiacente*) sorry

do'le|re *vi* ache, hurt; (*dispiacere*) regret. ~rsi *vr* regret; (*protestare*) complain; ~rsi di be sorry for

'dollaro *nm* dollar

'dolo *nm* Jur malice; (*truffa*) fraud

Dolo'miti *nfpl* le ~ the Dolomites

do'lore *nm* pain; (*morale*) sorrow. dolo'roso *a* painful

do'loso *a* malicious

do'manda *nf* question; (*richiesta*) request; (*scritta*) application; Comm demand; **fare una ~ (a qcno)** ask (sb) a question. ~ di impiego job application

doman'dar|e *vt* ask; (*esigere*) demand; ~e qcsa a qcno ask sb for sth. ~si *vr* wonder

do'mani *adv* tomorrow; ~ sera tomorrow evening ● nm il ~ the future; a ~ see you tomorrow

do'ma|re *vt* tame; fig control (*emozioni*). ~'tore *nm* tamer

domat'tina *adv* tomorrow morning

do'meni|ca *nf* Sunday. ~'cale *a* Sunday *attrib*

do'mestico, -a *a* domestic ● nm servant ● nf maid

domicili'are *a* arresti domiciliari Jur house arrest

domicili'arsi *vr* settle

domi'cilio *nm* domicile; (*abitazione*) home; **recapitiamo a ~** we do home deliveries

domi'na|re *vt* dominate; (*controllare*) control ● *vi* rule over; (*prevalere*) be dominant. ~rsi *vr* control oneself. ~'tore, ~'trice *nmf* ruler ~zi'one *nf* domination

do'minio *nm* control; Pol dominion; (*ambito*) field; di ~ pubblico common knowledge

don *nm inv* (*ecclesiastico*) Father

do'na|re *vt* give; donate (*sangue, organo*) ● *vi* ~re a (*giovare esteticamente*) suit. ~'tore, ~'trice *nmf* donor. ~zi'one *nf* donation

dondo'l|are *vt* swing; (*cullare*) rock ● *vi* sway. ~arsi *vr* swing. ~io *nm* rocking. 'dondolo *nm* swing; cavallo/sedia a dondolo rocking-horse/chair

dongio'vanni *nm inv* Romeo

'donna *nf* woman. ~ di servizio domestic help

don'naccia *nf pej* whore

donnai'olo *nm* philanderer

'donnola *nf* weasel

'dono *nm* gift

'dopo *prep* after; (*a partire da*) since ● *adv* after, afterwards; (*più tardi*) later; (*in seguito*) later on; ~ di me after me

dopo'barba *nm inv* aftershave

dopo'cena *nm inv* evening

dopodiché *adv* after which

dopodo'mani *adv* the day after tomorrow

dopogu'erra *nm inv* post-war period

dopo'pranzo *nm inv* afternoon

dopo'sci *a & nm inv* après-ski

doposcu'ola *nm inv* after-school activities *pl*

dopo-'shampoo *nm inv* conditioner ● *a inv* conditioning

dopo'sole *nm inv* aftersun cream ● *a inv* aftersun

dopo'tutto *adv* after all

doppi'aggio *nm* dubbing

doppia'mente *adv* (*in misura doppia*) doubly

doppi'a|re *vt* Naut double; Sport lap; Cinema dub. ~'tore, ~'trice *nmf* dubber 'doppio *a & adv* double. ~ clic *nm* Comput double click. ~ fallo *nm* Tennis double fault. ~ gioco *nm* double-dealing. ~ mento *nm* double chin. ~ senso *nm* double entendre. doppi vetri *nmpl* double glazing ●*nm* double, twice the quantity; Tennis doubles *pl*. ~ misto *Tennis* mixed doubles ●*adv* double

doppi'one *nm* duplicate

doppio'petto *a* double-breasted

dop'pista *nmf* Tennis doubles player

do'ra|re *vt* gild; *Culin* brown. ~to *a* gilt; *(color oro)* golden. ~'tura *nf* gilding

dormicchi'are *vi* doze

dormigli'one, -a *nmf* sleepyhead; *fig* lazy-bones

dor'mi|re *vi* sleep; *(essere addormentato)* be asleep; *fig* be asleep. ~ta *nf* good sleep. ~'tina *nf* nap. ~'torio *nm* dormitory

dormi'veglia **nm essere in ~** be half asleep

dor'sale *a* dorsal ●*nf (di monte)* ridge

'dorso *nm* back; *(di libro)* spine; *(di monte)* crest; *(nel nuoto)* backstroke

do'saggio *nm* dosage

do'sare *vt* dose; *fig* measure; ~ **le parole** weigh one's words

dosa'tore *nm* measuring jug

'dose *nf* dose; **in buona ~** *fig* in good measure. ~ **eccessiva** overdose

dossi'er *nm inv (raccolta di dati, fascicolo)* file

'dosso *nm (dorso)* back; **levarsi di ~ gli abiti** take off one's clothes

do'ta|re *vt* endow; *(di accessori)* equip. ~**to** *a (persona)* gifted; *(fornito)* equipped. ~**zi'one** *nf (attrezzatura)* equipment; **in ~zione** at one's disposal

'dote *nf* dowry; *(qualità)* gift

'dotto *a* learned ●*nm* scholar; *Anat* duct

dotto'rato *nm* doctorate. dot'tore, ~'ressa *nmf* doctor

dot'trina *nf* doctrine

'dove *adv* where; **di ~ sei?** where do you come from; **fin ~?** how far?; **per ~?** which way?

do've|re *vi (obbligo)* have to, must; **devo andare** I have to go, I must go; **devo venire anch'io?** do I have to come too?; **avresti dovuto dirmelo** you should have told me, you ought to have told me; **devo sedermi un attimo** I must sit down for a minute, I need to sit down for a minute; **dev'essere successo qualcosa** something must have happened; **come si deve** properly ●*vt (essere debitore di, derivare)* owe; **essere dovuto a** be due to ●*nm* duty; **per ~** out of duty. **dove'roso** *a* only right and proper

do'vunque *adv (dappertutto)* everywhere; *(in qualsiasi luogo)* anywhere ●*conj* wherever

do'vuto *a* due; *(debito)* proper

doz'zi|na *nf* dozen. ~'nale *a* cheap

dra'gare *vt* dredge

'drago *nm* dragon

'dramm|a *nm* drama. dram'matico *a* dramatic. ~atiz'zare *vt* dramatize. ~a'turgo *nm* playwright. dram'mone *nm (film)* tear-jerker

drappeggi'are *vt* drape. drap-'peggio *nm* drapery

drap'pello *nm Mil* squad; *(gruppo)* band

'drastico *a* drastic

dre'na|ggio *nm* drainage. ~re *vt* drain

drib|blare *vt (in calcio)* dribble. 'dribbling *nm inv (in calcio)* dribble

'dritta *nf (mano destra)* right hand; *Naut* starboard; *(informazione)* pointer, tip; **a ~ e a manca** *(dappertutto)* left, right and centre

'dritto *a* = **diritto** ●*nmf fam* crafty so-and-so

driz'zar|e *vt* straighten; (*rizzare*) prick up. **~si** *vr* straighten [up]; (*alzarsi*) raise

'dro|ga *nf* drug. **~'gare** *vt* drug. **~'garsi** *vr* take drugs. **~'gato, -a** *nmf* drug addict

droghe'ria *nf* grocery. **~'iere, -a** *nmf* grocer

drome'dario *nm* dromedary

'dubbi|o *a* doubtful; (*ambiguo*) dubious ●*nm* doubt; (*sospetto*) suspicion; **essere fuori ~o** be beyond doubt; **essere in ~o** be doubtful. **~'oso** *a* doubtful

dubi'ta|re *vi* doubt; **~re di** doubt; (*diffidare*) mistrust; **dubito che venga** I doubt whether he'll come. **~'tivo** *a* (*ambiguo*) ambiguous

'duca, du'chessa *nmf* duke; duchess

'due *a & nm* two

due'cento *a & nm* two hundred

du'ello *nm* duel

due'mila *a & nm* two thousand

due'pezzi *nm inv* (*bikini*) bikini

du'etto *nm* duo; *Mus* duet

'duna *nf* dune

'dunque *conj* therefore; (*allora*) well [then]

'duo *nm inv* duo; *Mus* duet

du'omo *nm* cathedral

'duplex *nm Teleph* party line

dupli'ca|re *vt* duplicate. **'duplice** *a* double; **in duplice** in duplicate

dura'mente *adv* (*lavorare*) hard; (*rimproverare*) harshly

du'rante *prep* during

du'r|are *vi* last; (*cibo:*) keep; (*resistere*) hold out. **~ata** *nf* duration. **~a'turo, ~evole** *a* lasting, enduring

du'rezza *nf* hardness; (*di carne*) toughness; (*di voce, padre*) harshness

'duro, -a *a* hard; (*persona, carne*) tough; (*voce*) harsh; (*pane*) stale; **tieni ~!** (*resistere*) hang in there!

●*nmf* (*persona*) tough person, toughie *fam*

du'rone *nm* hardened skin

'duttile *a* (*materiale*) ductile; (*carattere*) malleable

Ee

e, ed *conj* and

'ebano *nm* ebony

eb'bene *conj* well [then]

eb'brezza *nf* inebriation; (*euforia*) elation; **guida in stato di ~** drink-driving, drunken driving. **'ebbro** *a* inebriated; **ebbro di gioia** delirious with joy

'ebete *a* stupid

ebolliz'ione *nf* boiling

e'braico *a* Hebrew ●*nm* (*lingua*) Hebrew. **e'br|eo, -a** *a* Jewish ●*nmf* Jew; Jewess

'Ebridi *nfpl* le **~** the Hebrides

eca'tombe *nf* fare un'**~** wreak havoc

ecc *abbr* (**eccetera**) etc

ecce'den|te *a* (*peso, bagaglio*) excess. **~za** *nf* excess; (*d'avanzo*) surplus; **avere qcsa in ~za** have an excess of sth; **bagagli in ~za** excess baggage. **~za di cassa** surplus. **ec'cedere** *vt* exceed ●*vi* go too far; **eccedere nel mangiare** overeat; **eccedere nel bere** drink to excess

eccel'len|te *a* excellent. **~za** *nf* excellence; (*titolo*) Excellency; **per ~za** par excellence. **ec'cellere** *vi* excel (**in** at)

eccentricità *nf* eccentricity. **ec'centrico, -a** *a & nmf* eccentric

ecces'siva'mente *adv* excessively. **ec'cessivo** *a* excessive

ec'cesso *nm* excess; **andare agli eccessi** go to extremes; **all'~** to excess. **~ di velocità** speeding

ec'cetera *adv* et cetera

ec'cetto *prep* except; **~ che** (*a*

meno che) unless. **eccettu'are** *vt* except

eccezio'nal|e *a* exceptional. **~'mente** *adv* exceptionally; (*contrariamente alla regola*) as an exception

eccezi'one *nf* exception; *Jur* objection; **a ~ di** with the exception of

ecci'ta'mento *nm* excitement. **ecci'tante** *a* exciting; (*sostanza*) stimulant ● *nm* stimulant

ecci'ta|re *vt* excite. **~rsi** *vr* get excited. **~to** *a* excited

eccitazi'one *nf* excitement

ecclesi'astico *a* ecclesiastical ● *nm* priest

'ecco *adv* (*qui*) here; (*là*) there; **~!** exactly!; **~ fatto** there we are; **~ la tua borsa** here is your bag; **~ [li] mio figlio** there is my son; **~mi** here I am; **~ tutto** that is all

ec'come *adv* & *int* and how!

echeggi'are *vi* echo

e'clissi *nf inv* eclipse

'eco *nmf* (*pl m* **echi**) echo

ecogra'fia *nf* scan

ecolo'gia *nf* ecology. **eco'logico** *a* ecological; (*prodotto*) environmentally friendly

e commerci'ale *nf* ampersand

econo'mi|a *nf* economy; (*scienza*) economics; **fare ~ia** economize (*di* on). **eco'nomico** *a* economic; (*a buon prezzo*) cheap. **~ista** *nmf* economist. **~iz'zare** *vt/i* economize; save (*tempo, denaro*). **e'conomo, -a** *a* thrifty ● *nmf* (*di collegio*) bursar

é'cru *a inv* raw

'Ecu *nm inv* ECU, ecu

ec'zema *nm* eczema

ed *conj vedi* **e**

'edera *nf* ivy

e'dicola *nf* [newspaper] kiosk

edifi'cabile *a* (*area, terreno*) classified as suitable for development

edifi'cante *a* edifying

edifi'care *vt* build; (*indurre al bene*) edify

edi'ficio *nm* building; *fig* structure

e'dile *a* building *attrib*

edi'lizi|a *nf* building trade. **~o** *a* building *attrib*

edi'tore, -'trice *a* publishing ● *nmf* publisher; (*curatore*) editor. **~to'ria** *nf* publishing. **~tori'ale** *a* publishing ● *nm* (*articolo*) editorial, leader

edizi'one *nf* edition; (*di manifestazione*) performance. **~ ridotta** abridg[e]ment. **~ della sera** (*di telegiornale*) evening news

edu'ca|re *vt* educate; (*allevare*) bring up. **~'tivo** *a* educational. **~to** *a* polite. **~'tore, ~'trice** *nmf* educator. **~zi'one** *nf* education; (*di bambini*) upbringing; (*buone maniere*) [good] manners *pl.* **~zione fisica** physical education

e'felide *nf* freckle

effemi'nato *a* effeminate

efferve'scente *a* effervescent; (*frizzante*) fizzy; (*aspirina*) soluble

effettiva'mente *adv* **è troppo tardi – ~** it's too late – so it is

effet'tivo *a* actual; (*efficace*) effective; (*personale*) permanent; *Mil* regular ● *nm* (*somma totale*) sum total

ef'fet|to *nm* effect; (*impressione*) impression; **in ~i** in fact; **a tutti gli ~i** to all intents and purposes; **~i personali** personal belongings. **~u'are** *vt* effect; carry out (*controllo, sondaggio*). **~u'arsi** *vr* take place

effi'ca|ce *a* effective. **~ia** *nf* effectiveness

effici'en|te *a* efficient. **~za** *nf* efficiency

ef'fimero *a* ephemeral

effusi'one *nf* effusion

E'geo *nm* **l'~** the Aegean [Sea]

E'gitto *nm* Egypt. **egizi'ano, -a** *a* & *nmf* Egyptian

'egli *pers pron* he; **~ stesso** he himself

ego'centrico, -a *a* egocentric ● *nmf* egocentric person

ego'is|mo nm selfishness. **~ta** a selfish ● nmf selfish person. **~tico** a selfish

e'gregio a distinguished; **E~ Signore** Dear Sir

egua'litario a & nm egalitarian

eiaculazi'one nf ejaculation

elabo'ra|re vt elaborate; process ⟨dati⟩. **~to** a elaborate. **~zi'one** nf elaboration; ⟨di dati⟩ processing. **~zione [di] testi** word processing

elar'gire vt lavish

elastici|tà nf elasticity. **~z'zato** a ⟨stoffa⟩ elasticated. **e'lastico** a elastic; ⟨tessuto⟩ stretch; ⟨orario, mente⟩ flexible; ⟨persona⟩ easygoing ● nm elastic; ⟨fascia⟩ rubber band

ele'fante nm elephant

ele'gan|te a elegant. **~za** nf elegance

e'leggere vt elect. **eleg'gibile** a eligible

elemen'tare a elementary; **scuola ~** primary school

ele'mento nm element; **elementi** pl ⟨fatti⟩ data; ⟨rudimenti⟩ elements

ele'mosina nf charity; **chiedere l'~** beg. **elemosi'nare** vt/i beg

elen'care vt list

e'lenco nm list. **~ abbonati** telephone directory. **~ telefonico** telephone directory

elet'tivo a ⟨carica⟩ elective. **e'letto, -a** pp di **eleggere** ● a chosen ⟨nominato⟩ elected member; **per pochi eletti** for the chosen few

eletto'ra|le a electoral. **~to** nm electorate

elet'tore, -'trice nmf voter

elet'trauto nm garage for electrical repairs

elettri'cista nm electrician

elettri|cità nf electricity. **e'lettrico** a electric. **~z'zante** a ⟨notizia, gara⟩ electrifying. **~z'zare** vt fig electrify. **~z'zato** a fig electrified

elettrocardio'gramma nm electrocardiogram

e'lettrodo nm electrode

elettrodo'mestico nm [electrical] household appliance

elet'trone nm electron

elet'tronico, -a a electronic ● nf electronics

ele'va|re vt raise; ⟨promuovere⟩ promote; ⟨erigere⟩ erect; ⟨fig: migliorare⟩ better; **~ al quadrato/cubo** square/cube. **~rsi** vr rise; ⟨edificio⟩ stand. **~to** a high. **~zi'one** nf elevation

elezi'one nf election

'elica nf Naut screw, propeller; Aeron propeller; ⟨del ventilatore⟩ blade

eli'cottero nm helicopter

elimi'na|re vt eliminate. **~'toria** nf Sport preliminary heat. **~zi'one** nf elimination

é'li|te nf inv élite. **~'tista** a élitist

'ella pers pron she

el'lepi nm inv LP

elo'gi|are vt praise. **e'logio** nm praise; ⟨discorso, scritto⟩ eulogy

elo'quen|te a eloquent; fig telltale. **~za** nf eloquence

e'lu|dere vt elude; evade ⟨sorveglianza, controllo⟩. **~'sivo** a elusive

el'vetico a Swiss

emaci'ato a emaciated

'E-mail nf e-mail

ema'na|re vt give off; pass ⟨legge⟩ ● vi emanate. **~zi'one** nf giving off; ⟨di legge⟩ enactment

emanci'pa|re vt emancipate. **~rsi** vr become emancipated. **~to** a emancipated. **~zi'one** nf emancipation

emargi'na|to nm marginalized person. **~zi'one** nf marginalization

ema'toma nm haematoma

em'bargo nm embargo

em'ble|ma nm emblem. **~'matico** a emblematic

embo'lia nf embolism

embrio'nale a Biol, fig embryonic. **embri'one** nm embryo

emen|da|mento *nm* amendment. **~'dare** *vt* amend

emer'gen|te *a* emergent. **~za** *nf* emergency; **in caso di ~za** in an emergency

e'mergere *vi* emerge; ⟨sottomarino:⟩ surface; ⟨distinguersi⟩ stand out

e'merito *a* ⟨professore⟩ emeritus; **un ~ imbecille** a prize idiot

e'merso *pp di* **emergere**

e'messo *pp di* **emettere**

e'mettere *vt* emit; give out ⟨luce, suono⟩; let out ⟨grido⟩; ⟨mettere in circolazione⟩ issue

emi'crania *nf* migraine

emi'gra|re *vi* emigrate. **~to, -a** *nmf* immigrant. **~zi'one** *nf* emigration

emi'nen|te *a* eminent. **~za** *nf* eminence

e'miro *nm* emir

emis'fero *nm* hemisphere

emis'sario *nm* emissary

emissi'one *nf* emission; ⟨di denaro⟩ issue; ⟨trasmissione⟩ broadcast

emit'tente *a* issuing; ⟨trasmittente⟩ broadcasting ● *nf Radio* transmitter

emorra'gia *nf* haemorrhage

emor'roidi *nfpl* piles

emotività *nf* emotional make-up. **emo'tivo** *a* emotional

emozio'na|nte *a* exciting; ⟨commovente⟩ moving. **~re** *vt* excite; ⟨commuovere⟩ move. **~rsi** *vr* become excited; ⟨commuoversi⟩ be moved. **~to** *a* excited; ⟨commosso⟩ moved. **emozi'one** *nf* emotion; ⟨agitazione⟩ excitement

'empio *a* impious; ⟨spietato⟩ pitiless; ⟨malvagio⟩ wicked

em'pirico *a* empirical

em'porio *nm* emporium; ⟨negozio⟩ general store

emu'la|re *vt* emulate. **~zi'one** *nf* emulation

emulsi'one *nf* emulsion

en'ciclica *nf* encyclical

enciclope'dia *nf* encyclopaedia

encomi'are *vt* commend. **en'co-mio** *nm* commendation

en'demico *a* endemic

endo've|na *nf* intravenous injection. **~'noso** *a* intravenous; **per via ~nosa** intravenously

E.N.I.T. *nm abbr* (**Ente Nazionale Italiano per il Turismo**) Italian State Tourist Office

ener'getico *a* ⟨risorse, crisi⟩ energy *attrib*; ⟨alimento⟩ energy-giving

ener'gia *nf* energy. **e'nergico** *a* energetic; ⟨efficace⟩ strong

ener'gumeno *nm* Neanderthal

en'fasi *nf* emphasis

en'fatico *a* emphatic. **~z'zare** *vt* emphasize

e'nigma *nm* enigma. **enig'matico** *a* enigmatic. **enig'mistica** *nf* puzzles *pl*

en'nesimo *a Math* nth; *fam* umpteenth

e'norm|e *a* enormous. **~e'mente** *adv* massively. **~ità** *nf inv* enormity; ⟨assurdità⟩ absurdity

eno'teca *nf* wine-tasting shop

'ente *nm* board; ⟨società⟩ company; ⟨filosofia⟩ being

entità *nf inv* ⟨filosofia⟩ entity; ⟨gravità⟩ seriousness; ⟨dimensione⟩ extent

entou'rage *nm inv* entourage

en'trambi *a & pron* both

en'tra|re *vi* go in, enter; **~re in** go into; ⟨stare in, trovar posto in⟩ fit into; ⟨arruolarsi⟩ join; **~rci** ⟨avere a che fare⟩ have to do with; **tu che c'entri?** what has it got to do with you? **~ta** *nf* entry, entrance; **~te** *pl Comm* takings; ⟨reddito⟩ income *sg*

'entro *prep* ⟨tempo⟩ within

entro'terra *nm inv* hinterland

entusias'mante *a* fascinating, exciting

entusias'mar|e *vt* arouse enthusiasm in. **~si** *vr* be enthusiastic (**per** about)

entusi'as|mo *nm* enthusiasm. **~ta** *a* enthusiastic ● *nmf* enthusiast. **~tico** *a* enthusiastic

enume'ra|re *vt* enumerate. **~zi'one** *nf* enumeration

enunci'a|re *vt* enunciate. **~zi'one** *nf* enunciation

epa'tite *nf* hepatitis

'epico *a* epic

epide'mia *nf* epidemic

epi'dermide *nf* epidermis

Epifa'nia *nf* Epiphany

epi'gramma *nm* epigram

epil'es'sia *nf* epilepsy. **epi'lettico, -a** *a & nmf* epileptic

e'pilogo *nm* epilogue

epi'sodi|co *a* episodic; **caso ~co** one-off case. **~o** *nm* episode

e'piteto *nm* epithet

'epoca *nf* age; (*periodo*) period; **a quell'~** in those days; **auto d'~** vintage car

ep'pure *conj* [and] yet

epu'rare *vt* purge

equa'tore *nm* equator. **equatori'ale** *a* equatorial

equazi'one *nf* equation

e'questre *a* equestrian; **circo ~** circus

equi'latero *a* equilateral

equili'bra|re *vt* balance. **~to** *a* (*persona*) well-balanced. **equi'librio** *nm* balance; (*buon senso*) common sense; (*di bilancia*) equilibrium

equili'brismo *nm* **fare ~** do a balancing act

e'quino *a* horse *attrib*

equi'nozio *nm* equinox

equipaggia'mento *nm* equipment

equipaggi'are *vt* equip; (*di persone*) man

equi'paggio *nm* crew; *Aeron* cabin crew

equipa'rare *vt* make equal

é'quipe *nf inv* team

equità *nf* equity

equitazi'one *nf* riding

equiva'len|te *a & nm* equivalent. **~za** *nf* equivalence

equiva'lere *vi* **~ a** be equivalent to

equivo'care *vi* misunderstand

e'quivoco *a* equivocal; (*sospetto*) suspicious; **un tipo ~ a** a shady character ● *nm* misunderstanding

'equo *a* fair, just

'era *nf* era

'erba *nf* grass; (*aromatica, medicinale*) herb. **~ cipollina** chives *pl*. **er'baccia** *nf* weed. **er'baceo** *a* herbaceous

erbi'cida *nm* weed-killer

erbo'rist|a *nmf* herbalist. **~e'ria** *nf* herbalist's shop

er'boso *a* grassy

er'culeo *a* (*forza*) herculean

e'red|e *nmf* heir; heiress. **~ità** *nf inv* inheritance; *Biol* heredity. **~i'tare** *vt* inherit. **~itarietà** *nf* heredity. **~i'tario** *a* hereditary

ere'mita *nm* hermit

ere'sia *nf* heresy. **e'retico, -a** *a* heretical ● *nmf* heretic

e're|tto *pp* di **erigere** ● *a* erect. **~zi'one** *nf* erection; (*costruzione*) building

'erica *nf* heather

e'rigere *vt* erect; (*fig: fondare*) found

eri'tema *nm* (*cutaneo*) inflammation; (*solare*) sunburn

ermel'lino *nm* ermine

ermetica'mente *adv* hermetically. **er'metico** *a* hermetic; (*a tenuta d'aria*) airtight

'ernia *nf* hernia

e'rodere *vi* erode

e'ro|e *nm* hero. **~ico** *a* heroic. **~'ismo** *nm* heroism

ero'ga|re *vt* distribute; (*fornire*) supply. **~zi'one** *nf* supply

ero'ina *nf* heroine; (*droga*) heroin

erosi'one *nf* erosion

e'rotico *a* erotic. **ero'tismo** *nm* eroticism

er'rante *a* wandering. **er'rare** *vi* wander; (*sbagliare*) be mistaken

er'rato *a* (*sbagliato*) mistaken

'erre *nf* **~ moscia** burr

erronea'mente *adv* mistakenly

er'rore *nm* error, mistake; *(di stampa)* misprint; **essere in ~** be wrong

'erta *nf* **stare all'~** be on the alert

eru'dirsi *vr* get educated. **~to** *a* learned

erut'tare *vt* ⟨*vulcano:*⟩ erupt ● *vi* ⟨*ruttare*⟩ belch. **eruzi'one** *nf* eruption; *Med* rash

esacer'bare *vt* exacerbate

esage'ra|re *vi* exaggerate ● *vi* exaggerate; *(nel comportamento)* go over the top; **~re nel mangiare** eat too much. **~ta'mente** *adv* excessively. **~to** *a* exaggerated; *(prezzo)* exorbitant ● *nm* è un **~to** he exaggerates. **~zi'one** *nf* exaggeration; **è costato un'~zione** it cost the earth

esa'lare *vt/i* exhale

esal'ta|re *vt* exalt; *(entusiasmare)* elate. **~to** *a* ⟨*fanatico*⟩ fanatical ● *nm* fanatic. **~zi'one** *nf* exaltation; *(in discorso)* fervour

e'same *nm* examination, exam; **dare un ~** take an exam; **prendere in ~** examine. • **del sangue** blood test. **esami** *pl* **di maturità** ≈ A-levels

esami'na|re *vt* examine. **~tore**, **~trice** *nmf* examiner

e'sangue *a* bloodless

e'sanime *a* lifeless

esaspe'rante *a* exasperating

esaspe'ra|re *vt* exasperate. **~rsi** *vr* get exasperated. **~zi'one** *nf* exasperation

esat|ta'mente *adv* exactly. **~'tez-za** *nf* exactness; *(precisione)* precision; *(di risposta, risultato)* accuracy

e'satto *pp di* **esigere** ● *a* exact; *(risposta, risultato)* correct; *(orologio)* right; **hai l'ora esatta?** do you have the right time?; **sono le due esatte** it's two o'clock exactly

esat'tore *nm* collector

esau'dire *vt* grant; fulfil *(speranze)*

esauri'ente *a* exhaustive

esau'ri|re *vt* exhaust. **~rsi** *vr* ex-

haust oneself; *(merci ecc.)* run out. **~to** *a* exhausted; *(merci)* sold out; *(libro)* out of print; **fare il tutto ~to** *(spettacolo:)* play to a full house

'esca *nf* bait

escande'scen|za *nf* outburst; **dare in ~e** lose one's temper

escla'ma|re *vi* exclaim. **~tivo** *a* exclamatory. **~zi'one** *nf* exclamation

es'clu|dere *vt* exclude; rule out *(possibilità, ipotesi).* **~si'one** *nf* exclusion. **~'siva** *nf* exclusive right, sole right; **in ~siva** exclusive. **~siva'mente** *adv* exclusively. **~'sivo** *a* exclusive. **~so** *pp di* **escludere** ● **a non è ~so che ci sia** it's not out of the question that he'll be there

escogi'tare *vt* contrive

escre'mento *nm* excrement

escursi'one *nf* excursion; *(scorreria)* raid; *(di temperatura)* range

ese'cra|bile *a* abominable. **~re** *vt* abhor

esecu'tivo *a* & *nm* executive. **~'tore**, **~'trice** *nmf* executor; *Mus* performer. **~zi'one** *nf* execution; *Mus* performance

esegu'ire *vt* carry out; *Jur* execute; *Mus* perform

e'sempio *nm* example; **ad** *o* **per ~** for example; **dare l'~** set sb an example; **fare un ~** give an example. **esem'plare** *a* examplary ● *nm* specimen; *(di libro)* copy. **esemplifi'care** *vt* exemplify

esen'tar|e *vt* exempt. **~si** *vr* free oneself. **e'sente** *a* exempt. **esente da imposta** duty-free. **esente da IVA** VAT-exempt

esen'tasse *a* duty-free

e'sequie *nfpl* funeral rites

eser'cente *nmf* shopkeeper

eserci'ta|re *vt* exercise; *(addestrare)* train; *(fare uso di)* exert; *(professione)* practise. **~rsi** *vr* practise. **~zi'one** *nf* exercise; *Mil* drill

e'sercito *nm* army

eser'cizio *nm* exercise; (*pratica*) practice; *Comm* financial year; (*azienda*) business; **essere fuori ~** be out of practice

esi'bi|re *vt* show off; produce (*documenti*). **~rsi** *vr* *Theat* perform; *fig* show off. **~zi'one** *nf* *Theat* performance; (*di documenti*) production

esibizio'nis|mo *nm* showing off. **~ta** *nmf* exhibitionist

esi'gen|te *a* exacting; (*pignolo*) fastidious. **~za** *nf* demand; (*bisogno*) need. **e'sigere** *vt* demand; (*riscuotere*) collect

e'siguo *a* meagre

esila'ra|nte *a* exhilarating

'esile *a* slender; (*voce*) thin

esili'a|re *vt* exile. **~rsi** *vr* go into exile. **~to, -a** *a* exiled ● *nmf* exile. **e'silio** *nm* exile

e'simer|e *vt* release. **~si** *vr* **~si da** get out of

esi'sten|te *a* existing. **~za** *nf* existence. **~zi'ale** *a* existential. **~zia'lismo** *nm* existentialism

e'sistere *vi* exist

esi'tante *a* hesitating; (*voce*) faltering

esi'ta|re *vi* hesitate. **~zi'one** *nf* hesitation

'esito *nm* result; **avere buon ~** be a success

'esodo *nm* exodus

e'sofago *nm* oesophagus

esone'rare *vt* exempt. **e'sonero** *nm* exemption

esorbi'tante *a* exorbitant

esorciz'zare *vt* exorcize

esordi'ente *nmf* person making his/her début. **e'sordio** *nm* opening; (*di attore*) début. **esor'dire** *vi* début

esor'tare *vt* (*pregare*) beg; (*incitare*) urge

eso'terico *a* esoteric

e'sotico *a* exotic

espa'drillas *nfpl* espadrilles

es'pan|dere *vt* expand. **~dersi** *vr* expand; (*diffondersi*) extend. **~si'one** *nf* expansion. **~'sivo** *a* expansive; (*persona*) friendly

espatri'are *vi* leave one's country. **es'patrio** *nm* expatriation

espedi'ent|e *nm* expedient; **vivere di ~** I live by one's wits

es'pellere *vt* expel

esperi'enza *nf* experience; **parlare per ~enza** speak from experience. **~'mento** *nm* experiment

es'perto, -a *a & nmf* expert

espi'a|re *vt* atone for. **~'torio** *a* expiatory

espi'rare *vt/i* breathe out

espli'care *vt* carry on

explicita'mente *adv* explicitly. **es'plicito** *a* explicit

es'plodere *vi* explode ● *vt* fire

esplo'ra|re *vt* explore. **~'tore, ~'trice** *nmf* explorer; **giovane ~tore** boy scout. **~zi'one** *nf* exploration

esplosi'one *nf* explosion. **~'sivo** *a & nm* explosive

espo'nente *nm* exponent

es'por|re *vt* expose; display (*merci*); (*spiegare*) expound; exhibit (*quadri ecc*). **~si** *vr* (*compromettersi*) compromise oneself; (*al sole*) expose oneself; (*alle critiche*) lay oneself open

espor'ta|re *vt* export. **~'tore, ~'trice** *nmf* exporter. **~zi'one** *nf* export

esposizi'one *nf* (*mostra*) exhibition; (*in vetrina*) display; (*spiegazione ecc*) exposition; (*posizione, fotografia*) exposure. **es'posto** *pp* *di* **esporre** ● *a* exposed; **esposto a** (*rivolto*) facing ● *nm* *Jur ecc* statement

espressa'mente *adv* expressly; **non l'ha detto ~** he didn't put it in so many words

espressi'one *nf* expression. **~'sivo** *a* expressive

es'presso *pp di* **esprimere** ● *a* express ● *nm* (*lettera*) express letter; (*treno*) express train; (*caffè*) espresso; **per ~** (*spedire*) [by] express [post]

es'primer|e *vt* express. **~si** *vr* express oneself

espropri'a|re *vt* dispossess. **~zi'one** *nf* Jur expropriation. **es'proprio** *nm* expropriation

espulsi'one *nf* expulsion. **es'pulso** *pp di* **espellere**

es'senz|a *nf* essence. **~i'ale** *a* essential ● *nm* important thing. **~ial'mente** *a* essentially

'essere *vi* be; **c'è** there is; **ci sono** there are; **che ora è? – sono le dieci** what time is it? – it's ten o'clock; **chi è? – sono io** who is it? – it's me; **ci sono!** *(ho capito)* I've got it!; **ci siamo!** *(siamo arrivati)* here we are at last!; **è stato detto che** it has been said that; **siamo in due** there are two of us; **questa camicia è da lavare** this shirt is to be washed; **non è da te** it's not like you; **~ di** *(provenire da)* be from; **~ per** *(favorevole)* be in favour of; **se fossi in te,...** if I were you,...; **sarà!** if you say so!; **come sarebbe a dire?** what are you getting at? ● *v aux* have; *(in passivi)* be; **siamo arrivati** we have arrived; **ci sono stato ieri** I was there yesterday; **sono nato a Torino** I was born in Turin; **è riconosciuto come...** he is recognized as... ● *nm* being. **~ umano** human being. **~ vivente** living creature

essic'cato *a* dried

'esso, -a *pers pron* he, she; *(cosa, animale)* it

est *nm* east

'estasi *nf* ecstasy; **andare in ~ per** go into raptures over. **'~are** *vt* enrapture

e'state *nf* summer

e'sten|dere *vt* extend. **~dersi** *vr* spread; *(allungarsi)* stretch. **~si'one** *nf* extension; *(ampiezza)* expanse; Mus range. **~'sivo** *a* extensive

estenu'ante *a* exhausting

estenu'a|re *vt* wear out; deplete *(risorse, casse)*. **~rsi** *vr* wear oneself out

esteri'or|e *a* & *nm* exterior.

~'mente *adv* externally; *(di persone)* outwardly

esterna'mente *adv* on the outside

ester'nare *vt* express, show

e'sterno *a* external; **per uso ~** for external use only ● *nm* *(allievo)* day-boy; Archit exterior; *(scala)* outside; *(in film)* location shot

'estero *a* foreign ● *nm* foreign countries *pl*; **all'~** abroad

esterre'fatto *a* horrified

e'steso *pp di* **estendere** ● *a* extensive; *(diffuso)* widespread; **per ~** *(scrivere)* in full

e'stetic|a *nf* aesthetics *sg*. **~a'mente** *adv* aesthetically. **~o, -a** *a* aesthetic; *(chirurgia, chirurgo)* plastic. **este'tista** *nf* beautician

'estimo *nm* estimate

e'stin|guere *vt* extinguish. **~guersi** *vr* die out. **~to, -a** *pp di* **estinguere** ● *nmf* deceased. **~'tore** *nm* [fire] extinguisher. **~zi'one** *nf* extinction; *(di incendio)* putting out

estir'pa|re *vt* uproot; extract *(dente)*; *fig* eradicate *(crimine, malattia)*. **~zi'one** *nf* eradication; *(di dente)* extraction

e'stivo *a* summer

e'stor|cere *vt* extort. **~si'one** *nf* extortion. **~to** *pp di* **estorcere**

estradizi'one *nf* extradition

e'straneo, -a *a* extraneous; *(straniero)* foreign ● *nmf* stranger

estrani'ar|e *vt* estrange. **~si** *vr* become estranged

e'stra|rre *vt* extract; *(sorteggiare)* draw. **~tto** *pp di* **estrarre** ● *nm* extract; *(brano)* excerpt; *(documento)* abstract. **~tto conto** statement [of account], bank statement. **~zi'one** *nf* extraction; *(a sorte)* draw

estrema'mente *adv* extremely

estre'mis|mo *nm* extremism. **~ta** *nmf* extremist

estremità *nf inv* extremity; *(di una corda)* end ● *nfpl* Anat extremities

e'**stremo** *a* extreme; (*ultimo*) last; **misure estreme** drastic measures; l'**E~ Oriente** the Far East ● *nm* (*limite*) extreme. **estremi** *pl* (*di documento*) main points; (*di reato*) essential elements; **essere agli estremi** be at the end of one's tether

'**estro** *nm* (*disposizione artistica*) talent; (*ispirazione*) inspiration; (*capriccio*) whim. e'**stroso** *a* talented; (*capriccioso*) unpredictable

estro'**mettere** *vt* expel

estro'**verso** *a* extroverted ● *nm* extrovert

estu'**ario** *nm* estuary

esube'**rante** *a* exuberant. **~za** *nf* exuberance

'**esule** *nmf* exile

esul'**tante** *a* exultant

esul'**tare** *vi* rejoice

esu'**mare** *vt* exhume

e'**tà** *nf inv* age; **raggiungere la maggiore ~** come of age; **un uomo di mezz'~** a middle-aged man

'**etere** *nm* ether. e'**tereo** *a* ethereal

eterna'**mente** *adv* eternally

eternità *nf* eternity; **è un'~ che non la vedo** I haven't seen her for ages

e'**terno** *a* eternal; (*questione, problema*) age-old; **in ~** *fam* for ever

etero'**geneo** *a* diverse, heterogeneous

eterosessu'**ale** *nmf* heterosexual

'**etic|a** *nf* ethics. **~o** *a* ethical

eti'**chetta¹** *nf* label; (*con il prezzo*) price-tag

eti'**chetta²** *nf* (*cerimoniale*) etiquette

etichet'**tare** *vt* label

eti'**lometro** *nm* Breathalyzer®

etimolo'**gia** *nf* etymology

Eti'**opia** *nf* Ethiopia

'**etnico** *a* ethnic. etnolo'**gia** *nf* ethnology

e'**trusco** *a* & *nmf* Etruscan

'**ettaro** *nm* hectare

'**etto, etto'grammo** *nm* hundred grams, ≈ quarter pound

euca'**lipto** *nm* eucalyptus

eucari'**stia** *nf* Eucharist

eufe'**mismo** *nm* euphemism

eufo'**ria** *nf* elation; *Med* euphoria. eu'**forico** *a* elated; *Med* euphoric

Euro'**city** *nm* international Intercity

eurodepu'**tato** *nm* Euro MP, MEP

Eu'**ropa** *nf* Europe. euro'**peo, -a** *a* & *nmf* European

eutana'**sia** *nf* euthanasia

evacu'**a|re** *vt* evacuate. **~zi'one** *nf* evacuation

e'**vadere** *vt* evade; (*sbrigare*) deal with ● *vi* **~ da** escape from

evane'**scente** *a* vanishing

evan'**gelico** *a* evangelical. evan-ge'**lista** *nm* evangelist. **~o** *nm* = vangelo

evapo'**ra|re** *vi* evaporate. **~zi'one** *nf* evaporation

evasi'**one** *nf* escape; (*fiscale*) evasion; *fig* escapism. eva'**sivo** *a* evasive

e'**vaso** *pp di* evadere ● *nm* fugitive

eva'**sore** *nm* **~ fiscale** tax evader

eveni'**enza** *nf* eventuality

e'**vento** *nm* event

eventu'**al|e** *a* possible. **~ità** *nf inv* eventuality

evi'**dente** *a* evident; **è ~te che** it is obvious that. **~te'mente** *adv* evidently. **~za** *nf* evidence; **mettere in ~za** emphasize; **mettersi in ~za** make oneself conspicuous

evidenzi'**a|re** *vt* highlight. **~'tore** *nm* (*penna*) highlighter

evi'**tare** *vt* avoid; (*risparmiare*) spare

evo'**care** *vt* evoke

evo'**lu|to** *pp di* **evolvere** ● *a* evolved; (*progredito*) progressive; (*civiltà, nazione*) advanced; **una donna evoluta** a modern woman. **~zi'one** *nf* evolution; (*di ginnasta, aereo*) circle

e'**volver|e** *vt* develop. **~si** *vr* evolve

ev'**viva** *int* hurray; **~ il Papa!** long live the Pope!; **gridare ~** cheer

ex+ *pref* ex+, former

'extra a inv extra; (qualità) first-class ● nm inv extra

extracomuni'tario a non-EC

extraconiu'gale a extramarital

extrater'restre nmf extra-terrestrial

• •

Ff

fa[1] nm inv Mus (chiave, nota) F

fa[2] adv ago; **due mesi ~** two months ago

fabbi'sogno nm requirements pl, needs pl

'fabbri|ca nf factory

fabbri'cabile a (area, terreno) that can be built on

fabbri'cante nm manufacturer

fabbri'ca|re vt build; (produrre) manufacture; (fig: inventare) fabricate. **~to** nm building. **~zi'one** nf manufacturing; (costruzione) building

'fabbro nm blacksmith

fac'cend|a nf matter; **~e** pl (lavori domestici) housework sg. **~i'ere** nm wheeler-dealer

fac'chino nm porter

'facci|a nf face; (di foglio) side; **~ a ~a** face to face; **~a tosta** cheek; **voltar ~a** change sides; (di palazzo) opposite; **alla ~a di** (fam: a dispetto di) in spite of. **~'ata** nf façade; (di foglio) side; (fig: esteriorità) outward appearance

fa'ceto a facetious; **tra il serio e il ~** half joking

fa'chiro nm fakir

'facil|e a easy; (affabile) easygoing; **essere ~e alle critiche** be quick to criticize; **essere ~e al riso** laugh a lot; **~e a farsi** easy to do; **è ~e che piova** it's likely to rain. **~ità** nf inv ease; (disposizione) aptitude; **avere ~ità di parola** express oneself well

facili'ta|re vt facilitate. **~zi'one** nf facility; **~zioni** pl special terms

facil'mente adv (con facilità) easily; (probabilmente) probably

faci'lone a slapdash. **~'ria** nf slapdash attitude

facino'roso a violent

facoltà nf inv faculty; (potere) power. **~'tivo** a optional; **fermata ~tiva** request stop

facol'toso a wealthy

fac'simile nm facsimile

fac'totum nmf man/girl Friday, factotum

'faggio nm beech

fagi'ano nm pheasant

fagio'lino nm French bean

fagi'olo nm bean; **a ~** (arrivare, capitare) at the right time

fagoci'tare vt gobble up (società)

fa'gotto nm bundle; Mus bassoon

'faida nf feud

fai da te nm do-it-yourself, DIY

fal'cata nf stride

'falc|e nf scythe. **fal'cetto** nm sickle. **~i'are** vt cut; fig mow down. **~ia'trice** nf [lawn-]mower

'falco nm hawk

fal'cone nm falcon

'falda nf stratum; (di neve) flake; (di cappello) brim; (pendio) slope

fale'gname nm carpenter. **~'ria** nf carpentry

'falla nf leak

fal'lace a deceptive

'fallico a phallic

falli'mento a disastrous; Jur bankruptcy. **falli'mento** nm Fin bankruptcy; fig failure

fal'li|re vi Fin go bankrupt; fig fail ● vt miss (colpo). **~to, -a** a unsuccessful; Fin bankrupt ● nmf failure; Fin bankrupt

'fallo nm fault; (errore) mistake; Sport foul; (imperfezione) flaw; **senza ~** without fail

fa'lò nm inv bonfire

fal'sar|e vt alter; (falsificare) falsify. **~io, -a** nmf forger; (di documenti) counterfeiter

falsifi'ca|re vt fake; (contraffare)

forge. **~zi'one** nf (di documento) falsification

falsità nf falseness

'falso a false; (sbagliato) wrong; ⟨opera d'arte ecc⟩ fake; ⟨gioielli, oro⟩ imitation ● nm forgery; **giurare il ~** commit perjury

'fama nf fame; (reputazione) reputation

'fame nf hunger; **aver ~** be hungry; **fare la ~** barely scrape a living. **fa'melica** a ravenous

famige'rato a infamous

fa'miglia nf family

famili'are a family attrib; (ben noto) familiar; (senza cerimonie) informal ● nmf relative, relation **~tà** nf familiarity; (informalità) informality. **~iz'zarsi** vr familiarize oneself

fa'moso a famous

fa'nale nm lamp; Auto ecc light. **fanali** pl posteriori Auto rear lights

fa'natico, -a a fanatical; **essere ~ di calcio/cinema** fanatic about football/cinema ● nmf fanatic. **fana'tismo** nm fanaticism

fanci'ulla nf young girl. **~lezza** nf childhood. **~lo** nm young boy

fan'donia nf lie; **fandonie!** nonsense!

fan'fara nf fanfare; (complesso) brass band

fanfaro'nata nf brag. **fanfa'rone, -a** nmf braggart

fan'ghiglia nf mud. **'fango** nm mud. **fan'goso** a muddy

fannul'lone, -a nmf idler

fantasci'enza nf science fiction

fanta'sia nf fantasy; (immaginazione) imagination; (capriccio) fancy; (di tessuto) pattern. **~'oso** a ⟨stilista, ragazzo⟩ imaginative; (resoconto) improbable

fan'tasma nm ghost

fantasti'care vi day-dream. **~he'ria** nf day-dream. **fan'tastico** a fantastic; (racconto) fantasy

'fante nm infantryman; (nelle carte) jack. **~'ria** nm infantry

fan'tino nm jockey

fan'toccio nm puppet

fanto'matico a (inafferrabile) phantom attrib

fara'butto nm trickster

fara'ona nf (uccello) guinea-fowl

far'cire vt stuff; fill ⟨torta⟩. **~to a** (dolce) filled

far'dello nm bundle; fig burden

'fare vt do; make ⟨dolce, letto ecc⟩; (recitare la parte di) play; (trascorrere) spend; **~ una pausa/un sogno** have a break/a dream; **~ colpo su** impress; **~ paura a** frighten; **~ piacere a** please; **farla finita** put an end to it; **l'insegnante ~ a teacher**; **~ lo scemo** play the idiot; **~ una settimana al mare** spend a week at the seaside; **3 più 3 fa 6** 3 and 3 makes 6; **quanto fa?** – **fanno 10 000 lire** how much is it? – it's 10,000 lire; **far ~ qcsa a qcno** get sb to do sth; (costringere) make sb do sth; **~ vedere** show; **fammi parlare** let me speak; **niente a che ~ con** nothing to do with; **non c'è niente da ~** (per problema) there is nothing we/you/etc. can do; **fa caldo/buio** it's warm/dark; **non fa niente** it doesn't matter; **strada facendo** on the way. **farcela** (riuscire) manage ● vi **fai in modo di venire** try and come; **~ da** act as; **~ per** make as if to; **~ presto** be quick; **non fa per me** it's not for me ● nm way; **sul far del giorno** at daybreak. **farsi** vr (diventare) get; (sl: drogarsi) shoot up; **farsi avanti** come forward; **farsi i fatti propri** mind one's own business; **farsi la barba** shave; **farsi la villa** buy a villa; **farsi il ragazzo** fam find a boyfriend; **farsi due risate** have a laugh; **farsi male** hurt oneself; **farsi strada** (aver successo) make one's way in the world

fa'retto nm spot(light)

far'falla nf butterfly

farfal'lino nm (cravatta) bow tie

farfu'gliare vt mutter

fa'rina nf flour. **fari'nacei** nmpl starchy food sg

fa'ringe nf pharynx

fari'noso a ⟨neve⟩ powdery; ⟨mela⟩ soft; ⟨patata⟩ floury

farma'ceutico a pharmaceutical. ~**'cia** nf pharmacy; ⟨negozio⟩ chemist's [shop]. ~**cia di turno** duty chemist. ~**'cista** nmf chemist. **'farmaco** nm drug

'faro nm Auto headlight; Aeron beacon; ⟨costruzione⟩ lighthouse

'farsa nf farce

'fascia nf band; ⟨zona⟩ area; ⟨ufficiale⟩ sash; ⟨benda⟩ bandage. ~**'are** vt bandage; cling to ⟨fianchi⟩. ~**a'tura** nf dressing; ⟨azione⟩ bandaging

fa'scicolo nm file; ⟨di rivista⟩ issue; ⟨libretto⟩ booklet

'fascino nm fascination

'fascio nm bundle; ⟨di fiori⟩ bunch

fa'scismo nm fascism. ~**ta** nmf fascist

'fase nf phase

fa'stidi|o nm nuisance; ⟨scomodo⟩ inconvenience; **dar** ~**o a qcno** bother sb; ~**i** pl ⟨preoccupazioni⟩ worries; ⟨disturbi⟩ troubles. ~**'oso** a tiresome

'fasto nm pomp. **fa'stoso** a sumptuous

fa'sullo a bogus

'fata nf fairy

fa'ta|le a fatal; ⟨inevitabile⟩ fated

fata'l|ismo nm fatalism. ~**ista** nmf fatalist. ~**ità** nf inv fate; ⟨caso sfortunato⟩ misfortune. ~**'mente** adv inevitably

fa'tica nf effort; ⟨lavoro faticoso⟩ hard work; ⟨stanchezza⟩ fatigue; **a** ~ with great difficulty; **è** ~ **sprecata** it's a waste of time; **fare** ~ **a fare qcsa** find it difficult to do sth; **fare** ~ **a finire qcsa** struggle to finish sth. **fati'caccia** nf pain

fati'ca|re vi toil; ~**re a** ⟨stentare⟩ find it difficult to. ~**ta** nf effort;

⟨sfacchinata⟩ grind. **fati'coso** a tiring; ⟨difficile⟩ difficult

'fato nm fate

fat'taccio nm hum foul deed

fat'tezze nfpl features

fat'tibile a feasible

'fatto pp di **fare** ● a done, made; ~ **a mano/in casa** handmade/homemade ● nm fact; ⟨azione⟩ action; ⟨avvenimento⟩ event; **bada ai fatti tuoi!** mind your own business; **sa il** ~ **suo** he knows his business; **di** ~ in fact; **in** ~ **di** as regards

fat'to|re nm ⟨causa, Math⟩ factor; ⟨di fattoria⟩ farm manager. ~**'ria** nf farm; ⟨casa⟩ farmhouse

fatto'rino nm messenger [boy]

fattuc'chiera nf witch

fat'tura nf ⟨di stile⟩ cut; ⟨lavorazione⟩ workmanship; Comm invoice

fattu'ra|re vt invoice; ⟨adulterare⟩ adulterate. ~**to** nm turnover, sales pl. ~**zi'one** nf invoicing, billing

'fatuo a fatuous

'fauna nf fauna

fau'tore nm supporter

'fava nf broad bean

fa'vella nf speech

fa'villa nf spark

'favo|la nf fable; ⟨fiaba⟩ story; ⟨oggetto di pettegolezzi⟩ laughingstock; ⟨meraviglia⟩ dream. ~**'loso** a fabulous

fa'vore nm favour; **essere a** ~ **di** be in favour of; **per** ~ please; **di** ~ ⟨condizioni, trattamento⟩ preferential. ~**ggia'mento** nm Jur aiding and abetting. **favo'revole** a favourable. ~**vol'mente** adv favourably

favo'ri|re vt favour; ⟨promuovere⟩ promote; **vuol** ~**re?** ⟨a cena, pranzo⟩ will you have some?; ⟨entrare⟩ will you come in?. ~**to, -** **a** nmf favourite

fax nm inv fax. **fa'xare** vt fax

fazi'one nf faction

faziosità nf bias. **fazi'oso** nm sectarian

fazzolet'tino *nm* ~ [di carta] [paper] tissue

fazzo'letto *nm* handkerchief; (*da testa*) headscarf

feb'braio *nm* February

'febbre *nf* fever; **avere la ~** have *o* run a temperature. **~ da fieno** hay fever. **febbrici'tante** *a* feverish. **feb'brile** *a* feverish

'feccia *nf* dregs *pl*

'fecola *nf* potato flour

fecon'da\|re *vt* fertilize. **~'tore** *nm* fertilizer. **~zi'one** *nf* fertilization. **~zione artificiale** artificial insemination. **fe'condo** *a* fertile

'fede *nf* faith; (*fiducia*) trust; (*anello*) wedding-ring; **in buona/mala ~** in good/bad faith; **prestar ~ a** believe; **tener ~ alla parola** keep one's word. **fe'dele** *a* faithful ● *nmf* believer; (*seguace*) follower. **~l'mente** *adv* faithfully. **~ltà** *nf* faithfulness; **alta ~ltà** high fidelity

'federa *nf* pillowcase

fede'ra\|le *a* federal. **~'lismo** *nm* federalism. **~zi'one** *nf* federation

fe'dina *nf* **avere la ~ penale sporca/pulita** have a/no criminal record

'fegato *nm* liver; *fig* guts *pl*

'feice *nf* fern

fe'lic\|e *a* happy; (*fortunato*) lucky. **~ità** *nf* happiness

felici'ta\|rsi *vr* **~rsi con** congratulate. **~zi'oni** *nfpl* congratulations

fe'lino *a* feline

'felpa *nf* (*indumento*) sweatshirt

fel'pato *a* brushed; (*passo*) stealthy

'feltro *nm* felt; (*cappello*) felt hat

'femmin\|a *nf* female. **femmi'nile** *a* feminine; (*rivista, abbigliamento*) women's; (*sesso*) female ● *nm* feminine. **~ilità** *nf* femininity. **femmi'nismo** *nm* feminism

'femore *nm* femur

'fend\|ere *vt* split. **~i'tura** *nf* split; (*in roccia*) crack

feni'cottero *nm* flamingo

fenome'nale *a* phenomenal. **fe'nomeno** *nm* phenomenon

'feretro *nm* coffin

feri'ale *a* weekday; **giorno ~** weekday

'ferie *nfpl* holidays; (*di università, tribunale ecc*) vacation *sg*; **andare in ~** go on holiday

feri'mento *nm* wounding

fe'ri\|re *vt* wound; (*in incidente*) injure; *fig* hurt. **~rsi** *vr* injure oneself. **~ta** *nf* wound. **~to** *a* wounded ● *nm* wounded person; *Mil* casualty

'ferma *nf* *Mil* period of service

ferma'celli *nm inv* hairslide

ferma'carte *nm inv* paperweight

ferma'vatta *nm inv* tiepin

fer'maglio *nm* clasp; (*spilla*) brooch; (*per capelli*) hair slide

ferma'mente *adv* firmly

fer'ma\|re *vt* stop; (*fissare*) fix; *Jur* detain ● *vi* stop. **~rsi** *vr* stop. **~ta** *nf* stop. **~ta dell'autobus** bus-stop. **~ta a richiesta** request stop

fermen'ta\|re *vi* ferme. **~zi'one** *nf* fermentation. **fer'mento** *nm* ferment; (*lievito*) yeast

fer'mezza *nf* firmness

'fermo *a* still; (*veicolo*) stationary; (*stabile*) steady; (*orologio*) not working ● *nm* *Jur* detention; *Mech* catch; **in stato di ~** in custody

fe'roc\|e *a* ferocious; (*bestia*) wild; (*freddo, dolore*) unbearable. **~e'mente** *adv* fiercely, ferociously. **~ia** *nf* ferocity

fer'raglia *nf* scrap iron

ferra'gosto *nm* 15 August (*bank holiday in Italy*); (*periodo*) August holidays *pl*

ferra'menta *nfpl* ironmongery *sg*; **negozio di ~** ironmonger's

fer'ra\|re *vt* shoe (*cavallo*). **~to a ~to in** (*preparato in*) well up in

'ferreo *a* iron

'ferro *nm* iron; (*attrezzo*) tool; (*di chirurgo*) instrument; **bistecca ai ferri** grilled steak; **di ~** (*memoria*) excellent; (*alibi*) cast-iron; **salute**

di ~ iron constitution. ~ **battuto**
wrought iron. ~ **da calza** knitting
needle. ~ **di cavallo** horseshoe. ~
da stiro iron

ferro'vecchio nm scrap merchant
ferro'vi|a nf railway. ~**ario** a railway. ~**'ere** nm railwayman

fertil|e a fertile. ~**ità** nf fertility.
~**iz'zante** nm fertilizer

fer'vente a blazing; fig fervent

'fervere vi (preparativi:) be well
under way

'fervid|o a fervent; ~**i auguri** best
wishes

fer'vore nm fervour

fesse'ria nf nonsense

'fesso pp di **fendere** ● a cracked;
(fam: sciocco) foolish ● nm fam
(idiota) fool; **far** ~ **qcno** con sb

fes'sura nf crack; (per gettone ecc)
slot

'festa nf feast; (giorno festivo) holiday; (compleanno) birthday; (ricevimento) party; fig joy; **fare** ~ **a
qcno** welcome sb; **essere in** ~ be
on holiday; **far** ~ celebrate. ~**i'olga**
a festive

festeggia'mento nm celebration;
(manifestazione) festivity

festeggi'are vt celebrate; (accogliere festosamente) give a hearty
welcome to

fe'stino nm feast

festività nfpl festivities. **fe'stivo**
a holiday; (lieto) festive. **festivi**
nmpl public holidays

fe'stone nm (nel cucito) scallop,
scallop

fe'stoso a merry

fe'tente a evil smelling; fig revolting ● nmf fam bastard

fe'ticcio nm fetish

'feto nm foetus

fe'tore nm stench

'fetta nf slice; **a fette** sliced. ~
biscottata slices of crispy toast-
like bread

fet'tuccia nf tape; (con nome)
name tape

feu'dale a feudal. **'feudo** nm feud

FFSS abbr (**Ferrovie dello Stato**)
Italian state railways

fi'aba nf fairy-tale. **fia'besco** a
fairy-tale

fi'acc|a nf weariness; (indolenza)
laziness; **battere la** ~**a** be sluggish. **fiac'care** vt weaken. ~**o** a
weak; (indolente) slack; (stanco)
weary; (partita) dull

fi'acco|la nf torch. ~**lata** nf torch-
light procession

fi'ala nf phial

fi'amma nf flame; Naut pennant;
in fiamme aflame. **andare in
fiamme** go up in flames. ~
ossidrica blowtorch

fiam'ma|nte a flaming; **nuovo**
~**nte** brand new. ~**re** nf blaze

fiammeggi'are vi blaze

fiam'mifero nm match

fiam'mingo, -a a Flemish ● nmf
Fleming ● nm (lingua) Flemish

fianccheggi'are vt border; fig support

fi'anco nm side; (di persona) hip;
(di animale) flank; Mil wing; **al
mio** ~ by my side; ~ **a** ~
(lavorare) side by side

fi'asco nm flask; fig fiasco; **fare** ~
be a fiasco

fia'tare vi breathe; (parlare)
breathe a word

fi'ato nm breath; (vigore) stamina;
strumenti a ~ wind instruments;
senza ~ breathlessly; **tutto d'un
** ~ (bere, leggere) all in one go

'fibbia nf buckle

'fibra nf fibre; **fibre** pl (alimentari)
roughage. ~ **ottica** optical fibre

ficca'naso nmf nosey parker

fic'car|e vt thrust; drive (chiodo
ecc); (fam: mettere) shove. ~**si** vr
thrust oneself; (nascondersi) hide;
~**si nei guai** get oneself into trouble

fiche nf (gettone) chip

'fico nm (albero) fig-tree; (frutto)
fig. ~ **d'India** prickly pear

'fico, -a fam nmf cool sort ● a cool

fidanza'mento nm engagement

fidan'zar|si vr get engaged. **~to, -a** nmf (ufficiale) fiancé; fiancée

fi'da|rsi vr **~rsi di** trust. **~to** a trustworthy

'**fido** nm devoted follower; Comm credit

fi'duci|a nf confidence; **degno di ~a** trustworthy; **persona di ~a** reliable person; **di ~a** (fornitore, banca) regular, usual. **~'oso** a trusting

fi'ele nm bile; fig bitterness

fie'nile nm barn. fi'eno nm hay

fi'era nf fair

fie'rezza nf (dignità) pride. fi'ero a proud

fi'evole a faint; (luce) dim

'fifa nf fam jitters; **aver ~** have the jitters. fi'fone, -a nmf fam chicken

'figli|a nf daughter; **~a unica** only child. **~astra** nf stepdaughter. **~'astro** nm stepson. **~o** nm son; (generico) child. **~o di papà** spoilt brat. **~o unico** only child

figli'occi|a nf goddaughter. **~o** nm godson

figli'ol|a nf girl. **~'lanza** nf offspring. **~lo** nm boy

'**figo, -a** vedi fico, -a

fi'gura nf figure; (aspetto esteriore) shape; (illustrazione) illustration; **far bella/brutta ~** make a good/bad impression; **mi hai fatto fare una brutta ~** you made me look a fool; **che ~!** how embarrassing!. figu'raccia nf bad impression

figu'ra|re vt represent; (simboleggiare) symbolize; (immaginare) imagine • vi (far figura) cut a fine figure; (in lista) appear, figure. **~rsi** vr (immaginarsi) imagine; **~ti!** imagine that!; **posso? – [ma] ~ti!** may I? – of course!. **~'tivo** a figurative

figu'rina nf (da raccolta) ≈ cigarette card

figu|ri'nista nmf dress designer. **~'rino** nm fashion sketch. **~'rone** nm fare un **~rone** make an excellent impression

'fila nf line; (di soldati ecc) file; (di oggetti) row; (coda) queue; **di ~** in succession; **fare la ~** queue [up], stand in line Am; **in ~ indiana** single file

fila'mento nm filament

filantro'pia nf philanthropy

fi'lare vt spin; Naut pay out • vi (andarsene) run away; (liquido:) trickle; **fila!** fam scram!; **~ con** (fam: amoreggiare) go out with; **~ dritto** toe the line

filar'monica nf (orchestra) orchestra

fila'strocca nf rigmarole; (per bambini) nursery rhyme

filate'lia nf philately

fi'la|to a spun; (ininterrotto) running; (continuato) uninterrupted; **di ~to** (subito) immediately • nm yarn. **~'tura** nf spinning; (filanda) spinning mill

fil di 'ferro nm wire

fi'letto nm (bordo) border; (di vite) thread; Culin fillet

fili'ale a filial • nf Comm branch

fili'grana nf filigree; (su carta) watermark

film nm inv film. **~ giallo** thriller. **~ a lungo metraggio** feature film

fil'ma|re vt film. **~to** nm short film. fil'mino nm cine film

'filo nm thread; (tessile) yarn; (metallico) wire; (di lama) edge; (venatura) grain; (di perle) string; (d'erba) blade; (di luce) ray; **con un ~ di voce** in a whisper; **per e per segno** in detail; **fare il ~ a** qcno fancy sb; **perdere il ~** lose the thread. **~ spinato** barbed wire

'filobus nm inv trolleybus

filodiffusi'one nf rediffusion

fi'lone nm vein; (di pane) long loaf

filoso'fia nf philosophy. fi'losofo, -a nmf philosopher

fil'trare vt filter. 'filtro nm filter

'filza nf string

fin vedi fine, fino[1]

fi'na|le a final • nm end • nf Sport final. fina'lista nmf finalist. **~ità** nf inv finality; (scopo) aim.

~'**mente** *adv* at last; (*in ultimo*) finally

fi'nanz|a *nf* finance; ~i'ario a financial. ~i'ere *nm* financier; (*guardia di finanza*) customs officer. ~ia'mento *nm* funding

finanzi'a|re *vt* fund, finance. ~'tore, ~'trice *nmf* backer

finché *conj* until; (*per tutto il tempo che*) as long as

'fine a fine; (*sottile*) thin; ⟨*udito, vista*⟩ keen; (*raffinato*) refined ● *nf* end; alla ~ in the end; alla fin ~ after all; in fin dei conti when all's said and done; te lo dico a fin di bene I'm telling you for your own good; senza ~ endless ● *nm* aim. ~ settimana weekend

fi'nestra *nf* window. fine'strella *nf* di aiuto *Comput* help window, help box. fine'strino *nm* *Rail*, *Auto* window

fi'nezza *nf* fineness; (*sottigliezza*) thinness; (*raffinatezza*) refinement

'finger|e *vt* pretend; feign ⟨*affetto ecc*⟩. ~si *vr* pretend to be

fini'menti *nmpl* finishing touches; (*per cavallo*) harness *sg*

fini'mondo *nm* end of the world; *fig* pandemonium

fi'ni|re *vt/i* finish, end; (*smettere*) stop; (*diventare, andare a finire*) end up; ~scial stop it!. ~to a finished; (*abile*) accomplished. ~'tura *nf* finish

finlan'dese a Finnish ● *nmf* Finn ● *nm* (*lingua*) Finnish

Fin'landia *nf* Finland

'fino¹ *prep* ~ a till, until; (*spazio*) as far as; ~ all'ultimo to the last; fin da (*tempo*) since; (*spazio*) from; fin qui as far as here; fin troppo too much; ~ a che punto how far

'fino² a fine; (*acuto*) subtle; (*puro*) pure

fi'nocchio *nm* fennel; (*fam: omosessuale*) poof

fi'nora *adv* so far, up till now

'finta *nf* pretence, sham; *Sport* feint; far ~ di pretend to; far ~ di

niente act as if nothing had happened; per ~ (*per scherzo*) for a laugh

'fint|o, -a *pp di* fingere ● a false; (*artificiale*) artificial; fare il ~o tonto act dumb

finzi'one *nf* pretence

fi'occo *nm* bow; (*di neve*) flake; (*nappa*) tassel; coi fiocchi *fig* excellent. ~ di neve snowflake

fi'ocina *nf* harpoon

fi'oco a weak; (*luce*) dim

fi'onda *nf* catapult

fio'raio, -a *nmf* florist

fiorda'liso *nm* cornflower

fi'ordo *nm* fiord

fi'ore *nm* flower; (*parte scelta*) cream; fiori pl (*nelle carte*) clubs; a fior d'acqua on the surface of the water; fior di (*abbondanza*) a lot of; ha i nervi a fior di pelle his nerves are on edge; a fiori flowery

fioren'tino a Florentine

fio'retto *nm* (*scherma*) foil; *Relig* act of mortification

fio'rire *vi* flower; ⟨*albero:*⟩ blossom; *fig* flourish

fio'rista *nmf* florist

fiori'tura *nf* (*di albero*) blossoming

fi'otto *nm* scorrere a fiotti pour out; piove a fiotti the rain is pouring down

Fi'renze *nf* Florence

'firma *nf* signature; (*nome*) name

fir'ma|re *vt* sign. ~'tario, -a *nmf* signatory. ~to (*abito, borsa*) designer *attrib*

fisar'monica *nf* accordion

fi'scale a fiscal

fischi'are *vi* whistle ● *vt* whistle; (*in segno di disapprovazione*) boo

fischiet'ta|re *vt* whistle. ~io *nm* whistling

fischi'etto *nm* whistle. 'fischio *nm* whistle

'fisco *nm* treasury; (*tasse*) taxation; il ~ the taxman

'fisica *nf* physics

fisica'mente *adv* physically

'fisico, -a a physical ● *nmf* physicist ● *nm* physique

'fisima nf whim

fisio|lo'gia nf physiology. **~'logico** a physiological

fisiono'mia nf features, face; (di paesaggio) appearance

fisiotera'pi|a nf physiotherapy. **~sta** nmf physiotherapist

fis'sa|re vt fix, fasten; (guardare fissamente) stare at; arrange (appuntamento, ora). **~rsi** vr (stabilirsi) settle; (fissare lo sguardo) stare; **~rsi su** (ostinarsi) set one's mind on; **~rsi di fare qcsa** become obsessed with doing sth. **~to** nm (persona) person with an obsession. **~zi'one** nf fixation; (ossessione) obsession

'fisso a fixed; **un lavoro** ~ a regular job; **senza fissa dimora** of no fixed abode

'fitta nf sharp pain

fit'tizio a fictitious

'fitto[1] a thick; **~ di** full of ● nm depth

'fitto[2] nm (affitto) rent; **dare a** ~ let; **prendere a** ~ rent; (noleggiare) hire

fiu'mana nf swollen river; fig stream

fi'ume nm river; fig stream

fiu'tare vt smell. **fi'uto** nm [sense of] smell; fig nose

flac'cido a flabby

fla'cone nm bottle

fla'gello nm scourge

fla'grante a flagrant; **in** ~ in the act

fla'nella nf flannel

flash nm inv Journ newsflash

'flauto nm flute

'flebile a feeble

'flemma nf calm; Med phlegm. **flem'matico** a phlegmatic

fles'sibil|e a flexible. **~ità** nf flexibility

flessi'one nf (del busto in avanti) forward bend

'flesso pp di flettere

flessu'oso a supple

'flettere vt bend

flir'tare vi flirt

F.lli abbr (fratelli) Bros

'floppy disk nm inv floppy disk

'flora nf flora

'florido a flourishing

'floscio a limp; (flaccido) flabby

'flotta nf fleet. **flot'tiglia** nf flotilla

flu'ente a fluent

flu'ido nm fluid

flu'ire vi flow

fluore'scente a fluorescent

flu'oro nm fluorine

'flusso nm flow; Med flux; (del mare) flood[-tide]; ~ **e riflusso** ebb and flow

fluttu'ante a fluctuating

fluttu'a|re vi (prezzi, moneta:) fluctuate. **~zi'one** nf fluctuation

fluvi'ale a river

fo'bia nf phobia

'foca nf seal

fo'caccia nf (pane) flat bread; (dolce) ≈ raisin bread

fo'cale a (distanza, punto) focal. **focaliz'zare** vt get into focus (fotografia); focus (attenzione); define (problema)

'foce nf mouth

foco'laio nm Med focus; fig centre

foco'lare nm hearth; (caminetto) fireplace; Techn furnace

fo'coso a fiery

'foder|a nf lining; (di libro) dust-jacket; (di poltrona ecc) loose cover. **fode'rare** vt line; cover (libro). **~o** nm sheath

'foga nf impetuosity

'foggi|a nf fashion; (maniera) manner; (forma) shape. **~'are** vt mould

'fogli|a nf leaf; (di metallo) foil. **~'ame** nm foliage

fogli'etto nm (pezzetto di carta) piece of paper

'foglio nm sheet; (pagina) leaf. ~ **elettronico** Comput spreadsheet. ~ **rosa** provisional driving licence

'fogna nf sewer. **~'tura** nf sewerage

fo'lata nf gust

fol'clo|re nm folclore. **~'ristico** a folk; (bizzarro) weird

folgo'ra|re vi (splendere) shine ●vt (con un fulmine) strike. **~zi'one** nf (da fulmine, elettrica) electrocution; (idea) brainwave

'folgore nf thunderbolt

'folla nf crowd

'folle a mad; **in ~** Auto in neutral; **andare in ~** Auto coast

folle'mente adv madly

fol'lia nf madness; **alla ~** (amare) to distraction

'folto a thick

fomen'tare vt stir up

fond'ale nm Theat backcloth

fonda'men|ta nfpl foundations. **~'tale** a fundamental. **~to** nm (di principio, teoria) foundation

fon'da|re vt establish; base (ragionamento, accusa). **~to** a (ragionamento) well-founded. **~zi'one** nf establishment; **~zioni** pl (di edificio) foundations

fon'delli nmpl **prendere qcno per i ~** fam pull sb's leg

fon'dente a (cioccolato) dark

'fonder|e vt/i melt; (colori:) blend. **~si** vr melt; Comm merge. **fonde'ria** nf foundry

'fondi nmpl (denaro) funds; (di caffè) grounds

'fondo a deep; **è notte fonda** it's the middle of the night ●nm bottom; (fine) end; (sfondo) background; (indole) nature; (somma di denaro) fund; (feccia) dregs pl; **andare a ~** (nave:) sink; **da cima a ~** from beginning to end; **in ~** after all; **in ~ in ~** deep down; **fino in ~** right to the end; (capire) thoroughly. **~ d'investimento** investment trust

fondo'tinta nm foundation cream

fon'duta nf fondue made with cheese, milk and eggs

fo'netica nf phonetics. **~o** a phonetic

fon'tana nf fountain

'fonte nf spring; fig source ●nm font

fo'raggio nm forage

fo'rar|e vt pierce; punch (biglietto) ●vi puncture. **~si** vr (gomma, pallone:) go soft

'forbici nfpl scissors

for'bicine nfpl (per le unghie) nail scissors

for'bito a erudite

'forca nf fork; (patibolo) gallows pl

for'cella nf fork; (per capelli) hairpin

for'chet|ta nf fork. **~'tata** nf (quantità) forkful

for'cina nf hairpin

'forcipe nm forceps pl

for'cone nm pitchfork

fo'resta nf forest. **fore'stale** a forest attrib

foresti'ero, -a a foreign ●nmf foreigner

for'fait nm inv fixed price; **dare ~** (abbandonare) give up

'forfora nf dandruff

'forgi|a nf forge. **~'are** vt forge

'forma nf form; (sagoma) shape; Culin mould; (da calzolaio) last; **essere in ~** be in good form; **a ~ di** in the shape of; **forme** pl (del corpo) figure sg; (convenzioni) appearances

formag'gino nm processed cheese. **for'maggio** nm cheese

for'mal|e a formal. **~ità** nf inv formality. **~iz'zarsi** vr stand on ceremony. **~'mente** adv formally

for'ma|re vt form. **~rsi** vr form; (svilupparsi) develop. **~to** nm size; (di libro) format; **~to tessera** (fotografia) passport-size

format'tare vt format

formazi'one nf formation; Sport line-up. **~ professionale** vocational training

for'mica nf (also nm) anthill

'formica® nf (laminato plastico) Formica®

formico'l|are vi (braccio ecc.) tingle; **~are di** be swarming with; **mi ~a la mano** I have pins and needles in my hand. **~io** nm swarming; (di braccio ecc) pins and needles pl

formi'dabile a (tremendo) formidable; (eccezionale) tremendous

for'mina nf mould

for'moso a shapely

'formula nf formula. **formu'lare** vt formulate; (esprimere) express

for'nace nf furnace; (per laterizi) kiln

for'naio nm baker; (negozio) bakery

for'nello nm stove; (di pipa) bowl

for'ni|re vt supply (di with). **~'tore** nm supplier. **~'tura** nf supply

'forno nm oven; (panetteria) bakery; **al ~** roast. **~ a microonde** microwave [oven]

'foro nm hole; (romano) forum; (tribunale) [law] court

'forse adv perhaps, maybe; **essere in ~** be in doubt

forsen'nato, -a a mad ● nmf madman; madwoman

'forte a strong; (colore) bright; (suono) loud; (resistente) tough; (spesa) considerable; (dolore) severe; (pioggia) heavy; (a tennis, calcio) good; (fam: simpatico) great; (taglia) large ● adv strongly; (parlare) loudly; (veloce-mente) fast; (piovere) heavily ● nm (fortezza) fort; (specialità) strong point

for'tezza nf fortress; (forza morale) fortitude

fortifi'care vt fortify

for'tino nm Mil blockhouse

for'tuito a fortuitous; **incontro ~** chance encounter

for'tuna nf fortune; (successo) success; (buona sorte) luck. **atter-raggio di ~** forced landing; **per ~** be lucky; **buona ~!** good luck!; **di ~** makeshift; **per ~** luckily. **fortu'nato, -a** a lucky, fortunate. **~ta'mente** (impresa) successful. **~ta'mente** adv fortunately

fo'runcolo nm pimple; (grosso) boil

'forza nf strength; (potenza)

power; (fisica) force; **di ~** by force; **a ~ di** by dint of; **con ~** hard; **~! come on!**; **~ di volontà** will-power; **~ maggiore** circumstances beyond one's control; **la ~ pubblica** the police; **per ~** against one's will; (naturalmente) of course; **farsi ~** bear up; **mare ~ 8** force 8 gale; **bella ~!** fam big deal!. **le forze armate** the armed forces. **~ di gravità** [force of] gravity

for'za|re vt force; (scassare) break open; (sforzare) strain. **~to a** forced; (sorriso) strained ● nm convict

forzi'ere nm coffer

for'zuto a strong

fo'schia nf haze

'fosco a dark

fo'sfato nm phosphate

'fosforo nm phosphorus

'fossa nf pit; (tomba) grave. **~ biologica** cesspool. **fos'sato** nm (di fortificazione) moat

fos'setta nf dimple

'fossile nm fossil

'fosso nm ditch; Mil trench

'foto nf inv fam photo; **fare delle ~** take some photos

foto'cellula nf photocell

fotocomposizi'one nf filmsetting, photocomposition

foto'copi|a nf photocopy. **~'are** vt photocopy. **~a'trice** nf photocopier

foto'finish nm inv photo finish

foto'genico a photogenic

fotogra'f|are vt photograph. **~'fia** nf (arte) photography; (immagine) photograph; **fare ~fie** take photographs. **foto'grafico** a photographic; **macchina fotografica** camera. **fo'tografo, -a** nmf photographer

foto'gramma nm frame

fotomo'dello, -a nmf [photographer's] model

fotomon'taggio nm photomontage

fotoro'manzo nm photo story

'fotter|e vt (fam: rubare) nick; vulg fuck, screw. **~sene** vr vulg not give a fuck

fot'tuto a (fam: maledetto) bloody

fou'lard nm inv scarf

fra prep (in mezzo a due) between; (in un insieme) among; (tempo, distanza) in; **detto ~ noi** between you and me; **~ sé e sé** to oneself; **~ l'altro** what's more; **~ breve** soon; **~ quindici giorni** in two weeks' time; **~ tutti, siamo in venti** there are twenty of us altogether

fracas'sar|e vt smash. **~si** vr shatter

fra'casso nm din; (di cose che cadono) crash

'fradicio a (bagnato) soaked; (guasto) rotten; **ubriaco ~** blind drunk

'fragil|e a fragile; fig frail. **~ità** nf fragility; fig frailty

'fragola nf strawberry

fra'go|re nm uproar; (di cose rotte) clatter; (di tuono) rumble. **~'roso** a uproarious; (tuono) rumbling; (suono) clanging

fra'gran|te a fragrant. **~za** nf fragrance

frain'te|ndere vt misunderstand. **~ndersi** vr be at cross-purposes. **~so** pp di **fraintendere**

frammen'tario a fragmentary. **fram'mento** nm fragment

'frana nf landslide; (fam: persona) walking disaster area. **fra'nare** vi slide down

franca'mente adv frankly

fran'cese a French ● nmf Frenchman; Frenchwoman ● nm (lingua) French

'Francia nf France

'franco' a frank; Comm free; **farla franca** get away with sth

'franco² nm (moneta) franc

franco'bollo nm stamp

fran'gente nm (onda) breaker; (scoglio) reef; (fig: momento diffici-

le) crisis; **in quel ~** given the situation

'frangia nf fringe

fra'noso a subject to landslides

fran'toio nm olive-press

frantu'mar|e vt, **~si** vr shatter. **fran'tumi** nmpl splinters; **andare in frantumi** be smashed to smithereens

frappé nm inv milkshake

frap'por|re vt interpose. **~si** vr intervene

fra'sario nm vocabulary; (libro) phrase book

'frase nf sentence; (espressione) phrase. **~ fatta** cliché

'frassino nm ash[-tree]

frastagli'a|re vt make jagged. **~to** a jagged

frastor'nar|e vt daze. **~to** a dazed

frastu'ono nm racket

'frate nm friar; (monaco) monk

fratel'la|nza nf brotherhood. **~stro** nm half-brother

fra'tell|i nmpl (fratello e sorella) brother and sister. **~o** nm brother

fraterniz'zare vi fraternize. **fra'terno** a brotherly

frat'taglie nfpl (di pollo ecc) giblets

frat'tanto adv in the meantime

frat'tempo nm **nel ~** meanwhile, in the meantime

frat'tu|ra nf fracture. **~'rare** vt, **~'rarsi** vr break

fraudo'lento a fraudulent

frazi'one nf fraction; (borgata) hamlet

'freccia nf arrow; Auto indicator. **~'ata** nf (osservazione pungente) cutting remark

fredda'mente adv coldly

fred'dare vt cool; (fig: con sguardo, battuta) cut down; (uccidere) kill

fred'dezza nf coldness

'freddo a & nm cold; **aver ~** be cold; **fa ~** it's cold

freddo'loso a sensitive to cold, chilly

fred'dura nf pun

fre'ga|re vt rub; (fam: truffare)

cheat; (fam: rubare) swipe.
~rsene fam not give a damn; **chi
se ne frega!** what the heck!. **~si**
vr rub (occhi). **~ta** nf rub. **~ta
nf** fam (truffa) swindle; (delusione)
letdown

'fregio nm Archit frieze; (ornamento) decoration

fre'mente a quivering

'frem|ere vi quiver. **~ito** nm
quiver

fre'na|re vt brake; fig restrain;
hold back (lacrime, impazienza)
● vi brake. **~rsi** vr check oneself.
~ta nf fare una **~ta brusca** hit
the brakes

fre'nesia nf frenzy; (desiderio
smodato) craze. **fre'netico** a frenzied

'freno nm brake; fig check;
togliere il ~ release the brake;
usare il ~ apply the brake; **tenere
a ~** restrain. **~ a mano** handbrake

frequen'tare vt frequent; attend
(scuola ecc); mix with (persone)

fre'quen|te a frequent; **di ~te** frequently. **~za** nf frequency;
(assiduità) attendance

fre'schezza nf freshness; (di temperatura) coolness

'fresco a fresh; (temperatura)
cool; **stai ~!** you're for it! ● nm
coolness; **far ~** be cool; **mettere/
tenere in ~** put/keep in a cool
place

'fretta nf hurry, haste; **aver ~** be in
a hurry; **far ~ a qcno** hurry sb; **in
~ e furia** in a great hurry.
frettolosa'mente adv hurriedly.
fretto'loso a (persona) in a hurry;
(lavoro) rushed, hurried

fri'abile a crumbly

'friggere vt fry; **vai a farti ~!** get
lost! ● vi sizzle

friggi'trice nf chip pan

frigidità nf frigidity. **'frigido** a
frigid

fri'gnare vi whine

'frigo nm fridge

'frigo'bar nm inv minibar

frigo'rifero a refrigerating ● nm
refrigerator

fringu'ello nm chaffinch

frit'tata nf omelette

frit'tella nf fritter; (fam: macchia
d'unto) grease stain

'fritto pp di **friggere** ● a fried;
essere ~ be done for ● nm fried
food. **~ misto** mixed fried fish/
vegetables. **frit'tura** nf (pietanza)
fried dish

frivo'lezza nf frivolity. **'frivolo** a
frivolous

frizio'nare vt rub. **frizi'one** nf friction; Mech clutch; (di pelle) rub

friz'zante a fizzy; (vino) sparkling;
(aria) bracing

'frizzo nm gibe

fro'dare vt defraud

'frode nf fraud. **~ fiscale** tax evasion

'frollo a tender; (selvaggina) high;
(persona) spineless; **pasta frolla**
short[crust] pastry

'fronda nf [leafy] branch; fig rebellion. **fron'doso** a leafy

fron'tale a frontal; (scontro) head-on

'fronte nf forehead; (di edificio)
front; **di ~** opposite; **di ~ a** opposite, facing; (a paragone) compared with; **far ~** a face ● nm Mil,
Pol front. **~ggi'are** vt face

fronte'spizio nm title page

fronti'era nf frontier, border

fron'tone nm pediment

fron'zolo nm frill

'frotta nf swarm; (di animali) flock

frot'tola nf fib; **frottole** pl nonsense sg

fru'gale a frugal

fru'gare vi rummage ● vt search

frul'la|re vt Culin whisk ● vi (ali:)
whirr. **~to nm ~to di frutta** fruit
drink made with milk and crushed ice.
~'tore nm [electric] mixer.
frul'lino nm whisk

fru'mento nm wheat

frusci'are vi rustle

fru'scio *nm* rustle; *(radio, giradischi)* background noise; *(di acque)* murmur

'frusta *nf* whip; *(frullino)* whisk

fru'sta|re *vt* whip. ~ta *nf* lash.

fru'stino *nm* riding crop

fru'stra|re *vt* frustrate. ~to *a* frustrated. ~zi'one *nf* frustration

'frutt|a *nf* fruit; *(portata)* dessert. frut'tare *vi* bear fruit ● *vt* yield. frut'teto *nm* orchard. ~i'vendolo, -a *nmf* greengrocer. ~o *nm anche fig* fruit; *Fin* yield; ~i di bosco fruits of the forest. ~i di mare seafood *sg*. ~u'oso *a* profitable

f.to *abbr* (firmato) signed

fu *a* (defunto) late; il ~ signor Rossi the late Mr Rossi

fuci'la|re *vt* shoot. ~ta *nf* shot

fu'cile *nm* rifle

fu'cina *nf* forge

'fucsia *nf* fuchsia

'fuga *nf* escape; *(perdita)* leak; *Mus* fugue; darsi alla ~ take to flight

fu'gace *a* fleeting

fug'gevole *a* short-lived

fuggi'asco, -a *nmf* fugitive

fuggi'fuggi *nm* stampede

fug'gi|re *vi* flee; *(innamorati:)* elope; *fig* fly. ~'tivo, -a *nmf* fugitive

'fulcro *nm* fulcrum

ful'gore *nm* splendour

fu'liggine *nf* soot

fulmi'nar|e *vt* strike by lightning; *(con sguardo)* look daggers at; *(con scarica elettrica)* electrocute. ~si *vr* burn out. 'fulmine *nm* lightning. ful'mineo *a* rapid

'fulvo *a* tawny

fumai'olo *nm* funnel; *(di casa)* chimney

fu'ma|re *vt/i* smoke; *(in ebollizione)* steam. ~'tore, -'trice *nmf* smoker; non fumatori non-smoker, non-smoking

fu'metto *nm* comic strip; fumetti *pl* comics

'fumo *nm* smoke; *(vapore)* steam;

fig hot air; andare in ~ vanish.

fu'moso *a* *(ambiente)* smoky; *(discorso)* vague

fu'nambolo, -a *nmf* tightrope walker

'fune *nf* rope; *(cavo)* cable

'funebre *a* funeral; *(cupa)* gloomy

fune'rale *nm* funeral

fu'nereo *a* *(aria)* funereal

fu'nesto *a* sad

'fungere *vi* ~ da act as

'fungo *nm* mushroom; *Bot, Med* fungus

funico'lare *nf* funicular [railway]

funi'via *nf* cableway

funzio'nal|e *a* functional. ~ità *nf* functionality

funziona'mento *nm* functioning

funzio'nare *vi* work, function; ~ da *(fungere da)* act as

funzio'nario *nm* official

funzi'one *nf* function; *(carica)* office; *Relig* service; entrare in ~ take up office

fu'oco *nm* fire; *(fisica, fotografia)* focus; far ~ fire; dar ~ a set fire to; prendere ~ catch fire. fuochi *pl* d'artificio fireworks. ~ di paglia nine-days' wonder

fuorché *prep* except

fu'ori *adv* out; *(all'esterno)* outside; *(all'aperto)* outdoors; andare di ~ *(traboccare)* spill over; essere di sé be beside oneself; essere in ~ *(sporgere)* stick out; far ~ *fam* do in; ~ luogo *(inopportuno)* out of place; ~ mano out of the way; ~ moda old-fashioned; ~ pasto between meals; ~ pericolo out of danger; ~ questione out of the question; ~ uso out of use ● *nm* outside

fuori'bordo *nm* speedboat *(with outboard motor)*

fuori'classe *nmf inv* champion

fuorigi'oco *nm & adv* offside

fuori'legge *nmf* outlaw

fuori'serie *a* custom-made ● *nf* *Auto* custom-built model

fuori'strada *nm* off-road vehicle

fuorvi'are *vt* lead astray ●*vi* go astray

furbacchi'one *nm* crafty old devil

furbe'ria *nf* cunning. **fur'bizia** *nf* cunning

'furbo *a* cunning; (*intelligente*) clever; (*astuto*) shrewd; **bravo ~!** nice one!; **fare il ~** try to be clever

fu'rente *a* furious

fur'fante *nm* scoundrel

furgon'cino *nm* delivery van. **fur'gone** *nm* van

'furi|a *nf* fury; (*fretta*) haste; **a ~a di** by dint of. **~'bondo, ~'oso** *a* furious

fu'rore *nm* fury; (*veemenza*) frenzy; **far ~** be all the rage. **~ggi'are** *vi* be a great success

furtiva'mente *adv* covertly. **fur'tivo** *a* furtive

'furto *nm* theft; (*con scasso*) burglary; **commettere un ~** steal

'fusa *nfpl* **fare le ~** purr

fu'scello *nm* (*di legno*) twig; (*di paglia*) straw; **sei un ~** you're as light as a feather

fu'seaux *mpl* leggings

fu'sibile *nm* fuse

fusi'one *nf* fusion; *Comm* merger

'fuso *pp di* **fondere** ●*a* melted ●*nm* spindle; *a* ~ spindle-shaped. **~ orario** time zone

fusoli'era *nf* fuselage

fu'stagno *nm* corduroy

fu'stino *nm* (*di detersivo*) box

'fusto *nm* stem; (*tronco*) trunk; (*recipiente di metallo*) drum; (*di legno*) barrel

'futile *a* futile

fu'turo *a & nm* future

Gg

gab'bar|e *vt* cheat. **~si** *vr* **~si di** make fun of

'gabbia *nf* cage; (*da imballaggio*) crate. **~ degli imputati** dock. **~ toracica** rib cage

gabbi'ano *nm* [sea]gull

gabi'netto *nm* (*di medico*) consulting room; *Pol* cabinet; (*toletta*) lavatory; (*laboratorio*) laboratory

'gaffe *nf inv* blunder

gagli'ardo *a* vigorous

gai'ezza *nf* gaiety. **'gaio** *a* cheerful

'gala *nf* gala

ga'lante *a* gallant. **~'ria** *nf* gallantry. **galan'tuomo** *nm* (*pl* **galan-tuomini**) gentleman

ga'lassia *nf* galaxy

gala'teo *nm* [good] manners *pl*; (*trattato*) book of etiquette

gale'otto *nm* (*rematore*) galley-slave; (*condannato*) convict

ga'lera *nf* (*nave*) galley; *fam* prison

'galla *nf* *Bot* gall; **a ~** *adv* afloat; **venire a ~** surface

galleggi'ante *a* floating ●*nm* craft; (*boa*) float

galleggi'are *vi* float

galle'ria *nf* (*traforo*) tunnel; (*d'arte*) gallery; *Theat* circle; (*arcata*) arcade. **~ d'arte** art gallery

'Galles *nm* Wales. **gal'lese** *a* welsh ●*nm* Welshman; (*lingua*) Welsh ●*nf* Welshwoman

gal'letto *nm* cockerel; **fare il ~** show off

gal'lina *nf* hen

gal'lismo *nm* machismo

'gallo *nm* cock

gal'lone *nm* stripe; (*misura*) gallon

galop'pare *vi* gallop. **ga'loppo** *nm* gallop; **al galoppo** at a gallop

galvaniz'zare *vt* galvanize

'gamba *nf* leg; (*di lettera*) stem; **a quattro gambe** on all fours;

darsela a gambe take to one's heels; **essere in ~** (*essere forte*) be strong; (*capace*) be smart

gamba'letto *nm* pop sock

gambe'retto *nm* shrimp. '**gambero** *nm* prawn; (*di fiume*) crayfish

'**gambo** *nm* stem; (*di pianta*) stalk

'**gamma** *nf Mus* scale; *fig* range

ga'nascia *nf* jaw; **ganasce** *pl* **del freno** brake shoes

'**gancio** *nm* hook

'**ganghero** *nm* **uscire dai gangheri** *fig* get into a temper

'**gara** *nf* competition; (*di velocità*) race; **fare a ~** compete. **~ d'appalto** call for tenders

ga'rage *nm inv* garage

ga'ran|te *nmf* guarantor. **~'tire** *vt* guarantee; (*rendersi garante*) vouch for; (*assicurare*) assure. **~'zia** *nf* guarantee; **in ~zia** under guarantee

gar'ba|re *vi* like; **non mi garba** I don't like it. **~to** *a* courteous

'**garbo** *nm* courtesy; (*grazia*) grace; **con ~** graciously

gareggi'are *vi* compete

garga'nella *nf* **a ~** from the bottle

garga'rismo *nm* gargle; **fare i gargarismi** gargle

ga'rofano *nm* carnation

gar'rire *vi* chirp

'**garza** *nf* gauze

gar'zone *nm* boy. **~ di stalla** stable-boy

gas *nm inv* gas; **dare ~** *Auto* accelerate; **a tutto ~** flat out. **~ lacrimogeno** tear gas. **~ di scarico** *pl* exhaust fumes

gas'dotto *nm* natural gas pipeline

ga'solio *nm* diesel oil

ga'sometro *nm* gasometer

gas's|are *vt* aerate; (*uccidere col gas*) gas. **~ato** *a* gassy. **~oso, -a** *a* gassy; (*bevanda*) fizzy ● *nf* lemonade

'**gastrico** *a* gastric. **ga'strite** *nf* gastritis

gastro|no'mia *nf* gastronomy. **~'nomico** *a* gastronomic. **ga'stronomo, -a** *nmf* gourmet

'**gatta** *nf* **una ~ da pelare** a headache

gatta'buia *nf hum* clink

gat'tino, -a *nmf* kitten

'**gatto, -a** *nmf* cat. **~ delle nevi** snowmobile

gat'toni *adv* on all fours

ga'vetta *nf* mess tin; **fare la ~** rise through the ranks

gay *a inv* gay

'**gazza** *nf* magpie

gaz'zarra *nf* racket

gaz'zella *nf* gazelle; *Auto* police car

gaz'zetta *nf* gazette

gaz'zosa *nf* clear lemonade

'**geco** *nm* gecko

ge'la|re *vt/i* freeze. **~ta** *nf* frost

gela'ti|aio, -a *nmf* ice-cream seller; (*negozio*) ice-cream shop. **~e'ria** *nf* ice-cream parlour. **~i'era** *nf* ice-cream maker

gela'tina *nf* gelatine; (*dolce*) jelly. **~na di frutta** fruit jelly. **~'noso** *a* gelatinous

ge'lato *a* frozen ● *nm* ice-cream

'**gelido** *a* freezing

'**gelo** *nm* (*freddo intenso*) freezing cold; (*brina*) frost; *fig* chill

ge'lone *nm* chilblain

gelosa'mente *adv* jealously

gelo'sia *nf* jealousy. **ge'loso, -a** *a* jealous

'**geiso** *nm* mulberry[-tree]

gelso'mino *nm* jasmine

gemel'laggio *nm* twinning

ge'mello, -a *a* twin; (*di polsino*) cuff-link; **Gemelli** *pl Astr* Gemini *sg*

'**gem|ere** *vi* groan; (*tubare*) coo. **~ito** *nm* groan

'**gemma** *nf* gem; *Bot* bud

'**gene** *nm* gene

genealo'gia *nf* genealogy

gene'ral|e[1] *a* general; **spese ~i** overheads

gene'rale[2] *nm Mil* general

generalità *nf* (*qualità*) generality, general nature; **~ pl** (*dati personali*) particulars

generaliz'za|re *vt* generalize.

~zi'one *nf* generalization. **general'mente** *adv* generally

gene'ra|re *vt* give birth to; (*causare*) breed; *Techn* generate. **~'tore** *nm Techn* generator. **~zi'one** *nf* generation

'genere *nm* kind; *Biol* genus; *Gram* gender; (*letterario, artistico*) genre; (*prodotto*) product; **il ~ umano** mankind; **in ~** generally. **generi** *pl* **alimentari** provisions

generica'mente *adv* generically. **ge'nerico** *a* generic; **medico generico** general practitioner

'genero *nm* son-in-law

generosità *nf* generosity. **gene'roso** *a* generous

'genesi *nf* genesis

ge'netico, -a *a* genetic ● *nf* genetics

gen'giva *nf* gum

geni'ale *a* ingenious; (*congeniale*) congenial

'genio *nm* genius; **andare a ~ be** to one's taste. **~ civile** civil engineering. **~** [**militare**] Engineers

geni'tale *a* genital. **genitali** *nmpl* genitals

geni'tore *nm* parent

gen'naio *nm* January

'Genova *nf* Genoa

gen'taglia *nf* rabble

'gente *nf* people *pl*

gen'ti|le *a* kind; **G~e Signore** (*in lettere*) Dear Sir. **genti'lezza** *nf* kindness; **per gentilezza** (*per favore*) please. **~'mente** *adv* kindly. **~u'omo** (*pl* **~u'omini**) *nm* gentleman

genu'ino *a* genuine; (*cibo, prodotto*) natural

geogra'fia *nf* geography. **geo'grafico** *a* geographical. **ge'ogra-fo, -a** *nmf* geographer

geolo'gia *nf* geology. **geo'logico** *a* geological. **ge'ologo, -a** *nmf* geologist

ge'ometra *nmf* surveyor

geome|'tria *nf* geometry. **geo'metrico** *a* geometric[al]

ge'ranio *nm* geranium

gerar'chia *nf* hierarchy. **ge-'rarchico** hierarchic[al]

ge'rente *nm* manager ● *nf* manageress

'gergo *nm* slang; (*di professione ecc*) jargon

geria'tria *nf* geriatrics *sg*

Ger'mania *nf* Germany

'germe *nm* germ; (*fig: principio*) seed

germogli'are *vi* sprout. **ger-'moglio** *nm* sprout

gero'glifico *nm* hieroglyph

'gesso *nm* chalk; (*Med, scultura*) plaster

gestazi'one *nf* gestation

gestico'lare *vi* gesticulate

gesti'one *nf* management

ge'sti|re *vi* manage. **~si** *vr* budget one's time and money

'gesto *nm* gesture; (*azione pl* **gesta**) deed

ge'store *nm* manager

Gesù *nm* Jesus. **~ bambino** baby Jesus

gesu'ita *nm* Jesuit

get'ta|re *vt* throw; (*scagliare*) fling; (*emettere*) spout; *Techn, fig* cast; **~re via** throw away. **~rsi** *vr* throw oneself; **~rsi in** (*fiume:*) flow into. **~ta** *nf* throw; *Techn* casting

'getto *nm* throw; (*di liquidi, gas*) jet; **a ~ continuo** in a continuous stream; **di ~** straight off

getto'nato *a* (*canzone*) popular. **get'tone** *nm* token; (*per giochi*) counter

ghe'pardo *nm* cheetah

ghettiz'zare *vt* ghettoize. **'ghetto** *nm* ghetto

ghiacci'aio *nm* glacier

ghiacci'a|re *vt/i* freeze. **~to** *a* frozen; (*freddissimo*) ice-cold

ghi'acci|o *nm* ice; *Auto* black ice. **~'olo** *nm* icicle; (*gelato*) ice lolly

ghi'aia *nf* gravel

ghi'anda *nf* acorn

ghi'andola *nf* gland

ghigliot'tina *nf* guillotine

ghi'gnare vi sneer. **'ghigno** nm sneer

ghi'ot|to a greedy, gluttonous; (appetitoso) appetizing. **~tone, -a** nmf glutton. **~tone'ria** nf (qualità) gluttony; (cibo) tasty morsel

ghir'landa nf (corona) wreath; (di fiori) garland

'ghiro nm dormouse; **dormire come un ~** sleep like a log

'ghisa nf cast iron

già adv already; (un tempo) formerly; **~!** indeed!; **~ da ieri** since yesterday

gi'acca nf jacket. **~ a vento** windcheater

giacché conj since

giac'cone nm jacket

gia'cere vi lie

giaci'mento nm deposit. **~ di petrolio** oil deposit

gia'cinto nm hyacinth

gi'ada nf jade

giaggi'olo nm iris

giagu'aro nm jaguar

gial'lastro a yellowish

gi'allo a & nm yellow; **[libro] ~** thriller

Giap'pone nm Japan. **giappo'nese** a & nmf Japanese

giardi'naggio nm gardening. **~i'ere, -a** nmf gardener ● nf Auto estate car; (sottaceti) pickles pl

giar'dino nm garden. **~ d'infanzia** kindergarten. **~ pensile** roofgarden. **~ zoologico** zoo

giarretti'era nf garter

giavel'lotto nm javelin

gi'gante a gigantic ● nm giant. **~'tesco** a gigantic

gigantogra'fia nf blow-up

'giglio nm lily

gilè nm inv waistcoat

gin nm inv gin

gineco'lo'gia nf gynaecology. **~'logico** a gynaecological. **gine-'cologo, -a** nmf gynaecologist

gi'nepro nm juniper

gi'nestra nf broom

gingil'larsi vr fiddle; (perder tem-**

po) potter. **gin'gillo** nm plaything; (ninnolo) knick-knack

gin'nasio nm (scuola) ≈ grammar school

gin'nast|a nmf gymnast. **~ica** nf gymnastics; (esercizi) exercises pl

ginocchi'ata nf prendere una ~ bang one's knee

gi'nocchi|o nm (pl m ginocchi o f ginocchia) knee; **in ~o** on one's knees; **mettersi in ~o** kneel down; (per supplicare) go down on one's knees; **al ~o** (gonna) kneelength. **~'oni** adv kneeling

gio'ca|re vt/i play; (giocherellare) toy; (d'azzardo) gamble; (puntare) stake; (ingannare) trick. **~rsi la carriera** throw one's career away. **~'tore, ~'trice** nmf player; (d'azzardo) gambler

gio'cattolo nm toy

giocherel'|lare vi toy; (nervosamente) fiddle. **~one** a skittish

gi'oco nm game; (di bambini, Techn) play; (d'azzardo) gambling; (scherzo) joke; (insieme di pezzi ecc) set; **essere in ~** be at stake; **fare il doppio ~ con qcno** double-cross sb

giocoli'ere nm juggler

gio'coso a playful

gi'ogo nm yoke

gi'oia nf joy; (gioiello) jewel; (appellativo) sweetie

gioiell|e'ria nf jeweller's [shop]. **~i'ere** nm jeweller. **gioi'ello** nm jewel; **gioielli** pl jewellery

gioi'oso a joyous

gio'ire vi ~ **per** rejoice at

Gior'dania nf Jordan

giorna'laio, -a nmf newsagent, newsdealer

gior'nale nm [news]paper; (diario) journal. **~ di bordo** logbook. **~ radio** news bulletin

giornali'ero a daily ● nm (per sciare) day pass

giorna'lino nm comic

giorna'lismo nm journalism. **~ta** nmf journalist

giornal'mente *adv* daily

gior'nata *nf* day; **in ~** today; **vivere alla ~** live from day to day

gi'orno *nm* day; **al ~** per day; **al ~ d'oggi** nowadays; **di ~** by day; **in pieno ~** in broad daylight; **un ~ sì, un ~ no** every other day

gi'ostra *nf* merry-go-round

giova'mento *nm* **trarre ~ da** derive benefit from

gi'ova|ne *a* young; (*giovanile*) youthful ● *nm* youth, young man ● *nf* girl, young woman. **~'nile** *a* youthful. **~'notto** *nm* young man

gio'var|e *vi* **~e a** be a useful to; (*far bene a*) be good for. **~si** *vr* **~si di** avail oneself of

giovedì *nm inv* Thursday. **~ grasso** *last Thursday before Lent*

gioventù *nf* youth; (*i giovani*) young people *pl*

giovi'ale *a* jovial

giovi'nezza *nf* youth

gira'dischi *nm inv* record-player

gi'raffa *nf* giraffe; *Cinema* boom

gi'randola *nf* (*fuoco d'artificio*) Catherine wheel; (*giocattolo*) windmill; (*banderuola*) weathercock

gi'ra|re *vt* turn; (*andare intorno, visitare*) go round; *Cinema* endorse; *Cinema* shoot ● *vi* turn; (*aerei, uccelli:*) circle; (*andare in giro*) wander; **far ~re le scatole a qcno** *fam* drive sb round the twist; **~re al largo** steer clear. **~rsi** *vr* turn [round]; **mi gira la testa** I feel dizzy. **~ta** *nf* turn; *Comm* endorsement; (*in macchina ecc*) ride; **fare una ~ta** (*a piedi*) go for a walk; (*in macchina*) go for a ride

girar'rosto *nm* spit

gira'sole *nm* sunflower

gira'volta *nf* spin; *fig* U-turn

gi'rello *nm* (*per bambini*) babywalker; *Culin* topside

gi'revole *a* revolving

gi'rino *nm* tadpole

'giro *nm* turn; (*circolo*) circle; (*percorso*) round; (*viaggio*) tour; (*passeggiata*) short walk; (*in*

macchina) drive; (*in bicicletta*) ride; (*circolazione di denaro*) circulation; **nel ~ di un mese** within a month; **prendere in ~ qcno** pull sb's leg; **senza giri di parole** without beating about the bush; **a ~ di posta** by return mail. **~ d'affari** *Comm* turnover. **~ [della] manica** armhole. **giri** *pl* **al minuto** rpm. **~ turistico** sightseeing tour. **~ vita** waist measurement

giro'collo *nm* choker; **a ~** crewneck

gi'rone *nm* round

gironzo'lare *vi* wander about

giro'tondo *nm* ring-a-ring-o'-roses

girova'gare *vi* wander about.

gi'rovago *nm* wanderer

'gita *nf* trip; **andare in ~** go on a trip. **~ scolastica** school trip.

gi'tante *nmf* tripper

giù *adv* down; (*sotto*) below; (*dabbasso*) downstairs; **a testa in ~** (*a capofitto*) headlong; **essere ~** be down; (*di salute*) be run down; **~ di corda** down; **~ di lì, su per ~** more or less; **non andare ~ a qcno** stick in sb's craw

gi'ub|ba *nf* jacket; *Mil* tunic. **~'botto** *nm* bomber jacket, jerkin

giudi'care *vt* judge; (*ritenere*) consider

gi'udice *nm* judge. **~ conciliatore** justice of the peace. **~ di gara** umpire. **~ di linea** linesman

giu'dizi|o *nm* judg[e]ment; (*opinione*) opinion; (*senno*) wisdom; (*processo*) trial; (*sentenza*) sentence; **mettere ~o** become wise. **~'oso** *a* sensible

gi'ugno *nm* June

giu'menta *nf* mare

gi'unco *nm* reed

gi'ungere *vi* arrive; **~ a** (*riuscire*) succeed in ● *vt* (*unire*) join

gi'ungla *nf* jungle

gi'unta *nf* addition; *Mil* junta; **per ~** in addition. **~ comunale** district council

gi'unto *pp* di **giungere** ● *nm* *Mech* joint

giun'tura nf joint

giuo'care, giu'oco = **giocare, gioco**

giura'mento nm oath; **prestare ~** take the oath

giu'ra|re vt/i swear. **~to, -a** a sworn ● nmf juror

giu'ria nf jury

giu'ridico a legal

giurisdizi'one nf jurisdiction

giurispru'denza nf jurisprudence

giu'rista nmf jurist

giustifi'ca|re vt justify. **~zi'one** nf justification

giu'stizi|a nf justice. **~'are** vt execute. **~'ere** nm executioner

gi'usto a just, fair; (adatto) right; (esatto) exact ● nm (uomo retto) just man; (cosa giusta) right ● adv exactly; **~ ora** just now

glaci'ale a glacial

gla'diolo nm gladiolus

glassa nf Culin icing

gli def art mpl (before vowel and s + consonant, gn, ps, z) the; vedi **il** ● pron (a lui) [to] him; (a esso) [to] it; (a loro) [to] them

glice'rina nf glycerine

glicine nm wisteria

gli'e|lo, -a pron [to] him/her/them; (forma di cortesia) [to] you; **~ chiedo** I'll ask him/her/them/ you; **gliel'ho prestato** I've lent it to him/her/them/you. **~ne** (di ciò) [of] it; **~ne ho dato un po'** I gave him/her/them/you some

glo'ba|le a global; fig overall. **~'mente** adv globally

globo nm globe. **~ oculare** eyeball. **~ terrestre** globe

globulo nm globule; Med corpuscle. **~ bianco** white cell, white corpuscle. **~ rosso** red cell, red corpuscle

'glori|a nf glory. **~'arsi** vr ~**arsi di** be proud of. **~'oso** a glorious

glos'sario nm glossary

glu'cosio nm glucose

'gluteo nm buttock

'gnomo nm gnome

'gnorri nm fare lo **~** play dumb

'gobb|a nf hump. **~o, -a** a hunchbacked ● nmf hunchback

'goccia nf drop; (di sudore) bead; **è stata l'ultima ~a** it was the last straw. **~o'lare** vi drip. **~o'lio** nm dripping

go'der|e vi (sessualmente) come; **~e di** enjoy. **~sela** have a good time. **~si** vr ~**si qcsa** enjoy sth

godi'mento nm enjoyment

goffa'mente adv awkwardly. **'goffo** a awkward

'gola nf throat; (ingordigia) gluttony; Geog gorge; (di camino) flue; **avere mal di ~** have a sore throat; **far ~ a** tempt sb

golf nm inv jersey; Sport golf

'golfo nm gulf

golosità nf inv greediness; (cibo) tasty morsel. **go'loso** a greedy

'golpe nm inv coup

gomi'tata nf nudge

'gomito nm elbow; **alzare il ~** raise one's elbow

go'mitolo nm ball

'gomma nf rubber; (colla, da masticare) gum; (pneumatico) tyre. **~ da masticare** chewing gum

gommapi'uma nf foam rubber

gom'mista nm tyre specialist

gom'mone nm [rubber] dinghy

gom'moso a chewy

'gondol|a nf gondola. **~'iere** nm gondolier

gonfa'lone nm banner

gonfi'abile a inflatable

gonfi'ar|e vi swell ● vt blow up; pump up (pneumatico); (esagerare) exaggerate. **~si** vr swell; (acque:) rise. **'gonfio** a swollen; (pneumatico) inflated; **a gonfie vele** splendidly. **gonfi'ore** nm swelling

gongo'la|nte a overjoyed. **~re** vi be overjoyed

'gonna nf skirt. **~ pantalone** culottes pl

'gonzo nm simpleton

gorgheggi'are vi warble. **gor'gheggio** nm warble

'gorgo nm whirlpool

gorgogli'are *vi* gurgle

go'rilla *nm inv* gorilla; (*guardia del corpo*) bodyguard, minder

'gotico *a* & *nm* Gothic

gover'nante *nf* housekeeper

gover'na|re *vt* govern; (*dominare*) rule; (*dirigere*) manage; (*curare*) look after. **~'tivo** *a* government. **~'tore** *nm* governor

go'verno *nm* government; (*dominio*) rule; **al ~** in power

gracchi'are *vi* caw; (*fig: persona:*) screech

graci'dare *vi* croak

'gracile *a* delicate

gra'dasso *nm* braggart

gradata'mente *adv* gradually

gradazi'one *nf* gradation. **~ alcoolica** alcohol[ic] content

gra'devol|e *a* agreeable. **~'mente** *adv* pleasantly, agreeably

gradi'mento *nm* liking; **indice di ~** *Radio, TV* popularity rating; **non è di mio ~** it's not to my liking

gradi'nata *nf* flight of steps; (*di stadio*) stand; (*di teatro*) tiers *pl*

gra'dino *nm* step

gra'di|re *vt* like; (*desiderare*) wish. **~to** *a* pleasant; (*bene accetto*) welcome

'grado *nm* degree; (*rango*) rank; **di buon ~** willingly; **essere in ~ di fare qcsa** to be in a position to do sth; (*essere capace a*) be able to do sth

gradu'ale *a* gradual

gradu'a|re *vt* graduate. **~to** *a* graded; (*provvisto di scala graduata*) graduated ●*nm* *Mil* noncommissioned officer. **~'toria** *nf* list. **~zi'one** *nf* graduation

'graffa *nf* clip; (*segno grafico*) brace

graf'fetta *nf* staple

graffi'a|re *vt* scratch. **~'tura** *nf* scratch

'graffio *nm* scratch

gra'fia *nf* [hand]writing; (*ortografia*) spelling

'grafic|a *nf* graphics; **~a pubblici-**

taria commercial art. **~a'mente** *adv* in graphics, graphically. **~o** *a* graphic ●*nm* graph; (*persona*) graphic designer

gra'migna *nf* weed

gram'mati|ca *nf* grammar. **~'cale** *a* grammatical

'grammo *nm* gram[me]

gran *a vedi* **grande**

'grana *nf* grain; (*formaggio*) parmesan; (*fam: seccatura*) trouble; (*fam: soldi*) readies *pl*

gra'naio *nm* barn

gra'nat|a *nf* *Mil* grenade; (*frutto*) pomegranate. **~i'ere** *nm* *Mil* grenadier

Gran Bre'tagna *nf* Great Britain

'granchio *nm* crab; (*fig: errore*) blunder; **prendere un ~** make a blunder

grandango'lare *nm* wide-angle lens

'grande (*a volte* **gran**) *a* (*ampio*) large; (*grosso*) big; (*alto*) tall; (*largo*) wide; (*fig: senso morale*) grand; (*grandioso*) grand; (*adulto*) grown-up; **ho una gran fame** I'm very hungry; **fa un gran caldo** it is very hot; **in ~** on a large scale; **in gran parte** to a great extent; **non è un gran che** it is nothing much; **un gran ballo** a grand ball ●*nmf* (*persona adulta*) grown-up; (*persona eminente*) great man/woman. **~ggi'are** *vi* **~ggiare su** tower over; (*darsi arie*) show off

gran'dezza *nf* greatness; (*ampiezza*) largeness; (*larghezza*) width, breadth; (*dimensione*) size; (*fasto*) grandeur; (*prodigalità*) lavishness; **a ~ naturale** life-size

grandi'nare *vi* hail; **grandina** it's hailing. **'grandine** *nf* hail

grandiosità *nf* grandeur. **grandi'oso** *a* grand

gran'duca *nm* grand duke

gra'nello *nm* grain; (*di frutta*) pip

gra'nita *nf* crushed ice drink

gra'nito *nm* granite

'grano *nm* grain; (*frumento*) wheat

gran'turco *nm* maize

'granulo nm granule
'grappa nf grappa; (morsa) cramp
'grappolo nm bunch. ~ d'uva bunch of grapes
gras'setto nm bold [type]
gras'sezza nf fatness; (untuosità) greasiness
'grasso a fat; (cibo) fatty; (unto) greasy; (terreno) rich; (grossolano) coarse ●nm fat; (sostanza) grease. ~'soccio a plump
'grata nf grating. gra'tella, gra'ticola nf Culin grill
gra'tifica nf bonus. ~zi'one nf satisfaction
grati'na|re vt cook au gratin. ~to a au gratin
'gratis adv free
grati'tudine nf gratitude. 'grato a grateful; (gradito) pleasant
gratta'capo nm trouble
grattaci'elo nm skyscraper
grat'tar|e vt scratch; (raschiare) scrape; (grattugiare) grate; (fam: rubare) pinch ●vi grate. ~si vr scratch oneself
grat'tugi|a nf grater. ~'are vt grate
gratuita'mente adv free [of charge]. gra'tuito a free [of charge]; (ingiustificato) gratuitous
gra'vare vt burden ●vi ~ su weigh on
'grave a (pesante) heavy; (serio) serious; (difficile) hard; (voce, suono) low; (fonetica) grave; essere ~ (gravemente ammalato) be seriously ill. ~'mente adv seriously, gravely
gravi'danza nf pregnancy. 'gravido a pregnant
gravità nf seriousness; Phys gravity
gravi'tare vi gravitate
gra'voso a onerous
'grazi|a nf grace; (favore) favour; Jur pardon; entrare nelle ~e di qcno get into sb's good books. ~'are vt pardon

'grazie int thank you!, thanks!; ~ mille! many thanks!, thanks a lot!
grazi'oso a charming; (carino) pretty
'Grec|ia nf Greece. g~o, -a a & nmf Greek
'gregge nm flock
'greggio a raw ●nm (petrolio) crude [oil]
grembi'ale, grembi'ule nm apron
'grembo nm lap; (utero) womb; fig bosom
gre'mi|re vt pack. ~rsi vr become crowded (di with). ~to a packed
'gretto a stingy; (di vedute ristrette) narrow-minded
'grezzo a = greggio
gri'dare vi shout; (di dolore) scream; (animale:) cry ●vt shout
'grido nm (pl m gridi o f grida) shout, cry; (di animale) cry; l'ultimo ~ the latest fashion; scrittore di ~ celebrated writer
'grigio a & nm grey
'griglia nf grill; alla ~ grilled
gril'letto nm trigger
'grillo nm cricket; (fig: capriccio) whim
grimal'dello nm picklock
'grinfia nf fig clutch
'grin|ta nf grit. ~'toso a determined
'grinza nf wrinkle; (di stoffa) crease
grip'pare vi Mech seize
gris'sino nm bread-stick
'gronda nf eaves pl
gron'daia nf gutter
gron'dare vi pour; (essere bagnato fradicio) be dripping
'groppa nf back
'groppo nm knot; avere un ~ alla gola have a lump in one's throat
gros'sezza nf size; (spessore) thickness
gros'sista nmf wholesaler
'grosso a big, large; (spesso) thick; (grossolano) coarse; (grave) serious ●nm big part; (massa) bulk; farla grossa do a stupid thing

grosso|**lanità** *nf inv* (*qualità*) coarseness; (*di errore*) grossness; (*azione, parola*) coarse thing. **~'lano** *a* coarse; (*errore*) gross

grosso'modo *adv* roughly

'grotta *nf* cave, grotto

grot'tesco *a & nm* grotesque

grovi'era *nmf* Gruyère

gro'viglio *nm* tangle; *fig* muddle

gru *nf inv* (*uccello, edilizia*) crane

'gruccia *nf* (*stampella*) crutch; (*per vestito*) hanger

gru'gni|**re** *vi* grunt. **~to** *nm* grunt

'grugno *nm* snout

'grullo *a* silly

'grumo *nm* clot; (*di farina ecc*) lump. **gru'moso** *a* lumpy

'gruppo *nm* group; (*comitiva*) party. **~ sanguigno** blood group

gruvi'era *nmf* Gruyère

gruzzolo *nm* nest-egg

guada'gnare *vt* earn; gain (*tempo, forza ecc*). **gua'dagno** *nm* gain; (*profitto*) profit; (*entrate*) earnings *pl*

gu'ado *nm* ford; **passare a ~** ford

gua'ina *nf* sheath; (*busto*) girdle

gu'aio *nm* trouble; **che ~!** that's just brilliant!; **essere nei guai** be in a fix; **guai a te se lo tocchi!** don't you dare touch it!

gua'i|**re** *vi* yelp. **~to** *nm* yelp

gu'anci|**a** *nf* cheek. **~'ale** *nm* pillow

gu'anto *nm* glove. **guantoni** *pl* [**da boxe**] boxing gloves

guarda'coste *nm* coastguard

guarda'linee *nm inv Sport* linesman

guar'dar|**e** *vt* look at; (*osservare*) watch; (*badare a*) look after; (*dare su*) look out on ● *vi* look; (*essere orientato verso*) face. **~si** *vr* look at oneself; **~si da** beware of; (*astenersi*) refrain from

guarda'rob|**a** *nm inv* wardrobe; (*di locale pubblico*) cloakroom. **~'iere, -a** *nmf* cloakroom attendant

gu'ardia *nf* guard; (*poliziotto*) policeman; (*vigilanza*) watch; **es-** sere di ~ be on guard; (*medico:*) be on duty; **fare la ~ a** keep guard over; **mettere in ~ qcno** warn sb; **stare in ~** be on one's guard. **~ carceraria** prison warder. **~ del corpo** bodyguard, minder. **~ di finanza** ≈ Fraud Squad. **~ forestale** forest ranger. **~ medica** duty doctor

guardi'ano, -a *nmf* caretaker. **~ notturno** night watchman

guar'dingo *a* cautious

guardi'ola *nf* gatekeeper's lodge

guarigi'one *nf* recovery

gua'rire *vt* cure ● *vi* recover; (*ferita:*) heal [up]

guarnigi'one *nf* garrison

guar'ni|**re** *vt* trim; *Culin* garnish. **~zi'one** *nf* trimming; *Culin* garnish; *Mech* gasket

guasta'feste *nmf inv* spoilsport

gua'star|**e** *vt* spoil; (*rovinare*) ruin; break (*meccanismo*). **~si** *vr* spoil; (*andare a male*) go bad; (*tempo:*) change for the worse; (*meccanismo:*) break down. **gua'sto** *a* broken; (*ascensore, telefono*) out of order; (*auto*) broken down; (*cibo, dente*) bad ● *nm* breakdown; (*danno*) damage

guazza'buglio *nm* muddle

guaz'zare *vi* wallow

gu'ercio *a* cross-eyed

gu'err|**a** *nf* war; (*tecnica bellica*) warfare. **~ fredda** Cold War. **~ mondiale** world war. **~afon'daio** *nm* warmonger. **~eggi'are** *vi* wage war. **guer'resco** *a* (*di guerra*) war; (*bellicoso*) warlike. **~i'ero** *nm* warrior

guer'riglia *nf* guerrilla warfare. **~'ero, -a** *nmf* guerrilla

'gufo *nm* owl

'guglia *nf* spire

gu'ida *nf* guide; (*direzione*) guidance; (*comando*) leadership; *Auto* driving; (*tappeto*) runner; **~ a destra/sinistra** right-/left-hand drive. **~ telefonica** telephone directory. **~a turistica** tourist guide. **gui'dare** *vt* guide; *Auto* drive; steer (nave). **~a'tore**, **~a'trice** nmf driver

guin'zaglio nm leash

guiz'zare vi dart; (luce:) flash. **gu'izzo** nm dart; (di luce) flash

'guscio nm shell

gu'stare vt taste ● vi like. **'gusto** nm taste; (piacere) pleasure; **mangiare di gusto** eat heartily; **prenderci gusto** come to enjoy it, develop a taste for it. **gu'stoso** a tasty; fig delightful

guttu'rale a guttural

Hh

habitué nmf inv regular [customer]

ham'burger nm inv hamburger

'handicap nm inv Sport handicap

handicap'pare vt handicap. **~to**, **-a** nmf disabled person ●a disabled

'harem nm inv harem

'hascisc nm hashish

henné nm henna

hi-fi nm hi-fi

'hippy a hippy

hockey nm hockey. **~ su ghiaccio** ice hockey. **~ su prato** hockey

hollywoodi'ano a Hollywood attrib

ho'tel nm inv hotel

Ii

i def art mpl the; vedi **il**

i'ato nm hiatus

iber'na|re vi hibernate. **~zi'one** nf hibernation

i'bisco nm hibiscus

'ibrido a & nm hybrid

iceberg nm inv iceberg

i'cona nf icon

Id'dio nm God

i'dea nf idea; (opinione) opinion; (ideale) ideal; (indizio) inkling; (piccola quantità) hint; (intenzione) intention; **cambiare ~** change one's mind; **neanche per ~!** not on your life!; **chiarirsi le idee** get one's ideas straight. **~ fissa** obsession

ide'ale a & nm ideal. **~'lista** nmf idealist. **~liz'zare** vt idealize

ide'a|re vt conceive. **~'tore**, **~'trice** nmf originator

'idem adv the same

i'dentico a identical

identifi'cabile a identifiable

identifi'ca|re vt identify. **~zi'one** nf identification

identi'kit nm inv identikit®

identità nf inv identity

ideolo'gia nf ideology. **ideo'logico** a ideological

i'dillio a idyllic. **~o** nm idyll

idi'oma nm idiom. **idio'matico** a idiomatic

idi'ota a idiotic ● nmf idiot. **idio'zia** nf (cosa stupida) idiocy

idola'trare vt worship

idoleggi'are vt idolize. **'idolo** nm idol

idoneità nf suitability; Mil fitness; **esame di ~** qualifying examination. **i'doneo** a **idoneo a** suitable for; Mil fit for

i'drante nm hydrant

idra'ta|re vt hydrate; (cosmetico:) moisturize. **~nte** a (crema, gel) moisturizing. **~zi'one** nf moisturizing

i'draulico a hydraulic ● nm plumber

'idrico a water attrib

idrocar'buro nm hydrocarbon

idroe'lettrico a hydroelectric

i'drofilo a vedi **cotone**

i'drogeno nm hydrogen

idromas'saggio nm (sistema) whirlpool bath

idrovo'lante nm seaplane

i'ella nf fam bad luck; **portare ~** be

bad luck. **iel'lato** *a fam* jinxed, plagued by bad luck

i'ena *nf* hyena

i'eri *adv* yesterday; ~ **l'altro, l'altro** ~ the day before yesterday; ~ **pomeriggio** yesterday afternoon; **il giornale di** ~ yesterday's paper

ietta|'tore, -'trice *nmf* jinx. ~'**tura** *nf* (*sfortuna*) bad luck

igi'en|e *nf* hygiene. ~'**ico** *a* hygienic. **igie'nista** *nmf* hygienist

i'gnaro *a* unaware

i'gnobile *a* base; (*non onorevole*) dishonourable

igno'ran|te *a* ignorant ● *nmf* ignoramus. ~'**za** *nf* ignorance

igno'rare *vt* (*non sapere*) be unaware of; (*trascurare*) ignore

i'gnoto *a* unknown

il *def art m* the; **il latte fa bene** milk is good for you; **il signor Magnetti** Mr Magnetti; **il dottor Piazza** Dr Piazza; **ha il naso storto** he has a bent nose; **mettiti il cappello** put your hat on; **il lunedì** on Mondays; **il 1986** 1986; **5 000 lire il chilo** 5,000 lire the *o* a kilo

i'lar|e *a* merry. ~**ità** *nf* hilarity

illazi'one *nf* inference

ille'cita|mente *adv* illicitly. **il'lecito** *a* illicit

ille'gal|e *a* illegal. ~**ità** *nf* illegality. ~'**mente** *adv* illegally

illeg'gibile *a* illegible; (*libro*) unreadable

illegittimità *nf* illegitimacy. **ille'gittimo** *a* illegitimate

il'leso *a* unhurt

illette'rato, -a *a* & *nmf* illiterate

illi'bato *a* chaste

illimi'tato *a* unlimited

illivi'dire *vt* bruise ● *vi* (*per rabbia*) turn livid

il'logico *a* illogical

il'lud|ere *vt* deceive. ~**si** *vr* deceive oneself

illumi'na|re *vt* light [up]; *fig* enlighten; ~**re a giorno** floodlight. ~**rsi** *vr* light up. ~**zi'one** *nf* lighting; *fig* enlightenment

illumi'nismo *nm* Enlightenment

illusi'one *nf* illusion; **farsi illusioni** delude oneself

illusio'nis|mo *nm* conjuring. ~**ta** *nmf* conjurer

il'lu|so, -a *pp di* **illudere** ● *a* deluded ● *nmf* day-dreamer. ~'**sorio** *a* illusory

illu'stra|re *vt* illustrate. ~'**tivo** *a* illustrative. ~'**tore, -'trice** *nmf* illustrator. ~**zi'one** *nf* illustration

il'lustre *a* distinguished

imbacuc'ca|re *vt*, ~**rsi** *vr* wrap up. ~**to** *a* wrapped up

imbal'la|ggio *nm* packing. ~**re** *vt* pack; *Auto* race

imbalsa'ma|re *vt* embalm; stuff (*animale*). ~**to** *a* embalmed; (*animale*) stuffed

imbambo'lato *a* vacant

imbaraz'zante *a* embarrassing

imbaraz'za|re *vt* embarrass; (*ostacolare*) encumber. ~**to** *a* embarrassed

imba'razzo *nm* embarrassment; (*ostacolo*) hindrance; **trarre qcno d'**~ help sb out of a difficulty; **avere l'**~ **della scelta** be spoilt for choice. ~ **di stomaco** indigestion

imbarca'dero *nm* landing-stage

imbar'ca|re *vt* embark; (*fam: rimorchiare*) score. ~**rsi** *vr* embark, go on board. ~**rsi in** boat. ~**zi'one** *nf* boat. **im'barco** *nm* embarkation, boarding; (*banchina*) landing-stage

imba'sti|re *vt* tack; *fig* sketch. ~'**tura** *nf* tacking, basting

im'battersi *vr* ~ **in** run into

imbat'ti|bile *a* unbeatable. ~**uto** *a* unbeaten

imbavagli'are *vt* gag

imbec'cata *nf* *Theat* prompt

imbe'cille *a* stupid ● *nmf* *Med* imbecile

imbel'lire *vt* embellish

im'berbe *a* beardless; *fig* inexperienced

imbestia'li|re vi. **~si** vr fly into a rage. **~to** a enraged

im'bever|e vt imbue (**di** with). **~si** vr absorb

imbe'vi|bile a undrinkable. **~uto** a **~uto di** ⟨acqua⟩ soaked in; ⟨nozioni⟩ imbued with

imbian'ca|re vt whiten ● vi turn white. **~hino** nm house painter

imbizzar'rir|e vi, **~si** vr become restless; ⟨arrabbiarsi⟩ become angry

imboc'ca|re vt feed; ⟨entrare⟩ enter; fig prompt. **~tura** nf opening; ⟨ingresso⟩ entrance; ⟨Mus: di strumento⟩ mouthpiece. **im'bocco** nm entrance

imbo'scare vt hide. **~si** vr Mil shirk military service

imbo'scata nf ambush

imbottigli'are vt bottle. **~rsi** vr get snarled up in a traffic jam. **~to** a ⟨vino, acqua⟩ bottled

imbot'ti|re vt stuff; pad ⟨giacca⟩; Culin fill. **~rsi** vr **~rsi di** ⟨fig: di pasticche⟩ stuff oneself with. **~ta** nf quilt. **~to** a ⟨spalle⟩ padded; ⟨cuscino⟩ stuffed; ⟨panino⟩ filled. **~tura** nf stuffing; ⟨di giacca⟩ padding; Culin filling

imbracci'are vt shoulder ⟨fucile⟩

imbra'nato a clumsy

imbrat'tar|e vt mark. **~si** vr dirty oneself

imbroc'care vt hit; **~la giusta** hit the nail on the head

imbrogli|'are vt muddle; ⟨raggirare⟩ cheat. **~arsi** vr get tangled; ⟨confondersi⟩ get confused. **im-'broglio** nm tangle; ⟨pasticcio⟩ mess; ⟨inganno⟩ trick. **~'one, -a** nmf cheat

imbronci'a|re vi, **~rsi** vr sulk. **~to** a sulky

imbru'nire vi get dark; **all'~** at dusk

imbrut'tire vt make ugly ● vi become ugly

imbu'care vt post, mail; ⟨nel biliardo⟩ pot

imbur'rare vt butter

im'buto nm funnel

imi'ta|re vt imitate. **~'tore, ~'trice** nmf imitator, impersonator. **~zi-'one** nf imitation

immaco'lato a immaculate

immagazzi'nare vt store

immagi'na|re vt imagine; ⟨supporre⟩ suppose; **s'immagini!** imagine that!. **~rio** a imaginary. **~zi'one** nf imagination. **im'magine** nf image; ⟨rappresentazione, idea⟩ picture

imman'cabil|e a unfailing. **~-'mente** adv without fail

im'mane a huge; ⟨orribile⟩ terrible

imma'nente a immanent

immangi'abile a inedible

immatrico'la|re vt register. **~si** vr ⟨studente⟩ matriculate. **~zi'one** nf registration; ⟨di studente⟩ matriculation

immaturità nf immaturity. **imma-'turo** a unripe; ⟨persona⟩ immature; ⟨precoce⟩ premature

immedesi'mar|si **~rsi in** identify oneself with. **~zi'one** nf identification

immediata'mente adv immediately. **~'tezza** nf immediacy. **immedi'ato** a immediate

immemo'rabile a immemorial

immensa'mente adv enormously. **~ità** nf immensity. **im-'menso** a immense

immensu'rabile a immeasurable

im'merger|e vt immerse. **~si** in plunge; ⟨sommergibile:⟩ dive; **~si in** immerse oneself in

immeri'tato a undeserved. **~evole** a undeserving

immersi'one nf immersion; ⟨di sommergibile⟩ dive. **im'merso** pp di **immergere**

immi'gra|nte a & nmf immigrant. **~re** vi immigrate. **~to, -a** nmf immigrant. **~zi'one** nf immigration

immi'nen|te a imminent. **~za** nf imminence

immischi'ar|e vt involve. **~si** vr **~si in** meddle in

immis'sario nm tributary

immissi'one nf insertion
im'mobile a motionless
im'mobili nmpl real estate. ~'are
a società ~are building society,
savings and loan Am
immobili|tà nf immobility. ~z'za-
re vt immobilize; Comm tie up
immo'desto a immodest
immo'lare vt sacrifice
immondez'zaio nm rubbish tip.
immon'dizia nf filth; (spazzatura)
rubbish. **im'mondo** a filthy
immo'ral|e a immoral. ~ità nf im-
morality
immorta'lare vt immortalize. **im-
mor'tale** a immortal
immoti'vato a (gesto) unjustified
im'mun|e a exempt; Med immune.
~ità nf immunity. ~iz'zare vt im-
munize. ~izzazi'one nf immuni-
zation
immunodefici'enza nf immuno-
deficiency
immuso'ni|rsi vr sulk. ~to a
sulky
immu'ta|bile a unchangeable. ~to
a unchanging
impacchet'tare vt wrap up
impacci'a|re vt hamper; (distur-
bare) inconvenience; (imbarazzare) embarrass. ~to a embarrassed; (goffo) awkward. **im'paccio** nm embarrassment; (ostacolo)
hindrance; (situazione difficile)
awkward situation
im'pacco nm compress
impadro'nirsi vr ~ di take possession of; (fig: imparare) master
impa'gabile a priceless
impagi'na|re vt paginate. ~zi'one
nf pagination
impagli'are vt stuff (animale)
impa'lato a fig stiff
impalca'tura nf scaffolding; fig
structure
impalli'dire vi turn pale; (fig:
perdere d'importanza) pale into
insignificance
impa'nare vt Culin roll in
breadcrumbs
impanta'narsi vr get bogged down

impape'rarsi vr, **impappi'narsi**
vr falter, stammer
impa'rare vt learn
impareggi'abile a incomparable
imparen'ta|rsi vr ~ con become
related to. ~to a related
'impari a unequal; (dispari) odd
impar'tire vt impart
imparzi'al|e a impartial. ~ità nf
impartiality
impas'sibile a impassive
impa'sta|re vt Culin knead; blend
(colori). ~'tura nf kneading.
im'pasto nm Culin dough; (miscuglio) mixture
impastic'carsi vr pop pills
im'patto nm impact
impau'ri|re vt frighten. ~si vr be-
come frightened
im'pavido a fearless
impazi'en|te a impatient; ~te di
fare qcsa eager to do sth. ~'tirsi
vr lose patience. ~za nf impa-
tience
impaz'zata nf all'~ at breakneck
speed
impaz'zire vi go mad; (maionese:)
separate; **far** ~ **qcno** drive sb
mad; ~ **per** be crazy about; **da** ~
(mal di testa) blinding
impec'cabile a impeccable
impedi'mento nm hindrance;
(ostacolo) obstacle
impe'dire vt ~ **di** prevent from;
(impacciare) hinder; (ostruire)
obstruct; ~ **a qcno di fare qcsa**
prevent sb [from] doing sth
impe'gna|re vt (dare in pegno)
pawn; (vincolare) bind; (prenotare) reserve; (assorbire) take up.
~rsi vr apply oneself; ~rsi a fare
qcsa commit oneself to doing sth.
~'tiva nf referral. ~'tivo a binding;
(lavoro) demanding. ~ato a en-
gaged; Pol committed. **im'pegno**
nm engagement; Comm commit-
ment; (zelo) care
impel'lente a pressing
impene'trabile a impenetrable
impen'na|rsi vr (cavallo:) rear; fig
bristle. ~ta nf (di prezzi) sharp

rise; (*di cavallo*) rearing; (*di moto*) wheelie

impen'sa|bile *a* unthinkable. **~to** *a* unexpected

impensie'rir|e *vt*, **~si** *vr* worry

impe'rante *a* prevailing. **~re** *vi* reign; (*tendenza*) prevail, hold sway

impera'tivo *a & nm* imperative

impera'tore, -'trice *nm* emperor
● *nf* empress

impercet'tibile *a* imperceptible

imperdo'nabile *a* unforgivable

imper'fe|tto *a & nm* imperfect.
~zi'one *nf* imperfection

imperi'a|le *a* imperial. **~'lismo** *nm* imperialism. **~'lista** *a* imperialist. **~'listico** *a* imperialistic

imperi'oso *a* imperious; (*impellente*) urgent

impe'rizia *nf* lack of skill

imperme'abile *a* waterproof
● *nm* raincoat

imperni'ar|e *vt* pivot; (*fondare*) base. **~si** *vr* **su** be based on

im'pero *nm* empire; (*potere*) rule

imperscru'tabile *a* inscrutable

imperso'nale *a* impersonal

imperso'nare *vt* personify; (*interpretare*) act [the part of]

imper'territo *a* undaunted

imperti'nen|te *a* impertinent.
~za *nf* impertinence

impertur'ba|bile *a* imperturbable. **~to** *a* unperturbed

imperver'sare *vi* rage

im'pervio *a* inaccessible

impe'to *nm* impetus; (*impulso*) impulse; (*slancio*) transport.
~u'oso *a* impetuous; (*vento*) blustering

impet'tito *a* stiff

impian'tare *vt* install; set up (*azienda*)

impi'anto *nm* plant; (*sistema*) system; (*operazione*) installation. **~ radio** *Auto* car stereo system

impia'strare *vt* plaster; (*sporcare*) dirty. **impi'astro** *nm* poultice; (*persona noiosa*) bore; (*pasticcione*) cack-handed person

impic'car|e *vt* hang. **~si** *vr* hang oneself

impicci'arsi *vr* meddle. **im'piccio** *nm* hindrance; (*seccatura*) bother. **~'one, -a** *nmf* nosey parker

impie'ga|re *vt* employ; (*usare*) use; spend (*tempo, denaro*); *Fin* invest. **l'autobus ha ~to un'ora** it took the bus an hour. **~rsi** *vr* get [oneself] a job

impie'gatizio *a* clerical

impie'gato, -a *nmf* employee. **~ di banca** bank clerk. **impi'ego** *nm* employment; (*posto*) job; *Fin* investment

impieto'sir|e *vt* move to pity. **~si** *vr* be moved to pity

impie'trito *a* petrified

impigli'ar|e *vt* entangle. **~si** *vr* get entangled

impi'grir|e *vt* make lazy. **~si** *vr* get lazy

impla'cabile *a* implacable

impli'ca|re *vt* implicate; (*sottintendere*) imply. **~rsi** *vr* become involved. **~zi'one** *nf* implication

implicita'mente *adv* implicitly. **im'plicito** *a* implicit

implo'rar|e *vt* implore. **~zi'one** *nf* entreaty

impolve'rar|e *vt* cover with dust. **~rsi** *vr* get covered with dust. **~to** *a* dusty

impon'derabile *a* imponderable; (*causa, evento*) unpredictable

impo'nen|te *a* imposing. **~za** *nf* impressiveness

impo'nibile *a* taxable ● *nm* taxable income

impopo'lar|e *a* unpopular. **~ità** *nf* unpopularity

im'por|re *vt* impose; (*ordinare*) order. **~si** *vr* assert oneself; (*aver successo*) be successful; **~si di** (*prefiggersi di*) set oneself the task of

impor'tan|te *a* important ● *nm* important thing. **~za** *nf* importance

impor'ta|re *vt Comm, Comput* import; (*comportare*) cause ● *vi* matter; (*essere necessario*) be necessary. **non ~l** it doesn't matter!; **non me ne ~ niente!** I couldn't care less!. **~'trice** *nmf* importer. **~zi'one** *nf* importation; (*merce importata*) import

im'porto *nm* amount

importu'nare *vt* pester. **impor'tuno** *a* troublesome; (*inopportuno*) untimely

imposizi'one *nf* imposition; (*imposta*) tax

imposses'sarsi *vr* **~ di** seize

impos'sibile *a* impossible **● nm fare l'~e** do absolutely all one can. **~ità** *nf* impossibility

im'posta[1] *nf* tax; **~ sul reddito** income tax; **~ sul valore aggiunto** value added tax

im'posta[2] *nf* (*di finestra*) shutter

impo'stare *vt* (*progettare*) plan; (*basare*) base; *Mus* pitch; (*imbucare*) post, mail; set out (*domanda, problema*). **~zi'one** *nf* planning; (*di voce*) pitching

im'posto *pp di* **imporre**

impo'store, -a *nmf* impostor

impo'tente *a* powerless; *Med* impotent. **~za** *nf* powerlessness; *Med* impotence

impove'rire *vt* impoverish. **~si** *vr* become poor

imprati'cabile *a* impracticable; (*strada*) impassable

imprati'chire *vt* train. **~si** *vr* **~si in** *o* a get practice in

impre'care *vi* curse. **~zi'one** *nf* curse

impreci'sabile *a* indeterminable. **~ato** *a* indeterminate. **~i'one** *nf* inaccuracy. **impre'ciso** *a* inaccurate

impre'gnare *vt* impregnate; (*imbevere*) soak; *fig* imbue. **~si** *vr* become impregnated with

imprendi'tore, -'trice *nmf* entrepreneur. **~i'ale** *a* entrepreneurial

imprepa'rato *a* unprepared

im'presa *nf* undertaking; (*gesta*) exploit; (*azienda*) firm

impre'sario *nm* impresario; (*appaltatore*) contractor

imprescin'dibile *a* inescapable

impressio'nabile *a* impressionable. **~nte** *a* impressive; (*spaventoso*) frightening

impressio'nare *vt* impress; (*spaventare*) frighten; expose (*foto*). **~o'narsi** *vr* be affected; (*spaventarsi*) be frightened. **~'one** *nf* impression; (*sensazione*) sensation; (*impronta*) mark; **far ~one a qcno** upset sb

impressio'nismo *nm* impressionism. **~ta** *nmf* impressionist

im'presso *pp di* **imprimere ● a** printed

impre'stare *vt* lend

impreve'dibile *a* unforeseeable; (*persona*) unpredictable

imprevi'dente *a* improvident

impre'visto *a* unforeseen **● nm** unforeseen event; **salvo imprevisti** all being well

imprigio'namento *nm* imprisonment. **~'nare** *vt* imprison

im'primere *vt* impress; (*stampare*) print; (*comunicare*) impart

impro'babile *a* unlikely, improbable. **~ità** *nf* improbability

improdut'tivo *a* unproductive

im'pronta *nf* impression; *fig* mark. **~ digitale** fingerprint. **~ del piede** footprint

impro'perio *nm* insult; **improperi** *pl* abuse *sg*

im'proprio *a* improper

improvvisa'mente *adv* suddenly

improvvi'sare *vt/i* improvise. **~rsi** *vr* turn oneself into a. **~ta** *nf* surprise. **~to** *a* (*discorso*) unrehearsed. **~zi'one** *nf* improvisation

improv'viso *a* sudden; **all'~** unexpectedly

impru'dente *a* imprudent. **~za** *nf* imprudence

impu'gnare *vt* grasp; *Jur* contest. **~tura** *nf* grip; (*manico*) handle

impulsi'vità *nf* impulsiveness.

impul'sivo *a* impulsive

im'pulso *nm* impulse; **agire d'~** act on impulse

impune'mente *adv* with impunity. impu'nito *a* unpunished

impun'tarsi *vr fig* dig one's heels in

impun'tura *nf* stitching

impurità *nf inv* impurity. im'puro *a* impure

impu'tabile *a* attributable (**a** to)

impu'ta|re *vt* attribute; (*accusare*) charge. **~to, -a** *nmf* accused. **~zi'one** *nf* charge

imputri'dire *vi* rot

in *prep* in; (*moto a luogo*) to; (*su*) on; (*entro*) within; (*mezzo*) by; (*con materiale*) made of; **essere in casa/ufficio** be at home/at the office; **in mano/tasca** in one's hand/pocket; **andare in Francia/ campagna** go to France/the country; **salire in treno** get on the train; **versa la birra nel bicchiere** pour the beer into the glass; **in alto** up there; **in giornata** within the day; **nel 1997** in 1997; **una borsa in pelle** a bag made of leather, a leather bag; **in macchina** (*viaggiare, venire*) by car; **in contanti** [in] cash; **in vacanza** on holiday; **di giorno in giorno** from day to day; **se fossi in te** if I were you; **siamo in sette** there are seven of us

inabbor'dabile *a* unapproachable

i'nabile *a* incapable; (*fisicamente*) unfit. **~ità** *nf* incapacity

inabi'tabile *a* uninhabitable

inacces'sibile *a* inaccessible; (*persona*) unapproachable

inaccet'tabile *a* unacceptable. **~ità** *nf* unacceptability

inacer'bi|re *vt* embitter; exacerbate (*rapporto*). **~si** *vr* grow bitter

inaci'dir|e *vt* turn sour. **~si** *vr* go sour; (*persona:*) become embittered

ina'datto *a* unsuitable

inadegu'ato *a* inadequate

inadempi'ente *nmf* defaulter. **~'mento** *nm* nonfulfilment

inaffer'rabile *a* elusive

ina'la|re *vt* inhale. **~'tore** *nm* inhaler. **~zi'one** *nf* inhalation

inalbe'rar|e *vt* hoist. **~si** *vr* (*cavallo:*) rear [up]; (*adirarsi*) lose one's temper

inalte'rabile *a* unchangeable; (*colore*) fast. **~to** *a* unchanged

inami'da|re *vt* starch. **~to** *a* starched

inammis'sibile *a* inadmissible

inamovi'bile *a* irremovable

inani'mato *a* inanimate; (*senza vita*) lifeless

inappa'gabile *a* unsatisfiable. **~to** *a* unfulfilled

inappel'labile *a* final

inappe'tenza *nf* lack of appetite

inappli'cabile *a* inapplicable

inappun'tabile *a* faultless

inar'car|e *vt* arch; raise (*sopracciglia*). **~si** *vr* (*legno:*) warp; (*ripiano:*) sag; (*linea:*) curve

inari'dir|e *vt* parch; empty of feelings (*persona*). **~si** *vr* dry up; (*persona:*) become empty of feelings

inartico'lato *a* inarticulate

inaspetta'mente *adv* unexpectedly. inaspet'tato *a* unexpected

inaspri'mento *nm* (*di carattere*) embitterment; (*di conflitto*) worsening

ina'sprir|e *vt* embitter. **~si** *vr* become embittered

inattac'cabile *a* unassailable; (*irreprensibile*) irreproachable

inatten'dibile *a* unreliable. inat'teso *a* unexpected

inattività *nf* inactivity. inat'tivo *a* inactive

inattu'abile *a* impracticable

inau'dito *a* unheard of

inaugu'rale *a* inaugural; **viaggio ~** maiden voyage

inaugu'ra|re *vt* inaugurate; open (*mostra*); unveil (*statua*); christen (*lavastoviglie ecc*). **~zi'one** *nf* inauguration; (*di mostra*) opening; (*di statua*) unveiling

inavver'tenza *nf* inadvertence. **~ita'mente** *adv* inadvertently

incagli'ar|e *vi* ground ● *vt* hinder. **~si** *vr* run aground

incalco'labile *a* incalculable

incal'li|rsi *vr* grow callous; *(abituarsi)* become hardened. **~to** *a* callous; *(abituato)* hardened

incal'za|nte *a (ritmo)* driving; *(richiesta)* urgent. **~re** *vt* pursue; *fig* press

incame'rare *vt* appropriate

incammi'nar|e *vt* get going; *(fig: guidare)* set off. **~si** *vr* set out

incana'lar|e *vt* canalize; *fig* channel. **~si** *vr* converge on

incande'scen|te *a* incandescent; *(discussione)* burning. **~za** *nf* incandescence

incan'ta|re *vt* enchant. **~rsi** *vr* stand spellbound; *(incepparsi)* jam. **~'tore**, **~'trice** *nm* enchanter ● *nf* enchantress

incan'tesimo *nm* spell

incan'tevole *a* enchanting

in'canto *nm* spell; *fig* delight; *(asta)* auction; **come per ~** as if by magic

incanu'ti|re *vi* turn white. **~to** *a* white

inca'pace *a* incapable. **~ità** *nf* incapability

incapo'nirsi *vr* be set (**a fare** on doing)

incap'pare *vi* **~ in** run into

incappucci'arsi *vr* wrap up

incapricci'arsi *vr* **~ di** take a fancy to

incapsu'lare *vt* seal; crown *(dente)*

incarce'ra|re *vt* imprison. **~zi'one** *nf* imprisonment

incari'ca|re *vt* charge. **~rsi** *vr* take upon oneself; **me ne incarico io** I will see to it. **~to**, **~a** *in* charge ● *nmf* representative. **in'carico** *nm* charge; **per incarico di** on behalf of

incar'na|re *vt* embody. **~rsi** *vr* become incarnate. **~zi'one** *nf* incarnation

incarta'mento *nm* documents *pl.* **incar'tare** *vt* wrap up [in paper]

incasi'nato *a (fam: vita)* screwed up; *(stanza)* messed up

incas'sa|re *vt* pack; *Mech* embed; box in *(mobile, frigo)*; *(riscuotere)* cash; take *(colpo)*. **~to** *a* set; *(fiume)* deeply embanked. **in'casso** *nm* collection; *(introito)* takings *pl*

incasto'na|re *vt* set. **~'tura** *nf* setting. **~to** *a* embedded; *(anello)* in-set **(di** with)

inca'strar|e *vt* fit in; *(fam: in situazione)* corner. **~si** *vr* fit. **in'castro** *nm* joint; **a incastro** *(pezzi)* interlocking

incate'nare *vt* chain

incatra'mare *vt* tar

incatti'vire *vt* turn nasty

in'cauto *a* imprudent

inca'va|re *vt* hollow out. **~to** *a* hollow. **~'tura** *nf* hollow. **in'cavo** *nm* hollow; *(scanalatura)* groove

incavo'la|rsi *vr fam* get shirty. **~to** *a fam* shirty

incendi'ar|e *vt* set fire to; *fig* inflame. **~si** *vr* catch fire. **~io, -a** *a* incendiary; *(fig: discorso)* inflammatory; *(fig: bellezza)* sultry ● *nmf* arsonist. **in'cendio** *nm* fire. **incendio doloso** arson

incene'ri|re *vt* burn to ashes; *(cremare)* cremate. **~rsi** *vr* be burnt to ashes. **~'tore** *nm* incinerator

in'censo *nm* incense

incensu'rato *a* blameless; **essere ~** *Jur* have a clean record

incenti'vare *vt* motivate. **incen'tivo** *nm* incentive

incen'trarsi *vr* **~ su** centre on

incep'par|e *vt* block; *fig* hamper. **~si** *vr* jam

ince'rata *nf* oilcloth

incerot'tato *a* with a plaster on

incer'tezza *nf* uncertainty. **in'certo** *a* uncertain ● *nm* uncertainty

inces'sante *a* unceasing. **~'mente** *adv* incessantly

in'cest|o *nm* incest. **~u'oso** *a* incestuous

in'cetta *nf* buying up; **fare ~ di** stockpile

inchi'esta nf investigation
inchi'nare vt, **~si** vr bow. **in'chino** nm bow; (di donna) curtsy
inchio'dare vt nail; nail down ‹coperchio›; **~ a letto** ‹malattia:› confine to bed
inchi'ostro nm ink
inciam'pare vi stumble; **~ in** ‹imbattersi› run into. **inci'ampo** nm hindrance
inciden'tale a incidental
inci'den|**te** nm (episodio) incident; (infortunio) accident. **~za** nf incidence
in'cidere vt cut; (arte) engrave; (registrare) record ● vi **~ su** ‹gravare:› weigh upon
in'cinta a pregnant
incipi'ente a incipient
incipri'ar|**e** vt powder. **~si** vr powder one's face
in'circa adv **all'~** more or less
incisi'one nf incision; (arte) engraving; (acquaforte) etching; (registrazione) recording
inci'sivo a incisive ● nm (dente) incisor
in'ciso nm **per ~** incidentally
incita'mento nm incitement. **inci'tare** vt incite
inci'vil|**e** a uncivilized; (maleducato) impolite. **~tà** nf barbarism; (maleducazione) rudeness
incle'men|**te** a harsh. **~za** nf harshness
incli'nabile a reclining
incli'na|**re** vt tilt ● vi **~re a** be inclined to. **~rsi** vr list. **~to a** tilted; (terreno) sloping. **~zi'one** nf slope, inclination. **in'cline** a inclined
in'clu|**dere** vt include; (allegare) enclose. **~si'one** nf inclusion. **~sivo** a inclusive. **~so** pp di **includere** ● a included; (compreso) inclusive; (allegato) enclosed
incoe'ren|**te** a (contraddittorio) inconsistent. **~za** nf inconsistency
in'cognit|**a** nf unknown quantity. **~o** a unknown ● nm **in ~o** incognito

incol'lar|**e** vt stick; (con colla liquida) glue. **~si** vr stick to; **~si a qcno** stick close to sb
incolle'r|**irsi** vr lose one's temper. **~to** a enraged
incol'mabile a (differenza) unbridgeable; (vuoto) unfillable
incolon'nare vt line up
inco'lore a colourless
incol'pare vt blame
in'colto a uncultivated; (persona) uneducated
in'colume a unhurt
incom'ben|**te** a impending. **~za** nf task
in'combere vi **~ su** hang over; **~ a** (spettare) be incumbent on
incomo'dar|**e** vt inconvenience. **~si** vr trouble. **in'comodo** a uncomfortable; (inopportuno) inconvenient ● nm inconvenience
incompa'rabile a incomparable
incompa'tibil|**e** a incompatible. **~ità** nf incompatibility
incompe'ten|**te** a incompetent. **~za** nf incompetence
incompi'uto a unfinished
incom'pleto a incomplete
incompren'si|**bile** a incomprehensible. **~'one** nf lack of understanding; (malinteso) misunderstanding. **incom'preso** a misunderstood
inconce'pibile a inconceivable
inconcili'abile a irreconcilable
inconclu'dente a inconclusive; (persona) ineffectual
incondizio'nata'mente adv unconditionally. **~'nato** a unconditional
inconfes'sabile a unmentionable
inconfon'dibile a unmistakable
inconfu'tabile a irrefutable
incongru'ente a inconsistent
in'congruo a inadequate
inconsa'pevol|**e** a unaware; (inconscio) unconscious. **~'mente** adv unwittingly
in'conscio a & nm unconscious
inconscia'mente adv uncon-

sciously. in'conscio a & nm Psych
unconscious

inconsi'sten|te a insubstantial;
⟨notizia ecc⟩ unfounded. ~za nf
⟨di ragionamento, prove⟩ flimsi-
ness

inconso'labile a inconsolable

inconsu'eto a unusual

incon'sulto a rash

incontami'nato a uncontami-
nated

inconte'nibile a irrepressible

inconten'tabile a insatiable; ⟨esi-
gente⟩ hard to please

inconte'stabile a indisputable

inconti'nen|te a incontinent. ~za
nf incontinence

incon'tra|re vt meet; encounter,
meet with ⟨difficoltà⟩. ~si vr meet
⟨con qcno sb⟩

incon'trario: all'~ adv the other
way around; ⟨in modo sbagliato⟩
the wrong way around

incontra'sta|bile a incontrover-
tible. ~to a undisputed

in'contro nm meeting; Sport
match. ~ al vertice summit meeting ● prep ~ a towards; andare ~
a qn go to meet sb; fig meet sb half
way

inconveni'ente nm drawback

incoraggia'mento nm encour-
agement. ~ante a encouraging.
~'are vt encourage

incornici'a|re vt frame. ~'tura nf
framing

incoro'na|re vt crown. ~zi'one nf
coronation

incorpo'rar|e vt incorporate; ⟨me-
scolare⟩ blend. ~si vr blend; ⟨ter-
ritori:⟩ merge

incorreg'gibile a incorrigible

in'correre vt ~ in incur; ~ nel
pericolo di... run the risk of...

incorrut'tibile a incorruptible

incosci'en|te a unconscious;
⟨irresponsabile⟩ reckless ● nmf irresponsible person. ~za nf uncon-
sciousness; recklessness

inco'stan|te a changeable; ⟨per-

sona⟩ fickle. ~za nf changeable-
ness; ⟨di persona⟩ fickleness

incostituzio'nale a unconstitutional

incre'dibile a unbelievable, incredible

incredulità nf incredulity. in-
'credulo a incredulous

incremen'tare vt increase; ⟨inten-
sificare⟩ step up. incre'mento nm
increase. incremento demogra-
fico population growth

incresci'oso a regrettable

incre'spar|e vt ruffle; wrinkle
⟨tessuto⟩; make frizzy ⟨capelli⟩; ~e
la fronte frown. ~si vr ⟨acqua:⟩
ripple; ⟨tessuto:⟩ wrinkle; ⟨capel-
li:⟩ go frizzy

incrimi'na|re vt indict; fig incrimi-
nate. ~zi'one nf indictment

incri'na|re vt crack; fig affect
⟨amicizia⟩. ~rsi vr crack; ⟨amici-
zia:⟩ be affected. ~'tura nf crack

incroci'a|re vt cross ● vi Naut,
Aeron cruise. ~rsi vr cross.
~'tore nm cruiser

in'crocio nm crossing; ⟨di strade⟩
crossroads sg

incrol'labile a indestructible

incro'sta|re vt encrust. ~zi'one nf
encrustation

incuba'trice nf incubator.
~zi'one nf incubation

'incubo nm nightmare

in'cudine nf anvil

incu'rabile a incurable

incu'rante a careless

incurio'si|re vt make curious. ~si
vr become curious

incursi'one nf raid. ~ aerea air
raid

incurva'mento nm bending

incur'va|re vt, ~rsi vr bend.
~'tura nf bending

in'cusso pp di incutere

incusto'dito a unguarded

in'cutere vt arouse; ~ spavento a
qcno strike fear into sb

in'daco nm indigo

indaffa'rato a busy

inda'gare vt/i investigate

in'dagine *nf* research; (*giudiziaria*) investigation. **~ di mercato** market survey

indebi'tar|e *vt*, **~si** *vr* get into debt

in'debito *a* undue

indeboli'mento *nm* weakening

indebo'lir|e *vt*, **~si** *vr* weaken

inde'cen|te *a* indecent. **~za** *nf* indecency; (*vergogna*) disgrace

indeci'frabile *a* indecipherable

indecisi'one *nf* indecision. **inde'ciso** *a* undecided

inde'fesso *a* tireless

indefi'ni|bile *a* indefinable. **~to** *a* indefinite

indefor'mabile *a* crushproof

in'degno *a* unworthy

inde'lebile *a* indelible

indelica'tezza *nf* indelicacy; (*azione*) tactless act. **indeli'cato** *a* indiscreet; (*grossolano*) indelicate

indemoni'ato *a* possessed

in'denne *a* uninjured; (*da malattia*) unaffected. **~ità** *nf inv* allowance; (*per danni*) compensation. **~ità di trasferta** travel allowance. **~iz'zare** *vt* compensate. **~'nizzo** *nm* compensation

indero'gabile *a* binding

indescri'vibile *a* indescribable

indeside'rabile *a* undesirable. **~to** *a* (*figlio, ospite*) unwanted

indetermi'na|bile *a* indeterminable. **~'tezza** *nf* vagueness. **~to** *a* indeterminate

'India *nf* India. **i~'ano, -a** *a & nmf* Indian; **in fila i~ana** in single file

indiavo'lato *a* possessed; (*vivace*) wild

indi'ca|re *vt* show; indicate; (*col dito*) point at; (*far notare*) point out; (*consigliare*) advise. **~'tivo** *a* indicative ● *nm* Gram indicative. **~'tore** *nm* indicator; Techn gauge; (*prontuario*) directory. **~zi'one** *nf* indication; (*istruzione*) direction

'indice *nm* (*dito*) forefinger; (*lancetta*) pointer; (*di libro, statistica*) index; (*fig: segno*) sign

indi'cibile *a* inexpressible

indietreggi'are *vi* draw back; *Mil* retreat

indi'etro *adv* back, behind; **all'~** backwards; **avanti e ~** back and forth; **essere ~** be behind; (*mentalmente*) be backward; (*con pagamenti*) be in arrears; (*di orologio*) be slow; **fare marcia ~** reverse; **rimandare ~** send back; **rimanere ~** be left behind; **torna ~!** come back!

indi'feso *a* undefended; (*inerme*) helpless

indiffe'ren|te *a* indifferent; **mi è ~te** it is all the same to me. **~za** *nf* indifference

in'digeno, -a *a* indigenous ● *nmf* native

indi'gen|te *a* needy. **~za** *nf* poverty

indigesti'one *nf* indigestion. **indi'gesto** *a* indigestible

indi'gna|re *vt* make indignant. **~rsi** *vr* be indignant. **~to** *a* indignant. **~zi'one** *nf* indignation

indimenti'cabile *a* unforgettable

indipen'den|te *a* independent. **~te'mente** *adv* independently; **~temente dal tempo** regardless of the weather, whatever the weather. **~za** *nf* independence

in'dire *vt* announce

indiretta'mente *adv* indirectly. **indi'retto** *a* indirect

indiriz'zar|e *vt* address; (*mandare*) send; (*dirigere*) direct. **~si** *vr* direct one's steps. **indi'rizzo** *nm* address; (*direzione*) direction

indisci'plina *nf* lack of discipline. **~'nato** *a* undisciplined

indi'scre|to *a* indiscreet. **~zi'one** *nf* indiscretion

indiscrimi'nata'mente *adv* indiscriminately. **~'nato** *a* indiscriminate

indi'scusso *a* unquestioned

indiscu'ti|bile *a* unquestionable. **~'mente** *adv* unquestionably

indispen'sabile *a* essential, indispensable

indispet'tir|e *vt* irritate. **~si** *vr* get irritated

indi'spo|rre *vt* antagonize. **~sto** *pp di* **indisporre ● a** indisposed. **~sizi'one** *nf* indisposition

indisso'lubile *a* indissoluble

indissolubil'mente *adv* indissolubly

indistin'guibile *a* indiscernible

indistinta'mente *adv* without exception. **indi'stinto** *a* indistinct

indistrut'tibile *a* indestructible

indistur'bato *a* undisturbed

in'divia *nf* endive

individu'a|le *a* individual. **~'lista** *nmf* individualist. **~lità** *nf* individuality. **~re** *vt* individualize; *(localizzare)* locate; *(riconoscere)* single out

indi'viduo *nm* individual

indivi'sibile *a* indivisible. **indi'viso** *a* undivided

indizi'a|re *vt* throw suspicion on. **~to, -a** *a* suspected **●** *nmf* suspect. **in'dizio** *nm* sign; *Jur* circumstantial evidence

'indole *nf* nature

indo'len|te *a* indolent. **~za** *nf* indolence

indolenzi'mento *nm* stiffness

indolen'zi|rsi *vr* go stiff. **~to** *a* stiff

indo'lore *a* painless

indo'mani *nm* **l'~** the following day

Indo'nesia *nf* Indonesia

indo'rare *vt* gild

indos'sa|re *vt* wear; *(mettere addosso)* put on. **~'tore, ~'trice** *nmf* model

in'dotto *pp di* **indurre**

indottri'nare *vt* indoctrinate

indovi'n|are *vt* guess; *(predire)* foretell. **~ato** *a* successful; *(scelta)* well-chosen. **~ello** *nm* riddle. **indo'vino, -a** *nmf* fortune-teller

indubbia'mente *adv* undoubtedly. **in'dubbio** *a* undoubted

indugi'ar|e *vi*, **~si** *vr* linger. **in'dugio** *nm* delay

indul'gen|te *a* indulgent. **~za** *nf* indulgence

in'dul|gere *vi* **~gere a** indulge in. **~to** *pp di* **indulgere ●** *nm* *Jur* pardon

indu'mento *nm* garment; **indumenti** *pl* clothes

induri'mento *nm* hardening

indu'rir|e *vt*, **~si** *vr* harden

in'durre *vt* induce

in'dustri|a *nf* industry. **~'ale** *a* industrial **●** *nmf* industrialist

industrializ'za|re *vt* industrialize. **~to** *a* industrialized. **~zi'one** *nf* industrialization

industrial'mente *adv* industrially

industri'|arsi *vr* try one's hardest. **~'oso** *a* industrious

induzi'one *nf* induction

ine'bito *a* stunned

inebri'ante *a* intoxicating, exciting

inecce'pibile *a* unexceptionable

i'nedia *nf* starvation

i'nedito *a* unpublished

ineffi'cace *a* ineffective

ineffici'en|te *a* inefficient. **~za** *nf* inefficiency

ineguagli'abile *a* incomparable

inegu'ale *a* unequal; *(superficie)* uneven

inelut'tabile *a* inescapable

ine'rente *a* **~ a** concerning

i'nerme *a* unarmed; *fig* defenceless

inerpi'carsi *vr* su clamber up; *(pianta:)* climb up

i'ner|te *a* inactive; *Phys* inert. **~zia** *nf* inactivity; *Phys* inertia

inesat'tezza *nf* inaccuracy. **ine'satto** *a* inaccurate; *(erroneo)* incorrect; *(non riscosso)* uncollected

inesau'ribile *a* inexhaustible

inesi'sten|te *a* non-existent. **~za** *nf* non-existence

ineso'rabile *a* inexorable

inesperi'enza *nf* inexperience. **ine'sperto** *a* inexperienced

inespli'cabile *a* inexplicable

ine'sploso a unexploded
inespri'mibile a inexpressible
inesti'mabile a inestimable
inetti'tudine nf ineptitude. **i'netto**
a inept; **inetto a** unsuited to
ine'vaso a ⟨pratiche⟩ pending;
⟨corrispondenza⟩ unanswered
inevi'tabil|e a inevitable. **~'men-
te** adv inevitably
i'nezia nf trifle
infagot'tar|e vt wrap up. **~si** vr
wrap [oneself] up
infal'libile a infallible
infa'ma|re vt defame. **~'torio** a de-
famatory
in'fam|e a infamous; ⟨fam: orren-
do⟩ awful, shocking. **~ia** nf infamy
infan'garsi vr get muddy
infan'tile a ⟨letteratura, abbiglia-
mento⟩ children's; ⟨ingenuità⟩
childlike; pej childish
in'fanzia nf childhood; ⟨bambini⟩
children pl; **prima ~** infancy
infar'cire vt pepper ⟨discorso⟩ (di
with)
infari'na|re vt flour; **~re di** sprin-
kle with. **~'tura** nf fig smattering
in'farto nm coronary
infasti'dir|e vt irritate. **~si** vr get
irritated
infati'cabile a untiring
in'fatti conj as a matter of fact;
⟨veramente⟩ indeed
infatu'a|rsi vr become infatuated
(di with). **~to** a infatuated.
~zi'one nf infatuation
in'fausto a ill-omened
infe'condo a infertile
infe'del|e a unfaithful. **~tà** nf un-
faithfulness; **~** pl affairs
infe'lic|e a unhappy; ⟨inappropria-
to⟩ unfortunate; ⟨cattivo⟩ bad.
~ità nf unhappiness
infel'tri|rsi vr get matted. **~to** a
matted
inferi'or|e a ⟨più basso⟩ lower;
⟨qualità⟩ inferior ● nmf inferior.
~ità nf inferiority
inferme'ria nf infirmary; ⟨di nave⟩
sick-bay

infermi'er|a nf nurse. **~e** nm
[male] nurse
infermità nf sickness. **~ mentale**
mental illness. **in'fermo, -a** a sick
● nmf invalid
infer'nale a infernal; ⟨spaventoso⟩
hellish
in'ferno nm hell; **va all'~!** go to
hell!
infero'cirsi vr become fierce
inferri'ata nf grating
infervo'rar|e vt arouse enthusi-
asm in. **~si** vr get excited
infe'stare vt infest
infet'tar|e vt infect. **~arsi** vr be-
come infected. **~ivo** a infectious.
in'fetto a infected. **infezi'one** nf
infection
infiac'chir|e vt/i, **~si** vr weaken
infiam'mabile a [in]flammable
infiam'ma|re vt set on fire; Med,
fig inflame. **~rsi** vr catch fire; Med
become inflamed. **~zi'one** nf Med
inflammation
in'fido a treacherous
infie'rire vi ⟨imperversare⟩ rage; **~
su** attack furiously
in'figger|e vt drive. **~si** vr **~si in**
penetrate
infi'lar|e vt thread; ⟨mettere⟩ in-
sert; ⟨indossare⟩ put on. **~si** vr
slip on ⟨vestito⟩; **~si in** ⟨introdursi
in⟩ slip into
infil'tra|rsi vr infiltrate. **~zi'one**
nf infiltration; ⟨d'acqua⟩ seepage;
⟨Med: iniezione⟩ injection
infil'zare vt pierce; ⟨infilare⟩
string; ⟨conficcare⟩ stick
'infimo a lowest
in'fine adv finally; ⟨insomma⟩ in
short
infinità nf infinity; **un'~ di** masses
of. **~'mente** adv infinitely.
infi'nito a infinite; Gram infinitive ● nm infinite; Gram infinitive; Math infinity; **all'infinito**
endlessly
infinocchi'are vt fam hoodwink
infischi'arsi vr **~ di** not care
about; **me ne infischio** fam I
couldn't care less

in'fisso pp di **infiggere** ● nm fixture; (di porta, finestra) frame

infit'tire vt/i, ~si vr thicken

infla zi'one nf inflation

infles'sibile a inflexible. ~ità nf inflexibility

infles si'one nf inflexion

in'fli|ggere vt inflict. ~tto pp di **infliggere**

influ'en|te a influential. ~za nf influence; Med influenza

influen'za|bile a (mente, opinione) impressionable. ~re vt influence. ~to a (malato) with the flu

influ'ire vi ~ su influence

in'flusso nm influence

info'carsi vr catch fire; (viso:) go red; (discussione:) become heated

info'gnarsi vr fam get into a mess

infol'tire vt/i thicken

infon'dato a unfounded

in'fondere vt instil

infor'care vt fork up; get on (bici); put on (occhiali)

infor'male a informal

infor'ma|re vt inform. ~rsi vr inquire (di about). ~'tivo a informative.

infor'matic|a nf computing, IT. ~o a computer attrib

infor'ma|tivo a informative. infor'mato a informed; **male informa**'mato a informed; (di polizia) informer. ~'tore, ~'trice (di polizia) informer. ~zi'one nf information (solo sg); un'~zi'one a piece of information

in'forme a shapeless

infor'nare vt put into the oven

infortu'narsi vr have an accident.

infor'tu|nio nm accident. ~nio sul lavoro industrial accident. ~'nistica nf study of industrial accidents

infos'sa|rsi vr sink; (guance, occhi:) become hollow. ~to a sunken, hollow

infradici'ar|e vt drench. ~si vr get drenched; (diventare marcio) rot

infra'dito nm inv (scarpe) flip-flop

in'frang|ere vt break; (in mille pezzi) shatter. ~ersi vr break. ~'gibile a unbreakable

in'franto pp di **infrangere** ● a shattered; (fig: cuore) broken

infra'rosso a infra-red

infrastrut'tura nf infrastructure

infrazi'one nf offence

infredda'tura nf cold

infreddo'li|rsi vr feel cold. ~to a cold

infrut'tuoso a fruitless

infuo'ca|re vt make red-hot. ~to a burning

infu'ori adv all'~ outwards; all'~ di except

infuri'ar|e vi rage. ~rsi vr fly into a rage. ~to a blustering

infusi'one nf infusion. in'fuso pp di **infondere** ● nm infusion

Ing. abbr ingegnere

ingabbi'are vt cage; (fig: mettere in prigione) jail

ingaggi'are vt engage; sign up (calciatori ecc); begin (lotta, battaglia). in'gaggio nm engagement; (di calciatore) signing [up]

ingan'nar|e vt deceive; (essere infedele a) be unfaithful to. ~si vr deceive oneself; **se non m'inganno** if I am not mistaken

ingan'nevole a deceptive. in'ganno nm deceit; (frode) fraud

ingarbugli'ar|e vt entangle; (confondere) confuse. ~rsi vr get entangled; (confondersi) become confused. ~to a confused

inge'gnarsi vr do one's best

inge'gnere nm engineer. ingegne'ria nf engineering

in'gegno nm brains pl; (genio) genius; (abilità) ingenuity. ~sa'mente adv ingeniously

ingegnosità nf ingenuity. inge'gnoso a ingenious

ingelo'sir|e vt make jealous. ~si vr become jealous

in'gente a huge

ingenu'a|mente adv artlessly. ~ità nf ingenuousness. in'genuo a ingenuous; (credulone) naïve

inge'renza nf interference

inge'rire *vt* swallow

inges'sa|re *vt* put in plaster. ~'tura *nf* plaster

Inghil'terra *nf* England

inghiot'tire *vt* swallow

in'ghippo *nm* trick

ingial'li|re *vi*, ~rsi *vr* turn yellow. ~to *a* yellowed

ingigan'tir|e *vt* magnify ● *vi*, ~si *vr* grow to enormous proportions

inginocchi'ar|si *vr* kneel [down]. ~to *a* kneeling. ~'toio *nm* prie-dieu

ingioiel'larsi *vr* put on one's jewels

ingiù *adv* down; all'~ downwards; a testa ~ head downwards

ingi'un|gere *vt* order. ~zi'one *nf* injunction. ~zione di pagamento final demand

ingi'uri|a *nf* insult; (*torto*) wrong; (*danno*) damage. ~'are *vt* insult; (*fare un torto a*) wrong. ~'oso *a* insulting

ingiusta'mente *adv* unjustly, unfairly. ingiu'stizia *nf* injustice. ingi'usto *a* unjust, unfair

in'glese *a* English ● *nm* Englishman; (*lingua*) English ● *nf* Englishwoman

ingoi'are *vt* swallow

ingol'far|e *vt* flood (*motore*). ~si *vr* fig get involved; (*motore*) flood

ingom'bra|nte *a* cumbersome. ~re *vt* clutter up; fig cram (*mente*)

in'gombro *nm* encumbrance; essere d'~ be in the way

ingor'digia *nf* greed. in'gordo *a* greedy

ingor'gar|e *vt* block. ~si *vr* be blocked [up]. in'gorgo *nm* blockage; (*del traffico*) jam

ingoz'zar|e *vt* gobble up; (*nutrire eccessivamente*) stuff; fatten (*animali*). ~si *vr* stuff oneself (di with)

ingra'na|ggio *nm* gear; fig mechanism. ~re *vt* engage ● *vi* be in gear

ingrandi'mento *nm* enlargement

ingran'dire *vt* enlarge; (*esagera-*

re) magnify. ~rsi *vr* become larger; (*aumentare*) increase

ingras'sar|e *vt* fatten up; *Mech* grease ● *vi*, ~si *vr* put on weight

ingrati'tudine *nf* ingratitude. in'grato *a* ungrateful; (*sgradevole*) thankless

ingrazi'arsi *vr* ingratiate oneself with

ingredi'ente *nm* ingredient

in'gresso *nm* entrance; (*accesso*) admittance; (*sala*) hall; ~ gratuito/libero admission free; vietato l'~ no entry; no admittance

ingros'sar|e *vt* make big; (*gonfiare*) swell ● *vi*, ~si *vr* grow big; (*gonfiare*) swell

in'grosso: all'~ *adv* wholesale; (*pressappoco*) roughly

ingua'ribile *a* incurable

'inguine *nm* groin

ingurgi'tare *vt* gulp down

ini'bi|re *vt* inhibit; (*vietare*) forbid. ~to *a* inhibited. ~zi'one *nf* inhibition; (*divieto*) prohibition

iniet'tar|e *vt* inject. ~si di sangue (*occhi*:) become bloodshot. iniezi'one *nf* injection

inimic'arsi *vr* make an enemy of. inimi'cizia *nf* enmity

inimi'tabile *a* inimitable

interrot'ta|mente *adv* continuously. ~'rotto *a* continuous

iniquità *nf* iniquity. in'iquo *a* iniquitous

inizi'al|e *a & nf* initial. ~'mente *adv* initially

inizi'ar|e *vt* begin; (*avviare*) open; ~ qcno a qcsa initiate sb in sth ● *vi* begin

inizia'tiva *nf* initiative; prendere l'~ take the initiative

inizi'a|to, -a *a* initiated ● *nmf* initiate; gli ~ti the initiated. ~'tore, ~'trice *nmf* initiator. ~zi'one *nf* initiation

i'nizio *nm* beginning, start; dare ~ a start; avere ~ get under way

innaffi'a|re *vt* water. ~'toio *nm* watering-can

innal'zar|e vt raise; (*erigere*) erect. **~si** vr rise

innamo'ra|rsi vr fall in love (**di** with). **~ta** nf girl-friend. **~to** a in love ● nm boy-friend

in'nanzi adv (*stato in luogo*) in front; (*di tempo*) ahead; (*avanti*) forward; (*prima*) before; **d'ora ~** from now on ● prep (*prima*) before; **~ a** in front of. **~'tutto** adv first of all; (*soprattutto*) above all

in'nato a innate

inne'gabile a undeniable

innervo'sir|e vt make nervous. **~si** vr get irritated

inne'scare vt prime. **in'nesco** nm primer

inne'stare vt graft; *Mech* engage; (*inserire*) insert. **in'nesto** nm graft; *Mech* clutch; *Electr* connection

inne'vato a covered in snow

'inno nm hymn. **~ nazionale** national anthem

inno'cen|te a innocent **~te'mente** adv innocently. **~za** nf innocence.

in'nocuo a innocuous

inno'va|re vt make changes in. **~'tivo** a innovative. **~'tore** a trail-blazing. **~zi'one** nf innovation

innume'revole a innumerable

ino'doro a odourless

inoffen'sivo a harmless

inol'trar|e vt forward. **~si** vr advance

inol'trato a late

i'noltre adv besides

inon'da|re vt flood. **~zi'one** nf flood

inope'roso a idle

inoppor'tuno a untimely

inorgo'glir|e vt make proud. **~si** vr become proud

inorri'dire vt horrify ● vi be horrified

inospi'tale a inhospitable

inosser'vato a unobserved; (*non rispettato*) disregarded; **passare ~** go unnoticed

inossi'dabile a stainless

'inox a inv (*acciaio*) stainless

inqua'dra|re vt frame; *fig* put in context (*scrittore, problema*). **~rsi** vr fit into. **~'tura** nf framing

inqualifi'cabile a unspeakable

inquie'tar|e vt worry. **~si** get worried; (*impazientirsi*) get cross. **inqui'eto** a restless; (*preoccupato*) worried. **inquie'tudine** nf anxiety

inqui'lino, ~a nmf tenant

inquina'mento nm pollution

inqui'na|re vt pollute. **~to** a polluted

inqui'rente a *Jur* (*magistrato*) examining; **commissione ~** commission of enquiry

inqui'si|re vt/i investigate. **~to** a under investigation. **~'tore, ~'trice** a inquiring ● nmf inquisitor. **~zi'one** nf inquisition

insabbi'are vt shelve

insa'lat|a nf salad. **~a belga** endive. **~i'era** nf salad bowl

insa'lubre a unhealthy

insa'nabile a incurable

insangui'na|re vt cover with blood. **~to** a bloody

insapo'nare vt soap

insa'pore a tasteless. **~'rire** vt flavour

insa'puta nf all'~ **di** unknown to

insazi'abile a insatiable

insce'nare vt stage

inscin'dibile a inseparable

insedia'mento nm installation

insedi'ar|e vt install. **~si** vr install oneself

in'segna nf sign; (*bandiera*) flag; (*decorazione*) decoration; (*emblema*) insignia pl; (*stemma*) symbol. **~ luminosa** neon sign

insegna'mento nm teaching. **inse'gnante** a teaching ● nmf teacher

inse'gnare vt/i teach; **~ qcsa a qcno** teach sb sth

insegui'mento nmf pursuit

insegu'i|re vt pursue. **~'tore, ~'trice** nmf pursuer

inselvati'chir|e vt make wild ● vi, **~si** vr grow wild

insemi'na|re *vt* inseminate. **~zi'one** *nf* insemination. **~zione artifi'ciale** artificial insemination

insena'tura *nf* inlet

insen'sato *a* senseless; *(folle)* crazy

insen'sibil|e *a* insensitive; *(braccio ecc)* numb. **~ità** *nf* insensitivity

insepa'rabile *a* inseparable

inseri'mento *nm* insertion

inse'rir|e *vt* insert; place *(annuncio)*; *Electr* connect. **~si** *vr* **~si in** get into. **in'serto** *nm* file; *(in un film ecc)* insert

inservi'ente *nmf* attendant

inserzi'o|ne *nf* insertion; *(avviso)* advertisement. **~nista** *nmf* advertiser

insetti'cida *nm* insecticide

in'setto *nm* insect

insicu'rezza *nf* insecurity. **insi'curo** *a* insecure

in'sidi|a *nf* trick; *(tranello)* snare. **~'are** *vt/i* lay a trap for. **~'oso** *a* insidious

insi'eme *adv* together; *(contemporaneamente)* at the same time ● *prep* **~ a** [together] with ● *nm* whole; *(completo)* outfit; *Theat* ensemble; *Math* set; **nell'~** as a whole; **tutto ~** all together; *(bere)* at one go

in'signe *a* renowned

insignifi'cante *a* insignificant

insi'gnire *vt* decorate

insinda'cabile *a* final

insinu'ante *a* insinuating

insinu'a|re *vt* insinuate. **~rsi** *vr* penetrate; **~rsi in** *fig* creep into. **~zi'one** *nf* insinuation

in'sipido *a* insipid

insi'sten|te *a* insistent. **~te'mente** *adv* repeatedly. **~za** *nf* insistence. **in'sistere** *vi* insist; *(perseverare)* persevere

insoddisfa'cente *a* unsatisfactory

insoddi'sfa|tto *a* unsatisfied; *(scontento)* dissatisfied. **~zi'one** *nf* dissatisfaction

insoffe'ren|te *a* intolerant. **~za** *nf* intolerance

insolazi'one *nf* sunstroke

inso'len|te *a* rude, insolent. **~za** *nf* rudeness, insolence; *(commento)* insolent remark

in'solito *a* unusual

inso'lubile *a* insoluble

inso'luto *a* unsolved; *(non pagato)* unpaid

insol'venza *nf* insolvency

in'somma *adv* in short; **~!** well really!; *(così così)* so so

in'sonne *a* sleepless. **~ia** *nf* insomnia

insonno'lito *a* sleepy

insonoriz'zato *a* soundproofed

insoppor'tabile *a* unbearable

insor'genza *nf* onset

in'sorgere *vi* revolt, rise up; *(sorgere)* arise; *(difficoltà)* crop up

insormon'tabile *a* (ostacolo, difficoltà) insurmountable

in'sorto *pp di* **insorgere** ● *a* rebellious ● *nm* rebel

insospet'tabile *a* unsuspected

insospet'tir|e *vt* make suspicious ● *vi*, **~si** *vr* become suspicious

insoste'nibile *a* untenable; *(insopportabile)* unbearable

insosti'tuibile *a* irreplaceable

inspe'ra|bile *a* una sua vittoria è **~bile** there is no hope of him winning. **~to** *a* unhoped-for

inspie'gabile *a* inexplicable

inspi'rare *vt* breathe in

in'stabil|e *a* unstable; *(tempo)* changeable. **~ità** *nf* instability; *(di tempo)* changeability

instal'la|re *vt* install. **~rsi** *vr* settle in. **~zi'one** *nf* installation

instan'cabile *a* untiring

instau'ra|re *vt* found. **~rsi** *vr* become established. **~zi'one** *nf* foundation

instra'dare *vt* direct

insù *adv* **all'~** upwards

insubordinazi'one *nf* insubordination

insuc'cesso *nm* failure

insudici'ar|e *vt* dirty. **~si** *vr* get dirty

insuffici'en|te *a* insufficient; (*inadeguato*) inadequate ● *nf* *Sch* fail. **~za** *nf* insufficiency; (*inadeguatezza*) inadequacy; *Sch* fail. **~za cardiaca** heart failure. **~za di prove** lack of evidence

insu'lare *a* insular

insu'lina *nf* insulin

in'sulso *a* insipid; (*sciocco*) silly

insul'tare *vt* insult. **in'sulto** *nm* insult

insupe'rabile *a* insuperable; (*eccezionale*) incomparable

insurrezi'one *nf* insurrection

insussi'stente *a* groundless

intac'care *vt* nick; (*corrodere*) corrode; draw on ⟨*capitale*⟩; (*danneggiare*) damage

intagli'are *vt* carve. **in'taglio** *nm* carving

intan'gibile *a* untouchable

in'tanto *adv* meanwhile; (*per ora*) for the moment; (*avversativo*) but; **~ che** while

intarsi'a|re *vt* inlay. **~to** *a* **~to di** inset with. **in'tarsio** *nm* inlay

inta'sa|re *vt* clog; block ⟨*traffico*⟩. **~rsi** *vr* get blocked. **~to** *a* blocked

inta'scare *vt* pocket

in'tatto *a* intact

intavo'lare *vt* start

inte'gra|le *a* whole; **edizione ~le** unabridged edition; **pane ~le** wholemeal bread. **~l'mente** *adv* fully. **~nte** *a* integral. **'integro** *a* complete; (*retto*) upright

inte'gra|re *vt* integrate; (*aggiungere*) supplement. **~rsi** *vr* integrate. **~'tivo** *a* ⟨*corso*⟩ supplementary. **~zi'one** *nf* integration

integrità *nf* integrity

intelaia'tura *nf* framework

intel'letto *nm* intellect

intellettu'al|e *a* & *nmf* intellectual. **~'mente** *adv* intellectually

intelli'gen|te *a* intelligent. **~te-'mente** *adv* intelligently. **~za** *nf* intelligence

intelli'gibil|e *a* intelligible. **~'mente** *adv* intelligibly

intempe'ranza *nf* intemperance

intem'perie *nfpl* bad weather

inten'den|te *nm* superintendent. **~za** *nf* **~za di finanza** inland revenue office

in'tender|e *vt* (*comprendere*) understand; (*udire*) hear; (*avere intenzione*) intend; (*significare*) mean. **~sela con** have an understanding with; **~si** *vr* (*capirsi*) understand each other; **~si di** (*essere esperto*) have a good knowledge of

intendi'mento *nm* understanding; (*intenzione*) intention. **~'tore**, **~'trice** *nmf* connoisseur

intene'rir|e *vt* soften; (*commuovere*) touch. **~si** *vr* be touched

intensa'mente *adv* intensely

intensifi'car|e *vt*, **~si** *vr* intensify

intensità *nf inv* intensity. **inten-'sivo** *a* intensive. **in'tenso** *a* intense

inten'tare *vt* start up; **~ causa contro qcno** bring *o* institute proceedings against sb

in'tento *a* engrossed (**a** in) ● *nm* purpose

intenzio'nato *a* **essere ~ a fare qcsa** have the intention of doing sth

intenzio'nale *a* intentional. **intenzi'one** *nf* intention; **senza ~ne** unintentionally; **avere ~ne di fare qcsa** intend to do sth, have the intention of doing sth.

intera'gire *vi* interact

intera'mente *adv* completely, entirely

interat'tivo *a* interactive. **~zi'one** *nf* interaction

interca'lare[1] *nm* stock phrase

interca'lare[2] *vt* insert

intercambi'abile *a* interchangeable

interca'pedine *nf* cavity

inter'ce|dere *vi* intercede. **~ssi'o-ne** *nf* intercession

intercet'ta|re *vt* intercept; tap ⟨*telefono*⟩. **~zi'one** *nf* interception. **~zione telefonica** telephone tapping

inter'city nm inv inter-city

intercontinen'tale a intercontinental

inter'correre vi (tempo:) elapse; (esistere) exist

interco'stale a intercostal

inter'detto pp di **interdire** ● a astonished; (proibito) forbidden; **rimanere ~** be taken aback

inter'di|re vt forbid; Jur deprive of civil rights. **~zi'one** nf prohibition

interessa'mento nm interest

interes'sante a interesting; **essere in stato ~** be pregnant

interes'sa|re vt interest; (riguardare) concern ● vi **~re a** be a matter to. **~rsi** vr **~rsi a** take an interest in. **~rsi di** take care of. **~to, -a** nmf interested party ● a interested; **essere ~to** pej have an interest

inte'resse nm interest; **fare qcsa per ~** do sth out of self-interest

inter'faccia nf Comput interface

interfe'renza nf interference

interfe'ri|re vi interfere

interi'ora nfpl entrails

interi'ore a interior

inter'ludio nm interlude

intermedi'ario, -a a & nmf intermediary

inter'medio a in-between

inter'mezzo nm Theat, Mus intermezzo

intermi'nabile a interminable

intermit'ten|te a intermittent; (luce) flashing. **~za** nf luce a **~za** flashing light

interna'mento nm internment; (in manicomio) committal

inter'nare vt intern; (in manicomio) commit [to a mental institution]

in'terno a internal; Geog inland; (interiore) inner; (politica) national; **alunno ~** boarder ● nm interior; (di condominio) flat; Teleph extension; Cinema interior shot; **all'~** inside

internazio'nale a international

in'tero a whole, entire; (intatto) intact; (completo) complete; **per ~** in full

interpel'lare vt consult

inter'por|re vt place (ostacolo). **~si** vr come between

interpre'ta|re vt interpret; Mus perform; **~zi'one** nf interpretation; Mus performance. **in'terprete** nmf interpreter; Mus performer

inter'ra|re vt (seppellire) bury; plant (pianta, seme). **~to** nm basement

interro'ga|re vt question; Sch test; examine (studenti). **~'tivo** a interrogative; (sguardo) questioning; **punto ~tivo** question mark ● nm question. **~'torio** a & nm questioning. **~zi'one** nf Sch oral [test]

inter'romper|e vt interrupt; (sospendere) stop; cut off (collegamento). **~si** vr break off

interrut'tore nm switch

interruzi'one nf interruption; **senza ~** non-stop. **~ di gravidanza** termination of pregnancy

interse'ca|re vt, **~'carsi** vr intersect. **~zi'one** nf intersection

inter'stizio nm interstice

interur'ban|a nf long-distance call. **~o** a inter-city; **telefonata ~a** long-distance call

interval'lare vt space out. **inter'vallo** nm interval; (spazio) space; Sch break. **intervallo pubblicitario** commercial break

interve'nire vi intervene; (Med: operare) operate; **~ a** take part in. **inter'vento** nm intervention; (presenza) presence; (chirurgico) operation; **pronto intervento** emergency services

inter'vista nf interview. **~'tore, ~'trice** nmf interviewer

in'tes|a nf understanding; **cenno**

d'~a acknowledgement. ~o pp di **intendere** ●a **resta** ~o **che...** needless to say,...; ~il agreed!; ~o a meant to; **non darsi per** ~o refuse to understand

inte'sta|re vt head; write one's name and address at the top of (lettera); Comm register. ~**rsi a fare qcsa** take it into one's head to do sth. ~**'tario, -a** nmf holder. ~**zi'one** nf heading; (su carta da lettere) letterhead

intesti'nale a intestinal

inte'stino a (lotte) internal ●nm intestine

intima'mente adv (conoscere) intimately

inti'ma|re vt order; ~**re l'alt a qcno** order sb to stop. ~**zi'one** nf order

intimi'di|torio a threatening. ~**zi'one** nf intimidation

intimi'dire vt intimidate

intimità nf cosiness. 'i**ntimo** a intimate; (interno) innermost; (amico) close ●nm (amico) close friend; (dell'animo) heart

intimo'ri|re vt frighten. ~**rsi** vr get frightened. ~**to** a frightened

in'tingere vt dip

in'tingolo nm sauce; (pietanza) stew

intiriz'zi|re vt numb. ~**rsi a essere** ~**to** (dal freddo) be perished

intito'lar|e vt entitle; (dedicare) dedicate. ~**si** vr be called

intolle'rabile a intolerable

intona'care vt plaster. **in'tonaco** nm plaster

into'na|re vt start to sing; tune (strumento); (accordare) match. ~**rsi** vr match. ~**to** a (persona) able to sing in tune; (colore) matching

intonazi'one nf (inflessione) intonation; (ironico) tone

inton'ti|re vt (droga; gas:) make dizzy ●vi be dazed. ~**to** a dazed

intop'pare vi ~ in run into

in'toppo nm obstacle

in'torno adv around ●prep ~ a around; (circa) about

intorpi'di|re vt numb. ~**rsi** vr become numb. ~**to** a torpid

intossi'ca|re vt poison. ~**rsi** vr be poisoned. ~**zi'one** nf poisoning

intralci'are vt hamper

in'tralcio nm hitch; **essere d'~** be a hindrance (a to)

intrallaz'zare vi intrigue. **intral-'lazzo** nm racket

intramon'tabile a timeless

intramusco'lare a intramuscular

intransi'gen|te a intransigent, uncompromising. ~**za** nf intransigence

intransi'tivo a intransitive

intrappo'lato a **rimanere ~** be trapped

intrapren'den|te a enterprising. ~**za** nf initiative

intra'prendere vt undertake

intrat'tabile a very difficult

intratte'ner|e vt entertain. ~**ersi** vr linger. ~**i'mento** nm entertainment

intrave'dere vt catch a glimpse of; (presagire) foresee

intrecci'ar|e vt interweave; plait (capelli, corda); intertwine; (aggrovigliarsi) become tangled; ~**e le mani** clasp one's hands

in'treccio nm (trama) plot

in'trepido a intrepid

intri'cato a tangled

intri'gante a scheming; (affascinante) intriguing

intri'ga|re vt entangle; (incuriosire) intrigue ●vi intrigue, scheme. ~**rsi** vr meddle. **in'trigo** nm plot; **intrighi** pl intrigues

in'trinseco a intrinsic

in'triso a ~ **di** soaked in

intri'stirsi vr grow sad

intro'du|rre vt introduce; (inserire) insert; ~**rre a** (iniziare a) introduce to. ~**rsi** vr get in (in to). ~**t'tivo** a (pagine, discorso) introductory. ~**zi'one** nf introduction in'troito nm income, revenue; (incasso) takings pl

intro'metter|e vt introduce. ~si vr interfere; (interporsi) intervene. intromissi'one nf intervention

intro'vabile a that can't be found; (prodotto) unobtainable

intro'verso, -a a introverted ● nmf introvert

intrufo'larsi vr sneak in

in'truglio nm concoction

intrusi'one nf intrusion. in'truso, -a nmf intruder

intu'i|re vt perceive

intui'tiva'mente adv intuitively. ~'tivo a intuitive. in'tuito nm intuition. ~zi'one nf intuition

inuguagli'anza nf inequality

inu'mano a inhuman

inu'mare vt inter

inumi'dir|e vt dampen; moisten (labbra). ~si vr become damp

i'nutil|e a useless; (superfluo) unnecessary. ~ità nf uselessness

inutiliz'za|bile a unusable. ~to a unused

inutil'mente adv fruitlessly

inva'dente a intrusive

in'vadere vt invade; (affollare) overrun

invali'd|are vt invalidate. ~ità nf disability; Jur invalidity. in'valido, -a a invalid; (handicappato) disabled ● nmf disabled person

in'vano adv in vain

invari'abil|e a invariable

invari'ato a unchanged

invasi'one nf invasion. in'vaso pp di invadere. inva'sore a invading ● nm invader

invecchia'mento nm (di vino) maturation

invecchi'are vt/i age

in'vece adv instead; (anzi) but; ~ di instead of

inve'ire vi ~ contro inveigh against

inven'd|ibile a unsaleable. ~uto a unsold

inven'tare vt invent

inventari'are vt make an inventory of. inven'tario nm inventory

inven'tivo, -a a inventive ● nf inventiveness. ~'tore, ~'trice nmf inventor. ~zi'one nf invention

inver'nale a wintry. in'verno nm winter

invero'simile a improbable

inversa'mente adv inversely; ~ proporzionale in inverse proportion

inversi'one nf inversion; Mech reversal. in'verso a inverse; (opposto) opposite ● nm opposite

inverte'brato a ● nm invertebrate

inver'ti|re vt reverse; (capovolgere) turn upside down. ~to, -a nmf homosexual

investi'ga|re vt investigate. ~'tore nm investigator. ~zi'one nf investigation

investi'mento nm investment; (incidente) crash

inve'sti|re vt invest; (urtare) collide with; (travolgere) run over; ~re qcno di invest sb with. ~'tura nf investiture

invet'tiva nf invective

invi'a|re vt send. ~to, -a nmf envoy; (di giornale) correspondent

invidi|a nf envy. ~'are vt envy. ~'oso a envious

invigo'ri|re vt invigorate. ~si vr become strong

invin'cibile a invincible

in'vio nm dispatch; Comput enter

invio'labile a inviolable

invipe'ri|rsi vr get nasty. ~to a furious

invi'sibil|e a invisible. ~ità nf invisibility

invi'tante a (piatto, profumo) enticing

invi'ta|re vt invite. ~to, -a nmf guest. in'vito nm invitation

invo'ca|re vt invoke; (implorare) beg. ~zi'one nf invocation

invogli'ar|e vt tempt; (indurre) induce. ~si vr ~si di take a fancy to

involon|taria'mente adv involuntarily. ~'tario a involuntary

invol'tino *nm* Culin beef olive

in'volto *nm* parcel; ⟨*fagotto*⟩ bundle

in'volucro *nm* wrapping

invulne'rabile *a* invulnerable

inzacche'rare *vt* splash with mud

inzup'par|e *vt* soak; ⟨*intingere*⟩ dip. **~si** *vr* get soaked

'io *pers pron* I; **chi è?** – [**sono**] **~** who is it? – [it's] me; **l'ho fatto io** [**stesso**] I did it myself ● *nm* **l'~** the ego

i'odio *nm* iodine

l'onio *nm* lo **~** the Ionian [Sea]

i'osa: a ~ *adv* in abundance

iperat'tivo *a* hyperactive

ipermer'cato *nm* hypermarket

iper'metrope *a* long-sighted

ipersen'sibile *a* hypersensitive

ipertensi'one *nf* high blood pressure

ip'no|si *nf* hypnosis. **~tico** *a* hypnotic. **~'tismo** *nm* hypnotism. **~tiz'zare** *vt* hypnotize

ipoca'lorico *a* low-calorie

ipocon'driaco, -a *a & nmf* hypochondriac

ipocri'sia *nf* hypocrisy. **i'pocrita** *a* hypocritical ● *nmf* hypocrite

ipo'te|ca *nf* mortgage. **~'care** *vt* mortgage

i'potesi *nf inv* hypothesis; ⟨*caso, eventualità*⟩ eventuality. **ipo'teti-co** *a* hypothetical. **ipotiz'zare** *vt* hypothesize

'ippico, -a *a* horse *attrib* ● *nf* riding

ippo'castano *nm* horse-chestnut

ip'podromo *nm* racecourse

ippo'potamo *nm* hippopotamus

'ira *nf* anger. **~'scibile** *a* irascible

i'rato *a* irate

'iride *nf* Anat iris; ⟨*arcobaleno*⟩ rainbow

Ir'landa *nf* Ireland. **~da del Nord** Northern Ireland. **i~'dese** *a* Irish ● *nm* Irishman; ⟨*lingua*⟩ Irish ● *nf* Irishwoman

iro'nia *nf* irony. **i'ronico** *a* ironic[al]

irradi'a|re *vt/i* radiate. **~zi'one** *nf* radiation

irraggiun'gibile *a* unattainable

irragio'nevole *a* unreasonable; ⟨*speranza, timore*⟩ irrational; ⟨*assurdo*⟩ absurd

irrazio'nal|e *a* irrational. **~ità** *a* irrationality. **~'mente** *adv* irrationally

irre'ale *a* unreal. **~'listico** *a* unrealistic. **~liz'zabile** *a* unattainable. **~ltà** *nf* unreality

irrecupe'rabile *a* irrecoverable

irrego'lar|e *a* irregular. **~ità** *nf inv* irregularity

irremo'vibile *a fig* adamant

irrepa'rabile *a* irreparable

irrepe'ribile *a* not to be found; **sarò ~** I won't be contactable

irrepren'sibile *a* irreproachable

irrepri'mibile *a* irrepressible

irrequi'eto *a* restless

irresi'stibile *a* irresistible

irrespon'sabil|e *a* irresponsible. **~ità** *nf* irresponsibility

irrever'sibile *a* irreversible

irrevo'cabile *a* irrevocable

irricono'scibile *a* unrecognizable

irri'ga|re *vt* irrigate; ⟨*fiume:*⟩ flow through. **~zi'one** *nf* irrigation

irrigidi'mento *nm* stiffening

irrigi'dir|e *vt*, **~si** *vr* stiffen

irrile'vante *a* unimportant

irrime'diabile *a* irreparable

irripe'tibile *a* unrepeatable

irri'sorio *a* derisive; ⟨*differenza, particolare, somma*⟩ insignificant

irri'tabile *a* irritable. **~nte** *a* aggravating

irri'ta|re *vt* irritate. **~rsi** *vr* get annoyed. **~to** *a* irritated; ⟨*gola*⟩ sore. **~zi'one** *nf* irritation

irrobu'stir|e *vt* fortify. **~si** *vr* get stronger

ir'rompere *vi* burst ⟨**in** into⟩

irro'rare *vt* sprinkle

irru'ente *a* impetuous

irruzi'one *nf* fare **~ in** burst into

i'scritto, -a *pp di* **iscrivere** ● *a* registered ● *nmf* member; **per ~** in writing

i'scriver|e *vt* register. **~si** *vr* **si a** register at, enrol at ⟨*scuola*⟩; join

⟨*circolo ecc*⟩. **iscrizi'one** *nf* registration; ⟨*epigrafe*⟩ inscription

i'sla|mico *a* Islamic. **~'mismo** *nm* Islam

I'slan|da *nf* Iceland. **i~'dese** *a* Icelandic ● *nmf* Icelander

'isola *nf* island. **le isole britanniche** the British Isles. **~ pedonale** traffic island. **~ spartitraffico** traffic island. **iso'lano, -a** *a* insular ● *nmf* islander

iso'lante *a* insulating ● *nm* insulator

iso'la|re *vt* isolate; *Mech, Electr* insulate; ⟨*acusticamente*⟩ soundproof. **~to** *a* isolated ● *nm* ⟨*di appartamenti*⟩ block

ispes'sir|e *vt, ~si* *vr* thicken

is'petto'rato *nm* inspectorate. **ispet'tore** *nm* inspector. **ispezio'nare** *vt* inspect. **ispezi'one** *nf* inspection

'ispido *a* bristly

ispi'ra|re *vt* inspire; suggest ⟨*idea, soluzione*⟩. **~rsi** *vr* **~rsi a** be based on. **~to** *a* inspired. **~zi'one** *nf* inspiration; ⟨*idea*⟩ idea

Isra'el|e *nm* Israel. **i~i'ano, -a** *a* & *nmf* Israeli

is'sare *vt* hoist

istan'taneo, -a *a* instantaneous ● *nf* snapshot

i'stante *nm* instant; **all'~** instantly

i'stanza *nf* petition

i'sterico *a* hysterical. **iste'rismo** *nm* hysteria

isti'ga|re *vt* instigate; **~re qcno al male** incite sb to evil. **~'tore, ~'trice** *nmf* instigator. **~zi'one** *nf* instigation

istin'tiva'mente *adv* instinctively. **~'tivo** *a* instinctive. **i'stinto** *nm* instinct; **d'istinto** instinctively

istitu'ire *vt* institute; ⟨*fondare*⟩ found; initiate ⟨*manifestazione*⟩

isti'tu|to *nm* institute; ⟨*universitario*⟩ department; *Sch* secondary school. **~to di bellezza** beauty salon. **~'tore, ~'trice** *nmf* ⟨*insegnante*⟩ tutor; ⟨*fondatore*⟩ founder

istituzio'nale *a* institutional. **istituzi'one** *nf* institution

'istmo *nm* isthmus

'istrice *nm* porcupine

istru'i|re *vt* instruct; ⟨*addestrare*⟩ train; ⟨*informare*⟩ inform; *Jur* prepare. **~to** *a* educated

istrut'tivo *a* instructive. **~ore, ~rice** *nmf* instructor; **giudice ~ore** examining magistrate. **~oria** *nf Jur* investigation. **istruzi'one** *nf* education; ⟨*indicazione*⟩ instruction

I'tali|a *nf* Italy. **i~'ano, -a** *a* & *nmf* Italian

itine'rario *nm* route, itinerary

itte'rizia *nf* jaundice

'ittico *a* fishing *attrib*

I.V.A. *nf abbr* (**imposta sul valore aggiunto**) VAT

Jj

jack *nm inv* jack

jazz *nm* jazz. **jaz'zista** *nmf* jazz player

jeep *nf inv* jeep

'jolly *nm inv* ⟨*carta da gioco*⟩ joker

Jugo'slav|ia *nf* Yugoslavia. **j~o, -a** *a* & *nmf* Yugoslav[ian]

ju'niores *nmfpl Sport* juniors

Kk

ka'jal *nm inv* kohl

kara'oke *nm inv* karaoke

kara'te *nm* karate

kg *abbr* (**chilogrammo**) kg

km *abbr* (**chilometro**) km

l' *def art mf* (*before vowel*) the; *vedi* **il**

la *def art f*; *vedi* **il** ● *pron* (*oggetto, riferito a persona*) her; (*riferito a cosa, animale*) it; (*forma di cortesia*) you ● *nm inv* Mus (*chiave, nota*) A

là *adv* there; **di** ~ **la** (*in quel luogo*) in there; (*da quella parte*) that way; **eccolo là!** there he is!; **farsi più in là** (*far largo*) make way; **là dentro** in there; **là fuori** out there; [**ma**] **va là!** come off it!; **più in là** (*nel tempo*) later on; (*nello spazio*) further on

'labbro *nm* (*pl* **Anat labbra**) lip

labi'rinto *nm* labyrinth; (*di sentieri ecc*) maze

labora'torio *nm* laboratory; (*di negozio, officina ecc*) workshop

labori'oso *a* (*operoso*) industrious; (*faticoso*) laborious

labu'rista *a* Labour ● *nmf* member of the Labour Party

'lacca *nf* lacquer; (*per capelli*) hairspray, lacquer. **lac'care** *vt* lacquer

'laccio *nm* noose; (*lazo*) lasso; (*trappola*) snare; (*stringa*) lace

lace'rante *a* (*grido*) earsplitting

lace'rare *vt* tear; lacerate (*carne*). ~**rsi** *vr* tear. ~**zi'one** *f* laceration. **'lacero** *a* torn; (*cencioso*) ragged

la'conico *a* laconic

'lacri|ma *nf* tear; (*goccia*) drop. ~**mare** *vi* weep. ~**mevole** *a* tearjerking

lacri'mogeno *a* gas ~ tear gas

lacri'moso *a* tearful

la'cuna *nf* gap. **lacu'noso** *a* (*preparazione, resoconto*) incomplete

la'custre *a* lake *attrib*

'ladro, -a *nmf* thief; **al** ~**!** stop thief! ~**'cinio** *nm* theft. **la'druncolo** *nm* petty thief

'lager *nm inv* concentration camp

laggiù *adv* down there; (*lontano*) over there

'lagna *nf* (*fam: persona*) moaning Minnie; (*film*) bore

la'gna|nza *nf* complaint. ~**rsi** *vr* moan; (*protestare*) complain (**di** about). **la'gnoso** *a* (*persona*) moaning

'lago *nm* lake

la'guna *nf* lagoon

'laico, -a *a* lay; (*vita*) secular ● *nm* layman ● *nf* laywoman

'lama *nf* blade ● *nm inv* (*animale*) llama

lambic'carsi *vr* ~ **il cervello** rack one's brains

lam'bire *vt* lap

lamé *nm inv* lamé

lamen'tar|e *vt* lament. ~**si** *vr* moan. ~**si di** (*lagnarsi*) complain about

lamen'te|la *nf* complaint. ~**vole** *a* mournful; (*pietoso*) pitiful. **la'mento** *nm* moan

la'metta *nf* ~ [**da barba**] razor blade

lami'era *nf* sheet metal

'lamina *nf* foil. ~ **d'oro** gold leaf

lami'na|re *vt* laminate. ~**to** *a* laminated ● *nm* laminate; (*tessuto*) lamé

'lampa|da *nf* lamp. ~ **da abbronzante** sunlamp. ~ **da a pila** torch. ~**'dario** *nm* chandelier. ~**'dina** *nf* light bulb

lam'pante *a* clear

lampeggi'a|re *vi* flash. ~**tore** *nm* Auto indicator

lampi'one *nm* street lamp

'lampo *nm* flash of lightning; (*luce*) flash; **lampi** *pl* lightning *sg.* ~ **di genio** stroke of genius. [**cerniera**] ~ zip [fastener], zipper *Am*

lam'pone *nm* raspberry

'lana *nf* wool; **di** ~ woollen. ~ **d'acciaio** steel wool. ~ **vergine** new wool. ~ **di vetro** glass wool

lan'cetta *nf* pointer; *(di orologio)* hand

'lancia *nf (arma)* spear, lance; *Naut* launch

lanci'ar|e *vt* throw; *(da un aereo)* drop; launch *(missile, prodotto)*; give *(grido)*; **~e uno sguardo a** glance at. **~si** *vr* fling oneself; *(intraprendere)* launch out

lanci'nante *a* piercing

'lancio *nm* throwing; *(da aereo)* drop; *(di missile, prodotto)* launch. **~ del disco** discus [throwing]. **~ del giavellotto** javelin [throwing]. **~ del peso** putting the shot

'landa *nf* heath

'languido *a* languid

langu'ore *nm* languor

lani'ero *a* wool

lani'ficio *nm* woollen mill

lan'terna *nf* lantern; *(faro)* lighthouse

la'nugine *nf* down

lapi'dare *vt* stone; *fig* demolish

lapi'dario *a (conciso)* terse

'lapide *nf* tombstone; *(commemorativa)* memorial tablet

'lapis *nm inv* pencil

'lapsus *nm inv* lapse, error

'lardo *nm* lard

larga'mente *adv (ampiamente)* widely

lar'ghezza *nf* width, breadth; *fig* liberality. **~ di vedute** broadmindedness

'largo *a* wide; *(ampio)* broad; *(abito)* loose; *(liberale)* liberal; *(abbondante)* generous; **stare alla larga** keep away; **~ di manica** *fig* generous; **~ di spalle/vedute** broadshouldered/-minded ●*nm* width; **andare al ~** *Naut* go out to sea; **fare ~** make room; **farsi ~** make one's way; **al ~ di** off the coast of

'larice *nm* larch

la'ringe *nf* larynx. **larin'gite** *nf* laryngitis

'larva *nf* larva; *(persona emaciata)* shadow

la'sagne *nfpl* lasagna *sg*

lasciapas'sare *nm inv* pass

lasci'ar|e *vt* leave; *(rinunciare)* give up; *(rimetterci)* lose; *(smettere di tenere)* let go [of]; *(concedere)* let; **~e di fare qcsa** *(smettere)* stop doing sth; **lascia perdere!** forget it!; **lascialo venire, lascia che venga** let him come. **~si** *vr (reciproco)* leave each other, split up; **~si andare** let oneself go

'lascito *nm* legacy

'laser *a & nm inv (raggio)* ~ laser [beam]

lassa'tivo *a & nm* laxative

'lasso *nm* **~ di tempo** period of time

lassù *adv* up there

'lastra *nf* slab; *(di ghiaccio)* sheet; *(di metallo, Phot)* plate; *(radiografia)* X-ray [plate]

lastri'ca|re *vt* pave. **~to, 'lastrico** *nm* pavement; **sul lastrico** on one's beam-ends

la'tente *a* latent

late'rale *a* side *attrib*; *Med, Techn ecc* lateral; **via ~** side street

late'rizi *nmpl* bricks

lati'fondo *nm* large estate

la'tino *a & nm* Latin

lati'tan|te *a* in hiding ●*nmf* fugitive [from justice]

lati'tudine *nf* latitude

'lato *a (ampio)* broad; **in senso ~** broadly speaking ●*nm* side; *(aspetto)* aspect; **a ~ di** beside; **dal ~ mio** *(punto di vista)* for my part; **d'altro ~** *fig* on the other hand

la'tra|re *vi* bark. **~to** *nm* barking

'latta *nf* tin, can

lat'taio, -a *nm* milkman ●*nf* milkwoman

lat'tante *a* breast-fed ●*nmf* suckling

'latt|e *nm* milk. **~e acido** sour milk. **~e condensato** condensed milk. **~e detergente** cleansing milk. **~e in polvere** powdered milk. **~e scremato** skimmed milk. **~eo** *a* milky. **~e'ria** *nf* dairy. **~i'cini** *nmpl* dairy products. **~i'era** *nf* milk jug

lat'tina *nf* can

lat'tuga *nf* lettuce

'laure|a *nf* degree; **prendere la ~a** graduate. **~'ando, -a** *nmf* final-year student

laure'a|rsi *vr* graduate. **~to, -a** *a & nmf* graduate

'lauro *nm* laurel

'lauto *a* lavish; **~ guadagno** handsome profit

'lava *nf* lava

la'vabile *a* washable

la'vabo *nm* wash-basin

la'vaggio *nm* washing. **~ automatico** (*per auto*) carwash. **~ del cervello** brainwashing. **~ a secco** dry-cleaning

la'vagna *nf* slate; *Sch* blackboard

la'van|da *nf* wash; *Bot* lavender; **fare una ~a gastrica** have one's stomach pumped. **~'daia** *nf* washerwoman. **~de'ria** *nf* laundry. **~deria automatica** launderette

lavan'dino *nm* sink; (*hum: persona*) bottomless pit

lavapi'atti *nmf inv* dishwasher

la'var|e *vt* wash; **~e i piatti** wash up. **~si** *vr* wash, have a wash; **~si i denti** brush one's teeth; **~si le mani** wash one's hands

lava'secco *nmf inv* dry-cleaner's

lavasto'viglie *nf inv* dishwasher

la'vata *nf* wash; **darsi una ~** have a wash; **~ di capo** *fig* scolding

lava'tivo *a, nmf* idler

lava'trice *nf* washing-machine

lavo'rante *nmf* worker

lavo'ra|re *vi* work ● *vt* work; knead (*pasta ecc*); till (*la terra*); **~re a maglia** knit. **~'tivo** a working. **~to a** (*pietra, legno*) carved; (*cuoio*) tooled; (*metallo*) wrought. **~'tore, ~'trice** *nmf* worker ● *a* working. **~zi'one** *nf* manufacture; (*di terra*) working; (*artigianale*) workmanship; (*del terreno*) cultivation. **lavo'rio** *nm* intense activity

la'voro *nm* work; (*faticoso, sociale*) labour; (*impiego*) job; *Theat* play; **mettersi al ~** set to work (**su**

on). **~ a maglia** knitting. **~ nero** moonlighting. **~ straordinario** overtime. **~ a tempo pieno** full-time job. **lavori** *pl* **di casa** housework. **lavori** *pl* **in corso** roadworks. **lavori** *pl* **forzati** hard labour. **lavori** *pl* **stradali** roadworks

le *def art fpl* the; *vedi* **il ●** *pers pron* (*oggetto*) them; (*a lei*) her; (*forma di cortesia*) you

le'al|e *a* loyal. **~'mente** *adv* loyally. **~tà** *nf* loyalty

'lebbra *nf* leprosy

lecca 'lecca *nm inv* lollipop

leccapi'edi *nmf inv* bootlicker

lec'ca|re *vt* lick; *fig* suck up to. **~rsi** *vr* lick; (*fig: agghindarsi*) doll oneself up; **da ~rsi i baffi** mouth-watering. **~ta** *nf* lick

leccor'nia *nf* delicacy

'lecito *a* lawful; (*permesso*) permissible

'ledere *vt* damage; *Med* injure

'lega *nf* league; (*di metalli*) alloy; **far ~ con** qcno take up with sb

le'gaccio *nm* string; (*delle scarpe*) shoelace

le'gal|e *a* legal ● *nm* lawyer. **~ità** *nf* legality. **~iz'zare** *vt* authenticate; (*rendere legale*) legalize. **~'mente** *adv* legally

le'game *nm* tie; (*amoroso*) liaison; (*connessione*) link

lega'mento *nm* *Med* ligament

le'gar|e *vt* tie; tie up (*persona*); tie together (*due cose*); (*unire, rilegare*) bind; alloy (*metalli*); (*connettere*) connect; **~sela al dito** *fig* bear a grudge ● *vi* (*far lega*) get on well. **~si** *vr* bind oneself; **~si a** qcno become attached to sb

le'gato *nm* legacy; *Relig* legate

lega'tura *nf* tying; (*di libro*) binding

'legenda *nf* legend

'legge *nf* law; (*parlamentare*) act; **a norma di ~** by law

leg'genda *nf* legend; (*didascalia*) caption. **leggen'dario** *a* legendary

'leggere *vt/i* read

legge'r|ezza nf lightness; (frivolezza) frivolity; (incostanza) fickleness. **~'mente** adv slightly

leg'gero a light; (bevanda) weak; (lieve) slight; (frivolo) frivolous; (incostante) fickle; **alla leggera** frivolously

leg'gibile a (scrittura) legible; (stile) readable

leg'gio nm lectern; Mus music stand

legi'ferare vi legislate

legio'nario nm legionary. **legi'one** nf legion

legisla'tivo a legislative. **~'tore** nm legislator. **~'tura** nf legislature. **~zi'one** nf legislation

legittimità nf legitimacy. **le'gittimo** a legitimate; (giusto) proper; **legittima difesa** self-defence

legna nf firewood

le'gname nm timber

le'gnata nf blow with a stick

'legno nm wood; **di ~** wooden. **~ compensato** plywood. **le'gnoso** a woody

le'gume nm pod

'lei pers pron (soggetto) she; (oggetto, con prep) her; (forma di cortesia) you; **lo ha fatto ~ stessa** she did it herself

'lembo nm edge; (di terra) strip

'lemma nm headword

'lena nf vigour

le'nire vt soothe

lenta'mente adv slowly

'lente nf lens. **~ a contatto** contact lens. **~ d'ingrandimento** magnifying glass

len'tezza nf slowness

len'ticchia nf lentil

len'tiggine nf freckle

'lento a slow; (allentato) slack; (abito) loose

'lenza nf fishing-line

len'zuolo nm (pl f lenzuola) nm sheet

le'one nm lion; Astr Leo

leo'pardo nm leopard

'lepre nf hare

'lercio a filthy

'lesbica nf lesbian

lesi'nare vt grudge ● vi be stingy

lesio'nare vt damage. **lesi'one** nf lesion

'leso pp di ledere ● a injured

les'sare vt boil

'lessico nm vocabulary

'lesso a boiled ● nm boiled meat

'lesto a quick; (mente) sharp

le'tale a lethal

leta'maio nm dunghill; fig pigsty. **le'tame** nm dung

le'targ|ico a lethargic. **~o** nm lethargy; (di animali) hibernation

le'tizia nf joy

'lettera nf letter; **alla ~** literally; **~ maiuscola** capital letter; **~ minuscola** small letter; **lettere** pl (letteratura) literature sg; Univ Arts; **dottore in lettere** BA, Bachelor of Arts

lette'rale a literal

lette'rario a literary

lette'rato a well-read

lettera'tura nf literature

let'tiga nf stretcher

let'tino nm cot; Med couch

'letto nm bed. **~ a castello** bunkbed. **~ a una piazza** single bed. **~ a due piazze** double bed. **~ matrimoniale** double bed

letto'rato nm (corso) ≈ tutorial

let'tore, -'trice nmf reader; Univ language assistant ● nm Comput disk drive. **~ di CD-ROM** CD-Rom drive

let'tura nf reading

leuce'mia nf leukaemia

'leva nf lever; Mil call-up; **far ~** lever. **~ del cambio** gear lever

le'vante nm East; (vento) east wind

le'va|re vt (alzare) raise; (togliere) take away; (rimuovere) take off; (estrarre) pull out; **~re di mezzo qcsa** get sth out of the way. **~rsi** vr rise; (da letto) get up; **~rsi di mezzo, ~rsi dai piedi** get out of the way. **~ta** nf rising; (di posta) collection

leva'taccia *nf* fare una ~ get up at the crack of dawn

leva'toio *a* ponte ~ drawbridge

levi'ga|re *vt* smooth; ⟨con carta vetro⟩ rub down. **~to** *a* ⟨superficie⟩ polished

levri'ero *nm* greyhound

lezi'one *nf* lesson; *Univ* lecture; ⟨rimprovero⟩ rebuke

lezi'oso *a* ⟨stile, modi⟩ affected

li *pers pron mpl* them

lì *adv* there; **fin lì** as far as there; **giù di lì** thereabouts; **lì per lì** there and then

Li'bano *nm* Lebanon

'libbra *nf* ⟨peso⟩ pound

li'beccio *nm* south-west wind

li'bellula *nf* dragon-fly

libe'rale *a* liberal; ⟨generoso⟩ generous ● *nmf* liberal

libe'ra|re *vt* free; release ⟨prigioniero⟩; vacate ⟨stanza⟩; ⟨salvare⟩ rescue. **~rsi** *vr* ⟨stanza:⟩ become vacant; *Teleph* become free; ⟨da impegno⟩ get out of it; **~rsi di** get rid of. **~tore**, **~trice** *a* liberating ● *nmf* liberator. **~torio** *a* liberating. **~zi'one** *nf* liberation; **la L~zione** ⟨ricorrenza⟩ Liberation Day

'liber|o *a* free; ⟨strada⟩ clear. **~o docente** qualified university lecturer. **~o professionista** self-employed person. **~tà** *nf inv* freedom; ⟨di prigioniero⟩ release. **~tà provvisoria** *Jur* bail; **~tà** *pl* ⟨confidenze⟩ liberties

'liberty *nm & a inv* Art Nouveau

'Libi|a *nf* Libya. **l~co**, **-a** *a & nmf* Libyan

li'bidi|ne *nf* lust. **~'noso** *a* lustful. **li'bido** *nf* libido

libra'io *nm* bookseller

libre'ria *nf* ⟨negozio⟩ bookshop; ⟨mobile⟩ bookcase; ⟨biblioteca⟩ library

li'bretto *nm* booklet; *Mus* libretto. **~ degli assegni** cheque book. **~ di circolazione** logbook. **~ d'istruzioni** instruction booklet. **~ di risparmio** bankbook. **~ uni-**

versitario book held by students which records details of their exam performances

'libro *nm* book. **~ giallo** thriller. **~ paga** payroll

lice'ale *nmf* secondary-school student ● *a* secondary-school *attrib*

li'cenza *nf* licence; ⟨permesso⟩ permission; *Mil* leave; *Sch* school-leaving certificate; **essere in ~** be on leave

licenzia'mento *nm* dismissal

licenzi'a|re *vt* dismiss, sack *fam*. **~rsi** *vr* ⟨da un impiego⟩ resign; ⟨accomiatarsi⟩ take one's leave

li'ceo *nm* secondary school, high school. **~ classico** secondary school with an emphasis on humanities. **~ scientifico** secondary school with an emphasis on sciences

li'chene *nm* lichen

'lido *nm* beach

li'eto *a* glad; ⟨evento⟩ happy; **molto ~!** I pleased to meet you!

li'eve *a* light; ⟨debole⟩ faint; ⟨trascurabile⟩ slight

lievi'tare *vi* rise ● *vt* leaven. **li'evito** *nm* yeast. **lievito in polve-re** baking powder

'lifting *nm inv* face-lift

'ligio *a* essere **~ al dovere** have a sense of duty

'lilla *nf Bot* lilac ● *nm* ⟨colore⟩ lilac

'lima *nf* file

limacci'oso *a* slimy

li'mare *vt* file

'limbo *nm* limbo

li'metta *nf* nail-file

limi'ta|re *nm* threshold ● *vt* limit. **~rsi** *vr* **~rsi a fare qcsa** restrict oneself to doing sth; **~rsi in qcsa** cut down on sth. **~'tivo** *a* limiting. **~to** *a* limited. **~zi'one** *nf* limitation

'limite *nm* limit; ⟨confine⟩ boundary. **~ di velocità** speed limit

li'mitrofo *a* neighbouring

limo'nata *nf* ⟨bibita⟩ lemonade; ⟨succo⟩ lemon juice

li'mone nm lemon; (albero) lemon tree

'limpido a clear; (occhi) limpid

'lince nf lynx

linci'are vt lynch

'lindo a neat; (pulito) clean

'linea nf line; (di autobus, aereo) route; (di metro) line; (di abito) cut; (di auto, mobile) design; (fisico) figure; in ~ as the crow flies; è caduta la ~ I've been cut off; in ~ di massima as a rule; a grandi linee in outline; mantenere la ~ keep one's figure; in prima ~ in the front line; mettersi in ~ line up; nave di ~ liner; volo di ~ scheduled flight. ~ d'arrivo finishing line. ~ continua unbroken line

linea'menti nmpl features

line'are a linear; (discorso) to the point; (ragionamento) consistent

line'etta nf (tratto lungo) dash; (d'unione) hyphen

lin'gotto nm ingot

'lingu|a nf tongue; (linguaggio) language. ~'accia nf (persona) backbiter. ~'aggio nm language. ~'etta nf (di scarpa) tongue; (di strumento) reed; (di busta) flap

lingu'ist|a nmf linguist. ~ica nf linguistics sg. ~ico a linguistic

'lino nm Bot flax; (tessuto) linen

li'noleum nm linoleum

liofiliz'za|re vt freeze-dry. ~to a freeze-dried

liposuzi'one nf liposuction

lique'far|e vt, ~si vr liquefy; (sciogliersi) melt

liqui'da|re vt liquidate; settle (conto); pay off (debiti); clear (merce); (fam: uccidere) get rid of. ~zi'one nf liquidation; (di conti) settling; (di merce) clearance sale

'liquido a & nm liquid

liqui'rizia nf liquorice

li'quore nm liqueur; liquori pl (bevande alcooliche) liquors

'lira nf lira; Mus lyre

'lirico, -a a lyrical; (poesia) lyric;

(cantante, musica) opera attrib ● nf lyric poetry; Mus opera

'lisca nf fishbone; avere la ~ (fam: nel parlare) have a lisp

lisci'are vt smooth; (accarezzare) stroke. 'liscio a smooth; (capelli) straight; (liquore) neat; (acqua minerale) still; passarla liscia get away with it

'liso a worn [out]

'lista nf list; (striscia) strip. ~ di attesa waiting list; in ~ di attesa Aeron stand-by. ~ elettorale electoral register. ~ nera blacklist. ~ di nozze wedding list. li'stare vt edge; Comput list

li'stino nm list. ~ prezzi price list

Lit. abbr (lire italiane) Italian lire

'lite nf quarrel; (baruffa) row; Jur lawsuit

liti'gare vi quarrel. li'tigio nm quarrel. litigi'oso a quarrelsome

lito'rale a coastal ● nm coast

'litro nm litre

li'turgico a liturgical

li'vella nf level. ~ a bolla d'aria spirit level

livel'lar|e vt level. ~si vr level out

li'vello nm level; passaggio a ~ level crossing; sotto/sul ~ del mare below/above sea level

'livido a livid; (per il freddo) blue; (per una botta) black and blue ● nm bruise

Li'vorno nf Leghorn

'lizza nf lists pl; essere in ~ per qcsa be in the running for sth

lo def art m (before s + consonant, gn, ps, z) the; vedi il ● pron (riferito a persona) him; (riferito a cosa) it; non lo so I don't know

'lobo nm lobe

lo'cal|e a local ● nm (stanza) room; (treno) local train; ~i pl (edifici) premises. ~e notturno night-club. ~ità nf inv locality

localiz'zare vt localize; (trovare) locate

lo'canda nf inn

locan'dina nf bill, poster

loca'|tario, -a nmf tenant. ~'tore,

~'**trice** nm landlord ● nf landlady. ~**zi'one** nf tenancy

locomo'tiva nf locomotive. ~**zi'one** nf locomotion; **mezzi di** ~**zione** means of transport

'**loculo** nm burial niche

locuzi'one nf expression

lo'**dare** vt praise. '**lode** nf praise; **laurea con lode** first-class degree

'**loden** m inv (cappotto) loden coat

lo'**devole** a praiseworthy

'**lodola** nf lark

'**loggia** nf loggia; (massonica) lodge

loggi'one nm gallery, the gods

'**logica** nf logic

logica'mente adv (in modo logico) logically; (ovviamente) of course

'**logico** a logical

lo'**gistica** nf logistics sg

logo'rante a (esperienza) wearing

logo'ra|re vt wear out; (sciupare) waste. ~**rsi** vr wear out; (persona:) wear oneself out. **logo'rio** nm wear and tear. **lo'goro** a worn-out

lom'baggine nf lumbago

Lombar'dia nf Lombardy

lom'bata nf loin. '**lombo** nm Anat loin

lom'brico nm earthworm

'**Londra** nf London

lon'gevo a long-lived

longi'lineo a tall and slim

longi'tudine nf longitude

lontana'mente adv distantly; (vagamente) vaguely; **neanche** ~ not for a moment

lonta'nanza nf distance; (separazione) separation; **in** ~ in the distance

lon'tano a far; (distante) distant; (nel tempo) far-off, distant; (parente) distant; (vago) vague; (assente) absent; **più** ~ further ● adv far [away]; **da** ~ from a distance; **tenersi** ~ **da** keep away from

'**lontra** nf otter

lo'**quace** a talkative

'**lordo** a dirty; (somma, peso) gross

'**loro**[1] pron pl (soggetto) they; (oggetto) them; (forma di cortesia) you; **sta a** ~ it is up to them

'**loro**[2] (**il** ~ m, **la** ~ f, **i** ~ mpl, **le** ~ fpl) a their; (forma di cortesia) your; **un** ~ **amico** a friend of theirs; (forma di cortesia) a friend of yours ● pron theirs; (forma di cortesia) yours; **i** ~ their folk

lo'**sanga** nf lozenge; **a losanghe** diamond-shaped

'**losco** a suspicious

'**loto** nm lotus

'**lott|a** nf fight, struggle; (contrasto) conflict; Sport wrestling. **lot'tare** vi fight, struggle; Sport, fig wrestle. ~**a'tore** nm wrestler

lotte'ria nf lottery

'**lotto** nm [national] lottery; (porzione) lot; (di terreno) plot

lozi'one nf lotion

lubrifi'ca|nte a lubricating ● nm lubricant. ~**re** vt lubricate

luc'chetto nm padlock

lucci'ca|nte a sparkling. ~**re** vi sparkle. **lucci'chio** nm sparkle

'**luccio** nm pike

'**lucciola** nf glow-worm

'**luce** nf light; **far** ~ **su** shed light on; **dare alla** ~ give birth to. ~ **della luna** moonlight. **luci di posizione** sidelights. ~ **del sole** sunlight

lu'**cente** a shining. ~**'tezza** nf shine

lucer'nario nm skylight

lu'**certola** nf lizard

lucida'labbra nm inv lip gloss

luci'da|re vt polish. ~**'trice** nf [floor-]polisher. '**lucido** a shiny; (pavimento, scarpe) polished; (chiaro) clear; (persona, mente) lucid; (occhi) watery ● nm shine. **lucido [da scarpe]** [shoe] polish

lucra'tivo a lucrative. '**lucro** nm lucre

'**luglio** nm July

lu'gubre a gloomy

'**lui** pers pron (soggetto) he; (oggetto, con prep) him; **lo ha fatto** ~ **stesso** he did it himself

lu'maca nf (mollusco) snail; fig slowcoach

'**lume** nm lamp; (luce) light; **a ~ di candela** by candlelight

luminosità nf brightness. **lumi-'noso** a luminous; ⟨stanza, cielo ecc⟩ bright

'**luna** nf moon; **chiaro di ~** moonlight; **avere la ~ storta** be in a bad mood. **~ di miele** honeymoon

luna park nm inv fairground

lu'nare a lunar

lu'nario nm almanac; **sbarcare il ~** make both ends meet

lu'natico a moody

lunedì nm inv Monday

lu'netta nf half-moon [shape]

lun'gaggine nf slowness

lun'ghezza nf length. **~ d'onda** wavelength

'**lungi** adv ero [ben] **~ dall'imma-ginare che...** I never dreamt for a moment that...

lungimi'rante a far-sighted, far-seeing

'**lungo** a long; (diluito) weak; (lento) slow; **saperla lunga** be shrewd ● nm length; **di gran lunga** by far; **andare per le lunghe** drag on ● prep (durante) throughout; (per la lunghezza di) along

lungofi'ume nm riverside

lungo'lago nm lakeside

lungo'mare nm sea front

lungome'traggio nm feature film

lu'notto nm rear window

lu'ogo nm place; (punto preciso) spot; (passo d'autore) passage; **aver ~** take place; **dar ~ a** give rise to; **del ~** ⟨usanze⟩ local. **~ comune** platitude. **~ pubblico** public place

luogote'nente nm Mil lieutenant

lu'petto nm Cub [Scout]

'**lupo** nm wolf

'**luppolo** nm hop

'**lurido** a filthy. **luri'dume** nm filth

lu'singa nf flattery

lusin'gare vt flatter. **~arsi** vr flatter oneself; (illudersi) fool oneself. **~hi'ero** a flattering

lus'sa|re vt, **~rsi** vr dislocate. **~zi'one** nf dislocation

Lussem'burgo nm Luxembourg

'**lusso** nm luxury; **di ~** luxury attrib

lussu'oso a luxurious

lussureggi'ante a luxuriant

lu'strare vt polish

lu'strino nm sequin

'**lustro** a shiny ● nm sheen; fig prestige; (quinquennio) five-year period

'**lutt|o** nm mourning; **~o stretto** deep mourning. **~u'oso** a mournful

....

Mm

....

m abbr (metro) m

ma conj but; (eppure) yet; **ma!** (dubbio) I don't know; (indignazione) really!; **ma davvero?** really?; **ma sì!** why not!; (certo che sì) of course!

'macabro a macabre

macché int of course not!

macche'roni nmpl macaroni sg

macche'ronico a ⟨italiano⟩ broken

'**macchia¹** nf stain; (di diverso colore) spot; (piccola) speck; **senza ~** spotless

'**macchia²** (boscaglia) scrub; **darsi alla ~** take to the woods

macchi'a|re vt, **~rsi** vr stain. **~to** a ⟨caffè⟩ with a dash of milk; **~to di** (sporco) stained with

'**macchina** nf machine; (motore) engine; (automobile) car. **~ da cu-cire** sewing machine. **~ da presa** cine camera. **~ da scrivere** typewriter

macchinal'mente adv mechanically

macchi'nare vt plot

macchi'nario nm machinery

macchi'netta nf ⟨per i denti⟩ brace

macchi'nista *nm* Rail engine-driver; *Naut* engineer; *Theat* stagehand

macchi'noso *a* complicated

mace'donia *nf* fruit salad

macel'la|io *nm* butcher. **~re** *vt* slaughter, butcher. **macelle'ria** *nf* butcher's [shop]. **ma'cello** *nm* (*mattatoio*) slaughterhouse; *fig* shambles *sg*; **andare al macello** *fig* go to the slaughter; **mandare al macello** *fig* send to his/her death

mace'rar|e *vt* macerate; *fig* distress. **~si** *vr* be consumed

ma'cerie *nfpl* rubble *sg*; (*rottami*) debris *sg*

ma'cigno *nm* boulder

maci'lento *a* emaciated

'macina *nf* millstone

macinacaffè *nm inv* coffee mill

macina'pepe *nm inv* pepper mill

maci'na|re *vt* mill. **~to** *a* ground ● *nm* (*carne*) mince. **maci'nino** *nm* mill; (*hum: macchina*) old banger

maciul'lare *vt* (*stritolare*) crush

macrobiotic|a *nf* negozio di **~a** health-food shop. **~o** *a* macro-biotic

macro'scopico *a* macroscopic

macu'lato *a* spotted

'madido *a* **~ di** moist with

Ma'donna *nf* Our Lady

mador'nale *a* gross

'madre *nf* mother. **~'lingua** *a inv* inglese **~lingua** English native speaker. **~'patria** *nf* native land. **~'perla** *nf* mother-of-pearl

ma'drina *nf* godmother

maestà *nf* majesty

maestosità *nf* majesty. **mae'stoso** *a* majestic

mae'strale *nm* northwest wind

mae'stranza *nf* workers *pl*

mae'stria *nf* mastery

ma'estro, -a *nmf* teacher ● *nm* master; *Mus* maestro. **~ di cerimonie** master of ceremonies ● *a* (*principale*) chief; (*di grande abilità*) skilful

'mafi|a *nf* Mafia. **~'oso** *a* of the Mafia ● *nm* member of the Mafia, Mafioso

'maga *nf* sorceress

ma'gagna *nf* fault

ma'gari *adv* (*forse*) maybe ● *int* I wish! ● *conj* (*per esprimere desiderio*) if only; (*anche se*) even if

magazzini'ere *nm* storesman, warehouseman. **magaz'zino** *nm* warehouse; (*emporio*) shop; **grande magazzino** department store

'maggio *nm* May

maggio'lino *nm* May bug

maggio'rana *nf* marjoram

maggio'ranza *nf* majority

maggio'rare *vt* increase

maggior'domo *nm* butler

maggi'ore *a* (*di dimensioni, numero*) bigger, larger; (*superlativo*) biggest, largest; (*di età*) older; (*superlativo*) oldest; (*di importanza, Mus*) major; (*superlativo*) greatest; **la maggior parte di** most; **la maggior parte del tempo** most of the time ● *pron* (*di dimensioni*) the bigger, the larger; (*superlativo*) the biggest, the largest; (*di età*) the older; (*superlativo*) the oldest; (*di importanza*) the major; (*superlativo*) the greatest ● *nm* Mil major; Aeron squadron leader. **maggio'renne** *a* of age ● *nmf* adult

maggiori'tario *a* (*sistema*) first-past-the-post *attrib*. **~'mente** *adv* [all] the more; (*più di tutto*) most

'Magi *nmpl* **i re ~** the Magi

ma'gia *nf* (*trucco*) magic trick **magica'mente** *adv* magically. **'magico** *a* magic

magi'stero *nm* (*insegnamento*) teaching; (*maestria*) skill; **facoltà di ~** arts faculty

magi'strale *a* masterly; **istituto ~e** teachers' training college

magi'stra|to *nm* magistrate. **~'tura** *nf* magistrature. **la ~tura** the Bench

'magli|a *nf* stitch; (*lavoro ai ferri*) knitting; (*tessuto*) jersey; (*di rete*)

mesh; (di catena) link; (indumento)
vest; **fare la ~a** knit. **~a diritta**
knit. **~a rosa** (ciclismo) ≈ yellow
jersey. **~a rovescia** purl. **~e'ria** nf
knitwear. **~'etta** nf **~etta** [a **maniche corte**] tee-shirt. **~'ficio** nm
knitwear factory. **ma'glina** nf (tessuto) jersey

magli'one nm sweater

'magma nm magma

ma'gnanimo a magnanimous

ma'gnate nm magnate

ma'gnesi|a nf magnesia. **~o** nm
magnesium

ma'gne|te nm magnet. **~tico** a
magnetic. **~'tismo** nm magnetism

magne'tofono nm tape recorder

magnifi'cenza adv magnifi-
cently. **~'cenza** nf magnificence;
(generosità) munificence. **ma'gni-
fico** a magnificent; (generoso) munificent

ma'gnolia nf magnolia

'mago nm magician

ma'gone nm **avere il ~** be down;
mi è venuto il ~ I've got a lump in
my throat

'magr|a nf low water. **ma'grezza** nf
thinness. **~o** a thin; (carne) lean;
(scarso) meagre

'mai adv never; (inter, talvolta)
ever; **caso ~** if anything; **caso ~
tornasse** in case he comes back;
come ~? why?; **cosa ~?** what on
earth?; **~ più** never again; **più
che ~** more than ever; **quando
~?** whenever?; **quasi ~** hardly
ever

mai'ale nm pig; (carne) pork

mai'olica nf majolica

maio'nese nf mayonnaise

'mais nm maize

mai'uscol|a nf capital [letter]. **~o**
a capital

mal vedi **male**

'mala nf la **~** sl the underworld

mala'fede nf bad faith

malaf'fare nm **gente di ~** shady
characters pl

mala'lingua nf backbiter

mala'mente adv (ridotto) badly

malan'dato a in bad shape; (di salute) in poor health

ma'lanimo nm ill will

ma'lanno nm misfortune; (malattia) illness; **prendersi un ~** catch
something

mala'pena: a ~ adv hardly

ma'laria nf malaria

mala'ticcio a sickly

ma'lato, -a a ill, sick; (pianta) dis-
eased ● nmf sick person. **~ di
mente** mentally ill person.
malat'tia nf disease, illness; **ho
preso due giorni di malattia** I
had two days off sick. **malattia venerea** venereal disease

malaugu'rato a ill-omened.
malau'gurio nm bad o ill omen

mala'vita nf underworld

mala'voglia nf unwillingness; **di
~** unwillingly

malcapi'tato a wretched

malce'lato a ill-concealed

mal'concio a battered

malcon'tento nm discontent

malco'stume nm immorality

mal'destro a awkward; (inesperto)
inexperienced

maldi'cen|te a slanderous. **~za** nf
slander

maldi'sposto a ill-disposed

'male adv badly; **funzionare ~** not
work properly; **star ~** be ill; **star
~ a qcno** (vestito ecc:) not suit sb;
rimanerci ~ be hurt; **non c'è ~!**
not bad at all! ● nm evil; (dolore)
pain; (malattia) illness; (danno)
harm. **distinguere il bene dal ~**
know right from wrong; **andare a
~** go off; **aver ~ a** have a pain in;
dove hai ~? where does it hurt?;
far ~ a qcno (provocare dolore)
hurt sb; (cibo:) be bad for sb; **le
cipolle mi fanno ~** onions don't
agree with me; **mi fa ~ la schiena**
my back is hurting; **mal d'auto**
car-sickness. **mal di denti** toothache. **mal di gola** sore throat. **mal
di mare** sea-sickness; **avere il mal
di mare** be sea-sick. **mal di pan-**

cia stomach ache. **mal di testa** headache

male'detto *a* cursed; (*orribile*) awful

male'di|re *vt* curse. **~zi'one** *nf* curse; **~zione!** damn!

maledu|cata'mente *adv* rudely. **~'cato** *a* ill-mannered. **~cazi'one** *nf* rudeness

male'fatta *nf* misdeed

male'ficio *nm* witchcraft. **ma'lefico** *a* (*azione*) evil; (*nocivo*) harmful

maleodo'rante *a* foul-smelling

ma'lessere *nm* indisposition; *fig* uneasiness

ma'levolo *a* malevolent

malfa'mato *a* of ill repute

mal'fat|to *a* badly done; (*malformato*) ill-shaped. **~'tore** *nm* wrongdoer

mal'fermo *a* unsteady; (*salute*) poor

malfor'ma|to *a* misshapen. **~zi'one** *nf* malformation

malgo'verno *nm* misgovernment

mal'grado *prep* in spite of ● *conj* although

ma'lia *nf* spell

mali'gn|are *vi* malign. **~ità** *nf* malice; *Med* malignancy. **ma'ligno** *a* malicious; (*perfido*) evil; *Med* malignant

malinco'ni|a *nf* melancholy. **~ca'mente** *adv* melancholically. **malin'conico** *a* melancholy

malincu'ore: a ~ *adv* unwillingly, reluctantly

malinfor'mato *a* misinformed

malintenzio'nato, **~a** *nmf* miscreant

malin'teso *a* mistaken ● *nm* misunderstanding

ma'lizi|a *nf* malice; (*astuzia*) cunning; (*espediente*) trick. **~'oso** *a* malicious; (*birichino*) mischievous

malle'abile *a* malleable

mal'loppo *nm* fam loot

malme'nare *vt* ill-treat

mal'messo *a* (*vestito male*) shab-

bily dressed; (*casa*) poorly furnished; (*fig: senza soldi*) hard up

malnu'tri|to *a* undernourished. **~zi'one** *nf* malnutrition

'malo *a* in **~ modo** badly

ma'locchio *nm* evil eye

ma'lora *nf* ruin; **della ~** awful; **andare in ~** go to ruin

ma'lore *nm* illness; **essere colto da ~** be suddenly taken ill

malri'dotto *a* (*persona*) in a sorry state

mal'sano *a* unhealthy

'malta *nf* mortar

mal'tempo *nm* bad weather

'malto *nm* malt

maltrat|ta'mento *nm* ill-treatment. **~'tare** *vt* ill-treat

malu'more *nm* bad mood; **di ~** in a bad mood

mal'vagi|o *a* wicked. **~tà** *nf* wickedness

malversazi'one *nf* embezzlement

mal'visto *a* unpopular (**da** with)

malvi'vente *nm* criminal

malvolenti'eri *adv* unwillingly

malvo'lere *vt* **farsi ~** make oneself unpopular

'mamma *nf* mummy, mum; **~ mia!** good gracious!

mam'mella *nf* breast

mam'mifero *nm* mammal

'mammola *nf* violet

ma'nata *nf* handful; (*colpo*) slap

'manca *nf* vedi **manco**

manca'mento *nm* **avere un ~** faint

man'can|te *a* missing. **~za** *nf* lack; (*assenza*) absence; (*insufficienza*) shortage; (*fallo*) fault; (*imperfezione*) defect; **in ~za d'altro** failing all else; **sento la sua ~za** I miss him

man'care *vi* be lacking; (*essere assente*) be missing; (*venir meno*) fail; (*morire*) pass away; **~ di** be lacking in; **~ a** fail to keep (*promessa*); **mi manca casa** I miss home; **mi manchi** I miss you; **mi è mancato il tempo** I didn't have [the] time; **mi mancano**

1000 lire I'm 1,000 lire short; **quanto manca alla partenza?** how long before we leave?; **è mancata la corrente** there was a power failure; **sentirsi ~** feel faint; **sentirsi ~ il respiro** be unable to breathe [properly] ● *vt* miss *(bersaglio)*; **è mancato poco che cadesse** he nearly fell

'**manche** *nf inv* heat

man'chevole *a* defective

'**mancia** *nf* tip

manci'ata *nf* handful

man'cino *a* left-handed

'**manco, -a** *a* left ● *nf* left hand ● *adv (nemmeno)* not even

man'dante *nmf (di delitto)* instigator

manda'rancio *nm* clementine

man'dare *vt* send; *(emettere)* give off; utter *(suono)*; **~ a chiamare** send for; **~ avanti la casa** run the house; **~ giù** *(ingoiare)* swallow

manda'rino *nm Bot* mandarin

man'data *nf* consignment; *(di serratura)* turn; **chiudere a doppia ~** double lock

man'dato *nm (incarico)* mandate; *Jur* warrant; *(di pagamento)* money order. **~ di comparizione [in giudizio]** subpoena. **~ di perquisizione** search warrant

man'dibola *nf* jaw

mando'lino *nm* mandolin

'**mandorla** *nf* almond; **a ~la** *(occhi)* almond-shaped. **~'lato** *nm* nut brittle *(type of nougat)*. **~'lo** *nm* almond[-tree]

'**mandria** *nf* herd

maneg'gevole *a* easy to handle. **maneggi'are** *vt* handle

ma'neggio *nm* handling; *(intrigo)* plot; *(scuola di equitazione)* riding school

ma'nesco *a* quick to hit out

ma'netta *nf* hand lever; **manette** *pl* handcuffs

man'forte *nm* **dare ~ a** qcno support sb

manga'nello *nm* truncheon

manga'nese *nm* manganese

mange'reccio *a* edible

mangia'dischi® *nm inv* type of portable record player

mangia'fumo *a inv* **candela ~** air-purifier in the form of a candle

mangia'nastri *nm inv* cassette player

mangi'a|re *vt/i* eat; *(consumare)* eat up; *(corrodere)* eat away; take *(scacchi, carte ecc)*; *(cibo)* food; *(pasto)* meal. **~rsi** *vr* **~rsi le parole** mumble; **~rsi le unghie** bite one's nails

mangi'ata *nf* big meal; **farsi una bella ~ di...** feast on...

mangia'toia *nf* manger

mangi'ime *nm* fodder

mangi'one, -a *nmf fam* glutton

mangiucchi'are *vt* nibble

'**mango** *nm* mango

ma'nia *nf* mania. **~ di grandezza** delusions of grandeur. **~co, -a** *a* maniacal ● *nmf* maniac

'**manica** *nf* sleeve; *(fam: gruppo)* band; **a maniche lunghe** long-sleeved; **essere in maniche di camicia** be in shirt sleeves; **essere di ~ larga** be free with one's money. **~ a vento** wind sock

'**Manica** *nf* **la ~** the [English] Channel

manica'retto *nm* tasty dish

mani'chetta *nf* hose

mani'chino *nm (da sarto, vetrina)* dummy

'**manico** *nm* handle; *Mus* neck

mani'comio *nm* mental home; *(fam: confusione)* tip

mani'cotto *nm* muff; *Mech* sleeve

mani'cure *nf* manicure ● *nmf inv (persona)* manicurist

mani'e|ra *nf* manner; **in ~ra che** so that. **~'rato** *a* affected; *(stile)* mannered. **~'rismo** *nm* mannerism

manifat'tura *nf* manufacture; *(fabbrica)* factory

manife'stante *nmf* demonstrator

manife'sta|re *vt* show; *(esprimere)* express ● *vi* demonstrate. **~rsi** *vr* show oneself. **~zi'one** *nf* show;

(*espressione*) expression; (*sintomo*) manifestation; (*dimostrazione pubblica*) demonstration

mani'festo *a* evident ● *nm* poster; (*dichiarazione pubblica*) manifesto

ma'niglia *nf* handle; (*sostegno, in autobus ecc*) strap

manipo'la|re *vt* handle; (*massaggiare*) massage; (*alterare*) adulterate; *fig* manipulate. **~'tore, ~'trice** *nmf* manipulator. **~zi'one** *nf* handling; (*massaggio*) massage; (*alterazione*) adulteration; *fig* manipulation

mani'scalco *nm* smith

man'naia *nf* (*scure*) axe; (*da macellaio*) cleaver

man'naro *a* lupo *nm* **~** werewolf

'mano *nf* hand; (*strato di vernice ecc*) coat; **alla ~** informal; **fuori ~** out of the way; **man ~** little by little; **man ~ che** as; **sotto ~** to hand

mano'dopera *nf* labour

ma'nometro *nm* gauge

mano'mettere *vt* tamper with; (*violare*) violate

ma'nopola *nf* (*di apparecchio*) knob; (*guanto*) mitten; (*su pullman*) handle

mano'scritto *a* handwritten ● *nm* manuscript

mano'vale *nm* labourer

mano'vella *nf* handle; *Techn* crank

ma'no|vra *nf* manoeuvre; *Rail* shunting; **fare le ~vre** *Auto* manoeuvre. **~'vrabile** *a* fig easy to manipulate. **~'vrare** *vt* (*azionare*) operate; *fig* manipulate ⟨*persona*⟩ ● *vi* manoeuvre

manro'vescio *nm* slap

man'sarda *nf* attic

mansi'one *nf* task; (*dovere*) duty

mansu'eto *a* meek; ⟨*animale*⟩ docile

man'tell|a *nf* cape. **~o** *nm* cloak; (*soprabito, di animale*) coat; (*di neve*) mantle

mante'ner|e *vt* (*conservare*) keep;

(*in buono stato, sostentare*) maintain. **~si** *vr* **~si in forma** keep fit.

manteni'mento *nm* maintenance

'mantice *nm* bellows *pl*; (*di automobile*) hood

'manto *nm* cloak; (*coltre*) mantle

manto'vana *nf* (*di tende*) pelmet

manu'al|e *a* & *nm* manual. **~e d'uso** user manual. **~'mente** *adv* manually

ma'nubrio *nm* handle; (*di bicicletta*) handlebars *pl*; (*per ginnastica*) dumb-bell

manu'fatto *a* manufactured

manutenzi'one *nf* maintenance

'manzo *nm* steer; (*carne*) beef

'mappa *nf* map

mappa'mondo *nm* globe

mar *vedi* **mare**

ma'rasma *nm* fig decline

mara'to|na *nf* marathon. **~'neta** *nmf* marathon runner

'marca *nf* mark; *Comm* brand; (*fabbricazione*) make; (*scontrino*) ticket. **~ da bollo** revenue stamp

mar'ca|re *vt* mark; *Sport* score. **~ta'mente** *adv* markedly. **~to** *a* ⟨*tratto, accento*⟩ strong, marked. **~'tore** *nm* (*nel calcio*) scorer

mar'chese, -a *nm* marquis ● *nf* marchioness

marchi'are *vt* brand

'marchio *nm* brand; (*caratteristica*) mark. **~ di fabbrica** trademark. **~ registrato** registered trademark

'marcia *nf* march; *Auto* gear; *Sport* walk; **mettere in ~** put into gear; **mettersi in ~** start off. **~ funebre** funeral march. **~ indietro** reverse gear; **fare ~ indietro** reverse; *fig* back-pedal. **~ nuziale** wedding march

marciapi'ede *nm* pavement; (*di stazione*) platform

marci'a|re *vi* march; (*funzionare*) go, work. **~tore, ~'trice** *nmf* walker

'marcio *a* rotten ● *nm* rotten part; *fig* corruption. **mar'cire** *vi* go bad, rot '**marco** *nm* (*moneta*) mark

'**mare** *nm* sea; (*luogo di mare*) sea-side; **sul** ~ (*casa*) at the seaside; (*città*) on the sea; **in alto** ~ on the high seas; **essere in alto** ~ *fig* not know which way to turn. ~ **Adriatico** Adriatic Sea. **mar Ionio** Ionian Sea. **mar Mediterraneo** Mediterranean. **mar Tirreno** Tyrrhenian Sea

ma'**rea** *nf* tide; **una** ~ **di** hundreds of; **alta** ~ high tide; **bassa** ~ low tide

mareggi'**ata** *nf* [sea] storm

mare'**moto** *nm* tidal wave, seaquake

maresci'**allo** *nm* (*ufficiale*) marshal; (*sottufficiale*) warrant-officer

marga'**rina** *nf* margarine

marghe'**rita** *nf* marguerite. **margheri'tina** *nf* daisy

margi'**nal|e** *a* marginal. ~'**mente** *adv* marginally

'**margine** *nm* margin; (*orlo*) brink; (*bordo*) border. ~ **di errore** margin of error. ~ **di sicurezza** safety margin

ma'**rina** *nf* navy; (*costa*) seashore; (*quadro*) seascape. ~ **mercantile** merchant navy. ~ **militare** navy

mari'**naio** *nm* sailor

mari'**na|re** *vt* marinate; ~**re la scuola** play truant. ~**ta** *nf* marinade. ~**to** *a* Culin marinated

ma'**rino** *a* sea *attrib*, marine

mario'**netta** *nf* puppet

ma'**rito** *nm* husband

ma'**rittimo** *a* maritime

mar'**maglia** *nf* rabble

marmel'**lata** *nf* jam; (*di agrumi*) marmalade

mar'**mitta** *nf* pot; *Auto* silencer. ~ **catalitica** catalytic converter

'**marmo** *nm* marble

mar'**mocchio** *nm fam* brat

mar'**mor|eo** *a* marble. ~**iz'zato** *a* marbled

mar'**motta** *nf* marmot

Ma'**rocco** *nm* Morocco

ma'**roso** *nm* breaker

mar'**rone** *a* brown ● *nm* brown; (*castagna*) chestnut; **marroni** *pl* **canditi** marrons glacés

mar'**sina** *nf* tails *pl*

mar'**supio** *nm* (*borsa*) bumbag

marte'**dì** *nm inv* Tuesday. ~ **grasso** Shrove Tuesday

martel'**lante** *a* (*mal di testa*) pounding

martel'**la|re** *vt* hammer ● *vi* throb. ~**ta** *nf* hammer blow

martel'**letto** *nm* (*di giudice*) gavel

mar'**tello** *nm* hammer; (*di battente*) knocker. ~ **pneumatico** pneumatic drill

marti'**netto** *nm Mech* jack

'**martire** *nmf* martyr. mar'**tirio** *nm* martyrdom

'**martora** *nf* marten

martori'**are** *vt* torment

mar'**xis|mo** *nm* Marxism. ~**ta** *a* & *nmf* Marxist

marza'**pane** *nm* marzipan

marzi'**ale** *a* martial

marzi'**ano, -a** *nmf* Martian

'**marzo** *nm* March

masca'**lzone** *nm* rascal

ma'**scara** *nm inv* mascara

mascar'**pone** *nm full-fat cream cheese often used for desserts*

ma'**scella** *nf* jaw

'**mascher|a** *nf* mask; (*costume*) fancy dress; *Cinema, Theat* usher *m*, usherette *f*; (*nella commedia dell'arte*) stock character. ~**a antigas** gas mask. ~**a di bellezza** face pack. ~**a ad ossigeno** oxygen mask. ~**a'mento** *nm* masking; *Mil* camouflage. masche'**rare** *vt* mask; *fig* camouflage. ~**arsi** *vr* put on a mask; ~**arsi da** dress up as. ~**ata** *nf* masquerade

maschi'**accio** *nm* (*ragazza*) tomboy

ma'**schi|le** *a* masculine; (*sesso*) male ● *nm* masculine [gender]. ~'**lista** *a* sexist. '**maschio** *a* male; (*virile*) manly ● *nm* male; (*figlio*) son. **masco'lino** *a* masculine

ma'**scotte** *nf inv* mascot

maso'chis|mo *nm* masochism. **~ta** *a* & *nmf* masochist

'massa *nf* mass; *Electr* earth, ground *Am*; **comunicazioni di ~** mass media

massa'cra|nte *a* a gruelling. **~re** *vt* massacre. **mas'sacro** *nm* massacre; *fig* mess

massaggi'a|re *vt* massage. **mas'saggio** *nm* massage. **~'tore**, **~'trice** *nm* masseur ● *nf* masseuse

mas'saia *nf* housewife

masse'rizie *nfpl* household effects

mas'siccio *a* massive; *(oro ecc)* solid; *(corporatura)* heavy ● *nm* massif

'massim|a *nf* maxim; *(temperatura)* maximum. **~o** *a* greatest; *(quantità)* maximum, greatest ● *nm* il **~o** the maximum; **al ~o** at [the] most, as a maximum

'masso *nm* rock

mas'sone *nm* [Free]mason. **~'ria** Freemasonry

ma'stello *nm* wooden box for the grape or olive harvest

masti'care *vt* chew; *(borbottare)* mumble

'mastice *nm* mastic; *(per vetri)* putty

ma'stino *nm* mastiff

masto'dontico *a* gigantic

'mastro *nm* master; **libro ~** ledger

mastur'ba|rsi *vr* masturbate. **~zi'one** *nf* masturbation

ma'tassa *nf* skein

mate'matica *nf* mathematics, maths. **~o**, **-a** *a* mathematical ● *nmf* mathematician

materas'sino *nm* **~ gonfiabile** air bed

mate'rasso *nm* mattress. **~ a molle** spring mattress

ma'teria *nf* matter; *(materiale)* material; *(di studio)* subject. **~ prima** raw material

materi'a|le *a* material; *(grossolano)* coarse ● *nm* material. **~'lismo** *nm* materialism. **~'lista** *a* materialistic ● *nmf* materialist.

~liz'zarsi *vr* materialize. **~l'mente** *adv* physically

mater'nità *nf* motherhood; **ospedale di ~** maternity hospital

ma'terno *a* maternal; **lingua materna** mother tongue

ma'tita *nf* pencil

ma'trice *nf* matrix; *(origini)* roots *pl*; *Comm* counterfoil

ma'tricola *nf* *(registro)* register; *Univ* fresher

ma'trigna *nf* stepmother

matrimoni'ale *a* matrimonial; **vita ~** married life. **matri'monio** *nm* marriage; *(cerimonia)* wedding

ma'trona *nf* matron

'matta *nf* *(nelle carte)* joker

mattacchi'one, **-a** *nmf* rascal

matta'toio *nm* slaughterhouse

matte'rello *nm* rolling-pin

mat'ti|na *nf* morning; **la ~na** in the morning. **~'nata** *nf* morning; *Theat* matinée. **~ni'ero** *a* **essere ~niero** be an early riser. **~no** *nm* morning

'matto, **-a** *a* mad, crazy; *Med* insane; *(falso)* false; *(opaco)* matt; **~ da legare** barking mad; **avere una voglia matta di** be dying for ● *nmf* madman; madwoman

mat'tone *nm* brick; *(libro)* bore

matto'nella *nf* tile

mattu'tino *a* morning *attrib*

matu'rare *vt* ripen. **maturità** *nf* maturity; *Sch* school-leaving certificate. **ma'turo** *a* mature; *(frutto)* ripe

ma'tusa *nm* old fogey

mauso'leo *nm* mausoleum

maxi+ *pref* maxi+

'mazza *nf* club; *(martello)* hammer; *(da baseball, cricket)* bat. **~ da golf** golf-club. **maz'zata** *nf* blow

maz'zetta *nf* *(di banconote)* bundle

'mazzo *nm* bunch; *(carte da gioco)* pack

me *pers pron* me; **me lo ha dato** he gave it to me; **fai come me** do as I do; è più veloce di me he is faster than me o faster than I am

me'andro nm meander

M.E.C. nm abbr (Mercato Comune Europeo) EEC

mec'canica nf mechanics sg

meccanica'mente adv mechanically

mec'canico a mechanical ● nm mechanic. **mecca'nismo** nm mechanism

mèche nfpl [farsi] fare le ~ have one's hair streaked

me'daglia nf medal. **~'one** nm medallion; (gioiello) locket

me'desimo a same

'**media** nf average; Sch average mark; Math mean; **essere nella ~a** be in the mid-range. **~'ano** a middle ● nm (calcio) half-back

medi'ante prep by

medi'are vt act as intermediary in. **~'tore, ~'trice** nmf mediator; Comm middleman. **~zi'one** nf mediation

medica'mento nm medicine

medi'care vt treat; dress (ferita). **~zi'one** nf medication; (di ferita) dressing

medi'cina nf medicine. **~ina legale** forensic medicine. **~i'nale** a medicinal ● nm medicine

'**medico** a medical ● nm doctor. **~ generico** general practitioner. **~ legale** forensic scientist. **~ di turno** duty doctor

medie'vale a medieval

'**medio** a average; (punto) middle; (statura) medium ● nm (dito) middle finger

medi'ocre a mediocre; (scadente) poor

medio'evo nm Middle Ages pl

medi'tare vt meditate; (progettare) plan; (considerare attentamente) think over ● vi meditate. **~zi'one** nf meditation

mediter'raneo a Mediterranean; **il [mar] M~** the Mediterranean [Sea]

me'dusa nf jellyfish

me'gafono nm megaphone

mega'lattico a fam gigantic

mega'lomane nmf megalomaniac

me'gera nf hag

'**meglio** adv better; **tanto ~, ~ così** so much the better ● a better; (superlativo) best ● nmf best ● nf **avere la ~ su** have the better of; **fare qcsa alla [bell'e] ~** do sth as best one can ● nm **fare del proprio ~** do one's best; **fare qcsa il ~ possibile** make an excellent job of sth; **al ~** to the best of one's ability; **per il ~** for the best

'**mela** nf apple. **~ cotogna** quince

mela'grana nf pomegranate

mela'nina nf melanin

melan'zana nf aubergine, eggplant Am

me'lassa nf molasses sg

me'lenso a (persona, film) dull

mel'lifluo a (parole) honeyed; (voce) sugary

'melma nf slime. **mel'moso** a slimy

melo nm apple[-tree]

melo'dia nf melody. **me'lodico** a melodic. **~'oso** a melodious

melo'dramma nm melodrama. **~'matico** a melodramatic

melo'grano nm pomegranate tree

me'lone nm melon

mem'brana nf membrane

'**membro** nm member; (pl nf **membra** Anat) limb

memo'rabile a memorable

'**memore** a mindful; (riconoscente) grateful

me'moria nf memory; (oggetto ricordo) souvenir. **imparare a ~a** learn by heart. **~a permanente** Comput non-volatile memory. **~a tampone** Comput buffer. **~a volatile** Comput volatile memory; **memorie** pl (biografiche) memoirs. **~'ale** nm memorial. **~z'zare** vt memorize; Comput save, store

mena'dito: a ~ adv perfectly

me'nare vt lead; (fam: picchiare) hit

mendi'ca|nte *nmf* beggar. **~re** *vt/i* beg

menefre'ghista *a* devil-may-care

me'ningi *nfpl* **spremersi le ~** rack one's brains

menin'gite *nf* meningitis

me'nisco *nm* meniscus

'meno *adv* less; (*superlativo*) least; (*in operazioni, con temperatura*) minus; **far qcsa alla ~ peggio** do sth as best one can; **fare a ~ di qcsa** do without sth; **non posso fare a ~ di ridere** I can't help laughing; **~ male!** thank goodness!; **sempre ~** less and less; **venir ~** (*svenire*) faint; **venir ~ a qcno** (*coraggio:*) fail sb; **sono le tre ~ un quarto** it's a quarter to three; **che tu venga o ~** whether you're coming or not; **quanto ~** at least ● *a* inv less; (*con nomi plurali*) fewer ● *nm* least; *Math* minus sign; **il ~ possibile** as little as possible; **per lo ~** at least ● *prep* except [for] ● *conj* **a ~ che** unless

meno'ma|re *vt* (*incidente:*) maim. **~to** *a* disabled

meno'pausa *nf* menopause

'mensa *nf* table; *Mil* mess; *Sch*, *Univ* refectory

men'sil|e *a* monthly ● *nm* (*stipendio*) [monthly] salary; (*rivista*) monthly. **~ità** *nf* inv monthly salary. **~'mente** *adv* monthly

'mensola *nf* bracket; (*scaffale*) shelf

'menta *nf* mint. **~ peperita** peppermint

men'tal|e *a* mental. **~ità** *nf* inv mentality

'mente *nf* mind; **a ~ fredda** in cold blood; **venire in ~ a qcno** occur to sb; **mi è uscito di ~** it slipped my mind

men'tina *nf* mint

men'tire *vi* lie

'mento *nm* chin

'mentre *conj* (*temporale*) while; (*invece*) whereas

menù *nm* inv menu. **~ fisso** set menu. **~ a tendina** *Comput* pulldown menu

menzio'nare *vt* mention. **menzi-'one** *nf* mention

men'zogna *nf* lie

mera'viglia *nf* wonder; **a ~** marvellously; **che ~!** how wonderful!; **con mia grande ~** much to my amazement; **mi fa ~ che...** I am surprised that...

meravigli'ar|e *vt* surprise. **~si** *vr* **~si di** be surprised at

meravigli'osa'mente *adv* marvellously. **~'oso** *a* marvellous

mer'can|te *nm* merchant. **~teggi-'are** *vi* trade; (*sul prezzo*) bargain. **~'tile** *a* mercantile. **~'zia** *nf* merchandise, goods *pl* ● *nm* merchant ship

mer'cato *nm* market; *Fin* market [-place]. **a buon ~** (*comprare*) cheap[ly]; (*articolo*) cheap. **~ dei cambi** foreign exchange market. **M~ Comune [Europeo]** [European] Common Market. **~ coperto** covered market. **~ libero** free market. **~ nero** black market

'merce *nf* goods *pl*

mercé *nf* **alla ~ di** at the mercy of

merce'nario *a* & *nm* mercenary

merce'ria *nf* haberdashery; (*negozio*) haberdasher's

mercoledì *nm* inv Wednesday. **~ delle Ceneri** Ash Wednesday

mer'curio *nm* mercury

me'renda *nf* afternoon snack; **far ~** have an afternoon snack

meridi'ana *nf* sundial

meridi'ano *a* midday ● *nm* meridian

meridio'nale *a* southern ● *nmf* southerner. **meridi'one** *nm* south

me'ringa *nf* meringue. **~'gata** *nf* meringue pie

meri'tare *vt* deserve. **meri'tevole** *a* deserving

'meri|to *nm* merit; (*valore*) worth; **in ~to a** as to; **per ~to di** thanks to. **~'torio** *a* meritorious

mer'letto *nm* lace

'merlo nm blackbird

mer'luzzo nm cod

'mero a mere

meschine'ria nf meanness. me-'schino a wretched; (gretto) mean ● nm wretch

mesco|la'mento nm mixing. ~'lanza nf mixture

mesco'la|re vt mix; shuffle ⟨carte⟩; (confondere) mix up; blend ⟨tè, tabacco ecc⟩. ~rsi vr mix; (immischiarsi) meddle. ~ta nf (a carte) shuffle; Culin stir

'mese nm month

me'setto nm un ~ about a month

'messa[1] nf Mass

'messa[2] nf (il mettere) putting. ~ in moto Auto starting. ~ in piega (di capelli) set. ~ a punto adjustment. ~ in scena production. ~ a terra earthing, grounding Am

messag'gero nm messenger. mes-'saggio nm message

mes'sale nm missal

'messe nf harvest

Mes'sia nm Messiah

messi'cano, -a a e nmf Mexican

'Messico nm Mexico

messin'scena nf staging; fig act

'messo pp di mettere ● nm messenger

mesti'ere nm trade; (lavoro) job; essere del ~ be an expert, know one's trade

'mesto a sad

'mestola nf (di cuoco) ladle

mestru'a|le a menstrual. ~zi'one nf menstruation. ~zi'oni pl period

'meta nf destination; fig aim

metà nf inv half; (centro) middle; a ~ strada half-way; fare a ~ con qcno go halves with sb

metabo'lismo nm metabolism

meta'done nm methadone

meta'fisico a metaphysical

me'tafora nf metaphor. meta-'forico a metaphorical

me'talli|co a metallic. ~z'zato a ⟨grigio⟩ metallic

me'tall|o nm metal. ~ur'gia nf metallurgy

metal'meccanico a engineering ● nm engineering worker

meta'morfosi nf metamorphosis

me'tano nm methane. ~'dotto nm methane pipeline

meta'nolo nm methanol

me'teora nf meteor. meteo'rite nm meteorite

meteoro|lo'gia nf meteorology. ~'logico a meteorological

me'ticcio, -a nmf half-caste

meti'coloso a meticulous

me'todi|co a methodical. 'metodo nm method. ~olo'gia nf methodology

me'traggio nm length (in metres)

'metrico, -a a metric; (in poesia) metrical ● nf metrics sg

'metro nm (per nastro) tape measure ● nf inv (fam: metropolitana) tube Br, subway

me'tronomo nm metronome

metro'notte nmf inv night security guard

me'tropoli nf inv metropolis. ~'tana nf subway, underground Br. ~'tano a metropolitan

'metter|e vt put; (indossare) put on; (fam: installare) put in; ~e al mondo bring into the world; ~e da parte set aside; ~e fiducia inspire trust; ~e qcsa in chiaro make sth clear; ~e in mostra display; ~e a posto tidy up; ~e in vendita put up for sale; ~e su set up ⟨casa, azienda⟩; metter su famiglia start a family; ci ho messo un'ora it took me an hour; mettiamo che... let's suppose that... ~si vr (indossare) put on; (diventare) turn out; ~si a start to; ~si con qcno (fam: formare una coppia) start to go out with sb; ~si a letto go to bed; ~si a sedere sit down; ~si in viaggio set out

'mezza nf è la ~ it's half past twelve; sono le quattro e ~ it's half past four

mezza'luna *nf* half moon; (*simbolo islamico*) crescent; (*coltello*) two-handled chopping knife; **a ~** half-moon shaped

mezza'manica *nf* **a ~** (*maglia*) short-sleeved

mez'zano *a* middle

mezza'notte *nf* midnight

mezz'asta: a ~ *adv* at half mast

'mezzo *a* half; **di ~ mezza età** middle-aged; **~ bicchiere** half a glass; **una mezza idea** a vague idea; **siamo mezzi morti** we're half dead; **sono le quattro e ~** it's half past four. **mezz'ora** *nf* half an hour. **mezza pensione** *nf* half board. **mezza stagione** *nf* una **giacca di mezza stagione** a spring/autumn jacket ●*adv* (*a metà*) half ●*nm* (*metà*) half; (*centro*) middle; (*per raggiungere un fine*) means *sg*; **uno e ~** one and a half; **tre anni e ~** three and a half years; **in ~ a** in the middle of; **il giusto ~** the happy medium; **levare di ~** clear away; **per ~ di** by means of; **a ~ posta** by mail; **via di ~** *fig* halfway house; (*soluzione*) middle way. **mezzi** *pl* (*denaro*) means *pl*. **mezzi pubblici** public transport. **mezzi di trasporto** [means of] transport

mezzo'busto: a ~ *a foto, ritratto* half-length

mezzo'fondo *nm* middle-distance running

mezzogi'orno *nm* midday; (*sud*) South. **il M~** Southern Italy. **~ in punto** high noon

mi *pers pron me*; (*refl*) myself; **mi ha dato un libro** he gave me a book; **mi lavo le mani** I wash my hands; **eccomi** here I am ●*nm Mus* (*chiave, nota*) E

miago'l|are *vi* miaow. **~io** *nm* miaowing

'mica¹ *nf* mica

'mica² *adv fam* (*per caso*) by any chance; **hai ~ visto Paolo?** have you seen Paul, by any chance?;

non è ~ bello it is not at all nice; **~ male** not bad

'miccia *nf* fuse

micidi'ale *a* deadly

'micio *nm* pussy-cat

'microbo *nm* microbe

micro'cosmo *nm* microcosm

micro'fiche *nf inv* microfiche

micro'film *nm inv* microfilm

mi'crofono *nm* microphone

microorga'nismo *nm* microorganism

microproces'sore *nm* microprocessor

micro'scopi|o *nm* microscope. **~co** *a* microscopic

micro'solco *nm* (*disco*) long-playing record

mi'dollo *nm* (*pl f* midolla, *Anat*) marrow; **fino al ~** through and through. **~ osseo** bone marrow. **~ spinale** spinal cord

'mie, mi'ei *vedi* mio

mi'ele *nm* honey

mi'et|ere *vt* reap. **~i'trice** *nf Mech* harvester. **~i'tura** *nf* harvest

migli'aio *nm* (*pl f* migliaia) thousand. **a migliaia** in thousands

'miglio *nm Bot* millet; (*misura: pl f* miglia) mile

migliora'mento *nm* improvement

migliora'rare *vt/i* improve

migli'ore *a* better; (*superlativo*) the best ●*nmf* **il/la ~** the best

'mignolo *nm* little finger; (*del piede*) little toe

mi'gra|re *vi* migrate. **~zi'one** *nf* migration

'mila *vedi* mille

Mi'lano *nf* Milan

miliar'dario, -a *nm* millionaire; (*plurimiliardario*) billionaire ●*nf* millionairess; billionairess

mili'ardo *nm* billion

mili'are *a* **pietra ~** *nf* milestone

milio'nario, -a *nm* millionaire ●*nf* millionairess

mili'one *nm* million

milio'nesimo *a* millionth

mili'tante *a & nmf* militant

mili'tare *vi* **~ in** be a member of

⟨partito ecc⟩ ● a military ● nm soldier; **fare il ~** do one's military service. **~ di leva** National Serviceman

'**milite** nm soldier. **mil'izia** nf militia

'**mille** a & nm (pl **mila**) a o one thousand; **due/tre mila** two/three thousand; **~ grazie!** thanks a lot!

mille'foglie nm inv Culin vanilla slice

mil'lennio nm millennium

millepi'edi nm inv centipede

mil'lesimo a & nm thousandth

milli'grammo nm milligram

mil'limetro nm millimetre

'**milza** nf spleen

mi'mare vt mime ⟨persona⟩ ● vi mime

mi'metico a camouflage attrib

mimetiz'zar|e vt camouflage. **~si** vr camouflage oneself

'**mim|ica** nf mime. **~ico** a mimic. **~o** nm mime

mi'mosa nf mimosa

'**mina** nf mine; ⟨di matita⟩ lead

mi'naccia nf threat

minacci'|are vt threaten. **~'oso** a threatening

mi'nare vt mine; fig undermine

mina'tor|e nm miner. **~io** a threatening

mine'ra|le a & nm mineral. **~rio** a mining attrib

mi'nestra nf soup. **mine'strone** nm vegetable soup; ⟨fam: insieme confuso⟩ hotchpotch

mingher'lino a skinny

mini+ pref mini+

minia'tura nf miniature. **miniaturiz'zato** a miniaturized

mini'era nf mine

mini'golf nm miniature golf

mini'gonna nf miniskirt

minima'mente adv minimally

mini'market nm inv minimarket

minimiz'zare vt minimize

'**minimo** a least, slightest; ⟨il più basso⟩ lowest; ⟨salario, quantità ecc⟩ minimum ● nm minimum; **girare al ~** Auto idle

mini'stero nm ministry; ⟨governo⟩ government

mi'nistro nm minister. **M~ del Tesoro** Finance Minister, Chancellor of the Exchequer Br

mino'ranza nf minority attrib

mino'rato, -a a disabled ● nmf disabled person

mi'nore a ⟨gruppo, numero⟩ smaller; ⟨superlativo⟩ smallest; ⟨distanza⟩ shorter; ⟨superlativo⟩ shortest; ⟨prezzo⟩ lower; ⟨superlativo⟩ lowest; ⟨di età⟩ younger; ⟨superlativo⟩ youngest; ⟨di importanza⟩ minor; ⟨superlativo⟩ least important ● nmf younger; ⟨superlativo⟩ youngest; Jur minor; **il ~ dei mali** the lesser of two evils; **i minori di 14 anni** children under 14. **mino'renne** a under age ● nmf minor

minori'tario a minority attrib

minu'etto nm minuet

mi'nuscolo, -a a tiny ● nf small letter

mi'nuta nf rough copy

mi'nuto¹ a minute; ⟨persona⟩ delicate; ⟨ricerca⟩ detailed; ⟨pioggia, neve⟩ fine; **al ~** Comm retail

mi'nuto² nm ⟨di tempo⟩ minute; **spaccare il ~** be dead on time

mi'nuzi|a nf trifle. **~'oso** a detailed; ⟨persona⟩ meticulous

'**mio (il mio m, la mia f, i miei** mpl, **le mie** fpl) a poss my; **questa macchina è mia** this car is mine; **~ padre** my father; **un ~ amico** a friend of mine ● poss pron mine; **i miei** ⟨genitori ecc⟩ my folks

mi'ope a short-sighted. **mio'pia** nf short-sightedness

'**mira** nf aim; ⟨bersaglio⟩ target; **prendere la ~** take aim; **prendere di ~ qcno** have it in for sb

mi'racolo nm miracle. **~sa'mente** adv miraculously. **miraco'loso** a miraculous

mi'raggio nm mirage

mi'rar|e vi [take] aim. **~si** vr ⟨guardarsi⟩ look at oneself

mi'riade nf myriad

mi'rino nm sight; Phot view-finder

mir'tillo nm blueberry

mi'santropo, -a nmf misanthropist

mi'scela nf mixture; (di caffè, tabacco ecc) blend. **~'tore** nm (di acqua) mixer tap

miscel'lanea nf miscellany

'mischia nf scuffle; (nel rugby) scrum

mischi'ar|e vt mix; shuffle ⟨carte da gioco⟩. **~si** vr mix; (immischiarsi) interfere

misco'noscere vt not appreciate

mi'scuglio nm mixture; fig medley

mise'rabile a wretched

misera'mente adv (finire) miserably; (vivere) in abject poverty

mi'seria nf poverty; (infelicità) misery; **guadagnare una ~** earn a pittance; **porca ~!** hell!; **miserie** pl (disgrazie) misfortunes

miseri'cordi|a nf mercy. **~'oso** a merciful

'misero a (miserabile) wretched; (povero) poor; (scarso) paltry

mi'sfatto nm misdeed

mi'sogino nm misogynist

mis'saggio nm vision mixer

'missile nm missile

missio'nario, -a nmf missionary. **missi'one** nf mission

misteri|osa'mente adv mysteriously. **~'oso** a mysterious. **mi'stero** nm mystery

'misti|ca nf mysticism. **~'cismo** nm mysticism. **~co** a mystic[al] ● nm mystic

mistifi'ca|re vt distort ⟨verità⟩. **~zi'one** nf (della verità) distortion

'misto a mixed; **scuola mista** mixed or co-educational school ● nm mixture; **~ lana/cotone** wool/cotton mix

mi'sura nf measure; (dimensione) measurement; (taglia) size; (limite) limit; **su ~** ⟨abiti⟩ made to measure; (mobile) custom-made; **a ~** ⟨andare, calzare⟩ perfectly; a

~ che as. **~ di sicurezza** safety measure. **misu'rare** vt measure; try on ⟨indumenti⟩; (limitare) limit. **misu'rarsi** vr **misurarsi con** ⟨gareggiare⟩ compete with. **misu'rato** a measured. **misu'rino** nm measuring spoon

'mite a mild; (prezzo) moderate

'mitico a mythical

miti'gar|e vt mitigate. **~si** vr calm down; (clima:) become mild

mitiz'zare vt mythicize

'mito nm myth. **~lo'gia** nf mythology. **~'logico** a mythological

mi'tomane nmf compulsive liar

'mitra nf Relig mitre ● nm inv Mil machine-gun

mitragli'a|re vt machine-gun; **~re di domande** fire questions at. **~'trice** nf machine-gun

mit'tente nmf sender

mne'monico a mnemonic

mo' nm **a ~ di** by way of ⟨esempio, consolazione⟩

'mobile¹ a mobile; (volubile) fickle; (che si può muovere) movable; **beni mobili** personal estate; **squadra ~** flying squad

'mobile² nm piece of furniture; **mobili** pl furniture sg. **mo'bilia** nf furniture. **~li'ficio** nm furniture factory

mo'bilio nm furniture

mobilità nf mobility

mobili'ta|re vt mobilize. **~zi'one** nf mobilization

mocas'sino nm moccasin

mocci'oso, -a nmf brat

'moccolo nm (di candela) candleend; (moccio) snot

'moda nf fashion; **di ~** in fashion; **alla ~** ⟨musica, vestiti⟩ up-to-date; **fuori ~** unfashionable

modalità nf inv formality; **~ d'uso** instruction

mo'della nf model. **model'lare** vt model

model'li|no nm model. **~sta** nmf designer

mo'dello nm model; (stampo)

'modem nm inv modem; **mandare per ~** modem, send by modem

mode'ra|re vt moderate; (diminuire) reduce. **~rsi** vr control oneself. **~ta'mente** adv moderately **~to** a moderate. **~'tore, ~'trice** nmf (in tavola rotonda) moderator. **~zi'one** nf moderation

moderna|'mente adv (in modo moderno) in a modern style. **~iz'zare** vt modernize. **mo'derno** a modern

mo'dest|ia nf modesty. **~o** a modest

'modico a reasonable

mo'difica nf modification

modifi'ca|re vt modify. **~zi'one** nf modification

mo'dista nf milliner

'modo nm way; (garbo) manners pl; (occasione) chance; Gram mood; **ad ogni ~** anyhow; **di ~ che** so that; **fare in ~ di** try to; **in che ~** (inter) how; **in qualche ~** somehow; **in questo ~** like this; **di dire** idiom; **per ~ di dire** so to speak

modu'la|re vt modulate. **~zi'one** nf modulation. **~zione di frequenza** frequency modulation. **~'tore** nm **~'tore di frequenza** frequency modulator

'modulo nm form; (lunare, di comando) module. **~ continuo** continuous paper

'mogano nm mahogany

'mogio a dejected

'moglie nf wife

'mola nf millstone; Mech grindstone

mo'lare nm molar

'mole nf mass; (dimensione) size

mo'lecola nf molecule

mole'stare vt bother; (più forte) molest. **mo'lestia** nf nuisance. **mo'lesto** a bothersome

'molla nf spring; **molle** pl tongs

mol'lare vt let go; (fig: lasciare) leave; fam give (ceffone); Naut cast off ● vi cease; **mollala!** fam stop that!

'molle a soft; (bagnato) wet

mol'letta nf (per capelli) hair-grip; (per bucato) clothes-peg; **mollette** pl (per ghiaccio ecc) tongs

mol'lezz|a nf softness; **~e** pl fig luxury

mol'lica nf crumb

mol'lusco nm mollusc

'molo nm pier; (banchina) dock

mol'teplic|e a manifold; (numeroso) numerous. **~ità** nf multiplicity

moltipli'ca|re vt, **~rsi** vr multiply. **~'tore** nm multiplier. **~'trice** nf calculating machine. **~zi'one** nf multiplication

molti'tudine nf multitude

'molto a a lot of; (con negazione e interrogazione) much, a lot of; (con nomi plurali) many, a lot of; **non ~ tempo** not much time, not a lot of time ● adv very; (con verbi) a lot; (con avverbi) much; **~ stupido** very stupid; **mangiare ~** eat a lot; **~ più veloce** much faster; **non mangiare ~** not eat a lot, not eat much ● pron a lot; (molto tempo) a lot of time; (con negazione e interrogazione) much, a lot; (plurale) many; **non ne ho ~** I don't have much, I don't have a lot; **non ne ho molti** I don't have many, I don't have a lot; **non ci metterò ~** I won't be long; **fra non ~** before long; **molti** (persone) a lot of people; **eravamo in molti** there were a lot of us

momentanea'mente adv momentarily; **è ~ assente** he's not here at the moment. **momen'taneo** a momentary

mo'mento nm moment; **a momenti** (a volte) sometimes; (fra un momento) in a moment; **dal ~ che** since; **per il ~** for the time being; **da un ~ all'altro** (cambiare idea ecc) from one moment to the next; (aspettare qcno ecc) at any moment

'monac|a nf nun. **~o** nm monk

'**Monaco** *nm* Monaco ●*nf (di Baviera)* Munich

mo'**narca** *nm* monarch. **monar'chia** *nf* monarchy. ~**hico, -a** *a* monarchic ●*nmf* monarchist

mona'**stero** *nm (di monaci)* monastery; *(di monache)* convent. mo'**nastico** *a* monastic

monche'**rino** *nm* stump

'**monco** *a* maimed; *(fig: troncato)* truncated; ~ **di un braccio** one-armed

mon'**dano** *a* worldly; **vita mondana** social life

mondi'**ale** *a* world *attrib*; **di fama** ~ world-famous

'**mondo** *nm* world; **il bel** ~ fashionable society; **un** ~ *(molto)* a lot

mondovisi'**one** *nf* **in** ~ transmitted worldwide

mo'**nello, -a** *nmf* urchin

mo'**neta** *nf* coin; *(denaro)* money; *(denaro spicciolo)* [small] change. ~ **estera** foreign currency; ~ **legale** legal tender; ~ **unica** single currency. **mone'tario** *a* monetary

mongolfi'**era** *nf* hot air balloon

mo'**nile** *nm* jewel

'**monito** *nm* warning

moni'**tore** *nm* monitor

mo'**nocolo** *nm* monocle

monoco'**lore** *a Pol* one-party

mono'dose *a inv* individually packaged

monogra'**fia** *nf* monograph

mono'**gramma** *nm* monogram

mono'**kini** *nm inv* monokini

mono'**lingue** *a* monolingual

monolo'**cale** *nm* studio flat *Br*, studio apartment

mono'**logo** *nm* monologue

mono'**pattino** *nm* [child's] scooter

mono'**polio** *nm* monopoly. ~**o di Stato** state monopoly. ~**z'zare** *vt* monopolize

mono'**sci** *nm inv* monoski

monosil'**labico** *a* monosyllabic. mono'**sillabo** *nm* monosyllable

monoto'**nia** *nf* monotony. mo'**notono** *a* monotonous

---

mono'**uso** *a* disposable

monsi'**gnore** *nm* monsignor

mon'**sone** *nm* monsoon

monta'**carichi** *nm inv* hoist

mon'**taggio** *nm Mech* assembly; *Cinema* editing; **catena di** ~ production line

mon'**tagna** *nf* mountain; *(zona)* mountains *pl*. **montagne** *pl* **russe** big dipper. ~**gnoso** *a* mountainous. ~**'naro, -a** *nmf* highlander. ~**o** *a* mountain *attrib*

mon'**tante** *nm (di finestra, porta)* upright

mon'**tare** *vt/i* mount; get on *(veicolo)*; *(aumentare)* rise; *Mech* assemble; frame *(quadro)*; *Culin* whip; edit *(film)*; *(a cavallo)* ride; *fig* blow up; ~**rsi la testa** get bigheaded. ~**to, -a** *nmf* poser. ~**'tura** *nf Mech* assembling; *(di occhiali)* frame; *(di gioiello)* mounting; *fig* exaggeration

'**monte** *nm anche fig* mountain; **a** ~ up-stream; **andare a** ~ be ruined; **mandare a** ~ **qcsa** ruin sth. ~ **di pietà** pawnshop

monte'**premi** *nm inv* jackpot

mont'**gomery** *nm inv* duffle coat

mon'**tone** *nm* ram; **carne di** ~ mutton

montu'**oso** *a* mountainous

monumen'**tale** *a* monumental.

monu'**mento** *nm* monument

mo'**quette** *nf (tappeto)* fitted carpet

'**mora** *nf (del gelso)* mulberry; *(del rovo)* blackberry

mo'**rale** *a* moral ●*nf* morale *pl*; *(di storia)* moral ●*nm* morale. mora'**lista** *nmf* moralist. ~**ità** *nf* morality; *(condotta)* morals *pl*. ~**iz'zare** *vt/i* moralize. ~'**mente** *adv* morally

morbi'**dezza** *nf* softness

'**morbido** *a* soft

mor'**billo** *nm* measles *sg*

'**morbo** *nm* disease. ~**sità** *nf (qualità)* morbidity

mor'**boso** *a* morbid

mor'**dace** *a* cutting

mor'dente a biting. **'mordere** vt bite; (corrodere) bite into. **mordicchi'are** vt gnaw

mor'fina nf morphine. **morfi'nomane** nmf morphine addict

mori'bondo a dying; (istituzione) moribund

morige'rato a moderate

mo'rire vi die; fig die out; **fa un freddo da** ~ it's freezing cold, it's perishing; ~ **di noia** be bored to death; **c'era da** ~ **dal ridere** it was killingly or hilariously funny

mor'mone nmf Mormon

mormo'r|are vt/i murmur; (brontolare) mutter. ~**io** nm murmuring; (lamentela) grumbling

'moro a dark ● nm Moor

mo'roso a in arrears

'morsa nf vice; fig grip

'morse a alfabeto ~ Morse code

mor'setto nm clamp

morsi'care vt bite. **'morso** nm bite; (di cibo, briglia) bit; **i morsi della fame** hunger pangs

morta'della nf mortadella (type of salted pork)

mor'taio nm mortar

mor'tal|e a mortal; (simile a morte) deadly; **di una noia** ~ e deadly. ~**ità** nf mortality. ~'**mente** adv (ferito) fatally; (offeso) mortally

morta'retto nm firecracker

'morte nf death

mortifi'cante a mortifying

mortifi'ca|re vt mortify. ~**rsi** vr be mortified. ~**to** a mortified. ~**zi'one** nf mortification

'morto, -a pp di **morire** ● a dead; ~ **di freddo** frozen to death; **stanco** ~ dead tired ● nm dead man ● nf dead woman

mor'torio nm funeral

mo'saico nm mosaic

'Mosca nf Moscow

'mosca nf fly; (barba) goatee. ~ **cieca** blindman's buff

mo'scato a muscat; **noce moscata** nutmeg ● nm muscatel

mosce'rino nm midge; (fam: persona) midget

mo'schea nf mosque

moschi'cida a fly attrib

'moscio a limp; **avere l'erre moscia** not be able to say one's r's properly

mo'scone nm bluebottle; (barca) pedalo

'moss|a nf movement; (passo) move. ~**o** pp di **muovere** ● a (mare) rough; (capelli) wavy; (fotografia) blurred

mo'starda nf mustard

'mostra nf show; (d'arte) exhibition; **far** ~ **di** pretend; **in** ~ on show; **mettersi in** ~ make oneself conspicuous

mo'stra|re vt show; (indicare) point out; (spiegare) explain. ~**rsi** vr show oneself; (apparire) appear

'mostro nm monster; (fig: persona) genius; ~ **sacro** fig sacred cow

mostru'osa'mente adv tremendously. ~'**oso** a monstrous; (incredibile) enormous

mo'tel nm inv motel

moti'va|re vt cause; Jur justify. ~**to** a (persona) motivated. ~**zi'one** nf motivation; (giustificazione) justification

mo'tivo nm reason; (movente) motive; (in musica, letteratura) theme; (disegno) motif

'moto nm motion; (esercizio) exercise; (gesto) movement; (sommossa) rising ● nf inv (motocicletta) motor bike; **mettere in** ~ start (motore)

moto'carro nm three-wheeler

motoci'cl|etta nf motor cycle. ~**ismo** nm motorcycling. ~**ista** nmf motor-cyclist

moto'cros|s nm motocross. ~'**sista** nmf scrambler

moto'lancia nf motor launch

moto'nave nf motor vessel

mo'tore a motor ● nm motor, engine. **moto'retta** nf motor scooter.

moto'rino nm moped. **motorino d'avviamento** starter

motoriz'za|to a Mil motorized. **~zi'one** nf (ufficio) vehicle licensing office

moto'scafo nm motorboat

motove'detta nf patrol vessel

'motto nm motto; (facezia) witticism; (massima) saying

mountain bike nf inv mountain bike

mouse nm inv Comput mouse

mo'vente nm motive

movimenta|re vt enliven. **~to** a lively. movi'mento nm movement; **essere sempre in movimento** be always on the go

mozi'one nf motion

mozzafi'ato a inv nail-biting

moz'zare vt cut off; dock (coda); **~ il fiato a qcno** take sb's breath away

mozza'rella nf mozzarella, mild, white cheese

mozzi'cone nm (di sigaretta) stub

'mozzo nm Mech hub; Naut ship's boy ●a (coda) truncated; (testa) severed

'mucca nf cow. **morbo della ~ pazza** mad cow disease

'mucchio nm heap, pile; **un ~ di** fig lots of

'muco nm mucus

'muffa nf mould; **fare la ~** go mouldy. **muf'fire** vi go mouldy

muf'fole nfpl mittens

mug'gi|re vi (mucca:) moo, low; (toro:) bellow. **~to** nm moo; bellow; (azione) mooing; bellowing

mu'ghetto nm lily of the valley

mugo'lare vi whine; (persona:) moan. **mugo'lio** nm whining

mugu'gnare vt fam mumble

mulatti'era nf mule track

mu'latto, -a nmf mulatto

muli'nello nm (d'acqua) whirlpool; (di vento) eddy; (giocattolo) windmill

mu'lino nm mill. **~ a vento** windmill

'mulo nm mule

'multa nf fine. mul'tare vt fine

multico'lore a multicoloured

multi'lingue a multilingual

multi'media mpl multimedia

multimedi'ale a multimedia attrib

multimiliar'dario, -a nmf multimillionaire

multinazio'nale nf multinational

'multiplo a & nm multiple

multiproprietà nf inv time-share

multi'uso a (utensile) all-purpose

'mummia nf mummy

'mungere vt milk

mungi'tura nf milking

munici'pal|e a municipal. **~ità** nf inv town council. **muni'cipio** nm town hall

mu'nifico a munificent

mu'nire vt fortify; **~ di** (provvedere) supply with

muni'zioni nfpl ammunition sg

'munto pp di mungere

mu'over|e vt move; (suscitare) arouse. **~si** vr move; **muoviti!** hurry up!, come on!

'mura nfpl (cinta di città) walls

mu'raglia nf wall

mu'rale a mural; (pittura) wall attrib

mur'a|re vt wall up. **~'tore** nm bricklayer; (con pietre) mason; (operaio edile) builder. **~'tura** nf (di pietra) masonry, stonework; (di mattoni) brickwork

mu'rena nf moray eel

'muro nm wall; (di nebbia) bank; **a ~** (armadio) built-in. **~ portante** load-bearing wall. **~ del suono** sound barrier

'muschio nm Bot moss

musco'la|re a muscular. **~'tura** nf muscles pl. 'muscolo nm muscle

mu'seo nm museum

museru'ola nf muzzle

'musi|ca nf music. **~cal** nm inv musical. **~'cale** a musical. **~'cista** nmf musician

'muso nm muzzle; (pej: di persona) mug; (di aeroplano) nose; **fare il ~** sulk. mu'sone, -a nmf sulker

'mussola nf muslin

musul'mano, -a nmf Moslem

'muta nf (cambio) change; (di penne) moult; (di cani) pack; (per immersione subacquea) wetsuit

muta'mento nm change

mu'tan|de nfpl pants; (da donna) knickers. **~'doni** nmpl (da uomo) long johns; (da donna) bloomers

mu'tare vt change

mu'tevole a changeable

muti'la|re vt mutilate. **~to, -a** nmf disabled person. **~to di guerra** disabled ex-serviceman. **~zi'one** nf mutilation

mu'tismo nm dumbness; fig obstinate silence

'muto a dumb; (silenzioso) silent; (fonetica) mute

mutu|a nf [cassa nf] **~** sickness benefit fund. **~'ato, -a** nmf ≈ NHS patient

'mutuo[1] a mutual

'mutuo[2] nm loan; (per la casa) mortgage; **fare un ~** take out a mortgage. **~ ipotecario** mortgage

....

Nn

....

'nacchera nf castanet

'nafta nf naphtha; (per motori) diesel oil

'naia nf cobra; (sl: servizio militare) national service

'nailon nm nylon

'nanna nf (sl: infantile) byebyes; **andare a ~** go byebyes; **fare la ~** sleep

'nano, -a a & nmf dwarf

napole'tano, -a a & nmf Neapolitan

'Napoli nf Naples

'nappa nf tassel; (pelle) soft leather

narci'sis|mo nm narcissism. **~ta** a & nmf narcissist

nar'ciso nm narcissus

nar'cotico a & nm narcotic

na'rice nf nostril

narra|re vt tell. **~'tivo, -a** a narrative ● nf fiction. **~'tore, ~'trice** nmf narrator. **~zi'one** nf narration; (racconto) story

na'sale a nasal

'nasc|ere vi (venire al mondo) be born; (germogliare) sprout; (sorgere) rise; **~ere da** fig arise from. **~ita** nf birth. **~i'turo** nm unborn child

na'scondere vt hide. **~si** vr hide

nascon'di|glio nm hiding-place. **~no** nm hide-and-seek. **na'scosto** pp di nascondere ● a hidden; **di nascosto** secretly

na'sello nm (pesce) hake

'naso nm nose

'nastro nm ribbon; (di registratore ecc) tape. **~ adesivo** adhesive tape. **~ isolante** insulating tape. **~ trasportatore** conveyor belt

na'tal|e a (paese) of one's birth. **N~e** nm Christmas; **~i** pl parentage. **~ità** nf [number of] births. **nata'lizio** a (del Natale) Christmas attrib; (di nascita) of one's birth

na'tante a floating ● nm craft

'natica nf buttock

na'tio a native

Nativi'tà nf Nativity. **na'tivo, -a** a & nmf native

'nato pp di nascere ● a born; **uno scrittore ~** a born writer; **nata Rossi** née Rossi

NATO nf Nato, NATO

na'tura nf nature; **pagare in ~** pay in kind. **~ morta** still life

natu'ra|le a natural; **al ~le** (alimento) plain, natural; **lel** naturally, of course. **~'lezza** nf naturalness. **~liz'zare** vt naturalize. **~l'mente** adv (ovviamente) naturally, of course

natu'rista nmf naturalist

naufra'gare vi be wrecked; (persona:) be shipwrecked. **nau'fragio** nm shipwreck; fig wreck. **'naufrago, -a** nmf survivor

'nause|a nf nausea; **avere la ~a**

feel sick. **~a'bondo** *a* nauseating. **~'ante** *a* nauseating. **~'are** *vt* nauseate

'nautic|a *nf* navigation. **~o** *a* nautical

na'vale *a* naval

na'vata *nf* (*centrale*) nave; (*laterale*) aisle

'nave *nf* ship. **~ cisterna** tanker. **~ da guerra** warship. **~ spaziale** spaceship

na'vetta *nf* shuttle

navicella *nf* **~ spaziale** nose cone

navi'gabile *a* navigable

navi'ga|re *vi* sail; **~re in Internet** surf the Net. **~'tore, ~'trice** *mf* navigator. **~zi'one** *nf* navigation

na'viglio *nm* fleet; (*canale*) canal

nazio'na|le *a* national ● *nf Sport* national team. **~'lismo** *nm* nationalism. **~'lista** *nmf* nationalist **~lità** *nf inv* nationality. **~liz'zare** *vt* nationalize. **nazi'one** *nf* nation

na'zista *a nmf* Nazi

N.B. *abbr* (**nota bene**) N.B.

ne *pers pron* (*di lui*) about him; (*di lei*) about her; (*di loro*) about them; (*di ciò*) about it; (*da ciò*) from that; (*di un insieme*) of it; (*di un gruppo*) of them; **non ne conosco nessuno** I don't know any of them; **ne ho** I have some; **non ne ho più** I don't have any left ● *adv* from there; **ne vengo ora** I've just come from there; **me ne vado** I'm off

né *conj* né... né... neither... nor...; **non ne ho il tempo né la voglia** I don't have either the time or the inclination; **né tu né io vogliamo andare** neither you nor I want to go; **né l'uno né l'altro** neither [of them/us]

ne'anche *adv* (*neppure*) not even; (*senza neppure*) without even ● *conj* (*e neppure*) neither... nor; **non parlo inglese, e lui ~** I don't speak English, neither does he *o* and he doesn't either

'nebbi|a *nf* mist; (*in città, su strada*) fog. **~'oso** *a* misty; foggy

necessaria'mente *adv* necessarily. **neces'sario** *a* necessary

necessità *nf inv* necessity; (*bisogno*) need

necessi'tare *vi* **~ di** need; (*essere necessario*) be necessary

necro'logio *nm* obituary

ne'cropoli *nf inv* necropolis

ne'fando *a* wicked

ne'fasto *a* ill-omened

ne'ga|re *vt* deny; (*rifiutare*) refuse; **essere ~to per qcsa** be no good at sth. **~'tivo, -a** *a* negative ● *nf* negative. **~zi'one** *nf* negation; (*diniego*) denial; *Gram* negative

ne'gletto *a* neglected

~negli = **in** + **gli**

negli'gen|te *a* negligent. **~za** *nf* negligence

negozi'abile *a* negotiable

negozi'ante *nmf* dealer; (*bottegaio*) shopkeeper

negozi'a|re *vt* negotiate ● *vi* **~re in trade** in. **~ti** *nmpl* negotiations

ne'gozio *nm* shop

'negro, -a *a* Negro, black ● *nmf* Negro, black; (*scrittore*) ghost writer

'nei = **in** + **i**. **nel** = **in** + **il**. **'nella** = **in** + **la**. **'nelle** = **in** + **le**. **'nello** = **in** + **lo**

'nembo *nm* nimbus

ne'mico, -a *a* hostile ● *nmf* enemy

nem'meno *conj* not even

'nenia *nf* dirge; (*per bambini*) lullaby; (*piagnucolio*) wail

'neo *nm* mole; (*applicato*) beauty spot

neo+ *pref* neo+

neofa'scismo *nm* neofascism

neo'litico *a* Neolithic

neolo'gismo *nm* neologism

'neon *nm* neon

neo'nato, -a *a* newborn ● *nmf* newborn baby

neozelan'dese *a* New Zealand ● *nmf* New Zealander

nep'pure *conj* not even

'nerb|o *nm* (*forza*) strength; *fig* backbone. **~o'ruto** *a* brawny

ne'retto *nm* Typ bold [type]

'nero *a* black; (*fam:* arrabbiato) fuming ● *nm* black; **mettere ~ su bianco** put in writing

nerva'tura *nf* nerves *pl*; *Bot* veining; (*di libro*) band

'nervo *nm* nerve; *Bot* vein; **avere i nervi** be bad-tempered; **dare ai nervi a qcno** get on sb's nerves. **~'sismo** *nm* nerviness

ner'voso *a* nervous; (*irritabile*) bad-tempered; **avere il ~** be irritable; **esaurimento** *nm* **~** nervous breakdown

'nespol|a *nf* medlar. **~o** *nm* medlar[-tree]

'nesso *nm* link

nes'suno *a* no, not... any; (*qualche*) any; **non ho nessun problema** I don't have any problems, I have no problems; **non lo trovo da nessuna parte** I can't find it anywhere; **in nessun modo** on no account; **nessuna notizia?** any news? ● *pron* nobody, no one, not... anybody, not... anyone; (*qualcuno*) anybody, anyone; **hai delle domande? - nessuna** do you have any questions? - none; **di voi nessuno** none of you; **~ dei due** (*di voi due*) neither of you; **non ho visto ~ dei tuoi amici** I haven't seen any of your friends; **c'è ~?** is anybody there?

'nettare *nm* nectar

net'tare *vt* clean

net'tezza *nf* cleanliness. **~ urbana** cleansing department

'netto *a* clean; (*chiaro*) clear; *Comm* net; **di ~** just like that

nettur'bino *nm* dustman

neu'tral|e *a & nm* neutral. **~ità** *nf* neutrality. **~iz'zare** *vt* neutralize.

'neutro *a* neutral; *Gram* neuter ● *nm Gram* neuter

neu'trone *nm* neutron

'neve *nf* snow

nevi'|care *vi* snow; **~ca** it is snowing. **~cata** *nf* snowfall. **ne'vischio** *nm* sleet. **ne'voso** *a* snowy

nevral'gia *nf* neuralgia. **ne'vralgico** *a* neuralgic

ne'vro|si *nf inv* neurosis. **~tico** *a* neurotic

'nibbio *nm* kite

'nicchia *nf* niche

nicchi'are *vi* shilly-shally

'nichel *nm* nickel

nichi'lista *a & nmf* nihilist

nico'tina *nf* nicotine

nidi'ata *nf* brood. **'nido** *nm* nest; (*giardino d'infanzia*) crèche

ni'ente *pron* nothing, not... anything; (*qualcosa*) anything; **non ho fatto ~ di male** I didn't do anything wrong, I did nothing wrong; **grazie! - di ~!** thank you! - don't mention it!; **non serve a ~** it is no use; **vuoi ~?** do you want anything?; **da ~** (*poco importante*) minor; (*di poco valore*) worthless ● *a inv fam* **non ho ~ fame** I'm not the slightest bit hungry ● *adv* **non fa ~** (*non importa*) it doesn't matter; **per ~** at all; (*litigare*) over nothing; **~ affatto!** no way! ● *nm* **un bel ~** absolutely nothing

niente'meno, **niente'meno** *adv* **~ che** no less than ● *int* fancy that!

'ninfa *nf* nymph

nin'fea *nf* water-lily

ninna'nanna *nf* lullaby

'ninnolo *nm* plaything; (*fronzolo*) knick-knack

ni'pote *nm* (*di zii*) nephew; (*di nonni*) grandson, grandchild ● *nf* (*di zii*) niece; (*di nonni*) granddaughter, grandchild

'nisba *pron* (*sl: niente*) zilch

'nitido *a* neat; (*chiaro*) clear

ni'trato *nm* nitrate

ni'tri|re *vi* neigh. **~to** *nm* (*di cavallo*) neigh

n° *abbr* (**numero**) No

no *adv* no; (*con congiunzione*) not; **dire di no** say no; **credo di no** I don't think so; **perché no?** why not?; **io no** not me; **ha detto così, no?** he said so, didn't he?; **fa freddo, no?** it's cold, isn't it?

'**nobil**|e *a* noble ● *nm* noble, nobleman ● *nf* noble, noblewoman. **~l'are** *a* noble. **~tà** *nf* nobility

'**nocca** *nf* knuckle

nocci'ol|**a** *nf* hazelnut. **~o** *nm* (*albero*) hazel

'**nocciolo** *nm* stone; *fig* heart

'**noce** *nf* walnut ● *nm* (*albero*, *legno*) walnut. **~ moscata** nutmeg. **~'pesca** *nf* nectarine

no'**civo** *a* harmful

'**nodo** *nm* knot; *fig* lump; *Comput* node; **fare il ~ della cravatta** do up one's tie. **~ alla gola** lump in the throat. **no'doso** *a* knotty.

'**nodulo** *nm* nodule

'**noi** *pers pron* (*soggetto*) we; (*oggetto, con prep*) us; **chi è? – siamo ~** who is it? – it's us

'**noia** *nf* boredom; (*fastidio*) bother; (*persona*) bore; **dar ~** annoy

noi'altri *pers pron* we

noi'oso *a* boring; (*fastidioso*) tiresome

noleggi'are *vt* hire; (*dare a noleggio*) hire out; charter (*nave, aereo*). **no'leggio** *nm* hire; (*di nave, aereo*) charter. **'nolo** *nm* hire; *Naut* freight; **a nolo** for hire

'**nomade** *a* nomadic ● *nmf* nomad

'**nome** *nm* name; *Gram* noun; **a ~ di** in the name of; **di ~** by name; **farsi un ~** make a name for oneself. **~ di famiglia** surname. **~ da ragazza** maiden name. **no'mea** *nf* reputation

nomencla'tura *nf* nomenclature

no'mignolo *nm* nickname

'**nomina** *nf* appointment. **nomi'na-le** *a* nominal; *Gram* noun *attrib*

nomi'na|**re** *vt* name; (*menzionare*) mention; (*eleggere*) appoint. **~'tivo** *a* nominative; *Comm* registered ● *nm* nominative; (*nome*) name

non *adv* not; **~ ti amo** I do not don't love you; **~ c'è di che** not at all

nonché *conj* (*tanto meno*) let alone; (*e anche*) as well as

noncu'ran|**te** *a* nonchalant; (*negli-*

gente) indifferent. **~za** *nf* nonchalance; (*negligenza*) indifference

nondi'meno *conj* nevertheless

'**nonna** *nf* grandmother, grandma *fam*

'**nonno** *nm* grandfather, grandpa *fam*; **nonni** *pl* grandparents

non'nulla *nm inv* trifle

'**nono** *a & nm* ninth

nono'stante *prep* in spite of ● *conj* although

nontiscordardimé *nm inv* forget-me-not

nonvio'lento *a* nonviolent

nonvio'lenza *nf* nonviolence

nord *nm* north; **del ~** northern

nord-est *nm* northeast; **a ~** northeasterly

'**nordico** *a* northern

nordocciden'tale *a* northwestern

nordorien'tale *a* northeastern

nord-ovest *nm* northwest; **a ~** northwesterly

'**norma** *nf* rule; (*istruzione*) instruction; **a ~ di legge** according to law; **è buona ~** it's advisable

nor'mal|**e** *a* normal. **~ità** *nf* normality. **~iz'zare** *vt* normalize. **~'mente** *adv* normally

norve'gese *a & nmf* Norwegian. **Nor'vegia** *nf* Norway

nossi'gnore *adv* no way

nostal'gia *nf* (*di casa, patria*) homesickness; (*del passato*) nostalgia; **aver ~ di** be homesick; **aver ~ di qcno** miss sb. **no'stalgico, -a** *a* nostalgic ● *nmf* reactionary

no'strano *a* local; (*fatto in casa*) home-made

'**nostro** (**il nostro** *m*, **la nostra** *f*, **i nostri** *mpl*, **le nostre** *fpl*) *poss a* our; **quella macchina è nostra** that car is ours; **~ padre** our father; **un ~ amico** a friend of ours ● *poss pron* ours

'**nota** *nf* (*segno*) sign; (*comunicazione, commento, Mus*) note; (*conto*) bill; (*lista*) list; **degno di ~** noteworthy; **prendere ~** take note. **note** *pl* **caratteristiche** distinguishing marks

no'tabile a & nm notable

no'taio nm notary

no'ta|re vt (segnare) mark; (annotare) note down; (osservare) notice; **far ~re** qcsa point sth out; **farsi ~re** get oneself noticed. **~zi'one** nf marking; (annotazione) notation

'**notes** nm inv notepad

no'tevole a (degno di nota) remarkable; (grande) considerable

noti'fica nf notification. **notifi'care** vt notify; Comm advise. **~zi'one** nf notification

no'tizi|a nf una ~a a piece of news, some news; (informazione) a piece of information, some information; **le ~e** the news sg. **~'ario** nm news sg

'**noto** a [well-]known; **rendere ~** (far sapere) announce

notorietà nf fame; **raggiungere la ~** become famous. **no'torio** a well-known; pej notorious

not'tambulo nm night-bird

not'tata nf night; **far ~** stay up all night

'**notte** nf night; **di ~** at night; **bianca** sleepless night; **peggio che andar di ~** worse than ever. **~'tempo** adv at night

not'turno a nocturnal; (servizio ecc) night

no'vanta a & nm ninety

novan't|enne a & nmf ninety-year-old. **~esimo** a ninetieth. **~ina** nf about ninety. **'nove** a & nm nine. **nove'cento** a & nm nine hundred. **il N~cento** the twentieth century

no'vella nf short story

novel'lino, -a a inexperienced ● nmf novice, beginner. **no'vello** a new

no'vembre nm November

novità nf inv novelty; (notizie) news sg; **l'ultima ~** (moda) the latest fashion

novizi'ato nm Relig novitiate; (tirocinio) apprenticeship

nozi'one nf notion; **nozioni** pl rudiments

'**nozze** nfpl marriage sg; (cerimonia) wedding sg. **~ d'argento** silver wedding [anniversary]. **~ d'oro** golden wedding [anniversary]

'**nub|e** nf cloud. **~e tossica** toxic cloud. **~i'fragio** nm cloudburst

'**nubile** a unmarried ● nf unmarried woman

'**nuca** nf nape

nucle'are a nuclear

'**nucleo** nm nucleus; (unità) unit

nu'di|smo nm nudism. **~sta** nmf nudist. **~tà** nf inv nudity, nakedness

'**nudo** a naked; (spoglio) bare; **a occhio ~** to the naked eye

'**nugolo** nm large number

'**nulla** pron = niente; **da ~** worthless

nulla'osta nm inv permit

nulla'nente nm **i nullatenenti** the have-nots

nullità nf inv (persona) nonentity

'**nullo** a Jur null and void

nume'ra|bile a countable. **~le** a & nm numeral

nume'ra|re vt number. **~zi'one** nf numbering. **nu'merico** a numerical

'**numero** nm number; (romano, arabo) numeral; (di scarpe ecc) size; **dare i numeri** be off one's head. **~ cardinale** cardinal [number]. **~ decimale** decimal. **~ ordinale** ordinal [number]. **~ di telefono** phone number. **nume'roso** a numerous

'**nunzio** nm nuncio

nu'ocere vi **a** harm

nu'ora nf daughter-in-law

nuo'ta|re vi swim; fig wallow; **~re nell'oro** be stinking rich, be rolling in it. **nu'oto** nm swimming. **~'tore, ~'trice** nmf swimmer

nu'ov|a nf (notizie) news sg. **~a'mente** adv again. **~o** a new; **di ~o** again; **rimettere a ~o** give a new lease of life to

nutri'ente *a* nourishing. **~'mento** *nm* nourishment

nu'tri|re *vt* nourish; harbour ⟨*sentimenti*⟩. **~rsi** eat; **~rsi di** *fig* live on. **~tivo** *a* nourishing. **~zi'one** *nf* nutrition

'nuvola *nf* cloud. **nuvo'loso** *a* cloudy

nuzi'ale *a* nuptial; ⟨*vestito, anello ecc*⟩ wedding *attrib*

....

Oo

....

O *abbr* (**ovest**) W

o *conj* or; **~ l'uno ~ l'altro** one or the other, either

'oasi *nf inv* oasis

obbedi'ente ecc = **ubbidiente** ecc

obbli'ga|re *vt* force, oblige; **~rsi** *vr* **~rsi a** undertake to. **~to a** *a* obliged. **~'torio** *a* compulsory. **~zi'one** *nf* obligation; *Comm* bond. **'obbligo** *nm* obligation; (*dovere*) duty; **avere obblighi verso** be under an obligation to; **d'obbligo** obligatory

obbligatoria'mente *adv* **fare qcsa ~** be obliged to do sth; **bisogna ~ farlo** you absolutely have to do it

ob'bro|brio *nm* disgrace. **~'brioso** *a* disgraceful

obe'lisco *nm* obelisk

obe'rare *vt* overburden

obesità *nf* obesity. **o'beso** *a* obese

obiet'tare *vt/i* object; **~ su** object to

obiettiva'mente *adv* objectively. **~vità** *nf* objectivity. **obiet'tivo** *a* objective ● *nm* objective; (*scopo*) object

obie|t'tore *nm* objector. **~t'tore di coscienza** conscientious objector. **~zi'one** *nf* objection

obi'torio *nm* mortuary

o'blio *nm* oblivion

o'bliquo *a* oblique; *fig* underhand

oblite'rare *vt* obliterate

oblò *nm inv* porthole

'oboe *nm* oboe

obso'leto *a* obsolete

'oca *nf* (*pl* **oche**) goose; (*donna*) silly girl

occasio'nal|e *a* occasional. **~'mente** *adv* occasionally

occasi'one *nf* occasion; (*buon affare*) bargain; (*motivo*) cause; (*opportunità*) chance; **d'~** second-hand

occhi'aia *nf* eye socket; **occhiaie** *pl* shadows under the eyes

occhi'ali *nmpl* glasses, spectacles. **~ da sole** sunglasses. **~ da vista** glasses, spectacles

occhi'ata *nf* look; **dare un'~ a** have a look at

occhieggi'are *vt* ogle ● *vi* (*far capolino*) peep

occhi'ello *nm* buttonhole; (*asola*) eyelet

'occhio *nm* eye; **~!** watch out!; **a quattr'occhi** in private; **tenere d'~ qcno** keep an eye on sb; **a ~** [**e croce**] roughly; **chiudere un'~** turn a blind eye; **dare nell'~** attract attention; **pagare** *o* **spendere un ~** [**della testa**] pay an arm and a leg; **saltare agli occhi** be blindingly obvious. **~ nero** (*pesto*) black eye. **~ di pernice** (*callo*) corn. **~'lino** *nm* **fare l'~lino a qcno** wink at sb

occiden'tale *a* western ● *nmf* westerner. **occi'dente** *nm* west

oc'clu|dere *vt* obstruct. **~si'one** *nf* occlusion

occor'ren|te *a* necessary ● *nm* the necessary. **~za** *nf* need; **all'~za** if need be

oc'correre *vi* be necessary

occulta'mento *nm* **~ di prove** concealment of evidence

occul'ta|re *vt* hide. **~'ismo** *nm* occult. **oc'culto** *a* hidden; (*magico*) occult

occu'pante *nmf* occupier; (*abusivo*) squatter

occu'pa|re vt occupy; spend ⟨tempo⟩; take up ⟨spazio⟩; ⟨dar lavoro a⟩ employ. **~rsi** vr occupy oneself; ⟨trovare lavoro⟩ find a job; **~rsi di** ⟨badare⟩ look after. **~to** a engaged; ⟨persona⟩ busy; ⟨posto⟩ taken. **~zi'one** nf occupation; **trovarsi un'~zione** ⟨interesse⟩ find oneself something to do

o'ceano nm ocean. **~ Atlantico** Atlantic [Ocean]. **~ Pacifico** Pacific [Ocean]

'ocra nf ochre

ocu'lare a ocular; ⟨testimone, bagno⟩ eye attrib

ocula'tezza nf care. **ocu'lato** a ⟨scelta⟩ wise

ocu'lista nmf optician; ⟨per malattie⟩ ophthalmologist

od conj or

'ode nf ode

odi'are vt hate

odi'erno a of today; ⟨attuale⟩ present

'odi|o nm hatred; **avere in ~o** hate. **~'oso** a hateful

odo'ra|re vt smell; ⟨profumare⟩ perfume ● vi **~re di** smell of. **~to** nm sense of smell. **o'dore** nm smell; ⟨profumo⟩ scent; **c'è odore di...** there's a smell of...; **sentire odore di** smell; **odori** pl Culin herbs. **odo'roso** a fragrant

of'fender|e vt offend; ⟨ferire⟩ injure. **~si** vr take offence

offen'siv|a nf Mil offensive. **~o** a offensive

offe'rente nmf offerer; ⟨in aste⟩ bidder

offer'ta nf offer; ⟨donazione⟩ donation; Comm supply; ⟨nelle aste⟩ bid; **in ~a speciale** on special offer. **~o** pp di **offrire**

offe'sa nf offence. **~o** pp di **offendere** ● a offended

offici'are vi officiate

offi'cina nf workshop; **~ [meccanica]** garage

of'frir|e vt offer. **~si** vr offer oneself; ⟨occasione:⟩ present itself; **~si di fare qcsa** offer to do sth

offu'scar|e vt darken; fig dull ⟨memoria, bellezza⟩; blur ⟨vista⟩. **~si** vr darken; ⟨fig: memoria, bellezza:⟩ fade away; ⟨vista:⟩ become blurred

of'talmico a ophthalmic

oggettività nf objectivity. **ogget'tivo** a objective

og'getto nm object; ⟨argomento⟩ subject; **oggetti** pl smarriti lost property, lost and found Am

'oggi adv & nm today; ⟨al giorno d'oggi⟩ nowadays; **da ~ in poi** from today on; **~ a otto** a week today; **dall'~ al domani** overnight; **il giornale di ~** today's paper; **al giorno d'~** these days, nowadays. **~gi'orno** adv nowadays

'ogni a inv every; ⟨qualsiasi⟩ any; **~ tre giorni** every three days; **ad ~ costo** at any cost; **ad ~ modo** anyway; **~ cosa** everything; **~ tanto** now and then; **~ volta che** every time, whenever

o'gnuno pron everyone, everybody; **~ di voi** each of you

ohimè int oh dear!

'ola nf inv Mexican wave

O'lan|da nf Holland. **o~'dese** a Dutch ● nm Dutchman; ⟨lingua⟩ Dutch ● nf Dutchwoman

ole'andro nm oleander

ole'at|o a oiled; **carta ~a** greaseproof paper

oleo'dotto nm oil pipeline. **ole'oso** a oily

ol'fatto nm sense of smell

oli'are vt oil

oli'era nf cruet

olim'piadi nfpl Olympic Games. **o'limpico** a Olympic. **olim'pionico** a ⟨primato, squadra⟩ Olympic

'olio nm oil; **sott'~** in oil; **colori a ~** oils; **quadro a ~** oil painting. **~ di mais** corn oil. **~ d'oliva** olive oil. **~ di semi** vegetable oil. **~ solare** sun-tan oil

o'liv|a nf olive. **oli'vastro** a olive. **oli'veto** nm olive grove. **~o** nm olive tree

'olmo *nm* elm

oltraggi'are *vt* offend. ol'traggio *nm* offence

ol'tranza *nf* a ~ to the bitter end

'oltre *adv* (*di luogo*) further; (*di tempo*) longer ● *prep* (*di luogo*) over; (*di tempo*) later than; (*più di*) more than; (*in aggiunta*) besides; ~ **a** (*eccetto*) except, apart from; **per** ~ **due settimane** for more than two weeks; **una settimana e** ~ a week and more. **~'mare** *adv* overseas. **~'modo** *adv* extremely

oltrepas'sare *vt* go beyond; (*eccedere*) exceed

o'maggio *nm* homage; (*dono*) gift; **in** ~ **con** free with; **omaggi** *pl* (*saluti*) respects

ombeli'cale *a* umbilical; **cordone** ~ umbilical cord. **ombe'lico** *nm* navel

'ombra *nf* (*zona*) shade; (*immagine oscura*) shadow; **all'~a in** the shade. **~eggi'are** *vt* shade

om'brello *nm* umbrella. **ombrel'lone** *nm* beach umbrella

om'bretto *nm* eye-shadow

om'broso *a* shady; (*cavallo*) skittish

ome'lette *nf inv* omelette

ome'lia *nf Relig* sermon

omeopa'tia *nf* homoeopathy. **omeo'patico** *a* homoeopathic ● *nm* homoeopath

omertà *nf* conspiracy of silence

o'messo *pp di* omettere

o'mettere *vt* omit

omi'cid|a *a* murderous ● *nmf* murderer. **~io** *nm* murder. **~io colposo** manslaughter

omissi'one *nf* omission

omogeneiz'zato *a* homogenized. **omo'geneo** *a* homogeneous

omolo'gare *vt* approve

o'monimo, -a *nmf* namesake ● *nm* (*parola*) homonym

omosessu'al|e *a & nmf* homosexual. **~ità** *nf* homosexuality

On. *abbr* (**onorevole**) MP

'oncia *nf* ounce

'onda *nf* wave; **andare in** ~ *Radio*

go on the air. **a ondate** in waves. **onde** *pl* **corte** short wave. **onde** *pl* **lunghe** long wave. **onde** *pl* **medie** medium wave. **on'data** *nf* wave

'onde *conj* so that ● *pron* whereby

ondeggi'are *vi* wave; (*barca*) roll

ondu'la|torio *a* undulating. **~zi'one** *nf* undulation; (*di capelli*) wave

'oner|e *nm* burden. **~'oso** *a* onerous

onestà *nf* honesty; (*rettitudine*) integrity. o'nesto *a* honest; (*giusto*) just

'onice *nf* onyx

onnipo'tente *a* omnipotent

onnipre'sente *a* ubiquitous; *Rel* omnipresent

ono'mastico *nm* name-day

ono'ra|bile *a* honourable. **~re** *vt* (*fare onore a*) be a credit to; honour (*promessa*). **~rio** *a* honorary ● *nm* fee. **~rsi** *vr* **~rsi di** be proud of

o'nore *nm* honour; **in** ~ **di** (*festa, ricevimento*) in honour of; **fare** ~ **a** do justice to (*pranzo*); **farsi** ~ **in** excel in; **fare gli onori di casa** do the honours

ono'revole *a* honourable ● *nmf* Member of Parliament

onorifi'cenza *nf* honour; (*decorazione*) decoration. **ono'rifico** *a* honorary

'onta *nf* shame

O.N.U. *nf abbr* (**Organizzazione delle Nazioni Unite**) UN

o'paco *a* opaque; (*colori ecc*) dull; (*fotografia, rossetto*) matt

o'pale *nf* opal

'opera *nf* (*lavoro*) work; (*azione*) deed; *Mus* opera; (*teatro*) opera house; (*ente*) institution; **mettere in** ~ put into effect; **mettersi all'~** get to work; **opere** *pl* **pubbliche** public works. **~ d'arte** work of art. **~ lirica** opera

ope'raio, -a *a* working ● *nmf* worker; ~ **specializzato** skilled worker

ope'ra|re *vt Med* operate on; **farsi** **~re** have an operation ● *vi* operate; (agire) work. ~'tivo, ~'torio a operating attrib. ~'tore, ~'trice nmf operator; TV cameraman. ~tore turistico tour operator. ~zi'one nf operation; Comm transaction

ope'retta nf operetta

ope'roso a industrious

opini'one nf opinion; rimanere della propria ~ still feel the same way. ~ pubblica public opinion, vox pop

'oppio nm opium

oppo'nente a opposing ● nmf opponent

op'por|re vt oppose; (obiettare) object; ~re resistenza offer resistance. ~si vr ~si a oppose

opportu'ni|smo nm expediency. ~sta nmf opportunist. ~tà nf inv opportunity; (l'essere opportuno) timeliness. oppor'tuno a opportune; (adeguato) appropriate; ritenere opportuno fare qcsa think it appropriate to do sth; il momento opportuno the right moment

opposi'tore nm opposer. ~zi'one nf opposition; d'~zione (giornale, partito) opposition

op'posto pp di opporre ● a opposite; (opinioni) opposing ● nm opposite; all'~ on the contrary

oppres|si'one nf oppression. ~sivo a oppressive. op'presso pp di opprimere ● a oppressed. ~'sore nm oppressor

oppri'me|nte a oppressive. op'primere vt oppress; (gravare) weigh down

op'pure conj otherwise, or [else]; lunedì ~ martedì Monday or Tuesday

op'tare vi ~ per opt for

opu'lento a opulent

o'puscolo nm booklet; (pubblicitario) brochure

opzio'nale a optional. opzi'one nf option

'ora¹ nf time; (unità) hour; di buon'~ early; che ~ è?, che ore

sono? what time is it?; mezz'~ half an hour; a ore (lavorare, pagare) by the hour; 50 km all'~ 50 km an hour; a un'~ di macchina one hour by car; non vedo l'~ di vederti I can't wait to see you; fare le ore piccole stay up until the small hours. ~ d'arrivo arrival time. l'~ esatta Teleph speaking clock. ~ legale daylight saving time. ~ di punta, ore pl di punta peak time; (per il traffico) rush hour

'ora² adv now; (tra poco) presently; ~ come ~ just now, at the moment; d'~ in poi from now on; per ~ for the time being, for now; è ~ di finirla! that's enough now! ~ [dunque] now [then]; ~ che ci penso,... now that I come to think about it,...

o'racolo nm oracle

'orafo nm goldsmith

o'rale a & nm oral; per via ~ by mouth

ora'mai adv = ormai

o'rario a (tariffa) hourly; (segnale) time attrib; (velocità) per hour ● nm time; (tabella dell'orario) timetable, schedule Am; essere in ~ be on time; in senso ~ clockwise. ~ di chiusura closing time. ~ flessibile flexitime. ~ di sportello banking hours. ~ d'ufficio business hours. ~ di visita Med consulting hours

o'rata nf gilthead

ora'tore, -'trice nmf speaker

ora'torio, -a a oratorical ● nm Mus oratorio ● nmf oratory. orazi'one nf Relig prayer

'orbita nf orbit; Anat [eye-]socket

or'chestra nf orchestra; (parte del teatro) pit

orche'stra|le a orchestral ● nmf member of an/the orchestra. ~re vt orchestrate

orchi'dea nf orchid

'orco nm ogre

'orda nf horde

or'digno nm device; (arnese) tool. ~ esplosivo explosive device

ordi'nale a & a nm ordinal

ordina'mento nm order; (leggi) rules pl.

ordi'nanza nf (del sindaco) bylaw; d'~ (soldato) on duty

ordi'na|re vt (sistemare) arrange; (comandare) order; (prescrivere) prescribe; Relig ordain

ordi'nario a ordinary; (grossolano) common; (professore) with a permanent position; di ordinaria amministrazione routine ●nm ordinary; Univ professor

ordi'nato a (in ordine) tidy

ordinazi'one nf order; fare un'~ place an order

'ordine nm order; (di avvocati, medici) association; mettere in ~ put in order; tidy up (appartamento ecc); di prim'~ first-class; di terz'~e (film, albergo) third-rate; di ~ pratico/economico (problema) of a practical/economic nature; fino a nuovo ~ until further notice; parola d'~ password. ~ del giorno agenda. ordini sacri pl Holy Orders

or'dire vt (tramare) plot

orec'chino nm ear-ring

o'recchi|o nm (pl nf orecchie) ear; avere ~ o have a good ear; mi è giunto all'~o che... I've heard that...; parlare all'~o a qcno whisper in sb's ear; suonare a ~o play by ear; ~'oni pl Med mumps sg

o'refice nm jeweller. ~'ria nf (arte) goldsmith's art; (negozio) goldsmith's [shop]

'orfano, -a a orphan ●nmf orphan. ~'trofio nm orphanage

orga'netto nm barrel-organ; (a bocca) mouth-organ; (fisarmonica) accordion

or'ganico a organic ●nm personnel

orga'nismo nm organism; (corpo umano) body

orga'nista nmf organist

organiz'za|re vt organize. ~rsi vr get organized. ~'tore, ~'trice nmf organizer. ~zi'one nf organization

'organo nm organ

or'gasmo nm orgasm; fig agitation

'orgia nf orgy

or'gogli|o nm pride. ~'oso a proud

orien'tale a eastern; (cinese ecc) oriental

orienta'mento nm orientation; perdere l'~ lose one's bearings; senso dell'~ sense of direction

orien'ta|re vt orientate. ~rsi vr find one's bearings; (tendere) tend

ori'ente nm east. l'Estremo O~ the Far East. il Medio O~ the Middle East

o'rigano nm oregano

origi'na|le a original; (eccentrico) odd ●nm original. ~'lità nf originality. ~re vt/i originate. ~rio a (nativo) native

o'rigine nf origin; in ~ originally; aver ~ da originate from; dare ~ a give rise to

origli'are vi eavesdrop

o'rina nf urine. ori'nale nm chamber-pot. ori'nare vi urinate

ori'undo a native

orizzon'tale a horizontal

orizzon'tare vt = orientare. oriz'zonte nm horizon

or'la|re vt hem. ~'tura nf hem. 'orlo nm edge; (di vestito ecc) hem

'orma nf track; (di piede) footprint; (impronta) mark

or'mai adv by now; (passato) by then; (quasi) almost

ormeggi'are vt moor. or'meggio nm mooring

ormo'nale a hormonal. or'mone nm hormone

orna'mentale a ornamental. orna'mento nm ornament

or'na|re vt decorate. ~rsi vr deck oneself. ~to a (stile) ornate

ornitolo'gia nf ornithology

'**oro** nm gold; **d'~** gold; fig golden; **una persona d'~** a wonderful person

orologi'aio, -a nmf clockmaker, watchmaker

oro'logio nm (portatile) watch; (da tavolo, muro ecc) clock. **~ a pendolo** grandfather clock. **~ da polso** wrist-watch. **~ a sveglia** alarm clock

o'roscopo nm horoscope

or'rendo a awful, dreadful

or'ribile a horrible

orripi'lante a horrifying

or'rore nm horror; **avere qcsa in ~** hate sth

orsacchi'otto nm teddy bear

'**orso** nm bear; (persona scontrosa) hermit. **~ bianco** polar bear

or'taggio nm vegetable

or'tensia nf hydrangea

or'tica nf nettle. **orti'caria** nf nettle-rash

orticol'tura nf horticulture. '**orto** nm vegetable plot

orto'dosso a orthodox

ortogo'nale a perpendicular

orto'grafia nf spelling. **~'grafico** a spelling attrib

orto'lano nm market gardener; (negozio) greengrocer's

ortope'dia nf orthopaedics sg. **~'pedico** a orthopaedic ● nm orthopaedist

orzai'olo nm sty

or'zata nf barley-water

osan'nato a praised to the skies

o'sare vt/i dare; (avere audacia) be daring

oscenità nf inv obscenity. **o'sceno** a obscene

oscil'lare vi swing; (prezzi ecc) fluctuate; Tech oscillate; (fig: essere indeciso) vacillate. **~zi'one** nf swinging; (di prezzi) fluctuation; Tech oscillation

oscura'mento nm darkening; (fig: di vista, mente) dimming; (totale) black-out

oscu'r|are vt darken; fig obscure.

~arsi vr get dark. **~ità** nf darkness. **o'scuro** a dark; (triste) gloomy; (incomprensibile) obscure

ospe'dal|e nm hospital. **~i'ero** a hospital attrib

ospi'tal|e a hospitable. **~ità** nf hospitality. **~re** vt give hospitality to. **'ospite** nm (chi ospita) host; (chi viene ospitato) guest ● nf hostess; guest

o'spizio nm (per vecchi) [old people's] home

ossa'tura nf bone structure; (di romanzo) structure, framework. **'osseo** a bone attrib

ossequi'|are vt pay one's respects to. **os'sequio** nm homage; **ossequi** pl respects. **~'oso** a obsequious

osser'van|te a (cattolico) practising. **~za** nf observance

osser'va|re vt observe; (notare) notice; keep (ordine, silenzio). **~'tore, ~'trice** nmf observer. **~'torio** nm Astr observatory; Mil observation post. **~zi'one** nf observation; (rimprovero) reproach

ossessio'na|nte a haunting; (persona) nagging. **~re** vt obsess; (infastidire) nag. **ossessi'one** nf obsession; (assillo) pain in the neck. **osses'sivo** a obsessive. **os'sesso** a obsessed

os'sia conj that is

ossi'dabile a liable to tarnish

ossi'dar|e vt, **~si** vr oxidize

'**ossido** nm oxide. **~ di carbonio** carbon monoxide

os'sidrico a **fiamma ossidrica** blowlamp

ossige'nar|e vt oxygenate; (decolorare) bleach. **~si** vr fig put back on its feet (azienda); **~si i capelli** dye one's hair blonde **os'sigeno** nm oxygen

'**osso** nm (Anat: pl nf **ossa**) bone; (di frutto) stone

osso'buco nm marrowbone

os'suto a bony

ostaco'lare vt hinder, obstruct.

o'stacolo *nm* obstacle; *Sport* hurdle

o'staggio *nm* hostage; **prendere in ~** take hostage

o'stello *nm* ~ **della gioventù** youth hostel

osten'ta|re *vt* show off; ~**re indifferenza** pretend to be indifferent. ~**zi'one** *nf* ostentation

oste'ria *nf* inn

o'stetrico, -a *a* obstetric ● *nm* obstetrician

'ostia *nf* host; (*cialda*) wafer

'ostico *a* tough

o'stile *a* hostile. ~**ità** *nf inv* hostility

osti'na|rsi *vr* persist (**a** in). ~**to** *a* obstinate. ~**zi'one** *nf* obstinacy

ostra'cismo *nm* ostracism

'ostrica *nf* oyster

ostro'goto *nm* **parlare ~** talk double Dutch

ostru'i|re *vt* obstruct. ~**zi'one** *nf* obstruction

otorinolaringoi'atra *nmf* ear, nose and throat specialist

otta'gonale *a* octagonal. ot'ta-gono *nm* octagon

ot'tan|ta *a & nm* eighty. ~**tenne** *a & nmf* eighty-year-old. ~**tesimo** *a* eightieth. ~**tina** *nf* about eighty

ot'tav|a *nf* octave. ~**o** *a* eighth

otte'nere *vt* obtain; (*più comune*) get; (*conseguire*) achieve

'ottico, -a *a* optic[al] ● *nmf* optician ● *nf* (*scienza*) optics *sg*; (*di lenti ecc*) optics *pl*

otti'ma|le *a* optimum. ~'**mente** *adv* very well

otti'mis|mo *nm* optimism. ~**ta** *nmf* optimist. ~**tico** *a* optimistic

'ottimo *a* very good ● *nm* optimum

'otto *a & nm* eight

ot'tobre *nm* October

otto'cento *a & nm* eight hundred; **l'O~** the nineteenth century

ot'tone *nm* brass

ottuage'nario, -a *a & nmf* octogenarian

ottu'ra|re *vt* block; fill (*dente*). ~**rsi** *vr* clog. ~'**tore** *nm Phot* shutter. ~**zi'one** *nf* stopping; (*di dente*) filling

ot'tuso *pp di* ottundere ● *a* obtuse

o'vaia *nf* ovary

o'vale *a & nm* oval

o'vat|ta *nf* cotton wool. ~'**tato** *a* (*suono, passi*) muffled

ovazi'one *nf* ovation

over'dose *nf inv* overdose

'ovest *nm* west

o'vile *nm* sheep-fold. ~**no** *a* sheep attrib

ovo'via *nf* two-seater cable car

ovulazi'one *nf* ovulation

o'vunque *adv* = **dovunque**

ov'vero *conj* or; (*cioè*) that is

ovvia'mente *adv* obviously

ovvi'are *vi* ~ **a** qcsa counter sth. 'ovvio *a* obvious

ozi'are *vi* laze around. '**ozio** *nm* idleness; **stare in ozio** idle about. ozi'oso *a* idle; (*questione*) pointless

o'zono *nm* ozone; **buco nell'~** hole in the ozone layer

Pp

pa'ca|re *vt* quieten. ~**to** *a* quiet

pac'chetto *nm* packet; (*postale*) parcel, package; (*di sigarette*) pack, packet. **~ software** software package

'pacchia *nf* (*fam: situazione*) bed of roses

pacchia'nata *nf* **è una ~** it's so garish. pacchi'ano *a* garish

'pacco *nm* parcel; (*involto*) bundle. **~ regalo** gift-wrapped package

paccot'tiglia *nf* (*roba scadente*) junk, rubbish

'pace *nf* peace; **darsi ~** forget it; **fare ~ con** qcno make it up with sb; **lasciare in ~** qcno leave sb in peace

pachi'derma nm (animale) pachyderm

pachi'stano, -a nmf & a Pakistani

pacifi'ca|re vt reconcile; (mettere pace) pacify. **~zi'one** nf reconciliation

pa'cifico a pacific; (calmo) peaceful; **il P~** the Pacific

paci'fis|mo nm pacifism. **~ta** nmf pacifist

pacioc'cone, -a nmf fam chubbychops

pa'dano a **pianura padana** Po Valley

pa'del|la nf frying-pan; (per malati) bedpan. **~'lata** nf una **~lata** di a frying-panful of

padigli'one nm pavilion

'padr|e nm father; **~i** pl (antenati) forefathers. **pa'drino** nm godfather. **~e'nostro** nm **il ~e nostro** the Lord's Prayer. **~'terno** nm God Almighty

padro'nanza nf mastery. **~ di sé** self-control

pa'drone, -a nmf master; mistress; (datore di lavoro) boss; (proprietario) owner. **~ggi'are** vt master

pae'sag|gio nm scenery; (pittura) landscape. **~'gista** nmf landscape architect

pae'sano, -a a country ● nmf villager

pa'ese nm (nazione) country; (territorio) land; (villaggio) village; **il Bel P~** Italy; **va' a quel ~!** I get lost!; **Paesi pl Bassi** Netherlands

paf'futo a plump

'paga nf pay, wages pl

pa'gabile a payable

pa'gaia nf paddle

paga'mento nm payment; **a ~** (parcheggio) which you have to pay to use. **~ anticipato** Comm advance payment. **~ alla consegna** cash on delivery, COD

paga'nesimo nm paganism

pa'gano, -a a & nmf pagan

pa'gare vt/i pay; **~ da bere a qcno**

buy sb a drink; **te la faccio ~** you'll pay for this

pa'gella nf [school] report

'pagina nf page. **Pagine pl Gialle** Yellow Pages. **~ web** Comput web page

'paglia nf straw

pagliac'cetto nm (per bambini) rompers pl

pagliac'ciata nf farce

pagli'accio nm clown

pagli'aio nm haystack

pagli'ericcio nm straw mattress

pagli'etta nf (cappello) boater; (per pentole) steel wool

pagli'uzza nf wisp of straw; (di metallo) particle

pa'gnotta nf [round] loaf

pail'lette nf inv sequin

'paio nm (pl nf paia) pair; **un ~** (circa due) a couple; **un ~ di** (scarpe, forbici) a pair of

Paki'stan nm Pakistan

'pala nf shovel; (di remo, elica) blade; (di ruota) paddle

pala'fitta nf pile-dwelling

pala'sport nm inv indoor sports arena

pa'late nfpl **a ~** (fare soldi) hand over fist

pa'lato nm palate

palaz'zetto nm **~ dello sport** indoor sports arena

palaz'zina nf villa

pa'lazzo nm palace; (edificio) building. **~ delle esposizioni** exhibition centre. **~ di giustizia** law courts pl, courthouse. **~ dello sport** indoor sports arena

'palco nm (pedana) platform; Theat box. **~['scenico]** nm stage

pale'sar|e vt disclose. **~si** vr reveal oneself. **pa'lese** a evident

Pale'sti|na nf Palestine. **~'nese** nmf Palestinian

pa'lestra nf gymnasium, gym; (ginnastica) gymnastics pl

pa'letta nf paper; (per focolare) shovel. **~ [della spazzatura]** dustpan

pa'letto nm peg

'palio *nm* (*premio*) prize. il P~ horse-race held at Siena

paliz'zata *nf* fence

'palla *nf* ball; (*proiettile*) bullet; (*fam: bugia*) porkie; **che palle!** *vulg* this is a pain in the arse!. ~ di neve snowball. ~ al piede *fig* millstone round one's neck

pallaca'nestro *nf* basketball

palla'mano *nf* handball

pallanu'oto *nf* water polo

palla'volo *nf* volley-ball

palleggi'are *vi* (*calcio*) practise ball control; *Tennis* knock up

pallia'tivo *nm* palliative

'pallido *a* pale; **non ne ho la più pallida idea** I don't have the faintest idea

pal'lina *nf* (*di vetro*) marble

pal'lino *nm* avere il ~ del calcio be crazy about football

pallon'cino *nm* balloon; (*lanterna*) Chinese lantern; (*fam: etilometro*) Breathalyzer®

pal'lone *nm* ball; (*calcio*) football; (*aerostato*) balloon

pal'lore *nm* pallor

pal'loso *a sl* boring

pal'lottola *nf* pellet; (*proiettile*) bullet

'palma *nf Bot* palm. ~o *nm Anat* palm; (*misura*) hand's-breadth; **restare con un ~o di naso** feel disappointed

'palo *nm* pole; (*di sostegno*) stake; (*in calcio*) goalpost; **fare il ~** (*ladro*) keep a lookout. ~ della luce lamppost

palom'baro *nm* diver

pal'pare *vt* feel

'palpebra *nf* eyelid

palpi'ta|re *vi* throb; (*fremere*) quiver. **~zi'one** *nf* palpitation. 'palpito *nm* throb; (*del cuore*) beat

pa'lude *nf* marsh, swamp

palu'doso *a* marshy

pa'lustre *a* marshy; (*piante, uccelli*) marsh *attrib*

pam'pino *nm* vine leaf

pana'cea *nf* panacea

'panca *nf* bench; (*in chiesa*) pew

pancarré *nm* sliced bread

pan'cetta *nf Culin* bacon; (*di una certa età*) paunch

pan'chetto *nm* [foot]stool

pan'china *nf* garden seat; (*in calcio*) bench

'pancia *nf* belly, tummy *fam*; **mal di ~** stomach-ache; **metter su ~** develop a paunch; **a ~ in giù** lying face down. panci'era *nf* corset

panci'olle: **stare in ~** lounge about

panci'one *nm* (*persona*) pot belly

panci'otto *nm* waistcoat

pande'monio *nm* pandemonium

pan'doro *nm* kind of sponge cake traditionally eaten at Christmas

'pane *nm* bread; (*pagnotta*) loaf; (*di burro*) block. ~ a cassetta sliced bread. pan grattato breadcrumbs *pl*. ~ di segale rye bread. pan di Spagna sponge cake. ~ tostato toast

panet'te|ria *nf* bakery; (*negozio*) baker's [shop]. ~i'ere, -a *nmf* baker

panet'tone *nf* dome-shaped cake with sultanas and candied fruit eaten at Christmas

'panfilo *nm* yacht

pan'forte *nm* nougat-like spicy delicacy from Siena

'panico *nm* panic; **lasciarsi prendere dal ~** panic

pani'ere *nm* basket; (*cesta*) hamper

pani'ficio *nm* bakery; (*negozio*) baker's [shop]

pani'naro *nm sl* preppie

pa'nino *nm* [bread] roll. ~ imbottito filled roll. ~ al prosciutto ham roll. ~teca *nf* sandwich bar

'panna *nf* cream. ~ da cucina [single] cream. ~ montata whipped cream

'panne *nf Mech* in ~ broken down; **restare in ~** break down

pan'nello *nm* panel. ~ solare solar panel

'panno *nm* cloth; panni *pl* (*abiti*)

clothes; **mettersi nei panni di qcno** *fig* put oneself in sb's shoes

pan'nocchia *nf* (*di granoturco*) cob

panno'lino *nm* (*per bambini*) nappy; (*da donna*) sanitary towel

pano'rama *nm* panorama; *fig* overview. **~ico** *a* panoramic

pantacol'lant *nmpl* leggings

pantalon'cini *nmpl* ~ [**corti**] shorts

panta'loni *nmpl* trousers, pants *Am*

pan'tano *nm* bog

pan'tera *nf* panther; (*auto della polizia*) high-speed police car

pan'tofo|la *nf* slipper. **~'laio, -a** *nmf fig* stay-at-home

pan'zana *nf* fib

pao'nazzo *a* purple

'papa *nm* Pope

papà *nm inv* dad[dy]

pa'pale *a* papal

papa'lina *nf* skull-cap

papa'razzo *nm* paparazzo

pa'pato *nm* papacy

pa'pavero *nm* poppy

'paper|a *nf* (*errore*) slip of the tongue. **~o** *nm* gosling

papil'lon *nm inv* bow tie

pa'piro *nm* papyrus

'pappa *nf* (*per bambini*) pap

pappa'gallo *nm* parrot

pappa'molle *nmf* wimp

'para *nf* suole *nfpl* **di ~** crêpe soles

pa'rabola *nf* parable; (*curva*) parabola

para'bolico *a* parabolic

para'brezza *nm inv* windscreen, windshield *Am*

paracadu'tar|e *vt* parachute. **~si** *vr* parachute

paraca'du|te *nm inv* parachute. **~'tismo** *nm* parachuting. **~'tista** *nmf* parachutist

para'carro *nm* roadside post

paradi'siaco *a* heavenly

para'diso *nm* paradise. **~ terrestre** Eden, earthly paradise

parados'sale *a* paradoxical. **para'dosso** *nm* paradox

para'fango *nm* mudguard

paraf'fina *nf* paraffin

parafra'sare *vt* paraphrase

para'fulmine *nm* lightning-conductor

pa'raggi *nmpl* neighbourhood *sg*

parago'na|bile *a* comparable (a to). **~re** *vt* compare. **para'gone** *nm* comparison; **a paragone di** in comparison with

pa'ragrafo *nm* paragraph

pa'ra|lisi *nf inv* paralysis. **~'litico, -a** *a & nmf* paralytic. **~liz'zare** *vt* paralyse. **~liz'zato** *a* (*dalla paura*) transfixed

paral'lel|a *nf* parallel line. **~a'mente** *adv* in parallel. **~o** *a & nm* parallel; **~e** *pl* parallel bars. **~o'gramma** *nm* parallelogram

para'lume *nm* lampshade

para'medico *nm* paramedic

pa'rametro *nm* parameter

para'noi|a *nf* paranoia. **~co, -a** *a & nmf* paranoid

paranor'male *a* (*fenomeno, facoltà*) paranormal

para'occhi *nmpl* blinkers. **parao'recchie** *nm* earmuffs

para'petto *nm* parapet

para'piglia *nm* turmoil

para'plegico, -a *a & nmf* paraplegic

pa'rar|e *vt* (*addobbare*) adorn; (*riparare*) shield; save (*tiro, pallone*) ward off, parry (*schiaffo, pugno*) ● *vi* (*mirare*) lead up to. **~si** *vr* (*abbigliarsi*) dress up; (*da pioggia, pugni*) protect oneself; **~si dinanzi a qcno** appear in front of sb

para'sole *nm inv* parasol

paras'sita *a* parasitic ● *nm* parasite

parasta'tale *a* a government-controlled

pa'rata *nf* parade; (*in calcio*) save; (*in scherma, pugilato*) parry

para'urti *nm inv* *Auto* bumper, fender *Am*

para'vento *nm* screen

par'cella *nf* bill

parcheggi'a|re *vt* park. **par-**

'**cheggio** nm parking; (posteggio) carpark, parking lot Am. ~'**tore**, ~'**trice** nmf parking attendant. ~**tore abusivo** person who illegally earns money by looking after parked cars

par'**chimetro** nm parking-meter

'**parco**[1] a sparing; (moderato) moderate

'**parco**[2] nm park. ~ **di divertimenti** fun-fair. ~ **giochi** playground. ~ **naturale** wildlife park. ~ **nazionale** national park. ~ **regionale** [regional] wildlife park

pa'**recchi** a a good many ●pron several

pa'**recchio** a quite a lot of ●pron quite a lot ●adv rather; (parecchio tempo) a time

pareggi'**are** vt level; (eguagliare) equal; Comm balance ●vi draw

pa'**reggio** nm Comm balance; Sport draw

paren'**tado** nm relatives pl; (vincolo di sangue) relationship

pa'**rente** nmf relative. ~ **stretto** close relation

paren'**tela** nf relatives pl; (vincolo di sangue) relationship

pa'**rentesi** nf inv parenthesis; (segno grafico) bracket; (fig: pausa) break. ~ **pl graffe** curly brackets. ~ **quadre** square brackets. ~ **tonde** round brackets

pa'**reo** nm (copricapo) sarong; **a** ~ (gonna) wrap-around

pa'**rere**[1] nm opinion; **a mio** ~ in my opinion

pa'**rere**[2] vi seem; (pensare) think; **che te ne pare?** what do you think of it?; **pare di sì** it seems so

pa'**rete** nf wall; (in alpinismo) face. ~ **divisoria** partition wall

'**pari** a inv equal; (numero) even; **andare di** ~ **passo** keep pace; **essere** ~ be even o quits; **arrivare** ~ draw; ~ (copiare, ripetere) word for word; **fare** ~ **o dispari** toss a coin ●nmf inv equal, peer; **ragazza alla** ~ au pair [girl]; **mettersi in** ~ **con qcsa** catch up

with sth ●nm (titolo nobiliare) peer

Pa'**rigi** nf Paris

pa'**riglia** nf pair

pari'**tà** nf equality; Tennis deuce. ~'**tario** a parity attrib

parlamen'**tare** a parliamentary ●nmf Member of Parliament ●vi discuss. **parla'mento** nm Parliament. **il Parlamento europeo** the European Parliament

parlan'**tina** nf **avere la** ~ be a chatterbox

par'**la|re** vt/i speak, talk; (confessare) talk; ~ **bene/male di qcno** speak well/ill of somebody; **non parliamone più** let's forget about it; **non se ne parla nemmeno** don't even mention it!. ~**to** a (lingua) spoken. ~'**torio** nm parlour; (in prigione) visiting room

parlot'**tare** vi mutter. **parlot'tìo** nm muttering

parmigi'**ano** nm Parmesan

paro'**dia** nf parody

pa'**rola** nf (facoltà) speech; **è una** ~ **!** it is easier said than done!; **parole** pl (di canzone) words, lyrics; **rivolgere la** ~ **a** address; **dare a qcno la propria** ~ give sb one's word; **in parole povere** crudely speaking. **parole** pl **incrociate** crossword [puzzle] sg. ~ **d'onore** word of honour. ~ **d'ordine** password. **paro'laccia** nf swear-word

par'**quet** nm inv (pavimento) parquet flooring

par'**rocchi|a** nf parish. ~'**ale** a parish attrib. ~'**ano, -a** nmf parishioner. '**parr|oco** nm parish priest

par'**rucca** nf wig

parrucchi'**ere, -a** nmf hairdresser

parruc'**chino** nm toupée, hairpiece

parsi'**moni|a** nf thrift. ~'**oso** a thrifty

'**parso** pp di **parere**

'**parte** nf part; (lato) side; (partito) party; (porzione) share; **a** ~ apart from; **in** ~ in part; **la maggior** ~

di the majority of; **d'altra ~** on the other hand; **da ~** aside; (*in disparte*) to one side; **farsi da ~** stand aside; **da ~ di** from; (*per conto di*) on behalf of; **è gentile da ~ tua** it is kind of you; **fare una brutta ~ a qcno** behave badly towards sb; **da che ~ è...?** whereabouts is...?; **da una ~..., dall'altra...** on the one hand..., on the other hand...; **dall'altra ~ di** on the other side of; **da nessuna ~** nowhere; **da tutte le parti** (*essere*) everywhere; **da questa ~** (*in questa direzione*) this way; **da un anno a questa ~** for about a year now; **essere dalla ~ di qcno** be on sb's side; **prendere la parti di qcno** take sb's side; **essere ~ in causa** be involved; **fare ~ di** (*appartenere a*) be a member of; **rendere ~** a take part in. ~ **civile** plaintiff

parteci'pante *nmf* participant

parteci'pa|re *vi* **~re a** participate in, take part in; (*condividere*) share in. **~zi'one** *nf* participation; (*annuncio*) announcement; *Fin* shareholding; (*presenza*) presence. **par'tecipe** *a* participating

parteggi'are *vi* **~ per** side with

par'tenza *nf* departure; *Sport* start; **in ~** leaving for

parti'cella *nf* particle

parti'cipio *nm* participle

partico'lar|e *a* particular; (*privato*) private ●*nm* detail, particular; **fin nei minimi ~i** down to the smallest detail. **~eggi'ato** *a* detailed. **~ità** *nf inv* particularity; (*dettaglio*) detail

partigi'ano, -a *a & nmf* partisan

par'tire *vi* leave; (*aver inizio*) start; **a ~ da** [beginning] from

par'tita *nf* game; (*incontro*) match; *Comm* lot; (*contabilità*) entry. **~ di calcio** football match. **~ a carte** game of cards

par'tito *nm* party; (*scelta*) choice; (*occasione di matrimonio*) match;

---

per ~ preso out of sheer pigheadedness

'parto *nm* childbirth; **un ~ facile** an easy birth *o* labour; **dolori** *pl* **del ~** labour pains. **~ cesareo** Caesarean section. **~'rire** *vt* give birth to

par'venza *nf* appearance

parzi'al|e *a* partial. **~ità** *nf* partiality. **~'mente** *adv* (*non completamente*) partially; **~mente scremato** semi-skimmed

pasco'lare *vt* graze. **'pascolo** *nm* pasture

'Pasqua *nf* Easter. **pa'squale** *a* Easter *attrib*

'passa: e ~ *adv* (*e oltre*) plus

pas'sabile *a* passable

pas'saggio *nm* passage; (*traversata*) crossing; *Sport* pass; (*su veicolo*) lift; **essere di ~** be passing through. **~ a livello** level crossing, grade crossing *Am*. **~ pedonale** pedestrian crossing

passamon'tagna *nm inv* balaclava

pas'sante *nmf* passer-by ●*nm* (*di cintura*) loop ●*a Tennis* passing

passa'porto *nm* passport

pas'sa|re *vi* pass; (*attraversare*) pass through; (*far visita*) call; (*andare*) go; (*essere approvato*) be passed; **~re alla storia** go down in history; **mi è ~to di mente** it slipped my mind; **~re per un genio/idiota** be taken for a genius/an idiot; **farsi ~re per qcno** pass oneself off as sb ●*vt* (*far scorrere*) pass over; (*sopportare*) go through; (*al telefono*) put through; *Culin* strain; **~re di moda** go out of fashion; **le passo il signor Rossi** I'll put you through to Mr Rossi; **~rsela bene** be well off; **come te la passi?** how are you doing?. **~ta** *nf* (*di vernice*) coat; (*spolverata*) dusting; (*occhiata*) look

passa'tempo *nm* pastime

pas'sato *a* past; **l'anno ~** last year; **sono le tre passate** it's past *o* after three o'clock ● *nm* past; *Culin* purée; *Gram* past tense. ~ **prossimo** *Gram* present perfect. ~ **remoto** *Gram* [simple] past. ~ **di verdure** cream of vegetable soup

passaver'dure *nm inv* food mill

passeg'gero, -a *a* passing ● *nmf* passenger

passeggi'a|re *vi* walk, stroll. ~**ta** *nf* walk, stroll; (*luogo*) public walk; (*in bicicletta*) ride; **fare una ~ta** go for a walk

passeg'gino *nm* pushchair, stroller *Am*

pas'seggio *nm* walk; (*luogo*) promenade; **andare a ~** go for a walk; **scarpe da ~** walking shoes

passe-partout *nm inv* master-key

passe'rella *nf* gangway; *Aeron* boarding bridge; (*per sfilate*) catwalk

'passero *nm* sparrow. **passe'rotto** *nm* (*passero*) sparrow

pas'sibile *a* ~ **di** liable to

passio'nale *a* passionate. **passi'one** *nf* passion

pas'sivo *a* passive ● *nm* passive; *Comm* liabilities *pl*; **in ~** (*bilancio*) loss-making

'passo *nm* step; (*orma*) footprint; (*andatura*) pace; (*brano*) passage; (*valico*) pass; **a due passi da qui** a stone's throw away; **a ~ d'uomo** at walking pace; **di buon ~** at a spanking pace; **fare due passi** go for a stroll; **di pari ~** *fig* hand in hand. ~ **carrabile**, ~ **carraio** driveway

'past|a *nf* (*impasto per pane ecc*) dough; (*per dolci, pasticcino*) pastry; (*pastasciutta*) pasta; (*massa molle*) paste; *fig* nature. ~**a frolla** shortcrust pastry. **pa'stella** *nf* batter

pastasci'utta *nf* pasta

pa'stello *nm* pastel

pa'sticca *nf* pastille; (*fam: pastiglia*) pill

pasticc|e'ria *nf* cake shop, patisse-

rie; (*pasticcini*) pastries *pl*; (*arte*) confectionery

pasticci'are *vi* make a mess ● *vt* make a mess of

pasticci'ere, -a *nmf* confectioner

pastic'cino *nm* little cake

pastic'ci|o *nm Culin* pie; (*lavoro disordinato*) mess; **mettersi nei pasticci** get into trouble. ~**one, -a** *nmf* bungler ● *a* bungling

pasti'ficio *nm* pasta factory

pa'stiglia *nf Med* pill, tablet; (*di menta*) sweet. ~ **dei freni** brake pad

'pasto *nm* meal

pasto'rale *a* pastoral. **pa'store** *nm* shepherd; *Relig* pastor. **pastore tedesco** German shepherd, Alsatian

pastoriz'za|re *vt* pasteurize. ~**to** *a* pasteurized. ~**zi'one** *nf* pasteurization

pa'stoso *a* doughy; *fig* mellow

pa'stura *nf* pasture; (*per pesci*) bait

pa'tacca *nf* (*macchia*) stain; (*fig: oggetto senza valore*) piece of junk

pa'tata *nf* potato. **patate fritte** chips *Br*, French fries. **pata'tine** *nfpl* [potato] crisps, chips *Am*

pata'trac *nm inv* (*crollo*) crash

pâté *nm inv* pâté

pa'tella *nf* limpet

pa'tema *nm* anxiety

pa'tente *nf* licence. ~ **di guida** driving licence, driver's license *Am*

pater'na|le *nf* scolding. ~**lista** *nm* paternalist

paternità *nf* paternity. **pa'terno** *a* paternal; (*affetto ecc*) fatherly

pa'tetico *a* pathetic. **'pathos** *nm* pathos

pa'tibolo *nm* gallows *sg*

patina *nf* patina; (*sulla lingua*) coating

pa'ti|re *vt/i* suffer. ~**to, -a** *a* suffering ● *nm* fanatic. ~**to della musica** music lover

patolo'gia *nf* pathology. **pato'logico** *a* pathological

'patria *nf* native land

patri'arca *nm* patriarch

pa'trigno *nm* stepfather

patrimoni'ale *a* property *attrib.* **patri'monio** *nm* estate

patri'o|**ta** *nmf* patriot. **~tico** *a* patriotic. **~'tismo** *nm* patriotism

pa'trizio, -a *a* & *nmf* patrician

patro|**ci'nare** *vt* support. **~'cinio** *nm* support

patro'nato *nm* patronage. **pa'trono** *nm Relig* patron saint; *Jur* counsel

'patta' *nf (di tasca)* flap

'patta² *nf (pareggio)* draw

patteggia|**a'mento** *nm* bargaining. **~'are** *vt/i* negotiate

patti'naggio *nm* skating. **~ su ghiaccio** ice skating. **~ a rotelle** roller skating

patti'na|**re** *vi* skate; *(auto:)* skid. **~'tore, ~'trice** *nmf* skater. **'pattino** *nm* skate; *Aeron* skid. **pattino da ghiaccio** iceskate. **pattino a rotelle** roller-skate

'patto *nm* deal; *Pol* pact; **a ~ che** on condition that

pat'tuglia *nf* patrol. **~ stradale** patrol car; police motorbike, highway patrol *Am*

pattu'ire *vt* negotiate

pattumi'era *nf* dustbin, trashcan *Am*

pa'ura *nf* fear; *(spavento)* fright; **aver ~** be afraid; **mettere ~ a** frighten. **pau'roso** *a (che fa paura)* frightening; *(che ha paura)* fearful; *(fam: enorme)* awesome

'pausa *nf* pause; *(nel lavoro)* break; **fare una ~** pause; *(nel lavoro)* have a break

pavimen'ta|**re** *vt* pave *(strada)*. **~zi'one** *nf (operazione)* paving. **pavi'mento** *nm* floor

pa'vone *nm* peacock. **~ggi'arsi** *vr* strut

pazien'tare *vi* be patient

pazi'ente *a* & *nmf* patient. **~'mente** *adv* patiently. **pazi'enza** *nf* patience; **pazienza!** never mind!

'pazza *nf* madwoman. **~'mente** *adv* madly

paz'z|**esco** *a* foolish; *(esagerato)* crazy. **~ia** *nf* madness; *(azione)* [act of] folly. **'pazzo** *a* mad; *fig* crazy ● *nm* madman; **essere pazzo di/per** be crazy about; **pazzo di gioia** mad with joy; **da pazzi** *fam* crackpot; **darsi alla pazza gioia** live it up. **paz'zoide** *a* whacky

'pecca *nf* fault; **senza ~** flawless. **peccami'noso** *a* sinful

pec'ca|**re** *vi* sin; **~re di** be guilty of *(ingratitudine)*. **~to** *nm* sin; **~to che...** it's a pity that...; *[che]* **~to!** [what a] pity!. **~'tore, ~'trice** *nmf* sinner

'pece *nf* pitch

'peco|**ra** *nf* sheep. **~ra nera** black sheep. **~'raio** *nm* shepherd. **~'rella** *nf* cielo a **~relle** sky full of fluffy white clouds. **~'rino** *nm (formaggio)* sheep's milk cheese

peculi'ar|**e** *a* **~ di** peculiar to. **~ità** *nf inv* peculiarity

pe'daggio *nm* toll

pedago'gia *nf* pedagogy. **peda'gogico** *a* pedagogical

peda'lare *vi* pedal. **pe'dale** *nm* pedal. **pedalò** *nm inv* pedalo

pe'dana *nf* footrest; *Sport* springboard

pe'dante *a* pedantic. **~'ria** *nf* pedantry. **pedan'tesco** *a* pedantic

pe'data *nf (in calcio)* kick; *(impronta)* footprint

pede'rasta *nm* pederast

pe'destre *a* pedestrian

pedi'atra *nmf* paediatrician. **pedia'tria** *nf* paediatrics *sg*

pedi'cure *nm inv* chiropodist, podiatrist *Am* ● *nm (cura dei piedi)* pedicure

pedi'gree *nm inv* pedigree

pe'dina *nf (alla dama)* piece; *fig* pawn. **~'mento** *nm* shadowing. **pedi'nare** *vt* shadow

pe'dofilo, -a *nmf* paedophile

pedo'nale *a* pedestrian. **pe'done, -a** *nmf* pedestrian

peeling *nm inv* exfoliation treatment

'peggio *adv* worse; **~ per te!** too bad!; **~ di cosi** any worse; **la persona ~ vestita** the worst dressed person ●*a* worse; **niente di ~** nothing worse ●*nm* **il ~ è che...** the worst of it is that...; **pensare al ~** think the worst ●*nf* **alla ~** at worst; **avere la ~** get the worst of it; **alla meno ~** as best I can

peggiora'mento *nm* worsening

peggio'ra|re *vt* make worse, worsen ●*vi* get worse, worsen. **~tivo** *a* pejorative

peggi'ore *a* worse; (*superlativo*) worst; **nella ~ delle ipotesi** if the worst comes to the worst ●*nmf* **il/la ~** the worst

'pegno *nm* pledge; (*nei giochi di società*) forfeit; *fig* token

pelan'drone *nm* slob

pe'la|re *vt* (*spennare*) pluck; (*spellare*) skin; (*sbucciare*) peel; (*fam: spillare denaro*) fleece. **~rsi** *vr fam* lose one's hair. **~to** *a* bald. **~ti** *nmpl* (*pomodori*) peeled tomatoes

pel'lame *nm* skins *pl*

'pelle *nf* skin; (*cuoio*) leather; (*buccia*) peel; **avere la ~ d'oca** have goose-flesh

pellegri'naggio *nm* pilgrimage. **pelle'grino, -a** *nmf* pilgrim

pelle'rossa *nmf* Red Indian, Redskin

pellette'ria *nf* leather goods *pl*

pelli'cano *nm* pelican

pellicce'ria *nf* furrier's [shop]. **pel'liccia** *nf* fur; (*indumento*) fur coat. **~i'aio, -a** *nmf* furrier

pel'licola *nf* Phot, Cinema film. **~ [trasparente]** cling film

'pelo *nm* hair; (*di animale*) coat; (*di lana*) pile; **per un ~** by the skin of one's teeth; **cavarsela per un ~** have a narrow escape. **pe'loso** *a* hairy

'peltro *nm* pewter

pe'luche *nm inv* **giocattolo di ~** soft toy

pe'luria *nf* down

'pelvico *a* pelvic

'pena *nf* (*punizione*) punishment; (*sofferenza*) pain; (*dispiacere*) sorrow; (*disturbo*) trouble; **a mala ~** hardly; **mi fa ~** I pity him; **vale la ~ andare** it is worth [while] going. **~ di morte** death sentence

pe'nale *a* criminal; **diritto** *nm* **~e** criminal law. **~ità** *nf inv* penalty

penaliz'za|re *vt* penalize. **~zi'one** *nf* (*penalità*) penalty

pe'nare *vi* suffer; (*faticare*) find it difficult

pen'daglio *nm* pendant

pen'dant *nm inv* **fare ~ [con]** match

pen'den|te *a* hanging; Comm outstanding ●*nm* (*ciondolo*) pendant; **~ti** *pl* drop earrings. **~za** *nf* slope; Comm outstanding account

'pendere *vi* hang; (*superficie:*) slope; (*essere inclinato*) lean

pen'dio *nm* slope; **in ~** sloping

pendo'l|are *a* pendulum ●*nmf* commuter. **~ino** *nm* (*treno*) special, first class only, fast train

'pendolo *nm* pendulum

'pene *nm* penis

pene'trante *a* penetrating; (*freddo*) biting

pene'tra|re *vt/i* penetrate; (*trafiggere*) pierce ●*vt* (*odore:*) get into ●*vi* (*entrare furtivamente*) steal in. **~zi'one** *nf* penetration

penicil'lina *nf* penicillin

pe'nisola *nf* peninsula

peni'ten|te *a & nmf* penitent. **~za** *nf* penitence; (*punizione*) penance; (*in gioco*) forfeit. **~zi'ario** *nm* penitentiary

'penna *nf* (*da scrivere*) pen; (*di uccello*) feather. **~ a feltro** felt-tip[ped pen]. **~ a sfera** ball-point [pen]. **~ stilografica** fountain-pen

pen'nacchio *nm* plume

penna'rello *nm* felt-tip[ped pen]

pennel'la|re *vt* paint. **~ta** *nf* brushstroke. **pen'nello** *nm* brush; **a pennello** (*a perfezione*) perfectly

pen'nino *nm* nib

pen'none *nm* (*di bandiera*) flag-pole

pen'nuto *a* feathered

pe'nombra *nf* half-light

pe'noso *a* (*fam: pessimo*) painful

pen'sa|re *vi* think; **penso di si** I think so; **~re** a think of; remember to (*chiudere il gas ecc*); **pensa ai fatti tuoi!** mind your own business!; **ci penso io** I'll take care of it; **~re di fare qcsa** think of doing sth; **~re tra sé e sé** think to oneself ● *vt* think. **~ta** *nf* idea

pensi'e|ro *nm* thought; (*mente*) mind; (*preoccupazione*) worry; **stare in ~ro per** be anxious about. **~'roso** *a* pensive

'pensi|le *a* hanging; **giardino ~le** roof-garden ● *nm* (*mobile*) wall unit. **~'lina** *nf* (*di fermata d'autobus*) bus shelter

pensio'nante *nmf* boarder; (*ospite pagante*) lodger

pensio'nato, -a *nmf* pensioner ● *nm* (*per anziani*) [old folks'] home; (*per studenti*) hostel. **pensi'one** *nf* pension; (*albergo*) boarding-house; (*vitto e alloggio*) board and lodging; **andare in pensione** retire; **mezza pensione** half board. **pensione completa** full board

pen'soso *a* pensive

pen'tagono *nm* pentagon

Pente'coste *nf* Whitsun

penti'mento *nm* repentance

penti'r|si *vr* **~rsi di** repent of; (*rammaricarsi*) regret. **~'tismo** *nm* turning informant. **~to** *nm* Mafioso turned informant

'pentola *nf* saucepan; (*contenuto*) potful. **~ a pressione** pressure cooker

pe'nultimo *a* last but one, penultimate

pe'nuria *nf* shortage

penzo'l|are *vi* dangle. **~oni** *adv* dangling

pe'pa|re *vt* pepper. **~to** *a* peppery

'pepe *nm* pepper; **grano di ~** peppercorn. **~ in grani** whole pepper-

corns. **~ macinato** ground pepper

pepe'ro'n|ata *nf* peppers cooked in olive oil with onion, tomato and garlic. **~'cino** *nm* chilli pepper. **pepe'rone** *nm* pepper. **peperone verde** green pepper

pe'pita *nf* nugget

per *prep* for; (*attraverso*) through; (*stato in luogo*) in, on; (*distributivo*) per; (*mezzo, entro*) by; (*causa*) with; (*in qualità di*) as; **~ strada** on the street; **~ la fine del mese** by the end of the month; **in fila ~ due** in double file; **l'ho sentito ~ telefono** I spoke to him on the phone; **~ iscritto** in writing; **~ caso** by chance; **ho aspettato ~ ore** I've been waiting for hours; **~ tempo** in time; **~ sempre** forever; **~ scherzo** as a joke; **gridare ~ il dolore** scream with pain; **vendere ~ 10 milioni** sell for 10 million; **uno ~ volta** one at a time; **uno ~ uno** one by one; **venti ~ cento** twenty per cent; **~ fare qcsa** [in order to] do sth; **stare ~** be about to; **è troppo bello ~ essere vero** it's too good to be true

'pera *nf* pear; **farsi una ~** (*sl: di eroina*) shoot up

perbe'nis|mo *nm* prissiness. **~ta** *a inv* prissy

per'cento *adv* per cent. **percen-tu'ale** *nf* percentage

perce'pibile *a* perceivable; (*somma*) payable

perce'pi|re *vt* perceive; (*riscuotere*) cash

perce't'tibile *a* perceptible. **~zi'one** *nf* perception

perché *conj* (*in interrogazioni*) why; (*per il fatto che*) because; (*affinché*) so that; **~ non vieni** why don't you come?; **dimmi ~** tell me why; **~ no/si** because!; **la ragione ~ l'ho fatto** the reason [that] I did it, the reason why I did it; **è troppo difficile ~ lo possa capire** it's too difficult for me to understand ● *nm inv* reason

[why]; **senza un ~** without any reason

perciò *conj* so

per'correre *vt* cover ⟨*distanza*⟩; ⟨*viaggiare*⟩ travel. **per'corso** *pp di* percorrere ● *nm* ⟨*tragitto*⟩ course, route; ⟨*distanza*⟩ distance; ⟨*viaggio*⟩ journey

per'coss|a *nf* blow. **~o** *pp di* percuotere. **percu'otere** *vt* strike

percussi'o|ne *nf* percussion; **strumenti** *a* **~ne** percussion instruments. **~'nista** *nmf* percussionist

per'dente *nmf* loser

'perder|e *vt* lose; ⟨*sprecare*⟩ waste; ⟨*non prendere*⟩ miss; ⟨*fig: vizio*⟩ ruin; **~e** tempo waste time ● *vi* lose; ⟨*recipiente:*⟩ leak; **lascia ~e!** forget it!. **~si** *vr* get lost; ⟨*reciproco*⟩ lose touch

perdifi'ato: **a ~** *adv* ⟨*gridare*⟩ at the top of one's voice

perdigi'orno *nmf inv* idler

'perdita *nf* loss; ⟨*spreco*⟩ waste; ⟨*falla*⟩ leak; **a ~ d'occhio** as far as the eye can see. **~ di tempo** waste of time. **perdi'tempo** *nm* waste of time

perdo'nare *vt* forgive; ⟨*scusare*⟩ excuse. **per'dono** *nm* forgiveness; *Jur* pardon

perdu'rare *vi* last; ⟨*perseverare*⟩ persist

perduta'mente *adv* hopelessly. **per'duto** *pp di* perdere ● *a* lost; ⟨*rovinato*⟩ ruined

pe'renne *a* everlasting; *Bot* perennial; **nevi perenni** perpetual snow. **~'mente** *adv* perpetually

peren'torio *a* peremptory

per'fetto *a* perfect ● *nm* *Gram* perfect [tense]

perfezio'nar|e *vt* perfect; ⟨*migliorare*⟩ improve. **~si** *vr* improve oneself; ⟨*specializzarsi*⟩ specialize

perfezi'o|ne *nf* perfection; **alla ~ne** to perfection. **~'nismo** *nm* perfectionism. **~'nista** *nmf* perfectionist

per'fidia *nf* wickedness; ⟨*atto*⟩

wicked act. **'perfido** *a* treacherous; ⟨*malvagio*⟩ perverse

per'fino *adv* even

perfo'ra|re *vt* pierce; punch ⟨*schede*⟩; *Mech* drill. **~'tore, ~'trice** *nmf* punch-card operator ● *nm* perforator. **~zi'one** *nf* perforation; ⟨*di schede*⟩ punching

per'formance *nf inv* performance

perga'mena *nf* parchment

perico'lante *a* precarious; ⟨*azienda*⟩ shaky

pe'rico|lo *nm* danger; ⟨*rischio*⟩ risk; **mettere in ~lo** endanger. **~lo pubblico** danger to society. **~'loso** *a* dangerous

perife'ria *nf* periphery; ⟨*di città*⟩ outskirts *pl*; *fig* fringes *pl*

peri'ferica *nf* peripheral; ⟨*strada*⟩ ring road. **~o** *a* ⟨*quartiere*⟩ outlying

pe'rifrasi *nf inv* circumlocution

pe'rimetro *nm* perimeter

peri'odico *nm* periodical ● *a* periodical; ⟨*vento, mal di testa, Math*⟩ recurring. **pe'riodo** *nm* period; *Gram* sentence. **periodo di prova** trial period

peripe'zie *nfpl* misadventures

pe'rire *vi* perish

peri'scopio *nm* periscope

pe'ri|to, -a *a* skilled ● *nmf* expert

perito'nite *nf* peritonitis

pe'rizia *nf* skill; ⟨*valutazione*⟩ survey

'perla *nf* pearl. **per'lina** *nf* bead

perlo'meno *adv* at least

perlu'stra|re *vt* patrol. **~zi'one** *nf* patrol; **andare in ~zione** go on patrol

perma'loso *a* touchy

perma'ne|nte *a* permanent ● *nf* perm; **farsi [fare] la ~nte** have a perm. **~nza** *nf* permanence; ⟨*soggiorno*⟩ stay; **in ~nza** permanently. **~re** *vi* remain

perme'are *vt* permeate

per'messo *pp di* permettere ● *nm* permission; ⟨*autorizzazione*⟩ permit; *Mil* leave; **[è] ~?** ⟨*posso entrare?*⟩ may I come in?; ⟨*posso* *passare?*) excuse me. ~ **di lavoro** work permit

per'mettere *vt* allow, permit; **potersi** ~ **qcsa** (*finanziariamente*) be able to afford sth; **come si permette?** how dare you?. **permis'sivo** *a* permissive

permutazi'one *nf* exchange; *Math* permutation

per'nacchia *nf* (*sl:* con la bocca) raspberry *sl*

per'nic|e *nf* partridge. ~**i'oso** *a* pernicious

'perno *nm* pivot

pernot'tare *vi* stay overnight

'pero *nm* pear-tree

però *conj* but; (*tuttavia*) however

pero'rare *vt* plead

perpendico'lare *a* & *nf* perpendicular

perpe'trare *vt* perpetrate

perpetu'are *vt* perpetuate. **per'petuo** *a* perpetual

perplessità *nf inv* perplexity; (*dubbio*) doubt. **per'plesso** *a* perplexed

perqui'si|re *vt* search. ~**zi'one** *nf* search. ~**zione domiciliare** search of the premises

persecu'tore, -'trice *nmf* persecutor. ~**zi'one** *nf* persecution

persegu'ire *vt* pursue

persegui'tare *vt* persecute

perseve'ra|nte *a* persevering. ~**nza** *nf* perseverance. ~**re** *vi* persevere

persi'ano, -a *a* Persian ● *nf* (*di finestra*) shutter. **'persico** *a* Persian

per'sino *adv* = **perfino**

persi'sten|te *a* persistent. ~**za** *nf* persistence. **per'sistere** *vi* persist

'perso *pp di* **perdere** ● *a* lost; **a tempo** ~ in one's spare time

per'sona *nf* person; (*un tale*) somebody; **di** ~, **in** ~ in person, personally; **per** ~ per person, a head; **per interposta** ~ through an intermediary; **persone** *pl* people

perso'naggio *nm* (*persona di*

---

riguardo) personality; *Theat* ecc character

perso'nal|e *a* personal ● *nm* staff. ~**e di terra** ground crew. ~**ità** *nf inv* personality. ~**iz'zare** *vt* customize (*auto* ecc); personalize (*penna* ecc)

personifi'ca|re *vt* personify. ~**zi'one** *nf* personification

perspi'cac|e *a* shrewd. ~**ia** *nf* shrewdness

persua'dere *vt* convince; impress (*critici*); ~**dere qcno a fare qcsa** persuade sb to do sth. ~**si'one** *nf* persuasion. ~**'sivo** *a* persuasive. **persu'aso** *pp di* **persuadere**

per'tanto *conj* therefore

'pertica *nf* pole

perti'nente *a* relevant

per'tosse *nf* whooping cough

pertur'ba|re *vt* perturb. ~**rsi** *vr* be perturbed. ~**zi'one** *nf* disturbance. ~**zione atmosferica** atmospheric disturbance

per'va|dere *vt* pervade. ~**so** *pp di* **pervadere**

perven'ire *vi* reach; **far** ~ **qcsa a qcno** send sth to sb

pervers|i'one *nf* perversion. ~**ità** *nf* perversity. **per'verso** *a* perverse

perver'ti|re *vt* pervert. ~**to** *a* perverted ● *nm* pervert

per'vinca *nm* (*colore*) blue with a touch of purple

p. es. *abbr* (**per esempio**) e.g.

pesa *nf* weighing; (*bilancia*) weighing machine; (*per veicoli*) weighbridge

pe'sante *a* heavy; (*stomaco*) overfull ● *adv* (*vestirsi*) warmly. ~**'mente** *adv* (*cadere*) heavily. **pesan'tezza** *nf* heaviness

pe'sar|e *vt/i* weigh; ~**e su** *fig* lie heavy on; ~**e le parole** weigh one's words. ~**si** *vr* weigh oneself

'pesca[1] *nf* (*frutto*) peach

'pesca[2] *nf* fishing; **andare a** ~ go fishing. ~ **subacquea** underwater fishing. **pe'scare** *vt* (*andare a pesca di*) fish for; (*prendere*) catch;

(*fig: trovare*) fish out. **~'tore** *nm* fisherman

'**pesce** *nm* fish. **~ d'aprile!** April Fool!. **~ grosso** *fig* big fish. **~ piccolo** *fig* small fry. **~ rosso** goldfish. **~ spada** swordfish. **Pesci** *Astr* Pisces

pesce'cane *nm* shark

pesche'reccio *nm* fishing boat

pesche'ria *nf* fishmonger's [shop]. **~hi'era** *nf* fish-pond. **~i'vendolo** *nm* fishmonger

'**pesco** *nm* peach-tree

'**peso** *nm* weight; **essere di ~ per qcno** be a burden to sb; **di poco ~** (*senza importanza*) not very important; **non dare ~ a qcsa** not attach any importance to st^h

pessi'mis|mo *nm* pessimism. **~ta** *nmf* pessimist ●*a* pessimistic. '**pessimo** *a* very bad

pe'staggio *nm* beating-up. **pestare** *vt* tread on; (*schiacciare*) crush; (*picchiare*) beat; crush (*aglio, prezzemolo*)

'**peste** *nf* plague; (*persona*) pest

pe'stello *nm* pestle

pesti'cida *nm* pesticide. **pe'stifero** *a* (*fastidioso*) pestilential

pesti'len|za *nf* pestilence; (*fetore*) stench. **~zi'ale** *a* (*odore aria*) noxious

'**pesto** *a* ground; **occhio ~** black eye ● *nm* basil and garlic sauce

'**petalo** *nm* petal

pe'tardo *nm* banger

petizi'one *nf* petition; **fare una ~** draw up a petition

petroli'e|ra *nf* [oil] tanker. **~lifero** *a* oil-bearing. **pe'trolio** *nm* oil

pettego'lare *vi* gossip. **~lezzo** *nm* piece of gossip; **far ~lezzi** gossip

pet'tegolo, -a *a* gossipy ● *nmf* gossip

pettina|re *vt* comb. **~rsi** *vr* comb one's hair. **~tura** *nf* combing; (*acconciatura*) hair-style. '**pettine** *nm* comb

petti'nino *nm* (*fermaglio*) comb

petti'rosso *nm* robin [redbreast]

'**petto** *nm* chest; (*seno*) breast; **a doppio ~** double-breasted

petto'rale *nm* (*in gare sportive*) number.. **~'rina** *nf* (*di salopette*) bib. **~'ruto** *a* (*donna*) full-breasted; (*uomo*) broad-chested

petu'lante *a* impertinent

'**pezza** *nf* cloth; (*toppa*) patch; (*rotolo di tessuto*) roll

pez'zente *nmf* tramp; (*avaro*) miser

'**pezzo** *nm* piece; (*parte*) part; **un bel ~ d'uomo** a fine figure of a man; **un ~** (*di tempo*) some time; (*di spazio*) a long way; **al ~** (*costare*) each; **essere a pezzi** (*stanco*) be shattered; **fare a pezzi** tear to shreds. **~ grosso** bigwig

pia'cente *a* attractive

pia'ce|re *nm* pleasure; (*favore*) favour; **a ~re** as much as one likes; **per ~re!** please!; **~re [di conoscerla]** pleased to meet you!; **con ~re** with pleasure ● *vi* **la Scozia mi piace** I like Scotland; **mi piacciono i dolci** I like sweets; **faccio come mi pare e piace** I do as I please; **ti piace?** do you like it?; **lo spettacolo è piaciuto** the show was a success. **~vole** *a* pleasant

piaci'mento *nm* **a ~** as much as you like

pia'dina *nf* unleavened focaccia bread

pi'aga *nf* sore; *fig* scourge; (*fig: persona noiosa*) pain; (*fig: ricordo doloroso*) wound

piagni'steo *nm* whining

piagnuco'lare *vi* whimper

pi'alla *nf* plane. **pial'lare** *vt* plane

pi'ana *nf* (*pianura*) plane. **pianeggi'ante** *a* level

piane'rottolo *nm* landing

pia'neta *nm* planet

pi'angere *vi* cry; (*disperatamente*) weep ● *vt* (*lamentare*) lament; (*per un lutto*) mourn

pianifi'ca|re *vt* plan. **~zi'one** *nf* planning

pia'nista *nmf* *Mus* pianist

pi'ano *a* flat; *(a livello)* flush; *(regolare)* smooth; *(facile)* easy ● *adv* slowly; *(con cautela)* gently; **andarci ~** go carefully ● *nm* plain; *(di edificio)* floor; *(livello)* plane; *(progetto)* plan; *Mus* piano; **di primo ~** first-rate; **primo ~** *Phot* close-up; **in primo ~** in the foreground. **~ regolatore** town plan. **~ di studi** syllabus

piano'forte *nm* piano. **~ a coda** grand piano

piano'terra *nm inv* ground floor, first floor *Am*

pi'anta *nf* plant; *(del piede)* sole; *(disegno)* plan; **di sana ~** *(totalmente)* entirely; **in ~ stabile** permanently. **~gio'ne** *nf* plantation. **~ stradale** road map. **~gio'ne** *nf* plantation

piantagrane *nmf fam* **è un/una ~** he's/she's bolshie

pian'tar|e *vt* plant; *(conficcare)* drive; *(fam: abbandonare)* dump; **piantala!** *fam* stop it!. **~si** *vr* plant oneself; *(fam: lasciarsi)* leave each other

pianter'reno *nm* ground floor, first floor *Am*

pi'anto *pp di* **piangere** ● *nm* crying; *(disperato)* weeping; **(lacrime)** tears *pl*

pian|to'nare *vt* guard. **~'tone** *nm* guard

pia'nura *nf* plain

pi'astra *nf* plate; *(lastra)* slab; *Culin* griddle. **~ elettronica** circuit board. **~ madre** *Comput* motherboard

pia'strella *nf* tile

pia'strina *nf Mil* identity disc; *Med* platelet; *Comput* chip

platta'forma *nf* platform. **~ di lancio** launch pad

piat'tino *nm* saucer

pi'atto *a* flat ● *nm* plate; *(da portata, vivanda)* dish; *(portata)* course; *(parte piatta)* flat; *(di giradischi)* turntable; **piatti** *pl Mus* cymbals; **lavare i piatti** do the dishes, do the washing-up. **~ fondo** soup plate. **~ piano** [ordinary] plate

pi'azza *nf* square; *Comm* market; **letto a una ~** single bed; **letto a due piazze** double bed; **far ~ pulita** make a clean sweep. **~'forte** *nf* stronghold. **piaz'zale** *nm* large square. **~'mento** *nm (in classifica)* placing

piaz'za|re *vt* place. **~rsi** *vr* Sport be placed; **~rsi secondo** come second. **~to a** *(cavallo)* placed; **ben ~to** *(robusto)* well built

piaz'zista *nm* salesman

piaz'zuola *nf* **~ di sosta** pull-in

pic'cante *a* hot; *(pungente)* sharp; *(salace)* spicy

pic'carsi *vr (risentirsi)* take offence; **~ di** *(vantarsi di)* claim to

'picche *nfpl (carte)* spades

picchet'tare *vt* stake; *(scioperanti:)* picket. **pic'chetto** *nm* picket

picchi'a|re *vt* beat, hit ● *vi (bussare)* knock; *Aeron* nosedive; **~re in testa** *(motore:)* knock. **~ta** *nf* beating; *Aeron* nosedive; **scendere in ~ta** nosedive

picchiet'tare *vt* tap; *(punteggiare)* spot

picchiet'tio *nm* tapping

'picchio *nm* woodpecker

pic'cino *a* tiny; *(gretto)* mean; *(di poca importanza)* petty ● *nm* little one, child

picci'one *nm* pigeon

'picco *nm* peak; **a ~** vertically; **colare a ~** sink

'piccolo, -a *a* small, little; *(di età)* young; *(di statura)* short; *(gretto)* petty ● *nmf* child, little one; **da ~** as a child

pic'co|ne *nm* pickaxe. **~zza** *nf* ice axe

pic'nic *nm inv* picnic

pi'docchio *nm* louse

piè *nm inv* **~ di pagina** at the foot of the page; **saltare a ~ pari** skip

pi'ede *nm* foot; **a piedi** on foot; **andare a piedi** walk; **a piedi nudi** barefoot; **a ~ libero** free; **in piedi**

standing; **alzarsi in piedi** stand up; **in punta di piedi** on tiptoe; **ai piedi di** ⟨montagna⟩ at the foot of; **prendere** ~ fig gain ground; ⟨moda:⟩ catch on; **mettere in piedi** ⟨allestire⟩ set up; **togliti dai piedi!** get out of the way!. ~ **di porco** ⟨strumento⟩ jemmy

pie'dino nm fare ~ a qcno fam play footsie with sb

piedi'stallo nm pedestal

pi'ega nf ⟨piegatura⟩ fold; ⟨di gonna⟩ pleat; ⟨di pantaloni⟩ crease; ⟨grinza⟩ wrinkle; ⟨andamento⟩ turn; **non fare una** ~ ⟨ragionamento:⟩ be flawless

pie'ga|re vt fold; ⟨flettere⟩ bend ● vi bend. **~rsi** vr bend. **~rsi a** fig yield to. **~tura** nf folding

pieghet'ta|re vt pleat. **~to** a pleated. **pie'ghevole** a pliable; ⟨tavolo⟩ folding ● nm leaflet

piemon'tese a Piedmontese

pi'en|a nf ⟨di fiume⟩ flood; ⟨folla⟩ crowd. **~o** a full; ⟨massiccio⟩ solid; **in ~a estate** in the middle of summer; **a ~i voti** ⟨diplomarsi⟩ ≈ with A-grades, with first class honours ● nm ⟨colmo⟩ height; ⟨carico⟩ full load; **in ~o** ⟨completamente⟩ fully; **fare il ~o** ⟨di benzina⟩ fill up

pie'none nm c'era il ~ the place was packed

pietà nf pity; ⟨misericordia⟩ mercy; **senza ~** ⟨persona⟩ pitiless; ⟨spietatamente⟩ pitilessly; **avere ~ di** qcno take pity on sb; **far ~** ⟨far pena⟩ be pitiful

pie'tanza nf dish

pie'toso a pitiful, merciful; ⟨fam: pessimo⟩ terrible

pi'etr|a nf stone. **~a dura** semi-precious stone. **~a preziosa** precious stone. **~a dello scandalo** cause of the scandal. **pie'trame** nm stones pl. **~ifi'care** vt petrify. **pie'trina** nf ⟨di accendino⟩ flint. **pie'troso** a stony

piffero nm fife

pigi'ama nm pyjamas pl

'pigia 'pigia nm inv crowd, crush. **pigi'are** vt press

pigi'one nf rent; **dare a** ~ let, rent out; **prendere a** ~ rent

pigli'are vt ⟨fam: afferrare⟩ catch. **'piglio** nm air

pig'mento nm pigment

pig'meo, -a a & nmf pygmy

'pigna nf cone

pi'gnolo a pedantic

pigo'lare vi chirp. **pigo'lio** nm chirping

pi'grizia nf laziness. **'pigro** a lazy; ⟨intelletto⟩ slow

'pila nf pile; Electr battery; ⟨fam: lampadina tascabile⟩ torch; ⟨vasca⟩ basin; **a pile** battery operated, battery powered

pi'lastro nm pillar

'pillola nf pill; **prendere la** ~ be on the pill

pi'lone nm pylon; ⟨di ponte⟩ pier

pi'lota nmf pilot ● nm Auto driver. **pilo'tare** vt pilot; drive ⟨auto⟩

pinaco'teca nf art gallery

'Pinco Pallino nm so-and-so

pi'neta nf pine-wood

ping-'pong nm table tennis, ping-pong fam

'pingue a fat. **~'edine** nf fatness

pingu'ino nm penguin; ⟨gelato⟩ choc ice on a stick

'pinna nf fin; ⟨per nuotare⟩ flipper

'pino nm pine[-tree]. **pi'nolo** nm pine kernel. ~ **marittimo** cluster or maritime pine

'pinta nf pint

'pinza nf pliers pl; Med forceps pl

pin'za|re vt ⟨con pinzatrice⟩ staple. **~'trice** nf stapler

pin'zette nfpl tweezers pl

pinzi'monio nm sauce for crudités

'pio a pious; ⟨benefico⟩ charitable

pi'oggia nf rain; ⟨fig: di pietre, insulti⟩ hail, shower; **sotto la** ~ in the rain. ~ **acida** acid rain

pi'olo nm ⟨di scala⟩ rung

piom'ba|re vi fall heavily; **~re su** fall upon ● vt fill ⟨dente⟩. **~'tura** nf ⟨di dente⟩ filling. **piom'bino** nm

(*sigillo*) [lead] seal; (*da pesca*) sinker; (*in gonne*) weight
pi'ombo nm lead; (*sigillo*) [lead] seal; **a ~** plumb; **senza ~** (*benzina*) lead-free
pioni'ere, -a nmf pioneer
pi'oppo nm poplar
pio'vano a **acqua piovana** rainwater
pi'ov|ere vi rain; **~e** it's raining; **~iggi'nare** vi drizzle. **pio'voso** a rainy
'pipa nf pipe
pipì nf **fare [la] ~** pee, piddle; **andare a fare [la] ~** go for a pee
pipi'strello nm bat
pi'ramide nf pyramid
pi'ranha nm inv piranha
pi'rat|a nm pirate. **~a della strada** road-hog ●a inv pirate. **~e'ria** nf piracy
piro'etta nf pirouette
pi'rofil|a nf (*tegame*) oven-proof dish. **~o** a heat-resistant
pi'romane nmf pyromaniac
pi'roscafo nm steamer. **~ di linea** liner
pisci'are vi vulg piss
pi'scina nf swimming pool. **~ coperta** indoor swimming pool. **~ scoperta** outdoor swimming pool
pi'sello nm pea; (*fam: pene*) willie
piso'lino nm nap; **fare un ~** have a nap
'pista nf track; Aeron runway; (*orma*) footprint; (*sci*) slope, piste. **~ d'atterraggio** airstrip. **~ da ballo** dance floor. **~ ciclabile** cycle track
pi'stacchio nm pistachio
pi'stola nf pistol; (*per spruzzare*) spray-gun. **~ a spruzzo** paint spray
pi'stone nm piston
pi'tone nm python
pit'to|re, -'trice nmf painter. **~'resco** a picturesque. **pit'torico** a pictorial
pit'tu|ra nf painting. **~'rare** vt paint
più adv more; (*superlativo*) most;

Math plus; **~ importante** more important; **il ~ importante** the most important; **~ caro** dearer; **il ~ caro** the dearest; **di ~** more; **una coperta in ~** an extra blanket; **non ho ~ soldi** I don't have any more money; **non vive ~ a Milano** he no longer lives in Milan, he doesn't live in Milan any longer; **~ o meno** more or less; **il ~ lentamente possibile** as slow as possible; **per di ~** what's more; **mai ~!** never again!; **~ di** more than; **sempre ~** more and more ●a more; (*superlativo*) most; **~ tempo** more time; **la classe con ~ alunni** the class with most pupils; **~ volte** several times ●a più most; Math plus sign; **il ~ è fatto** the worst is over; **parlare del ~ e del meno** make small talk; **i ~** the majority
piucceper'fetto nm pluperfect
pi'uma nf feather. **piu'maggio** nm plumage. **piu'mino** nm (*di cigni*) down; (*copriletto*) eiderdown; (*per cipria*) powder-puff; (*per spolverare*) feather duster; (*giacca*) down jacket. **piu'mone**® nm duvet, continental quilt
piut'tosto adv rather; (*invece*) instead
pi'vello nm fam greenhorn
'pizza nf pizza; Cinema reel.
pizza'iola nf slices of beef in tomato sauce, oregano and anchovies
pizze'ria nf pizza restaurant, pizzeria
pizzi'c|are vt pinch; (*pungere*) sting; (*di sapore*) taste sharp; (*fam: sorprendere*) catch; Mus pluck ●vi scratch; (*cibo*) be spicy **'pizzico** nm, **~otto** nm pinch
'pizzo nm lace; (*di montagna*) peak
pla'car|e vt placate; assuage (*fame, dolore*). **~si** vr calm down
'placca nf plate; (*commemorativa, dentale*) plaque; Med patch
plac'ca|re vt plate. **~to a ~to d'argento** silver-plated. **~to d'oro** gold-plated. **~'tura** nf plating

pla'centa *nf* placenta

'placido *a* placid

plagi'are *vt* plagiarize; pressure ⟨*persona*⟩. 'plagio *nm* plagiarism

plaid *nm inv* tartan rug

pla'nare *vi* glide

'plancia *nf Naut* bridge; ⟨*passerella*⟩ gangplank

plane'tario *a* planetary ●*nm* planetarium

pla'smare *vt* mould

'plastic|a *nf* ⟨*arte*⟩ plastic art; *Med* plastic surgery; ⟨*materia*⟩ plastic. ~o *a* plastic ●*nm* plastic model

'platano *nm* plane[-tree]

pla'tea *nf* stalls *pl*; ⟨*pubblico*⟩ audience

'platino *nm* platinum

pla'tonico *a* platonic

plau'sibil|e *a* plausible. ~ità *nf* plausibility

ple'baglia *nf pej* mob

pleni'lunio *nm* full moon

'plettro *nm* plectrum

pleu'rite *nf* pleurisy

'plico *nm* packet; **in ~ a parte** under separate cover

plissé *a inv* plissé; ⟨*gonna*⟩ accordeon-pleated

plo'tone *nm* platoon; ⟨*di ciclisti*⟩ group. ~ **d'esecuzione** firing-squad

'plumbeo *a* leaden

plu'ral|e *a & nm* plural; **al ~e** in the plural. ~ità *nf* ⟨*maggioranza*⟩ majority

pluridiscipli'nare *a* multidisciplinary

plurien'nale *a* ~ **esperienza** many years' experience

pluripar'titico *a Pol* multi-party

plu'tonio *nm* plutonium

pluvi'ale *a* rain *attrib*

pneu'matico *a* pneumatic ●*nm* tyre

pneu'monia *nf* pneumonia

po' *vedi* poco

po'chette *nf inv* clutch bag

po'chino *nm* un ~ a little bit

'poco *a* little; ⟨*tempo*⟩ short; ⟨*con nomi plurali*⟩ few ●*pron* little;

⟨*poco tempo*⟩ a short time; ⟨*plurale*⟩ few ●*nm* little; **un po'** a little [bit]; **un po' di** a little, some; ⟨*con nomi plurali*⟩ a few; **a ~ a ~** little by little; **fra ~** soon; **per ~** ⟨*a poco prezzo*⟩ cheap; ⟨*quasi*⟩ nearly; **~ fa** a little while ago; **sono arrivato da ~** I have just arrived; **un bel po'** quite a lot; **un ~ di buono** a shady character ●*adv* ⟨*con verbi*⟩ not much; ⟨*con avverbi*⟩ not very; **parla ~** he doesn't speak much; **lo conosco ~** I don't know him very well; **~ spesso** not very often

po'dere *nm* farm

pode'roso *a* powerful

'podio *nm* dais; *Mus* podium

po'dis|mo *nm* walking. ~ta *nmf* walker

po'e|ma *nm* poem. ~'sia *nf* poetry; ⟨*componimento*⟩ poem. ~ta *nm* poet. ~'tessa *nf* poetess. ~tico *a* poetic

poggiapi'edi *nm inv* footrest

poggi'a|re *vt* lean; ⟨*posare*⟩ place ●*vi* ~re su be based on. ~'testa *nm inv* head-rest

'poggio *nm* hillock

poggi'olo *nm* balcony

'poi *adv* ⟨*dopo*⟩ then; ⟨*più tardi*⟩ later [on]; ⟨*finalmente*⟩ finally. **d'ora in ~** from now on; **questa ~!** well I

poiché *conj* since

pois *nm inv* **a ~** a polka-dot

'poker *nm* poker

po'lacco, -a *a* Polish ●*nmf* Pole ●*nm* ⟨*lingua*⟩ Polish

po'lar|e *a* polar. ~iz'zare *vt* polarize

'polca *nf* polka

po'lemic|a *nf* controversy. ~ca-'mente *adv* controversially. ~co *a* controversial. ~z'zare *vi* engage in controversy

po'lenta *nf* cornmeal porridge

poli'clinico *nm* general hospital

poli'estere *nm* polyester

poliga'mia *nf* polygamy. po'liga-mo *a* polygamous

polio[mie'lite] *nf* polio[myelitis]

'polipo *nm* polyp

poli'sti'rolo *nm* polystyrene

poli'tecnico *nm* polytechnic

po'litic|a *nf* politics *sg*; ⟨*linea di condotta*⟩ policy; **fare** **~a** be in politics. **~o, -a** *a* political ● *nmf* politician

poliva'lente *a* catch-all

poli'zi|a *nf* police. **~a giudiziaria** ≈ Criminal Investigation Department, CID. **~a stradale** traffic police. **~'esco** *a* police *attrib*; ⟨*romanzo, film*⟩ detective *attrib*. **~'otto** *nm* policeman

'polizza *nf* policy

pol'la|io *nm* chicken run; (*fam*: *luogo chiassoso*) mad house. **~me** *nm* poultry. **~'strello** *nm* spring chicken. **~stro** *nm* cockerel

'pollice *nm* thumb; (*unità di misura*) inch

'polline *nm* pollen; **allergia al ~** hay fever

polli'vendolo, -a *nmf* poulterer

'pollo *nm* chicken; (*fam*: *sempliciotto*) simpleton. **~ arrosto** roast chicken

polmo|'nare *a* pulmonary. pol'mone *nm* lung. **polmone d'acciaio** iron lung. **~'nite** *nf* pneumonia

'polo *nm* pole; *Sport* polo; ⟨*maglietta*⟩ polo top. **~ nord** North Pole. **~ sud** South Pole

Po'lonia *nf* Poland

'polpa *nf* pulp

pol'paccio *nm* calf

polpa'strello *nm* fingertip

pol'pet|ta *nf* meatball. **~'tone** *nm* meat loaf

'polpo *nm* octopus

pol'poso *a* fleshy

pol'sino *nm* cuff

'polso *nm* pulse; *Anat* wrist; *fig* authority; **avere ~** be strict

pol'tiglia *nf* mush

pol'trire *vi* lie around

pol'tron|a *nf* armchair; *Theat* seat in the stalls. **~e** *a* lazy

'polve|re *nf* dust; (*sostanza polverizzata*) powder; **in ~re** powdered; **sapone in ~re** soap powder. **~re**

da sparo gun powder. **~'rina** *nf* (*medicina*) powder. **~riz'zare** *vt* pulverize; (*nebulizzare*) atomize. **~'rone** *nm* cloud of dust. **~'roso** *a* dusty

po'mata *nf* ointment, cream

po'mello *nm* knob; (*guancia*) cheek

pomeridi'ano *a* afternoon *attrib*; **alle tre pomeridiane** at three in the afternoon, at three p.m. pome'riggio *nm* afternoon

'pomice *nf* pumice

'pomo *nm* (*oggetto*) knob. **~ d'Adamo** Adam's apple

pomo'doro *nm* tomato

'pompa *nf* pump; (*sfarzo*) pomp. **pompe** *pl* **funebri** (*funzione*) funeral. pom'pare *vt* pump; (*gonfiare d'aria*) pump up; (*fig: esagerare*) exaggerate; **pompare fuori** pump out

pom'pelmo *nm* grapefruit

pompi'ere *nm* fireman; **i pompieri** the fire brigade

pom'pon *nm inv* pompom

pom'poso *a* pompous

ponde'rare *vt* ponder

po'nente *nm* west

'ponte *nm* bridge; *Naut* deck; (*impalcatura*) scaffolding; **fare il ~** *fig* make a long weekend of it

pon'tefice *nm* pontiff

pontifi'ca|re *vi* pontificate. **~to** *nm* pontificate

ponti'ficio *a* papal

pon'tile *nm* jetty

popò *nf inv fam* pooh

popo'lano *a* of the [common] people

popo'la|re *a* popular; (*comune*) common ● *vt* populate. **~rsi** *vr* get crowded. **~rità** *nf* popularity. **~zi'one** *nf* population. '**popolo** *nm* people. **popo'loso** *a* populous

'poppa *nf* *Naut* stern; (*mammella*) breast; **a ~** astern

pop'pa|re *vt* suck. **~ta** *nf* (*pasto*) feed. **~'toio** *nm* [feeding-]bottle

popu'lista *nmf* populist

por'cata *nf* load of rubbish; **porcate** *pl* (*fam: cibo*) junk food

porcel'lana *nf* porcelain, china

porcel'lino *nm* piglet. ~ **d'India** guinea-pig

porche'ria *nf* dirt; (*fig: cosa orrenda*) piece of filth; (*fam: robaccia*) rubbish

por'cile *nm* pigsty. **~no** *a* pig *attrib* ●**nm** (*fungo*) edible mushroom. '**porco** *nm* pig; (*carne*) pork

porco'spino *nm* porcupine

'porgere *vt* give; (*offrire*) offer; **porgo distinti saluti** (*in lettera*) I remain, yours sincerely

porno|gra'fia *nf* pornography. **~'grafico** *a* pornographic

'poro *nm* pore. **po'roso** *a* porous

'porpora *nf* purple

'porre *vt* put; (*collocare*) place; (*supporre*) suppose; ask (*domanda*); present (*candidatura*); **poniamo il caso che...** let us suppose that...; **~re fine** *o* **termine a** put an end to. **~si** *vr* put oneself; **~si a sedere** sit down; **~si in cammino** set out

'porro *nm* Bot leek; (*verruca*) wart

'porta *nf* door; Sport goal; (*di città*) gate; Comput port. **~ a** ~ door-to-door; **mettere alla** ~ show sb the door. **~ di servizio** tradesmen's entrance

portaba'gagli *nm inv* (*facchino*) porter; (*di treno ecc*) luggage rack; Auto boot, trunk Am; (*sul tetto di un'auto*) roof rack

portabot'tiglie *nm inv* bottle rack, wine rack

porta'cenere *nm inv* ashtray

portachi'avi *nm inv* keyring

porta'cipria *nm inv* compact

portadocu'menti *nm inv* document wallet

porta'erei *nf inv* aircraft carrier

portafi'nestra *nf* French window

porta'foglio *nm* wallet; (*per documenti*) portfolio; (*ministero*) ministry

portafor'tuna *nm inv* lucky charm ●*a inv* lucky

portagi'oie *nm inv* jewellery box

por'tale *nm* door

portama'tite *nm inv* pencil case

porta'mento *nm* carriage; (*condotta*) behaviour

porta'mina *nm inv* propelling pencil

portamo'nete *nm inv* purse

por'tante *a* bearing *attrib*

portaom'brelli *nm inv* umbrella stand

porta'pacchi *nm inv* roof rack; (*su bicicletta*) luggage rack

porta'penne *nm inv* pencil case

por'tare *vt* (*verso chi parla*) bring; (*lontano da chi parla*) take; (*sorreggere*, Math) carry; (*condurre*) lead; (*indossare*) wear; (*sopportare*) bear. **~rsi** *vr* (*trasferirsi*) move; (*comportarsi*) behave; **~si bene/male gli anni** look young/old for one's age

porta'viste *nm inv* magazine rack

porta'sci *nm inv* ski rack

portasiga'rette *nm inv* cigarettecase

porta'spilli *nm inv* pin-cushion

por'ta|ta *nf* (*di pranzo*) course; Auto carrying capacity; (*di arma*) range; (*fig: abilità*) capability; **a ~ta di mano** within reach; **alla ~ta di tutti** accessible to all; (*finanziariamente*) within everybody's reach. **por'tatile** *a* & *nm* portable. **~to** *a* (*indumento*) worn; (*dotato*) gifted; **essere ~to per qcsa** have a gift for sth; **essere ~to a** (*tendere a*) be inclined to. **~tore**, **~trice** *nmf* bearer; **al ~tore** to the bearer. **~tore di handicap** disabled person

portatovagli'olo *nm* napkin ring

portau'ovo *nm inv* egg-cup

porta'voce *nm inv* spokesman ●*nf inv* spokeswoman

por'tento *nm* marvel; (*persona dotata*) prodigy

'portico *nm* portico

porti'er|a *nf* door; (*tendaggio*)

door curtain. **~e** *nm* porter, door-man; *Sport* goalkeeper. **~e di notte** night porter

porti'n|aio, -a *nmf* caretaker, concierge. **~e'ria** *nf* concierge's room; (*di ospedale*) porter's lodge

'porto *pp di* **porgere ●** *nm* harbour; (*complesso*) port; (*vino*) port [wine]; (*spesa di trasporto*) carriage; **andare in ~** succeed. **~ d'armi** gun licence

Porto'g|allo *nm* Portugal. **p~hese** *a & nmf* Portuguese

por'tone *nm* main door

portu'ale *nm* dockworker, docker

porzi'one *nf* portion

'posa *nf* laying; (*riposo*) rest; *Phot* exposure; (*atteggiamento*) pose; **mettersi in ~** pose

po'sa|re *vt* put; (*giù*) put [down] **●** *vi* (*poggiare*) rest; (*per una ritratto*) pose; (*sostare*) rest; *Aeron* land. **~ta** *nf* piece of cutlery; **~te** *pl* cutlery *sg.* **~to** *a* sedate

po'scritto *nm* postscript

posi'tivo *nm* a positive

posizio'nare *vt* position

posizi'one *nf* position; **farsi in ~** get ahead

posolo'gia *nf* dosage

po'spo|rre *vt* place after; (*posticipare*) postpone. **~sto** *pp di* **posporre**

posse'd|ere *vt* possess, own. **~i'mento** *nm* possession

posses'sivo *a* possessive. **pos'sesso** *nm* ownership; (*bene*) possession. **~'sore** *nm* owner

pos'sibil|e *a* possible; **il più presto ~e** as soon as possible **●** *nm* **fare [tutto] il ~e** do one's best. **~ità** *nf inv* possibility; (*occasione*) chance **●** *nfpl* (*mezzi*) means

possi'dente *nmf* land-owner

'posta *nf* post, mail; (*ufficio postale*) post office; (*al gioco*) stake; **spese di ~** postage; **per ~** by post, by mail; **la ~ in gioco è...** *fig* what's at stake is...; **a bella ~** on purpose; **Poste e Telecomunica-**

zioni, *pl* [Italian] Post Office. **~ elettronica** electronic mail, e-mail. **~ elettronica vocale** voice-mail

posta'giro *nm* postal giro

po'stale *a* postal

postazi'one *nf* position

postda'tare *vt* postdate (*assegno*)

posteggi'a|re *vt/i* park. **~'trice** *nmf* parking attendant. **po'steggio** *nm* car-park, parking lot *Am*; (*di taxi*) taxi-rank

'posteri *nmpl* descendants. **~'ore** *a* rear; (*nel tempo*) later **●** *nm fam* posterior, behind. **~tà** *nf* posterity

po'sticcio *a* artificial; (*baffi, barba*) false **●** *nm* hair-piece

postici'pare *vt* postpone

po'stilla *nf* note; *Jur* rider

po'stino *nm* postman, mailman *Am*

'posto *pp di* **porre ●** *nm* place; (*spazio*) room; (*impiego*) job; *Mil* post; (*sedile*) seat; **a/fuori ~** in/out of place; **prendere ~** take up room; **sul ~** on-site; **essere a ~** (*casa, libri*) be tidy; **mettere a ~** tidy (*stanza*); **fare ~** a make room for; **al ~ di** (*invece di*) in place of, instead of. **~ di blocco** check-point. **~ di guida** driving seat. **~ di lavoro** workstation. **posti** *pl* **in piedi** standing room. **~ di polizia** police station. **posti** *pl* **a sedere** seating

post-partum *a* post-natal

'postumo *a* posthumous **●** *nm* after-effect

po'tabile *a* drinkable; **acqua ~** drinking water

po'tare *vt* prune

po'tassio *nm* potassium

po'ten|te *a* powerful; (*efficace*) potent. **~za** *nf* power; (*efficacia*) potency. **~zi'ale** *a & nm* potential

po'tere *nm* power; **al ~** in power **●** *vi* can, be able to; **posso entrare?** can I come in?; (*formale*) may I come in?; **posso fare qualche cosa?** can I do something?; **che tu possa essere felice!** may you be happy!; **non ne posso più** (*sono stanco*) I can't go on; (*sono stufo*) I can't take any more; **può darsi** perhaps; **può darsi che sia vero** perhaps it's true; **potrebbe aver ragione** he could be right, he might be right; **avresti potuto telefonare** you could have phoned, you might have phoned; **spero di poter venire** I hope to be able to come; **senza poter telefonare** without being able to phone

potestà *nf inv* power

'pover|o, -a *a* poor; (*semplice*) plain ● *nm* poor man ● *nf* poor woman; **i ~i** the poor. **~tà** *nf* poverty

'pozza *nf* pool. **poz'zanghera** *nf* puddle

'pozzo *nm* well; (*minerario*) pit. **~ petrolifero** oil-well

PP.TT. *abbr* (**Poste e Telegrafi**) [Italian] Post Office

prag'matico *a* pragmatic

prali'nato *a* (*mandorla, gelato*) praline-coated

pram'matica *nf* **essere di ~** be customary

pran'zare *vi* dine; (*a mezzogiorno*) lunch. **'pranzo** *nm* dinner; (*a mezzogiorno*) lunch. **pranzo di nozze** wedding breakfast

'prassi *nf* standard procedure

prate'ria *nf* grassland

'prati|ca *nf* practice; (*esperienza*) experience; (*documentazione*) file; **avere ~ca di qcsa** be familiar with sth; **far ~ca** gain experience; **fare le pratiche per** gather the necessary papers for. **~'cabile** *a* practicable; (*strada*) passable. **~ca'mente** *adv* practically. **~'cante** *nmf* apprentice; *Relig* [regular] church-goer

prati'care *vt* practise; (*frequentare*) associate with; (*fare*) make

praticità *nf* practicality. **'pratico** *a* practical; (*esperto*) experienced; **essere pratico di qcsa** know about sth

'prato *nm* meadow; (*di giardino*) lawn

pre'ambolo *nm* preamble

preannunci'are *vt* give advance notice of

preavvi'sare *vt* forewarn. **preav'viso** *nm* warning

pre'cario *a* precarious

precauzi'one *nf* precaution; (*cautela*) care

prece'den|te *a* previous ● *nm* precedent. **~te'mente** *adv* previously. **~za** *nf* precedence; (*di veicoli*) right of way; **dare la ~za** give way. **pre'cedere** *vt* precede

pre'cetto *nm* precept

precipi'ta|re *vt* **~re le cose** precipitate events; **~re qcno nella disperazione** cast sb into a state of despair ● *vi* fall headlong; (*situazione, eventi*) come to a head. **~rsi** *vr* (*gettarsi*) throw oneself; (*affrettarsi*) rush; **~rsi a fare qcsa** rush to do sth. **~zi'one** *nf* (*fretta*) haste; (*atmosferica*) precipitation. **precipi'toso** *a* hasty; (*avventato*) reckless; (*caduta*) headlong

preci'pizio *nm* precipice; **a ~** headlong

precisa'mente *adv* precisely

preci'sa|re *vt* specify; (*spiegare*) clarify. **~zi'one** *nf* clarification

precisi'one *nf* precision. **pre'ciso** *a* precise; (*ore*) sharp; (*identico*) identical

pre'clu|dere *vt* preclude. **~so** *pp di* **precludere**

pre'coc|e *a* precocious; (*prematuro*) premature. **~ità** *nf* precociousness

precon'cetto *a* preconceived ● *nm* prejudice

pre'correre *vt* **~ere i tempi** be ahead of one's time

precur'sore *nm* forerunner, precursor

'preda *nf* prey; (*bottino*) booty; **essere in ~ al panico** be panic-stricken; **in ~ alle fiamme** engulfed in flames. **pre'dare** *vt* plunder. **~tore** *nm* predator

predeces'sore *nmf* predecessor

pre'del|la *nf* platform. **~'lino** *nm* step

predesti'na|re *vt* predestine. **~to** *a Relig* predestined, preordained

predetermi'nato *a* predetermined, preordained

pre'detto *pp di* **predire**

'predica *nf* sermon; *fig* lecture

predi'ca|re *vt* preach. **~to** *nm* predicate

predi'let|to, -a *pp di* **prediligere** ● *a* favourite ● *nmf* pet. **~zi'one** *nf* predilection. **predi'ligere** *vt* prefer

pre'dire *vt* foretell

predi'spo|rre *vt* arrange. **~rsi** *vr* **~rsi a** prepare oneself for. **~sizi'one** *nf* predisposition; (*al disegno ecc*) bent (**a** for). **~sto** *pp di* **predisporre**

predizi'one *nf* prediction

predomi'na|nte *a* predominant. **~re** *vi* predominate. **predo'minio** *nm* predominance

pre'done *nm* robber

prefabbri'cato *a* prefabricated ● *nm* prefabricated building

prefazi'one *nf* preface

prefe'renz|a *nf* preference; **di ~a** preferably. **~i'ale** *a* preferential; **corsia ~iale** bus and taxi lane

prefe'ribile *a* preferable. **~'mente** *adv* preferably

prefe'ri|re *vt* prefer. **~to, -a** *a & nmf* favourite

pre'fet|to *nm* prefect. **~'tura** *nf* prefecture

pre'figgersi *vr* be determined

pre'fisso *pp di* **prefiggere** ● *nm* prefix; *Teleph* [dialling] code

pre'gare *vt/i* pray; (*supplicare*) beg; **farsi ~** need persuading

pre'gevole *a* valuable

preghi'era *nf* prayer; (*richiesta*) request

pregi'ato *a* esteemed; (*prezioso*) valuable. **'pregio** *nm* esteem; (*va-*

lore) value; (*di persona*) good point; **di pregio** valuable

pregiudi'ca|re *vt* prejudice; (*danneggiare*) harm. **~to** *a* prejudiced ● *nm* *Jur* previous offender

pregiu'dizio *nm* prejudice; (*danno*) detriment

'prego *int* (*non c'è di che*) don't mention it!; (*per favore*) please; **~?** I beg your pardon?

pregu'stare *vt* look forward to

prei'storia *nf* prehistory. **prei'storico** *a* prehistoric

pre'lato *nm* prelate

prela'vaggio *nm* prewash

preleva'mento *nm* withdrawal. **prele'vare** *vt* withdraw (*denaro*); collect (*merci*); *Med* take. **preli'e-vo** *nm* (*di soldi*) withdrawal. **prelievo di sangue** blood sample

prelimi'nare *a* preliminary ● *nm* **preliminari** *pl* preliminaries

pre'ludio *nm* prelude

prema'man *nm inv* maternity dress ● *a* maternity *attrib*

prematrimoni'ale *a* premarital

prema'turo, -a *a* premature ● *nmf* premature baby

premedi'ta|re *vt* premeditate. **~zi'one** *nf* premeditation

'premere *vt* press; *Comput* hit (*tasto*) ● *vi* **~ a** (*importare*) matter to; **mi preme sapere** I want to know; **~ su** press on; push (*pulsante*)

pre'messa *nf* introduction

pre'me|sso *pp di* **premettere**. **~sso che** bearing in mind that. **~ttere** *vt* put forward; (*mettere prima*) put before.

premi'a|re *vt* give a prize to; (*ricompensare*) reward. **~zi'one** *nf* prize giving

premi'nente *a* pre-eminent

'premio *nm* prize; (*ricompensa*) reward; *Comm* premium. **~ di consolazione** booby prize

premoni'tore *a* (*sogno, segno*) premonitory. **~zi'one** *nf* premonition

premu'nir|e *vt* fortify. **~si** *vr* take

protective measures; **~si di** provide oneself with; **~si contro** protect oneself against

pre'mura nf (fretta) hurry; (cura) care. **~'roso** a thoughtful

prena'tale a antenatal

'prender|e vt take; (afferrare) seize; catch (treno, malattia, ladro, pesce); have (cibo, bevanda); (far pagare) charge; (assumere) take on; (ottenere) get; (occupare) take up; **~e informazioni** make inquiries; **~e a calci/pugni** kick/punch; **che ti prende?** what's got into you?; **quanto prende?** what do you charge?; **~e una persona per un'altra** mistake a person for someone else; (attecchire) take root; (rapprendersi) set; **~e a destra/sinistra** turn right/left; **~e a fare qcsa** start doing sth. **~si** vr **~si a pugni** come to blows; **~si cura di** take care of (ammalato); **~sela** take it to heart

prendi'sole nm sundress

preno'ta|re vt book, reserve. **~to a** booked, reserved **~zi'one** nf booking, reservation

'prensile a prehensile

preoccu'pante a alarming

preoccu'pa|re vt worry. **~rsi** vr **~rsi** worry (di about); **~rsi di fare qcsa** take the trouble to do sth. **~to a** (ansioso) worried. **~zi'one** nf worry; (apprensione) concern

prepa'ra|re vt prepare. **~rsi** vr get ready. **~tivi** nmpl preparations. **~to** nm (prodotto) preparation. **~'torio** a preparatory. **~zi'one** nf preparation

prepensiona'mento nm early retirement

prepon-de'ran|te a predominant. **~za** nf prevalence

pre'porre vt place before

preposizi'one nf preposition

pre'posto pp di **preporre** ● a **~ a** (addetto a) in charge of

prepo'ten|te a overbearing

● nmf bully. **~za** nf high-handedness

preroga'tiva nf prerogative

'presa nf taking; (conquista) capture; (stretta) hold; (di cemento ecc) setting; Electr socket; (pizzico) pinch; **essere alle prese con** be struggling o grappling with; **a ~ rapida** (cemento, colla) quick-setting; **fare ~ su** influence sb. **~ d'aria** air vent. **~ in giro** leg-pull. **~ multipla** adaptor

pre'sagio nm omen. **presa'gire** vt foretell

'presbite a long-sighted

presbiteri'ano, -a a & nmf Presbyterian. **presbi'terio** nm presbytery

pre'scelto a selected

pre'scindere vi **~ da** leave aside; **a ~ da** apart from

presco'lare a **in età ~** pre-school

pre'scritto pp di **prescrivere**

pre'scrivere vt prescribe. **~zi'one** nf prescription; (norma) rule

preselezi'one nf **chiamare qcno in ~** call sb via the operator

presen'ta|re vt present; (far conoscere) introduce; show (documento); (inoltrare) submit. **~rsi** vr present oneself; (farsi conoscere) introduce oneself; (a ufficio) attend; (alla polizia ecc) report; (come candidato) stand; run; (occasione:) occur; **~rsi bene/male** (persona:) make a good/bad impression; (situazione:) look good/bad. **~'tore, -'trice** nmf presenter; (di notizie) announcer. **~zi'one** nf presentation; (per conoscersi) introduction

pre'sente a present; (attuale) current; (questo) this; **aver ~** remember ● nm present; **i presenti** those present ● nm **allegato alla ~** (in lettera) enclosed

presenti'mento nm foreboding

pre'senza nf presence; (aspetto) appearance; **in ~ di, alla ~ di** in the presence of; **di bella ~** personable. **~ di spirito** presence of mind

presenzi'are vi **~ a** attend

pre'sepe nm, **pre'sepio** nm crib

preser'va|re vt preserve; (*proteggere*) protect (**da** from). **~tivo** a condom. **~zi'one** nf preservation

'**preside** nm headmaster; Univ dean ●nf headmistress; Univ dean

presi'den|te nm chairman; Pol president ●nf chairwoman; Pol president. **~ del consiglio [dei ministri]** Prime Minister. **~ della repubblica** President of the Republic. **~za** nf presidency; (*di assemblea*) chairmanship. **~zi'ale** a presidential

presidi'are vt garrison. **pre'sidio** nm garrison

presi'edere vt preside over

'**preso** pp di **prendere**

'**pressa** nf Mech press

pres'sante a urgent

pressap'poco adv about

pres'sare vt press

pressi'one nf pressure; **far ~ su** put pressure on. **~ del sangue** blood pressure

'**presso** prep near; (*a casa di*) with; (*negli indirizzi*) care of, c/o; (*lavorare*) for ●**pressi** nmpl: **nei pressi di...** in the neighbourhood o vicinity of...

pressoché adv almost

pressuriz'za|re vt pressurize. **~to** a pressurized

prestabi'li|re vt arrange in advance. **~to** a agreed

prestam'pato a printed ●nm (*modulo*) form

pre'stante a good-looking

pre'sta|re vt lend; **~e attenzione** pay attention; **~e aiuto** lend a hand; **farsi ~** borrow (**da** from). **~si** vr (*frase:*) lend itself; (*persona:*) offer

prestazi'one nf performance; **prestazioni** pl (*servizi*) services

prestigia'tore, -'trice nmf conjurer

pre'stigio nm prestige; **gioco di ~o** conjuring trick. **~'oso** nm prestigious

pre'stito nm loan; **dare in ~** lend; **prendere in ~** borrow

'**presto** adv soon; (*di buon'ora*) early; (*in fretta*) quickly; **a ~** see you soon; **al più ~** as soon as possible; **~ o tardi** sooner or later; **far ~** be quick

pre'sumere vt presume; (*credere*) think

presu'mibile a **è ~ che...** presumably,...

pre'sunto a (*colpevole*) presumed

presun|tu'oso a presumptuous ●nmf presumptuous person. **~zi'one** nf presumption

presup'po|rre vt suppose; (*richiedere*) presuppose. **~sizi'one** nf presupposition. **~sto** nm essential requirement

'**prete** nm priest

preten'dente nmf pretender ●nm (*corteggiatore*) suitor

pre'ten|dere vt (*sostenere*) claim; (*esigere*) demand ●vi **~dere a** (*esigere*) make a claim to; **~dere di** (*esigere*) demand to. **~si'one** nf pretension. **~zi'oso** a pretentious

pre'te|sa nf pretension; (*esigenza*) claim; **senza ~e** unpretentious. **~o** pp di **pretendere**

pre'testo nm pretext

pre'tore nm magistrate

pretta'mente adv decidedly

pre'tura nf magistrate's court

preva'le|nte a prevalent. **~nte'mente** adv primarily. **~nza** nf prevalence. **~re** vi prevail

pre'valso pp di **prevalere**

preve'dere vt foresee; forecast (*tempo*); (*legge ecc:*) provide for

preve'nire vt precede; (*evitare*) prevent; (*avvertire*) forewarn

preven|ti'vare vt estimate; (*aspettarsi*) budget for. **~'tivo** a preventive ●nm Comm estimate

preve'nu|to a forewarned; (*mal disposto*) prejudiced. **~zi'one** nf prevention; (*preconcetto*) prejudice

previ'den|te *a* provident. **~za** *nf* foresight. **~za sociale** social security, welfare *Am*. **~zi'ale** *a* provident

'previo *a* **~ pagamento** on payment

previsi'one *nf* forecast; **in ~ di** in anticipation of

pre'visto *pp di* prevedere ● *a* foreseen ● *nm* **più/meno/prima del ~** more/less/earlier than expected

prezi'oso *a* precious

prez'zemolo *nm* parsley

'prezzo *nm* price. **~ di fabbrica** factory price. **~ all'ingrosso** wholesale price. **[a] metà ~** half price

prigi'on|e *nf* prison; (*pena*) imprisonment. **prigio'nia** *nf* imprisonment. **~i'ero, -a** *a* imprisoned ● *nmf* prisoner

'prima *adv* before; (*più presto*) earlier; (*in primo luogo*) first; **~, finiamo questo** let's finish this first; **puoi venire ~?** (*di giorni*) can't you come any sooner?; (*di ore*) can't you come any earlier?; **~ o poi** sooner or later; **quanto ~** as soon as possible ● *prep* **~ di** before; **~ d'ora** before now ● *conj* **~ che** before **~** *nf* first class; *Theat* first night; *Auto* first [gear]

pri'mario *a* primary; (*principale*) principal

pri'mat|e *nm* primate. **~o** *nm* supremacy; *Sport* record

prima've'ra *nf* spring. **~rile** *a* spring *attrib*

primeggi'are *vi* excel

primi'tivo *a* primitive; (*originario*) original

pri'mizie *nfpl* early produce *sg*

'primo *a* first; (*fondamentale*) principal, (*precedente di due*) former; (*iniziale*) early; (*migliore*) best ● *nm* first; **primi** *pl* (*i primi giorni*) the beginning; **in un ~ tempo** at first. **prima copia** master copy

primo'genito, -a *a* & *nmf* firstborn

primordi'ale *a* primordial

'primula *nf* primrose

princi'pale *a* main ● *nm* head, boss *fam*

princi'pato *nm* principality. **'principe** *nm* prince. **principe ereditario** crown prince. **~'pesco** *a* princely. **~'pessa** *nf* princess

principi'ante *nmf* beginner

prin'cipio *nm* beginning; (*concetto*) principle; (*causa*) cause; **per ~** on principle

'prisma *nm* prism

pri'va|re *vt* deprive. **~rsi** *vr* deprive oneself

privatizzazi'one *nf* privatization. **pri'vato, -a** *a* private ● *nmf* private citizen

privazi'one *nf* deprivation

privilegi'are *vt* privilege; (*considerare più importante*) favour. **privi'legio** *nm* privilege

'privo *a* **~ di** devoid of; (*mancante*) lacking in

pro *prep* for ● *nm* advantage; **a che ~?** what's the point?; **il ~ e il contro** the pros and cons

pro'babil|e *a* probable. **~ità** *nf inv* probability. **~'mente** *adv* probably

pro'ble|ma *nm* problem. **~'matico** *a* problematic

pro'boscide *nf* trunk

procacci'ar|e *vt*, **~si** *vr* obtain

pro'cace *a* (*ragazza*) provocative

pro'ced|ere *vi* proceed; (*iniziare*) start; **~ere contro** *Jur* start legal proceedings against. **~i'mento** *nm* process; *Jur* proceedings *pl*. **proce'dura** *nf* procedure

proces'sare *vt* *Jur* try

processi'one *nf* procession

pro'cesso *nm* process; *Jur* trial

proces'sore *nm* *Comput* processor

processu'ale *a* trial

pro'cinto *nm* essere in ~ di be about to

pro'clama *nm* proclamation

procla'mare *vt* proclaim. ~zi'one *nf* proclamation

procrasti'nare *vt liter* postpone

procreazi'one *nf* procreation

pro'cura *nf* power of attorney; per ~ by proxy

procu'rare *vt/i* procure; (*causare*) cause; (*cercare*) try. ~'tore *nm* attorney. P~tore Generale Attorney General. ~tore legale lawyer. ~tore della repubblica public prosecutor

'prode *a* brave. pro'dezza *nf* bravery

prodi'gare *vt* lavish. ~si *vr* do one's best

pro'digio *nm* prodigy. ~'oso *a* prodigious

pro'dotto *nm* pp di produrre ● *nm* product. prodotti agricoli farm produce *sg.* ~ derivato by-product. ~ interno lordo gross domestic product. ~ nazionale lordo gross national product

pro'durre *vt* produce. ~rsi *vr* (*attore*) play; (*accadere*) happen. ~ttività *nf* productivity. ~'tivo *a* productive. ~'tore, ~'trice *nmf* producer. ~zi'one *nf* production

profa'nare *vt* desecrate. ~zi'one *nf* desecration. pro'fano *a* profane

profe'rire *vt* utter

Prof.essa *abbr* (Professoressa) Prof.

profes'sare *vt* profess; practise (*professione*)

professio'nale *a* professional

professi'one *nf* profession; libera ~ne profession. ~'nismo *nm* professionalism. ~'nista *nmf* professional

profes'sore, -'essa *nmf Sch* teacher; *Univ* lecturer; (*titolare di cattedra*) professor

pro'feta *nm* prophet. ~tico *a* prophetic. ~tiz'zare *vt* prophesy. ~'zia *nf* prophecy

pro'ficuo *a* profitable

profi'lare *vt* outline; (*ornare*) border; *Aeron* streamline. ~si *vr* stand out

profi'lattico *a* prophylactic ● *nm* condom

pro'filo *nm* profile; (*breve studio*) outline; di ~ in profile

profit'tare *vi* ~ di (*avvantaggiarsi*) profit by; (*approfittare*) take advantage of. pro'fitto *nm* profit; (*vantaggio*) advantage

profonda'mente *adv* deeply, profoundly. ~ità *nf inv* depth

pro'fondo *a* deep; *fig* profound; (*cultura*) great

'profugo, -a *nmf* refugee

profu'mare *vt* perfume. ~si *vr* put on perfume

profumata'mente *adv* pagare ~ pay through the nose

profu'mato *a* (*fiore*) fragrant; (*fazzoletto ecc*) scented

profume'ria *nf* perfumery. pro'fumo *nm* perfume, scent

profusi'one *nf* profusion; a ~ in profusion. pro'fuso *pp di* profondere ● *a* profuse

proget'tare *vt* plan. ~'tista *nmf* designer. pro'getto *nm* plan; (*di lavoro importante*) project. progetto di legge bill

prog'nosi *nf inv* prognosis; in ~ riservata on the danger list

pro'gramma *nm* programme; *Comput* program. ~ scolastico syllabus

program'mare *vt* programme; *Comput* program. ~'tore, ~'trice *nmf* [computer] programmer. ~zi'one *nf* programming

progre'dire *vi* [make] progress

progres'sione *nf* progression. ~'sivo *a* progressive. pro'gresso *nm* progress

proi'bire *vt* forbid. ~'tivo *a* prohibitive. ~to *a* forbidden. ~zi'one *nf* prohibition

proiet'tare *vt* project; show (*film*). ~t'tore *nm* projector; *Auto* headlight

proi'ettile *nm* bullet

proiezi'one *nf* projection

'prole *nf* offspring. **proletari'ato** *nm* proletariat. **prole'tario** *a & nm* proletarian

prolife'rare *vi* proliferate. **pro'lifico** *a* prolific

pro'lisso *a* verbose, prolix

'prologo *nm* prologue

pro'lunga *nf Electr* extension

prolun'gar|e *vt* prolong; *(allungare)* lengthen; extend *(contratto, scadenza)*. ~**si** *vr* continue; *(~si su (dilungarsi))* dwell upon

prome'moria *nm* memo; *(per se stessi)* reminder, note; *(formale)* memorandum

pro'me|ssa *nf* promise. ~**sso** *pp di* promettere. ~**ttere** *vt/i* promise

promet'tente *a* promising

promi'nente *a* prominent

promiscuità *nf* promiscuity. **pro'miscuo** *a* promiscuous

promon'torio *nm* promontory

pro'mo|sso *pp di* **promuovere** ● *a Sch* who has gone up a year; *Univ* who has passed an exam. ~**'tore**, ~**'trice** *nmf* promoter

promozio'nale *a* promotional. **promozi'one** *nf* promotion

promul'gare *vt* promulgate

promu'overe *vt* promote; *Sch* move up a class

proni'pote *nm (di bisnonno)* great-grandson; *(di prozio)* great-nephew ● *nf (di bisnonno)* great-granddaughter; *(di prozio)* great-niece

pro'nome *nm* pronoun

pronosti'care *vt* forecast, predict. **pro'nostico** *nm* forecast

pron'tezza *nf* readiness; *(rapidità)* quickness

'pronto *a* ready; *(rapido)* quick; ~**!** *Teleph* hallo!; **tenersi ~** be ready **(per** for**); pronti, via! (in gare** ready! steady! go!. ~ **soccorso** first aid; *(in ospedale)* accident and emergency

prontu'ario *nm* handbook

pro'nuncia *nf* pronunciation

pronunci'a|re *vt* pronounce; *(dire)*

utter; deliver *(discorso)*. ~**rsi** *vr (su un argomento)* give one's opinion. ~**to** *a* pronounced; *(prominente)* prominent

pro'nunzia *ecc =* **pronuncia** *ecc*

propa'ganda *nf* propaganda

propa'ga|re *vt* propagate. ~**rsi** *vr* spread. ~**zi'one** *nf* propagation

prope'deutico *a* introductory

pro'pen|dere *vi* ~**dere per** be in favour of. ~**si'one** *nf* inclination, propensity. ~**so** *pp di* propendere ● *a* **essere ~so a fare qcsa** be inclined to do sth

propi'nare *vt* administer

pro'pizio *a* favourable

propo'nimento *nm* resolution

pro'por|re *vt* propose; *(suggerire)* suggest. ~**si** *vr* set oneself *(obiettivo, meta)*; ~**si di** intend to

proporzio'na|le *a* proportional. ~**re** *vt* proportion. ~**to** *a* proportioned. **proporzi'one** *nf* proportion

pro'posito *nm* purpose; **a ~** by the way; **a ~ di** with regard to; **di ~** *(apposta)* on purpose; **capitare a ~**, **giungere a ~** come at just the right time

proposizi'one *nf* clause; *(frase)* sentence

pro'post|a *nf* proposal. ~**o** *pp di* proporre

proprietà *nf inv* property; *(diritto)* ownership; *(correttezza)* propriety. ~ **immobiliare** property. ~ **privata** private property. **proprie'taria** *nf* owner; *(di casa affittata)* landlady. **proprie'tario** *nm* owner; *(di casa affittata)* landlord

'proprio *a* one's [own]; *(caratteristico)* typical; *(appropriato)* proper ● *adv* just; *(veramente)* really; **non ~** not really, not exactly; *(affatto)* not... at all ● *pron* one's own ● *nm* one's [own]; **lavorare in ~** be one's own boss; **mettersi in ~** set up on one's own

propul|si'one *nf* propulsion. ~**'sore** *nm* propeller

'proroga *nf* extension

proro'ga|bile *a* extendable. ~re *vt* extend

pro'rompere *vi* burst out

'prosa *nf* prose. pro'saico *a* prosaic

pro'scio|gliere *vt* release; *Jur* acquit. ~lto *pp di* prosciogliere

prosciu'gar|e *vt* dry up; *(bonificare)* reclaim. ~si *vr* dry up

prosci'utto *nm* ham. ~ cotto cooked ham. ~ crudo type of dry-cured ham, Parma ham

pro'scri|tto, -a *pp di* proscrivere ● *nmf* exile

prosecuzi'one *nf* continuation

prosegui'mento *nm* continuation; buon ~! *(viaggio)* have a good journey!; *(festa)* enjoy the rest of the party!

prosegu'ire *vt* continue ● *vi* go on, continue

prospe'r|are *vi* prosper. ~ità *nf* prosperity. 'prospero *a* prosperous; *(favorevole)* favourable. ~oso *a* flourishing; *(ragazza)* buxom

prospet'tar|e *vt* show. ~si *vr* seem

prospet'tiva *nf* perspective; *(panorama)* view; *fig* prospect. pro'spetto *nm* *(vista)* view; *(facciata)* façade; *(tabella)* table

prospici'ente *a* facing

prossima'mente *adv* soon

prossimità *nf* proximity

'prossimo, -a *a* near; *(seguente)* next; *(molto vicino)* close; l'anno ~ next year ● *nmf* neighbour

prosti'tu|ta *nf* prostitute. ~zi'one *nf* prostitution

pro'stra|re *vt* prostrate. ~rsi *vr* prostrate oneself. ~to *a* prostrate

protago'nista *nmf* protagonist

pro'te|ggere *vt* protect; *(favorire)* favour

prote'ina *nf* protein

pro'tender|e *vt* stretch out. ~si *vr* *(in avanti)* lean out. pro'teso *pp di* protendere

pro'te|sta *nf* protest; *(dichiarazione)* protestation. ~'stante *a & nmf* Protestant. ~'stare *vt/i* protest

prote|t'tivo *a* protective. ~tto *pp*

di proteggere. ~t'tore, ~t'trice *nmf* protector; *(sostenitore)* patron ● *nm* *(di prostituta)* pimp. ~zi'one *nf* protection

protocol'lare *a* *(visita)* protocol ● *vt* register

proto'collo *nm* protocol; *(registro)* register; carta ~ official stamped paper

pro'totipo *nm* prototype

pro'tra|rre *vt* protract; *(differire)* postpone. ~rsi *vr* go on, continue. ~tto *pp di* protrarre

protube'ran|te *a* protuberant. ~za *nf* protuberance

'prova *nf* test; *(dimostrazione)* proof; *(tentativo)* try; *(di abito)* fitting; *Sport* heat; *Theat* rehearsal; *(bozza)* proof; fino a ~ contraria until I'm told otherwise; in ~ *(assumere)* for a trial period; mettere alla ~ put to the test. ~ generale dress rehearsal

pro'var|e *vt* *(dimostrare)* prove; *(tentare)* try; try on *(abiti ecc)*; *(sentire)* feel; *Theat* rehearse. ~si *vr* try

proveni'enza *nf* origin. prove'nire *vi* provenire da come from

pro'vento *nm* proceeds *pl*

prove'nuto *pp di* provenire

pro'verbio *nm* proverb

pro'vetta *nf* test-tube; bambino in ~ test-tube baby

pro'vetto *a* skilled

pro'vinci|a *nf* province; *(strada)* B road, secondary road. ~'ale *a* provincial; strada ~ale B road, secondary road

pro'vino *nm* specimen; *Cinema* screen test

provo'can|te *a* provocative. ~re *vt* provoke; *(causare)* cause. ~'tore, ~'trice *nmf* trouble-maker. ~'torio *a* provocative. ~zi'one *nf* provocation

provve'der|e *vi* ~ere a provide for. ~i'mento *nm* measure; *(previdenza)* precaution

provvi'denz|a *nf* providence. ~i'ale *a* providential

provvigione | puntata

provvigi'one *nf Comm* commission

provvi'sorio *a* provisional

prov'vista *nf* supply

pro'zio, -a *nm* great-uncle ● *nf* great-aunt

'prua *nf* prow

pru'den|te *a* prudent. **~za** *nf* prudence; **per ~za** as a precaution

'prudere *vi* itch

'prugn|a *nf* plum. **~a secca** prune. **~o** *nm* plum[-tree]

prurigi'noso *a* itchy. **pru'rito** *nm* itch

pseu'donimo *nm* pseudonym

psica'na|lisi *nf* psychoanalysis. **~'lista** *nmf* psychoanalyst. **~liz'zare** *vt* psychoanalyse

'psiche *nf* psyche

psichi'a|tra *nmf* psychiatrist. **~'tria** *nf* psychiatry. **~trico** *a* psychiatric

'psichico *a* mental

psico|lo'gia *nf* psychology. **~'logico** *a* psychological. **psi'cologo, -a** *nmf* psychologist

psico'patico, -a *a* psychopathic ● *nmf* psychopath

PT *abbr* (Posta e Telecomunicazioni) PO

pubbli'ca|re *vt* publish. **~zi'one** *nf* publication. **~zioni** *pl* (*di matrimonio*) banns

pubbli'cista *nmf* Journ correspondent

pubblicità *nf inv* publicity, advertising; (*annuncio*) advertisement, advert; **fare ~ a qcsa** advertise sth; **piccola ~** small advertisements. **pubblici'tario** *a* advertising

'pubblico *a* public; **scuola pubblica** state school ● *nm* public; (*spettatori*) audience; **grande ~** general public. **Pubblica Sicurezza** Police. **~ ufficiale** civil servant

'pube *nm* pubis

pubertà *nf* puberty

pu'dico *a* modest. **pu'dore** *nm* modesty

pue'rile *a* children's; *pej* childish

pugi'lato *nm* boxing. **'pugile** *nm* boxer

pugna'la|re *vt* stab. **~ta** *nf* stab. **pu'gnale** *nm* dagger

'pugno *nm* fist; (*colpo*) punch; (*manciata*) fistful; (*fig: numero limitato*) handful; **dare un ~ a** punch

'pulce *nf* flea; (*microfono*) bug

pul'cino *nm* chick; (*nel calcio*) junior

pu'ledra *nf* filly

pu'ledro *nm* colt

pu'li|re *vt* clean. **~re a secco** dry-clean. **~to** *a* clean. **~'tura** *nf* cleaning. **~'zia** *nf* (*il pulire*) cleaning; (*l'essere pulito*) cleanliness; **~zie** *pl* housework; **fare le ~zie** do the cleaning

'pullman *nm inv* bus, coach; (*urbano*) bus

pul'mino *nm* minibus

'pulpito *nm* pulpit

pul'sante *nm* button; *Electr* [push-]button. **~ di accensione** on/off switch

pul'sa|re *vi* pulsate. **~zi'one** *nf* pulsation

pul'viscolo *nm* dust

'puma *nm inv* puma

pun'gente *a* prickly; (*insetto*) stinging; (*odore ecc*) sharp

'punger|e *vt* prick; (*insetto:*) sting. **~si un dito** prick one's finger

pungi'glione *nm* sting

pu'ni|re *vt* punish. **~'tivo** *a* punitive. **~zi'one** *nf* punishment; *Sport* free kick

'punta *nf* point; (*estremità*) tip; (*di monte*) peak; (*un po'*) pinch; *Sport* forward; **doppie punte** (*di capelli*) split ends

pun'tare *vt* point; (*spingere con forza*) push; (*scommettere*) bet; (*fam: appuntare*) fasten ● *vi* **~ su** *fig* rely on; **~ verso** (*dirigersi*) head for; **~ a** aspire to

punta'spilli *nm inv* pincushion

pun'tat|a *nf* (*di una storia*) instalment; (televisiva) episode; (al gioco) stake, bet; (breve visita) flying visit; **a ~e** serialized, in instalments; **fare una ~a a/in** pop over to (luogo)

punteggia'tura nf punctuation
pun'teggio nm score
puntel'lare vt prop. **pun'tello** nm prop
pun'tigli|o nm spite; (ostinazione) obstinacy. **~'oso** a punctilious, pernickety pej
pun'tin|a nf (da disegno) drawing pin, thumb tack Am; (di giradischi) stylus. **~o** nm dot; **a ~o** perfectly; (cotto) a T
'punto nm point; (in cucito, Med) stitch; (in punteggiatura) full stop; **in che ~?** where, exactly?; **di ~ in bianco** all of a sudden; **due punti** colon; **in ~** sharp; **mettere a ~** put right; fig fine tune; tune up (motore); **essere sul ~ di fare qcsa** be about to do sth, be on the point of doing sth. **punti** pl **cardinali** points of the compass. **~ debole** blind spot. **~ esclamativo** exclamation mark. **~ interrogativo** question mark. **~ nero** Questa blackhead. **~ di riferimento** landmark; (per la qualità) benchmark. **~ di vendita** point of sale. **~ e virgola** semicolon. **~ di vista** point of view
puntu'al|e a punctual. **~ità** nf punctuality. **~'mente** adv punctually, on time
pun'tura nf (di insetto) sting; (di ago ecc) prick; Med puncture; (iniezione) injection; (fitta) stabbing pain
punzecchi'are vt prick; fig tease
'pupa nf doll. **pu'pazzo** nm puppet. **pupazzo di neve** snowman
pup'illa nf Anat pupil
pu'pillo, -a nmf (di professore) favourite
purché conj provided
'pure adv too, also; (concessivo) **fate ~!** please do! ● conj (tuttavia)

yet; (anche se) even if; **pur di** just to
purè nm inv purée. **~ di patate** mashed potatoes, creamed potatoes
pu'rezza nf purity
'purga nf purge. **pur'gante** nm laxative. **pur'gare** vt purge
purga'torio nm purgatory
purifi'care vt purify
puri'tano, -a a & nmf Puritan
'puro a pure; (vino ecc) undiluted; **per ~ caso** by sheer chance, purely by chance
puro'sangue a & nm thoroughbred
pur'troppo adv unfortunately
pus nm pus. **'pustola** nf pimple
puti'ferio nm uproar
putre'far|e vi, **~si** vr putrefy
'putrido a putrid
put'tana nf vulg whore
'puzza nf = puzzo
puz'zare vi stink; **~ di bruciato** fig smell fishy
'puzzo nm stink, bad smell. **~la** nf polecat. **~'lente** a stinking
p.zza abbr (piazza) Sq.

Qq

qua adv here; **da un anno in ~** for the last year; **da quando in ~?** since when?; **di ~** this way; **di ~ di** on this side of; **~ dentro** in here; **~ sotto** under here; **~ vicino** near here; **~ e là** here and there
qua'derno nm exercise book; (per appunti) notebook
quadrango'lare a (forma) quadrangular. **qua'drangolo** nm quadrangle
qua'drante nm quadrant; (di orologio) dial
qua'dra|re vt square; (contabilità) balance ● vi fit in. **~to** a square; (equilibrato) level-headed ● nm

square; (*pugilato*) ring; **al ~to** squared

quadret'tato *a* squared; (*carta*) graph *attrib*. **qua'dretto** *nm* square; (*piccolo quadro*) small picture; **a quadretti** (*tessuto*) check

quadricro'mia *nf* four-colour printing

quadrien'nale *a* (*che dura quattro anni*) four-year

quadri'foglio *nm* four-leaf clover

quadri'latero *nm* quadrilateral

quadri'mestre *nm* four-month period

'quadro *nm* picture, painting; (*quadrato*) square; (*fig: scena*) sight; (*tabella*) table; *Theat* scene; *Comm* executive panel; *pl* (*carte*) diamonds; **a quadri** (*tessuto, giacca, motivo*) check. **quadri** *pl* **direttivi** senior management

qua'drupede *nm* quadruped

quaggiù *adv* down here

'quaglia *nf* quail

'qualche *a* (*alcuni*) a few, some; (*un certo*) some; (*in interrogazioni*) any; **ho ~ problema** I have a few problems, I have some problems; **~ tempo fa** some time ago; **hai ~ libro italiano?** have you any Italian books?; **posso prendere ~ libro?** can I take some books?; **in ~ modo** somehow; **in ~ posto** somewhere; **~ volta** sometimes; **~ cosa = qualcosa**

qual'cosa *pron* something; (*in interrogazioni*) anything; **~'altro** something else; **vuoi ~'altro?** would you like anything else?; **~a di strano** something strange; **vuoi ~a da mangiare?** would you like something to eat?

qual'cuno *pron* someone, somebody; (*in interrogazioni*) anyone, anybody; (*alcuni*) some; (*in interrogazioni*) any; **c'è ~?** is anybody in?; **qualcun altro** someone else, somebody else; **c'è qualcun altro che aspetta?** is anybody else waiting?; **ho letto ~ dei suoi libri** I've read some of his books; **cono-**

sci ~ dei suoi amici? do you know any of his friends?

'quale *a* which; (*indeterminato*) what; (*come*) as, like; **~ macchina è la tua?** which car is yours?; **~ motivo avrà di parlare così?** what reason would he have to speak like that?; **~ onore!** what an honour!; **città quali Venezia** towns like Venice; **~ che sia la tua opinione** whatever you may think ● *pron inter* which [one]; **~ preferisci?** which [one] do you prefer? ● *pron rel* **il/la ~** (*persona*) who; (*animale, cosa*) that, which; (*oggetto: con prep*) whom; (*animale, cosa*) which; **ho incontrato tua madre, la ~ mi ha detto...** I met your mother, who told me...; **l'ufficio nel ~ lavoro** the office in which I work; **l'uomo con il ~ parlavo** the man to whom I was speaking ● *adv* (*come*) as

qua'lifica *nf* qualification; (*titolo*) title

qualifi'ca|re *vt* qualify; (*definire*) define. **~rsi** *vr* be placed. **~'tivo** *a* qualifying. **~to** *a* (*operaio*) semiskilled. **~zi'one** *nf* qualification

qualità *nf inv* quality; (*specie*) kind; **in ~** in one's capacity as. **~tiva'mente** *adv* qualitatively. **~'tivo** *a* qualitative

qua'lora *conj* in case

qual'siasi, **qua'lunque** *a* any; (*non importa quale*) whatever; (*ordinario*) ordinary; **dammi una penna ~** give me any pen [whatsoever]; **farei ~ cosa** I would do anything; **~ cosa io faccia** whatever I do; **~ persona** anyone; **in ~ caso** in any case; **uno ~** any one, whichever; **l'uomo qualunque** the man in the street; **vivo in una casa ~** I live in an ordinary house

qualunqu'ismo *nm* lack of political views

'quando *conj* & *adv* when; **da ~ ti ho visto** since I saw you; **da ~ esci con lui?** how long have you been going out with him?; **da ~ in qua?** since when?; **~... ~...** sometimes..., sometimes...

quantifi'care *vt* quantify

quantità *nf inv* quantity; **una ~ di** *(gran numero)* a great deal of. **~tiva'mente** *adv* quantitatively. **~'tivo** *nm* amount ● *a* quantitative

'**quanto** *a inter* how much; *(con nomi plurali)* how many; *(in esclamazione)* what a lot of; **~ tempo?** how long?; **quanti anni hai?** how old are you? ● *a rel* as much... as; *(con nomi plurali)* as many... as; **prendi ~ denaro ti serve** take as much money as you need; **prendi quanti libri vuoi** take as many books as you like ● *pron inter* how much; *(quanto tempo)* how long; *(plurale)* how many; **quanti ne abbiamo oggi?** what date is it today?, what's the date today? ● *pron rel* as much as; *(quanto tempo)* as long as; *(plurale)* as many as; **prendine ~/quanti ne vuoi** take as much/as many as you like; **stai ~ vuoi** stay as long as you like; **questo è ~** that's it ● *adv inter* how much; *(quanto tempo)* how long; **~ sei alto?** how tall are you?; **~ hai aspettato?** how long did you wait for?; **~ costa?** how much is it?; **~ mi dispiace!** I'm so sorry!; **~ è bello!** how nice! ● *adv rel* as much as; **lavoro ~ posso** I work as much as I can; **è tanto intelligente ~ bello** he's as intelligent as he's good-looking; **in ~** *(in qualità di)* as; *(poiché)* since; **in ~ a me** as far as I'm concerned; **per ~** however; **per ~ ne sappia** as far as I know; **per ~ mi riguarda** as far as I'm concerned; **per ~ mi sia simpatico** much as I like him; **~ a** as for; **~ prima** *(al più presto)* as soon as possible

quan'tunque *conj* although

qua'ranta *a & nm* forty

quaran'tena *nf* quarantine

quaran'tenne *a* forty-year-old. **~io** *nm* period of forty years

quaran'tesimo *a* fortieth. **~ina** *nf* una **~ina** about forty

qua'resima *nf* Lent

quar'tetto *nm* quartet

quarti'ere *nm* district; *Mil* quarters *pl.* **~ generale** headquarters

quarto *a* fourth ● *nm* fourth; *(quarta parte)* quarter; **le sette e un ~** a quarter past seven. **quarti** *pl* **di finale** quarterfinals. **~ d'ora** quarter of an hour. **quar'tultimo**, **-a** *nmf* fourth from the end, fourth last

'quarzo *nm* quartz

'quasi *adv* almost, nearly; **~ mai** hardly ever ● *conj (come se)* as if; **~ ~ sto a casa** I'm tempted to stay home

quassù *adv* up here

'quatto *a* crouching; *(silenzioso)* silent; **starsene ~ ~** keep very quiet

quat'tordici *a & nm* fourteen

quat'trini *nmpl* money *sg*, dosh *sg fam*

'quattro *a & nm* four; **dirne ~ a qcno** give sb a piece of one's mind; **farsi in ~ (per qcno/per fare qcsa)** go to a lot of trouble (for sb/ to do sth); **in ~ e quattr'otto** in a flash. **~ per ~** *nm inv Auto* four-wheel drive [vehicle]

quat'trocchi: a ~ *adv* in private

quattro'cento *a & nm* four hundred; **il ~cento** the fifteenth century

quattro'mila *a & nm* four thousand

'quell|o *a* that *(pl* those); **quell'albero** that tree; **quegli alberi** those trees; **quel cane** that dog; **quei cani** those dogs ● *pron* that [one] *(pl* those [ones]); **~o lì** that one over there; **~o che** the one that; *(ciò che)* what; **quelli che** the ones that, those that; **~o a destra** the one on the right

'quercia *nf* oak

que'rela *nf* [legal] action

quere'lare vt bring an action against

que'sito nm question

questio'nario nm questionnaire

quest'ione nf question; (faccenda) matter; (litigio) quarrel; **in ~** in doubt; **è fuori ~** it's out of the question; **è ~ di vita o di morte** it's a matter of life and death

'questo a this (pl these) ● pron this [one] (pl these [ones]); **~o qui, ~o qua** this one here; **~ è quello che a detto** that's what he said; **per ~o** for this or that reason. **quest'oggi** today

que'store nm chief of police

que'stura nf police headquarters pl

qui adv here; **da ~ in poi** from now on; **fin ~** (di tempo) up till now, until now; **~ dentro** in here; **~ sotto** under here; **~ vicino** near here ● nm **~ pro quo** misunderstanding

quie'scienza nf trattamento di **~** retirement package

quie'tanza nf receipt

quie'tar|e vt calm. **~si** vr quieten down

quie'et|e nf quiet; disturbo della **~e pubblica** breach of the peace. **~o** a quiet

'quindi adv then ● conj therefore

'quindi|ci a & nm fifteen. **~cina** nf **una ~cina** about fifteen; **una ~cina di giorni** a fortnight Br, two weeks pl

quinquen'nale a (che dura cinque anni) five-year. **quin'quennio** nm [period of] five years

quin'tale nm a hundred kilograms

'quinte nfpl Theat wings

quin'tetto nm quintet

'quinto a fifth

quin'tuplo a quintuple

qui'squiglia nf **perdersi in quisquiglie** get bogged down in details

'quota nf (rata) instalment; (altitudine) height; Aeron altitude, height; (ippica) odds pl; per-

dere ~ lose altitude; **prendere ~** gain altitude. **~ di iscrizione** entry fee

quo'tar|e vt Comm quote. **~o a** quoted; **essere ~to in Borsa** be quoted on the Stock Exchange. **~zi'one** nf quotation

quotidi|ana'mente adv daily. **~'ano** a daily; (ordinario) everyday ● nm daily [paper]

quozi'ente nm quotient. **~ d'intelligenza** intelligence quotient, IQ

Rr

ra'barbaro nm rhubarb

'rabbia nf rage; (ira) anger; Med rabies sg; **che ~!** what a nuisance!; **mi fa ~** it makes me angry

rab'bino nm rabbi

rabbiosa'mente adv furiously. **rabbi'oso** a hot-tempered; Med rabid; (violento) violent

rabbo'nir|e vt pacify. **~si** vr calm down

rabbrivi'dire vi shudder; (di freddo) shiver

rabbui'arsi vr become dark

raccapez'zar|e vt put together. **~si** vr see one's way ahead

raccapricci'ante a horrifying

raccatta'palle nm inv ball boy ● nf inv ball girl

raccat'tare vt pick up

rac'chetta nf racket. **~ da ping pong** table-tennis bat. **~ da sci** ski stick, ski pole. **~ da tennis** tennis racket

'racchio a fam ugly

racchi'udere vt contain

rac'cogli|ere vt pick; (da terra) pick up; (mietere) harvest; (collezionare) collect; (radunare) gather; win (voti ecc); (dare asilo a) take in. **~ersi** vr gather; (concentrarsi) collect one's thoughts. **~'mento** nm concentration.

~'tore, ~'trice *nmf* collector ● *nm* (*cartella*) ring-binder

rac'colto, -a *pp di* raccogliere ● *a* (*rannicchiato*) hunched; (*intimo*) cosy; (*concentrato*) engrossed ● *nm* (*mietitura*) harvest ● *nf* collection; (*di scritti*) compilation; (*del grano ecc*) harvesting; (*adunata*) gathering

raccoman'dabile *a* recommendable; poco ~ (*persona*) shady

raccoman'da|re *vt* recommend; (*affidare*) entrust. ~rsi *vr* (*implorare*) beg. ~ta *nf* registered letter; ~ta con ricevuta di ritorno recorded delivery. ~-espresso *nf guaranteed next-day delivery of recorded items*. ~zi'one *nf* recommendation

raccon'tare *vt* tell. rac'conto *nm* story

raccorci'are *vt* shorten

raccor'dare *vt* join. rac'cordo *nm* connection; (*stradale*) feeder. **raccordo anulare** ring road. **raccordo ferroviario** siding

ra'chitico *a* rickety; (*poco sviluppato*) stunted

racimo'lare *vt* scrape together

'racket *nm inv* racket

'radar *nm* radar

raddol'cir|e *vt* sweeten; *fig* soften. ~si *vr* become milder; (*carattere:*) mellow

raddoppi'are *vt* double. **rad'doppio** *nm* doubling

raddriz'zare *vt* straighten

'rader|e *vt* shave; graze (*muro*); ~e al suolo raze [to the ground]. ~si *vr* shave

radi'are *vt* strike off; ~ **dall'albo** strike off

radia|'tore *nm* radiator. ~zi'one *nf* radiation

'radica *nf* briar

radi'cale *a* radical ● *nm Gram* root; *Pol* radical

ra'dicchio *nm* chicory

ra'dice *nf* root; mettere [le] radici *fig* put down roots. ~ quadrata square root

'radio *nf inv* radio; via ~ by radio. ~ a transistor transistor radio ● *nm Chem* radium

radioama'tore, -'trice *nmf* [radio] ham

radioascolta'tore, -'trice *nmf* listener

radioat|tività *nf* radioactivity. ~'tivo *a* radioactive

radio'cro|naca *nf* radio commentary; fare la ~naca di commentate on. ~'nista *nmf* radio reporter

radiodiffusi'one *nf* broadcasting

radiogra|'fare *vt* X-ray. ~'fia *nf* X-ray [photograph]; (*radiologia*) radiography; fare una ~fia (*paziente:*) have an X-ray; (*dottore:*) take an X-ray

radio'fonico *a* radio *attrib*

radio'lina *nf* transistor

radi'ologo, -a *nmf* radiologist

radi'oso *a* radiant

radio'sveglia *nf* radio alarm

radio'taxi *nm inv* radio taxi

radiote'lefono *nm* radiotelephone; (*privato*) cordless [phone]

radiotelevi'sivo *a* broadcasting *attrib*

'rado *a* sparse; (*non frequente*) rare; di ~ seldom

radu'nar|e *vt*, ~si *vr* gather [together]. ra'duno *nm* meeting; *Sport* rally

ra'dura *nf* clearing

'rafano *nm* horseradish

raffazzo'nato *a* (*discorso, lavoro*) botched

raf'fermo *a* stale

'raffica *nf* gust; (*di armi da fuoco*) burst; (*di domande*) barrage

raffigu'ra|re *vt* represent. ~zi'one *nf* representation

raffi'na|re *vt* refine. ~ta'mente *adv* elegantly. ~'tezza *nf* refinement. ~to *a* refined. raffine'ria *nf* refinery

rafforza|'mento *nm* reinforcement; (*di muscolatura*) strengthening. ~re *vt* reinforce. ~'tivo *nm Gram* intensifier

raffredda'mento *nm* (*processo*) cooling

raffred'd|are *vt* cool. **~arsi** *vr* get cold; (*prendere un raffreddore*) catch a cold. **~ore** *nm* cold. **~ore da fieno** hay fever

raf'fronto *nm* comparison

'rafia *nf* raffia

Rag. *abbr* ragioniere

ra'gaz|za *nf* girl; (*fidanzata*) girlfriend. **~za alla pari** au pair [girl]. **~'zata** *nf* prank. **~zo** *nm* boy; (*fidanzato*) boyfriend; **da ~zo** (*da giovane*) as a boy

ragge'lar|e *vt fig* freeze. **~si** *vr fig* turn to ice

raggi'ante *a* radiant; **~ di successo** flushed with success

raggi'era *nf* **a ~** with a pattern like spokes radiating from a centre

'raggio *nm* ray; *Math* radius; (*di ruota*) spoke; (*d'azione*) range. **~ laser** laser beam

raggi'rare *vt* trick. **rag'giro** *nm* trick

raggi'un|gere *vt* reach; (*conseguire*) achieve. **~'gibile** *a* (*luogo*) within reach

raggomito'lar|e *vt* wind. **~si** *vr* curl up

raggranel'lare *vt* scrape together

raggrin'zir|e *vt*, **~si** *vr* wrinkle

raggrup|pa'mento *nm* (*gruppo*) group; (*azione*) grouping. **~'pare** *vt* group together

ragguagli'are *vt* compare; (*informare*) inform. **raggu'aglio** *nm* comparison; (*informazione*) information

ragguar'devole *a* considerable

'ragia *nf* resin; **acqua ~** turpentine

ragiona'mento *nm* reasoning; (*discussione*) discussion. **ragio'nare** *vi* reason; (*discutere*) discuss

ragi'one *nf* reason; (*ciò che è giusto*) right; **a ~** *o* **a torto** rightly or wrongly; **aver ~** be right; **perdere la ~** go out of one's mind;

a ragion veduta after due consideration

ragione'ria *nf* accountancy

ragio'nevol|e *a* reasonable. **~'mente** *adv* reasonably

ragioni'ere, -a *nmf* accountant

ragli'are *vi* bray

'raglio *nm* bray

ragna'tela *nf* cobweb. **'ragno** *nm* spider

ragù *nm inv* meat sauce

RAI *nf abbr* (**Radio Audizioni Italiane**) Italian public broadcasting company

ralle'gra|re *vt* gladden. **~rsi** *vr* rejoice; **~rsi con qcno** congratulate sb. **~'menti** *nmpl* congratulations

rallenta'mento *nm* slowing down

rallen'ta|re *vt/i* slow down; (*allentare*) slacken. **~rsi** *vr* slow down. **~'tore** *nm* (*su strada*) speed bump; **al ~tore** in slow motion

raman'zina *nf* reprimand

ra'marro *nm* type of lizard

ra'mato *a* (*capelli*) copper[-coloured]

'rame *nm* copper

ramifi'ca|re *vi*, **~rsi** *vr* branch out; (*strada:*) branch. **~zi'one** *nf* ramification

rammari'carsi *vr* **~ di** regret; (*lamentarsi*) complain (**di** about). **ram'marico** *nm* regret

rammen'dare *vt* darn. **ram'mendo** *nm* darning

rammen'tar|e *vt* remember; **~e qcsa a qcno** (*richiamare alla memoria*) remind sb of sth. **~si** *vr* remember

rammol'li|re *vt* soften. **~rsi** *vr* go soft. **~to, -a** *nmf* wimp

'ramo *nm* branch. **~'scello** *nm* twig

'rampa *nf* (*di scale*) flight. **~ d'accesso** slip road. **~ di lancio** launch[ing] pad

ram'pante *a* **giovane ~** yuppie

rampi'cante *a* climbing ● *nm Bot* creeper

ram'pollo *nm hum* brat; (*discendente*) descendant

ram'pone *nm* harpoon; (*per scarpe*) crampon

'rana *nf* frog; (*nel nuoto*) breaststroke; **uomo ~** frogman

'rancido *a* rancid

ran'core *nm* resentment

ran'dagio *a* stray

'rango *nm* rank

rannicchi'arsi *vr* huddle up

rannuvola'mento *nm* clouding over. **rannuvo'larsi** *vr* cloud over

ra'nocchio *nm* frog

ranto'lare *vi* wheeze. **'rantolo** *nm* wheeze; (*di moribondo*) deathrattle

'rapa *nf* turnip

ra'pace *a* rapacious; (*uccello*) predatory

ra'pare *vt* crop

'rapida *nf* rapids *pl.* **~'mente** *adv* rapidly

rapidità *nf* speed

'rapido *a* swift ● *nm* (*treno*) express [train]

rapi'mento *nm* (*crimine*) kidnapping

ra'pina *nf* robbery; **~ a mano armata** armed robbery. **~ in banca** bank robbery. **rapi'nare** *vt* rob. **~'tore** *nm* robber

ra'pi|re *vt* abduct; (*a scopo di riscatto*) kidnap; (*estasiare*) ravish. **~'tore, ~'trice** *nmf* kidnapper

rappacifi'ca|re *vt* pacify. **~rsi** *vr* be reconciled, make it up. **~zi'one** *nf* reconciliation

rappor'tare *vt* reproduce (*disegno*); (*confrontare*) compare

rap'porto *nm* report; (*connessione*) relation; (*legame*) relationship; *Math, Techn* ratio; **rapporti** *pl* relationship; **essere in buoni rapporti** be on good terms. **~ di amicizia** friendship. **~ di lavoro** working relationship. **rapporti** *pl* **sessuali** sexual intercourse

rap'prendere *vr* set; (*latte:*) curdle

rappre'saglia *nf* reprisal

rappresen'tan|te *nmf* representa-

tive. **~te di classe** class representative. **~te di commercio** sales representative, [sales] rep *fam.* **~za** *nf* delegation; *Comm* agency; **spese** *pl* **di ~za** entertainment expenses; **di ~za** (*appartamento ecc*) company

rappresen'ta|re *vt* represent; *Theat* perform. **~'tivo** *a* representative. **~zi'one** *nf* representation; (*spettacolo*) performance

rap'preso *pp di* **rapprendersi**

rapso'dia *nf* rhapsody

'raptus *nm inv* fit of madness

rara'mente *adv* rarely, seldom

rare'fa|re *vt*, **~rsi** *vr* rarefy. **~tto** *a* rarefied

rarità *nf inv* rarity. **'raro** *a* rare

ra'sar|e *vt* shave; trim (*siepe ecc*). **~si** *vr* shave

raschia'mento *nm* *Med* curettage

raschi'are *vt* scrape; (*togliere*) scrape off

rasen'tare *vt* go close to. **ra'sente** *prep* very close to

'raso *pp di* **radere** ● *a* smooth; (*colmo*) full to the brim; (*barba*) close-cropped; **~ terra** close to the ground; **un cucchiaio ~** a level spoonful ● *nm* satin

ra'soio *nm* razor

ras'segna *nf* review; (*mostra*) exhibition; (*musicale, cinematografica*) festival; **passare in ~** review; *Mil* inspect

rasse'gna|re *vt* present. **~rsi** *vr* resign oneself. **~to** *a* (*persona, aria, tono*) resigned. **~zi'one** *nf* resignation

rassere'nar|e *vt* clear; *fig* cheer up. **~si** *vr* become clear; *fig* cheer up

rasset'tare *vt* tidy up; (*riparare*) mend

rassicu'ra|nte *a* (*persona, parole, presenza*) reassuring. **~re** *vt* reassure. **~zi'one** *nf* reassurance

rasso'dare *vt* harden; *fig* strengthen

rassomiglia'nza *nf* resemblance. **~re** *vi* **~re a** resemble

rastrella'mento *nm* (*di fieno*) raking; (*perlustrazione*) combing. **rastrel'lare** *vt* rake; (*perlustrare*) comb

rastrelli'era *nf* rack; (*per biciclette*) bicycle rack; (*scolapiatti*) [plate] rack. **ra'strello** *nm* rake

'rata *nf* instalment; **pagare a rate** pay by instalments; **comprare qcsa a rate** buy sth on hire purchase, buy sth on the installment plan *Am.* **rate'ale** *a* by instalments; **pagamento rateale** payment by instalments

rate'are, rateiz'zare *vt* divide into instalments

ra'tifica *nf Jur* ratification

ratifi'care *vt Jur* ratify

'ratto *nm* abduction; (*roditore*) rat

rattop'pare *vt* patch. **rat'toppo** *nm* patch

rattrap'pir|e *vt* make stiff. **~si** *vr* become stiff

rattri'star|e *vt* sadden. **~si** *vr* become sad

rau'cedine *nf* hoarseness. **'rauco** *a* hoarse

rava'nello *nm* radish

ravi'oli *nmpl* ravioli *sg*

ravve'dersi *vr* mend one's ways

ravvicina'mento *nm* (*tra persone*) reconciliation; *Pol* rapprochement

ravvici'nar|e *vt* bring closer; (*riconciliare*) reconcile. **~si** *vr* be reconciled

ravvi'sare *vt* recognize

ravvi'var|e *vt* revive; *fig* brighten up. **~si** *vr* revive

'rayon *nm* rayon

razio'cinio *nm* rational thought; (*buon senso*) common sense

razio'nal|e *a* rational. **~ità** *nf* (*raziocinio*) rationality; (*di ambiente*) functional nature. **~iz'zare** *vt* rationalize (*programmi, metodi, spazio*). **~'mente** *adv* (*con raziocinio*) rationally

razio'nare *vt* ration. **razi'one** *nf* ration

'razza *nf* race; (*di cani ecc*) breed; (*genere*) kind; **che ~ di idiota!** *fam* what an idiot!

raz'zia *nf* raid

razzi'ale *a* racial

raz'zis|mo *nm* racism. **~ta** *a* & *nmf* racist

'razzo *nm* rocket. **~ da segnalazione** flare

razzo'lare *vi* (*polli:*) scratch about

re *nm inv* king; *Mus* (*chiave, nota*) D

rea'gire *vi* react

re'ale *a* real; (*di re*) royal

rea'lis|mo *nm* realism. **~ta** *nmf* realist; (*fautore del re*) royalist

realistica'mente *adv* realistically. **rea'listico** *a* realistic

realiz'zabile *a* (*programma*) feasible

realiz'za|re *vt* (*attuare*) carry out, realize; *Comm* make; score (*gol, canestro*); (*rendersi conto di*) realize. **~rsi** *vr* come true; (*nel lavoro ecc*) fulfil oneself. **~zi'one** *nf* realization; (*di sogno, persona*) fulfilment. **~zione scenica** production

rea'lizzo *nm* (*vendita*) proceeds *pl*; (*riscossione*) yield

real'mente *adv* really

realtà *nf inv* reality. **~ virtuale** virtual reality

re'ato *nm* crime, criminal offence

reat'tivo *a* reactive

reat'tore *nm* reactor; *Aeron* jet [aircraft]

reazio'nario, -a *a* & *nmf* reactionary

reazi'one *nf* reaction. **~ a catena** chain reaction

'rebus *nm inv* rebus; (*enigma*) puzzle

recapi'tare *vt* deliver. **re'capito** *nm* address; (*consegna*) delivery. **recapito a domicilio** home delivery. **recapito telefonico** contact telephone number

re'car|e *vt* bear; (*produrre*) cause. **~si** *vr* go

re'cedere *vi* recede; *fig* give up

recensi'one *nf* review

recen'si|re *vt* review. **~ore** *nm* reviewer

re'cente *a* recent; **di ~** recently. **~'mente** *adv* recently

recessi'one *nf* recession

reces'sivo *a* Biol recessive. **re'cesso** *nm* recess

re'cidere *vt* cut off

reci'divo, -a *a* Med recurrent ● *nmf* repeat offender

recin'tare *vt* close off. **re'cinto** *nm* enclosure; (*per animali*) pen; (*per bambini*) play-pen. **~zi'one** *nf* (*muro*) wall; (*rete*) wire fence; (*cancellata*) railings *pl*

recipi'ente *nm* container

re'ciproco, -a *a* reciprocal

re'ciso *pp di* recidere

'recita *nf* performance. **reci'tare** *vt* recite; Theat act; play (*ruolo*). **~zi'one** *nf* recitation; Theat acting

recla'mare *vi* protest ● *vt* claim

ré'clame *nf inv* advertising; (*avviso pubblicitario*) advertisement

re'clamo *nm* complaint; **ufficio reclami** complaints department or office

recli'na|bile *a* reclining; **sedile ~bile** reclining seat. **~re** *vt* tilt (*sedile*); lean (*capo*)

reclusi'one *nf* imprisonment. **re'cluso, -a** *a* secluded ● *nmf* prisoner

'recluta *nf* recruit

reclu|ta'mento *nm* recruitment. **~'tare** *vt* recruit

'record *nm inv* record ● *a inv* (*cifra*) record *attrib*

recrimi'na|re *vi* recriminate. **~zi'one** *nf* recrimination

recupe'rare *vt* recover. **re'cupero** *nm* recovery; **corso di recupero** additional classes; **minuti di recupero** Sport injury time

redargu'ire *vt* rebuke

re'datto *pp di* redigere

redat'tore, -'trice *nmf* editor; (*di testo*) writer

redazi'one *nf* (*ufficio*) editorial office; (*di testi*) editing

reddi'tizio *a* profitable

'reddito *nm* income. **~ imponibile** taxable income

re'den|to *pp di* redimere. **~'tore** *nm* redeemer. **~zi'one** *nf* redemption

re'digere *vt* write; draw up (*documento*)

re'dimer|e *vt* redeem. **~si** *vr* redeem oneself

'redini *nfpl* reins

'reduce *a* **~ da** back from ● *nmf* survivor

refe'rendum *nm inv* referendum

refe'renza *nf* reference

refet'torio *nm* refectory

refrat'tario *a* refractory; **essere ~ a** have no aptitude for

refrige'ra|re *vt* refrigerate. **~zi'one** *nf* refrigeration

refur'tiva *nf* stolen goods *pl*

rega'lare *vt* give

re'gale *a* regal

re'galo *nm* present, gift

re'gata *nf* regatta

reg'gen|te *nmf* regent. **~za** *nf* regency

'regger|e *vt* (*sorreggere*) bear; (*tenere in mano*) hold; (*dirigere*) run; (*governare*) govern; Gram take ● *vi* (*resistere*) hold out; (*durare*) last; *fig* stand. **~si** *vr* stand

'reggia *nf* royal palace

reggi'calze *nm inv* suspender belt

reggi'mento *nm* regiment; (*fig: molte persone*) army

reggi'petto, reggi'seno *nm* bra

re'gia *nf* Cinema direction; Theat production

re'gime *nm* regime; (*dieta*) diet; Mech speed. **~ militare** military regime

re'gina *nf* queen

'regio *a* royal

regio'na|le *a* regional. **~'lismo** *nm* (*parola*) regionalism

regi'one *nf* region

re'gista nmf Cinema director; Theat, TV producer

regi'stra|re vt register; Comm enter; (incidere su nastro) tape, record; (su disco) record. **~'tore** nm recorder; (magnetofono) tape-recorder. **~tore di cassa** cash register. **~zi'one** nf registration; Comm entry; (di programma) recording

re'gistro nm register; (ufficio) registry. **~ di cassa** ledger

re'gnare vi reign

'regno nm kingdom; (sovranità) reign. **R~ Unito** United Kingdom

'regola nf rule; **essere in ~** be in order; (persona:) have one's papers in order. **rego'labile** a (meccanismo) adjustable. **~'mento** nm regulation; Comm settlement. **~mento di conti** settling of scores

rego'la|re a regular ● vt regulate; (ridurre, moderare) limit; (sistemare) settle. **~si** vr (agire) act; (moderarsi) control oneself. **~ità** nf inv regularity. **~iz'zare** vt regularize (debito)

rego'la|ta nf **darsi una ~ta** pull oneself together. **~'tore**, **~'trice** a piano **~'tore** urban development plan

'regolo nm ruler

regre'dire vi Biol, Psych regress

regres|si'one nf regression. **~'sivo** a regressive. **re'gresso** nm decline

reinseri'mento nm (di persona) reintegration

reinser'irsi vr (in ambiente) reintegrate

reinte'grare vt restore

relativa'mente adv relatively; **~ a** as regards. **relatività** nf relativity. **rela'tivo** a relative

rela'tore, **-'trice** nmf (in una conferenza) speaker

re'lax nm relaxation

relazi'one nf relation[ship]; (rapporto amoroso) [love] affair; (reso-

conto) report; **pubbliche relazioni** pl public relations

rele'gare vt relegate

religi'o|ne nf religion. **~so, -a** a religious ● nm monk ● nf nun

re'liquia nf relic. **~'ario** nm reliquary

re'litto nm wreck

re'ma|re vi row. **~'tore**, **~'trice** nmf rower

remini'scenza nf reminiscence

remissi'one nf remission; (sottomissione) submissiveness. **remis-'sivo** a submissive

'remo nm oar

'remora nf **senza remore** without hesitation

re'moto a remote

remune'ra|re vt remunerate. **~'tivo** a remunerative. **~zi'one** nf remuneration

'rende|re vt (restituire) return; (esprimere) render; (fruttare) yield; (far diventare) make. **~si** vr become; **~si conto di qcsa** realize sth; **~si utile** make oneself useful

rendi'conto nm report

rendi'mento nm rendering; (produzione) yield

'rendita nf income; (dello Stato) revenue; **vivere di ~** fig rest on one's laurels

'rene nm kidney. **~ artificiale** kidney machine

'reni nfpl (schiena) back

reni'tente a **essere ~ a** (consigli di qcno) be unwilling to accept

'renna nf reindeer (pl inv); (pelle) buckskin

'Reno nm Rhine

'reo, -a a guilty ● nmf offender

re'parto nm department; Mil unit

repel'lente a repulsive

repen'taglio nm **mettere a ~** risk

repen'tino a sudden

repe'ribile a available; **non è ~** (perduto) it's not to be found

repe'rire vt trace (fondi)

re'perto nm **~ archeologico** find

reper'torio nm repertory; (elenco)

index; **immagini** pl **di ~** archive footage

'replica nf reply; (obiezione) objection; (copia) replica; Theat repeat performance. **repli'care** vt reply; Theat repeat

repor'tage nm inv report

repres|si'one nf repression. **~'sivo** a repressive. **re'presso** pp di **reprimere. re'primere** vt repress

re'pubbli|ca nf republic. **~'cano, -a** a & nmf republican

repu'tare vt consider

reputazi'one nf reputation

requi'sire vt requisition. **~to** nm requirement

requisi'toria nf (arringa) closing speech

requisizi'one nf requisition

'resa nf surrender; Comm rendering. **~ dei conti** rendering of accounts

'residence nm inv residential hotel

resi'den|te a & nmf resident. **~za** nf residence; (soggiorno) stay. **~zi'ale** a residential; **zona ~ziale** residential district

re'siduo a residual ● nm remainder

'resina nf resin

resi'sten|te a resistant; **~te all'acqua** water-resistant. **~za** nf resistance; (fisica) stamina; Electr resistor; **la R~za** the Resistance

re'sistere vi **~ [a]** resist; (a colpi, scosse) stand up to; **~ alla pioggia/al vento** be rain-/wind-resistant

'reso pp di **rendere**

reso'conto nm report

respin'gente nm Rail buffer

re'spin|gere vt repel; (rifiutare) reject; (bocciare) fail. **~to** pp di **respingere**

respi'ra|re vt/i breathe. **~'tore** nm respirator. **~'tore [a tubo]** snorkel **~'torio** a respiratory. **~zi'one** nf breathing; Med respiration. **~zione bocca a bocca** mouth-to-mouth rescuscitation, kiss of life.

re'spiro nm breath; (il respirare) breathing; fig respite

respon'sabile a responsible (**di** for); Jur liable ● nmf person responsible. **~ della produzione** production manager. **~ità** nf inv responsibility; Jur liability. **~iz'zare** vt give responsibility to

re'sponso nm response

'ressa nf crowd

re'stante a remaining ● nm remainder

re'stare vi = **rimanere**

restau'ra|re vt restore. **~'tore, ~'trice** nf restorer. **~zi'one** nf restoration. **re'stauro** nm (riparazione) repair

re'stio a restive; **~ a** reluctant to

restitu'ire vt return; (reintegrare) restore. **~zi'one** nf return; Jur restitution

'resto nm remainder; (saldo) balance; (denaro) change; **resti** pl (avanzi) remains; **del ~** besides

re'string|ere vt contract; take in (vestiti); (limitare) restrict; shrink (stoffa). **~si** vr contract; (farsi più vicini) close up; (stoffa:) shrink. **restringi'mento** nm (di tessuto) shrinkage

restrit'tivo a (legge, clausola) restrictive. **~zi'one** nf restriction

resurrezi'one nf resurrection

resusci'tare vt/i revive

re'tata nf round-up

'rete nf net; (sistema) network; (televisiva) channel; (in calcio, hockey) goal; fig trap; (per la spesa) string bag. **~ locale** Comput local [area] network, LAN. **~ stradale** road network. **~ televisiva** television channel

reti'cen|te a reticent. **~za** nf reticence

retico'lato nm grid; (rete metallica) wire netting. **re'ticolo** nm network

'retina nf retina

re'tina nf (per capelli) hair net

re'torico, -a a rhetorical; **domanda retorica** rhetorical question ● nf rhetoric

retribu|ire *vt* remunerate. **~zi·one** *nf* remuneration

'retro *adv* behind; **vedi ~** see over ● *nm inv* back. **~ di copertina** outside back cover

retroat'tivo *a* retroactive

retro·ce|dere *vi* retreat ● *vt Mil* demote; *Sport* relegate. **~ssi·one** *nf Sport* relegation

retroda'tare *vt* backdate

re'trogrado *a* retrograde; *fig* old-fashioned; *Pol* reactionary

retrogu'ardia *nf Mil* rearguard

retro'marcia *nf* reverse [gear]

retro'scena *nm inv Theat* backstage; *fig* background details *pl*

retrospet'tivo *a* retrospective

retro'stante *a* **il palazzo ~** the building behind

retrovi'sore *nm* rear-view mirror

'retta[1] *nf Math* straight line; *(di collegio, pensionato)* fee

'retta[2] *nf* **dar ~ a qcno** take sb's advice

rettango'lare *a* rectangular. **ret·'tangolo** *a* right-angled ● *nm* rectangle

ret'tifi|ca *nf* rectification. **~'care** *vt* rectify

'rettile *nm* reptile

retti'lineo *a* rectilinear; *(retto)* upright ● *nm Sport* back straight

retti'tudine *nf* rectitude

'retto *pp di* **reggere** ● *a* straight; *fig* upright; *(giusto)* correct; **angolo ~** right angle

ret'tore *nm Relig* rector; *Univ* chancellor

reu'matico *a* rheumatic

reuma'tismi *nmpl* rheumatism

reve'rendo *a* reverend

rever'sibile *a* reversible

revisio'nare *vt* revise; *Comm* audit; *Auto* overhaul. **revisi·one** *nf* revision; *Comm* audit; *Auto* overhaul. **revi'sore** *nm (di conti)* auditor; *(di bozze)* proof-reader; *(di traduzioni)* revisor

re'vival *nm inv* revival

'revoca *nf* repeal. **revo'care** *vt* repeal

riabili'ta|re *vt* rehabilitate. **~zi·one** *nf* rehabilitation

riabitu'ar|e *vt* reaccustom. **~si** *vr* reaccustom oneself

riac'cender|e *vt* rekindle *(fuoco)*. **~si** *vr (luce:)* come back on

riacqui'stare *vt* buy back; regain *(libertà, prestigio)*; recover *(vista, udito)*

riaggancia're *vt* replace *(ricevitore)*. **~ la cornetta** hang up ● *vi* hang up

riallac'ciare *vt* refasten; reconnect *(corrente)*; renew *(amicizia)*

rial'zare *vt* raise ● *vi* rise. **ri'alzo** *nm* rise

riani'mar|e *vt Med* resuscitate; *(ridare forza) a* revive; *(ridare coraggio) a* cheer up. **~si** *vr* regain consciousness; *(riprendere forza)* revive; *(riprendere coraggio)* cheer up

riaper'tura *nf* reopening

ria'prir|e *vt, i,* **~si** *vr* reopen

ri'armo *nm* rearmament

rias'sumere *vt (ricapitolare)* resume

riassun'tivo *a* summarizing. **rias·'sunto** *pp di* **riassumere** ● *nm* summary

riaver|e *vt* get back; regain *(salute, vista)*. **~si** *vr* recover

riavvici'nar|e *vt* reconcile *(paesi, persone)*. **~si** *vr (riconciliarsi)* be reconciled, make it up

riba'dire *vt (confermare)* reaffirm

ri'balta *nf* flap; *Theat* footlights *pl*; *fig* limelight

ribal'tabile *a* tip-up

ribal'tar|e *vt/i.* **~si** *vr* tip over; *Naut* capsize

ribas'sare *vt* lower ● *vi* fall. **ri'basso** *nm* fall; *(sconto)* discount

ri'battere *vt (a macchina)* retype; *(controbattere)* deny ● *vi* answer back

ribel'lar|si *vr* rebel. **ri'belle** *a* rebellious ● *nmf* rebel. **~'lione** *nf* rebellion '**ribes** nm inv (rosso) redcurrant; (nero) blackcurrant

ribol'lire vi (fermentare) ferment; fig seethe

ri'brezzo nm disgust; **far ~ a** disgust

rica'dere vi fall back; (nel peccato ecc) lapse; (pendere) hang [down]; **~ su** (riversarsi) fall on. **rica'duta** nf relapse

rical'care vt trace

ricalci'trante a recalcitrant

rica'ma|re vt embroider. **~to a** embroidered

ri'cambi nmpl spare parts

ricambi'are vt return; reciprocate (sentimento); **~ qcsa a qcno** repay sb for sth. **ri'cambio** nm replacement; Biol metabolism; **pezzo di ricambio** Mech spare [part]

ri'camo nm embroidery

ricapito'la|re vt sum up. **~zi'one** nf summary, recap fam

ri'carica nf (di sveglia) rewinding

ricari'care vt reload (macchina fotografica, fucile, camion); recharge (batteria); Comput reboot

ricat'ta|re vt blackmail. **~tore, ~trice** nmf blackmailer. **ri'catto** nm blackmail

rica'va|re vt get; (ottenere) obtain; (dedurre) draw. **~to** nm proceeds pl. **ri'cavo** nm proceeds pl

'ricca nf rich woman. **~'mente** adv lavishly

ric'chezza nf wealth; fig richness; **ricchezze** pl riches

'**riccio** a curly ● nm curl; (animale) hedgehog. **~ di mare** sea-urchin. **~lo** nm curl. **~luto** a curly. **ricci'uto** a (barba) curly

'**ricco** a rich ● nm rich man

ri'cerca nf search; (indagine) investigation; (scientifica) research; Sch project

ricer'ca|re vt search for; (fare ricerche su) research. **~ta** nf wanted woman. **~'tezza** nf refinement. **~to a** sought-after; (raffina-

to) refined; (affettato) affected ● nm (polizia) wanted man

ricetrasmit'tente nf transceiver

ri'cetta nf Med prescription; Culin recipe

ricet'tacolo nm receptacle

ricet'tario nm (di cucina) recipe book

ricetta|'tore, -'trice nmf fence, receiver of stolen goods. **~zi'one** nf receiving [stolen goods]

rice'vente a (apparecchio, stazione) receiving ● nmf receiver

ri'cev|ere vt receive; (dare il benvenuto) welcome; (di albergo) accommodate. **~i'mento** nm receiving; (accoglienza) welcome; (trattenimento) reception

ricevi'tor|e nm receiver. **~ia** nf **~ia del lotto** agency authorized to sell lottery tickets

rice'vuta nf receipt. **~ fiscale** tax receipt

ricezi'one nf Radio, TV reception

richia'mare vt (al telefono) call back; (far tornare) recall; (rimproverare) rebuke; (attirare) draw; **~ alla mente** call to mind. **richi'amo** nm recall; (attrazione) call

richi'edere vt ask for; (di nuovo) ask again for; **~ a qcno di fare qcsa** ask o request sb to do sth. **richi'esta** nf request; Comm demand

ri'chiud|ere vt shut again, close again. **~si** vr (ferita:) heal

rici'claggio nm recycling

rici'clar|e vt recycle. **~si** vr retrain; (cambiare lavoro) change one's line of work

'**ricino** nm **olio di ~** castor oil

ricogni'zi'one nf Mil reconnaissance

ri'colmo a full

ricominci'are vt/i start again

ricompa'rire vi reappear

ricom'pen|sa nf reward. **~'sare** vt reward

ricom'por|re vt (riscrivere) rewrite; (ricostruire) reform; Typ reset. **~si** *vr* regain one's composure

riconcili'a|re *vt* reconcile. **~rsi** *vr* be reconciled. **~zi'one** *nf* reconciliation

ricono'scen|te *a* grateful. **~za** *nf* gratitude

rico'nosc|ere *vt* recognize; (*ammettere*) acknowledge. **~i'mento** *nm* recognition; (*ammissione*) acknowledgement; (*per la polizia*) identification. **~i'uto** *a* recognized

riconqui'stare *vt Mil* retake, reconquer

riconside'rare *vt* rethink

rico'prire *vt* re-cover; (*rivestire*) coat; (*di insulti*) shower (**di** with); hold ⟨*carica*⟩

ricor'dar|e *vt* remember; (*richiamare alla memoria*) recall; (*far ricordare*) remind; (*rassomigliare*) look like. **~si** *vr* **~si** [**di**] remember. **ri'cordo** *nm* memory; (*oggetto*) memento; (*di viaggio*) souvenir; **ricordi** *pl* (*memorie*) memoirs

ricor'ren|te *a* recurrent. **~za** *nf* recurrence; (*anniversario*) anniversary

ri'correre *vi* recur; (*accadere*) occur; ⟨*data*⟩ fall; **~ a** have recourse to; (*rivolgersi a*) turn to. **ri'corso** *pp* *di* **ricorrere** ● *nm* recourse; *Jur* appeal

ricostitu'ente *nm* tonic

ricostitu'ire *vt* re-establish

ricostru'i|re *vt* reconstruct. **~zi'one** *nf* reconstruction

ricove'ra|re *vt* give shelter to; **~re in ospedale** admit to hospital, hospitalize. **~to, -a** *nmf* hospital patient. **ri'covero** *nm* shelter; (*ospizio*) home

ricre'a|re *vt* re-create; (*ristorare*) restore. **~rsi** *vr* amuse oneself. **~'tivo** *a* recreational. **~zi'one** *nf* recreation; *Sch* break

ri'credersi *vr* change one's mind

ricupe'rare *vt* recover; rehabilitate ⟨*tossicodipendente*⟩; **~ il tem-**

po perduto make up for lost time.

ri'cupero *nm* recovery; (*di tossicodipendente*) rehabilitation; (*salvataggio*) rescue; [**minuti** *nmpl* **di**] **ricupero** injury time

ri'curvo *a* bent

ridacchi'are *vi* giggle

ri'dare *vt* give back, return

ri'dente *a* (*piacevole*) pleasant

'ridere *vi* laugh; **~ di** (*deridere*) laugh at

ri'detto *pp* *di* **ridire**

ridicoliz'zare *vt* ridicule. **ri'dicolo** *a* ridiculous

ridimensio'nare *vt* reshape; *fig* see in the right perspective

ri'dire *vt* repeat; (*criticare*) find fault with; **trova sempre da ~** he's always finding fault

ridon'dante *a* redundant

ri'dotto *pp* *di* **ridurre** ● *nm Theat* foyer ● *a* reduced

ri'du|rre *vt* reduce. **~rsi** *vr* diminish. **~rsi a** be reduced to. **~t'tivo** *a* reductive. **~zi'one** *nf* reduction; (*per cinema, teatro*) adaptation

rieducazi'one *nf* (*di malato*) rehabilitation

riem'pi|re *vt* fill [up]; fill in ⟨*moduli ecc*⟩. **~rsi** *vr* fill [up]. **~'tivo** *a* filling ● *nm* filler

rien'tranza *nf* recess

rien'trare *vi* go/come back in; (*tornare*) return; (*piegare indentro*) recede; **~ in** (*far parte*) fall within. **ri'entro** *nm* return; (*di astronave*) re-entry

riepilo'gare *vt* recapitulate. **rie'pilogo** *nm* roundup

riesami'nare *vt* reappraise

ri'essere *vi* **ci risiamo!** here we go again!

riesu'mare *vt* exhume

rievo'ca|re *vt* (*commemorare*) commemorate. **~zi'one** *nf* (*commemorazione*) commemoration

rifaci'mento *nm* remake

ri'fa|re *vt* do again; (*creare*) make again; (*riparare*) repair; (*imitare*) imitate; make ⟨*letto*⟩. **~rsi** *vr* (*rimettersi*) recover; (*vendicarsi*) get even; **~rsi una vita/carriera** make a new life/career for oneself; **~rsi il trucco** touch up one's makeup; **~rsi** di make up for. **~tto** pp di **rifare**

riferi'mento nm reference

rife'rir|e vt report; **~e a** attribute to ● vi make a report. **~si** vr **~si a** refer to

rifi'lare vt (tagliare a filo) trim; (fam: affibbiare) saddle

rifi'ni|re vt finish off. **~'tura** nf finish

rifio'rire vi blossom again; fig flourish again

rifiu'tare vt refuse. **rifi'uto** nm refusal; **rifiuti** pl (immondizie) rubbish sg. **rifiuti** pl urbani urban waste sg

riflessi'one nf reflection; (osservazione) remark. **rifles'sivo** a thoughtful; Gram reflexive

ri'flesso pp di **riflettere** ● nm (luce) reflection; Med reflex; **per ~** indirectly

ri'fletter|e vt reflect ● vi think. **~si** vr be reflected

riflet'tore nm reflector; (proiettore) searchlight

ri'flusso nm ebb

rifoci'l|are vt restore. **~si** vr liter, hum take some refreshment

ri'fondere vt (rimborsare) refund

ri'forma nf reform; Relig reformation; Mil exemption on medical grounds

rifor'ma|re vt re-form; (migliorare) reform; Mil declare unfit for military service. **~to** a (chiesa) Reformed. **~'tore, ~'trice** nmf reformer. **~'torio** nf reformatory. **rifor'mista** a reformist

riforni'mento nm supply; (scorta) stock; (di combustibile) refuelling; **stazione** nf **di ~** petrol station

rifor'nir|e vt **~e di** provide with. **~si** vr restock, stock up (**di** with)

ri'fra|ngere vt refract. **~tto** pp di **rifrangere**. **~zi'one** nf refraction

rifu'gire vi **~ da** fig shun

rifu'gi|arsi vr take refuge. **~to, ~a** nmf refugee

ri'fugio nm shelter; (nascondiglio) hideaway

'**riga** nf line; (fila) row; (striscia) stripe; (scriminatura) parting; (regolo) rule; **a righe** (stoffa) striped; (quaderno) ruled; **mettersi in ~** line up

ri'gagnolo nm rivulet

ri'gare vt rule (foglio) ● vi **~ dritto** behave well

rigatti'ere nm junk dealer

rigene'rare vt regenerate

riget'tare vt (gettare indietro) throw back; (respingere) reject; (vomitare) throw up. **ri'getto** nm rejection

ri'ghello nm ruler

rigi'da'mente adv rigidly. **~ità** nf rigidity; (di clima) severity; (severità) strictness. '**rigido** a rigid; (freddo) severe; (severo) strict

rigi'rar|e vt turn again; (ripercorrere) go round; fig twist (argomentazione) ● vi walk about. **~si** vr turn round; (nel letto) turn over. **ri'giro** nm (imbroglio) trick

'**rigo** nm line; Mus staff

ri'goglio nm bloom. **~'oso** a luxuriant

ri'gonfio a swollen

ri'gore nm rigours pl; **a ~** strictly speaking; **calcio di ~** penalty [kick]; **area di ~** penalty area; **essere di ~** be compulsory

rigo|rosa'mente adv (giudicare) severely. **~'roso** a (severo) strict; (scrupoloso) rigorous

rigua'gnare vt regain (quota, velocità)

riguar'dar|e vt look at again; (considerare) regard; (concernere) concern; **per quanto riguarda** with regard to. **~si** vr take care of oneself. **rigu'ardo** nm care; (considerazione) consideration; **nei ~i di** towards; **riguardo a** with regard to

ri'gurgito nm regurgitation

rilanci'are vt throw back (palla);

(di nuovo) throw again; increase *(offerta)*; revive *(moda)*; relaunch *(prodotto)* ● *vi (a carte)* raise the stakes

rilasci'ar|e *vt (concedere)* grant; *(liberare)* release; issue *(documento)*. **~si** *vr* relax. **ri'lascio** *nm* release; *(di documento)* issue

rilassa'mento *nm (relax)* relaxation

rilas'sa|re *vt, ~rsi vr* relax. **~to** *a (ambiente)* relaxed

rile'ga|re *vt* bind *(libro)*. **~to** *a* bound. **~'tura** *nf* binding

ri'leggere *vt* reread

ri'lento: a ~ *adv* slowly

rileva'mento *nm* survey; *Comm* buyout

rile'vante *a* considerable

rile'va|re *vt (trarre)* get; *(mettere in evidenza)* point out; *(notare)* notice; *(topografia)* survey; *Comm* take over; *Mil* relieve. **~zi'one** *nf (statistica)* survey

rili'evo *nm* relief; *Geog* elevation; *(topografia)* survey; *(importanza)* importance; *(osservazione)* remark; **mettere in ~ qcsa** point sth out

rilut'tan|te *a* reluctant. **~za** *nf* reluctance

'rima *nf* rhyme; **far ~ con qcsa** rhyme with sth

riman'dare *vt (posporre)* postpone; *(mandare indietro)* send back; *(mandare di nuovo)* send again; *(far ridare un esame)* make resit an examination. **ri'mando** *nm* return; *(in un libro)* cross-reference

rima'nen|te *a* remaining ● *nm* remainder. **~za** *nf* remainder; **~ze** *pl* remnants

rima'ne|re *vi* stay, remain; *(essere d'avanzo)* be left; *(venirsi a trovare)* be; *(restare stupito)* be astonished; *(restare d'accordo)* agree

rimar'chevole *a* remarkable

ri'mare *vt/i* rhyme

rimargi'nar|e *vt, ~si vr* heal

ri'masto *pp di* **rimanere**

rima'sugli *nmpl (di cibo)* leftovers

rimbal'zare *vi* rebound; *(proiettile:)* ricochet; **far ~** bounce. **rim'balzo** *nm* rebound; *(di proiettile)* ricochet

rimbam'bi|re *vi* be in one's dotage ● *vt* stun. **~to** *a* in one's dotage

rimboc'care *vt* turn up; roll up *(maniche)*; tuck in *(coperte)*

rimbom'bare *vi* resound

rimbor'sare *vt* reimburse, repay. **rim'borso** *nm* reimbursement, repayment. **rimborso spese** reimbursement of expenses

rime'diare *vi* **~ a** a remedy; make up for *(errore)*; *(procurare)* scrape up. **ri'medio** *nm* remedy

rimesco'lare *vt* mix [up]; shuffle *(carte)*; *(rivangare)* rake up

ri'messa *nf (locale per veicoli)* garage; *(per aerei)* hangar; *(per autobus)* depot; *(di denaro)* remittance; *(di merci)* consignment

ri'messo *pp di* **rimettere**

ri'metter|e *vt (a posto)* put back; *(restituire)* return; *(affidare)* entrust; *(perdonare)* remit; *(rimandare)* put off; *(vomitare)* bring up; **~ci** *(fam: perdere)* lose [out]. **~si** *vr (ristabilirsi)* recover; *(tempo:)* clear up; **~si a** start again

'rimmel® *nm inv* mascara

rimoder'nare *vt* modernize

rimon'tare *vt (risalire)* go up; *Mech* reassemble ● *vi* remount; **~** *a (risalire)* go back to

rimorchi'are *vt* tow; *fam* pick up *(ragazza)*. **~'tore** *nm* tug[boat]. **ri'morchio** *nm* tow; *(veicolo)* trailer

ri'morso *nm* remorse

rimo'stranza *nf* complaint

rimozi'one *nf* removal; *(da un incarico)* dismissal. **~ forzata** *illegally parked vehicles removed at owner's expense*

rim'pasto *nm Pol* reshuffle

rimpatri'are *vt/i* repatriate. **rim'patrio** *nm* repatriation

rim'pian|gere *vt* regret. **~to** *pp di* **rimpiangere** ● *nm* regret

rimpiat'tino *nm* hide-and-seek

rimpiaz'zare *vt* replace

rimpiccio'lire *vi* become smaller

rimpinz'ar|e *vt* ~**e** di stuff with. ~**si** *vr* stuff oneself

rimprove'rare *vt* reproach; ~ qcsa a qcno reproach sb for sth. **rim'provero** *nm* reproach

rimugi'nare *vt* rummage; *fig* ~ **su** brood over

rimune'ra|re *vt* remunerate. ~**'tivo** *a* remunerative. ~**zi'one** *nf* remuneration

ri'muovere *vt* remove

ri'nascere *vi* be reborn, be born again

rinascimen'tale *a* Renaissance. **Rinasci'mento** *nm* Renaissance

ri'nascita *nf* rebirth

rincal'zare *vt* (sostenere) support; (rimboccare) tuck in. **rin'calzo** *nm* support; **rincalzi** *pl Mil* reserves

rincantucci'arsi *vr* hide oneself away in a corner

rinca'rare *vt* increase the price of ●*vi* become more expensive. **rin'caro** *nm* price increase

rinca'sare *vi* return home

rinchi'uder|e *vt* shut up. ~**si** *vr* shut oneself up

rin'correre *vt* run after

rin'cors|a *nf* run-up. ~**o** *pp di* **rincorrere**

rin'crescere *vi* mi rincresce di non... I'm sorry o I regret that I can't...; **se non ti** ~**e** if you don't mind. ~**i'mento** *nm* regret. ~**i'uto** *pp di* **rincrescere**

rincreti'nire *vi* be stupid

rincu'lare *vi* (arma:) recoil; (cavallo:) shy. **rin'culo** *nm* recoil

rincuo'rar|e *vt* encourage. ~**si** *vr* take heart

rinfacci'are *vt* ~ qcsa a qcno throw sth in sb's face

rinfor'zar|e *vt* strengthen; (rendere più saldo) reinforce. ~**si** *vr* become stronger. **rin'forzo** *nm* reinforcement; *fig* support

rinfran'care *vt* reassure

rinfre'scante *a* cooling

rinfre'scar|e *vt* cool; (rinnovare) freshen up ● *vi* get cooler. ~**si** *vr* freshen [oneself] up. **rin'fresco** *nm* light refreshment; (ricevimento) party

rin'fusa *nf* alla ~ at random

ringhi'are *vi* snarl

ringhi'era *nf* railing; (di scala) banisters *pl*

ringiova'nire *vt* rejuvenate (pelle, persona); (vestito:) make look younger ● *vi* become young again; (sembrare) look young again

ringrazi|a'mento *nm* thanks *pl*. ~**'are** *vt* thank

rinne'ga|re *vt* disown. ~**to, -a** *nmf* renegade

rinnova'mento *nm* renewal; (di edifici) renovation

rinno'var|e *vt* renew; renovate (edifici). ~**si** *vr* be renewed; (ripetersi) recur, happen again. **rin'novo** *nm* renewal

rinoce'ronte *nm* rhinoceros

rino'mato *a* renowned

rinsal'dare *vt* consolidate

rinsa'vire *vi* come to one's senses

rinsec'chi|re *vi* shrivel up. ~**to** *a* shrivelled up

rinta'narsi *vr* hide oneself away; (animale:) retreat into its den

rintoc'care *vi* (campana:) toll; (orologio:) strike. **rin'tocco** *nm* toll; (di orologio) stroke

rinton'ti|re *vt* anche *fig* stun. ~**to** *a* (stordito) dazed

rintracci'are *vt* trace

rintro'nare *vt* stun ● *vi* boom

ri'nuncia *nf* renunciation

rinunci'a|re *vi* ~**re a** renounce, give up. ~**'tario** *a* defeatist

ri'nunzia, rinunzi'are = rinuncia, rinunciare

rinveni'mento *nm* (di reperti) discovery; (di refurtiva) recovery. **rinve'nire** *vt* find ● *vi* (riprendere i sensi) come round; (ridiventare fresco) revive

rinvi'are *vt* put off; (mandare indietro) return; (in libro) refer; ~ **a giudizio** indict

rin'vio nm Sport goal kick; (in libro) cross-reference; (di appuntamento) postponement; (di merce) return

rio'nale a local. **ri'one** nm district

riordi'nare vt tidy [up]; (ordinare di nuovo) reorder; (riorganizzare) reorganize

riorganiz'zare vt reorganize

ripa'gare vt repay

ripa'ra|re vt (proteggere) shelter, protect; (aggiustare) repair; (porre rimedio) remedy ●vi ~re a make up for. ~rsi vr take shelter. ~to a (luogo) sheltered. ~zi'one nf repair; fig reparation. **ri'paro** nm shelter; (rimedio) remedy

ripar'ti|re vt (dividere) divide ●vi leave again. ~zi'one nf division

ripas'sa|re vt recross; (rivedere) revise ●vi pass again. ~ta nf (di vernice) second coat. **ri'passo** nm (di lezione) revision

ripensa'mento nm second thoughts pl

ripen'sare vi (cambiare idea) change one's mind; ~ a think of; **ripensaci!** think again!

riper'correre vt (con la memoria) go back over

riper'cosso pp di **ripercuotere**

ripercu'oter|e vt strike again. ~si vr (suono:) reverberate; ~si su (fig: avere conseguenze) impact on. **ripercussi'one** nf repercussion

ripe'scare vt fish out (oggetti)

ripe'tente nmf student repeating a year

ri'pet|ere vt repeat. ~ersi vr (evento:) recur. ~izi'one nf repetition; (di lezione) revision; (lezione privata) private lesson. ~uta'mente adv repeatedly

ri'piano nm (di scaffale) shelf; (terreno pianeggiante) terrace

ri'picca nf fare qcsa per ~a do sth out of spite. ~o nm spite

'ripido a steep

ripie'ga|re vt refold; (abbassare) lower ●vi (indietreggiare) retreat.

~si vr bend; (sedile:) fold. **ripi'ego** nm expedient; (via d'uscita) way out

ripi'eno a full; Culin stuffed ●nm filling; Culin stuffing

ripopo'lar|e vt repopulate. ~si vr be repopulated

ri'porre vt put back; (mettere da parte) put away; (collocare) place; repeat (domanda)

ripor'ta|re vt (restituire) bring/ take back; (riferire) report; (subire) suffer; Math carry; win (vittoria); transfer (disegno). ~rsi vr go back; (riferirsi) refer. **ri'porto** nm cane da riporto gun dog

ripo'sante a (colore) restful, soothing

ripo'sa|re vi rest ●vt put back. ~rsi vr rest. ~to a (mente) fresh. **ri'poso** nm rest; andare a riposo retire; riposo! Mil at ease!; **giorno di riposo** day off

ripo'stiglio nm cupboard

ri'posto pp di **riporre**

ri'prender|e vt take again; (prendere indietro) take back; (riconquistare) recapture; (ricuperare) recover; (ricominciare) resume; (rimproverare) reprimand; take in (cucitura); Cinema shoot. ~si vr recover; (correggersi) correct oneself

ri'presa nf resumption; (ricupero) recovery; Theat revival; Cinema shot; Auto acceleration; Mus repeat. ~ aerea bird's-eye view

ripresen'tar|e vt resubmit (domanda, certificato). ~si vr (a ufficio) go/come back again; (come candidato) stand o run again; (occasione:) arise again

ri'preso pp di **riprendere**

ripristi'nare vt restore

ripro'dotto pp di **riprodurre**

ripro'du|rre vt, ~rsi vr reproduce. ~t'tivo a reproductive. ~zi'one nf reproduction

ripro'mettersi vr (intendere) intend

ri'prova nf confirmation

ripudi'are *vt* repudiate

ripu'gnan|te *a* repugnant. **~za** *nf* disgust. **ripu'gnare** *vi* **ripugnare a** a disgust

ripu'li|re *vt* clean [up]; *fig* polish. **~ta** *nf* darsi una **~ta** have a wash and brushup

ripuls|i'one *nf* repulsion. **~'ivo** *a* repulsive

ri'quadro *nm* square; (*pannello*) panel

ri'sacca *nf* undertow

ri'saia *nf* rice field, paddy field

risa'lire *vt* go back up ● *vi* **~ a** (*nel tempo*) go back to; (*essere datato a*) date back to, go back to

risal'tare *vi* (*emergere*) stand out. **ri'salto** *nm* prominence; (*rilievo*) relief

risa'nare *vt* heal; (*bonificare*) reclaim

risa'puto *a* well-known

risarci'mento *nm* compensation. **risar'cire** *vt* indemnify

ri'sata *nf* laugh

riscalda'mento *nm* heating. **~ autonomo** central heating (*for one flat*)

riscal'dar|e *vt* heat; warm (*persona*). **~si** *vr* warm up

riscat'tar|e *vt* ransom. **~si** *vr* redeem oneself. **ri'scatto** *nm* ransom; (*morale*) redemption

rischia'rar|e *vt* light up; brighten (*colore*). **~si** *vr* light up; (*cielo*): clear up

rischi|'are *vt* risk ● *vi* run the risk. **'rischio** *nm* risk. **~'oso** *a* risky

risciac'quare *vt* rinse. **risci-'acquo** *nm* rinse

riscon'trare *vt* (*confrontare*) compare; (*verificare*) check; (*rilevare*) find. **ri'scontro** *nm* comparison; check; (*Comm: risposta*) reply

ri'scossa *nf* revolt; (*riconquista*) recovery

riscossi'one *nf* collection

ri'scosso *pp di* **riscuotere**

riscu'oter|e *vt* shake; (*percepire*)

draw; (*ottenere*) gain; cash (*assegno*). **~si** *vr* rouse oneself

risen'ti|re *vt* hear again; (*provare*) feel ● *vi* **~re di** feel the effect of. **~rsi** *vr* (*offendersi*) take offence. **~to** *a* resentful

ri'serbo *nm* reserve; **mantenere il ~** remain tight-lipped

ri'serva *nf* reserve; (*di caccia, pesca*) preserve; *Sport* substitute, reserve. **~ di caccia** game reserve. **~ indiana** Indian reservation. **~ naturale** wildlife reserve

riser'va|re *vt* reserve; (*prenotare*) book; (*per occasione*) keep. **~rsi** *vr* (*ripromettersi*) plan for oneself (*cambiamento*). **~'tezza** *nf* reserve. **~to** *a* reserved

ri'siedere *vi* **~ a** reside in

'riso[1] *pp di* **ridere** ● *nm* (*pl inv* **risa**) laughter; (*singolo*) laugh. **~'lino** *nm* giggle

'riso[2] *nm* (*cereale*) rice

ri'solto *pp di* **risolvere**

risolu'tezza *nf* determination. **riso'luto** *a* resolute, determined. **~zi'one** *nf* resolution

ri'solver|e *vt* resolve; *Math* solve. **~si** *vr* (*decidersi*) decide; **~si in** turn into

riso'na|nza *nf* resonance; **aver ~nza** arouse great interest. **~re** *vi* resound; (*rimbombare*) echo

ri'sorgere *vi* rise again

risorgi'mento *nm* revival; (*storico*) Risorgimento

ri'sorsa *nf* resource; (*espediente*) resort

ri'sorto *pp di* **risorgere**

ri'sotto *nm* risotto

ri'sparmi *nmpl* (*soldi*) savings

risparmi|'are *vt* save; (*salvare*) spare. **~'tore**, **~'trice** *nmf* saver **ri'sparmio** *nm* saving

rispecchi'are *vt* reflect

rispet'tabile *a* respectable. **~ità** *nf* respectability

rispet'tare *vt* respect; **farsi ~** command respect

rispet'tivo *a* respective

ri'spetto nm respect; **~ a** as regards; (in paragone a) compared to

rispet|tosa'mente adv respectfully. **~'toso** a respectful

risplen'dente a shining. **ri'splendere** vi shine

rispon'den|te a **~te a** in keeping with. **~za** nf correspondence

ri'spondere vt answer; (rimbeccare) answer back; (obbedire) respond; **~ a** reply to; **~ di** (rendersi responsabile) answer for

ri'spost|a nf answer, reply; (reazione) response. **~o** pp di **rispondere**

'**rissa** nf brawl. **ris'soso** a pugnacious

ristabi'lir|e vt re-establish. **~si** vr (in salute) recover

rista'gnare vi stagnate; (sangue:) coagulate. **ri'stagno** nm stagnation

ri'stampa nf reprint; (azione) reprinting. **ristam'pare** vt reprint

risto'rante nm restaurant

risto'ra|re vt refresh. **~rsi** vr liter take some refreshment; (riposarsi) take a rest. **~'tore**, **~'trice** nmf (proprietario di ristorante) restaurateur; (fornitore) caterer ● a refreshing. **ri'storo** nm refreshment; (sollievo) relief

ristret'tezza nf narrowness; (povertà) poverty; **vivere in ristrettezze** live in straitened circumstances

ri'stretto pp di **restringere** ● a narrow; (condensato) condensed; (limitato) restricted; **di idee ristrette** narrow-minded

ristruttu'rare vt restructure, reorganize (ditta); refurbish (casa)

risucchi'are vt suck in. **ri'succhio** nm whirlpool; (di corrente) undertow

risul'ta|re vi result; (riuscire) turn out. **~to** nm result

risuo'nare vi (grida, parola:) echo; Phys resonate

risurrezi'one nf resurrection

risusci'tare vt resuscitate; fig revive ● vi return to life

risvegli'ar|e vt reawaken (interesse). **~si** vr wake up; (natura:) awake; (desiderio:) be aroused. **ri'sveglio** nm waking up; (dell'interesse) revival; (del desiderio) arousal

ri'svolto nm (di giacca) lapel; (di pantaloni) turn-up, cuff Am; (di manica) cuff; (di tasca) flap; (di libro) inside flap

ritagli'are vt cut out. **ri'taglio** nm cutting; (di stoffa) scrap

ritar'da|re vi be late; (orologio:) be slow ● vt delay; (progresso:) (differire) postpone. **~'tario**, **-a** nmf late-comer. **~to** a Psych retarded

ri'tardo nm delay; **essere in ~** be late; (volo:) be delayed

ri'tegno nm reserve

rite'n|ere vt retain; deduct (somma); (credere) believe. **~uta** nf (sul salario) deduction

riti'ra|re vt throw back (palla); (prelevare) withdraw; (riscuotere) draw; collect (pacco). **~rsi** vr withdraw; (stoffa:) shrink; (da attività) retire; (marea:) recede. **~ta** nf retreat; (WC) toilet. **ri'tiro** nm withdrawal; Relig retreat; (da attività) retirement. **ritiro bagagli** baggage reclaim

'**ritmo** nm rhythm

'**rito** nm rite; **di ~** customary

ritoc'care vt (correggere) touch up. **ri'tocco** nm retouch

ritor'nare vi return; (andare/venire indietro) go/come back; (ricorrere) recur; (ridiventare) become again

ritor'nello nm refrain

ri'torno nm return

ritorsi'one nf retaliation

ri'trarre vt (ritirare) withdraw; (distogliere) turn away; (rappresentare) portray

ritrat'ta|re vt deal with again; retract (dichiarazione). **~zi'one** nf withdrawal, retraction

ritrat'tista nmf portrait painter.
ri'tratto pp di **ritrarre** ● nm portrait

ritro'sia nf shyness. **ri'troso** a backward; (timido) shy; **a ritroso** backwards; **ritroso** a reluctant to

ritrova'mento nm (azione) finding
ritro'va|re vt find [again]; regain ⟨salute⟩. **~rsi** vr meet; (di nuovo) meet again; (capitare) find oneself; (raccapezzarsi) see one's way. **~to** nm discovery. **ri'trovo** nm meeting-place; (notturno) nightclub

'**ritto** a upright; (diritto) straight
ritu'ale a & nm ritual
riunifi'ca|re vt reunify. **~rsi** vr be reunited. **~zl'one** nf reunification
riuni'one nf meeting; (fra amici) reunion

rlu'nir|e vt (unire) join together; (radunare) gather. **~si** vr be reunited; (adunarsi) meet

riusc'i|re vi (aver successo) succeed; (in matematica ecc) be good (in at); (aver esito) turn out; **le è riuscito simpatico** she found him likeable. **~ta** nf (esito) result; (successo) success

'**riva** nf (di mare, lago) shore; (di fiume) bank
ri'val|e nmf rival. **~ità** nf inv rivalry
rivalutazi'one nf revaluation
rivan'gare vt dig up again
rive'dere vt see again; revise ⟨lezione⟩; (verificare) check
rive'la|re vt reveal. **~rsi** vr (dimostrarsi) turn out. **~'tore** a revealing ● nm Techn detector. **~zi'one** nf revelation
ri'vendere vt resell
rivendi'ca|re vt claim. **~zi'one** nf claim
ri'vendi|ta nf (negozio) shop. **~'tore, ~'trice** nmf retailer. **~'tore autorizzato** authorized dealer
ri'verbero nm reverberation; (bagliore) glare

rive'renza nf reverence; (inchino) curtsy; (di uomo) bow
rive'rire vt respect; (ossequiare) pay one's respects to
river'sar|e vt pour. **~si** vr ⟨fiume:⟩ flow
river'sibile a reversible
rivesti'mento nm covering
rive'sti|re vt (rifornire di abiti) clothe; (ricoprire) cover; (internamente) line; hold ⟨carica⟩. **~rsi** vr get dressed again; (per una festa) dress up
rivi'era nf coast; **la ~ ligure** the Italian Riviera
ri'vincita nf Sport return match; (vendetta) revenge
rivi'suto pp di **rivivere**
ri'vista nf review; (pubblicazione) magazine; Theat revue; **passare in ~** review
ri'vivere vi come to life again; (riprendere le forze) revive ● vt relive
ri'volger|e vt turn; (indirizzare) address; **~e da** (distogliere) turn away from. **~si** vr turn round; **~si a** (indirizzarsi) turn to
ri'volta nf revolt
rivol'tante a disgusting
rivol'ta|re vt turn [over]; (mettendo l'interno verso l'esterno) turn inside out; (sconvolgere) upset. **~rsi** vr (ribellarsi) revolt
rivol'tella nf revolver
ri'volto pp di **rivolgere**
rivoluzio'nar|e vt revolutionize. **~io, -a** a & nmf revolutionary.
rivoluzi'one nf revolution; (fig: disordine) chaos
riz'zar|e vt raise; (innalzare) erect; prick up ⟨orecchie⟩. **~si** vr stand up; ⟨capelli:⟩ stand on end; ⟨orecchie:⟩ prick up
'**roba** nf stuff; (personale) belongings pl, stuff; (faccenda) thing; (sl: droga) drugs pl; **~ da matti!** absolute madness!. **~ da mangiare** food, things to eat
ro'baccia nf rubbish

ro'bot *nm inv* robot. ~iz'zato *a* robotic

robu'stezza *nf* sturdiness, robustness; (*forza*) strength. ro'busto *a* sturdy, robust; (*forte*) strong

'rocca *nf* fortress. ~'forte *nf* stronghold

roc'chetto *nm* reel

'roccia *nf* rock

ro'daggio *nm* running in. ~re *vt* run in

'roderle *vt* gnaw; (*corrodere*) corrode. ~si *vr* ~si da (*logorarsi*) be consumed with. rodi'tore *nm* rodent

rodo'dendro *nm* rhododendron

'rogna *nf* scabies *sg*; *fig* nuisance

ro'gnone *nm* Culin kidney

'rogo *nm* (*supplizio*) stake; (*per cadaveri*) pyre

'Roma *nf* Rome

Roma'nia *nf* Romania

ro'manico *a* Romanesque

ro'mano, -a *a & nmf* Roman

romanti'cismo *nm* romanticism. ro'mantico *a* romantic

ro'manza *nf* romance. ~'zato *a* romanticized. ~'zesco *a* fictional; (*stravagante*) wild, unrealistic. ~zi'ere *nm* novelist

ro'manzo *nm* Romance *nm* novel. ~ d'appendice serial story. ~ giallo thriller

'rombo *nm* rumble; *Math* rhombus; (*pesce*) turbot

'romperle *vt* break; break off (*relazione*); non ~e [le scatole]! (*fam: seccare*) don't be a pain [in the neck]!. ~si *vr* break; ~si una gamba break one's leg

rompi'capo *nm* nuisance; (*indovinello*) puzzle

rompi'collo *nm* daredevil; a ~ at breakneck speed

rompighi'accio *nm* ice-breaker

rompi'scatole *nmf inv fam* pain

'ronda *nf* rounds *pl*

ron'della *nf* Mech washer

'rondine *nf* swallow

ron'done *nm* swift

ron'fare *vi* (*russare*) snore

ron'zare *vi* buzz; ~ attorno a qcno *fig* hang about sb

ron'zino *nm* jade

ron'zio *nm* buzz

'rosa *nf* rose. ~ dei venti wind rose ● *a & nm* (*colore*) pink. ro'saio *nm* rose-bush

ro'sario *nm* rosary

ro'sato *a* rosy ● *nm* (*vino*) rosé

'roseo *a* pink

ro'seto *nm* rose garden

rosicchi'are *vt* nibble; (*rodere*) gnaw

rosma'rino *nm* rosemary

'roso *pp di* rodere

roso'lare *vt* brown

roso'lia *nf* German measles

ro'sone *nm* rosette; (*apertura*) rose-window

'rospo *nm* toad

ros'setto *nm* (*per labbra*) lipstick

'rosso *a & nm* red; passare con il ~ jump a red light. ~ d'uovo [egg] yolk. ros'sore *nm* redness; (*della pelle*) flush

rosticce'ria *nf* shop selling cooked meat and other prepared food

ro'tabile *a* strada ~ carriageway

ro'taia *nf* rail; (*solco*) rut

ro'ta|re *vt/i* rotate. ~zi'one *nf* rotation

rote'are *vt/i* roll

ro'tella *nf* small wheel; (*di mobile*) castor

roto'lar|e *vt/i* roll. ~si *vr* roll [about]. 'rotolo *nm* roll; andare a rotoli go to rack and ruin

rotondità *nf* (*qualità*) roundness; ~ *pl* (*curve femminili*) curves. ro'tondo, -a *a* round ● *nf* (*spiazzo*) terrace

ro'tore *nm* rotor

'rotta[^1] *nf Naut, Aeron* course; far ~ per make course for; fuori ~ off course

'rotta[^2] *nf* a ~ di collo at breakneck speed; essere in ~ con be on bad terms with

rot'tame *nm* scrap; *fig* wreck

'rotto *pp di* rompere ● *a* broken; (*stracciato*) torn

[^1]: 1
[^2]: 2

rot'tura nf break; **che ~ di scatole!** fam what a pain!
'rotula nf kneecap
rou'lette nf inv roulette
rou'lotte nf inv caravan, trailer
Am
rou'tine nf inv routine; **di ~**
(operazioni, controlli) routine
ro'vente a scorching
'rovere nm (legno) oak
rovesci'ar|e vt (buttare a terra)
knock over; (sottosopra) turn upside down; (rivoltare) turn inside
out; spill (liquido); overthrow
(governo); reverse (situazione).
~si vr (capovolgersi) overturn;
(riversarsi) pour. **ro'vescio** a (contrario) reverse; **alla rovescia**
(capovolto) upside down; (con
l'interno all'esterno) inside out
● nm reverse; (nella maglia) purl;
(di pioggia) downpour; Tennis
backhand
ro'vina nf ruin; (crollo) collapse
rovi'na|re vt ruin; (guastare)
spoil ● vi crash. **~rsi** vr be ruined. **~to**
a (oggetto) ruined. **rovi'noso** a ru-
inous
rovi'stare vt ransack
'rovo nm bramble
'rozzo a rough
R.R. abbr (ricevuta di ritorno) return receipt for registered mail
'ruba nf andare a **~** sell like hot
cakes
ru'bare vt steal
rubi'netto nm tap, faucet Am
ru'bino nm ruby
ru'brica nf (in giornale) column;
(in programma televisivo) TV report; (quaderno con indice) address book. **~ telefonica** telephone and address book
'rude a rough
'rudere nm ruin
rudimen'tale a rudimentary. **rudi-
'menti** nmpl rudiments
ruffi'an|a nf procuress. **~o** nm
pimp; (adulatore) bootlicker
'ruga nf wrinkle
'ruggine nf rust; **fare la ~** go rusty

rug'gi|re vi roar. **~to** nm roar
rugi'ada nf dew
ru'goso a wrinkled
rul'lare vi roll; Aeron taxi
rul'lino nm film
rul'lio nm rolling; Aeron taxiing
'rullo nm roll; Techn roller
rum nm inv rum
ru'meno, -a a & nmf Romanian
rumi'nare vt ruminate
ru'mor|e nm noise; fig rumour.
~eggi'are vi rumble. **rumo'roso**
a noisy; (sonoro) loud
ru'olo nm role; Theat role; **di ~**
on the staff
ru'ota nf wheel; andare a **~ libera**
free-wheel. **~ di scorta** spare
wheel
'rupe nf cliff
ru'rale a rural
ru'scello nm stream
'ruspa nf bulldozer
rus'sare vi snore
'Russ|ia nf Russia. **r~o,-o** a & nmf
Russian; (lingua) Russian
'rustico a rural; (carattere) rough
rut'tare vi belch. **'rutto** nm belch
'ruvido a coarse
ruzzo'l|are vi tumble down. **~one**
nm tumble; **cadere ruzzoloni**
tumble down

*****

Ss

*****

'sabato nm Saturday
'sabbi|a nf sand. **~e** pl mobili
quicksand. **~'oso** a sandy
sabo'ta|ggio nm sabotage. **~'tore**,
~'trice nmf saboteur
'sacca nf bag. **~ da viaggio** travel-
ling-bag
sacca'rina nf saccharin
sac'cente a pretentious ● nmf
know-all
saccheggi'a|re vt sack; hum raid

(*frigo*). **~'tore**, **~'trice** *nmf* plunderer. **sac'cheggio** *nm* sack

sac'chetto *nm* bag

'sacco *nm* sack; *Anat* sac; **mettere nel ~** *fig* swindle; **un ~** (*moltissimo*) a lot; **un ~ di** (*gran quantità*) lots of. **~ a pelo** sleeping-bag

sacer'do|te *nm* priest. **~zio** *nm* priesthood

sacra'mento *nm* sacrament

sacrifi'ca|re *vt* sacrifice. **~rsi** *vr* sacrifice oneself. **~to a** (*non valorizzato*) wasted. **sacri'ficio** *nm* sacrifice

sacri'legio *nm* sacrilege. **sa'crilego** *a* sacrilegious

'sacro *a* sacred ● *nm Anat* sacrum

sacro'santo *a* sacrosanct

'sadico, -a *a* sadistic ● *nmf* sadist. **sa'dismo** *nm* sadism

sa'etta *nf* arrow

sa'fari *nm inv* safari

'saga *nf* saga

sa'gace *a* shrewd

sag'gezza *nf* wisdom

saggi'are *vt* test

'saggio[1] *nm* (*scritto*) essay; (*prova*) proof; (*di metallo*) assay; (*campione*) sample; (*esempio*) example

'saggio[2] *a* wise ● *nm* (*persona*) sage

sag'gistica *nf* non-fiction

Sagit'tario *nm Astr* Sagittarius

'sagoma *nf* shape; (*profilo*) outline; **che ~!** *fam* what a character!. **sago'mato** *a* shaped

'sagra *nf* festival

sagre'|stano *nm* sacristan. **~'stia** *nf* sacristy

'sala *nf* hall; (*stanza*) room; (*salotto*) living room. **~ d'attesa** waiting room. **~ da ballo** ballroom. **~ d'imbarco** departure lounge. **~ macchine** engine room. **~ operatoria** operating theatre *Br*, operating room *Am*. **~ parto** delivery room. **~ da pranzo** dining room

sa'lame *nm* salami

sala'moia *nf* brine

sa'lare *vt* salt

sa'lario *nm* wages *pl*

sa'lasso *nm* **essere un ~** *fig* cost a fortune

sala'tini *nmpl* savouries (*eaten with aperitifs*)

sa'lato *a* salty; (*costoso*) dear

sal'ciccia *nf* = **salsiccia**

sal'dar|e *vt* weld; set (*osso*); pay off (*debito*); settle (*conto*); **~e a stagno** solder. **~si** *vr* (*Med: osso*) knit

salda'trice *nf* welder; (*a stagno*) soldering iron

salda'tura *nf* weld; (*azione*) welding; (*di osso*) knitting

'saldo *a* firm; (*resistente*) strong ● *nm* (*di conto*) settlement; (*svendita*) sale; *Comm* balance

'sale *nm* salt; **restare di ~** be struck dumb [with astonishment]. **~ fine** table salt. **~ grosso** cooking salt. **sali** *pl* **e tabacchi** tobacconist's shop

'salice *nm* willow. **~ piangente** weeping willow

sali'ente *a* outstanding; **i punti salienti di un discorso** the main points of a speech

sali'era *nf* salt-cellar

sa'lina *nf* salt-works *sg*

sa'li|re *vi* go/come up; (*levarsi*) rise; (*su treno ecc*) get on; (*in macchina*) get in ● *vt* go/come up (*scale*). **~ta** *nf* climb; (*aumento*) rise; **in ~ta** uphill

sa'liva *nf* saliva

'salma *nf* corpse

'salmo *nm* psalm

sal'mone *nm* & *a inv* salmon

sa'lone *nm* hall; (*salotto*) living room; (*di parrucchiere*) salon. **~ di bellezza** beauty parlour

salo'pette *nf inv* dungarees *pl*

salot'tino *nm* bower

sa'lotto *nm* drawing room; (*soggiorno*) sitting room; (*mobili*) [three-piece] suite; **fare ~** chat

sal'pare *vt/i* sail; **~ l'ancora** weigh anchor

'salsa *nf* sauce. **~ di pomodoro** tomato sauce

sal'sedine *nf* saltiness

sal'siccia nf sausage

salsi'era nf sauce-boat

sal'ta|re vi jump; (venir via) come off; (balzare) leap; (esplodere) blow up ● vt fuori spring from nowhere; ⟨oggetto cercato:⟩ turn up; **è ~to fuori che...** it emerged that...; **~re fuori con...** come out with...; **~re in aria** blow up; **~re in mente** spring to mind ● vt jump [over]; skip ⟨pasti, lezioni⟩; Culin sauté. **~to a** Culin sautéed

saltel'lare vi hop; (di gioia) skip

saltim'banco nm acrobat

'salto nm jump; (balzo) leap; (dislivello) drop; (fig: omissione, lacuna) gap; **fare un ~ da** (visitare) drop in on; **in un ~** fig in a jiffy. **~ in alto** high jump. **~ con l'asta** pole-vault. **~ in lungo** long jump. **~ pagina** Comput page down

saltuaria'mente adv occasionally. **saltu'ario** a desultory; **lavoro saltuario** casual work

sa'lubre a healthy

salume'ria nf delicatessen. **sa'lumi** nmpl cold cuts

salu'tare vt greet; (congedandosi) say goodbye to; (portare i saluti a) give one's regards to; Mil salute ● a healthy

sa'lute nf health; **~!** (dopo uno starnuto) bless you!; (a un brindisi) cheers!

sa'luto nm greeting; (di addio) goodbye; Mil salute; **saluti** pl (ossequi) regards

'salva nf salvo; **sparare a salve** fire blanks

salvada'naio nm money box

salva'gente nm lifebelt; (a giubbotto) life-jacket; (ciambella) rubber ring; (spartitraffico) traffic island

salvaguar'dare vt safeguard. **salvagu'ardia** nf safeguard

sal'var|e vt save; (proteggere) protect. **~si** vr save oneself

salva'slip nm inv panty-liner

salva'taggio nm rescue; Naut salvage; Comput saving; **battello di ~taggio** lifeboat. **~'tore**, **~'trice** nmf saviour

sal'vezza nf safety; Relig salvation

'salvia nf sage

salvi'etta nf serviette

'salvo a safe ● prep except [for] ● conj **~ che** (a meno che) unless; (eccetto che) except that

samari'tano, -a a & nmf Samaritan

sam'buco nm elder

san nm S~ **Francesco** Saint Francis

sa'nare vt heal

sana'torio nm sanatorium

san'cire vt sanction

'sandalo nm sandal; Bot sandalwood

'sangu|e nm blood; **al ~e** ⟨carne⟩ rare; **farsi cattivo ~e per** worry about; **occhi iniettati di ~e** bloodshot eyes. **~e freddo** composure; **a ~e freddo** in cold blood. **~'igno** a blood

sangui'naccio nm Culin black pudding

sangui'nante a bleeding

sangui'nar|e vi bleed. **~io** a bloodthirsty

sangui'noso a bloody

sangui'suga nf leech

sa'nità nf soundness; (salute) health. **~ mentale** sanity, mental health

sani'tario a sanitary; **Servizio S~** National Health Service

'sano a sound; (salutare) healthy; **~ di mente** sane; **~ come un pesce** as fit as a fiddle

San Sil'vestro nm New Year's Eve

santifi'care vt sanctify

'santo a holy; (con nome proprio) saint ● nm saint. **san'tone** nm guru. **santu'ario** nm sanctuary

sanzi'one nf sanction

sa'pere vt know; (essere capace di) be able to; (venire a sapere) hear; **saperla lunga** know a thing or two ● vi **~ di** know about; (aver sapore di) taste of; (aver odore di) smell of; **saperci fare** have the know-how ● *nm* knowledge

sapi'en|**te** *a* wise; (*esperto*) expert ● *nm* (*uomo colto*) sage. **~za** *nf* wisdom

sa'pone *nm* soap. **~ da bucato** washing soap. **sapo'netta** *nf* bar of soap

sa'pore *nm* taste. **saporita'mente** *adv* (*dormire*) soundly. **sapo'rito** *a* tasty

sapu'tello, -a *a & nm sl* know-all, know-it-all *Am*

saraci'nesca *nf* roller shutter

sar'cas|**mo** *nm* sarcasm. **~tico** *a* sarcastic

Sar'degna *nf* Sardinia

sar'dina *nf* sardine

'sardo, -a *a & nmf* Sardinian

sar'donico *a* sardonic

'sarto, -a *nm* tailor ● *nf* dressmaker. **~'ria** *nf* tailor's; dressmaker's; (*arte*) couture

sas'sata *nf* blow with a stone; **prendere a sassate** stone. **'sasso** *nm* stone; (*ciottolo*) pebble

sassofo'nista *nmf* saxophonist. **sas'sofono** *nm* saxophone

sas'soso *a* stony

'Satana *nm* Satan. **sa'tanico** *a* satanic

sa'tellite *a inv & nm* satellite

sati'nato *a* glossy

'satira *nf* satire. **sa'tirico** *a* satirical

satu'ra|**re** *vt* saturate. **~zi'one** *nf* saturation. **'saturo** *a* saturated; (*pieno*) full

'sauna *nf* sauna

savoi'ardo *nm* (*biscotto*) sponge finger

sazi'ar|**e** *vt* satiate. **~si** *vr* **~si di** *fig* grow tired of

sazietà *nf* **mangiare a ~** eat one's fill. **'sazio** *a* satiated

sbaciucchi'ar|**e** *vt* smother with kisses. **~si** *vr* kiss and cuddle

sbada'ta|**ggine** *nf* carelessness; **è stata una ~ggine** it was careless. **~'mente** *adv* carelessly. **sba'dato** *a* careless

sbadigli'are *vi* yawn. **sba'diglio** *nm* yawn

sba'fa|**re** *vt* sponge. **~ta** *nf sl* nosh

'sbafo *nm* sponging; **a ~** (*gratis*) without paying

sbagli'ar|**e** *vi* make a mistake; (*aver torto*) be wrong ● *vt* make a mistake in; **~e strada** go the wrong way; **~e numero** get the number wrong; *Teleph* dial a wrong number. **~si** *vr* make a mistake. **'sbaglio** *nm* mistake; **per sbaglio** by mistake

sbal'l|**are** *vt* unpack; *fam* screw up (*conti*) ● *vi fam* go crazy. **~ato** *a* (*squilibrato*) unbalanced. **'sballo** *nm fam* scream; (*per droga*) trip; **da sballo** *sl* terrific

sballot'tare *vt* toss about

sbalor'di|**re** *vt* stun ● *vi* be stunned. **~'tivo** *a* amazing. **~to** *a* stunned

sbal'zare *vt* throw; (*da una carica*) dismiss ● *vi* bounce; (*saltare*) leap. **'sbalzo** *nm* bounce; (*sussulto*) jolt; (*di temperatura*) sudden change; **a sbalzi** in spurts; **a sbalzo** (*lavoro a rilievo*) embossed

sban'care *vt* bankrupt; **~ il banco** break the bank

sbanda'mento *nm Auto* skid; *Naut* list; *fig* going off the rails

sban'da|**re** *vi Auto* skid; *Naut* list. **~rsi** *vr* (*disperdersi*) disperse. **~ta** *nf* skid; *Naut* list; **prendere una ~ta per** get a crush on. **~to, -a** *a* mixed-up ● *nmf* mixed-up person

sbandie'rare *vt* wave; *fig* display

sbarac'care *vt/i* clear up

sbaragli'are *vt* rout. **sba'raglio** *nm* rout; **mettere allo sbaraglio** rout

sbaraz'zar|**e** *vt* clear. **~si** *vr* **~si di** get rid of

sbaraz'zino, -a *a* mischievous ● *nmf* scamp

sbar'ba|**re** *vt*, **~si** *vr* shave

sbar'care *vt/i* disembark; **~ il lunario** make ends meet. **'sbarco** *nm* landing; (*di merci*) unloading

'sbarra *nf* bar; (*di passaggio a li-*

vello) barrier. ~'**mento** nm barricade. **sbar'rare** vt bar; ⟨*ostruire*⟩ block; cross ⟨*assegno*⟩; ⟨*spalancare*⟩ open wide

sbatacchi'are vt/i sl bang, slam

'**sbatter|e** vt bang; slam, bang ⟨*porta*⟩; ⟨*urtare*⟩ knock; Culin beat; flap ⟨*ali*⟩; shake ⟨*tappeto*⟩ ●vi bang; ⟨*porta:*⟩ slam, bang. ~**si** vr rush around; ~**sene il capo** sl not give a damn about sth.

sbat'tuto a tossed; Culin beaten; fig run down

sba'va|re vi dribble; ⟨*colore:*⟩ smear. ~'**tura** nf smear; **senza** ~'**ture** fig faultless

sbelli'carsi vr ● **dalle risa** split one's sides ⟨with laughter⟩

'**sberla** nf slap

sbia'di|re vt/i, ~**rsi** vr fade. ~**to** a faded; fig colourless

sbian'car|e vt/i, ~**si** vr whiten

sbi'eco a slanting; **di** ~ on the slant; ⟨*guardare*⟩ sidelong; **guardare qcno di** ~ look askance at sb; **tagliare di** ~ cut on the bias

sbigot'ti|re vt dismay ● vi, ~**rsi** vr be dismayed. ~**to** a dismayed

sbilanci'ar|e vt unbalance ● vi ⟨*perdere l'equilibrio*⟩ overbalance. ~**si** vr lose one's balance

sbirci'a|re vt cast sidelong glances at. ~'**ta** nf furtive glance. **~'tina** nf **dare una** ~'**tina** a sneak a glance at

sbizzar'rirsi vr satisfy one's whims

sbloc'care vt unblock; Mech release; decontrol ⟨*prezzi*⟩

sboc'care vi ~ **in** ⟨*fiume:*⟩ flow into; ⟨*strada:*⟩ lead to; ⟨*folla:*⟩ pour into

sboc'cato a foul-mouthed

sbocci'are vi blossom

'**sbocco** nm flowing; ⟨*foce*⟩ mouth; Comm outlet

sbolo'gnare vt fam get rid of

'**sbornia** nf **prendere una ~** get drunk

sbor'sare vt pay out

sbot'tare vi burst out

sbotto'nar|e vt unbutton. ~**si** vr ⟨*fam: confidarsi*⟩ open up; ~**si la camicia** unbutton one's shirt

sbra'carsi vr put on something more comfortable; ~ **dalle risate** fam kill oneself laughing

sbracci'a|rsi vr wave one's arms. ~**to** a bare-armed; ⟨*abito*⟩ sleeveless

sbrai'tare vi bawl

sbra'nare vt tear to pieces

bricio'lar|e vt, ~**si** vr crumble

sbri'ga|re vt expedite; ⟨*occuparsi di*⟩ attend to. ~**rsi** vr be quick. ~'**tivo** a quick

sbrindel'la|re vt tear to shreds. ~**to** a in rags

sbro'dolare vt stain. ~**one** nm messy eater, dribbler

'**sbronza** nf **prendersi una ~a** get tight. **sbron'zarsi** vr get tight. ~**o** a ⟨*ubriaco*⟩ tight

sbruffo'nata nf boast. **sbruf'fone, -a** nmf boaster

sbu'care vi come out

sbucci'ar|e vt peel; shell ⟨*piselli*⟩. ~**si** vr graze oneself

sbuf'fare vi snort; ⟨*per impazienza*⟩ fume. '**sbuffo** nm puff

'**scabbia** nf scabies sg

sca'broso a rough; fig difficult; ⟨*scena*⟩ indecent

scacci'are vt chase away

'**scacc|o** nm check; ~**hi** pl ⟨*gioco*⟩ chess; ⟨*pezzi*⟩ chessmen; **dare ~o matto** a chessmate; **a ~hi** ⟨*tessuto*⟩ checked. ~**hi'era** nf chess-board

sca'dente a shoddy

sca'de|nza nf ⟨*di contratto*⟩ expiry; Comm maturity; ⟨*di progetto*⟩ deadline; **a breve/lunga ~nza** short-/long-term. ~**re** vi expire; ⟨*valore:*⟩ decline; ⟨*debito:*⟩ be due.

sca'duto a ⟨*biglietto*⟩ out-of-date

sca'fandro nm diving suit; ⟨*di astronauta*⟩ spacesuit

scaf'fale nm shelf; ⟨*libreria*⟩ bookshelf

'**scafo** nm hull

scagion'are vt exonerate

'**scaglia** nf scale; (di sapone) flake; (scheggia) chip

scagli'ar|e vt fling. ~**si** vr fling oneself; ~**si contro** fig rail against

scaglio'nare vt space out. ~'**one** nm group; **a** ~**oni** in groups. ~**one di reddito** tax bracket

'**scala** nf staircase; (portatile) ladder; (Mus, misura, fig) scale; **scale** pl stairs. ~ **mobile** escalator; (dei salari) cost of living index

sca'la|re vt climb; layer (capelli); (detrarre) deduct. ~**ta** nf climb; (dell'Everest ecc) ascent; **fare delle** ~**te** go climbing. ~'**tore**, ~'**trice** nmf climber

scalca'gnato a down at heel

scalci'are vi kick

scalci'nato a shabby

scalda'bagno nm water heater

scalda'muscoli nm inv legwarmer

scal'dar|e vt heat. ~**si** vr warm up; (eccitarsi) get excited

scal'fi|re vt scratch. ~**t'tura** nf scratch

scali'nata nf flight of steps. **sca'lino** nm step; (di scala a pioli) rung

scalma'narsi vr get worked up

'**scalo** nm slipway; Aeron, Naut port of call; **fare** ~ **a** call at; Aeron land at

sca'lo|gna nf bad luck. ~'**gnato** a unlucky

scalop'pina nf escalope

scal'pello nm chisel

scalpi'tare vi paw the ground; fig champ at the bit

'**scalpo** nm scalp

scal'pore nm noise; **far** ~ fig cause a sensation

scal'trezza nf shrewdness. **scal'trirsi** vr get shrewder. '**scaltro** a shrewd

scal'zare vt bare the roots of (albero); fig undermine; (da una carica) oust

'**scalzo** a & adv barefoot

scambi'are vt exchange; ~**are**

qcno per qualcun altro mistake sb for somebody else. ~'**evole** a reciprocal

'**scambio** nm exchange; Comm trade; **libero** ~ free trade

scamosci'ato a suede

scampa'gnata nf trip to the country

scampa'nato a (gonna) flared

scampanel'lata nf [loud] ring

scam'pare vt save; (evitare) escape; **scamparla bella** have a lucky escape. '**scampo** nm escape

'**scampolo** nm remnant

scanala'tura nf groove

scandagli'are vt sound

scanda'listico a sensational

scandaliz'zare vt scandalize. ~**iz'zarsi** vr be scandalized

'**scanda|lo** nm scandal. ~'**loso** a (somma ecc) scandalous; (fortuna) outrageous

Scandi'navia nf Scandinavia. **scandi'navo, -a** a & nmf Scandinavian

scan'dire vt scan (verso); pronounce clearly (parole)

scan'nare vt slaughter

scanneriz'zare vt Comput scan

scansafa'tiche nmf inv lazybones sg

scan'sar|e vt shift; (evitare) avoid. ~**si** vr get out of the way

scansi'one nf Comput scanning

'**scanso** nm **a** ~ **di** in order to avoid; **a** ~ **di equivoci** to avoid any misunderstanding

scanti'nato nm basement

scanto'nare vi turn the corner; (svignarsela) sneak off

scanzo'nato a easy-going

scapacci'one nm smack

scape'strato a dissolute

'**scapito** nm loss; **a** ~ **di** to the detriment of

'**scapola** nf shoulder-blade

'**scapolo** nm bachelor

scappa'mento nm Auto exhaust

scap'par|e vi escape; (andarsene) dash [off]; (sfuggire) slip; **mi** ~ **da ridere!** I want to burst out laughing; **mi ~ la pipì** I'm bursting, I need a pee. **~ta** *inf* short visit. **~'tella** *nf* escapade; (*infedeltà*) fling. **~'toia** *nf* way out

scappel'lotto *nm* cuff

scara'bocchio *nm* scribble

scara'faggio *nm* cockroach

scara'mantico *a* (*gesto*) to ward off the evil eye

scara'muccia *nf* skirmish

scarabocchi'are *vt* scribble

scaraven'tare *vt* hurl

scarce'rare *vt* release [from prison]

scardi'nare *vt* unhinge

'scarica *nf* discharge; (*di arma da fuoco*) volley; *fig* shower

scari'ca|re *vt* discharge; unload (*arma, merci*); *fig* unburden. **~rsi** *vr* (*fiume*) flow; (*orologio, batteria*) run down; (*fig* unwind. **~'tore** *nm* loader; (*di porto*) docker. **'scarico** *a* unloaded; (*vuoto*) empty; (*orologio*) run-down; (*batteria*) flat; *fig* untroubled ● *nm* unloading; (*di rifiuti*) dumping; (*di acqua*) draining; (*di sostanze inquinanti*) discharge; (*luogo*) [rubbish] dump; *Auto* exhaust; (*tubo*) waste pipe

scarlat'tina *nf* scarlet fever

scar'latto *a* scarlet

'scarno *a* thin; (*fig: stile*) bare

sca'ro|gna *nf* *fam* bad luck. **~'gnato** *a* *fam* unlucky

'scarpa *nf* shoe; (*fam: persona*) dead loss. **scarpe** *pl* **da ginnastica** trainers, gym shoes

scar'pata *nf* slope; (*burrone*) escarpment

scarpi'nare *vi* hike

scar'pone *nm* boot. **scarponi** *pl* **da sci** ski boot. **scarponi** *pl* **da trekking** walking boots

scarroz'zare *vt/i* drive around

scarseggi'are *vi* be scarce; **~ di** (*mancare*) be short of

scar'sezza *nf* scarcity, shortage. **scarsità** *nf* shortage. **'scarso** *a* scarce; (*manchevole*) short

scarta'mento *nm* *Rail* gauge. **~ ridotto** narrow gauge

scar'tare *vt* discard; unwrap (*pacco*); (*respingere*) reject ● *vi* (*deviare*) swerve. **'scarto** *nm* scrap; (*in carte*) discard; (*deviazione*) swerve; (*distacco*) gap

scar'toffie *nfpl* bumf, bumph

scas'sa|re *vt* break. **~to** *a* *fam* clapped out

scassi'nare *vt* force open

scassina'tore, -'trice *nmf* burglar. **'scasso** *nm* (*furto*) housebreaking

scate'na|re *vt* *fig* stir up. **~rsi** *vr* break out; (*fig: temporale*:) break; (*fam: infiammarsi*) get excited. **~to** *a* crazy

'scatola *nf* box; (*di latta*) can, tin *Br*; **in ~** (*cibo*) canned, tinned *Br*; **rompere le scatole a qcno** get on sb's nerves

scat'tare *vi* (*balzare*) spring up; (*adirarsi*) lose one's temper; take (*foto*). **'scatto** *nm* (*balzo*) spring; (*d'ira*) outburst; (*di telefono*) unit; (*dispositivo*) release; **a scatti** jerkily; **di scatto** suddenly

scatu'rire *vi* spring

scaval'care *vt* jump over (*muretto*); climb over (*muro*); (*fig: superare*) overtake

sca'vare *vt* dig (*buca*); dig up (*tesoro*); excavate (*città sepolta*). **'scavo** *nm* excavation

scazzot'tata *nf* *fam* punch-up

'scegliere *vt* choose, select

scelle'rato *a* wicked

'scel|ta *nf* choice; (*di articoli*) range; **...a ~a** (*in menù*) choice of...; **prendine una a ~a** take your choice o pick; **di prima ~a** top-grade, choice. **~o** *pp di* **scegliere** ● *a* select; (*merce ecc*) choice

sce'mare *vt/i* diminish

sce'menza *nf* silliness; (*azione*) silly thing to do/say. **'scemo** *a* silly

'scempio *nm* havoc; (*fig: di pae-*

saggio) ruination; **fare ~ di** play havoc with

'**scena** *nf* scene; *(palcoscenico)* stage; **entrare in ~** go/come on; *fig* enter the scene; **fare ~** put on an act; **fare una ~** make a scene; **andare in ~** *Theat* be staged, be put on. **sce'nario** *nm* scenery

sce'nata *nf* row, scene

'**scendere** *vi* go/come down; *(da treno, autobus)* get off; *(da macchina)* get out; *(strada:)* slope; *(notte, prezzi:)* fall ● *vt* go/come down *(scale)*

sceneggia'a|re *vt* dramatize. **~to** *nm* television serial. **~'tura** *nf* screenplay

'**scenico** *a* scenic

scervel'la|rsi *vr* rack one's brains. **~to** *a* brainless

'**sceso** *pp di* **scendere**

scetti'cismo *nm* scepticism. '**scettico, -a** *a* sceptical ● *nmf* sceptic

'**scettro** *nm* sceptre

'**scheda** *nf* card. **~ elettorale** ballot-paper. **~ di espansione** *Comput* expansion card. **~ perfo'rata** punch card. **~ telefonica** phonecard. **sche'dare** *vt* file. **sche'dario** *nm* (*mobile*) filing cabinet

sche'dina *nf* ≈ pools coupon; **giocare la ~** do the pools

scheggi'a|re *nf* fragment; *(di legno)* splinter. **~'arsi** *vr* chip; *(legno:)* splinter

scheletro *nm* skeleton

'**schema** *nm* diagram; *(abbozzo)* outline. **sche'matico** *a* schematic. **~tiz'zare** *vt* schematize

scherma *nf* fencing

scher'mirsi *vr* protect oneself

'**schermo** *nm* screen; **grande ~** big screen

scher'nire *vt* mock. '**scherno** *nm* mockery

scher'zare *vi* joke; *(giocare)* play

'**scherzo** *nm* joke; *(trucco)* trick; *(effetto)* play; *Mus* scherzo; **fare uno ~ a** qcno play a joke on sb;

per ~ for fun; **stare allo ~** take a joke. **scher'zoso** *a* playful

schiaccia'noci *nm inv* nutcrackers *pl*

schiacci'ante *a* damning

schiacci'are *vt* crush; *Sport* smash; press *(pulsante)*; crack *(noce)*; **~ un pisolino** grab forty winks

schiaffeggi'are *vt* slap. **schi'affo** *nm* slap; **dare uno schiaffo a** slap

schiamaz'zare *vi* make a racket; *(galline:)* cackle

schian'tar|e *vt* break. **~si** *vr* crash ● *vi* **schianto dalla fatica** I'm wiped out. '**schianto** *nm* crash; *fam* knock-out; *(divertente)* scream

schia'rir|e *vt* clear; *(sbiadire)* fade ● *vi*, **~si** *vr* brighten up; **~si la gola** clear one's throat

schiavitù *nf* slavery. **schi'avo, -a** *nmf* slave

schi'ena *nf* back; **mal di ~** backache. **schie'nale** *nm* *(di sedia)* back

schi'er|a *nf* *Mil* rank; *(moltitudine)* crowd. **~a'mento** *nm* lining up

schie'rar|e *vt* draw up. **~si** *vr* draw up; **~si con** *(parteggiare)* side with

schiet'tezza *nf* frankness. **schi'etto** *a* frank; *(puro)* pure

schi'fezza *nf* **una ~** rubbish. **schifil'toso** *a* fussy. '**schifo** *nm* disgust; **mi fa schifo** it makes me sick. **schi'foso** *a* disgusting; *(di cattiva qualità)* rubbishy

schioc'care *vt* crack; snap *(dita)*. **schi'occo** *nm* *(di frusta)* crack; *(di bacio)* smack; *(di dita, lingua)* click

schi'oppo *nm* **ad un tiro di ~** a stone's throw away

schi'uder|e *vt*, **~si** *vr* open

schi'u|ma *nf* foam; *(di sapone)* lather; *(feccia)* scum. **~ma da barba** shaving foam. **~'mare** *vt* skim ● *vi* foam

schi'uso *pp di* **schiudere**

schi'vare *vt* avoid. **'schivo** *a* bashful

schizo'frenico *a* schizophrenic

schiz'zare *vt* squirt; *(inzaccherare)* splash; *(abbozzare)* sketch ● *vi* spurt; **~ via** scurry away

schiz'zato, -a *a & nmf sl* loony

schizzi'noso *a* squeamish

'schizzo *nm* squirt; *(di fango)* splash; *(abbozzo)* sketch

sci *nm inv* ski; *(sport)* skiing. **~ d'acqua** water-skiing

'scia *nf* wake; *(di fumo ecc)* trail

sci'abola *nf* sabre

sciabor'dare *vt/i* lap

scia'callo *nm* jackal; *fig* profiteer

sciac'quar|e *vt* rinse. **~si** *vr* rinse oneself. **sci'acquo** *nm* mouth-wash

scia'gura *nf* disaster. **~'rato** *a* unfortunate; *(scellerato)* wicked

scialac'quare *vt* squander

scia'lare *vi* spend money like water

sci'albo *a* pale; *fig* dull

sci'alle *nm* shawl

scia'luppa *nf* dinghy. **~ di salvataggio** lifeboat

sci'ame *nm* swarm

sci'ampo *nm* shampoo

scian'cato *a* lame

sci'are *vi* ski

sci'arpa *nf* scarf

sci'atica *nf Med* sciatica

scia'tore, -'trice *nmf* skier

sci'atto *a* slovenly; *(stile)* careless. **sciat'tone, -a** *nmf* slovenly person

scienti'fico *a* scientific

scien'z|a *nf* science; *(sapere)* knowledge. **~'ato, -a** *nmf* scientist

'scimmi|a *nf* monkey. **~ot'tare** *vt* ape

scimpanzé *nm inv* chimpanzee, chimp

scimu'nito *a* idiotic

'scinder|e *vt*, **~si** *vr* split

scin'tilla *nf* spark. **scintil'lante** *a* sparkling. **scintil'lare** *vi* sparkle

scioc'ca|nte *a* shocking. **~re** *vt* shock

scioc'chezza *nf* foolishness; *(assurdità)* nonsense. **sci'occo** *a* foolish

sci'oglier|e *vt* untie; undo, untie *(nodo)*; *(liberare)* release; *(liquefare)* melt; dissolve *(contratto, qcsa nell'acqua)*; loosen up *(muscoli)*. **~si** *vr* release oneself; *(liquefarsi)* melt; *(contratto:)* be dissolved; *(pastiglia:)* dissolve

scioglilingua *nm inv* tongue-twister

scio'lina *nf* wax

sciol'tezza *nf* agility; *(disinvoltura)* ease

sci'olto *pp di* **sciogliere** ● *a* loose; *(agile)* agile; *(disinvolto)* easy; **versi sciolti** blank verse *sg*

sciope'ra|nte *nmf* striker. **~re** *vi* go on strike, strike. **sciopero** *nm* strike. **sciopero a singhiozzo** on-off strike

sciori'nare *vt fig* show off

scip'pa|re *vt fam* snatch. **~'tore, ~'trice** *nmf* bag snatcher. **'scippo** *nm* bag-snatching

sci'rocco *nm* sirocco

sscirop'pato *a* *(frutta)* in syrup. **sci'roppo** *nm* syrup

'scisma *nm* schism

scissi'one *nf* division

'scisso *pp di* **scindere**

sciu'par|e *vt* spoil; *(sperperare)* waste. **~si** *vr* get spoiled; *(deperire)* wear oneself out. **sciu'pìo** *nm* waste

scivo'l|are *vi* slide; *(involontariamente)* slip. **'scivolo** *nm* slide; *Techn* chute. **~oso** *a* slippery

scle'rosi *nf* sclerosis

scoc'care *vt* shoot ● *vi* *(scintilla:)* shoot out; *(ora:)* strike

scocci'a|re *vt* *(dare noia a)* bother. **~rsi** *vr* be bothered. **~to** *a fam* narked. **~'tore, ~'trice** *nmf* bore. **~'tura** *nf* nuisance

sco'della *nf* bowl

scodinzo'lare *vi* wag its tail

scogli'era *nf* cliff; *(a flor d'acqua)*

reef. '**scoglio** *nm* rock; (*fig: ostacolo*) stumbling block

scoi'attolo *nm* squirrel

scola|'pasta *nm inv* colander. **~pi'atti** *nm inv* dish drainer

sco'lara *nf* schoolgirl

sco'lare *vt* drain; strain (*pasta, verdura*) ● *vi* drip

sco'laro *nm* schoolboy. **~'resca** *nf* pupils *pl*. **~stico** *a* school *attrib*

scoli'osi *nf* curvature of the spine

scol'la|re *vt* cut away the neck of (*abito*); (*staccare*) unstick. **~to** *a* (*abito*) low-necked. **~'tura** *nf* neckline

'**scolo** *nm* drainage

scolo'ri|re *vt*, **~rsi** *vr* fade. **~to** *a* faded

scol'pire *vt* carve; (*imprimere*) engrave

scombi'nare *vt* upset

scombus'solare *vt* muddle up

scom'messa *nf* bet. **~o** *pp di* **scommettere**. **scom'mettere** *vt* bet

scomo'dar|e *vt*, **~si** *vr* trouble. **scomodità** *nf* discomfort. '**scomodo** *a* uncomfortable ● *nm* **essere di scomodo a qcno** be a trouble to sb

scompa'rire *vi* disappear; (*morire*) pass on. **scom'parsa** *nf* disappearance; (*morte*) passing, death. **scom'parso, -a** *pp di* **scomparire** ● *nmf* departed

scomparti'mento *nm* compartment. **scom'parto** *nm* compartment

scom'penso *nm* imbalance

scompigli'are *vt* disarrange. **scom'piglio** *nm* confusion

scom'po|rre *vt* take to pieces; (*fig: turbare*) upset. **~rsi** *vr* get flustered, lose one's composure. **~sto** *pp di* **scomporre** ● *a* (*sguaiato*) unseemly; (*disordinato*) untidy

sco'muni|ca *nf* excommunication. **~'care** *vt* excommunicate

sconcer'ta|re *vt* disconcert; (*rendere perplesso*) bewilder. **~to** *a* disconcerted; bewildered

scon'cezza *nf* obscenity. '**sconcio** *a* (*osceno*) dirty ● *nm* **è uno sconcio che...** it's a disgrace that...

sconclusio'nato *a* incoherent

scon'dito *a* unseasoned; (*insalata*) with no dressing

sconfes'sare *vt* disown

scon'figgere *vt* defeat

sconfi'na|re *vi* cross the border; (*in proprietà privata*) trespass. **~to** *a* unlimited

scon'fitt|a *nf* defeat. **~o** *pp di* **sconfiggere**

scon'forto *nm* dejection

sconge'lare *vt* thaw out (*cibo*), defrost

scongiu'rare *vt* beseech; (*evitare*) avert. **~'uro** *nm* **fare gli scongiuri** touch wood, knock on wood *Am*

scon'nesso *pp di* **sconnettere** ● *a fig* incoherent. **scon'nettere** *vt* disconnect

sconosci'uto, -a *a* unknown ● *nmf* stranger

sconquas'sare *vt* smash; (*sconvolgere*) upset

sconside'rato *a* inconsiderate

sconsigli'a|bile *a* not advisable. **~re** *vt* advise against

sconso'lato *a* disconsolate

scon'ta|re *vt* discount; (*dedurre*) deduct; (*pagare*) pay off; serve (*pena*). **~to** *a* discount; (*ovvio*) expected; **~to del 10%** with 10% discount; **dare qcsa per ~to** take for granted

scon'tento *a* displeased ● *nm* discontent

'**sconto** *nm* discount; **fare uno ~** give a discount

scon'trarsi *vr* clash; (*urtare*) collide

scon'trino *nm* ticket; (*di cassa*) receipt

scon'tro *nm* clash; (*urto*) collision

scon'troso *a* unsociable

sconveni'ente *a* unprofitable; (*scorretto*) unseemly

sconvol'gente *a* mind-blowing

scon'vol|gere *vt* upset; (*mettere in disordine*) disarrange. **~gi'mento**

nm upheaval. **~to** *pp di* **sconvolgere** ● *a* distraught

'**scopa** *nf* broom. **sco'pare** *vt* sweep; *vulg* shag, screw

scoperchi'are *vt* take the lid off ⟨*pentola*⟩; take the roof off ⟨*casa*⟩

sco'pert|a *nf* discovery. **~o** *pp di* **scoprire** ● *a* uncovered; ⟨*senza riparo*⟩ exposed; ⟨*conto*⟩ overdrawn; ⟨*spoglio*⟩ bare

'**scopo** *nm* aim; **allo ~ di** in order to

scoppi'are *vi* burst; *fig* break out. **scoppiet'tare** *vi* crackle. '**scoppio** *nm* burst; ⟨*di guerra*⟩ outbreak; ⟨*esplosione*⟩ explosion

sco'prire *vt* discover; ⟨*togliere la copertura a*⟩ uncover

scoraggi'ante *a* discouraging

scoraggi'a|re *vt* discourage. **~rsi** *vr* lose heart

scor'butico *a* peevish

scorcia'toia *nf* short cut

'**scorcio** *nm* ⟨*di epoca*⟩ end; ⟨*di cielo*⟩ patch; ⟨*in arte*⟩ foreshortening; **di ~** ⟨*vedere*⟩ from an angle. **~ panoramico** panoramic view

scor'da|re *vt*, **~rsi** *vr* forget. **~to a** *Mus* out of tune

sco'reggi|a *nf fam* fart. **~'are** *vi fam* fart

'**scorgere** *vt* make out; ⟨*notare*⟩ notice

scoria *nf* waste; ⟨*di metallo, carbone*⟩ slag; **scorie** ⟨*pl* **radioattive** radioactive waste

scor'nato *a fig* hangdog. '**scorno** *nm* humiliation

scorpacci'ata *nf* bellyful; **fare una ~ di** stuff oneself with

scorpi'one *nm* scorpion; *Astr* Scorpio

scorraz'zare *vi* run about

'**scorrere** *vt* ⟨*dare un'occhiata*⟩ glance through ● *vi* run; ⟨*scivolare*⟩ slide; ⟨*fluire*⟩ flow; *Comput* scroll. **scor'revole** *a* **porta scorrevole** sliding door

scorre'ria *nf* raid

scorret'tezza *nf* ⟨*mancanza di educazione*⟩ bad manners *pl*. **scor-**

'**retto** *a* incorrect; ⟨*sconveniente*⟩ improper

scorri'banda *nf* raid; *fig* excursion

'**scors|a** *nf* glance. **~o** *pp di* **scorrere** ● *a* last

scor'soio *a* **nodo ~** noose

'**scort|a** *nf* escort; ⟨*provvista*⟩ supply. **~'tare** *vt* escort

scor'te|se *a* discourteous. **~'sia** *nf* discourtesy

scorti'ca|re *vt* skin. **~'tura** *nf* graze

'**scorto** *pp di* **scorgere**

'**scorza** *nf* peel; ⟨*crosta*⟩ crust; ⟨*corteccia*⟩ bark

sco'sceso *a* steep

'**scoss|a** *nf* shake; *Electr*, *fig* shock; **prendere la ~** get an electric shock. **~ elettrica** electric shock. **~ sismica** earth tremor

'**scosso** *pp di* **scuotere** ● *a* shaken; ⟨*sconvolto*⟩ upset

sco'stante *a* off-putting

sco'sta|re *vt* push away. **~rsi** *vr* stand aside

scostu'mato *a* dissolute; ⟨*maleducato*⟩ ill-mannered

scot'tante *a* ⟨*argomento*⟩ dangerous

scot'ta|re *vt* scald ● *vi* burn; ⟨*bevanda*⟩ be too hot; ⟨*sole, pentola*⟩ be very hot. **~rsi** *vr* burn oneself; ⟨*al sole*⟩ get sunburnt; *fig* get one's fingers burnt. **~'tura** *nf* burn; ⟨*da liquido*⟩ scald; **~tura solare** sunburn; *fig* painful experience

'**scotto** *a* overcooked

sco'vare *vt* ⟨*scoprire*⟩ discover

'**Scoz|ia** *nf* Scotland. **~'zese** *a* Scottish ● *nmf* Scot

scre'dito *nm* discredit

scredi'tare *vt* discredit

scre'mare *vt* skim

screpo'la|re *vt*, **~rsi** *vr* crack. **~to** *a* ⟨*labbra*⟩ chapped. **~'tura** *nf* crack

screzi'ato *a* speckled

'**screzio** *nm* disagreement

scribac|chi'are *vt* scribble. **~'chino, -a** *nmf* scribbler; ⟨*impiegato*⟩ penpusher

scricchio'l|are *vi* creak. **~io** *nm* creaking

'scricciolo *nm* wren

'scrigno *nm* casket

scrimina'tura *nf* parting

'scrit|ta *nf* writing; *(su muro)* graffiti. **~to** *pp di* **scrivere ●a** written **●***nm* writing; *(lettera)* letter. **~toio** *nm* writing-desk. **~'tore, ~'trice** *nmf* writer. **~'tura** *nf* writing; *Relig* scripture

scrittu'rare *vt* engage

scriva'nia *nf* desk

'scrivere *vt* write; *(descrivere)* write about; **~ a macchina** type

scroc'c|are *vt* **~are a** sponge off. **'scrocco** *nm fam* a scrocco *fam* without paying; **vivere a scrocco** sponge off other people. **~one, -a** *nmf* sponger

'scrofa *nf* sow

scrol'lar|e *vt* shake; **~e le spalle** shrug one's shoulders. **~si** *vr* shake oneself; **~si qcsa di dosso** shake sth off

scrosci'are *vi* roar; *(pioggia:)* pelt down. **'scroscio** *nm* roar; *(di pioggia)* pelting; **uno scroscio di applausi** thunderous applause

scro'star|e *vt* scrape. **~si** *vr* peel off

'scrupo|lo *nm* scruple; *(diligenza)* care; **senza scrupoli** unscrupulous, without scruples. **~'loso** *a* scrupulous

scru'tare *vt* scan; *(indagare)* search. **~'tore** *nm (alle elezioni)* returning officer

scruti'nare *vt* scrutinize. **scru'tinio** *nm (di voti alle elezioni)* poll; *Sch* assessment of progress

scu'cire *vt* unstitch; **scuci i soldi!** *fam* cough up [the money!]

scude'ria *nf* stable

scu'detto *nm Sport* championship shield

'scudo *nm* shield

sculacci'are *vt* spank. **~'ata** *nf* spanking. **~'one** *nm* spanking

scule'tare *vi* wiggle one's hips

scul'tore, -'trice *nm* sculptor **●***nf* sculptress. **~'tura** *nf* sculpture

scu'ola *nf* school. **~ elementare** primary school. **~ guida** driving school. **~ materna** day nursery. **~ media** secondary school. **~ media [inferiore]** secondary school (*10-13*). **~ [media] superiore** secondary school (*13-18*). **~ dell'obbligo** compulsory education

scu'oter|e *vt* shake. **~si** *vr (destarsi)* rouse oneself; **~si di dosso** shake off

'scure *nf* axe

scu'reggia *nf fam* fart. **scureggi'are** *vi fam* fart

'scuro *a* dark **●***nm* darkness; *(imposta)* shutter

scur'rile *a* scurrilous

'scusa *nf* excuse; *(giustificazione)* apology; **chiedere ~** apologize; **chiedo ~!** I'm sorry!

scu'sar|e *vt* excuse. **~si** *vr* **~si** apologize (**di** for); **[mi] scusi!** excuse me!; *(chiedendo perdono)* [I'm] sorry!

sdebi'tarsi *vr (disobbligarsi)* repay a kindness

sde'gna|re *vt* despise. **~rsi** *vr* get angry. **~to** *a* indignant. **'sdegno** *nm* disdain. **sde'gnoso** *a* disdainful

sden'tato *a* toothless

sdolci'nato *a* sentimental, schmaltzy

sdoppi'are *vt* halve

sdrai'arsi *vr* lie down. **'sdraio** *nm [sedia a] sdraio** deckchair

sdrammatiz'zare *vi* provide some comic relief

sdruccio'l|are *vi* slither. **~evole** *a* slippery

se *conj* if; *(interrogativo)* whether, if; **se mai** *(caso mai)* if need be; **se mai telefonasse,...** should he call,..., if he calls,...; **se no** otherwise, or else; **se non altro** at least, if nothing else; **se pur** *(sebbene)* even though; *(anche se)* even if; **non so se sia vero** I don't know whether it's true, I don't know if it's true; **come se** as if; **se lo avessi saputo prima!** if only I had known before!; **e se andassimo fuori a cena?** how about going out for dinner? ● *nm inv* if

sé *pers pron* oneself; *(lui)* himself; *(lei)* herself; *(esso, essa)* itself; *(loro)* themselves; **l'ha fatto da sé** he did it himself; **ha preso i soldi con sé** he took the money with him; **si sono tenuti le notizie per sé** they kept the news to themselves

seb'bene *conj* although

'secca *nf* shallows *pl*; **in ~** *(nave)* aground

sec'cante *a* annoying

sec'ca|re *vt* dry; *(importunare)* annoy ● *vi* dry up. **~rsi** *vr* dry up; *(irritarsi)* get annoyed; *(annoiarsi)* get bored. **~'tore, ~'trice** *nmf* nuisance. **~'tura** *nf* bother

secchi'ello *nm* pail

'secchio *nm* bucket. **~ della spaz-zatura** rubbish bin, trash can *Am*

'secco, -a *a* dry; *(disseccato)* dried; *(magro)* thin; *(brusco)* curt; *(preciso)* sharp; **restare a ~** be left penniless; **restarci ~** *(fam: morire di colpo)* be killed on the spot ● *nm (siccità)* drought; **lavare a ~** dry-clean

secessi'one *nf* secession

seco'lare *a* age-old; *(laico)* secular.

'secolo *nm* century; *(epoca)* age; **è un secolo che non lo vedo** *fam* I haven't seen him for ages *o* yonks

se'cond|a *nf* Sch, Rail second class; *Auto* second [gear]. **~o** *a* second ● *nm* second; *(secondo piatto)* main course ● *prep* according to; **~o me** in my opinion

secondo'genito, -a *a & nm* second-born

secrezi'one *nf* secretion

'sedano *nm* celery

seda'tivo *a & nm* sedative

'sede *nf* seat; *(centro)* centre; *Relig* see; *Comm* head office. **~ sociale** registered office

seden'tario *a* sedentary

se'der|e *vi* sit. **~si** *vr* sit down ● *nm (deretano)* bottom

'sedia *nf* chair. **~ a dondolo** rocking chair. **~ a rotelle** wheelchair

sedi'cente *a* self-styled

'sedici *a & nm* sixteen

se'dile *nm* seat

sedizi'o|ne *nf* sedition. **~so** *a* seditious

se'dotto *pp di* sedurre

sedu'cente *a* seductive; *(allettante)* enticing

se'durre *vt* seduce

se'duta *nf* session; *(di posa)* sitting. **~ stante** *adv* here and now

seduzi'one *nf* seduction

'sega *nf* saw; *vulg* wank

'segala *nf* rye

se'gare *vt* saw

sega'tura *nf* sawdust

'seggio *nm* seat. **~ elettorale** polling station

seggio'l|a *nf* chair. **~ino** *nm* seat; *(da bambino)* child's seat. **~'one** *nm (per bambini)* high chair

seggio'via *nf* chair lift

seghe'ria *nf* sawmill

se'ghetto *nm* hacksaw

seg'mento *nm* segment

segna'lar|e *vt* signal; *(annunciare)* announce; *(indicare)* point out. **~si** *vr* distinguish oneself

se'gnale *nm* signal; *(stradale)* sign. **~le acustico** beep. **~le orario** time signal. **~letica** *nf* signals *pl*. **~letica stradale** road signs *pl*

segna'libro *nm* bookmark

se'gnar|e *vt* mark; *(prendere nota)* note; *(indicare)* indicate; *Sport* score. **~si** *vr* cross oneself. **'segno** *nm* sign; *(traccia, limite)* mark; *(bersaglio)* target; **far segno** *(col capo)* nod; *(con la mano)* beckon. **segno zodiacale** birth sign

segre'ga|re *vt* segregate. **~zi'one** *nf* segregation

segretari'ato *nm* secretariat

segre'tario, -a *nmf* secretary. **~ comunale** town clerk

segrete'ria *nf (uffico)* [administrative] office; *(segretariato)* secretariat. **~ telefonica** answering machine, answerphone

segre'tezza *nf* secrecy

se'greto *a & nm* secret; **in ~** in secret

segu'ace *nmf* follower

segu'ente *a* following, next

se'gugio *nm* bloodhound

segu'ire *vt/i* follow; *(continuare)* continue

segu'itare *vt/i* continue

'seguito *nm* retinue; *(sequela)* series; *(continuazione)* continuation; **di ~** in succession; **in ~** later on; **in ~ a** following; **al ~** in his/her wake; *(a causa di)* owing to; **fare ~ a** *Comm* follow up

'sei *a & nm* six. **sei'cento** *a & nm* six hundred; **il Seicento** the seventeenth century. **sei'mila** *a & nm* six thousand

sel'ciato *nm* paving

selet'tivo *a* selective. **selezio'nare** *vt* select. **selezi'one** *nf* selection

'sella *nf* saddle. **sel'lare** *vt* saddle

seltz *nm* soda water

'selva *nf* forest

selvag'gina *nf* game

sel'vaggio, -a *a* wild; *(primitivo)* savage ● *nmf* savage

sel'vatico *a* wild

se'maforo *nm* traffic lights *pl*

se'mantica *nf* semantics *sg*

sem'brare *vi* seem; *(assomigliare)* look like; **che te ne sembra?** what do you think?; **mi sembra che...** I think...

'seme *nm* seed; *(di mela)* pip; *(di carte)* suit; *(sperma)* semen

se'mestre *nm* half-year

semi'cerchio *nm* semicircle

semifi'nale *nf* semifinal

semi'freddo *nm* ice cream and sponge dessert

'semina *nf* sowing

semi'nare *vt* sow; *fam* shake off *(inseguitori)*

semi'nario *nm* seminar; *Relig* seminary

seminter'rato *nm* basement

se'mitico *a* Semitic

sem'mai *conj* in case ● *adv* **è lui, ~, che...** if anyone, it's him who...

'semola *nf* bran. **semo'lino** *nm* semolina

'semplice *a* simple; **in parole semplici** in plain words. **~'cemente** *adv* simply. **~'ciotto, -a** *nmf* simpleton. **~'cistico** *a* simplistic. **~'cità** *nf* simplicity. **~fi'care** *vt* simplify

'sempre *adv* always; *(ancora)* still; **per ~** for ever

sempre'verde *a & nm* evergreen

'senape *nf* mustard

se'nato *nm* senate. **sena'tore** *nm* senator

se'nile *a* senile. **~ità** *nf* senility

'senno *nm* sense

'seno *nm (petto)* breast; *Math* sine; **in ~ a** in the bosom of

sen'sato *a* sensible

sensazi|o'nale *a* sensational. **~'o'ne** *nf* sensation

sen'sibil|e *a* sensitive; *(percepibile)* perceptible; *(notevole)* considerable. **~ità** *nf* sensitivity. **~iz'zare** *vt* make more aware (a of)

sensi'tivo, -a *a* sensory ● *nmf* sensitive person; *(medium)* medium

'senso *nm* sense; *(significato)* meaning; *(direzione)* direction; **far ~ a qcno** make sb shudder; **non ha ~** it doesn't make sense; **senza ~** meaningless; **perdere i sensi** lose consciousness; **~ dell'umorismo** sense of humour. **~ unico** *(strada)* one-way; **~ vietato** no entry

sensu'al|e *a* sensual. **~ità** *nf* sensuality

sen'tenz|a *nf* sentence; *(massima)* saying. **~i'are** *vi* *Jur* pass judgment

senti'ero *nm* path

sentimen'tale *a* sentimental. **senti'mento** *nm* feeling

senti'nella *nf* sentry

sen'ti|re *vt* feel; *(udire)* hear; *(ascoltare)* listen to; *(gustare)* taste;

(*odorare*) smell ● *vi* feel; (*udire*) hear; **~re caldo/freddo** feel hot/cold. **~rsi** *vr* feel; **~rsi di fare qcsa** feel like doing sth; **~rsi bene** feel well; **~rsi poco bene** feel unwell; **~rsela di fare qcsa** feel up to doing sth. **~to** *a* (*sincero*) sincere; **per ~to dire** by hearsay

sen'tore *nm* inkling

'**senza** *prep* without; **~ correre** without running; **senz'altro** certainly; **~ ombrello** without an umbrella

senza'tetto *nm inv* i **~** the homeless

sepa'ra|re *vt* separate. **~rsi** *vr* separate; (*amici:*) part; **~rsi da** be separated from. **~ta'mente** *adv* separately. **~zi'one** *nf* separation

se'pol|cro *nm* sepulchre. **~to** *pp di* **seppellire**. **~'tura** *nf* burial

seppel'lire *vt* bury

'**seppia** *nf* cuttle fish; **nero di ~** sepia

sep'pure *conj* even if

se'quenza *nf* sequence

seque'strare *vt* (*rapire*) kidnap; *Jur* impound; (*confiscare*) confiscate. **se'questro** *nm* Jur impounding; (*di persona*) kidnap[ping]

'**sera** *nf* evening; **di ~** in the evening. **se'rale** *a* evening. **se'rata** *nf* evening; (*ricevimento*) party

ser'bare *vt* keep; harbour (*odio*); cherish (*speranza*)

serba'toio *nm* tank. **~ d'acqua** water tank; (*per una città*) reservoir

'**serbo, -a** *a a & nmf* Serbian ● *nm* (*lingua*) Serbian; **mettere in ~** put aside

sere'nata *nf* serenade

serenità *nf* serenity. **se'reno** *a* serene; (*cielo*) clear

ser'gente *nm* sergeant

seria'mente *adv* seriously

'**serie** *nf inv* series; (*complesso*) set; *Sport* division; **fuori ~** custom-

built; **produzione in ~** mass production; **di ~ B** second-rate

serietà *nf* seriousness.

'**serio** *a* serious; (*degno di fiducia*) reliable; **sul serio** seriously; (*davvero*) really

ser'mone *nm* sermon

'**serpe** *nf liter* viper. **~ggi'are** *vi* meander; (*diffondersi*) spread

ser'pente *nm* snake. **~ a sonagli** rattlesnake

'**serra** *nf* greenhouse; **effetto ~** greenhouse effect

ser'randa *nf* shutter

ser'ra|re *vt* shut; (*stringere*) tighten; (*incalzare*) press on. **~'tura** *nf* lock

ser'vi|re *vt* serve; (*al ristorante*) wait on ● *vi* serve; (*essere utile*) be of use; **non serve** it's no good. **~rsi** *vr* (*di cibo*) help oneself; **~si da** buy from; **~si di** use

servitù *nf inv* servitude; (*personale di servizio*) servants *pl*

servizi'evole *a* obliging

ser'vizio *nm* service; (*da caffè ecc*) set; (*di cronaca, sportivo*) report; **servizi** *pl* bathroom; **essere di ~** be on duty; **fare ~** (*autobus ecc.*) run; **fuori ~** (*bus*) not in service; (*ascensore*) out of order; **~ compreso** service charge included. **~ in camera** room service. **~ civile** civilian duties done instead of national service. **~ militare** military service. **~ pubblico** utility company. **~ al tavolo** waiter service

'**servo, -a** *nmf* servant

servo'sterzo *nm* power steering

ses'san|ta *a & nm* sixty. **~'tina** *nf* **una ~tina** about sixty

sessi'one *nf* session

'**sesso** *nm* sex

sessu'al|e *a* sexual. **~ità** *nf* sexuality

'**sesto**[1] *a* sixth

'**sesto**[2] *nm* (*ordine*) order

'**seta** *nf* silk

setacci'are *vt* sieve. **se'taccio** *nm* sieve

'**sete** *nf* thirst; **avere ~** be thirsty

'setola nf bristle

'setta nf sect

set'tan|ta a & nm seventy. **~'tina** nf una **~tina** about seventy

'sette a & nm seven. **~'cento** a & nm seven hundred; **il S~cento** the eighteenth century

set'tembre nm September

settentri|o'nale a northern ●nmf northerner. **~'one** nm north

setti'ma|na nf week. **~'nale** a & nm weekly

'settimo a seventh

set'tore nm sector

severità nf severity. **se'vero** a severe; (rigoroso) strict

se'vizi|a nf torture; **se'vizie** pl torture sg. **~'are** vt torture

sezio'nare vt divide; Med dissect. **sezi'one** nf section; (reparto) department; Med dissection

sfaccen'dato a idle

sfacchi'na|re vi toil. **~ta** nf drudgery

sfacciа'taggine nf cheek, insolence. **~'ato** a cheeky, fresh Am

sfa'celo nm ruin; **in ~** in ruins

sfal'darsi vr flake off

sfa'mar|e vt feed. **~si** vr satisfy one's hunger, eat one's fill

sfar'zo nm pomp. **~'zoso** a sumptuous

sfa'sato a fam confused; ⟨motore:⟩ which needs tuning

sfasci'ar|e vt unbandage; (fracassare) smash. **~rsi** vr fall to pieces. **~to** a beat-up

sfa'tare vt explode

sfati'cato a lazy

sfavil'la|nte a sparkling. **~re** vi sparkle

sfavo'revole a unfavourable

sfavo'rire vt disadvantage, put at a disadvantage

'sfer|a nf sphere. **~ico** a spherical

sfer'rare vt unshoe ⟨cavallo⟩; (scagliare) land

sfer'zare vt whip

sfian'carsi vr wear oneself out

sfi'bra|re vt exhaust. **~to** a exhausted

'sfida nf challenge. **sfi'dare** vt challenge

sfi'duci|a nf mistrust. **~'ato** a discouraged

'sfiga nf vulg bloody bad luck

sfigu'rare vt disfigure ●vi (far cattiva figura) look out of place

sfilacci'ar|e vt, **~si** vr fray

sfi'la|re vt unthread; (togliere di dosso) take off ●vi ⟨truppe:⟩ march past; (in parata) parade. **~rsi** vr come unthreaded; ⟨collant:⟩ ladder; take off ⟨pantaloni⟩. **~ta** nf parade; (sfilza) series. **~ta di moda** fashion show

'sfilza nf (di errori, domande) string

'sfinge nf sphinx

sfi'nito a worn out

sfio'rare vt skim; touch on ⟨argomento⟩

sfio'rire vi wither; ⟨bellezza:⟩ fade

'sfitto a vacant

'sfizio nm whim, fancy; **togliersi uno ~** satisfy a whim

sfo'cato a out of focus

sfoci'are vi **~ in** flow into

sfode'ra|re vt draw ⟨pistola, spada⟩. **~to** a unlined

sfo'gar|e vt vent. **~si** vr give vent to one's feelings

sfoggi'are vt/i show off. **'sfoggio** nm show, display; **fare sfoggio di** show off

'sfoglia nf sheet of pastry; **pasta ~** puff pastry

sfogli'are vt leaf through

'sfogo nm outlet; fig outburst; Med rash; **dare ~ a** give vent to

sfolgo'ra|nte a blazing. **~re** vi blaze

sfol'lare vt clear ●vi Mil be evacuated

sfol'tire vt thin [out]

sfon'dare vt break down ●vi (aver successo) make a name for oneself

'sfondo nm background

sfor'ma|re vt pull out of shape ⟨tasche⟩. **~rsi** vr lose its shape; ⟨persona:⟩ lose one's figure. **~to** nm Culin flan

sfor'nito *a* ~ **di** *(negozio)* out of
sfor'tuna *nf* bad luck. **~ta'mente** *adv* unfortunately. **sfortu'nato** *a* unlucky

sfor'zar|e *vt* force. **~si** *vr* try hard. **'sforzo** *nm* effort; *(tensione)* strain
'sfottere *vt sl* tease
sfracel'larsi *vr* smash
sfrat'tare *vt* evict. **'sfratto** *nm* eviction
sfrecci'are *vi* flash past
sfregi'a|re *vt* slash. **~to** *a* scarred **'sfregio** *nm* slash
sfre'na|rsi *vr* run wild. **~to** *a* wild
sfron'tato *a* shameless
sfrutta'mento *nm* exploitation. **sfrut'tare** *vt* exploit
sfug'gente *a* elusive; *(mento)* receding
sfug'gi|re *vi* escape; **~re a** escape [from]; **mi sfugge** it escapes me; **mi è sfuggito di mano** I lost hold of it ● *vt* avoid. **~ta** *nf* **di ~ta** in passing
sfu'ma|re *vi (svanire)* vanish; *(colore:)* shade off ● *vt* soften *(colore)*. **~'tura** *nf* shade
sfuri'ata *nf* outburst [of anger]
sga'bello *nm* stool
sgabuz'zino *nm* cupboard
sgam'bato *a (costume da bagno)* high-cut
sgambet'tare *vi* kick one's legs; *(camminare)* trot. **sgam'betto** *nm* **fare lo sgambetto a qcno** trip sb up
sganasci'arsi *vr* ~ **dalle risa** roar with laughter
sganci'ar|e *vt* unhook; *Rail* uncouple; drop *(bombe)*; *fam* cough up *(denaro)*. **~si** *vr* become unhooked; *fig* get away
sganghe'rato *a* ramshackle
sgar'bato *a* rude. **'sgarbo** *nm* discourtesy; **fare uno sgarbo a** qcno be rude
sgargi'ante *a* garish
sgar'rare *vi* be wrong; *(da regola)* stray from the straight and narrow. **'sgarro** *nm* mistake, slip

sgattaio'lare *vi* sneak away; ~ **via** decamp
sghignaz'zare *vi* laugh scornfully, sneer
sgob'b|are *vi* slog; *(fam: studente:)* swot. **~one, -a** *nmf* slogger; *(fam: studente)* swot
sgoccio'lare *vi* drip
sgo'larsi *vr* shout oneself hoarse
sgomb[e]'rare *vt* clear [out]. **'sgombro** *a* clear ● *nm (trasloco)* removal; *(pesce)* mackerel
sgomen'tar|e *vt* dismay. **~si** *vr* be dismayed. **sgo'mento** *nm* dismay
sgomi'nare *vt* defeat
sgom'mata *nf* screech of tyres
sgonfi'ar|e *vt* deflate. **~si** *vr* go down. **'sgonfio** *a* flat
'sgorbio *nm* scrawl; *(fig: vista sgradevole)* sight
sgor'gare *vi* gush [out] ● *vt* flush out, unblock *(lavandino)*
sgoz'zare *vt* ~ **qcno** cut sb's throat
sgra'd|evole *a* disagreeable. **~ito** *a* unwelcome
sgrammati'cato *a* ungrammatical
sgra'nare *vt* shell *(piselli)*; open wide *(occhi)*
sgran'chir|e *vt*, **~si** *vr* stretch
sgranocchi'are *vt* munch
sgras'sare *vt* remove the grease from
sgrazi'ato *a* ungainly
sgreto'lar|e *vt*, **~si** *vr* crumble
sgri'da|re *vt* scold. **~ta** *nf* scolding
sgros'sare *vt* rough-hew *(marmo)*; *fig* polish
sguai'ato *a* coarse
sgual'cire *vt* crumple
sgual'drina *nf* slut
sgu'ardo *nm* look; *(breve)* glance
'sguattero, -a *nmf* skivvy
sguaz'zare *vi* splash; *(nel fango)* wallow
sguinzagli'are *vt* unleash
sgusci'are *vt* shell ● *vi (sfuggire)* slip away; ~ **fuori** slip out
shake'rare *vt* shake
si *pers pron (riflessivo)* oneself; *(lui)*

himself; (*lei*) herself; (*esso, essa*) itself; (*loro*) themselves; (*reciproco*) each other; (*tra più di due*) one another; (*impersonale*) you, one; **lavarsi** wash [oneself]; **si è lavata** she washed [herself]; **lavarsi le mani** wash one's hands; **si è lavata le mani** she washed her hands; **si è mangiato un pollo intero** he ate an entire chicken by himself; **incontrarsi** meet each other; **la gente si aiuta a vicenda** people help one another; **non si sa mai** you never know, one never knows *fml*; **queste cose si dimenticano facilmente** these things are easily forgotten ● *nm* (*chiave, nota*) B

sì *adv* yes

'sia¹ *vedi* **essere**

'sia² *conj* ~...~... (*entrambi*) both...and...; (*o l'uno o l'altro*) either...or...~ **che venga**, ~ **che non venga** whether he comes or not; **scegli** ~ **questo** ~ **quello** choose either this one or that one; **voglio** ~ **questo che quello** I want both this one and that one

sia'mese *a* Siamese

sibi'lare *vi* hiss. **'sibilo** *nm* hiss

si'cario *nm* hired killer

sicché *conj* (*perciò*) so [that]; (*allora*) then

siccità *nf* drought

sic'come *conj* as

Si'cili|a *nf* Sicily. **s~'ano, -a** *a e nmf* Sicilian

si'cura *nf* safety catch; (*di portiera*) child-proof lock. ~'**mente** *adv* definitely

sicu'rezza *nf* (*certezza*) certainty; (*salvezza*) safety; **uscita di** ~ emergency exit

si'curo *a* (*non pericoloso*) safe; (*certo*) sure; (*saldo*) steady; *Comm* sound ● *adv* certainly ● *nm* safety; **al** ~ safe; **andare sul** ~ play [it] safe; **di** ~ definitely; **di** ~, **sarà arrivato** he must have arrived

siderur'gia *nf* iron and steel industry. **side'rurgico** *a* iron and steel *attrib*

'sidro *nm* cider

si'epe *nf* hedge

si'ero *nm* serum

sieroposi'tivo *a* HIV positive

si'esta *nf* afternoon nap, siesta

si'fone *nm* siphon

Sig. *abbr* (*signore*) Mr

Sig.a *abbr* (*signora*) Mrs, Ms

siga'retta *nf* cigarette; **pantaloni a** ~ drainpipes

'sigaro *nm* cigar

Sigg. *abbr* (*signori*) Messrs

sigil'lare *vt* seal. **si'gillo** *nm* seal

'sigla *nf* initials *pl.* ~ **musicale** signature tune. **si'glare** *vt* initial

Sig.na *abbr* (*signorina*) Miss, Ms

signifi'ca|re *vt* mean. ~'**tivo** *a* significant. ~**to** *nm* meaning

si'gnora *nf* lady; (*davanti a nome proprio*) Mrs; (*non sposata*) Miss; (*in lettere ufficiali*) Dear Madam; **il signor Venè e** ~ Mr and Mrs Venè

si'gnore *nm* gentleman; *Relig* lord; (*davanti a nome proprio*) Mr; (*in lettere ufficiali*) Dear Sir. **signo'rile** *a* gentlemanly; (*di lusso*) luxury

signo'rina *nf* young lady; (*seguito da nome proprio*) Miss

silenzia'tore *nm* silencer

si'lenzi|o *nm* silence. ~'**oso** *a* silent

silhou'ette *nf* silhouette, outline

si'licio *nm* **piastrina di** ~ silicon chip

sili'cone *nm* silicone

'sillaba *nf* syllable

silu'rare *vt* torpedo. **si'luro** *nm* torpedo

simboleggi'are *vt* symbolize

sim'bolico *a* symbolic[al]

'simbolo *nm* symbol

similarità *nf inv* similarity

'simil|e *a* similar; (*tale*) such; ~**e** *a* ● *nm* (*il prossimo*) fellow man. ~'**mente** *adv* similarly. ~'**pelle** *nf* Leatherette®

simme'tria *nf* symmetry. **sim'metrico** *a* symmetric[al]

simpa'ti|a _nf_ liking; (_compenetrazione_) sympathy; **prendere qcno in** ~**a** take a liking to sb. **sim'patico** _a_ nice. **~iz'zante** _a_ well-wisher. **~iz'zare** _vt_ **~izzare con** take a liking to; **~izzare per** qcsa/qcno lean towards sth/sb

sim'posio _nm_ symposium

simu'la|re _vt_ simulate; feign (_amicizia, interesse_). **~zi'one** _nf_ simulation

simul'tane|a _nf_ in ~**a** simultaneously. **~o** _a_ simultaneous

sina'goga _nf_ synagogue

sincerità _nf_ sincerity. **sin'cero** _a_ sincere

'**sincope** _nf_ syncopation; _Med_ fainting fit

sincron'ia _nf_ synchronization; **in** ~ with synchronized timing

sincroniz'za|re _vt_ synchronize. **~zi'one** _nf_ synchronization

sinda'ca|le _a_ [trade] union, [labor] union _Am_. **~lista** _nmf_ trade unionist; labor union member _Am_. **~re** _vt_ inspect. **~to** _nm_ [trade] union, [labor] union _Am_; (_associazione_) syndicate

'**sindaco** _nm_ mayor

'**sindrome** _nf_ syndrome

sinfo'nia _nf_ symphony. **sin'fonico** _a_ symphonic

singhioz'za|re _vi_ (_di pianto_) sob. **~'ozzo** _nm_ hiccup; (_di pianto_) sob; **avere il ~ozzo** have the hiccups

singo'lar|e _a_ singular ● _nm_ singular. **~'mente** _adv_ individually; (_stranamente_) peculiarly

'**singolo** _a_ single ● _nm_ individual; _Tennis_ singles _pl_

si'nistra _nf_ left; **a** ~ on the left; **girare a** ~ turn to the left; **con la guida a** ~ (_auto_) with left-hand drive

sini'strato _a_ injured

si'nistr|o, -a _a_ left[-hand]; (_avverso_) sinister ● _nm_ accident ● _nf_ left [hand]; _Pol_ left ● _nf_ wing

'**sino** _prep_ = **fino** '

si'nonimo _a_ synonymous ● _nm_ synonym

sin'ta|ssi _nf_ syntax. **~ttico** _a_ syntactic[al]

'**sintesi** _nf_ synthesis; (_riassunto_) summary

sin'teti|co _a_ synthetic; (_conciso_) summary. **~z'zare** _vt_ summarize

sintetizza'tore _nm_ synthesizer

sinto'matico _a_ symptomatic.

'**sintomo** _nm_ symptom

sinto'nia _nf_ tuning; **in** ~ on the same wavelength

sinu'oso _a_ (_strada_) winding

sinu'site _nf_ sinusitis

si'pario _nm_ curtain

si'rena _nf_ siren

'**Siri|a** _nf_ Syria. **s~'ano, -a** _a_ & _nmf_ Syrian

si'ringa _nf_ syringe

'**sismico** _a_ seismic

si'stem|a _nm_ system. **S~a Monetario Europeo** European Monetary System. **~a operativo** _Comput_ operating system

siste'ma|re _vt_ (_mettere_) put; tidy up (_casa, camera_); (_risolvere_) sort out; (_procurare lavoro a_) fix up with a job; (_trovare alloggio a_) find accommodation for; (_sposare_) marry off; (_fam: punire_) sort out. **~rsi** _vr_ settle down; (_trovare un lavoro_) find a job; (_trovare alloggio_) find accommodation; (_sposarsi_) marry. **~tico** _a_ systematic. **~zi'one** _nf_ arrangement; (_di questione_) settlement; (_lavoro_) job; (_alloggio_) accommodation; (_matrimonio_) marriage

'**sito** _nm_ site. ~ **web** _Comput_ web site

situ'are _vt_ place

situazi'one _nf_ situation

ski-'lift _nm_ ski tow

slacci'are _vt_ unfasten

slanci'a|rsi _vr_ hurl oneself. **~to** _a_ slender. '**slancio** _nm_ impetus; (_impulso_) impulse

sla'vato _a_ (_carnagione, capelli_) fair

'**slavo** _a_ Slav[onic]

sle'al|e _a_ disloyal. **~tà** _nf_ disloyalty

sle'gare _vt_ untie

'**slitta** _nf_ sledge, sleigh. **~'mento**

nm (*di macchina*) skid; (*fig: di riunione*) postponement
slit'ta|re *vi* Auto skid; (*riunione:*) be put off. **~ta** *nf* skid
slit'tino *nm* toboggan
'slogan *nm inv* slogan
slo'ga|re *vt* dislocate. **~rsi** *vr* **~rsi una caviglia** sprain one's ankle. **~'tura** *nf* dislocation
sloggi'are *vt* dislodge ● *vi* move out
Slo'vacchia *nf* Slovakia
Slo'venia *nf* Slovenia
smacchi'a|re *vt* clean. **~'tore** *nm* stain remover
'smacco *nm* humiliating defeat
smagli'ante *a* dazzling
smagli'a|rsi *vr* (*calza:*) ladder *Br*, run. **~'tura** *nf* ladder *Br*, run
smalizi'ato *a* cunning
smal'ta|re *vt* enamel; glaze (*ceramica*); varnish (*unghie*). **~to** *a* enamelled
smalti'mento *nm* disposal; (*di merce*) selling off. **~ rifiuti** waste disposal; (*di grassi*) burning off
smal'tire *vt* burn off; (*merce*) sell off; *fig* get through (*corrispondenza*); **~ la sbornia** sober up
'smalto *nm* enamel; (*di ceramica*) glaze; (*per le unghie*) nail varnish
'smani|a *nf* fidgets *pl*; (*desiderio*) longing. **~'are** *vi* have the fidgets; **~are per** long for. **~'oso** *a* restless
smantel|la'mento *nm* dismantling. **~'lare** *vt* dismantle
smarri'mento *nm* loss; (*psicologico*) bewilderment
smar'ri|re *vt* lose; (*temporaneamente*) mislay. **~rsi** *vr* get lost; (*turbarsi*) be bewildered
smasche'rar|e *vt* unmask. **~si** *vr* (*tradirsi*) give oneself away
SME *nm abbr* (**Sistema Monetario Europeo**) EMS
smemo'rato, -a *a* forgetful ● *nmf* scatterbrain
smen'ti|re *vt* deny. **~ta** *nf* denial
sme'raldo *nm* & *a* emerald

smerci'are *vt* sell off
smerigli'a|to *a* emery; **vetro ~** frosted glass. **sme'riglio** *nm* emery
'smesso *pp di* smettere ● *a* (*abiti*) cast-off
smett|ere *vt* stop; stop wearing (*abiti*); **~ila!** stop it!
smidol'lato *a* spineless
sminu'i|re *vt* diminish. **~si** *vr fig* belittle oneself
sminuz'zare *vt* crumble; (*fig: analizzare*) analyse in detail
smista'mento *nm* clearing; (*postale*) sorting. **smi'stare** *vt* sort; Mil post
smisu'rato *a* boundless; (*esorbitante*) excessive
smobili'ta|re *vt* demobilize. **~zi'one** *nf* demobilization
smo'dato *a* immoderate
smog *nm* smog
'smoking *nm inv* dinner jacket, tuxedo *Am*
smon'tabile *a* jointed
smon'tar|e *vt* take to pieces; (*scoraggiare*) dishearten ● *vi* (*da veicolo*) get off; (*da cavallo*) dismount; (*dal servizio*) go off duty. **~si** *vr* lose heart
smorfi|a *nf* grimace; (*moina*) simper; **fare ~e** make faces. **~'oso** *a* affected
smorto *a* pale; (*colore*) dull
smor'zare *vt* dim (*luce*); tone down (*colori*); deaden (*suoni*); quench (*sete*)
smosso *pp di* smuovere
smotta'mento *nm* landslide
smunto *a* emaciated
smu'over|e *vt* shift; (*commuovere*) move. **~si** *vr* move; (*commuoversi*) be moved
smus'sar|e *vt* round off; (*fig: attenuare*) tone down. **~si** *vr* go blunt
snatu'rato *a* inhuman
snel'li|re *vt* slim down. **~si** *vr* slim [down]. **'snello** *a* slim
sner'vante *a* enervating
sner'va|re *vt* enervate. **~rsi** *vr* get exhausted

sni'dare vt drive out

snif'fare vt snort

snob'bare vt snub. **sno'bismo** nm snobbery

snoccio'lare vt stone; fig blurt out

sno'da|re vt untie; (sciogliere) loosen. **~rsi** vr come untied; ⟨strada:⟩ wind. **~to** a ⟨persona⟩ double-jointed; ⟨dita⟩ flexible

so'ave a gentle

sobbal'zare vi jerk; (trasalire) start. **sob'balzo** nm jerk; (trasalimento) start

sobbar'carsi vr ~ **a** undertake

sobbor'go nm suburb

sobil'la|re vt stir up

'sobrio a sober

soc'chiu|dere vt half-close. **~so** pp di **socchiudere** ● a ⟨occhi⟩ half-closed; ⟨porta⟩ ajar

soc'combere vi succumb

soc'cor|rere vt assist. **~so** pp di **soccorrere** ● nm assistance; **soccorsi** pl rescuers; (dopo disastro) relief workers. **~so stradale** breakdown service

socialdemo'cra|tico, -a a Social Democratic ● nmf Social Democrat. **~'zia** nf Social Democracy

soci'ale a social

socia'li|smo nm Socialism. **~sta** a & nmf Socialist. **~z'zare** vi socialize

società nf inv society; Comm company. **~ per azioni** plc. **~ a responsabilità limitata** limited liability company

soci'evole a sociable

'socio, -a nmf member; Comm partner

sociolo'gia nf sociology. **socio-'logico** a sociological

'soda nf soda

soddisfa'cente a satisfactory

soddi'sfa|re vt/i satisfy; meet ⟨richiesta⟩; make amends for ⟨offesa⟩. **~tto** pp di **soddisfare** ● a satisfied. **~zi'one** nf satisfaction

'sodo a hard; fig firm; ⟨uovo⟩ hard-boiled ● adv hard; **dormire ~**

sleep soundly ● nm **venire al ~** get to the point

sofà nm inv sofa

soffe'ren|te a ⟨malato⟩ ill. **~za** nf suffering

soffer'mar|si vr pause; **~ su** dwell on

sof'ferto pp di **soffrire**

soffi'a|re vt blow; reveal ⟨segreto⟩; (rubare) pinch fam ● vi blow. **~ta** nf fig sl tip-off

'soffice a soft

'soffio nm puff; Med murmur

sof'fitt|a nf attic. **~o** nm ceiling

soffoca'mento nm suffocation

soffo'ca|nte a suffocating. **~re** vt/i suffocate; (con cibo) choke; fig stifle

sof'friggere vt fry lightly

sof'frire vt/i suffer; (sopportare) bear; **~ di** suffer from

sof'fritto pp di **soffriggere**

sof'fuso a ⟨luce⟩ soft

sofisti'ca|re vt ⟨adulterare⟩ adulterate ● vi (sottilizzare) quibble. **~to** a sophisticated

sogget'tiva'mente adv subjectively. **~'tivo** a subjective

sog'getto nm subject ● a subject; **essere ~ a** be subject to

soggezi'one nf subjection; (rispetto) awe

sogghi'gnare vi sneer. **sog'ghigno** nm sneer

soggio'gare vt subdue

soggior'nare vi stay. **soggi'orno** nm stay; (stanza) living room

soggi'ungere vt add

'soglia nf threshold

'sogliola nf sole

so'gna|re vt/i dream; **~re a occhi aperti** daydream. **~'tore, ~'trice** nmf dreamer. **'sogno** nm dream; **fare un sogno** have a dream; **neanche per sogno!** not at all!

'soia nf soya

sol nm Mus ⟨chiave, nota⟩ G

so'laio nm attic

sola'mente adv only

so'lar|e a ⟨energia, raggi⟩ solar;

⟨crema⟩ sun attrib. **~ium** nm inv solarium

sol'care vt plough. **'solco** nm furrow; ⟨di ruota⟩ track; ⟨di nave⟩ wake; ⟨di disco⟩ groove

sol'dato nm soldier

'soldo nm **non ha un ~ he** hasn't got a penny to his name; **senza un ~** penniless; **soldi** pl ⟨denaro⟩ money sg

'sole nm sun; ⟨luce del sole⟩ sun[light]; **al ~** in the sun; **prendere il ~** sunbathe

soleggi'ato a sunny

so'lenn|e a solemn. **~ità** nf solemnity

so'lere vi be in the habit of; **come si suol dire** as they say

sol'fato nm sulphate

soli'da|le a in agreement. **~rietà** nf solidarity

solidifi'car|e vt/i, **~si** vr solidify

solidità nf solidity; ⟨di colori⟩ fastness. **'solido** a solid; ⟨robusto⟩ sturdy; ⟨colore⟩ fast ● nm solid

soli'loquio nm soliloquy

so'lista a solo ● nmf soloist

solita'mente adv usually

soli'tario a solitary; ⟨isolato⟩ lonely ● nm ⟨brillante⟩ solitaire; ⟨gioco di carte⟩ patience, solitaire

'solito a usual; **essere ~ fare qcsa** be in the habit of doing sth ● nm usual; **di ~** usually

soli'tudine nf solitude

solleci'ta|re vt speed up; urge ⟨persona⟩. **~zi'one** nf ⟨richiesta⟩ request; ⟨preghiera⟩ entreaty

sol'leci|to a prompt ● nm reminder. **~'tudine** nf promptness; ⟨interessamento⟩ concern

solle'one nm noonday sun; ⟨periodo⟩ dog days of summer

solleti'care vt tickle. **sol'letico** nm tickling; **fare il solletico a qcno** tickle sb; **soffrire il solletico** be ticklish

solleva'mento nm **~ pesi** weightlifting

solle'var|e vt lift; ⟨elevare⟩ raise;

⟨confortare⟩ comfort. **~si** vr rise; ⟨riaversi⟩ recover

solli'evo nm relief

'solo, -a a alone; ⟨isolato⟩ lonely; ⟨unico⟩ only; Mus solo; **da ~** by myself/yourself/himself etc ● nmf **il ~, la sola** the only one ● nm Mus solo ● adv only

sol'stizio nm solstice

sol'tanto adv only

so'lubile a soluble; ⟨caffè⟩ instant

soluzi'one nf solution; Comm payment

sol'vente a & nm solvent; **~ per unghie** nail polish remover

'soma nf **bestia da ~** beast of burden

so'maro nm ass; Sch dunce

so'matico a somatic

somigli'an|te a similar. **~za** nf resemblance

somigli'ar|e vi **~e** a resemble. **~si** vr be alike

'somma nf sum; Math addition

som'mare vt add; ⟨totalizzare⟩ add up

som'mario a & nm summary

som'mato a **tutto ~** all things considered

sommeli'er nm inv wine waiter

som'mer|gere vt submerge. **~'gibile** nm submarine. **~so** pp di sommergere

som'messo a soft

sommini'stra|re vt administer. **~zi'one** nf administration

sommità nf inv summit

'sommo a highest; fig supreme ● nm summit

som'mossa nf rising

sommozza'tore nm frogman

so'naglio nm bell

so'nata nf sonata; fig fam beating

'sonda nf Mech drill; ⟨spaziale, Med⟩ probe. **son'daggio** nm drilling; ⟨spaziale, Med⟩ probe; ⟨indagine⟩ survey. **sondaggio d'opinioni** opinion poll. **son'dare** vt sound; ⟨investigare⟩ probe

so'netto nm sonnet

sonnambu'lismo nm sleepwalking. **son'nambulo, -a** *nmf* sleep-walker

sonnecchi'are *vi* doze

son'nifero *nm* sleeping-pill

'**sonno** *nm* sleep; **aver** ~ be sleepy. ~**lenza** *nf* sleepiness

so'noro *a* resonant; (*rumoroso*) loud; (*onde, scheda*) sound *attrib*

sontu'oso *a* sumptuous

sopo'rifero *a* soporific

sop'palco *nm* platform

soppe'rire *vi* ~ **a qcsa** provide for sth

soppe'sare *vt* weigh up (*situazione*)

soppi'atto: di ~ *adv* furtively

soppor'ta|re *vt* support; (*tollerare*) stand; bear (*dolore*)

soppressi'one *nf* removal; (*di legge*) abolition; (*di diritti, pubblicazione*) suppression; (*annullamento*) cancellation. **sop'presso** *pp di* **sopprimere**

sop'primere *vt* get rid of; abolish (*legge*); suppress (*diritti, pubblicazione*); (*annullare*) cancel

'**sopra** *adv* on top; (*più in alto*) higher [up]; (*al piano superiore*) upstairs; (*in testo*) above; **mettilo lì** ~ put it up there; **di** ~ upstairs; **dormirci** ~ *fig* sleep on it; **pensarci** ~ think about it; **vedi** ~ see above ● *prep* ~ [**a**] on; (*senza contatto, oltre*) over; (*riguardo a*) about; **è** ~ **al tavolo,** è ~ **il tavolo** it's on the table; **il quadro è appeso** ~ **al camino** the picture is hanging over the fireplace; **il ponte passa** ~ **all'autostrada** the bridge crosses over the motorway; **è caduto** ~ **il tetto** it fell on the roof; **l'uno** ~ **l'altro** one on top of the other; (*senza contatto*) one above the other; **abita** ~ **di me** he lives upstairs from me; **i bambini** ~ **i dieci anni** (children over ten; **20°** ~ **lo zero** 20° above zero; ~ **il livello del mare** above sea level; **rifletti** ~ **quello che è successo** think about what happened; **non ha nessuno** ~ **di sé** he has no-

body above him; **al di** ~ **di** over ● *nm* **il [di]** ~ the top

so'prabito *nm* overcoat

soprac'ciglio *nm* (*pl* pl **sopracciglia**) eyebrow

sopracco'per|ta *nf* (*di letto*) bedspread; (*di libro*) [dust-]jacket. ~**tina** *nf* book jacket

soprad'detto *a* above-mentioned

sopraele'vata *nf* elevated railway

sopraf'fa|re *vt* overwhelm. ~**tto** *pp di* **sopraffare**. ~**zi'one** *nf* abuse of power

sopraf'fino *a* excellent; (*gusto, udito*) highly refined

soprag'giungere *vi* (*accadere*) turn up; (*persona:*) happen

soprallu'ogo *nm* inspection

sopram'mobile *nm* ornament

soprannatu'rale *a & nm* supernatural

sopran'nom|e *nm* nickname. ~**i'nare** *vt* nickname

so'prano *nmf* soprano

soprappensi'ero *adv* lost in thought

sopras'salto *nm* **di** ~ with a start

soprasse'dere *vi* ~ **a** postpone

soprat'tutto *adv* above all

sopravvalu'tare *vt* overvalue

soprav've'nire *vi* turn up; (*accadere*) happen. ~**'vento** *nm fig* upper hand

sopravvis'suto *pp di* **sopravvivere**. ~**'venza** *nf* survival. **sopravvivere** *vi* survive; **sopravvivere a** outlive (*persona*)

soprinten'den|te *nmf* supervisor; (*di museo ecc*) keeper. ~**za** *nf* supervision; (*ente*) board

so'pruso *nm* abuse of power

soq'quadro *nm* **mettere a** ~ turn upside down

sor'betto *nm* sorbet

sor'bire *vt* sip; *fig* put up with

'sordido *a* sordid; (*avaro*) stingy

sor'dina *nf* mute; **in** ~ *fig* on the quiet

sordità *nf* deafness. '**sordo, -a** *a* deaf; (*rumore, dolore*) dull ● *nmf*

deaf person. **sordo'muto, -a** *a*
deaf-and-dumb ● *nmf* deaf mute
so'rel|la *nf* sister. **~'lastra** *nf* step-
sister
sor'gente *nf* spring; ⟨*fonte*⟩ source
'**sorgere** *vi* rise; *fig* arise
sormon'tare *vt* surmount
sorni'one *a* sly
sorpas'sa|re *vt* surpass; ⟨*eccedere*⟩
exceed; overtake, pass *Am* ⟨*veicolo*⟩. **~to** *a* old-fashioned. **sor'passo** *nm* overtaking, passing *Am*
sorpren'dente *a* surprising;
⟨*straordinario*⟩ remarkable
sor'prendere *vt* surprise; ⟨*cogliere
in flagrante*⟩ catch
sor'pres|a *nf* surprise; **di ~ a** by
surprise. **~o** *pp di* **sorprendere**
sor're|ggere *vt* support; ⟨*tenere*⟩
hold up. **~ggersi** *vr* support oneself. **~tto** *pp di* **sorreggere**
sorri'dente *a* smiling
sor'ri|dere *vi* smile. **~so** *pp di*
sorridere ● *nm* smile
sorseggi'are *vt* sip. '**sorso** *nm* sip;
⟨*piccola quantità*⟩ drop
'**sorta** *nf* sort; **di ~** whatever; **ogni
~ di** all sorts of
'**sorte** *nf* fate; ⟨*caso imprevisto*⟩
chance; **tirare a ~** draw lots.
~ggi'are *vt* draw lots for.
sor'teggio *nm* draw
sorti'legio *nm* witchcraft
sor'ti|re *vi* come out. **~ta** *nf Mil*
sortie; ⟨*battuta*⟩ witticism
'**sorto** *pp di* **sorgere**
sorvegli'an|te *nmf* keeper; ⟨*con-
trollore*⟩ overseer. **~za** *nf* watch;
Mil ecc surveillance
sorvegli'are *vt* watch over;
⟨*controllare*⟩ oversee; ⟨*polizia:*⟩
watch, keep under surveillance
sorvo'lare *vt* fly over; *fig* skip
'**sosia** *nm inv* double
so'spen|dere *vt* hang; ⟨*interrom-
pere*⟩ stop; ⟨*privare di una carica*⟩
suspend. **~si'one** *nf* suspension
so'speso *pp di* **sospendere** ● *a*
⟨*impiegato, alunno*⟩ suspended; **~
a** hanging from; **~ a un filo** *fig*

hanging by a thread ● *nm* **in ~**
pending; ⟨*emozionato*⟩ in suspense
sospet'tare *vt* suspect. **so'spetto**
a suspicious; **persona sospet-
ta** suspicious person ● *nm* suspicion; ⟨*persona*⟩ suspect. **~'toso** *a*
suspicious
so'spin|gere *vt* drive. **~to** *pp di*
sospingere
sospi'rare *vi* sigh ● *vt* long for.
so'spiro *nm* sigh
'**sosta** *nf* stop; ⟨*pausa*⟩ pause; **senza ~** non-stop; **"divieto di ~"** "no
parking"
sostan'tivo *nm* noun
so'stanz|a *nf* substance; **~e** *pl*
⟨*patrimonio*⟩ property *sg*; **in ~a** to
sum up. **~'l'oso** *a* substantial;
~l'oso *a* ⟨*cibo*⟩ nourishing
so'stare *vi* stop; ⟨*fare una pausa*⟩
pause
so'stegno *nm* support
soste'ne|re *vt* support; ⟨*sopporta-
re*⟩ bear; ⟨*resistere*⟩ withstand;
⟨*affermare*⟩ maintain; ⟨*nutrire*⟩
sustain; sit ⟨*esame*⟩; **~e le spese**
meet the costs. **~si** *vr* support
oneself
sosteni'tore, -'trice *nmf* supporter
sostenta'mento *nm* maintenance
soste'nuto *a* ⟨*stile*⟩ formal; ⟨*prezzi, velocità*⟩ high
sostitu'ir|e *vt* substitute (a for),
replace (con with). **~si** *vr* **~si a**
replace
sosti'tu|to, -a *nmf* replacement,
stand-in ● *nm* ⟨*surrogato*⟩ substitute. **~zi'one** *nf* substitution
sotta'ceto *a* pickled; **sottaceti** *pl*
pickles
sot'tana *nf* petticoat; ⟨*di prete*⟩ cas-
sock
sotter'fugio *nm* subterfuge; **di ~**
secretly
sotter'raneo *a* underground ● *nm*
cellar
sotter'rare *vt* bury
sottigli'ezza *nf* slimness; *fig*
subtlety
sot'til|e *a* thin; ⟨*udito, odorato*⟩

keen; ⟨*osservazione, distinzione*⟩
subtle. **~iz'zare** *vi* split hairs
sottin'tendere *vt* imply. **~so** *pp
di* **sottintendere** ● *nm* allusion;
senza ~si openly ● *a* implied
'sotto *adv* below; ⟨*più in basso*⟩
lower [down]; ⟨*al di sotto*⟩ underneath; ⟨*al piano di sotto*⟩ downstairs; **è lì ~** it's underneath; **~ ~**
deep down; ⟨*di nascosto*⟩ on the
quiet; **di ~** downstairs; **mettersi
~** *fig* get down to it; **mettere ~**
⟨*fam: investire*⟩ knock down; **fatti
~!** *fam* get stuck in! ● *prep* **~**
[a] under; ⟨*al di sotto di*⟩
under[neath]; **abita ~ di me** he
lives downstairs from me; **i
bambini ~ i dieci anni** children
under ten; **20° ~ zero** 20° below
zero; **~ il livello del mare** below
sea level; **la pioggia** in the rain;
~ Elisabetta I under Elizabeth I;
~ calmante under sedation; **~**
condizione che... on condition
that...; **~ giuramento** under oath;
~ sorveglianza under surveillance; **~ Natale/gli esami** around
Christmas/exam time; **al di ~ di**
under; **andare ~ i 50 all'ora** do
less than 50km an hour ● *nm* **il
[di] ~** the bottom
sotto'banco *adv* under the counter
sottobicchi'ere *nm* coaster
sotto'bosco *nm* undergrowth
sotto'braccio *adv* arm in arm
sotto'fondo *nm* background
sottoline'are *vt* underline; *fig*
stress
sot'tolio *adv* in oil
sotto'mano *adv* within reach
sottoma'rino *a & nm* submarine
sotto'messo *pp di* **sottomettere**
● *a* ⟨*remissivo*⟩ submissive
sotto'mettere *vt* submit; subdue
⟨*popolo*⟩. **~si** *vr* submit. **sotto-
missi'one** *nf* submission
sottopa'gare *vt* underpay
sottopas'saggio *nm* underpass;
⟨*pedonale*⟩ subway
sotto'porre *vt* submit; ⟨*costringe-*

re⟩ subject. **~si** *vr* submit oneself;
~si a undergo. **sotto'posto** *pp di*
sottoporre
sotto'scala *nm* cupboard under
the stairs
sotto'scritto *pp di* **sottoscrivere**
● *nm* undersigned
sotto'scrivere *vt* sign; ⟨*approvare*⟩ sanction, subscribe to. **~zi'one**
nf ⟨*petizione*⟩ petition; ⟨*approvazione*⟩ sanction; ⟨*raccolta di denaro*⟩ appeal
sottosegre'tario *nm* undersecre-
tary
sotto'sopra *adv* upside down
sotto'stante *a* ⟨*la strada*⟩ **~** the
road below
sottosu'olo *nm* subsoil
sottosvi'luppato *a* underdevel-
oped. **~'luppo** *nm* underdevelop-
ment
sotto'terra *adv* underground
sotto'titolo *nm* subtitle
sottovalu'tare *vt* underestimate
sotto'veste *nf* slip
sotto'voce *adv* in a low voice
sottovu'oto *a* vacuum-packed
sot'trarre *vt* remove; embezzle
⟨*fondi*⟩; *Math* subtract. **~rsi** *vr*
~rsi a escape from; avoid ⟨*responsabilità*⟩. **~tto** *pp di* **sottrarre**.
~zi'one *nf* removal; ⟨*di fondi*⟩ embezzlement; *Math* subtraction
sottuffici'ale *nm* non-commis-
sioned officer; *Naut* petty officer
sou'brette *nf inv* showgirl
so'vietico, **-a** *a & nmf* Soviet
sovraccari'care *vt* overload. **so-
vrac'carico** *a* overloaded (**di** with)
● *nm* overload
sovraffati'carsi *vr* overexert oneself
sovrannatu'rale *a & nm =* **soprannaturale**
so'vrano, **-a** *a* sovereign; *fig* supreme ● *nmf* sovereign
sovrap'porre *vt* superimpose.
~si *vr* overlap. **sovrapposizi'one**
nf superimposition
sovra'stare *vt* dominate; ⟨*fig: pericolo:*⟩ hang over

sovrinten'den|te, ~za = soprin-
tendente, soprintendenza

sovru'mano *a* superhuman

sovvenzi'one *nf* subsidy

sovver'sivo *a* subversive

'sozzo *a* filthy

S.p.A. *abbr* (**società per azioni**)
plc

spac'ca|re *vt* split; chop (*legna*).
~rsi *vr* split. ~'tura *nf* split

spacci'a|re *vt* deal in, push
(*droga*); ~re qcsa per qcsa pass
sth off as sth; essere ~to be done
for, be a goner. ~rsi *vr* ~rsi per
pass oneself off as. ~'tore, ~'trice
nmf (*di droga*) pusher; (*di denaro
falso*) distributor of forged bank
notes. 'spaccio *nm* (*di droga*)
dealer, pusher; (*negozio*) shop

'spacco *nm* split

spac'cone, -a *nmf* boaster

'spada *nf* sword. ~c'cino *nm*
swordsman

spadroneggi'are *vi* act the boss

spae'sato *a* disorientated

spa'ghetti *nmpl* spaghetti *sg*

spa'ghetto *nm* (*fam: spavento*)
fright

'Spagna *nf* Spain

spa'gnolo, -a *a* Spanish ● *nmf*
Spaniard ● *nm* (*lingua*) Spanish

'spago *nm* string; dare ~ a qcno
encourage sb

spa'ato *a* odd

spalan'ca|re *vt*, ~rsi *vr* open
wide. ~to *a* wide open

spa'lare *vt* shovel

'spall|a *nf* shoulder; (*di comico*)
straight man; ~e *pl* (*schiena*)
back; alle ~e di qcno (*ridere*) behind sb's back. ~eggi'are *vt* back
up

spal'letta *nf* parapet

spalli'era *nf* back; (*di letto*) head-
board; (*ginnastica*) wall bars *pl*

spal'lina *nf* strap; (*imbottitura*)
shoulder pad

spal'mare *vt* spread

'spander|e *vt* spread; (*versare*)
spill. ~si *vr* spread

spappo'lare *vt* crush

spa'ra|re *vt/i* shoot; ~rle grosse
talk big. ~ta *nf fam* tall story.
~'toria *nf* shooting

sparec'chiare *vt* clear

spa'reggio *nm* Comm deficit;
Sport play-off

'sparg|ere *vt* scatter; (*diffondere*)
spread; shed (*lacrime, sangue*).
~ersi *vr* spread. ~'imento *nm*
scattering; (*di lacrime, sangue*)
shedding; ~imento di sangue
bloodshed

spa'ri|re *vi* disappear; ~scil get
lost!. ~zi'one *nf* disappearance

spar'lare *vi* ~ di run down

'sparo *nm* shot

sparpagli'ar|e *vt*, ~si *vr* scatter

'sparso *pp di* spargere ● *a* scat-
tered; (*sciolto*) loose

spar'tire *vt* share out; (*separare*)
separate

sparti'traffico *nm inv* traffic island; (*di autostrada*) central reservation, median strip *Am*

spartizi'one *nf* division

spa'ruto *a* gaunt; (*gruppo*) small;
(*peli, capelli*) sparse

sparvi'ero *nm* sparrow-hawk

spasi'ma|nte *nm hum* admirer.
~re *vi* suffer agonies

'spasimo *nm* spasm

spa'smodico *a* spasmodic

spas'sar|si *vr* amuse oneself;
~sela have a good time

spassio'nato *a* (*osservatore*) dispassionate, impartial

'spasso *nm* fun; essere uno ~ be
hilarious; andare a ~ go for a
walk. spas'soso *a* hilarious

'spatola *nf* spatula

spau'racchio *nm* scarecrow; *fig*
bugbear. spau'rire *vt* frighten

spa'valdo *a* defiant

spaventa'passeri *nm inv* scarecrow

spaven'tar|e *vt* frighten, scare.
~si *vr* be frightened, be scared.
spa'vento *nm* fright. spaven'toso
a frightening; (*fam: enorme*) incredible

spazi'ale *a* spatial; *(cosmico)* space *attrib*

spazi'are *vt* space out ● *vi* range

spazien'tirsi *vr* lose [one's] patience

'spazi|o *nm* space. **~'oso** *a* spacious

spazzaca'mino *nm* chimney sweep

spaz'z|are *vt* sweep; **~are via** sweep away; *(fam: mangiare)* devour. **~a'tura** *nf (immondizia)* rubbish. **~ino** *nm* road sweeper; *(netturbino)* dustman

'spazzo|la *nf* brush; *(di tergicristallo)* blade. **~'lare** *vt* brush. **~'lino** *nm* small brush. **~lino da denti** toothbrush. **~'lone** *nm* scrubbing brush

specchi'arsi *vr* look at oneself in a/the mirror; *(riflettersi)* be mirrored; **~ in qcno** model oneself on sb

specchi'etto *nm* **~ retrovisore** driving mirror

'specchio *nm* mirror

speci'a|le *a* special ● *nm* TV special [programme]. **~'lista** *nmf* specialist. **~lità** *nf inv* speciality, specialty *Am*

specializ'za|re *vt*, **~rsi** *vr* specialize. **~to** *a (operaio)* skilled

special'mente *adv* especially

'specie *nf inv (scientifico)* species; *(tipo)* kind; **fare ~ a** surprise

specifi'care *vt* specify. **spe'cifico** *a* specific

specu'lare[1] *vi* speculate; **~ su** *(indagare)* speculate on; *Fin* speculate in

specu'lare[2] *a* mirror *attrib*

specula'tore, -'trice *nmf* speculator. **~zi'one** *nf* speculation

spe'di|re *vt* send. **~to** *pp di* spedire ● *a* quick; *(parlata)* fluent. **~zi'one** *nf (di lettere ecc)* dispatch; *Comm* consignment; *(scientifica)* expedition

'spegner|e *vt* put out; turn off *(gas, luce)*; switch off *(motore)*;

slake *(sete)*. **~si** *vr* go out; *(morire)* pass away

spelacchi'ato *a (tappeto)* threadbare; *(cane)* mangy

spe'lar|e *vt* skin *(coniglio)*. **~si** *vr (cane)* moult

speleolo'gia *nf* potholing, speleology

spel'lar|e *vt* skin; *fig* fleece. **~si** *vr* peel off

spe'lonca *nf* cave; *fig* dingy hole

spendacci'one, -a *nmf* spendthrift

'spendere *vt* spend; **~ fiato** waste one's breath

spen'nare *vt* pluck; *fam* fleece *(cliente)*

spennel'lare *vt* brush

spensie'ra'tezza *nf* lightheartedness. **~'rato** *a* carefree

'spento *pp di* spegnere ● *a* off; *(gas)* out; *(smorto)* dull

spe'ranza *nf* hope; **pieno di ~** hopeful; **senza ~** hopeless

spe'rare *vt* hope for; *(aspettarsi)* expect ● *vi* **~ in** trust in; **spero di si** I hope so

'sper|dersi *vr* get lost. **~'duto** *a* lost; *(isolato)* secluded

spergi'uro, -a *nmf* perjurer ● *nm* perjury

speri'co'lato *a* swashbuckling

sperimen'ta|le *a* experimental. **~re** *vt* experiment with; test *(resistenza, capacità, teoria)*. **~zi'one** *nf* experimentation

'sperma *nm* sperm

spe'rone *nm* spur

sperpe'rare *vt* squander. **'sperpe'ro** *nm* waste

'spes|a *nf* expense; *(acquisto)* purchase; **andare a far ~e** go shopping; **fare la ~a** do the shopping; **fare le ~e di** pay for. **~e** *pl* bancarie bank charges. **~e a carico del destinatario** carriage forward. **~e di spedizione** shipping costs. **spesato** *a* all-expenses-paid. **~o** *pp di* spendere

'spesso[1] *a* thick

'spesso[2] *adv* often

spes'sore nm thickness; (fig: consistenza) substance

spet'tabile a (Comm abbr **Spett.**) **S~ ditta Rossi** Messrs Rossi

spettaco|'lare a spectacular. **spet'tacolo** nm spectacle; (rappresentazione) show. **~'loso** a spectacular

spet'tare vi ~ **a** be up to; (diritto:) be due to

spetta'tore, -'trice nmf spectator; **spettatori** pl (di cinema ecc) audience sg

spetteggo'lare vi gossip

spetti'nar|e vt ~**e qcno** ruffle sb's hair. **~si** vr ruffle one's hair

spet'trale a ghostly. **'spettro** nm ghost; Phys spectrum

'spezie nfpl spices

spez'zar|e vt, **~si** vr break

spezza'tino nm stew

spez'zato nm coordinated jacket and trousers

spezzet'tare vt break into small pieces

'spia nf spy; (della polizia) informer; (di porta) peep-hole; **fare la ~** sneak. **~ [luminosa]** light. **~ dell'olio oil** [warning] light

spiacci'care vt squash

spia'ce|nte a sorry. **~vole** a unpleasant

spi'aggia nf beach

spia'nare vt level; (rendere liscio) smooth; roll out (pasta); raze to the ground (edificio)

spi'ano nm **a tutto ~** flat out

spian'tato a fig penniless

spi'are vt spy on; wait for (occasione ecc)

spiattel'lare vt blurt out; shove (oggetto)

spiaz'zare vt wrong-foot

spi'azzo nm (radura) clearing

spic'ca|re vt ~**re un salto** jump; **~re il volo** take flight ● vi stand out. **~to** a marked

'spicchio nm (di agrumi) segment; (di aglio) clove

spicci'a|rsi vr hurry up. **~'tivo** a speedy

'spicciolo a (comune) banal; (denaro, 10 000 lire) in change. **spiccioli** pl change sg

'spicco nm relief; **fare ~** stand out

'spider nmf inv open-top sports car

spie'dino nm kebab. **spi'edo** nm spit; **allo spiedo** on a spit, spit-roasted

spie'ga|re vt explain; open out (cartina); unfurl (vele). **~rsi** vr explain oneself; (vele, bandiere:) unfurl. **~zi'one** nf explanation

spiegaz'zato a crumpled

spie'tato a ruthless

spiffe'rare vt blurt out ● vi (vento:) whistle. **'spiffero** nm (corrente d'aria) draught

'spiga nf spike; Bot ear

spigli'ato a self-possessed

'spigolo nm edge; (angolo) corner

'spilla nf (gioiello) brooch. **~ da balia** safety pin. **~ di sicurezza** safety pin

spil'lare vt tap

'spillo nm pin. **~ di sicurezza** safety pin; (in arma) safety catch

spil'lorcio a stingy

spilun'gone, -a nmf beanpole

'spina nf thorn; (di pesce) bone; Electr plug. **~ dorsale** spine

spi'naci nmpl spinach

spi'nale a spinal

spi'nato a (filo) barbed; (pianta) thorny

spi'nello nm fam joint

'spinger|e vt push; fig drive. **~si** vr (andare) proceed

spi'noso a thorny

'spint|a nf push; (violenta) thrust; fig spur. **~o** pp di **spingere**

spio'naggio nm espionage, spying

spio'vente a (tetto) sloping

spi'overe vi liter stop raining; (ricadere) fall; (scorrere) flow down

'spira nf coil

spi'raglio nm small opening; (soffio d'aria) breath of air; (raggio di luce) gleam of light

spi'rale a ~ nf spiral; (negli

orologi) hairspring; (anticoncezionale) coil

spi'rare vi (soffiare) blow; (morire) pass away

spiri'tato a possessed; (espressione) wild. **~ismo** nm spiritualism. **'spirito** nm spirit; (arguzia) wit; (intelletto) mind; **fare lo spirito** to be witty; **sotto spirito** in brandy. **~o'saggine** nf witticism. **spiri'toso** a witty

spiritu'ale a spiritual

splen'dente a shining

splen|dere vi shine. **~dido** a splendid. **~'dore** nm splendour

spode'stare vt dispossess; depose (re)

'spoglia nf (di animale) skin; **spoglie** pl (salma) mortal remains; (bottino) spoils

spogli|a're vt strip; (svestire) undress; (fare lo spoglio di) go through. **~'rello** nm strip-tease. **~rsi** vr strip, undress. **~'toio** nm dressing room; Sport changing room; (guardaroba) cloakroom, checkroom Am. **'spoglio** a undressed; (albero, muro) bare ● nm (scrutinio) perusal

'spola nf shuttle; **fare la ~** shuttle

spol'pare vt take the flesh off; fig fleece

spolve'rare vt dust; fam devour (cibo)

'sponda nf (di mare, lago) shore; (di fiume) bank; (bordo) edge

sponsoriz'zare vt sponsor

spon'taneo a spontaneous

spopo'lar|e vt depopulate ● vi (avere successo) draw the crowds. **~si** vr become depopulated

sporadica'mente adv sporadically. **spo'radico** a sporadic

sporcacci'one, -a nmf dirty pig

spor|c'are vt dirty; (macchiare) soil. **~arsi** vr get dirty. **~izia** nf dirt. **'sporco** a dirty; **avere la coscienza sporca** have a guilty conscience ● nm dirt

spor'gen|te a jutting. **~za** nf projection

'sporger|e vt stretch out; **~e querela contro** take legal action against ● vi jut out. **~si** vr lean out

sport nm inv sport

'sporta nf shopping basket

spor'tello nm door; (di banca ecc) window. **~ automatico** cash dispenser

spor'tivo, -a a sports attrib; (persona) sporty ● nm sportsman ● nf sportswoman

'sporto pp di sporgere

'sposa nf bride. **~'lizio** nm wedding

spo'sa|re vt marry; fig espouse. **~rsi** vr get married; (vino:) go (con with). **~to** a married. **'sposo** nm bridegroom; **sposi** pl [novelli] newlyweds

spos'satezza nf exhaustion. **spos'sato** a exhausted, worn out

spo'sta|re vt move; (cambiare) change. **~rsi** vr move. **~to, -a** ill-adjusted ● nmf (disadattato) misfit

'spranga nf bar. **spran'gare** vt bar

'sprazzo nm (di colore) splash; (di luce) flash; fig glimmer

spre'care vt waste. **'spreco** nm waste

spre'g|evole a despicable. **~ia'tivo** a pejorative. **'spregio** nm contempt

spregiudi'cato a unscrupulous

'spremer|e vt squeeze. **~si** vr **~si le meningi** rack one's brains

spremia'grumi nm lemon squeezer

spre'muta nf juice. **~ d'arancia** fresh orange [juice]

sprez'zante a contemptuous

sprigio'nar|e vt emit. **~si** vr burst out

spriz'zare vt/i spurt; be bursting with (salute, gioia)

sprofon'dar|e vi sink; (crollare) collapse. **~si** vr **~si in** sink into; fig be engrossed in

spro'nare vt spur on. **'sprone** nm spur; (sartoria) yoke

sproporzio|'nato *a* disproportion-ate. **~'one** *nf* disproportion

sproposi'tato *a* full of blunders; ⟨*enorme*⟩ huge. **spro'posito** *nm* blunder; ⟨*eccesso*⟩ excessive amount; **a sproposito** inopportunely

sprovve'duto *a* unprepared; **~ di** lacking in

sprov'visto *a* **~ di** out of; lacking in ⟨*fantasia, pazienza*⟩; **alla sprovvista** unexpectedly

spruz'za|re *vt* sprinkle; ⟨*vaporizzare*⟩ spray; ⟨*inzaccherare*⟩ spatter. **~'tore** *nm* spray; **'spruzzo** *nm* spray; ⟨*di fango*⟩ splash

spudo|ra'tezza *nf* shamelessness. **~'rato** *a* shameless

'spugna *nf* sponge; ⟨*tessuto*⟩ towelling. **spu'gnoso** *a* spongy

'spuma *nf* foam; ⟨*schiuma*⟩ froth; *Culin* mousse. **spu'mante** *nm* sparkling wine, spumante. **spumeggi'are** *vi* foam

spun'ta|re *vt* ⟨*rompere la punta di*⟩ break the point of; trim ⟨*capelli*⟩; **~rla** *fig* win ● *vi* ⟨*pianta:*⟩ sprout; ⟨*capelli:*⟩ begin to grow; ⟨*sorgere*⟩ rise; ⟨*apparire*⟩ appear. **~rsi** *vr* get blunt. **~ta** *nf* trim

spun'tino *nm* snack

'spunto *nm* cue; *fig* starting point; **dare ~** a give rise to

spur'gar|e *vt* purge. **~si** *vr Med* expectorate

spu'tare *vt/i* spit; **~ sentenze** pass judgment. **'sputo** *nm* spit

'squadra *nf* ⟨*gruppo*⟩ team, squad; ⟨*di polizia ecc*⟩ squad; ⟨*da disegno*⟩ square. **squa'drare** *vt* square; ⟨*guardare*⟩ look up and down

squa'dri|glia *nf*, **~one** *nm* squadron

squagli'ar|e *vt*, **~si** *vr* melt; **~sela** ⟨*fam: svignarsela*⟩ steal out

squa'lifi|ca *nf* disqualification. **~'care** *vt* disqualify

'squallido *a* squalid. **squal'lore** *nm* squalor

'squalo *nm* shark

'squama *nf* scale; ⟨*di pelle*⟩ flake

squa'ma|re *vt* scale. **~arsi** *vr* ⟨*pelle:*⟩ flake off. **~'moso** *a* scaly; ⟨*pelle*⟩ flaky

squarcia'gola: a ~ *adv* at the top of one's voice

squarci'a|re *vt* rip. **'squarcio** *nm* rip; ⟨*di ferita, in nave*⟩ gash; ⟨*di cielo*⟩ patch

squar'tare *vt* quarter; dismember ⟨*animale*⟩

squattri'nato *a* penniless

squili'bra|re *vt* unbalance. **~to, -a** *a* unbalanced ● *nmf* lunatic. **squi'librio** *nm* imbalance

squil'la|nte *a* shrill. **~re** *vi* ⟨*campana:*⟩ peal; ⟨*tromba:*⟩ blare; ⟨*telefono:*⟩ ring. **'squillo** *nm* blare; *Teleph* ring. ⟨*ragazza*⟩ call girl

squi'sito *a* exquisite

squit'tire *vi* ⟨*pappagallo, fig:*⟩ squawk; ⟨*topo:*⟩ squeak

sradi'care *vt* uproot; eradicate ⟨*vizio, male*⟩

sragio'nare *vi* rave

srego|la'tezza *nf* dissipation. **~'lato** *a* inordinate; ⟨*dissoluto*⟩ dissolute

s.r.l. *abbr* ⟨**società a responsabilità limitata**⟩ Ltd

sroto'lare *vt* uncoil

SS *abbr* ⟨**strada statale**⟩ national road

'stabile *a* stable; ⟨*permanente*⟩ lasting; ⟨*saldo*⟩ steady; **compagnia** *Theat* repertory company ● *nm* ⟨*edificio*⟩ building

stabili'mento *nm* factory; ⟨*industriale*⟩ plant; ⟨*edificio*⟩ establishment. **~ balneare** lido

stabi'li|re *vt* establish; ⟨*decidere*⟩ decide. **~rsi** *vr* settle. **~tà** *nf* stability

stabiliz'za|re *vt* stabilize. **~rsi** *vr* stabilize. **~'tore** *nm* stabilizer

stac'car|e *vt* detach; pronounce clearly ⟨*parole*⟩; ⟨*separare*⟩ separate; turn off ⟨*corrente*⟩; **~e gli occhi da** take one's eyes off ● *vi* ⟨*fam: finire di lavorare*⟩ knock off. **~si** *vr* come off; **~si da** break away from ⟨*partito, famiglia*⟩

staccio'nata nf fence

'stacco nm gap

'stadio nm stadium

'staffa nf stirrup

staf'fetta nf dispatch rider

stagio'nale a seasonal

stagio'na|re vt season ⟨legno⟩; mature ⟨formaggio⟩. **~to** a ⟨legno⟩ seasoned; ⟨formaggio⟩ matured

stagi'one nf season; **alta/bassa ~** high/low season

stagli'arsi vr stand out

sta'gna|nte a stagnant. **~re** vt ⟨saldare⟩ solder; ⟨chiudere ermeticamente⟩ seal ● vi ⟨acqua:⟩ stagnate. **'stagno** a ⟨a tenuta d'acqua⟩ watertight ● nm ⟨acqua ferma⟩ pond; ⟨metallo⟩ tin

sta'gnola nf tinfoil

stalag'mite nf stalagmite

stalat'tite nf stalactite

'stal|la nf stable; ⟨per buoi⟩ cowshed. **~i'ere** nm groom

stal'lone nm stallion

sta'mani, stamat'tina adv this morning

stam'becco nm ibex

stam'berga nf hovel

'stampa nf Typ printing; ⟨giornali, giornalisti⟩ press; ⟨riproduzione⟩ print

stam'pa|nte nf printer. **~nte ad aghi** dot matrix printer. **~nte laser** laser printer. **~re** vt print. **~'tello** nm block letters pl

stam'pella nf crutch

'stampo nm mould; **di vecchio ~** ⟨persona⟩ of the old school

sta'nare vt drive out

stan'car|e vt tire; ⟨annoiare⟩ bore. **~si** vr get tired

stan'chezza nf tiredness. **'stanco** a tired; **stanco di** ⟨stufo⟩ fed up with. **stanco morto** dead tired, knackered fam

'standard a & nm inv standard. **~iz'zare** vt standardize

'stan|ga nf bar; ⟨persona⟩ beanpole. **~gata** nf fig blow; ⟨fam: nel calcio⟩ big kick; **prendere una ~gata** ⟨fam: agli esami, economi-**

ca⟩ come a cropper. **stan'ghetta** nf ⟨di occhiali⟩ leg

sta'notte nf tonight; ⟨la notte scorsa⟩ last night

'stante prep on account of; **a sé ~** separate

stan'tio a stale

stan'tuffo nm piston

'stanza nf room; ⟨metrica⟩ stanza

stanzi'are vt allocate

stap'pare vt uncork

'stare vi ⟨essere⟩ stay; ⟨abitare⟩ live; ⟨con gerundio⟩ be; **sto solo cinque minuti** I'll stay only five minutes; **sto in piazza Peyron** I live in Peyron Square; **sta dormendo** he's sleeping; **~ a** ⟨attenersi⟩ keep to; ⟨spettare⟩ be up to; **~ bene** ⟨economicamente⟩ be well off; ⟨di salute⟩ be well; ⟨addirsi⟩ suit; **~ dietro a** ⟨seguire⟩ follow; ⟨sorvegliare⟩ keep an eye on; ⟨corteggiare⟩ run after; **~ in piedi** stand; **~ per** be about to; **ben ti sta!** it serves you right!; **come stai/sta?** how are you?; **lasciar ~** leave alone; **starci** ⟨essere contenuto⟩ go into; ⟨essere d'accordo⟩ agree; **il 3 nel 12 ci sta 4 volte** 3 into 12 goes 4; **non sa ~ agli scherzi** he can't take a joke; **~ su** ⟨con la schiena⟩ sit up straight; **~ sulle proprie** keep oneself to oneself. **starsene** vr ⟨rimanere⟩ stay

starnu'tire vi sneeze. **star'nuto** nm sneeze

sta'sera adv this evening, tonight

sta'tale a state attrib ● nmf state employee ● nf ⟨strada⟩ main road, trunk road

'statico a static

sta'tista nm statesman

sta'tistic|a nf statistics sg. **~o** a statistical

'stato pp di **essere, stare** ● nm state; ⟨posizione sociale⟩ position; Jur status. **~ d'animo** frame of mind. **~ civile** marital status. **S~ Maggiore** Mil General Staff. **Stati pl Uniti [d'America]** United States [of America] '**statua** *nf* statue

statuni'tense *a* United States *attrib*, US *attrib* ● *nmf* citizen of the United States, US citizen

sta'tura *nf* height; **di alta ~** tall; **di bassa ~** short

sta'tuto *nm* statute

stazio'nario *a* stationary

stazi'one *nf* station; (*città*) resort. **~ balneare** seaside resort. **~ ferroviaria** railway station *Br*, train station. **~ di servizio** petrol station *Br*, service station. **~ termale** spa

'**stecca** *nf* stick; (*di ombrello*) rib; (*da biliardo*) cue; *Med* splint; (*di sigarette*) carton; (*di reggiseno*) stiffener

stec'cato *nm* fence

stec'chito *a* skinny; (*rigido*) stiff; (*morto*) stone cold dead

'**stella** *nf* star; **salire alle stelle** ⟨*prezzi:*⟩ rise sky-high. **~ alpina** edelweiss. **~ cadente** shooting star. **~ filante** streamer. **~ di mare** starfish

stel'la|re *a* star *attrib*; (*grandezza*) stellar. **~to** *a* starry

'**stelo** *nm* stem; **lampada** *nf* **a ~** standard lamp

'**stemma** *nm* coat of arms

stempi'ato *a* bald at the temples

sten'dardo *nm* standard

'**stender|e** *vt* spread out; (*appendere*) hang out; (*distendere*) stretch [out]; (*scrivere*) write down. **~si** *vr* stretch out

stendibian'che'ria *nm inv*, **stendi'tolo** *nm* clothes horse

stenodat'tilogra'fia *nf* shorthand typing. **~'lografo**, *a nmf* shorthand typist

stenogra'f|are *vt* take down in shorthand. **~ia** *nf* shorthand

sten'ta|re *vi* **~re a** find it hard to. **~to** *a* laboured. '**stento** *nm* (*fatica*) effort; **a stento** with difficulty; **stenti** *pl* hardships, privations

'**sterco** *nm* dung

stereo['fonico] *a* stereo[phonic]

stereoti'pato *a* stereotyped; ⟨*sor-*

riso⟩ insincere. **stere'otipo** *nm* stereotype

steril|e *a* sterile; ⟨*terreno*⟩ barren. **~ità** *nf* sterility. **~iz'zare** *vt* sterilize. **~izzazi'one** *nf* sterilization

ster'lina *nf* pound; **lira ~** [pound] sterling

stermi'nare *vt* exterminate

stermi'nato *a* immense

ster'minio *nm* extermination

'**sterno** *nm* breastbone

ste'roide *nm* steroid

ster'zare *vi* steer. '**sterzo** *nm* steering

'**steso** *pp di* **stendere**

'**stesso** *a* same; **io ~** myself; **tu ~** yourself; **me ~** myself; **se ~** himself; **in quel momento ~** at that very moment; **dalla stessa regina** (*in persona*) by the Queen herself; **tuo fratello ~ dice che hai torto** even your brother says you're wrong; **coi miei stessi occhi** with my own eyes ● *pron* **lo ~** the same one; (*la stessa cosa*) the same; **fa lo ~** it's all the same; **ci vado lo ~** I'll go just the same

ste'sura *nf* drawing up; (*documento*) draft

stick **colla a ~** glue stick; **deodorante a ~** stick deodorant

'**stigma** *nm* stigma. **~te** *nfpl* stigmata

sti'lare *vt* draw up

'**stil|e** *nm* style. **~e libero** (*nel nuoto*) freestyle, crawl. **sti'lista** *nmf* stylist. **~iz'zato** *a* stylized

stil'lare *vi* ooze

stilo'grafic|a *nf* fountain pen. **~o** *a* **penna** a fountain pen

'**stima** *nf* esteem; (*valutazione*) estimate. **sti'mare** *vt* esteem; (*valutare*) estimate; (*ritenere*) consider

stimo'la|nte *a* stimulating ● *nm* stimulant. **~re** *vt* stimulate; (*incitare*) incite

'**stimolo** *nm* stimulus; (*fitta*) pang

'**stinco** *nm* shin

'**stinger|e** *vt/i* fade. **~si** *vr* fade.

'**stinto** *pp di* **stingere**

sti'par|e vt cram. ~**si** vr crowd together

stipendi'ato a salaried ● nm salaried worker. **sti'pendio** nm salary

'stipite nm doorpost

stipu'la|re vt stipulate. ~**zi'one** nf stipulation; (accordo) agreement

stira'mento nm sprain

sti'ra|re vt iron; (distendere) stretch. ~**rsi** vr (distendersi) stretch; pull (muscolo). ~**tura** nf ironing. **'stiro** nm **ferro da stiro** iron

'stirpe nf stock

stiti'chezza nf constipation. **'stitico** a constipated

'stiva nf Naut hold

sti'vale nm boot. **stivali** pl **di gomma** Wellington boots, Wellingtons

'stizza nf anger

stiz'zi|re vt irritate. ~**rsi** vr become irritated. ~**to** a irritated. **stiz'zoso** a peevish

stocca'fisso nm stockfish

stoc'cata nf stab; (battuta pungente) gibe

'stoffa nf material; fig stuff

'stola nf stole

'stolto a foolish

stoma'chevole a revolting

'stomaco nm stomach; **mal di ~** stomach-ache

sto'na|re vt/i sing/play out of tune ● vi (non intonarsi) clash. ~**to** a out of tune; (discordante) clashing; (confuso) bewildered. ~**tura** nf false note; (discordanza) clash

'stoppia nf stubble

stop'pino nm wick

stop'poso a tough

'storcer|e vt, ~**si** vr twist

stor'di|re vt stun; (intontire) daze. ~**rsi** vr dull one's senses. ~**to** a stunned; (intontito) dazed; (sventato) heedless

'storia nf history; (racconto, bugia) story; (pretesto) excuse; **senza storie** no fuss!; **fare [delle] storie** make a fuss

'storico, -a a historical; (di importanza storica) historic ● nmf historian

stori'one nm sturgeon

'stormo nm flock

'storno nm starling

storpi'a|re vt cripple; mangle (parole). ~**'tura** nf deformation. **'storpio,** a a crippled ● nmf cripple

'stort|a nf (distorsione) sprain; **prendere una ~a alla caviglia** sprain one's ankle. ~**o** pp di **storcere** ● a crooked; (ritorto) twisted; (gambe) bandy; fig wrong

sto'viglie nfpl crockery sg

'strabico a cross-eyed; **essere ~** be cross-eyed, have a squint.

strabili'ante a astonishing

stra'bismo nm squint

straboc'care vi overflow

stra'carico a overloaded

stracci'|are vt tear; (fam: vincere) thrash. ~**'ato** a torn; (persona) in rags; (prezzi) slashed; **a un prezzo ~ato** dirt cheap. **'straccio** a torn ● nm rag; (strofinaccio) cloth ~**'one** nm tramp

stra'cotto a overdone; (fam: innamorato) head over heels ● nm stew

'strada nf road; (di città) street; (fig: cammino) way; **essere fuori ~** be on the wrong track; **fare ~** lead the way; **farsi ~** make one's way. ~ **maestra** main road. ~ **a senso unico** one-way street. ~ **senza uscita** blind alley. **stra'dale** a road attrib

strafalci'one nm blunder

stra'fare vi overdo it, overdo things

stra'foro: di ~ adv on the sly

strafot'ten|te a arrogant. ~**za** nf arrogance

'strage nf slaughter

'straicio nm (parte) extract

stralu'na|re vt ~**re gli occhi** open one's eyes wide. ~**to** a (occhi) staring; (persona) distraught

stramaz'zare vi fall heavily

strambe'ria nf oddity. **'strambo** a strange

strampa'lato a odd

stra'nezza nf strangeness

strango'lare vt strangle

strani'ero, -a a foreign ● nmf foreigner

'strano a strange

straordi|naria'mente adv extraordinarily. **~'nario** a extraordinary; (notevole) remarkable; (edizione) special; **lavoro ~nario** overtime; **treno ~nario** special train

strapaz'zar|e vt ill-treat; scramble (uova). **~si** vr tire oneself out. **stra'pazzo** nm strain; **da strapazzo** fig worthless

strapi'eno a overflowing

strapi'ombo nm projection; **a ~** sheer

strap'par|e vt tear; (per distruggere) tear up; pull out (dente, capelli); (sradicare) pull up; (estorcere) wring. **~si** vr get torn; (allontanarsi) tear oneself away. **'strappo** nm tear; (strattone) jerk; (fam: passaggio) lift; **fare uno strappo alla regola** make an exception to the rule. **~ muscolare** muscle strain

strapun'tino nm folding seat

strari'pare vi flood

strasci'c|are vt trail; shuffle (piedi); drawl (parole). **'strascico** nm train; fig after-effect

strass nm inv rhinestone

strata'gemma nm stratagem

strate'gia nf strategy. **stra'tegico** a strategic

'strato nm layer; (di vernice ecc) coat, layer; (roccioso, sociale) stratum. **~'sfera** nf stratosphere. **~'sferico** a stratospheric; fig sky-high

stravac'car|si vr fam slouch. **~to** a fam slouching

strava'gan|te a extravagant; (eccentrico) eccentric. **~za** nf extravagance; (eccentricità) eccentricity

stra'vecchio a ancient

strave'dere vt **~ per** worship

stravizi'are vi indulge oneself. **stra'vizio** nm excess

stra'volg|ere vt twist; (turbare) upset. **~i'mento** nm twisting. **stra'volto** a distraught; (fam: stanco) done in

strazi'a|nte a heartrending; (dolore) agonizing. **~re** vt grate on (orecchie); break (cuore). **'strazio** nm agony; **essere uno strazio** be agony; **che strazio!** fam it's awful!

'strega nf witch. **stre'gare** vt bewitch. **stre'gone** nm wizard

'stregua nf **alla ~ di** like

stre'ma|re vt exhaust. **~to** a exhausted

'stremo nm **ridotto allo ~** at the end of one's tether

'strenuo a strenuous

strepi'tare vi make a din. **'strepito** nm noise. **~'toso** a noisy; fig resounding

stres'sa|nte a (lavoro, situazione) stressful. **~to** a stressed [out]

'stretta nf grasp; (dolore) pang; **essere alle strette** be in dire straits; **mettere alle strette qcno** have sb's back up against the wall. **~ di mano** handshake

stret'tezza nf narrowness; **stret'tezze** pl (difficoltà finanziarie) financial difficulties

'stret|to pp di **stringere** ● a narrow; (serrato) tight; (vicino) close; (dialetto) broad; (rigoroso) strict; **lo ~to necessario** the bare minimum ● nm Geog strait. **~'toia** nf bottleneck; (fam: difficoltà) tight spot

stri'a|to a striped. **~'tura** nf streak

stri'dente a strident

'stridere vi squeak; fig clash. **'stridore** nm screech

'stridulo a shrill

strigli'a|re vt groom. **~ta** nf grooming; fig dressing down

stril'l|are vi/t scream. **'strillo** nm scream

strimin'zito *a* skimpy; (*magro*) skinny

strimpel'lare *vt* strum

'strin|ga *nf* lace; *Comput* string. **~'gato** *a fig* terse

stringer|e *vt* press; (*serrare*) squeeze; (*tenere stretto*) hold tight; take in (*abito*); (*comprimere*) be tight; (*restringere*) tighten; **~e la mano a** shake hands with ● *vi* (*premere*) press. **~si** *vr* (*accostarsi*) draw close (**a** to); (*avvicinarsi*) squeeze up

'striscia *nf* strip; (*riga*) stripe. **strisce** *pl* [**pedonali**] zebra crossing *sg*

strisci'ar|e *vi* crawl; (*sfiorare*) graze ● *vt* drag (*piedi*). **~si** *vr* **~si a** a rub against. **'striscio** *nm* graze; *Med* smear; **colpire di striscio** graze

strisci'one *nm* banner

strito'lare *vt* grind

striz'zare *vt* squeeze; (*torcere*) wring [out]; **~ l'occhio** wink

'strofa *nf* strophe

strofi'naccio *nm* cloth; (*per spolverare*) duster. **~ da cucina** tea towel

strofi'nare *vt* rub

stromboz'zare *vt* boast about ● *vi* hoot

stromboz'zata *nf* (*di clacson*) hoot

stron'care *vt* cut off; (*reprimere*) crush; (*criticare*) tear to shreds

'stronzo *nm vulg* shit

stropicci'are *vt* rub; crumple (*vestito*)

stroz'za|re *vt* strangle. **~'tura** *nf* strangling; (*di strada*) narrowing

strozzi'naggio *nm* loan-sharking

stroz'zino *nm pej* usurer; (*truffatore*) shark

strug'gente *a* all-consuming

'struggersi *vr* liter pine [away]

strumen'tale *a* instrumental

strumentaliz'zare *vt* make use of

strumentazi'one *nf* instrumentation

stru'mento *nm* instrument; (*arnese*) tool. **~ a corda** string instru-ment. **~ musicale** musical instru-ment

strusci'are *vt* rub

'strutto *nm* lard

strut'tura *nf* structure. **struttu'rale** *a* structural

struttu'rare *vt* structure

strutturazi'one *nf* structuring

'struzzo *nm* ostrich

stuc'care *vt* stucco

stuc'chevole *a* nauseating

'stucco *nm* stucco

stu'den|te, -'essa *nmf* student; (*di scuola*) schoolboy; schoolgirl. **~'tesco** *a* student; (*di scolaro*) school *attrib*

studi'are *vt* study. **~si** *vr* **~si di** try to

'studio *nm* studying; (*stanza, ricerca*) study; (*di artista, TV ecc*) studio; (*di professionista*) office. **~'oso, -a** *a* studious ● *nmf* scholar

'stufa *nf* stove. **~ elettrica** electric fire

stu'fare *vt Culin* stew; (*dare fastidio*) bore. **~rsi** *vr* get bored. **~to** *nm* stew

'stufo *a* bored; **essere ~ di** be fed up with

stu'oia *nf* mat

stupefa'cente *a* amazing ● *nm* drug

stu'pendo *a* stupendous

stupi'd|aggine *nf* (*azione*) stupid thing; (*cosa da poco*) nothing. **~ata** *nf* stupid thing. **~ità** *nf* stu-pidity. **'stupido** *a* stupid

stu'pir|e *vt* astonish ● *vi*, **~si** *vr* be astonished. **stu'pore** *nm* amaze-ment

stu'pra|re *vt* rape. **~'tore** *nm* rap-ist. **'stupro** *nm* rape

sturalavan'dini *nm inv* plunger

stu'rare *vt* uncork; unblock (*lavandino*)

stuzzica'denti *nm inv* toothpick

stuzzi'care *vt* prod [at]; pick (*denti*); poke (*fuoco*); (*molestare*) tease; whet (*appetito*)

stuzzi'chino *nm Culin* appetizer

su *prep* on; *(senza contatto)* over; *(riguardo a)* about; *(circa, intorno a)* about; around; **le chiavi sono sul tavolo** the keys are on the table; **il quadro è appeso sul camino** the picture is hanging over the fireplace; **un libro sull'antico Egitto** a book on o about Ancient Egypt; **costa sulle 50 000 lire** it costs about 50,000 lire; **decidere sul momento** decide at the time; **su commissione** on commission; **su due piedi** on the spot; **uno su dieci** one out of ten ● *adv (sopra)* up; *(al piano di sopra)* upstairs; *(addosso)* on; **ho su il cappotto** I've got my coat on; **in su** *(guardare)* up; **dalla vita in su** from the waist up; **su!** come on!

su'bacqueo *a* underwater

subaffit'tare *vt* sublet. **subaf'fitto** *nm* sublet

subal'terno *a & nm* subordinate

sub'buglio *nm* turmoil

sub'conscio *a & nm* subconscious

subdola'mente *adv* deviously.
'subdolo *a* devious, underhand

suben'trare *vi (circostanze:)* come up; **~ a** take the place of

su'bire *vt* undergo; *(patire)* suffer

subis'sare *vt fig* **~ di** overwhelm with

'subito *adv* at once; **~ dopo** straight after

su'blime *a* sublime

subodo'rare *vt* suspect

subordi'nato, -a *a & nmf* subordinate

subur'bano *a* suburban

suc'cederle *vi (accadere)* happen; **~e a** succeed; *(venire dopo)* follow; **~e al trono** succeed to the throne. **~si** *vr* happen one after the other

successi'one *nf* succession; **in ~** in succession

succesiva'mente *adv* subsequently. **~'sivo** *a* successive

suc'cesiso *pp di* **succedere** ● *nm* success; *(esito)* outcome; *(disco ecc)* hit. **~'sone** *nm* huge success

succes'sore *nm* successor

succhi'are *vt* suck [up]

suc'cinto *a (conciso)* concise; *(abito)* scanty

'succo *nm* juice; *(fig* essence); **~ di frutta** fruit juice. **suc'coso** *a* juicy

suc'cube *nm* **essere ~ di** qcno be totally dominated by sb

succu'lento *a* succulent

succur'sale *nf* branch [office]

sud *nm* south; **del ~** southern

su'dare *vi* sweat, perspire; *(faticare)* sweat blood; **~re freddo** be in a cold sweat. **~ta** *nf* anche *fig* sweat. **~'ticcio** *a* sweaty. **~to** *a* sweaty

sud'detto *a* above-mentioned

'suddito, -a *nmf* subject

suddi'viderle *vt* subdivide. **~si'one** *nf* subdivision

su'd-est *nm* southeast

'sudicio *a* dirty, filthy. **~'ume** *nm* dirt, filth

sudorazi'one *nf* perspiring. **su'dore** *nm* sweat, perspiration; *fig* sweaty

su'd-ovest *nm* southwest

suffici'enite *a* sufficient; *(presuntuoso)* conceited ● *nm* bare essentials *pl*; *Sch* pass mark. **~za** *nf* sufficiency; *(presunzione)* conceit; *Sch* pass; **a ~za** enough

suf'fisso *nm* suffix

suf'fragio *nm (voto)* vote. **~ universale** universal suffrage

suggeri'mento *nm* suggestion

sugge'rirle *vt* suggest; *Theat* prompt. **~'tore, ~'trice** *nmf Theat* prompter

suggestiona'bile *a* suggestible

suggestio'naire *vt* influence. **~to** *a* influenced. **suggesti'one** *nf* influence

sugge'stivo *a* suggestive; *(musica ecc)* evocative

'sughero *nm* cork

'sugli = **su** + **gli**

'sugo *nm (di frutta)* juice; *(di carne)* gravy; *(salsa)* sauce; *(sostanza)* substance

'sui = **su** + **i**

sui'cid|a a suicidal ● nmf suicide.
suici'darsi vr commit suicide. **~io**
nm suicide

su'ino a **carne suina** pork ● nm
swine

sul = **su** + **il**. **'sullo** = **su** + **lo**. **'sulla**
= **su** + **la**. **'sulle** = **su** + **le**

sul'ta|na nf sultana. **~nina** a **uva**
~nina sultana. **~no** nm sultan

'sunto nm summary

'suo, -a poss a **il ~, i suoi** his; (di
cosa, animale) its; (forma di
cortesia) your; **la sua, le sue** hers;
(di cosa, animale) its; (forma di
cortesia) your; **questa macchina**
è sua this car is his/hers; **~ padre**
his/her/your father; **un ~ amico**
a friend of his/hers/yours ● poss
pron **il ~, i suoi** his; (di cosa,
animale) its; (forma di cortesia)
yours; **la sua, le sue** hers; (di cosa
animale) its; (forma di cortesia)
yours; **i suoi** his/her folk

su'ocera nf mother-in-law

su'ocero nm father-in-law

su'ola nf sole

su'olo nm ground; (terreno) soil

suo'na|re vt/i Mus play; ring
⟨campanello⟩; sound ⟨allarme,
clacson⟩; ⟨orologio:⟩ strike. **~tore,**
~trice nmf player. **suone'ria** nf
alarm. **su'ono** nm sound

su'ora nf nun; **Suor Maria** Sister
Maria

superal'colico nm spirit ● a **be-**
vande pl **superalcoliche** spirits

supera'mento nm (di timidezza)
overcoming; (di esame) success (di
in)

supe'rare vt surpass; (eccedere) exceed; (vincere) overcome; overtake, pass Am ⟨veicolo⟩; pass
⟨esame⟩

su'perbia nf haughtiness. **~o** a
haughty; (magnifico) superb

super'donna nf superwoman

superdo'tato a highly gifted

superfici'al|e a superficial ● nmf
superficial person. **~ità** nf super-
ficiality. **super'ficie** nf surface;
(area) area

su'perfluo a superfluous

superi'or|e a superior; (di grado)
senior; (più elevato) higher; (so-
vrastante) upper; (al di sopra)
above ● nmf superior. **~ità** nf
superiority

superla'tivo a & nm superlative

supermer'cato nm supermarket

super'sonico a supersonic

su'perstite a surviving ● nmf survivor

superstizi'o|ne nf superstition.
~so a superstitious

super'strada nf toll-free motorway

supervisi'one nf supervision.
~'sore nm supervisor

su'pino a supine

suppel'lettili nfpl furnishings

suppergiù adv about

supplemen'tare a additional,
supplementary

supple'mento nm supplement; **~**
rapido express train supplement

sup'plen|te a temporary ● nmf
Sch supply teacher. **~za** nf temporary post

'suppli|ca nf plea; (domanda) peti-
tion. **~'care** vt beg. **~'chevole** a
imploring

sup'plire vt replace ● vi **~ a**
(compensare) make up for

sup'plizio nm torture

sup'porre vt suppose

sup'porto nm support

supposizi'one nf supposition

sup'posta nf suppository

sup'posto pp di **supporre**

suprema'zia nf supremacy. **su-**
'premo a supreme

sur'fare vi **~ in Internet** surf the
Net

surge'la|re vt deep-freeze. **~ti**
nmpl frozen food sg. **~to** a frozen

surrea'lismo nm surrealism. **~ta**
nmf surrealist

surriscal'dare vt overheat

surro'gato nm substitute

suscet'tibil|e a touchy. **~ità** nf
touchiness

susci'tare *vt* stir up; arouse ⟨*ammirazione ecc*⟩

su'sin|a *nf* plum. **~o** *nm* plumtree

su'spense *nf* suspense

sussegu'ente *a* subsequent. **~ir-si** *vr* follow one after the other

sussidi'ar|e *vt* subsidize. **~io** *a* subsidiary. **sus'sidio** *nm* subsidy; ⟨*aiuto*⟩ aid. **sussidio di disoccupazione** unemployment benefit

sussi'ego *nm* haughtiness

sussi'stenza *nf* subsistence. **sus'sistere** *vi* subsist; ⟨*essere valido*⟩ hold good

sussul'tare *vi* start. **sus'sulto** *nm* start

sussur'rare *vt* whisper. **sus'surro** *nm* whisper

su'tu|ra *nf* suture. **~'rare** *vt* suture

sva'gar|e *vt* amuse. **~si** *vr* amuse oneself. **'svago** *nm* relaxation; ⟨*divertimento*⟩ amusement

svaligi'are *vt* rob; burgle ⟨*casa*⟩

svalu'ta|re *vt* devalue; *fig* underestimate. **~rsi** *vr* lose value. **~zi'one** *nf* devaluation

svam'pito *a* absent-minded

sva'nire *vi* vanish

svantaggi'ato *a* at a disadvantage; ⟨*bambino, paese*⟩ disadvantaged. **svan'taggio** *nm* disadvantage; **essere in svantaggio** *Sport* be losing; **in svantaggio di tre punti** three points down; **~'oso** *a* disadvantageous

svapo'rare *vi* evaporate

svari'ato *a* varied

sva'sato *a* flared

'svastica *nf* swastika

sve'dese *a & nm* ⟨*lingua*⟩ Swedish ● *nmf* Swede

'sveglia *nf* ⟨*orologio*⟩ alarm [clock]; **~!** get up!; **mettere la ~** set the alarm [clock]

svegli'ar|e *vt* wake up; *fig* awaken. **~si** *vr* wake up. **'sveglio** *a* awake; ⟨*di mente*⟩ quick-witted

sve'lare *vt* reveal

svel'tezza *nf* speed; *fig* quick-wittedness

svel'tir|e *vt* quicken. **~si** *vr* ⟨*per-*

sona:⟩ liven up. **'svelto** *a* quick; ⟨*slanciato*⟩ svelte; **alla svelta** quickly

'svend|ere *vt* undersell. **~ita** *nf* [clearance] sale

sveni'mento *nm* fainting fit. **sve'nire** *vi* faint

sven'ta|re *vt* foil. **~to** *a* thoughtless ● *nmf* thoughtless person

'sventola *nf* slap; **orecchie** *nfpl* **a ~** protruding ears

svento'lare *vt/i* wave

sven'trare *vt* disembowel; *fig* demolish ⟨*edificio*⟩

sven'tura *nf* misfortune. **sventu-'rato** *a* unfortunate

sve'nuto *pp di* **svenire**

svergo'gnato *a* shameless

sver'nare *vi* winter

sve'stir|e *vt* undress. **~si** *vr* undress, get undressed

'Svezia *nf* Sweden

svezza'mento *nm* weaning. **svez-'zare** *vt* wean

svi'ar|e *vt* divert; ⟨*corrompere*⟩ lead astray. **~si** *vr fig* go astray

svico'lare *vi* turn down a side street; ⟨*fig: dalla questione ecc*⟩ evade the issue; ⟨*fig: da una persona*⟩ dodge out of the way

svi'gnarsela *vr* slip away

svi'lire *vt* debase

svilup'par|e *vt*, **~si** *vr* develop. **svi'luppo** *nm* development; **paese in via di sviluppo** developing country

svinco'lar|e *vt* release; clear ⟨*merce*⟩. **~si** *vr* free oneself. **'svincolo** *nm* clearance; ⟨*di autostrada*⟩ exit

svi'sce|rare *vt* gut; *fig* dissect. **~'rato** *a* ⟨*amore*⟩ passionate; ⟨*ossequioso*⟩ obsequious

'svista *nf* oversight

svi'tare *vt* unscrew. **~to** *a* ⟨*fam: matto*⟩ cracked, nutty

Svizzer|a *nf* Switzerland. **s~o, -a** *a & nmf* Swiss

svogli'a|tezza *nf* half-heartedness. **~to** *a* lazy

svolaz'za|nte *a* ⟨*capelli*⟩ windswept. **~re** *vi* flutter

'svolger|e vt unwind; unwrap ⟨pacco⟩; ⟨risolvere⟩ solve; ⟨portare a termine⟩ carry out; ⟨sviluppare⟩ develop. **~si** vr ⟨accadere⟩ take place. **svolgi'mento** nm course; ⟨sviluppo⟩ development

'svolta nf turning; fig turning-point. **svol'tare** vi turn

'svolto pp di **svolgere**

svuo'tare vt empty [out]

Tt

tabac'c|aio, -a nmf tobacconist. **~he'ria** nf tobacconist's ⟨which also sells stamps, postcards etc⟩. **ta'bacco** nm tobacco

ta'bel|la nf table; ⟨lista⟩ list. **~la dei prezzi** price list. **~'lina** nf Math multiplication table. **~'lone** nm wall chart. **~lone del canestro** backboard

taber'nacolo nm tabernacle

tabù a & nm inv taboo

tabu'lato nm Comput [data] printout

'tacca nf notch; **di mezza ~** ⟨attore, giornalista⟩ second-rate

tac'cagno a fam stingy

tac'cheggio nm shoplifting

tac'chetto nm Sport stud

tac'chino nm turkey

tacci'are vt **~ qcno di qcsa** accuse sb of sth

'tacco nm heel; **alzare i tacchi** take to one's heels; **scarpe senza ~** flat shoes. **tacchi** pl **a spillo** stiletto heels

taccu'ino nm notebook

ta'cere vi be silent ● vt say nothing about; **mettere a ~ qcsa** ⟨scandalo⟩ hush sth up; **mettere a ~ qcno** silence sb

ta'chimetro nm speedometer

'tacito a silent; ⟨inespresso⟩ tacit. **taci'turno** a taciturn

ta'fano nm horsefly

taffe'ruglio nm scuffle

'taglia nf ⟨riscatto⟩ ransom; ⟨ricompensa⟩ reward; ⟨statura⟩ height; ⟨misura⟩ size. **~ unica** one size

taglia'carte nm inv paperknife

taglia'erba nm inv lawn-mower

tagliafu'oco a inv **porta ~** fire door; **striscia ~** fire break

tagli'ando nm coupon; **fare il ~** ≈ put one's car in for its MOT

tagli'ar|e vt cut; ⟨attraversare⟩ cut across; ⟨interrompere⟩ cut off; ⟨togliere⟩ cut out; carve ⟨carne⟩; mow ⟨erba⟩; **farsi ~ i capelli** have a haircut ● vi cut. **~si** vr cut oneself; **~si i capelli** have a haircut

taglia'telle nfpl tagliatelle sg, thin, flat strips of egg pasta

taglieggi'are vt extort money from

tagli'ent|e a sharp ● nm cutting edge. **~re** nm chopping board

'taglio nm cut; ⟨il tagliare⟩ cutting; ⟨di stoffa⟩ length; ⟨parte tagliente⟩ edge; **a doppio ~** double-edged. **~ cesareo** Caesarean section

tagli'ola nf trap

tagli'one nm **legge del ~** an eye for an eye and a tooth for a tooth

tagliuz'zare vt cut into small pieces

tail'leur nm inv ⟨lady's⟩ suit

talassotera'pia nf thalasso-therapy

'talco nm talcum powder

'tale a such a; ⟨con nomi plurali⟩ such; **c'è un ~ disordine** there is such a mess; **non accetto tali scuse** I won't accept such excuses; **il rumore era ~ che non si sentiva nulla** there was so much noise you couldn't hear yourself think; **il ~ giorno** on such and such a day; **quel tal signore** that gentleman; **il ~ quale** just like ● pron un ~ someone; **quel ~** that man; **il tal dei tali** such and such a person

ta'lento nm talent

tali'smano nm talisman

tallo'nare vt be hot on the heels of

tallon'cino nm coupon

tal'lone nm heel

tal'mente adv so

ta'lora adv = talvolta

'talpa nf mole

tal'volta adv sometimes

tamburel'lare vi (con le dita) drum; (pioggia:) beat, drum. **tambu'rello** nm tambourine. **tambu'rino** nm drummer. **tam'buro** nm drum

Ta'migi nm Thames

tampona'mento nm Auto collision; (di ferita) dressing; (di falla) plugging. ~ **a catena** pile-up. **tampo'nare** vt (urtare) crash into; (otturare) plug. **tam'pone** nm swab; (per timbri) pad; (per mestruazioni) tampon; (per treni, Comput) buffer

'tana nf den

'tanfo nm stench

'tanga nm inv tanga

tan'gen|te a tangent ● nf tangent; (somma) bribe. ~'**topoli** nf widespread corruption in Italy in the early 90s. ~**zi'ale** nf orbital road

tan'gibile a tangible

'tango nm tango

tan'tino: un ~ adv a little [bit]

'tanto a [so] much; (con nomi plurali) [so] many, [such] a lot of; ~ **tempo** [such] a long time; **non ha tanta pazienza** he doesn't have much patience; ~ **tempo quanto ti serve** as much time as you need; **non è** ~ **intelligente quanto suo padre** he's not as intelligent as his father; **tanti amici quanti parenti** as many friends as relatives ● pron much; (plurale) many; (tanto tempo) a long time; **è un uomo come tanti** he's just an ordinary man; **tanti** (molte persone) many people; **non ci vuole così** ~ it doesn't take that long; ~ **quanto** as much as; **tanti quanti** as many as ● conj (comunque) anyway, in any case ● adv (così) so; (con verbi) so much; ~ **debole**

so weak; **è** ~ **ingenuo da crederle** he's naive enough to believe her; **di** ~ **in** ~ every now and then; ~ **l'uno come l'altro** both; ~ **quanto** as much as; **tre volte** ~ three times as much; **una volta** ~ once in a while; ~ **meglio così!** so much the better!; **tant'è** so much so; ~ **per cambiare** for a change

'tappa nf stop; (parte di viaggio) stage

tappa'buchi nm inv stopgap

tap'par|e vt plug; cork (bottiglia); ~**e la bocca a qcno** fam shut sb up. ~**si** vr ~**si gli occhi** cover one's eyes; ~**si il naso** hold one's nose; ~**si le orecchie** put one's fingers in one's ears

tappa'rella nf fam roller blind

tap'pe|tino nm mat; Comput mouse mat. ~ **antiscivolo** safety bathmat

tap'peto nm carpet; (piccolo) rug; **andare a** ~ (pugilato:) hit the canvas; **mandare qcno al** ~ knock sb down

tappez'z|are vt paper (pareti); (rivestire) cover. ~**e'ria** nf tapestry; (di carta) wallpaper; (arte) upholstery. ~**i'ere** nm upholsterer; (imbianchino) decorator

'tappo nm plug; (di sughero) cork; (di metallo, per penna) top; (fam: persona piccola) dwarf. ~ **di sughero** cork

'tara nf (difetto) flaw; (ereditaria) hereditary defect; (peso) tare

ta'rantola nf tarantula

ta'ra|re vt calibrate (strumento). ~**to** a Comm discounted; Techn calibrated; Med with a hereditary defect; fam crazy

tarchi'ato a stocky

tar'dare vi be late ● vt delay

'tard|i adv late; **al più** ~**i** at the latest; **più** ~**i** later [on]; **sul** ~**i** late in the day; **far** ~**i** (essere in ritardo) be late; (con gli amici) stay up late; **a più** ~**i** see you later. **tar'divo** a late; (bambino) retarded. ~**o** a slow; (tempo) late

'targ|a *nf* plate; *Auto* numberplate. **~a di circolazione** numberplate.

tar'gato *a* un'auto targata... a car with the registration number... **~'hetta** *nf (su porta)* nameplate; *(sulla valigia)* name tag

ta'rif|fa *nf* rate, tariff. **~'fario** *nm* price list

tar'larsi *vr* get wormeaten. **'tarlo** *nm* woodworm

'tarma *nf* moth. **tar'marsi** *vr* get moth-eaten

ta'rocco *nm* tarot; **ta'rocchi** *pl* tarot

tartagli'are *vi* stutter

'tartaro *a & nm* tartar

tarta'ruga *nf* tortoise; *(di mare)* turtle; *(per pettine ecc)* tortoise-shell

tartas'sare *vt (angariare)* harass

tar'tina *nf* canapé

tar'tufo *nm* truffle

'tasca *nf* pocket; *(in borsa)* compartment; **da ~** pocket *attrib*; **avere le tasche piene di qcsa** *fam* have had a bellyful of sth. **~ da pasticciere** icing bag

ta'scabile *a* pocket *attrib* ● *nm* paperback

tasca'pane *nm inv* haversack

ta'schino *nm* breast pocket

'tassa *nf* tax; *(discrizione ecc)* fee; *(doganale)* duty. **~ di circolazione** road tax. **~ d'iscrizione** registration fee

tas'sametro *nm* taximeter

tas'sare *vt* tax

tassa|tiva'mente *adv* without question. **~'tivo** *a* peremptory

tassazi'one *nf* taxation

tas'sello *nm* wedge; *(di stoffa)* gusset

tassì *nm inv* taxi. **tas'sista** *nmf* taxi driver

'tasso[1] *nm Bot* yew; *(animale)* badger

'tasso[2] *nm Comm* rate. **~ di cambio** exchange rate. **~ di interesse** interest rate

ta'stare *vt* feel; *(sondare)* sound; **~**

il terreno *fig* test the water or the ground

tasti'e|ra *nf* keyboard. **~'rista** *nmf* keyboarder

'tasto *nm* key; *(tatto)* touch. **~ delicato** *fig* touchy subject. **~ funzione** *Comput* function key. **~ tabulatore** tab key

ta'stoni: **a ~** *adv* gropingly

'tattica *nf* tactics *pl*

'tattico *a* tactical

'tatto *nm (senso)* touch; *(accortezza)* tact; **aver ~** be tactful

tatu'aggio *nm* tattoo. **~re** *vt* tattoo

'tavola *nf* table; *(illustrazione)* plate; *(asse)* plank. **~ calda** snackbar

tavo'lato *nm* boarding; *(pavimento)* wood floor

tavo'letta *nf* bar; *(medicinale)* tablet; **andare a ~** *Auto* drive flat out

tavo'lino *nm* small table

'tavolo *nm* table. **~ operatorio** *Med* operating table

tavo'lozza *nf* palette

'tazza *nf* cup; *(del water)* bowl. **~ da caffè/tè** coffee-cup/teacup

taz'zina *nf* **~ da caffè** espresso coffee cup

T.C.I. *abbr* **(Touring Club Italiano)** Italian Touring Club

te *pers pron* you; **te l'ho dato** I gave it to you

tè *nm inv* tea

tea'trale *a* theatrical

te'atro *nm* theatre. **~ all'aperto** open-air theatre. **~ di posa** *Cinema* set. **~ tenda** marquee for theatre performances

'tecnico, -a *a* technical ● *nmf* technician ● *nf* technique

tec'nigrafo *nm* drawing board

tecno|lo'gia *nf* technology. **~'logico** *a* technological

te'desco, -a *a & nmf* German

tedi|o *nm* tedium. **~'oso** *a* tedious

te'game *nm* saucepan

'teglia *nf* baking tin

'tegola *nf* tile; *fig* blow

tei'era *nf* teapot

tek nm teak

'**tela** nf cloth; (per quadri, vele) canvas; Theat curtain. ~ **cerata** oilcloth. ~ **di lino** linen

te'laio nm (di bicicletta, finestra) frame; Auto chassis; (per tessere) loom

tele'camera nf television camera

teleco|man'dato a remote-controlled, remote control attrib. ~'**mando** nm remote control

Telecom Italia nf Italian State telephone company

telecomunicazi'oni nfpl telecommunications

tele'cro|naca nf [television] commentary. ~**naca diretta** live [television] coverage. ~'**naca registrata** recording. ~'**nista** nmf television commentator

tele'ferica nf cableway

telefo'na|re vt/i [telephone, ring. ~**ta** nf call. ~**ta interurbana** long-distance call

telefonica'mente adv by [tele]phone

tele'fo|nico a [tele]phone attrib. ~'**nino** nm mobile [phone]. ~'**nista** nmf operator

te'lefono nm [tele]phone. ~ **senza filo** cordless [phone]. ~ **a gettoni** pay phone, coin-box. ~ **interno** internal telephone. ~ **a schede** cardphone

telegior'nale nm television news sg

telegra'fare vt telegraph. **tele'grafico** a telegraphic; (risposta) monosyllabic; **sii telegrafico** keep it brief

tele'gramma nm telegram

tele'matica nf data communications, telematics

teleno'vela nf soap opera

teleobiet'tivo nm telephoto lens

telepa'tia nf telepathy

telero'manzo nm television serial

tele'schermo nm television screen

tele'scopio nm telescope

teleselezi'one nf subscriber trunk dialling, STD; **chiamare in ~** dial direct

telespetta'tore, -'**trice** nmf viewer

tele'text® nm Teletext®

tele'video nm videophone

televisi'one nf television; **guardare la ~** watch television

televi'sivo a television attrib; **operatore ~** television cameraman; **apparecchio ~** television set

televi'sore nm television [set]

'**tema** nm theme; Sch essay. **te'matica** nf main theme

teme'rario a reckless

te'mere vt be afraid of, fear ● vi be afraid, fear

tem'paccio nm filthy weather

temperama'tite nm inv pencil-sharpener

tempera'mento nm temperament

tempe'ra|re vt temper; sharpen (matita). ~**to** a temperate. ~'**tura** nf temperature. ~'**tura ambiente** room temperature

tempe'rino nm penknife

tem'pe|sta nf storm. ~**sta di neve** snowstorm. ~**sta di sabbia** sandstorm

tempe|stiva'mente adv quickly. ~'**stivo** a timely. ~'**stoso** a stormy

'**tempia** nf Anat temple

'**tempio** nm Relig temple

tem'pismo nm timing

'**tempo** nm time; (atmosferico) weather; Mus tempo; Gram tense; (di film) part; (di partita) half; **a suo ~** in due course; **~ fa** some time ago; **un ~** once; **ha fatto il suo ~** it's superannuated. ~ **supplementare** Sport extra time, overtime Am. ~'**rale** a temporal ● nm [thunder]storm. ~**rale'mente** adv temporarily. ~'**raneo** a temporary. ~**reggi'are** vi play for time

tem'prare vt temper

te'nac|e a tenacious. ~**ia** nf tenacity

te'naglia nf pincers pl
'**tenda** nf curtain; (per campeggio) tent; (tendone) awning. ~ **a ossigeno** oxygen tent
ten'denza nf tendency. **~ial-'mente** adv by nature. **~i'oso** a tendentious
'**tendere** vt (allargare) stretch [out]; (tirare) tighten; (porgere) hold out; fig lay (trappola) ● vi ~ **a** aim at; (essere portato a) tend to
'**tendine** nm tendon
ten'do|ne nm awning; (di circo) tent. **~poli** nf inv tent city
'**tenebre** nfpl darkness. **tene-'broso** a gloomy
te'nente nm lieutenant
tenera'mente adv tenderly
te'ner|e vt hold; (mantenere) keep; (gestire) run; (prendere) take; (seguire) follow; (considerare) consider ● vi hold; **~ci a, ~e a** be keen on; **~e per** support (squadra). **~si** vr hold on (**a** to); (in una condizione) keep oneself; (seguire) stick to; **~si indietro** stand back
tene'rezza nf tenderness. '**tenero** a tender
'**tenia** nf tapeworm
'**tennis** nm tennis. ~ **da tavolo** table tennis. **ten'nista** nmf tennis player
te'nore nm standard; Mus tenor; **a ~ di legge** by law. **~ di vita** standard of living
tensi'one nf tension; Electr voltage; **alta ~** high voltage
ten'tacolo nm tentacle
ten'ta|re vt attempt; (sperimentare) try; (indurre in tentazione) tempt. **~'tivo** nm attempt. **~zi'one** nf temptation
tenten|na'mento nm wavering. **~'nare** vi waver
'**tenue** a fine; (debole) weak; (esiguo) small; (leggero) slight
te'nuta nf (capacità) capacity; (Sport: resistenza) stamina; (possedimento) estate; (divisa) uniform; (abbigliamento) clothes pl; **a**

~ d'aria airtight. **~ di strada** road holding

teolo'gia nf theology. **teo'logico** a theological. **te'ologo** nm theologian
teo'rema nm theorem
teo'ria nf theory
teorica'mente adv theoretically. **te'orico** a theoretical
te'pore nm warmth
'**teppa** nf mob. **tep'pismo** nm hooliganism. **tep'pista** nm hooligan
tera'peutico a therapeutic. **tera-'pia** nf therapy
tergicri'stallo nm windscreen wiper, windshield wiper Am
tergilu'notto nm rear windscreen wiper
tergiver'sare vi hesitate
'**tergo** nm **a ~** behind; **segue a ~** please turn over, PTO
ter'male a thermal; **stazione ~** spa. '**terme** nfpl thermal baths
'**termico** a thermal
termi'na|le a & nm terminal; **malato ~ le** terminally ill person. **~re** vt/i finish, end. '**termine** nm (limite) limit; (fine) end; (condizione, espressione) term
terminolo'gia nf terminology
ter'mite nf termite
termoco'perta nf electric blanket
ter'mometro nm thermometer
'**termos** nm inv thermos®
termosi'fone nm radiator; (sistema) central heating
ter'mostato nm thermostat
'**terra** nf earth; (regione) land; (terreno) ground; (argilla) clay; (cosmetico) dark face powder (which gives the impression of a tan); **a ~** (sulla costa) ashore; (installazioni) onshore; **per ~** on the ground; **sotto ~** underground. **~'cotta** nf terracotta; **vasellame di ~cotta** earthenware. **~'ferma** nf dry land. **~pl'eno** nm embankment
ter'razza nf. **~o** nm balcony
terremo'tato, -a a (zona) affected by an earthquake ● nmf earth-

quake victim. **terre'moto** *nm* earthquake

ter'reno *a* earthly ●*nm* ground; (*suolo*) soil; (*proprietà terriera*) land; **perdere/guadagnare ~** lose/gain ground. **~ di gioco** playing field

ter'restre *a* terrestrial; **esercito ~** land forces *pl*

ter'ribil|e *a* terrible. **~'mente** *adv* terribly

ter'riccio *nm* potting compost

terrifi'cante *a* terrifying

territori'ale *a* territorial. **terri'to-rio** *nm* territory

ter'rore *nm* terror

terro'ris|mo *nm* terrorism. **~ta** *nmf* terrorist

terroriz'zare *vt* terrorize

'terso *a* clear

ter'zetto *nm* trio

terzi'ario *a* tertiary

'terzo *a* third; **di terz'ordine** ⟨*locale, servizio*⟩ third-rate; **fare il ~ grado** a qn give sb the third degree; **la terza età** the third age ●*nm* third; **terzi** *pl* *Jur* third party *sg*. **ter'zultimo, -a** *a* & *nmf* third from last

'tesa *nf* brim

'teschio *nm* skull

'tesi *nf inv* thesis

'teso *pp* di **tendere** ●*a* taut; *fig* tense

tesor|e'ria *nf* treasury. **~i'ere** *nm* treasurer

te'soro *nm* treasure; (*tesoreria*) treasury

'tessera *nf* card; (*abbonamento all'autobus*) season ticket

'tessere *vt* weave; hatch ⟨*complotto*⟩

tesse'rino *nm* travel card

'tessile *a* textile. **tessili** *nmpl* textiles; (*operai*) textile workers

tessi'tore, -'trice *nmf* weaver. **~'tura** *nf* weaving

tes'suto *nm* fabric; *Anat* tissue

'testa *nf* head; (*cervello*) brain; **essere in ~** a be ahead of; **in ~** *Sport* in the lead; **~ o croce?**

heads or tails?; **fare ~ o croce** have a toss-up to decide

'testa-'coda *nm inv* **fare un ~** spin right round

testa'mento *nm* will; **T~** *Relig* Testament

testar'daggine *nf* stubbornness.

te'stardo *a* stubborn

te'stata *nf* head; (*intestazione*) heading; (*colpo*) butt

'teste *nmf* witness

te'sticolo *nm* testicle

testi'mon|e *nmf* witness. **~e oculare** eye witness

testi'monial *nmf inv* celebrity who promotes a brand of cosmetics

testimoni'anza *nf* testimony; **falsa ~anza** *Jur* perjury. **~'are** *vt* testify to ●*vi* testify, give evidence

'testo *nm* text; **far ~** be an authority

te'stone, -a *mf* blockhead

testu'ale *a* textual

'tetano *nm* tetanus

'tetro *a* gloomy

tetta'rella *nf* teat

'tetto *nm* roof. **~ apribile** ⟨*di auto*⟩ sunshine roof. **tet'toia** *nf* roofing. **tet'tuccio** *nm* **tettuccio apribile** sun-roof

'Tevere *nm* Tiber

ti *pers pron* you; (*riflessivo*) yourself; **ti ha dato un libro** he gave you a book; **lavati le mani** wash your hands; **eccoti!** here you are!; **sbrigati!** hurry up!

ti'ara *nf* tiara

tic *nm inv* tic

ticchet't|are *vi* tick. **~io** *nm* ticking

'ticchio *nm* tic; (*ghiribizzo*) whim

'ticket *nm inv* (*per farmaco, esame*) amount paid by National Health patients

tiepida'mente *adv* half-heartedly.

ti'epido *a* anche *fig* lukewarm

ti'fare *vi* **~ per** shout for. **'tifo** *nm* *Med* typhus; **fare il tifo per** *fig* be a fan of

tifoi'dea *nf* typhoid

ti'fone *nm* typhoon

ti'foso, -a nmf fan

'tiglio nm lime

ti'grato a gatto ~ tabby [cat]

'tigre nf tiger

'tilde nmf tilde

tim'ballo nm Culin pie

tim'brare vt stamp; **~ il cartellino** clock in/out

'timbro nm stamp; (di voce) tone

timida'mente adv timidly, shyly. **timi'dezza** nf timidity, shyness. **'timido** a timid, shy

'timo nm thyme

ti'mon|e nm rudder. **~'iere** nm helmsman

ti'more nm fear; (soggezione) awe. **timo'roso** a timorous

'timpano nm eardrum; Mus kettledrum

ti'nello nm dining-room

'tinger|e vt dye; (macchiare) stain. **~si** vi (viso, cielo:) be tinged (di with); **~si i capelli** have one's hair dyed; (da solo) dye one's hair

'tino nm, **ti'nozza** nf tub

'tint|a nf dye; (colore) colour; **in ~a unita** plain. **~a'rella** nf fam suntan

tintin'nare vi tinkle

'tinto pp di **tingere**. **~'ria** nf (negozio) cleaner's. **tin'tura** nf dyeing; (colorante) dye.

'tipico a typical

'tipo nm type; (fam: individuo) chap, guy

tipogra'fia nf printery; (arte) typography. **tipo'grafico** a typographic[al]. **ti'pografo** nm printer

tip tap nm tap dancing

ti'raggio nm draught

tiramisù nm inv dessert made of coffee-soaked sponge, eggs, Marsala, cream and cocoa powder

tiran|neggi'are vt tyrannize. **~'nia** nf tyranny. **ti'ranno, -a** a tyrannical ● nmf tyrant

tirapi'edi nm inv pej hanger-on

ti'rar|e vt pull; (gettare) throw; kick (palla); (sparare) fire; (tracciare) draw; (stampare) print ● vi pull; (vento:) blow; (abito:) be

tight; (sparare) fire; **~e avanti** get by; **~e su** (crescere) bring up; (da terra) pick up; **tirar su col naso** sniffle. **~si** vr **~si indietro** fig back out, pull out

tiras'segno nm target shooting; (alla fiera) rifle range

ti'rata nf (strattone) pull, tug; **in una ~** in one go

tira'tore nm shot. **~ scelto** marksman

tira'tura nf printing; (di giornali) circulation; (di libri) [print] run

tirchie'ria nf meanness. **'tirchio** a mean

tiri'tera nf spiel

'tiro nm (traino) draught; (lancio) throw; (sparo) shot; (scherzo) trick. **~ con l'arco** archery. **~ alla fune** tug-of-war. **~ a segno** rifle-range

tiro'cinio nm apprenticeship

ti'roide nf thyroid

Tir'reno nm **il [mar] ~** the Tyrrhenian Sea

ti'sana nf herb[al] tea

tito'lar|e a regular ● nmf principal; (proprietario) owner; (calcio) regular player

'titolo nm title; (accademico) qualification; Comm security; **a ~ di** as; **a ~ di favore** as a favour. **titoli** pl **di studio** qualifications

titu'ba|nte a hesitant. **~nza** nf hesitation. **~re** vi hesitate

tivù nf inv fam TV, telly

'tizio nm fellow

tiz'zone nm brand

toc'cante a touching

toc'ca|re vt touch; touch on (argomento); (tastare) feel; (riguardare) concern ● vi **~re a** (capitare) happen to; **mi tocca aspettare** I'll have to wait; **tocca a te** it's your turn; (da pagare da bere) it's your round

tocca'sana nm inv cure-all

'tocco nm touch; (di pennello, orologio) stroke; (di pane ecc) chunk ● a fam crazy, touched

'toga *nf* toga; *(accademica, di magi-strato)* gown

'toglier|e *vt* take off *(coperta)*; take away *(bambino da scuola, sete, Math)*; take out, remove *(dente)*; **~e qcsa di mano a qcno** take sth away from sb; **~e qcno dai guai** get sb out of trouble; **ciò non toglie che...** nevertheless... **~si** *vr* take off *(abito)*; **~si la vita** take one's [own] life; **togliti dai piedi!** get out of here!

toi'lette *nf inv*, **to'letta** *nf* toilet; *(mobile)* dressing table

tolle'ra|nte *a* tolerant. **~nza** *nf* tolerance. **~re** *vt* tolerate

'tolto *pp di* togliere

to'maia *nf* upper

'tomba *nf* grave, tomb

tom'bino *nm* manhole cover

'tombola *nf* bingo; *(caduta)* tumble

'tomo *nm* tome

'tonaca *nf* habit

tonalità *nf inv* Mus tonality

'tondo *a* round ● *nm* circle

'tonfo *nm* thud; *(in acqua)* splash

'tonico *a & nm* tonic

toni'fi care *vt* brace

tonnel'la ggio *nm* tonnage. **~ta** *nf* ton

'tonno *nm* tuna [fish]

'tono *nm* tone

ton'sil la *nf* tonsil. **~'lite** *nf* tonsillitis

'tonto *a fam* thick

top *nm inv (indumento)* sun-top

to'pazio *nm* topaz

'topless *nm inv* in **~** topless

'topo *nm* mouse. **~ di biblioteca** *fig* bookworm

topogra'fia *nf* topography. **topo-'grafico** *a* topographic[al]

to'ponimo *nm* place name

'toppa *nf (rattoppo)* patch; *(serra-tura)* keyhole

to'race *nm* chest. **to'racico** *a* tho-racic; **gabbia toracica** rib cage

'torba *nf* peat

'torbido *a* cloudy; *fig* troubled

'torcer|e *vt* twist; wring [out] *(biancheria)*. **~si** *vr* twist

'torchio *nm* press

'torcia *nf* torch

torci'collo *nm* stiff neck

'tordo *nm* thrush

to'rero *nm* bullfighter

To'rino *nf* Turin

tor'menta *nf* snowstorm

tormen'tare *vt* torment. **tor'men-to** *nm* torment

torna'conto *nm* benefit

tor'nado *nm* tornado

tor'nante *nm* hairpin bend

tor'nare *vi* return, go/come back; *(ridiventare)* become again; *(con-to:)* add up; **~ a sorridere** become happy again

tor'neo *nm* tournament

'tornio *nm* lathe

'torno **togliersi di ~** get out of the way

'toro *nm* bull; *Astr* Taurus

tor'pedine *nf* torpedo. **~i'era** *nf* torpedo boat

tor'pore *nm* torpor

'torre *nf* tower; *(scacchi)* castle. **~ di controllo** control tower

torrefazi'one *nf* roasting

tor'rente *nm* torrent, mountain stream; *(fig: di lacrime)* flood. **~zi'ale** *a* torrential

tor'retta *nf* turret

'torrido *a* torrid

torri'one *nm* keep

tor'rone *nm* nougat

'torso *nm* torso; *(di mela, pera)* core; **a ~ nudo** bare-chested

'torsolo *nm* core

'torta *nf* cake; *(crostata)* tart

tortel'lini *nmpl* tortellini, *small packets of pasta stuffed with pork, ham, Parmesan and nutmeg*

torti'era *nf* baking tin

tor'tino *nm* pie

'torto *pp di* torcere ● *a* twisted ● *nm* wrong; *(colpa)* fault; **aver ~** be wrong; **a ~** wrongly

'tortora *nf* turtle-dove

tortu'oso *a* winding; *(ambiguo)* tortuous

tor'tu|ra nf torture. **~'rare** vt torture

'torvo a grim

to'sare vt shear

tosa'tura nf shearing

To'scana nf Tuscany

'tosse nf cough

'tossico a toxic ● nm poison. **tossi'comane** nmf drug addict, drug user

tos'sire vi cough

tosta'pane nm inv toaster

to'stare vt toast ⟨pane⟩; roast ⟨caffè⟩

'tosto adv ⟨subito⟩ soon ● a chiefly cool

tot a inv **una cifra ~** such and such a figure ● nm **un ~** so much

to'tale a & nm total. **~ità** nf entirety; **la ~ità dei presenti** all those present

totali'tario a totalitarian

totaliz'zare vt total; score ⟨punti⟩

total'mente adv totally

'totano nm squid

toto'calcio nm ≈ [football] pools pl

tournée nf inv tour

to'vaglia nf tablecloth. **~'etta** nf ~**etta [all'americana]** place mat. **~'olo** nm napkin

'tozzo a squat ● nm **~ di pane** stale piece of bread

tra = **fra**

trabal'la|nte a staggering; ⟨sedia⟩ rickety, wonky. **~re** vi stagger; ⟨veicolo:⟩ jolt

tra'biccolo nm fam contraption; ⟨auto⟩ jalopy

traboc'care vi overflow

trabocchetto nm trap

tracan'nare vt gulp down

'traccia nf track; ⟨orma⟩ footstep; ⟨striscia⟩ trail; ⟨residuo⟩ trace; fig sign. **~'are** vt trace; sketch out ⟨schema⟩; draw ⟨linea⟩. **~'ato** nm ⟨schema⟩ layout

tra'chea nf windpipe

tra'colla nf shoulder-strap; **borsa a ~** shoulder-bag

tra'collo nm collapse

tradi'mento nm betrayal; Pol treason

tra'di|re vt betray; be unfaithful to ⟨moglie, marito⟩. **~'tore**, **~'trice** nmf traitor

tradizio'na|le a traditional. **~'lista** nmf traditionalist. **~l'mente** adv traditionally. **tradizi'one** nf tradition

tra'dotto pp di **tradurre**

tra'du|rre vt translate. **~t'tore**, **~t'trice** nmf translator. **~ttore elettronico** electronic phrasebook. **~zi'one** nf translation

tra'ente a breathless

tra'ente nm Comm drawer

traffi'ca|nte nmf dealer. **~nte di droga** [drug] pusher. **~re** vi ⟨affaccendarsi⟩ busy oneself; **~re in** pej traffic in. **'traffico** nm traffic; Comm trade

tra'figgere vt stab; ⟨straziare⟩ pierce

tra'fila nf fig rigmarole

trafo'rare vt bore, drill. **tra'foro** nm boring; ⟨galleria⟩ tunnel

trafu'gare vt steal

tra'gedia nf tragedy

traghet'tare vt ferry. **tra'ghetto** nm ferrying; ⟨nave⟩ ferry

tragica'mente adv tragically. **'tragico** a tragic ● nm ⟨autore⟩ tragedian

tra'gitto nm journey; ⟨per mare⟩ crossing

tragu'ardo nm finishing post; ⟨meta⟩ goal

traiet'toria nf trajectory

trai'nare vt drag; ⟨rimorchiare⟩ tow

tralasci'are vt interrupt; ⟨omettere⟩ leave out

'tralcio nm Bot shoot

tra'liccio nm ⟨graticcio⟩ trellis

tram nm inv tram, streetcar Am

'trama nf weft; ⟨di film ecc⟩ plot

traman'dare vt hand down

tra'mare vt weave; ⟨macchinare⟩ plot

tram'busto nm turmoil, hullaballoo

trame'stio *nm* bustle

tramez'zino *nm* sandwich

tra'mezzo *nm* partition

'**tramite** *prep* through ● *nm* link; **fare da ~** act as go-between

tramon'tana *nf* north wind

tramon'tare *vi* set; *(declinare)* decline. **tra'monto** *nm* sunset; *(declino)* decline

tramor'tire *vt* stun ● *vi* faint

trampo'lino *nm* springboard; *(per lo sci)* ski-jump

'**trampolo** *nm* stilt

tramu'tare *vt* transform

'**trancia** *nf* shears *pl*; *(fetta)* slice

tra'nello *nm* trap

trangugi'are *vt* gulp down, gobble up

'**tranne** *prep* except

tranquilla'mente *adv* peacefully

tranquil'lante *nm* tranquillizer

tranquil'li|tà *nf* calm; *(di spirito)* tranquillity. **~z'zare** *vt* reassure. **tran'quillo** *a* quiet; *(pacifico)* peaceful; *(coscienza)* easy

transat'lantico *a* transatlantic ● *nm* ocean liner

tran'sa|tto *pp di* **transigere**. **~zi'one** *nf* Comm transaction

tran'senna *nf* *(barriera)* barrier

tran'sigere *vi* reach an agreement; *(cedere)* yield

transi'ta|bile *a* passable. **~re** *vi* pass

transi'tivo *a* transitive

'**transi|to** *nm* transit; **diritto di ~to** right of way; **"divieto di ~to"** "no thoroughfare". **~'torio** *a* transitory. **~zi'one** *nf* transition

tran'tran *nm fam* routine

tranvi'ere *nm* tram driver, streetcar driver *Am*

'**trapano** *nm* drill

trapas'sare *vt* go [right] through ● *vi* *(morire)* pass away

trape'lare *vi* *(liquido, fig:)* leak out

tra'pezio *nm* trapeze; *Math* trapezium

trapian|'tare *vt* transplant. **~'anto** *nm* transplant

'**trappola** *nf* trap

tra'punta *nf* quilt

'trarre *vt* draw; *(ricavare)* obtain; **~ in inganno** deceive

trasa'lire *vi* start

trasan'dato *a* shabby

trasbor'dare *vt* transfer; *Naut* tran[s]ship ● *vi* change. **tra'sbordo** *nm* trans[s]hipment

tra'scende|re *vt* transcend ● *vi* *(eccedere)* go too far

trasci'nar|e *vt* drag; *(fig: entusiasmo:)* carry away. **~si** *vr* drag oneself

tra'scorrere *vt* spend ● *vi* pass

tra'scri|tto *pp di* **trascrivere**. **~vere** *vt* transcribe. **~zi'one** *nf* transcription

trascu'ra|bile *a* negligible. **~re** *vt* neglect; *(non tenere conto di)* disregard. **~'tezza** *nf* negligence. **~to** *a* negligent; *(curato male)* neglected; *(nel vestire)* slovenly

traseco'lato *a* amazed

trasferi'mento *nm* transfer; *(trasloco)* move

trasfe'ri|re *vt* transfer. **~rsi** *vr* move

tra'sferta *nf* transfer; *(indennità)* subsistence allowance; *Sport* away match; **in ~** *(impiegato)* on secondment; **giocare in ~** play away

trasfigu'rare *vt* transfigure

trasfor'ma|re *vt* transform; *(in rugby)* convert. **~'tore** *nm* transformer. **~zi'one** *nf* transformation; *(in rugby)* conversion

trasfor'mista *nmf (artista)* quick-change artist

trasfusi'one *nf* transfusion

trasgre'dire *vt* disobey; *Jur* infringe

trasgredi'trice *nf* transgressor

trasgres|si'one *nf* infringement. **~'sivo** *a* intended to shock. **~'sore** *nm* transgressor

tra'slato *a* metaphorical

traslo'car|e *vt* move ● *vi*, **~si** *vr* move house. **tra'sloco** *nm* removal

tra'smesso pp di **trasmettere**

tra'smett|ere vt pass on; TV, Radio broadcast; Techn, Med transmit. **~i'tore** nm transmitter

trasmis'si|bile a transmissible. **~'one** nf transmission; TV, Radio programme

trasmit'tente nm transmitter ● nf broadcasting station

traso'gna|re vi day-dream. **~to** a dreamy

traspa'ren|te a transparent. **~za** nf transparency; **in ~za** against the light. **traspa'rire** vi show [through]

traspi'ra|re vi perspire; fig transpire. **~zi'one** nf perspiration

tra'sporre vt transpose

traspor'tare vt transport; **lasciar-si ~ da** get carried away by. **tra'sporto** nm transport; (passione) passion

trastul'lar|e vt amuse. **~si** vr amuse oneself

trasu'dare vi ooze with ● vi sweat

trasver'sale a transverse

trasvo'la|re vt fly over ● vi **~re su** fig skim over. **~ta** nf crossing [by air]

tratta nf (traffico illegale) trade; Comm draft

trat'tabile a or nearest offer, o.n.o.

tratta'mento nm treatment. **~ di riguardo** special treatment

trat'ta|re vt treat; (commerciare in) deal in; (negoziare) negotiate ● vi **~re di** deal with. **~rsi** vr **di che si tratta?** what is it about?; **si tratta di...** it's about... **~'tive** nfpl negotiations. **~to** nm treaty; (opera scritta) treatise

tratteggi'are vt outline; (descrivere) sketch

tratte'ner|e vt (far restare) keep; hold (respiro, in questura); hold back (lacrime, riso); (frenare) restrain; (da paga) withhold; **sono stato trattenuto** (ritardato) I was o got held up. **~si** vr restrain oneself; (fermarsi) stay; **~si su** (indugiare) dwell on. **tratteni'mento** nm entertainment; (ricevimento) party

tratte'nuta nf (deduction)

trat'tino nm dash; (in parole composte) hyphen

'tratto pp di **trarre** ● nm (di spazio, tempo) stretch; (di penna) stroke; (linea) line; (brano) passage; **tratti** pl (lineamenti) features; **a tratti** at intervals; **a un ~** suddenly

trat'tore nm tractor

tratto'ria nf restaurant

'trauma nm trauma. **trau'matico** a traumatic. **~tiz'zare** vt traumatize

tra'vaglio nm labour; (angoscia) anguish

trava'sare vt decant

'trave nf beam

tra'veggole nfpl **avere le ~** be seeing things

tra'versa nf crossbar; **è una ~ di Via Roma** it's off Via Roma, it crosses via Roma

traver'sa|re vt cross. **~ta** nf crossing

traver'sie nfpl misfortunes

traver'sina nf Rail sleeper

tra'vers|o a crosswise ● adv di **~o** crossways; **andare di ~o** (cibo:) go down the wrong way; **cammi-nare di ~o** not walk in a straight line; **guardare qcno di ~o** look askance at sb. **~'one** nm (in calcio) cross

travesti'mento nm disguise

trave'stir|e vt disguise. **~rsi** vr disguise oneself. **~to** a disguised ● nm transvestite

travi'ar|e vt lead astray

travi'sare vt distort

travol'gente a overwhelming

tra'vol|gere vt sweep away; (sopraffare) overwhelm. **~to** pp di **travolgere**

trazi'one nf traction. **~ anterio-re/posteriore** front-/rear-wheel drive

tre a & nm three

trebbi'a|re vt thresh

'treccia nf plait, braid

tre'cento *a* & *nm* three hundred; **il T~** the fourteenth century

tredi'cesima *nf* extra month's salary paid as a Christmas bonus

'tredici *a* & *nm* thirteen

'tregua *nf* truce; *fig* respite

tre'mare *vi* tremble; *(di freddo)* shiver. trema'rella *nf fam* jitters *pl*

tremenda'mente *adv* terribly. tre'mendo *a* terrible; **ho una fame tremenda** I'm terribly hungry

tremen'tina *nf* turpentine

tre'mila *a* & *nm* three thousand

'tremito *nm* tremble

tremo'lare *vi* shake; *(luce:)* flicker. tre'more *nm* trembling

tre'nino *nm* miniature railway

'treno *nm* train

'tren|ta *a* & *nm* thirty; **~ta e lode** top marks. **~tatré giri** *nm inv* LP. **~'tenne** *a* & *nmf* thirty-year-old. **~'tesimo** *a* & *nm* thirtieth. **~'tina** *nf* **una ~tina di** about thirty

trepi'dare *vi* be anxious. 'trepido *a* anxious

treppi'ede *nm* tripod

'tresca *nf* intrigue; *(amorosa)* affair

'trespolo *nm* perch

triango'lare *a* triangular. tri'angolo *nm* triangle

tri'bale *a* tribal

tribo'la|re *vi (soffrire)* suffer; *(fare fatica)* go through all kinds of trials and tribulations. **~zi'one** *nf* tribulation

tribù *nf inv* tribe

tri'buna *nf* tribune; *(per uditori)* gallery; *Sport* stand. **~ coperta** stand

tribu'nale *nm* court

tribu'tare *vt* bestow

tribu'tario *a* tax *attrib*. tri'buto *nm* tribute; *(tassa)* tax

tri'checo *nm* walrus

tri'ciclo *nm* tricycle

trico'lore *a* three-coloured ● *nm (bandiera)* tricolour

tri'dente *nm* trident

trien'nale *a (ogni tre anni)* three-yearly; *(lungo tre anni)* three-year. tri'ennio *nm* three-year period

tri'foglio *nm* clover

trifo'lato *a* a sliced thinly and cooked with olive oil, parsley and garlic

'triglia *nf* mullet

trigonome'tria *nf* trigonometry

tril'lare *vi* trill

trilo'gia *nf* trilogy

tri'mestre *nm* quarter; *Sch* term

'trina *nf* lace

trin'ce|a *nf* trench. **~'rare** *vt* entrench

trincia'pollo *nm inv* poultry shears *pl*

trinci'are *vt* cut up

Trinità *nf* Trinity

'trio *nm* trio

trion'fa|le *a* triumphal. **~nte** *a* triumphant. **~re** *vi* triumph; **~re su** triumph over. tri'onfo *nm* triumph

tripli'care *vt* triple. 'triplice *a* triple; **in triplice [copia]** in triplicate. 'triplo *a* treble ● *nm* **il triplo (di)** three times as much (as)

'trippa *nf* tripe; *(fam: pancia)* belly

'trist|e *a* sad; *(luogo)* gloomy. tri'stezza *nf* sadness. **~o** *a* wicked; *(meschino)* miserable

trita'carne *nm inv* mincer. **~ghi'accio** *nm inv* ice-crusher

tri'ta|re *vt* mince. 'trito *a* **trito e ritrito** well-worn, trite

'trittico *nm* triptych

tritu'rare *vt* chop finely

triumvi'rato *nm* triumvirate

tri'vella *nf* drill. trivel'lare *vt* drill

trivi'ale *a* vulgar

tro'feo *nm* trophy

'trogolo *nm (per maiali)* trough

'troia *nf* sow; *vulg* bitch; *(sessuale)* whore

'tromba *nf* trumpet; *Auto* horn; *(delle scale)* well. **~ d'aria** whirlwind

trom'bare *vt vulg* screw; *(fam: in esame)* fail

trom'b|etta *nm* toy trumpet. **~one** *nm* trombone

trom'bosi *nf* thrombosis

tron'care *vt* sever; truncate ⟨parola⟩

'tronco *a* truncated; **licenziare in ~** fire on the spot ● *nm* trunk; ⟨di strada⟩ section. **tron'cone** *nm* stump

troneggi'are *vi* **~ su** tower over

'trono *nm* throne

tropi'cale *a* tropical. **'tropico** *nm* tropic

'troppo *a* too much; ⟨con nomi plurali⟩ too many ● *pron* too much; ⟨plurale⟩ too many; ⟨troppo tempo⟩ too long; **troppi** ⟨troppa gente⟩ too many people ● *adv* too; ⟨con verbi⟩ too much; **~ stanco** too tired; **ho mangiato ~** I ate too much; **hai fame? – non ~** are you hungry? – not very; **sentirsi di ~** feel unwanted

'trota *nf* trout

trot'tare *vi* trot. **trotterel'lare** *vi* trot along; ⟨bimbo:⟩ toddle

'trotto *nm* trot; **andare al ~** trot

'trottola *nf* [spinning] top; ⟨movimento⟩ spin

troupe *nf inv* **~ televisiva** camera crew

tro'vare *vt* find; ⟨scoprire⟩ find out; ⟨incontrare⟩ meet; ⟨ritenere⟩ think; **andare a ~re** go and see. **~rsi** *vr* find oneself; ⟨luogo:⟩ be; ⟨sentirsi⟩ feel. **~ta** *nf* bright idea. **~ta pubblicitaria** advertising gimmick

truc'care *vt* make up; ⟨falsificare⟩ fix *sl*. **~rsi** *vr* make up. **~tore, ~trice** *nmf* make-up artist

'trucco *nm* ⟨cosmetico⟩ make-up; ⟨imbroglio⟩ trick

'truce *a* fierce; ⟨delitto⟩ appalling

truci'dare *vt* slay

truci'olo *nm* shaving

trucu'lento *a* truculent

'truffa *nf* fraud. **truf'fare** *vt* swindle. **~'tore, ~trice** *nmf* swindler

'truppa *nf* troops *pl*; ⟨gruppo⟩ group

tu *pers pron* you; **sei tu?** is that you?; **l'hai fatto tu?** did you do it

yourself?; **a tu per tu** in private; **darsi del tu** *use the familiar* tu

'tuba *nf Mus* tuba; ⟨cappello⟩ top hat

tu'bare *vi* coo

tuba'tura, tubazi'one *nf* piping

tubazi'oni *nf* piping *sg*, pipes

tuberco'losi *nf* tuberculosis

tu'betto *nm* tube

tu'bino *nm* ⟨vestito⟩ shift

'tubo *nm* pipe; *Anat* canal; **non ho capito un ~** *fam* I understood zilch. **~ di scappamento** exhaust [pipe]

tubo'lare *a* tubular

tuf'fare *vt* plunge. **~rsi** *vr* dive. **~'tore, ~'trice** *nmf* diver

'tuffo *nm* dive; ⟨bagno⟩ dip; **ho avuto un ~ al cuore** my heart missed a beat. **~ di testa** dive

'tufo *nm* tufa

tu'gurio *nm* hovel

tuli'pano *nm* tulip

'tulle *nm* tulle

tume'fatto *a* swollen. **~zi'one** *nf* swelling. **'tumido** *a* swollen

tu'more *nm* tumour

tumulazi'one *nf* burial

tu'multo *nm* turmoil; ⟨sommossa⟩ riot. **~u'oso** *a* uproarious

'tunica *nf* tunic

Tuni'sia *nf* Tunisia

'tunnel *nm inv* tunnel

'tuo (il **~** *m*, **la tua** *f*, **i ~i** *mpl*, **le tue** *fpl*) *poss a* your; **è tua questa macchina?** is this car yours?; **un ~ amico** a friend of yours; **~ padre** your father ● *poss pron* yours; **i tuoi** your folks

tuo'nare *vt* thunder. **tu'ono** *nm* thunder

tu'orlo *nm* yolk

tu'racciolo *nm* stopper; ⟨di sughero⟩ cork

tu'rare *vt* stop; cork ⟨bottiglia⟩. **~si** *vr* become blocked; **~si le orecchie** stick one's fingers in one's ears; **~si il naso** hold one's nose

turba'mento *nm* disturbance; ⟨sconvolgimento⟩ upsetting. **~ del-**

la quiete pubblica breach of the peace

tur'bante nm turban

tur'ba|re vt upset. **~rsi** vr get upset. **~to** a upset

tur'bina nf turbine

turbi'nare vi whirl. **'turbine** nm whirl. **turbine di vento** whirlwind

turbo'len|to a turbulent. **~za** nf turbulence

turboreat'tore nm turbo-jet

tur'chese a & nmf turquoise

Tur'chia nf Turkey

tur'chino a & nm deep blue

'turco, -a a Turkish ● nmf Turk ● nm (lingua) Turkish; fig double Dutch; **fumare come un ~** smoke like a chimney; **bestemmiare come un ~** swear like a trooper

tu'ris|mo nm tourism. **~ta** nmf tourist. **~tico** a tourist attrib

'turno nm turn; **a ~** in turn; **di ~** on duty; **fare a ~** take turns. **~ di notte** night shift

'turp|e a base. **~i'loquio** nm foul language

'tuta nf overalls pl; Sport tracksuit. **~ da ginnastica** tracksuit. **~ da lavoro** overalls pl. **~ mimetica** camouflage. **~ spaziale** spacesuit. **~ subacquea** wetsuit

tu'tela nf Jur guardianship; (protezione) protection. **tute'lare** vt protect

tu'tina nf sleepsuit; (da danza) leotard

tu'tore, -'trice nmf guardian

'tutta nf **mettercela ~ per fare qcsa** go flat out for sth

tutta'via conj nevertheless, still

'tutto a whole; (con nomi plurali) all; (ogni) every; **tutta la classe** the whole class, all the class; **tutti gli alunni** all the pupils; **a tutta velocità** at full speed; **ho aspettato ~ il giorno** I waited all day [long]; **in ~ il mondo** all over the world; **noi tutti** all of us; **era tutta contenta** she was delighted; **tutti e due** both; **tutti e tre** all three ● pron all; (tutta la gente)

everybody; (tutte le cose) everything; (qualunque cosa) anything; **l'ho mangiato ~** I ate it all; **le ho lavate tutte** I washed them all; **raccontami ~** tell me everything; **lo sanno tutti** everybody knows; **è capace di ~** he's capable of anything; **~ compreso** all in; **del ~ quite**; **in ~ altogether** ● adv completely; **tutt'a un tratto** all at once; **tutt'altro** not at all; **tutt'altro che** anything but ● nm whole; **tentare il ~ per ~** go for broke. **~'fare** a inv & nmf [impiegato] ~ general handyman; **donna** ~ general maid

tut'tora adv still

tutù nm inv tutu, ballet dress

tv nf inv TV

Uu

ubbidi'en|te a obedient. **~za** nf obedience. **ubbi'dire** vi ~ (a) obey

ubi'ca|to a located. **~zi'one** nf location

ubria'car|e vt get drunk. **~si** vr get drunk; **~si di** fig become intoxicated with

ubria'chezza nf drunkenness; **in stato di ~** inebriated

ubri'a|co, -a a drunk; **~ fradicio** dead o blind drunk ● nmf drunk

ubria'cone nm drunkard

uccelli'era nf aviary. **uc'cello** nm bird; (vulg: pene) cock

uc'cider|e vt kill. **~si** vr kill oneself

ucci|si'one nf killing. **uc'ciso** pp di **uccidere**. **~'sore** nm killer

u'dente a **i non udenti** the hearing-impaired

u'dibile a audible

udi'enza nf audience; (colloquio) interview; Jur hearing

u'di|re vt hear. **~'tivo** a auditory. **~to** nm hearing. **~'tore, ~'trice**

nmf listener; *Sch* unregistered student *(allowed to sit in on lectures)*. ~'**torio** *nm* audience

'**uffa** *int (con impazienza)* come on!; *(con tono seccato)* damn!

uffici'al|e *a* official ● *nm* officer; *(funzionario)* official; **pubblico** ~**e** public official. ~**e giudiziario** clerk of the court. ~**iz'zare** *vt* make official, officialize

uf'ficio *nm* office; *(dovere)* duty. ~ **di collocamento** employment office. ~ **informazioni** information office. ~ **del personale** personnel department. ~**sa'mente** *adv* unofficially

uffici'oso *a* unofficial

'**ufo**[1] *nm inv* UFO

'**ufo**[2]: **a** ~ *adv* without paying

uggi'oso *a* boring

uguagli'a|nza *nf* equality. ~**re** *vt* make equal; *(essere uguale)* equal; *(livellare)* level. ~**rsi** *vr* ~**rsi a** compare oneself to

ugu'al|e *a* equal; *(lo stesso)* the same; *(simile)* like. ~'**mente** *adv* equally; *(malgrado tutto)* all the same

'**ulcera** *nf* ulcer

uli'veto *nm* olive grove

ulteri'or|e *a* further. ~'**mente** *adv* further

ultima'mente *adv* lately

ulti'ma|re *vt* complete. ~**tum** *nm inv* ultimatum

ulti'missime *nfpl Journ* stop press, latest news *sg*

'**ultimo** *a* last; *(notizie ecc)* latest; *(più lontano)* farthest; *fig* ultimate ● *nm* last; **fino all'**~ to the last; **per** ~ at the end; **l'**~ **piano** the top floor

ultrà *nmf inv Sport* fanatical supporter

ultramo'derno *a* ultramodern

ultra'rapido *a* extra-fast

ultrasen'sibile *a* ultrasensitive

ultra's|onico *a* ultrasonic. ~**u'o-no** *nm* ultrasound

ultrater'reno *a (vita)* after death

ultravio'letto *a* ultraviolet

ulu'la|re *vi* howl. ~**to** *nm* howling; **gli** ~**ti** the howls, the howling

umana'mente *adv (trattare)* humanely; ~ **impossibile** not humanly possible

uma'nesimo *nm* humanism

umani|tà *nf* humanity. ~'**tario** *a* humanitarian. **u'mano** *a* human; *(benevolo)* humane

umidifica'tore *nm* humidifier

umidità *nf* dampness; *(di clima)* humidity. **'umido** *a* damp; *(mani, occhi)* moist ● *nm* dampness; **in umido** *Culin* stewed

'umile *a* humble

umili'a|nte *a* humiliating. ~**re** *vt* humiliate. ~**rsi** *vr* humble oneself. ~**zi'one** *nf* humiliation.

umiltà *nf* humility. **umil'mente** *adv* humbly

u'more *nm* humour; *(stato d'animo)* mood; **di cattivo/buon** ~ **in** a bad/good mood

umo'ris|mo *nm* humour. ~**ta** *nmf* humorist. ~**tico** *a* humorous

un *indef art* a; *(davanti a vocale o h muta)* an; *vedi* **uno**

una *indef art f* a; *vedi* **un**

u'nanim|e *a* unanimous. ~**e'men-te** *adv* unanimously. ~**ità** *nf* unanimity; **all'**~**ità** unanimously

unci'nato *a* hooked; *(parentesi)* angle

unci'netto *nm* crochet hook

un'cino *nm* hook

'undici *a & nm* eleven

'unger|e *vt* grease; *(sporcare)* get greasy; *Relig* anoint; *(blandire)* flatter. ~**si** *vr (con olio solare)* oil oneself; ~**si le mani** get one's hands greasy

unghe'rese *a & nmf* Hungarian. **Unghe'ria** *nf* Hungary; *(lingua)* Hungarian

'unghi|a *nf* nail; *(di animale)* claw. ~'**ata** *nf (graffio)* scratch

ungu'ento *nm* ointment

unica'mente *adv* only. **'unico** *a* only; *(singolo)* single; *(incomparabile)* unique

unifi'ca|re vt unify. **~zi'one** nf unification

unifor'mar|e vt level. **~si** vr conform (**a** to)

uni'form|e a & nf uniform. **~ità** nf uniformity

unilate'rale a unilateral

uni'one nf union; (*armonia*) unity.
U~ Europea European Union.
U~ Monetaria Europea European Monetary Union. **~ sinda-
cale** trade union, labor union *Am*.
U~ Sovietica Soviet Union

u'ni|re vt unite; (*collegare*) join;
blend (*colori ecc*). **~rsi** vr unite;
(*collegarsi*) join

'**unisex** a inv unisex

unità nf inv university. **~ di misura** unit of
measurement. **~ di misura** unit of
measurement. **~rio** a unitary

univer'sal|e a universal. **~iz'zare**
vt universalize. **~'mente** adv universally

università nf inv university. **~rio,
-a** a university attrib ● nmf (*insegnante*) university lecturer; (*studente*) undergraduate

uni'verso nm universe

uno, -a indef art (*before* s + *consonant, gn, ps, z*) a ● pron one; a ~ a
~ one by one; l'~ e l'altro both [of
them]; né l'~ né l'altro neither [of
them]; ~ di noi one of us; ~ fa
quello che può you do what you
can ● a, one ● nm (*numerale*)
one; (*un tale*) some man ● nf some
woman

'**unt|o** pp di **ungere** ● a greasy
● nm grease. **~u'oso** a greasy.
unzi'one nf l'**Estrema Unzione**
Extreme Unction

u'omo nm (pl **uomini**) man. ~
d'affari business man. ~ **di fiducia** right-hand man. ~ **di Stato**
statesman

u'ovo nm (pl nf **uova**) egg. ~ **in camicia** poached egg. ~ **alla coque**
boiled egg. ~ **di Pasqua** Easter
egg. ~ **sodo** hard-boiled egg. ~
strapazzato scrambled egg

ura'gano nm hurricane

u'ranio nm uranium

urba'n|esimo nm urbanization.
~ista nmf town planner. **~istica**
nf town planning. **~istico** a urban. **urbanizzazi'one** nf urbaniza-
tion. **ur'bano** a urban; (*cortese*)
urbane

ur'gen|te a urgent. **~te'mente** adv
urgently. **~za** nf urgency; **in caso
d'~za** in an emergency; **d'~za**
(*misura, chiamata*) emergency

'**urgere** vi be urgent

u'rina nf urine. **uri'nare** vi urinate

ur'lare vi shout, yell; (*cane, vento:*)
howl. '**urlo** nm (pl nm **urli**, nf **urla**)
shout; (*di cane, vento*) howling

'urna nf urn; (*elettorale*) ballot box;
andare alle urne go to the polls

urrà int hurrah!

U.R.S.S. nf abbr (**Unione delle Re-
pubbliche Socialiste Sovietiche**)
USSR

ur'tar|e vt knock against; (*scon-
trarsi*) bump into; fig irritate. **~si**
vr collide; fig clash

'**urto** nm knock; (*scontro*) crash;
(*contrasto*) conflict; fig clash; **d'~**
(*misure, terapia*) shock

usa e getta a inv (*rasoio, siringa*)
throw-away, disposable

u'sanza nf custom; (*moda*) fashion

u'sa|re vt use; (*impiegare*) employ;
(*esercitare*) exercise; **~re fare
qcsa** be in the habit of doing sth
● vi (*essere di moda*) be fashionable; **non si usa più** it's out of
fashion; (*attrezzatura, espressione:*) it's not used any more. **~to** a
used; (*non nuovo*) second-hand

U.S.A. nmpl abbr US[A] sg

u'scente a (*presidente*) outgoing

usci'ere nm usher. '**uscio** nm door

u'sci|re vi come out; (*andare fuori*)
go out; (*sfuggire*) get out; (*essere
sorteggiato*) come up; (*giornale:*)
come out; **~re da** Comput exit
from, quit; **~re di strada** leave the
road. **~ta** nf exit, way out; (*spesa*)
outlay; (*di autostrada*) junction;
(*battuta*) witty remark; **essere in**

libera **~ta** be off duty. **~ta di servizio** back door. **~ta di sicurezza** emergency exit

usi'gnolo nm nightingale

'uso nm use; (abitudine) custom; (usanza) usage; **fuori ~** out of use; **per ~ esterno** (medicina) for external use only

U.S.S.L. nf abbr (**Unità Socio-Sanitaria Locale**) local health centre

ustio'nare vr burn oneself. **~to, -a** nmf burns case ● a burnt. usti'one nf burn

usu'ale a usual

usufru'ire vi **~ di** take advantage of

u'sura nf usury. usu'raio nm usurer

usur'pare vt usurp

u'tensile nm tool; Culin utensil; **cassetta degli utensili** tool box

u'tente nmf user. **~ finale** end user

u'tenza nf (utenti) users pl. **~ finale** end users

ute'rino a uterine. 'utero nm womb

'utile a useful ● nm Comm profit. **~ità** nf usefulness, utility; Comput utility. **~i'taria** nf Auto small car. **~i'tario** a utilitarian

utiliz'za|re vt utilize. **~zi'one** nf utilization. uti'lizzo nm (utilizzazione) use

uto'pistico a Utopian

'uva nf grapes pl; **chicco d'~** grape. **~ passa** raisins pl. **~ sultanina** currants pl

----

Vv

----

va'cante a vacant

va'canza nf holiday; (posto vacante) vacancy. **essere in ~** be on holiday

'vacca nf cow. **~ da latte** dairy cow

vacci'nare vt vaccinate. **~inazi'one** nf vaccination. vac'cino nm vaccine

vacil'lante a tottering; (oggetto) wobbly; (luce) flickering; fig wavering. **~re** vi totter; (oggetto:) wobble; (luce:) flicker; fig waver

'vacuo a (vano) vain; fig empty ● nm vacuum

vagabon'dare vi wander. vaga'bondo, -a a (cane) stray; **gente vagabonda** tramps pl ● nmf tramp

va'gare vi wander

vagheggi'are vt long for

va'gi|na nf vagina. **~'nale** a vaginal

va'gire vi whimper. **~to** nm whimper

'vaglia nm inv money order. **~ bancario** bank draft. **~ postale** postal order

vagli'are vt sift; fig weigh

'vago a vague

vagon'cino nm (di funivia) car

va'gone nm (per passeggeri) carriage; (per merci) wagon. **~ letto** sleeper. **~ ristorante** restaurant car

vai'olo nm smallpox

va'langa nf avalanche

va'lente a skilful

va'le|re vi be worth; (contare) count; (regola:) apply (per to); (essere valido) be valid; **far ~e i propri diritti** assert one's rights; **farsi ~e** assert oneself; **non vale!** that's not fair!; **tanto vale che me ne vada** I might as well go ● vt **~re qcsa a qcno** (procurare) earn sb sth; **~ne la pena** be worth it; **vale la pena di vederlo** it's worth seeing; **~si di** avail oneself of

valeri'ana nf valerian

va'levole a valid

vali'care vt cross. 'valico nm pass

vali'dità nf validity; **con ~ illimitata** valid indefinitely

'valido a valid; (efficace) efficient; (contributo) valuable

valige'ria *nf* (*fabbrica*) leather factory; (*negozio*) leather goods shop

va'ligia *nf* suitcase; **fare le valigie** pack; (*fig* pack one's bags. **~ diplomatica** diplomatic bag

val'lata *nf* valley. **'valle** *nf* valley; **a valle** downstream

val'lett|a *nf* TV assistant. **~o** *nm* valet; *TV* assistant

val'lone *nm* (*valle*) deep valley

va'lor|e *nm* value, worth; (*merito*) merit; (*coraggio*) valour; **~i** *pl Comm* securities; **di ~e** (*oggetto*) valuable; **oggetti** *pl* **di ~e** valuables; **senza ~e** worthless. **~iz'zare** *vt* (*mettere in valore*) use to advantage; (*aumentare di valore*) increase the value of; (*migliorare l'aspetto di*) enhance

valo'roso *a* courageous

'valso *pp di* **valere**

va'luta *nf* currency. **~ estera** foreign currency

valu'ta|re *vt* value; weigh up (*situazione*). **~rio** *a* (*mercato, norme*) currency. **~zi'one** *nf* valuation

'valva *nf* valve. **'valvola** *nf* valve; *Electr* fuse

'valzer *nm inv* waltz

vam'pata *nf* blaze; (*di calore*) blast; (*al viso*) flush

vam'piro *nm* vampire; *fig* bloodsucker

vana'mente *adv* (*inutilmente*) in vain

van'da|lico *a* atto **~lico** act of vandalism. **~'lismo** *nm* vandalism. **'vandalo** *nm* vandal

vaneggi'are *vi* rave

'vanga *nf* spade. **van'gare** *vt* dig

van'gelo *nm* Gospel; (*fam: verità*) gospel [truth]

vanifi'care *vt* nullify

va'nigli|a *nf* vanilla. **~'ato** *a* (*zucchero*) vanilla *attrib*

vanil'lina *nf* vanillin

vanità *nf* vanity. **vani'toso** *a* vain

'vano *a* vain ● *nm* (*stanza*) room; (*spazio vuoto*) hollow

van'taggi|o *nm* advantage; *Sport* lead; *Tennis* advantage; **trarre ~o**

da qcsa derive benefit from sth. **~'oso** *a* advantageous

van't|are *vt* praise; (*possedere*) boast. **~arsi** *vr* boast. **~e'ria** *nf* boasting. **'vanto** *nm* boast

'vanvera *nf* **a ~** at random; **parlare a ~** talk nonsense

va'por|e *nm* steam; (*di benzina, cascata*) vapour; **a ~e** steam *attrib*; **al ~e** *Culin* steamed. **~e acqueo** steam, water vapour; **battello a ~e** steamboat. **vapo'retto** *nm* ferry. **~i'era** *nf* steam engine

vaporiz'za|re *vt* vaporize. **~'tore** *nm* spray

vapo'roso *a* (*vestito*) filmy; **capelli vaporosi** big hair *sg*

va'rare *vt* launch

var'care *vt* cross. **'varco** *nm* passage; **aspettare al varco** lie in wait

vari'abil|e *a* changeable, variable ● *nf* variable. **~ità** *nf* changeableness, variability

vari'a|nte *nf* variant. **~re** *vt/i* vary; **~re di umore** change one's mood. **~zi'one** *nf* variation

va'rice *nf* varicose vein

vari'cella *nf* chickenpox

vari'coso *a* varicose

varie'gato *a* variegated

varietà *nf inv* variety ● *nm inv* variety show

'vario *a* varied; (*al pl, parecchi*) various; **vari** *pl* (*molti*) several; **varie ed eventuali** any other business

vario'pinto *a* multicoloured

'varo *nm* launch

va'saio *nm* potter

'vasca *nf* tub; (*piscina*) pool; (*lunghezza*) length. **~ da bagno** bath

va'scello *nm* vessel

va'schetta *nf* tub

vase'lina *nf* Vaseline®

vasel'lame *nm* china. **~ d'oro/ d'argento** gold/silver plate

'vaso *nm* pot; (*da fiori*) vase; *Anat* vessel; (*per cibi*) jar. **~ da notte** chamber pot

vas'soio *nm* tray

vastità *nf* vastness. **'vasto** *a* vast; **di vaste vedute** broad-minded

Vati'cano *nm* Vatican

vattela'pesca *adv fam* God knows!

ve *pers pron* you; **ve l'ho dato** I gave it to you

vecchia *nf* old woman. **vecchi'aia** *nf* old age. **'vecchio** *a* old ● *nmf* old man; **i vecchi** old people

vece *nf* **in ~ di** in place of; **fare le veci di qcno** take sb's place

ve'dente *a* **i non vedenti** the visually handicapped

ve'der|e *vt/i* see; **far ~e** show; **farsi ~e** show one's face; **non vedo l'ora di...** I can't wait to....
~si *vr* see oneself; *(reciproco)* see each other

ve'detta *nf (luogo)* lookout; *Naut* patrol vessel

vedovo, -a *nm* widower ● *nf* widow

ve'duta *nf* view

vee'mente *a* vehement

vege'ta|le *a & nm* vegetable. **~li'ano** *a & nmf* vegan. **~re** *vi* vegetate. **~ri'ano, -a** *a & nmf* vegetarian. **~zi'one** *nf* vegetation

'vegeto *a vedi* **vivo**

veg'gente *nmf* clairvoyant

'veglia *nf* watch; **fare la ~** keep watch. **~ funebre** vigil

vegli'are *vi* be awake; **~are su** watch over. **~one** *nm* **~one di capodanno** New Year's Eve celebration

ve'icolo *nm* vehicle

'vela *nf* sail; *Sport* sailing; **far ~** set sail

ve'la|re *vt* veil; *(fig: nascondere)* hide. **~rsi** *vr (vista:)* mist over; *(voce:)* go husky. **~ta'mente** *adv* indirectly; **~to** *a* veiled; *(occhi)* misty; *(collant)* sheer

'velcro® *nm* velcro®

veleggi'are *vi* sail

ve'leno *nm* poison. **vele'noso** *a* poisonous

veli'ero *nm* sailing ship

ve'lina *nf (carta)* ~ tissue paper; *(copia)* carbon copy

ve'lista *nm* yachtsman ● *nf* yachtswoman

ve'livolo *nm* aircraft

velle'i|tà *nf inv* foolish ambition. **~'tario** *a* unrealistic

'vello *nm* fleece

vellu'tato *a* velvety. **vel'luto** *nm* velvet. **velluto a coste** corduroy

'velo *nm* veil; *(di zucchero, cipria)* dusting; *(tessuto)* voile

ve'loc|e *a* fast. **~e'mente** *adv* quickly. **velo'cista** *nmf Sport* sprinter. **~ità** *nf inv* speed; *(Auto: marcia)* gear. **~ità di crociera** cruising speed. **~iz'zare** *vt* speed up

ve'lodromo *nm* cycle track

'vena *nf* vein; **essere in ~ di** be in the mood for

ve'nale *a* venal; *(persona)* mercenary, venal

ve'nato *a* grainy

vena'torio *a* a hunting *attrib*

vena'tura *nf (di legno)* grain; *(di foglia, marmo)* vein

ven'demmi|a *nf* grape harvest. **~'are** *vt* harvest

'vender|e *vt* sell. **~si** *vr* sell oneself; **vendesi** for sale

ven'detta *nf* revenge

vendi'ca|re *vt* avenge. **~rsi** *vr* get one's revenge. **~'tivo** *a* vindictive

'vendi|ta *nf* sale; **in ~ta** on sale. **~ta all'asta** sale by auction. **~ta al dettaglio** retailing. **~ta all'ingrosso** wholesaling. **~ta al minuto** retailing. **~ta porta a porta** door-to-door selling. **~'tore, ~'trice** *nmf* seller. **~'tore ambulante** hawker, pedlar

vene'ra|bile, ~ndo *a* venerable

vene'rare *vt* revere

venerdì *nm inv* Friday. **V~ Santo** Good Friday

'Venere *nf* Venus. **ve'nereo** *a* venereal

Ve'nezi|a *nf* Venice. **v~'ano, -a** *a & nmf* Venetian ● *nf (persiana)* Venetian blind; *Culin* sweet bun

veni'ale *a* venial

ve'nire *vi* come; *(riuscire)* turn out; *(costare)* cost; *(in passivi)* be; ~ a sapere learn; ~ **in mente** occur; ~ **meno** *(svenire)* faint; ~ **meno a un contratto** go back on a contract; ~ **via** come away; *(staccarsi)* come off; **mi viene da piangere** I feel like crying; **vieni a prendermi** come and pick me up

ven'taglio *nm* fan

ven'tata *nf* gust [of wind]; *fig* breath

ven'te|nne *a & nmf* twenty-year-old. **~simo** *a & nm* twentieth. **'venti** *a & nm* twenty

venti'la|re *vt* air. **~'tore** *nm* fan. **~zi'one** *nf* ventilation

ven'tina *nf* **una** ~ *(circa venti)* about twenty

ventiquat'trore *nf inv (valigia)* overnight case

'vento *nm* wind; **farsi** ~ fan oneself

ven'tosa *nf* sucker

ven'toso *a* windy

'ventre *nm* stomach. **ven'triloquo** *nm* ventriloquist

ven'tura *nf* fortune; **andare alla** ~ trust to luck

ven'turo *a* next

ve'nuta *nf* coming

vera'mente *adv* really

ve'randa *nf* veranda

verb'al|e *a* verbal ● *nm (di riunione)* minutes *pl.* **~'mente** *adv* verbally

'verbo *nm* verb. ~ **ausiliare** auxiliary [verb]

'verde *a* green ● *nm* green; *(vegetazione)* greenery; *(semaforo)* green light; **essere al** ~ be broke. ~ **oliva** olive green. ~ **pisello** pea green. **~'rame** *nm* verdigris

ver'detto *nm* verdict

ver'dura *nf* vegetables *pl*; **una** ~ a vegetable

'verga *nf* rod

vergi'n|ale *a* virginal. **'vergine** *nf* virgin; *Astr* Virgo ● *a* virgin; *(cassetta)* blank. **~ità** *nf* virginity

ver'gogna *nf* shame; *(timidezza)* shyness

vergo'gn|arsi *vr* feel ashamed; *(essere timido)* feel shy. **~oso** *a* ashamed; *(timido)* shy; *(disonorevole)* shameful

ve'rifica *nf* check. **verifi'cabile** *a* verifiable

verifi'car|e *vt* check. **~si** *vr* come true

ve'rismo *nm* realism

verit'à *nf* truth. **~i'ero** *a* truthful

'verme *nm* worm. ~ **solitario** tapeworm

ver'miglio *a & nm* vermilion

ver'mut *nm inv* vermouth

ver'nacolo *nm* vernacular

ver'nic|e *nf* paint; *(trasparente)* varnish; *(pelle)* patent leather; *fig* veneer; **"vernice fresca"** "wet paint". **~i'are** *vt* paint; *(con vernice trasparente)* varnish. **~la'tura** *nf* painting; *(strato)* paintwork; *fig* veneer

'vero *a* true; *(autentico)* real; *(perfetto)* perfect; **è** ~**?** is that so?; ~ **e proprio** full-blown; **sei stanca,** ~**?** you're tired, aren't you ● *nm* truth; *(realtà)* life

verosimigli'anza *nf* probability. **vero'simile** *a* probable

ver'ruca *nf* wart; *(sotto la pianta del piede)* verruca

versa'mento *nm* *(pagamento)* payment; *(in banca)* deposit

ver'sante *nm* slope

ver'sa|re *vt* pour; *(spargere)* shed; *(rovesciare)* spill; pay *(denaro)*. **~rsi** *vr* spill; *(sfociare)* flow

ver'satil|e *a* versatile. **~ità** *nf* versatility

ver'setto *nm* verse

versi'one *nf* version; *(traduzione)* translation; **"~ integrale"** "unabridged version"; **"~ ridotta"** "abridged version"

'verso¹ *nm* verse; *(grido)* cry; *(gesto)* gesture; *(senso)* direction; *(modo)* manner; **fare il** ~ **a** qcno ape sb; **non c'è** ~ **di** there is no way of

'**verso**² *prep* towards; *(nei pressi di)* round about; ~ **dove?** which way?

'**vertebra** *nf* vertebra

'**vertere** *vi* ~ **su** focus on

verti'cal|e *a* vertical; *(in parole crociate)* down ● *nm* vertical ● *nf* handstand. ~'**mente** *adv* vertically

'**vertice** *nm* summit; *Math* vertex; **conferenza al** ~ summit conference

ver'**tigine** *nf* dizziness; *Med* vertigo. **vertigini** *pl* giddy spells; **aver le vertigini** feel dizzy

vertigi|**nosa'mente** *adv* dizzily. ~'**noso** *a* dizzy; *(velocità)* breakneck; *(prezzi)* sky-high; *(scollatura)* plunging

ve'**scica** *nf* bladder; *(sulla pelle)* blister

'**vescovo** *nm* bishop

'**vespa** *nf* wasp

vespasi'ano *nm* urinal

'**vespro** *nm* vespers *pl*

ves'**sillo** *nm* standard

ve'**staglia** *nf* dressing gown

'**vest|e** *nf* dress; *(rivestimento)* covering; **in** ~**e di** in the capacity of; **in** ~**e ufficiale** in an official capacity. ~'**ario** *nm* clothing

ve'**stibolo** *nm* hall

ve'**stigio** *nm* (*pl nm* **vestigi**, *pl nf* **vestigia**) trace

ve'**sti|re** *vt* dress. ~**rsi** *vr* get dressed. ~**ti** *pl* clothes. ~**to** *a* dressed ● *nm* (*da uomo*) suit; *(da donna)* dress

vete'**rano**, -*a* *a & nmf* veteran

veteri'**naria** *nf* veterinary science

veteri'**nario** *a* veterinary ● *nm* veterinary surgeon

'**veto** *nm inv* veto

ve'**tra|io** *nm* glazier. ~**ta** *nf* big window; *(in chiesa)* stained-glass window; *(porta)* glass door. ~**to** *a* glazed. **vetre'ria** *nf* glass works

ve'**tri|na** *nf* [shop-]window; *(mobile)* display cabinet. ~'**nista** *nmf* window dresser

vetri'olo *nm* vitriol

'**vetro** *nm* glass; *(di finestra, porta)* pane. ~**resina** *nf* fibreglass

'**vetta** *nf* peak

vet'**tore** *nm* vector

vetto'vaglie *nfpl* provisions

vet'**tura** *nf* coach; *(ferroviaria)* carriage; *Auto* car. **vettu'rino** *nm* coachman

vezzeggi|a|re *vt* fondle. ~'**tivo** *nm* pet name. '**vezzo** *nm* habit; *(attrattiva)* charm; **vezzi** *pl* *(moine)* affectation *sg*. **vez'zoso** *a* charming; *pej* affected

vi *pers pron* you; *(riflessivo)* yourselves; *(reciproco)* each other; *(tra più persone)* one another; **vi ho dato un libro** I gave you a book; **lavatevi le mani** wash your hands; **eccovi!** here you are! ● *adv* = **ci**

'**via**¹ *nf* street, road; *fig* way; *Anat* tract; **in** ~ **di** in the course of; **per** ~ **di** on account of; ~ ~ **che** as; **per** ~ **aerea** by airmail

'**via**² *adv* away; *(fuori)* out; **andar** ~ go away; **e così** ~ and so on; ● ~ **dicendo** and whatnot ● *int* ~**! **go away!; *Sport* go!; *(andiamo)* come on! ● *nm* starting signal

viabilità *nf* road conditions *pl*; *(rete)* road network; *(norme)* road and traffic laws *pl*

via'card *nf inv* motorway card

via'dotto *nm* viaduct

viaggi|a|re *vi* travel. ~'**tore**, ~'**trice** *nmf* traveller

vi'**aggio** *nm* journey; *(breve)* trip; **buon** ~**! **safe journey!, have a good trip!; **fare un** ~ go on a journey. ~ **di nozze** honeymoon

vi'**ale** *nm* avenue; *(privato)* drive

vi'**vai** *nm* coming and going

vi'**bra|nte** *a* vibrant. ~**re** *vi* vibrate; *(fremere)* quiver. ~**zi'one** *nf* vibration

vi'**cario** *nm* vicar

'**vice**+ *pref* vice+

'**vice** *nm* deputy. ~**diret'tore** *nm* assistant manager

vi'**cenda** *nf* event; **a** ~ *(fra due)* each other; *(a turno)* in turn[s]

vice'versa *adv* vice versa

vici'na|nza *nf* nearness; **~nze** *pl* (*paraggi*) neighbourhood. **~to** *nm* neighbourhood; (*vicini*) neighbours *pl*

vi'cino, -a *a* near; (*accanto*) next ● *adv* near, close. **~ a** *prep* near [to] ● *nmf* neighbour. **~ di casa** nextdoor neighbour

vicissi'tudine *nf* vicissitude

'vicolo *nm* alley

'video *nm* video. **~'camera** *nf* camcorder. **~cas'setta** *nf* video cassette

videoci'tofono *nm* video entry phone

video'clip *nm inv* video clip

videogi'oco *nm* video game

videoregistra'tore *nm* video-recorder

video'teca *nf* video library

video'tel® *nm* = Videotex®

videotermi'nale *nm* visual display unit, VDU

vidi'mare *vt* authenticate

vie'ta|re *vt* forbid; **sosta ~ta** no parking; **~to fumare** no smoking; **~to ai minori di 18 anni** prohibited to children under the age of 18

vi'gente *a* in force. **'vigere** *vi* be in force

vigi'la|nte *a* vigilant. **~nza** *nf* vigilance. **~re** *vt* keep an eye on ● *vi* keep watch

'vigile *a* watchful ● *nm* = [urbano] policeman. **~ del fuoco** fireman

vi'gilia *nf* eve

vigliacche'ria *nf* cowardice. **vigli'acco, -a** *a* cowardly ● *nmf* coward

'vigna *nf*, **vi'gneto** *nm* vineyard

vi'gnetta *nf* cartoon

vi'gore *nm* vigour; **entrare in ~** come into force. **vigo'roso** *a* vigorous

'vile *a* cowardly; (*abietto*) vile

'villa *nf* villa

vil'laggio *nm* village. **~ turistico** holiday village

vil'lano *a* rude ● *nm* boor; (*contadino*) peasant

villeggi'a|nte *nmf* holiday-maker. **~re** *vi* spend one's holidays. **~'tura** *nf* holiday[s] [*pl*], vacation *Am*

vil'l|etta *nf* small detached house. **~ino** *nm* detached house

viltà *nf* cowardice

'vimine *nm* wicker

'vinc|ere *vt* win; (*sconfiggere*) beat; (*superare*) overcome. **~ita** *nf* win; (*somma vinta*) winnings *pl*. **~i'tore, ~i'trice** *nmf* winner

vinco'la|nte *a* binding. **~re** *vt* bind; *Comm* tie up. **'vincolo** *nm* bond

vi'nicolo *a* wine *attrib*

vinil'pelle® *nm* Leatherette®

'vino *nm* wine. **~ spumante** sparkling wine. **~ da taglio** blending wine. **~ da tavola** table wine

'vinto *pp di* **vincere**

vi'ola *nf Bot* violet; *Mus* viola. **vio'laceo** *a* purplish; (*labbra*) blue

vio'la|re *vt* violate. **~zi'one** *nf* violation. **~zione di domicilio** breaking and entering

violen'tare *vt* rape

violente'mente *adv* violently

vio'len|to *a* violent. **~za** *nf* violence. **~za carnale** rape

vio'letta *nf* violet

vio'letto *a & nm* (*colore*) violet

violi'nista *nmf* violinist. **vio'lino** *nm* violin. **violon'cello** *nm* cello

vi'ottolo *nm* path

'vipera *nf* viper

vi'raggio *nm Phot* toning; *Naut*, *Aeron* turn. **~re** *vi* turn; **~re di bordo** veer

virgo'la *nf* comma. **~ette** *nfpl* inverted commas

vi'ril|e *a* virile; (*da uomo*) manly. **~ità** *nf* virility; manliness

virtù *nf inv* virtue; **in ~ di** (*legge*) under. **~'ale** *a* virtual. **~'oso** *a* virtuous ● *nm* virtuoso

viru'lento *a* virulent

'virus *nm inv* virus

visa'gista *nmf* beautician

visce'rale *a* visceral; *(odio)* deep-seated; *(reazione)* gut

'viscere *nm* internal organ ● *nfpl* guts

vischi|o *nm* mistletoe. **~'oso** *a* viscous; *(appiccicoso)* sticky

'viscido *a* slimy

vi'sconte *nm* viscount. **~'essa** *nf* viscountess

vi'scoso *a* viscous

vi'sibile *a* visible

visi'bilio *nm* profusion; **andare in ~** go into ecstasies

visibilità *nf* visibility

visi'era *nf* *(di elmo)* visor; *(di berretto)* peak

visio'nare *vt* examine; *Cinema* screen. **visi'one** *nf* vision; **prima visione** *Cinema* first showing

'visit|a *nf* visit; *(breve)* call; *Med* examination; **fare ~a a qcno** pay sb a visit. **~a di controllo** *Med* checkup. **visi'tare** *vt* visit; *(brevemente)* call on; *Med* examine; **~a'tore, ~a'trice** *nmf* visitor

vi'sivo *a* visual

'viso *nm* face

vi'sone *nm* mink

'vispo *a* lively

vis'suto *pp di* vivere ● *a* experienced

'vist|a *nf* sight; *(veduta)* view; **a ~a d'occhio** *(crescere)* visibly; *(estendersi)* as far as the eye can see; **in ~a di** in view of; **perdere di ~a qcno** lose sight of sb; *fig* lose touch with sb. **~o** *pp di* **vedere** ● *nm* visa. **vi'stoso** *a* showy; *(notevole)* considerable

visu'ale *a* visual. **~izza'tore** *nm* *Comput* display, VDU. **~izzazi'one** *nf* *Comput* display

'vita *nf* life; *(durata della vita)* lifetime; *Anat* waist; **a ~** for life; **essere in fin di ~** be at death's door; **essere in ~** be alive

vi'tale *a* vital. **~ità** *nf* vitality

vita'lizio *a* life *attrib* ● *nm* [life] annuity

vita'min|a *nf* vitamin. **~iz'zato** *a* vitamin-enriched

'vite *nf Mech* screw; *Bot* vine

vi'tello *nm* calf; *Culin* veal; *(pelle)* calfskin

vi'ticcio *nm* tendril

viticol'tore *nm* wine grower. **~ura** *nf* wine growing

'vitreo *a* vitreous; *(sguardo)* glassy

'vittima *nf* victim

'vitto *nm* food; *(pasti)* board. ● **e alloggio** board and lodging

vit'toria *nf* victory

vittori'ano *a* Victorian

vittori'oso *a* victorious

vi'uzza *nf* narrow lane

'viva *int* hurrah!; **~ la Regina!** long live the Queen!

vi'vac|e *a* vivacious; *(mente)* lively; *(colore)* bright. **~ità** *nf* vivacity; *(di mente)* liveliness; *(di colore)* brightness. **~iz'zare** *vt* liven up

vi'vaio *nm* nursery; *(per pesci)* pond; *fig* breeding ground

viva'mente *adv* *(ringraziare)* warmly

vi'vanda *nf* food; *(piatto)* dish

vi'vente *a* living ● *nmpl* **i viventi** the living

'vivere *vi* live; **~ di** live on ● *vt* *(passare)* go through ● *nm* life

'viveri *nmpl* provisions

'vivido *a* vivid

vivisezi'one *nf* vivisection

'vivo *a* alive; *(vivente)* living; *(vivace)* lively; *(colore)* bright; **~ e vegeto** alive and kicking; **farsi ~** keep in touch; *(arrivare)* turn up ● *nm* **colpire qcno sul ~** cut sb to the quick; **dal ~** *(trasmissione)* live; *(disegnare)* from life; **i vivi** the living

vizi'are *vt* spoil *(bambino ecc)*; *(guastare)* vitiate. **~'ato** *a* spoilt; *(aria)* stale. **'vizio** *nm* vice; *(cattiva abitudine)* bad habit; *(difetto)* flaw. **~'oso** *a* dissolute; *(difettoso)* faulty; **circolo ~oso** vicious circle

vocabo'lario *nm* dictionary;

(*lessico*) vocabulary. **vo'cabolo** *nm* word

vo'cale *a* vocal ● *nf* vowel. **vo-'calico** *a* ⟨*corde*⟩ vocal; ⟨*suono*⟩ vowel *attrib*

vocazi'one *nf* vocation

'voce *nf* voice; (*diceria*) rumour; (*di bilancio, dizionario*) entry

voci'are *vi* (*spettegolare*) gossip ● *nm* buzz of conversation

vocife'rare *vi* shout; **si vocifera che...** it is rumoured that...

'vogia *nf* rowing; (*lena*) enthusiasm; (*moda*) vogue; **essere in ~a** be in fashion. **vo'gare** *vi* row. **~a'tore** *nm* oarsman; (*attrezzo*) rowing machine

'vogl|ia *nf* desire; (*volontà*) will; (*della pelle*) birthmark; **aver ~a di fare qcsa** feel like doing sth. **~oso** *a* ⟨*occhi, persona*⟩ covetous

'voi *pers pron you;* **siete ~?** is that you?; **l'avete fatto ~?** did you do it yourself?. **~a'ltri** *pers pron* you

vo'iano *nm* shuttlecock; *Mech* flywheel

vo'lante *a* flying; ⟨*foglio*⟩ loose ● *nm* steering-wheel

volan'tino *nm* leaflet

vo'la|re *vi* fly. **~ta** *nf Sport* final sprint; **di ~ta** in a rush

vo'latile *a* (*liquido*) volatile ● *nm* bird

volée *nf inv Tennis* volley

vo'lente *a* **~ o nolente** whether you like it or not

volente'roso *a* willing

volenti'eri *adv* willingly; **~!** with pleasure!

vo'lere *vt* want; (*chiedere di*) ask for; (*aver bisogno di*) need; **vuole che lo faccia io** he wants me to do it; **fai come vuoi** do as you like; **se tuo padre vuole, ti porto al cinema** if your father agrees, I'll take you to the cinema; **vorrei un caffè** I'd like a coffee; **la leggenda vuole che...** legend has it that...; **la vuoi smettere?** will you stop that!; **senza ~** without meaning to; **voler bene/male a qcno** love/

have something against sb; **voler dire** mean; **ci vuole il latte** we need milk; **ci vuole tempo/pazienza** it takes time/patience; **volerne a** have a grudge against; **vuoi...vuoi...** either...or... ● *nm* will; **voleri** *pl* wishes

vol'gar|e *a* vulgar; (*popolare*) common. **~ità** *nf inv* vulgarity. **~iz'zare** *vt* popularize. **~'mente** *adv* (*grossolanamente*) vulgarly, coarsely; (*comunemente*) commonly

'volger|e *vt/i* turn. **~si** *vr* turn [round]. **~si a** (*dedicarsi*) take up

voli'era *nf* aviary

voli'tivo *a* strong-minded

'volo *nm* flight; **al ~** ⟨*fare qcsa*⟩ quickly; ⟨*prendere qcsa*⟩ in midair; **alzarsi in ~** ⟨*uccello:*⟩ take off; **in ~** airborne. **~ di linea** scheduled flight. **~ nazionale** domestic flight. **~ a vela** gliding.

volontà *nf inv* will; (*desiderio*) wish; **a ~** ⟨*mangiare*⟩ as much as you like. **~ria'mente** *adv* voluntarily. **volon'tario** *a* voluntary ● *nm* volunteer

volonte'roso *a* willing

'volpe *nf* fox

volt *nm inv* volt

'volta *nf* time; (*turno*) turn; (*curva*) bend; *Archit* vault; **4 volte** 4 **times** 4; **a volte** sometimes; **c'era una ~...** once upon a time, there was...; **una ~** once; **due volte** twice; **tre/quattro volte** three/ four times; **una ~ per tutte** once and for all; **uno per ~** one at a time; **uno alla ~** one at a time; **alla ~ di** in the direction of

volta'faccia *nm inv* volte-face

vol'taggio *nm* voltage

vol'ta|re *vt/i* turn; (*rigirare*) turn round; (*rivoltare*) turn over; **~re pagina** *fig* forget the past. **~rsi** *vr* turn [round]

volta'stomaco *nm* nausea; *fig* disgust

volteggi'are *vi* circle; (*ginnastica*) vault

'volto pp di volgere ● nm face; **mi ha mostrato il suo vero ~** he revealed his true colours

vo'lubile a fickle

vo'lum|e nm volume. **~i'noso** a voluminous

voluta'mente adv deliberately

voluttu|osità nf voluptuousness. **~'oso** a voluptuous

vomi'tare vt vomit, be sick. **vomi'tevole** a nauseating. **'vomito** nm vomit.

'vongola nf clam

vo'race a voracious. **~'mente** adv voraciously

vo'ragine nf abyss

'vortice nm whirl; (gorgo) whirlpool; (di vento) whirlwind

'vostro (il ~ m, la vostra f, i vostri mpl, le vostre fpl) poss a your; **è vostra questa macchina?** is this car yours?; **un ~ amico** a friend of yours; **~ padre** your father ● poss pron yours; **i vostri** your folks

vo'ta|nte nmf voter. **~re** vi vote. **~zi'one** nf voting; Sch marks pl. **'voto** nm vote; Sch mark; Relig vow

vs. abbr Comm (vostro) yours

vul'canico a volcanic. **vul'cano** nm volcano

vulne'rabil|e a vulnerable. **~ità** nf vulnerability

vuo'tare vt, **vuo'tarsi** vr empty

vu'oto a empty; (non occupato) vacant; **~ di** (sprovvisto) devoid of ● nm empty space; Phys vacuum; fig void; **assegno a ~** dud cheque; **sotto ~** (prodotto) vacuum-packed; **a perdere** no deposit. **~ d'aria** air pocket

Ww

W abbr (viva) long live

'wafer nm inv (biscotto) wafer

walkie-'talkie nm inv walkie-talkie

watt nm inv watt

WC nm WC

'western a inv cowboy attrib ● nm Cinema western

Xx

X, x a raggi pl X X-rays; **il giorno X** D-day

xenofo'bia nf xenophobia. **xe'nofobo, -a** a xenophobic ● nmf xenophobe

xe'res nm inv sherry

xi'lofono nm xylophone

Yy

yacht nm inv yacht

yen nm inv Fin yen

'yoga nm yoga; (praticante) yogi

'yogurt nm inv yoghurt. **~i'era** nf yoghurt-maker

Zz

zaba[gl]i'one nm zabaglione (dessert made from eggs, wine or marsala and sugar)

zaf'fata nf whiff; (di fumo) cloud

zaffe'rano nm saffron

zaf'firo nm sapphire

'zaino nm rucksack

'**zampa** *nf* leg; **a quattro zampe** 〈*animale*〉 four-legged; 〈*carponi*〉 on all fours. **zampe** *pl* **di gallina** crow's feet

zampil'li|ante *a* spurting. **~re** *vi* spurt. **zam'pillo** *nm* spurt

zam'pogna *nf* bagpipe

zam'pone *nm* stuffed pig's trotter with lentils

'**zanna** *nf* fang; (*di elefante*) tusk

zan'zar|a *nf* mosquito. **~i'era** *nf* (*velo*) mosquito net; (*su finestra*) insect screen

'**zappa** *nf* hoe. **zap'pare** *vt* hoe

zat'tera *nf* raft

zatte'roni *nmpl* (*scarpe*) wedge shoes

za'vorra *nf* ballast; *fig* dead wood

'zazzera *nf* mop of thick hair

'**zebra** *nf* zebra; **zebre** *pl* (*passaggio pedonale*) zebra crossing

'**zecca**[1] *nf* mint; **nuovo di ~** brand-new

'**zecca**[2] *nf* (*parassita*) tick

zec'chino *nm* sequin; **oro ~** pure gold

ze'lante *a* zealous. '**zelo** *nm* zeal

'**zenit** *nm* zenith

zen'zero *nm* ginger

'**zeppa** *nf* wedge

'**zeppo** *a* packed full; **pieno ~ di** crammed *o* packed with

zer'bino *nm* doormat

'**zero** *nm* zero, nought; (*in calcio*) nil; *Tennis* love; **due a ~** (*in partite*) two nil; **ricominciare da ~** *fig* start again from scratch

'**zeta** *nf* zed, zee *Am*

'**zia** *nf* aunt

zibel'lino *nm* sable

'**zigomo** *nm* cheek-bone

zig'zag *nm inv* zigzag; **andare a ~** zigzag

zim'bello *nm* decoy; (*oggetto di scherno*) laughing-stock

'**zinco** *nm* zinc

'**zingaro, -a** *nmf* gypsy

'**zio** *nm* uncle

zi'tel|la *nf* spinster; *pej* old maid. **~'lona** *nf pej* old maid

zit'tire *vi* fall silent ● *vt* silence.

'**zitto** *a* silent; **sta' zitto!** keep quiet!

ziz'zania *nf* (*discordia*) discord; **seminare ~** cause trouble

'**zoccolo** *nm* clog; (*di cavallo*) hoof; (*di terra*) clump; (*di parete*) skirting board, baseboard *Am*; (*di colonna*) base

zodia'cale *a* of the zodiac. **zo'diaco** *nm* zodiac

'**zolfo** *nm* sulphur

'**zolla** *nf* clod; (*di zucchero*) lump

zol'letta *nf* sugar cube, sugar lump

'**zombi** *nmf inv fig* zombie

'**zona** *nf* zone; (*area*) area. **~ di depressione** area of low pressure. **~ disco** area for parking discs only. **~ pedonale** pedestrian precinct. **~ verde** green belt

'**zonzo** *adv* **andare a ~** stroll about

zoo *nm inv* zoo

zoolo'gia *nf* zoology. **zoo'logico** *a* zoological. **zo'ologo, -a** *nmf* zoologist

zoo sa'fari *nm inv* safari park

zoppi'ca|nte *a* limping; *fig* shaky. **~re** *vi* limp; (*essere debole*) be shaky. '**zoppo, -a** *a* lame ● *nmf* cripple

zoti'cone *nm* boor

'**zucca** *nf* marrow; (*fam: testa*) head; (*fam: persona*) thickie

zucche'r|are *vt* sugar. **~i'era** *nf* sugar bowl. **~i'ficio** *nm* sugar refinery. **zucche'rino** *a* sugary ● *nm* sugar cube, sugar lump

'**zucchero** *nm* sugar. **~ di canna** cane sugar. **~ vanigliato** vanilla sugar. **~ a velo** icing sugar. **zucche'roso** *a fig* honeyed

zuc'chin|a *nf*, **~o** *nm* courgette, zucchini *Am*

zuc'cone *nm* blockhead

'**zuffa** *nf* scuffle

zufo'lare *vt/i* whistle

zu'mare *vi* zoom

'**zuppa** *nf* soup. **~ inglese** *Am* trifle

zup'petta *nf* **fare ~** [**con**] dunk

zup'piera *nf* soup tureen

'**zuppo** *a* soaked

Numbers/Numeri

Cardinal numbers/ Numeri cardinali

0	zero	zero
1	one	uno
2	two	due
3	three	tre
4	four	quattro
5	five	cinque
6	six	sei
7	seven	sette
8	eight	otto
9	nine	nove
10	ten	dieci
11	eleven	undici
12	twelve	dodici
13	thirteen	tredici
14	fourteen	quattordici
15	fifteen	quindici
16	sixteen	sedici
17	seventeen	diciassette
18	eighteen	diciotto
19	nineteen	diciannove
20	twenty	venti
21	twenty-one	ventuno
22	twenty-two	ventidue
30	thirty	trenta
40	forty	quaranta
50	fifty	cinquanta
60	sixty	sessanta
70	seventy	settanta
80	eighty	ottanta
90	ninety	novanta
100	a hundred	cento
101	a hundred and one	centouno
110	a hundred and ten	centodieci
200	two hundred	duecento
1,000	a thousand	mille
10,000	ten thousand	diecimila
100,000	a hundred thousand	centomila
1,000,000	a million	un milione

Ordinal numbers/ Numeri ordinali

1st	first	primo
2nd	second	secondo
3rd	third	terzo
4th	fourth	quarto
5th	fifth	quinto
6th	sixth	sesto
7th	seventh	settimo
8th	eighth	ottavo
9th	ninth	nono
10th	tenth	decimo
11th	eleventh	undicesimo
20th	twentieth	ventesimo
21st	twenty-first	ventunesimo
30th	thirtieth	trentesimo
40th	fortieth	quarantesimo
50th	fiftieth	cinquantesimo
100th	hundredth	centesimo
1,000th	thousandth	millesimo

Phrasefinder/Trovafrasi

Useful phrases

Frasi utili

yes, please
no, thank you
sorry
excuse me
you're welcome
I'm sorry, I don't understand

sì, grazie
no, grazie
scusa
mi scusi
prego
scusi, non capisco

Meeting people

Incontri

hello/goodbye
how do you do?
how are you?
nice to meet you

ciao/arrivederci
come sta?
come stai?
piacere

Asking questions

Fare domande

do you speak English/Italian?
what's your name?
where are you from?
where is…?
can I have…?
would you like…?
do you mind if…?

parli inglese/italiano?
come ti chiami?
di dove sei?
dov'è…?
posso avere…?
vuoi…?
le dispiace se…?

Statements about yourself

Presentarsi

my name is…
I'm English/Italian
I don't speak Italian/English
very well
I'm here on holiday
I live near York/Pisa

mi chiamo…
sono inglese/italiano
non parlo molto bene
l'italiano/l'inglese
sono qui in vacanza
abito vicino a York/Pisa

Emergencies

Emergenze

can you help me, please?
I'm lost
I'm ill
call an ambulance/the Police
watch out!

mi può aiutare, per favore?
mi sono perso
sto male
chiami un'ambulanza/la polizia
attenzione!

❶ Going Places

On the road

where's the nearest garage/petrol station (US filling station)?

what's the best way to get there?

I've got a puncture

I'd like to hire a bike/car

I'm looking for somewhere to park

there's been an accident

my car's broken down

the car won't start

Sulla strada

dov'è la stazione di servizio più vicina?

qual è la strada migliore per arrivarci?

ho bucato

vorrei noleggiare una bicicletta/una macchina

sto cercando parcheggio

c'è stato un incidente

ho la macchina in panne

la macchina non parte

By rail

where can I buy a ticket?

what time is the next train to York/Milan?

do I have to change?

can I take my bike on the train?

which platform for the train to Bath/Florence?

there's a train to London at 10 o'clock

a single/return to Birmingham/Turin, please

I'd like a cheap day-return/an all-day ticket

I'd like to reserve a seat

In treno

dove si fanno i biglietti?

a che ora è il prossimo treno per York/Milano?

devo cambiare?

posso portare la bicicletta sul treno?

da quale binario parte il treno per Bath/Firenze?

c'è un treno per Londra alle 10

un biglietto di sola andata/di andata e ritorno per Birmingham/Torino, per favore

vorrei un biglietto giornaliero di andata e ritorno a tariffa ridotta

vorrei prenotare un posto

At the airport

when's the next flight to Paris/Rome?

what time do I have to check in?

where do I check in?

I'd like to confirm my flight

I'd like a window seat/an aisle seat

I want to change/cancel my reservation

All'aeroporto

quand'è il prossimo volo per Parigi/Roma?

a che ora si fa il check-in?

dov'è il check-in?

vorrei confermare il mio volo

vorrei un posto accanto al finestrino/di corridoio

voglio cambiare/annullare la mia prenotazione

Getting there

could you tell me the way to the castle?

how long will it take to get there?

how far is it from here?

which bus do I take for the cathedral?

can you tell me where to get off?

how much is the fare to the town centre (US center)?

what time is the last bus?

how do I get to the airport?

where's the nearest under-ground (US subway) station?

can you call me a taxi, please?

take the first turning right

turn left at the traffic lights/ just past the church

I'll take a taxi

Chiedere e dare indicazioni

può indicarmi la strada per il castello?

quanto ci vuole per arrivarci?

quanto dista da qui?

quale autobus devo prendere per andare al duomo?

può dirmi dove devo scendere?

quant'è la tariffa per il centro?

a che ora è l'ultimo autobus?

come si arriva all'aeroporto?

dov'è la metropolitana più vicina?

può chiamarmi un taxi, per favore?

prenda la prima svolta a destra

al semaforo giri a sinistra/ appena dopo la chiesa

prenderò un taxi

❷ Keeping in touch

On the phone	Al telefono
where can I buy a phone card?	dove si comprano le schede telefoniche?
may I use your phone?	posso usare il telefono?
do you have a mobile?	ha il telefonino?
what is the code for Venice/ Sheffield?	qual è il prefisso di Venezia/ Sheffield?
I want to make a phone call	vorrei fare una telefonata
I'd like to reverse the charges (US call collect)	vorrei fare una telefonata a carico del destinatario
the line's engaged (US busy)	è occupato
there's no answer	non risponde nessuno
hello, this is Natalie	pronto, sono Natalie
is Richard there, please?	c'è Richard, per favore?
who's calling?	chi parla?
sorry, wrong number	ha sbagliato numero
just a moment, please	un attimo, prego
would you like to hold?	vuole attendere in linea?
please tell him/her I called	gli/le dica che ho chiamato, per favore
I'd like to leave a message for him/her	vorrei lasciare un messaggio
I'll try again later	riproverò più tardi
please tell her that Clare called	le dica che ha chiamato Clare
can he/she ring me back?	mi può richiamare?
my home number is…	il mio numero è…
my business number is…	il mio numero al lavoro è…
my fax number is…	il mio numero di fax è…
we were cut off	è caduta la linea

Writing	Corrispondenza
what's your address?	qual è il tuo indirizzo?
here's my business card	questo è il mio biglietto da visita
where is the nearest post office?	dov'è l'ufficio postale più vicino?
could I have a stamp for the UK/Italy, please?	mi dà un francobollo per la Gran Bretagna/l'Italia, per favore?
I'd like stamps for two postcards to the USA, please	vorrei due francobolli per cartolina per gli Stati Uniti, per favore
I'd like to send a parcel/a telegram	vorrei spedire un pacco/mandare un telegramma

On line	Internet
are you on the Internet?	sei su Internet?
what's your e-mail address?	qual è il tuo indirizzo di posta elettronica?
we could send it by e-mail	possiamo spedirlo con la posta elettronica
I'll e-mail it to you on Thursday	te lo mando per posta elettronica giovedì
I looked it up on the Internet	l'ho cercato su Internet
the information is on their website	le informazioni si trovano sul sito web

Meeting up	Appuntamenti
what shall we do this evening?	cosa facciamo stasera?
where shall we meet?	dove ci diamo appuntamento?
I'll see you outside the café at 6 o'clock	ci vediamo davanti al bar alle 6
see you later	a più tardi
I can't today, I'm busy	oggi non posso, sono impegnato

❸ Food and drink

Booking a restaurant | Prenotare un ristorante

can you recommend a good restaurant?	può consigliarmi un buon ristorante?
I'd like to reserve a table for four	vorrei prenotare un tavolo per quattro
a reservation for tomorrow evening at eight o'clock	una prenotazione per domani sera alle otto
I booked a table for two	ho prenotato un tavolo per due

Ordering | Ordinare

could we see the menu/wine list, please?	possiamo avere il menù/la carta dei vini, per favore?
do you have a vegetarian/children's menu?	avete un menù vegetariano/per bambini?
could we have some more bread/wine?	possiamo avere dell'altro pane/vino?
could I have the bill (US check)?	il conto, per favore
a bottle of mineral water, please	una bottiglia d'acqua minerale, per favore
as a starter ... and to follow ...	come antipasto ... e poi ...
a black/white coffee	un caffè/un caffè macchiato
we'd like to pay separately	conti separati, per favore

Reading a menu | Leggere il menù

cover charge	coperto
starters	antipasti
soups/first courses	minestre/primi piatti
main courses	secondi piatti
dish/soup of the day	piatto/minestra del giorno
salads/choice of vegetables	insalate/verdure a scelta
meat/game and poultry	carne/selvaggina e pollame
side dishes	contorni
desserts	dolci
drinks	bevande

Any complaints?

there's a mistake in the bill (US check)	c'è un errore nel conto
the meat isn't cooked/ is overdone	la carne è poco/troppo cotta
that's not what I ordered	non avevo ordinato questo
we are waiting to be served	stiamo aspettando che ci servano
we are still waiting for our drinks	stiamo ancora aspettando da bere
my coffee is cold	il caffè è freddo
the wine is not chilled	il vino non è fresco

Lamentele?

Food shopping

where is the nearest super-market?	dov'è il supermercato più vicino?
is there a baker's/butcher's near here?	c'è una panetteria/macelleria qui vicino?
can I have a carrier bag	mi dà un sacchetto di plastica
how much is it?	quant'è?
I'll have that one/this one	prendo quello/questo

Fare la spesa

On the shopping list

I'd like some bread	vorrei del pane
that's all, thank you	nient'altro, grazie
a bit more/less, please	un po' di più/meno, grazie
that's enough, thank you	basta così, grazie
100 grams of salami/cheese	un etto di salame/formaggio
half a kilo of tomatoes	mezzo chilo di pomodori
a packet of tea	un pacchetto di tè
a carton/litre of milk	un cartone/litro di latte
a can/bottle of beer	una lattina/bottiglia di birra

La lista della spesa

❹ Places to stay

Camping | In campeggio

can we pitch our tent here?	possiamo montare la tenda qui?
can we park our caravan here?	possiamo parcheggiare la roulotte qui?
what are the facilities like?	che attrezzature ci sono?
how much is it per night?	quant'è a notte?
where do we park the car?	dov'è il parcheggio?
we're looking for a campsite	stiamo cercando un campeggio
this is a list of local campsites	questo è l'elenco dei campeggi della zona
we go on a camping holiday every year	andiamo in campeggio tutti gli anni

At the hotel | In albergo

I'd like a double/single room with bath	vorrei una camera doppia/singola con bagno
we have a reservation in the name of Morris	abbiamo prenotato a nome Morris
we'll be staying three nights, from Friday to Sunday	ci fermiamo tre notti, da venerdì a domenica
how much does the room cost?	quant'è la camera?
I'd like to see the room, please	vorrei vedere la camera, per favore
what time is breakfast?	a che ora è la colazione?
can I leave this in your safe?	posso lasciare questo nella cassaforte?
bed and breakfast	camera e prima colazione
we'd like to stay another night	vorremmo fermarci un'altra notte
please call me at 7:30	mi chiami alle 7.30, per favore
are there any messages for me?	ci sono messaggi per me?

Hostels	Ostelli
could you tell me where the youth hostel is?	mi sa dire dov'è l'ostello della gioventù?
what time does the hostel close?	a che ora chiude l'ostello?
I'm staying in a hostel	alloggio in un ostello
the hostel we're staying in is great value	l'ostello in cui alloggiamo è molto conveniente
I know a really good hostel in Dublin	conosco un ottimo ostello a Dublino
I'd like to go backpacking in Australia	mi piacerebbe girare l'Australia con zaino e sacco a pelo

Rooms to let	In affitto
I'm looking for a room with a reasonable rent	vorrei affittare una camera a prezzo modico
I'd like to rent an apartment for a few weeks	vorrei affittare un appartamento per qualche settimana
where do I find out about rooms to let?	dove posso informarmi su camere in affitto?
what's the weekly rent?	quant'è l'affitto alla settimana?
I'm staying with friends at the moment	al momento alloggio presso amici
I rent an apartment on the outskirts of town	affitto un appartamento in periferia
the room's fine—I'll take it	la camera mi piace, la prendo
the deposit is one month's rent in advance	la caparra è di un mese d'affitto

❺ Shopping and money

At the bank | In banca

I'd like to change some money	vorrei cambiare dei soldi
I want to change some lire into pounds	vorrei cambiare delle lire in sterline
do you take Eurocheques?	accettate Eurochèque?
what's the exchange rate today?	quant'è il tasso di cambio oggi?
I prefer traveller's cheques (US traveler's checks) to cash	preferisco i traveller's cheque al contante
I'd like to transfer some money from my account	vorrei fare un bonifico
I'll get some money from the cash machine	prenderò dei soldi dal bancomat®
I'm with another bank	ho il conto in un'altra banca

Finding the right shop | Il negozio giusto

where's the main shopping district?	dov'è la zona commerciale principale?
where's a good place to buy sunglasses/shoes?	qual è il posto migliore per comprare occhiali da sole/scarpe?
where can I buy batteries/postcards?	dove posso comprare pile/cartoline?
where's the nearest chemist/bookshop?	dov'è la farmacia/libreria più vicina?
is there a good food shop around here?	c'è un buon negozio di generi alimentari qui vicino?
what time do the shops open/close?	a che ora aprono/chiudono i negozi?
where can I hire a car?	dove posso noleggiare una macchina?
where did you get those?	dove le/li hai comprati?
I'm looking for presents for my family	sto cercando dei regalini per la mia famiglia
we'll do all our shopping on Saturday	faremo la spesa sabato
I love shopping	adoro fare spese

Are you being served?

how much does that cost?	
can I try it on?	
can you keep it for me?	
could you wrap it for me, please?	
can I pay by credit card/cheque (US check)?	
do you have this in another colour (US color)?	
could I have a bag, please?	
I'm just looking	
I'll think about it	
I'd like a receipt, please	
I need a bigger/smaller size	
I take a size 10/a medium	
it doesn't suit me	
I'm sorry, I don't have any change/anything smaller	
that's all, thank you	

Nei negozi

quanto costa quello?
posso provarlo?
me lo mette da parte?
me lo incarta, per favore?

posso pagare con la carta di credito/un assegno?
c'è in altri colori?

mi dà un sacchetto, per favore?
sto solo dando un'occhiata
ci devo pensare
mi dà lo scontrino, per favore?
mi serve la taglia più grande/piccola
porto la 42/la media
non mi sta bene
mi dispiace, non ho spiccioli/biglietti più piccoli
nient'altro, grazie

Changing things

can I have a refund?
can you mend it for me?
can I speak to the manager?
it doesn't work
I'd like to change it, please
I bought this here yesterday

Cambiare un acquisto

rimborsate i soldi?
può ripararlo?
posso parlare con il direttore?
non funziona
vorrei cambiarlo, per favore
l'ho comprato qui ieri

➏ Sport and leisure

Keeping fit

where can we play
football/squash?

where is the local sports centre
(US center)?

what's the charge per day?

is there a reduction for
children/a student discount?

I'm looking for a swimming
pool/tennis court

you have to be a member

I play tennis on Mondays

I would like to go fishing/riding

I want to do aerobics

I love swimming/rollerblading

we want to hire skis/
snowboards

Tenersi in forma

dove possiamo giocare a
calcio/squash?

dov'è il centro sportivo della
zona?

quant'è la tariffa giornaliera?

c'è uno sconto per bambini/
studenti?

sto cercando una piscina/
un campo da tennis

bisogna essere soci

gioco a tennis di lunedì

vorrei andare a pescare/
a cavallo

vorrei fare aerobica

mi piace nuotare/pattinare

vorremmo noleggiare degli
sci/snowboard

Watching sport

is there a football match on
Sunday?

which teams are playing?

where can I get tickets?

I'd like to see a rugby/football
match

my favourite (US favorite) team
is…

let's watch the match on TV

Assistere a un incontro sportivo

c'è una partita di calcio
domenica?

quali squadre giocano?

dove si comprano i biglietti?

mi piacerebbe vedere una
partita di rugby/calcio

la mia squadra preferita è…

guardiamo la partita in TV

Going to the cinema/theatre/club

what's on?

Andare al cinema/a teatro/in discoteca

cosa danno?

when does the box office open/close?	a che ora apre/chiude il botteghino?
what time does the concert/performance start?	a che ora inizia il concerto/lo spettacolo?
when does it finish?	a che ora finisce?
are there any seats left for tonight?	ci sono dei posti per stasera?
how much are the tickets?	quanto costano i biglietti?
where can I get a programme (US program)?	dove si comprano i programmi?
I want to book tickets for tonight's performance	vorrei prenotare dei biglietti per lo spettacolo di stasera
I'll book seats in the circle	prenoterò dei posti in galleria
I'd rather have seats in the stalls	preferirei dei posti in platea
somewhere in the middle, but not too far back	dei posti al centro, ma non troppo distanti
four, please	quattro, per favore
for Saturday	per sabato
we'd like to go to a club	vorremmo andare in discoteca
I go clubbing every weekend	vado in discoteca tutti i fine settimana

Hobbies | ## Hobby

do you have any hobbies?	che hobby hai?
what do you do at the weekend?	cosa fai il fine settimana?
I like yoga/listening to music	mi piace lo yoga/ascoltare musica
I spend a lot of time surfing the Net	passo molto tempo a navigare in Internet
I read a lot	leggo molto
I collect comic books	faccio collezione di fumetti

❼ Good timing

Telling the time

could you tell me the time?
what time is it?
it's 2 o'clock
at about 8 o'clock
at 9 o'clock tomorrow
from 10 o'clock onwards
at 8 a.m./p.m.
at 5 o'clock in the morning/afternoon
it's five past/quarter past/half past one
it's twenty-five to/quarter to/five to one
a quarter /three quarters of an hour

Dire l'ora

mi dice che ore sono?
che ora è?
sono le due
verso le otto
domani mattina alle nove
dalle dieci in poi
alle otto di mattina/di sera
alle cinque del mattino/di sera

è l'una e cinque/e un quarto/e mezza
è l'una meno venticinque/meno un quarto/meno cinque
un quarto/tre quarti d'ora

Days and dates

Sunday, Monday, Tuesday, Wednesday, Thursday, Friday, Saturday

January, February, March, April, May, June, July, August, September, October, November, December

what's the date?
it's the second of June
we meet up every Monday
she comes on Tuesdays
we're going away in August
it was the first of April
on November 8th

Giorni, mesi e date

domenica, lunedì, martedì, mercoledì, giovedì, venerdì, sabato

gennaio, febbraio, marzo, aprile, maggio, giugno, luglio, agosto, settembre, ottobre, novembre, dicembre

quanti ne abbiamo oggi?
è il due giugno
ci incontriamo ogni lunedì
viene di martedì
saremo via ad agosto
era il primo aprile
l'otto novembre

Public holidays and special days	Festività
Bank holiday	festa civile
Bank holiday Monday	festa civile che cade di lunedì
long weekend	ponte
New Year's Day (Jan 1)	Capodanno (1 gennaio)
Epiphany (Jan 6)	Epifania (la Befana: 6 gennaio)
St Valentine's Day (Feb 14)	San Valentino (14 febbraio)
Shrove Tuesday/Pancake Day	martedì grasso
Ash Wednesday	mercoledì delle Ceneri
St Joseph's Day (Mar 19)	San Giuseppe (19 marzo)
Mother's Day	Festa della mamma
Palm Sunday	domenica delle Palme
Maundy Thursday	giovedì grasso
Good Friday	venerdì santo
Easter Day	Pasqua
Easter Monday	lunedì dell'Angelo (pasquetta)
Anniversary of the liberation of Italy in 1945	anniversario della Liberazione (25 aprile)
May Day (May 1)	Festa del lavoro (1 maggio)
Father's Day	Festa del papà
Independence Day (Jul 4)	anniversario dell'Indipendenza (4 luglio)
Assumption (Aug 15)	Assunzione (ferragosto: 15 agosto)
Halloween (Oct 31)	vigilia d'Ognissanti
All Saints' Day (Nov 1)	Ognissanti (1 novembre)
Thanksgiving	giorno del Ringraziamento
Christmas Eve (Dec 24)	vigilia di Natale (24 dicembre)
Christmas Day (Dec 25)	Natale (25 dicembre)
Boxing Day (Dec 26)	Santo Stefano (26 dicembre)
New Year's Eve (Dec 31)	San Silvestro (31 dicembre)

❽ Conversion charts/Tabelle di conversione

Length/Lunghezze

inches/pollici	0.39	3.9	7.8	11.7	15.6	19.7	39
cm/centimetri	1	10	20	30	40	50	100

Distance/Distanze

miles/miglia	0.62	6.2	12.4	18.6	24.9	31	62
km/kilometri	1	10	20	30	40	50	100

Weight/Pesi

pounds/libbre	2.2	22	44	66	88	110	220
kg/kilogrammi	1	10	20	30	40	50	100

Capacity/Capacità

gallons/galloni	0.22	2.2	4.4	6.6	8.8	11	22
litres/litri	1	10	20	30	40	50	100

Temperature/Temperature

°C	0	5	10	15	20	25	30	37	38	40
°F	32	41	50	59	68	77	86	98.4	100	104

Clothing and shoe sizes/Taglie e numeri di scarpe

Women's clothing sizes/Abbigliamento femminile

UK	8	10	12	14	16	18
US	6	8	10	12	14	16
Italy	40	42	44	46	48	50

Men's clothing sizes/Abbigliamento maschile

UK/US	36	38	40	42	44	46
Italy	46	48	50	52	54	56

Men's and women's shoes/Scarpe da uomo e da donna

UK women	3	4	5	6	7	7.5	8		
UK men					6	7	8	9	10
US	5.5	6.5	7.5	8.5	9.5	10.5	11.5	12.5	13.5
Italy	36	37	38	39	40	41	42	43	44

Aa

A /eɪ/ n Mus la m inv

a /ə/, accentato /eɪ/ (davanti a una vocale **an**) indef art un m, una f; (before s + consonant, gn, ps and z) uno; (before feminine noun starting with a vowel) un' (each) a; **I am a lawyer** sono avvocato; **a tiger is a feline** la tigre è un felino; **a knife and fork** un coltello e una forchetta; **a Mr Smith is looking for you** un certo signor Smith ti sta cercando; **£2 a kilo/a head** due sterline al chilo/a testa

aback /ə'bæk/ adv **be taken ~** essere preso in contropiede

abandon /ə'bændən/ vt abbandonare; (give up) rinunciare a ●n abbandono m. **~ed** a abbandonato

abashed /ə'bæʃt/ a imbarazzato

abate /ə'beɪt/ vi calmarsi

abattoir /'æbətwɑː(r)/ n mattatoio m

abbey /'æbɪ/ n abbazia f

abbreviat|e /ə'briːvɪeɪt/ vt abbreviare. **~ion** /-'eɪʃn/ n abbreviazione f

abdicat|e /'æbdɪkeɪt/ vi abdicare ● vt rinunciare a. **~ion** /-'keɪʃn/ n abdicazione f

abdomen /'æbdəmən/ n addome m. **~inal** /-'dɒmɪnl/ a addominale

abduct /əb'dʌkt/ vt rapire. **~ion** /-ʌkʃn/ n rapimento m

aberration /æbə'reɪʃn/ n aberrazione f

abet /ə'bet/ vt (pt/pp **abetted**) **aid and ~** Jur essere complice di

abeyance /ə'beɪəns/ n **in ~** in sospeso; **fall into ~** cadere in disuso

abhor /əb'hɔː(r)/ vt (pt/pp **abhorred**) aborrire. **~rence** /-'hɒrəns/ n orrore m

abide /ə'baɪd/ vt (pt/pp **abided**)

(tolerate) sopportare ● **abide by** vi rispettare. **~ing** a perpetuo

ability /ə'bɪlətɪ/ n capacità f inv

abject /'æbdʒekt/ a (poverty) degradante; (apology) umile; (coward) abietto

ablaze /ə'bleɪz/ a in fiamme; **be ~ with light** risplendere di luci

able /'eɪbl/ a capace, abile; **be ~ to do sth** poter fare qcsa; **were you ~ to...?** sei riuscito a...? **~-'bodied** a robusto; Mil abile

ably /'eɪblɪ/ adv abilmente

abnormal /æb'nɔːml/ a anormale. **~ity** /-'mælətɪ/ n anormalità f inv. **~ly** adv in modo anormale

aboard /ə'bɔːd/ adv & prep a bordo

abolish /ə'bɒlɪʃ/ vt abolire. **~ition** /æbə'lɪʃn/ n abolizione f

abomina|ble /ə'bɒmɪnəbl/ a abominevole

Aborigine /æbə'rɪdʒəni/ n aborigeno, -a mf d'Australia

abort /ə'bɔːt/ vt fare abortire; fig annullare. **~ion** /-ɔːʃn/ n aborto m; **have an ~ion** abortire. **~ive** /-tɪv/ a (attempt) infruttuoso

abound /ə'baʊnd/ vi abbondare; **~ in** abbondare in

about /ə'baʊt/ adv (here and there) [di] qua e [di] là; (approximately) circa; **be ~** (illness, tourists:) essere in giro; **be up and ~** essere alzato; **leave sth lying ~** lasciare in giro qcsa ● prep (concerning) su; (in the region of) intorno a; (here and there in) per; **what is the book/the film ~?** di cosa parla il libro/il film?; **he wants to see you - what ~?** ti vuole vedere - a che proposito?; **talk/know ~** parlare/sapere di; **I know nothing ~ it** non ne so niente; **~ 5 o'clock** intorno alle 5; **travel ~ the world**

viaggiare per il mondo; **be ~ to do sth** stare per fare qcsa; **how ~ going to the cinema?** e se andassimo al cinema?

about: **~·'face** n, **~·'turn** n dietro front m inv

above /ə'bʌv/ adv & prep sopra; **~ all** soprattutto

above: **~·'board** a onesto. **~·'mentioned** a suddetto

abrasive /ə'breɪsɪv/ a abrasivo; ⟨remark⟩ caustico ●n abrasivo m

abreast /ə'brest/ adv fianco a fianco; **come ~ of** allinearsi con; **keep ~ of** tenersi al corrente di

abridged /ə'brɪdʒd/ a ridotto

abroad /ə'brɔːd/ adv all'estero

abrupt /ə'brʌpt/ a brusco

abscess /'æbsɪs/ n ascesso m

abscond /əb'skɒnd/ vi fuggire

absence /'æbsəns/ n assenza f; ⟨lack⟩ mancanza f

absent[1] /'æbsənt/ a assente

absent[2] /æb'sent/ vt **~ oneself** essere assente

absentee /æbsən'tiː/ n assente mf

absent-minded /æbsənt'maɪndɪd/ a distratto

absolute /'æbsəluːt/ a assoluto; **an ~ idiot** un perfetto idiota. **~ly** adv assolutamente; ⟨fam: indicating agreement⟩ esattamente

absolution /æbsə'luːʃn/ n assoluzione f

absolve /əb'zɒlv/ vt assolvere

absorb /əb'sɔːb/ vt assorbire; **~ed in** assorto in. **~ent** /-ənt/ a assorbente

absorption /əb'sɔːpʃn/ n assorbimento m; ⟨in activity⟩ concentrazione f

abstain /əb'steɪn/ vi astenersi (**from** da)

abstemious /əb'stiːmɪəs/ a moderato

abstention /əb'stenʃn/ n Pol astensione f

abstinence /'æbstɪnəns/ n astinenza f

abstract /'æbstrækt/ a astratto

●n astratto m; ⟨summary⟩ estratto m

absurd /əb'sɜːd/ a assurdo. **~ity** n assurdità f inv

abundan|ce /ə'bʌndəns/ n abbondanza f. **~t** a abbondante

abuse[1] /ə'bjuːz/ vt ⟨misuse⟩ abusare di; ⟨insult⟩ insultare; ⟨ill-treat⟩ maltrattare

abuse[2] /ə'bjuːs/ n abuso m; ⟨verbal⟩ insulti mpl; ⟨ill-treatment⟩ maltrattamento m. **~ive** /-ɪv/ a offensivo

abut /ə'bʌt/ vi (pt/pp **abutted**) confinare (**onto** con)

abysmal /ə'bɪzml/ a fam pessimo; ⟨ignorance⟩ abissale

abyss /ə'bɪs/ n abisso m

academic /ækə'demɪk/ a teorico; ⟨qualifications, system⟩ scolastico; **be ~** ⟨person:⟩ avere predisposizione allo studio ●n docente mf universitario, -a

academy /ə'kædəmɪ/ n accademia f; ⟨of music⟩ conservatorio m

accede /ək'siːd/ vi **~ to** accedere a ⟨request⟩; salire a ⟨throne⟩

accelerat|e /ək'seləreɪt/ vt/i accelerare. **~ion** /-'reɪʃn/ n accelerazione f. **~or** n Auto acceleratore m

accent /'æksənt/ n accento m

accentuate /ək'sentjʊeɪt/ vt accentuare

accept /ək'sept/ vt accettare. **~able** /-əbl/ a accettabile. **~ance** n accettazione f

access /'ækses/ n accesso m. **~ible** /-'sesɪbl/ a accessibile

accession /ək'seʃn/ n ⟨to throne⟩ ascesa f al trono

accessory /ək'sesərɪ/ n accessorio m; Jur complice mf

accident /'æksɪdənt/ n incidente m; ⟨chance⟩ caso m; **by ~** per caso; ⟨unintentionally⟩ senza volere; **I'm sorry, it was an ~** mi dispiace, non l'ho fatto apposta. **~al** /-'dentl/ a ⟨meeting⟩ casuale; ⟨death⟩ incidentale; ⟨unintentional⟩ involontario. **~ally** adv per caso; (*unintentionally*) inavvertitamente

acclaim /əˈkleɪm/ *n* acclamazione *f* ● *vt* acclamare (**as** come)

acclimatize /əˈklaɪmətaɪz/ *vt* become ~d acclimatarsi

accolade /ˈækəleɪd/ *n* riconoscimento *m*

accommodat|e /əˈkɒmədeɪt/ *vt* ospitare; (*oblige*) favorire. ~ing *a* accomodante. ~ion /-ˈdeɪʃn/ *n* (*place to stay*) sistemazione *f*

accompan|iment /əˈkʌmpənɪmənt/ *n* accompagnamento *m*. ~ist *n* *Mus* accompagnatore, -trice *mf*

accompany /əˈkʌmpənɪ/ *vt* (*pt/pp* -ied) accompagnare

accomplice /əˈkʌmplɪs/ *n* complice *mf*

accomplish /əˈkʌmplɪʃ/ *vt* (*achieve*) concludere; realizzare ⟨*aim*⟩. ~ed *a* dotato; (*fact*) compiuto. ~ment *n* realizzazione *f*; (*achievement*) risultato *m*; (*talent*) talento *m*

accord /əˈkɔːd/ *n* (*treaty*) accordo *m*; **with one** ~ tutti d'accordo; **of his own** ~ di sua spontanea volontà. ~ance *n* in ~ance with in conformità di o a

according /əˈkɔːdɪŋ/ adv ~ **to** secondo. ~**ly** *adv* di conseguenza

accordion /əˈkɔːdɪən/ *n* fisarmonica *f*

accost /əˈkɒst/ *vt* abbordare

account /əˈkaʊnt/ *n* conto *m*; (*report*) descrizione *f*; (*of eyewitness*) resoconto *m*; ~**s** *pl* Comm conti *mpl*; **on** ~ di a causa di; **on no** ~ per nessun motivo; **on this** ~ per questo motivo; **on my** ~ per causa mia; **of no** ~ di nessuna importanza; **take into** ~ tener conto di ● **account for** *vi* (*explain*) spiegare; (*person:*) render conto di; (*constitute*) costituire. ~**ability** *n* responsabilità *f* *inv*. ~**able** *a* responsabile (**for** di)

accountant /əˈkaʊntənt/ *n* (book-

keeper) contabile *mf*; (*consultant*) commercialista *mf*

accredited /əˈkredɪtɪd/ *a* accreditato

accrue /əˈkruː/ *vi* (*interest:*) maturare

accumulat|e /əˈkjuːmjʊleɪt/ *vt* accumulare ● *vi* accumularsi. ~**ion** /-ˈleɪʃn/ *n* accumulazione *f*

accura|cy /ˈækjʊrəsɪ/ *n* precisione *f*. ~**te** /-rət/ *a* preciso. ~**tely** *adv* con precisione

accusation /ækjuˈzeɪʃn/ *n* accusa *f*

accusative /əˈkjuːzətɪv/ *a* & *n* ~ [**case**] Gram accusativo *m*

accuse /əˈkjuːz/ *vt* accusare; ~ **sb of doing sth** accusare qcno di fare qcsa. ~**d** *n* the ~**d** l'accusato *m*, l'accusata *f*

accustom /əˈkʌstəm/ *vt* abituare (**to** a); **grow** *or* **get** ~**ed to** abituarsi a. ~**ed** *a* abituato

ace /eɪs/ *n* Cards asso *m*; (*tennis*) ace *m* *inv*

ache /eɪk/ *n* dolore *m* ● *vi* dolere, far male; ~ **all over** essere tutto indolenzito

achieve /əˈtʃiːv/ *vt* ottenere ⟨*success*⟩; realizzare ⟨*goal, ambition*⟩. ~**ment** *n* (*feat*) successo *m*

acid /ˈæsɪd/ *a* acido ● *n* acido *m*. ~**ity** /əˈsɪdətɪ/ *n* acidità *f*. ~ **rain** *n* pioggia *f* acida

acknowledge /əkˈnɒlɪdʒ/ *vt* riconoscere; rispondere a ⟨*greeting*⟩; far cenno di aver notato ⟨*sb's presence*⟩. ~ **receipt of** accusare ricevuta di. ~**ment** *n* riconoscimento *m*; **send an** ~**ment of a letter** confermare il ricevimento di una lettera

acne /ˈæknɪ/ *n* acne *f*

acorn /ˈeɪkɔːn/ *n* ghianda *f*

acoustic /əˈkuːstɪk/ *a* acustico. ~**s** *npl* acustica *fsg*

acquaint /əˈkweɪnt/ *vt* ~ **sb with** metter qcno al corrente di; **be** ~**ed with** conoscere ⟨*person*⟩; essere a conoscenza di ⟨*fact*⟩. ~**ance** *n* (*person*) conoscente *mf*; **make**

sb's **~ance** fare la conoscenza di qcno

acquiesce /ˌækwɪˈes/ vi acconsentire (**to, in** a). **~nce** n acquiescenza f

acquire /əˈkwaɪə(r)/ vt acquisire

acquisit|ion /ækwɪˈzɪʃn/ n acquisizione f. **~ive** /əˈkwɪzətɪv/ a avido

acquit /əˈkwɪt/ vt (pt/pp **acquitted**) assolvere; **~ oneself well** cavarsela bene. **~tal** n assoluzione f

acre /ˈeɪkə(r)/ n acro m (= 4 047 m²)

acrid /ˈækrɪd/ a acre

acrimon|ious /ækrɪˈməʊnɪəs/ a aspro. **~y** /ˈækrɪmənɪ/ n asprezza f

acrobat /ˈækrəbæt/ n acrobata mf. **~ic** /-ˈbætɪk/ a acrobatico

across /əˈkrɒs/ adv dall'altra parte; (wide) in larghezza; (not lengthwise) attraverso; (in crossword) orizzontale; **come ~ sth** imbattersi in qcsa; **go ~** attraversare ● prep (crosswise) di traverso su; (on the other side of) dall'altra parte di

act /ækt/ n atto m; (in variety show) numero m; **put on an ~** fam fare scena ● vi agire; (behave) comportarsi; Theat recitare; (pretend) fingere; **~ as** fare da ● vt recitare (role). **~ing** a (deputy) provvisorio ● n Theat recitazione f; (profession) teatro m. **~ing profession** n professione f dell'attore

action /ˈækʃn/ n azione f; Mil combattimento m; Jur azione f legale; **out of ~** (machine:) fuori uso; **take ~** agire. **~ 'replay** n replay m inv

activ|e /ˈæktɪv/ a attivo. **~ely** adv attivamente. **~ity** /-ˈtɪvətɪ/ n attività f inv

act|or /ˈæktə(r)/ n attore m. **~ress** n attrice f

actual /ˈæktʃʊəl/ a (real) reale. **~ly** adv in realtà

acumen /ˈækjʊmən/ n acume m

acupuncture /ˈækjʊ-/ n agopuntura f

acute /əˈkjuːt/ a acuto; (shortage, hardship) estremo

AD abbr (**Anno Domini**) d.C.

ad /æd/ n fam pubblicità f inv

adamant /ˈædəmənt/ a categorico (**that** sul fatto che)

adapt /əˈdæpt/ vt adattare (play) ● vi adattarsi. **~ability** /-əˈbɪlətɪ/ n adattabilità f. **~able** /-əbl/ a adattabile

adaptation /ædæpˈteɪʃn/ n Theat adattamento m

adapter, adaptor /əˈdæptə(r)/ n adattatore m; (two-way) presa f multipla

add /æd/ vt aggiungere; Math addizionare ● vi addizionare; **~ to** (fig: increase) aggravare. **add up** vt addizionare (figures) ● vi addizionare; **~ up to** ammontare a; **it doesn't ~ up** fig non quadra

adder /ˈædə(r)/ n vipera f

addict /ˈædɪkt/ n tossicodipendente mf; fig fanatico, -a mf

addict|ed /əˈdɪktɪd/ a assuefatto (**to** a); **~ed to drugs** tossicodipendente; **he's ~ed to television** è videodipendente. **~ion** /-ɪkʃn/ n dipendenza f; (to drugs) tossicodipendenza f. **~ive** /-ɪv/ a **be ~ive** dare assuefazione

addition /əˈdɪʃn/ n Math addizione f; (thing added) aggiunta f; **in ~** in aggiunta. **~al** a supplementare. **~ally** adv in più

additive /ˈædɪtɪv/ n additivo m

address /əˈdres/ n indirizzo m; (speech) discorso m; **form of ~** formula f di cortesia ● vt indirizzare; (speak to) rivolgersi a (person); tenere un discorso a (meeting). **~ee** /ædreˈsiː/ n destinatario, -a mf

adenoids /ˈædənɔɪdz/ npl adenoidi fpl

adept /ˈædept/ a & n esperto, -a mf (**at** in)

adequate /ˈædɪkwət/ a adeguato. **~ly** adv adeguatamente

adhere /ədˈhɪə(r)/ vi aderire; **~ to** attenersi a (principles, rules)

adhesive /əd'hiːsɪv/ a adesivo ● n adesivo m

adjacent /ə'dʒeɪsənt/ a adiacente

adjective /'ædʒɪktɪv/ n aggettivo m

adjoin /ə'dʒɔɪn/ vt essere adiacente a. **~ing** a adiacente

adjourn /ə'dʒɜːn/ vt/i aggiornare (**until** a). **~ment** n aggiornamento m

adjudicate /ə'dʒuːdɪkeɪt/ vi decidere; (*in competition*) giudicare

adjust /ə'dʒʌst/ vt modificare; regolare (*focus, sound etc*) ● vi adattarsi. **~able** /-əbl/ a regolabile. **~ment** n adattamento m; Techn regolamento m

ad lib /æd'lɪb/ a improvvisato ● adv a piacere ● n (pt/pp ad libbed) fam improvvisare

administer /əd'mɪnɪstə(r)/ vt amministrare; somministrare (*medicine*)

administration /ədmɪnɪ'streɪʃn/ n amministrazione f; Pol governo m. **~or** /əd'mɪnɪstreɪtə(r)/ n amministratore, -trice f

admirable /'ædmərəbl/ a ammirevole

admiral /'ædmərəl/ n ammiraglio m

admiration /ædmə'reɪʃn/ n ammirazione f

admire /əd'maɪə(r)/ vt ammirare. **~r** n ammiratore, -trice mf

admissible /əd'mɪsɪbl/ a ammissibile

admission /əd'mɪʃn/ n ammissione f; (*to hospital*) ricovero m; (*entry*) ingresso m

admit /əd'mɪt/ vt (pt/pp admitted) (*let in*) far entrare; (*to hospital*) ricoverare; (*acknowledge*) ammettere ● vi **~ to sth** ammettere qcsa. **~tance** n ammissione f; **'no ~tance'** 'vietato l'ingresso'. **~tedly** adv bisogna riconoscerlo

admonish /əd'mɒnɪʃ/ vt ammonire

ado /ə'duː/ n **without more ~** senza ulteriori indugi

adolescence /ædə'lesns/ n adolescenza f. **~t** a & n adolescente mf

adopt /ə'dɒpt/ vt adottare; Pol scegliere (*candidate*). **~ion** /-ɒpʃn/ n adozione f. **~ive** /-ɪv/ a adottivo

adorable /ə'dɔːrəbl/ a adorabile. **~ation** /ædə'reɪʃn/ n adorazione f

adore /ə'dɔː(r)/ vt adorare

adrenalin /ə'drenəlɪn/ n adrenalina f

Adriatic /eɪdrɪ'ætɪk/ a & n **the ~ [Sea]** il mare Adriatico, l'Adriatico m

adrift /ə'drɪft/ a alla deriva; **be ~** andare alla deriva; **come ~** staccarsi

adroit /ə'drɔɪt/ a abile

adulation /ædjʊ'leɪʃn/ n adulazione f

adult /'ædʌlt/ n adulto, -a mf

adulterate /ə'dʌltəreɪt/ vt adulterare (*wine*)

adultery /ə'dʌltərɪ/ n adulterio m

advance /əd'vɑːns/ n avanzamento m; Mil avanzata f; (*payment*) anticipo m; **in ~** in anticipo ● vi avanzare; (*make progress*) fare progressi ● vt avanzare (*theory*); promuovere (*cause*); anticipare (*money*). **~ booking** n prenotazione f [in anticipo]. **~d** a avanzato. **~ment** n promozione f

advantage /əd'vɑːntɪdʒ/ n vantaggio m; **take ~ of** approfittare di. **~ous** /ædvən'teɪdʒəs/ a vantaggioso

advent /'ædvent/ n avvento m

adventure /əd'ventʃə(r)/ n avventura f. **~ous** /-rəs/ a avventuroso

adverb /'ædvɜːb/ n avverbio m

adversary /'ædvəsərɪ/ n avversario, -a mf

adverse /'ædvɜːs/ a avverso. **~ity** /-'vɜːsətɪ/ n avversità f

advert /'ædvɜːt/ n fam = **advertisement**

advertise /'ædvətaɪz/ vt reclamizzare; mettere un annuncio per (*job, flat*) ● vi fare pubblicità; (*for job, flat*) mettere un annuncio

advertisement /əd'vɜ:tɪsmənt/ n pubblicità f inv; (in paper) inserzione f, annuncio m

advertis|er /'ædvətaɪzə(r)/ n (in newspaper) inserzionista mf. **~ing** n pubblicità f ● attrib pubblicitario

advice /əd'vaɪs/ n consigli mpl; **piece of ~** consiglio m

advisable /əd'vaɪzəbl/ a consigliabile

advis|e /əd'vaɪz/ vt consigliare; (inform) avvisare; **~e sb to do sth** consigliare a qcno di fare qcsa; **~e sb against sth** sconsigliare qcsa a qcno. **~er** n consulente mf. **~ory** a consultivo

advocate¹ /'ædvəkət/ n (supporter) fautore, -trice mf

advocate² /'ædvəkeɪt/ vt propugnare

aerial /'eərɪəl/ a aereo ● n antenna f

aerobics /eə'rəʊbɪks/ n aerobica f sg

aero|drome /'eərədrəʊm/ n aerodromo m. **~plane** n aeroplano m

aerosol /'eərəsɒl/ n bomboletta f spray

aesthetic /i:s'θetɪk/ a estetico

afar /ə'fɑ:(r)/ adv from **~** da lontano

affable /'æfəbl/ a affabile

affair /ə'feə(r)/ n affare m; (scandal) caso m; (sexual) relazione f

affect /ə'fekt/ vt influire su; (emotionally) colpire; (concern) riguardare. **~ation** /æfek'teɪʃn/ n affettazione f. **~ed** a affettato

affection /ə'fekʃn/ n affetto m. **~ate** /-ət/ a affettuoso

affiliated /ə'fɪlɪeɪtɪd/ a affiliato

affinity /ə'fɪnətɪ/ n affinità f inv

affirm /ə'fɜ:m/ vt affermare; Jur dichiarare solennemente

affirmative /ə'fɜ:mətɪv/ a affermativo ● n in the **~** affermativamente

afflict /ə'flɪkt/ vt affliggere. **~ion** /-ɪkʃn/ n afflizione f

affluen|ce /'æflʊəns/ n agiatezza f. **~t** a agiato

afford /ə'fɔ:d/ vt be able to **~** sth potersi permettere qcsa. **~able** /-əbl/ a abbordabile

affray /ə'freɪ/ n rissa f

affront /ə'frʌnt/ n affronto m

afield /ə'fi:ld/ adv **further ~** più lontano

afloat /ə'fləʊt/ a a galla

afoot /ə'fʊt/ **there's something ~** si sta preparando qualcosa

aforesaid /ə'fɔ:sed/ a Jur suddetto

afraid /ə'freɪd/ a **be ~** aver paura; **I'm ~ not** purtroppo no; **I'm ~ so** temo di sì; **I'm ~ I can't help you** mi dispiace, ma non posso esserle d'aiuto

afresh /ə'freʃ/ adv da capo

Africa /'æfrɪkə/ n Africa f. **~n** a & n africano, -a f

after /'ɑ:ftə(r)/ adv dopo; **the day ~** il giorno dopo; **be ~** cercare ● prep dopo; **~ all** dopotutto; **the day ~ tomorrow** dopodomani ● conj dopo che

after: **~-effect** n conseguenza f. **~math** /-mɑ:θ/ n conseguenze fpl; **the ~math of war** il dopoguerra; **in the ~math of** nel periodo successivo a. **~'noon** n pomeriggio m; **good ~noon!** buon giorno! **~-sales service** n servizio m assistenza clienti. **~shave** n [lozione f] dopobarba m inv. **~thought** n added as an **~thought** aggiunto in un secondo momento; **~wards** adv in seguito

again /ə'gem/ adv di nuovo; [then] **~** (besides) inoltre; (on the other hand) d'altra parte; **~ and ~** continuamente

against /ə'gemst/ prep contro

age /eɪdʒ/ n età f inv; (era) era f; **~s** fam secoli; **what ~ are you?** quanti anni hai?; **be under ~** non avere l'età richiesta; **be two years of ~** ha due anni ● vt/i (pres p ageing) invecchiare

aged¹ /eɪdʒd/ a **~ two** di due anni

aged² /'eɪdʒɪd/ a anziano ● n the ~ pl gli anziani

ageless /'eɪdʒlɪs/ a senza età

agency /'eɪdʒənsɪ/ n agenzia f; **have the ~ for** essere un concessionario di

agenda /ə'dʒendə/ n ordine m del giorno; **on the ~** all'ordine del giorno; fig in programma

agent /'eɪdʒənt/ n agente mf

aggravat|e /'ægrəveɪt/ vt aggravare; (annoy) esasperare. **~ion** /-'veɪʃn/ n aggravamento m; (annoyance) esasperazione f

aggregate /'ægrɪgət/ a totale ● n totale m; **on ~** nel complesso

aggress|ion /ə'greʃn/ n aggressione f. **~ive** /-sɪv/ a aggressivo. **~iveness** n aggressività f. **~or** n aggressore m

aggro /'ægrəʊ/ n fam aggressività f; (problems) grane fpl

aghast /ə'gɑːst/ a inorridito

agil|e /'ædʒaɪl/ a agile. **~ity** /ə'dʒɪlətɪ/ n agilità f

agitat|e /'ædʒɪteɪt/ vt mettere in agitazione; (shake) agitare ● vi fig **~e for** creare delle agitazioni per. **~ed** a agitato. **~ion** /-'teɪʃn/ n agitazione f. **~or** n agitatore, -trice mf

agnostic /æg'nɒstɪk/ n agnostico, -a mf

ago /ə'gəʊ/ adv fa; **a long time/a month ~** molto tempo/un mese fa

agog /ə'gɒg/ a eccitato

agoniz|e /'ægənaɪz/ vi angosciarsi (over per). **~ing** a angosciante

agony /'ægənɪ/ n agonia f; (mental) angoscia f; **be in ~** avere dei dolori atroci

agree /ə'griː/ vt accordarsi su; ~ **to do sth** accettare di fare qcsa; ~ **that** essere d'accordo [sul fatto] che ● vi essere d'accordo; (figures:) concordare; (reach agreement) mettersi d'accordo; (get on) andare d'accordo; (consent) acconsentire (to a); **it doesn't ~ with me** mi fa male; ~ **with sth** (approve of) approvare qcsa

agreeable /ə'griːəbl/ a gradevole; (willing) d'accordo

agreed /ə'griːd/ a convenuto

agreement /ə'griːmənt/ n accordo m; **in ~** d'accordo

agricultur|al /ægrɪ'kʌltʃərəl/ a agricolo. **~e** /'ægrɪkʌltʃə(r)/ n agricoltura f

aground /ə'graʊnd/ adv **run ~** (ship:) arenarsi

ahead /ə'hed/ adv avanti; **be ~ of** essere davanti a; fig essere avanti rispetto a; **draw ~** passare davanti (of a); **get ~** (in life) riuscire; **go ~!** fai pure!; **look ~** pensare all'avvenire; **plan ~** fare progetti per l'avvenire

aid /eɪd/ n aiuto m; **in ~ of** a favore di ● vt aiutare

aide /eɪd/ n assistente mf

Aids /eɪdz/ n AIDS m

ail|ing /'eɪlɪŋ/ a malato. **~ment** n disturbo m

aim /eɪm/ n mira f; fig scopo m; **take ~** prendere la mira ● vt puntare (gun) (at contro) ● vi mirare; ~ **to do sth** aspirare a fare qcsa. **~less** a, **~lessly** adv senza scopo

air /eə(r)/ n aria f; **be on the ~** (programme:) essere in onda; **put on ~s** darsi delle arie; **by ~** in aereo; (airmail) per via aerea ● vt arieggiare; far conoscere (views)

air: **~-bed** n materassino m [gonfiabile]. **~-conditioned** a con aria condizionata. **~-conditioning** n aria f condizionata. **~craft** n aereo m. **~craft carrier** n portaerei f inv. **~fare** n tariffa f aerea. **~field** n campo m d'aviazione. **~force** n aviazione f. **~freshener** n deodorante m per l'ambiente. **~gun** n fucile m pneumatico. **~hostess** n hostess f inv. **~letter** n aerogramma m. **~line** n compagnia f aerea. **~lock** n bolla f d'aria. **~mail** n posta f aerea. **~plane** n Am aereo m. **~pocket** n vuoto m d'aria. **~port** n aeroporto m. **~raid** n incursione f aerea. **~raid shelter** n rifugio m an-

tiaereo. **~ship** *n* dirigibile *m*.
~tight *a* ermetico. **~ traffic** *n*
traffico *m* aereo. **~-traffic con-
troller** *n* controllore *m* di volo.
~worthy *a* idoneo al volo

airy /'eərɪ/ *a* (**-ier, -iest**) arieggiato;
⟨*manner*⟩ noncurante

aisle /aɪl/ *n* corridoio *m*; (*in
supermarket*) corsia *f*; (*in church*)
navata *f*

ajar /ə'dʒɑ:(r)/ *a* socchiuso

akin /ə'kɪn/ *a* ~ to simile a

alacrity /ə'lækrɪtɪ/ *n* alacrità *f inv*

alarm /ə'lɑ:m/ *n* allarme *m*; **set
the ~** (*of alarm-clock*) mettere la
sveglia ● *vt* allarmare. **~ clock** *n*
sveglia *f*

alas /ə'læs/ *int* ahimè

album /'ælbəm/ *n* album *m inv*

alcohol /'ælkəhɒl/ *n* alcool *m*. **~ic**
/-'hɒlɪk/ *a* alcolico ● *n* alcolizzato,
-a *mf*. **~ism** *n* alcolismo *m*

alcove /'ælkəʊv/ *n* alcova *f*

alert /ə'lɜ:t/ *a* sveglio; ⟨*watchful*⟩
vigile ● *n* segnale *m* d'allarme;
be on the ~ stare allerta ● *vt*
allertare

algae /'ældʒi:/ *npl* alghe *fpl*

algebra /'ældʒɪbrə/ *n* algebra *f*

Algeria /æl'dʒɪərɪə/ *n* Algeria *f*.
~n *a* & *n* algerino, -a *mf*

alias /'eɪlɪəs/ *n* pseudonimo *m*
● *adv* alias

alibi /'ælɪbaɪ/ *n* alibi *m inv*

alien /'eɪlɪən/ *a* straniero; *fig* estraneo ● *n* straniero, -a *mf*; (*from
space*) alieno, -a *mf*

alienat|e /'eɪlɪəneɪt/ *vt* alienare.
~ion /-'neɪʃn/ *n* alienazione *f*

alight[1] /ə'laɪt/ *vi* scendere; ⟨*bird:*⟩
posarsi

alight[2] /ə'laɪt/ *a* **be ~** essere in fiamme;
set ~ dar fuoco a

align /ə'laɪn/ *vt* allineare. **~ment** *n*
allineamento *m*; **out of ~ment**
non allineato

alike /ə'laɪk/ *a* simile; **be ~** rassomigliarsi ● *adv* in modo simile;
look ~ rassomigliarsi; **summer
and winter ~** sia d'estate che d'inverno

alimony /'ælɪmənɪ/ *n* alimenti *mpl*

alive /ə'laɪv/ *a* vivo; **~ with** bruli-
cante di; **~ to** sensibile a; **~ and
kicking** vivo e vegeto

alkali /'ælkəlaɪ/ *n* alcali *m*

all /ɔ:l/ *a* tutto; **~ the children, ~
children** tutti i bambini; **~ day**
tutto il giorno; **he refused ~ help**
ha rifiutato qualsiasi aiuto; **for ~
that** (*nevertheless*) nonostante;
in ~ sincerity in tutta sincerità;
be ~ for essere favorevole a
● *pron* tutto; **~ of you/them** tutti
voi/loro; **~ of it** tutto; **~ of the
town** tutta la città; **in ~** in tutto;
in ~ tutto sommato; **most of ~**
più di ogni altra cosa; **once and
for ~** una volta per tutte ● *adv*
completamente; **~ but** quasi; **~ at
once** (*at the same time*) tutto in
una volta; **~ at once, ~ of a
sudden** all'improvviso; **~ too
soon** troppo presto; **~ the same**
(*nevertheless*) nonostante; **~ the
better** meglio ancora; **she's
not ~ that good an actress** non è
poi così brava come attrice; **~ in**
in tutto; *fam* esausto; **thirty/three
~** (*in sport*) trenta/tre pari; **~
over** (*finished*) tutto finito; (*everywhere*) dappertutto; **it's ~ right** (*I
don't mind*) non fa niente; **I'm ~
right** (*not hurt*) non ho niente; **~
right!** va bene!

allay /ə'leɪ/ *vt* placare ⟨*suspicions,
anger*⟩

allegation /ælɪ'geɪʃn/ *n* accusa *f*

allege /ə'ledʒ/ *vt* dichiarare. **~d** *a*
presunto. **~dly** /-ɪdlɪ/ *adv* a quanto si dice

allegiance /ə'li:dʒəns/ *n* fedeltà *f*

allegor|ical /ælɪ'gɒrɪkl/ *a* allegori-
co. **~y** /'ælɪgərɪ/ *n* allegoria *f*

allerg|ic /ə'lɜ:dʒɪk/ *a* allergico. **~y**
/'ælədʒɪ/ *n* allergia *f*

alleviate /ə'li:vɪeɪt/ *vt* alleviare

alley /'ælɪ/ *n* vicolo *m*; (*for
bowling*) corsia *f*

alliance /ə'laɪəns/ *n* alleanza *f*

allied /'ælaɪd/ *a* alleato; (*fig:
related*) connesso (**to** a)

alligator /'ælɪgeɪtə(r)/ n alligatore m

allocat|e /'æləkeɪt/ vt assegnare; distribuire (resources). **~ion** /-'keɪʃn/ n assegnazione f; (of resources) distribuzione f

allot /ə'lɒt/ vt (pt/pp allotted) distribuire. **~ment** n distribuzione f; (share) parte f; (land) piccolo lotto m di terreno

allow /ə'laʊ/ vt permettere; (grant) accordare; (reckon on) contare; (agree) ammettere; **~ for** tener conto di; **~ sb to do sth** permettere a qcno di fare qcsa; **you are not ~ed to...** è vietato...

allowance /ə'laʊəns/ n sussidio m; (Am: pocket money) paghetta f; (for petrol etc) indennità f inv; (of luggage, duty free) limite m; **make ~s for** essere indulgente verso (sb); tener conto di (sth)

alloy /'ælɔɪ/ n lega f

allude /ə'luːd/ vi alludere

allusion /ə'luːʒn/ n allusione f

ally¹ /'ælaɪ/ n alleato, -a mf

ally² /ə'laɪ/ vt (pt/pp -ied) alleare; **~ oneself with** allearsi con

almighty /ɔːl'maɪtɪ/ a (fam: big) mega inv ● n the A~ l'Onnipotente m

almond /'ɑːmənd/ n mandorla f; (tree) mandorlo m

almost /'ɔːlməʊst/ adv quasi

alone /ə'ləʊn/ a solo; **leave me ~!** lasciami in pace!; **let ~** (not to mention) figurarsi ● adv da solo

along /ə'lɒŋ/ prep lungo ● adv **~ with** assieme a; **all ~** tutto il tempo; **come ~!** (hurry up) vieni qui!; **I'll be ~ in a minute** arrivo tra un attimo; **move ~** spostarsi; **move ~!** circolare!

along'side adv lungo bordo ● prep lungo; **work ~ sb** lavorare fianco a fianco con qcno

aloof /ə'luːf/ a distante

aloud /ə'laʊd/ adv ad alta voce

alphabet /'ælfəbet/ n alfabeto m. **~ical** /-'betɪkl/ a alfabetico

alpine /'ælpaɪn/ a alpino

Alps /ælps/ npl Alpi fpl

already /ɔːl'redɪ/ adv già

Alsatian /æl'seɪʃn/ n (dog) pastore m tedesco

also /'ɔːlsəʊ/ adv anche; **~, I need...** [e] inoltre, ho bisogno di...

altar /'ɔːltə(r)/ n altare m

alter /'ɔːltə(r)/ vt cambiare; aggiustare (clothes) ● vi cambiare. **~ation** /-'reɪʃn/ n modifica f

alternate¹ /'ɔːltəneɪt/ vi alternarsi ● vt alternare

alternate² /ɔːl'tɜːnət/ a alterno; **on ~ days** a giorni alterni

'alternating current n corrente f alternata

alternative /ɔːl'tɜːnətɪv/ a alternativo ● n alternativa f. **~ly** adv alternativamente

although /ɔːl'ðəʊ/ conj benché, sebbene

altitude /'æltɪtjuːd/ n altitudine f

altogether /ɔːltə'geðə(r)/ adv (in all) in tutto; (completely) completamente; **I'm not ~ sure** non sono del tutto sicuro

altruistic /æltrʊ'ɪstɪk/ a altruistico

aluminium /æljʊ'mɪnɪəm/ n, Am **aluminum** /ə'luːmɪnəm/ n alluminio m

always /'ɔːlweɪz/ adv sempre

am /æm/ see **be**

a.m. abbr (ante meridiem) del mattino

amalgamate /ə'mælgəmeɪt/ vt fondere ● vi fondersi

amass /ə'mæs/ vt accumulare

amateur /'æmətə(r)/ n non professionista mf, pej dilettante mf ● attrib dilettante; **~ dramatics** filodrammatica f. **~ish** a dilettantesco

amaze /ə'meɪz/ vt stupire. **~d** a stupito. **~ment** n stupore m

amazing /ə'meɪzɪŋ/ a incredibile

ambassador /æm'bæsədə(r)/ n ambasciatore, -trice mf

amber /'æmbə(r)/ n ambra f ● a (colour) ambra inv

ambidextrous /ˌæmbɪˈdekstrəs/ a ambidestro

ambience /ˈæmbɪəns/ n atmosfera f

ambigu|ity /æmbɪˈgjuːətɪ/ n ambiguità f inv. ~**ous** /-ˈbɪgjʊəs/ a ambiguo

ambiti|on /æmˈbɪʃn/ n ambizione f; (aim) aspirazione f. ~**ous** /-ʃəs/ a ambizioso

ambivalent /æmˈbɪvələnt/ a ambivalente

amble /ˈæmbl/ vi camminare senza fretta

ambulance /ˈæmbjʊləns/ n ambulanza f

ambush /ˈæmbʊʃ/ n imboscata f ● vt tendere un'imboscata a

amenable /əˈmiːnəbl/ a conciliante; ~ **to** sensibile a

amend /əˈmend/ vt modificare. ~**ment** n modifica f. ~**s** npl make ~**s** fare ammenda (for di, per)

amenities /əˈmiːnətɪz/ npl comodità fpl

America /əˈmerɪkə/ n America f. ~**n** a & n americano, -a mf

amiable /ˈeɪmɪəbl/ a amabile

amicable /ˈæmɪkəbl/ a amichevole

amiss /əˈmɪs/ a there's something ~ c'è qualcosa che non va ● adv take sth ~ prendersela (a male); it won't come ~ non sarebbe sgradito

ammonia /əˈməʊnɪə/ n ammoniaca f

ammunition /æmjʊˈnɪʃn/ n munizioni fpl

amnesia /æmˈniːzɪə/ n amnesia f

amnesty /ˈæmnəstɪ/ n amnistia f

among[st] /əˈmʌŋ[st]/ prep tra, fra

amoral /eɪˈmɒrəl/ a amorale

amorous /ˈæmərəs/ a amoroso

amount /əˈmaʊnt/ n quantità f inv; (sum of money) importo m ● vi to ~ **to** ammontare a; fig equivalere a

amp /æmp/ n ampère m inv

amphibi|an /æmˈfɪbɪən/ n anfibio m. ~**ous** /-ɪəs/ a anfibio

amphitheatre /ˈæmfɪ-/ n anfiteatro m

ampl|e /ˈæmpl/ a (large) grande; (proportions) ampio; (enough) largamente sufficiente

amplif|ier /ˈæmplɪfaɪə(r)/ n amplificatore m. ~**y** /-faɪ/ vt (pt/pp -ied) amplificare (sound)

amputat|e /ˈæmpjʊteɪt/ vt amputare. ~**ion** /-ˈteɪʃn/ n amputazione f

amuse /əˈmjuːz/ vt divertire. ~**ment** n divertimento m. ~**ment arcade** n sala f giochi

amusing /əˈmjuːzɪŋ/ a divertente

an /ən/, accentato /æn/ see **a**

anaem|ia /əˈniːmɪə/ n anemia f. ~**ic** a anemico

anaesthetic /ænəsˈθetɪk/ n anestesia f

anaesthet|ist /əˈniːsθətɪst/ n anestesista mf

analog[ue] /ˈænəlɒg/ a analogico

analogy /əˈnælədʒɪ/ n analogia f

analyse /ˈænəlaɪz/ vt analizzare

analysis /əˈnæləsɪs/ n analisi f inv

analyst /ˈænəlɪst/ n analista mf

analytical /ænəˈlɪtɪkl/ a analitico

anarch|ist /ˈænəkɪst/ n anarchico, -a mf. ~**y** n anarchia f

anatom|ical /ænəˈtɒmɪkl/ a anatomico. ~**ically** adv anatomicamente. ~**y** /əˈnætəmɪ/ n anatomia f

ancest|or /ˈænsestə(r)/ n antenato, -a mf. ~**ry** n antenati mpl

anchor /ˈæŋkə(r)/ n ancora f ● vi gettar l'ancora ● vt ancorare

anchovy /ˈæntʃəvɪ/ n acciuga f

ancient /ˈeɪnʃənt/ a antico; fam vecchio

ancillary /ænˈsɪlərɪ/ a ausiliario

and /ənd/, accentato /ænd/ conj e; **two ~ two** due più due; **six hundred ~ two** seicentodue; **more ~ more** sempre più; **nice ~ warm** bello caldo; **try ~ come** cerca di venire; **go ~ get** vai a prendere

anecdote /ˈænɪkdəʊt/ n aneddoto m

anew /ə'nju:/ *adv* di nuovo

angel /'emdʒl/ *n* angelo *m*. **~ic** /æn'dʒelɪk/ *a* angelico

anger /'æŋgə(r)/ *n* rabbia *f* ● *vt* far arrabbiare

angle[1] /'æŋgl/ *n* angolo *m*; *fig* angolazione *f*; **at an ~** storto

angle[2] *vi* pescare con la lenza; **~ for** *fig* cercare di ottenere. **~r** *n* pescatore, -trice *mf*

Anglican /'æŋglɪkən/ *a & n* anglicano, -a *mf*

Anglo-Saxon /æŋgləʊ'sæksn/ *a & n* anglo-sassone *mf*

angr|y /'æŋgrɪ/ *a* (**-ier, -iest**) arrabbiato; **get ~y** arrabbiarsi; **~y with** *or* **at sb** arrabbiato con qcno; **~y at** *or* **about sth** arrabbiato per qcsa. **~ily** *adv* rabbiosamente

anguish /'æŋgwɪʃ/ *n* angoscia *f*

angular /'æŋgjʊlə(r)/ *a* angolare

animal /'ænɪml/ *a & n* animale *m*

animate[1] /'ænɪmət/ *a* animato

animat|e[2] /'ænɪmeɪt/ *vt* animare. **~ed** *a* animato; (*person*) vivace. **~ion** /-'meɪʃn/ *n* animazione *f*

animosity /ænɪ'mɒsətɪ/ *n* animosità *f inv*

ankle /'æŋkl/ *n* caviglia *f*

annex /ə'neks/ *vt* annettere

annex[e] /'æneks/ *n* annesso *m*

annihilat|e /ə'naɪəleɪt/ *vt* annientare. **~ion** /-'leɪʃn/ *n* annientamento *m*

anniversary /ænɪ'vɜ:sərɪ/ *n* anniversario *m*

announce /ə'naʊns/ *vt* annunciare. **~ment** *n* annuncio *m*. **~r** *n* annunciatore, -trice *mf*

annoy /ə'nɔɪ/ *vt* dare fastidio a; **get ~ed** essere infastidito. **~ance** *n* seccatura *f*; (*anger*) irritazione *f*. **~ing** *a* fastidioso

annual /'ænjʊəl/ *a* annuale; (*income*) annuo ● *n Bot* pianta *f* annua; (*children's book*) almanacco *m*

annuity /ə'nju:ətɪ/ *n* annualità *f inv*

annul /ə'nʌl/ *vt* (*pt/pp* **annulled**) annullare

anomaly /ə'nɒməlɪ/ *n* anomalia *f*

anonymous /ə'nɒnɪməs/ *a* anonimo

anorak /'ænəræk/ *n* giacca *f* a vento

anorexi|a /ænə'reksɪə/ *n* anoressia *f*. **~ic** *a* anoressico

another /ə'nʌðə(r)/ *a & pron*; **[one]** un altro, un'altra; **in ~ way** diversamente; **one ~** l'un l'altro

answer /'ɑ:nsə(r)/ *n* risposta *f*; (*solution*) soluzione *f* ● *vt* rispondere a (*person, question, letter*); esaudire (*prayer*); **~ the door** aprire la porta; **~ the telephone** rispondere al telefono ● *vi* rispondere; **~ back** ribattere; **~ for** rispondere di. **~able** /-əbl/ *a* responsabile; **be ~able to sb** rispondere a qcno. **~ing machine** *n Teleph* segreteria *f* telefonica

ant /ænt/ *n* formica *f*

antagonis|m /æn'tægənɪzm/ *n* antagonismo *m*. **~tic** /-'nɪstɪk/ *a* antagonistico

antagonize /æn'tægənaɪz/ *vt* provocare l'ostilità di

Antarctic /æn'tɑ:ktɪk/ *n* Antartico *m* ● *a* antartico

antenatal /æntɪ'neɪtl/ *a* prenatale

antenna /æn'tenə/ *n* antenna *f*

anthem /'ænθəm/ *n* inno *m*

anthology /æn'θɒlədʒɪ/ *n* antologia *f*

anthropology /ænθrə'pɒlədʒɪ/ *n* antropologia *f*

anti-'aircraft /æntɪ-/ *a* antiaereo

antibiotic /æntɪbaɪ'ɒtɪk/ *n* antibiotico *m*

'antibody *n* anticorpo *m*

anticipat|e /æn'tɪsɪpeɪt/ *vt* prevedere; (*forestall*) anticipare. **~ion** /-'peɪʃn/ *n* anticipo *m*; (*excitement*) attesa *f*

anti'climax *n* delusione *f*

anti'clockwise *a & adv* in senso antiorario

antics /'æntɪks/ *npl* gesti *mpl* buffi

anti'cyclone *n* anticiclone *m*

antidote /'æntɪdəʊt/ *n* antidoto *m*

'antifreeze *n* antigelo *m*

antipathy /æn'tɪpəθɪ/ n antipatia f

antiquated /'æntɪkweɪtɪd/ a antiquato

antique /æn'tiːk/ a antico ● n antichità f inv. ~ **dealer** n antiquario, -a mf

antiquity /æn'tɪkwətɪ/ n antichità f

anti-Semitic /æntɪsɪ'mɪtɪk/ a antisemita

anti'septic a & n antisettico m

anti'social a (behaviour) antisociale; (person) asociale

anti'virus program n Comput programma m di antivirus

antlers /'æntləz/ npl corna fpl

anus /'eɪnəs/ n ano m

anxiety /æŋ'zaɪətɪ/ n ansia f

anxious /'æŋkʃəs/ a ansioso. ~**ly** adv con ansia

any /'enɪ/ a (no matter which) qualsiasi, qualunque; **have we ~ wine/biscuits?** abbiamo del vino/ dei biscotti?; **have we ~ jam/ apples?** abbiamo della marmellata/delle mele?; ~ **colour/number you like** qualsiasi colore/numero ti piaccia; **we don't have ~ wine/biscuits** non abbiamo vino/ biscotti; **I don't have ~ reason to lie** non ho nessun motivo per mentire; **for ~ reason** per qualsiasi ragione ● pron (some) ne; (no matter which) qualsiasi; **I don't want ~ [of it]** non ne voglio [nessuno]; **there aren't ~** non ce ne sono; **have we ~?** ne abbiamo?; **have you read ~ of her books?** hai letto qualcuno dei suoi libri? ● adv **I can't go ~ quicker** non posso andare più in fretta; **is it ~ better?** va un po' meglio?; **would you like ~ more?** ne vuoi ancora?; **I can't eat ~ more** non posso mangiare più di niente

'anybody pron chiunque; (after negative) nessuno; **I haven't seen ~** non ho visto nessuno

'anyhow adv ad ogni modo, comunque; (badly) non importa come

'anyone pron = anybody

'anything pron qualche cosa, qualcosa; (no matter what) qualsiasi cosa; (after negative) niente; **take/ buy ~ you like** prendi/compra quello che vuoi; **I don't remember ~** non mi ricordo niente; **he's ~ but stupid** è tutto, ma non stupido; **I'll do ~ but that** farò qualsiasi cosa, tranne quello

'anyway adv ad ogni modo, comunque

'anywhere adv dovunque; (after negative) da nessuna parte; **put it ~** mettilo dove vuoi; **I can't find it ~** non lo trovo da nessuna parte; ~ **else** da qualch'altra parte; (after negative) da nessun'altra parte; **I don't want to go ~ else** non voglio andare da nessun'altra parte

apart /ə'pɑːt/ adv lontano; **live ~** vivere separati; **100 miles ~** lontani 100 miglia; ~ **from** a parte; **you can't tell them ~** non si possono distinguere; **joking ~** scherzi a parte

apartment /ə'pɑːtmənt/ n (Am: flat) appartamento m; **in my ~** a casa mia

apathy /'æpəθɪ/ n apatia f

ape /eɪp/ n scimmia f ● vt scimmiottare

aperitif /ə'perətiːf/ n aperitivo m

aperture /'æpətʃə(r)/ n apertura f

apex /'eɪpeks/ n vertice m

apiece /ə'piːs/ adv ciascuno

apologetic /əpɒlə'dʒetɪk/ a (air, remark) di scusa; **be ~** essere spiacente

apologize /ə'pɒlədʒaɪz/ vi scusarsi (for per)

apology /ə'pɒlədʒɪ/ n scusa f; fig **an ~ for a dinner** una specie di cena

apostle /ə'pɒsl/ n apostolo m

apostrophe /ə'pɒstrəfɪ/ n apostrofo m

appal /ə'pɔːl/ vt (pt/pp **appalled**) sconvolgere. **~ling** a sconvolgente

apparatus /æpə'reɪtəs/ n apparato m

apparent /ə'pærənt/ a evidente; (seeming) apparente. **~ly** adv apparentemente

apparition /æpə'rɪʃn/ n apparizione f

appeal /ə'piːl/ n appello m; (attraction) attrattiva f ● vi fare appello; **~ to** (be attractive to) attrarre. **~ing** a attraente

appear /ə'pɪə(r)/ vi apparire; (seem) sembrare; (publication:) uscire; Theat esibirsi. **~ance** n apparizione f; (look) aspetto m; **to all ~ances** a giudicare dalle apparenze; **keep up ~ances** salvare le apparenze

appease /ə'piːz/ vt placare

appendicitis /əpendɪ'saɪtɪs/ n appendicite f

appendix /ə'pendɪks/ n (pl **-ices** /-ɪsiːz/) (of book) appendice f; (pl **-es**) Anat appendice f

appetite /'æpɪtaɪt/ n appetito m

appetizer /'æpɪtaɪzə(r)/ n stuzzichino m. **~ing** a appetitoso

applaud /ə'plɔːd/ vt/i applaudire. **~se** n applauso m

apple /'æpl/ n mela f. **~-tree** n melo m

appliance /ə'plaɪəns/ n attrezzo m; [**electrical**] **~** elettrodomestico m

applicable /ə'plɪkəbl/ a **be ~ to** essere valido per; **not ~** (on form) non applicabile

applicant /'æplɪkənt/ n candidato, -a mf

application /æplɪ'keɪʃn/ n applicazione f; (request) domanda f; (for job) candidatura f. **~ form** n modulo m di domanda

applied /ə'plaɪd/ a applicato

apply /ə'plaɪ/ vt (pt/pp **-ied**) applicare; **~ oneself** applicarsi ● vi applicarsi; (law:) essere applicabile; **~ to** (ask) rivolgersi a; **~ for** fare domanda per (job etc)

appoint /ə'pɔɪnt/ vt nominare; fissare (time). **~ment** n appuntamento m; (to job) nomina f; (job) posto m

appraisal /ə'preɪz(ə)l/ n valutazione f

appreciable /ə'priːʃəbl/ a sensibile

appreciate /ə'priːʃɪeɪt/ vt apprezzare; (understand) comprendere ● vi (increase in value) aumentare di valore. **~ion** /-'eɪʃn/ n (gratitude) riconoscenza f; (enjoyment) apprezzamento m; (understanding) comprensione f; (in value) aumento m. **~ive** /-ətɪv/ a riconoscente

apprehend /æprɪ'hend/ vt arrestare

apprehension /æprɪ'henʃn/ n arresto m; (fear) apprensione f. **~ive** /-sɪv/ a apprensivo

apprentice /ə'prentɪs/ n apprendista mf. **~ship** n apprendistato m

approach /ə'prəʊtʃ/ n avvicinamento m; (to problem) approccio m; (access) accesso m; **make ~es to** fare degli approcci con ● vi avvicinarsi ● vt avvicinarsi a; (with request) rivolgersi a; affrontare (problem). **~able** /-əbl/ a accessibile

appropriate¹ /ə'prəʊprɪət/ a appropriato

appropriate² /ə'prəʊprɪeɪt/ vt appropriarsi di

approval /ə'pruːvl/ n approvazione f; **on ~** in prova

approve /ə'pruːv/ vt approvare ● vi **~ of** approvare (sth); avere una buona opinione di (sb). **~ing** a (smile, nod) d'approvazione

approximate /ə'prɒksɪmət/ a approssimativo. **~ly** adv approssimativamente

approximation /əprɒksɪ'meɪʃn/ n approssimazione f

apricot /'eɪprɪkɒt/ n albicocca f

April /'eɪprəl/ n aprile m; **~ Fool's Day** il primo d'aprile

apron /'eɪprən/ n grembiule m

apt /æpt/ *a* appropriato; **be ~ to do sth** avere tendenza a fare qcsa
aptitude /'æptɪtjuːd/ *n* disposizione *f*. **~ test** *n* test *m inv* attitudinale
aqualung /'ækwəlʌŋ/ *n* autorespiratore *m*
aquarium /ə'kweərɪəm/ *n* acquario *m*
Aquarius /ə'kweərɪəs/ *n Astr* Acquario *m*
aquatic /ə'kwætɪk/ *a* acquatico
Arab /'ærəb/ *a* & *n* arabo, -a *mf*. **~ian** /ə'reɪbɪən/ *a* arabo
Arabic /'ærəbɪk/ *a* arabo; **~ numerals** numeri *mpl* arabici ● *n* arabo *m*
arable /'ærəbl/ *a* coltivabile
arbitrary /'ɑːbɪtrərɪ/ *a* arbitrario
arbitrat|e /'ɑːbɪtreɪt/ *vi* arbitrare. **~ion** /-'treɪʃn/ *n* arbitraggio *m*
arc /ɑːk/ *n* arco *m*
arcade /ɑː'keɪd/ *n* portico *m*; (*shops*) galleria *f*
arch /ɑːtʃ/ *n* arco *m*; (*of foot*) dorso *m* del piede
archaeological /ɑːkɪə'lɒdʒɪkl/ *a* archeologico
archaeolog|ist /ɑːkɪ'ɒlədʒɪst/ *n* archeologo, -a *mf*. **~y** *n* archeologia *f*
archaic /ɑː'keɪɪk/ *a* arcaico
arch|bishop /ɑːtʃ-/ *n* arcivescovo *m*
arch-enemy *n* acerrimo nemico *m*
architect /'ɑːkɪtekt/ *n* architetto *m*. **~ural** /ɑː'kɪtektʃərəl/ *a* architettonico
architecture /'ɑːkɪtektʃə(r)/ *n* architettura *f*
archives /'ɑːkaɪvz/ *npl* archivi *mpl*
archiving /'ɑːkaɪvɪŋ/ *n Comput* archiviazione *f*
archway /'ɑːtʃweɪ/ *n* arco *m*
Arctic /'ɑːktɪk/ *a* artico ● *n* **the ~** l'Artico
ardent /'ɑːdənt/ *a* ardente
arduous /'ɑːdjʊəs/ *a* arduo
are /ɑː(r)/ *see* **be**
area /'eərɪə/ *n* area *f*; (*region*) zona

f; (*fig: field*) campo *m*. **~ code** *n* prefisso *m* [telefonico]
arena /ə'riːnə/ *n* arena *f*
aren't /ɑːnt/ = **are not** *see* **be**
Argentina /ɑːdʒən'tiːnə/ *n* Argentina *f*
Argentinian /-'tɪnɪən/ *a* & *n* argentino, -a *mf*
argue /'ɑːgjuː/ *vi* litigare (**about** su); (*debate*) dibattere; **don't ~!** non discutere! ● *vt* (*debate*) dibattere; (*reason*) ~ **that** sostenere che
argument /'ɑːgjʊmənt/ *n* argomento *m*; (*reasoning*) ragionamento *m*; **have an ~** litigare. **~ative** /-'mentətɪv/ *a* polemico
aria /'ɑːrɪə/ *n* aria *f*
arid /'ærɪd/ *a* arido
Aries /'eəriːz/ *n Astr* Ariete *m*
arise /ə'raɪz/ *vi* (*pt* **arose**, *pp* **arisen**) (*opportunity, need, problem:*) presentarsi; (*result*) derivare
aristocracy /ærɪ'stɒkrəsɪ/ *n* aristocrazia *f*
aristocrat /'ærɪstəkræt/ *n* aristocratico, -a *mf*. **~ic** /-'krætɪk/ *a* aristocratico
arithmetic /ə'rɪθmətɪk/ *n* aritmetica *f*
arm /ɑːm/ *n* braccio *m*; (*of chair*) bracciolo *m*; **~s** *pl* (*weapons*) armi *fpl*; **~ in ~** a braccetto; **up in ~s** *fam* furioso (**about** per) ● *vt* armare
armaments /'ɑːməmənts/ *npl* armamenti *mpl*
armchair *n* poltrona *f*
armed /ɑːmd/ *a* armato; **~ forces** forze *fpl* armate; **~ robbery** rapina *f* a mano armata
armistice /'ɑːmɪstɪs/ *n* armistizio *m*
armour /'ɑːmə(r)/ *n* armatura *f*. **~ed** *a* (*vehicle*) blindato
armpit *n* ascella *f*
army /'ɑːmɪ/ *n* esercito *m*; **join the ~** arruolarsi
aroma /ə'rəʊmə/ *n* aroma *f*. **~tic** /ærə'mætɪk/ *a* aromatico
arose /ə'rəʊz/ *see* **arise**

around /əˈraʊnd/ *adv* intorno; **all ~** tutt'intorno; **I'm not from ~ here** non sono di qui; **he's not ~** non c'è ● *prep* intorno a; in giro per *⟨room, shops, world⟩*

arouse /əˈraʊz/ *vt* svegliare; *⟨sexually⟩* eccitare

arrange /əˈreɪndʒ/ *vt* sistemare *⟨furniture, books⟩*; organizzare *⟨meeting⟩*; fissare *⟨date, time⟩*; **~ to do sth** combinare di fare qcsa. **~ment** *n* (*of furniture*) sistemazione *f*; *Mus* arrangiamento *m*; (*agreement*) accordo; (*of flowers*) composizione *f*; **make ~ments** prendere disposizioni

arrears /əˈrɪəz/ *npl* arretrati *mpl*; **be in ~** essere in arretrato; **paid in ~** pagato a lavoro eseguito

arrest /əˈrest/ *n* arresto *m*; **under ~** in stato d'arresto ● *vt* arrestare

arrival /əˈraɪvl/ *n* arrivo *m*; **new ~s** *pl* nuovi arrivati *mpl*

arrive /əˈraɪv/ *vi* arrivare; **~ at** *fig* raggiungere

arrogan|ce /ˈærəgəns/ *n* arroganza *f*. **~t** *a* arrogante

arrow /ˈærəʊ/ *n* freccia *f*

arse /ɑːs/ *n* *vulg* culo *m*

arsenic /ˈɑːsənɪk/ *n* arsenico *m*

arson /ˈɑːsn/ *n* incendio *m* doloso. **~ist** /-sənɪst/ *n* incendiario, -a *mf*

art /ɑːt/ *n* arte *f*. **~s and crafts** *pl* artigianato *m*; **the A~s** *pl* l'arte *f*; **A~s degree** *Univ* laurea *f* in Lettere

artery /ˈɑːtərɪ/ *n* arteria *f*

artful /ˈɑːtfl/ *a* scaltro

'art gallery *n* galleria *f* d'arte

arthritis /ɑːˈθraɪtɪs/ *n* artrite *f*

artichoke /ˈɑːtɪtʃəʊk/ *n* carciofo *m*

article /ˈɑːtɪkl/ *n* articolo *m*; **~ of clothing** capo *m* d'abbigliamento

articulate¹ /ɑːˈtɪkjʊlət/ *a* *⟨speech⟩* chiaro; **be ~** esprimersi bene

articulate² /ɑːˈtɪkjʊleɪt/ *vt* scandire *⟨words⟩*. **~d lorry** *n* autotreno *m*

artifice /ˈɑːtɪfɪs/ *n* artificio *m*

artificial /ɑːtɪˈfɪʃl/ *a* artificiale.

~ly *adv* artificialmente; *⟨smile⟩* artificiosamente

artillery /ɑːˈtɪlərɪ/ *n* artiglieria *f*

artist /ˈɑːtɪst/ *n* artista *mf*

artiste /ɑːˈtiːst/ *n* *Theat* artista *mf*

artistic /ɑːˈtɪstɪk/ *a* artistico

as /æz/ *conj* come; (*since*) siccome; (*while*) mentre; **as he grew older** diventando vecchio; **as you get to know her** conoscendola meglio; **young as she is** per quanto sia giovane ● *prep* come; **as a friend** come amico; **as a child** da bambino; **as a foreigner** in quanto straniero; **disguised as** travestito da ● *adv* **as well** (*also*) anche; **as soon as I get home** [non] appena arrivo a casa; **as quick as you** veloce quanto te; **as quick as you can** più veloce che puoi; **as far as** *(distance)* fino a; **as far as I'm concerned** per quanto mi riguarda; **as long as** finché; *(provided that)* purché

asbestos /æzˈbestɒs/ *n* amianto *m*

ascend /əˈsend/ *vi* salire ● *vt* salire a *⟨throne⟩*

Ascension /əˈsenʃn/ *n* *Relig* Ascensione *f*

ascent /əˈsent/ *n* ascesa *f*

ascertain /æsəˈteɪn/ *vt* accertare

ascribe /əˈskraɪb/ *vt* attribuire

ash¹ /æʃ/ *n* (*tree*) frassino *m*

ash² *n* cenere *f*

ashamed /əˈʃeɪmd/ *a* **be/feel ~** vergognarsi

ashore /əˈʃɔː(r)/ *adv* a terra; **go ~** sbarcare

ash: ~tray *n* portacenere *m*. **A~ Wednesday** *n* mercoledì *m inv* delle Ceneri

Asia /ˈeɪʒə/ *n* Asia *f*. **~n** *a & n* asiatico, -a *mf*. **~tic** /eɪʒɪˈætɪk/ *a* asiatico

aside /əˈsaɪd/ *adv* **take sb ~** prendere qcno a parte; **put sth ~** mettere qcsa da parte; **~ from you** *Am* a parte te

ask /ɑːsk/ *vt* fare *⟨question⟩*; (*invite*) invitare; **~ sb sth** domandare *or* chiedere qcsa a qcno; **~ sb**

to do sth domandare *or* chiedere a qcno di fare qcsa ● *vi* ~ **about sth** informarsi su qcsa; ~ **after** chiedere [notizie] di; ~ **for** chiedere ⟨*sth*⟩; chiedere di ⟨*sb*⟩; ~ **for trouble** *fam* andare in cerca di guai. **ask in** *vt* ~ **sb in** invitare qcno ad entrare. **ask out** *vt* ~ **sb out** chiedere a qcno di uscire

askance /ə'skɑːns/ *adv* **look** ~ **at sb/sth** guardare qcno/qcsa di traverso

askew /ə'skjuː/ *a & adv* di traverso

asleep /ə'sliːp/ *a* **be** ~ dormire; **fall** ~ addormentarsi

asparagus /ə'spærəgəs/ *n* asparagi *mpl*

aspect /'æspekt/ *n* aspetto *m*

aspersions /ə'spɜːʃnz/ *npl* **cast** ~ **on** diffamare

asphalt /'æsfælt/ *n* asfalto *m*

asphyxia /əs'fɪksɪə/ *n* asfissia *f*. ~**te** /əs'fɪksɪeɪt/ *vt* asfissiare. ~**tion** /-'eɪʃn/ *n* asfissia *f*

aspirations /æspə'reɪʃnz/ *npl* aspirazioni *fpl*

aspire /ə'spaɪə(r)/ *vi* ~ **to** aspirare a

ass /æs/ *n* asino *m*

assailant /ə'seɪlənt/ *n* assalitore, -trice *mf*

assassin /ə'sæsɪn/ *n* assassino, -a *mf*. ~**ate** *vt* assassinare. ~**ation** /-'neɪʃn/ *n* assassinio *m*

assault /ə'sɔːlt/ *n* *Mil* assalto *m*; *Jur* aggressione *f* ● *vt* aggredire

assemble /ə'sembl/ *vi* radunarsi ● *vt* radunare; *Techn* montare

assembly /ə'semblɪ/ *n* assemblea *f*; *Sch* assemblea *f* giornaliera di alunni e professori di una scuola; *Techn* montaggio *m*. ~ **line** catena *f* di montaggio

assent /ə'sent/ *n* assenso *m* ● *vi* acconsentire

assert /ə'sɜːt/ *vt* asserire; far valere ⟨*one's rights*⟩; ~ **oneself** farsi valere. ~**ion** /-ɜːʃn/ *n* asserzione *f*. ~**ive** /-tɪv/ *a* **be** ~**ive** farsi valere

assess /ə'ses/ *vt* valutare; ⟨*for tax purposes*⟩ stabilire l'imponibile

di. ~**ment** *n* valutazione *f*; ⟨*of tax*⟩ accertamento *m*

asset /'æset/ *n* ⟨*advantage*⟩ vantaggio *m*; ⟨*person*⟩ elemento *m* prezioso. ~**s** *pl* beni *mpl*; ⟨*on balance sheet*⟩ attivo *msg*

assign /ə'saɪn/ *vt* assegnare. ~**ment** *n* ⟨*task*⟩ incarico *m*

assimilate /ə'sɪmɪleɪt/ *vt* assimilare; integrare ⟨*person*⟩

assist /ə'sɪst/ *vt/i* assistere; ~ **sb to do sth** assistere qcno nel fare qcsa. ~**ance** *n* assistenza *f*. ~**ant** *a* ~**ant manager** vicedirettore, -trice *mf* ● *n* assistente *mf*; ⟨*in shop*⟩ commesso, -a *mf*

associat|e[1] /ə'səʊʃɪeɪt/ *vt* associare (**with** a); **be** ~**ed with sth** ⟨*involved in*⟩ essere coinvolto in qcsa ● *vi* ~**e with** frequentare. ~**ion** /-ʃɪ-/ *n* associazione *f*. **A**~**ion** 'Football *n* ⟨*gioco m del*⟩ calcio *m*

associate[2] /ə'səʊʃɪət/ *a* associato ● *n* collega *mf*; ⟨*member*⟩ socio, -a *mf*

assort|ed /ə'sɔːtɪd/ *a* assortito. ~**ment** *n* assortimento *m*

assum|e /ə'sjuːm/ *vt* presumere; assumere ⟨*control*⟩; ~**e office** entrare in carica; ~**ing that you're right,...** ammettendo che tu abbia ragione,...

assumption /ə'sʌmpʃn/ *n* supposizione *f*; **on the** ~ **that** partendo dal presupposto che; **the A**~ *Relig* l'Assunzione *f*

assurance /ə'ʃʊərəns/ *n* assicurazione *f*; ⟨*confidence*⟩ sicurezza *f*

assure /ə'ʃʊə(r)/ *vt* assicurare. ~**d** *a* sicuro

asterisk /'æstərɪsk/ *n* asterisco *m*

astern /ə'stɜːn/ *adv* a poppa

asthma /'æsmə/ *n* asma *f*. ~**tic** /-'mætɪk/ *a* asmatico

astonish /ə'stɒnɪʃ/ *vt* stupire. ~**ing** *a* stupefacente. ~**ment** *n* stupore *m*

astound /ə'staʊnd/ *vt* stupire

astray /ə'streɪ/ *adv* **go** ~ smarrirsi; (*morally*) uscire dalla retta via; **lead ~** traviare

astride /əˈstraɪd/ *adv* [a] cavalcioni ● *prep* a cavalcioni di

astrolog|er /əˈstrɒlədʒə(r)/ *n* astrologo, -a *mf*. **~y** *n* astrologia *f*

astronaut /ˈæstrənɔːt/ *n* astronauta *mf*

astronom|er /əˈstrɒnəmə(r)/ *n* astronomo, -a *mf*. **~ical** /æstrəˈnɒmɪkl/ *a* astronomico. **~y** *n* astronomia *f*

astute /əˈstjuːt/ *a* astuto

asylum /əˈsaɪləm/ *n* [political] ~ asilo *m* politico; [lunatic] ~ manicomio *m*

at /ət/, *accentato* /æt/ *prep* a; **at the station/the market** alla stazione/al mercato; **at the office/the bank** in ufficio/banca; **at the beginning** all'inizio; **at John's** da John; **at the hairdresser's** dal parrucchiere; **at home** a casa; **at work** al lavoro; **at school** a scuola; **at a party/wedding** a una festa/un matrimonio; **at 1 o'clock** all'una; **at 50 km an hour** ai 50 all'ora; **at Christmas/Easter** a Natale/Pasqua; **at times** talvolta; **two at a time** due alla volta; **good at languages** bravo nelle lingue; **at sb's request** su richiesta di qcno; **are you at all worried?** sei preoccupato?

ate /et/ *see* **eat**

atheist /ˈeɪθɪɪst/ *n* ateo, -a *mf*

athlet|e /ˈæθliːt/ *n* atleta *mf*. **~ic** /-ˈletɪk/ *a* atletico. **~ics** /-ˈletɪks/ *n* atletica *fsg*

Atlantic /ətˈlæntɪk/ *a & the* ~ [Ocean] l'[Oceano *m*] Atlantico *m*

atlas /ˈætləs/ *n* atlante *m*

atmospher|e /ˈætməsfɪə(r)/ *n* atmosfera *f*. **~ic** /-ˈferɪk/ *a* atmosferico

atom /ˈætəm/ *n* atomo *m*. **~ bomb** *n* bomba *f* atomica

atomic /əˈtɒmɪk/ *a* atomico

atone /əˈtəʊn/ *vi* **~ for** pagare per. **~ment** *n* espiazione *f*

atrocious /əˈtrəʊʃəs/ *a* atroce; (*fam: meal, weather*) abominevole

atrocity /əˈtrɒsɪtɪ/ *n* atrocità *f inv*

attach /əˈtætʃ/ *vt* attaccare; attribuire (*importance*); **be ~ed to** *fig* essere attaccato a

attaché /əˈtæʃeɪ/ *n* addetto *m*. **~ case** *n* ventiquattrore *f inv*

attachment /əˈtætʃmənt/ *n* (*affection*) attaccamento *m*; (*accessory*) accessorio *m*

attack /əˈtæk/ *n* attacco *m*; (*physical*) aggressione *f* ● *vt* attaccare; (*physically*) aggredire. **~er** *n* assalitore, -trice *mf*; (*critic*) detrattore, -trice *mf*

attain /əˈteɪn/ *vt* realizzare (*ambition*); raggiungere (*success, age, goal*)

attempt /əˈtempt/ *n* tentativo *m* ● *vt* tentare

attend /əˈtend/ *vt* essere presente a; (*go regularly to*) frequentare; (*doctor:*) avere in cura ● *vi* essere presente; (*pay attention*) prestare attenzione. **attend to** *vt* occuparsi di; (*in shop*) servire. **~ance** *n* presenza *f*. **~ant** *n* guardiano, -a *mf*

attention /əˈtenʃn/ *n* attenzione *f*; **~!** *Mil* attenti!; **pay ~** prestare attenzione; **need ~** aver bisogno di attenzioni; (*skin, hair, plant:*) dover essere curato; (*car, tyres:*) dover essere riparato; **for the ~ of** all'attenzione di

attentive /əˈtentɪv/ *a* (*pupil, audience*) attento

attest /əˈtest/ *vt/i* attestare

attic /ˈætɪk/ *n* soffitta *f*

attitude /ˈætɪtjuːd/ *n* atteggiamento *m*

attorney /əˈtɜːnɪ/ *n* (*Am: lawyer*) avvocato *m*; **power of ~** delega *f*

attract /əˈtrækt/ *vt* attirare. **~ion** /-ækʃn/ *n* attrazione *f*; (*feature*) attrattiva *f*. **~ive** /-tɪv/ *a* (*person*) attraente; (*proposal, price*) allettante

attribute[1] /ˈætrɪbjuːt/ *n* attributo *m*

attribut|e[2] /əˈtrɪbjuːt/ *vt* attribuire

attrition /əˈtrɪʃn/ n war of ~ guerra f di logoramento

aubergine /ˈəʊbəʒiːn/ n melanzana f

auburn /ˈɔːbən/ a castano ramato

auction /ˈɔːkʃn/ n asta f ● vt vendere all'asta. **~eer** /-ʃəˈnɪə(r)/ n banditore m

audaci|ous /ɔːˈdeɪʃəs/ a sfacciato; (daring) audace. **~ty** /-ˈdæsətɪ/ n sfacciataggine f; (daring) audacia f

audible /ˈɔːdəbl/ a udibile

audience /ˈɔːdɪəns/ n Theat pubblico m; TV telespettatori mpl; Radio ascoltatori mpl; (meeting) udienza f

audio /ˈɔːdɪəʊ/: **~tape** n audiocassetta f. **~ typist** n dattilografo, -a mf (che trascrive registrazioni). **~visual** a audiovisivo

audit /ˈɔːdɪt/ n verifica f del bilancio ● vt verificare

audition /ɔːˈdɪʃn/ n audizione f ● vi fare un'audizione

auditor /ˈɔːdɪtə(r)/ n revisore m di conti

auditorium /ɔːdɪˈtɔːrɪəm/ n sala f

augment /ɔːɡˈment/ vt aumentare

augur /ˈɔːɡə(r)/ vi ~ **well**/**ill** essere di buon/cattivo augurio

August /ˈɔːɡəst/ n agosto m

aunt /ɑːnt/ n zia f

au pair /əʊˈpeə(r)/ n ~ [**girl**] ragazza f alla pari

aura /ˈɔːrə/ n aura f

auspices /ˈɔːspɪsɪz/ npl **under the** ~ **of** sotto l'egida di

auspicious /ɔːˈspɪʃəs/ a di buon augurio

auster|e /ɒˈstɪə(r)/ a austero. **~ity** /-ˈterətɪ/ n austerità f

Australia /ɒˈstreɪlɪə/ n Australia f. **~n** a & n australiano, -a mf

Austria /ˈɒstrɪə/ n Austria f. **~n** a & n austriaco, -a mf

authentic /ɔːˈθentɪk/ a autentico. **~ate** vt autenticare. **~ity** /-ˈtɪsətɪ/ n autenticità f

author /ˈɔːθə(r)/ n autore m

authoritarian /ɔːθɒrɪˈteərɪən/ a autoritario

authoritative /ɔːˈθɒrɪtətɪv/ a autorevole; (manner) autoritario

authority /ɔːˈθɒrətɪ/ n autorità f; (permission) autorizzazione f; **be in** ~ **over** avere autorità su

authorization /ɔːθəraɪˈzeɪʃn/ n autorizzazione f

authorize /ˈɔːθəraɪz/ vt autorizzare

autobi|ography /ɔːtə-/ n autobiografia f

autocratic /ɔːtəˈkrætɪk/ a autocratico

autograph /ˈɔːtə-/ n autografo m

automate /ˈɔːtəmeɪt/ vt automatizzare

automatic /ɔːtəˈmætɪk/ a automatico ● n (car) macchina f col cambio automatico; (washing machine) lavatrice f automatica. **~ally** adv automaticamente

automation /ɔːtəˈmeɪʃn/ n automazione f

automobile /ˈɔːtəməbiːl/ n automobile f

autonom|ous /ɔːˈtɒnəməs/ a autonomo. **~y** n autonomia f

autopsy /ˈɔːtpsɪ/ n autopsia f

autumn /ˈɔːtəm/ n autunno m. **~al** /-ˈtʌmnl/ a autunnale

auxiliary /ɔːɡˈzɪlɪərɪ/ a ausiliario ● n ausiliare m

avail /əˈveɪl/ n **to no** ~ invano ● vi ~ **oneself of** approfittare di

available /əˈveɪləbl/ a disponibile; (book, record etc) in vendita

avalanche /ˈævəlɑːnʃ/ n valanga f

avarice /ˈævərɪs/ n avidità f

avenge /əˈvendʒ/ vt vendicare

avenue /ˈævənjuː/ n viale m; fig strada f

average /ˈævərɪdʒ/ a medio; (mediocre) mediocre ● n media f; **on** ~ in media ● vt (sales, attendance etc) raggiungere una media di. **average out at** vt risultare in media

averse /əˈvɜːs/ a **not be** ~**e to sth**

non essere contro qcsa. **~ion**
/-ɜːʃn/ n avversione f **(to** per)

avert /əˈvɜːt/ vt evitare ⟨crisis⟩; distogliere ⟨eyes⟩

aviary /ˈeɪvɪərɪ/ n uccelliera f

aviation /eɪvɪˈeɪʃn/ n aviazione f

avid /ˈævɪd/ a avido **(for** di); ⟨reader⟩ appassionato

avocado /ævəˈkɑːdəʊ/ n avocado m

avoid /əˈvɔɪd/ vt evitare. **~able** /-əbl/ a evitabile

await /əˈweɪt/ vt attendere

awake /əˈweɪk/ a sveglio; **wide ~** completamente sveglio ● vi ⟨pt **awoke**, pp **awoken**⟩ svegliarsi

awaken /əˈweɪkn/ vt svegliare. **~ing** n risveglio m

award /əˈwɔːd/ n premio m; ⟨medal⟩ riconoscimento m; ⟨of prize⟩ assegnazione f ● vt assegnare; ⟨hand over⟩ consegnare

aware /əˈweə(r)/ a **be ~ of** ⟨sense⟩ percepire; ⟨know⟩ essere conscio di; **become ~ of** accorgersi di; ⟨learn⟩ venire a sapere di; **be ~ that** rendersi conto che. **~ness** n percezione f; ⟨knowledge⟩ consapevolezza f

awash /əˈwɒʃ/ a inondato **(with** di)

away /əˈweɪ/ adv via; **go/stay ~** andare/stare via; **he's ~ from his desk/the office** non è alla sua scrivania/in ufficio; **far ~** lontano; **four kilometres ~** a quattro chilometri; **play ~** Sport giocare fuori casa. **~ game** n partita f fuori casa

awe /ɔː/ n soggezione f

awful /ˈɔːfl/ a terribile. **~ly** adv /ˈɔːf(ʊ)lɪ/ terribilmente; ⟨pretty⟩ estremamente

awhile /əˈwaɪl/ adv per un po'

awkward /ˈɔːkwəd/ a ⟨movement⟩ goffo; ⟨moment, situation⟩ imbarazzante; ⟨time⟩ scomodo. **~ly** adv ⟨move⟩ goffamente; ⟨say⟩ con imbarazzo

awning /ˈɔːnɪŋ/ n tendone m

awoke(n) /əˈwəʊk(ən)/ see **awake**

awry /əˈraɪ/ adv storto

---

avert | back

axe /æks/ n scure f ● vt ⟨pres p **axing**⟩ fare dei tagli a ⟨budget⟩; sopprimere ⟨jobs⟩; annullare ⟨project⟩

axis /ˈæksɪs/ n ⟨pl **axes** /-siːz/⟩ asse m

axle /ˈæksl/ n Techn asse m

ay[e] /aɪ/ adv sì ● n sì m invar

Bb

B /biː/ n Mus si m

BA n abbr Bachelor of Arts

babble /ˈbæbl/ vi farfugliare; ⟨stream⟩ gorgogliare

baby /ˈbeɪbɪ/ n bambino, -a mf; ⟨fam: darling⟩ tesoro m

baby: ~ carriage n Am carrozzina f. **~ish** a bambinesco. **~-sit** vi fare da baby-sitter. **~-sitter** n baby-sitter mf

bachelor /ˈbætʃələ(r)/ n scapolo m; **B~ of Arts/Science** laureato, -a mf in lettere/in scienze

back /bæk/ n schiena f; ⟨of horse, hand⟩ dorso m; ⟨of chair⟩ schienale m; ⟨of house, cheque, page⟩ retro m; ⟨in football⟩ difesa f; **at the ~** in fondo; **in the ~** Auto dietro; **~ to front** ⟨sweater⟩ il davanti di dietro; **at the ~ of beyond** in un posto sperduto ● a posteriore; ⟨taxes, payments⟩ arretrato ● adv indietro; ⟨returned⟩ di ritorno; **turn/ move ~** tornare/spostarsi indietro; **put it ~ here/there** rimettilo qui/là; **~ at home** di ritorno a casa; **I'll be ~ in five minutes** torno fra cinque minuti; **I'm just ~** sono appena tornato; **when do you want the book ~?** quando rivuoi il libro?; **pay ~** ripagare ⟨sb⟩; restituire ⟨money⟩; **~ in power** di nuovo al potere ● vt ⟨support⟩ sostenere; ⟨with money⟩ finanziare; puntare su ⟨horse⟩; ⟨cover the back of⟩ rivestire il retro di ●*vi Auto* fare retromarcia. **back down** *vi* battere in ritirata. **back in** *vi Auto* entrare in retromarcia; ⟨*person:*⟩ entrare camminando all'indietro. **back out** *vi Auto* uscire in retromarcia; ⟨*person:*⟩ uscire camminando all'indietro; *(fig:* tirarsi indietro **(of** da). **back up** *vi* sostenere; confermare ⟨*person's alibi*⟩; *Comput* fare una copia di salvataggio di; **be ~ed up** ⟨*traffic:*⟩ essere congestionato ●*vi Auto* fare retromarcia.

back: **~ache** *n* mal *m* di schiena. **~bencher** *n* parlamentare *mf* ordinario, -a. **~biting** *n* maldicenza *f*. **~bone** *n* spina *f* dorsale. **~chat** *n* risposta *f* impertinente. **~date** *vt* retrodatare ⟨*cheque*⟩; **~dated to** valido a partire da. **~ 'door** *n* porta *f* di servizio

backer /'bækə(r)/ *n* sostenitore, -trice *mf*; ⟨*with money*⟩ finanziatore, -trice *mf*

back: **~'fire** *vi Auto* avere un ritorno di fiamma; *(fig: plan)* fallire. **~ground** *n* sfondo *m*; *(environment)* ambiente *m*. **~hand** *n (tennis)* rovescio *m*. **~'handed** *a* ⟨*compliment*⟩ implicito. **~'hander** *n (fam: bribe)* bustarella *f*

backing /'bækɪŋ/ *n (support)* supporto *m*; *(material)* riserva *f*; *Mus* accompagnamento *m*; **~ group** gruppo *m* d'accompagnamento

back: **~lash** *n fig* reazione *f* opposta. **~log** *n* **~log of work** lavoro *m* arretrato. **~ 'seat** *n* sedile *m* posteriore. **~side** *n fam* fondoschiena *m inv*. **~slash** *n Typ* barra *f* retroversa. **~stage** *a & adv* dietro le quinte. **~stroke** *n* dorso *m*. **~-up** *n* rinforzi *mpl*; *Comput* riserva *f*; **~-up copy** *n Comput* copia *f* di riserva

backward /'bækwəd/ *a (step)* indietro; ⟨*child*⟩ lento nell'apprendimento; ⟨*country*⟩ arretrato ●*adv* **~s** *(also Am:* **~)** indietro; *(fall, walk)* all'indietro; **~s and forwards** avanti e indietro

back: **~water** *n fig* luogo *m* allo scarto. **~ 'yard** *n* cortile *m*

bacon /'beɪkn/ *n* ≈ pancetta *f*

bacteria /bæk'tɪərɪə/ *npl* batteri *mpl*

bad /bæd/ *a* ⟨**worse, worst**⟩ cattivo; ⟨*weather, habit, news, accident*⟩ brutto; ⟨*apple etc*⟩ marcio; **the light is ~** non c'è una buona luce; **use ~ language** dire delle parolacce; **feel ~** sentirsi male; *(feel guilty)* sentirsi in colpa; **have a ~ back** avere dei problemi alla schiena; **smoking is ~ for you** fumare fa male; **go ~** andare a male; **that's just too ~!** pazienza!; **not ~** niente male

bade /bæd/ *see* **bid**

badge /bædʒ/ *n* distintivo *m*

badger /'bædʒə(r)/ *n* tasso *m* ●*vt* tormentare

badly /'bædlɪ/ *adv* male; ⟨*hurt*⟩ gravemente; **~ off** povero; **~ behaved** maleducato; **need ~** estremamente bisogno di

bad-'mannered *a* maleducato

badminton /'bædmɪntn/ *n* badminton *m*

bad-'tempered *a* irascibile

baffle /'bæfl/ *vt* confondere

bag /bæg/ *n* borsa *f*; *(of paper)* sacchetto *m*; **old ~** *sl* megera *f*; **~s under the eyes** occhiaie *fpl*; **~s of** *fam* un sacco di

baggage /'bægɪdʒ/ *n* bagagli *mpl*

baggy /'bægɪ/ *a* ⟨*clothes*⟩ ampio

'bagpipes *npl* cornamusa *f*

Bahamas /bə'hɑːməz/ *npl* **the ~** le Bahamas

bail /beɪl/ *n* cauzione *f*; **on ~** su cauzione ●**bail out** *n Naut* aggottare; **~ sb out** *Jur* pagare la cauzione per qcno ●*vi Aeron* paracadutarsi

bait /beɪt/ *n* esca *f* ●*vt* innescare; *(fig: torment)* tormentare

bake /beɪk/ *vt* cuocere al forno; *(make)* fare ●*vi* cuocersi al forno

baker /'beɪkə(r)/ *n* fornaio, -a *mf*, panettiere, -a *mf*; **~'s [shop]** panetteria *f.* **~y** *n* panificio *m*, forno *m*

baking /'beɪkɪŋ/ *n* cottura *f* al forno. **~-powder** *n* lievito *m* in polvere. **~tin** *n* teglia *f*

balance /'bæləns/ *n* equilibrio *m*; *Comm* bilancio *m*; (*outstanding sum*) saldo *m*; [**bank**] ~ saldo *m*; **be** *or* **hang in the ~** *fig* essere in sospeso ● *vt* bilanciare; equilibrare ⟨*budget*⟩; *Comm* fare il bilancio di ⟨*books*⟩ ● *vi* bilanciarsi; *Comm* essere in pareggio. **~d** *a* equilibrato. **~ sheet** *n* bilancio *m* [d'esercizio]

balcony /'bælkənɪ/ *n* balcone *m*

bald /bɔːld/ *a* ⟨*person*⟩ calvo; ⟨*tyre*⟩ liscio; ⟨*statement*⟩ nudo e crudo; **go ~** perdere i capelli

balding /'bɔːldɪŋ/ *a* **be ~ing** stare perdendo i capelli. **~ness** *n* calvizie *f*

bale /beɪl/ *n* balla *f*

baleful /'beɪlfl/ *a* malvagio; (*sad*) triste

balk /bɔːlk/ *vt* ostacolare ● *vi* **~ at** ⟨*horse*⟩ impennarsi davanti a; *fig* tirarsi indietro davanti a

Balkans /'bɔːlkənz/ *npl* Balcani *mpl*

ball[1] /bɔːl/ *n* palla *f*; (*football*) pallone *m*; (*of yarn*) gomitolo *m*; **on the ~** *fam* sveglio

ball[2] *n* (*dance*) ballo *m*

ballad /'bæləd/ *n* ballata *f*

ballast /'bæləst/ *n* zavorra *f*

ball-bearing *n* cuscinetto *m* a sfera

ballerina /bælə'riːnə/ *n* ballerina *f* [classica]

ballet /'bæleɪ/ *n* balletto *m*; (*art form*) danza *f*; **~ dancer** *n* ballerino, -a *mf* [classico, -a]

ballistic /bə'lɪstɪk/ *a* balistico. **~s** *n* balistica *fsg*

balloon /bə'luːn/ *n* pallone *m*; *Aeron* mongolfiera *f*

ballot /'bælət/ *n* votazione *f*. **~-box** *n* urna *f*. **~-paper** *n* scheda *f* di votazione

ball: **~point** ['pen'] *n* penna *f* a sfera. **~room** *n* sala *f* da ballo

---

balm /bɑːm/ *n* balsamo *m*

balmy /'bɑːmɪ/ *a* (**-ier, -iest**) mite; (*fam: crazy*) strampalato

Baltic /'bɔːltɪk/ *a* & *n* **the ~** [Sea] il [mar] Baltico

bamboo /bæm'buː/ *n* bambù *m inv*

bamboozle /bæm'buːzl/ *vt* (*fam: mystify*) confondere

ban /bæn/ *n* proibizione *f* ● *vt* (*pt/pp* **banned**) proibire; **~ from** espellere da ⟨*club*⟩; **she was ~ned from driving** le hanno ritirato la patente

banal /bə'nɑːl/ *a* banale. **~ity** /-'nælətɪ/ *n* banalità *f inv*

banana /bə'nɑːnə/ *n* banana *f*

band /bænd/ *n* banda *f*; (*stripe*) nastro *m*; (*Mus: pop group*) complesso *m*; (*Mus: brass*) ~ banda *f*; *Mil* fanfara *f* ● **band together** *vi* riunirsi

bandage /'bændɪdʒ/ *n* benda *f* ● *vt* fasciare ⟨*limb*⟩

b. & b. *abbr* bed and breakfast

bandit /'bændɪt/ *n* bandito *m*

band: **~stand** *n* palco *m* coperto (dell'orchestra). **~wagon** *n* **jump on the ~wagon** *fig* seguire la corrente

bandy[1] /'bændɪ/ *vt* (*pt/pp* **-ied**) scambiarsi ⟨*words*⟩. **bandy about** *vt* far circolare

bandy[2] *a* (**-ier, -iest**) **be ~** avere le gambe storte

bang /bæŋ/ *n* (*noise*) fragore *m*; (*of gun, firework*) scoppio *m*; (*blow*) colpo *m* ● *adv* **~ in the middle of** *fam* proprio nel mezzo di; **go ~** ⟨*gun:*⟩ sparare; ⟨*balloon:*⟩ esplodere ● *int* bum! ● *vt* battere ⟨*fist*⟩; battere su ⟨*table*⟩; sbattere ⟨*door, head*⟩ ● *vi* scoppiare; ⟨*door:*⟩ sbattere

banger /'bæŋə(r)/ *n* (*firework*) petardo *m*; (*fam: sausage*) salsiccia *f*; **old ~** (*fam: car*) macinino *m*

bangle /'bæŋgl/ *n* braccialetto *m*

banish /'bænɪʃ/ *vt* bandire

banisters /'bænɪstəz/ *npl* ringhiera *fsg*

bank[1] /bæŋk/ *n* (*of river*) sponda *f*;

(slope) scarpata *f* ● *vi Aeron* inclinarsi in virata

bank² *n* banca *f* ● *vt* depositare in banca ● *vi* ~ **with** avere un conto [bancario] presso. **bank on** *vt* contare su

'**bank account** *n* conto *m* in banca

'**bank card** *n* carta *f* assegno.

banker /'bæŋkə(r)/ *n* banchiere *m*

bank: ~ '**holiday** *n* giorno *m* festivo. ~**ing** *n* bancario *m*. ~ **manager** *n* direttore, -trice *mf* di banca. ~**note** *n* banconota *f*

bankrupt /'bæŋkrʌpt/ *a* fallito; **go** ~ fallire ● *n* persona *f* che ha fatto fallimento ● *vt* far fallire. ~**cy** *n* bancarotta *f*

banner /'bænə(r)/ *n* stendardo *m*; *(of demonstrators)* striscione *m*.

banns /bænz/ *npl Relig* pubblicazioni *fpl* [di matrimonio]

banquet /'bæŋkwɪt/ *n* banchetto *m*

banter /'bæntə(r)/ *n* battute *fpl* di spirito

baptism /'bæptɪzm/ *n* battesimo *m*

Baptist /'bæptɪst/ *a* & *n* battista *mf*

baptize /bæp'taɪz/ *vt* battezzare

bar /bɑː(r)/ *n* sbarra *f*; *Jur* ordine *m* degli avvocati; *(of chocolate)* tavoletta *f*; *(café)* bar *m inv*; *(counter)* banco *m*; *Mus* battuta *f*; *(fig: obstacle)* ostacolo *m*; ~ **of** soap/gold saponetta *f*/lingotto *m* d'oro; **behind** ~**s** *fam* dietro le sbarre ● *vt* *(pt/pp* **barred**) sbarrare *(way)*; sprangare *(door)*; escludere *(person)* ● *prep* tranne; ~ **none** in assoluto

barbarian /bɑː'beərɪən/ *n* barbaro, -a *mf*

barbar|ic /bɑː'bærɪk/ *a* barbarico. ~**ity** *n* barbarie *f inv*. ~**ous** /'bɑː:bərəs/ *a* barbaro

barbecue /'bɑː:bɪkjuː/ *n* barbecue *m inv*; *(party)* grigliata *f*, barbecue *m inv* ● *vt* arrostire sul barbecue

barbed /bɑːbd/ *a* ~ **wire** filo *m* spinato

barber /'bɑː:bə(r)/ *n* barbiere *m*

barbiturate /bɑː'bɪtjʊrət/ *n* barbiturico *m*

'**bar code** *n* codice *m* a barre

bare /beə(r)/ *a* a nudo; *(tree, room)* spoglio; *(floor)* senza moquette ● *vt* scoprire; mostrare *(teeth)*

bare: ~**back** *adv* senza sella. ~**faced** *a* sfacciato. ~**foot** *adv* scalzo. ~**headed** *a* a capo scoperto

barely /'beəlɪ/ *adv* appena

bargain /'bɑːgɪn/ *n* *(agreement)* patto *m*; *(good buy)* affare *m*; **into the** ~ per di più ● *vi* contrattare; *(haggle)* trattare. **bargain for** *vt* *(expect)* aspettarsi

barge /bɑːdʒ/ *n* barcone *m* ● **barge** *in vi fam* *(to room)* piombare dentro; *(into conversation)* interrompere bruscamente. ~ **into** *vt* piombare dentro a *(room)*; venire addosso a *(person)*

baritone /'bærɪtəʊn/ *n* baritono *m*

bark¹ /bɑːk/ *n* *(of tree)* corteccia *f*

bark² /bɑːk/ *n* abbaiamento *m* ● *vi* abbaiare

barley /'bɑːlɪ/ *n* orzo *m*

bar: ~**maid** *n* barista *f*. ~**man** *n* barista *m*

barmy /'bɑːmɪ/ *a fam* strampalato

barn /bɑːn/ *n* granaio *m*

barometer /bə'rɒmɪtə(r)/ *n* barometro *m*

baron /'bærn/ *n* barone *m*. ~**ess** *n* baronessa *f*

baroque /bə'rɒk/ *a* & *n* barocco *m*

barracks /'bærəks/ *npl* caserma *fsg*

barrage /'bærɑːʒ/ *n* *Mil* sbarramento *m*; *(fig: of criticism)* sfilza *f*

barrel /'bærl/ *n* barile *m*, botte *f*; *(of gun)* canna *f*. ~**-organ** *n* organetto *m* [a cilindro]

barren /'bærn/ *a* sterile; *(landscape)* brullo

barricade /bærɪ'keɪd/ *n* barricata *f* ● *vt* barricare

barrier /'bærɪə(r)/ *n* barriera *f*; *Rail* cancello *m*; *fig* ostacolo *m*

barring /'bɑːrɪŋ/ *prep* ~ **accidents** tranne imprevisti

barrister /'bærɪstə(r)/ *n* avvocato *m*

barrow /'bærəʊ/ *n* carretto *m*; (wheel~) carriola *f*

barter /'bɑːtə(r)/ *vi* barattare (for con)

base /beɪs/ *n* base *f* ● *a* vile ● *vt* basare; **be ~d on** basarsi su

base: **~ball** *n* baseball *m*. **~less** *a* infondato. **~ment** *n* seminterrato *m*. **~ment flat** *n* appartamento *m* nel seminterrato

bash /bæʃ/ *n* colpo *m* [violento] ● *vt* colpire [violentemente]; (dent) ammaccare; **~ed** in *a* ammaccato

bashful /'bæʃfl/ *a* timido

basic /'beɪsɪk/ *a* di base; (condition, requirement) basilare; (living conditions) povero; **my Italian is pretty ~** il mio italiano è abbastanza rudimentale; **the ~s** (of language, science) i rudimenti; (essentials) l'essenziale *m*. **~ally** *adv* fondamentalmente

basil /'bæzɪl/ *n* basilico *m*

basilica /bə'zɪlɪkə/ *n* basilica *f*

basin /'beɪsn/ *n* bacinella *f*; (wash-hand ~) lavabo *m*; (for food) recipiente *m*; Geog bacino *m*

basis /'beɪsɪs/ *n* (pl **-ses** /-siːz/) base *f*

bask /bɑːsk/ *vi* crogiolarsi

basket /'bɑːskɪt/ *n* cestino *m*. **~ball** *n* pallacanestro *f*

Basle /bɑːl/ *n* Basilea *f*

bass /beɪs/ *a* basso; **~ voice** voce *f* di basso ● *n* basso *m*

bastard /'bɑːstəd/ *n* (illegitimate child) bastardo. *a* *mf*; sl figlio *m* di puttana

bastion /'bæstɪən/ *n* bastione *m*

bat¹ /bæt/ *n* mazza *f*; (for table tennis) racchetta *f*; **off one's own ~** fam tutto da solo ● *vt* (pt/pp **batted**) battere; **she didn't ~ an eyelid** fig non ha battuto ciglio

bat² *n* Zool pipistrello *m*

batch /bætʃ/ *n* gruppo *m*; (of goods) partita *f*; (of bread) infornata *f*

bated /'beɪtɪd/ *a* **with ~ breath** col fiato sospeso

bath /bɑːθ/ *n* (pl **~s** /bɑːðz/) bagno *m*; (tub) vasca *f* da bagno; **~s** *pl* piscina *f*; **have a ~** fare un bagno ● *vt* fare il bagno a

bathe /beɪð/ *n* bagno *m* ● *vi* fare il bagno ● *vt* lavare (wound). **~r** *n* bagnante *mf*

bathing /'beɪðɪŋ/ *n* bagni *mpl*. **~-cap** *n* cuffia *f*. **~-costume** *n* costume *m* da bagno

bath: **~-mat** *n* tappetino *m* da bagno. **~-robe** *n* accappatoio *m*. **~-room** *n* bagno *m*. **~-towel** *n* asciugamano *m* da bagno

baton /'bætn/ *n* Mus bacchetta *f*

battalion /bə'tælɪən/ *n* battaglione *m*

batter /'bætə(r)/ *n* Culin pastella *f*; **~ed** *a* (car) malandato; (wife, baby) maltrattato

battery /'bætərɪ/ *n* batteria *f*; (of torch, radio) pila *f*

battle /'bætl/ *n* battaglia *f*; fig lotta *f* ● *vi* fig lottare

battle: **~field** *n* campo *m* di battaglia. **~ship** *n* corazzata *f*

bawdy /'bɔːdɪ/ *a* (-ier, -iest) piccante

bawl /bɔːl/ *vt/i* urlare

bay¹ /beɪ/ *n* Geog baia *f*

bay² *n* **keep at ~** tenere a bada

bay³ *n* Bot alloro *m*. **~-leaf** *n* foglia *f* d'alloro

bayonet /'beɪənɪt/ *n* baionetta *f*

bay window *n* bay window *f* inv (grande finestra sporgente)

bazaar /bə'zɑː(r)/ *n* bazar *m* inv

BC *abbr* (before Christ) a.C.

be /biː/ *vi* (pres **am, are, is, are**; pt **was, were**; pp **been**) essere; **he is a teacher** è insegnante, fa l'insegnante; **what do you want to be?** cosa vuoi fare?; **be quiet!** sta' zitto!; **I am cold/hot** ho freddo/caldo; **it's cold/hot, isn't it?** fa freddo/caldo, vero?; **how are you?** come stai?; **I am well** sto bene; **there is** c'è; **there are** ci sono; **I have been to Venice** sono stato a

Venezia; **has the postman been?** è passato il postino?; **you're coming too, aren't you?** vieni anche tu, no?; **it's yours, is it?** è tuo, vero?; **was John there? - yes, he was** c'era John? - sì; **John wasn't there - yes he was!** John non c'era - sì che c'era!; **three and three are six** tre più tre fanno sei; **he is five** ha cinque anni; **that will be £10, please** fanno 10 sterline, per favore; **how much is it?** quanto costa?; **that's £5 you owe me** mi devi 5 sterline ●v *aux* **I am coming/reading** sto venendo/leggendo; **I'm staying** (*not leaving*) resto; **I am being lazy** sono pigro; **I was thinking of you** stavo pensando a te; **you are not to tell him** non devi dirgielo; **you are to do that immediately** devi farlo subito ● *passive* essere; **I have been robbed** sono stato derubato

beach /biːtʃ/ *n* spiaggia *f*. **~wear** *n* abbigliamento *m* da spiaggia

bead /biːd/ *n* perlina *f*

beak /biːk/ *n* becco *m*

beaker /'biːkə(r)/ *n* coppa *f*

beam /biːm/ *n* trave *f*; (*of light*) raggio *m* ●*vi* irradiare; (*person:*) essere raggiante. **~ing** *a* raggiante

bean /biːn/ *n* fagiolo *m*; (*of coffee*) chicco *m*

bear[1] /beə(r)/ *n* orso *m*

bear[2] *v* (*pt* **bore**, *pp* **borne**) ●*vt* (*endure*) sopportare; mettere al mondo ⟨*child*⟩; (*carry*) portare; **~ in mind** tenere presente ●*vi* **~ left/right** andare a sinistra/a destra. **bear with** *vt* aver pazienza con. **~able** /-əbl/ *a* sopportabile

beard /bɪəd/ *n* barba *f*. **~ed** *a* barbuto

bearer /'beərə(r)/ *n* portatore, -trice *mf*; (*of passport*) titolare *mf*

bearing /'beərɪŋ/ *n* portamento *m*; *Techn* cuscinetto *m* [a sfera]; **have a ~ on** avere attinenza con; **get one's ~s** orientarsi

beast /biːst/ *n* bestia *f*; (*fam: person*) animale *m*

beat /biːt/ *n* battito *m*; (*rhythm*) battuta *f*; (*of policeman*) giro *m* d'ispezione ●*v* (*pt* **beat**, *pp* **beaten**) *vt* battere; picchiare ⟨*person*⟩; **~ it!** *fam* darsela a gambe!; **it ~s me why...** *fam* non capisco proprio perché... **beat up** *vt* picchiare

beat|en /'biːtn/ *a* **off the ~en track** fuori mano. **~ing** *n* batosta *f*; **get a ~ing** (*with fists*) essere preso a pugni; (*team, player:*) prendere una batosta

beautician /bjuː'tɪʃn/ *n* estetista *mf*

beauti|ful /'bjuːtɪfl/ *a* bello. **~fully** *adv* splendidamente

beauty /'bjuːtɪ/ *n* bellezza *f*. **~ parlour** *n* istituto *m* di bellezza. **~ spot** *n* neo *m* di; (*place*) luogo *m* pittoresco

beaver /'biːvə(r)/ *n* castoro *m*

became /br'keɪm/ *see* **become**

because /br'kɒz/ *conj* perché; **you didn't tell me, I...** poiché non me lo hai detto,... ● *adv* **~ of** a causa di

beck /bek/ *n* **at the ~ and call of** completa disposizione di

beckon /'bekn/ *vt/i* **~ [to]** chiamare con un cenno

become /br'kʌm/ *v* (*pt* **became**, *pp* **become**) ●*vt* diventare ● *vi* diventare; **what has ~e of her?** che ne è di lei? **~ing** *a* ⟨*clothes*⟩ bello

bed /bed/ *n* letto *m*; (*of sea, lake*) fondo *m*; (*layer*) strato *m*; (*of flowers*) aiuola *f*; **in ~** a letto; **go to ~** andare a letto; **~ and breakfast** pensione *f* familiare in cui il prezzo della camera comprende la prima colazione. **~clothes** *npl* lenzuola *fpl* e coperte *fpl*. **~ding** *n* biancheria *f* per il letto, materasso e guanciali

bedlam /'bedləm/ *n* baraonda *f*

bedraggled /br'drægld/ *a* inzaccherato

bed: ~**ridden** *a* costretto a letto. ~**room** *n* camera *f* da letto

bedside *n* at his ~ al suo capezzale. ~ **lamp** *n* abat-jour *m inv.* ~**table** *n* comodino *m*

bed: ~**sit** *n*, ~**sitter** *n*, ~**sitting-room** *n* = *camera f ammobiliata fornita di cucina.* ~**spread** *n* copriletto *m*. ~**time** *n* l'ora *f* di andare a letto

bee /bi:/ *n* ape *f*

beech /bi:tʃ/ *n* faggio *m*

beef /bi:f/ *n* manzo *m*. ~**burger** *n* hamburger *m inv*

bee: ~**hive** *n* alveare *m*. ~**line** *n* make a ~**line** for *fam* precipitarsi verso

been /bi:n/ *see* **be**

beer /bɪə(r)/ *n* birra *f*

beetle /'bi:tl/ *n* scarafaggio *m*

beetroot /'bi:tru:t/ *n* barbabietola *f*

before /bɪ'fɔ:(r)/ *prep* prima di; **the day ~ yesterday** ieri l'altro; **~ long** fra poco ● *adv* prima; **never ~ have I seen...** non ho mai visto prima...; **~ that** prima; **~ going** prima di andare ● *conj* (*time*) prima che; **~ you go** prima che tu vada. **~hand** *adv* in anticipo

befriend /bɪ'frend/ *vt* trattare da amico

beg /beg/ *v* (*pt/pp* **begged**) *vi* mendicare ● *vt* pregare; chiedere ⟨*favour, forgiveness*⟩

began /bɪ'gæn/ *see* **begin**

beggar /'begə(r)/ *n* mendicante *mf*; **poor ~!** povero cristo!

begin /bɪ'gɪn/ *vt/i* (*pt* **began**, *pp* **begun**, *pres p* **beginning**) cominciare. ~**ner** *n* principiante *mf*. ~**ning** *n* principio *m*

begonia /bɪ'gəʊnɪə/ *n* begonia *f*

begrudge /bɪ'grʌdʒ/ *vt* (*envy*) essere invidioso di; dare malvolentieri ⟨*money*⟩

begun /bɪ'gʌn/ *see* **begin**

behalf /bɪ'hɑ:f/ *n* **on ~ of** a nome di; **on my ~** a nome mio

behave /bɪ'heɪv/ *vi* comportarsi; ~ **[oneself]** comportarsi bene

behaviour /bɪ'heɪvjə(r)/ *n* comportamento *m*; (*of prisoner, soldier*) condotta *f*

behead /bɪ'hed/ *vt* decapitare

behind /bɪ'haɪnd/ *prep* dietro; **be ~ sth** *fig* stare dietro qcsa ● *adv* dietro, indietro; (*late*) in ritardo; **a long way ~** molto indietro ● *n fam* didietro *m*. ~**hand** *adv* indietro

beholden /bɪ'həʊldn/ *a* obbligato (**to** verso)

beige /beɪʒ/ *a* & *n* beige *m inv*

being /'bi:ɪŋ/ *n* essere *m*; **come into ~** nascere

belated /bɪ'leɪtɪd/ *a* tardivo

belch /beltʃ/ *vi* ruttare ● *vt* ~ **[out]** eruttare ⟨*smoke*⟩

belfry /'belfrɪ/ *n* campanile *m*

Belgian /'beldʒən/ *a* & *n* belga *mf*

Belgium /'beldʒəm/ *n* Belgio *m*

belief /bɪ'li:f/ *n* fede *f*; (*opinion*) convinzione *f*

believable /bɪ'li:vəbl/ *a* credibile

believe /bɪ'li:v/ *vt/i* credere. ~**r** *n Relig* credente *mf*; **be a great ~r in** credere fermamente in

belittle /bɪ'lɪtl/ *vt* sminuire ⟨*person, achievements*⟩

bell /bel/ *n* campana *f*; (*on door*) campanello *m*

belligerent /bɪ'lɪdʒərənt/ *a* belligerante; (*aggressive*) bellicoso

bellow /'beləʊ/ *vi* gridare a squarciagola; (*animal*) muggire

bellows /'beləʊz/ *npl* (*for fire*) soffietto *msg*

belly /'belɪ/ *n* pancia *f*

belong /bɪ'lɒŋ/ *vi* appartenere (**to** a); (**be member**) essere socio (**to** di). ~**ings** *npl* cose *fpl*

beloved /bɪ'lʌvɪd/ *a* & *n* amato, -a *mf*

below /bɪ'ləʊ/ *prep* sotto; (*with numbers*) al di sotto di ● *adv* sotto, di sotto; *Naut* sotto coperta; **see ~** guardare qui di seguito

belt /belt/ *n* cintura *f*; (*area*) zona *f*; *Techn* cinghia *f* ● *vi* ~ **along** (*fam: rush*) filare velocemente ● *vt* (*fam: hit*) picchiare

bemused /bɪˈmjuːzd/ a confuso

bench /bentʃ/ n panchina f; (work~) piano m da lavoro; **the B~** Jur la magistratura

bend /bend/ n curva f; (of river) ansa f ● v (pt/pp **bent**) ● vt piegare ● vi piegarsi; (road:) curvare; ~ **[down]** chinarsi. **bend over** vi inchinarsi

beneath /bɪˈniːθ/ prep sotto, di sotto di; **he thinks it's ~ him** fig pensa che sia sotto al suo livello ● adv giù

benediction /benɪˈdɪkʃn/ n Relig benedizione f

benefactor /ˈbenɪfæktə(r)/ n benefattore, -trice mf

beneficial /benɪˈfɪʃl/ a benefico

beneficiary /benɪˈfɪʃərɪ/ n beneficiario, -a mf

benefit /ˈbenɪfɪt/ n vantaggio m; (allowance) indennità f inv ● v (pt/pp -**fited**, pp p -**fiting**) ● vt giovare a ● vi trarre vantaggio (**from** da)

benevolen|ce /bɪˈnevələns/ n benevolenza f. **~t** a benevolo

benign /bɪˈnaɪn/ a benevolo; Med benigno

bent /bent/ see **bend** ● a (person) ricurvo; (distorted) curvato; (fam: dishonest) corrotto; **be ~ on doing sth** essere ben deciso a fare qcsa ● n predisposizione f

be|queath /bɪˈkwiːθ/ vt lasciare in eredità. **~quest** /-ˈkwest/ n lascito m

bereave|d /bɪˈriːvd/ n **the ~d** pl i familiari del defunto. **~ment** n lutto m

bereft /bɪˈreft/ a ~ **of** privo di

beret /ˈbereɪ/ n berretto m

berry /ˈberɪ/ n bacca f

berserk /bəˈsɜːk/ a **go ~** diventare una belva

berth /bɜːθ/ n (bed) cuccetta f; (anchorage) ormeggio m ● vi ormeggiare

beseech /bɪˈsiːtʃ/ vt (pt/pp **beseeched** or **besought**) supplicare

beside /bɪˈsaɪd/ prep accanto a; ~ **oneself** fuori di sé

besides /bɪˈsaɪdz/ prep oltre a ● adv inoltre

besiege /bɪˈsiːdʒ/ vt assediare

besought /bɪˈsɔːt/ see **beseech**

best /best/ a migliore; **the ~ part of a year** la maggior parte dell'anno; ~ **before** Comm preferibilmente prima di ● n **the ~** il meglio; (person) il/la migliore; **at ~** tutt'al più; **all the ~!** tanti auguri!; **do one's ~** fare del proprio meglio; **to the ~ of my knowledge** per quel che ne so; **make the ~ of it** cogliere il lato buono della cosa ● adv meglio, nel modo migliore; **as ~ I could** meglio che potevo. **~ 'man** n testimone m

bestow /bɪˈstəʊ/ vt conferire (**on** a)

best'seller n bestseller m inv

bet /bet/ n scommessa f ● v (pt/pp **bet** or **betted**) scommettere

betray /bɪˈtreɪ/ vt tradire. **~al** n tradimento m

better /ˈbetə(r)/ a migliore, meglio; **get ~** migliorare; (after illness) rimettersi ● adv meglio; ~ **off** meglio; (wealthier) più ricco; **all the ~** tanto meglio; **the sooner the ~** prima è, meglio è; **I've thought ~ of it** ci ho ripensato; **you'd ~ stay** faresti meglio a restare; **I'd ~ not** è meglio che non lo faccia ● vt migliorare; ~ **oneself** migliorare le proprie condizioni

'betting shop n ricevitoria f (dell'allibratore)

between /bɪˈtwiːn/ prep fra, tra; ~ **you and me** detto fra di noi; ~ **us** (together) tra me e te ● adv **[in]** ~ in mezzo; (time) frattempo

beverage /ˈbevərɪdʒ/ n bevanda f

beware /bɪˈweə(r)/ vi guardarsi (**of** da); ~ **of the dog!** attenti al cane!

bewilder /bɪˈwɪldə(r)/ vt disorientare; **~ed** perplesso. **~ment** n perplessità f

beyond /bɪˈjɒnd/ prep oltre; ~

reach irraggiungibile; ~ **doubt** senza alcun dubbio; ~ **belief** da non credere; **it's ~ me** *fam* non riesco proprio a capire ●*adv* più in là

bias /'baɪəs/ *n* (*preference*) preferenza *f*; *pej* pregiudizio *m* ●*vt* (*pt/pp* **biased**) (*influence*) influenzare. ~**ed** *a* parziale

bib /bɪb/ *n* bavaglino *m*

Bible /'baɪbl/ *n* Bibbia *f*

biblical /'bɪblɪkl/ *a* biblico

bicarbonate /baɪ'kɑ:bənət/ ~ **of soda** bicarbonato *m* di sodio

biceps /'baɪseps/ *n* bicipite *m*

bicker /'bɪkə(r)/ *vi* litigare

bicycle /'baɪsɪkl/ *n* bicicletta *f* ●*vi* andare in bicicletta

bid¹ /bɪd/ *n* offerta *f*; (*attempt*) tentativo *m* ●*vt/i* (*pt/pp* **bid**, *pres p* **bidding**) offrire; (*in cards*) dichiarare

bid² *vt* (*pt* **bade** *or* **bid**, *pp* **bidden** *or* **bid**, *pres p* **bidding**) *liter* (*command*) comandare; ~ **sb welcome** dare il benvenuto a qcno

bidder /'bɪdə(r)/ *n* offerente *mf*

bide /baɪd/ *vt* ~ **one's time** aspettare il momento buono

biennial /baɪ'enɪəl/ *a* biennale

bifocals /baɪ'fəʊklz/ *npl* occhiali *mpl* bifocali

big /bɪg/ *a* (**bigger, biggest**) grande; (*brother, sister*) più grande; (*fam: generous*) generoso ●*adv* **talk ~** *fam* sparare le grosse

bigam|ist /'bɪgəmɪst/ *n* bigamo, -a *mf*. ~**y** *n* bigamia *f*

'big-head *n fam* gasato, -a *mf*

big-'headed *a fam* gasato

bigot /'bɪgət/ *n* fanatico, -a *mf*. ~**ed** *a* di mentalità ristretta

'bigwig *n fam* pezzo *m* grosso

bike /baɪk/ *n fam* bici *f inv*

bikini /bɪ'ki:nɪ/ *n* bikini *m inv*

bile /baɪl/ *n* bile *f*

bilingual /baɪ'lɪŋgwəl/ *a* bilingue

bill¹ /bɪl/ *n* fattura *f*; (*in restaurant etc*) conto *m*; (*poster*) manifesto *m*; *Pol* progetto *m* di legge; (*Am: note*) biglietto *m* di banca ●*vt* fatturare

bill² *n* (*beak*) becco *m*

'billfold *n Am* portafoglio *m*

billiards /'bɪljədz/ *n* biliardo *m*

billion /'bɪljən/ *n* (*thousand million*) miliardo *m*; (*old-fashioned Br: million million*) mille miliardi *mpl*

billy-goat /'bɪlɪ-/ *n* caprone *m*

bin /bɪn/ *n* bidone *m*

bind /baɪnd/ *vt* (*pt/pp* **bound**) legare (**to** a); (*bandage*) fasciare; *Jur* obbligare. ~**ing** *a* (*promise, contract*) vincolante ●*n* (*of book*) rilegatura *f*; (*on ski*) attacco *m* [di sicurezza]

binge /bɪndʒ/ *n fam* **have a ~** fare baldoria; (*eat a lot*) abbuffarsi ●*vi* abbuffarsi (**on** di)

binoculars /bɪ'nɒkjʊləz/ *npl* [**pair of**] ~ binocolo *msg*

bio'chemist /baɪəʊ-/ *n* biochimico, -a *mf*. ~**ry** *n* biochimica *f*

biodegradable /-dɪ'greɪdəbl/ *a* biodegradabile

biograph|er /baɪ'ɒgrəfə(r)/ *n* biografo, -a *mf*. ~**y** *n* biografia *f*

biological /baɪə'lɒdʒɪkl/ *a* biologico

biolog|ist /baɪ'ɒlədʒɪst/ *n* biologo, -a *mf*. ~**y** *n* biologia *f*

birch /bɜ:tʃ/ *n* (*tree*) betulla *f*

bird /bɜ:d/ *n* uccello *m*; (*fam: girl*) ragazza *f*

Biro® /'baɪrəʊ/ *n* biro *f inv*

birth /bɜ:θ/ *n* nascita *f*

birth: ~ certificate *n* certificato *m* di nascita. ~**control** *n* controllo *m* delle nascite. ~**day** *n* compleanno *m*. ~**mark** *n* voglia *f*. ~**rate** *n* natalità *f*

biscuit /'bɪskɪt/ *n* biscotto *m*

bisect /baɪ'sekt/ *vt* dividere in due [parti]

bishop /'bɪʃəp/ *n* vescovo *m*; (*in chess*) alfiere *m*

bit¹ /bɪt/ *n* pezzo *m*; (*smaller*) pezzetto *m*; (*for horse*) morso *m*; *Comput bit m inv*; **a ~ of** un pezzo di (*cheese, paper*); un po' di (*time, rain, silence*); ~ **by** ~ poco a poco; **do one's** ~ fare la propria parte

bit[2] *see* **bite**

bitch /bɪtʃ/ *n* cagna *f*; *sl* stronza *f*. **~y** *a* velenoso

bit|e /baɪt/ *n* morso *m*; *(insect ~)* puntura *f*; *(mouthful)* boccone *m* ● *vt* *(pt* **bit***, pp* **bitten***)* mordere; **~e one's nails** mangiarsi le unghie ● *vi* mordere; *(insect:)* pungere. **~ing** *a* *(wind, criticism)* pungente; *(remark)* mordace

bitter /ˈbɪtə(r)/ *a* amaro ● *n Br* birra *f* amara. **~ly** *adv* amaramente; **it's ~ly cold** c'è un freddo pungente. **~ness** *n* amarezza *f*

bitty /ˈbɪtɪ/ *a Br fam* frammentario

bizarre /bɪˈzɑː(r)/ *a* bizzarro

blab /blæb/ *vi* *(pt/pp* **blabbed***)* spifferare

black /blæk/ *a* nero; **be ~ and blue** essere pieno di lividi ● *n* nero, -a *mf* ● *vt* boicottare *(goods)*. **black out** *vt* cancellare ● *vi* *(lose consciousness)* perdere coscienza

black: **~berry** *n* mora *f.* **~bird** *n* merlo *m.* **~board** *n Sch* lavagna *f.* **~currant** *n* ribes *m inv* nero; **~'eye** *n* occhio *m* nero. **~'ice** *n* ghiaccio *m* *(sulla strada).* **~leg** *n Br* crumiro *m.* **~list** *vt* mettere sulla lista nera. **~mail** *n* ricatto *m* ● *vt* ricattare. **~mailer** *n* ricattatore, -trice *mf.* **~ market** *n* mercato *m* nero. **~out** *n* blackout *m inv*; **have a ~out** *Med* perdere coscienza. **~smith** *n* fabbro *m*

bladder /ˈblædə(r)/ *n Anat* vescica *f*

blade /bleɪd/ *n* lama *f*; *(of grass)* filo *m*

blame /bleɪm/ *n* colpa *f* ● *vt* dare la colpa a; **~ sb for doing sth** dare la colpa a qcno per aver fatto qcsa; **no one is to ~** non è colpa di nessuno. **~less** *a* innocente

blanch /blɑːntʃ/ *vi* sbiancare ● *vt Culin* sbollentare

blancmange /bləˈmɒnʒ/ *n* biancomangiare *m inv*

bland /blænd/ *a* *(food)* insipido; *(person)* insulso

blank /blæŋk/ *a* bianco; *(look)* vuoto ● *n* spazio *m* vuoto; *(cartridge)* a salve. **~ 'cheque** *n* assegno *m* in bianco

blanket /ˈblæŋkɪt/ *n* coperta *f*

blank 'verse *n* versi *mpl* sciolti

blare /bleə(r)/ *vi* suonare a tutto volume. **blare out** *vt* far risuonare ● *vi* *(music, radio:)* strillare

blasé /ˈblɑːzeɪ/ *a* vissuto, blasé *inv*

blaspheme /blæsˈfiːm/ *vi* bestemmiare

blasphem|ous /ˈblæsfəməs/ *a* blasfemo. **~y** *n* bestemmia *f*

blast /blɑːst/ *n* *(gust)* raffica *f*; *(sound)* scoppio *m* ● *vt* *(with explosive)* far saltare ● *int sl* maledizione!. **~ed** *a sl* maledetto

blast: **~furnace** *n* altoforno *m.* **~-off** *n* *(of missile)* lancio *m*

blatant /ˈbleɪtənt/ *a* sfacciato

blaze /bleɪz/ *n* incendio *m*; **a ~ of colour** un'esplosione *f* di colori ● *vi* ardere

blazer /ˈbleɪzə(r)/ *n* blazer *m inv*

bleach /bliːtʃ/ *n* decolorante *m*; *(for cleaning)* candeggina *f* ● *vt* sbiancare; ossigenare *(hair)*

bleak /bliːk/ *a* desolato; *(fig: prospects, future)* tetro

bleary-eyed /ˈblɪərˈaɪd/ *a* **look ~** avere gli occhi assonnati

bleat /bliːt/ *vi* belare ● *n* belato *m*

bleed /bliːd/ *v* *(pt/pp* **bled***)* ● *vi* sanguinare ● *vt* spurgare *(brakes, radiator)*

bleep /bliːp/ *n* bip *m* ● *vi* suonare ● *vt* chiamare *(col cercapersone) (doctor)*. **~er** *n* cercapersone *m inv*

blemish /ˈblemɪʃ/ *n* macchia *f*

blend /blend/ *n* *(of tea, coffee, whisky)* miscela *f*; *(of colours)* insieme *m* ● *vt* mescolare ● *vi* *(colours, sounds:)* fondersi *(with con).* **~er** *n Culin* frullatore *m*

bless /bles/ *vt* benedire. **~ed** /ˈblesɪd/ *a also sl* benedetto. **~ing** *n* benedizione *f*

blew /bluː/ *see* **blow**[2]

blight /blaɪt/ n Bot ruggine f ● vt far avvizzire ⟨plants⟩

blind[1] /blaɪnd/ a cieco; **the ~** npl i ciechi mpl; **~ man/woman** cieco/cieca ● vt accecare

blind[2] n [roller] ~ avvolgibile m; [Venetian] ~ veneziana f

blind: ~ 'alley n vicolo m cieco. ~fold a be ~fold avere gli occhi bendati ● n benda f ● vt bendare gli occhi a. ~ly adv ciecamente. ~ness n cecità f

blink /blɪŋk/ vi sbattere le palpebre; ⟨light:⟩ tremolare

blinkered /'blɪŋkəd/ adj fig be ~ avere i paraocchi

blinkers /'blɪŋkəz/ npl paraocchi mpl

bliss /blɪs/ n Rel beatitudine f; ⟨happiness⟩ felicità f. ~ful a beato; ⟨happy⟩ meraviglioso

blister /'blɪstə(r)/ n Med vescica f; (in paint) bolla f ● vi ⟨paint:⟩ formare una bolla/delle bolle

blitz /blɪts/ n bombardamento m aereo; **have a ~ on sth** fig darci sotto con qcsa

blizzard /'blɪzəd/ n tormenta f

bloated /'bləʊtɪd/ a gonfio

blob /blɒb/ n goccia f

bloc /blɒk/ n Pol blocco m

block /blɒk/ n blocco m; (building) isolato m; (building ~) cubo m (per giochi di costruzione); ~ of flats palazzo m ● vt bloccare. **block up** vt bloccare

blockade /blɒ'keɪd/ n blocco m ● vt bloccare

blockage /'blɒkɪdʒ/ n ostruzione f

block: ~head n fam testone, -a mf. ~ 'letters npl stampatello m

bloke /bləʊk/ n fam tizio m

blonde /blɒnd/ a biondo ● n bionda f

blood /blʌd/ n sangue m

blood: ~ bath n bagno m di sangue. ~ count n esame m emocromocitometrico. ~ donor n donatore m di sangue. ~ group n gruppo m sanguigno. ~hound n segugio m. ~poisoning n setti-

cemia f. ~ pressure n pressione f del sangue. ~shed n spargimento m di sangue. ~shot a iniettato di sangue. ~ sports npl sport mpl cruenti. ~stained a macchiato di sangue. ~stream n sangue m. ~ test n analisi f del sangue. ~thirsty a assetato di sangue. ~ transfusion n trasfusione f del sangue

bloody /'blʌdɪ/ a (-ier, -iest) insanguinato; sl maledetto ● adv sl ~ easy/difficult facile/difficile da matti. ~-'minded a scorbutico

bloom /bluːm/ n fiore m; **in ~** ⟨flower:⟩ sbocciato; ⟨tree:⟩ in fiore ● vi fiorire; fig essere in forma smagliante

bloom|er /'bluːmə(r)/ n fam papera f. ~ing a fam maledetto. ~ers npl mutandoni mpl (da donna)

blossom /'blɒsəm/ n fiori mpl (d'albero); (single one) fiore m ● vi sbocciare

blot /blɒt/ n also fig macchia f ● **blot out** vt (pt/pp blotted) fig cancellare

blotch /blɒtʃ/ n macchia f. ~y a chiazzato

'blotting-paper n carta f assorbente

blouse /blaʊz/ n camicetta f

blow[1] /bləʊ/ n colpo m

blow[2] v (pt blew, pp blown) ● vi ⟨wind:⟩ soffiare; ⟨fuse:⟩ saltare ● vt (fam: squander) sperperare; ~ one's nose soffiarsi il naso. **blow away** vt far volar via ⟨papers⟩ ● vi ⟨papers:⟩ volare via. **blow down** vt abbattere ● vi abbattersi al suolo. **blow out** vt (extinguish) spegnere. **blow over** vi ⟨storm:⟩ passare; ⟨fuss, trouble:⟩ dissiparsi. **blow up** vt (inflate) gonfiare; (enlarge) ingrandire ⟨photograph⟩; (by explosion) far esplodere ● vi esplodere

blow: ~-dry vt asciugare col fon. ~lamp n fiamma f ossidrica

blown /bləʊn/ see blow[2]

'blowtorch n fiamma f ossidrica

blowy /'bləʊɪ/ *a* ventoso

blue /bluː/ *a* (*pale*) celeste; (*navy*) blu *inv*; (*royal*) azzurro; **~ with cold** livido per il freddo ● *n* blu *m inv*; **have the ~s** essere giù [di tono]; **out of the ~** inaspettatamente

blue: **~bell** *n* giacinto *m* di bosco. **~berry** *n* mirtillo *m*. **~bottle** *n* moscone *m*. **~ film** *n* film *m inv* a luci rosse. **~print** *n fig* riferimento *m*

bluff /blʌf/ *n* bluff *m inv* ● *vi* bluffare

blunder /'blʌndə(r)/ *n* gaffe *f inv* ● *vi* fare una/delle gaffe

blunt /blʌnt/ *a* spuntato; (*person*) reciso. **~ly** *adv* schiettamente

blur /blɜː(r)/ *n* **it's all a ~** *fig* è tutto un insieme confuso ● *vt* (*pt/pp* **blurred**) rendere confuso. **~red** *a* (*vision*, *photo*) sfocato

blurb /blɜːb/ *n* soffietto *m* editoriale

blurt /blɜːt/ *vt* **~ out** spifferare

blush /blʌʃ/ *n* rossore *m* ● *vi* arrossire

blusher /'blʌʃə(r)/ *n* fard *m*

bluster /'blʌstə(r)/ *n* sbruffonata *f*. **~y** *a* (*wind*) furioso; (*day*, *weather*) molto tempestoso

boar /bɔː(r)/ *n* cinghiale *m*

board /bɔːd/ *n* tavola *f*; (*for notices*) tabellone *m*; (*committee*) assemblea *f*; (*of directors*) consiglio *m*; **full ~** *Br* pensione *f* completa; **half ~** *Br* mezza pensione *f*; **~ and lodging** vitto e alloggio *m*; **go by the ~** *fam* andare a monte ● *vt Naut*, *Aviat* salire a bordo di ● *vi* (*passengers:*) salire a bordo. **board up** *vt* sbarrare con delle assi. **board with** *vt* stare a pensione da.

boarder /'bɔːdə(r)/ *n* pensionante *mf*; convittore, -trice *mf*

board: **~-game** *n* gioco *m* da tavolo. **~ing-house** *n* pensione *f*. **~ing-school** *n* collegio *m*

boast /bəʊst/ *vi* vantarsi (**about** di). **~ful** *a* vanaglorioso

boat /bəʊt/ *n* barca *f*; (*ship*) nave *f*. **~er** *n* (*hat*) paglietta *f*

bob /bɒb/ *n* (*hairstyle*) caschetto *m* ● *vi* (*pt/pp* **bobbed**) (*also* **~ up and down**) andare su e giù

'bob-sleigh *n* bob *m inv*

bode /bəʊd/ *vi* **well/ill** essere di buono/cattivo augurio

bodily /'bɒdɪlɪ/ *a* fisico ● *adv* (*forcibly*) fisicamente

body /'bɒdɪ/ *n* corpo *m*; (*organization*) ente *m*; (*amount: of poems etc*) quantità *f*. **~guard** *n* guardia *f* del corpo. **~work** *n Auto* carrozzeria *f*

bog /bɒg/ *n* palude *f* ● *vt* (*pt/pp* **bogged**) **get ~ged down** impantanarsi

boggle /'bɒgl/ *vi* **the mind ~s** non posso neanche immaginarlo

bogus /'bəʊgəs/ *a* falso

boil[1] /bɔɪl/ *n Med* foruncolo *m*

boil[2] *n* **bring/come to the ~** portare/arrivare a ebollizione ● *vt* [far] bollire ● *vi* bollire; (*fig: with anger*) ribollire; **the water or kettle's ~ing** l'acqua bolle. **boil down to** *vt fig* ridursi a. **boil over** *vi* straboccare (*bollendo*). **boil up** *vt* far bollire

boiler /'bɔɪlə(r)/ *n* caldaia *f*. **~suit** *n* tuta *f*

'boiling point *n* punto *m* di ebollizione

boisterous /'bɔɪstərəs/ *a* chiassoso

bold /bəʊld/ *a* audace ● *n Typ* neretto *m*. **~ness** *n* audacia *f*

bollard /'bɒlɑːd/ *n* colonnina *m* di sbarramento al traffico

bolster /'bəʊlstə(r)/ *n* cuscino *m* (*lungo e rotondo*) ● *vt* **~ [up]** sostenere

bolt /bəʊlt/ *n* (*for door*) catenaccio *m*; (*for fixing*) bullone *m* ● *vt* fissare (*con i bulloni*) (**to** a); chiudere col chiavistello (*door*); ingurgitare (*food*) ● *vi* svignarsela; (*horse:*) scappar via ● *adv* **~ upright** diritto come un fuso

bomb /bɒm/ n bomba f ● vt bombardare

bombard /bɒm'bɑːd/ vt also fig bombardare

bombastic /bɒm'bæstɪk/ a ampolloso

bomb|er /'bɒmə(r)/ n Aviat bombardiere m; (person) dinamitardo m. **~er jacket** giubbotto m, bomber m inv. **~shell** n (fig: news) bomba f

bond /bɒnd/ n fig legame m; Comm obbligazione f ● vt (glue:) attaccare

bondage /'bɒndɪdʒ/ n schiavitù f

bone /bəʊn/ n osso m; (of fish) spina f ● vt disossare (meat); togliere le spine da (fish). **~-dry** a secco

bonfire /'bɒn-/ n falò m inv. **~ night** festa della notte del 5 novembre con fuochi d'artificio e falò

bonnet /'bɒnɪt/ n cuffia f; (of car) cofano m

bonus /'bəʊnəs/ n (individual) gratifica f; (production ~) premio m; (life insurance) dividendo m; **a ~** fig qualcosa in più

bony /'bəʊnɪ/ a (-ier, -iest) ossuto; (fish) pieno di spine

boo /buː/ interj to surprise or frighten) bu! ● vt/i fischiare

boob /buːb/ n (fam: mistake) gaffe f inv; (breast) tetta f ● vi fam fare una gaffe

book /bʊk/ n libro m; (of tickets) blocchetto m; (of tickets) blocchetto m; **~s** Comm tenere la contabilità; **be in sb's bad/good ~s** essere nel libro nero/nelle grazie di qcno ● vt (reserve) prenotare; (for offence) multare ● vi (reserve) prenotare

book: **~case** n libreria f. **~ends** npl reggilibri mpl. **~ing-office** n biglietteria f. **~keeping** n contabilità f. **~let** n opuscolo m. **~maker** n allibratore m. **~mark** n segnalibro m. **~seller** n libraio, -a mf. **~shop** n libreria f. **~worm** n topo m di biblioteca

boom /buːm/ n Comm boom m inv;

(upturn) impennata f; (of thunder, gun) rimbombo m ● vi (thunder, gun:) rimbombare; fig prosperare

boon /buːn/ n benedizione f

boor /bʊə(r)/ n zoticone m. **~ish** a maleducato

boost /buːst/ n spinta f ● vt stimolare (sales); sollevare (morale); far crescere (hopes). **~er** n Med dose f supplementare

boot /buːt/ n stivale m; (up to ankle) stivaletto m; (football) scarpetta f; (climbing) scarpone m; Auto portabagagli m inv ● vt Comput inizializzare

booth /buːð/ n (Teleph, voting) cabina f; (at market) bancarella f

'boot-up n Comput boot m inv

booty /'buːtɪ/ n bottino m

booze /buːz/ n fam alcolici mpl. **~-up** n bella bevuta f

border /'bɔːdə(r)/ n bordo m; (frontier) frontiera f; (in garden) bordura f ● vi **~ on** confinare con; fig essere ai confini di (madness). **~line** n linea f di demarcazione. **~line case** caso m dubbio

bore¹ /bɔː(r)/ see **bear²**

bore² vt Techn forare

bor|e³ /bɔː(r)/ n (of gun) calibro m; (person) seccatore, -trice mf; (thing) seccatura f ● vt annoiare. **~edom** n noia f. **be ~ed (to tears or to death)** annoiarsi (da morire). **~ing** a noioso

born /bɔːn/ pp be ~ nascere; **I was ~ in 1966** sono nato nel 1966 ● a nato; **a ~ liar/actor** un bugiardo/attore nato

borne /bɔːn/ see **bear²**

borough /'bʌrə/ n municipalità f inv

borrow /'bɒrəʊ/ vt prendere a prestito (from da); **can I ~ your pen?** mi presti la tua penna?

bosom /'bʊzm/ n seno m

boss /bɒs/ n direttore, -trice mf ● vt (also ~ about) comandare a bacchetta. **~y** a autoritario

botanical /bə'tænɪkl/ a botanico

botan|ist /'bɒtǝnɪst/ n botanico, -a mf. **~y** n botanica f

botch /bɒtʃ/ vt fare un pasticcio con

both /bǝʊθ/ adj & pron tutti e due, entrambi ● adv **~ men and women** entrambi uomini e donne; **~ [of] the children** tutti e due i bambini; **they are ~ dead** sono morti entrambi; **~ of them** tutti e due

bother /'bɒðǝ(r)/ n preoccupazione f; (minor trouble) fastidio m; **it's no ~** non c'è problema ● int fam che seccatura! ● vt (annoy) dare fastidio a; (disturb) disturbare ● vi preoccuparsi (about di); **don't ~** lascia perdere

bottle /'bɒtl/ n bottiglia f; (baby's) biberon m inv ● vt imbottigliare. **bottle up** vt fig reprimere

bottle: ~ bank n contenitore m per la raccolta del vetro. **~-neck** n fig ingorgo m. **~-opener** n apribottiglie m inv

bottom /'bɒtm/ a ultimo; **the ~ shelf** l'ultimo scaffale in basso ● n (of container) fondo m; (of river) fondale m; (of hill) piedi mpl; (buttocks) sedere m; **at the ~ of the page** in fondo alla pagina; **get to the ~ of** fig vedere cosa c'è sotto. **~less** a senza fondo

bough /baʊ/ n ramoscello m

bought /bɔ:t/ see **buy**

boulder /'bǝʊldǝ(r)/ n masso m

bounce /baʊns/ vi rimbalzare; ⟨fam: cheque:⟩ essere respinto ● vt far rimbalzare ⟨ball⟩

bouncer /'baʊnsǝ(r)/ n fam buttafuori m inv

bound¹ /baʊnd/ n balzo m ● vi balzare

bound² see **bind** ● a **~ for** ⟨ship⟩ diretto a; **be ~ to do** (likely) dovere fare per forza; (obliged) essere costretto a fare

boundary /'baʊndǝrɪ/ n limite m

boundless a illimitato

bounds /baʊndz/ npl fig limiti mpl; **out of ~** fuori dai limiti

bouquet /bʊ'keɪ/ n mazzo m di fiori; (of wine) bouquet m

bourgeois /'bʊǝʒwɑ:/ a pej borghese

bout /baʊt/ n Med attacco m; Sport incontro m

bow¹ /bǝʊ/ n (weapon) arco m; Mus archetto m; (knot) nodo m

bow² /baʊ/ n inchino m ● vi inchinarsi ● vt piegare ⟨head⟩

bow³ /baʊ/ n Naut prua f

bowel /'baʊǝl/ n intestino m; **~s** pl intestini mpl

bowl¹ /bǝʊl/ n (for soup, cereal) scodella f; (of pipe) fornello m

bowl² n (ball) boccia f ● vt lanciare ● vi Cricket servire; (in bowls) lanciare. **bowl over** vt buttar giù; (fig: leave speechless) lasciar senza parole

bow-legged /bǝʊ'legd/ a dalle gambe storte

bowler¹ /'bǝʊlǝ(r)/ n Cricket lanciatore m; Bowls giocatore m di bocce

bowler² n **~ [hat]** bombetta f

bowling /'bǝʊlɪŋ/ n gioco m delle bocce. **~-alley** n pista f da bowling

bowls /bǝʊlz/ n gioco m delle bocce

bow-'tie /bǝʊ-/ n cravatta f a farfalla

box¹ /bɒks/ n scatola f; Theat palco m

box² vi Sport fare il pugile ● vt **~ sb's ears** dare uno scappaccione a qcno

box|er /'bɒksǝ(r)/ n pugile m. **~ing** n pugilato m. **B~ing Day** n [giorno m di] Santo Stefano m

box: ~-office n Theat botteghino m. **~-room** n Br sgabuzzino m

boy /bɔɪ/ n ragazzo m; (younger) bambino m

boycott /'bɔɪkɒt/ n boicottaggio m ● vt boicottare

boy: ~friend n ragazzo m. **~ish** a da ragazzino

bra /brɑ:/ n reggiseno m

brace /breɪs/ n sostegno m; (dental) apparecchio m; **~s** npl bretelle *fpl* ● *vt* ~ oneself *fig* farsi forza (**for** per affrontare)

bracelet /'breislɪt/ *n* braccialetto *m*

bracing /'breisɪŋ/ *a* tonificante

bracken /'brækn/ *n* felce *f*

bracket /'brækɪt/ *n* mensola *f*; (*group*) categoria *f*; *Typ* parentesi *f inv* ● *vt* mettere fra parentesi

brag /bræg/ *vi* (*pt/pp* **bragged**) vantarsi (**about** di)

braid /breɪd/ *n* (*edging*) passamano *m*

braille /breɪl/ *n* braille *m*

brain /breɪn/ *n* cervello *m*; ~**s** *pl* *fig* testa *fsg*

brain: ~**child** *n* invenzione *f* personale. ~ **dead** *a* *Med* celebralmente morto; *fig fam* senza cervello. ~**less** *a* senza cervello. ~**wash** *vt* fare il lavaggio del cervello a. ~**wave** *n* lampo *m* di genio

brainy /'breɪnɪ/ *a* (**-ier**, **-iest**) intelligente

braise /breɪz/ *vt* brasare

brake /breɪk/ *n* freno *m* ● *vi* frenare. ~**-light** *n* stop *m inv*

bramble /'bræmbl/ *n* rovo *m*; (*fruit*) mora *f*

bran /bræn/ *n* crusca *f*

branch /brɑːntʃ/ *n* also *fig* ramo *m*; *Comm* succursale *f* ● *vi* (*road:*) biforcarsi. **branch off** *vi* biforcarsi. **branch out** ~ **out into** allargare le proprie attività nel ramo di

brand /brænd/ *n* marca *f*; (*on animal*) marchio *m* ● *vt* marcare 〈*animal*〉; *fig* tacciare (**as** di)

brandish /'brændɪʃ/ *vt* brandire

brand-'new *a* nuovo fiammante

brandy /'brændɪ/ *n* brandy *m inv*

brash /bræʃ/ *a* sfrontato

brass /brɑːs/ *n* ottone *m*; **the** ~ *Mus* gli ottoni *mpl*; **top** ~ *fam* pezzi *mpl* grossi. ~ **band** *n* banda *f* (*di soli ottoni*)

brassiere /'bræzɪə(r)/ *n* *fml*, *Am* reggipetto *m*

brat /bræt/ *n* *pej* marmocchio, -a *mf*

bravado /brə'vɑːdəʊ/ *n* bravata *f*

brave /breɪv/ *a* coraggioso ● *vt* affrontare. ~**ry** /-ərɪ/ *n* coraggio *m*

brawl /brɔːl/ *n* rissa *f* ● *vi* azzuffarsi

brawn /brɔːn/ *n* *Culin* ≈ soppressata *f*

brawny /'brɔːnɪ/ *a* muscoloso

brazen /'breɪzn/ *a* sfrontato

brazier /'breɪzɪə(r)/ *n* braciere *m*

Brazil /brə'zɪl/ *n* Brasile *m*. ~**ian** *a* & *n* brasiliano, -a *mf*. ~ **nut** *n* noce *f* del Brasile

breach /briːtʃ/ *n* (*of law*) violazione *f*; (*gap*) breccia *f*; (*fig: in party*) frattura *f*; ~ **of contract** inadempienza *f* di contratto; ~ **of the peace** violazione *f* della quiete pubblica ● *vt* recedere 〈*contract*〉

bread /bred/ *n* pane *m*; **a slice of** ~ **and butter** una fetta di pane imburrato

bread: ~ **bin** *n* cassetta *f* portapane *inv*. ~**crumbs** *npl* briciole *fpl*; *Culin* pangrattato *m*. ~**line** *n* **be on the** ~**line** essere povero in canna

breadth /bredθ/ *n* larghezza *f*

'bread-winner *n* quello, -a *mf* che porta i soldi a casa

break /breɪk/ *n* rottura *f*; (*interval*) intervallo *m*; (*interruption*) interruzione *f*; (*fam: chance*) opportunità *f* ● *v* (*pt* **broke**, *pp* **broken**) ● *vt* rompere; (*interrupt*) interrompere; ~ **one's arm** rompersi un braccio ● *vi* rompersi; 〈*day:*〉 spuntare; 〈*storm:*〉 scoppiare; 〈*news:*〉 diffondersi; 〈*boy's voice:*〉 cambiare. **break away** *vi* scappare; *fig* chiudere (**from** con). **break down** *vi* 〈*machine, car:*〉 guastarsi; (*emotionally*) cedere (*psicologicamente*) ● *vt* sfondare 〈*door*〉; ripartire 〈*figures*〉. **break into** *vt* introdursi (*con la forza*) in; forzare 〈*car*〉. **break off** *vt* rompere 〈*engagement*〉 ● *vi* (*part of whole:*) rompersi. **break out** *vi* 〈*fight, war:*〉 scoppiare. **break up** *vt* far cessare 〈*fight*〉; disperdere 〈crowd〉 ● vi 〈crowd:〉 disperdersi; 〈couple:〉 separarsi; **Sch** iniziare le vacanze

break|able /'breɪkəbl/ a fragile. **~age** /-ɪdʒ/ n rottura f. **~down** n (of car, machine) guasto m; **Med** esaurimento m nervoso; (of figures) analisi f inv. **~er** n 〈wave〉 frangente m

breakfast /'brekfəst/ n [prima] colazione f

break: **~through** n scoperta f. **~water** n frangiflutti m inv

breast /brest/ n seno m. **~-feed** vt allattare [al seno]. **~-stroke** n nuoto m a rana

breath /breθ/ n respiro m, fiato m; **out of ~** senza fiato

breathalyse /'breθəlaɪz/ vt sottoporre alla prova [etilica] del palloncino. **~r®** n Br alcoltest m inv

breathe /briːð/ vt/i respirare. **breathe in** vi inspirare ● vt respirare 〈scent, air〉. **breathe out** vt/i espirare

breath|er /'briːðə(r)/ n pausa f. **~ing** n respirazione f

breath /breθ/: **~less** a senza fiato. **~-taking** a mozzafiato. **~ test** n prova [etilica] del palloncino

bred /bred/ see **breed**

breed /briːd/ n razza f ● v (pt/pp **bred**) ● vt allevare; (give rise to) generare ● vi riprodursi. **~er** n allevatore, -trice m/f. **~ing** n allevamento m; fig educazione f

breeze /briːz/ n brezza f. **~y** a ventoso

brew /bruː/ n infuso m ● vt mettere in infusione 〈tea〉; produrre 〈beer〉 ● vi fig 〈trouble:〉 essere nell'aria. **~er** n birraio m. **~ery** n fabbrica f di birra

bribe /braɪb/ n (money) bustarella f; (large sum of money) tangente f ● vt corrompere. **~ry** /-ərɪ/ n corruzione f

brick /brɪk/ n mattone m. **'~layer** n muratore ● **brick up** vt murare

bridal /'braɪdl/ a nuziale

bride /braɪd/ n sposa f. **~groom** n sposo m. **~smaid** n damigella f d'onore

bridge¹ /brɪdʒ/ n ponte m; (of nose) setto m nasale; (of spectacles) ponticello m ● vt fig colmare 〈gap〉

bridge² n Cards bridge m

bridle /'braɪdl/ n briglia f

brief¹ /briːf/ a breve

brief² n istruzioni fpl; (Jur: case) causa f ● vt dare istruzioni a; **Jur** affidare la causa a. **~case** n cartella f

brief|ing /'briːfɪŋ/ n briefing m inv. **~ly** adv brevemente. **~ly,...** in breve,... **~ness** n brevità f

briefs /briːfs/ npl slip m inv

brigade /brɪ'geɪd/ n brigata f. **~ier** /-ə'dɪə(r)/ n generale m di brigata

bright /braɪt/ a 〈metal, idea〉 brillante; 〈day, room, future〉 luminoso; (clever) intelligente; **~ red** rosso m acceso

bright|en /'braɪtn/ v **~en [up]** ● vt ravvivare; rallegrare 〈person〉 ● vi 〈weather:〉 schiarirsi; 〈face:〉 illuminarsi; 〈person:〉 rallegrarsi. **~ly** adv 〈shine〉 intensamente; 〈smile〉 allegramente. **~ness** n luminosità f; (intelligence) intelligenza f

brilliance /'brɪljəns/ n luminosità f; (of person) genialità f

brilliant /'brɪljənt/ a (very good) eccezionale; (very intelligent) brillante; 〈sunshine〉 splendente

brim /brɪm/ n bordo m; (of hat) tesa f ● **brim over** vi (pt/pp **brimmed**) traboccare

brine /braɪn/ n salamoia f

bring /brɪŋ/ vt (pt/pp **brought**) portare 〈person, object〉. **bring about** vt causare. **bring along** vt portare [con sé]. **bring back** vt restituire 〈sth borrowed〉; reintrodurre 〈hanging〉; fare ritornare in mente 〈memories〉. **bring down** vt portare giù; fare cadere 〈government〉; fare abbassare 〈price〉.

bring off vt ~ sth off riuscire a fare qcsa. **bring on** vt 〈cause〉 provocare. **bring out** vt 〈emphasize〉 mettere in evidenza; pubblicare 〈book〉. **bring round** vt portare; 〈persuade〉 convincere; far rinvenire 〈unconscious person〉. **bring up** vt 〈vomit〉 rimettere; allevare 〈children〉; tirare fuori 〈question, subject〉

brink /brɪŋk/ n orlo m

brisk /brɪsk/ a svelto; 〈person〉 sbrigativo; 〈trade, business〉 redditizio; 〈walk〉 a passo spedito

bristle /ˈbrɪsl/ n setola f ● vi ~ling **with** pieno di. **~ly** a 〈chin〉 ispido

Brit|ain /ˈbrɪtn/ n Gran Bretagna f. **~ish** a britannico; 〈ambassador〉 della Gran Bretagna ● npl the **~ish** il popolo britannico. **~on** n cittadino, -a britannico, -a mf

brittle /ˈbrɪtl/ a fragile

broach /brəʊtʃ/ vt toccare 〈subject〉

broad /brɔːd/ a ampio; 〈hint〉 chiaro; 〈accent〉 marcato. **two metres ~** largo due metri; **in ~ daylight** in pieno giorno. **~ beans** npl fave fpl

broadcast n trasmissione f ● vt/i (pt/pp **-cast**) trasmettere. **~er** n giornalista mf radiotelevisivo. **~ing** n diffusione f radiotelevisiva; **be in ~ing** lavorare per la televisione/radio

broaden /ˈbrɔːdn/ vt allargare ● vi allargarsi

broadly /ˈbrɔːdlɪ/ adv largamente; **~ [speaking]** generalmente

broad-minded a di larghe vedute

broccoli /ˈbrɒkəlɪ/ n inv broccoli mpl

brochure /ˈbrəʊʃə(r)/ n opuscolo m; 〈travel ~〉 dépliant m inv

broke /brəʊk/ see break ● a fam al verde

broken /ˈbrəʊkn/ see break ● a rotto; 〈fig: marriage〉 fallito. **~ English** inglese m stentato. **~-hearted** a affranto

broker /ˈbrəʊkə(r)/ n broker m inv

brolly /ˈbrɒlɪ/ n fam ombrello m

bronchitis /brɒŋˈkaɪtɪs/ n bronchite f

bronze /brɒnz/ n bronzo m ● attrib di bronzo

brooch /brəʊtʃ/ n spilla f

brood /bruːd/ n covata f; 〈hum: children〉 prole f ● vi fig rimuginare

brook /brʊk/ n ruscello m

broom /bruːm/ n scopa f. **~stick** n manico m di scopa

broth /brɒθ/ n brodo m

brothel /ˈbrɒθl/ n bordello m

brother /ˈbrʌðə(r)/ n fratello m

brother: ~-in-law n (pl **~s-in-law**) cognato m. **~ly** a fraterno

brought /brɔːt/ see bring

brow /braʊ/ n fronte f; 〈of hill〉 cima f

browbeat vt (pt **-beat**, pp **-beaten**) intimidire

brown /braʊn/ a marrone; castano 〈hair〉 ● n marrone m ● vt rosolare 〈meat〉 ● vi 〈meat:〉 rosolarsi. **~ paper** n carta f da pacchi

Brownie /ˈbraʊnɪ/ n coccinella f 〈negli scout〉

browse /braʊz/ vi 〈read〉 leggicchiare; 〈in shop〉 curiosare

bruise /bruːz/ n livido m; 〈on fruit〉 ammaccatura f ● vt ammaccare 〈fruit〉; **~ one's arm** farsi un livido sul braccio. **~d** a contuso

brunette /bruːˈnet/ n bruna f

brunt /brʌnt/ n **bear the ~ of** sth subire maggiormente qcsa

brush /brʌʃ/ n spazzola f; 〈with long handle〉 spazzolone m; 〈for paint〉 pennello m; 〈bushes〉 boscaglia f; 〈fig: conflict〉 breve scontro m ● vt spazzolare 〈hair〉; lavarsi 〈teeth〉; scopare 〈stairs, floor〉. **brush against** vt sfiorare. **brush aside** vt ignorare. **brush off** vt spazzolare; 〈with hands〉 togliere; ignorare 〈criticism〉. **brush up** vt/i fig **~ up [on]** rinfrescare

brusque /brʊsk/ a brusco

Brussels /ˈbrʌslz/ n Bruxelles f. **~**

sprouts *npl* cavoletti *mpl* di Bruxelles

brutal /'bruːtl/ *a* brutale. **~ity** /-'tælətɪ/ *n* brutalità *f* pl

brute /bruːt/ *n* bruto *m*. **~ force** *n* forza *f* bruta

BSc *n abbr* **Bachelor of Science**

BSE *n abbr* (**bovine spongiform encephalitis**) encefalite *f* bovina spongiforme

bubble /'bʌbl/ *n* bolla *f*; (*in drink*) bollicina *f*

buck[1] /bʌk/ *n* maschio *m* del cervo; (*rabbit*) maschio *m* del coniglio ●*vi* (*horse*:) saltare a quattro zampe. **buck up** *vi fam* tirarsi su; (*hurry*) sbrigarsi

buck[2] *n Am fam* dollaro *m*

buck[3] *n* **pass the ~** scaricare la responsabilità

bucket /'bʌkɪt/ *n* secchio *m*

buckle /'bʌkl/ *n* fibbia *f* ●*vt* allacciare ●*vi* (*shelf*:) piegarsi; (*wheel*:) storcersi

bud /bʌd/ *n* bocciolo *m*

Buddhism /'bʊdɪzm/ *n* buddismo *m*. **~t** *a & n* buddista *mf*

buddy /'bʌdɪ/ *n fam* amico, -a *mf*

budge /bʌdʒ/ *vt* spostare ●*vi* spostarsi

budgerigar /'bʌdʒərɪgɑː(r)/ *n* cocorita *f*

budget /'bʌdʒɪt/ *n* bilancio *m*; (*allotted to specific activity*) budget *m inv* ●*vi* (*pt/pp* **budgeted**) prevedere le spese; **~ for** sth includere qcsa nelle spese previste

buff /bʌf/ *a* (*colour*) [color] camoscio ●*n fam* fanatico, -a *mf*

buffalo /'bʌfələʊ/ *n* (*inv or pl* **-es**) bufalo *m*

buffer /'bʌfə(r)/ *n Rail* respingente *m*; *old — fam* vecchio bacucco *m*. **~ zone** *n* zona *f* cuscinetto

buffet[1] /'bʊfeɪ/ *n* buffet *m inv*

buffet[2] /'bʌfɪt/ *vt* (*pt/pp* **buffeted**) sferzare

buffoon /bə'fuːn/ *n* buffone, -a *mf*

bug /bʌg/ *n* (*insect*) insetto *m*; *Comput* bug *m inv*; (*fam: device*) cimice *f* ●*vt* (*pt/pp* **bugged**)

fam installare le microspie in (*room*); mettere sotto controllo (*telephone*); (*fam: annoy*) scocciare

buggy /'bʌgɪ/ *n* **[baby]** ~ passeggino *m*

bugle /'bjuːgl/ *n* tromba *f*

build /bɪld/ *n* (*of person*) corporatura *f* ●*vt/i* (*pt/pp* **built**) costruire. **build on** *vt* aggiungere (*extra storey*); sviluppare (*previous work*). **build up** *vt* ~ **up one's strength** rimettersi in forza ●*vi* (*pressure, traffic*:) aumentare; (*excitement, tension*:) crescere

builder /'bɪldə(r)/ *n* (*company*) costruttore *m*; (*worker*) muratore *m*

building /'bɪldɪŋ/ *n* edificio *m*. **~ site** *n* cantiere *m* [di costruzione]. **~ society** *n* istituto *m* di credito immobiliare

built-up /bɪlt-/ *n* (*of age etc*) accumulo *m*; *fig* battage *m inv* pubblicitario

built /bɪlt/ *see* **build**. **~-in** *a* (*unit*) a muro; (*fig: feature*) incorporato. **~-up area** *n Auto* centro *m* abitato

bulb /bʌlb/ *n* bulbo *m*; *Electr* lampadina *f*

bulge /bʌldʒ/ *n* rigonfiamento *m* ●*vi* esser gonfio (**with** di); (*stomach, wall*:) sporgere; (*eyes, with surprise*:) uscire dalle orbite. **~ing** *a* gonfio; (*eyes*:) sporgente

bulk /bʌlk/ *n* volume *m*; (*greater part*) grosso *m*; **in ~** in grande quantità; (*loose*) sfuso. **~y** *a* voluminoso

bull /bʊl/ *n* toro *m*

bulldog *n* bulldog *m inv*

bulldozer /'bʊldəʊzə(r)/ *n* bulldozer *m inv*

bullet /'bʊlɪt/ *n* pallottola *f*

bulletin /'bʊlɪtɪn/ *n* bollettino *m*. **~ board** *n Comput* bacheca *f* elettronica

bullet-proof *a* antiproiettile *inv*; (*vehicle*) blindato

bullfight *n* corrida *f*. **~er** *n* torero *m*

bullion /'bʊlɪən/ n gold ~ oro m in lingotti

bullock /'bʊlək/ n manzo m

bull: **~ring** n arena f; **~'s-eye** n centro m del bersaglio; **score a ~'s-eye** fare centro

bully /'bʊlɪ/ n prepotente mf ● vt fare il/la prepotente con. **~ing** n prepotenze fpl

bum[1] /bʌm/ n sl sedere m

bum[2] n Am fam vagabondo, -a mf ● **bum around** vi fam vagabondare

bumble-bee /'bʌmbl-/ n calabrone m

bump /bʌmp/ n botta f; (swelling) bozzo m, gonfiore m; (in road) protuberanza f ● vt sbattere. **bump into** vt sbattere contro; (meet) imbattersi in. **bump off** vt fam far fuori

bumper /'bʌmpə(r)/ n Auto paraurti m inv ● a abbondante

bumpkin /'bʌmpkɪn/ n **country ~** zoticone, -a mf

bumptious /'bʌmpʃəs/ a presuntuoso

bumpy /'bʌmpɪ/ a (road) accidentato; (flight) turbolento

bun /bʌn/ n focaccina f (dolce); (hair) chignon m inv

bunch /bʌntʃ/ n (of flowers, keys) mazzo m; (of bananas) casco m; (of people) gruppo m; **~ of grapes** grappolo m d'uva

bundle /'bʌndl/ n fascio m; (of money) mazzetta f; **a ~ of nerves** fam un fascio di nervi ● vt ~ [up] affastellare

bung /bʌŋ/ vt fam (throw) buttare. **bung up** vt (block) otturare

bungalow /'bʌŋgələʊ/ n bungalow m inv

bungle /'bʌŋgl/ vt fare un pasticcio di

bunion /'bʌnjən/ n Med callo m all'alluce

bunk /bʌŋk/ n cuccetta f. **~-beds** npl letti mpl a castello

bunny /'bʌnɪ/ n fam coniglietto m

buoy /bɔɪ/ n boa f

buoyan|cy /'bɔɪənsɪ/ n galleggiabilità f. **~t** a (boat) galleggiante; (water) che aiuta a galleggiare

burden /'bɜːdn/ n carico m ● vt caricare. **~some** /-səm/ a gravoso

bureau /'bjʊərəʊ/ n (pl -x /-əʊz/ or **~s**) (desk) scrivania f; (office) ufficio m

bureaucracy /bjʊə'rɒkrəsɪ/ n burocrazia f

bureaucrat /'bjʊərəkræt/ n burocrate mf. **~ic** /-'krætɪk/ a burocratico

burger /'bɜːgə(r)/ n hamburger m inv

burglar /'bɜːglə(r)/ n svaligiatore, -trice mf. **~ alarm** n antifurto m inv

burglar|ize /'bɜːgləraɪz/ vt Am svaligiare. **~y** n furto m con scasso

burgle /'bɜːgl/ vt svaligiare

Burgundy /'bɜːgəndɪ/ n Borgogna f

burial /'berɪəl/ n sepoltura f. **~ ground** cimitero m

burlesque /bɜː'lesk/ n parodia f

burly /'bɜːlɪ/ a (-ier, -iest) corpulento

Burm|a /'bɜːmə/ n Birmania f. **~ese** /-'miːz/ a & n birmano, -a mf

burn /bɜːn/ n bruciatura f ● v (pt/pp **burnt** or **burned**) ● vt bruciare● vi bruciare. **burn down** vt/i bruciare. **burn out** vi fig esaurirsi. **~er** n (on stove) bruciatore m

burnish /'bɜːnɪʃ/ vt lucidare

burnt /bɜːnt/ see **burn**

burp /bɜːp/ n fam rutto m ● vi fam ruttare

burrow /'bʌrəʊ/ n tana f ● vt scavare (hole)

bursar /'bɜːsə(r)/ n economo, -a mf. **~y** n borsa f di studio

burst /bɜːst/ n (of gunfire, energy, laughter) scoppio m; (of speed) scatto m ● v (pt/pp **burst**) ● vt far scoppiare ● vi scoppiare; **~ into tears** scoppiare in lacrime; **she ~ into the room** ha fatto irruzione nella stanza. **burst out** vi **~ out laughing/crying** scoppiare a ridere/piangere

bury /'berɪ/ vt (pt/pp **-ied**) seppellire; (hide) nascondere

bus /bʌs/ n autobus m inv, pullman m inv; (long distance) pullman m inv, corriera f

bush /bʊʃ/ n cespuglio m; (land) boscaglia f. **~y** a (**-ier, -iest**) folto

busily /'bɪzɪlɪ/ adv con grande impegno

business /'bɪznɪs/ n affare m; Comm affari mpl; (establishment) attività f di commercio; **on ~** per affari; **he has no ~** to non ha alcun diritto di; **mind one's own ~** farsi gli affari propri; **that's none of your ~** non sono affari tuoi. **~like** a efficiente. **~man** n uomo m d'affari. **~woman** n donna f d'affari

busker /'bʌskə(r)/ n suonatore, -trice mf ambulante

'bus station n stazione f degli autobus

'bus-stop n fermata f d'autobus

bust[^1] /bʌst/ n busto m; (chest) petto m

bust[^2] a fam rotto; **go ~** fallire ● v (pt/pp **busted** or **bust**) fam ● vt far scoppiare ● vi scoppiare

bustle /'bʌsl/ n (activity) trambusto m ● **bustle about** vi affannarsi. **~ing** a animato

'bust-up n fam lite f

busy /'bɪzɪ/ a (**-ier, -iest**) occupato; (day, time) intenso; (street) affollato; (with traffic) pieno di traffico; **be ~ doing** essere occupato a fare ● vt **~ oneself** darsi da fare

'busybody n ficcanaso mf inv

but /bʌt/, atono /bət/ conj ma ● prep eccetto, tranne; **nobody ~ you** nessuno tranne te; **~ for** (without) se non fosse stato per; **the last ~ one** il penultimo; **the next ~ one** il secondo ● adv (only) soltanto; **there were ~ two** ce n'erano soltanto due

butcher /'bʊtʃə(r)/ n macellaio m; **~'s [shop]** macelleria f ● vt macellare; fig massacrare

butler /'bʌtlə(r)/ n maggiordomo m

butt /bʌt/ n (of gun) calcio m; (of cigarette) mozzicone m; (for water) barile m; (fig: target) bersaglio m ● vt dare una testata a; (goat:) dare una cornata a. **butt in** vi interrompere

butter /'bʌtə(r)/ n burro m ● vt imburrare. **butter up** vt fam arruffianarsi

butter: ~cup n ranuncolo m. **~fingers** nsg fam **~fingers** avere le mani di pasta frolla. **~fly** n farfalla f

buttocks /'bʌtəks/ npl natiche fpl

button /'bʌtn/ n bottone m ● vt ~ [up] abbottonare ● vi abbottonarsi. **~hole** n occhiello m, asola f

buttress /'bʌtrɪs/ n contrafforte m

buxom /'bʌksəm/ a formosa

buy /baɪ/ n **good/bad ~** buon/cattivo acquisto m ● vt (pt/pp **bought**) comprare; **~ sb a drink** pagare da bere a qcno; **I'll ~ this one** (drink) questo, lo offro io. **~er** n compratore, -trice mf

buzz /bʌz/ n ronzio m; **give sb a ~** fam (on phone) dare un colpo di telefono a qcno; (excite) mettere in fermento qcno ● vi ronzare ● vt **~ sb** chiamare qcno col cicalino. **buzz off** vi fam levarsi di torno

buzzer /'bʌzə(r)/ n cicalino m

by /baɪ/ prep (near, next to) vicino a; (at the latest) per; **by Mozart** di Mozart; **he was run over by a bus** è stato investito da un autobus; **by oneself** da solo; **by the sea** al mare; **by sea** via mare; **by car/bus** in macchina/autobus; **by day/night** di giorno/notte; **by the hour/metre** a ore/metri; **six metres by four** sei metri per quattro; **he won by six metres** ha vinto di sei metri; **I missed the train by a minute** ho perso il treno per un minuto; **I'll be home by six** sarò a casa per le sei; **by this time next week** a quest'ora tra una settimana; **he rushed by me** mi è

passato accanto di corsa ● *adv*
she'll be here by and by sarà qui
fra poco; **by and large** in complesso

bye[-bye] /baɪ['baɪ]/ *int fam* ciao

by: **~-election** *n elezione f straordi-
naria indetta per coprire una cari-
ca rimasta vacante in Parlamento.
~gone *a* passato. **~-law** *n* legge *f*
locale. **~pass** *n* circonvallazione
f; *Med* by-pass *m inv* ● *vt* evitare.
~-product *n* sottoprodotto *m*.
~stander *n* spettatore, -trice *mf*.
~word *n* **be a ~word for** essere
sinonimo di

Cc

cab /kæb/ *n* taxi *m inv*; *(of lorry,
train)* cabina *f*

cabaret /'kæbəreɪ/ *n* cabaret *m inv*

cabbage /'kæbɪdʒ/ *n* cavolo *m*

cabin /'kæbɪn/ *n (of plane, ship)* cabina *f*; *(hut)* capanna *f*

cabinet /'kæbɪnɪt/ *n* armadietto
m; [display] ~ vetrina *f*; **C~** *Pol*
consiglio *m* dei ministri. **~-maker**
n ebanista *m*

cable /'keɪbl/ *n* cavo *m*. ~ **railway**
n funicolare *f*. ~ **television** *n* televisione *f* via cavo

cache /kæʃ/ *n* nascondiglio *m*; ~
of arms deposito *m* segreto di
armi

cackle /'kækl/ *vi* ridacchiare

cactus /'kæktəs/ *n (pl* -**ti** /-taɪ/ *or*
-**tuses**) cactus *m inv*

caddie /'kædɪ/ *n* portabastoni *m
inv*

caddy /'kædɪ/ *n* [tea-]~ barattolo
m del tè

cadet /kə'det/ *n* cadetto *m*

cadge /kædʒ/ *vt/i fam* scroccare

Caesarean /sɪ'zeərɪən/ *n* parto *m*
cesareo

café /'kæfeɪ/ *n* caffè *m inv*

cafeteria /kæfə'tɪərɪə/ *n* tavola *f*
calda

caffeine /'kæfiːn/ *n* caffeina *f*

cage /keɪdʒ/ *n* gabbia *f*

cagey /'keɪdʒɪ/ *a fam* riservato
(about su)

cajole /kə'dʒəʊl/ *vt* persuadere
con le lusinghe

cake /keɪk/ *n* torta *f*; *(small)* pasticcino *m*. **~d** *a* incrostato **(with**
di)

calamity /kə'læmətɪ/ *n* calamità *f
inv*

calcium /'kælsɪəm/ *n* calcio *m*

calculat|e /'kælkjʊleɪt/ *vt* calcola-
re. **~ing** *a fig* calcolatore. **~ion**
/-'leɪʃn/ *n* calcolo *m*. **~or** *n* calco-
latrice *f*

calendar /'kælɪndə(r)/ *n* calenda-
rio *m*

calf[1] /kɑːf/ *n (pl* **calves**) vitello *m*

calf[2] *n (pl* **calves**) *Anat* polpac-
cio *m*

calibre /'kælɪbə(r)/ *n* calibro *m*

call /kɔːl/ *n* grido *m*; *Teleph* telefonata *f*; *(visit)* visita *f*; **be on** ~
(doctor:) essere di guardia ● *vt*
chiamare; indire *(strike)*; **be ~ed**
chiamarsi ● *vi* chiamare; ~ **[in or
round)** passare. **call back** *vt/i* richiamare. **call for** *vt (ask for)* chiedere; *(require)* richiedere; *(fetch)*
passare a prendere. **call off** *vt* richiamare *(dog)*; disdire *(meeting)*;
revocare *(strike)*. **call on** *vt* chiamare; *(appeal to)* fare un appello
a; *(visit)* visitare. **call out** *vt* chiamare ad alta voce *(names)* ● *vi*
chiamare ad alta voce. **call together** *vt* riunire. **call up** *vt Mil*
chiamare alle armi; *Teleph* chiamare

call: **~-box** *n* cabina *f* telefonica.
~er *n* visitatore, -trice *mf*; *Teleph*
persona *f* che telefona. **~ing** *n* vocazione *f*

callous /'kæləs/ *a* insensibile

'call-up *n Mil* chiamata *f* alle armi

calm /kɑːm/ *a* calmo ● *n* calma *f*.
calm down *vt* calmare ● *vi* calmarsi. **~ly** *adv* con calma

calorie /'kælərɪ/ n caloria f
calves /kɑ:vz/ npl see **calf¹ & ²**
camber /'kæmbə(r)/ n curvatura f
Cambodia /kæm'bəʊdɪə/ n Cambogia f. **~n** a & n cambogiano, -a mf
camcorder /'kæmkɔ:də(r)/ n videocamera f
came /keɪm/ see **come**
camel /'kæml/ n cammello m
camera /'kæmərə/ n macchina f fotografica; TV telecamera f. **~man** n operatore m [televisivo], cameraman m inv
camouflage /'kæməflɑ:ʒ/ n mimetizzazione f ● vt mimetizzare
camp /kæmp/ n campeggio f; Mil campo m ● vi campeggiare; Mil accamparsi
campaign /kæm'peɪn/ n campagna f ● vi fare una campagna
camp: **~-bed** n letto m da campo. **~er** n campeggiatore, -trice mf; Auto camper m inv. **~ing** n campeggio m. **~site** n campeggio m
campus /'kæmpəs/ n (pl **-puses**) Univ città f universitaria, campus m inv
can¹ /kæn/ n (for petrol) latta f; (tin) scatola f; **~ of beer** lattina f di birra ● vt mettere in scatola
can² /kæn/, atono /kən/ v aux (pres **can**; pt **could**) (be able to) potere; (know how to) sapere; **I cannot** or **can't go** non posso andare; **he could not** or **couldn't go** non poteva andare; **she can't swim** non sa nuotare; **I ~ smell something burning** sento odor di bruciato
Canad|a /'kænədə/ n Canada m. **~ian** /kə'neɪdɪən/ a & n canadese mf
canal /kə'næl/ n canale m
Canaries /kə'neərɪz/ npl Canarie fpl
canary /kə'neərɪ/ n canarino m
cancel /'kænsl/ v (pt/pp **cancelled**) ● vt disdire (meeting, newspaper); revocare (contract, order); annullare (reservation, appointment, stamp). **~lation**

/-ə'leɪʃn/ n (of meeting, contract) revoca f; (in hotel, restaurant, for flight) cancellazione f
cancer /'kænsə(r)/ n cancro m; **C~** Astr Cancro m. **~ous** /-rəs/ a canceroso
candelabra /kændə'lɑ:brə/ n candelabro m
candid /'kændɪd/ a franco
candidate /'kændɪdət/ n candidato, -a mf
candle /'kændl/ n candela f. **~stick** n portacandele m inv
candour /'kændə(r)/ n franchezza f
candy /'kændɪ/ n Am caramella f; **a [piece of] ~** una caramella. **~floss** /-flɒs/ n zucchero m filato
cane /keɪn/ n (stick) bastone m; Sch bacchetta f ● vt prendere a bacchettate (pupil)
canine /'keɪnaɪn/ a canino. **~ tooth** n canino m
canister /'kænɪstə(r)/ n barattolo m (di metallo)
cannabis /'kænəbɪs/ n cannabis f
canned /kænd/ a in scatola; **~ music** fam musica f registrata
cannibal /'kænɪbl/ n cannibale mf. **~ism** n cannibalismo m
cannon /'kænən/ n inv cannone m. **~-ball** n palla f di cannone
cannot /'kænɒt/ see **can²**
canny /'kænɪ/ a astuto
canoe /kə'nu:/ n canoa f ● vi andare in canoa
'can-opener n apriscatole m inv
canopy /'kænəpɪ/ n baldacchino f; (of parachute) calotta f
can't /kɑ:nt/ = **cannot** see **can²**
cantankerous /kæn'tæŋkərəs/ a stizzoso
canteen /kæn'ti:n/ n mensa f; **~ of cutlery** servizio m di posate
canter /'kæntə(r)/ vi andare a piccolo galoppo
canvas /'kænvəs/ n tela f; (painting) dipinto m su tela
canvass /'kænvəs/ vi Pol fare propaganda elettorale. **~ing** n sollecitazione f di voti

337

canyon /'kænjən/ n canyon m inv

cap /kæp/ n berretto m; (nurse's) cuffia f; (top, lid) tappo m ● vt (pt/pp **capped**) (fig: do better than) superare

capability /keipə'biləti/ n capacità f

capable /'keipəbl/ a capace; (skilful) abile; **be ~e of doing sth** essere capace di fare qcsa. **~y** adv con abilità

capacity /kə'pæsəti/ n capacità f; (function) qualità f; **in my ~ as** in qualità di

cape[1] /keip/ n (cloak) cappa f

cape[2] n Geog capo m

caper[1] /'keipə(r)/ vi saltellare ● n fam birichinata f

caper[2] n Culin cappero m

capital /'kæpitl/ n (town) capitale f; (money) capitale m; (letter) lettera f maiuscola. **~ city** n capitale f

capital|ism /'kæpitəlizm/ n capitalismo m. **~ist** /-ist/ a & n capitalista mf. **~ize** /-aiz/ vi **~ize on** fig trarre vantaggio da. **~ 'letter** n lettera f maiuscola. **~ 'punishment** n pena f capitale

capitulat|e /kə'pitjuleit/ vi capitolare. **~ion** /-'leiʃn/ n capitolazione f

capricious /kə'priʃəs/ a capriccioso

Capricorn /'kæprikɔːn/ n Astr Capricorno m

capsize /kæp'saiz/ vi capovolgersi ● vt capovolgere

capsule /'kæpsjul/ n capsula f

captain /'kæptin/ n capitano m ● vt comandare (team)

caption /'kæpʃn/ n intestazione f; (of illustration) didascalia f

captivate /'kæptiveit/ vt incantare

captiv|e /'kæptiv/ a prigioniero; **hold/take ~e** tenere/fare prigioniero ● n prigioniero, -a mf. **~ity** /-'tivəti/ n prigionia f; (animals) cattività f

capture /'kæptʃə(r)/ n cattura f ● vt catturare; attirare (attention)

car /kɑː(r)/ n macchina f; **by ~** in macchina

carafe /kə'ræf/ n caraffa f

caramel /'kærəmel/ n (sweet) caramella f al mou; Culin caramello m

carat /'kærət/ n carato m

caravan /'kærəvæn/ n roulotte f inv; (horse-drawn) carovana f

carbohydrate /kɑːbə'haidreit/ n carboidrato m

carbon /'kɑːbən/ n carbonio m

carbon: **~ copy** n copia f in carta carbone; (fig: person) ritratto m. **~ di'oxide** n anidride f carbonica. **~ paper** n carta f carbone

carburettor /kɑːbjʊ'retə(r)/ n carburatore m

carcass /'kɑːkəs/ n carcassa f

card /kɑːd/ n (for birthday, Christmas etc) biglietto m di auguri; (playing ~) carta f [da gioco]; (membership ~) tessera f; (business ~) biglietto m da visita; (credit ~) carta f di credito; Comput scheda f

cardboard n cartone m. **~ 'box** n scatola f di cartone; (large) scatolone m

card-game n gioco m di carte

cardiac /'kɑːdiæk/ a cardiaco

cardigan /'kɑːdigən/ n cardigan m inv

cardinal /'kɑːdinl/ a cardinale; **~ number** numero m cardinale ● n Relig cardinale m

card 'index n schedario m

care /keə(r)/ n cura f; (caution) attenzione f; (worry) preoccupazione f; **~ of** (on letter abbr c/o) presso; **take ~** (be cautious) fare attenzione; **bye, take ~** ciao, stammi bene; **take ~ of** occuparsi di; **be taken into ~** essere preso in custodia da un ente assistenziale ● vi **~ about** interessarsi di; **~ for** (feel affection for) volere bene a; (look after) aver cura di; **I don't ~ for chocolate** non mi piace il cioccolato; **I don't ~** non me ne importa; **who ~s?** chi se ne frega?

career /kə'riə(r)/ n carriera f;

(*profession*) professione *f* ● *vi* andare a tutta velocità

care: **~free** *a* spensierato. **~ful** *a* attento; (*driver*) prudente. **~fully** *adv* con attenzione. **~less** *a* irresponsabile; (*in work*) trascurato; (*work*) fatto con poca cura; (*driver*) distratto. **~lessly** *adv* negligentemente. **~lessness** *n* trascuratezza *f*. **~r** *n* persona *f* che accudisce a un anziano o a un malato

caress /kəˈres/ *n* carezza *f* ● *vt* accarezzare

'**caretaker** *n* custode *mf*; (*in school*) bidello *m*

'**car ferry** *n* traghetto *m* (*per il trasporto di auto*)

cargo /ˈkɑːɡəʊ/ *n* (*pl* **-es**) carico *m*

Caribbean /kærɪˈbiːən/ *n* **the ~** (*sea*) il Mar dei Caraibi ● *a* caraibico

caricature /ˈkærɪkətjʊə(r)/ *n* caricatura *f*

caring /ˈkeərɪŋ/ *a* (*parent*) premuroso; (*attitude*) altruista; **the ~ professions** le attività assistenziali

carnage /ˈkɑːnɪdʒ/ *n* carneficina *f*

carnal /ˈkɑːnl/ *a* carnale

carnation /kɑːˈneɪʃn/ *n* garofano *m*

carnival /ˈkɑːnɪvl/ *n* carnevale *m*

carnivorous /kɑːˈnɪvərəs/ *a* carnivoro

carol /ˈkærəl/ *n* [**Christmas**] **~** canzone *f* natalizia

carp¹ /kɑːp/ *n inv* carpa *f*

carp² *vi* **~ at** trovare da ridire su

'**car park** *n* parcheggio *m*

carpent|er /ˈkɑːpɪntə(r)/ *n* falegname *m*. **~ry** *n* falegnameria *f*

carpet /ˈkɑːpɪt/ *n* tappeto *m*; (*wall-to-wall*) moquette *f inv* ● *vt* mettere la moquette in (*room*)

'**car phone** *n* telefono *m* in macchina

carriage /ˈkærɪdʒ/ *n* carrozza *f*; (*of goods*) trasporto *m*; (*cost*) spese *fpl* di trasporto; (*bearing*) portamento *m*; **~way** *n* strada *f* carreg-

zabile; **north-bound ~way** carreggiata *f* nord

carrier /ˈkærɪə(r)/ *n* (*company*) impresa *f* di trasporti; Aeron compagnia *f* di trasporto aereo; (*of disease*) portatore *m*. **~ [bag]** *n* borsa *f* [per la spesa]

carrot /ˈkærət/ *n* carota *f*

carry /ˈkærɪ/ *v* (*pt/pp* **-ied**) ● *vt* portare; (*transport*) trasportare; **get carried away** *fam* lasciarsi prender la mano ● *vi* (*sound:*) trasmettersi. **carry off** *vt* portare via; vincere (*prize*). **carry on** *vi* continuare; (*fam: make scene*) fare delle storie; **~ on with sth** continuare qcsa; **~ on with sb** *fam* intendersela con qcno ● *vt* mantenere (*business*). **carry out** *vt* portare fuori; eseguire (*instructions, task*); mettere in atto (*threat*); effettuare (*experiment, survey*)

'**carry-cot** *n* porte-enfant *m inv*

cart /kɑːt/ *n* carretto *m* ● *vt* (*fam: carry*) portare

cartilage /ˈkɑːtɪlɪdʒ/ *n* Anat cartilagine *f*

carton /ˈkɑːtn/ *n* scatola *f* di cartone; (*for drink*) cartone *m*; (*of cream, yoghurt*) vasetto *m*; (*of cigarettes*) stecca *f*

cartoon /kɑːˈtuːn/ *n* vignetta *f*; (*strip*) vignette *fpl*; (*film*) cartone *m* animato; (*in art*) bozzetto *m*. **~ist** *n* vignettista *f*; (*for films*) disegnatore, -trice *mf* di cartoni animati

cartridge /ˈkɑːtrɪdʒ/ *n* cartuccia *f*; (*for film*) bobina *f*; (*of record player*) testina *f*

carve /kɑːv/ *vt* scolpire; tagliare (*meat*)

carving /ˈkɑːvɪŋ/ *n* scultura *f*. **~-knife** *n* trinciante *m*

'**car wash** *n* autolavaggio *m inv*

case¹ /keɪs/ *n* caso *m*; **in any ~** in ogni caso; **in that ~** in questo caso; **just in ~** per sicurezza; **in ~ he comes** nel caso in cui venisse

case² /keɪs/ *n* (*container*) scatola *f*;

(crate) cassa *f*; *(for spectacles)* astuccio *m*; *(suitcase)* valigia *f*; *(for display)* vetrina *f*

cash /kæʃ/ *n* denaro *m* contante; *(fam: money)* contanti *mpl*; **pay [in]** ~ pagare in contanti; ~ **on delivery** pagamento alla consegna ● *vt* incassare *(cheque)*. ~ **desk** *n* cassa *f*

cashier /kæ'ʃɪə(r)/ *n* cassiere, -a *mf*

'**cash register** *n* registratore *m* di cassa

casino /kə'si:nəʊ/ *n* casinò *m* *inv*

casket /'kɑ:skɪt/ *n* scrigno *m*; *(Am: coffin)* bara *f*

casserole /'kæsərəʊl/ *n* casseruola *f*; *(stew)* stufato *m*

cassette /kə'set/ *n* cassetta *f*. ~ **recorder** *n* registratore *m* *(a cassette)*

cast /kɑ:st/ *n* *(mould)* forma *f*; *Theat* cast *m* *inv*; *(plaster)* ~ *Med* ingessatura *f* ● *vt* *(pt/pp* **cast**) dare *(vote)*; *Theat* assegnare le parti *(play)*; fondere *(metal)*; *(throw)* gettare; ~ **an actor** dare a un attore il ruolo di; ~ **a glance at** lanciare uno sguardo a. **cast off** *vi Naut* sganciare gli ormeggi ● *vt* *(in knitting)* diminuire. **cast on** *vt* *(in knitting)* avviare

castaway /'kɑ:stəweɪ/ *n* naufrago, -a *mf*

caste /kɑ:st/ *n* casta *f*

caster /'kɑ:stə(r)/ *n* *(wheel)* rotella *f*. ~ **sugar** *n* zucchero *m* raffinato

cast 'iron *n* ghisa *f*

cast-'iron *a* di ghisa; *fig* solido

castle /'kɑ:sl/ *n* castello *m*; *(in chess)* torre *f*

'**cast-offs** *npl* abiti *mpl* smessi

castor /'kɑ:stə(r)/ *n* *(wheel)* rotella *f*. ~ **oil** *n* olio *m* di ricino. ~ **sugar** *n* zucchero *m* raffinato

castrat|e /kæ'streɪt/ *vt* castrare. ~**ion** /-eɪʃn/ *n* castrazione *f*

casual /'kæʒʊəl/ *a* *(chance)* casuale; *(remark)* senza importanza; *(glance)* di sfuggita; *(attitude, approach)* disinvolto; *(chat)* infor-

male; *(clothes)* casual *inv*; *(work)* saltuario; ~ **wear** abbigliamento *m* casual. ~**ly** *adv* *(dress)* casual; *(meet)* casualmente

casualty /'kæʒʊəltɪ/ *n* *(injured person)* ferito *m*; *(killed)* vittima *f*. ~ **[department]** *n* pronto soccorso *m*

cat /kæt/ *n* gatto *m*; *pej* arpia *f*

catalogue /'kætəlɒg/ *n* catalogo *m* ● *vt* catalogare

catalyst /'kætəlɪst/ *n Chem & fig* catalizzatore *m*

catalytic /kætə'lɪtɪk/ *a* ~ **converter** *Auto* marmitta *f* catalitica

catapult /'kætəpʌlt/ *n* catapulta *f*; *(child's)* fionda *f* ● *vt* *fig* catapultare

cataract /'kætərækt/ *n Med* cataratta *f*

catarrh /kə'tɑ:(r)/ *n* catarro *m*

catastroph|e /kə'tæstrəfɪ/ *n* catastrofe *f*. ~**ic** /kætə'strɒfɪk/ *a* catastrofico

catch /kætʃ/ *n* *(of fish)* pesca *f*; *(fastener)* fermaglio *m*; *(on door)* fermo *m*; *(on window)* gancio *m*; *(fam: snag)* tranello *m* ● *v* *(pt/pp* **caught**) ● *vt* acchiappare *(ball)*; *(grab)* afferrare; prendere *(illness, fugitive, train)*; ~ **a cold** prendersi un raffreddore; ~ **sight of** scorgere; **I caught him stealing** l'ho sorpreso mentre rubava; ~ **one's finger in the door** chiudersi il dito nella porta; ~ **sb's eye** *or* **attention** attirare l'attenzione di qcno ● *vi* *(fire:)* prendere; *(get stuck)* impigliarsi. **catch on** *vi* *fam* *(understand)* afferrare; *(become popular)* diventare popolare. **catch up** *vt* raggiungere ● *vi* recuperare; *(runner:)* riguadagnare terreno; ~ **up with** raggiungere *(sb)*; mettersi in pari con *(work)*

catching /'kætʃɪŋ/ *a* contagioso

catch: ~**-phrase** *n* tormentone *m*. ~**word** *n* slogan *m* *inv*

catchy /'kætʃɪ/ *a* **(-ier, -iest)** orecchiabile

categor|ical /ˌkætɪˈgɒrɪkl/ a categorico. **~y** /ˈkætɪgərɪ/ n categoria f

cater /ˈkeɪtə(r)/ vi **~ for** provvedere a ⟨needs⟩; fig venire incontro alle esigenze di. **~ing** n ⟨trade⟩ ristorazione f; ⟨food⟩ rinfresco m

caterpillar /ˈkætəpɪlə(r)/ n bruco m

cathedral /kəˈθiːdrl/ n cattedrale f

Catholic /ˈkæθəlɪk/ a & n cattolico, -a mf. **~ism** /kəˈθɒlɪsɪzm/ n cattolicesimo m

cat's eyes npl catarifrangente msg ⟨inserito nell'asfalto⟩

cattle /ˈkætl/ npl bestiame msg

catty /ˈkætɪ/ a (-ier, -iest) dispettoso

catwalk /ˈkætwɔːk/ n passerella f

caught /kɔːt/ see **catch**

cauliflower /ˈkɒlɪˌflaʊə(r)/ n cavolfiore m

cause /kɔːz/ n causa f ● vt causare; **~ sb to do sth** far fare qcsa a qcno

'causeway n strada f sopraelevata

caustic /ˈkɔːstɪk/ a caustico

caution /ˈkɔːʃn/ n cautela f; ⟨warning⟩ ammonizione f ● vt mettere in guardia; Jur ammonire

cautious /ˈkɔːʃəs/ a cauto

cavalry /ˈkævlrɪ/ n cavalleria f

cave /keɪv/ n caverna f ● **cave in** vi ⟨roof:⟩ crollare; ⟨fig: give in⟩ capitolare

cavern /ˈkævən/ n caverna f

caviare /ˈkævɪɑː(r)/ n caviale m

caving /ˈkeɪvɪŋ/ n speleologia f

cavity /ˈkævətɪ/ n cavità f inv; ⟨in tooth⟩ carie f inv

cavort /kəˈvɔːt/ vi saltellare

CD n CD m inv. **~ player** n lettore m [di] compact

CD-Rom /siːdiːˈrɒm/ n CD-Rom m inv. **~ drive** n lettore m [di] CD-Rom

cease /siːs/ n **without ~** incessantemente ● vt/i cessare. **~-fire** n cessate il fuoco m inv. **~less** a incessante

cedar /ˈsiːdə(r)/ n cedro m

cede /siːd/ vt cedere

ceiling /ˈsiːlɪŋ/ n soffitto m; fig tetto m [massimo]

celebrat|e /ˈselɪbreɪt/ vt festeggiare ⟨birthday, victory⟩ ● vi far festa. **~ed** a celebre (**for** per). **~ion** /-ˈbreɪʃn/ n celebrazione f

celebrity /sɪˈlebrɪtɪ/ n celebrità f

celery /ˈselərɪ/ n sedano m

celiba|cy /ˈselɪbəsɪ/ n celibato m. **~te** a ⟨man⟩ celibe; ⟨woman⟩ nubile

cell /sel/ n cella f; Biol cellula f

cellar /ˈselə(r)/ n scantinato m; ⟨for wine⟩ cantina f

cellist /ˈtʃelɪst/ n violoncellista mf

cello /ˈtʃeləʊ/ n violoncello m

Cellophane® /ˈseləfeɪn/ n cellofan m inv

cellular phone /seljʊləˈfəʊn/ n [telefono m] cellulare m

celluloid /ˈseljʊlɔɪd/ n celluloide f

Celsius /ˈselsɪəs/ a Celsius

Celt /kelt/ n celta mf. **~ic** a celtico

cement /sɪˈment/ n cemento m; ⟨adhesive⟩ mastice m ● vt cementare; fig consolidare

cemetery /ˈsemətrɪ/ n cimitero m

censor /ˈsensə(r)/ n censore m ● vt censurare. **~ship** n censura f

censure /ˈsenʃə(r)/ vt biasimare

census /ˈsensəs/ n censimento m

cent /sent/ n ⟨coin⟩ centesimo m

centenary /senˈtiːnərɪ/ n, Am **centennial** /senˈtenɪəl/ n centenario m

center /ˈsentə(r)/ n Am = **centre**

centi|grade /ˈsentɪ-/ a centigrado. **~metre** n centimetro m. **~pede** /-piːd/ n centopiedi m inv

central /ˈsentrl/ a centrale. **~ heating** n riscaldamento m autonomo. **~ize** vt centralizzare. **~ly** adv al centro; **~ly heated** con riscaldamento autonomo. **~ reservation** n Auto banchina f spartitraffico

centre /ˈsentə(r)/ n centro m ● v (pt/pp **centred**) ● vt centrare ● vi **~ on** fig incentrarsi su. **~-'forward** n centravanti m inv

centrifugal /sentrɪ'fjuːgl/ *a* ~ **force** forza *f* centrifuga

century /'sentʃərɪ/ *n* secolo *m*

ceramic /sɪ'ræmɪk/ *a* ceramico. ~**s** *n* (*art*) ceramica *fsg*; (*objects*) ceramiche *fpl*

cereal /'sɪərɪəl/ *n* cereale *m*

cerebral /'serɪbrl/ *a* cerebrale

ceremoni|al /serɪ'məʊnɪəl/ *a* da cerimonia ● *n* cerimoniale *m*. ~**ious** /-ɪəs/ *a* cerimonioso

ceremony /'serɪmənɪ/ *n* cerimonia *f*

certain /'sɜːtn/ *a* certo; **for** ~ di sicuro; **make** ~ accertarsi; **he is** ~ **to win** è certo di vincere; **it's not** ~ **whether he'll come** non è sicuro che venga. ~**ly** *adv* certamente; ~**ly not!** no di certo! ~**ty** *n* certezza *f*; **it's a** ~**ty** è una cosa certa

certificate /sə'tɪfɪkət/ *n* certificato *m*

certify /'sɜːtɪfaɪ/ *vt* (*pt/pp* **-ied**) certificare; (*declare insane*) dichiarare malato di mente

cessation /se'seɪʃn/ *n* cessazione *f*

cesspool /'ses-/ *n* pozzo *m* nero

cf *abbr* (*compare*) cf, cfr

chafe /tʃeɪf/ *vt* irritare

chain /tʃeɪn/ *n* catena *f* ● *vt* incatenare (*prisoner*); attaccare con la catena (*dog*) (**to** a). **chain up** *vt* legare alla catena (*dog*)

chain: ~ **re'action** reazione *f* a catena. ~**-smoke** *vi* fumare una sigaretta dopo l'altra. ~**-smoker** *n* fumatore, -trice *mf* accanito, -a. ~ **store** *n* negozio *m* appartenente a una catena

chair /tʃeə(r)/ *n* sedia *f*; *Univ* cattedra *f* ● *vt* presiedere. ~**-lift** *n* seggiovia *f*. ~**man** *n* presidente *m*

chalet /'ʃæleɪ/ *n* chalet *m inv*; (*in holiday camp*) bungalow *m inv*

chalice /'tʃælɪs/ *n Relig* calice *m*

chalk /tʃɔːk/ *n* gesso *m*. ~**y** *a* gessoso

challeng|e /'tʃælɪndʒ/ *n* sfida *f*; *Mil* intimazione *f* ● *vt* sfidare; *Mil* intimare il chi va là a; *fig* mettere in dubbio (*statement*). ~**er** *n* sfi-

dante *mf*. ~**ing** *a* (*job*) impegnativo

chamber /'tʃeɪmbə(r)/ *n* **C**~ **of Commerce** camera *f* di commercio

chamber: ~**maid** *n* cameriera *f* [d'albergo]. ~ **music** *n* musica *f* da camera

chamois[1] /'ʃæmwɑː/ *n inv* (*animal*) camoscio *m*

chamois[2] /'ʃæmɪ/ *n* ~[-**leather**] [pelle *f* di] camoscio *m*

champagne /ʃæm'peɪn/ *n* champagne *m inv*

champion /'tʃæmpɪən/ *n Sport* campione *m*; (*of cause*) difensore, difenditrice *mf* ● *vt* (*defend*) difendere; (*fight for*) lottare per. ~**ship** *n Sport* campionato *m*

chance /tʃɑːns/ *n* caso *m*; (*possibility*) possibilità *f*; (*opportunity*) occasione *f*; **by** ~ per caso; **take a** ~ provarci; **give sb a second** ~ dare un'altra possibilità a qcno ● *attrib* fortuito ● *vt* **I'll** ~ **it** *fam* corro il rischio

chancellor /'tʃɑːnsələ(r)/ *n* cancelliere *m*; *Univ* rettore *m*; **C**~ **of the Exchequer** ≈ ministro *m* del tesoro

chancy /'tʃɑːnsɪ/ *a* rischioso

chandelier /ʃændə'lɪə(r)/ *n* lampadario *m*

change /tʃeɪndʒ/ *n* cambiamento *m*; (*money*) resto *m*; (*small coins*) spiccioli *mpl*; **for a** ~ tanto per cambiare; **a** ~ **of clothes** un cambio di vestiti; **the** ~ [**of life**] la menopausa ● *vt* cambiare; (*substitute*) scambiare (**for** con). ~ **one's clothes** cambiarsi [i vestiti]; ~ **trains** cambiare treno ● *vi* cambiare; (~ *clothes*) cambiarsi; **all** ~! stazione terminale!

changeable /'tʃeɪndʒəbl/ *a* mutevole; (*weather*) variabile

'changing-room *n* camerino *m*; (*for sports*) spogliatoio *m*

channel /'tʃænl/ *n* canale *m*; **the** [**English**] **C**~ la Manica; **the C**~ **Islands** le Isole del Canale ● *vt* (*pt/pp* **channelled**) ~ one's energies into sth convogliare le proprie energie in qcsa

chant /tʃɑːnt/ *n* cantilena *f*; (*of demonstrators*) slogan *m inv* di protesta ● *vt* cantare; ⟨*demonstrators:*⟩ gridare

chao|s /ˈkeɪɒs/ *n* caos *m*. **~tic** /-ˈɒtɪk/ *a* caotico

chap /tʃæp/ *n fam* tipo *m*

chapel /ˈtʃæpl/ *n* cappella *f*

chaperon /ˈʃæpərəʊn/ *n* chaperon *f inv* ● *vt* fare da chaperon a ⟨*sb*⟩

chaplain /ˈtʃæplɪn/ *n* cappellano *m*

chapped /tʃæpt/ *a* ⟨*skin, lips*⟩ screpolato

chapter /ˈtʃæptə(r)/ *n* capitolo *m*

char[1] /tʃɑː(r)/ *n fam* donna *f* delle pulizie

char[2] *vt* (*pt/pp* **charred**) (*burn*) carbonizzare

character /ˈkærɪktə(r)/ *n* carattere *m*; (*in novel, play*) personaggio *m*; **quite a ~** *fam* un tipo particolare

characteristic /kærɪktəˈrɪstɪk/ *a* caratteristico ● *n* caratteristica *f*. **~ally** *adv* tipicamente

characterize /ˈkærɪktəraɪz/ *vt* caratterizzare

charade /ʃəˈrɑːd/ *n* farsa *f*

charcoal /ˈtʃɑː-/ *n* carbonella *f*

charge /tʃɑːdʒ/ *n* (*cost*) prezzo *m*; *Electr, Mil* carica *f*; *Jur* accusa *f*; **free of ~** gratuito; **be in ~** essere responsabile (**of** di); **take ~** assumersi la responsabilità; **take ~** of occuparsi di ● *vt* far pagare ⟨*fee*⟩; far pagare a ⟨*person*⟩; *Electr, Mil* caricare; *Jur* accusare (**with** di); **~ sb for sth** far pagare qcsa a qcno; **~ it to my account** lo addebiti sul mio conto ● *vt* (*attack*) caricare

chariot /ˈtʃærɪət/ *n* cocchio *m*

charisma /kəˈrɪzmə/ *n* carisma *m*. **~tic** /kærɪzˈmætɪk/ *a* carismatico

charitable /ˈtʃærɪtəbl/ *a* caritatevole; (*kind*) indulgente

charity /ˈtʃærətɪ/ *n* carità *f*; (*organization*) associazione *f* di bene-

ficenza; **concert given for ~** concerto *m* di beneficenza; **live on ~** vivere di elemosina

charm /tʃɑːm/ *n* fascino *m*; (*object*) ciondolo *m* ● *vt* affascinare. **~ing** *a* affascinante

chart /tʃɑːt/ *n* carta *f* nautica; (*table*) tabella *f*

charter /ˈtʃɑːtə(r)/ *n* – **[flight]** [volo *m*] charter *m inv* ● *vt* noleggiare. **~ed accountant** *n* commercialista *mf*

charwoman /ˈtʃɑː-/ *n* donna *f* delle pulizie

chase /tʃeɪs/ *n* inseguimento *m* ● *vt* inseguire. **chase away** *or* **off** *vt* cacciare via

chasm /ˈkæz(ə)m/ *n* abisso *m*

chassis /ˈʃæsɪ/ *n* (*pl* **chassis** /-sɪz/) telaio *m*

chaste /tʃeɪst/ *a* casto

chastity /ˈtʃæstətɪ/ *n* castità *f*

chat /tʃæt/ *n* chiacchierata *f*; **have a ~ with** fare quattro chiacchiere con ● *vi* (*pt/pp* **chatted**) chiacchierare. **~ show** *n* talk show *m inv*

chatter /ˈtʃætə(r)/ *n* chiacchiere *fpl* ● *vi* chiacchierare; ⟨*teeth:*⟩ battere. **~box** *n fam* chiacchierone, -a *mf*

chatty /ˈtʃætɪ/ *a* (**-ier, -iest**) chiacchierone; ⟨*style*⟩ familiare

chauffeur /ˈʃəʊfə(r)/ *n* autista *mf*

chauvin|ism /ˈʃəʊvɪnɪzm/ *n* sciovinismo *m*. **~ist** *n* sciovinista *mf*. **male ~ist** *n fam* maschilista *m*

cheap /tʃiːp/ *a* a buon mercato; (*rate*) economico; (*vulgar*) grossolano; (*of poor quality*) scadente ● *adv* a buon mercato. **~ly** *adv* a buon mercato

cheat /tʃiːt/ *n* imbroglione, -a *mf*; (*at cards*) baro *m* ● *vt* imbrogliare; **~ sb out of sth** sottrarre qcsa a qcno con l'inganno ● *vi* imbrogliare; (*at cards*) barare. **cheat on** *vt fam* tradire ⟨*wife*⟩

check[1] /tʃek/ *n* ⟨*pattern*⟩ a quadri ● *n* disegno *m* a quadri

check² n verifica f; (of tickets) controllo m; (in chess) scacco m; (Am: bill) conto m; (Am: cheque) assegno m; (Am: tick) segnetto m; **keep a ~ on** controllare; **keep in ~** tenere sotto controllo ● vt verificare; controllare (tickets); (restrain) contenere; (stop) bloccare ● vi controllare; **~ on sth** controllare qcsa. **check in** vi registrarsi all'arrivo (in albergo); Aeron fare il check-in ● vt registrare all'arrivo (in albergo). **check out** vi (of hotel) saldare il conto ● vt (fam: investigate) controllare. **check up** vi accertarsi; **~ up on** prendere informazioni su

check|ed /tʃekt/ a a quadri. **~ers** n Am dama f

check: ~-in n (in airport: place) banco m accettazione, check-in m inv; **~-in time** check-in m inv. **~ mark** n Am segnetto m. **~mate** int scacco matto! **~-out** n (in supermarket) cassa f. **~-room** n Am deposito m bagagli. **~-up** n Med visita f di controllo, check-up m inv

cheek /tʃiːk/ n guancia f; (impudence) sfacciataggine f. **~y** a sfacciato

cheep /tʃiːp/ vi pigolare

cheer /tʃɪə(r)/ n evviva m inv; **three ~s** tre urrà; **~s!** salute!; (goodbye) arrivederci!; (thanks) grazie! ● vt/i acclamare. **cheer up** vt tirare su [di morale] ● vi tirarsi su [di morale]; **~ up!** su con la vita!. **~ful** a allegro. **~fulness** n allegria f. **~ing** n acclamazione f

cheerio /tʃɪərɪˈəʊ/ int fam arrivederci

'**cheerless** a triste, tetro

cheese /tʃiːz/ n formaggio m. **~cake** n dolce m al formaggio

chef /ʃef/ n cuoco, -a mf, chef mf inv

chemical /ˈkemɪkl/ a chimico ● n prodotto m chimico

chemist /ˈkemɪst/ n (pharmacist) farmacista mf; (scientist) chimico,

-a mf; **~'s [shop]** farmacia f. **~ry** n chimica f

cheque /tʃek/ n assegno m. **~-book** n libretto m degli assegni. **~ card** n carta f assegni

cherish /ˈtʃerɪʃ/ vt curare teneramente; (love) avere caro; nutrire (hope)

cherry /ˈtʃerɪ/ n ciliegia f; (tree) ciliegio m

cherub /ˈtʃerəb/ n cherubino m

chess /tʃes/ n scacchi mpl

chess: ~board n scacchiera f. **~-man** n pezzo m degli scacchi. **~player** n scacchista mf

chest /tʃest/ n petto m; (box) cassapanca f

chestnut /ˈtʃesnʌt/ n castagna f; (tree) castagno m

chest of 'drawers n cassettone m

chew /tʃuː/ vt masticare. **~ing-gum** n gomma f da masticare

chic /ʃiːk/ a chic inv

chick /tʃɪk/ n pulcino m; (fam: girl) ragazza f

chicken /ˈtʃɪkn/ n pollo m ● attrib (soup, casserole) di pollo ● a fam fifone ● **chicken out** vi fam **he ~ed out** gli è venuta fifa. **~pox** n varicella f

chicory /ˈtʃɪkərɪ/ n cicoria f

chief /tʃiːf/ a principale ● n capo m. **~ly** adv principalmente

chilblain /ˈtʃɪlbleɪn/ n gelone m

child /tʃaɪld/ n (pl **~ren**) bambino, -a mf; (son/daughter) figlio, -a mf

child: ~birth n parto m. **~hood** n infanzia f. **~ish** a infantile. **~ishness** n puerilità f. **~less** a senza figli. **~like** a ingenuo. **~minder** n baby-sitter mf inv

children /ˈtʃɪldrən/ see **child**

Chile /ˈtʃɪlɪ/ n Cile m. **~an** a & n cileno, -a mf

chill /tʃɪl/ n freddo m; (illness) infreddatura f ● vt raffreddare

chilli /ˈtʃɪlɪ/ n (pl -es) = **[pepper]** peperoncino m

chilly /ˈtʃɪlɪ/ a freddo

chime /tʃaɪm/ vi suonare

chimney /ˈtʃɪmnɪ/ n camino m.

~-pot *n* comignolo *m*. **~-sweep** *n* spazzacamino *m*

chimpanzee /tʃɪmpænˈziː/ *n* scimpanzé *m inv*

chin /tʃɪn/ *n* mento *m*

china /ˈtʃaɪnə/ *n* porcellana *f*

China *n* Cina *f*. **~ese** /-ˈniːz/ *a* & *n* cinese *mf*; (*language*) cinese *m*; **the ~ese** *pl* i cinesi

chink[1] /tʃɪŋk/ *n* (*slit*) fessura *f*

chink[2] *n* (*noise*) tintinnio *m*

chip /tʃɪp/ *n* (*fragment*) scheggia *f*; (*in china, paintwork*) scheggiatura *f*; Comput chip *m inv*; (*in gambling*) fiche *f inv*; **~s** *pl* Br Culin patatine *fpl* fritte; Am Culin patatine *fpl* ● *vt* (*pt/pp* **chipped**) (*damage*) scheggiare. **chip in** *vi fam* intromettersi; (*with money*) contribuire. **~ped** *a* (*damaged*) scheggiato

chiropod|ist /kɪˈrɒpədɪst/ *n* podiatra *mf inv*. **~y** *n* podiatria *f*

chirp /tʃɜːp/ *vi* cinguettare; ⟨*cricket:*⟩ fare cri cri. **~y** *a fam* pimpante

chisel /ˈtʃɪzl/ *n* scalpello *m*

chival|rous /ˈʃɪvlrəs/ *a* cavalleresco. **~ry** *n* cavalleria *f*

chives /tʃaɪvz/ *npl* erba *f* cipollina

chlorine /ˈklɔːriːn/ *n* cloro *m*

chloroform /ˈklɔːrəfɔːm/ *n* cloroformio *m*

chock-a-block /tʃɒkəˈblɒk/, **chock-full** /tʃɒkˈfʊl/ *a* pieno zeppo

chocolate /ˈtʃɒkələt/ *n* cioccolato *m*; (*drink*) cioccolata *f*; **a ~** un cioccolatino

choice /tʃɔɪs/ *n* scelta *f* ● *a* scelto

choir /ˈkwaɪə(r)/ *n* coro *m*. **~boy** *n* corista *m*

choke /tʃəʊk/ *n* Auto aria *f* ● *vt/i* soffocare

cholera /ˈkɒlərə/ *n* colera *m*

cholesterol /kəˈlestərɒl/ *n* colesterolo *m*

choose /tʃuːz/ *vt/i* (*pt* **chose**, *pp* **chosen**) scegliere; **as you ~** come vuoi

choos[e]y /ˈtʃuːzɪ/ *a fam* difficile

chop /tʃɒp/ *n* (*blow*) colpo *m* (*d'ascia*); Culin costata *f* ● *vt* (*pt/pp* **chopped**) tagliare. **chop down** *vt* abbattere (*tree*). **chop off** *vt* spaccare

chop|per /ˈtʃɒpə(r)/ *n* accetta *f*; *fam* elicottero *m*. **~py** *a* increspato

'chopsticks *npl* bastoncini *mpl* cinesi

choral /ˈkɔːrəl/ *a* corale

chord /kɔːd/ *n* Mus corda *f*

chore /tʃɔː(r)/ *n* corvé *f inv*; (*household*) **~s** faccende *fpl* domestiche

choreograph|er /kɒrɪˈɒɡrəfə(r)/ *n* coreografo, -a *mf*. **~y** /-ɪ/ *n* coreografia *f*

chortle /ˈtʃɔːtl/ *vi* ridacchiare

chorus /ˈkɔːrəs/ *n* coro *m*; (*of song*) ritornello *m*

chose, chosen /tʃəʊz, ˈtʃəʊzn/ *see* **choose**

Christ /kraɪst/ *n* Cristo *m*

christen /ˈkrɪsn/ *vt* battezzare. **~ing** *n* battesimo *m*

Christian /ˈkrɪstʃən/ *a* & *n* cristiano, -a *mf*. **~ity** /-stɪˈænətɪ/ *n* cristianesimo *m*. **~ name** *n* nome *m* di battesimo

Christmas /ˈkrɪsməs/ *n* Natale *m* ● *attrib* di Natale. **'~ card** *n* biglietto *m* d'auguri di Natale. **~ 'Day** *n* il giorno di Natale. **~ 'Eve** *n* la vigilia di Natale. **'~ present** *n* regalo *m* di Natale. **~ 'pudding** *n* dolce *m* natalizio a base di frutta candita e liquore. **'~ tree** *n* albero *m* di Natale

chrome /krəʊm/ *n*, **chromium** /ˈkrəʊmɪəm/ *n* cromo *m*

chromosome /ˈkrəʊməsəʊm/ . *n* cromosoma *m*

chronic /ˈkrɒnɪk/ *a* cronico

chronicle /ˈkrɒnɪkl/ *n* cronaca *f*

chronological /krɒnəˈlɒdʒɪkl/ *a* cronologico. **~ly** *adv* ⟨*ordered*⟩ in ordine cronologico

chrysanthemum /krɪˈsænθəməm/ *n* crisantemo *m*

chubby /'tʃʌbɪ/ a (**-ier, -iest**) paffuto

chuck /tʃʌk/ vt fam buttare. **chuck out** vt fam buttare via 〈object〉; buttare fuori 〈person〉

chuckle /'tʃʌkl/ vi ridacchiare

chug /tʃʌg/ vi (pt/pp **chugged**) **the train ~ged out of the station** il treno è uscito dalla stazione sbuffando

chum /tʃʌm/ n amico, -a mf. **~my** a fam **be ~my with** essere amico di

chunk /tʃʌŋk/ n grosso pezzo m

church /tʃɜːtʃ/ n chiesa f. **~yard** n cimitero m

churlish /'tʃɜːlɪʃ/ a sgarbato

churn /tʃɜːn/ vt **churn out** sfornare

chute /ʃuːt/ n scivolo m; (for rubbish) canale m di scarico

CID n abbr (**Criminal Investigation Department**) polizia f giudiziaria

cider /'saɪdə(r)/ n sidro m

cigar /sɪ'gɑː(r)/ n sigaro m

cigarette /sɪgə'ret/ n sigaretta f

cine-camera /'sɪnɪ-/ n cinepresa f

cinema /'sɪnɪmə/ n cinema m inv

cinnamon /'sɪnəmən/ n cannella f

circle /'sɜːkl/ n cerchio m; Theat galleria f; **in a ~** in cerchio ● vt girare intorno a; cerchiare 〈mistake〉 ● vi descrivere dei cerchi

circuit /'sɜːkɪt/ n circuito m; (lap) giro m; **~ board** n circuito m stampato. **~ous** /sə'kjuːɪtəs/ a **~ous route** percorso m lungo e indiretto

circular /'sɜːkjʊlə(r)/ a circolare ● n circolare f

circulat|e /'sɜːkjʊleɪt/ vt far circolare ● vi circolare. **~ion** /-'leɪʃn/ n circolazione f; (of newspaper) tiratura f

circumcis|e /'sɜːkəmsaɪz/ vt circoncidere. **~ion** /-'sɪʒn/ n circoncisione f

circumference /sə'kʌmfərəns/ n conconferenza f

circumstance /'sɜːkəmstəns/ n circostanza f; **~s** pl (financial) condizioni fpl finanziarie

circus /'sɜːkəs/ n circo m

CIS n abbr (**Commonwealth of Independent States**) CSI f

cistern /'sɪstən/ n (tank) cisterna f; (of WC) serbatoio m

cite /saɪt/ vt citare

citizen /'sɪtɪzn/ n cittadino, -a mf; (of town) abitante mf. **~ship** n cittadinanza f

citrus /'sɪtrəs/ n ~ [**fruit**] agrume m

city /'sɪtɪ/ n città f inv; **the C~** la City (di Londra)

civic /'sɪvɪk/ a civico

civil /'sɪvl/ a civile

civilian /sɪ'vɪljən/ a civile; **in ~ clothes** in borghese ● n civile mf

civilization /sɪvɪlaɪ'zeɪʃn/ n civiltà f inv. **~e** /'sɪvɪlaɪz/ vt civilizzare

civil: ~ **'servant** n impiegato, -a statale. **C~ 'Service** n pubblica amministrazione f

clad /klæd/ a vestito (**in** di)

claim /kleɪm/ n richiesta f; (right) diritto m; (assertion) dichiarazione f; **lay ~ to sth** rivendicare qcsa ● vt richiedere; reclamare 〈lost property〉; rivendicare 〈ownership〉; **~ that** sostenere che. **~ant** n richiedente mf

clairvoyant /kleə'vɔɪənt/ n chiaroveggente mf

clam /klæm/ n Culin vongola f ● **clam up** vi (pt/pp **clammed**) zittirsi

clamber /'klæmbə(r)/ vi arrampicarsi

clammy /'klæmɪ/ a (**-ier, -iest**) appiccicaticcio

clamour /'klæmə(r)/ n (protest) rimostranza f ● vi ~ **for** chiedere a gran voce

clamp /klæmp/ n morsa f ● vt ammorsare; Auto mettere i ceppi bloccaruote a. **clamp down** vi fam essere duro; **~ down on** reprimere

clan /klæn/ n clan m inv

clandestine /klæn'destɪn/ *a* clandestino

clang /klæŋ/ *n* suono *m* metallico.
~**er** *n fam* gaffe *f inv*

clank /klæŋk/ *n* rumore *m* metallico

clap /klæp/ *n* **give sb a** ~ applaudire qcno; ~ **of thunder** tuono *m*
● *vt/i* (*pt/pp* **clapped**) applaudire;
~ **one's hands** applaudire. ~**ping**
n applausi *mpl*

clari|fication /klærɪfɪ'keɪʃn/ *n*
chiarimento *m*. ~**fy** /'klærɪfaɪ/ *vt/i*
(*pt/pp* **-ied**) chiarire

clarinet /klærɪ'net/ *n* clarinetto *m*

clarity /'klærətɪ/ *n* chiarezza *f*

clash /klæʃ/ *n* scontro *m*; (*noise*)
fragore *m* ● *vi* scontrarsi; (*colours:*) stonare; (*events:*) coincidere

clasp /klɑːsp/ *n* chiusura *f* ● *vt* agganciare; (*hold*) stringere

class /klɑːs/ *n* classe *f*; (*lesson*) corso *m* ● *vt* classificare

classic /'klæsɪk/ *a* classico ● *n*
classico *m*; ~**s** *pl Univ* lettere *fpl*
classiche. ~**al** *a* classico

classi|fication /klæsɪfɪ'keɪʃn/ *n*
classificazione *f*. ~**fy** /'klæsɪfaɪ/ *vt*
(*pt/pp* **-ied**) classificare

classroom *n* aula *f*

classy /'klɑːsɪ/ *a* (**-ier, -iest**) *fam*
d'alta classe

clatter /'klætə(r)/ *n* fracasso *m*
● *vi* far fracasso

clause /klɔːz/ *n* clausola *f*; *Gram*
proposizione *f*

claustrophob|ia /klɔːstrə'fəʊbɪə/
n claustrofobia *f*

claw /klɔː/ *n* artiglio *m*; (*of crab,
lobster & Techn*) tenaglia *f* ● *vt*
(*cat:*) graffiare

clay /kleɪ/ *n* argilla *f*

clean /kliːn/ *a* pulito, lindo ● *adv*
completamente ● *vt* pulire (*shoes,
windows*); ~ **one's teeth** lavarsi i
denti; **have a coat** ~**ed** portare
un cappotto in lavanderia. **clean
up** *vt* pulire ● *vi* far pulizia

cleaner /'kliːnə(r)/ *n* uomo *m*/donna *f* delle pulizie; (*substance*) de-

tersivo *m*; **[dry]** ~**'s** lavanderia *f*,
tintoria *f*

cleanliness /'klenlɪnɪs/ *n* pulizia *f*

cleanse /klenz/ *vt* pulire. ~**r** *n* detergente *m*

clean-shaven *a* sbarbato

cleansing cream /klenz-/ *n* latte
m detergente

clear /klɪə(r)/ *a* chiaro; (*conscience*) pulito; (*road*) libero; (*profit, advantage, majority*) netto; (*sky*) sereno; (*water*) limpido;
(*glass*) trasparente; **make sth** ~
mettere qcsa in chiaro; **have I
made myself** ~? mi sono fatto capire?; **five** ~ **days** cinque giorni
buoni ● *adv* **stand** ~ **of** allontanarsi da; **keep** ~ **of** tenersi alla
larga da ● *vt* sgombrare (*room,
street*); sparecchiare (*table*); (*acquit*) scagionare; (*authorize*) autorizzare; scavalcare senza toccare
(*fence, wall*); guadagnare (*sum of
money*); passare (*Customs*); ~
one's throat schiarirsi la gola
● *vi* (*face, sky:*) rasserenarsi;
(*fog:*) dissiparsi. **clear away** *vt*
metter via. **clear off** *vi fam* filar
via. **clear out** *vt* sgombrare ● *vi
fam* filar via. **clear up** *vt* (*tidy*)
mettere a posto; chiarire
(*mystery*) ● *vi* (*weather:*) schiarirsi

clearance /'klɪərəns/ *n* (*space*)
spazio *m* libero; (*authorization*)
autorizzazione *f*; (*Customs*) sdoganamento *m*. ~ **sale** *n* liquidazione *f*

clear|ing /'klɪərɪŋ/ *n* radura *f*. ~**ly**
adv chiaramente. ~ **way** *n Auto*
strada *f* con divieto di sosta

cleavage /'kliːvɪdʒ/ *n* (*woman's*)
décolleté *m inv*

cleft /kleft/ *n* fenditura *f*

clench /klentʃ/ *vt* serrare

clergy /'klɜːdʒɪ/ *npl* clero *m*.
~**man** *n* ecclesiastico *m*

cleric /'klerɪk/ *n* ecclesiastico *m*.
~**al** *a* impiegatizio; *Relig* clericale

clerk /klɑːk/, *Am* /klɜːk/ *n* impiegáto, -a *mf*; (*Am: shop assistant*) commesso, -a *mf*

clever /'klevə(r)/ *a* intelligente; (*skilful*) abile

cliché /'kli:ʃeɪ/ *n* cliché *m inv*

click /klɪk/ *vi* scattare ● *n* Comput click *m*. **click on** *vt* Comput cliccare su

client /'klaɪənt/ *n* cliente *mf*

clientele /kli:ɒn'tel/ *n* clientela *f*

cliff /klɪf/ *n* scogliera *f*

climate /'klaɪmət/ *n* clima *f*. **~ic** /-'mætɪk/ *a* climatico

climax /'klaɪmæks/ *n* punto *m* culminante

climb /klaɪm/ *n* salita *f* ● *vt* scalare (*mountain*); arrampicarsi su (*ladder, tree*) ● *vi* arrampicarsi; (*rise*) salire; (*road*) salire. **climb down** *vi* scendere; (*from ladder, tree*) scendere; *fig* tornare sui propri passi

climber /'klaɪmə(r)/ *n* alpinista *mf*; (*plant*) rampicante *m*

clinch /klɪntʃ/ *vt fam* concludere (*deal*) ● *n* (*in boxing*) clinch *m inv*

cling /klɪŋ/ *vi* (*pt/pp* clung) aggrapparsi; (*stick*) aderire. **~ film** *n* pellicola *f* trasparente

clinic /'klɪnɪk/ *n* ambulatorio *m*. **~al** *a* clinico

clink /klɪŋk/ *n* tintinnio *m*; (*fam: prison*) galera *f* ● *vi* tintinnare

clip[1] /klɪp/ *n* fermaglio *m*; (*jewellery*) spilla *f* ● *vt* (*pt/pp* clipped) attaccare

clip[2] *n* (*extract*) taglio *m* ● *vt* obliterare (*ticket*). **~board** *n* fermabloc *m inv*. **~pers** *npl* (*for hair*) rasoio *m*; (*for hedge*) tosasiepi *m inv*; (*for nails*) tronchesina *f*. **~ping** *n* (*from newspaper*) ritaglio *m*

clique /kli:k/ *n* cricca *f*

cloak /kləʊk/ *n* mantello *m*. **~room** *n* guardaroba *m inv*; (*toilet*) bagno *m*

clock /klɒk/ *n* orologio *m*; (*fam: speedometer*) tachimetro *m* ● **clock in** *vi* attaccare. **clock out** *vi* staccare

clock: **~ tower** *n* torre *f* dell'orologio. **~wise** *a & adv* in senso orario. **~work** *n* meccanismo *m*

clod /klɒd/ *n* zolla *f*

clog /klɒg/ *n* zoccolo *m* ● *vt* (*pt/pp* clogged) **~** [up] intasare (*drain*); inceppare (*mechanism*) ● *vi* (*drain*) intasarsi

cloister /'klɔɪstə(r)/ *n* chiostro *m*

clone /kləʊn/ *n* clone *m*

close[1] /kləʊs/ *a* vicino; (*friend*) intimo; (*weather*) afoso; **have a ~ shave** *fam* scamparla bella; **be ~ to sb** essere unito a qcno ● *adv* vicino; **~ by** vicino; **it's ~ on five o'clock** sono quasi le cinque

close[2] /kləʊz/ *n* fine *f* ● *vt* chiudere ● *vi* chiudersi; (*shop:*) chiudere. **close down** *vt* chiudere ● *vi* (*TV station:*) interrompere la trasmissione; (*factory:*) chiudere

closely /'kləʊslɪ/ *adv* da vicino; (*watch, listen*) attentamente

closet /'klɒzɪt/ *n Am* armadio *m*

close-up /'kləʊs-/ *n* primo piano *m*

closure /'kləʊʒə(r)/ *n* chiusura *f*

clot /klɒt/ *n* grumo *m*; (*fam: idiot*) tonto, -a *mf* ● *vi* (*pt/pp* clotted) (*blood:*) coagularsi

cloth /klɒθ/ *n* (*fabric*) tessuto *m*; (*duster etc*) straccio *m*

clothe /kləʊð/ *vt* vestire

clothes /kləʊðz/ *npl* vestiti *mpl*, abiti *mpl*. **~brush** *n* spazzola *f* per abiti. **~line** *n* corda *f* stendibiancheria

clothing /'kləʊðɪŋ/ *n* abbigliamento *m*

cloud /klaʊd/ *n* nuvola *f* ● **cloud over** *vi* rannuvolarsi. **~burst** *n* acquazzone *m*

cloudy /'klaʊdɪ/ *a* (**-ier, -iest**) nuvoloso; (*liquid*) torbido

clout /klaʊt/ *n fam* colpo *m*; (*influence*) impatto *m* (**with** su) ● *vt fam* colpire

clove /kləʊv/ *n* chiodo *m* di garofano; **~ of garlic** spicchio *m* d'aglio

clover /'kləʊvə(r)/ *n* trifoglio *m*

clown /klaʊn/ *n* pagliaccio *m* ● *vi* **~** [about] fare il pagliaccio

club /klʌb/ n club m inv; (weapon) clava f; Sport mazza f; ~s pl (Cards) fiori mpl ●v (pt/pp **clubbed**) ●vt bastonare. **club together** vi unirsi

cluck /klʌk/ vi chiocciare

clue /klu:/ n indizio m; (in crossword) definizione f; **I haven't a ~** fam non ne ho idea

clump /klʌmp/ n gruppo m

clumsiness /'klʌmzɪnɪs/ n goffaggine f

clumsy /'klʌmzɪ/ a (-ier, -iest) maldestro; (tool) scomodo; (remark) senza tatto

clung /klʌŋ/ see **cling**

cluster /'klʌstə(r)/ n gruppo m ●vi raggrupparsi (**round** intorno a)

clutch /klʌtʃ/ n stretta f; Auto frizione f; **be in sb's ~s** essere in balia di qcno ●vt stringere; (grab) afferrare ●vi ~ **at** afferrare

clutter /'klʌtə(r)/ n caos m ●vt ~ [**up**] ingombrare

c/o abbr (**care of**) c/o, presso

coach /kəʊtʃ/ n pullman m inv; Rail vagone m; (horse-drawn) carrozza f; Sport allenatore, -trice mf ●vt fare esercitare; Sport allenare

coagulate /kəʊˈægjʊleɪt/ vi coagularsi

coal /kəʊl/ n carbone m

coalition /kəʊəˈlɪʃn/ n coalizione f

'coal-mine n miniera f di carbone

coarse /kɔ:s/ a grossolano; (joke) spinto

coast /kəʊst/ n costa f ●vi (freewheel) scendere a ruota libera; Auto scendere in folle. **~al** a costiero. **~er** n (mat) sottobicchiere m inv

coast: **~guard** n guardia f costiera. **~line** n litorale m

coat /kəʊt/ n cappotto m; (of animal) manto m; (of paint) mano f; **~ of arms** stemma m ●vt coprire; (with paint) ricoprire. **~-hanger** n gruccia f. **~-hook** n gancio m [appendiabiti]

coating /'kəʊtɪŋ/ n rivestimento m; (of paint) stato m

coax /kəʊks/ vt convincere con le moine

cob /kɒb/ n (of corn) pannocchia f

cobble /'kɒbl/ vt ~ **together** raffazzonare. **~r** n ciabattino m

'cobblestones npl ciottolato msg

cobweb /'kɒb-/ n ragnatela f

cocaine /kəˈkeɪn/ n cocaina f

cock /kɒk/ n gallo m; (any male bird) maschio m ●vt sollevare il grilletto di (gun); ~ **its ears** (animal): drizzare le orecchie

cockerel /'kɒkərəl/ n galletto m

cock-'eyed a fam storto; (absurd) assurdo

cockle /'kɒkl/ n cardio m

cockney /'kɒknɪ/ n (dialect) dialetto m londinese; (person) abitante mf dell'est di Londra

cock: **~pit** n Aeron cabina f. **~roach** /-rəʊtʃ/ n scarafaggio m. **~tail** n cocktail m inv. **~-up** n sl **make a ~-up** fare un casino (**of** con)

cocky /'kɒkɪ/ a (-ier, -iest) fam presuntuoso

cocoa /'kəʊkəʊ/ n cacao m

coconut /'kəʊkənʌt/ n noce f di cocco

cocoon /kəˈku:n/ n bozzolo m

COD abbr (**cash on delivery**) pagamento m alla consegna

cod /kɒd/ n inv merluzzo m

code /kəʊd/ n codice m. **~d** a codificato

coedu'cational /kəʊ-/ a misto

coerc|e /kəʊˈɜːs/ vt costringere. **~ion** /-'ɜːʃn/ n coercizione f

coe'xist vi coesistere. **~ence** n coesistenza f

coffee /'kɒfɪ/ n caffè m inv

coffee: **~-grinder** n macinacaffè m inv. **~-pot** n caffettiera f. **~-table** n tavolino m

coffin /'kɒfɪn/ n bara f

cog /kɒg/ n Techn dente m (di ruota)

cogent /'kəʊdʒənt/ a convincente

cog-wheel n ruota f dentata

cohabit /kəʊˈhæbɪt/ vi Jur convivere

coherent /kəʊˈhɪərənt/ a coerente; ⟨when speaking⟩ logico

coil /kɔɪl/ n rotolo m; Electr bobina f; ~s pl spire fpl ● vt ~ [up] avvolgere

coin /kɔɪn/ n moneta f ● vt coniare ⟨word⟩

coincide /kəʊɪnˈsaɪd/ vi coincidere

coinciden|ce /kəʊˈɪnsɪdəns/ n coincidenza f. ~'tal /-ˈdentl/ a casuale. ~tally adv casualmente

Coke® n Coca[-cola]® f

coke /kəʊk/ n [carbone m] coke m

cold /kəʊld/ a freddo; I'm ~ ho freddo ● n freddo m; Med raffreddore m

cold: ~-'blooded a spietato. ~-'hearted a insensibile. ~·ly adv fig freddamente. ~ meat n salumi mpl. ~ness n freddezza f

coleslaw /ˈkəʊlslɔː/ n insalata f di cavolo crudo, cipolle e carote in maionese

colic /ˈkɒlɪk/ n colica f

collaborat|e /kəˈlæbəreɪt/ vi collaborare; ~e on sth collaborare in qcsa. ~ion /-ˈreɪʃn/ n collaborazione f; ⟨with enemy⟩ collaborazionismo m. ~or n collaboratore, -trice mf; ⟨with enemy⟩ collaborazionista m

collaps|e /kəˈlæps/ n crollo m ● vi ⟨person⟩ svenire; ⟨roof, building⟩ crollare. ~ible a pieghevole

collar /ˈkɒlə(r)/ n colletto m; ⟨for animal⟩ collare m. ~-bone n clavicola f

colleague /ˈkɒliːɡ/ n collega mf

collect /kəˈlekt/ vt andare a prendere ⟨person⟩; ritirare ⟨parcel, tickets⟩; riscuotere ⟨taxes⟩; raccogliere ⟨rubbish⟩; ⟨as hobby⟩ collezionare ● vi riunirsi ● adv call ~ Am telefonare a carico del destinatario. ~ed /-ɪd/ a controllato

collection /kəˈlekʃn/ n collezione f; ⟨in church⟩ questua f; ⟨of rubbish⟩ raccolta f; ⟨of post⟩ levata f

collective /kəˈlektɪv/ a collettivo

collector /kəˈlektə(r)/ n ⟨of stamps etc⟩ collezionista mf

college /ˈkɒlɪdʒ/ n istituto m parauniversitario; C~ of... Scuola f di...

collide /kəˈlaɪd/ vi scontrarsi

colliery /ˈkɒljərɪ/ n miniera f di carbone

collision /kəˈlɪʒn/ n scontro m

colloquial /kəˈləʊkwɪəl/ a colloquiale. ~ism n espressione f colloquiale

cologne /kəˈləʊn/ n colonia f

colon /ˈkəʊlən/ n due punti mpl; Anat colon m inv

colonel /ˈkɜːnl/ n colonnello m

colonial /kəˈləʊnɪəl/ a coloniale

colon|ize /ˈkɒlənaɪz/ vt colonizzare. ~y n colonia f

colossal /kəˈlɒsl/ a colossale

colour /ˈkʌlə(r)/ n colore m; ⟨complexion⟩ colorito m; ~s pl ⟨flag⟩ bandiera fsg; off ~ fam giù di tono ● vt colorare; ~ [in] colorare ● vi ⟨blush⟩ arrossire

colour: ~ bar n discriminazione f razziale. ~-blind a daltonico. ~ed a colorato; ⟨person⟩ di colore ● n ⟨person⟩ persona f di colore. ~-fast a dai colori resistenti. ~ film n film m inv a colori. ~-ful a pieno di colore. ~-less a incolore. ~ television n televisione f a colori

colt /kəʊlt/ n puledro m

column /ˈkɒləm/ n colonna f. ~ist /-nɪst/ n giornalista mf che cura una rubrica

coma /ˈkəʊmə/ n coma m inv

comb /kəʊm/ n pettine m; ⟨for wearing⟩ pettinino m ● vt pettinare; ⟨fig: search⟩ setacciare; ~ one's hair pettinarsi i capelli

combat /ˈkɒmbæt/ n combattimento m ● vt ⟨pt/pp combated⟩ combattere

combination /kɒmbɪˈneɪʃn/ n combinazione f

combine[1] /kəm'baɪn/ vt unire; ~ **a job with being a mother** conciliare il lavoro con il ruolo di madre ● vi ⟨chemical elements:⟩ combinarsi

combine[2] /'kɒmbaɪn/ n Comm associazione f ● [**harvester**] n mietitrebbia f

combustion /kəm'bʌstʃn/ n combustione f

come /kʌm/ vi ⟨pt **came**, pp **come**⟩ venire; **where do you ~ from?** da dove vieni?; ~ **to** arrivare a; **that ~s to £10** fanno 10 sterline; ~ **in money** ricevere dei soldi; ~ **true/open** verificarsi/aprirsi; ~ **first** arrivare primo; fig venire prima di tutto; ~ **in two sizes** esistere in due misure; **the years to ~** gli anni a venire; **how ~?** fam come mai? **come about** vi succedere. **come across** vi ~ **across as being** fam dare l'impressione di essere ● vt ⟨find⟩ imbattersi in. **come along** vi venire; ⟨job, opportunity:⟩ presentarsi; ⟨progress⟩ andare bene. **come apart** vi smontarsi; ⟨break⟩ rompersi. **come away** vi venir via; ⟨button, fastener:⟩ staccarsi. **come back** vi ritornare. **come by** vi passare ● vt ⟨obtain⟩ avere. **come down** vi scendere. ~ **down to** ⟨reach⟩ arrivare a. **come in** vi entrare; ⟨in race⟩ arrivare; ⟨tide:⟩ salire. **come in for** vi ~ **in for criticism** essere criticato. **come off** vi staccarsi; ⟨take place⟩ essere; ⟨succeed⟩ riuscire. **come on** vi ⟨make progress⟩ migliorare; ~ **on!** ⟨hurry⟩ dai!; ⟨indicating disbelief⟩ ma va là!. **come out** vi venir fuori; ⟨book, sun:⟩ uscire; ⟨stain:⟩ andar via. **come over** vi venire. **come round** vi venire; ⟨after fainting⟩ riaversi; ⟨change one's mind⟩ farsi convincere. **come to** vi ⟨after fainting⟩ riaversi. **come up** vi salire; ⟨sun:⟩ sorgere; ⟨plant:⟩ crescere; **something came up** ⟨I was

prevented⟩ ho avuto un imprevisto. **come up with** vt tirar fuori

'come-back n ritorno m

comedian /kə'miːdɪən/ n comico m

'come-down n passo m indietro

comedy /'kɒmədɪ/ n commedia f

comet /'kɒmɪt/ n cometa f

come-uppance /kʌm'ʌpəns/ n **get one's ~** fam avere quel che si merita

comfort /'kʌmfət/ n benessere m; ⟨consolation⟩ conforto m ● vt confortare

comfortabl|e /'kʌmfətəbl/ a comodo; **be ~e** ⟨person:⟩ stare comodo; ⟨fig: in situation⟩ essere a proprio agio; ⟨financially⟩ star bene. ~**y** adv comodamente

'comfort station n Am bagno m pubblico

comfy /'kʌmfɪ/ a fam comodo

comic /'kɒmɪk/ a comico ● n comico, -a m/f; ⟨periodical⟩ fumetto m. ~**al** a comico. ~ **strip** n striscia f di fumetti

coming /'kʌmɪŋ/ n venuta f; ~**s and goings** viavai m

comma /'kɒmə/ n virgola f

command /kə'mɑːnd/ n comando m; ⟨order⟩ ordine m; ⟨mastery⟩ padronanza f ● vt ordinare; comandare ⟨army⟩

commandeer /kɒmən'dɪə(r)/ vt requisire

command|er /kə'mɑːndə(r)/ n comandante m. ~**ing** a ⟨view⟩ imponente; ⟨lead⟩ dominante. ~**ing officer** n comandante m. ~**ment** n comandamento m

commemorat|e /kə'meməreɪt/ vt commemorare. ~**ion** /-'reɪʃn/ n commemorazione f. ~**ive** /-ətɪv/ a commemorativo

commence /kə'mens/ vt/i cominciare. ~**ment** n inizio m

commend /kə'mend/ vt complimentarsi con ⟨on per⟩; ⟨recommend⟩ raccomandare ⟨to a⟩. ~**able** /-əbl/ a lodevole

commensurate /kə'menʃərət/ *a* proporzionato (**with** a)

comment /'kɒment/ *n* commento *m* ● *vi* fare commenti (**on** su)

commentary /'kɒməntri/ *n* commento *m*; [**running**] ~ (*on radio, TV*) cronaca *f* diretta

commentate /'kɒmenteɪt/ *vt* ~ **on** *TV, Radio* fare la cronaca di. **~or** *n* cronista *mf*

commerce /'kɒmɜːs/ *n* commercio *m*

commercial /kə'mɜːʃl/ *a* commerciale ● *n TV* pubblicità *f inv*. **~ize** *vt* commercializzare

commiserate /kə'mɪzəreɪt/ *vi* esprimere il proprio rincrescimento (**with** a)

commission /kə'mɪʃn/ *n* commissione *f*; **receive one's** ~ *Mil* essere promosso ufficiale; **out of** ~ fuori uso ● *vt* commissionare

commissionaire /kəmɪʃə'neə(r)/ *n* portiere *m*

commissioner /kə'mɪʃənə(r)/ *n* commissario *m*

commit /kə'mɪt/ *vt* (*pt/pp* **committed**) commettere; (*to prison, hospital*) affidare (**to** a); impegnare (*funds*); ~ **oneself** impegnarsi. **~ment** *n* impegno *m*; (*involvement*) compromissione *f*. **~ted** *a* impegnato

committee /kə'mɪtɪ/ *n* comitato *m*

commodity /kə'mɒdətɪ/ *n* prodotto *m*

common /'kɒmən/ *a* comune; (*vulgar*) volgare ● *n* prato *m* pubblico; **have in** ~ avere in comune; **House of C~s** Camera *f* dei Comuni. **~er** *n* persona *f* non nobile

common: **~ law** *n* diritto *m* consuetudinario. **~ly** *adv* comunemente. **C~ 'Market** *n* Mercato *m* Comune. **~place** *a* banale. **~-room** *n* sala *f* dei professori/degli studenti. **~ 'sense** *n* buon senso *m*

commotion /kə'məʊʃn/ *n* confusione *f*

communal /'kɒmjʊnl/ *a* comune

communicate /kə'mjuːnɪkeɪt/ *vt/i* comunicare

communication /kəmjuːnɪ'keɪʃn/ *n* comunicazione *f*; (*of disease*) trasmissione *f*; **be in** ~ **with sb** essere in contatto con qcno; **~s** *pl* (*technology*) telecomunicazioni *fpl*. **~ cord** *n* fermata *f* d'emergenza

communicative /kə'mjuːnɪkətɪv/ *a* comunicativo

Communion /kə'mjuːnɪən/ *n* [**Holy**] ~ comunione *f*

communiqué /kə'mjuːnɪkeɪ/ *n* comunicato *m*

Communis|m /'kɒmjʊnɪzm/ *n* comunismo *m*. **~t** /-ɪst/ *a & n* comunista *mf*

community /kə'mjuːnətɪ/ *n* comunità *f*. **~ centre** *n* centro *m* sociale

commute /kə'mjuːt/ *vi* fare il pendolare ● *vt Jur* commutare. **~r** *n* pendolare *mf*

compact[1] /kəm'pækt/ *a* compatto

compact[2] /'kɒmpækt/ *n* portacipria *m inv*. **~ disc** *n* compact disc *m inv*

companion /kəm'pænjən/ *n* compagno, -a *mf*. **~ship** *n* compagnia *f*

company /'kʌmpəni/ *n* compagnia *f*; (*guests*) ospiti *mpl*. **~ car** *n* macchina *f* della ditta

comparable /'kɒmpərəbl/ *a* paragonabile

comparative /kəm'pærətɪv/ *a* comparativo; (*relative*) relativo ● *n Gram* comparativo *m*. **~ly** *adv* relativamente

compare /kəm'peə(r)/ *vt* paragonare (**with/to** a) ● *vi* essere paragonato

comparison /kəm'pærɪsn/ *n* paragone *m*

compartment /kəm'pɑːtmənt/ *n* compartimento *m*; *Rail* scompartimento *m*

compass /'kʌmpəs/ *n* bussola *f*. **~es** *npl*, **pair of ~es** compasso *msg*

compassion /kəm'pæʃn/ *n* compassione f. **~ate** /-fənət/ a compassionevole

compatible /kəm'pætəbl/ a compatibile

compatriot /kəm'pætrɪət/ n compatriota mf

compel /kəm'pel/ vt (pt/pp **compelled**) costringere. **~ling** a (reason) inconfutabile

compensat|e /'kɒmpənseɪt/ vt risarcire ● vi **~e for** fig compensare di. **~ion** /-'seɪʃn/ n risarcimento m; (fig: comfort) consolazione f

compère /'kɒmpeə(r)/ n presentatore, -trice mf

compete /kəm'piːt/ vi competere; (take part) partecipare

competen|ce /'kɒmpɪtəns/ n competenza f. **~t** a competente

competition /kɒmpə'tɪʃn/ n concorrenza f; (contest) gara f

competitive /kəm'petɪtɪv/ a competitivo; **~ prices** prezzi mpl concorrenziali

competitor /kəm'petɪtə(r)/ n concorrente mf

complacen|cy /kəm'pleɪsənsɪ/ n compiacimento m. **~t** a compiaciuto

complain /kəm'pleɪn/ vi lamentarsi (about di); (formally) reclamare; **~ of** Med accusare. **~t** n lamentela f; (formal) reclamo m; Med disturbo m

complement¹ /'kɒmplɪmənt/ n complemento m

complement² /'kɒmplɪment/ vt complementare; **~ each other** complementarsi a vicenda. **~ary** /-'mentərɪ/ a complementare

complete /kəm'pliːt/ a completo; (utter) finito ● vt completare; compilare (form). **~ly** adv completamente

completion /kəm'pliːʃn/ n fine f

complex /'kɒmpleks/ a complesso ● n complesso m

complexion /kəm'plekʃn/ n carnagione f

complexity /kəm'pleksətɪ/ n complessità f inv

compliance /kəm'plaɪəns/ n accettazione f; (with rules) osservanza f; **in ~ with** in osservanza a (law); conformemente a (request)

complicat|e /'kɒmplɪkeɪt/ vt complicare. **~ed** a complicato. **~ion** /-'keɪʃn/ n complicazione f

compliment /'kɒmplɪmənt/ n complimento m; **~s** pl omaggi mpl ● vt complimentare. **~ary** /-'mentərɪ/ a complimentoso; (given free) in omaggio

comply /kəm'plaɪ/ vi (pt/pp **-ied**) **~ with** conformarsi a

component /kəm'pəʊnənt/ a & n **~ [part]** componente m

compose /kəm'pəʊz/ vt comporre; **~ oneself** ricomporsi; **be ~d of** essere composto da. **~d** a (calm) composto. **~r** n compositore, -trice mf

composition /kɒmpə'zɪʃn/ n composizione f; (essay) tema m

compost /'kɒmpɒst/ n composta f

composure /kəm'pəʊʒə(r)/ n calma f

compound /'kɒmpaʊnd/ a composto. **~ fracture** n frattura f esposta. **~ 'interest** n interesse m composto ● n Chem composto m; Gram parola f composta; (enclosure) recinto m

comprehen|d /kɒmprɪ'hend/ vt comprendere. **~sible** /-'hensəbl/ a comprensibile. **~sion** /-'henʃn/ n comprensione f

comprehensive /kɒmprɪ'hensɪv/ a & n comprensivo. **~ [school]** n scuola f media in cui gli allievi hanno capacità d'apprendimento diverse. **~ insurance** n Auto polizza f casco

compress¹ /'kɒmpres/ n compressa f

compress² /kəm'pres/ vt comprimere; **~ed air** aria f compressa

comprise /kəm'praɪz/ vt comprendere; (form) costituire

compromise /'kɒmprəmaɪz/ n compromesso m ● vt compromettere ● vi fare un compromesso

compuls|ion /kəm'pʌlʃn/ n desiderio m irresistibile. **~ive** /-sɪv/ a Psych patologico. **~ive eating** voglia f ossessiva di mangiare. **~ory** /-sərɪ/ a obbligatorio

comput|er /kəm'pju:tə(r)/ n computer m inv. **~erize** vt computerizzare. **~ing** n informatica f

comrade /'kɒmreɪd/ n camerata m; Pol compagno, -a mf. **~ship** n cameratismo m

con¹ /kɒn/ see **pro**

con² n fam fregatura f ● vt (pt/pp **conned**) fam fregare

concave /'kɒnkeɪv/ a concavo

conceal /kən'si:l/ vt nascondere

concede /kən'si:d/ vt (admit) ammettere; (give up) rinunciare a; lasciar fare (goal)

conceit /kən'si:t/ n presunzione f. **~ed** a presuntuoso

conceivable /kən'si:vəbl/ a concepibile

conceive /kən'si:v/ vt Biol concepire ● vi aver figli. **conceive of** vt fig concepire

concentrat|e /'kɒnsəntreɪt/ vt concentrare ● vi concentrarsi. **~ion** /-'treɪʃn/ n concentrazione f. **~ion camp** n campo m di concentramento

concept /'kɒnsept/ n concetto m. **~ion** /kən'sepʃn/ n concezione f; (idea) idea f

concern /kən'sɜ:n/ n preoccupazione f; Comm attività f inv ● vt (be about, affect) riguardare; (worry) preoccupare; **be ~ed about** essere preoccupato per; **~ oneself with** preoccuparsi di; **as far as I am ~ed** per quanto mi riguarda. **~ing** prep riguardo a

concert /'kɒnsət/ n concerto m. **~ed** /-sɜ:tɪd/ a concertato

concertina /kɒnsə'ti:nə/ n piccola fisarmonica f

'concertmaster n Am primo violino m

concerto /kən'tʃeətəʊ/ n concerto m

concession /kən'seʃn/ n conces-

sione f; (reduction) sconto m. **~ary** a (reduced) scontato

conciliation /kənsɪlɪ'eɪʃn/ n conciliazione f

concise /kən'saɪs/ a conciso

conclu|de /kən'klu:d/ vt concludere ● vi concludersi. **~ding** a finale

conclusion /kən'klu:ʒn/ n conclusione f; **in ~** per concludere

conclusive /kən'klu:sɪv/ a definitivo. **~ly** adv in modo definitivo

concoct /kən'kɒkt/ vt confezionare; fig inventare. **~ion** /-ɒkʃn/ n mistura f; (drink) intruglio m

concourse /'kɒŋkɔ:s/ n atrio m

concrete /'kɒŋkri:t/ a concreto ● n calcestruzzo m

concur /kən'kɜ:(r)/ vi (pt/pp **concurred**) essere d'accordo

concurrently /kən'kʌrəntlɪ/ adv contemporaneamente

concussion /kən'kʌʃn/ n commozione f cerebrale

condemn /kən'dem/ vt condannare; dichiarare inagibile (building). **~ation** /kɒndem'neɪʃn/ n condanna f

condensation /kɒnden'seɪʃn/ n condensazione f

condense /kən'dens/ vt condensare; Phys condensare ● vi condensarsi. **~d milk** n latte m condensato

condescend /kɒndɪ'send/ vi degnarsi. **~ing** a condiscendente

condition /kən'dɪʃn/ n condizione f; **on ~ that** a condizione che ● vt Psych condizionare; Gram condizionale ● n Gram condizionale m. **~er** n balsamo m; (for fabrics) ammorbidente m

condolences /kən'dəʊlənsɪz/ npl condoglianze fpl

condom /'kɒndəm/ n preservativo m

condo[minium] /'kɒndə('mɪnɪəm)/ n Am condominio m

condone /kən'dəʊn/ vt passare sopra a

conducive /kən'dju:sɪv/ *a* be ~ to contribuire a

conduct[1] /'kɒndʌkt/ *n* condotta *f*

conduct[2] /kən'dʌkt/ *vt* condurre; dirigere (*orchestra*); **~or** *n* direttore *m* d'orchestra; (*of bus*) bigliettaio *m*; *Phys* conduttore *m*. **~ress** *n* bigliettaia *f*

cone /kəʊn/ *n* cono *m*; *Bot* pigna *f*; *Auto* birillo *m* **● cone off** *vt* **be ~d off** *Auto* essere chiuso da birilli

confectioner /kən'fekʃənə(r)/ *n* pasticciere, -a *mf*. **~y** *n* pasticceria *f*

confederation /kənfedə'reɪʃn/ *n* confederazione *f*

confer /kən'fɜ:(r)/ *v* (*pt/pp* **conferred**) **●** *vt* conferire (**on** a) **●** *vi* (*discuss*) conferire

conference /'kɒnfərəns/ *n* conferenza *f*

confess /kən'fes/ *vt* confessare **●** *vi* confessare; *Relig* confessarsi. **~ion** /-eʃn/ *n* confessione *f*. **~ional** /-eʃənəl/ *n* confessionale *m*. **~or** *n* confessore *m*

confetti /kən'feti/ *n* coriandoli *mpl*

confide /kən'faɪd/ *vt* confidare. **confide in** *vt* **~ in sb** fidarsi di qcno

confidence /'kɒnfidəns/ *n* (*trust*) fiducia *f*; (*self-assurance*) sicurezza *f* di sé; (*secret*) confidenza *f*; **in ~** in confidenza. **~ trick** *n* truffa *f*

confident /'kɒnfidənt/ *a* fiducioso; (*self-assured*) sicuro di sé. **~ly** *adv* con aria fiduciosa

confidential /kɒnfi'denʃl/ *a* confidenziale

confine /kən'faɪn/ *vt* rinchiudere; (*limit*) limitare; **be ~d to bed** essere confinato a letto. **~d** *a* (*space*) limitato. **~ment** *n* detenzione *f*; *Med* parto *m*

confines /'kɒnfaɪnz/ *npl* confini *mpl*

confirm /kən'fɜ:m/ *vt* confermare; *Relig* cresimare. **~ation** /kɒnfə'meɪʃn/ *n* conferma *f*; *Relig*

cresima *f*. **~ed** *a* incallito; **~ed bachelor** scapolo *m* impenitente

confiscat|e /'kɒnfiskeɪt/ *vt* confiscare. **~ion** /-'keɪʃn/ *n* confisca *f*

conflict[1] /'kɒnflɪkt/ *n* conflitto *m*

conflict[2] /kən'flɪkt/ *vi* essere in contraddizione. **~ing** *a* contraddittorio

conform /kən'fɔ:m/ *vi* (*person*:) conformarsi; (*thing*:) essere conforme (**to** a). **~ist** *n* conformista *mf*

confound /kən'faʊnd/ *a* fam maledetto

confront /kən'frʌnt/ *vt* affrontare; **the problems ~ing us** i problemi che dobbiamo affrontare. **~ation** /kɒnfrʌn'teɪʃn/ *n* confronto *m*

confus|e /kən'fju:z/ *vt* confondere. **~ing** *a* che confonde. **~ion** /-ju:ʒn/ *n* confusione *f*

congeal /kən'dʒi:l/ *vi* (*blood*:) coagularsi

congenial /kən'dʒi:nɪəl/ *a* congeniale

congenital /kən'dʒenɪtl/ *a* congenito

congest|ed /kən'dʒestɪd/ *a* congestionato. **~ion** /-estʃn/ *n* congestione *f*

congratulat|e /kən'grætjʊleɪt/ *vt* congratularsi con (**on** per). **~ions** /-'eɪʃnz/ *npl* congratulazioni *fpl*

congregat|e /'kɒŋgrɪgeɪt/ *vi* radunarsi. **~ion** /-'geɪʃn/ *n* *Relig* assemblea *f*

congress /'kɒŋgres/ *n* congresso *m*. **~man** *n* *Am Pol* membro *m* del congresso

conical /'kɒnɪkl/ *a* conico

conifer /'kɒnɪfə(r)/ *n* conifera *f*

conjecture /kən'dʒektʃə(r)/ *n* congettura *f*

conjugal /'kɒndʒʊgl/ *a* coniugale

conjugat|e /'kɒndʒʊgeɪt/ *vt* coniugare. **~ion** /-'geɪʃn/ *n* coniugazione *f*

conjunction /kən'dʒʌŋkʃn/ *n* congiunzione *f*; **in ~ with** insieme a

conjunctivitis /kəndʒʌŋktɪ'vaɪtɪs/ *n* congiuntivite *f*

conjur|e /'kʌndʒə(r)/ vi ~ing tricks npl giochi mpl di prestigio. ~or n prestigiatore, -trice mf. **conjure up** vt evocare ⟨image⟩; tirar fuori dal nulla ⟨meal⟩

conk /kɒŋk/ vi ~ out fam ⟨machine:⟩ guastarsi; ⟨person:⟩ crollare

'con-man n fam truffatore m

connect /kə'nekt/ vt collegare; **be ~ed with** avere legami con; ⟨be related to⟩ essere imparentato con; **be well ~ed** aver conoscenze influenti ● vi essere collegato **(with** a); ⟨train:⟩ fare coincidenza

connection /kə'nekʃn/ n ⟨between ideas⟩ nesso m; ⟨in travel⟩ coincidenza f; Electr collegamento m; **in ~ with** con riferimento a. **~s** pl ⟨people⟩ conoscenze fpl

connoisseur /kɒnə'sɜ:(r)/ n intenditore, -trice mf

conquer /'kɒŋkə(r)/ vt conquistare; fig superare ⟨fear⟩. **~or** n conquistatore m

conquest /'kɒŋkwest/ n conquista f

conscience /'kɒnʃəns/ n coscienza f

conscientious /kɒnʃɪ'enʃəs/ a coscienzioso. **~ ob'jector** n obiettore m di coscienza

conscious /'kɒnʃəs/ a conscio; ⟨decision⟩ meditato; **[fully]** ~ cosciente; **be/become ~ of sth** rendersi conto di qcsa. **~ly** adv consapevolmente. **~ness** n consapevolezza f; Med conoscenza f

conscript¹ /'kɒnskrɪpt/ n coscritto m

conscript² /kən'skrɪpt/ vt Mil chiamare alle armi. **~ion** /-ɪpʃn/ n coscrizione f, leva f

consecrat|e /'kɒnsɪkreɪt/ vt consacrare. **~ion** /-'kreɪʃn/ n consacrazione f

consecutive /kən'sekjʊtɪv/ a consecutivo

consensus /kən'sensəs/ n consenso m

consent /kən'sent/ n consenso m ● vi acconsentire

consequen|ce /'kɒnsɪkwəns/ n conseguenza f; ⟨importance⟩ importanza f. **~t** a conseguente. **~tly** adv di conseguenza

conservation /kɒnsə'veɪʃn/ n conservazione f. **~ist** n fautore, -trice mf della tutela ambientale

conservative /kən'sɜ:vətɪv/ a conservativo; ⟨estimate⟩ ottimistico. **C~** Pol a conservatore ● n conservatore, -trice mf

conservatory /kən'sɜ:vətrɪ/ n spazio m chiuso da vetrate adiacente alla casa

conserve /kən'sɜ:v/ vt conservare

consider /kən'sɪdə(r)/ vt considerare; **~ doing sth** considerare la possibilità di fare qcsa. **~able** /-əbl/ a considerevole. **~ably** adv considerevolmente

consider|ate /kən'sɪdərət/ a pieno di riguardo. **~ately** adv con riguardo. **~ation** /-'reɪʃn/ n considerazione f; ⟨thoughtfulness⟩ attenzione f; ⟨respect⟩ riguardo m; ⟨payment⟩ compenso m; **take sth into ~ation** prendere qcsa in considerazione. **~ing** prep considerando

consign /kən'saɪn/ vt affidare. **~ment** n consegna f

consist /kən'sɪst/ vi ~ **of** consistere di

consisten|cy /kən'sɪstənsɪ/ n coerenza f; ⟨density⟩ consistenza f. **~t** a coerente; ⟨loyalty⟩ costante. **~tly** adv coerentemente; ⟨late, loyal⟩ costantemente

consolation /kɒnsə'leɪʃn/ n consolazione f. **~ prize** n premio m di consolazione

console /kən'səʊl/ vt consolare

consolidate /kən'sɒlɪdeɪt/ vt consolidare

consonant /'kɒnsənənt/ n consonante f

consort /kən'sɔ:t/ vi ~ **with** frequentare

consortium /kən'sɔ:tɪəm/ n consorzio m

conspicuous /kən'spɪkjʊəs/ a facilmente distinguibile

conspiracy /kən'spɪrəsɪ/ n cospirazione f

conspire /kən'spaɪə(r)/ vi cospirare

constable /'kʌnstəbl/ n agente m [di polizia]

constant /'kʌnstənt/ a costante. **~ly** adv costantemente

constellation /kʌnstə'leɪʃn/ n costellazione f

consternation /kʌnstə'neɪʃn/ n costernazione f

constipat|ed /'kʌnstɪpeɪtɪd/ a stitico. **~ion** /-'peɪʃn/ n stitichezza f

constituency /kən'stɪtjʊənsɪ/ n area f elettorale di un deputato nel Regno Unito

constituent /kən'stɪtjʊənt/ n costituente m; Pol elettore, -trice mf

constitut|e /'kʌnstɪtju:t/ vt costituire. **~ion** /-'tju:ʃn/ n costituzione f. **~ional** /-'tju:ʃənl/ a costituzionale

constrain /kən'streɪn/ vt costringere. **~t** n costrizione f; (restriction) restrizione f; (strained manner) disagio m

construct /kən'strʌkt/ vt costruire. **~ion** /-ʌkʃn/ n costruzione f; **under ~ion** in costruzione. **~ive** /-ɪv/ a costruttivo

construe /kən'stru:/ vt interpretare

consul /'kʌnsl/ n console m. **~ar** /'kʌnsjʊlə(r)/ a consolare. **~ate** /'kʌnsjʊlət/ n consolato m

consult /kən'sʌlt/ vt consultare. **~ant** n consulente mf; Med specialista mf. **~ation** /kʌnsl'teɪʃn/ n consultazione f; Med consulto m

consume /kən'sju:m/ vt consumare. **~r** n consumatore, -trice mf. **~r goods** npl beni mpl di consumo. **~er organization** n organizzazione f per la tutela dei consumatori

consumerism /kən'sju:mərɪzm/ n consumismo m

consummate /'kʌnsəmeɪt/ vt consumare

consumption /kən'sʌmpʃn/ n consumo m

contact /'kʌntækt/ n contatto m; (person) conoscenza f ● vt mettersi in contatto con. **~ lenses** npl lenti fpl a contatto

contagious /kən'teɪdʒəs/ a contagioso

contain /kən'teɪn/ vt contenere; **~ oneself** controllarsi. **~er** n recipiente m; (for transport) container m inv

contaminat|e /kən'tæmɪneɪt/ vt contaminare. **~ion** /-'neɪʃn/ n contaminazione f

contemplat|e /'kʌntəmpleɪt/ vt contemplare; (consider) considerare; **~e doing sth** considerare di fare qcsa. **~ion** /-'pleɪʃn/ n contemplazione f

contemporary /kən'tempərərɪ/ a & n contemporaneo, -a mf

contempt /kən'tempt/ n disprezzo m; **beneath ~** più che vergognoso; **~ of court** oltraggio m alla Corte. **~ible** /-əbl/ a spregevole. **~uous** /-tjʊəs/ a sprezzante

contend /kən'tend/ vi ~ **with** occuparsi di ● vt (assert) sostenere. **~er** n concorrente mf

content¹ /'kʌntent/ n contenuto m

content² /kən'tent/ a soddisfatto ● vt ~ **oneself** accontentarsi (with di). **~ed** a soddisfatto. **~edly** adv con aria soddisfatta

contention /kən'tenʃn/ n (assertion) opinione f

contentment /kən'tentmənt/ n soddisfazione f

contents /'kʌntents/ npl contenuto m

contest¹ /'kʌntest/ n gara f

contest² /kən'test/ vt contestare (statement); impugnare (will); Pol (candidates:) contendersi; (one candidate:) aspirare a. **~ant** n concorrente mf

context /ˈkɒntekst/ n contesto m

continent /ˈkɒntɪnənt/ n continente m; **the C~** l'Europa f continentale

continental /kɒntɪˈnentl/ a continentale. **~ breakfast** n prima colazione f a base di pane, burro, marmellata, croissant, ecc. **~ quilt** n piumone m

contingency /kənˈtɪndʒənsɪ/ n eventualità f inv

continual /kənˈtɪnjʊəl/ a continuo

continuation /kəntɪnjʊˈeɪʃn/ n continuazione f

continue /kənˈtɪnjuː/ vt continuare; **~ doing** or **to do sth** continuare a fare qcsa; **to be ~d** continua ●vi continuare. **~d** a continuo

continuity /kɒntɪˈnjuːətɪ/ n continuità f

continuous /kənˈtɪnjʊəs/ a continuo

contort /kənˈtɔːt/ vt contorcere. **~ion** /-ɔːʃn/ n contorsione f. **~ionist** n contorsionista mf

contour /ˈkɒntʊə(r)/ n contorno m; (line) curva f di livello

contraband /ˈkɒntrəbænd/ n contrabbando m

contraception /kɒntrəˈsepʃn/ n contraccezione f. **~tive** /-tɪv/ n contraccettivo m

contract¹ /ˈkɒntrækt/ n contratto m

contract² /kənˈtrækt/ vi (get smaller) contrarsi ●vt contrarre ⟨illness⟩. **~ion** /-ækʃn/ n contrazione f. **~or** n imprenditore, -trice mf

contradict /kɒntrəˈdɪkt/ vt contraddire. **~ion** /-ɪkʃn/ n contraddizione f. **~ory** a contraddittorio

contra-flow /ˈkɒntrəfləʊ/ n utilizzazione f di una corsia nei due sensi di marcia durante lavori stradali

contralto /kənˈtræltəʊ/ n contralto m

contraption /kənˈtræpʃn/ n fam aggeggio m

contrary¹ /ˈkɒntrərɪ/ a contrario

●adv **~ to** contrariamente a ●n contrario m; **on the ~** al contrario

contrary² /kənˈtreərɪ/ a disobbediente

contrast¹ /ˈkɒntrɑːst/ n contrasto m

contrast² /kənˈtrɑːst/ vt confrontare ●vi contrastare. **~ing** a contrastante

contravene /kɒntrəˈviːn/ vt trasgredire. **~tion** /-ˈvenʃn/ n trasgressione f

contribute /kənˈtrɪbjuːt/ vt/i contribuire. **~ion** /kɒntrɪˈbjuːʃn/ n contribuzione f; (what is contributed) contributo m. **~or** n contributore, -trice f

contrive /kənˈtraɪv/ vt escogitare; **~ to do sth** riuscire a fare qcsa

control /kənˈtrəʊl/ n controllo m; **~s** pl (of car, plane) comandi mpl; **get out of ~** sfuggire al controllo ●vt (pt/pp **controlled**) controllare; **~ oneself** controllarsi

controversial /kɒntrəˈvɜːʃl/ a controverso. **~y** /ˈkɒntrəvɜːsɪ/ n controversia f

conurbation /kɒnɜːˈbeɪʃn/ n conurbazione f

convalesce /kɒnvəˈles/ vi essere in convalescenza

convalescent /kɒnvəˈlesənt/ a convalescente. **~ home** n convalescenziario m

convector /kənˈvektə(r)/ n **~ [heater]** convettore m

convene /kənˈviːn/ vt convocare ●vi riunirsi

convenience /kənˈviːnɪəns/ n convenienza f; [public] **~** gabinetti mpl pubblici; **with all modern ~s** con tutti i comfort

convenient /kənˈviːnɪənt/ a comodo; **be ~ for sb** andar bene per qcno; **if it is ~ [for you]** se ti va bene. **~ly** adv comodamente; **~ly located** in una posizione comoda

convent /ˈkɒnvənt/ n convento m

convention /kənˈvenʃn/ n convenzione f; (assembly) convegno m. **~al** a convenzionale

converge /kən'vɜːdʒ/ vi convergere

conversant /kən'vɜːsənt/ a **~ with** pratico di

conversation /kɒnvə'seɪʃn/ n conversazione f. **~al** a di conversazione. **~alist** n conversatore, -trice mf

converse¹ /kən'vɜːs/ vi conversare

converse² /'kɒnvɜːs/ n inverso m. **~ly** adv viceversa

conversion /kən'vɜːʃn/ n conversione f

convert¹ /'kɒnvɜːt/ n convertito, -a mf

convert² /kən'vɜːt/ vt convertire (into in); sconsacrare (church). **~ible** /-əbl/ a convertibile • n Auto macchina f decappottabile

convex /'kɒnveks/ a convesso

convey /kən'veɪ/ vt portare; trasmettere (idea, message). **~or belt** n nastro m trasportatore

convict¹ /'kɒnvɪkt/ n condannato, -a mf

convict² /kən'vɪkt/ vt giudicare colpevole. **~ion** /-ɪkʃn/ n condanna f; (belief) convinzione f; **previous ~ion** precedente m penale

convince /kən'vɪns/ vt convincere. **~ing** a convincente

convivial /kən'vɪvɪəl/ a conviviale

convoluted /'kɒnvəluːtɪd/ a contorto

convoy /'kɒnvɔɪ/ n convoglio m

convulse /kən'vʌls/ vt sconvolgere; **be ~ed with laughter** contorcersi dalle risa. **~ion** /-ʌlʃn/ n convulsione f

coo /kuː/ vi tubare

cook /kʊk/ n cuoco, -a mf • vt cucinare; **is it ~ed?** è cotto?; **~ the books** fam truccare i libri contabili • vi (food:) cuocere; (person:) cucinare. **~book** n libro m di cucina

cooker /'kʊkə(r)/ n cucina f; (apple) mela f da cuocere. **~y** n cucina f. **~y book** n libro m di cucina

cookie /'kʊkɪ/ n Am biscotto m

cool /kuːl/ a fresco; (calm) calmo; (unfriendly) freddo • n fresco m • vt rinfrescare • vi rinfrescarsi. **~-box** n borsa f termica. **~ness** n freddezza f

coop /kuːp/ n stia f • vt **~ up** rinchiudere

co-operat|e /kəʊ'ɒpəreɪt/ vi cooperare. **~ion** /-'reɪʃn/ n cooperazione f

co-operative /kəʊ'ɒpərətɪv/ a cooperativo • n cooperativa f

co-opt /kəʊ'ɒpt/ vt eleggere

co-ordinat|e /kəʊ'ɔːdmeɪt/ vt coordinare. **~ion** /-'neɪʃn/ n coordinazione f

cop /kɒp/ n fam poliziotto m

cope /kəʊp/ vi fam farcela; **can she ~ by herself?** ce la fa da sola?; **~ with** farcela con

copious /'kəʊpɪəs/ a abbondante

copper¹ /'kɒpə(r)/ n rame m; **~s** pl monete fpl da uno o due pence • attrib di rame

copper² n fam poliziotto m

coppice /'kɒpɪs/ n, **copse** /kɒps/ n boschetto m

copulat|e /'kɒpjʊleɪt/ vi accoppiarsi. **~ion** /-'leɪʃn/ n copulazione f

copy /'kɒpɪ/ n copia f • vt (pt/pp -ied) copiare

copy: ~right n diritti mpl d'autore. **~-writer** n copywriter mf inv

coral /'kɒrəl/ n corallo m

cord /kɔːd/ n corda f; (thinner) cordoncino m; (fabric) velluto m a coste; **~s** pl pantaloni mpl di velluto a coste

cordial /'kɔːdɪəl/ a cordiale • n analcolico m

cordon /'kɔːdn/ n cordone m (di persone) • **cordon off** vt mettere un cordone (di persone) intorno a

corduroy /'kɔːdərɔɪ/ n velluto m a coste

core /kɔː(r)/ n (of apple, pear) tor-

solo m; (*fig: of organization*) cuore m; (*of problem, theory*) nocciolo m
cork /kɔːk/ n sughero m; (*for bottle*) turacciolo m. **~screw** n cavatappi m inv
corn¹ /kɔːn/ n grano m; (*Am: maize*) granturco m
corn² n Med callo m
cornea /ˈkɔːnɪə/ n cornea f
corned beef /kɔːndˈbiːf/ n manzo m sotto sale
corner /ˈkɔːnə(r)/ n angolo m; (*football*) calcio m d'angolo, corner m inv ● vt fig bloccare; Comm accaparrarsi (*market*)
cornet /ˈkɔːnɪt/ n Mus cornetta f; (*for ice-cream*) cono m
corn: ~flour n, Am **~starch** farina f di granturco
corny /ˈkɔːnɪ/ a (-ier, -iest) ⟨*fam: joke, film*⟩ scontato; ⟨*person*⟩ banale; (*sentimental*) sdolcinato
coronary /ˈkɒrənərɪ/ a coronario ● n **~ [thrombosis]** trombosi f coronarica
coronation /kɒrəˈneɪʃn/ n incoronazione f
coroner /ˈkɒrənə(r)/ n coroner m inv (*nel diritto britannico, ufficiale incaricato delle indagini su morti sospette*)
corporal¹ /ˈkɔːpərəl/ n Mil caporale m
corporal² a corporale; **~ punishment** punizione f corporale
corporate /ˈkɔːpərət/ a ⟨*decision, policy, image*⟩ aziendale; **~ life** la vita in un'azienda
corporation /kɔːpəˈreɪʃn/ n ente m; (*of town*) consiglio m comunale
corps /kɔː(r)/ n (pl **corps** /kɔːz/) corpo m
corpse /kɔːps/ n cadavere m
corpulent /ˈkɔːpjʊlənt/ a corpulento
corpuscle /ˈkɔːpʌsl/ n globulo m
correct /kəˈrekt/ a corretto; **be ~** ⟨*person*⟩ aver ragione; **~!** esatto! ● vt correggere. **~ion** /-ekʃn/ n correzione f. **~ly** adv correttamente

correlation /kɒrɪˈleɪʃn/ n correlazione f
correspond /kɒrɪˈspɒnd/ vi corrispondere (**to** a); (*two things:*) corrispondere; (*write*) scriversi. **~ence** n corrispondenza f. **~ent** n corrispondente mf. **~ing** a corrispondente. **~ingly** adv in modo corrispondente
corridor /ˈkɒrɪdɔː(r)/ n corridoio m
corroborate /kəˈrɒbəreɪt/ vt corroborare
corro|de /kəˈrəʊd/ vt corrodere ● vi corrodersi. **~sion** /-ˈrəʊʒn/ n corrosione f
corrugated /ˈkɒrəgeɪtɪd/ a ondulato. **~ iron** n lamiera f ondulata
corrupt /kəˈrʌpt/ a corrotto ● vt corrompere. **~ion** /-ʌpʃn/ n corruzione f
corset /ˈkɔːsɪt/ n & **-s** pl busto m
Corsica /ˈkɔːsɪkə/ n Corsica f. **~n** a & n corso, -a mf
cortège /kɔːˈteɪʒ/ n [**funeral**] corteo m funebre
cosh /kɒʃ/ n randello m
cosmetic /kɒzˈmetɪk/ a cosmetico ● n **~s** pl cosmetici mpl
cosmic /ˈkɒzmɪk/ a cosmico
cosmonaut /ˈkɒzmənɔːt/ n cosmonauta mf
cosmopolitan /kɒzməˈpɒlɪtən/ a cosmopolita
cosmos /ˈkɒzmɒs/ n cosmo m
cosset /ˈkɒsɪt/ vt coccolare
cost /kɒst/ n costo m; **~s** pl Jur spese fpl processuali; **at all ~s** a tutti i costi; **I learnt to my ~** ho imparato a mie spese ● vt (pt/pp **cost**) costare; **it ~ me £20** mi è costato 20 sterline ● vt (pt/pp **costed**) **~ [out]** stabilire il prezzo di
costly /ˈkɒstlɪ/ a (-ier, -iest) costoso
cost: ~ of living n costo m della vita. **~ price** n prezzo m di costo
costume /ˈkɒstjuːm/ n costume m. **~ jewellery** n bigiotteria f
cosy /ˈkəʊzɪ/ a (-ier, -iest) ⟨*pub,*

chat) intimo; **it's nice and ~ in here** si sta bene qui

cot /kɒt/ *n* lettino *m*; (*Am: campbed*) branda *f*

cottage /ˈkɒtɪdʒ/ *n* casetta *f.* **~ 'cheese** *n* fiocchi *mpl* di latte

cotton /ˈkɒtn/ *n* cotone *m* ● *attrib* di cotone ● **cotton on** *vi fam* capire

cotton 'wool *n* cotone *m* idrofilo

couch /kaʊtʃ/ *n* divano *m.* ~ **potato** *n* pantofolaio, -a *mf*

couchette /kuːˈʃet/ *n* cuccetta *f*

cough /kɒf/ *n* tosse *f* ● *vi* tossire. **cough up** *vt/i* sputare; (*fam: pay*) sborsare

'**cough mixture** *n* sciroppo *m* per la tosse

could /kʊd/, *atono* /kəd/ *v aux* (*see also* can²) **~ I have a glass of water?** potrei avere un bicchier d'acqua?; **I ~n't do it even if I wanted to** non potrei farlo nemmeno se lo volessi; **I ~n't care less** non potrebbe importarmene di meno; **he ~n't have done it without help** non avrebbe potuto farlo senza aiuto; **you ~ have phoned** avresti potuto telefonare

council /ˈkaʊnsl/ *n* consiglio *m.* ~ **house** *n* casa *f* popolare

councillor /ˈkaʊnsələ(r)/ *n* consigliere, -a *mf*

'**council tax** *n* imposta *f* locale sugli immobili

counsel /ˈkaʊnsl/ *n* consigli *mpl*; *Jur* avvocato *m* ● *vt* (*pt/pp* counselled) consigliare a (*person*). ~**lor** *n* consigliere, -a *mf*

count¹ /kaʊnt/ *n* (*nobleman*) conte *m*

count² *n* conto *m*; **keep ~** tenere il conto ● *vt/i* contare. **count on** *vt* contare su

countdown /ˈkaʊntdaʊn/ *n* conto *m* alla rovescia

countenance /ˈkaʊntənəns/ *n* espressione *f* ● *vt* approvare

counter¹ /ˈkaʊntə(r)/ *n* banco *m*; (*in games*) gettone *m*

counter² *adv* **~ to** contro, in con-

trasto a; **go ~ to sth** andare contro qcsa ● *vt/i* opporre (*measure, effect*); parare (*blow*)

'**counter'act** *vt* neutralizzare

'**counter-attack** *n* contrattacco *m*

'**counter-'espionage** *n* controspionaggio *m*

'**counterfeit** /-fɪt/ *a* contraffatto ● *n* contraffazione *f* ● *vt* contraffare

'**counterfoil** *n* matrice *f*

'**counterpart** *n* equivalente *mf*

counter-pro'ductive *a* controproduttivo

'**countersign** *vt* controfirmare

countess /ˈkaʊntɪs/ *n* contessa *f*

countless /ˈkaʊntlɪs/ *a* innumerevole

country /ˈkʌntrɪ/ *n* nazione *f*, paese *m*; (*native land*) patria *f*; (*countryside*) campagna *f*; **in the ~** in campagna; **go to the ~** andare in campagna; *Pol* indire le elezioni politiche. ~**man** *n* uomo *m* di campagna; (*fellow ~man*) compatriota *m.* ~**side** *n* campagna *f*

county /ˈkaʊntɪ/ *n* contea *f* (*unità amministrativa britannica*)

coup /kuː/ *n* Pol colpo *m* di stato

couple /ˈkʌpl/ *n* coppia *f*; **a ~ of** un paio di

coupon /ˈkuːpɒn/ *n* tagliando *m*; (*for discount*) buono *m* sconto

courage /ˈkʌrɪdʒ/ *n* coraggio *m.* ~**ous** /kəˈreɪdʒəs/ *a* coraggioso

courgette /kʊəˈʒet/ *n* zucchino *m*

courier /ˈkʊrɪə(r)/ *n* corriere *m*; (*for tourists*) guida *f*

course /kɔːs/ *n* Sch corso *m*; Naut rotta *f*; Culin portata *f*; (*for golf*) campo *m*; **~ of treatment** Med serie *f* inv di cure; **of ~** naturalmente; **in the ~ of** durante; **in due ~** a tempo debito

court /kɔːt/ *n* tribunale *m*; Sport campo *m*; **take sb to ~** citare qcno in giudizio ● *vt* fare la corte a (*woman*); sfidare (*danger*); ~**ing** **couples** coppiette *fpl*

courteous /ˈkɜːtɪəs/ *a* cortese

courtesy /ˈkɜːtəsɪ/ *n* cortesia *f*

court: ~ **'martial** n (pl ~**s martial**) corte f marziale ● ~**-martial** vt (pt ~**-martialled**) portare davanti alla corte marziale; ~**yard** n cortile m

cousin /'kʌzɪn/ n cugino, -a mf

cove /kəʊv/ n insenatura f

cover /'kʌvə(r)/ n copertura f; (of cushion, to protect sth) fodera f; (of book, magazine) copertina f; **take** ~ mettersi al riparo; **under separate** ~ a parte ● vt coprire; foderare ⟨cushion⟩; Journ fare un servizio su. **cover up** vt coprire; fig soffocare ⟨scandal⟩

coverage /'kʌvərɪdʒ/ n Journ **it got a lot of** ~ i media gli hanno dedicato molto spazio

cover: ~ **charge** n coperto m. ~**ing** n copertura f; (for floor) rivestimento m; ~**ing letter** lettera f d'accompagnamento. ~**-up** n messa f a tacere

covet /'kʌvɪt/ vt bramare

cow /kaʊ/ n vacca f, mucca f

coward /'kaʊəd/ n vigliacco, -a mf. ~**ice** /-ɪs/ n vigliaccheria f. ~**ly** a da vigliacco

'cowboy n cowboy m inv; fam buffone m

cower /'kaʊə(r)/ vi acquattarsi

'cowshed n stalla f

cox /kɒks/ n, **coxswain** /'kɒksn/ n timoniere, -a mf

coy /kɔɪ/ a falsamente timido; ⟨flirtatiously⟩ civettuolo; **be** ~ **about sth** essere evasivo a qcsa

crab /kræb/ n granchio m

crack /kræk/ n (in wall) crepa f; (in china, glass, bone) incrinatura f; (noise) scoppio m; (fam: joke) battuta f; **have a** ~ (try) fare un tentativo ● a (fam: best) di prim'ordine ● vt incrinare ⟨china, glass⟩; schiacciare ⟨nut⟩; decifrare ⟨code⟩; fam risolvere ⟨problem⟩; ~ **a joke** fam fare una battuta ● vi ⟨china, glass:⟩ incrinarsi; ⟨whip:⟩ schioccare. **crack down** vi fam prendere seri provvedimenti.

crack down on vt fam prendere seri provvedimenti

cracked /krækt/ a ⟨plaster⟩ crepato; ⟨skin⟩ screpolato; ⟨rib⟩ incrinato; (fam: crazy) svitato

cracker /'krækə(r)/ n (biscuit) cracker m inv; (firework) petardo m; [**Christmas**] ~ tubo m di cartone colorato contenente una sorpresa

crackers /'krækəz/ a fam matto

crackle /'krækl/ vi crepitare

cradle /'kreɪdl/ n culla f

craft¹ /krɑːft/ n inv ⟨boat⟩ imbarcazione f

craft² n mestiere m; ⟨technique⟩ arte f. ~**sman** n artigiano m

crafty /'krɑːftɪ/ a (-ier, -iest) astuto

crag /kræg/ n rupe f. ~**gy** a scosceso; ⟨face⟩ dai lineamenti marcati

cram /kræm/ v (pt/pp crammed) ● vt stipare (**into** in) ● vi (for exams) sgobbare

cramp /kræmp/ n crampo m. ~**ed** a ⟨room⟩ stretto; ⟨handwriting⟩ appiccicato

crampon /'kræmpən/ n rampone m

cranberry /'krænbərɪ/ n Culin mirtillo m rosso

crane /kreɪn/ n (at docks, bird) gru f inv ● vt ~ **one's neck** allungare il collo

crank¹ /kræŋk/ n tipo, -a mf strampalato, -a

crank² n Techn manovella f. ~**shaft** n albero m a gomiti

cranky /'kræŋkɪ/ a strampalato; (Am: irritable) irritabile

cranny /'krænɪ/ n fessura f

crash /kræʃ/ n (noise) fragore m; Auto, Aeron incidente m; Comm crollo m ● vi schiantarsi (**into** contro); ⟨plane:⟩ precipitare ● vt schiantare ⟨car⟩

crash: ~ **course** n corso m intensivo. ~**helmet** n casco m. ~**-landing** n atterraggio m di fortuna

crate /kreɪt/ n (for packing) cassa f

crater /'kreɪtə(r)/ n cratere m

crave /kreɪv/ vt morire dalla voglia di. **~ing** n voglia f smodata

crawl /krɔːl/ n (swimming) stile m libero; **do the ~** nuotare a stile libero; **at a ~** a passo di lumaca ● vi andare carponi; **~ with** brulicare di. **~er lane** n Auto corsia f riservata al traffico lento

crayon /'kreɪən/ n pastello m a cera; (pencil) matita f colorata

craze /kreɪz/ n mania f

crazy /'kreɪzɪ/ a (**-ier**, **-iest**) matto; **be ~ about** andar matto per

creak /kriːk/ n scricchiolio m ● vi scricchiolare

cream /kriːm/ n crema f; (fresh) panna f ● a (colour) [bianco] panna inv ● vt Culin sbattere. **~ 'cheese** n formaggio m cremoso. **~y** a cremoso

crease /kriːs/ n piega f ● vt stropicciare ● vi stropicciarsi. **~-resistant** a che non si stropiccia

creat|e /kriː'eɪt/ vt creare. **~ion** /-'eɪʃn/ n creazione f. **~ive** /-tɪv/ a creativo. **~or** n creatore, -trice mf

creature /'kriːtʃə(r)/ n creatura f

crèche /kreʃ/ n asilo m nido

credentials /krɪ'denʃlz/ npl credenziali fpl

credibility /kredə'bɪlətɪ/ n credibilità f

credible /'kredəbl/ a credibile

credit /'kredɪt/ n credito m; (honour) merito m; **take the ~ for** prendersi il merito di ● vt (pt/pp credited) accreditare; **~ sb with** accreditare qcsa a qcno; fig attribuire qcsa a qcno. **~able** /-əbl/ a lodevole

credit: **~ card** n carta f di credito. **~or** n creditore, -trice m

creed /kriːd/ n credo m inv

creek /kriːk/ n insenatura f; (Am: stream) torrente m

creep /kriːp/ vi (pt/pp crept) muoversi furtivamente ● n fam tipo m

viscido. **~er** n pianta f rampicante. **~y** a che fa venire i brividi

cremate /krɪ'meɪt/ vt cremare. **~ion** /-eɪʃn/ n cremazione f

crematorium /kremə'tɔːrɪəm/ n crematorio m

crêpe /kreɪp/ n (fabric) crespo m

crept /krept/ see **creep**

crescent /'kresənt/ n mezzaluna f

cress /kres/ n crescione m

crest /krest/ n cresta f; (coat of arms) cimiero m

Crete /kriːt/ n Creta f

crevasse /krɪ'væs/ n crepaccio m

crevice /'krevɪs/ n crepa f

crew /kruː/ n equipaggio m; (gang) équipe f inv. **~ cut** n capelli mpl a spazzola. **~ neck** n girocollo m

crib[1] /krɪb/ n (for baby) culla f

crib[2] vt/i (pt/pp cribbed) fam copiare

crick /krɪk/ n **~ in the neck** torcicollo m

cricket[1] /'krɪkɪt/ n (insect) grillo m

cricket[2] n cricket m. **~er** n giocatore m di cricket

crime /kraɪm/ n crimine m; (criminality) criminalità f

criminal /'krɪmɪnl/ a criminale; (law, court) penale ● n criminale mf

crimson /'krɪmzn/ a cremisi inv

cringe /krɪndʒ/ vi (cower) acquattarsi; (at bad joke etc) fare una smorfia

crinkle /'krɪŋkl/ vt spiegazzare ● vi spiegazzarsi

cripple /'krɪpl/ n storpio, -a mf ● vt storpiare; fig danneggiare. **~d** a (person) storpio; (ship) danneggiato

crisis /'kraɪsɪs/ n (pl **-ses** /-siːz/) crisi f inv

crisp /krɪsp/ a croccante; (air) frizzante; (style) incisivo. **~bread** n crostini mpl di pane. **~s** npl patatine fpl

criterion /kraɪ'tɪərɪən/ n (pl **-ria** /-rɪə/) criterio m

critic /'krɪtɪk/ n critico, -a mf. **~al**

a critico. **~ally** *adv* in modo critico; **~ally ill** gravemente malato

criticism /ˈkrɪtɪsɪzm/ *n* critica *f*; **he doesn't like ~** non ama le critiche

criticize /ˈkrɪtɪsaɪz/ *vt* criticare

croak /krəʊk/ *vi* gracchiare; ⟨*frog:*⟩ gracidare

crochet /ˈkrəʊʃeɪ/ *n* lavoro *m* all'uncinetto ● *vt* fare all'uncinetto. **~hook** *n* uncinetto *m*

crock /krɒk/ *n fam* **old ~** ⟨*person*⟩ rudere *m*; ⟨*car*⟩ macinino *m*

crockery /ˈkrɒkərɪ/ *n* terrecotte *fpl*

crocodile /ˈkrɒkədaɪl/ *n* coccodrillo *m*. **~ tears** lacrime *fpl* di coccodrillo

crocus /ˈkrəʊkəs/ *n* (*pl* **-es**) croco *m*

crony /ˈkrəʊnɪ/ *n* compare *m*

crook /krʊk/ *n* ⟨*fam: criminal*⟩ truffatore, -trice *mf*

crooked /ˈkrʊkɪd/ *a* storto; ⟨*limb*⟩ storpiato; ⟨*fam: dishonest*⟩ disonesto

crop /krɒp/ *n* raccolto *m*; *fig* quantità *f inv* ● *v* (*pt/pp* **cropped**) ● *vt* coltivare. **crop up** *vi fam* presentarsi

croquet /ˈkrəʊkeɪ/ *n* croquet *m*

croquette /krəʊˈket/ *n* crocchetta *f*

cross /krɒs/ *a* ⟨*annoyed*⟩ arrabbiato; **talk at ~ purposes** fraintendersi ● *n* croce *f*; *Bot*, *Zool* incrocio *m* ● *vt* sbarrare ⟨*cheque*⟩; incrociare ⟨*road, animals:*⟩; **~ oneself** farsi il segno della croce; **~ one's arms** incrociare le braccia; **~ one's legs** accavallare le gambe; **keep one's fingers ~ed for sb** tenere le dita incrociate per qcno; **it ~ed my mind** mi è venuto in mente ● *vi* ⟨*go across*⟩ attraversare; ⟨*lines:*⟩ incrociarsi. **cross out** *vt* depennare

cross: **~bar** *n* ⟨*of goal*⟩ traversa *f*; ⟨*on bicycle*⟩ canna *f*. **~'country** *n* *Sport* corsa *f* campestre. **~ex'amine** *vt* sottoporre a contro-

interrogatorio. **~-exami'nation** *n* controinterrogatorio *m*. **~-eyed** *a* strabico. **~-fire** *n* fuoco *m* incrociato. **~ing** *n* ⟨*for pedestrians*⟩ passaggio *m* pedonale; ⟨*sea journey*⟩ traversata *f*. **~-reference** *n* rimando *m*. **~-roads** *n* incrocio *m*. **~-section** *n* sezione *f*; ⟨*of community*⟩ campione *m*. **~-wise** *adv* in diagonale. **~-word** *n* **~word [puzzle]** parole *fpl* crociate

crotchet /ˈkrɒtʃɪt/ *n* *Mus* semiminima *f*

crotchety /ˈkrɒtʃɪtɪ/ *a* irritabile

crouch /kraʊtʃ/ *vi* accovacciarsi

crow /krəʊ/ *n* corvo *m*; **as the ~ flies** in linea d'aria ● *vi* cantare. **~bar** *n* piede *m* di porco

crowd /kraʊd/ *n* folla *f* ● *vt* affollare ● *vi* affollarsi. **~ed** /ˈkraʊdɪd/ *a* affollato

crown /kraʊn/ *n* corona *f* ● *vt* incoronare; incapsulare ⟨*tooth*⟩

crucial /ˈkruːʃl/ *a* cruciale

crucifix /ˈkruːsɪfɪks/ *n* crocifisso *m*

crucif'ixion /kruːsɪˈfɪkʃn/ *n* crocifissione *f*. **~y** /ˈkruːsɪfaɪ/ *vt* (*pt/pp* **-ied**) crocifiggere

crude /kruːd/ *a* ⟨*oil*⟩ greggio; ⟨*language*⟩ crudo; ⟨*person*⟩ rozzo

cruel /ˈkruːəl/ *a* (**crueller**, **cruellest**) crudele (**to** verso). **~ly** *adv* con crudeltà. **~ty** *n* crudeltà *f*

cruise /kruːz/ *n* crociera *f* ● *vi* fare una crociera; ⟨*car:*⟩ andare a velocità di crociera. **~r** *n* *Mil* incrociatore *m*; ⟨*motor boat*⟩ motoscafo *m*. **~ing speed** *n* velocità *m inv* di crociera

crumb /krʌm/ *n* briciola *f*

crumb|le /ˈkrʌmbl/ *vt* sbriciolare ● *vi* sbriciolarsi; ⟨*building, society:*⟩ sgretolarsi. **~ly** *a* friabile

crumple /ˈkrʌmpl/ *vt* spiegazzare ● *vi* spiegazzarsi

crunch /krʌntʃ/ *n fam* **when it comes to the ~** quando si viene al dunque ● *vt* sgranocchiare ● *vi* ⟨*snow:*⟩ scricchiolare

crusade /kru:'seɪd/ n crociata f. **~r** n crociato m

crush /krʌʃ/ n (crowd) calca f; **have a ~ on sb** essersi preso una cotta per qcno ● vt schiacciare; sgualcire (clothes)

crust /krʌst/ n crosta f

crutch /krʌtʃ/ n gruccia f; Anat inforcatura f

crux /krʌks/ n fig punto m cruciale

cry /kraɪ/ n grido m; **have a ~** farsi un pianto; **a far ~ from** fig tutta un'altra cosa rispetto a ● vi (pt/pp **cried**) (weep) piangere; (call) gridare

crypt /krɪpt/ n cripta f. **~ic** a criptico

crystal /'krɪstl/ n cristallo m; (glassware) cristalli mpl. **~lize** vi (become clear) concretizzarsi

cub /kʌb/ n (animal) cucciolo m; C~ [Scout] lupetto m

Cuba /'kju:bə/ n Cuba f

cubby-hole /'kʌbɪ-/ n (compartment) scomparto m; (room) ripostiglio m

cub|e /kju:b/ n cubo m. **~ic** a cubico

cubicle /'kju:bɪkl/ n cabina f

cuckoo /'koku:/ n cuculo m. **~ clock** n orologio m a cucù

cucumber /'kju:kʌmbə(r)/ n cetriolo m

cuddl|e /'kʌdl/ vt coccolare ● vi **~e up to** starsene accoccolato insieme a ● n **have a ~e** (child:) farsi coccolare; (lovers:) abbracciarsi. **~y** a tenerone; (wanting cuddles) coccolone. **~y 'toy** n peluche m inv

cudgel /'kʌdʒl/ n randello m

cue¹ /kju:/ n segnale m; Theat battuta f d'entrata

cue² n (in billiards) stecca f. **~ ball** n pallino m

cuff /kʌf/ n polsino m; (Am: turn-up) orlo m; (blow) scapaccione m; **off the ~** improvvisando ● vt dare una pacca a. **~-link** n gemello m

cul-de-sac /'kʌldəsæk/ n vicolo m cieco

culinary /'kʌlɪnərɪ/ a culinario

cull /kʌl/ vt scegliere (flowers); (kill) selezionare e uccidere

culminat|e /'kʌlmɪnet/ vi culminare. **~ion** /-'neɪʃn/ n culmine m

culottes /kju:'lɒts/ npl gonna fsg pantalone

culprit /'kʌlprɪt/ n colpevole mf

cult /kʌlt/ n culto m

cultivate /'kʌltɪvet/ vt coltivare; fig coltivari (person)

cultural /'kʌltʃərəl/ a culturale

culture /'kʌltʃə(r)/ n cultura f. **~d** a colto

cumbersome /'kʌmbəsəm/ a ingombrante

cumulative /'kju:mjʊlətɪv/ a cumulativo

cunning /'kʌnɪŋ/ a astuto ● n astuzia f

cup /kʌp/ n tazza f; (prize, of bra) coppa f

cupboard /'kʌbəd/ n armadio m. **~ love** fam amore m interessato

Cup 'Final n finale f di coppa

Cupid /'kju:pɪd/ n Cupido m

curable /'kjʊərəbl/ a curabile

curate /'kjʊərət/ n curato m

curator /kjʊə'reɪtə(r)/ n direttore, -trice mf (di museo)

curb /kɜ:b/ vt tenere a freno

curdle /'kɜ:dl/ vi coagularsi

cure /kjʊə(r)/ n cura f ● vt curare; (salt) mettere sotto sale; (smoke) affumicare

curfew /'kɜ:fju:/ n coprifuoco m

curio /'kjʊərɪəʊ/ n curiosità f inv

curiosity /kjʊərɪ'ɒsətɪ/ n curiosità f

curious /'kjʊərɪəs/ a curioso. **~ly** adv (strangely) curiosamente

curl /kɜ:l/ n ricciolo m ● vt arricciare ● vi arricciarsi. **curl up** vi raggomitolarsi

curler /kɜ:lə(r)/ n bigodino m

curly /'kɜ:lɪ/ a (-ier, -iest) riccio

currant /'kʌrənt/ n (dried) uvetta f

currency /'kʌrənsɪ/ n valuta f; (of

word) ricorrenza *f*; **foreign ~** valuta *f* estera

current /ˈkʌrənt/ *a* corrente ● *n* corrente *f*. **~ affairs** *or* **events** *npl* attualità *fsg*. **~ly** *adv* attualmente

curriculum /kəˈrɪkjʊləm/ *n* programma *m* di studi. **~ vitae** /ˈviːtaɪ/ *n* curriculum vitae *m inv*

curry /ˈkʌrɪ/ *n* curry *m inv*; (*meal*) piatto *m* cucinato nel curry ● *vt* (*pt/pp* **-ied**) **~ favour with sb** cercare d'ingraziarsi qcno

curse /kɜːs/ *n* maledizione *f*; (*oath*) imprecazione *f* ● *vt* maledire ● *vi* imprecare

cursor /ˈkɜːsə(r)/ *n* cursore *m*

cursory /ˈkɜːsərɪ/ *a* sbrigativo

curt /kɜːt/ *a* brusco

curtail /kɜːˈteɪl/ *vt* ridurre

curtain /ˈkɜːtn/ *n* tenda *f*; *Theat* sipario *m*

curtsy /ˈkɜːtsɪ/ *n* inchino *m* ● *vi* (*pt/pp* **-ied**) fare l'inchino

curve /kɜːv/ *n* curva *f* ● *vi* curvare; **~ to the right/left** curvare a destra/sinistra. **~d** *a* curvo

cushion /ˈkʊʃn/ *n* cuscino *m* ● *vt* attutire; (*protect*) proteggere

cushy /ˈkʊʃɪ/ *a* (**-ier, -iest**) *fam* facile

custard /ˈkʌstəd/ *n* (*liquid*) crema *f* pasticciera

custodian /kʌˈstəʊdɪən/ *n* custode *mf*

custody /ˈkʌstədɪ/ *n* (*of child*) custodia *f*; (*imprisonment*) detenzione *f* preventiva

custom /ˈkʌstəm/ *n* usanza *f*; *Jur* consuetudine *f*; *Comm* clientela *f*. **~ary** *a* (*habitual*) abituale; **it's ~ to...** è consuetudine.... **~er** *n* cliente *mf*

customs /ˈkʌstəmz/ *npl* dogana *f*. **~ officer** *n* doganiere *m*

cut /kʌt/ *n* (*with knife etc, of clothes*) taglio *m*; (*reduction*) riduzione *f*; (*in public spending*) taglio *m* ● *vt/i* (*pt/pp* **cut**, *pres p* **cutting**) tagliare; (*reduce*) ridurre; **~ one's finger** tagliarsi il dito; **~ sb's hair**

tagliare i capelli a qcno ● *vi* (*with cards*) alzare. **cut back** *vt* tagliare (*hair*); potare (*hedge*); (*reduce*) ridurre. **cut down** *vt* abbattere (*tree*); (*reduce*) ridurre. **cut off** *vt* tagliar via; (*disconnect*) interrompere; *fig* isolare; **I was ~ off** *Teleph* la linea è caduta. **cut out** *vt* ritagliare; (*delete*) eliminare; **be ~ out for** essere tagliato per; **~ it out!** *fam* dacci un taglio!. **cut up** *vt* (*slice*) tagliare a pezzi

'cut-back *n* riduzione *f*; (*in government spending*) taglio *m*

cute /kjuːt/ *a fam* (*in appearance*) carino; (*clever*) acuto

cuticle /ˈkjuːtɪkl/ *n* cuticola *f*

cutlery /ˈkʌtlərɪ/ *n* posate *fpl*

cutlet /ˈkʌtlɪt/ *n* cotoletta *f*

'cut-price *a* a prezzo ridotto; (*shop*) che fa prezzi ridotti

'cut-throat *a* spietato

cutting /ˈkʌtɪŋ/ *a* (*remark*) tagliente ● *n* (*from newspaper*) ritaglio *m*; (*of plant*) talea *f*

CV *n abbr* curriculum vitae

cyanide /ˈsaɪənaɪd/ *n* cianuro *m*

cybernetics /saɪbəˈnetɪks/ *n* cibernetica *f*

cycl|e /ˈsaɪkl/ *n* ciclo *m*; (*bicycle*) bicicletta *f*, bici *f inv fam* ● *vi* andare in bicicletta. **~ing** *n* ciclismo *m*. **~ist** *n* ciclista *mf*

cyclone /ˈsaɪkləʊn/ *n* ciclone *m*

cylind|er /ˈsɪlɪndə(r)/ *n* cilindro *m*. **~rical** /-ˈlɪndrɪkl/ *a* cilindrico

cymbals /ˈsɪmblz/ *npl Mus* piatti *mpl*

cynic /ˈsɪnɪk/ *n* cinico, -a *mf*. **~al** *a* cinico. **~ism** /-sɪzm/ *n* cinismo *m*

cypress /ˈsaɪprəs/ *n* cipresso *m*

Cypriot /ˈsɪprɪət/ *n* cipriota *mf*

Cyprus /ˈsaɪprəs/ *n* Cipro *m*

cyst /sɪst/ *n* ciste *f*. **~itis** /-ˈstaɪtɪs/ *n* cistite *f*

Czech /tʃek/ *a* ceco; **~ Republic** Repubblica *f* Ceca ● *n* ceco, -a *mf*

Czechoslovak /tʃekəˈsləʊvæk/ *a* cecoslovacco. **~ia** /-ˈvækɪə/ *n* Cecoslovacchia *f*

Dd

dab /dæb/ n colpetto m; **a ~ of** un pochino di ● vt (pt/pp **dabbed**) toccare leggermente (eyes). **dab on** vt mettere un po' di (paint etc)

dabble /'dæbl/ vi **~ in sth** fig occuparsi di qcsa a tempo perso

dachshund /'dækshund/ n bassotto m

dad[dy] /'dæd[ɪ]/ n fam papà m inv, babbo m

daddy-'long-legs n zanzarone m [dei boschi]; (Am: spider) ragno m

daffodil /'dæfədil/ n giunchiglia f

daft /dɑːft/ a sciocco

dagger /'dægə(r)/ n stiletto m

dahlia /'deɪlɪə/ n dalia f

daily /'deɪlɪ/ a giornaliero ● adv giornalmente ● n (newspaper) quotidiano m; (fam: cleaner) donna f delle pulizie

dainty /'deɪntɪ/ a (-ier, -iest) grazioso; (movement) delicato

dairy /'deərɪ/ n caseificio m; (shop) latteria f. **~ cow** n mucca f da latte. **~ products** npl latticini mpl

dais /'deɪɪs/ n pedana f

daisy /'deɪzɪ/ n margheritina f; (larger) margherita f

dale /deɪl/ n liter valle f

dam /dæm/ n diga f ● vt (pt/pp **dammed**) costruire una diga su

damage /'dæmɪdʒ/ n danno m (**to** a); **~es** pl Jur risarcimento msg ● vt danneggiare; fig nuocere a. **~ing** a dannoso

dame /deɪm/ n liter dama f; Am sl donna f

damn /dæm/ a fam maledetto ● adv (lucky, late) maledettamente ● n **I don't care a ~** fam non me ne frega un accidente ● vt dannare. **~ation** /-'neɪʃn/ n dannazione f ● int fam accidenti!

damp /dæmp/ a umido ● n umidità f ● vt = **dampen**

damp|en /'dæmpən/ vt inumidire; fig raffreddare (enthusiasm). **~ness** n umidità f

dance /dɑːns/ n ballo m ● vt/i ballare. **~-hall** n sala f da ballo. **~ music** n musica f da ballo

dancer /'dɑːnsə(r)/ n ballerino, -a mf

dandelion /'dændɪlaɪən/ n dente m di leone

dandruff /'dændrʌf/ n forfora f

Dane /deɪn/ n danese mf; **Great ~** danese m

danger /'deɪndʒə(r)/ n pericolo m; **in/out of ~** in/fuori pericolo. **~ous** /-rəs/ a pericoloso. **~ously** adv pericolosamente. **~ously ill** in pericolo di vita

dangle /'dæŋgl/ vi penzolare ● vt far penzolare

Danish /'deɪnɪʃ/ a & n danese m. **~ 'pastry** n dolce m a base di pasta sfoglia contenente pasta di mandorle, mele ecc

dank /dæŋk/ a umido e freddo

Danube /'dænjuːb/ n Danubio m

dare /deə(r)/ vt/i osare; (challenge) sfidare (**to** a); **~ [to] do sth** osare fare qcsa; **I ~ say!** molto probabilmente! ● n sfida f. **~-devil** n spericolato, -a mf

daring /'deərɪŋ/ a audace ● n audacia f

dark /dɑːk/ a buio; **~ blue/brown** blu/marrone scuro; **it's getting ~** sta cominciando a fare buio; **~ horse** fig (in race, contest) vincitore m imprevisto; (not much known about) misterioso m; **keep sth ~** fig tenere qcsa nascosto ● n **after ~** col buio; **in the ~** al buio; **keep sb in the ~** fig tenere qcno all'oscuro

dark|en /'dɑːkn/ vt oscurare ● vi oscurarsi. **~ness** n buio m

'dark-room n camera f oscura

darling /'dɑːlɪŋ/ a adorabile; **my ~ Joan** carissima Joan ● n tesoro m

darn /dɑːn/ vt rammendare. **~ing-needle** n ago m da rammendo

dart /dɑːt/ n dardo m; (in sewing) pince f inv; ~s sg (game) freccette fpl ● vi lanciarsi

dartboard /ˈdɑːtbɔːd/ n bersaglio m [per freccette]

dash /dæʃ/ n Typ trattino m; (in Morse) linea f; **a ~ of milk** un goccio di latte; **make a ~ for** lanciarsi verso ● vi **I must ~** devo scappare ● vt far svanire ⟨hopes⟩. **dash off** vi scappar via ● vt (write quickly) buttare giù. **dash out** vi uscire di corsa

'dashboard n cruscotto m

dashing /ˈdæʃɪŋ/ a (bold) ardito; (in appearance) affascinante

data /ˈdeɪtə/ npl & sg dati mpl. **~base** n base [di] dati f, database m inv. **~comms** /ˈkɒmz/ n telematica f. **~processing** n elaborazione f [di] dati

date¹ /deɪt/ n (fruit) dattero m

date² n data f; (meeting) appuntamento m; **to ~** fino ad oggi; **out of ~** (not fashionable) fuori moda; (expired) scaduto; (information) non aggiornato; **make a ~ with sb** dare un appuntamento a qcno; **be up to ~** essere aggiornato ● vt/i datare; (go out with) uscire con. **date back to** vi risalire a

dated /ˈdeɪtɪd/ a fuori moda; ⟨language⟩ antiquato

'date-line n linea f [del cambiamento] di data

daub /dɔːb/ vt imbrattare ⟨walls⟩

daughter /ˈdɔːtə(r)/ n figlia f. **~-in-law** n (pl **~s-in-law**) nuora f

daunt /dɔːnt/ vt scoraggiare; **nothing ~ed** senza scoraggiarsi. **~less** a intrepido

dawdle /ˈdɔːdl/ vi bighellonare; (over work) cincischiarsi

dawn /dɔːn/ n alba f; **at ~** all'alba ● vi albeggiare; **it ~ed on me** fig mi è apparso chiaro

day /deɪ/ n giorno m; (whole day) giornata f; (period) epoca f; **these ~s** oggigiorno; **in those ~s** a quei tempi; **it's had its ~** fam ha fatto il suo tempo

day: **~break** n **at ~break** allo spuntar del giorno. **~-dream** n sogno m ad occhi aperti ● vi sognare ad occhi aperti. **~light** n luce f diretto m di andata e ritorno con validità giornaliera. **~time** n giorno m; **in the ~time** di giorno

daze /deɪz/ n **in a ~** stordito; fig sbalordito. **~d** a stordito; fig sbalordito

dazzle /ˈdæzl/ vt abbagliare

deacon /ˈdiːkn/ n diacono m

dead /ded/ a morto; (numb) intorpidito; **~ body** morto m; **~ centre** pieno centro m ● adv **~ tired** stanco morto; **~ slow/easy** lentissimo/facilissimo; **you're ~ right** hai perfettamente ragione; **~ stop** ~ fermarsi di colpo; **be ~ on time** essere in perfetto orario ● n **the ~** pl i morti; **in the ~ of night** nel cuore della notte

deaden /ˈdedn/ vt attutire ⟨sound⟩; calmare ⟨pain⟩

dead: **~ 'end** n vicolo m cieco. **~ 'heat** n **it was a ~ heat** è finita a pari merito. **~line** n scadenza f. **~lock** n **reach ~lock** fig giungere a un punto morto

deadly /ˈdedlɪ/ a (-ier, -iest) mortale; (fam: dreary) barboso; **~ sins** peccati mpl capitali

deadpan /ˈdedpæn/ a impassibile; ⟨humour⟩ all'inglese

deaf /def/ a sordo; **~ and dumb** sordomuto. **~-aid** n apparecchio m acustico

deaf|en /ˈdefn/ vt assordare; (permanently) render sordo. **~ening** a assordante. **~ness** n sordità f

deal /diːl/ n (agreement) patto m; (in business) accordo m; **whose ~?** (in cards) a chi tocca dare le carte?; **a good** o **great ~** molto; **get a raw ~** fam ricevere un trattamento ingiusto ● vt (pt/pp dealt /delt/) (in cards) dare; **~ sb a blow** dare un colpo a qcno. **deal in** vt trattare in. **deal out** vt ⟨hand *out*) distribuire. **deal with** *vt* (*handle*) occuparsi di; trattare con ⟨*company*⟩; (*be about*) trattare di; **that's been ~t with** è stato risolto

deal|er /'di:lə(r)/ *n* commerciante *mf*; (*in drugs*) spacciatore, -trice *mf*. **~ings** *npl* **have ~ings with** avere a che fare con

dean /di:n/ *n* decano *m*; *Univ* ≈ preside *mf* di facoltà

dear /dɪə(r)/ *a* caro; (*in letter*) Caro; (*formal*) Gentile ● *n* caro, -a *mf* ● *int* **oh ~!** Dio mio!. **~ly** *adv* ⟨*love*⟩ profondamente; ⟨*pay*⟩ profumatamente

dearth /dɜ:θ/ *n* penuria *f*

death /deθ/ *n* morte *f*. **~ certificate** *n* certificato *m* di morte. **~ duty** *n* tassa *f* di successione

deathly /'deθlɪ/ *a* ~ **silence** silenzio *m* di tomba ● *adv* ~ **pale** di un pallore cadaverico

death: ~ penalty *n* pena *f* di morte. **~-trap** *n* trappola *f* mortale

debar /dɪ'bɑ:(r)/ *vt* (*pt/pp* **debarred**) escludere

debase /dɪ'beɪs/ *vt* degradare

debatable /dɪ'beɪtəbl/ *a* discutibile

debate /dɪ'beɪt/ *n* dibattito *m* ● *vt* discutere; (*in formal debate*) dibattere ● *vi* ~ **whether to...** considerare se...

debauchery /dɪ'bɔ:tʃərɪ/ *n* dissolutezza *f*

debility /dɪ'bɪlɪtɪ/ *n* debilitazione *f*

debit /'debɪt/ *n* debito *m* ● *vt* (*pt/pp* **debited**) *Comm* addebitare ⟨*sum*⟩

debris /'debri:/ *n* macerie *fpl*

debt /det/ *n* debito *m*; **be in ~** avere dei debiti. **~or** *n* debitore, -trice *mf*

début /'deɪbu:/ *n* debutto *m*

decade /'dekeɪd/ *n* decennio *m*

decaden|ce /'dekədəns/ *n* decadenza *f*. **~t** *a* decadente

decaffeinated /di:'kæfɪneɪtɪd/ *a* decaffeinato

decant /dɪ'kænt/ *vt* travasare. **~er** *n* caraffa *f* (*di cristallo*)

decapitate /dɪ'kæpɪteɪt/ *vt* decapitare

decay /dɪ'keɪ/ *n* (*also fig*) decadenza *f*; ⟨*rot*⟩ decomposizione *f*; (*of tooth*) carie *f inv* ● *vi* imputridire; ⟨*rot*⟩ decomporsi; ⟨*tooth:*⟩ cariarsi

deceased /dɪ'si:st/ *a* defunto ● *n* **the ~d** il defunto; la defunta

deceit /dɪ'si:t/ *n* inganno *m*. **~ful** *a* falso

deceive /dɪ'si:v/ *vt* ingannare

December /dɪ'sembə(r)/ *n* dicembre *m*

decency /'di:sənsɪ/ *n* decenza *f*

decent /'di:sənt/ *a* decente; (*respectable*) rispettabile; **very ~ of you** molto gentile da parte tua. **~ly** *adv* decentemente; (*kindly*) gentilmente

decentralize /di:'sentrəlaɪz/ *vt* decentralizzare

decept|ion /dɪ'sepʃn/ *n* inganno *m*. **~ive** /-tɪv/ *a* ingannevole. **~ively** *adv* ingannevolmente; **it looks ~ively easy** sembra facile, ma non lo è

decibel /'desɪbel/ *n* decibel *m inv*

decide /dɪ'saɪd/ *vt* decidere ● *vi* decidere (**on** di)

decided /dɪ'saɪdɪd/ *a* risoluto. **~ly** *adv* risolutamente; (*without doubt*) senza dubbio

deciduous /dɪ'sɪdjʊəs/ *a* a foglie decidue

decimal /'desɪml/ *a* decimale ● *n* numero *m* decimale. **~ 'point** *n* virgola *f*

decimate /'desɪmeɪt/ *vt* decimare

decipher /dɪ'saɪfə(r)/ *vt* decifrare

decision /dɪ'sɪʒn/ *n* decisione *f*

decisive /dɪ'saɪsɪv/ *a* decisivo

deck¹ /dek/ *vt* abbigliare

deck² *n* *Naut* ponte *m*; **on ~** in coperta; **top ~** (*of bus*) piano *m* di sopra; **~ of cards** mazzo *m*. **~-chair** *n* [sedia *f* a] sdraio *f inv*

declaration /deklə'reɪʃn/ *n* dichiarazione *f*

declare /dɪ'kleə(r)/ *vt* dichiarare; **anything to ~?** niente da dichiarare?

declension /dɪ'klenʃn/ *n* declinazione *f*

decline /dɪ'klaɪn/ *n* declino *m* • *vt also Gram* declinare • *vi* (*decrease*) diminuire; ⟨*health*:⟩ deperire; ⟨*say no*⟩ rifiutare

decode /di:'kəʊd/ *vt* decifrare; *Comput* decodificare

decompose /di:kəm'pəʊz/ *vi* decomporsi

décor /'deɪkɔ:(r)/ *n* decorazione *f*; (*including furniture*) arredamento *m*

decorat|e /'dekəreɪt/ *vt* decorare; (*paint*) pitturare; (*wallpaper*) tappezzare. **~ion** /-'reɪʃn/ *n* decorazione *f*. **~ive** /-rətɪv/ *a* decorativo. **~or** *n* painter and **~or** imbianchino *m*

decorum /dɪ'kɔ:rəm/ *n* decoro *m*

decoy[1] /'di:kɔɪ/ *n* esca *f*

decoy[2] /dɪ'kɔɪ/ *vt* adescare

decrease[1] /'di:kri:s/ *n* diminuzione *f*

decrease[2] /dɪ'kri:s/ *vt/i* diminuire

decree /dɪ'kri:/ *n* decreto *m* • *vt* (*pt/pp* **decreed**) decretare

decrepit /dɪ'krepɪt/ *a* decrepito

dedicat|e /'dedɪkeɪt/ *vt* dedicare. **~ed** *a* ⟨*person*⟩ scrupoloso. **~ion** /-'keɪʃn/ *n* dedizione *f*; (*in book*) dedica *f*

deduce /dɪ'dju:s/ *vt* dedurre (**from** da)

deduct /dɪ'dʌkt/ *vt* dedurre

deduction /dɪ'dʌkʃn/ *n* deduzione *f*

deed /di:d/ *n* azione *f*; *Jur* atto *m* di proprietà

deem /di:m/ *vt* ritenere

deep /di:p/ *a* profondo; **go off the ~ end** *fam* arrabbiarsi

deepen /'di:pn/ *vt* approfondire; scavare più profondamente ⟨*trench*⟩ • *vi* approfondirsi; ⟨*fig: mystery*:⟩ infittirsi

deep-'freeze *n* congelatore *m*

deeply /'di:plɪ/ *adv* profondamente

deer /dɪə(r)/ *n inv* cervo *m*

deface /dɪ'feɪs/ *vt* sfigurare ⟨*picture*⟩; deturpare ⟨*monument*⟩

defamat|ion /defə'meɪʃn/ *n* diffamazione *f*. **~ory** /-'fæmətərɪ/ *a* diffamatorio

default /dɪ'fɔ:lt/ *n* ⟨*Jur: non-payment*⟩ morosità *f*; (*failure to appear*) contumacia *f*; **win by ~** *Sport* vincere per abbandono dell'avversario. **in ~ of** per mancanza di • *a* **~ drive** *Comput* lettore *m* di default • *vi* (*not pay*) venir meno a un pagamento

defeat /dɪ'fi:t/ *n* sconfitta *f* • *vt* sconfiggere; (*frustrate*) vanificare ⟨*attempts*⟩; **that ~s the object** questo fa fallire l'obiettivo

defect[1] /dɪ'fekt/ *vi Pol* fare defezione

defect[2] /'di:fekt/ *n* difetto *m*. **~ive** /dɪ'fektɪv/ *a* difettoso

defence /dɪ'fens/ *n* difesa *f*. **~less** *a* indifeso

defend /dɪ'fend/ *vt* difendere; (*justify*) giustificare. **~ant** *n Jur* imputato, -a *mf*

defensive /dɪ'fensɪv/ *a* difensivo • *n* difensiva *f*; **on the ~** sulla difensiva

defer /dɪ'fɜ:(r)/ *vt* (*pt/pp* **deferred**) • *vt* (*postpone*) rinviare • *vi* **~ to sb** rimettersi a qcno

deferen|ce /'defərəns/ *n* deferenza *f*. **~tial** /-'renʃl/ *a* deferente

defian|ce /dɪ'faɪəns/ *n* sfida *f*; **in ~ce of** sfidando. **~t** *a* ⟨*person*⟩ ribelle; ⟨*gesture, attitude*⟩ di sfida. **~tly** *adv* con aria di sfida

deficien|cy /dɪ'fɪʃənsɪ/ *n* insufficienza *f*. **~t** *a* insufficiente; **be ~t in** mancare di

deficit /'defɪsɪt/ *n* deficit *m inv*

defile /dɪ'faɪl/ *vt fig* contaminare

define /dɪ'faɪn/ *vt* definire

definite /'defɪnɪt/ *a* definito; (*certain*) definitivo; ⟨*answer, yes*⟩ definitivo; (*improvement, difference*) netto; **he was ~ about it** è stato chiaro in proposito. **~ly** *adv* sicuramente

definition /defɪ'nɪʃn/ *n* definizione *f*

definitive /dɪ'fɪnətɪv/ *a* definitivo

deflat|e /dɪ'fleɪt/ vt sgonfiare. **~ion** /-eɪʃn/ n Comm deflazione f

deflect /dɪ'flekt/ vt deflettere

deform|ed /dɪ'fɔ:md/ a deforme. **~ity** n deformità f inv

defraud /dɪ'frɔ:d/ vt defraudare

defrost /di:'frɒst/ vt sbrinare ⟨fridge⟩; scongelare ⟨food⟩

deft /deft/ a abile

defunct /dɪ'fʌŋkt/ a morto e sepolto; ⟨law⟩ caduto in disuso

defuse /di:'fju:z/ vt disinnescare; calmare ⟨situation⟩

defy /dɪ'faɪ/ vt (pt/pp -ied) ⟨challenge⟩ sfidare; resistere a ⟨attempt⟩; ⟨not obey⟩ disobbedire a

degenerate¹ /dɪ'dʒenəreɪt/ vi degenerare; **~ into** fig degenerare in

degenerate² /dɪ'dʒenərət/ a degenerato

degrading /dɪ'greɪdɪŋ/ a degradante

degree /dɪ'gri:/ n grado m; Univ laurea f; **20 ~s** 20 gradi; **not to the same ~** non allo stesso livello

dehydrate /di:'haɪdreɪt/ vt disidratare. **~d** /-ɪd/ a disidratato

de-ice /di:'aɪs/ vt togliere il ghiaccio da

deign /deɪn/ vi **~ to do sth** degnarsi di fare qcsa

deity /'di:ɪtɪ/ n divinità f inv

dejected /dɪ'dʒektɪd/ a demoralizzato

delay /dɪ'leɪ/ n ritardo m; **without ~** senza indugio ● vt ritardare; **be ~ed** ⟨person:⟩ essere trattenuto; ⟨train, aircraft:⟩ essere in ritardo ● vi indugiare

delegate¹ /'delɪgət/ n delegato, -a f

delegat|e² /'delɪgeɪt/ vt delegare. **~ion** /-'geɪʃn/ n delegazione f

delet|e /dɪ'li:t/ vt cancellare. **~ion** /-i:ʃn/ n cancellatura f

deliberate¹ /dɪ'lɪbərət/ a deliberato; ⟨slow⟩ posato. **~ly** adv deliberatamente; ⟨slowly⟩ in modo posato

deliberat|e² /dɪ'lɪbəreɪt/ vt/i deliberare. **~ion** /-'reɪʃn/ n deliberazione f

delicacy /'delɪkəsɪ/ n delicatezza f; ⟨food⟩ prelibatezza f

delicate /'delɪkət/ a delicato

delicatessen /delɪkə'tesn/ n negozio m di specialità gastronomiche

delicious /dɪ'lɪʃəs/ a delizioso

delight /dɪ'laɪt/ n piacere m ● vt deliziare ● vi **~ in** dilettarsi con. **~ed** a lieto. **~ful** a delizioso

delinquen|cy /dɪ'lɪŋkwənsɪ/ n delinquenza f. **~t** a delinquente ● n delinquente mf

deli|rious /dɪ'lɪrɪəs/ a be **~rious** delirare; ⟨fig: very happy⟩ essere pazzo di gioia. **~rium** /-rɪəm/ n delirio m

deliver /dɪ'lɪvə(r)/ vt consegnare; recapitare ⟨post, newspaper⟩; tenere ⟨speech⟩; dare ⟨message⟩; tirare ⟨blow⟩; ⟨set free⟩ liberare; **~ a baby** far nascere un bambino. **~ance** n liberazione f. **~y** n consegna f; ⟨of post⟩ distribuzione f; Med parto m; **cash on ~y** pagamento m alla consegna

delude /dɪ'lu:d/ vt ingannare; **~ oneself** illudersi

deluge /'delju:dʒ/ n diluvio m ● vt ⟨fig: with requests etc⟩ inondare

delusion /dɪ'lu:ʒn/ n illusione f

de luxe /də'lʌks/ a di lusso

delve /delv/ vi **~ into** ⟨into pocket etc⟩ frugare in; ⟨into notes, the past⟩ fare ricerche in

demand /dɪ'mɑ:nd/ n richiesta f; Comm domanda f; **in ~** richiesto; **on ~** a richiesta ● vt esigere ⟨of/from da⟩. **~ing** a esigente

demarcation /di:mɑ:'keɪʃn/ n demarcazione f

demean /dɪ'mi:n/ vt **~ oneself** abbassarsi ⟨to a⟩

demeanour /dɪ'mi:nə(r)/ n comportamento m

demented /dɪ'mentɪd/ a demente

demise /dɪ'maɪz/ n decesso m

demister /di:'mɪstə(r)/ n Auto sbrinatore m

demo /'deməʊ/ n (pl **~s**) fam ma-

nifestazione f; **~ disk** Comput
demodisk m inv
democracy /dɪˈmɒkrəsɪ/ n demo-
crazia f
democrat /ˈdeməkræt/ n democra-
tico, -a mf. **~ic** /-ˈkrætɪk/ a demo-
cratico
demo|lish /dɪˈmɒlɪʃ/ vt demolire.
~lition /deməˈlɪʃn/ n demolizio-
ne f
demon /ˈdiːmən/ n demonio m
demonstrat|e /ˈdemənstreɪt/ vt di-
mostrare; fare una dimostrazione
sull'uso di ⟨appliance⟩ ● vi Pol
manifestare. **~ion** /-ˈstreɪʃn/ n dimostrazione f; Pol manifestazione f
demonstrative /dɪˈmɒnstrətɪv/ a
Gram dimostrativo; **be ~** essere
espansivo
demonstrator /ˈdemənstreɪtə(r)/
n Pol manifestante mf; ⟨for prod-
uct⟩ dimostratore, -trice mf
demoralize /dɪˈmɒrəlaɪz/ vt de-
moralizzare
demote /dɪˈməʊt/ vt retrocedere di
grado; Mil degradare
demure /dɪˈmjʊə(r)/ a schivo
den /den/ n tana f; ⟨room⟩ rifugio m
denial /dɪˈnaɪəl/ n smentita f
denim /ˈdenɪm/ n [tessuto m] jeans
m; **~s** pl [blue]jeans mpl
Denmark /ˈdenmɑːk/ n Danimar-
ca f
denomination /dɪnɒmɪˈneɪʃn/ n
Relig confessione f; ⟨money⟩ valore f
denounce /dɪˈnaʊns/ vt denunciare
dens|e /dens/ a denso; ⟨crowd,
forest⟩ fitto; ⟨stupid⟩ ottuso. **~ely**
adv ⟨populated⟩ densamente.
~ely wooded fittamente ricoperto di alberi. **~ity** n densità f inv;
⟨of forest⟩ fittezza f
dent /dent/ n ammaccatura f ● vt
ammaccare. **~ed** a ammaccato
dental /ˈdentl/ a dei denti;
⟨treatment⟩ dentistico; ⟨hygiene⟩
dentale. **~ surgeon** n odontoiatra
mf, medico m dentista

dentist /ˈdentɪst/ n dentista mf.
~ry n odontoiatria f
dentures /ˈdentʃəz/ npl dentiera
fsg
denunciation /dɪnʌnsɪˈeɪʃn/ n de-
nuncia f
deny /dɪˈnaɪ/ vt ⟨pt/pp -ied⟩ negare; ⟨officially⟩ smentire; **~ sb sth**
negare qcsa a qcno
deodorant /diːˈəʊdərənt/ n deodorante m
depart /dɪˈpɑːt/ vi ⟨plane, train⟩
partire; ⟨liter: person⟩ andare via;
⟨deviate⟩ allontanarsi **⟨from** da⟩
department /dɪˈpɑːtmənt/ n reparto m; Pol ministero m; ⟨of
company⟩ sezione f; Univ diparti-
mento m. **~ store** n grande magazzino m
departure /dɪˈpɑːtʃə(r)/ n partenza f; ⟨from rule⟩ allontanamento
m; **new ~** svolta f
depend /dɪˈpend/ vi dipendere ⟨on
da⟩; ⟨rely⟩ contare ⟨on su⟩; **it all
~s** dipende; **~ing on what he
says** a seconda di quello che dice.
~able /-əbl/ a fidato. **~ant** n persona f a carico. **~ence** n dipen-
denza f. **~ent** a dipendente ⟨on da⟩
depict /dɪˈpɪkt/ vt ⟨in writing⟩ dipingere; ⟨with picture⟩ rappresentare
depilatory /dɪˈpɪlətərɪ/ n ⟨cream⟩
crema f depilatoria
deplete /dɪˈpliːt/ vt ridurre;
totally ~d completamente esaurito
deplor|able /dɪˈplɔːrəbl/ a deplo-
revole. **~e** vt deplorare
deploy /dɪˈplɔɪ/ vt Mil spiegare
● vi schierarsi
deport /dɪˈpɔːt/ vt deportare.
~ation /diːpɔːˈteɪʃn/ n deportazio-
ne f
depose /dɪˈpəʊz/ vt deporre
deposit /dɪˈpɒzɪt/ n deposito m;
⟨against damage⟩ cauzione f; ⟨first
instalment⟩ acconto m ● vt ⟨pt/pp
deposited⟩ depositare. **~ account** n libretto m di risparmio;

(*without instant access*) conto *m* vincolato

depot /'depǝʊ/ *n* deposito *m*; *Am Rail* stazione *f* ferroviaria

deprav|e /dɪ'preɪv/ *vt* depravare. **~ed** *a* depravato. **~ity** /-'prævǝtɪ/ *n* depravazione *f*

depreciat|e /dɪ'priːʃɪeɪt/ *vi* deprezzarsi. **~ion** /-'eɪʃn/ *n* deprezzamento *m*

depress /dɪ'pres/ *vt* deprimere; (*press down*) premere. **~ed** *a* depresso; **~ed area** zona *f* depressa. **~ing** *a* deprimente. **~ion** /-eʃn/ *n* depressione *f*

deprivation /deprɪ'veɪʃn/ *n* privazione *f*

deprive /dɪ'praɪv/ *vt* **~ sb of qcsa** privare qcno di qcsa. **~d** *a* (*area, childhood*) disagiato

depth /depθ/ *n* profondità *f*; **in ~** (*study, analyse*) in modo approfondito; **in the ~s of winter** in pieno inverno; **be out of one's ~** (*in water*) non toccare il fondo; *fig* sentirsi in alto mare

deputation /depjʊ'teɪʃn/ *n* deputazione *f*

deputize /'depjʊtaɪz/ *vi* **~ for** fare le veci di

deputy /'depjʊtɪ/ *n* vice *mf*; (*temporary*) sostituto, -a *mf* ●*attrib* **~ leader** ≈ vicesegretario, -a *mf*; **~ chairman** vicepresidente *mf*

derail /dɪ'reɪl/ *vt* **be ~ed** (*train*) essere deragliato. **~ment** *n* deragliamento *m*

deranged /dɪ'reɪndʒd/ *a* squilibrato

derelict /'derǝlɪkt/ *a* abbandonato

deri|de /dɪ'raɪd/ *vt* deridere. **~sion** /-'rɪʒn/ *n* derisione *f*

derisory /dɪ'raɪsǝrɪ/ *a* (*laughter*) derisorio; (*offer*) irrisorio

derivation /derɪ'veɪʃn/ *n* derivazione *f*

derivative /dɪ'rɪvǝtɪv/ *a* derivato ●*n* derivato *m*

derive /dɪ'raɪv/ *vt* (*obtain*) derivare; **be ~d from** (*word:*) derivare da

dermatologist /dɜːmǝ'tɒlǝdʒɪst/ *n* dermatologo, -a *mf*

derogatory /dɪ'rɒgǝtrɪ/ *a* (*comments*) peggiorativo

descend /dɪ'send/ *vi* scendere ●*vt* scendere da; **be ~ed from** discendere da. **~ant** *n* discendente *mf*

descent /dɪ'sent/ *n* discesa *f*; (*lineage*) origine *f*

describe /dɪ'skraɪb/ *vt* descrivere

description /dɪ'skrɪpʃn/ *n* descrizione *f*; **they had no help of any ~tion** non hanno avuto proprio nessun aiuto. **~tive** /-tɪv/ *a* descrittivo; (*vivid*) vivido

desecrat|e /'desɪkreɪt/ *vt* profanare. **~ion** /-'kreɪʃn/ *n* profanazione *f*

desert[1] /'dezǝt/ *n* deserto ●*a* deserto; **~ island** isola *f* deserta

desert[2] /dɪ'zɜːt/ *vt* abbandonare ●*vi* disertare. **~ed** *a* deserto. **~er** *n* Mil disertore *m*. **~ion** /-'zɜːʃn/ *n* Mil diserzione *f*; (*of family*) abbandono *m*

deserts /dɪ'zɜːts/ *npl* **get one's just ~** ottenere ciò che ci si merita

deserv|e /dɪ'zɜːv/ *vt* meritare. **~ing** *a* meritevole; **~ing cause** opera *f* meritoria

design /dɪ'zaɪn/ *n* progettazione *f*; (*fashion, appearance*) design *m inv*; (*pattern*) modello *m*; (*aim*) proposito *m* ●*vt* progettare; disegnare (*clothes, furniture, model*); **be ~ed for** essere fatto per

designat|e /'dezɪgneɪt/ *vt* designare. **~ion** /-'neɪʃn/ *n* designazione *f*

designer /dɪ'zaɪnǝ(r)/ *n* progettista *mf*; (*of clothes*) stilista *mf*; (*Theat: of set*) scenografo, -a *mf*

desirable /dɪ'zaɪǝrǝbl/ *a* desiderabile

desire /dɪ'zaɪǝ(r)/ *n* desiderio *m* ●*vt* desiderare

desk /desk/ *n* scrivania *f*; (*in school*) banco *m*; (*in hotel*) reception *f inv*; (*cash ~*) cassa *f*. **~top 'publishing** *n* desktop publishing *m*, editoria *f* da tavolo

desolat|e /ˈdesələt/ *a* desolato. **~ion** /-ˈleɪʃn/ *n* desolazione *f*

despair /dɪˈspeə(r)/ *n* disperazione *f*; **in ~** disperato; ⟨say⟩ per disperazione ● *vi* **I ~ of that boy** quel ragazzo mi fa disperare

desperat|e /ˈdespərət/ *a* disperato; **be ~e** ⟨criminal:⟩ essere un disperato; **be ~e for sth** morire dalla voglia di. **~ely** *adv* disperatamente; **he said ~ely** ha detto, disperato. **~ion** /-ˈreɪʃn/ *n* disperazione *f*; **in ~ion** per disperazione

despicable /dɪˈspɪkəbl/ *a* disprezzevole

despise /dɪˈspaɪz/ *vt* disprezzare

despite /dɪˈspaɪt/ *prep* malgrado

despondent /dɪˈspɒndənt/ *a* abbattuto

despot /ˈdespɒt/ *n* despota *m*

dessert /dɪˈzɜːt/ *n* dolce *m*. **~ spoon** *n* cucchiaio *m* da dolce

destination /destɪˈneɪʃn/ *n* destinazione *f*

destine /ˈdestɪn/ *vt* destinare; **be ~d for sth** essere destinato a qcsa

destiny /ˈdestɪnɪ/ *n* destino *m*

destitute /ˈdestɪtjuːt/ *a* bisognoso

destroy /dɪˈstrɔɪ/ *vt* distruggere. **~er** *n* Naut cacciatorpediniere *m*

destruc|tion /dɪˈstrʌkʃn/ *n* distruzione *f*. **~tive** /-tɪv/ *a* distruttivo; ⟨fig: criticism⟩ negativo

detach /dɪˈtætʃ/ *vt* staccare. **~able** /-əbl/ *a* separabile. **~ed** *a* distaccato; **~ed house** villetta *f*

detachment /dɪˈtætʃmənt/ *n* distacco *m*; Mil distaccamento *m*

detail /ˈdiːteɪl/ *n* particolare *m*, dettaglio *m*; **in ~** particolareggiatamente ● *vt* esporre con tutti i particolari; Mil assegnare. **~ed** *a* particolareggiato, dettagliato

detain /dɪˈteɪn/ *vt* ⟨police:⟩ trattenere; ⟨delay⟩ far ritardare. **~ee** /diːteɪˈniː/ *n* detenuto, -a *f*

detect /dɪˈtekt/ *vt* individuare; ⟨perceive⟩ percepire. **~ion** /-ekʃn/ *n* scoperta *f*

detective /dɪˈtektɪv/ *n* investigato-

re, -trice *mf*. **~ story** *n* racconto *m* poliziesco

detector /dɪˈtektə(r)/ *n* ⟨for metal⟩ metal detector *m inv*

detention /dɪˈtenʃn/ *n* detenzione *f*; Sch punizione *f*

deter /dɪˈtɜː(r)/ *vt* (pt/pp **deterred**) impedire; **~ sb from doing sth** impedire a qcno di fare qcsa

detergent /dɪˈtɜːdʒənt/ *n* detersivo *m*

deteriorat|e /dɪˈtɪərɪəreɪt/ *vi* deteriorarsi. **~ion** /-ˈreɪʃn/ *n* deterioramento *m*

determination /dɪtɜːmɪˈneɪʃn/ *n* determinazione *f*

determine /dɪˈtɜːmɪn/ *vt* ⟨ascertain⟩ determinare; **~ to** ⟨resolve⟩ decidere di. **~d** *a* deciso

deterrent /dɪˈterənt/ *n* deterrente *m*

detest /dɪˈtest/ *vt* detestare. **~able** /-əbl/ *a* detestabile

detonat|e /ˈdetəneɪt/ *vt* far detonare ● *vi* detonare. **~or** *n* detonatore *m*

detour /ˈdiːtʊə(r)/ *n* deviazione *f*

detract /dɪˈtrækt/ *vi* **~ from** sminuire ⟨merit⟩; rovinare ⟨pleasure, beauty⟩

detriment /ˈdetrɪmənt/ *n* **to the ~ of** a danno di. **~al** /-ˈmentl/ *a* dannoso

deuce /djuːs/ *n* Tennis deuce *m inv*

devaluation /diːvæljʊˈeɪʃn/ *n* svalutazione *f*

de'value *vt* svalutare ⟨currency⟩

devastat|e /ˈdevəsteɪt/ *vt* devastare. **~ed** *a* fam sconvolto. **~ing** *a* devastante; ⟨news⟩ sconvolgente. **~ion** /-ˈsteɪʃn/ *n* devastazione *f*

develop /dɪˈveləp/ *vt* sviluppare; contrarre ⟨illness⟩; ⟨add to value of⟩ valorizzare ⟨area⟩ ● *vi* svilupparsi; **~ into** diventare. **~er** *n* ⟨property⟩ **~er** imprenditore, -trice *mf* edile

de'veloping country *n* paese *m* in via di sviluppo

development /dɪˈveləpmənt/ *n*

sviluppo *m*; *(of vaccine etc)* messa *f* a punto

deviant /'di:vɪənt/ *a* deviato

deviat|e /'di:vɪeɪt/ *vi* deviare. **~ion** /-'eɪʃn/ *n* deviazione *f*

device /dɪ'vaɪs/ *n* dispositivo *m*

devil /'devl/ *n* diavolo *m*

devious /'di:vɪəs/ *a (a person)* subdolo; *(route)* tortuoso

devise /dɪ'vaɪz/ *vt* escogitare

devoid /dɪ'vɔɪd/ *a* **~ of** privo di

devolution /di:və'lu:ʃn/ *n (of power)* decentramento *m*

devot|e /dɪ'vəʊt/ *vt* dedicare. **~ed** *a (daughter etc)* affezionato; be **~ed to sth** consacrarsi a qcsa. **~ee** /devə'ti:/ *n* appassionato, -a *mf*

devotion /dɪ'vəʊʃn/ *n* dedizione *f*; **~s** *pl Relig* devozione *fsg*

devour /dɪ'vaʊə(r)/ *vt* divorare

devout /dɪ'vaʊt/ *a* devoto

dew /dju:/ *n* rugiada *f*

dexterity /dek'sterətɪ/ *n* destrezza *f*

diabet|es /daɪə'bi:ti:z/ *n* diabete *m*. **~ic** /-'betɪk/ *a* diabetico ● *n* diabetico, -a *mf*

diabolical /daɪə'bɒlɪkl/ *a* diabolico

diagnose /daɪəg'nəʊz/ *vt* diagnosticare

diagnosis /daɪəg'nəʊsɪs/ *n (pl -oses* /-si:z/) diagnosi *f inv*

diagonal /daɪ'ægənl/ *a* diagonale ● *n* diagonale *f*

diagram /'daɪəgræm/ *n* diagramma *m*

dial /'daɪəl/ *n (of clock, machine)* quadrante *m*; *Teleph* disco *m* combinatore ● *v* (*pt/pp* **dialled**) ● *vi Teleph* fare il numero; **~ direct** chiamare in teleselezione ● *vt* fare *(number)*

dialect /'daɪəlekt/ *n* dialetto *m*

dialling /'daɪəlɪŋ/ **~ code** *n* prefisso *m*. **~ tone** *n* segnale *m* di linea libera

dialogue /'daɪəlɒg/ *n* dialogo *m*

'dial tone *n Am Teleph* segnale *m* di linea libera

diameter /daɪ'æmɪtə(r)/ *n* diametro *m*

diametrically /daɪə'metrɪklɪ/ *adv* **~ opposed** diametralmente opposto

diamond /'daɪəmənd/ *n* diamante *m*, brillante *m*; *(shape)* losanga *f*; **~s** *pl (in cards)* quadri *mpl*

diaper /'daɪəpə(r)/ *n Am* pannolino *m*

diaphragm /'daɪəfræm/ *n* diaframma *m*

diarrhoea /daɪə'ri:ə/ *n* diarrea *f*

diary /'daɪərɪ/ *n (for appointments)* agenda *f*; *(for writing in)* diario *m*

dice /daɪs/ *n inv* dadi *mpl* ● *vt Culin* tagliare a dadini

dicey /'daɪsɪ/ *a fam* rischioso

dictat|e /dɪk'teɪt/ *vt/i* dettare. **~ion** /-eɪʃn/ *n* dettato *m*

dictator /dɪk'teɪtə(r)/ *n* dittatore *m*. **~ial** /-tə'tɔ:rɪəl/ *a* dittatoriale. **~ship** *n* dittatura *f*

dictionary /'dɪkʃənrɪ/ *n* dizionario *m*

did /dɪd/ *see* **do**

didactic /dɪ'dæktɪk/ *a* didattico

diddle /'dɪdl/ *vt fam* gabbare

didn't /'dɪdnt/ = **did not**

die /daɪ/ *vi (pres p* **dying**) morire **(of** di); **be dying to do sth** *fam* morire dalla voglia di fare qcsa. **die down** *vi* calmarsi; *(fire, flames:)* spegnersi. **die out** *vi* estinguersi; *(custom:)* morire

diesel /'di:zl/ *n* diesel *m*

diet /'daɪət/ *n* regime *m* alimentare; *(restricted)* dieta *f*; **be on a ~** essere a dieta ● *vi* essere a dieta

differ /'dɪfə(r)/ *vi* differire; *(disagree)* non essere d'accordo

difference /'dɪfrəns/ *n* differenza *f*; *(disagreement)* divergenza *f*

different /'dɪfrənt/ *a* diverso, differente; *(various)* diversi; **be ~ from** essere diverso da

differential /dɪfə'renʃl/ *a* differenziale ● *n* differenziale *m*

differentiate /dɪfə'renʃɪeɪt/ *vt* distinguere **(between** fra); *(dis-*

criminate) discriminare (**between** fra); (*make differ*) differenziare

differently /'dɪfrəntlɪ/ *adv* in modo diverso; **~ from** diversamente da

difficult /'dɪfɪkəlt/ *a* difficile. **~n** difficoltà *f inv*; **with ~y** con difficoltà

diffuse[1] /dɪ'fju:s/ *a* diffuso; (*wordy*) prolisso

diffuse[2] /dɪ'fju:z/ *vt* Phys diffondere

dig /dɪg/ *n* (*poke*) spinta *f*; (*remark*) frecciata *f*; Archaeol scavo *m*; **~s** *pl fam* camera *fsg* ammobiliata ● *vt/i* (*pt/pp* dug, *pres p* digging) scavare (*hole*); vangare (*garden*); (*thrust*) conficcare; **~ sb in the ribs** dare una gomitata a qcno. **dig out** *vt fig* tirar fuori. **dig up** *vt* scavare (*garden, street, object*); sradicare (*plant*); (*fig: find*) scovare

digest[1] /'daɪdʒest/ *n* compendio *m*

digest[2] /daɪ'dʒest/ *vt* digerire. **~ible** *a* digeribile. **~ion** /-estʃn/ *n* digestione *f*

digger /'dɪgə(r)/ *n* Techn scavatrice *f*

digit /'dɪdʒɪt/ *n* cifra *f*; (*finger*) dito *m*

digital /'dɪdʒɪtl/ *a* digitale; **~ clock** orologio *m* digitale

dignified /'dɪgnɪfaɪd/ *a* dignitoso

dignitary /'dɪgnɪtərɪ/ *n* dignitario *m*

dignity /'dɪgnɪtɪ/ *n* dignità *f*

digress /daɪ'gres/ *vi* divagare. **~ion** /-eʃn/ *n* digressione *f*

dike /daɪk/ *n* diga *f*

dilapidated /dɪ'læpɪdeɪtɪd/ *a* cadente

dilate /daɪ'leɪt/ *vi* dilatarsi

dilemma /dɪ'lemə/ *n* dilemma *m*

dilettante /dɪlɪ'tæntɪ/ *n* dilettante *mf*

dilly-dally /'dɪlɪdælɪ/ *vi* (*pt/pp* -ied) *fam* tentennare

dilute /daɪ'lu:t/ *vt* diluire

dim /dɪm/ *a* (**dimmer, dimmest**) debole (*light*); (*dark*) scuro; (*prospect, chance*) scarso; (*indis*-

tinct) impreciso; (*fam: stupid*) tonto ● *vt/i* (*pt/pp* dimmed) affievolire. **~ly** *adv* (*see, remember*) indistintamente; (*shine*) debolmente

dime /daɪm/ *n Am* moneta *f* da dieci centesimi

dimension /daɪ'menʃn/ *n* dimensione *f*

diminish /dɪ'mɪnɪʃ/ *vt/i* diminuire

diminutive /dɪ'mɪnjʊtɪv/ *a* minuscolo ● *n* diminutivo *m*

dimple /'dɪmpl/ *n* fossetta *f*

din /dɪn/ *n* baccano *m*

dine /daɪn/ *vi* pranzare. **~ r** *n* (*Am: restaurant*) tavola *f* calda; the last **~ r in the restaurant** l'ultimo cliente nel ristorante

dinghy /'dɪŋgɪ/ *n* dinghy *m*; (*inflatable*) canotto *m* pneumatico

dingy /'dɪndʒɪ/ *a* (**-ier, -iest**) squallido e tetro

dining /'daɪnɪŋ/: **~car** *n* carrozza *f* ristorante. **~room** *n* sala *f* da pranzo. **~table** *n* tavolo *m* da pranzo

dinner /'dɪnə(r)/ *n* cena *f*; (*at midday*) pranzo *m*. **~jacket** *n* smoking *m inv*

dinosaur /'daɪnəsɔ:(r)/ *n* dinosauro *m*

dint /dɪnt/ *n* **by ~ of** a forza di

diocese /'daɪəsɪs/ *n* diocesi *f inv*

dip /dɪp/ *n* (*in ground*) inclinazione *f*; Culin salsina *f*; **go for a ~** andare a fare una nuotata ● *v* (*pt/pp* dipped) ● *vt* (*in liquid*) immergere; abbassare (*head, headlights*) ● *vi* (*land:*) formare un avvallamento. **dip into** *vt* scorrere (*book*)

diphtheria /dɪf'θɪərɪə/ *n* difterite *f*

diphthong /'dɪfθɒŋ/ *n* dittongo *m*

diploma /dɪ'pləʊmə/ *n* diploma *m*

diplomacy /dɪ'pləʊməsɪ/ *n* diplomazia *f*

diplomat /'dɪpləmæt/ *n* diplomatico, -a *mf*. **~ic** /-'mætɪk/ *a* diplomatico. **~ically** *adv* con diplomazia

dip-stick *n* Auto astina *f* dell'olio

dire /'daɪə(r)/ *a* (*situation, consequences*) terribile

direct /dɪ'rekt/ a diretto ● adv direttamente ● vt (aim) rivolgere ⟨attention, criticism⟩; (control) dirigere; fare la regia di ⟨film, play⟩; ~ sb (show the way) indicare la strada a qcno; ~ sb to do sth ordinare a qcno di fare qcsa. ~ 'current n corrente m continua

direction /dɪ'rekʃn/ n direzione f; ⟨of play, film⟩ regia f; ~s pl indicazioni fpl

directly /dɪ'rektlɪ/ adv direttamente; (at once) immediatamente ● conj [non] appena

director /dɪ'rektə(r)/ n Comm direttore, -trice mf; ⟨of play, film⟩ regista mf

directory /dɪ'rektərɪ/ n elenco m; Teleph elenco m [telefonico]; ⟨of streets⟩ stradario m

dirt /dɜːt/ n sporco m; ~ cheap fam a [un] prezzo stracciato

dirty /'dɜːtɪ/ a (-ier, -iest) sporco; ~ trick brutto scherzo m; ~ word parolaccia f ● vt (pt/pp -ied) sporcare

disa|bility /dɪsə'bɪlətɪ/ n infermità f inv. ~abled /dɪ'seɪbld/ a invalido

disad'van|tage n svantaggio m; at a ~tage in una posizione di svantaggio. ~taged a svantaggiato. ~tageous a svantaggioso

disa'gree vi non essere d'accordo; ~ with ⟨food⟩ far male a

disa'greeable a sgradevole

disa'greement n disaccordo m; ⟨quarrel⟩ dissidio m

disal'low vt annullare ⟨goal⟩

disap'pear vi scomparire. ~ance n scomparsa f

disap'point vt deludere; I'm ~ed sono deluso. ~ing a deludente. ~ment n delusione f

disap'proval n disapprovazione f

disap'prove vi disapprovare; ~ of sb/sth disapprovare qcno/qcsa

dis'arm vt disarmare ● vi Mil disarmarsi. ~ament n disarmo m. ~ing a ⟨frankness etc⟩ disarmante

disar'ray n in ~ in disordine

disast|er /dɪ'zɑːstə(r)/ n disastro m. ~rous /-rəs/ a disastroso

dis'band vt scogliere; smobilitare ⟨troops⟩ ● vi scogliersi; ⟨regiment⟩ essere smobilitato

disbe'lief n incredulità f; in ~ con incredulità

disc /dɪsk/ n disco m; ⟨CD⟩ compact disc m inv

discard /dɪ'skɑːd/ vt scartare; ⟨throw away⟩ eliminare; scaricare ⟨boyfriend⟩

discern /dɪ'sɜːn/ vt discernere. ~ible a discernibile. ~ing a perspicace

dis'charge¹ n Electr scarica f; ⟨dismissal⟩ licenziamento m; Mil congedo m; ⟨Med: of blood⟩ emissione f; ⟨of cargo⟩ scarico m

dis'charge² vt scaricare ⟨battery, cargo⟩; ⟨dismiss⟩ licenziare; Mil congedare; Jur assolvere ⟨accused⟩; dimettere ⟨patient⟩ ● vi Electr scaricarsi

disciple /dɪ'saɪpl/ n discepolo m

disciplinary /'dɪsɪplɪnərɪ/ a disciplinare

discipline /'dɪsɪplɪn/ n disciplina f ● vt disciplinare; ⟨punish⟩ punire

'disc jockey n disc jockey m inv

dis'claim vt disconoscere. ~er n rifiuto m

dis'close vt svelare. ~ure n rivelazione f

disco /'dɪskəʊ/ n discoteca f

dis'colour vt scolorire ● vi scolorirsi

dis'comfort n scomodità f; fig disagio m

disconcert /dɪskən'sɜːt/ vt sconcertare

discon'nect vt disconnettere

disconsolate /dɪs'kɒnsələt/ a sconsolato

discon'tent n scontentezza f. ~ed a scontento

discon'tinue vt cessare, smettere; Comm sospendere la produzione di; ~d line fine f serie

'discord n discordia f; Mus dissonanza f. **~ant** /dɪˈskɔːdənt/ a **~ant note** nota f discordante

discothèque /ˈdɪskətek/ n discoteca f

'discount¹ n sconto m

dis'count² vt (not believe) non credere a; (leave out of consideration) non tener conto di

dis'courage vt scoraggiare; (dissuade) dissuadere

'discourse n discorso m

dis'courteous a scortese

discover /dɪˈskʌvə(r)/ vt scoprire. **~y** n scoperta f

dis'credit n discredito m ● vt (pt/pp **discredited**) screditare

discreet /dɪˈskriːt/ a discreto

discrepancy /dɪˈskrepənsɪ/ n discrepanza f

discretion /dɪˈskreʃn/ n discrezione f

discriminat|e /dɪˈskrɪmɪneɪt/ vi discriminare (against contro); **~e between** distinguere tra. **~ing** a esigente. **~ion** /-ˈneɪʃn/ n discriminazione f; (quality) discernimento m

discus /ˈdɪskəs/ n disco m

discuss /dɪˈskʌs/ vt discutere; (examine critically) esaminare. **~ion** /-ʌʃn/ n discussione f

disdain /dɪsˈdeɪn/ n sdegno f ● vt sdegnare. **~ful** a sdegnoso

disease /dɪˈziːz/ n malattia f. **~d** a malato

disem'bark vi sbarcare

disen'chant vt disincantare. **~ment** n disincanto m

disen'gage vt disimpegnare; disinnestare (clutch)

disen'tangle vt districare

dis'favour n sfavore m

dis'figure vt deformare

dis'grace n vergogna f; **I am in ~** sono caduto in disgrazia; **it's a ~** è una vergogna. **~ful** a vergognoso

disgruntled /dɪsˈɡrʌntld/ a malcontento

disguise /dɪsˈɡaɪz/ n travestimento m; **in ~** travestito ● vt contraf-

fare (voice); dissimulare (emotions); **~d as** travestito da

disgust /dɪsˈɡʌst/ n disgusto m; **in ~ con** aria disgustata ● vt disgustare. **~ing** a disgustoso

dish /dɪʃ/ n piatto m; **do the ~es** lavare i piatti ● **dish out** vt (serve) servire; (distribute) distribuire. **dish up** vt servire

'dishcloth n strofinaccio m

dis'hearten vt scoraggiare

dishevelled /dɪˈʃevld/ a scompigliato

dis'honest a disonesto. **~y** n disonestà f

dis'honour n disonore m ● vt disonorare (family); non onorare (cheque). **~able** a disonorevole. **~ably** adv in modo disonorevole

'dishwasher n lavapiatti f inv

disil'lusion vt disilludere. **~ment** n disillusione f

disin'fect vt disinfettare. **~ant** n disinfettante m

disin'herit vt diseredare

disin'tegrate vi disintegrarsi

disin'terested a disinteressato

dis'jointed a sconnesso

disk /dɪsk/ n Comput disco m; (diskette) dischetto m

dis'like n avversione f; **your likes and ~s** i tuoi gusti ● vt **I ~ him/it** non mi piace; **I don't ~ him/it** non mi dispiace

dislocate /ˈdɪsləkeɪt/ vt slogare; **~ one's shoulder** slogarsi una spalla

dis'lodge vt sloggiare

dis'loyal a sleale. **~ty** n slealtà f

dismal /ˈdɪzməl/ a (person) abbacchiato; (news, weather) deprimente; (performance) mediocre

dismantle /dɪsˈmæntl/ vt smontare (tent, machine); fig smantellare

dis'may n sgomento m. **~ed** a sgomento

dis'miss vt licenziare (employee); (reject) scartare (idea, suggestion). **~al** n licenziamento m

dis'mount vi smontare

diso'bedien|ce n disubbidienza f. **~t** a disubbidiente

dis'obey vt disubbidire a ⟨rule⟩ ● vi disubbidire

dis'order n disordine m; Med disturbo m. **~ly** a disordinato; ⟨crowd⟩ turbolento; **~ly conduct** turbamento m della quiete pubblica

dis'organized a disorganizzato

dis'orientate vt disorientare

dis'own vt disconoscere

disparaging /dɪ'spærɪdʒɪŋ/ a sprezzante

disparity /dɪ'spærəti/ n disparità f inv

dispassionate /dɪ'spæʃənət/ a spassionato

dispatch /dɪ'spætʃ/ n Comm spedizione f; ⟨Mil, report⟩ dispaccio m; **with ~** con prontezza ● vt spedire; ⟨kill⟩ spedire al creatore

dispel /dɪ'spel/ vt (pt/pp **dispelled**) dissipare

dispensable /dɪ'spensəbl/ a dispensabile

dispensary /dɪ'spensəri/ n farmacia f

dispense /dɪ'spens/ vt distribuire; **~ with** fare a meno di; **dispensing chemist** farmacista mf; ⟨shop⟩ farmacia f. **~r** n ⟨device⟩ distributore m

dispers|al /dɪ'spɜ:sl/ n disperzione f. **~e** /dɪ'spɜ:s/ vt disperdere ● vi disperdersi

dispirited /dɪ'spɪrɪtɪd/ a scoraggiato

dis'place vt spostare; **~d person** profugo, -a mf

display /dɪ'spleɪ/ n mostra f; Comm esposizione f; ⟨of feelings⟩ manifestazione f; pej ostentazione f, Comput display m inv ● vt mostrare; esporre ⟨goods⟩; manifestare ⟨feeling⟩; Comput visualizzare

dis'please vt non piacere a; **be ~d with** essere scontento di

dis'pleasure n malcontento m

disposable /dɪ'spəʊzəbl/ a ⟨throwaway⟩ usa e getta; ⟨income⟩ disponibile

disposal /dɪ'spəʊzl/ n ⟨getting rid of⟩ eliminazione f; **be at sb's ~** essere a disposizione di qcno

dispose /dɪ'spəʊz/ vi **~ of** ⟨get rid of⟩ disfarsi di; **be well ~d** essere ben disposto (**to** verso)

disposition /dɪspə'zɪʃn/ n disposizione f; ⟨nature⟩ indole f

disproportionate /dɪsprə'pɔ:ʃənət/ a sproporzionato

dis'prove vt confutare

dispute /dɪ'spju:t/ n disputa f; ⟨industrial⟩ contestazione f ● vt contestare ⟨statement⟩

disqualifi'cation n squalifica f; ⟨from driving⟩ ritiro m della patente

dis'qualify vt (pt/pp **-ied**) escludere; Sport squalificare; **~ sb from driving** ritirare la patente a qcno

disquieting /dɪs'kwaɪətɪŋ/ a allarmante

disre'gard n mancanza f di considerazione ● vt ignorare

disre'pair n fall into **~** deteriorarsi; **in a state of ~** in cattivo stato

dis'reputable a malfamato

disre'pute n discredito m; **bring sb into ~** rovinare la reputazione a qcno

disre'spect n mancanza f di rispetto. **~ful** a irrispettoso

disrupt /dɪs'rʌpt/ vt creare scompiglio in; sconvolgere ⟨plans⟩. **~ion** /-ʌpʃn/ n scompiglio m; ⟨of plans⟩ sconvolgimento m. **~ive** /-tɪv/ a ⟨person, behaviour⟩ indisciplinato

dissatis'faction n malcontento m

dis'satisfied a scontento

dissect /dɪ'sekt/ vt sezionare. **~ion** /-ekʃn/ n dissezione f

dissent /dɪ'sent/ n dissenso m ● vi dissentire

dissertation /dɪsə'teɪʃn/ n tesi f inv

dis'service n **do sb/oneself a ~** rendere un cattivo servizio a qcno/se stesso

dissident /'dɪsɪdənt/ n dissidente mf

dis'similar a dissimile (**to** da)

dissociate /dɪ'səʊʃɪet/ vt dissociare; ~ **oneself from** dissociarsi da

dissolute /'dɪsəluːt/ a dissoluto

dissolution /dɪsə'luːʃn/ n scioglimento m

dissolve /dɪ'zɒlv/ vt dissolvere ● vi dissolversi

dissuade /dɪ'sweɪd/ vt dissuadere

distance /'dɪstəns/ n distanza f; **it's a short ~ from here to the station** la stazione non è lontana da qui; **in the ~** in lontananza; **from a ~** da lontano

distant /'dɪstənt/ a distante; (relative) lontano

dis'taste n avversione f. **~ful** a spiacevole

distil /dɪ'stɪl/ vt (pt/pp **distilled**) distillare. **~lation** /-'leɪʃn/ n distillazione f. **~lery** /-ərɪ/ n distilleria f

distinct /dɪ'stɪŋkt/ a chiaro; (different) distinto. **~ion** /-ɪŋkʃn/ n distinzione f; Sch massimo m dei voti. **~ive** /-tɪv/ a caratteristico. **~ly** adv chiaramente

distinguish /dɪ'stɪŋwɪʃ/ vt/i distinguere; ~ **oneself** distinguersi. **~ed** a rinomato; (appearance) distinto; (career) brillante

distort /dɪ'stɔːt/ vt distorcere. **~ion** /-ɔːʃn/ n distorsione f

distract /dɪ'strækt/ vt distrarre. **~ed** /-ɪd/ a assente; (fam: worried) preoccupato. **~ing** a che distoglie. **~ion** /-ækʃn/ n distrazione f; (despair) disperazione f; **drive sb to ~** portare qcno alla disperazione

distraught /dɪ'strɔːt/ a sconvolto

distress /dɪ'stres/ n angoscia f; (pain) sofferenza f; (danger) difficoltà f ● vt sconvolgere; (sadden) affliggere. **~ing** a penoso; (shocking) sconvolgente. **~ signal** n segnale m di richiesta di soccorso

distribute /dɪ'strɪbjuːt/ vt distri-

buire. **~ion** /-'bjuːʃn/ n distribuzione f. **~or** n distributore m

district /'dɪstrɪkt/ n regione f; Admin distretto m. **~ nurse** n infermiere, -a mf che fa visite a domicilio

dis'trust n sfiducia f ● vt non fidarsi di. **~ful** a diffidente

disturb /dɪ'stɜːb/ vt disturbare; (emotionally) turbare; spostare (papers). **~ance** n disturbo m; **~ances** (pl: rioting etc) disordini mpl. **~ed** a turbato; [mentally] **~ed** malato di mente. **~ing** a inquietante

dis'used a non utilizzato

ditch /dɪtʃ/ n fosso m ● vt (fam: abandon) abbandonare (plan, car); piantare (lover)

dither /'dɪðə(r)/ vi titubare

divan /dɪ'væn/ n divano m

dive /daɪv/ n tuffo m; Aeron picchiata f; (fam: place) bettola f ● vi tuffarsi; (when in water) immergersi; Aeron scendere in picchiata; (fam: rush) precipitarsi

diver /'daɪvə(r)/ n (from board) tuffatore, -trice mf; (scuba) sommozzatore, -trice mf; (deep sea) palombaro m

diverge /daɪ'vɜːdʒ/ vi divergere. **~gent** /-ənt/ a divergente

diverse /daɪ'vɜːs/ a vario

diversify /daɪ'vɜːsɪfaɪ/ vt/i (pt/pp -ied) diversificare

diversion /daɪ'vɜːʃn/ n deviazione f; (distraction) diversivo m

diversity /daɪ'vɜːsətɪ/ n varietà f

divert /daɪ'vɜːt/ vt deviare (traffic); distogliere (attention)

divest /daɪ'vest/ vt privare (**of** di)

divide /dɪ'vaɪd/ vt dividere (**by** per); **six ~d by two** sei diviso due ● vi dividersi

dividend /'dɪvɪdend/ n dividendo m; **pay ~s** fig ripagare

divine /dɪ'vaɪn/ a divino

diving /'daɪvɪŋ/ n (from board) tuffi mpl; (scuba) immersione f. **~-board** n trampolino m. **~ mask**

n maschera *f* [subacquea]. **~-suit** *n* muta *f*; (*deep sea*) scafandro *m*

divinity /dɪˈvɪnətɪ/ *n* divinità *f inv*; (*subject*) teologia *f*; (*at school*) religione *f*

divisible /dɪˈvɪzɪbl/ *a* divisibile (**by** per)

division /dɪˈvɪʒn/ *n* divisione *f*; (*in sports league*) serie *f*

divorce /dɪˈvɔːs/ *n* divorzio *m* ● *vt* divorziare da. **~d** *a* divorziato; **get ~d** divorziare

divorcee /dɪvɔːˈsiː/ *n* divorziato, -a *mf*

divulge /daɪˈvʌldʒ/ *vt* rendere pubblico

DIY *n abbr* do-it-yourself

dizziness /ˈdɪzɪnɪs/ *n* giramenti *mpl* di testa

dizzy /ˈdɪzɪ/ *a* (**-ier, -iest**) vertiginoso; **I feel ~** mi gira la testa

do /duː/ *n* (*pl* **dos** *or* **do's**) *fam* festa *f* ● *v* (3 *sg pres tense* **does**; *pt* **did**; *pp* **done**) ● *vt* fare; (*fam: cheat*) fregare; **be done** *Culin* essere cotto; **well done** bravo; *Culin* ben cotto; **do the flowers** sistemare i fiori; **do the washing up** lavare i piatti; **do one's hair** farsi i capelli ● *vi* (*be suitable*) andare; (*be enough*) bastare; **this will do** questo va bene; **that will do!** basta così!; **do well/badly** cavarsela bene/male; **how is he doing?** come sta? ● *v aux* **do you speak Italian?** parli italiano?; **you don't like him, do you?** non ti piace, vero?; (*expressing astonishment*) non dirmi che ti piace!; **yes, I do** sì; (*emphatic*) invece sì; **no, I don't** no, I don't; **I don't smoke** non fumo; **don't you/doesn't he?** vero?; **so do I** anch'io; **do come in, John** entra, John; **how do you do?** piacere. **do away with** *vt* abolire (*rule*). **do for** *vt* **done for** *fam* rovinato. **do in** *vt* (*fam: kill*) uccidere; farsi male a (*back*); **done in** *fam* esausto. **do up** *vt* (*fasten*) abbottonare; (*renovate*) rimettere a nuovo; (*wrap*) avvolgere. **do with** *vt*

could do with a spanner mi ci vorrebbe una chiave inglese. **do without** *vt* fare a meno di

docile /ˈdəʊsaɪl/ *a* docile

dock[1] /dɒk/ *n Jur* banco *m* degli imputati

dock[2] *n Naut* bacino *m* ● *vi* entrare in porto; (*spaceship:*) congiungersi. **~er** *n* portuale *m*. **~s** *npl* porto *m*. **~yard** *n* cantiere *m* navale

doctor /ˈdɒktə(r)/ *n* dottore *m*, dottoressa *f* ● *vt* alterare (*drink*); castrare (*cat*). **~ate** /-ət/ *n* dottorato *m*

doctrine /ˈdɒktrɪn/ *n* dottrina *f*

document /ˈdɒkjʊmənt/ *n* documento *m*. **~ary** /-ˈmentərɪ/ *a* documentario ● *n* documentario *m*

doddery /ˈdɒdərɪ/ *a fam* barcollante

dodge /dɒdʒ/ *n fam* trucco *m* ● *vt* schivare (*blow*); evitare (*person*) ● *vi* scansarsi; **~ out of the way** scansarsi

dodgems /ˈdɒdʒəmz/ *npl* autoscontro *msg*

dodgy /ˈdɒdʒɪ/ *a* (**-ier, -iest**) (*fam: dubious*) sospetto

doe /dəʊ/ *n* femmina *f* (*di daino, renna, lepre*); (*rabbit*) coniglia *f*

does /dʌz/ *see* **do**

doesn't /ˈdʌznt/ = **does not**

dog /dɒg/ *n* cane *m* ● *vt* (*pt/pp* **dogged**) (*illness, bad luck:*) perseguitare

dog: **~-biscuit** *n* biscotto *m* per cani. **~-collar** *n* collare *m* (*per cani*); *Relig fam* collare *m* del prete. **~-eared** *a* con le orecchie

dogged /ˈdɒgɪd/ *a* ostinato

'dog house *n* **in the ~** *fam* in disgrazia

dogma /ˈdɒgmə/ *n* dogma *m*. **~tic** /-ˈmætɪk/ *a* dogmatico

'dogsbody *n fam* tirapiedi *mf inv*

doily /ˈdɔɪlɪ/ *n* centrino *m*

do-it-yourself /duːɪtjəˈself/ *n* fai da te *m*, bricolage *m*. **~ shop** *n* negozio *m* di bricolage

doldrums /ˈdɒldrəmz/ *npl* **be in**

the ~ essere giù di corda; (business:) essere in fase di stasi

dole /dəʊl/ n sussidio m di disoccupazione; **be on the ~** essere disoccupato ● **dole out** vt distribuire

doleful /'dəʊlfl/ a triste

doll /dɒl/ n bambola f ● **doll oneself up** vt fam mettersi in ghingheri

dollar /'dɒlə(r)/ n dollaro m

dollop /'dɒləp/ n fam cucchiaiata f

dolphin /'dɒlfɪn/ n delfino m

dome /dəʊm/ n cupola f

domestic /də'mestɪk/ a domestico; Pol interno; Comm nazionale. **~ animal** n animale m domestico

domesticated /də'mestɪkeɪtd/ a (animal) addomesticato

domestic: ~ flight n volo m nazionale. **~ 'servant** n domestico, -a mf

dominant /'dɒmɪnənt/ a dominante

dominate /'dɒmɪneɪt/ vt/i dominare. **~ion** /-'neɪʃn/ n dominio m

domineering /dɒmɪ'nɪərɪŋ/ a autoritario

dominion /də'mɪnjən/ n Br Pol dominion m inv

domino /'dɒmɪnəʊ/ n (pl -es) tessera f del domino; **~es** sg (game) domino m

don¹ /dɒn/ vt (pt/pp donned) liter indossare

don² n docente m/f universitario, -a

donate /dəʊ'neɪt/ vt donare. **~ion** /-eɪʃn/ n donazione f

done /dʌn/ see do

donkey /'dɒŋkɪ/ n asino m; **~'s years** fam anni mpl. **~-work** n sgobbata f

donor /'dəʊnə(r)/ n donatore, -trice mf

don't /dəʊnt/ = **do not**

doodle /'du:dl/ vi scarabocchiare

doom /du:m/ n destino m; (ruin) rovina f ● vt be **~ed** [to failure] essere destinato al fallimento; **~ed** (ship) destinato ad affondare

door /dɔ:(r)/ n porta f; (of car) portiera f; **out of ~s** all'aperto

door: ~man n portiere m. **~mat** n zerbino m. **~step** n gradino m della porta. **~way** n vano m della porta

dope /dəʊp/ n fam (drug) droga f leggera; (information) indiscrezioni fpl; (idiot) idiota mf ● vt drogare; Sport dopare

dopey /'dəʊpɪ/ a fam addormentato

dormant /'dɔ:mənt/ a latente; (volcano) inattivo

dormer /'dɔ:mə(r)/ n ~ [window] abbaino m

dormitory /'dɔ:mɪtərɪ/ n dormitorio m

dormouse /'dɔ:-/ n ghiro m

dosage /'dəʊsɪdʒ/ n dosaggio m

dose /dəʊs/ n dose f

doss /dɒs/ vi sl accamparsi. **~er** n barbone, -a mf. **~house** n dormitorio m pubblico

dot /dɒt/ n punto m; **at 8 o'clock on the ~** alle 8 in punto

dote /dəʊt/ vi ~ on stravedere per

dotted /'dɒtɪd/ a ~ **line** linea f punteggiata; **be ~ with** essere punteggiato di

dotty /'dɒtɪ/ a (-ier, -iest) fam tocco; (idea) folle

double /'dʌbl/ a doppio ● adv **cost ~** costare il doppio; **see ~** vedere doppio; **~ the amount** la quantità doppia ● n doppio m; (person) sosia m inv; **~s** pl Tennis doppio m; **at the ~** di corsa ● vt raddoppiare; (fold) piegare in due ● vi raddoppiare. **double back** vi (go back) fare dietro front. **double up** vi (bend) piegare in due (**with** per); (share) dividere una stanza

double: ~'bass n contrabbasso m. **~ 'bed** n letto m matrimoniale. **~-breasted** a a doppio petto. **~-'chin** n doppio mento m. **~-'cross** vt ingannare. **~-'decker** n autobus m inv a due piani. **~ 'Dutch** n fam ostrogoto m. **~ 'glazing** n doppiovetro m. **~ 'room** n camera f doppia

doubly /'dʌblɪ/ adv doppiamente

doubt /daut/ n dubbio m ● vt dubitare di. ~**ful** a dubbio; (having doubts) in dubbio. ~**fully** adv con aria dubbiosa. ~**less** adv indubbiamente

dough /dəu/ n pasta f. (for bread) impasto m; (fam: money) quattrini mpl. ~**nut** n bombolone m, krapfen m inv

douse /daus/ vt spegnere

dove /dʌv/ n colomba f. ~**tail** n Techn incastro m a coda di rondine

dowdy /'daudɪ/ a (-ier, -iest) trasandato

down[1] /daun/ n (feathers) piumino m

down[2] adv giù; go/come ~ scendere; ~ there laggiù; sales are ~ le vendite sono diminuite; £50 ~ 50 sterline d'acconto; ~ 10% ridotto del 10%; ~ with..! abbasso..! ● prep walk ~ the road camminare per strada; ~ the stairs giù per le scale; fall ~ the stairs cadere giù dalle scale; get that ~ you! fam butta giù!; be ~ the pub fam essere al pub ● vt bere tutto d'un fiato (drink)

down: ~**-and-'out** n spiantato, -a mf. ~**cast** a abbattuto. ~**fall** n caduta f; (of person) rovina f. ~'**grade** vt (in seniority) degradare. ~**-'hearted** a scoraggiato. ~'**hill** adv in discesa; **go** ~**hill** fig essere in declino. ~ **payment** n deposito m. ~'**pour** n acquazzone m. ~'**right** a (absolute) totale; (lie) bell'e buono; (idiot) perfetto ● adv (completely) completamente. ~'**stairs** adv al piano di sotto ● a /'-/ del piano di sotto. ~'**stream** adv a valle. ~**-to-'earth** a (person) con i piedi per terra. ~**town** adv Am in centro. ~**trodden** a oppresso. ~**ward[s]** a verso il basso; (slope) in discesa ● adv verso il basso

dowry /'dauri/ n dote f

doze /dəuz/ n sonnellino m ● vi

sonnecchiare. **doze off** vi assopirsi

dozen /'dʌzn/ n dozzina f; ~**s of books** libri a dozzine

Dr abbr **doctor**

drab /dræb/ a spento

draft[1] /drɑːft/ n abbozzo m; Comm cambiale f; Am Mil leva f ● vt abbozzare; Am Mil arruolare

draft[2] n Am = **draught**

drag /dræg/ n fam scocciatura f; in ~ fam (man) travestito da donna ● vt (pt/pp **dragged**) trascinare; dragare (river). **drag on** vi (time, meeting:) trascinarsi

dragon /'drægən/ n drago m. ~**-fly** n libellula f

drain /dreɪn/ n tubo m di scarico; (grid) tombino m; **be a ~ on sb's finances** prosciugare le finanze di qcno ● vt drenare (land, wound); scolare (liquid, vegetables); svuotare (tank, glass, person) ● vi ~ [away] andar via

drain|age /'dreɪnɪdʒ/ n (system) drenaggio m; (of land) scolo m. ~**ing board** n scolapiatti m inv. ~**pipe** n tubo m di scarico

drake /dreɪk/ n maschio m dell'anatra

drama /'drɑːmə/ n arte f drammatica; (play) opera f teatrale; (event) dramma m

dramatic /drə'mætɪk/ a drammatico

dramat|ist /'dræmətɪst/ n drammaturgo, -a mf. ~**-ize** vt adattare per il teatro; fig drammatizzare

drank /dræŋk/ see **drink**

drape /dreɪp/ n Am tenda f ● vt appoggiare (**over** su)

drastic /'dræstɪk/ a drastico; ~**ally** adv drasticamente

draught /drɑːft/ n corrente f [d'aria]; ~**s** sg (game) [gioco m della] dama f sg

draught: ~ **beer** n birra f alla spina. ~**sman** n disegnatore, -trice mf

draughty /'drɑːftɪ/ *a* a pieno di correnti d'aria: **it's ~** c'è corrente

draw /drɔː/ *n* (*attraction*) attrazione *f*; *Sport* pareggio *m*; (*in lottery*) sorteggio *m* ● *v* (*pt* **drew**, *pp* **drawn**) ● *vt* tirare; (*attract*) attirare; disegnare (*picture*); tracciare (*line*); ritirare (*money*); **~** tirare a sorte ● *vi* (*tea:*) essere in infusione; *Sport* pareggiare; **~ near** avvicinarsi. **draw back** *vt* tirare indietro; ritirare (*hand*); tirare (*curtains*) ● *vi* (*recoil*) tirarsi indietro. **draw in** *vt* ritrarre (*claws etc*) ● *vi* (*train:*) arrivare; (*days:*) accorciarsi. **draw out** *vt* (*pull out*) tirar fuori; ritirare (*money*) ● *vi* (*train:*) partire; (*days:*) allungarsi. **draw up** *vt* redigere (*document*); accostare (*chair*); **~ oneself up to one's full height** farsi grande ● *vi* (*stop*) fermarsi

draw: **~back** *n* inconveniente *m*. **~bridge** *n* ponte *m* levatoio

drawer /drɔː(r)/ *n* cassetto *m*

drawing /'drɔːɪŋ/ *n* disegno *m*

drawing: **~board** *n* tavolo *m* da disegno; *fig* **go back to the ~board** ricominciare da capo. **~pin** *n* puntina *f*. **~room** *n* salotto *m*

drawl /drɔːl/ *n* strascicata *f* cata

drawn /drɔːn/ *see* **draw**

dread /dred/ *n* terrore *m* ● *vt* aver il terrore di

dreadful /'dredfʊl/ *a* terribile. **~ly** *adv* terribilmente

dream /driːm/ *n* sogno *m* ● *attrib* di sogno ● *vt/i* (*pt/pp* **dreamt** /dremt/ *or* **dreamed**) sognare (*about/of* di)

dreary /'drɪərɪ/ *a* (**-ier**, **-iest**) tetro; (*boring*) monotono

dredge /dredʒ/ *vt/i* dragare

dregs /dregz/ *npl* feccia *fsg*

drench /drentʃ/ *vt* **get ~ed** inzupparsi; **~ed** zuppo

dress /dres/ *n* (*woman's*) vestito *m*; (*clothing*) abbigliamento *m* ● *vt*

vestire; (*decorate*) adornare; *Culin* condire; *Med* fasciare; **~ oneself**, **get ~ed** vestirsi ● *vi* vestirsi

dress up *vi* mettersi elegante; (*in disguise*) travestirsi (**as** da)

dress: **~ circle** *n* *Theat* prima galleria *f*. **~er** *n* (*furniture*) credenza *f*; (*Am: dressing-table*) toilette *f*

dressing /'dresɪŋ/ *n* *Culin* condimento *m*; *Med* fasciatura *f*

dressing: **~-gown** *n* vestaglia *f*. **~-room** *n* (*in gym*) spogliatoio *m*; *Theat* camerino *m*. **~-table** *n* toilette *f inv*

dress: **~maker** *n* sarta *f*. **~ rehearsal** *n* prova *f* generale

dressy /'dresɪ/ *a* (**-ier**, **-iest**) elegante

drew /druː/ *see* **draw**

dribble /'drɪbl/ *vi* gocciolare; (*baby:*) sbavare; *Sport* dribblare

dribs and drabs /drɪbzən'dræbz/ *npl* **in ~** alla spicciolata

dried /draɪd/ *a* (*food*) essiccato

drier /'draɪə(r)/ *n* asciugabiancheria *m inv*

drift /drɪft/ *n* movimento *m* lento; (*of snow*) cumulo *m*; (*meaning*) senso *m* ● *vi* (*off course*) andare alla deriva; (*snow:*) accumularsi; (*fig: person:*) procedere senza meta. **drift apart** *vi* (*people:*) allontanarsi l'uno dall'altro

drill /drɪl/ *n* trapano *m*; *Mil* esercitazione *f* ● *vt* trapanare; *Mil* fare esercitare ● *vi* *Mil* esercitarsi; **~ for oil** trivellare in cerca di petrolio

drily /'draɪlɪ/ *adv* seccamente

drink /drɪŋk/ *n* bevanda *f*; (*alcoholic*) bicchierino *m*; **have a ~** bere qualcosa; **a ~ of water** un po' d'acqua ● *vt/i* (*pt* **drank**, *pp* **drunk**) bere. **drink up** *vt* finire ● *vi* finire il bicchiere

drink|able /'drɪŋkəbl/ *a* potabile. **~er** *n* bevitore, **-trice** *mf*

drinking-water *n* acqua *f* potabile

drip /drɪp/ *n* gocciolamento *m*; (*drop*) goccia *f*; *Med* flebo *f inv*;

(fam: person) mollaccione, -a *mf* ● *vi (pt/pp* dripped) gocciolare. ~-'dry *a* che non si stira. ~ping *n (from meat)* grasso *m* d'arrosto ● *a* ~ping [wet] fradicio

drive /draɪv/ *n (in car)* giro *m*; *(entrance)* viale *m*; *(energy)* grinta *f*; *Psych* pulsione *f*; *(organized effort)* operazione *f*; *Techn* motore *m*; *Comput* lettore *m* ● *v (pt* drove, *pp* driven) ● *vt* portare *(person by car)*; guidare *(car)*; *(Sport: hit)* mandare; *Techn* far funzionare; ~ **sb mad** far diventare matto qcno ● *vi* guidare. **drive at** *vt* **what are you driving at?** dove vuoi arrivare? **drive away** *vt* portare via in macchina; *(chase)* cacciare ● *vi* andare via in macchina. **drive in** *vt* piantare *(nail)* ● *vi* arrivare [in macchina]. **drive off** *vt* portare via in macchina; *(chase)* cacciare ● *vi* andare via in macchina. **drive on** *vi* proseguire *(in macchina)*. **drive up** *vi* arrivare *(in macchina)*

drivel /'drɪvl/ *n fam* sciocchezze *fpl*

driven /'drɪvn/ *see* **drive**

driver /'draɪvə(r)/ *n* guidatore, -trice *mf*; *(of train)* conducente *mf*

driving /'draɪvɪŋ/ *a ‹rain›* violento; *‹force›* motore ● *n* guida *f*

driving: ~ **lesson** *n* lezione *f* di guida. ~ **licence** *n* patente *f* di guida. ~ **school** *n* scuola *f* guida. ~ **test** *n* esame *m* di guida

drizzle /'drɪzl/ *n* pioggerella *f* ● *vi* piovigginare

drone /drəʊn/ *n (bee)* fuco *m*; *(sound)* ronzio *m*

droop /druːp/ *vi* abbassarsi; *‹flowers›* afflosciarsi

drop /drɒp/ *n (of liquid)* goccia *f*; *(fall)* caduta *f*; *(in price, temperature)* calo *m* ● *v (pt/pp* dropped) ● *vt* far cadere; sganciare *‹bomb›*; *(omit)* omettere; *(give up)* abbandonare ● *vi* cadere; *‹price, temperature, wind›* calare; *‹ground›* essere in pendenza. **drop in** *vi* passare. **drop off** *vt* depositare *‹person›* ● *vi* cadere; *(fall asleep)*

assopirsi. **drop out** *vi* cadere; *(of race, society)* ritirarsi; ~ **out of school** lasciare la scuola

'drop-out *n* persona *f* contro il sistema sociale

droppings /'drɒpɪŋz/ *npl* sterco *m*

drought /draʊt/ *n* siccità *f*

drove /drəʊv/ *see* **drive**

droves /drəʊvz/ *npl* **in** ~ in massa

drown /draʊn/ *vi* annegare ● *vt* annegare; coprire *‹noise›*; **he was** ~**ed** è annegato

drowsy /'draʊzɪ/ *a* sonnolento

drudgery /'drʌdʒərɪ/ *n* lavoro *m* pesante e noioso

drug /drʌg/ *n* droga *f*; *Med* farmaco *m*; **take** ~**s** drogarsi ● *vt (pt/pp* drugged) drogare

drug: ~ **addict** *n* tossicomane, -a *mf*. ~ **dealer** *n* spacciatore, -trice *mf* [di droga]. ~**gist** *n Am* farmacista *mf*. ~**store** *n Am* negozio *m* di generi vari, inclusi medicinali, che funge anche da bar; *(dispensing)* farmacia *f*

drum /drʌm/ *n* tamburo *m*; *(for oil)* bidone *m*; ~**s** *(pl: in pop-group)* batteria *f* ● *v (pt/pp* drummed) ● *vi* suonare il tamburo; *(in pop-group)* suonare la batteria ● *vt* ~ **sth into sb** ripetere qcsa a qcno cento volte. ~**mer** *n* percussionista *mf*; *(in pop-group)* batterista *mf*. ~**stick** *n* bacchetta *f*; *(of chicken, turkey)* coscia *f*

drunk /drʌŋk/ *see* **drink** ● *a* ubriaco; **get** ~ ubriacarsi ● *n* ubriaco, -a *mf*

drunk|ard /'drʌŋkəd/ *n* ubriacone, -a *mf*. ~**en** *a* ubriaco; ~**en driving** guida *f* in stato di ebbrezza

dry /draɪ/ *a* (drier, driest) asciutto; *‹climate, country›* secco ● *vt/i (pt/pp* dried) asciugare; ~ **one's eyes** asciugarsi le lacrime. **dry up** *vi* seccarsi; *‹fig: source›* prosciugarsi; *(fam: be quiet)* stare zitto; *(do dishes)* asciugare i piatti

dry: ~-'**clean** *vt* pulire a secco. ~-'**clean'er's** *n (shop)* tintoria *f*. ~**ness** *n* secchezza *f*

DTP n abbr (**desktop publishing**) desktop publishing m

dual /'dju:əl/ a doppio

dual: ~ **'carriageway** n strada f a due carreggiate. ~-**'purpose** a a doppio uso

dub /dʌb/ vt (pt/pp **dubbed**) doppiare ⟨film⟩; ⟨name⟩ soprannominare

dubious /'dju:bɪəs/ a dubbio; **be ~ about** avere dei dubbi riguardo

duchess /'dʌtʃɪs/ n duchessa f

duck /dʌk/ n anatra f ● vt ⟨in water⟩ immergere; ~ **one's head** abbassare la testa ● vi abbassarsi. ~**ling** n anatroccolo m

duct /dʌkt/ n condotto m; Anat dotto m

dud /dʌd/ fam a Mil disattivato; ⟨coin⟩ falso; ⟨cheque⟩ a vuoto ● n (banknote) banconota f falsa

due /dju:/ a dovuto; **be ~** essere previsto; **the baby is ~ next week** il bambino dovrebbe nascere la settimana prossima; ~ **to** (owing to) a causa di; **be ~ to** (causally) essere dovuto a; **I'm ~ to...** dovrei...; **in ~ course** a tempo debito ● adv ~ **north** direttamente a nord

duel /'dju:əl/ n duello m

dues /dju:z/ npl quota f [di iscrizione]

duet /dju:'et/ n duetto m

dug /dʌg/ see **dig**

duke /dju:k/ n duca m

dull /dʌl/ a ⟨overcast, not bright⟩ cupo; ⟨not shiny⟩ opaco; ⟨sound⟩ soffocato; ⟨boring⟩ monotono; ⟨stupid⟩ ottuso ● vt intorpidire ⟨mind⟩; attenuare ⟨pain⟩

duly /'dju:lɪ/ adv debitamente

dumb /dʌm/ a muto; ⟨fam: stupid⟩ ottuso. ~-**founded** /dʌm'faʊndɪd/ a sbigottito

dummy /'dʌmɪ/ n (tailor's) manichino m; ⟨for baby⟩ succhiotto m; ⟨model⟩ riproduzione f

dump /dʌmp/ n ⟨for refuse⟩ scarico m; ⟨fam: town⟩ mortorio m; **be down in the ~s** fam essere de-

presso ● vt scaricare; ⟨fam: put down⟩ lasciare; ⟨fam: get rid of⟩ liberarsi di

dumpling /'dʌmplɪŋ/ n gnocco m

dunce /dʌns/ n zuccone, -a mf

dune /dju:n/ n duna f

dung /dʌŋ/ n sterco m

dungarees /dʌŋgə'ri:z/ npl tuta f sg

dungeon /'dʌndʒən/ n prigione f sotterranea

duo /'dju:əʊ/ n duo m inv; Mus duetto m

duplicate¹ /'dju:plɪkət/ a doppio ● n duplicato m; ⟨document⟩ copia f; **in ~** in duplicato

duplicat|e² /'dju:plɪkeɪt/ vt fare un duplicato di; ⟨research:⟩ essere una ripetizione di ⟨work⟩

durable /'djʊərəbl/ a resistente; durevole ⟨basis, institution⟩

duration /djʊə'reɪʃn/ n durata f

duress /djʊə'res/ n costrizione f; **under ~** sotto minaccia

during /'djʊərɪŋ/ prep durante

dusk /dʌsk/ n crepuscolo m

dust /dʌst/ n polvere f ● vt spolverare; ⟨sprinkle⟩ cospargere ⟨cake⟩ ⟨with di⟩ ● vi spolverare

dust: ~**bin** n pattumiera f. ~-**cart** n camion m della nettezza urbana. ~**er** n strofinaccio m. ~-**jacket** n sopraccoperta f. ~-**man** n spazzino m. ~-**pan** n paletta f per la spazzatura

dusty /'dʌstɪ/ a (-ier, -iest) polveroso

Dutch /dʌtʃ/ a olandese; **go ~** fam fare alla romana ● n ⟨language⟩ olandese m; **the ~** pl gli olandesi. ~**man** n olandese m

dutiable /'dju:tɪəbl/ a soggetto a imposta

dutiful /'dju:tɪfl/ a rispettoso

duty /'dju:tɪ/ n dovere m; ⟨task⟩ compito m; ⟨tax⟩ dogana f; **be on ~** essere di servizio. ~-**free** a esente da dogana

duvet /'du:veɪ/ n piumone m

dwarf /dwɔ:f/ n (pl -**s** or **dwarves**) nano, -a mf ● vt rimpicciolire

dwell /dwel/ *vi* (*pt/pp* **dwelt**) *liter* dimorare. **dwell on** *vt fig* soffermarsi su. **~ing** *n* abitazione *f*

dwindle /ˈdwɪndl/ *vi* diminuire

dye /daɪ/ *n* tintura *f* ● *vt* (*pres p* **dyeing**) tingere

dying /ˈdaɪɪŋ/ *see* **die²**

dynamic /daɪˈnæmɪk/ *a* dinamico

dynamite /ˈdaɪnəmaɪt/ *n* dinamite *f*

dynamo /ˈdaɪnəməʊ/ *n* dinamo *f inv*

dynasty /ˈdɪnəstɪ/ *n* dinastia *f*

dysentery /ˈdɪsəntrɪ/ *n* dissenteria *f*

dyslex|ia /dɪsˈleksɪə/ *n* dislessia *f*. **~ic** *a* dislessico

• •

Ee

• •

each /iːtʃ/ *a* ogni ● *pron* ognuno; **£1 ~** una sterlina ciascuno; **they love/hate ~ other** si amano/odiano; **we lend ~ other money** ci prestiamo i soldi

eager /ˈiːgə(r)/ *a* ansioso (**to do** di fare); (*pupil*) avido di sapere. **~ly** *adv* (*wait*) ansiosamente; (*offer*) premurosamente. **~ness** *n* premura *f*

eagle /ˈiːgl/ *n* aquila *f*

ear¹ /ɪə(r)/ *n* (*of corn*) spiga *f*

ear² *n* orecchio *m*. **~ache** *n* mal *m* d'orecchi. **~drum** *n* timpano *m*

earl /ɜːl/ *n* conte *m*

early /ˈɜːlɪ/ *a* (**-ier, -iest**) (*before expected time*) in anticipo; (*spring*) prematuro; (*reply*) pronto; (*works, writings*) primo; **be here ~!** sii puntuale!; **you're ~!** sei in anticipo!; **~ morning walk** passeggiata *f* mattutina; **in the ~ morning** la mattina presto; **in the ~ spring** all'inizio della primavera; **~ retirement** prepensionamento ● *adv* presto; (*ahead of*

time) in anticipo; **~ in the morning** la mattina presto

'earmark *vt* riservare (**for** a)

earn /ɜːn/ *vt* guadagnare; (*deserve*) meritare

earnest /ˈɜːnɪst/ *a* serio ● *n* **in ~** sul serio. **~ly** *adv* con aria seria

earnings /ˈɜːnɪŋz/ *npl* guadagni *mpl*; (*salary*) stipendio *m*

ear: **~phones** *npl* cuffia *fsg*. **~ring** *n* orecchino *m*. **~shot** *n* **within ~shot** a portata d'orecchio; **he is out of ~shot** non può sentire

earth /ɜːθ/ *n* terra *f* **where/what on ~?** dove/che diavolo? ● *vt Electr* mettere a terra

earthenware /ˈɜːθn-/ *n* terraglia *f*

earthly /ˈɜːθlɪ/ *a* terrestre; **be no ~ use** *fam* essere perfettamente inutile

'earthquake *n* terremoto *m*

earthy /ˈɜːθɪ/ *a* terroso; (*coarse*) grossolano

earwig /ˈɪəwɪg/ *n* forbicina *f*

ease /iːz/ *n* **at ~** a proprio agio; **at ~!** *Mil* riposo!; **ill at ~** a disagio; **with ~** con facilità ● *vt* calmare (*pain*); alleviare (*tension, shortage*); (*slow down*) rallentare; (*loosen*) allentare ● *vi* (*pain, situation, wind*) calmarsi

easel /ˈiːzl/ *n* cavalletto *m*

easily /ˈiːzɪlɪ/ *adv* con facilità; **~ the best** certamente il migliore

east /iːst/ *n* est *m*; **to the ~ of** a est di ● *a* dell'est ● *adv* verso est

Easter /ˈiːstə(r)/ *n* Pasqua *f*. **~ egg** *n* uovo *m* di Pasqua

east|erly /ˈiːstəlɪ/ *a* da levante. **~ern** *a* orientale. **~ward[s]** /-wəd[z]/ *adv* verso est

easy /ˈiːzɪ/ *a* (**-ier, -iest**) facile; **take it** *or* **things ~** prendersela con calma; **take it ~!** (*don't get excited*) calma!; **go ~ with** andarci piano con

easy: **~ chair** *n* poltrona *f*. **~'going** *a* conciliante; **too ~-going** troppo accomodante

eat /iːt/ *vt/i* (*pt* **ate**, *pp* **eaten**) man-

eatable | effervescent

giare. **eat into** vt intaccare. **eat up** vt mangiare tutto ⟨food⟩; fig inghiottire ⟨profits⟩

eat|able /'i:tbl/ a mangiabile. **~er** n ⟨apple⟩ mela f da tavola; **be a big ~er** ⟨person:⟩ essere una buona forchetta

eau-de-Cologne /əʊdəkə'ləʊn/ n acqua f di Colonia

eaves /i:vz/ npl cornicione msg. **~drop** vi ⟨pt/pp **~dropped**⟩ origliare; **~drop on** ascoltare di nascosto

ebb /eb/ n ⟨tide⟩ riflusso m; **at a low ~** fig a terra ● vi rifluire; fig declinare

ebony /'ebənɪ/ n ebano m

EC n abbr **(European Community)** CE f

eccentric /ɪk'sentrɪk/ a & n eccentrico, -a f

ecclesiastical /ɪkli:zɪ'æstɪkl/ a ecclesiastico

echo /'ekəʊ/ n ⟨pl **-es**⟩ eco f or m ● v ⟨pt/pp **echoed**, pres p **echoing**⟩ ● vt echeggiare; ripetere ⟨words⟩ ● vi risuonare **(with** di⟩

eclipse /ɪ'klɪps/ n Astr eclissi f inv ● vt fig eclissare

ecolog|ical /i:kə'lɒdʒɪkl/ a ecologico. **~y** /ɪ'kɒlədʒɪ/ n ecologia f

economic /i:kə'nɒmɪk/ a economico. **~al** a economico. **~ally** adv economicamente; **(thriftily)** in economia. **~s** n economia f

economist /ɪ'kɒnəmɪst/ n economista mf

economize /ɪ'kɒnəmaɪz/ vi economizzare **(on** su⟩

economy /ɪ'kɒnəmɪ/ n economia f

ecstasy /'ekstəsɪ/ n estasi f inv; ⟨drug⟩ ecstasy f

ecstatic /ɪk'stætɪk/ a estatico

ecu /'eɪkju:/ n ecu m inv

eczema /'eksɪmə/ n eczema m

edge /edʒ/ n bordo m; ⟨of knife⟩ filo m; ⟨of road⟩ ciglio m; **(on** ⟨person:⟩⟩ sono nervi tesi; **have the ~ on** fam avere un vantaggio su ● vt bordare. **edge forward** vi avanzare lentamente

edgeways /'edʒweɪz/ adv di fianco; **I couldn't get a word in ~** non ho potuto infilare neanche mezza parola nel discorso

edging /'edʒɪŋ/ n bordo m.

edgy /'edʒɪ/ a nervoso

edible /'edɪbl/ a commestibile; **this pizza's not ~** questa pizza è immangiabile

edict /'i:dɪkt/ n editto m

edify /'edɪfaɪ/ vt ⟨pt/pp **-ied**⟩ edificare. **~ing** a edificante

edit /'edɪt/ vt ⟨pt/pp **edited**⟩ far la revisione di ⟨text⟩; curare l'edizione di ⟨anthology, dictionary⟩; dirigere ⟨newspaper⟩; montare ⟨film⟩; editare ⟨tape⟩. **~ed by** ⟨book⟩ a cura di

edition /ɪ'dɪʃn/ n edizione f.

editor /'edɪtə(r)/ n ⟨of anthology, dictionary⟩ curatore, -trice mf; ⟨of newspaper⟩ redattore, -trice mf; ⟨of film⟩ responsabile mf del montaggio

editorial /edɪ'tɔːrɪəl/ a redazionale ● n Journ editoriale m

educate /'edjʊkeɪt/ vt istruire; educare ⟨public, mind⟩; **be ~d at Eton** essere educato a Eton. **~d** a istruito

education /edjʊ'keɪʃn/ n istruzione f; ⟨culture⟩ cultura f, educazione f. **~al** a istruttivo; ⟨visit⟩ educativo; ⟨publishing⟩ didattico

eel /i:l/ n anguilla f

eerie /'ɪərɪ/ a **(-ier, -iest)** inquietante

effect /ɪ'fekt/ n effetto m; **in ~** in effetti; **take ~** ⟨law:⟩ entrare in vigore; ⟨medicine:⟩ fare effetto ● vt effettuare

effective /ɪ'fektɪv/ a efficace; ⟨striking⟩ che colpisce; ⟨actual⟩ di fatto; **~ from** in vigore a partire da. **~ly** adv efficacemente; ⟨actually⟩ di fatto. **~ness** n efficacia f

effeminate /ɪ'femɪnət/ a effeminato

effervescent /efə'vesnt/ a effervescente

efficiency /ɪˈfɪʃənsɪ/ n efficienza f; (of machine) rendimento m
efficient /ɪˈfɪʃənt/ a efficiente. **~ly** adv efficientemente
effort /ˈefət/ n sforzo m; **make an ~** sforzarsi. **~less** a facile. **~lessly** adv con facilità
effrontery /ɪˈfrʌntərɪ/ n sfrontatezza f
effusive /ɪˈfjuːsɪv/ a espansivo; (speech) caloroso
e.g. abbr (exempli gratia) per es.
egalitarian /ɪɡælɪˈteərɪən/ a egalitario
egg[1] /eg/ vt ~ **on** fam incitare
egg[2] n uovo m. **~cup** n portauovo m inv. **~head** n fam intellettuale mf. **~shell** n guscio m d'uovo. **~timer** n clessidra f per misurare il tempo di cottura delle uova
ego /ˈiːɡəʊ/ n ego m. **~centric** /-ˈsentrɪk/ a egocentrico. **~ism** n egoismo m. **~ist** n egoista mf. **~tism** n egotismo m. **~tist** n egotista mf
Egypt /ˈiːdʒɪpt/ n Egitto m. **~ian** /ɪˈdʒɪpʃn/ a & n egiziano, -a mf
eiderdown /ˈaɪdə-/ n (quilt) piumino m
eigh|t /eɪt/ a otto ● n otto m. **~'teen** a diciotto. **~'teenth** a diciottesimo
eighth /eɪtθ/ a ottavo ● n ottavo m
eightieth /ˈeɪtɪθ/ a ottantesimo
eighty /ˈeɪtɪ/ a ottanta
either /ˈaɪðə(r)/ a & pron ~ [of them] l'uno o l'altro; **I don't like ~** [of them] non mi piace né l'uno né l'altro; **on ~ side** da tutte e due le parti ● adv **I don't ~** nemmeno io; **I don't like John or his brother ~** non mi piace John e nemmeno suo fratello ● conj ~ **John or his brother will be there** ci saranno o John o suo fratello; **I don't like ~ John or his brother** non mi piacciono né John né suo fratello; **~ you go to bed or [else]...** o vai a letto o [altrimenti]...

eject /ɪˈdʒekt/ vt eiettare (pilot); espellere (tape, drunk)
eke /iːk/ vt ~ **out** far bastare; (increase) arrotondare; **~ out a living** arrangiarsi
elaborate[1] /ɪˈlæbərət/ a elaborato
elaborate[2] /ɪˈlæbəreɪt/ vi entrare nei particolari (**on** di)
elapse /ɪˈlæps/ vi trascorrere
elastic /ɪˈlæstɪk/ a elastico ● n elastico m. **~ 'band** n elastico m
elasticity /ɪlæˈstɪsətɪ/ n elasticità f
elated /ɪˈleɪtɪd/ a esultante
elbow /ˈelbəʊ/ n gomito m
elder[1] /ˈeldə(r)/ n (tree) sambuco m
elder[2] a maggiore ● n the ~ il/la maggiore. **~ly** a anziano. **~est** a maggiore ● n the ~est il/la maggiore
elect /ɪˈlekt/ a the **president** ~ il futuro presidente ● vt eleggere; **~ to do sth** decidere di fare qcsa. **~ion** /-ekʃn/ n elezione f
elector /ɪˈlektə(r)/ n elettore, -trice mf. **~al** a elettorale; **~al roll** liste fpl elettorali. **~ate** /-rət/ n elettorato m
electric /ɪˈlektrɪk/ a elettrico
electrical /ɪˈlektrɪkl/ a elettrico; **~ engineering** elettrotecnica f
electric: ~ 'blanket n termocoperta f. ~ 'fire n stufa f elettrica
electrician /ɪlekˈtrɪʃn/ n elettricista m
electricity /ɪlekˈtrɪsətɪ/ n elettricità f
electrify /ɪˈlektrɪfaɪ/ vt (pt/pp -ied) elettrificare; fig elettrizzare. **~ing** a fig elettrizzante
electrocute /ɪˈlektrəkjuːt/ vt fulminare; (execute) giustiziare sulla sedia elettrica
electrode /ɪˈlektrəʊd/ n elettrodo m
electron /ɪˈlektrɒn/ n elettrone m
electronic /ɪlekˈtrɒnɪk/ a elettronico. **~ mail** n posta f elettronica. **~s** n elettronica f
elegance /ˈelɪɡəns/ n eleganza f
elegant /ˈelɪɡənt/ a elegante
elegy /ˈelɪdʒɪ/ n elegia f

element /'elɪmənt/ n elemento m. **~ary** /-'mentərɪ/ a elementare

elephant /'elɪfənt/ n elefante m

elevat|e /'elɪveɪt/ vt elevare. **~ion** /-'veɪʃn/ n elevazione f; (height) altitudine f; (angle) alzo m

elevator /'elɪveɪtə(r)/ n Am ascensore m

eleven /ɪ'levn/ a undici ● n undici m. **~th** a undicesimo; at the **~th hour** fam all'ultimo momento

elf /elf/ n (pl elves) elfo m

elicit /ɪ'lɪsɪt/ vt ottenere

eligible /'elɪdʒəbl/ a eleggibile; **~ young man** buon partito; **be ~** for aver diritto a

eliminate /ɪ'lɪmɪneɪt/ vt eliminare

élite /eɪ'liːt/ n fior fiore m

ellip|se /ɪ'lɪps/ n ellisse f. **~tical** a ellittico

elm /elm/ n olmo m

elocution /elə'kjuːʃn/ n elocuzione f

elope /ɪ'ləʊp/ vi fuggire [per sposarsi]

eloquen|ce /'eləkwəns/ n eloquenza f. **~t** a eloquente. **~tly** adv con eloquenza

else /els/ adv altro; **who ~?** e chi altro?; **he did of course, who ~?** l'ha fatto lui e chi, se no?; **nothing ~** nient'altro; **or ~** altrimenti; **someone ~** qualcun altro; **somewhere ~** da qualche altra parte; **anyone ~** chiunque altro; (as question) nessun'altro?; **anything ~** qualunque altra cosa; (as question) altro?. **~where** adv altrove

elucidate /ɪ'luːsɪdeɪt/ vt delucidare

elude /ɪ'luːd/ vt eludere; (avoid) evitare; **the name ~s me** il nome mi sfugge

elusive /ɪ'luːsɪv/ a elusivo

emaciated /ɪ'meɪsɪeɪtɪd/ a emaciato

e-mail /'iːmeɪl/ n posta f elettronica ● vt spedire via posta elettronica

emanate /'eməneɪt/ vi emanare

emancipat|ed /ɪ'mænsɪpeɪtɪd/ a emancipato. **~ion** /-'peɪʃn/ n emancipazione f; (of slaves) liberazione f

embankment /ɪm'bæŋkmənt/ n argine m; Rail massicciata f

embargo /em'bɑːgəʊ/ n (pl -es) embargo m

embark /ɪm'bɑːk/ vi imbarcarsi; **~ on** intraprendere. **~ation** /emba:-'keɪʃn/ n imbarco m

embarrass /em'bærəs/ vt imbarazzare. **~ed** a imbarazzato. **~ing** a imbarazzante. **~ment** n imbarazzo m

embassy /'embəsɪ/ n ambasciata f

embedded /ɪm'bedɪd/ a (in concrete) cementato; (traditions, feelings) radicato

embellish /ɪm'belɪʃ/ vt abbellire

embers /'embəz/ npl brace fpl

embezzle /ɪm'bezl/ vt appropriarsi indebitamente di. **~ment** n appropriazione f indebita

embitter /ɪm'bɪtə(r)/ vt amareggiare

emblem /'embləm/ n emblema m

embody /ɪm'bɒdɪ/ vt (pt/pp -ied) incorporare; **~ what is best in...** rappresentare quanto c'è di meglio di...

emboss /ɪm'bɒs/ vt sbalzare (metal); stampare in rilievo (paper). **~ed** a in rilievo

embrace /ɪm'breɪs/ n abbraccio m ● vt abbracciare ● vi abbracciarsi

embroider /ɪm'brɔɪdə(r)/ vt ricamare (design); fig abbellire. **~y** n ricamo m

embryo /'embrɪəʊ/ n embrione m

emerald /'emərəld/ n smeraldo m

emerge /ɪ'mɜːdʒ/ vi emergere; (come into being: nation) nascere; (sun, flowers) spuntare fuori. **~gence** /-əns/ n emergere m; (of new country) nascita f

emergency /ɪ'mɜːdʒənsɪ/ n emergenza f; **in an ~** in caso di emergenza. **~ exit** n uscita f di sicurezza

emery /'emərɪ/: **~ board** n limetta f [per le unghie]

emigrant /'emɪgrənt/ n emigrante mf

emigrat|e /'emɪgreɪt/ vi emigrare. **~ion** /-'greɪʃn/ n emigrazione f

eminent /'emɪnənt/ a eminente. **~ly** adv eminentemente

emission /ɪ'mɪʃn/ n emissione f; (of fumes) esalazione f

emit /ɪ'mɪt/ vt (pt/pp **emitted**) emettere; esalare (fumes)

emotion /ɪ'məʊʃn/ n emozione f. **~al** a denso di emozione; (person, reaction) emotivo; **become ~al** avere una reazione emotiva

emotive /ɪ'məʊtɪv/ a emotivo

empathize /'empəθaɪz/ vi **~ with sb** immedesimarsi nei problemi di qcno

emperor /'empərə(r)/ n imperatore m

emphasis /'emfəsɪs/ n enfasi f; **put the ~ on sth** accentuare qcsa

emphasize /'emfəsaɪz/ vt accentuare (word, syllable); sottolineare (need)

emphatic /ɪm'fætɪk/ a categorico

empire /'empaɪə(r)/ n impero m

empirical /em'pɪrɪkl/ a empirico

employ /em'plɔɪ/ vt impiegare; fig usare (tact). **~ee** /emplɔɪ'iː/ n impiegato, -a mf. **~er** n datore m di lavoro. **~ment** n occupazione f; (work) lavoro m. **~ment agency** n ufficio m di collocamento

empower /ɪm'paʊə(r)/ vt autorizzare; (enable) mettere in grado

empress /'emprɪs/ n imperatrice f

empties /'emptɪz/ npl vuoti mpl

emptiness /'emptɪnɪs/ n vuoto m

empty /'emptɪ/ a vuoto; (promise, threat) vano ● v (pt/pp **-ied**) ● vt vuotare (con-tainer) ● vi vuotarsi

emulate /'emjʊleɪt/ vt emulare

emulsion /ɪ'mʌlʃn/ n emulsione f

enable /ɪ'neɪbl/ vt **~ sb to** mettere qcno in grado di

enact /ɪ'nækt/ vt Theat rappresentare; decretare (law)

enamel /ɪ'næml/ n smalto m ● vt (pt/pp **enamelled**) smaltare

enchant /ɪn'tʃɑːnt/ vt incantare.

~ing a incantevole. **~ment** n incanto m

encircle /ɪn'sɜːkl/ vt circondare

enclave /'enkleɪv/ n enclave f inv; fig territorio m

enclos|e /ɪn'kləʊz/ vt circondare (land); (in letter) allegare (**with** a). **~ed** a (space) chiuso; (in letter) allegato. **~ure** /-ʒə(r)/ n (at zoo) recinto m; (in letter) allegato m

encompass /ɪn'kʌmpəs/ vt (include) comprendere

encore /'ɒŋkɔː(r)/ n & int bis m inv

encounter /ɪn'kaʊntə(r)/ n incontro m; (battle) scontro m ● vt incontrare

encourag|e /ɪn'kʌrɪdʒ/ vt incoraggiare; promuovere (the arts, independence). **~ment** n incoraggiamento m; (of the arts) promozione f. **~ing** a incoraggiante; (smile) di incoraggiamento

encroach /ɪn'krəʊtʃ/ vi **~ on** invadere (land, privacy); abusare di (time); interferire con (rights)

encumber /ɪn'kʌmbə(r)/ vt **~ered with** essere carico di (children, suitcases); ingombro di (furniture). **~rance** /-rəns/ n peso m

encyclop[a]ed|ia /ɪnsaɪklə'piːdɪə/ n enciclopedia f. **~ic** a enciclopedico

end /end/ n fine f; (of box, table, piece of string) estremità f; (of town, room) parte f; (purpose) fine m; **in the ~** alla fine; **at the ~ of May** alla fine di maggio; **at the ~ of the street/garden** in fondo alla strada/al giardino; **on ~** (upright) in piedi; **for days on ~** per giorni e giorni; **for six days on ~** per sei giorni di fila; **put an ~ to sth** mettere fine a qcsa; **make ~s meet** fam sbarcare il lunario; **no ~ of** fam un sacco di ● vt/vi finire. **end up** vi finire; **~ up doing sth** finire col fare qcsa

endanger /ɪn'deɪndʒə(r)/ vt rischiare (one's life); mettere a repentaglio (sb else, success of sth)

endear|ing /ɪn'dɪərɪŋ/ a accattivante. **~ment** n term of **~ment** vezzeggiativo m

endeavour /ɪnˈdevə(r)/ n tentativo m ● vi sforzarsi (**to** di)

ending /ˈendɪŋ/ n fine f; Gram desinenza f

endive /ˈendaɪv/ n indivia f

endless /ˈendlɪs/ a interminabile; ⟨patience⟩ infinito. **~ly** adv continuamente; ⟨patient⟩ infinitamente

endorse /enˈdɔːs/ vt girare ⟨cheque⟩; ⟨sports personality:⟩ fare pubblicità a ⟨product⟩; appoggiare ⟨plan⟩. **~ment** n (of cheque) girata f; (of plan) conferma f; (on driving licence) registrazione f su patente di un'infrazione

endow /ɪnˈdaʊ/ vt dotare

endur|able /ɪnˈdjʊərəbl/ a sopportabile. **~ance** /-rəns/ n resistenza f; **it is beyond ~ance** è insopportabile

endur|e /ɪnˈdjʊə(r)/ vt sopportare ● vi durare. **~ing** a duraturo

'end user n utente m finale

enemy /ˈenəmɪ/ n nemico, -a mf ● attrib nemico

energetic /enəˈdʒetɪk/ a energico

energy /ˈenədʒɪ/ n energia f

enforce /ɪnˈfɔːs/ vt far rispettare ⟨law⟩. **~d** a forzato

engage /ɪnˈgeɪdʒ/ vt assumere ⟨staff⟩; Theat ingaggiare; Auto ingranare ⟨gear⟩ ● vi Techn ingranare; **~ in** impegnarsi in. **~d** a (in use, busy) occupato; ⟨person⟩ impegnato; (to be married) fidanzato; **get ~d** fidanzarsi (**to** con); **~d tone** Teleph segnale m di occupato. **~ment** n fidanzamento m; (appointment) appuntamento m; Mil combattimento m; **~ment ring** anello m di fidanzamento

engaging /ɪnˈgeɪdʒɪŋ/ a attraente

engender /ɪnˈdʒendə(r)/ vt fig generare

engine /ˈendʒɪn/ n motore m; Rail locomotrice f. **~-driver** n macchinista m

engineer /endʒɪˈnɪə(r)/ n ingegnere m; (service, installation) tecnico m; Naut, Am Rail macchinista m ● vt fig architettare. **~ing** n ingegneria f

England /ˈɪŋglənd/ n Inghilterra f

English /ˈɪŋglɪʃ/ a inglese; **the ~ Channel** la Manica ● n (language) inglese m; **the ~ pl** gli inglesi. **~man** n inglese m. **~woman** n inglese f

engrave /ɪnˈgreɪv/ vt incidere. **~ing** n incisione f

engross /ɪnˈgrəʊs/ vt **~ed in** assorto in

engulf /ɪnˈgʌlf/ vt ⟨fire, waves:⟩ inghiottire

enhance /ɪnˈhɑːns/ vt accrescere ⟨beauty, reputation⟩; migliorare ⟨performance⟩

enigma /ɪˈnɪgmə/ n enigma m. **~tic** /enɪgˈmætɪk/ a enigmatico

enjoy /ɪnˈdʒɔɪ/ vt godere di ⟨good health⟩; **~ oneself** divertirsi; **I ~ cooking/painting** mi piace cucinare/dipingere; **~ your meal** buon appetito. **~able** /-əbl/ a piacevole. **~ment** n piacere m

enlarge /ɪnˈlɑːdʒ/ vt ingrandire ● vi **~ upon** dilungarsi su. **~ment** n ingrandimento m

enlighten /ɪnˈlaɪtn/ vt illuminare. **~ed** a progressista. **~ment** n **The E~ment** l'Illuminismo m

enlist /ɪnˈlɪst/ vt Mil reclutare; **~ sb's help** farsi aiutare da qcno ● vi Mil arruolarsi

enliven /ɪnˈlaɪvn/ vt animare

enmity /ˈenmɪtɪ/ n inimicizia f

enormity /ɪˈnɔːmətɪ/ n enormità f

enormous /ɪˈnɔːməs/ a enorme. **~ly** adv estremamente; ⟨grateful⟩ infinitamente

enough /ɪˈnʌf/ a & n abbastanza; **I didn't bring ~ clothes** non ho portato abbastanza vestiti; **have you had ~?** (to eat/drink) hai mangiato/bevuto abbastanza?; **I've had ~! fam** ne ho abbastanza!; **is that ~?** basta?; **that's ~!** basta così!; **£50 isn't ~** 50 sterline non sono sufficienti ● adv abbastanza;

you're not working fast ~ non lavori abbastanza in fretta; **funnily ~** stranamente

enquir|e /ɪn'kwaɪə(r)/ *vi* domandare; **~e about** chiedere informazioni su. **~y** *n* domanda *f*; *(investigation)* inchiesta *f*

enrage /ɪn'reɪdʒ/ *vt* fare arrabbiare

enrich /ɪn'rɪtʃ/ *vt* arricchire; *(improve)* migliorare *(vocabulary)*

enrol /ɪn'rəʊl/ *vi* *(pt/pp* **-rolled)** *(for exam, in club)* iscriversi **(for, in** a). **~ment** *n* iscrizione *f*

ensemble /ɒn'sɒmbl/ *n* *(clothing & Mus)* complesso *m*

enslave /ɪn'sleɪv/ *vt* render schiavo

ensu|e /ɪn'sju:/ *vi* seguire; **the ~ing discussion** la discussione che ne è seguita

ensure /ɪn'ʃʊə(r)/ *vt* assicurare; **~ that** *(person:)* assicurarsi che; *(measure:)* garantire che

entail /ɪn'teɪl/ *vt* comportare; **what does it ~?** in che cosa consiste?

entangle /ɪn'tæŋgl/ *vt* **get ~d in** rimanere impigliato in; *fig* rimanere coinvolto in

enter /'entə(r)/ *vt* entrare in; iscrivere *(horse, runner in race)*; cominciare *(university)*; partecipare a *(competition)*; *Comput* immettere *(data)*; *(write down)* scrivere ● *vi* entrare; *Theat* entrare in scena; *(register as competitor)* iscriversi; *(take part)* partecipare **(in** a)

enterpris|e /'entəpraɪz/ *n* impresa *f*; *(quality)* iniziativa *f*. **~ing** *a* intraprendente

entertain /entə'teɪn/ *vt* intrattenere; *(invite)* ricevere; nutrire *(ideas, hopes)*; prendere in considerazione *(possibility)* ● *vi* intrattenersi; *(have guests)* ricevere. **~er** *n* artista *mf*. **~ing** *a* *(person)* di gradevole compagnia; *(evening, film, play)* divertente. **~ment** *n* *(amusement)* intrattenimento *m*

enthral /ɪn'θrɔ:l/ *vt* *(pt/pp* **en-**thralled)** **be ~led** essere affascinato **(by** da)

enthusias|m /ɪn'θju:zɪæzm/ *n* entusiasmo *m*. **~t** *n* entusiasta *mf*. **~tic** /-'æstɪk/ *a* entusiastico

entice /ɪn'taɪs/ *vt* attirare. **~ment** *n* *(incentive)* incentivo *m*

entire /ɪn'taɪə(r)/ *a* intero; **I'm not ~ly satisfied** non sono completamente soddisfatto. **~ty** /-rəti/ *n* **in its ~ty** nell'insieme

entitle /ɪn'taɪtld/ *a* *(book)* intitolato; **be ~ to sth** aver diritto a qcsa

entitlement /ɪn'taɪtlmənt/ *n* diritto *m*

entity /'entɪtɪ/ *n* entità *f*

entrance[1] /'entrəns/ *n* entrata *f*; *Theat* entrata *f* in scena; *(right to enter)* ammissione *f*; **'no ~'** ingresso vietato'. **~ examination** esame *m* di ammissione. **~ fee** *n* **how much is the ~ fee?** quanto costa il biglietto di ingresso?

entrance[2] /ɪn'trɑ:ns/ *vt* estasiare

entrant /'entrənt/ *n* concorrente *mf*

entreat /ɪn'tri:t/ *vt* supplicare

entrenched /ɪn'trentʃt/ *a* *(ideas, views)* radicato

entrust /ɪn'trʌst/ *vt* **~ sb with sth, ~ sth to sb** affidare qcsa a qcno

entry /'entrɪ/ *n* ingresso *m*; *(way in)* entrata *f*; *(in directory etc)* voce *f*; *(in appointment diary)* appuntamento *m*; **no ~** ingresso vietato; *Auto* accesso vietato. **~ form** *n* modulo *m* di ammissione. **~ visa** *n* visto *m* di ingresso

enumerate /ɪ'nju:məreɪt/ *vt* enumerare

enunciate /ɪ'nʌnsɪeɪt/ *vt* enunciare

envelop /ɪn'veləp/ *vt* *(pt/pp* **enveloped)** avviluppare

envelope /'envələʊp/ *n* busta *f*

enviable /'envɪəbl/ *a* invidiabile

envious /'envɪəs/ *a* invidioso. **~ly** *adv* con invidia

environment /ɪn'vaɪrənmənt/ n ambiente m

environmental /ɪnvaɪrən'mentl/ a ambientale. **~ist** n ambientalista mf. **~ly** adv **~ly friendly** che rispetta l'ambiente

envisage /ɪn'vɪzɪdʒ/ vt prevedere

envoy /'envɔɪ/ n inviato, -a

envy /'envɪ/ n invidia ● vt (pt/pp **-ied**) **~ sb sth** invidiare qcno per qcsa

enzyme /'enzaɪm/ n enzima m

epic /'epɪk/ a epico ● n epopea f

epidemic /epɪ'demɪk/ n epidemia f

epilep|sy /'epɪlepsɪ/ n epilessia f. **~tic** /-'leptɪk/ a & n epilettico, -a mf

epilogue /'epɪlɒg/ n epilogo m

episode /'epɪsəʊd/ n episodio m

epitaph /'epɪtɑ:f/ n epitaffio m

epithet /'epɪθet/ n epiteto m

epitom|e /ɪ'pɪtəmɪ/ n epitome f. **~ize** vt essere il classico esempio di

epoch /'i:pɒk/ n epoca f

equal /'i:kwl/ a ⟨parts, amounts⟩ uguale; **of ~ height** della stessa altezza; **be ~ to the task** essere a l'altezza del compito ● n pari m inv ● vt (pt/pp **equalled**) ⟨be same in quantity as⟩ essere pari a; ⟨rival⟩ uguagliare; **5 plus 5 ~s 10** 5 più 5 [è] uguale a 10. **~ity** /ɪ'kwɒlətɪ/ n uguaglianza f

equalize /'i:kwəlaɪz/ vi Sport pareggiare. **~r** n Sport pareggio m

equally /'i:kwəlɪ/ adv ⟨divide⟩ in parti uguali; **~ intelligent** della stessa intelligenza; **~,...** allo stesso tempo...

equanimity /ekwə'nɪmətɪ/ n equanimità f

equat|e /ɪ'kweɪt/ vt **~e sth with sth** equiparare qcsa a qcsa. **~ion** /-eɪʒn/ n Math equazione f

equator /ɪ'kweɪtə(r)/ n equatore m

equestrian /ɪ'kwestrɪən/ a equestre

equilibrium /i:kwɪ'lɪbrɪəm/ n equilibrio m

equinox /'i:kwɪnɒks/ n equinozio m

equip /ɪ'kwɪp/ vt (pt/pp **equipped**) equipaggiare; attrezzare ⟨kitchen, office⟩. **~ment** n attrezzatura f

equitable /'ekwɪtəbl/ a giusto

equity /'ekwɪtɪ/ n ⟨justness⟩ equità f; Comm azioni fpl

equivalent /ɪ'kwɪvələnt/ a equivalente; **be ~ to** equivalere a ● n equivalente m

equivocal /ɪ'kwɪvəkl/ a equivoco

era /'ɪərə/ n età f; ⟨geological⟩ era f

eradicate /ɪ'rædɪkeɪt/ vt eradicare

erase /ɪ'reɪz/ vt cancellare. **~r** n gomma f [da cancellare]; ⟨for blackboard⟩ cancellino m

erect /ɪ'rekt/ a eretto ● vt erigere. **~ion** /-ekʃn/ n erezione f

ero|de /ɪ'rəʊd/ vt ⟨water:⟩ erodere; ⟨acid:⟩ corrodere. **~sion** /-əʊʒn/ n erosione f; ⟨by acid⟩ corrosione f

erotic /ɪ'rɒtɪk/ a erotico. **~ism** /-tɪsɪzm/ n erotismo m

err /ɜ:(r)/ vi errare; ⟨sin⟩ peccare

errand /'erənd/ n commissione f

erratic /ɪ'rætɪk/ a irregolare; ⟨person, moods⟩ imprevedibile; ⟨exchange rate⟩ incostante

erroneous /ɪ'rəʊnɪəs/ a erroneo

error /'erə(r)/ n errore m; **in ~** per errore

erudit|e /'erʊdaɪt/ a erudito. **~ion** /-'dɪʃn/ n erudizione f

erupt /ɪ'rʌpt/ vi eruttare; ⟨spots:⟩ spuntare; ⟨fig: in anger⟩ dare in escandescenze. **~ion** /-ʌpʃn/ n eruzione f; fig scoppio m

escalat|e /'eskəleɪt/ vi intensificarsi ● vt intensificare. **~ion** /-'leɪʃn/ n escalation f inv. **~or** n scala f mobile

escapade /'eskəpeɪd/ n scappatella f

escape /ɪ'skeɪp/ n fuga f; ⟨from prison⟩ evasione f; **have a narrow ~** cavarsela per un pelo ● vi ⟨prisoner:⟩ evadere (**from** da); sfuggire (**from sb** alla sorveglianza di qcno); ⟨animal:⟩ scappare; ⟨gas:⟩ fuoriuscire ● vt **~ notice**

passare inosservato; **the name ~s me** mi sfugge il nome

escapism /ɪˈskeɪpɪzm/ n evasione f [dalla realtà]

escort¹ /ˈeskɔːt/ n (of person) accompagnatore, -trice mf; Mil etc scorta f

escort² /ɪˈskɔːt/ vt accompagnare; Mil etc scortare

Eskimo /ˈeskɪməʊ/ n esquimese mf

esoteric /esəˈterɪk/ a esoterico

especial /ɪˈspeʃl/ a speciale. **~ly** adv specialmente; (kind) particolarmente

espionage /ˈespɪənɑːʒ/ n spionaggio m

essay /ˈeseɪ/ n saggio m; Sch tema f

essence /ˈesns/ n essenza f; **in ~** in sostanza

essential /ɪˈsenʃl/ a essenziale ● npl the **~s** l'essenziale m. **~ly** adv essenzialmente

establish /ɪˈstæblɪʃ/ vt stabilire (contact, lead); fondare (firm); (prove) accertare; **~ oneself as** affermarsi come. **~ment** n (firm) azienda f; **the E~ment** l'ordine m costituito

estate /ɪˈsteɪt/ n tenuta f; (possessions) patrimonio m; (housing) quartiere m residenziale. **~ agent** n agente m immobiliare. **~ car** n giardiniera f

esteem /ɪˈstiːm/ n stima f ● vt stimare; (consider) giudicare

estimate¹ /ˈestɪmət/ n valutazione f; Comm preventivo m; **at a rough ~** a occhio e croce

estimate² /ˈestɪmeɪt/ vt stimare. **~ion** /-ˈmeɪʃn/ n (esteem) stima f; **in my ~ion** (judgement) a mio giudizio

estuary /ˈestjʊərɪ/ n estuario m

etc /etˈsetərə/ abbr (et cetera) ecc

etching /ˈetʃɪŋ/ n acquaforte f

eternal /ɪˈtɜːnl/ a eterno

eternity /ɪˈtɜːnətɪ/ n eternità f

ethic /ˈeθɪk/ n etica f. **~al** a etico. **~s** n etica f

Ethiopia /iːθɪˈəʊpɪə/ n Etiopia f

ethnic /ˈeθnɪk/ a etnico

etiquette /ˈetɪket/ n etichetta f

EU n abbr (European Union) UE f

eucalyptus /juːkəˈlɪptəs/ n eucalipto m

eulogy /ˈjuːlədʒɪ/ n elogio m

euphemism /ˈjuːfəmɪzm/ n eufemismo m. **~tic** /-ˈmɪstɪk/ a eufemistico

euphoria /juːˈfɔːrɪə/ n euforia f

Euro- /ˈjʊərəʊ-/ pref **~cheque** n eurochèque m inv. **~dollar** n eurodollaro m

Europe /ˈjʊərəp/ n Europa f

European /jʊərəˈpɪən/ a europeo; **~ Community** Comunità f Europea; **~ n** Unione f Europea ● n europeo, -a mf

evacuate /ɪˈvækjʊeɪt/ vt evacuare (building, area). **~ion** /-ˈeɪʃn/ n evacuazione f

evade /ɪˈveɪd/ vt evadere (taxes); evitare (the enemy, authorities); **~ the issue** evitare l'argomento

evaluate /ɪˈvæljʊeɪt/ vt valutare

evangelical /iːvænˈdʒelɪkl/ a evangelico. **~list** /ɪˈvændʒəlɪst/ n evangelista m

evaporate /ɪˈvæpəreɪt/ vi evaporare; fig svanire. **~ion** /-ˈreɪʃn/ n evaporazione f

evasion /ɪˈveɪʒn/ n evasione f

evasive /ɪˈveɪsɪv/ a evasivo

eve /iːv/ n liter vigilia f

even /ˈiːvn/ a (level) piatto; (same, equal) uguale; (regular) regolare; (number) pari; **get ~ with** vendicarsi di; **now we're ~** adesso siamo pari ● adv anche, ancora; **~ if** anche se; **~ so** con tutto ciò; **not ~** nemmeno; **~ bigger/hotter** ancora più grande/caldo ● vt **~ the score** Sport pareggiare. **even out** vi livellarsi. **even up** vt livellare

evening /ˈiːvnɪŋ/ n sera f; (whole evening) serata f; **this ~** stasera; **in the ~** la sera. **~ class** n corso m serale. **~ dress** n (man's) abito m scuro; (woman's) abito m da sera

evenly /ˈiːvnlɪ/ adv (distributed) uniformemente; (breathe) regolarmente; ⟨divided⟩ in uguali parti

event /ɪ'vent/ n avvenimento m; ⟨function⟩ manifestazione f; Sport gara f; **in the ~ of** nell'eventualità di; **in the ~** alla fine. **~ful** a movimentato

eventual /ɪ'ventʃʊəl/ a **the ~ winner was...** alla fine il vincitore è stato.... **~ity** /-'ælətɪ/ n eventualità f. **~ly** adv alla fine; **~ly!** finalmente!

ever /'evə(r)/ adv mai; **I haven't ~..**. non ho mai...; **for ~** per sempre; **hardly ~** quasi mai; **~ since** da quando; ⟨since that time⟩ da allora; **~ so** fam veramente

'evergreen sempreverde m

ever'lasting a eterno

every /'evrɪ/ a ogni; **~ one** ciascuno; **~ other day** un giorno sì un giorno no

every: **~body** pron tutti pl. **~day** a quotidiano, di ogni giorno. **~one** pron tutti pl; **~one else** tutti gli altri. **~thing** pron tutto; **~thing else** tutto il resto. **~where** adv dappertutto; ⟨wherever⟩ dovunque

evict /ɪ'vɪkt/ vt sfrattare. **~ion** /-ɪkʃn/ n sfratto m

eviden|ce /'evɪdəns/ n evidenza f; Jur testimonianza f; **give ~ce** testimoniare. **~t** a evidente. **~tly** adv evidentemente

evil /'i:vl/ a cattivo ● n male m

evocative /ɪ'vɒkətɪv/ a evocativo; **be ~ of** evocare

evoke /ɪ'vəʊk/ vt evocare

evolution /i:və'lu:ʃn/ n evoluzione f

evolve /ɪ'vɒlv/ vt evolvere ● vi evolversi

ewe /ju:/ n pecora f

exacerbate /ɪg'zæsəbeɪt/ vt esacerbare ⟨situation⟩

exact /ɪg'zækt/ a esatto ● vt esigere. **~ing** a esigente. **~itude** /-ɪtju:d/ n esattezza f. **~ly** adv esattamente; **not ~ly** non proprio. **~ness** n precisione f

exaggerat|e /ɪg'zædʒəreɪt/ vt/i esagerare. **~ion** /-'reɪʃn/ n esagerazione f

exam /ɪg'zæm/ n esame m

examination /ɪgzæmɪ'neɪʃn/ n esame m; ⟨of patient⟩ visita f

examine /ɪg'zæmɪn/ vt esaminare; visitare ⟨patient⟩. **~r** n Sch esaminatore, -trice mf

example /ɪg'zɑ:mpl/ n esempio m; **for ~** per esempio; **make an ~ of sb** punire qcno per dare un esempio; **be an ~ to sb** dare il buon esempio a qcno

exasperat|e /ɪg'zæspəreɪt/ vt esasperare. **~ion** /-'reɪʃn/ n esasperazione f

excavat|e /'ekskəveɪt/ vt scavare; Archaeol fare gli scavi di. **~ion** /-'veɪʃn/ n scavo m

exceed /ɪk'si:d/ vt eccedere. **~ingly** adv estremamente

excel /ɪk'sel/ v (pt/pp **excelled**) ● vi eccellere ● vt **~ oneself** superare se stessi

excellen|ce /'eksələns/ n eccellenza f. **E~cy** n ⟨title⟩ Eccellenza f. **~t** a eccellente

except /ɪk'sept/ prep eccetto, tranne; **~ for** eccetto, tranne; **~ that...** eccetto che... ● vt eccettuare. **~ing** prep eccetto, tranne

exception /ɪk'sepʃn/ n eccezione f; **take ~ to** fare obiezioni a. **~al** a eccezionale. **~ally** adv eccezionalmente

excerpt /'eksɜ:pt/ n estratto m

excess /ɪk'ses/ n eccesso m; **in ~ of** oltre. **~ baggage** n bagaglio m in eccedenza. **~ 'fare** n supplemento m

excessive /ɪk'sesɪv/ a eccessivo. **~ly** adv eccessivamente

exchange /ɪks'tʃeɪndʒ/ n scambio m; Teleph centrale f; Comm cambio m; ⟨stock⟩ borsa f valori; **in ~ in** cambio (for di) ● vt scambiare (for con); cambiare ⟨money⟩. **~ rate** n tasso m di cambio

exchequer /ɪks'tʃekə(r)/ n Pol tesoro m

excise¹ /'eksaɪz/ n dazio m; ~ **duty** dazio m

excise² /ek'saɪz/ vt recidere

excitable /ɪk'saɪtəbl/ a eccitabile

excit|e /ɪk'saɪt/ vt eccitare. ~**ed** a eccitato; **get** ~**ed** eccitarsi. ~**edly** adv tutto eccitato. ~**ement** n eccitazione f. ~**ing** a eccitante; ⟨story, film⟩ appassionante; ⟨holiday⟩ entusiasmante

exclaim /ɪk'skleɪm/ vt/i esclamare

exclamation /ekskləˈmeɪʃn/ n esclamazione f. ~ **mark** n, Am ~ **point** n punto m esclamativo

exclu|de /ɪk'sklu:d/ vt escludere. ~**ding** pron escluso. ~**sion** /-ʒn/ n esclusione f

exclusive /ɪk'sklu:sɪv/ a ⟨rights, club⟩ esclusivo; ⟨interview⟩ in esclusiva; ~ **of...** ...escluso. ~**ly** adv esclusivamente

excommunicate /ekskə'mju:nɪkeɪt/ vt scomunicare

excrement /'ekskrɪmənt/ n escremento m

excruciating /ɪk'skru:ʃɪeɪtɪŋ/ a atroce ⟨pain⟩; ⟨fam: very bad⟩ spaventoso

excursion /ɪk'skɜ:ʃn/ n escursione f

excusable /ɪk'skju:zəbl/ a perdonabile

excuse¹ /ɪk'skju:s/ n scusa f

excuse² /ɪk'skju:z/ vt scusare; ~ **from** esonerare da; ~ **me!** (to get attention) scusi!; (to get past) permesso!, scusi!; (indignant) come ha detto?

ex-di'rectory a **be** ~ non figurare sull'elenco telefonico

execute /'eksɪkju:t/ vt eseguire; (put to death) giustiziare; attuare ⟨plan⟩

execution /eksɪ'kju:ʃn/ n esecuzione f; (of plan) attuazione f. ~**er** n boia m inv

executive /ɪg'zekjʊtɪv/ a esecutivo ● n dirigente mf; Pol esecutivo m

executor /ɪg'zekjʊtə(r)/ n Jur esecutore, -trice mf

exemplary /ɪg'zemplərɪ/ a esemplare

exemplify /ɪg'zemplɪfaɪ/ vt (pt/pp -ied) esemplificare

exempt /ɪg'zempt/ a esente ● vt esentare (from da). ~**ion** /-empʃn/ n esenzione f

exercise /'eksəsaɪz/ n esercizio m; Mil esercitazione f; physical ~**s** ginnastica f; **take** ~ fare del moto ● vt esercitare ⟨muscles, horse⟩; portare a spasso ⟨dog⟩; mettere in pratica ⟨skills⟩ ● vi esercitarsi. ~ **book** n quaderno m

exert /ɪg'zɜ:t/ vt esercitare; ~ **oneself** sforzarsi. ~**ion** /-ʒ:ʃn/ n sforzo m

exhale /eks'heɪl/ vt/i esalare

exhaust /ɪg'zɔ:st/ n Auto scappamento m; (pipe) tubo m di scappamento; ~ **fumes** fumi mpl di scarico m ● vt esaurire. ~**ed** a esausto. ~**ing** a estenuante; ⟨climate, person⟩ sfibrante. ~**ion** /-ɔ:stʃn/ n esaurimento m. ~**ive** /-ɪv/ a fig esauriente

exhibit /ɪg'zɪbɪt/ n oggetto m esposto; Jur reperto m ● vt esporre; fig dimostrare

exhibition /eksɪ'bɪʃn/ n mostra f; (of strength, skill) dimostrazione f. ~**ist** n esibizionista mf

exhibitor /ɪg'zɪbɪtə(r)/ n espositore, -trice mf

exhilarat|ed /ɪg'zɪləreɪtɪd/ a rallegrato. ~**ing** a stimolante; ⟨mountain air⟩ tonificante. ~**ion** /-'reɪʃn/ n allegria f

exhort /ɪg'zɔ:t/ vt esortare

exhume /eks'zju:m/ vt esumare

exile /'eksaɪl/ n esilio m; (person) esule mf ● vt esiliare

exist /ɪg'zɪst/ vi esistere. ~**ence** /-əns/ n esistenza f; **in** ~ esistente; **be in** ~**ence** esistere. ~**ing** a attuale

exit /'eksɪt/ n uscita f; Theat uscita f di scena ● vi Theat uscire di scena; Comput uscire

exonerate /ɪg'zɒnəreɪt/ vt esonerare

exorbitant /ɪg'zɔːbɪtənt/ a esorbitante

exorcize /'eksɔːsaɪz/ vt esorcizzare

exotic /ɪg'zɒtɪk/ a esotico

expand /ɪk'spænd/ vt espandere ● vi espandersi; Comm svilupparsi; (metal:) dilatarsi; ~ **on** (fig: explain better) approfondire

expans|e /ɪk'spæns/ n estensione f. ~**ion** /-ænʃn/ n espansione f; Comm sviluppo m; (of metal) dilatazione f. ~**ive** /-ɪv/ a espansivo

expatriate /eks'pætrɪət/ n espatriato, -a mf

expect /ɪk'spekt/ vt aspettare (letter, baby); (suppose) pensare; (demand) esigere; **I ~ so** penso di si; **be ~ing** essere in stato interessante

expectan|cy /ɪk'spektənsɪ/ n aspettativa f. ~**t** a in attesa; ~**t mother** donna f incinta. ~**tly** adv con impazienza

expectation /ekspek'teɪʃn/ n aspettativa f, speranza f

expedient /ɪk'spiːdɪənt/ a conveniente ● n espediente m

expedition /ekspɪ'dɪʃn/ n spedizione f. ~**ary** a Mil di spedizione

expel /ɪk'spel/ vt (pt/pp **expelled**) espellere

expend /ɪk'spend/ vt consumare. ~**able** /-əbl/ a sacrificabile

expenditure /ɪk'spendɪtʃə(r)/ n spesa f

expense /ɪk'spens/ n spesa f; **business ~s** pl spese fpl; **at my ~** a mie spese; **at the ~ of** fig a spese di

expensive /ɪk'spensɪv/ a caro, costoso. ~**ly** adv costosamente

experience /ɪk'spɪərɪəns/ n esperienza f ● vt provare (sensation); avere (problem). ~**d** a esperto

experiment /ɪk'sperɪmənt/ n esperimento ● /-ment/ vi sperimentare. ~**al** /-'mentl/ a sperimentale

expert /'ekspɜːt/ a & n esperto, -a mf. ~**ly** adv abilmente

expertise /ekspɜː'tiːz/ n competenza f

expire /ɪk'spaɪə(r)/ vi scadere

expiry /ɪk'spaɪərɪ/ n scadenza f. ~ **date** n data f di scadenza

explain /ɪk'spleɪn/ vt spiegare

explana|tion /eksplə'neɪʃn/ n spiegazione f. ~**tory** /ɪk'splænətərɪ/ a esplicativo

expletive /ɪk'spliːtɪv/ n imprecazione f

explicit /ɪk'splɪsɪt/ a esplicito. ~**ly** adv esplicitamente

explode /ɪk'spləʊd/ vi esplodere ● vt fare esplodere

exploit¹ /'eksplɔɪt/ n impresa f

exploit² /ɪk'splɔɪt/ vt sfruttare. ~**ation** /eksplɔɪ'teɪʃn/ n sfruttamento m

explora|tion /eksplə'reɪʃn/ n esplorazione f. ~**tory** /ɪk'splɒrətərɪ/ a esplorativo

explore /ɪk'splɔː(r)/ vt esplorare; fig studiare (implications). ~**r** n esploratore, -trice mf

explos|ion /ɪk'spləʊʒn/ n esplosione f. ~**ive** /-sɪv/ a & n esplosivo m

exponent /ɪk'spəʊnənt/ n esponente mf

export /'ekspɔːt/ n esportazione f ● vt /-'spɔːt/ esportare. ~**er** n esportatore, -trice mf

expose /ɪk'spəʊz/ vt esporre; (reveal) svelare; smascherare (traitor etc). ~**ure** /-ʒə(r)/ n esposizione f; Med esposizione f prolungata al freddo/caldo; (of crimes) smascheramento m; **24 ~ures** Phot 24 pose

expound /ɪk'spaʊnd/ vt esporre

express /ɪk'spres/ a espresso ● adv (send) per espresso ● n (train) espresso m ● vt esprimere; ~ **oneself** esprimersi. ~**ion** /-ʃn/ n espressione f. ~**ive** /-ɪv/ a espressivo. ~**ly** adv espressamente

expulsion /ɪk'spʌlʃn/ n espulsione f

exquisite /ek'skwɪzɪt/ a squisito

ex-'serviceman n ex-combattente m

extend /ɪk'stend/ vt prolungare

〈*visit, road*〉; prorogare 〈*visa, contract*〉; ampliare 〈*building, knowledge*〉; 〈*stretch out*〉 allungare; tendere 〈*hand*〉 ● *vi* 〈*garden, knowledge:*〉 estendersi

extension /ɪk'stenʃn/ *n* prolungamento *m*; 〈*of visa, contract*〉 proroga *f*; 〈*of treaty*〉 ampliamento *m*; 〈*part of building*〉 annesso *m*; 〈*length of cable*〉 prolunga *f*; *Teleph* interno *m*; **~ 226** interno 226

extensive /ɪk'stensɪv/ *a* ampio, vasto. **~ly** *adv* ampiamente

extent /ɪk'stent/ *n* 〈*scope*〉 portata *f*; **to a certain ~** fino a un certo punto; **to such an ~ that...** fino al punto che...

extenuating /ɪk'stenjʊeɪtɪŋ/ *a* **~ circumstances** attenuanti *fpl*

exterior /ɪk'stɪərɪə(r)/ *a* & *n* esterno *m*

exterminat|e /ɪk'stɜːmɪneɪt/ *vt* sterminare. **~ion** /-'neɪʃn/ *n* sterminio *m*

external /ɪk'stɜːnl/ *a* esterno; **for ~ use only** *Med* per uso esterno. **~ly** *adv* esternamente

extinct /ɪk'stɪŋkt/ *a* estinto. **~ion** /-ɪŋkʃn/ *n* estinzione *f*

extinguish /ɪk'stɪŋgwɪʃ/ *vt* estinguere. **~er** *n* estintore *m*

extort /ɪk'stɔːt/ *vt* estorcere. **~ion** /-ɔːʃn/ *n* estorsione *f*

extortionate /ɪk'stɔːʃənət/ *a* esorbitante

extra /'ekstrə/ *a* in più; 〈*train*〉 straordinario; **an ~ £10** 10 sterline extra, 10 sterline in più ● *adv* in più; 〈*especially*〉 più; **pay ~** pagare in più, pagare extra; **~ strong/busy** fortissimo/occupatissimo ● *n* *Theat* comparsa *f*; **~s** *pl* extra *mpl*

extract¹ /'ekstrækt/ *n* estratto *m*

extract² /ɪk'strækt/ *vt* estrarre 〈*tooth, oil*〉; strappare 〈*secret*〉; ricavare 〈*truth*〉. **~or** [**fan**] *n* aspiratore *m*

extradit|e /'ekstrədaɪt/ *Jur* *vt* estradare. **~ion** /-'dɪʃn/ *n* estradizione *f*

extra'marital *a* extraconiugale

extraordinar|y /ɪk'strɔːdɪnərɪ/ *a* straordinario. **~ily** /-ɪlɪ/ *adv* straordinariamente

extravagan|ce /ɪk'strævəgəns/ *n* 〈*with money*〉 prodigalità *f*; 〈*of behaviour*〉 stravaganza *f*. **~t** *a* spendaccione; 〈*bizarre*〉 stravagante; 〈*claim*〉 esagerato

extrem|e /ɪk'striːm/ *a* estremo ● *n* estremo *m*; **in the ~e** al massimo. **~ely** *adv* estremamente. **~ist** *n* estremista *mf*

extremity /ɪk'stremətɪ/ *n* 〈*end*〉 estremità *f inv*

extricate /'ekstrɪkeɪt/ *vt* districare

extrovert /'ekstrəvɜːt/ *n* estroverso, -a *mf*

exuberant /ɪg'zjuːbərənt/ *a* esuberante

exude /ɪg'zjuːd/ *vt also fig* trasudare

exult /ɪg'zʌlt/ *vi* esultare

eye /aɪ/ *n* occhio *m*; 〈*of needle*〉 cruna *f*; **keep an ~ on** tener d'occhio; **see ~ to ~** aver le stesse idee ● *vt* 〈*pt/pp* **eyed**, *pres p* **ey[e]ing**〉 guardare

eye: **~ball** *n* bulbo *m* oculare. **~brow** *n* sopracciglio *m* 〈*pl* sopracciglia *f*〉. **~lash** *n* ciglio *m* 〈*pl* ciglia *f*〉. **~lid** *n* palpebra *f*. **~-opener** *n* rivelazione *f*. **~-shadow** *n* ombretto *m*. **~sight** *n* vista *f*. **~sore** *n fam* pugno *m* nell'occhio. **~witness** *n* testimone *mf* oculare

Ff

fable /'feɪbl/ *n* favola *f*

fabric /'fæbrɪk/ *n also fig* tessuto *m*

fabrication /fæbrɪ'keɪʃn/ *n* invenzione *f*; 〈*manufacture*〉 fabbricazione *f*

fabulous /'fæbjʊləs/ *a fam* favoloso

façade /fəˈsɑːd/ n (of building, person) facciata f

face /feɪs/ n faccia f, viso m; (grimace) smorfia f; (surface) faccia f; (of clock) quadrante m; **pull ~s** far boccacce; **in the ~ of** di fronte a; **on the ~ of it** in apparenza ● vt essere di fronta a; (confront) affrontare; **~ north** (house:) dare a nord; **~ the fact that** arrendersi al fatto che. **face up to** vt accettare (facts); affrontare (person)

face: **~-flannel** n ≈ guanto m di spugna. **~less** a anonimo. **~-lift** n plastica f facciale

facet /ˈfæsɪt/ n sfaccettatura f, fig aspetto m

facetious /fəˈsiːʃəs/ a spiritoso. **~ remarks** spiritosaggini mpl

face value (of money) valore m nominale; **take sb/sth at ~** fermarsi alle apparenze

facial /ˈfeɪʃl/ a facciale ● n trattamento m di bellezza al viso

facile /ˈfæsaɪl/ a semplicistico

facilitate /fəˈsɪlɪteɪt/ vt rendere possibile; (make easier) facilitare

facility /fəˈsɪlətɪ/ n facilità f; **~ies** pl (of area, in hotel etc) attrezzature fpl

facing /ˈfeɪsɪŋ/ prep **~ the sea** (house) che dà sul mare; **the person ~ me** la persona di fronte a me

facsimile /fækˈsɪmɪlɪ/ n facsimile m

fact /fækt/ n fatto m; **in ~** infatti

faction /ˈfækʃn/ n fazione f

factor /ˈfæktə(r)/ n fattore m

factory /ˈfæktərɪ/ n fabbrica f

factual /ˈfæktʃʊəl/ a be **~** attenersi ai fatti. **~ly** adv (inaccurate) dal punto di vista dei fatti

faculty /ˈfækltɪ/ n facoltà f inv

fad /fæd/ n capriccio m

fade /feɪd/ vi sbiadire; (sound, light:) affievolirsi; (flower:) appassire. **fade in** vt cominciare in dissolvenza (picture). **fade out** vt finire in dissolvenza (picture)

fag /fæg/ n (chore) fatica f; (fam: cigarette) sigaretta f; (Am sl: homosexual) frocio m. **~ end** n fam cicca f

fagged /fægd/ a **~ out** fam stanco morto

Fahrenheit /ˈfærənhaɪt/ a Fahrenheit

fail /feɪl/ n **without ~** senz'altro ● vi (attempt:) fallire; (eyesight, memory:) indebolirsi; (engine, machine:) guastarsi; (marriage:) andare a rotoli; (in exam) essere bocciato; **~ to do** sth non fare qcsa; **I tried but I ~ed** ho provato ma non ci sono riuscito ● vt non superare (exam); bocciare (candidate); (disappoint) deludere; **words ~ me** mi mancano le parole

failing /ˈfeɪlɪŋ/ n difetto m ● prep **~ that** altrimenti

failure /ˈfeɪljə(r)/ n fallimento m; (mechanical) guasto m; (person) incapace mf

faint /feɪnt/ a leggero; (memory) vago; **feel ~** sentirsi mancare ● n svenimento m ● vi svenire

faint: **~-hearted** a timido. **~ly** adv (slightly) leggermente. **~ness** n (physical) debolezza f

fair¹ /feə(r)/ n fiera f

fair² a (hair, person) biondo; (skin) chiaro; (weather) bello; (just) giusto; (quite good) discreto; Sch abbastanza bene; **a ~ amount** abbastanza ● adv **play ~** fare un gioco pulito. **~ly** adv con giustizia; (rather) discretamente, abbastanza. **~ness** n giustizia f. **~ play** n fair play m inv

fairy /ˈfeərɪ/ n fata f; **~ story**, **~-tale** n fiaba f

faith /feɪθ/ n fede f; (trust) fiducia f; **in good/bad ~** in buona/mala fede

faithful /ˈfeɪθfl/ a fedele. **~ly** adv fedelmente; **yours ~ly** distinti saluti. **~ness** n fedeltà f

'faith-healer n guaritore, -trice mf

fake /feɪk/ a falso ● n falsificazione f; (person) impostore m ● vt falsificare; (pretend) fingere

falcon /ˈfɔːlkən/ n falcone m

fall /fɔːl/ n caduta f; (in prices) ribasso m; (Am: autumn) autunno m; **have a ~** fare una caduta ● vi (pt fell, pp fallen) cadere; (night:) scendere; **~ in love** innamorarsi. **fall about** vi (with laughter) morire dal ridere. **fall back on** vt ritornare su. **fall for** vt fam innamorarsi di (person); cascarci (sth, trick). **fall down** vi cadere; (building:) crollare. **fall in** vi caderci dentro; (collapse) crollare; Mil mettersi in riga; **~ in with** concordare su (suggestion, plan). **fall off** vi cadere; (diminish) diminuire. **fall out** vi (quarrel) litigare; **his hair is ~ing out** perde i capelli. **fall over** vi cadere. **fall through** vi (plan:) andare a monte

fallacy /ˈfæləsɪ/ n errore m

fallible /ˈfæləbl/ a fallibile

'fall-out n pioggia f radioattiva

false /fɔːls/ a falso; **~ bottom** doppio fondo m; **~ start** Sport falsa partenza f; **~hood** n menzogna f. **~ness** n falsità f

false 'teeth npl dentiera f

falsify /ˈfɔːlsɪfaɪ/ vt (pt/pp -ied) falsificare

falter /ˈfɔːltə(r)/ vi vacillare; (making speech) esitare

fame /feɪm/ n fama f

familiar /fəˈmɪljə(r)/ a familiare; **be ~ with** (know) conoscere. **~ity** /-lɪˈærɪtɪ/ n familiarità f. **~ize** vt familiarizzare; **~ize oneself with** familiarizzarsi con

family /ˈfæməlɪ/ n famiglia f

family: ~ al'lowance n assegni mpl familiari. **~ 'doctor** n medico m di famiglia. **~ 'life** n vita f familiare. **~ 'planning** n pianificazione f familiare. **~ 'tree** n albero m genealogico

famine /ˈfæmɪn/ n carestia f

famished /ˈfæmɪʃt/ a **be ~** fam avere una fame da lupo

famous /ˈfeɪməs/ a famoso

fan¹ /fæn/ n ventilatore m; (handheld) ventaglio m ● vt (pt/pp fanned) far vento a; **~ oneself** sventagliarsi; fig **~ the flames** soffiare sul fuoco. **fan out** vi spiegarsi a ventaglio

fan² n (admirer) ammiratore, -trice mf; Sport tifoso m; (of Verdi etc) appassionato, -a mf

fanatic /fəˈnætɪk/ n fanatico, -a mf. **~al** a fanatico. **~ism** /-sɪzm/ n fanatismo m

'fan belt n cinghia f per ventilatore

fanciful /ˈfænsɪfl/ a fantasioso

fancy /ˈfænsɪ/ n fantasia f; **I've taken a real ~ to him** mi è molto simpatico; **as the ~ takes you** come ti pare ● a [a] fantasia ● vt (pt/pp -ied) (believe) credere; (fam: want) aver voglia di; **he fancies you** fam gli piaci; **~ that!** ma guarda un po'! **~ 'dress** n costume m (per maschera)

fanfare /ˈfænfeə(r)/ n fanfara f

fang /fæŋ/ n zanna f; (of snake) dente m

fan: ~ heater n termoventilatore m. **~light** n lunetta f

fantasize /ˈfæntəsaɪz/ vi fantasticare. **~tic** /-ˈtæstɪk/ a fantastico. **~y** n fantasia f

far /fɑː(r)/ adv lontano; (much) molto; **by ~** di gran lunga; **~ away** lontano; **as ~ as the church** fino alla chiesa; **how ~ is it from here?** quanto dista da qui?; **as ~ as I know** per quanto io sappia ● a (end, side) altro; **the F~ East** l'Estremo Oriente m

farce /fɑːs/ n farsa f. **~ical** a ridicolo

fare /feə(r)/ n tariffa f; (food) vitto m. **~-dodger** /-dɒdʒə(r)/ n passeggero, -a mf senza biglietto

farewell /feəˈwel/ int liter addio! ● n addio m

far-'fetched a improbabile

farm /fɑːm/ n fattoria f ● vi fare

l'agricoltore ● *vt* coltivare ⟨*land*⟩.
~er *n* agricoltore *m*

farm: **~house** *n* casa *f* colonica.
~ing *n* agricoltura *f*. **~yard** *n* aia *f*

far: **~·'reaching** *a* di larga portata. **~·'sighted** *a* *fig* prudente;
(*Am: long-sighted*) presbite

fart /fɑːt/ *n* scoreggia *f* ● *vi*
scoreggiare

farther /'fɑːðə(r)/ *adv* più lontano
● *a* **at the ~ end of** all'altra estremità *f*

fascinat|e /'fæsɪneɪt/ *vt* affascina-
re. **~ing** *a* affascinante. **~ion**
/-'neɪʃn/ *n* fascino *m*

fascis|m /'fæʃɪzm/ *n* fascismo *m*.
~t *n* fascista *mf* ● *a* fascista

fashion /'fæʃn/ *n* moda *f*; (*manner*)
maniera *f* ● *vt* modellare. **~able**
/-əbl/ *a* di moda; **be ~able** essere
alla moda. **~ably** *adv* alla moda

fast¹ /fɑːst/ *a* veloce; ⟨*colour*⟩ indelebile; **be ~** ⟨*clock*⟩ andare avanti
● *adv* velocemente; (*firmly*) saldamente; **~er!** più in fretta!; **be ~
asleep** dormire profondamente

fast² *n* digiuno *m* ● *vi* digiunare

fasten /'fɑːsn/ *vt* allacciare; chiudere ⟨*window*⟩; (*stop flapping*)
mettere un fermo a ● *vi* allacciar-
si. **~er**, **~ing** *n* chiusura *f*

fastidious /fə'stɪdɪəs/ *a* esigente

fat /fæt/ *a* (**fatter, fattest**) ⟨*person,
cheque*⟩ grasso ● *n* grasso *m*

fatal /'feɪtl/ *a* mortale; ⟨*error*⟩ fata-
le. **~ism** /-təlɪzm/ *n* fatalismo *m*.
~ist /-təlɪst/ *n* fatalista *mf*. **~ity**
/fə'tælətɪ/ *n* morte *f*. **~ly** *adv* mor-
talmente

fate /feɪt/ *n* destino *m*. **~ful** *a*
fatidico

'fat-head *n* *fam* zuccone, -a *mf*

father /'fɑːðə(r)/ *n* padre *m*; **F~
Christmas** Babbo *m* Natale ● *vt*
generare ⟨*child*⟩

father: **~hood** *n* paternità *f*.
~-in-law *n* (*pl* **~s-in-law**) suocero
m. **~ly** *a* paterno

fathom /'fæðəm/ *n* *Naut* braccio
m ● *vt* **~ [out]** comprendere

fatigue /fə'tiːg/ *n* fatica *f* ●

fatten /'fætn/ *vt* ingrassare ⟨*animal*⟩. **~ing** *a* **a cream is ~ing** la
panna fa ingrassare

fatty /'fætɪ/ *a* grasso ● *n* *fam* cic-
cione, -a *mf*

fatuous /'fætjʊəs/ *a* fatuo

faucet /'fɔːsɪt/ *n* *Am* rubinetto *m*

fault /fɔːlt/ *n* difetto *m*; *Geol* faglia
f; *Tennis* fallo *m*; **be at ~** avere
torto; **find ~ with** trovare da ridire su; **it's your ~** è colpa tua ● *vt*
criticare. **~less** *a* impeccabile

faulty /'fɔːltɪ/ *a* difettoso

fauna /'fɔːnə/ *n* fauna *f*

favour /'feɪvə(r)/ *n* favore *m*; **be in
~ of sth** essere a favore di qcsa;
do sb a ~ fare un piacere a qcno
● *vt* (*prefer*) preferire. **~able**
/-əbl/ *a* favorevole

favourit|e /'feɪvərɪt/ *a* preferito
● *n* preferito, -a *mf*; *Sport* favorito,
-a *mf*. **~ism** *n* favoritismo *m*

fawn /fɔːn/ *a* fulvo ● *n* ⟨*animal*⟩
cerbiatto *m*

fax /fæks/ *n* (*document, machine*)
fax *m inv*; **by ~** per fax ● *vt*
faxare. **~ machine** *n* fax *m inv*.
~-modem *n* modem-fax *m inv*,
fax-modem *m inv*

fear /fɪə(r)/ *n* paura *f*; **no ~!** *fam*
vai tranquillo! ● *vt* temere ● *vi* **~
for sth** temere per qcsa

fear|ful /'fɪəfl/ *a* pauroso; (*awful*)
terribile. **~less** *a* impavido.
~some /-səm/ *a* spaventoso

feas|ibility /fiːzɪ'bɪlɪtɪ/ *n* pratica-
bilità *f*. **~ible** *a* fattibile; (*possible*) probabile

feast /fiːst/ *n* festa *f*; (*banquet*)
banchetto *m* ● *vi* banchettare. **~
on** godersi

feat /fiːt/ *n* impresa *f*

feather /'feðə(r)/ *n* piuma *f*

feature /'fiːtʃə(r)/ *n* (*quality*) caratteristica *f*; *Journ* articolo *m*;
~s (*pl: of face*) lineamenti *mpl*
● *vt* (*film etc*) avere come protagonista ● *vi* (*on a list etc*) comparire. **~
film** *n* lungometraggio *m*

February /'februərɪ/ *n* febbraio *m*

fed /fed/ *see* **feed** ● a **be ~ up** *fam* essere stufo (**with** di)

federal /'fed(ə)rəl/ *a* federale

federation /fedə'reɪʃn/ *n* federazione *f*

fee /fiː/ *n* tariffa *f*; (*lawyer's, doctor's*) onorario *m*; (*for membership, school*) quota *f*

feeble /'fiːbl/ *a* debole; (*excuse*) fiacco

feed /fiːd/ *n* mangiare *m*; (*for baby*) pappa *f* ● *v* (*pt/pp* **fed**) ● *vt* dar da mangiare a (*animal*); (*support*) nutrire; **~ sth into sth** inserire qcsa in qcsa ● *vi* mangiare

'feedback *n* controreazione *f*; (*of information*) reazione *f*, feedback *m*

feel /fiːl/ *v* (*pt/pp* **felt**) ● *vt* sentire; (*experience*) provare; (*think*) pensare; (*touch: searching*) tastare; (*touch: for texture*) toccare ● *vi* **~ soft/hard** essere duro/morbido al tatto; **~ hot/hungry** aver caldo/fame; **~ ill** sentirsi male; **I don't ~ like it** non ne ho voglia; **how do you ~ about it?** (*opinion*) che te ne pare?; **it doesn't ~ right** non mi sembra giusto. **~er** *n* (*of animal*) antenna *f*; **put out ~ers** *fig* tastare il terreno. **~ing** *n* sentimento *m*; (*awareness*) sensazione *f*

feet /fiːt/ *see* **foot**

feign /feɪn/ *vt* simulare

feline /'fiːlaɪn/ *a* felino

fell[1] /fel/ *vt* (*knock down*) abbattere

fell[2] *see* **fall**

fellow /'feləʊ/ *n* (*of society*) socio *m*; (*fam: man*) tipo *m*

fellow: **~-'countryman** *n* compatriota *m*. **~-men** *npl* prossimi *mpl*. **~ship** *n* cameratismo *m*; (*group*) associazione *f*; *Univ* incarico *m* di ricercatore, -trice

felony /'felənɪ/ *n* delitto *m*

felt[1] /felt/ *see* **feel**

felt[2] *n* feltro *m*. **~[-tipped] 'pen** /[-tɪpt]/ *n* pennarello *m*

female /'fiːmeɪl/ *a* femminile; **the ~ antelope** l'antilope femmina ● *n* femmina *f*

femin|ine /'femmɪn/ *a* femminile ● *n* *Gram* femminile *m*. **~inity** /-'nɪnətɪ/ *n* femminilità *f*. **~ist** *a* & *n* femminista *f*

fenc|e /fens/ *n* recinto *m*; (*fam: person*) ricettatore *m* ● *vi* *Sport* tirar di scherma. **fence in** *vt* chiudere in un recinto. **~er** *n* schermidore *m*. **~ing** *n* steccato *m*; *Sport* scherma *f*

fend /fend/ *vi* **~ for oneself** badare a se stesso. **fend off** *vt* parare; difendersi da (*criticisms*)

fender /'fendə(r)/ *n* parafuoco *m* *inv*; (*Am: on car*) parafango *m*

fennel /'fenl/ *n* finocchio *m*

ferment[1] /'fɜːment/ *n* fermento *m*

ferment[2] /fə'ment/ *vi* fermentare ● *vt* far fermentare. **~ation** /fɜːmen'teɪʃn/ *n* fermentazione *f*

fern /fɜːn/ *n* felce *f*

feroc|ious /fə'rəʊʃəs/ *a* feroce. **~ity** /-'rɒsɪtɪ/ *n* ferocia *f*

ferret /'ferɪt/ *n* furetto *m* ● **ferret out** *vt* scovare

ferry /'ferɪ/ *n* traghetto *m* ● *vt* traghettare

fertil|e /'fɜːtaɪl/ *a* fertile. **~ity** /fɜː'tɪlətɪ/ *n* fertilità *f*

fertilize /'fɜːtɪlaɪz/ *vt* fertilizzare (*land, ovum*). **~r** *n* fertilizzante *m*

fervent /'fɜːvənt/ *a* fervente

fervour /'fɜːvə(r)/ *n* fervore *m*

fester /'festə(r)/ *vi* suppurare

festival /'festɪvl/ *n* *Mus, Theat* festival *m*; *Relig* festa *f*

festive /'festɪv/ *a* festivo; **~ season** periodo *m* delle feste natalizie. **~ities** /fe'stɪvətɪz/ *npl* festeggiamenti *mpl*

festoon /fe'stuːn/ *vt* **~ with** ornare di

fetch /fetʃ/ *vt* andare/venire a prendere; (*be sold for*) raggiungere [il prezzo di]

fetching /'fetʃɪŋ/ *a* attraente

fête /feɪt/ *n* festa *f* ● *vt* festeggiare

fetish /'fetɪʃ/ *n* feticcio *m*

fetter /'fetə(r)/ *vt* incatenare

fettle /'fetl/ n **in fine ~** in buona forma

feud /fjuːd/ n faida f

feudal /'fjuːdl/ a feudale

fever /'fiːvə(r)/ n febbre f. **~ish** a febbricitante; *fig* febbrile

few /fjuː/ a pochi; **every ~ days** ogni due o tre giorni; **a ~ people** alcuni; **~er reservations** meno prenotazioni; **the ~est number** il numero più basso ● pron pochi; **~ of us** pochi di noi; **a ~** alcuni; **quite a ~** parecchi; **~er than last year** meno dell'anno scorso

fiancé /fɪ'ɒnseɪ/ n fidanzato m. **~e** n fidanzata f

fiasco /fɪ'æskəʊ/ n fiasco m

fib /fɪb/ n storia f; **tell a ~** raccontare una storia

fibre /'faɪbə(r)/ n fibra f. **~glass** n fibra f di vetro

fickle /'fɪkl/ a incostante

fiction /'fɪkʃn/ n **[works of] ~** narrativa f; *(fabrication)* finzione f. **~al** a immaginario

fictitious /fɪk'tɪʃəs/ a fittizio

fiddle /'fɪdl/ n *fam* violino m; *(cheating)* imbroglio m ● vi gingillarsi **(with** con) ● vt *fam* truccare *(accounts)*

fiddly /'fɪdlɪ/ a intricato

fidelity /fɪ'delətɪ/ n fedeltà f

fidget /'fɪdʒɪt/ vi agitarsi. **~y** a agitato

field /fiːld/ n campo m

field: **~ events** npl atletica f*sg* leggera. **~-glasses** npl binocolo m*sg.* **F~ 'Marshal** n feldmaresciallo m. **~work** n ricerche f*pl* sul terreno

fiend /fiːnd/ n demonio m

fierce /fɪəs/ a feroce. **~ness** n ferocia f

fiery /'faɪərɪ/ a **(-ier, -iest)** focoso

fifteen /fɪf'tiːn/ a & n quindici m. **~th** a quindicesimo

fifth /fɪfθ/ a quinto

fiftieth /'fɪftɪəθ/ a cinquantesimo

fifty /'fɪftɪ/ a cinquanta

fig /fɪg/ n fico m

fight /faɪt/ n lotta f; *(brawl)* zuffa f;

(argument) litigio m; *(boxing)* incontro m ● v *(pt/pp* fought) ● vt *also fig* combattere ● vi combattere; *(brawl)* azzuffarsi; *(argue)* litigare. **~er** n combattente m*f;* *Aeron* caccia m *inv.* **~ing** n combattimento m

figment /'fɪgmənt/ n **it's a ~ of your imagination** questo è tutta una tua invenzione

figurative /'fɪgjərətɪv/ a *(sense)* figurato; *(art)* figurativo

figure /'fɪgə(r)/ n *(digit)* cifra f; *(carving, sculpture, illustration, form)* figura f; *(body shape)* linea f; **~ of speech** modo m di dire ● vi *(appear)* figurare ● vt *(Am: think)* pensare. **figure out** vt dedurre; capire *(person)*

figure: **~-head** n figura f simbolica. **~ skating** n pattinaggio m artistico

filament /'fɪləmənt/ n filamento m

file¹ /faɪl/ n scheda f; *(set of documents)* incartamento m; *(folder)* cartellina f; *Comput* file m *inv* ● vt archiviare *(documents)*

file² n *(line)* fila f; **in single ~** in fila

file³ n *Techn* lima f ● vt limare

filing cabinet /'faɪlɪŋkæbɪnət/ n schedario m, classificatore m

filings /'faɪlɪŋz/ npl limatura f*sg*

fill /fɪl/ n **eat one's ~** mangiare a sazietà ● vt riempire; otturare *(tooth)* ● vi riempirsi. **fill in** vt compilare *(form).* **fill out** vt compilare *(form).* **fill up** vi *(room, tank:)* riempirsi; *Auto* far il pieno ● vt riempire

fillet /'fɪlɪt/ n filetto m ● vt *(pt/pp* filleted) disossare

filling /'fɪlɪŋ/ n *Culin* ripieno m; *(of tooth)* piombatura f. **~ station** n stazione f di rifornimento

filly /'fɪlɪ/ n puledra f

film /fɪlm/ n *Cinema* film m *inv;* *Phot* pellicola f; **[cling] ~** pellicola f per alimenti ● vt/i filmare. **~ star** n star f *inv,* divo, -a m*f*

filter /'fɪltə(r)/ n filtro m ● vt filtrare. **filter through** vi ⟨news:⟩ trapelare. **~ tip** n filtro m; ⟨cigarette⟩ sigaretta f col filtro

filth /filθ/ n sudiciume m. **~y** a (-ier, -iest) sudicio; ⟨word⟩ sconcio

fin /fin/ n pinna f

final /'faɪnl/ a finale; ⟨conclusive⟩ decisivo ● n Sport finale f; **~s** pl Univ esami mpl finali

finale /fɪ'nɑːlɪ/ n finale m

finalist /'faɪnəlɪst/ n finalista mf. **~ity** /-'nælətɪ/ n finalità f

finalize /'faɪnəlaɪz/ vt mettere a punto ⟨text⟩; definire ⟨agreement⟩. **~ly** adv ⟨at last⟩ finalmente; ⟨at the end⟩ alla fine; ⟨to conclude⟩ per finire

finance /'faɪnæns/ n finanza f ● vt finanziare

financial /faɪ'nænʃl/ a finanziario

finch /fɪntʃ/ n fringuello m

find /faɪnd/ n scoperta f ● vt ⟨pt/pp found⟩ trovare; ⟨establish⟩ scoprire; **~ sb guilty** Jur dichiarare qcno colpevole. **find out** vt scoprire ● vi ⟨enquire⟩ informarsi

findings /'faɪndɪŋz/ npl conclusioni fpl

fine¹ /faɪn/ n ⟨penalty⟩ multa f ● vt multare

fine² a bello; ⟨slender⟩ fine; **he's ~** ⟨in health⟩ sta bene. **~ arts** npl belle arti fpl. ● adv bene; **that's cutting it** ~ non ci lascia molto tempo ● int [va] bene. **~ly** adv ⟨cut⟩ finemente

finery /'faɪnərɪ/ n splendore m

finesse /fɪ'nes/ n finezza f

finger /'fɪŋgə(r)/ n dito m ⟨pl dita f⟩ ● vt tastare

finger: **~-mark** n ditata f. **~-nail** n unghia f. **~-print** n impronta f digitale. **~-tip** n punta f del dito; **have sth at one's ~tips** sapere qcsa a menadito; ⟨close at hand⟩ avere qcsa a portata di mano

finicky /'fɪnɪkɪ/ a ⟨person⟩ pignolo; ⟨task⟩ intricato

finish /'fɪnɪʃ/ n fine f; ⟨finishing line⟩ traguardo m; ⟨of product⟩ finitura f; **have a good ~** ⟨runner:⟩

avere un buon finale ● vt finire; **~ reading** finire di leggere ● vi finire

finite /'faɪnaɪt/ a limitato

Finland /'fɪnlənd/ n Finlandia f

Finn /fɪn/ n finlandese mf. **~ish** a finlandese ● n ⟨language⟩ finnico m

fiord /fjɔːd/ n fiordo m

fir /fɜː(r)/ n abete m

fire /'faɪə(r)/ n fuoco m; ⟨forest, house⟩ incendio m; **be on ~** bruciare; **catch ~** prendere fuoco; **set ~ to** dar fuoco a; **under ~** sotto il fuoco ● vt cuocere ⟨pottery⟩; sparare ⟨shot⟩; tirare ⟨gun⟩; ⟨fam: dismiss⟩ buttar fuori ● vi sparare ⟨at a⟩

fire: **~ alarm** n allarme m antincendio. **~-arm** n arma f da fuoco. **~ brigade** n vigili mpl del fuoco. **~-engine** n autopompa f. **~-escape** n uscita f di sicurezza. **~ extinguisher** n estintore m. **~-man** n pompiere m, vigile m del fuoco. **~-place** n caminetto m. **~side** n by or at the **~side** accanto al fuoco. **~ station** n caserma f dei pompieri. **~-wood** n legna f ⟨da ardere⟩. **~-work** n fuoco m d'artificio; **~works** pl ⟨display⟩ fuochi mpl d'artificio

'firing squad n plotone m d'esecuzione

firm¹ /fɜːm/ n ditta f, azienda f

firm² a fermo; ⟨soil⟩ compatto; ⟨stable, properly fixed⟩ solido; ⟨resolute⟩ risoluto. **~ly** adv ⟨hold⟩ stretto; ⟨say⟩ con fermezza

first /fɜːst/ a & n primo, -a mf; **at ~** all'inizio; **who's ~?** chi è il primo?; **from the ~** ⟨fin⟩ dall'inizio ● adv ⟨arrive, leave⟩ per primo; ⟨beforehand⟩ prima; ⟨in listing⟩ prima di tutto, innanzitutto

first: **~ aid** n pronto soccorso m. **~-'aid kit** n cassetta f di pronto soccorso. **~-class** a di prima'ordine; Rail di prima classe ● adv ⟨travel⟩ in prima classe. **~ 'floor** n primo piano m; ⟨Am: ground floor⟩

pianterreno *m*. **~ly** *adv* in primo luogo. **~ name** *n* nome *m* di battesimo. **~rate** *a* ottimo

fish /fɪʃ/ *n* pesce *m* ● *vt/i* pescare. **fish out** *vt* tirar fuori

fish: ~bone *n* lisca *f*. **~erman** *n* pescatore *m*. **~farm** *n* vivaio *m*. **~ 'finger** *n* bastoncino *m* di pesce

fishing /'fɪʃɪŋ/ *n* pesca *f*. **~ boat** *n* peschereccio *m*. **~rod** *n* canna *f* da pesca

fish: ~monger /-mʌŋgə(r)/ *n* pescivendolo *m*. **~slice** *n* paletta *f* per fritti. **~y** *a* ⟨*fam: suspicious*⟩ sospetto

fission /'fɪʃn/ *n* Phys fissione *f*

fist /fɪst/ *n* pugno *m*

fit[1] /fɪt/ *n* ⟨*attack*⟩ attacco *m*; ⟨*of rage*⟩ accesso *m*; ⟨*of generosity*⟩ slancio *m*

fit[2] *a* (**fitter**, **fittest**) ⟨*suitable*⟩ adatto; ⟨*healthy*⟩ in buona salute; Sport in forma; **be ~ to do** essere in grado di fare qcsa; **~ to eat** buono da mangiare; **keep ~** tenersi in forma

fit[3] *n* ⟨*of clothes*⟩ taglio *m*; **it's a good ~** ⟨*coat etc:*⟩ ti/le sta bene ● *v* (*pt/pp* **fitted**) ● *vi* (*be the right size*) andare bene; **it won't ~** ⟨*no room*⟩ non ci sta ● *vt* (*fix*) applicare (**to** a); (*install*) installare; **it doesn't ~ me** ⟨*coat etc:*⟩ non mi va bene; **~ with** fornire di. **fit in** *vi* ⟨*person:*⟩ adattarsi; **it won't ~ in** ⟨*no room*⟩ non ci sta ● *vt* (*in schedule, vehicle*) trovare un buco per

fit|ful /'fɪtfl/ *a* irregolare. **~fully** *adv* a sprazzi. **~ments** *npl* (*in house*) impianti *mpl* fissi. **~ness** *n* (*suitability*) capacità *f*; [*physical*] **~ness** forma *f*, fitness *m*

fitted: ~ 'carpet *n* moquette *f* inv. **~ 'cupboard** *n* armadio *m* a muro; (*smaller*) armadietto *m* a muro. **~ 'kitchen** *n* cucina *f* componibile. **~ 'sheet** *n* lenzuolo *m* con angoli

fitter /'fɪtə(r)/ *n* installatore, -trice *mf*

fitting /'fɪtɪŋ/ *a* appropriato ● *n* (*of clothes*) prova *f*; Techn montaggio *m*; **~s** *pl* accessori *mpl*. **~ room** *n* camerino *m*

five /faɪv/ *a & n* cinque *m*. **~r** *n fam* biglietto *m* da cinque sterline

fix /fɪks/ *n* ⟨*sl: drugs*⟩ pera *f*; **be in a ~** *fam* essere nei guai ● *vt* fissare; (*repair*) aggiustare; preparare ⟨*meal*⟩. **fix up** *vt* fissare ⟨*meeting*⟩

fixation /fɪk'seɪʃn/ *n* fissazione *f*

fixed /fɪkst/ *a* fisso

fixture /'fɪkstʃə(r)/ *n* Sport incontro *m*; **~s and fittings** impianti *mpl* fissi

fizz /fɪz/ *vi* frizzare

fizzle /'fɪzl/ *vi* **~ out** finire in nulla

fizzy /'fɪzɪ/ *a* gassoso. **~ drink** *n* bibita *f* gassata

flabbergasted /'flæbəga:stɪd/ *a* **~** rimanere a bocca aperta

flabby /'flæbɪ/ *a* floscio

flag[1] /flæg/ *n* bandiera *f* ● **flag down** *vt* (*pt/pp* **flagged**) far segno di fermarsi a ⟨*taxi*⟩

flag[2] *vi* (*pt/pp* **flagged**) cedere

flag-pole *n* asta *f* della bandiera

flagrant /'fleɪgrənt/ *a* flagrante

flagship *n* Naut nave *f* ammiraglia; *fig* fiore *m* all'occhiello

flagstone *n* pietra *f* da lastricare

flair /fleə(r)/ *n* ⟨*skill*⟩ talento *m*; ⟨*style*⟩ stile *m*

flake /fleɪk/ *n* fiocco *m* ● *vi* **~ [off]** cadere in fiocchi

flaky /'fleɪkɪ/ *a* a scaglie. **~ pastry** *n* pasta *f* sfoglia

flamboyant /flæm'bɔɪənt/ *a* ⟨*personality*⟩ brillante; ⟨*tie*⟩ sgargiante

flame /fleɪm/ *n* fiamma *f*

flammable /'flæməbl/ *a* infiammabile

flan /flæn/ *n* ⟨*fruit*⟩ crostata *f*

flank /flæŋk/ *n* fianco *m* ● *vt* fiancheggiare

flannel /'flæn(ə)l/ *n* flanella *f*; (*for washing*) ≈ guanto *m* di spugna;

(*trousers*) pantaloni *mpl* di flanella

flannelette /flænə'let/ *n* flanella *f* di cotone

flap /flæp/ *n* (*of pocket, envelope*) risvolto *m*; (*of table*) ribalta *f*; **in a ~** *fam* in grande agitazione ●*v* (*pt/pp* **flapped**) ●*vi* sbattere; *fam* agitarsi ●*vt* ~ **its wings** battere le ali

flare /fleə(r)/ *n* fiammata *f*; (*device*) razzo *m* ●**flare up** *vi* (*rash:*) venire fuori; (*fire:*) fare una fiammata; (*person, situation:*) esplodere. **~d** *a* (*garment*) svasato

flash /flæʃ/ *n* lampo *m*; **in a ~** in un attimo ●*vi* lampeggiare; **~ past** passare con un bolide ●*vt* lanciare (*smile*); **~ one's headlights** lampeggiare; **~ a torch at** puntare una torcia su

flash: **~back** *n* scena *f* retrospettiva. **~bulb** *n* *Phot* flash *m inv*. **~er** *n* *Auto* lampeggiatore *m*. **~light** *n* *Phot* flash *m inv*; (*Am: torch*) torcia *f* [elettrica]. **~y** *a* vistoso

flask /flɑːsk/ *n* fiasco *m*; (*vacuum* ~) termos *m inv*

flat /flæt/ *a* (**flatter, flattest**) piatto; (*refusal*) reciso; (*beer*) sgasato; (*battery*) scarico; (*tyre*) a terra; **A ~** *Mus* la bemolle ●*n* appartamento *m*; *Mus* bemolle *m*; (*puncture*) gomma *f* a terra

flat: **~ 'feet** *npl* piedi *mpl* piatti. **~fish** *n* pesce *m* piatto. **~ly** *adv* (*refuse*) categoricamente. **~ rate** *n* tariffa *f* unica.

flatten /'flætn/ *vt* appiattire

flatter /'flætə(r)/ *vt* adulare. **~ing** *a* (*comments*) lusinghiero; (*colour, dress*) che fa sembrare più bello. **~y** *n* adulazione *f*

flat 'tyre *n* gomma *f* a terra

flaunt /flɔːnt/ *vt* ostentare

flautist /'flɔːtɪst/ *n* flautista *mf*

flavour /'fleɪvə(r)/ *n* sapore *m* ●*vt* condire; **chocolate ~ed** al sapore di cioccolato. **~ing** *n* condimento *m*

flaw /flɔː/ *n* difetto *m*. **~less** *a* perfetto

flax /flæks/ *n* lino *m*. **~en** *a* (*hair*) biondo platino

flea /fliː/ *n* pulce *m*. **~ market** *n* mercato *m* delle pulci

fleck /flek/ *n* macchiolina *f*

fled /fled/ *see* **flee**

flee /fliː/ *vt/i* (*pt/pp* **fled**) fuggire (**from** da)

fleec|e /fliːs/ *n* pelliccia *f* ●*vt* *fam* spennare. **~y** *a* (*lining*) felpato

fleet /fliːt/ *n* flotta *f*; (*of cars*) parco *m*

fleeting /'fliːtɪŋ/ *a* **catch a ~ glance of sth** intravedere qcsa; **for a ~ moment** per un attimo

flesh /fleʃ/ *n* carne *f*; **in the ~** in persona. **~y** *a* carnoso

flew /fluː/ *see* **fly²**

flex¹ /fleks/ *vt* flettere (*muscle*)

flex² /fleks/ *n* *Electr* filo *m*

flexib|ility /fleksɪ'bɪlətɪ/ *n* flessibilità *f*. **~le** *a* flessibile

'flexitime /'fleksɪ-/ *n* orario *m* flessibile

flick /flɪk/ *vt* dare un buffetto a; **~ sth off sth** togliere qcsa da qcsa con un colpetto. **flick through** *vt* sfogliare

flicker /'flɪkə(r)/ *vi* tremolare

flier /'flaɪə(r)/ *n* = **flyer**

flight¹ /flaɪt/ *n* (*fleeing*) fuga *f*; **take ~** darsi alla fuga

flight² /flaɪt/ *n* (*flying*) volo *m*; **~ of stairs** rampa *f*

flight: **~ path** *n* traiettoria *f* di volo. **~ recorder** *n* registratore *m* di volo

flighty /'flaɪtɪ/ *a* (**-ier, -iest**) frivolo

flimsy /'flɪmzɪ/ *a* (**-ier, -iest**) (*material*) leggero; (*shelves*) poco robusto; (*excuse*) debole

flinch /flɪntʃ/ *vi* (*wince*) sussultare; (*draw back*) ritirarsi; **~ from a task** *fig* sottrarsi a un compito

fling /flɪŋ/ *n* **have a ~** (*fam: affair*) aver un'avventura ●*vt* (*pt/pp* **flung**) gettare

flint /flɪnt/ *n* pietra *f* focaia; (*for lighter*) pietrina *f*

flip /flɪp/ *v* ⟨*pt/pp* **flipped**⟩ ● *vt* dare un colpetto a; buttare in aria ⟨*coin*⟩ ● *vi fam* uscire dai gangheri; ⟨*go mad*⟩ impazzire. **flip through** *vt* sfogliare

flippant /ˈflɪpənt/ *a* irriverente

flipper /ˈflɪpə(r)/ *n* pinna *f*

flirt /flɜːt/ *n* civetta *f* ● *vi* flirtare

flirtat|ion /flɜːˈteɪʃn/ *n* flirt *m inv*. **~ious** /-ʃəs/ *a* civettuolo

flit /flɪt/ *vi* ⟨*pt/pp* **flitted**⟩ volteggiare

float /fləʊt/ *n* galleggiante *m*; ⟨*in procession*⟩ carro *m*; ⟨*money*⟩ riserva *f* di cassa ● *vi* galleggiare; *Fin* fluttuare

flock /flɒk/ *n* gregge *m*; ⟨*of birds*⟩ stormo *m* ● *vi* affollarsi

flog /flɒg/ *vt* ⟨*pt/pp* **flogged**⟩ bastonare; ⟨*fam: sell*⟩ vendere

flood /flʌd/ *n* alluvione *f*; ⟨*of river*⟩ straripamento *m*; ⟨*fig: of replies, letters, tears*⟩ diluvio *m*; **be in ~** ⟨*river:*⟩ essere straripato ● *vt* allagare ● *vi* ⟨*river:*⟩ straripare

'floodlight *n* riflettore *m* ● *vt* ⟨*pt/pp* **floodlit**⟩ illuminare con riflettori

floor /flɔː(r)/ *n* pavimento *m*; ⟨*storey*⟩ piano *m*; ⟨*for dancing*⟩ pista *f* ● *vt* ⟨*baffle*⟩ confondere; ⟨*knock down*⟩ stendere ⟨*person*⟩

floor: ~ board *n* asse *f* del pavimento. **~-polish** *n* cera *f* per il pavimento. **~ show** *n* spettacolo *m* di varietà

flop /flɒp/ *n fam* ⟨*failure*⟩ tonfo *m*; *Theat* fiasco *m* ● *vi* ⟨*pt/pp* **flopped**⟩ ⟨*fam: fail*⟩ far fiasco. **flop down** *vi* accasciarsi

floppy /ˈflɒpɪ/ *a* floscio. **~ disk** *n* floppy disk *m inv*. **~ [disk] drive** *n* lettore di floppy *m*

flora /ˈflɔːrə/ *n* flora *f*

floral /ˈflɔːrəl/ *a* floreale

Florence /ˈflɒrəns/ *n* Firenze *f*

florid /ˈflɒrɪd/ *a* ⟨*complexion*⟩ florido; ⟨*style*⟩ troppo ricercato

florist /ˈflɒrɪst/ *n* fioriao, -a *mf*

flounce /flaʊns/ *n* balza *f* ● *vi* **~ out** uscire con aria melodrammatica

flounder¹ /ˈflaʊndə(r)/ *vi* dibattersi; ⟨*speaker:*⟩ impappinarsi

flounder² *n* ⟨*fish*⟩ passera *f* di mare

flour /ˈflaʊə(r)/ *n* farina *f*

flourish /ˈflʌrɪʃ/ *n* gesto *m* drammatico; ⟨*scroll*⟩ ghirigoro *m* ● *vi* prosperare ● *vt* brandire

floury /ˈflaʊərɪ/ *a* farinoso

flout /flaʊt/ *vt* fregarsene di ⟨*rules*⟩

flow /fləʊ/ *n* flusso *m* ● *vi* scorrere; ⟨*hang loosely*⟩ ricadere

flower /ˈflaʊə(r)/ *n* fiore *m* ● *vi* fiorire

flower: ~-bed *n* aiuola *f*. **~ed** *a* a fiori. **~pot** *n* vaso *m* [per i fiori]. **~y** *a* fiorito

flown /fləʊn/ *see* **fly²**

flu /fluː/ *n* influenza *f*

fluctuat|e /ˈflʌktjʊeɪt/ *vi* fluttuare. **~ion** /-ˈeɪʃn/ *n* fluttuazione *f*

fluent /ˈfluːənt/ *a* spedito; **speak ~ Italian** parlare correntemente l'italiano. **~ly** *adv* speditamente

fluff /flʌf/ *n* peluria *f*. **~y** *a* ⟨*-ier, -iest*⟩ vaporoso; ⟨*toy*⟩ di peluche

fluid /ˈfluːɪd/ *a* fluido ● *n* fluido *m*

fluke /fluːk/ *n* colpo *m* di fortuna

flung /flʌŋ/ *see* **fling**

flunk /flʌŋk/ *vt Am fam* essere bocciato in

fluorescent /flʊəˈresnt/ *a* fluorescente

fluoride /ˈflʊəraɪd/ *n* fluoruro *m*

flurry /ˈflʌrɪ/ *n* ⟨*snow*⟩ raffica *f*; *fig* agitazione *f*

flush /flʌʃ/ *n* ⟨*blush*⟩ [vampata *f* di] rossore *m* ● *vi* arrossire ● *vt* lavare con un getto d'acqua; **~ the toilet** tirare l'acqua ● *a* a livello (**with** di); ⟨*fam: affluent*⟩ a soldi

flustered /ˈflʌstəd/ *a* in agitazione; **get ~** mettersi in agitazione

flute /fluːt/ *n* flauto *m*

flutter /ˈflʌtə(r)/ *n* battito *m* ● *vi* svolazzare

flux /flʌks/ *n* **in a state of ~** in uno stato di flusso

fly¹ /flaɪ/ *n* ⟨*pl* **flies**⟩ mosca *f*

fly² *v* ⟨*pt* **flew**, *pp* **flown**⟩ ● *vi* volare; ⟨go by plane⟩ andare in aereo; ⟨flag:⟩ sventolare; ⟨rush⟩ precipitarsi; ~ **open** spalancarsi ● vt pilotare ⟨plane⟩; trasportare ⟨in aereo⟩ ⟨troops, supplies⟩; volare con ⟨Alitalia etc⟩

fly³ n & **flies** pl ⟨on trousers⟩ patta f

flyer /'flaɪə(r)/ n aviatore m; ⟨leaflet⟩ volantino m

flying /'flaɪɪŋ/: ~ **buttress** n arco m rampante. ~ **colours**: **with ~ colours** a pieni voti. ~ **saucer** n disco m volante. ~ **'start** n **get off to a ~ start** fare un'ottima partenza. ~ **'visit** n visita f lampo

fly: ~ **leaf** n risguardo m. ~**over** n cavalcavia m inv

foal /fəʊl/ n puledro m

foam /fəʊm/ n schiuma f; ⟨synthetic⟩ gommapiuma® f ● vi spumare; ~ **at the mouth** far la bava alla bocca. ~**rubber** n gommapiuma® f

fob /fɒb/ vt ⟨pt/pp **fobbed**⟩ ~ **sth off** affibbiare qcsa ⟨on sb a qcno⟩; ~ **sb off** liquidare qcno

focal /'fəʊkl/ a focale

focus /'fəʊkəs/ n fuoco m; **in ~** a fuoco; **out of ~** sfocato ● v ⟨pt/pp **focused** or **focussed**⟩ ● vt fig concentrare ⟨on su⟩ ● vi Phot ~**on** mettere a fuoco; fig concentrarsi ⟨on su⟩

fodder /'fɒdə(r)/ n foraggio m

foe /fəʊ/ n nemico, -a f

foetus /'fiːtəs/ n ⟨pl **-tuses**⟩ feto m

fog /fɒg/ n nebbia f

fogey /'fəʊgɪ/ n **old** ~ persona f antiquata

foggy /'fɒgɪ/ a ⟨**foggier, foggiest**⟩ nebbioso; **it's ~** c'è nebbia

'fog-horn n sirena f da nebbia

foil¹ /fɔɪl/ n lamina f di metallo

foil² vt ⟨thwart⟩ frustrare

foil³ n ⟨sword⟩ fioretto m

foist /fɔɪst/ vt appioppare ⟨on sb a qcno⟩

fold¹ /fəʊld/ n ⟨for sheep⟩ ovile m

fold² n piega f ● vt piegare; ~ **one's arms** incrociare le braccia ● vi piegarsi; ⟨fail⟩ crollare. **fold up** vt

ripiegare ⟨chair⟩ ● vi essere pieghevole; ⟨fam: business⟩ collassare

folder /'fəʊldə(r)/ n cartella f. ~**ing** a pieghevole

foliage /'fəʊlɪɪdʒ/ n fogliame m

folk /fəʊk/ npl gente f; **my ~s** ⟨family⟩ i miei; **hello there ~s** ciao a tutti

folk: ~**dance** n danza f popolare. ~**lore** n folclore m. ~**song** n canto m popolare

follow /'fɒləʊ/ vt/i seguire; **it doesn't ~** non è necessariamente cosi; ~ **suit** fig fare lo stesso; **as ~s** come segue. **follow up** vt fare seguito a ⟨letter⟩

follower /'fɒləʊə(r)/ n seguace mf. ~**ing** a seguente ● n seguito m; ⟨supporters⟩ seguaci mpl ● prep in seguito a

folly /'fɒlɪ/ n follia f

fond /fɒnd/ a affezionato; ⟨hope⟩ vivo; **be ~ of** essere appassionato di ⟨music⟩; **I'm ~ of...** ⟨food, person⟩ mi piace moltissimo...

fondle /'fɒndl/ vt coccolare

fondness /'fɒndnɪs/ n affetto m; ⟨for things⟩ amore m

font /fɒnt/ n fonte f battesimale; Typ carattere m di stampa

food /fuːd/ n cibo m; ⟨for animals, groceries⟩ mangiare m; **let's buy some ~** compriamo qualcosa da mangiare

food: ~ **mixer** n frullatore m. ~ **poisoning** n intossicazione f alimentare.~ **processor** n tritatutto m inv elettrico

fool¹ /fuːl/ n sciocco, -a mf; **she's no ~** non è una stupida; **make a ~ of oneself** rendersi ridicolo ● vt prendere in giro ● vi ~ **around** giocare; ⟨husband, wife:⟩ avere l'amante

fool² n Culin crema f

fool|**hardy** a temerario. ~**ish** a stolto. ~**ishly** adv scioccamente. ~**ishness** n sciocchezza f. ~**proof** a facilissimo

foot /fʊt/ n ⟨pl **feet**⟩ piede m; ⟨of

animal) zampa *f*; *(measure)* piede *m* (= 30,48 *cm)*; **on ~ a piedi; on one's feet** in piedi; **put one's ~ in it** *fam* fare una gaffe

foot: ~**-and-'mouth disease** *n* afta *f* epizootica. ~**ball** *n* calcio *m*; *(ball)* pallone *m*. ~**baller** *n* giocatore *m* di calcio. ~**ball pools** *npl* totocalcio *m*. ~**brake** *n* freno *m* a pedale. ~**bridge** *n* passerella *f*. ~**hills** *npl* colline *fpl* pedemontane. ~**hold** *n* punto *m* d'appoggio. ~**ing** *n* **lose one's ~ing** perdere l'appiglio; **on an equal ~ing** in condizioni di parità. ~**man** *n* valletto *m*. ~**note** *n* nota *f* a piè di pagina. ~**path** *n* sentiero *m*. ~**print** *n* orma *f*. ~**step** *n* passo *m*; **follow in sb's ~steps** *fig* seguire l'esempio di qcno. ~**stool** *n* sgabellino *m*. ~**wear** *n* calzature *fpl*

for /fə(r)/, accentato /fɔː(r)/ *prep* per; ~ **this reason** per questa ragione; **I have lived here ~ ten years** vivo qui da dieci anni; ~ **supper** per cena; ~ **all that** nonostante questo; **what ~?** a che scopo?; **send ~ a doctor** chiamare un dottore; **fight ~ a cause** lottare per una causa; **go ~ a walk** andare a fare una passeggiata; **there's no need ~ you to go** non c'è bisogno che tu vada; **it's not ~ me to say** non sta a me dirlo; **now you're ~ it** ora sei nei pasticci ● *conj* poiché, perché

forage /'fɒrɪdʒ/ *n* foraggio *m* ● *vi* ~ **for** cercare

forbade /fə'bæd/ *see* **forbid**

forbear|ance /fɔː'beərəns/ *n* pazienza *f*. ~**ing** *a* tollerante

forbid /fə'bɪd/ *vt* (*pt* **forbade**, *pp* **forbidden**) proibire. ~**ding** *a* *(prospect)* che spaventa; *(stern)* severo

force /fɔːs/ *n* forza *f*; **in ~** in vigore; *(in large numbers)* in massa; **come into ~** entrare in vigore; **the [armed] ~s** *pl* le forze armate ● *vt* forzare; ~ **sth on sb** *(decision)* imporre qcsa a qcno;

(drink) costringere qcno a fare qcsa

forced /fɔːst/ *a* forzato

force: ~**'feed** *vt* (*pt/pp* **-fed**) nutrire a forza. ~**ful** *a* energico. ~**fully** *adv* *(say, argue)* con forza

forceps /'fɔːseps/ *npl* forcipe *f*

forcible /'fɔːsɪbl/ *a* forzato

ford /fɔːd/ *n* guado *m* ● *vt* guadare

fore /fɔː(r)/ *n* **to the ~** in vista; **come to the ~** salire alla ribalta

fore: ~**arm** *n* avambraccio *m*. ~**boding** /-'bəʊdɪŋ/ *n* presentimento *m*. ~**cast** *n* previsione *f* ● *vt* (*pt/pp* ~**cast**) prevedere. ~**court** *n* cortile *m* anteriore. ~**fathers** *npl* antenati *mpl*. ~**finger** *n* [dito *m*] indice *m*. ~**front** *n* **be in the ~front** essere all'avanguardia. ~**gone** *a* **be a ~gone conclusion** essere una cosa scontata. ~**ground** *n* primo piano *m*. ~**head** /'fɔːhed, 'fɒrɪd/ *n* fronte *f*. ~**hand** *n* *Tennis* diritto *m*

foreign /'fɒrən/ *a* straniero; *(trade)* estero; *(not belonging)* estraneo; **he is ~** è uno straniero. ~ **currency** *n* valuta *f* estera. ~**er** *n* straniero, -a *mf*. ~ **language** *n* lingua *f* straniera

Foreign: ~ **Office** *n* ministero *m* degli [affari] esteri. ~ **'Secretary** *n* ministro *m* degli esteri

fore: ~**man** *n* caporeparto *m*. ~**most** *a* principale ● *adv* **first and ~most** in primo luogo. ~**name** *n* nome *m* di battesimo

forensic /fə'rensɪk/ *a* ~ **medicine** medicina *f* legale

'forerunner *n* precursore *m*

fore'see *vt* (*pt* **-saw**, *pp* **-seen**) prevedere. ~**able** /-əbl/ *a* **in the ~able future** in futuro per quanto si possa prevedere

'foresight *n* previdenza *f*

forest /'fɒrɪst/ *n* foresta *f*. ~**er** *n* guardia *f* forestale

fore'stall *vt* prevenire

forestry /'fɒrɪstrɪ/ *n* silvicoltura *f*

'foretaste *n* pregustazione *f*

fore'tell *vt* (*pt/pp* **-told**) predire

forever /fəˈrevə(r)/ *adv* per sempre; **he's ~ complaining** si lamenta sempre

fore·warn *vt* avvertire

foreword /ˈfɔːwɜːd/ *n* prefazione *f*

forfeit /ˈfɔːfɪt/ *n* (*in game*) pegno *m*; *Jur* penalità *f* ● *vt* perdere

forgave /fəˈgeɪv/ *see* forgive

forge¹ /fɔːdʒ/ *vi* **~ ahead** ⟨*runner:*⟩ lasciarsi indietro gli altri; *fig* farsi strada

forge² *n* fucina *f* ● *vt* fucinare; (*counterfeit*) contraffare. **~ r** *n* contraffattore *m*. **~ry** *n* contraffazione *f*

forget /fəˈget/ *vt/i* (*pt* **-got**, *pp* **-gotten**, *pres p* **-getting**) dimenticare; dimenticarsi di ⟨*language, skill*⟩. **~ful** *a* smemorato. **~fulness** *n* smemoratezza *f*. **~me-not** *n* non-ti-scordar-di-mé *m inv*. **~table** /-əbl/ *a* ⟨*day, film*⟩ da dimenticare

forgive /fəˈgɪv/ *vt* (*pt* **-gave**, *pp* **-given**) **~ sb for sth** perdonare qcno per qcsa. **~ness** *n* perdono *m*

forgo /fɔːˈgəʊ/ *vt* (*pt* **-went**, *pp* **-gone**) rinunciare a

forgot(ten) /fəˈgɒt(n)/ *see* forget

fork /fɔːk/ *n* forchetta *f*; (*for digging*) forca *f*; (*in road*) bivio *m* ● *vi* ⟨*road:*⟩ biforcarsi; **~ right** prendere a destra. **fork out** *vt fam* sborsare

fork-lift ˈtruck *n* elevatore *m*

forlorn /fəˈlɔːn/ *a* ⟨*look*⟩ perduto; ⟨*place*⟩ derelitto; **~ hope** speranza *f* vana

form /fɔːm/ *n* forma *f*; (*document*) modulo *m*; *Sch* classe *f* ● *vt* formare; formulare ⟨*opinion*⟩ ● *vi* formarsi

formal /ˈfɔːml/ *a* formale. **~ity** /-ˈmælɪtɪ/ *n* formalità *f inv*. **~ly** *adv* in modo formale; (*officially*) ufficialmente

format /ˈfɔːmæt/ *n* formato *m* ● *vt* formattare ⟨*disk, page*⟩

formation /fɔːˈmeɪʃn/ *n* formazione *f*

formative /ˈfɔːmətɪv/ *a* **~ years** anni *mpl* formativi

former /ˈfɔːmə(r)/ *a* precedente; (*PM, colleague*) ex; **the ~, the latter** il primo, l'ultimo. **~ly** *adv* precedentemente; (*in olden times*) in altri tempi

formidable /ˈfɔːmɪdəbl/ *a* formidabile

formula /ˈfɔːmjʊlə/ *n* (*pl* **-ae** /-liː/ *or* **-s**) formula *f*

formulate /ˈfɔːmjʊlərt/ *vt* formulare

forsake /fəˈseɪk/ *vt* (*pt* **-sook** /-sʊk/, *pp* **-saken**) abbandonare

fort /fɔːt/ *n* *Mil* forte *m*

forte /ˈfɔːteɪ/ *n* [pezzo *m*] forte *m*

forth /fɔːθ/ *adv* **back and ~** avanti e indietro; **and so ~** e così via

forth· **~'coming** *a* prossimo; (*communicative*) communicativo; **no response was ~** non arrivava nessuna risposta. **~right** *a* schietto. **~'with** *adv* immediatamente

fortieth /ˈfɔːtɪɪθ/ *a* quarantesimo

fortification /fɔːtɪfɪˈkeɪʃn/ *n* fortificazione *f*

fortify /ˈfɔːtɪfaɪ/ *vt* (*pt/pp* **-ied**) fortificare; *fig* rendere forte

fortnight /ˈfɔːtnaɪt/ *n* *Br* n quindicina *f*. **~ly** *a* bimensile ● *adv* ogni due settimane

fortress /ˈfɔːtrɪs/ *n* fortezza *f*

fortuitous /fɔːˈtjuːɪtəs/ *a* fortuito

fortunate /ˈfɔːtʃənət/ *a* fortunato; **that's ~!** meno male!. **~ly** *adv* fortunatamente

fortune /ˈfɔːtʃuːn/ *n* fortuna *f*. **~-teller** *n* indovino, -a *mf*

forty /ˈfɔːtɪ/ *a* & *n* quaranta *m*

forum /ˈfɔːrəm/ *n* foro *m*

forward /ˈfɔːwəd/ *adv* avanti; (*towards the front*) in avanti ● *a* in avanti; (*presumptuous*) sfacciato ● *n* *Sport* attaccante *m*. ● *vt* inoltrare ⟨*letter*⟩; spedire ⟨*goods*⟩. **~s** *adv* avanti

fossil /ˈfɒsl/ *n* fossile *m*. **~ized** *a* fossile; ⟨*ideas*⟩ fossilizzato

foster /ˈfɒstə(r)/ *vt* allevare ⟨*child*⟩

~-child n figlio, -a mf in affidamento. **~-mother** n madre f affidataria

fought /fɔːt/ see **fight**

foul /faʊl/ a ⟨smell, taste⟩ cattivo; ⟨air⟩ viziato; ⟨language⟩ osceno; ⟨mood, weather⟩ orrendo; **~ play** Jur delitto m ● n Sport fallo m ● vt inquinare ⟨water⟩; Sport commettere un fallo contro; ⟨nets, rope:⟩ impigliarsi in. **~-smelling** a puzzo

found¹ /faʊnd/ see **find**

found² vt fondare

foundation /faʊn'deɪʃn/ n ⟨basis⟩ fondamento m; ⟨charitable⟩ fondazione f; **~s** pl ⟨of building⟩ fondamenta fpl; **lay the ~-stone** porre la prima pietra

founder¹ /'faʊndə(r)/ n fondatore, -trice mf

founder² vi ⟨ship:⟩ affondare

foundry /'faʊndrɪ/ n fonderia f

fountain /'faʊntɪn/ n fontana f. **~-pen** n penna f stilografica

four /fɔː(r)/ a & n quattro m

four-'poster n letto m a baldacchino. **~-some** /'fɔːsəm/ n quartetto m. **~teen** a & n quattordici m. **~teenth** a quattordicesimo

fourth /fɔːθ/ a quarto

fowl /faʊl/ n pollame m

fox /fɒks/ n volpe f ● vt ⟨puzzle⟩ ingannare

foyer /'fɔɪeɪ/ n Theat ridotto m; (in hotel) salone m d'ingresso

fraction /'frækʃn/ n frazione f

fracture /'fræktʃə(r)/ n frattura f ● vt fratturare ● vi fratturarsi

fragile /'frædʒaɪl/ a fragile

fragment /'frægmənt/ n frammento m. **~ary** a frammentario

fragran|ce /'freɪɡrəns/ n fragranza f. **~t** a fragrante

frail /freɪl/ a gracile

frame /freɪm/ n ⟨of picture, door, window⟩ cornice f; ⟨of spectacles⟩ montatura f; Anat ossatura f; ⟨structure, of bike⟩ telaio m; **~ of mind** stato m d'animo ● vt incorniciare ⟨picture⟩; fig formulare;

⟨sl: incriminate⟩ montare. **~work** n struttura f

franc /fræŋk/ n franco m

France /frɑːns/ n Francia f

franchise /'fræntʃaɪz/ n Pol diritto m di voto; Comm franchigia f

frank¹ /fræŋk/ vt affrancare ⟨letter⟩

frank² a franco. **~ly** adv francamente

frankfurter /'fræŋkfɜːtə(r)/ n würstel m inv

frantic /'fræntɪk/ a frenetico; **be ~ with worry** essere agitatissimo. **~ally** adv freneticamente

fraternal /frə'tɜːnl/ a fraterno

fraud /frɔːd/ n frode f; ⟨person⟩ impostore m. **~ulent** /-jʊlənt/ a fraudolento

fraught /frɔːt/ a **~ with** pieno di

fray¹ /freɪ/ n mischia f

fray² vi sfilacciarsi

frayed /freɪd/ a ⟨cuffs⟩ sfilacciato; ⟨nerves⟩ a pezzi

freak /friːk/ n fenomeno m; ⟨person⟩ scherzo m di natura; ⟨fam: weird person⟩ tipo m strambo ● a anormale. **~ish** a strambo

freckle /'frekl/ n lentiggine f. **~d** a lentigginoso

free /friː/ a ⟨freer, freest⟩ libero; ⟨ticket, copy⟩ gratuito; ⟨lavish⟩ generoso; **~ of charge** gratuito; **set ~** liberare ● vt ⟨pt/pp **freed**⟩ liberare

free: **~dom** n libertà f. **~hand** adv a mano libera. **~hold** n proprietà f ⟨fondiaria⟩ assoluta. **~ 'kick** n calcio m di punizione. **~ lance** a & adv indipendente. **~ly** adv liberamente; ⟨generously⟩ generosamente; **I ~ly admit that...** devo ammettere che... **F~mason** n massone m. **~-range** a **~-range egg** uovo m di gallina ruspante. **~'sample** n campione m gratuito. **~style** n stile m libero. **~way** n Am autostrada f. **~'wheel** vi ⟨car:⟩ ⟨in neutral⟩ andare in folle; ⟨with engine switched off⟩ andare a motore spento; ⟨*bicycle:*⟩ andare a ruota libera

freez|e /friːz/ *vt* (*pt* **froze**, *pp* **frozen**) gelare; bloccare ⟨*wages*⟩ ● *vi* ⟨*water:*⟩ gelare; **it's ~ing** si gela; **my hands are ~ing** ho le mani congelate

freez|er /ˈfriːzə(r)/ *n* freezer *m inv*, congelatore *m*. **~ing** *a* gelido ● *n* **below ~ing** sotto zero

freight /freɪt/ *n* carico *m*. **~er** *n* nave *f* da carico. **~ train** *n Am* treno *m* merci

French /frentʃ/ *a* francese ● *n* ⟨*language*⟩ francese *m*; **the ~** *pl* i francesi *mpl*

French: **~ 'beans** *npl* fagiolini *mpl* [verdi]. **~ 'bread** *n* filone *m* (*di pane*). **~ 'fries** *npl* patate *fpl* fritte. **~man** *n* francese *m*. **~ 'window** *n* porta-finestra *f*. **~woman** *n* francese *f*

frenzied /ˈfrenzɪd/ *a* frenetico

frenzy /ˈfrenzɪ/ *n* frenesia *f*

frequency /ˈfriːkwənsɪ/ *n* frequenza *f*

frequent¹ /ˈfriːkwənt/ *a* frequente. **~ly** *adv* frequentemente

frequent² /frɪˈkwent/ *vt* frequentare

fresco /ˈfreskəʊ/ *n* affresco *m*

fresh /freʃ/ *a* fresco; (*new*) nuovo; (*Am: cheeky*) sfacciato. **~ly** *adv* di recente

freshen /ˈfreʃn/ *vi* ⟨*wind:*⟩ rinfrescare. **freshen up** *vi* dare una rinfrescata a ● *vi* rinfrescarsi

freshness /ˈfreʃnɪs/ *n* freschezza *f*

'freshwater *a* di acqua dolce

fret /fret/ *vi* (*pt/pp* **fretted**) inquietarsi. **~ful** *a* irritabile

'fretsaw *n* seghetto *m* da traforo

friar /ˈfraɪə(r)/ *n* frate *m*

friction /ˈfrɪkʃn/ *n* frizione *f*

Friday /ˈfraɪdeɪ/ *n* venerdì *m inv*

fridge /frɪdʒ/ *n* frigo *m*

fried /fraɪd/ *see* **fry** ● *a* fritto; **~ egg** uovo *m* fritto

friend /frend/ *n* amico. *a mf*. **~ly** *a* (**-ier**, **-iest**) ⟨*relations*, *meeting*, *match*⟩ amichevole; ⟨*neighbour-*

hood, *smile*⟩ piacevole; ⟨*software*⟩ di facile uso; **be ~ly with** essere amico di. **~ship** *n* amicizia *f*

frieze /friːz/ *n* fregio *m*

fright /fraɪt/ *n* paura *f*; **take ~** spaventarsi

frighten /ˈfraɪtn/ *vt* spaventare. **~ed** *a* spaventato; **be ~ed** aver paura (**of** di). **~ing** *a* spaventoso

frightful /ˈfraɪtfl/ *a* terribile

frigid /ˈfrɪdʒɪd/ *a* frigido. **~ity** /-ˈdʒɪdɪtɪ/ *n* freddezza *f*; *Psych* frigidità *f*

frill /frɪl/ *n* volant *m inv*. **~y** *a* ⟨*dress*⟩ con tanti volant

fringe /frɪndʒ/ *n* frangia *f*; (*of hair*) frangetta *f*; (*fig: edge*) margine *m*. **~ benefits** *npl* benefici *mpl* supplementari

frisk /frɪsk/ *vt* (*search*) perquisire

frisky /ˈfrɪskɪ/ *a* (**-ier**, **-iest**) vispo

fritter /ˈfrɪtə(r)/ *n* frittella *f*. ● **fritter away** *vt* sprecare

frivol|ity /frɪˈvɒlətɪ/ *n* frivolezza *f*. **~ous** /ˈfrɪvələs/ *a* frivolo

frizzy /ˈfrɪzɪ/ *a* crespo

fro /frəʊ/ *see* **to**

frock /frɒk/ *n* abito *m*

frog /frɒg/ *n* rana *f*. **~man** *n* uomo *m* rana

frolic /ˈfrɒlɪk/ *vi* (*pt/pp* **frolicked**) ⟨*lambs:*⟩ sgambettare; ⟨*people:*⟩ folleggiare

from /frɒm/ *prep* da; **~ Monday** lunedì; **~ that day** da quel giorno; **he's ~ London** è di Londra; **this is a letter ~ my brother** questa è una lettera di mio fratello; **documents ~ the 16th century** documenti del XVI secolo; **made ~** fatto con; **she felt ill ~ fatigue** si sentiva male dalla stanchezza; **~ now on** d'ora in poi

front /frʌnt/ *n* parte *f* anteriore; (*fig: organization etc*) facciata *f*; (*of garment*) davanti *m*; (*sea~*) lungomare *m*; *Mil*, *Pol*, *Meteorol* fronte *m*; **in ~** davanti a; **in or at the ~** davanti; **to the ~** avanti ● *a* davanti; ⟨*page*, *row*, *wheel*⟩ anteriore

frontal /ˈfrʌntl/ *a* frontale

front: ~ **'door** n porta f d'entrata. ~ **'garden** n giardino m davanti

frontier /frʌntɪə(r)/ n frontiera f

front-wheel 'drive n trazione f anteriore

frost /frɒst/ n gelo m; (hoar~) brina f. ~**bite** n congelamento m. ~**bitten** a congelato

frost|ed /frɒstɪd/ a ~**ed glass** vetro m smerigliato. ~**ily** adv gelidamente. ~**ing** n Am Culin glassa f. ~**y** a also fig gelido

froth /frɒθ/ n schiuma f ●vi far schiuma. ~**y** a schiumoso

frown /fraʊn/ n cipiglio m ●vi aggrottare le sopracciglia. **frown on** vt disapprovare

froze /frəʊz/ see **freeze**

frozen /frəʊzn/ see **freeze** ●a (corpse, hand) congelato; (wastes) gelido; Culin surgelato; **I'm** ~ sono gelato. ~ **food** n surgelati mpl

frugal /fruːgl/ a frugale

fruit /fruːt/ n frutto m; (collectively) frutta f; **eat more** ~ mangia più frutta. ~ **cake** n dolce m con frutta candita

fruit|erer /fruːtərə(r)/ n fruttivendolo, -a mf. ~**ful** a fig fruttuoso

fruition /fruːˈɪʃn/ n **come to** ~ dare dei frutti

fruit: ~ **juice** n succo m di frutta. ~**less** a infruttuoso. ~ **machine** n macchinetta f mangiasoldi. ~ **'salad** n macedonia f [di frutta]

frumpy /frʌmpɪ/ a scialbo

frustrat|e /frʌˈstreɪt/ vt frustrare; rovinare (plans). ~**ing** a frustrante. ~**ion** /-eɪʃn/ n frustrazione f

fry¹ /fraɪ/ vt/i (pt/pp **fried**) friggere

fry² /fraɪ/ n inv **small** ~ fig pesce m piccolo

frying pan n padella f

fuck /fʌk/ vulg vt/i scopare ●int cazzo. ~**ing** a del cazzo

fuddy-duddy /fʌdɪdʌdɪ/ n fam matusa mf inv

fudge /fʌdʒ/ n caramella f a base di zucchero, burro e latte

fuel /fjuːəl/ n carburante m; fig nutrimento m ●vt fig alimentare

fugitive /fjuːdʒɪtɪv/ n fuggiasco, -a mf

fugue /fjuːg/ n Mus fuga f

fulfil /fʊlˈfɪl/ vt (pt/pp **-filled**) soddisfare (conditions, need); realizzare (dream, desire); ~ **oneself** realizzarsi. ~**ling** a soddisfacente. ~**ment** n **sense of** ~**ment** senso m di appagamento

full /fʊl/ a pieno (**of** di); (detailed) esauriente; (bus, hotel) completo; (skirt) ampio; **at** ~ **speed** a tutta velocità; **in** ~ **swing** in pieno fervore ●n **in** ~ per intero

full: ~ **'moon** n luna f piena. ~**-scale** a (model) in scala reale; (alert) di massima gravità. ~ **'stop** n punto m. ~**-'time** a & adv a tempo pieno

fully /fʊlɪ/ adv completamente; (in detail) dettagliatamente; ~ **booked** (hotel, restaurant) tutto prenotato

fumble /fʌmbl/ vi ~ **in** rovistare in; ~ **with** armeggiare con; ~ **for one's keys** rovistare alla ricerca delle chiavi

fume /fjuːm/ vi (be angry) essere furioso

fumes /fjuːmz/ npl fumi mpl; (from car) gas mpl di scarico

fumigate /fjuːmɪgeɪt/ vt suffumicare

fun /fʌn/ n divertimento m; **for** ~ per ridere; **make** ~ **of** prendere in giro; **have** ~ divertirsi

function /fʌŋkʃn/ n funzione f; (event) cerimonia f ●vi funzionare; ~ **as** (serve as) funzionare da. ~**al** a funzionale

fund /fʌnd/ n fondo m; fig pozzo m; ~**s** pl fondi mpl ●vt finanziare

fundamental /fʌndəˈmentl/ a fondamentale

funeral /fjuːnərəl/ n funerale m

funeral: ~ **directors** n impresa f di pompe funebri. ~ **home** Am, ~ **parlour** n camera f ardente.

march n marcia f funebre. **~ service** n rito m funebre

'funfair n luna park m inv

fungus /'fʌŋgəs/ n (pl -gi /-gaɪ/) fungo m

funicular /fjuː'nɪkjʊlə(r)/ n funicolare f

funnel /'fʌnl/ n imbuto m; (on ship) ciminiera f

funnily /'fʌnɪlɪ/ adv comicamente; (oddly) stranamente; **~ enough** strano a dirsi

funny /'fʌnɪ/ a (-ier, -iest) buffo; (odd) strano. **~ business** n affare m losco

fur /fɜː(r)/ n pelo m; (for clothing) pelliccia f; (in kettle) deposito m. **~ 'coat** n pelliccia f

furious /'fjʊərɪəs/ a furioso

furnace /'fɜːnɪs/ n fornace f

furnish /'fɜːnɪʃ/ vt ammobiliare (flat); fornire (supplies). **~ed** a **~ed room** stanza f ammobiliata. **~ings** npl mobili mpl

furniture /'fɜːnɪtʃə(r)/ n mobili mpl

furred /fɜːd/ a (tongue) impastato

furrow /'fʌrəʊ/ n solco m

furry /'fɜːrɪ/ a (animal) peloso; (toy) di peluche

further /'fɜːðə(r)/ a (additional) ulteriore; **at the ~ end** all'altra estremità; **until ~ notice** fino a nuovo avviso ● adv più lontano; **~,...** inoltre,...; **~ off** più lontano ● vt promuovere

further: **~ edu'cation** n ≈ formazione f parauniversitaria. **~'more** adv per di più

furthest /'fɜːðɪst/ a più lontano ● adv più lontano

furtive /'fɜːtɪv/ a furtivo

fury /'fjʊərɪ/ n furore m

fuse[1] /fjuːz/ n (of bomb) detonatore m; (cord) miccia f

fuse[2] /fjuːz/ vt (Electr) fondere; (Electr) far saltare ● vi fondersi; (Electr) saltare; **the lights have ~d** sono saltate le luci. **~-box** n scatola f dei fusibili

fuselage /'fjuːzəlɑːʒ/ n Aeron fusoliera f

fusion /'fjuːʒn/ n fusione f

fuss /fʌs/ n storie fpl; **make a ~** fare storie; **make a ~ of** colmare di attenzioni ● vi fare storie

fussy /'fʌsɪ/ a (-ier, -iest) (person) difficile da accontentare; (clothes etc) pieno di fronzoli

fusty /'fʌstɪ/ a che odora di stantio; (smell) di stantio

futile /'fjuːtaɪl/ a inutile. **~ity** /-'tɪlətɪ/ n futilità f

future /'fjuːtʃə(r)/ a & n futuro; **in ~** in futuro. **~ perfect** futuro m anteriore

futuristic /fjuːtʃə'rɪstɪk/ a futuristico

fuzz /fʌz/ n **the ~** (sl: police) la pula

fuzzy /'fʌzɪ/ a (-ier, -iest) (hair) crespo; (photo) sfuocato

Gg

gab /gæb/ n fam **have the gift of the ~** avere la parlantina

gabble /'gæb(ə)l/ vi parlare troppo in fretta

gad /gæd/ vi (pt/pp gadded) **~ about** andarsene in giro

gadget /'gædʒɪt/ n aggeggio m

Gaelic /'geɪlɪk/ a & n gaelico m

gaffe /gæf/ n gaffe f inv

gag /gæg/ n bavaglio m; (joke) battuta f ● vt (pt/pp gagged) imbavagliare

gaily /'geɪlɪ/ adv allegramente

gain /geɪn/ n guadagno m; (increase) aumento m ● vt acquisire; **~ weight** aumentare di peso; **~ access** accedere ● vi (clock:) andare avanti. **~ful** a **~ful employment** lavoro m remunerato

gait /geɪt/ n andatura f

gala /'gɑːlə/ n gala f; **swimming ~** manifestazione f di nuoto ● attrib di gala

galaxy /'gæləksɪ/ n galassia f
gale /geɪl/ n bufera f
gall /gɔːl/ n (impudence) impudenza f
gallant /'gælənt/ a coraggioso; (chivalrous) galante. **~ry** n coraggio m
'**gall-bladder** n cistifellea f
gallery /'gælərɪ/ n galleria f
galley /'gælɪ/ n (ship's kitchen) cambusa f; **~** [**proof**] bozza f in colonna
gallivant /'gælɪvænt/ vi fam andare in giro
gallon /'gælən/ n gallone m (= 4,5 l; Am = 3,7 l)
gallop /'gæləp/ n galoppo m ● vi galoppare
gallows /'gæləʊz/ n forca f
'**gallstone** n calcolo m biliare
galore /ɡə'lɔː(r)/ adv a bizzeffe
galvanize /'gælvənaɪz/ vt Techn galvanizzare; fig stimolare (**into** a)
gambit /'gæmbɪt/ n prima mossa f
gambl|e /'gæmbl/ n (risk) azzardo m ● vi giocare; (on Stock Exchange) speculare; **~e on** (rely) contare su. **~er** n giocatore, -trice mf [d'azzardo]. **~ing** n gioco m [d'azzardo]
game /geɪm/ n gioco m; (match) partita f; (animals, birds) selvaggina f; **~s** Sch ≈ ginnastica f ● a (brave) coraggioso; **are you ~?** ti va?; **be ~ for** essere pronto per. **~keeper** n guardacaccia m inv
gammon /'gæmən/ n coscia f di maiale
gamut /'gæmət/ n fig gamma f
gander /'gændə(r)/ n oca f maschio
gang /gæŋ/ n banda f; (of workmen) squadra f ● **gang up** vi far comunella (**on** contro)
gangling /'gæŋlɪŋ/ a spilungone
gangrene /'gæŋgriːn/ n cancrena f
gangster /'gæŋstə(r)/ n gangster m inv
gangway /'gæŋweɪ/ n passaggio m; Naut, Aeron passerella f

gaol /dʒeɪl/ n carcere m ● vt incarcerare. **~er** n carceriere m
gap /gæp/ n spazio m; (in ages, between teeth) scarto m; (in memory) vuoto m; (in story) punto m oscuro
gap|e /geɪp/ vi stare a bocca aperta; (be wide open) spalancarsi; **~e at** guardare a bocca aperta. **~ing** a aperto
garage /'gæraːʒ/ n garage m inv; (for repairs) meccanico m; (for petrol) stazione f di servizio
garbage /'gaːbɪdʒ/ n immondizia f; (nonsense) idiozie fpl. **~ can** n Am bidone m dell'immondizia
garbled /'gaːbld/ a confuso
garden /'gaːdn/ n giardino m; [**public**] **~s** pl giardini mpl pubblici ● vi fare giardinaggio. **~ centre** n negozio m di piante e articoli da giardinaggio. **~er** n giardiniere, -a mf. **~ing** n giardinaggio m
gargle /'gaːgl/ n gargarismo m ● vi fare gargarismi
gargoyle /'gaːgɔɪl/ n gargouille f
garish /'geərɪʃ/ a sgargiante
garland /'gaːlənd/ n ghirlanda f
garlic /'gaːlɪk/ n aglio m. **~ bread** n pane m condito con aglio
garment /'gaːmənt/ n indumento m
garnish /'gaːnɪʃ/ n guarnizione f ● vt guarnire
garrison /'gærɪsn/ n guarnigione f
garter /'gaːtə(r)/ n giarrettiera f; (Am: for men's socks) reggicalze m inv da uomo
gas /gæs/ n gas m inv; (Am fam: petrol) benzina f ● v (pt/pp **gassed**) ● vt asfissiare ● vi fam blaterare. **~ cooker** n cucina f a gas. **~ 'fire** n stufa f a gas
gash /gæʃ/ n taglio m ● vt tagliare
gasket /'gæskɪt/ n Techn guarnizione f
gas: ~ mask n maschera f antigas. **~meter** n contatore m del gas
gasoline /'gæsəliːn/ n Am benzina f

gasp /gɑːsp/ vi avere il fiato mozzato

'**gas station** n Am distributore m di benzina

gastric /'gæstrɪk/ a gastrico. **~ 'flu** n influenza f gastro-intestinale. **~ 'ulcer** n ulcera f gastrica

gastronomy /gæ'strɒnəmɪ/ n gastronomia f

gate /geɪt/ n cancello m; (at airport) uscita f

gâteau /'gætəʊ/ n torta f

gate: **~crash** vt entrare senza invito a. **~crasher** n intruso, -a f. **~way** n ingresso m

gather /'gæðə(r)/ vt raccogliere; (conclude) dedurre; (in sewing) arricciare; **~ speed** acquistare velocità; **~ together** radunare ⟨people, belongings⟩; (obtain gradually) acquistare ● vi ⟨people:⟩ radunarsi. **~ing** n family **~ing** ritrovo m di famiglia

gaudy /'gɔːdɪ/ a (-ier, -iest) pacchiano

gauge /geɪdʒ/ n calibro m; Rail scartamento m; (device) indicatore m ● vt misurare; fig stimare

gaunt /gɔːnt/ a (thin) smunto

gauze /gɔːz/ n garza f

gave /geɪv/ see give

gawky /'gɔːkɪ/ a (-ier, -iest) sgraziato

gawp /gɔːp/ vi = [at] fam guardare con aria da ebete

gay /geɪ/ a gaio; (homosexual) omosessuale; ⟨bar, club⟩ gay

gaze /geɪz/ n sguardo m fisso ● vi guardare; **~ at** fissare

GB abbr (Great Britain) GB

gear /gɪə(r)/ n equipaggiamento m; Techn ingranaggio m; Auto marcia f; **in ~** con la marcia innestata; **change ~** cambiare marcia ● vt finalizzare (**to** a)

gear: **~box** n Auto scatola f del cambio. **~lever**, Am **~shift** n leva f del cambio

geese /giːs/ see goose

geezer /'giːzə(r)/ n sl tipo m

gel /dʒel/ n gel m inv

gelatine /'dʒelətɪn/ n gelatina f

gelignite /'dʒelɪgnaɪt/ n gelatina esplosiva f

gem /dʒem/ n gemma f

Gemini /'dʒemɪnaɪ/ n Astr Gemelli mpl

gender /'dʒendə(r)/ n Gram genere m

gene /dʒiːn/ n gene m

genealogy /dʒiːnɪ'ælədʒɪ/ n genealogia f

general /'dʒenrəl/ a generale ● n generale m; **in ~** in generale. **~ e'lection** n elezioni fpl politiche

generalization /dʒenrəlaɪ'zeɪʃn/ n generalizzazione f. **~e** /'dʒenrəlaɪz/ vi generalizzare

generally /'dʒenrəlɪ/ adv generalmente

general prac'titioner n medico m generico

generate /'dʒenəreɪt/ vt generare

generation /dʒenə'reɪʃn/ n generazione f

generator /'dʒenəreɪtə(r)/ n generatore m

generic /dʒɪ'nerɪk/ a **~ term** termine m generico

generosity /dʒenə'rɒsɪtɪ/ n generosità f

generous /'dʒenərəs/ a generoso. **~ly** adv generosamente

genetic /dʒɪ'netɪk/ a genetico. **~ engineering** n ingegneria f genetica. **~s** n genetica f

Geneva /dʒɪ'niːvə/ n Ginevra f

genial /'dʒiːnɪəl/ a gioviale

genitals /'dʒenɪtlz/ npl genitali mpl

genitive /'dʒenɪtɪv/ a & n **[case]** genitivo m

genius /'dʒiːnɪəs/ n (pl -uses) genio m

genocide /'dʒenəsaɪd/ n genocidio m

genre /'ʒɑ̃rə/ n genere m [letterario]

gent /dʒent/ n fam signore m; **the ~s** sg il bagno per uomini

genteel /dʒen'tiːl/ a raffinato

gentle /'dʒentl/ a delicato; ⟨breeze, tap, slope⟩ leggero
gentleman /'dʒentlmən/ n signore m; (well-mannered) gentiluomo m
gent|leness /'dʒentlnɪs/ n delicatezza f. **~ly** adv delicatamente
genuine /'dʒenjʊɪn/ a genuino. **~ly** adv ⟨sorry⟩ sinceramente
geograph|ical /dʒɪəˈgræfɪkl/ a geografico. **~y** /dʒɪˈɒgrəfɪ/ n geografia f
geological /dʒɪəˈlɒdʒɪkl/ a geologico
geolog|ist /dʒɪˈɒlədʒɪst/ n geologo, -a mf. **~y** n geologia f
geometr|ic[al] /dʒɪəˈmetrɪk(l)/ a geometrico. **~y** /dʒɪˈɒmɪtrɪ/ n geometria f
geranium /dʒəˈreɪnɪəm/ n geranio m
geriatric /dʒerɪˈætrɪk/ a geriatrico; **~ ward** n reparto m geriatria. **~s** n geriatria f
germ /dʒɜːm/ n germe m; **~s** pl microbi mpl
German /'dʒɜːmən/ n & a tedesco, -a mf; (language) tedesco m
Germanic /dʒəˈmænɪk/ a germanico
German: ~ 'measles n rosolia f. **~ 'shepherd** n pastore m tedesco
Germany /'dʒɜːmənɪ/ n Germania f
germinate /'dʒɜːmɪneɪt/ vi germogliare
gesticulate /dʒeˈstɪkjʊleɪt/ vi gesticolare
gesture /'dʒestʃə(r)/ n gesto m
get /get/ v (pt/pp got, pp Am also gotten, pres p getting) ●vt (receive) ricevere; (obtain) ottenere; (buy, catch, fetch) prendere; (transport, deliver to airport etc) portare; (reach on telephone) trovare; (fam: understand) comprendere; preparare ⟨meal⟩; **~ sb to do sth** far fare qcsa a qcno ●vi (become) ~ (become) diventare; **~ tired/bored/angry** stancarsi/annoiarsi/arrabbiarsi; **I'm ~ting hungry** mi sta venendo fame; **~**

dressed/married vestirsi/sposarsi; **~ sth ready** preparare qcsa; **~ nowhere** non concludere nulla; **this is ~ting us nowhere** questo non ci è di nessun aiuto; **~ to** (reach) arrivare a. **get at** vt (criticize) criticare; **I see what you're ~ting at** ho capito cosa vuoi dire; **what are you ~ting at?** dove vuoi andare a parare?. **get away** vi (leave) andarsene; (escape) scappare. **get back** vi tornare ●vt (recover) riavere; **~ one's own back** rifarsi. **get by** vi passare; (manage) cavarsela. **get down** vi scendere; **~ down to work** mettersi al lavoro ●vt (depress) buttare giù. **get in** vi entrare ●vt mettere dentro ⟨washing⟩; far venire ⟨plumber⟩. **get off** vi scendere; (from work) andarsene; Jur essere assolto; **~ off the bus/one's bike** scendere dal pullman/dalla bici ●vt (remove) togliere. **get on** vi salire; (be on good terms) andare d'accordo; (make progress) andare avanti; (in life) riuscire; **~ on the bus/one's bike** salire sul pullman/sulla bici; **how are you ~ting on?** come va?. **get out** vi uscire; (of car) scendere; **~ out!** fuori!; **~ out of** (avoid doing) evitare ●vt togliere ⟨cork, stain⟩. **get over** vi andare di là ●vt fig riprendersi da ⟨illness⟩. **get round** vt aggirare ⟨rule⟩; rigirare ⟨person⟩ ●vi **I never ~ round to it** non mi sono mai deciso a farlo. **get through** vi (on telephone) prendere la linea. **get up** vi alzarsi; (climb) salire; **~ up a hill** salire su una collina
get: ~away n fuga f. **~-up** n tenuta f
geyser /'giːzə(r)/ n scaldabagno m; Geol geyser m inv
ghastly /'gɑːstlɪ/ a (-ier, -iest) terribile; **feel ~** sentirsi da cani
gherkin /'gɜːkɪn/ n cetriolino m
ghetto /'getəʊ/ n ghetto m

ghost /gəʊst/ n fantasma m. **~ly** a spettrale

ghoulish /'gu:lɪʃ/ a macabro

giant /'dʒaɪənt/ n gigante m ● a gigante

gibberish /'dʒɪbərɪʃ/ n stupidaggini fpl

gibe /dʒaɪb/ n malignità fpl

giblets /'dʒɪblɪts/ npl frattaglie fpl

giddiness /'gɪdɪnɪs/ n vertigini fpl

giddy /'gɪdɪ/ a (-ier, -iest) vertiginoso; **feel** ~ avere le vertigini

gift /gɪft/ n dono m; (to charity) donazione f. **~ed** /-ɪd/ a dotato. **~-wrap** vt impacchettare in carta da regalo

gig /gɪg/ n Mus fam concerto m

gigantic /dʒaɪ'gæntɪk/ a gigantesco

giggle /'gɪgl/ n risatina f ● vi ridacchiare

gild /gɪld/ vt dorare

gills /gɪlz/ npl branchia fsg

gilt /gɪlt/ a dorato ● n doratura f. **~-edged stock** n investimento m sicuro

gimmick /'gɪmɪk/ n trovata f

gin /dʒɪn/ n gin m inv

ginger /'dʒɪndʒə(r)/ a rosso fuoco inv; (cat) rosso ● n zenzero m. **~ ale** n, **~ beer** n bibita f allo zenzero. **~bread** n panpepato m

gingerly /'dʒɪndʒəlɪ/ adv con precauzione

gipsy /'dʒɪpsɪ/ n = **gypsy**

giraffe /dʒɪ'rɑ:f/ n giraffa f

girder /'gɜ:də(r)/ n Techn trave f

girl /gɜ:l/ n ragazza f; (female child) femmina f. **~friend** n amica f; (of boy) ragazza f. **~ish** a da ragazza

giro /'dʒaɪərəʊ/ n bancogiro m; (cheque) sussidio m di disoccupazione

girth /gɜ:θ/ n circonferenza f

gist /dʒɪst/ n **the ~** la sostanza

give /gɪv/ n elasticità f ● v (pt gave, pp given) ● vt dare; (as present) regalare (to a); fare (lecture, present, shriek); donare (blood); ~ **birth** partorire ● vi (to charity) fare delle donazioni;

(yield) cedere. **give away** vt dar via; (betray) tradire; (distribute) assegnare; ~ **away the bride** portare la sposa all'altare. **give back** vt restituire. **give in** vt consegnare ● vi (yield) arrendersi. **give off** vt emanare. **give over** vi ~ **over!** piantala!. **give up** vt rinunciare a; ~ **oneself up** arrendersi ● vi rinunciare. **give way** vi cedere; Auto dare la precedenza; (collapse) crollare

given /'gɪvn/ see **give** ● a ~ **name** nome m di battesimo

glacier /'glæsɪə(r)/ n ghiacciaio m

glad /glæd/ a contento (**of** di). **~den** /'glædn/ vt rallegrare

glade /gleɪd/ n radura f

gladly /'glædlɪ/ adv volentieri

glamorize /'glæməraɪz/ vt rendere affascinante. **~ous** a affascinante

glamour /'glæmə(r)/ n fascino m

glance /glɑ:ns/ n sguardo m ● vi ~ **at** dare un'occhiata a. **glance up** vi alzare gli occhi

gland /glænd/ n glandola f

glandular /'glændjʊlə(r)/ a ghiandolare. **~ fever** n Med mononucleosi f

glare /gleə(r)/ n bagliore m; (look) occhiataccia f ● vi ~ **at** dare un'occhiataccia a

glaring /'gleərɪŋ/ a sfolgorante; (mistake) madornale

glass /glɑ:s/ n vetro m; (for drinking) bicchiere m; **~es** (pl: spectacles) occhiali mpl. **~y** a vitreo

glaze /gleɪz/ n smalto m ● vt mettere i vetri a (door, window); smaltare (pottery); Culin spennellare. **~d** a (eyes) vitreo

glazier /'gleɪzɪə(r)/ n vetraio m

gleam /gli:m/ n luccichio m ● vi luccicare

glean /gli:n/ vt racimolare (information)

glee /gli:/ n gioia f. **~ful** a gioioso

glen /glen/ n vallone m

glib /glɪb/ a pej insincero

glid|e /glaɪd/ vi scorrere; (*through the air*) planare. **~er** n aliante m

glimmer /'glɪmə(r)/ n barlume m ● vi emettere un barlume

glimpse /glɪmps/ n occhiata f; **catch a ~ of** intravedere ● vt intravedere

glint /glɪnt/ n luccichio m ● vi luccicare

glisten /'glɪsn/ vi luccicare

glitter /'glɪtə(r)/ vi brillare

gloat /gləʊt/ vi gongolare (**over** su)

global /'gləʊbl/ a mondiale

globe /gləʊb/ n globo m; (*map*) mappamondo m

gloom /gluːm/ n oscurità f; (*sadness*) tristezza f. **~y** adv (*sadly*) con aria cupa

gloomy /'gluːmɪ/ a (**-ier, -iest**) cupo

glorify /'glɔːrɪfaɪ/ vt (*pt/pp* **-ied**) glorificare; **a ~ied waitress** niente più che una cameriera

glorious /'glɔːrɪəs/ a splendido; (*deed, hero*) glorioso

glory /'glɔːrɪ/ n gloria f; (*splendour*) splendore m. **~ in** vi (*pt/pp* **-ied**) vantarsi di

gloss /glɒs/ n lucentezza f. **~ paint** n vernice f lucida ● **gloss over** vt sorvolare su

glossary /'glɒsərɪ/ n glossario m

glossy /'glɒsɪ/ a (**-ier, -iest**) lucido; **~ [magazine]** rivista f femminile

glove /glʌv/ n guanto m. **~ compartment** n Auto cruscotto m

glow /gləʊ/ n splendore m; (*in cheeks*) rossore m; (*of candle*) luce f soffusa ● vi risplendere; (*candle:*) brillare; (*person:*) avvampare. **~ing** a ardente; (*account*) entusiastico

'glow-worm n lucciola f

glucose /'gluːkəʊs/ n glucosio m

glue /gluː/ n colla f ● vt (*pres p* **gluing**) incollare

glum /glʌm/ a (**glummer, glummest**) tetro

glut /glʌt/ n eccesso m

glutton /'glʌtən/ n ghiottone, -a

mf. **~ous** /-əs/ a ghiotto. **~y** n ghiottoneria f

gnarled /nɑːld/ a nodoso

gnash /næʃ/ vt **~ one's teeth** digrignare i denti

gnat /næt/ n moscerino m

gnaw /nɔː/ vt rosicchiare

gnome /nəʊm/ n gnomo m

go /gəʊ/ n (*pl* **goes**) energia f; (*attempt*) tentativo m; **on the go** in movimento; **at one go** in una sola volta; **it's your go** tocca a te; **make a go of it** riuscire ● vi (*pt* **went**, *pp* **gone**) andare; (*leave*) andare via; (*vanish*) sparire; (*become*) diventare; (*be sold*) vendersi; **go and see** andare a vedere. **go swimming/shopping** andare a nuotare/fare spese; **where's the time gone?** come ha fatto il tempo a volare così?; **it's all gone** è finito; **be going to do** stare per fare; **I'm not going to** non ne ho nessuna intenzione; **to go** (*Am:* hamburgers etc) da asporto; **a coffee to go** un caffè da portar via. **go about** vi andare in giro. **go away** vi andarsene. **go back** vi ritornare. **go by** vi passare. **go down** vi andare giù; (*sun:*) tramontare; (*ship:*) affondare; (*swelling:*) diminuire. **go for** vt andare a prendere; andare a cercare (*doctor*); (*choose*) optare per; (*fam: attack*) aggredire; **he's not the kind I go for** non è il genere che mi attira. **go in** vi entrare. **go in for** vt partecipare a (*competition*); darsi a (*tennis*). **go off** vi andarsene; (*alarm:*) scattare; (*gun, bomb:*) esplodere; (*food, milk:*) andare a male; **go off well** riuscire. **go on** vi andare avanti; **what's going on?** cosa succede? **go on at** vt fam scocciare. **go out** vi uscire; (*light, fire:*) spegnersi. **go over** vi andare ● vt (*check*) controllare. **go round** vi andare in giro; (*visit*) andare; (*turn*) girare; **is there enough to go round?** ce n'è abbastanza per tutti? **go through** vi (*bill, proposal:*) passare ● vt (*suffer*) subire; (check) controllare; (read) leggere. **go under** vi passare sotto; (ship, swimmer:) andare sott'acqua; (fail) fallire. **go up** vi salire; (Theat: curtain:) aprirsi. **go with** vt accompagnare. **go without** vt fare a meno di (supper, sleep) vi fare senza

goad /gəʊd/ vt spingere (**into** a); (taunt) spronare

'**go-ahead** a (person, company) intraprendente ● n okay m

goal /gəʊl/ n porta f; (point scored) gol m inv; (in life) obiettivo m; **score a ~** segnare. **~ie** fam, **~keeper** n portiere m. **~post** n palo m

goat /gəʊt/ n capra f

gobble /'gɒbl/ vt ~ [**down, up**] tranguggiare

'**go-between** n intermediario, -a mf

God, god /gɒd/ n Dio m, dio m

god: **~child** n figlioccio, -a f. **~-daughter** n figlioccia f. **~dess** n dea f. **~father** n padrino m. **~-fearing** a timorato di Dio. **~forsaken** a dimenticato da Dio. **~mother** n madrina f. **~parents** npl padrino m e madrina f. **~send** n manna f. **~son** n figlioccio m

go-getter /'gəʊgetə(r)/ n ambizioso, -a mf

goggle /'gɒgl/ vi fam ~ **at** fissare con gli occhi sgranati. **~s** npl occhiali mpl; (of swimmer) occhialini mpl [da piscina]; (of worker) occhiali mpl protettivi

going /'gəʊɪŋ/ a (price, rate) corrente; ~ **concern** azienda f florida ● n it's **hard** ~ è una faticaccia; **while the** ~ **is good** finché si può. **~s-on** npl avvenimenti mpl

gold /gəʊld/ n oro m ● a d'oro

golden /'gəʊldn/ a dorato. '**handshake** n buonuscita f (al termine di un rapporto di lavoro). **~ mean** n giusto mezzo m. '**wedding** n nozze fpl d'oro

gold: **~fish** n inv pesce m rosso. **~mine** n miniera f d'oro.

~plated a placcato d'oro. **~smith** n orefice m

golf /gɒlf/ n golf m

golf: **~club** n circolo m di golf; (implement) mazza f da golf. **~course** n campo m di golf. **~er** n giocatore, -trice mf di golf

gondola /'gɒndələ/ n gondola f. **~lier** /-'lɪə(r)/ n gondoliere m

gone /gɒn/ see **go**

gong /gɒŋ/ n gong m inv

good /gʊd/ a (better, best) buono; (child, footballer, singer) bravo; (holiday, film) bello; **~ at** bravo in; **a ~ deal of anger** molta rabbia; **as ~ as** (almost) quasi; **~ morning, ~ afternoon** buon giorno; **~ evening** buona sera; **~ night** buonanotte; **have a ~ time** divertirsi ● n bene m; **for ~** per sempre; **do ~** far del bene; **do sb ~** far bene a qcno; **it's no ~** è inutile; **be up to no ~** combinare qualcosa

goodbye /gʊd'baɪ/ int arrivederci

good: **~-for-nothing** n buono, -a mf a nulla. **G~ 'Friday** n Venerdì m Santo

good: **~-'looking** a bello. **~-'natured** a be **~-natured** avere un buon carattere

goodness /'gʊdnɪs/ n bontà f; **my ~!** santo cielo!; **thank ~!** grazie al cielo!

goods /gʊdz/ npl prodotti mpl. **~ train** n treno m merci

goodwill /gʊd'wɪl/ n buona volontà f; Comm avviamento m

goody /'gʊdɪ/ n (fam: person) buono m. **~-goody** n santarellino, -a mf

gooey /'gu:ɪ/ a fam appiccicaticcio; fig sdolcinato

goof /gu:f/ vi fam cannare

goose /gu:s/ n (pl **geese**) oca f

gooseberry /'gʊzbərɪ/ n uva f spina

goose /gu:s/: **~-flesh** n, **~-pimples** npl pelle fsg d'oca

gore[1] /gɔ:(r)/ n sangue m

gore[2] vt incornare

gorge /gɔːdʒ/ n Geog gola f ● vt ~ oneself ingozzarsi

gorgeous /ˈgɔːdʒəs/ a stupendo

gorilla /gəˈrɪlə/ n gorilla m inv

gormless /ˈgɔːmlɪs/ a fam stupido

gorse /gɔːs/ n ginestrone m

gory /ˈgɔːrɪ/ a (-ier, -iest) cruento

gosh /gɒʃ/ int fam caspita

gospel /ˈgɒspl/ n vangelo m. ~ truth n sacrosanta verità f

gossip /ˈgɒsɪp/ n pettegolezzi mpl; (person) pettegolo, -a mf ● vi pettegolare. ~y a pettegolo

got /gɒt/ see get; have ~ avere; have ~ to do sth dover fare qcsa

Gothic /ˈgɒθɪk/ a gotico

gotten /ˈgɒtn/ Am see get

gouge /gaʊdʒ/ vt ~ out cavare

gourmet /ˈgʊəmeɪ/ n buongustaio, -a mf

gout /gaʊt/ n gotta f

govern /ˈgʌv(ə)n/ vt/i governare; (determine) determinare

government /ˈgʌvnmənt/ n governo m. ~al /-ˈmentl/ a governativo

governor /ˈgʌvənə(r)/ n governatore m; (of school) membro m di consiglio di istituto; (of prison) direttore, -trice mf; (fam: boss) capo m

gown /gaʊn/ n vestito m; Univ, Jur toga f

GP n abbr general practitioner

grab /græb/ vt (pt/pp grabbed) ~ [hold of] afferrare

grace /greɪs/ n grazia f; (before meal) benedicite m inv; with good ~ volentieri; three days' ~ tre giorni di proroga. ~ful a aggraziato. ~fully adv con grazia

gracious /ˈgreɪʃəs/ a cortese; (elegant) lussuoso

grade /greɪd/ n livello m; Comm qualità f; Sch voto m; (Am Sch: class) classe f; Am = gradient ● vt Comm classificare; Sch dare il voto a. ~ crossing n Am passaggio m a livello

gradient /ˈgreɪdɪənt/ n pendenza f

gradual /ˈgrædʒʊəl/ a graduale. ~ly adv gradualmente

graduate¹ /ˈgrædʒʊət/ n laureato, -a mf

graduate² /ˈgrædʒʊeɪt/ vi Univ laurearsi

graduation /grædʒʊˈeɪʃn/ n laurea f

graffiti /grəˈfiːtɪ/ npl graffiti mpl

graft /grɑːft/ n (Bot, Med) innesto m; (Med: organ) trapianto m; (fam: hard work) duro lavoro m; (fam: corruption) corruzione f ● vt innestare; trapiantare (organ)

grain /greɪn/ n (of sand, salt) granello m; (of rice) chicco m; (cereals) cereali mpl; (in wood) venatura f; it goes against the ~ fig è contro la mia/sua natura

gram /græm/ n grammo m

grammar /ˈgræmə(r)/ n grammatica f. ~ school n ≈ liceo m

grammatical /grəˈmætɪkl/ a grammaticale

granary /ˈgrænərɪ/ n granaio m

grand /grænd/ a grandioso; fam eccellente

grandad /ˈgrændæd/ n fam nonno m

'grandchild n nipote mf

'granddaughter n nipote f

grandeur /ˈgrændʒə(r)/ n grandiosità f

'grandfather n nonno m. ~ clock n pendolo m (che poggia a terra)

grandiose /ˈgrændɪəʊs/ a grandioso

grand: **~mother** n nonna f. **~parents** npl nonni mpl. **~ pi'ano** n pianoforte m a coda. **~son** n nipote m. **~stand** n tribuna f

granite /ˈgrænɪt/ n granito m

granny /ˈgrænɪ/ n fam nonna f

grant /grɑːnt/ n (money) sussidio m; Univ borsa f di studio ● vt accordare; (admit) ammettere; take sth for ~ed dare per scontato qcsa

granulated /ˈgrænjʊleɪtɪd/ a ~ sugar zucchero m semolato

granule /ˈgrænjuːl/ n granello m

grape /greɪp/ n acino m; ~s pl uva f sg

grapefruit /'greɪp-/ n inv pompelmo m

graph /grɑ:f/ n grafico m

graphic /'græfɪk/ a grafico; (vivid) vivido. ~s n grafica f

graph paper n carta f millimetrata

grapple /'græpl/ vi ~ with also fig essere alle prese con

grasp /grɑ:sp/ n stretta f; (understanding) comprensione f ● vt afferrare. ~ing a avido

grass /grɑ:s/ n erba f; at the ~ roots alla base. ~hopper n cavalletta f. ~land n prateria f

grassy /'grɑ:sɪ/ a erboso

grate¹ /greɪt/ n grata f

grate² vt Culin grattugiare ● vi stridere

grateful /'greɪtfl/ a grato. ~ly adv con gratitudine

grater /'greɪtə(r)/ n Culin grattugia f

gratif|y /'grætɪfaɪ/ vt (pt/pp -ied) appagare. ~ied a appagato. ~ying a appagante

grating /'greɪtɪŋ/ n grata f

gratis /'grɑ:tɪs/ adv gratis

gratitude /'grætɪtju:d/ n gratitudine f

gratuitous /grə'tju:ɪtəs/ a gratuito

gratuity /grə'tju:ɪtɪ/ n gratifica f

grave¹ /greɪv/ a grave

grave² n tomba f

gravel /'grævl/ n ghiaia f

grave: ~stone n lapide f. ~yard n cimitero m

gravitate /'grævɪteɪt/ vi gravitare

gravity /'grævɪtɪ/ n gravità f

gravy /'greɪvɪ/ n sugo m della carne

gray /greɪ/ a Am = grey

graze¹ /greɪz/ vi (animal:) pascolare

graze² n escoriazione f ● vt (touch lightly) sfiorare; (scrape) escoriare; sbucciarsi (knee)

grease /gri:s/ n grasso m ● vt un-

gere. ~-proof 'paper n carta f oleata

greasy /'gri:sɪ/ a (-ier, -iest) untuoso; (hair, skin) grasso

great /greɪt/ a grande; (fam: marvellous) eccezionale

great: ~-'aunt n prozia f. G~ 'Britain n Gran Bretagna f. ~-'grandchildren npl pronipoti mpl. ~-'grandfather n bisnonno m. ~-'grandmother n bisnonna f

greatly /'greɪtlɪ/ adv enormemente. ~ness n grandezza f

great-'uncle n prozio m

Greece /gri:s/ n Grecia f

greed /gri:d/ n avidità f; (for food) ingordigia f

greedily /'gri:dɪlɪ/ adv avidamente; (eat) con ingordigia

greedy /'gri:dɪ/ a (-ier, -iest) avido; (for food) ingordo

Greek /gri:k/ a & n greco, -a mf; (language) greco m

green /gri:n/ a verde; (fig: inexperienced) immaturo ● n verde m; ~s pl verdura f; the G~s pl Pol i verdi. ~ belt n zona f verde intorno a una città. ~ card n Auto carta f verde

greenery /'gri:nərɪ/ n verde m

green fingers npl have ~ ~ avere il pollice verde

greenfly /'gri:nflaɪ/ n afide m

green: ~grocer n fruttivendolo, -a mf. ~house n serra f. ~house effect n effetto m serra. ~ light n fam verde m

greet /gri:t/ vt salutare; (welcome) accogliere. ~ing n saluto m; (welcome) accoglienza f. ~ings card n biglietto m d'auguri

gregarious /grɪ'geərɪəs/ a gregario; (person) socievole

grenade /grɪ'neɪd/ n granata f

grew /gru:/ see grow

grey /greɪ/ a grigio; (hair) bianco ● n grigio m. ~hound n levriero m

grid /grɪd/ n griglia f; (on map) reticolato m; Electr rete f

grief /griːf/ n dolore m; **come to ~** ⟨plans:⟩ naufragare

grievance /ˈɡriːvəns/ n lamentela f

grieve /griːv/ vt addolorare ● vi essere addolorato

grill /grɪl/ n graticola f; ⟨for grilling⟩ griglia f; **mixed ~** grigliata f mista ● vt/i cuocere alla griglia; ⟨interrogate⟩ sottoporre al terzo grado

grille /grɪl/ n grata f

grim /grɪm/ a (**grimmer, grimmest**) arcigno; ⟨determination⟩ accanito

grimace /ɡrɪˈmeɪs/ n smorfia f ● vi fare una smorfia

grime /graɪm/ n sudiciume m

grimy /ˈgraɪmɪ/ a (**-ier, -iest**) sudicio

grin /grɪn/ n sorriso m ● vi ⟨pt/pp **grinned**⟩ fare un gran sorriso

grind /graɪnd/ n ⟨fam: hard work⟩ sfacchinata f ● vt ⟨pt/pp **ground**⟩ macinare; affilare ⟨knife⟩; ⟨Am: mince⟩ tritare; **~ one's teeth** digrignare i denti

grip /grɪp/ n presa f; fig controllo m; ⟨bag⟩ borsone m; **get a ~ of oneself** controllarsi ● vt ⟨pt/pp **gripped**⟩ afferrare; ⟨tyres:⟩ far presa su; tenere avvinto ⟨attention⟩

gripe /graɪp/ vi ⟨fam: grumble⟩ lagnarsi

gripping /ˈgrɪpɪŋ/ a avvincente

grisly /ˈgrɪzlɪ/ a (**-ier, -iest**) raccapricciante

gristle /ˈgrɪsl/ n cartilagine f

grit /grɪt/ n graniglia f; ⟨for roads⟩ sabbia f; ⟨courage⟩ coraggio m ● vt ⟨pt/pp **gritted**⟩ spargere sabbia su ⟨road⟩; **~ one's teeth** serrare i denti

grizzle /ˈgrɪzl/ vi piagnucolare

groan /grəʊn/ n gemito m ● vi gemere

grocer /ˈgrəʊsə(r)/ n droghiere, a m/f; **~'s** ⟨shop⟩ drogheria f. **~ies** npl generi mpl alimentari

groggy /ˈgrɒgɪ/ a (**-ier, -iest**) stordito; ⟨unsteady⟩ barcollante

groin /grɔɪn/ n Anat inguine m

groom /gruːm/ n sposo m; ⟨for horse⟩ stalliere m ● vt strigliare ⟨horse⟩; fig preparare; **well-~ed** ben curato

groove /gruːv/ n scanalatura f

grope /grəʊp/ vi brancolare; **~ for** cercare a tastoni

gross /grəʊs/ a obeso; ⟨coarse⟩ volgare; ⟨glaring⟩ grossolano; ⟨salary, weight⟩ lordo ● n inv grossa f. **~ly** adv ⟨very⟩ enormemente

grotesque /grəʊˈtesk/ a grottesco

grotto /ˈgrɒtəʊ/ n (pl **-es**) grotta f

grotty /ˈgrɒtɪ/ a (**-ier, -iest**) ⟨fam: flat, street⟩ squallido

ground[1] /graʊnd/ see **grind**

ground[2] n terra f; Sport terreno m; ⟨reason⟩ ragione f; **~s** pl ⟨park⟩ giardini mpl; ⟨of coffee⟩ fondi mpl ● vi ⟨ship:⟩ arenarsi ● vt bloccare a terra ⟨aircraft⟩; Am Electr mettere a terra

ground~: ~ floor n pianterreno m. **~ing** n base f. **~less** a infondato. **~sheet** n telone m impermeabile. **~work** n lavoro m di preparazione

group /gruːp/ n gruppo m ● vt raggruppare ● vi raggrupparsi

grouse[1] /graʊs/ n inv gallo m cedrone

grouse[2] vi fam brontolare

grovel /ˈgrɒvl/ vi ⟨pt/pp **grovelled**⟩ strisciare. **~ling** a leccapiedi inv

grow /grəʊ/ v ⟨pt **grew**, pp **grown**⟩ ● vi crescere; ⟨become⟩ diventare; ⟨unemployment, fear:⟩ aumentare; ⟨town:⟩ ingrandirsi ● vt coltivare; **~ one's hair** farsi crescere i capelli. **grow up** vi crescere; ⟨town:⟩ svilupparsi

growl /graʊl/ n grugnito m ● vi ringhiare

grown /grəʊn/ see **grow** ● a adulto. **~-up** a & n adulto, -a m/f

growth /grəʊθ/ n crescita f; ⟨increase⟩ aumento m; Med tumore m

grub /grʌb/ n larva f; (fam: food) mangiare m

grubby /'grʌbɪ/ a (-ier, -iest) sporco

grudge /grʌdʒ/ n rancore m; **bear sb a ~e** portare rancore a qcno ● vt dare a malincuore. **~ing** a reluttante. **~ingly** adv a malincuore

gruelling /'gru:əlɪŋ/ a estenuante

gruesome /'gru:səm/ a macabro

gruff /grʌf/ a burbero

grumble /'grʌmbl/ vi brontolare (**at** contro)

grumpy /'grʌmpɪ/ a (-ier, -iest) scorbutico

grunt /grʌnt/ n grugnito m ● vi fare un grugnito

guarant|ee /gærən'ti:/ n garanzia f ● vt garantire. **~or** n garante mf

guard /gɑ:d/ n guardia f; (security) guardiano m; (on train) capotreno m; Techn schermo m protettivo; **be on ~** essere di guardia ● vt sorvegliare; (protect) proteggere. **guard against** vt guardarsi da. **~-dog** n cane m da guardia

guarded /'gɑ:dɪd/ a guardingo

guardian /'gɑ:dɪən/ n (of minor) tutore, -trice mf

guerrilla /gə'rɪlə/ n guerrigliero, -a mf. **~ warfare** n guerriglia f

guess /ges/ n supposizione f ● vt indovinare ● vi indovinare; (Am: suppose) supporre. **~work** n supposizione f

guest /gest/ n ospite mf; (in hotel) cliente mf. **~-house** n pensione f

guffaw /gʌ'fɔ:/ n sghignazzata f ● vi sghignazzare

guidance /'gaɪdns/ n guida f; (advice) consigli mpl

guide /gaɪd/ n guida f; [Girl] G~ giovane esploratrice f ● vt guidare. **~book** n guida f turistica

guided /'gaɪdɪd/ a **~ missile** missile m teleguidato; **~ tour** giro m guidato

guide: **~-dog** n cane m per ciechi. **~lines** npl direttive fpl

guild /gɪld/ n corporazione f

guile /gaɪl/ n astuzia f

guillotine /'gɪlətiːn/ n ghigliottina f; (for paper) taglierina f

guilt /gɪlt/ n colpa f. **~ily** adv con aria colpevole

guilty /'gɪltɪ/ a (-ier, -iest) colpevole; **have a ~ conscience** avere la coscienza sporca

guinea-pig /'gɪnɪ-/ n porcellino m d'India; (fig: used for experiments) cavia f

guise /gaɪz/ n **in the ~ of** sotto le spoglie di

guitar /gɪ'tɑ:(r)/ n chitarra f. **~ist** n chitarrista mf

gulf /gʌlf/ n Geog golfo m; fig abisso m

gull /gʌl/ n gabbiano m

gullet /'gʌlɪt/ n esofago m; (throat) gola f

gullible /'gʌlɪbl/ a credulone

gully /'gʌlɪ/ n burrone m; (drain) canale m di scolo

gulp /gʌlp/ n azione f di deglutire; (of food) boccone m; (of liquid) sorso m ● vi deglutire. **gulp down** vt tranguggiare (food); scolarsi (liquid)

gum¹ /gʌm/ n Anat gengiva f

gum² n gomma f; (chewing-gum) gomma f da masticare, chewing-gum m inv ● vt (pt/pp gummed) ingommare (**to** a)

gummed /gʌmd/ see **gum²** ● a (label) adesivo

gumption /'gʌmpʃn/ n fam buon senso m

gun /gʌn/ n pistola f; (rifle) fucile m; (cannon) cannone m ● **gun down** vt (pt/pp gunned) freddare

gun: **~fire** n spari mpl; (of cannon) colpi mpl [di cannone]. **~man** uomo m armato

gun: **~powder** n polvere f da sparo. **~shot** n colpo m [di pistola]

gurgle /'gɜ:gl/ n gorgoglare f; (baby:) fare degli urletti

gush /gʌʃ/ vi sgorgare; (enthuse) parlare con troppo entusiasmo (**over** di). **gush out** vi sgorgare

~ing *a* eccessivamente entusiastico

gust /gʌst/ *n* (of wind) raffica *f*

gusto /'gʌstəʊ/ *n* **with ~** con trasporto

gusty /'gʌsti/ *a* ventoso

gut /gʌt/ *n* intestino *m*; **~s** *pl* pancia *f*; (*fam: courage*) fegato *m* ● *vt* (*pt/pp* gutted) *Culin* svuotare delle interiora; **~ted by fire** sventrato da un incendio

gutter /'gʌtə(r)/ *n* canale *m* di scolo; (*on roof*) grondaia *f*, *fig* bassifondi *mpl*

guttural /'gʌtərəl/ *a* gutturale

guy /gaɪ/ *n fam* tipo *m*, tizio *m*

guzzle /'gʌzl/ *vt* ingozzarsi con (*food*); **he's ~d the lot** si è sbafato tutto

gym /dʒɪm/ *n fam* palestra *f*; (*gymnastics*) ginnastica *f*

gymnasium /dʒɪm'neɪzɪəm/ *n* palestra *f*

gymnast /'dʒɪmnæst/ *n* ginnasta *mf*. **~ics** /-'næstɪks/ *n* ginnastica *f*

gym: ~ shoes *npl* scarpe *fpl* da ginnastica. **~-slip** *n Sch* grembiule *m* (*da bambina*)

gynaecolog|ist /gaɪnɪ'kɒlədʒɪst/ *n* ginecologo, -a *mf*. **~y** *n* ginecologia *f*

gypsy /'dʒɪpsɪ/ *n* zingaro, -a *mf*

gyrate /dʒaɪ'reɪt/ *vi* roteare

Hh

haberdashery /hæbə'dæʃərɪ/ *n* merceria *f*, *Am* negozio *m* d'abbigliamento da uomo

habit /'hæbɪt/ *n* abitudine *f*; (*Relig: costume*) tonaca *f*; **be in the ~ of doing sth** avere l'abitudine di fare qcsa

habitable /'hæbɪtəbl/ *a* abitabile

habitat /'hæbɪtæt/ *n* habitat *m inv*

habitation /hæbɪ'teɪʃn/ *n* **unfit for human ~** inagibile

habitual /hə'bɪtjʊəl/ *a* abituale; (*smoker, liar*) inveterato. **~ly** *adv* regolarmente

hack[1] /hæk/ *n* (*writer*) scribacchino, -a *mf*

hack[2] *vt* tagliare; **~ to pieces** tagliare a pezzi

hackneyed /'hæknɪd/ *a* trito [e ritrito]

'hacksaw *n* seghetto *m*

had /hæd/ *see* **have**

haddock /'hædək/ *n inv* eglefino *m*

haemorrhage /'hemərɪdʒ/ *n* emorragia *f*

haemorrhoids /'hemərɔɪdz/ *npl* emorroidi *fpl*

hag /hæg/ *n* **old ~** vecchia befana *f*

haggard /'hægəd/ *a* sfatto

haggle /'hægl/ *vi* contrattare (**over** per)

hail[1] /heɪl/ *vt* salutare; far segno a (*taxi*) ● *vi* **~ from** provenire da

hail[2] *n* grandine *f* ● *vi* grandinare. **~stone** *n* chicco *m* di grandine. **~storm** *n* grandinata *f*

hair /heə(r)/ *n* capelli *mpl*; (*on body, of animal*) pelo *m*

hair: ~brush *n* spazzola *f* per capelli. **~cut** *n* taglio *m* di capelli; **have a ~cut** farsi tagliare i capelli. **~do** *n fam* pettinatura *f*. **~dresser** *n* parrucchiere, -a *mf*. **~dryer** *n* fon *m inv*; (*with hood*) casco *m* [asciugacapelli]. **~grip** *n* molletta *f*. **~pin** *n* forcina *f*. **~pin 'bend** *n* tornante *m*, curva *f* a gomito. **~-raising** *a* terrificante. **~style** *n* acconciatura *f*

hairy /'heərɪ/ *a* (**-ier, -iest**) peloso; (*fam: frightening*) spaventoso

hale /heɪl/ *a* **~ and hearty** in piena forma

half /hɑːf/ *n* (*pl* **halves**) metà *f inv*; **cut in ~** tagliare a metà; **one and a ~** uno e mezzo; **~ a dozen** mezza dozzina; **~ an hour** mezz'ora ● *a* mezzo; **[at] ~ price** [a] metà prezzo ● *adv* a metà; **~ past two** le due e mezza

half: ~ board *n* mezza pensione *f*. **~-'hearted** *a* esitante. **~-'hourly** *a*

& *adv* ogni mezz'ora. ~ '**mast** *n* at ~ **mast** a mezz'asta. ~ **measures** *npl* mezze misure *fpl*. '~-**open** a socchiuso. ~-'**term** *n* vacanza *f* di metà trimestre. '~-**time** *n Sport* intervallo *m*. ~**way** a the ~**way mark/stage** il livello intermedio ● *adv* a metà strada; **get** ~**way** *fig* arrivare a metà. ~**wit** *n* idiota *mf*

hall /hɔːl/ *n* (*entrance*) ingresso *m*; (*room*) sala *f*; (*mansion*) residenza *f* di campagna; ~ **of residence** *Univ* casa *f* dello studente

'**hallmark** *n* marchio *m* di garanzia; *fig* marchio *m*

hallo /həˈləʊ/ *int* ciao!; (*on telephone*) pronto!; **say** ~ **to** salutare

Hallowe'en /hæləʊˈiːn/ *n* vigilia *f* d'Ognissanti *e* notte delle streghe, celebrata soprattutto dai bambini

hallucination /həluːsɪˈneɪʃn/ *n* allucinazione *f*

halo /ˈheɪləʊ/ *n* (*pl* -**es**) aureola *f*; *Astr* alone *m*

halt /hɔːlt/ *n* alt *m inv*; **come to a** ~ fermarsi; (*traffic*:) bloccarsi ● *vi* fermarsi; ~! alt! ● *vt* fermare. ~**ing** a esitante

halve /hɑːv/ *vt* dividere a metà; (*reduce*) dimezzare

ham /hæm/ *n* prosciutto *m*; *Theat* attore, -trice *mf* da strapazzo

hamburger /ˈhæmbɜːgə(r)/ *n* hamburger *m inv*

hamlet /ˈhæmlɪt/ *n* paesino *m*

hammer /ˈhæmə(r)/ *n* martello *m* ● *vt* martellare ● *vi* ~ **at/on** picchiare a

hammock /ˈhæmək/ *n* amaca *f*

hamper[1] /ˈhæmpə(r)/ *n* cesto *m*; [*gift*] ~ cestino *m*

hamper[2] *vt* ostacolare

hamster /ˈhæmstə(r)/ *n* criceto *m*

hand /hænd/ *n* mano *f*; (*of clock*) lancetta *f*; (*writing*) scrittura *f*; (*worker*) manovale *m*; **at** ~, **to** ~ a portata di mano; **on the one** ~ da un lato; **on the other** ~ d'altra parte; **out of** ~ incontrollabile; (*summarily*) su due piedi; **give sb a** ~ dare una mano a qcno ● *vt*

porgere. **hand down** *vt* tramandare. **hand in** *vt* consegnare. **hand out** *vt* distribuire. **hand over** *vt* passare; (*to police*) consegnare

hand: ~**bag** *n* borsa *f* (*da signora*). ~**book** *n* manuale *m*. ~**brake** *n* freno *m* a mano. ~**cuffs** *npl* manette *fpl*. ~**ful** *n* manciata *f*; **be** [**quite**] **a** ~**ful** *fam* essere difficile da tenere a freno

handicap /ˈhændɪkæp/ *n* handicap *m inv*. ~**ped** *a* **mentally/physically** ~**ped** mentalmente/fisicamente handicappato

handi|**craft** /ˈhændɪkrɑːft/ *n* artigianato *m*. ~**work** *n* opera *f*

handkerchief /ˈhæŋkətʃɪf/ *n* (*pl* ~**s** & -**chieves**) fazzoletto *m*

handle /ˈhændl/ *n* manico *m*; (*of door*) maniglia *f*; **fly off the** ~ *fam* perdere le staffe ● *vt* maneggiare; occuparsi di (*problem, customer*); prendere (*difficult person*); trattare (*subject*). ~**bars** *npl* manubrio *m*

hand: ~**luggage** *n* bagaglio *m* a mano. ~**made** a fatto a mano. ~**out** *n* (*at lecture*) foglio *m* informativo; (*fam: money*) elemosina *f*. ~**rail** *n* corrimano *m*. ~**shake** *n* stretta *f* di mano

handsome /ˈhænsəm/ a bello; (*fig: generous*) generoso

hand: ~**stand** *n* verticale *f*. ~**writing** *n* calligrafia *f*. ~-'**written** a scritto a mano

handy /ˈhændɪ/ a (-**ier**, -**iest**) utile; (*person*) abile; **have/keep** ~ avere/tenere a portata di mano. ~**man** *n* tuttofare *m inv*

hang /hæŋ/ *vt* (*pt/pp* **hung**) appendere (*picture*); (*pt/pp* **hanged**) impiccare (*criminal*); ~ **oneself** impiccarsi ● *vi* (*pt/pp* **hung**) pendere; (*hair*:) scendere ● *n* **get the** ~ **of it** *fam* afferrare. **hang about** *vi* gironzolare. **hang on** *vi* tenersi stretto; (*fam: wait*) aspettare; *Teleph* restare in linea. **hang on to** *vt* tenersi stretto a; (*keep*) tenere. **hang out** *vi* spuntare; **where**

does he usually ~ out? *fam* dove
bazzica di solito? ●*vt* stendere
⟨*washing*⟩. **hang up** *vt* appendere;
Teleph riattaccare ●*vi* essere appeso; *Teleph* riattaccare

hangar /'hæŋə(r)/ *n* Aeron hangar
m inv

hanger /'hæŋə(r)/ *n* gruccia *f*.
~-on *n* leccapiedi *mf*

hang: **~-glider** *n* deltaplano *m*.
~-gliding *n* deltaplano *m*. **~man**
n boia *m*. **~-over** *n fam* postumi
mpl da sbornia. **~-up** *n fam* complesso *m*

hanker /'hæŋkə(r)/ *vi* ~ **after sth**
smaniare per qcsa

hanky /'hæŋkɪ/ *n fam* fazzoletto *m*

hanky-panky /hæŋkɪ'pæŋkɪ/ *n*
fam qualcosa *m* di losco

haphazard /hæp'hæzəd/ *a* a
casaccio

happen /'hæpn/ *vi* capitare, succedere; **as it ~s** per caso; **I ~ed to
meet him** mi è capitato di incontrarlo; **what has ~ed to him?**
cosa gli è capitato?; ⟨*person:*⟩
che fine ha fatto? **~ing** *n* avvenimento *m*

happily /'hæpɪlɪ/ *adv* felicemente; ⟨*fortunately*⟩ fortunatamente.
~ness *n* felicità *f*

happy /'hæpɪ/ *a* (**-ier, -iest**) contento, felice. **~-go-lucky** *a* spensierato

harass /'hærəs/ *vt* perseguitare.
~ed *a* stressato. **~ment** *n* persecuzione *f*; **sexual ~ment** molestie
fpl sessuali

harbour /'ha:bə(r)/ *n* porto *m* ●*vt*
dare asilo a; nutrire ⟨*grudge*⟩

hard /ha:d/ *a* duro; ⟨*question,
problem*⟩ difficile; **~ of hearing**
duro d'orecchi; **be ~ on** sb
⟨*person:*⟩ essere duro con qcno
●*adv* ⟨*work*⟩ duramente; ⟨*pull,
hit, rain, snow*⟩ forte; **~ hit by
unemployment** duramente colpito dalla disoccupazione; **take sth
~** non accettare qcsa; **think ~!**
pensaci bene!; **try ~** mettercela
tutta; **try ~er** metterci più impe-

gno; **~ done by** *fam* trattato ingiustamente

hard: **~-back** *n* edizione *f* rilegata.
~-boiled *a* ⟨*egg*⟩ sodo. **~ copy** *n*
copia *f* stampata. **~ disk** *n* hard
disk *m inv*, disco *m* rigido

harden /'ha:dn/ *vt/i* indurirsi

hard: **~-'headed** *a* ⟨*businessman*⟩
dal sangue freddo. **~-'hearted** *a*
dal cuore duro. **~ line** *n* linea *f*
dura; **~ lines!** che sfortuna!.
~-line *a* duro. **~-liner** *n* fautore,
-trice *mf* della linea dura. **~ luck**
n sfortuna *f*

hardly /'ha:dlɪ/ *adv* appena; **~ly**
ever quasi mai. **~ness** *n* durezza
f. **~ship** *n* avversità *f inv*

hard: **~ 'shoulder** *n* Auto corsia
f d'emergenza. **~ up** *a fam* a
corto di soldi; **~ up for sth** a
corto di qcsa. **~ware** *n* ferramenta *fpl*; Comput hardware *m
inv*. **~-wearing** *a* resistente.
~-working *a* **be ~-working** essere un gran lavoratore

hardy /'ha:dɪ/ *a* (**-ier, -iest**) dal fisico resistente; ⟨*plant*⟩ che sopporta
il gelo

hare /heə(r)/ *n* lepre *f*. **~-brained** *a
fam* ⟨*scheme*⟩ da scervellati

hark /ha:k/ *vi* **~ back to** *fig* ritornare su

harm /ha:m/ *n* male *m*; ⟨*damage*⟩
danni *mpl*; **out of ~'s way** in un
posto sicuro; **it won't do any ~**
non farà certo male a ●*vt* far male
a; ⟨*damage*⟩ danneggiare. **~ful** *a*
dannoso. **~less** *a* innocuo

harmonica /ha:'mɒnɪkə/ *n* armonica *f* [a bocca]

harmonious /ha:'məʊnɪəs/ *a* armonioso. **~ly** *adv* in armonia

harmon|**ize** /'ha:mənaɪz/ *vt/i fig* armonizzare. **~y** *n* armonia *f*

harness /'ha:nɪs/ *n* finimenti *mpl*;
⟨*of parachute*⟩ imbracatura *f* ●*vt*
bardare ⟨*horse*⟩; sfruttare ⟨*resources*⟩

harp /ha:p/ *n* arpa *f* ●**harp on** *vi
fam* insistere ⟨**about** su⟩. **~ist** *n*
arpista *mf*

harpoon /hɑːˈpuːn/ *n* arpione *m*
harpsichord /ˈhɑːpsɪkɔːd/ *n* clavicembalo *m*
harrowing /ˈhærəʊɪŋ/ *a* straziante
harsh /hɑːʃ/ *a* duro; *(light)* abbagliante. **~ness** *n* durezza *f*
harvest /ˈhɑːvɪst/ *n* raccolta *f*; *(of grapes)* vendemmia *f*; *(crop)* raccolto *m* ● *vt* raccogliere
has /hæz/ *see* **have**
hash /hæʃ/ *n* **make a ~ of** *fam* fare un casino con
hashish /ˈhæʃiːʃ/ *n* hascisc *m*
hassle /ˈhæsl/ *n fam* rottura *f* ● *vt* rompere le scatole a
haste /heɪst/ *n* fretta *f*
hast|y /ˈheɪstɪ/ *a* (**-ier, -iest**) frettoloso; *(decision)* affrettato. **~ily** *adv* frettolosamente
hat /hæt/ *n* cappello *m*
hatch[1] /hætʃ/ *n (for food)* sportello *m* passavivande; *Naut* boccaporto *m*
hatch[2] *vi* **~[out]** rompere il guscio; *(egg:)* schiudersi ● *vt* covare; tramare *(plot)*
'hatchback *n* tre/cinque porte *m inv*; *(door)* porta *f* del bagagliaio
hatchet /ˈhætʃɪt/ *n* ascia *f*
hate /heɪt/ *n* odio *m* ● *vt* odiare. **~ful** *a* odioso
hatred /ˈheɪtrɪd/ *n* odio *m*
haught|y /ˈhɔːtɪ/ *a* (**-ier, -iest**) altezzoso. **~ily** *adv* altezzosamente
haul /hɔːl/ *n (fish)* pescata *f*; *(loot)* bottino *m*; *(pull)* tirata *f* ● *vt* tirare; trasportare *(goods)* ● *vi* **~ on** tirare. **~age** /-ɪdʒ/ *n* trasporto *m*. **~ier** /-ɪə(r)/ *n* autotrasportatore *m*
haunt /hɔːnt/ *n* ritrovo *m* ● *vt* frequentare; *(linger in the mind)* perseguitare; **this house is ~ed** questa casa è abitata da fantasmi
have /hæv/ *vt* (*3 sg pres tense* **has**; *pt/pp* **had**) avere; fare *(breakfast, bath, walk etc)*; **~ a drink** bere qualcosa; **~ lunch/dinner** pranzare/cenare; **~ a rest** riposarsi; **I had my hair cut** mi sono tagliata i capelli; **we had the house painted** abbiamo fatto tinteggiare

la casa; **I had it made** l'ho fatto fare; **~ to do sth** dover fare qcsa; **~ him telephone me tomorrow** digli di telefonarmi domani; **he has** *or* **he's got two houses** ha due case; **you've got the money, ~n't you?** hai i soldi, no? ● *v aux* avere; *(with verbs of motion & some others)* essere; **I ~ seen him** l'ho visto; **he has never been there** non ci è mai stato. **have on** *vt (be wearing)* portare; *(dupe)* prendere in giro; **I've got something on tonight** ho un impegno stasera. **have out** *vt* – **it out with sb** chiarire le cose con qcno ● *npl* **the ~s and the ~-nots** i ricchi e i poveri
haven /ˈheɪvn/ *n fig* rifugio *m*
haversack /ˈhævə-/ *n* zaino *m*
havoc /ˈhævək/ *n* strage *f*; **play ~ with** *fig* scombussolare
haw /hɔː/ *see* **hum**
hawk /hɔːk/ *n* falco *m*
hay /heɪ/ *n* fieno *m*. **~ fever** *n* raffreddore *m* da fieno. **~stack** *n* pagliaio *m*
'haywire *a fam* **go ~** dare i numeri; *(plans:)* andare all'aria
hazard /ˈhæzəd/ *n (risk)* rischio *m* ● *vt* rischiare; **~ a guess** azzardare un'ipotesi. **~ous** /-əs/ *a* rischioso. **~ [warning] lights** *npl Auto* luci *fpl* d'emergenza
haze /heɪz/ *n* foschia *f*
hazel /ˈheɪz(ə)l/ *n* nocciolo *m*; *(colour)* [color *m*] nocciola *m*. **~-nut** *n* nocciola *f*
haz|y /ˈheɪzɪ/ *a* (**-ier, -iest**) nebbioso; *(fig: person)* confuso; *(memories)* vago
he /hiː/ *pron* lui; **he's tired** è stanco; **I'm going but he's not** io vengo, ma lui no
head /hed/ *n* testa *f*; *(of firm)* capo *m*; *(of primary school)* direttore, -trice *mf*; *(of secondary school)* preside *mf*; *(on beer)* schiuma *f*; **be off one's ~** essere fuori di testa; **have a good ~ for business** avere il senso degli affari; **have a good ~**

for heights non soffrire di vertigini; **10 pounds a ~** 10 sterline a testa; **20 ~ of cattle** 20 capi di bestiame; **~ first** a capofitto; **~ over heels in love** innamorato pazzo; **~s or tails?** testa o croce? ● *vt* essere a capo di; essere in testa a ‹list›; colpire di testa ‹ball› ● *vi* **~ for** dirigersi verso.

head: **~ache** n mal m di testa. **~dress** n acconciatura f. **~er** /'hedə(r)/ n rinvio m di testa; (dive) tuffo m di testa. **~hunter** n cacciatore, -trice mf di teste. **~ing** n (in list etc) titolo m. **~lamp** n Auto fanale m. **~land** n promontorio m. **~light** n Auto fanale m. **~line** n titolo m. **~long** a & adv a capofitto. **~'master** n (of primary school) direttore m; (of secondary school) preside m. **~'mistress** n (of primary school) direttrice f; (of secondary school) preside f. **~ office** n sede f centrale. **~on** a (collision) frontale ● adv frontalmente. **~phones** npl cuffie fpl. **~quarters** npl sede fsg; Mil quartier m generale msg. **~rest** n poggiatesta m inv. **~room** n sottotetto m; (of bridge) altezza f libera di passaggio. **~scarf** n foulard m inv, fazzoletto m. **~strong** a testardo. **~waiter** n capocameriere m. **~way** n progresso m. **~wind** n vento m di prua

heady /'hedɪ/ a che dà alla testa

heal /hiːl/ vt/i guarire

health /helθ/ n salute f

health: ~ farm n centro m di rimessa in forma. **~ foods** npl alimenti mpl macrobiotici. **~-food shop** n negozio m di macrobiotica. **~ insurance** n assicurazione f contro malattie

health|y /'helθɪ/ a (-ier, -iest) sano. **~ily** adv in modo sano

heap /hiːp/ n mucchio m; **~s of** fam un sacco di ● vt ~ [up] ammucchiare; **~ed teaspoon** un cucchiaino abbondante

hear /hɪə(r)/ vt/i (pt/pp **heard**) sentire; **~, ~!** bravo! **~ from** vi aver notizie di. **hear of** vi sentir parlare di; **he would not ~ of it** non ne ha voluto sentir parlare

hearing /'hɪərɪŋ/ n udito m; Jur udienza f. **~-aid** n apparecchio m acustico

'hearsay n **from ~** per sentito dire

hearse /hɜːs/ n carro m funebre

heart /hɑːt/ n cuore m; **~s** pl (in cards) cuori mpl; **by ~** a memoria

heart: ~ache n pena f. **~ attack** n infarto m. **~beat** n battito m cardiaco. **~break** n afflizione f. **~breaking** a straziante. **~broken** a be **~broken** avere il cuore spezzato. **~burn** n mal m di stomaco. **~en** vt rincuorare. **~felt** a di cuore

hearth /hɑːθ/ n focolare m

heart|ily /'hɑːtɪlɪ/ adv di cuore; (eat) con appetito; **be ~ily sick of sth** non poterne più di qcsa. **~less** a spietato. **~-searching** n esame m di coscienza. **~-to-~** n conversazione f a cuore aperto ● a a cuore aperto. **~y** a caloroso; (meal) copioso; (person) gioviale

heat /hiːt/ n calore m; Sport prova f eliminatoria ● vt scaldare ● vi scaldarsi. **~ed** a (swimming pool) riscaldato; (discussion) animato. **~er** n (for room) stufa f; (for water) boiler m inv; Auto riscaldamento m

heath /hiːθ/ n brughiera f

heathen /'hiːðn/ a & n pagano, -a mf

heather /'heðə(r)/ n erica f

heating /'hiːtɪŋ/ n riscaldamento m

heat: ~-stroke n colpo m di sole. **~ wave** n ondata f di calore

heave /hiːv/ vt/i tirare; (lift) tirare su; (fam: throw) gettare; emettere (sigh) ● vi tirare

heaven /'hev(ə)n/ n paradiso m; **~ help you if...** Dio ti scampi se...; **H~s!** santo cielo!. **~ly** a celeste; fam delizioso

heav|y /'hevɪ/ a (**-ier, -iest**) pesante; ⟨traffic⟩ intenso; ⟨rain, cold⟩ forte; **be a ~y smoker/drinker** essere un gran fumatore/bevitore. **~ily** adv pesantemente; ⟨smoke, drink etc⟩ molto. **~yweight** n peso m massimo

Hebrew /'hi:bru:/ a ebreo

heckle /'hekl/ vt interrompere di continuo. **~r** n disturbatore, -trice mf

hectic /'hektɪk/ a frenetico

hedge /hedʒ/ n siepe f ● vi fig essere evasivo. **~hog** n riccio m

heed /hi:d/ n **pay ~ to** prestare ascolto a ● vt prestare ascolto a. **~less** a noncurante

heel¹ /hi:l/ n tallone m; (of shoe) tacco m; **take to one's ~s** fam darsela a gambe

heel² vi ~ **over** Naut inclinarsi

hefty /'heftɪ/ a (**-ier, -iest**) massiccio

heifer /'hefə(r)/ n giovenca f

height /haɪt/ n altezza f; (of plane) altitudine f; (of season, fame) culmine m. **~en** vt fig accrescere

heir /eə(r)/ n erede mf. **~ess** n ereditiera f. **~loom** n cimelio m di famiglia

held /held/ see **hold²**

helicopter /'helɪkɒptə(r)/ n elicottero m

hell /hel/ n inferno m; **go to ~!** sl va' al diavolo! ● int porca miseria!

hello /hə'ləʊ/ int & n = **hallo**

helm /helm/ n timone m; **at the ~** fig al timone

helmet /'helmɪt/ n casco m

help /help/ n aiuto m; (employee) aiuto m domestico; **that's no ~** non è d'aiuto ● vt aiutare; **oneself** vr servirsi di qcsa.; **~ yourself** (at table) serviti pure; **I could not ~ laughing** non ho potuto trattenermi dal ridere; **it cannot be ~ed** non c'è niente da fare; **I can't ~ it** non ci posso far niente ● vi aiutare

help|er /'helpə(r)/ n aiutante mf. **~ful** a ⟨person⟩ di aiuto; ⟨advice⟩

utile. **~ing** n porzione f. **~less** a (unable to manage) incapace; (powerless) impotente

helter-skelter /heltə'skeltə(r)/ adv in fretta e furia ● n scivolo m a spirale nei luna park

hem /hem/ n orlo m ● vt (pt/pp **hemmed**) orlare. **hem in** vt intrappolare

hemisphere /'hemɪ-/ n emisfero m

hemp /hemp/ n canapa f

hen /hen/ n gallina f; (any female bird) femmina f

hence /hens/ adv (for this reason) quindi. **~'forth** adv d'ora innanzi

henchman /'hentʃmən/ n pej tirapiedi m

hen: **~-party** n fam festa f di addio al celibato per sole donne. **~pecked** a tiranneggiato dalla moglie

her /hɜ:(r)/ poss a il suo m, la sua f, i suoi mpl, le sue fpl. **~ mother/ father** sua madre/suo padre ● pers pron (direct object) la; (indirect object) le; (after prep) lei; **I know ~** la conosco; **give ~ the money** dalle i soldi; **give it to ~** daglielo; **I came with ~** sono venuto con lei; **it's ~** è lei; **I've seen ~** l'ho vista; **I've seen ~, but not him** ho visto lei, ma non lui

herald /'herəld/ vt annunciare

herb /hɜ:b/ n erba f

herbal /'hɜ:b(ə)l/ a alle erbe; **~ tea** tisana f

herbs /hɜ:bz/ npl (for cooking) aromi mpl [da cucina]; (medicinal) erbe fpl

herd /hɜ:d/ n gregge m ● vt (tend) sorvegliare; (drive) far muovere; fig ammassare

here /hɪə(r)/ adv qui, qua; **in ~** dentro; **come/bring ~** vieni/porta qui; **~ is..., ~ are...** ecco...; **~ you are!** ecco qua!. **~'after** adv in futuro. **~by** adv con la presente

heredit|ary /hə'redɪtərɪ/ a ereditario. **~y** n eredità f

here|sy /'herəsɪ/ n eresia f. **~tic** n eretico, -a mf

here'with adv Comm con la presente

heritage /'herɪtɪdʒ/ n eredità f

hermetic /hə:'metɪk/ a ermetico. **~ally** adv ermeticamente

hermit /'hɜːmɪt/ n eremita mf

hernia /'hɜːnɪə/ n ernia f

hero /'hɪərəʊ/ n (pl **-es**) eroe m

heroic /hɪ'rəʊɪk/ a eroico

heroin /'herəʊɪn/ n eroina f (droga)

heroine /'herəʊɪn/ n eroina f. **~ism** n eroismo m

heron /'herən/ n airone m

herring /'herɪŋ/ n aringa f

hers /hɜːz/ poss pron il suo m, la sua f, i suoi mpl, le sue fpl; **a friend of ~** un suo amico; **friends of ~** dei suoi amici; **that is ~** questo è suo; (as opposed to mine) quello è il suo

her'self pers pron (reflexive) si; (emphatic) lei stessa; (after prep) sé, se stessa; **she poured ~ a drink** si è versata da bere; **she told me so ~** me lo ha detto lei stessa; **she's proud of ~** è fiera di sé; **by ~** da sola

hesitant /'hezɪtənt/ a esitante. **~ly** adv con esitazione

hesitate /'hezɪteɪt/ vi esitare. **~ion** /-'teɪʃn/ n esitazione f

het /het/ a ~ **up** fam agitato

hetero'sexual /hetərəʊ-/ a eterosessuale

hexagon /'heksəgən/ n esagono m. **~al** /hek'sægənl/ a esagonale

hey /heɪ/ int ehi

heyday /'heɪ-/ n tempi mpl d'oro

hi /haɪ/ int ciao!

hiatus /haɪ'eɪtəs/ n (pl **-tuses**) iato m

hibernate /'haɪbəneɪt/ vi andare in letargo. **~ion** /-'neɪʃn/ n letargo m

hiccup /'hɪkʌp/ n singhiozzo m; (fam: hitch) intoppo m. ● vi fare un singhiozzo

hid /hɪd/, **hidden** /'hɪdn/ see hide²

hide¹ /haɪd/ n (leather) pelle f (di animale)

hide² vt (pt **hid**, pp **hidden**)

nascondere. ● vi nascondersi. **~-and-seek** n play **~-and-seek** giocare a nascondino

hideous /'hɪdɪəs/ a orribile

'hide-out n nascondiglio m

hiding¹ /'haɪdɪŋ/ n (fam: beating) bastonata f; (defeat) batosta f

hiding² n go into **~** sparire dalla circolazione

hierarchy /'haɪərɑːkɪ/ n gerarchia f

hieroglyphics /haɪərə'glɪfɪks/ npl geroglifici mpl

hi-fi /'haɪfaɪ/ n fam stereo m, hi-fi m inv ● a fam ad alta fedeltà

higgledy-piggledy /hɪgldɪ'pɪgldɪ/ adv alla rinfusa

high /haɪ/ a alto; (meat) che comincia ad andare a male; (wind) forte; (on drugs) fatto; **it's ~ time we did something about it** è ora di fare qualcosa in proposito ● adv in alto; **~ and low** in lungo e in largo ● n massimo m; (temperature) massima f; **be on a ~** fam essere fatto

high: ~brow a & n intellettuale mf. **~ chair** n seggiolone m. **~er education** n formazione f universitaria. **~'-handed** a dispotico. **~'-heeled** a coi tacchi alti. **~ heels** npl tacchi mpl alti. **~ jump** n salto m in alto

highlight /'haɪlaɪt/ n fig momento m clou; **~s** pl (in hair) mèche fpl ● vt (emphasize) evidenziare. **~er** n (marker) evidenziatore m

highly /'haɪlɪ/ adv molto; **speak ~ of** lodare; **think ~ of** avere un'alta opinione di. **~'-strung** a nervoso

Highness /'haɪnɪs/ n altezza f; **Your ~** Sua Altezza

high: ~-rise a (building) molto alto ● n edificio m molto alto. **~ school** n ≈ scuola f superiore. **~ season** n alta stagione f. **~ street** n strada f principale. **~ tea** n pasto m pomeridiano servito insieme al tè. **~ tide** n alta marea f. **~way code** n codice m stradale

hijack /'haɪdʒæk/ vt dirottare ● n

dirottamento m. **~er** n dirottatore, -trice mf

hike /haɪk/ n escursione f a piedi ● vi fare un'escursione a piedi. **~r** n escursionista mf

hilarious /hɪˈleərɪəs/ a esilarante

hill /hɪl/ n collina f; (mound) collinetta f; (slope) altura f

hill: **~side** n pendio m. **~y** a collinoso

hilt /hɪlt/ n impugnatura f; **to the ~** (fam: support) fino in fondo; (mortgaged) fino al collo

him /hɪm/ pers pron (direct object) lo; (indirect object) gli; (with prep) lui; **I know ~** lo conosco; **give ~ the money** dagli i soldi; **give it to ~** daglielo; **I spoke to ~** gli ho parlato; **it's ~** è lui; **she loves ~** lo ama; **she loves ~, not you** ama lui, non te. **~'self** pers pron (reflexive) si; (emphatic) lui stesso; (after prep) sé, se stesso; **he poured ~ a drink** si è versato da bere; **he told me so ~self** me lo ha detto lui stesso; **he's proud of ~self** è fiero di sé; **by ~self** da solo

hind /haɪnd/ a posteriore

hind|er /ˈhɪndə(r)/ vt intralciare. **~rance** /-rəns/ n intralcio m

hindsight /ˈhaɪnd-/ n **with ~** con il senno del poi

Hindu /ˈhɪndu:/ n indù mf inv ● a indù. **~ism** n induismo m

hinge /hɪndʒ/ n cardine m ● vi **~ on** fig dipendere da

hint /hɪnt/ n (clue) accenno m; (advice) suggerimento m; (indirect suggestion) allusione f; (trace) tocco m ● vt ~ **that...** far capire che... ● vi **~ at** alludere a

hip /hɪp/ n fianco m

hippie /ˈhɪpɪ/ n hippy mf inv

hippo /ˈhɪpəʊ/ n ippopotamo m

hip 'pocket n tasca f posteriore

hippopotamus /hɪpəˈpɒtəməs/ n (pl -muses or -mi /-maɪ/) ippopotamo m

hire /ˈhaɪə(r)/ vt affittare; assumere (person); ~ **[out]** affittare ● n noleggio m; **'for ~'** 'affittasi'. ~

car n macchina f a noleggio. **~ purchase** n acquisto m rateale

his /hɪz/ poss a il suo m, la sua f; suoi mpl, le sue fpl; ~ **mother/father** sua madre/suo padre ● poss pron il suo m, la sua f; i suoi mpl, le sue fpl; **a friend of ~** un suo amico; **friends of ~** dei suoi amici; **that is ~** questo è suo; (as opposed to mine) questo è il suo

hiss /hɪs/ n sibilo m; (of disapproval) fischio m ● vt fischiare ● vi sibilare; (in disapproval) fischiare

historian /hɪˈstɔ:rɪən/ n storico, -a mf

historic /hɪˈstɒrɪk/ a storico. **~al** a storico. **~ally** adv storicamente

history /ˈhɪstərɪ/ n storia f; **make ~** passare alla storia

hit /hɪt/ n (blow) colpo m; (fam: success) successo m; **score a direct ~** (missile:) colpire in pieno ● vt/i (pt/pp hit, pres p hitting) colpire; ~ **one's head on the table** battere la testa contro il tavolo; **the car ~ the wall** la macchina ha sbattuto contro il muro; ~ **the roof** fam perdere le staffe

hit off vi ~ **it off** andare d'accordo. **hit on** vt fig trovare

hitch /hɪtʃ/ n intoppo m; **technical ~** problema m tecnico ● vt attaccare; ~ **a lift** chiedere un passaggio. **hitch up** vt tirarsi su (trousers). **~-hike** vi fare l'autostop. **~-hiker** n autostoppista mf

hit-or-'miss a on a very ~ **basis** all'improvvisata

hither /ˈhɪðə(r)/ adv ~ **and thither** di qua e di là. **~to** adv finora

hive /haɪv/ n alveare m; ~ **of industry** fucina f di lavoro ● **hive off** vt Comm separare

hoard /hɔ:d/ n provvista f; (of money) gruzzolo m ● vt accumulare

hoarding /ˈhɔ:dɪŋ/ n palizzata f; (with advertisements) tabellone m per manifesti pubblicitari

hoarse /hɔːs/ a rauco. **~ly** adv con voce rauca. **~ness** n raucedine f

hoax /həʊks/ n scherzo m; *(false alarm)* falso allarme m. **~er** n burlone, -a mf

hob /hɒb/ n piano m di cottura

hobble /'hɒbl/ vi zoppicare

hobby /'hɒbɪ/ n hobby m inv. **~-horse** n fig fissazione f

hockey /'hɒkɪ/ n hockey m

hoe /həʊ/ n zappa f

hog /hɒg/ n maiale m • vt (pt/pp hogged) fam monopolizzare

hoist /hɔɪst/ n montacarichi m inv; *(fam: push)* spinta f in su • vt sollevare; innalzare *(flag)*; issare *(anchor)*

hold[1] /həʊld/ n Naut, Aeron stiva f

hold[2] n presa f; *(fig: influence)* ascendente m; get **~** of trovare; procurarsi *(information)* • vt (pt/pp held) vt tenere; *(container:)* contenere; essere titolare di *(licence, passport)*; trattenere *(breath, suspect)*; mantenere vivo *(interest)*; *(retain)* mantenere; **~** sb's hand tenere qcno per mano; **~** one's tongue tenere la bocca chiusa; **~** sb responsible considerare qcno responsabile; **~** that *(believe)* ritenere che • vi tenere; *(weather, luck:)* durare; *(offer:)* essere valido; Teleph restare in linea; **I don't ~ with the idea that** fam non sono d'accordo sul fatto che. **hold back** vt rallentare • vi esitare. **hold down** vt tenere a bada *(sb)*. **hold on** vi *(wait)* attendere; Teleph restare in linea. **hold on to** vt aggrapparsi a; *(keep)* tenersi. **hold out** vt porgere *(hand)*; fig offrire *(possibility)* • vi *(resist)* resistere. **hold up** vt tenere su; *(delay)* rallentare; *(rob)* assalire; **~** one's head up fig tenere la testa alta

hold: ~all n borsone m. **~er** n titolare mf; *(of record)* detentore, -trice mf; *(container)* astuccio m. **~ing** n *(land)* terreno m in affitto.

Comm azioni fpl. **~up** n ritardo m; *(attack)* rapina f a mano armata

hole /həʊl/ n buco m

holiday /'hɒlɪdeɪ/ n vacanza f; *(public)* giorno m festivo; *(day off)* giorno m di ferie; **go on ~** andare in vacanza • vi andare in vacanza. **~maker** n vacanziere mf

holiness /'həʊlɪnɪs/ n santità f; **Your H~** Sua Santità

Holland /'hɒlənd/ n Olanda f

hollow /'hɒləʊ/ a cavo; *(promise)* a vuoto; *(voice)* assente; *(cheeks)* infossato • n cavità f inv; *(in ground)* avvallamento m

holly /'hɒlɪ/ n agrifoglio m

holocaust /'hɒləkɔːst/ n olocausto m

hologram /'hɒləgræm/ n ologramma m

holster /'həʊlstə(r)/ n fondina f

holy /'həʊlɪ/ a (**-ier, -est**) santo; *(water)* benedetto. **H~ Ghost** or **Spirit** n Spirito m Santo. **H~ Scriptures** npl sacre scritture fpl. **H~ Week** n settimana f santa

homage /'hɒmɪdʒ/ n omaggio m; **pay ~** a rendere omaggio a

home /həʊm/ n casa f; *(for children)* istituto m; *(for old people)* casa f di riposo; *(native land)* patria f • adv at **~** a casa; *(football)* in casa; **feel ~** sentirsi a casa propria; **come/go ~** venire/andare a casa; **drive a nail ~** piantare un chiodo a fondo • a domestico; *(movie, video)* casalingo; *(team)* ospitante; Pol nazionale

home: ~ ad'dress n indirizzo m di casa. **~ com'puter** n computer m inv da casa. **H~ Counties** npl contee fpl intorno a Londra. **~ game** n gioco m in casa. **~ help** n aiuto m domestico *(per persone non autosufficienti)*. **~land** n patria f. **~less** a senza tetto

homely /'həʊmlɪ/ a (**-ier, -iest**) semplice; *(atmosphere)* familiare; *(Am: ugly)* bruttino

home: ~-'made *a* fatto in casa. **H~ Office** *n Br* ministero *m* degli interni. **H~ 'Secretary** *n Br* ministro *m* degli interni. **~sick** *a* **be ~sick** avere nostalgia (**for**) di. **~sickness** *n* nostalgia *f* di casa. ~'**town** *n* città *f inv* natia. **~ward** *a* di ritorno • *adv* verso casa. **~work** *n Sch* compiti *mpl*

homicide /'hɒmɪsaɪd/ *n* (*crime*) omicidio *m*

homoeopath|ic /həʊmɪə'pæθɪk/ *a* omeopatico. **~y** /-'ɒpəθɪ/ *n* omeopatia *f*

homogeneous /hɒmə'dʒiːnɪəs/ *a* omogeneo

homo'sexual *a* & *n* omosessuale *mf*

honest /'ɒnɪst/ *a* onesto; (*frank*) sincero. **~ly** *adv* onestamente; (*frankly*) sinceramente; **~ly!** ma insomma!. **~y** *n* onestà *f*; (*frankness*) sincerità *f*

honey /'hʌnɪ/ *n* miele *m*; (*fam: darling*) tesoro *m*

honey: **~comb** *n* favo *m*. **~moon** *n* luna *f* di miele. **~suckle** *n* caprifoglio *m*

honk /hɒŋk/ *vi Aut* clacsonare

honorary /'ɒnərərɪ/ *a* onorario

honour /'ɒnə(r)/ *n* onore *m* • *vt* onorare. **~able** /-əbl/ *a* onorevole. **~ably** *adv* con onore. **~s degree** *n* ≈ diploma *m* di laurea

hood /hʊd/ *n* cappuccio *m*; (*of pram*) tettuccio *m*; (*over cooker*) cappa *f*; *Am* cofano *m*

hoodlum /'huːdləm/ *n* teppista *m*

'hoodwink *vt fam* infinocchiare

hoof /huːf/ *n* (*pl* **~s** *or* **hooves**) zoccolo *m*

hook /hʊk/ *n* gancio *m*; (*for fishing*) amo *m*; **off the ~** *Teleph* staccato; *fig* fuori pericolo • *vt* agganciare • *vi* agganciarsi

hook|ed /hʊkt/ *a* (*nose*) adunco **~ed on** (*fam: drugs*) dedito a; **be ~ed on skiing** essere un fanatico dello sci. **~er** *n Am sl* battona *f*

hookey /'hʊkɪ/ *n* **play ~** *Am fam* marinare la scuola

hooligan /'huːlɪɡən/ *n* teppista *mf*. **~ism** *n* teppismo *m*

hoop /huːp/ *n* cerchio *m*

hooray /hʊ'reɪ/ *int* & *n* = hurrah

hoot /huːt/ *n* colpo *m* di clacson; (*of siren*) ululato *m*; (*of owl*) grido *m* • *vi* (*owl:*) gridare; (*car:*) clacsonare; (*siren:*) ululare; (*jeer*) fischiare. **~er** *n* (*of factory*) sirena *f*; *Auto* clacson *m inv*

hoover® /'huːvə(r)/ *n* aspirapolvere *m inv* • *vt* passare l'aspirapolvere su (*carpet*); passare l'aspirapolvere su (*room*)

hop /hɒp/ *n* saltello *m* • *vi* (*pt/pp* **hopped**) saltellare; **~ it!** *fam* tela!. **hop in** *vi fam* saltar su

hope /həʊp/ *n* speranza *f* • *vi* sperare (**for** in); **I ~ so/not** spero di sì/no • *vt* **~ that** sperare che

hope|ful /'həʊpfl/ *a* pieno di speranza; (*promising*) promettente; **be ~ful that** avere buone speranze che. **~fully** *adv* con speranza; (*it is hoped*) se tutto va bene. **~less** *a* senza speranze; (*useless*) impossibile; (*incompetent*) incapace. **~lessly** *adv* disperatamente; (*inefficient, lost*) completamente. **~lessness** *n* disperazione *f*

horde /hɔːd/ *n* orda *f*

horizon /hə'raɪzn/ *n* orizzonte *m*

horizontal /hɒrɪ'zɒntl/ *a* orizzontale

hormone /'hɔːməʊn/ *n* ormone *m*

horn /hɔːn/ *n* corno *m*; *Auto* clacson *m inv*

horny /'hɔːnɪ/ *a* calloso; *fam* arrapato

horoscope /'hɒrəskəʊp/ *n* oroscopo *m*

horrible /'hɒrɪbl/ *a* orribile. **~y** *adv* spaventosamente

horrid /'hɒrɪd/ *a* orrendo

horrific /hə'rɪfɪk/ *a* raccapricciante; (*fam: accident, prices, story*) terrificante

horrify /'hɒrɪfaɪ/ *vt* (*pt/pp* **-ied**) far inorridire; **I was horrified** ero sconvolto. **~ing** *a* terrificante

horror /ˈhɒrə(r)/ n orrore m. **~ film** n film m dell'orrore

hors-d'œuvre /ɔːˈdɜːvr/ n antipasto m

horse /hɔːs/ n cavallo m

horse: **~back** n on **~back** a cavallo. **~man** n cavaliere m. **~play** n gioco m pesante. **~power** n cavallo m [vapore]. **~racing** n corse fpl di cavalli. **~shoe** n ferro m di cavallo

horti'cultural /hɔːtɪ-/ a di orticoltura.

'horticulture n orticoltura f

hose /həʊz/ n (pipe) manichetta f ● **hose down** vt lavare con la manichetta

hospice /ˈhɒspɪs/ n (for the terminally ill) ospedale m per i malati in fase terminale

hospitab|le /hɒˈspɪtəbl/ a ospitale. **~y** adv con ospitalità

hospital /ˈhɒspɪtl/ n ospedale m

hospitality /hɒspɪˈtælətɪ/ n ospitalità f

host¹ /həʊst/ n **a ~ of** una moltitudine di

host² n ospite m

host³ n Relig ostia f

hostage /ˈhɒstɪdʒ/ n ostaggio m; **hold sb ~** tenere qcno in ostaggio

hostel /ˈhɒstl/ n ostello m

hostess /ˈhəʊstɪs/ n padrona f di casa; Aeron hostess f inv

hostile /ˈhɒstaɪl/ a ostile

hostilit|y /hɒˈstɪlətɪ/ n ostilità f. **~ies** pl ostilità fpl

hot /hɒt/ a (hotter, hottest) caldo; (spicy) piccante; **I am** or **feel ~** ho caldo; **it is ~** fa caldo

'hotbed n fig focolaio m

hotchpotch /ˈhɒtʃpɒtʃ/ n miscuglio m

'hot-dog n hot dog m inv

hotel /həʊˈtel/ n albergo m. **~ier** /-ɪə(r)/ n albergatore, -trice mf

hot: **~head** n persona f impetuosa. **~house** n serra f. **~ly** adv fig accanitamente. **~plate** n piastra f riscaldante. **~ tap** n rubinetto m dell'acqua calda. **~-tempered** a ira-

scibile. **~-water bottle** n borsa f dell'acqua calda

hound /haʊnd/ n cane m da caccia ● vt fig perseguire

hour /ˈaʊə(r)/ n ora f. **~ly** a ad ora; (pay, rate) a ora ● adv ogni ora

house¹ /haʊs/ n casa f; Pol camera f; Theat sala f; **at my ~** a casa mia, da me

house² /haʊz/ vt alloggiare (person)

house /haʊs/: **~boat** n casa f galleggiante. **~breaking** n furto m con scasso. **~hold** n casa f, famiglia f. **~holder** n capo m di famiglia. **~keeper** n governante f di casa. **~keeping** n governo m della casa; (money) soldi mpl per le spese di casa. **~plant** n pianta f da appartamento. **~trained** a che non sporca in casa. **~warming** [party] n festa f di inaugurazione della nuova casa. **~wife** n casalinga f. **~work** n lavoro m domestico

housing /ˈhaʊzɪŋ/ n alloggio m. **~ estate** n zona f residenziale

hovel /ˈhɒvl/ n tugurio m

hover /ˈhɒvə(r)/ vi librarsi; (linger) indugiare. **~craft** n hovercraft m inv

how /haʊ/ adv come; **~ are you?** come stai?; **~ about a coffee/going on holiday?** che ne diresti di un caffè/di andare in vacanza?; **~ do you do?** molto lieto!; **~ old are you?** quanti anni hai?; **~ long** quanto tempo; **~ many** quanti; **~ much** quanto; **~ often** ogni quanto; and **~!** eccome!; **~ odd!** che strano!

how'ever adv (nevertheless) comunque; **~ small** per quanto piccolo

howl /haʊl/ n ululato m ● vi ululare; (cry, with laughter) singhiozzare. **~er** n fam strafalcione m

HP n abbr **hire purchase**; n abbr (horse power) C.V.

hub /hʌb/ n mozzo m; fig centro m

hubbub /ˈhʌbʌb/ n baccano m

'hub-cap n coprimozzo m

huddle /'hʌdl/ vi ~ **together** rannicchiarsi

hue¹ /hju:/ n colore m

hue² n ~ **and cry** clamore m

huff /hʌf/ n **be in/go into a** ~ fare il broncio

hug /hʌg/ n abbraccio m ● vt (pt/pp **hugged**) abbracciare; (keep close to) tenersi vicino a

huge /hju:dʒ/ a enorme

hulking /'hʌlkɪŋ/ a fam grosso

hull /hʌl/ n Naut scafo m

hullo /hə'ləʊ/ int = **hallo**

hum /hʌm/ n ronzio m ● v (pt/pp **hummed**) ● vt canticchiare ● vi (motor:) ronzare; fig fervere (di attività); ~ **and haw** esitare

human /'hju:mən/ a umano ● n essere m umano. ~ '**being** n essere m umano

humane /hju:'meɪn/ a umano

humanitarian /hju:mænɪ'teərɪən/ a & n umanitario, -a mf

humanit|y /hju:'mænətɪ/ n umanità f; ~**ies** pl Univ dottrine fpl umanistiche

humble /'hʌmbl/ a umile ● vt umiliare

'**humdrum** a noioso

humid /'hju:mɪd/ a umido. ~**ifier** /-'mɪdɪfaɪə(r)/ n umidificatore m. ~**ity** /-'mɪdətɪ/ n umidità f

humiliat|e /hju:'mɪlɪeɪt/ vt umiliare. ~**ion** /-'eɪʃn/ n umiliazione f

humility /hju:'mɪlətɪ/ n umiltà f

humorous /'hju:mərəs/ a umoristico. ~**ly** adv con spirito

humour /'hju:mə(r)/ n umorismo m; (mood) umore m; **have a sense of** ~ avere il senso dell'umorismo ● vt compiacere

hump /hʌmp/ n protuberanza f; (of camel, hunchback) gobba f

hunch /hʌntʃ/ n (idea) intuizione f

'**hunch|back** n gobbo, -a mf. ~**ed** a ~**ed up** incurvato

hundred /'hʌndrəd/ a **one** ~ cento ● n cento m; ~**s of** centinaia di. ~**th** a centesimo ● n centesimo m. ~**weight** n cinquanta chili m

hung /hʌŋ/ see **hang**

Hungarian /hʌŋ'geərɪən/ n & a ungherese mf; (language) ungherese m

Hungary /'hʌŋgərɪ/ n Ungheria f

hunger /'hʌŋgə(r)/ n fame f. ~-**strike** n sciopero m della fame m

hungr|y /'hʌŋgrɪ/ a (-**ier**, -**iest**) affamato; **be** ~**y** aver fame. ~**ily** adv con appetito

hunk /hʌŋk/ n (grosso) pezzo m

hunt /hʌnt/ n caccia f ● vt andare a caccia di (animal); dare la caccia a (criminal) ● vi andare a caccia; ~ **for** cercare. ~**er** n cacciatore m. ~**ing** n caccia f

hurdle /'hɜːdl/ n Sport & fig ostacolo m. ~**r** n ostacolista mf

hurl /hɜːl/ vt scagliare

hurrah /hʊ'rɑː/, **hurray** /hʊ'reɪ/ int urrà! ● n urrà m

hurricane /'hʌrɪkən/ n uragano m

hurried /'hʌrɪd/ a affrettato; (job) fatto in fretta. ~**ly** adv in fretta

hurry /'hʌrɪ/ n fretta f; **be in a** ~ aver fretta ● vi (pt/pp -**ied**) affrettarsi. **hurry up** vi sbrigarsi ● vt fare sbrigare (person); accelerare (things)

hurt /hɜːt/ v (pt/pp **hurt**) ● vt far male a; (offend) ferire ● vi far male; **my leg** ~**s** mi fa male la gamba. ~**ful** a fig offensivo

hurtle /'hɜːtl/ vi ~ **along** andare a tutta velocità

husband /'hʌzbənd/ n marito m

hush /hʌʃ/ n silenzio m ● **hush up** vt mettere a tacere. ~**ed** a (voice) sommesso. ~**-**'**hush** a fam segretissimo

husky /'hʌskɪ/ a (-**ier**, -**iest**) (voice) rauco

hustle /'hʌsl/ vt affrettare ● n attività f incessante; ~ **and bustle** trambusto m

hut /hʌt/ n capanna f

hybrid /'haɪbrɪd/ a ibrido ● n ibrido m

hydrant /'haɪdrənt/ n [**fire**] ~ idrante m

hydraulic /haɪ'drɔːlɪk/ a idraulico

hydroe'lectric /haɪdrəʊ-/ a idro-elettrico

hydrofoil /'haɪdrə-/ n aliscafo m

hydrogen /'haɪdrədʒən/ n idrogeno m

hyena /haɪ'iːnə/ n iena f

hygiene /'haɪdʒiːn/ n igiene m. **~ic** /haɪ'dʒiːnɪk/ a igienico

hymn /hɪm/ n inno m. **~-book** n libro m dei canti

hypermarket /'haɪpəmɑːkɪt/ n ipermercato m

hyphen /'haɪfn/ n lineetta f. **~ate** vt unire con lineetta

hypno|sis /hɪp'nəʊsɪs/ n ipnosi f. **~tic** /-'nɒtɪk/ a ipnotico

hypno|tism /'hɪpnətɪzm/ n ipnotismo m. **~tist** /-tɪst/ n ipnotizzatore, -trice m f. **~tize** vt ipnotizzare

hypochondriac /haɪpə'kɒndriæk/ a ipocondriaco ● n ipocondriaco, -a m f

hypocrisy /hɪ'pɒkrəsɪ/ n ipocrisia f

hypocrit|e /'hɪpəkrɪt/ n ipocrita m f. **~ical** /-'krɪtɪkl/ a ipocrita

hypodermic /haɪpə'dɜːmɪk/ a & n **~ [syringe]** siringa f ipodermica

hypothe|sis /haɪ'pɒθəsɪs/ n ipotesi f inv. **~tical** /-ə'θetɪkl/ a ipotetico. **~tically** adv in teoria; ⟨speak⟩ per ipotesi

hyster|ia /hɪ'stɪərɪə/ n isterismo m. **~ical** /-'sterɪkl/ a isterico. **~ically** adv istericamente; **~ically funny** da morir dal ridere. **~ics** /hɪ'sterɪks/ npl attacco m isterico

••••••••••••••••••••••••••••••

Ii

I /aɪ/ pron io; **I'm tired** sono stanco; **he's going, but I'm not** lui va, ma io no

ice /aɪs/ n ghiaccio m ● vt glassare ⟨cake⟩. **ice over/up** vi ghiacciarsi

ice: **~ age** n era f glaciale. **~-axe** n piccozza f per il ghiaccio. **~berg** /-bɜːg/ n iceberg m inv. **~box** n Am frigorifero m. **~-cream** n gelato m. **~-cream parlour** n gelateria f. **~-cube** n cubetto m di ghiaccio. **~ hockey** n hockey m su ghiaccio

Iceland /'aɪslənd/ n Islanda f. **~er** n islandese m f; **~ic** /-'lændɪk/ a & n islandese m

ice: **~-lolly** n ghiacciolo m. **~ rink** n pista f di pattinaggio. **~ skater** n pattinatore, -trice m f sul ghiaccio. **~ skating** n pattinaggio m su ghiaccio

icicle /'aɪsɪkl/ n ghiacciolo m

icing /'aɪsɪŋ/ n glassa f. **~ sugar** n zucchero m a velo

icon /'aɪkɒn/ n icona f

ic|y /'aɪsɪ/ a (**-ier, -iest**) ghiacciato; fig gelido. **~ily** adv gelidamente

idea /aɪ'dɪə/ n idea f; **I've no ~!** non ne ho idea!

ideal /aɪ'dɪəl/ a ideale ● n ideale m. **~ism** n idealismo m. **~ist** n idealista m f. **~istic** /-'lɪstɪk/ a idealistico. **~ize** vt idealizzare. **~ly** adv idealmente

identical /aɪ'dentɪkl/ a identico

identi|fication /aɪdentɪfɪ'keɪʃn/ n identificazione f; (proof of identity) documento m di riconoscimento. **~fy** /aɪ'dentɪfaɪ/ vt (pt/pp **-ied**) identificare

identikit® /aɪ'dentɪkɪt/ n identikit m inv

identity /aɪ'dentətɪ/ n identità f inv. **~ card** n carta f d'identità

ideolog|ical /aɪdɪə'lɒdʒɪkl/ a ideologico. **~y** /aɪdɪ'ɒlədʒɪ/ n ideologia f

idiom /'ɪdɪəm/ n idioma f. **~atic** /-'mætɪk/ a idiomatico

idiosyncrasy /ɪdɪə'sɪŋkrəsɪ/ n idiosincrasia f

idiot /'ɪdɪət/ n idiota m f. **~ic** /-'ɒtɪk/ a idiota

idle /'aɪd(ə)l/ a ⟨lazy⟩ pigro, ozioso; ⟨empty⟩ vano; ⟨machine⟩ fermo ● vi oziare; ⟨engine⟩ girare a vuo-

to. **~eness** n ozio m. **~y** adv ozio-
samente

idol /'aɪdl/ n idolo m. **~ize**
/'aɪdəlaɪz/ vt idolatrare

idyllic /ɪ'dɪlɪk/ a idillico

i.e. abbr (**id est**) cioè

if /ɪf/ conj se; **as if** come se

ignite /ɪg'naɪt/ vt dar fuoco a ● vi
prender fuoco

ignition /ɪg'nɪʃn/ n Auto accensione f. **~ key** n chiave f d'accensione

ignoramus /ɪgnə'reɪməs/ n ignorante mf

ignoran|ce /'ɪgnərəns/ n ignoran-
za f. **~t** a (lacking knowledge)
ignaro; (rude) ignorante

ignore /ɪg'nɔː(r)/ vt ignorare

ill /ɪl/ a ammalato; **feel ~ at ease**
sentirsi a disagio ● adv male ● n
male m. **~-advised** a avventato.
~-bred a maleducato

illegal /ɪ'liːgl/ a illegale

illegib|le /ɪ'ledʒɪbl/ a illeggibile

illegitima|cy /ɪlɪ'dʒɪtɪməsɪ/ n ille-
gittimità f. **~te** /-mət/ a illegitti-
mo

illicit /ɪ'lɪsɪt/ a illecito

illitera|cy /ɪ'lɪtərəsɪ/ n analfabeti-
smo m. **~te** /-rət/ a & n analfabeta
mf

illness /'ɪlnɪs/ n malattia f

illogical /ɪ'lɒdʒɪkl/ a illogico

ill-treat /ɪl'triːt/ vt maltrattare.
~ment n maltrattamento m

illuminat|e /ɪ'luːmɪneɪt/ vt illumi-
nare. **~ing** a chiarificatore. **~ion**
/-'neɪʃn/ n illuminazione f

illusion /ɪ'luːʒn/ n illusione f; **be
under the ~ that** avere l'illusione
che

illusory /ɪ'luːsərɪ/ a illusorio

illustrat|e /'ɪləstreɪt/ vt illustrare.
~ion /-'streɪʃn/ n illustrazione f.
~or n illustratore, -trice mf

illustrious /ɪ'lʌstrɪəs/ a illustre

ill 'will n malanimo m

image /'ɪmɪdʒ/ n immagine f;
(exact likeness) ritratto m

imagin|able /ɪ'mædʒɪnəbl/ a im-
maginabile. **~ary** /-ərɪ/ a immaginario

imaginat|ion /ɪmædʒɪ'neɪʃn/ n
immaginazione f, fantasia f; **it's
your ~ion** è solo una tua idea.
~ive /ɪ'mædʒɪnətɪv/ a fantasioso.
~ively adv con fantasia or immaginazione

imagine /ɪ'mædʒɪn/ vt immaginare; (wrongly) inventare

im'balance n squilibrio m

imbecile /'ɪmbəsiːl/ n imbecille mf

imbibe /ɪm'baɪb/ vt ingerire

imbue /ɪm'bjuː/ vt **~d with** impre-
gnato di

imitat|e /'ɪmɪteɪt/ vt imitare. **~ion**
/-'teɪʃn/ n imitazione f. **~or** n imitatore, -trice mf

immaculate /ɪ'mækjʊlət/ a immacolato. **~ly** adv immacolato

imma'terial a (unimportant) irrilevante

imma'ture a immaturo

immediate /ɪ'miːdɪət/ a immediato; (relative) stretto; **in the ~
vicinity** nelle immediate vicinanze. **~ly** adv immediatamente; **~ly
next to** subito accanto a ● conj
[non] appena

immemorial /ɪmɪ'mɔːrɪəl/ a **from
time ~** da tempo immemorabile

immense /ɪ'mens/ a immenso

immers|e /ɪ'mɜːs/ vt immergere;
be ~ed in fig essere immerso in.
~ion /-ɜːʃn/ n immersione f. **~ion
heater** n scaldabagno m elettrico

immigrant /'ɪmɪgrənt/ n immi-
grante mf

immigrat|e /'ɪmɪgreɪt/ vi immigra-
re. **~ion** /-'greɪʃn/ n immigrazio-
ne f

imminent /'ɪmɪnənt/ a imminente

immobile /ɪ'məʊbaɪl/ a immobile.
~ize /-bɪlaɪz/ vt immobilizzare

immoderate /ɪ'mɒdərət/ a smodato

immodest /ɪ'mɒdɪst/ a immodesto

immoral /ɪ'mɒrəl/ a immorale.
~ity /ɪmə'rælɪtɪ/ n immoralità f

immortal /ɪ'mɔːtl/ a immortale.
~ity /-'tælɪtɪ/ n immortalità f.
~ize vt immortalare

immovable /ɪˈmuːvəbl/ *a fig* irremovibile

immune /ɪˈmjuːn/ *a* immune (**to/from** da). **~ system** *n* sistema *m* immunitario

immunity /ɪˈmjuːnəti/ *n* immunità *f*

immuniz|e /ˈɪmjʊnaɪz/ *vt* immunizzare

imp /ɪmp/ *n* diavoletto *m*

impact /ˈɪmpækt/ *n* impatto *m*

impair /ɪmˈpeə(r)/ *vt* danneggiare

impale /ɪmˈpeɪl/ *vt* impalare

impart /ɪmˈpɑːt/ *vt* impartire

im'parti|al *a* imparziale. **~'ality** *n* imparzialità *f*

im'passable *a* impraticabile

impasse /æmˈpɑːs/ *n fig* impasse *f inv*

impassioned /ɪmˈpæʃnd/ *a* appassionato

im'passive *a* impassibile

im'patien|ce *n* impazienza *f*. **~t** *a* impaziente. **~tly** *adv* impazientemente

impeccabl|e /ɪmˈpekəbl/ *a* impeccabile. **~y** *adv* in modo impeccabile

impede /ɪmˈpiːd/ *vt* impedire

impediment /ɪmˈpedɪmənt/ *n* impedimento *m*; (*in speech*) difetto *m*

impel /ɪmˈpel/ *vt* (*pt/pp* **impelled**) costringere; **feel ~led** to sentire l'obbligo di

impending /ɪmˈpendɪŋ/ *a* imminente

impenetrable /ɪmˈpenɪtrəbl/ *a* impenetrabile

imperative /ɪmˈperətɪv/ *a* imperativo ● *n Gram* imperativo *m*

imper'ceptible *a* impercettibile

im'perfect *a* imperfetto; (*faulty*) difettoso ● *n Gram* imperfetto *m*. **~ion** /-ˈfekʃn/ *n* imperfezione *f*

imperial /ɪmˈpɪərɪəl/ *a* imperiale. **~ism** *n* imperialismo *m*. **~ist** *n* imperialista *m*

imperious /ɪmˈpɪərɪəs/ *a* imperioso

im'personal *a* impersonale

impersonat|e /ɪmˈpɜːsəneɪt/ *vt* impersonare. **~or** *n* imitatore, -trice *mf*

impertinen|ce /ɪmˈpɜːtɪnəns/ *n* impertinenza *f*. **~t** *a* impertinente

imperturbable /ɪmpəˈtɜːbəbl/ *a* imperturbabile

impervious /ɪmˈpɜːvɪəs/ *a* **~ to** *fig* indifferente a

impetuous /ɪmˈpetjʊəs/ *a* impetuoso. **~ly** *adv* impetuosamente

impetus /ˈɪmpɪtəs/ *n* impeto *m*

implacable /ɪmˈplækəbl/ *a* implacabile

im'plant[1] *vt* trapiantare; *fig* inculcare

'implant[2] *n* trapianto *m*

implement[1] /ˈɪmplɪmənt/ *n* attrezzo *m*

implement[2] /ˈɪmplɪment/ *vt* mettere in atto

implicat|e /ˈɪmplɪkeɪt/ *vt* implicare. **~ion** /-ˈkeɪʃn/ *n* implicazione *f*; **by ~ion** implicitamente

implicit /ɪmˈplɪsɪt/ *a* implicito; (*absolute*) assoluto

implore /ɪmˈplɔː(r)/ *vt* implorare

imply /ɪmˈplaɪ/ *vt* (*pt/pp* **-ied**) implicare; **what are you ~ing?** che cosa vorresti insinuare?

impo'lite *a* sgarbato

import[1] /ˈɪmpɔːt/ *n Comm* importazione *f*

import[2] /ɪmˈpɔːt/ *vt* importare

importan|ce /ɪmˈpɔːtəns/ *n* importanza *f*. **~t** *a* importante

importer /ɪmˈpɔːtə(r)/ *n* importatore, -trice *mf*

impos|e /ɪmˈpəʊz/ *vt* imporre (**on** a) ● *vi* imporsi; **~e on** abusare di. **~ing** *a* imponente. **~ition** /ɪmpəˈzɪʃn/ *n* imposizione *f*

impossi'bility *n* impossibilità *f*

im'possible *a* impossibile

impostor /ɪmˈpɒstə(r)/ *n* impostore, -trice *mf*

impoten|ce /ˈɪmpətəns/ *n* impotenza *f*. **~t** *a* impotente

impound /ɪmˈpaʊnd/ *vt* confiscare

impoverished /ɪmˈpɒvərɪʃt/ *a* impoverito

im'practicable a impraticabile

im'practical a non pratico

impre'cise a impreciso

impregnable /ɪm'prɛgnəbl/ a imprendibile

impregnate /'ɪmprɛgneɪt/ vt impregnare (with di); Biol fecondare

im'press vt imprimere; fig colpire (positivamente); ~ sth [up]on sb fare capire qcsa a qcno

impression /ɪm'prɛʃn/ n impressione f; (imitation) imitazione f. ~able a (child, mind) influenzabile. ~ism n impressionismo m. ~ist n imitatore, -trice mf; (artist) impressionista mf

impressive /ɪm'prɛsɪv/ a imponente

'imprint¹ n impressione f

im'print² vt imprimere; ~ed on my mind impresso nella mia memoria

im'prison vt incarcerare. ~ment n reclusione f

im'probable a improbabile

impromptu /ɪm'prɒmptjuː/ a improvvisato

im'proper a (use) improprio; (behaviour) scorretto. ~ly adv scorrettamente

impro'priety n scorrettezza f

improve /ɪm'pruːv/ vt/i migliorare. **improve** [up]on vt perfezionare. ~ment /-mənt/ n miglioramento m

improvis|e /'ɪmprəvaɪz/ vt/i improvvisare

im'prudent a imprudente

impuden|ce /'ɪmpjʊdəns/ n sfrontatezza f. ~t a sfrontato

impuls|e /'ɪmpʌls/ n impulso m; on [an] ~e impulsivamente. ~ive /-'pʌlsɪv/ a impulsivo

impunity /ɪm'pjuːnətɪ/ n with ~ impunemente

im'pur|e a impuro. ~ity n impurità f inv; ~ities pl impurità fpl

impute /ɪm'pjuːt/ vt imputare (to a)

in /ɪn/ prep in; (with names of towns) a; **in the garden** in giardi-

no; **in the street** in or per strada; **in bed/hospital** a letto/all'ospedale; **in the world** nel mondo; **in the rain** sotto la pioggia; **in the sun** al sole; **in this heat** con questo caldo; **in summer/winter** in estate/inverno; **in 1995** nel 1995; **in the evening** la sera; **he's arriving in two hours time** arriva fra due ore; **deaf in one ear** sordo da un orecchio; **in the army** nell'esercito; **in English/Italian** in inglese/italiano; **in ink/pencil** a penna/matita; **in red** (dressed, circled) di rosso; **the man in the raincoat** l'uomo con l'impermeabile; **in a soft/loud voice** a voce bassa/alta; **one in ten people** una persona su dieci; **in doing this,** ~ nel far questo,...; **in itself** in sé; **in that** in quanto ● adv (at home) a casa; (indoors) dentro; **he's not in yet** non è ancora arrivato; **in there/here** lì/qui dentro; **ten in all** dieci in tutto; **day in, day out** giorno dopo giorno; **have it in for sb** fam avercela con qcno; **send him in** fallo entrare; **come in** entrare; **bring in the washing** portare dentro i panni ● a (fam: in fashion) di moda ● n **the ins and outs** i dettagli

ina'bility n incapacità f

inac'cessible a inaccessibile

in'accura|cy n inesattezza f. ~te a inesatto

in'ac|tive a inattivo. ~'tivity n inattività f

in'adequate a inadeguato. ~ly adv inadeguatamente

inad'missible a inammissibile

inadvertently /ɪnəd'vɜːtntlɪ/ adv inavvertitamente

inad'visable a sconsigliabile

inane /ɪ'neɪn/ a stupido

in'animate a esanime

in'applicable a inapplicabile

inap'propriate a inadatto

inar'ticulate a inarticolato

inat'tentive a disattento

in'audib|le a impercettibile

inaugural /ɪˈnɔːgjʊrəl/ a inaugurale

inaugurat|e /ɪˈnɔːgjʊreɪt/ vt inaugurare. **~ion** /-ˈreɪʃn/ n inaugurazione f

inau'spicious a infausto

inborn /ˈɪnbɔːn/ a innato

inbred /ɪnˈbred/ a congenito

incalculable /ɪnˈkælkjʊləbl/ a incalcolabile

in'capable a incapace

incapacitate /ɪnkəˈpæsɪteɪt/ vt rendere incapace

incarnat|e /ɪnˈkɑːnət/ a **the devil ~** il diavolo in carne e ossa

incendiary /ɪnˈsendɪərɪ/ a incendiario

incense¹ /ˈɪnsens/ n incenso m

incense² /ɪnˈsens/ vt esasperare

incentive /ɪnˈsentɪv/ n incentivo m

incessant /ɪnˈsesənt/ a incessante

incest /ˈɪnsest/ n incesto m

inch /ɪntʃ/ n pollice m (= 2.54 cm) ● vi **~ forward** avanzare gradatamente

inciden|ce /ˈɪnsɪdəns/ n incidenza f. **~t** n incidente m

incidental /ɪnsɪˈdentl/ a incidentale; **~ expenses** spese fpl accessorie. **~ly** adv incidentalmente; (by the way) a proposito

incinerat|e /ɪnˈsɪnəreɪt/ vt incenerire. **~or** n inceneritore m

incision /ɪnˈsɪʒn/ n incisione f

incisive /ɪnˈsaɪsɪv/ a incisivo

incisor /ɪnˈsaɪzə(r)/ n incisivo m

incite /ɪnˈsaɪt/ vt incitare. **~ment** n incitamento m

inclination /ɪnklɪˈneɪʃn/ n inclinazione f

incline¹ /ɪnˈklaɪn/ vt inclinare; **be ~d to do sth** essere propenso a fare qcsa

incline² /ˈɪnklaɪn/ n pendio m

inclu|de /ɪnˈkluːd/ vt includere. **~ding** prep incluso. **~sion** /-uːʒn/ n inclusione f

inclusive /ɪnˈkluːsɪv/ a incluso; **~ of** comprendente; **be ~ of** comprendere ● adv incluso

incognito /ɪnkɒgˈniːtəʊ/ adv incognito

inco'herent a incoerente; (because drunk etc) incomprensibile

income /ˈɪnkʌm/ n reddito m. **~ tax** n imposta f sul reddito

'incoming a in arrivo. **~ tide** n marea f montante

in'comparable a incomparabile

incompati'bility n incompatibilità f

incom'patible a incompatibile

incom'peten|ce n incompetenza f. **~t** a incompetente

incom'plete a incompleto

incompre'hensible a incomprensibile

incon'ceivable a inconcepibile

incon'clusive a inconcludente

incongruous /ɪnˈkɒŋgrʊəs/ a contrastante

inconsequential /ɪnkɒnsɪˈkwenʃl/ a senza importanza

incon'siderate a trascurabile

incon'sistency n incoerenza f

incon'sistent a incoerente; **be ~ with** non essere coerente con. **~ly** adv in modo incoerente

inconsolable /ɪnkənˈsəʊləbl/ a inconsolabile

incon'spicuous a non appariscente. **~ly** adv modestamente

inconti'nen|ce /ɪnˈkɒntɪnəns/ n incontinenza f. **~t** a incontinente

inconven|ience /ɪnkənˈviːnɪəns/ n scomodità f; (drawback) inconveniente m; **put sb to ~** disturbare qcno. **~t** a scomodo; (time, place) inopportuno. **~tly** adv in modo inopportuno

incorporate /ɪnˈkɔːpəreɪt/ vt incorporare; (contain) comprendere

incor'rect a incorretto. **~ly** adv scorrettamente

incorrigible /ɪnˈkɒrɪdʒəbl/ a incorreggibile

incorruptible /ɪnkəˈrʌptəbl/ a incorruttibile

increase¹ /ˈɪnkriːs/ n aumento m; **on the ~** in aumento

increas|e² /ɪnˈkriːs/ vt/i aumentare. **~ing** *a (impatience etc)* crescente; *(numbers)* in aumento. **~ingly** *adv* sempre più

in'credible *a* incredibile

incredulous /ɪn'kredjʊləs/ *a* incredulo

increment /'ɪnkrɪmənt/ *n* incremento *m*

incriminate /ɪn'krɪmɪneɪt/ *vt Jur* incriminare

incubat|e /'ɪŋkjʊbeɪt/ *vt* incubare. **~ion** /-'beɪʃn/ *n* incubazione *f*. **~ion period** *n Med* periodo *m* di incubazione. **~or** *n (for baby)* incubatrice *f*

incumbent /ɪn'kʌmbənt/ *a* **be ~ on sb** incombere a qcno

incur /ɪn'kɜː/ *vt (pt/pp incurred)* incorrere; contrarre *(debts)*

in'curable *a* incurabile

incursion /ɪn'kɜːʃn/ *n* incursione *f*

indebted /ɪn'detɪd/ *a* obbligato (**to** verso)

in'decent *a* indecente

inde'cision *n* indecisione *f*

inde'cisive *a* indeciso. **~ness** *n* indecisione *f*

indeed /ɪn'diːd/ *adv (in fact)* difatti; **yes ~!** sì, certamente!; **I am/do** veramente!; **very much ~** moltissimo; **thank you very much ~** grazie infinite; **~?** davvero?

indefatigable /ɪndɪ'fætɪɡəbl/ *a* instancabile

inde'finable *a* indefinibile

in'definite *a* indefinito. **~ly** *adv* indefinitamente; *(postpone)* a tempo indeterminato

indelible /ɪn'delɪbl/ *a* indelebile

indemnity /ɪn'demnɪtɪ/ *n* indennità *f inv*

indent¹ /'ɪndent/ *n Typ* rientranza *f* dal margine

indent² /ɪn'dent/ *vt Typ* fare rientrare dal margine. **~ation** /-'teɪʃn/ *n (notch)* intaccatura *f*

inde'penden|ce *n* indipendenza *f*. **~t** *a* indipendente. **~tly** *adv* indipendentemente

indescribable /ɪndɪ'skraɪbəbl/ *a* indescrivibile

indestructible /ɪndɪ'strʌktəbl/ *a* indistruttibile

indeterminate /ɪndɪ'tɜːmɪnət/ *a* indeterminato

index /'ɪndeks/ *n* indice *m*

index: ~ card *n* scheda *f*. **~ finger** *n* dito *m* indice. **~-linked** *a (pension)* legato al costo della vita

India /'ɪndɪə/ *n* India *f*. **~n** *a* indiano; *(American)* indiano [d'America] ● *n* indiano, -a *mf*; *(American)* indiano, -a *mf* [d'America], pellerossa *mf inv*

indicat|e /'ɪndɪkeɪt/ *vt* indicare; *(register)* segnare ● *vi Auto* mettere la freccia. **~ion** /-'keɪʃn/ *n* indicazione *f*

indicative /ɪn'dɪkətɪv/ *a* **be ~ of** essere indicativo di ● *n Gram* indicativo *m*

indicator /'ɪndɪkeɪtə(r)/ *n Auto* freccia *f*

indict /ɪn'daɪt/ *vt* accusare. **~ment** *n* accusa *f*

in'differen|ce *n* indifferenza *f*. **~t** *a* indifferente; *(not good)* mediocre

indigenous /ɪn'dɪdʒɪnəs/ *a* indigeno

indi'gest|ible *a* indigesto. **~ion** *n* indigestione *f*

indigna|nt /ɪn'dɪɡnənt/ *a* indignato. **~ntly** *adv* con indignazione. **~tion** /-'neɪʃn/ *n* indignazione *f*

in'dignity *n* umiliazione *f*

indi'rect *a* indiretto. **~ly** *adv* indirettamente

indi'screet *a* indiscreto

indis'cretion *n* indiscrezione *f*

indiscriminate /ɪndɪ'skrɪmɪnət/ *a* indiscriminato. **~ly** *adv* senza distinzione

indi'spensable *a* indispensabile

indisposed /ɪndɪ'spəʊzd/ *a* indisposto

indisputable /ɪndɪ'spjuːtəbl/ *a* indisputabile

indi'stinct *a* indistinto

indistinguishable /ɪndɪˈstɪŋgwɪʃəbl/ *a* indistinguibile

individual /ɪndɪˈvɪdjʊəl/ *a* individuale ● *n* individuo *m*. ~**ity** /-ˈæləti/ *n* individualità *f*

indi·visible *a* indivisibile

indoctrinate /ɪnˈdɒktrɪneɪt/ *vt* indottrinare

indomitable /ɪnˈdɒmɪtəbl/ *a* indomito

indoor /ˈɪndɔː(r)/ *a* interno; ⟨shoes⟩ per casa; ⟨plant⟩ da appartamento; ⟨swimming pool etc⟩ coperto. ~**s** /-ˈdɔːz/ *adv* dentro

induce /ɪnˈdjuːs/ *vt* indurre (**to** a); ⟨produce⟩ causare. ~**ment** *n* ⟨incentive⟩ incentivo *m*

indulge /ɪnˈdʌldʒ/ *vt* soddisfare; viziare ⟨child⟩ ● *vi* ~ **in** concedersi. ~**nce** /-əns/ *n* lusso *m*; ⟨leniency⟩ indulgenza *f*. ~**nt** *a* indulgente

industrial /ɪnˈdʌstrɪəl/ *a* industriale; **take** ~ **action** scioperare. ~**ist** *n* industriale *mf*. ~**ized** *a* industrializzato

industr|ious /ɪnˈdʌstrɪəs/ *a* industrioso. ~**y** /ˈɪndəstrɪ/ *n* industria *f*; ⟨zeal⟩ operosità *f*

inebriated /ɪˈniːbrɪeɪtɪd/ *a* ebbro

in'edible *a* immangiabile

ineffective *a* inefficace

ineffectual /ɪnɪˈfektʃʊəl/ *a* inutile; ⟨person⟩ inconcludente

inefficien|cy *n* inefficienza *f*. ~**t** *a* inefficiente

in'eligible *a* inadatto

inept /ɪˈnept/ *a* inetto

ine'quality *n* ineguaglianza *f*

inert /ɪˈnɜːt/ *a* inerte. ~**ia** /ɪˈnɜːʃə/ *n* inerzia *f*

inescapable /ɪnɪˈskeɪpəbl/ *a* inevitabile

inestimable /ɪnˈestɪməbl/ *a* inestimabile

inevitab|le /ɪnˈevɪtəbl/ *a* inevitabile. ~**y** *adv* inevitabilmente

ine'xact *a* inesatto

inex'cusable *a* imperdonabile

inexhaustible /ɪnɪgˈzɔːstəbl/ *a* inesauribile

inexorable /ɪnˈeksərəbl/ *a* inesorabile

inex'pensive *a* poco costoso

inex'perience *n* inesperienza *f*. ~**d** *a* inesperto

inexplicable /ɪnɪkˈsplɪkəbl/ *a* inesplicabile

in'fallible *a* infallibile

infam|ous /ˈɪnfəməs/ *a* infame; ⟨person⟩ famigerato. ~**y** *n* infamia *f*

infan|cy /ˈɪnfənsɪ/ *n* infanzia *f*; **in its** ~**cy** *fig* agli inizi. ~**t** *n* bambino, -a *mf* piccolo, -a. ~**tile** *a* infantile

infantry /ˈɪnfəntrɪ/ *n* fanteria *f*

infatuat|ed /ɪnˈfætʃʊeɪtɪd/ *a* infatuato (**with** di). ~**ion** *n* infatuazione *f*

infect /ɪnˈfekt/ *vt* infettare; **become** ~**ed** ⟨wound:⟩ infettarsi. ~**ion** /-ˈfekʃn/ *n* infezione *f*. ~**ious** /-ˈfekʃəs/ *a* infettivo

infer /ɪnˈfɜː(r)/ *vt* ⟨pt/pp **inferred**⟩ dedurre (**from** da); ⟨imply⟩ implicare. ~**ence** /ˈɪnfərəns/ *n* deduzione *f*

inferior /ɪnˈfɪərɪə(r)/ *a* inferiore; ⟨goods⟩ scadente; ⟨in rank⟩ subalterno ● *n* inferiore *mf*; ⟨in rank⟩ subalterno, -a *mf*

inferiority /ɪnfɪərɪˈɒrəti/ *n* inferiorità *f*. ~ **complex** *n* complesso *m* di inferiorità

infern|al /ɪnˈfɜːnl/ *a* infernale. ~**o** *n* inferno *m*

in'fertile *a* sterile. ~**tility** *n* sterilità *f*

infest /ɪnˈfest/ *vt* **be** ~**ed with** essere infestato di

infi'delity *n* infedeltà *f*

infighting /ˈɪnfaɪtɪŋ/ *n* *fig* lotta *f* per il potere

infiltrate /ˈɪnfɪltreɪt/ *vt* infiltrare; *Pol* infiltrarsi in

infinite /ˈɪnfɪnət/ *a* infinito

infinitive /ɪnˈfɪnətɪv/ *n* *Gram* infinito *m*

infinity /ɪnˈfɪnətɪ/ *n* infinità *f*

infirm /ɪnˈfɜːm/ *a* debole. ~**ary** *n* infermeria *f*. ~**ity** *n* debolezza *f*

inflame /ɪnˈfleɪm/ *vt* infiammare. **~d** a infiammato; **become ~d** infiammarsi

in'flammable *a* infiammabile

inflammation /ɪnfləˈmeɪʃn/ *n* infiammazione *f*

inflammatory /ɪnˈflæmətrɪ/ *a* incendiario

inflatable /ɪnˈfleɪtəbl/ *a* gonfiabile

inflat|e /ɪnˈfleɪt/ *vt* gonfiare. **~ion** /-eɪʃn/ *n* inflazione *f*. **~ionary** /-eɪʃənərɪ/ *a* inflazionario

in'flexible *a* inflessibile

inflexion /ɪnˈflekʃn/ *n* inflessione *f*

inflict /ɪnˈflɪkt/ *vt* infliggere (**on** a)

influenc|e /ˈɪnflʊəns/ *n* influenza *f* ● *vt* influenzare. **~tial** /-ˈenʃl/ *a* influente

influenza /ɪnflʊˈenzə/ *n* influenza *f*

influx /ˈɪnflʌks/ *n* affluenza *f*

inform /ɪnˈfɔːm/ *vt* informare; **keep sb ~ed** tenere qcno al corrente ● *vi* **~ against** denunciare

in'for|mal *a* informale; ⟨*agreement*⟩ ufficioso. **~mally** *adv* in modo informale. **~'mality** *n* informalità *f inv*

informant /ɪnˈfɔːmənt/ *n* informatore, -trice *mf*

information /ɪnfəˈmeɪʃn/ *n* informazioni *fpl*; **a piece of ~ion** un'informazione. **~ion highway** *n* autostrada *f* telematica. **~ion technology** *n* informatica *f*. **~ive** /ɪnˈfɔːmətɪv/ *a* informativo; ⟨*film, book*⟩ istruttivo

informer /ɪnˈfɔːmə(r)/ *n* informatore, -trice *mf*; *Pol* delatore, -trice *mf*

infra-'red /ɪnfrə-/ *a* infrarosso

infrastructure /ˈɪnfrəstrʌktʃə(r)/ *n* infrastruttura *f*

infringe /ɪnˈfrɪndʒ/ *vt* **~ on** usurpare. **~ment** *n* violazione *f*

infuriat|e /ɪnˈfjʊərɪeɪt/ *vt* infuriare. **~ing** *a* esasperante

infusion /ɪnˈfjuːʒn/ *n* ⟨*drink*⟩ infusione *f*; ⟨*of capital, new blood*⟩ afflusso *m*

ingenious /ɪnˈdʒiːnɪəs/ *a* ingegnoso

ingenuity /ɪndʒɪˈnjuːətɪ/ *n* ingegnosità *f*

ingenuous /ɪnˈdʒenjʊəs/ *a* ingenuo

ingot /ˈɪŋɡət/ *n* lingotto *m*

ingrained /ɪnˈɡreɪnd/ *a* ⟨*in person*⟩ radicato; ⟨*dirt*⟩ incrostato

ingratiate /ɪnˈɡreɪʃɪeɪt/ *vt* **~ oneself with sb** ingraziarsi qcno

in'gratitude *n* ingratitudine *f*

ingredient /ɪnˈɡriːdɪənt/ *n* ingrediente *m*

ingrowing /ˈɪnɡrəʊɪŋ/ *a* ⟨*nail*⟩ incarnito

inhabit /ɪnˈhæbɪt/ *vt* abitare. **~ant** *n* abitante *mf*

inhale /ɪnˈheɪl/ *vt* aspirare; *Med* inalare ● *vi* inspirare; ⟨*when smoking*⟩ aspirare. **~r** *n* ⟨*device*⟩ inalatore *m*

inherent /ɪnˈhɪərənt/ *a* inerente

inherit /ɪnˈherɪt/ *vt* ereditare. **~ance** /-əns/ *n* eredità *f inv*

inhibit /ɪnˈhɪbɪt/ *vt* inibire. **~ed** *a* inibito. **~ion** /-ˈbɪʃn/ *n* inibizione *f*

inho'spitable *a* inospitale

in'human *a* disumano

initial /ɪˈnɪʃl/ *a* iniziale ● *n* iniziale *f* ● *vt* (*pt/pp* **initialled**) siglare. **~ly** *adv* all'inizio

initiat|e /ɪˈnɪʃɪeɪt/ *vt* iniziare. **~ion** /-ˈeɪʃn/ *n* iniziazione *f*

initiative /ɪˈnɪʃətɪv/ *n* iniziativa *f*

inject /ɪnˈdʒekt/ *vt* iniettare. **~ion** /-ekʃn/ *n* iniezione *f*

injur|e /ˈɪndʒə(r)/ *vt* ferire; ⟨*wrong*⟩ nuocere. **~y** *n* ferita *f*; ⟨*wrong*⟩ torto *m*

in'justice *n* ingiustizia *f*; **do sb an ~** giudicare qcno in modo sbagliato

ink /ɪŋk/ *n* inchiostro *m*

inkling /ˈɪŋklɪŋ/ *n* sentore *m*

inlaid /ɪnˈleɪd/ *a* intarsiato

inland /ˈɪnlənd/ *a* interno ● *adv* all'interno. **I~ Revenue** *n* fisco *m*

in-laws /ˈɪnlɔːz/ *npl fam* parenti *mpl* acquisiti

inlay /ˈɪnleɪ/ *n* intarsio *m*

inlet /ˈɪnlet/ *n* insenatura *f*; *Techn* entrata *f*

inmate /'ɪnmeɪt/ n (of hospital) degente mf; (of prison) carcerato, -a mf

inn /ɪn/ n locanda f

innate /ɪ'neɪt/ a innato

inner /'ɪnə(r)/ a interno. ~**most** a il più profondo. ~ **tube** camera f d'aria

'innkeeper n locandiere, -a mf

innocen|ce /'ɪnəsns/ n innocenza f. ~**t** a innocente

innocuous /ɪ'nɒkjʊəs/ a innocuo

innovat|e /'ɪnəveɪt/ vi innovare. ~**ion** /-'veɪʃn/ n innovazione f. ~**ive** /'ɪnəvətɪv/ a innovativo. ~**or** /'ɪnəveɪtə(r)/ n innovatore, -trice mf

innuendo /ɪnjʊ'endəʊ/ n (pl -es) insinuazione f

innumerable /ɪ'njuːmərəbl/ a innumerevole

inoculat|e /ɪ'nɒkjʊleɪt/ vt vaccinare. ~**ion** /-'leɪʃn/ n vaccinazione f

inoffensive /ɪnə'fensɪv/ a inoffensivo

inoperable /ɪn'ɒpərəbl/ a inoperabile

inopportune /ɪn'ɒpətjuːn/ a inopportuno

inordinate /ɪ'nɔːdɪnət/ a smodato

inorganic /ɪnɔː'gænɪk/ a inorganico

'in-patient n degente mf

input /'ɪnpʊt/ n input m inv, ingresso m

inquest /'ɪnkwest/ n inchiesta f

inquir|e /ɪn'kwaɪə(r)/ vi informarsi (**about** su); ~**e into** far indagini su ● vt domandare. ~**y** n domanda f, (investigation) inchiesta f

inquisitive /ɪn'kwɪzətɪv/ a curioso

inroad /'ɪnrəʊd/ n **make** ~**s into** intaccare ⟨savings⟩; cominciare a risolvere ⟨problem⟩

in'sane a pazzo; fig insensato

in'sanitary a malsano

in'sanity n pazzia f

insatiable /ɪn'seɪʃəbl/ a insaziabile

inscri|be /ɪn'skraɪb/ vt iscrivere. ~**ption** /-'skrɪpʃn/ n iscrizione f

inscrutable /ɪn'skruːtəbl/ a impenetrabile

insect /'ɪnsekt/ n insetto m.

~**icide** /-'sektɪsaɪd/ n insetticida m

inse'cure a malsicuro; ⟨fig: person⟩ insicuro. ~**ity** n mancanza f di sicurezza

insemination /ɪnsemɪ'neɪʃn/ n inseminazione f

in'sensitive a insensibile

in'separable a inseparabile

insert[1] /'ɪnsɜːt/ n inserto m

insert[2] /ɪn'sɜːt/ vt inserire. ~**ion** /-ʒ:ʃn/ n inserzione f

inside /ɪn'saɪd/ n interno m. ~**s** npl fam pancia f ● attrib Aut ~ **lane** n corsia f interna ● adv dentro; ~ **out** a rovescio; (thoroughly) a fondo ● prep dentro; (of time) entro

insidious /ɪn'sɪdɪəs/ a insidioso

insight /'ɪnsaɪt/ n intuito m (**into** per); **an** ~ **into** un quadro di

insignia /ɪn'sɪgnɪə/ npl insegne fpl

insig'nificant a insignificante

insin'cer|e a poco sincero. ~**ity** /-'serɪtɪ/ n mancanza f di sincerità

insinuat|e /ɪn'sɪnjʊeɪt/ vt insinuare. ~**ion** /-'eɪʃn/ n insinuazione f

insipid /ɪn'sɪpɪd/ a insipido

insist /ɪn'sɪst/ vi insistere (**on** per) ● vt ~ **that** insistere che. ~**ence** n insistenza f. ~**ent** a insistente

insole n soletta f

insolen|ce /'ɪnsələns/ n insolenza f. ~**t** a insolente

in'soluble a insolubile

in'solven|cy n insolvenza f. ~**t** a insolvente

insomnia /ɪn'sɒmnɪə/ n insonnia f

inspect /ɪn'spekt/ vt ispezionare; controllare ⟨ticket⟩. ~**ion** /-ekʃn/ n ispezione f; (of ticket) controllo m. ~**or** n ispettore, -trice mf; (of tickets) controllore m

inspiration /ɪnspə'reɪʃn/ n ispirazione f

inspire /ɪn'spaɪə(r)/ vt ispirare

insta'bility n instabilità f

install /ɪn'stɔːl/ vt installare. ~**ation** /-stə'leɪʃn/ n installazione f

instalment /ɪn'stɔːlmənt/ n Comm

rata f; (of serial) puntata f; (of publication) fascicolo m

instance /'ɪnstəns/ n (case) caso m; (example) esempio m; **in the first ~** in primo luogo; **for ~** per esempio

instant /'ɪnstənt/ a immediato; Culin espresso ● n istante m. **~aneous** /-'teɪnɪəs/ a istantaneo

instant 'coffee n caffè m in solubile

instantly /'ɪnstəntlɪ/ adv immediatamente

instead /ɪn'sted/ adv invece; **~ of doing** anziché fare; **~ of me** al mio posto; **~ of going** invece di andare

'instep n collo m del piede

instigat|e /'ɪnstɪgeɪt/ vt istigare. **~ion** /-'geɪʃn/ n istigazione f; **at his ~ion** dietro suo suggerimento. **~or** n istigatore, -trice mf

instil /ɪn'stɪl/ vt (pt/pp instilled) inculcare (into in)

instinct /'ɪnstɪŋkt/ n istinto m. **~ive** /ɪn'stɪŋktɪv/ a istintivo

institut|e /'ɪnstɪtjuːt/ n istituto m ● vt istituire (scheme); iniziare (search); intentare (legal action). **~ion** /-'tjuːʃn/ n istituzione f; (home for elderly) istituto m per anziani; (for mentally ill) istituto m per malati di mente

instruct /ɪn'strʌkt/ vt istruire; (order) ordinare. **~ion** /-ʌkʃn/ n istruzione f; **~s** (orders) ordini mpl. **~ive** /-ɪv/ a istruttivo. **~or** n istruttore, -trice mf

instrument /'ɪnstrəmənt/ n strumento m. **~al** /-'mentl/ a strumentale; **be ~al in** contribuire a. **~alist** n strumentista mf

insu'bordi|nate a insubordinato. **~nation** /-'neɪʃn/ n insubordinazione f

in'sufferable a insopportabile

insuf'ficient a insufficiente

insular /'ɪnsjʊlə(r)/ a fig gretto

insulat|e /'ɪnsjʊleɪt/ vt isolare. **~ing tape** n nastro m isolante. **~ion** /-'leɪʃn/ n isolamento m

insulin /'ɪnsjʊlɪn/ n insulina f

insult¹ /'ɪnsʌlt/ n insulto m

insult² /ɪn'sʌlt/ vt insultare

insuperable /ɪn'suːpərəbl/ a insuperabile

insur|ance /ɪn'ʃʊərəns/ n assicurazione f. **~e** vt assicurare

insurrection /ɪnsə'rekʃn/ n insurrezione f

intact /ɪn'tækt/ a intatto

'intake n immissione f; (of food) consumo m

in'tangible a intangibile

integral /'ɪntɪgrəl/ a integrale

integrat|e /'ɪntɪgreɪt/ vt integrare ● vi integrarsi. **~ion** /-'greɪʃn/ n integrazione f

integrity /ɪn'tegrətɪ/ n integrità f

intellect /'ɪntəlekt/ n intelletto m. **~ual** /-'lektjʊəl/ a & n intellettuale mf

intelligen|ce /ɪn'telɪdʒəns/ n intelligenza f; Mil informazioni fpl. **~t** a intelligente

intelligentsia /ɪntelɪ'dʒentsɪə/ n intellighenzia f

intelligible /ɪn'telɪdʒəbl/ a intelligibile

intend /ɪn'tend/ vt destinare; (have in mind) aver intenzione di; **be ~ed for** essere destinato a. **~ed** a (effect) voluto ● n my **~ed** fam il mio/la mia fidanzato, -a

intense /ɪn'tens/ a intenso; (person) dai sentimenti intensi. **~ly** adv intensamente; (very) estremamente

intensi|fication /ɪntensɪfɪ'keɪʃn/ n intensificazione f. **~fy** /-'tensɪfaɪ/ v (pt/pp -ied) ● vt intensificare ● vi intensificarsi

intensity /ɪn'tensətɪ/ n intensità f

intensive /ɪn'tensɪv/ a intensivo. **~ care** (for people in coma) rianimazione f; **~ care [unit]** terapia f intensiva

intent /ɪn'tent/ a intento; **~ on** (absorbed in) preso da; **be ~ on doing sth** essere intento a fare qcsa ● n intenzione f; **to all ~s**

and purposes a tutti gli effetti.
~ly adv attentamente

intention /ɪnˈtenʃn/ n intenzione f.
~al a intenzionale. **~ally** adv intenzionalmente

inter'acti|on n cooperazione f.
~ve a interattivo

intercede /ɪntəˈsiːd/ vi intercedere (**on behalf of** a favore di)

intercept /ɪntəˈsept/ vt intercettare

'interchange n scambio m; Auto raccordo m [autostradale]

inter'changeable a interscambiabile

intercom /ˈɪntəkɒm/ n citofono m

'intercourse n (sexual) rapporti mpl [sessuali]

interest /ˈɪntrəst/ n interesse m; **have an ~ in** Comm essere cointeressato in; **be of ~** essere interessante; **~ rate** n tasso m di interesse ● vt interessare. **~ed** a interessato. **~ing** a interessante

interface /ˈɪntəfeɪs/ n interfaccia f ● vt interfacciare ● vi interfacciarsi

interfere /ɪntəˈfɪə(r)/ vi interferire; **~ with** interferire con. **~nce** /-əns/ n interferenza f

interim /ˈɪntərɪm/ a temporaneo; **~ payment** acconto m ● n **in the ~** nel frattempo

interior /ɪnˈtɪərɪə(r)/ a interiore ● n interno m. **~ designer** n arredatore, -trice mf

interject /ɪntəˈdʒekt/ vt intervenire. **~ion** /-ekʃn/ n Gram interiezione f; (remark) intervento m

interloper /ˈɪntələʊpə(r)/ n intruso, -a mf

interlude /ˈɪntəluːd/ n intervallo m

inter'marry vi sposarsi tra parenti; (different groups:) contrarre matrimoni misti

intermediary /ɪntəˈmiːdɪərɪ/ n intermediario, -a mf

intermediate /ɪntəˈmiːdɪət/ a intermedio

interminable /ɪnˈtɜːmɪnəbl/ a interminabile

intermission /ɪntəˈmɪʃn/ n intervallo m

intermittent /ɪntəˈmɪtənt/ a intermittente

intern /ɪnˈtɜːn/ vt internare

internal /ɪnˈtɜːnl/ a interno. **~ly** adv internamente; (deal with) all'interno

inter'national a internazionale ● n (game) incontro m internazionale; (player) competitore, -trice mf in gare internazionali. **~ly** adv internazionalmente

Internet /ˈɪntənet/ n Internet m

internist /ɪnˈtɜːnɪst/ n Am internista mf

internment /ɪnˈtɜːnmənt/ n internamento m

'interplay n azione f reciproca

interpret /ɪnˈtɜːprɪt/ vt interpretare ● vi fare l'interprete. **~ation** /-ˈteɪʃn/ n interpretazione f. **~er** n interprete mf

interre'lated (facts) in correlazione

interrogat|e /ɪnˈterəgeɪt/ vt interrogare. **~ion** /-ˈgeɪʃn/ n interrogazione f; (by police) interrogatorio m

interrogative /ɪntəˈrɒgətɪv/ a & n **~ [pronoun]** interrogativo m

interrupt /ɪntəˈrʌpt/ vt/i interrompere. **~ion** /-ˈʌpʃn/ n interruzione f

intersect /ɪntəˈsekt/ vi intersecarsi ● vt intersecare. **~ion** /-ekʃn/ n intersezione f; (of street) incrocio m

interspersed /ɪntəˈspɜːst/ a **~ with** inframmezzato di

inter'twine vi attorcigliarsi

interval /ˈɪntəvl/ n intervallo m; **bright ~s** pl schiarite fpl

interven|e /ɪntəˈviːn/ vi intervenire. **~tion** /-ˈvenʃn/ n intervento m

interview /ˈɪntəvjuː/ n Journ intervista f; (for job) colloquio m [di lavoro] ● vt intervistare. **~er** n intervistatore, -trice mf

intestin|e /ɪnˈtestɪn/ n intestino m. **~al** a intestinale

intimacy /ˈɪntɪməsɪ/ n intimità f

intimate[1] /ˈɪntɪmət/ a intimo. **~ly** adv intimamente

intimate[2] /ˈɪntɪmeɪt/ vt far capire; (imply) suggerire

intimidat|e /ɪnˈtɪmɪdeɪt/ vt intimidire. **~ion** /-ˈdeɪʃn/ n intimidazione f

into /ˈɪntə/, di fronte a una vocale /ˈɪntʊ/ prep dentro, in; **go ~ the house** andare dentro [casa] o in casa; **be ~** (fam: like) essere appassionato di; **I'm not ~ that** questo non mi piace; **7 ~ 21 goes 3** il 7 nel 21 ci sta 3 volte; **translate ~ French** tradurre in francese; **get ~ trouble** mettersi nei guai

in'tolerable a intollerabile

in'toleran|ce n intolleranza f. **~t** a intollerante

intonation /ɪntəˈneɪʃn/ n intonazione f

intoxicat|ed /ɪnˈtɒksɪkeɪtɪd/ a inebriato. **~ion** /-ˈkeɪʃn/ n ebbrezza f

intractable /ɪnˈtræktəbl/ a intrattabile; (problem) insolubile

intransigent /ɪnˈtrænzɪdʒənt/ a intransigente

in'transitive a intransitivo

intravenous /ɪntrəˈviːnəs/ a endovenoso. **~ly** adv per via endovenosa

intrepid /ɪnˈtrepɪd/ a intrepido

intricate /ˈɪntrɪkət/ a complesso

intrigue /ɪnˈtriːg/ n intrigo m ●vt intrigare ●vi tramare. **~ing** a intrigante

intrinsic /ɪnˈtrɪnsɪk/ a intrinseco

introduce /ɪntrəˈdjuːs/ vt presentare; (bring in, insert) introdurre

introduct|ion /ɪntrəˈdʌkʃn/ n introduzione f; (to person) presentazione f; (to book) prefazione f. **~ory** /-tərɪ/ a introduttivo

introspective /ɪntrəˈspektɪv/ a introspettivo

introvert /ˈɪntrəvɜːt/ n introverso, -a mf

intru|de /ɪnˈtruːd/ vi intrometter-

si. **~der** n intruso, -a mf. **~sion** /-uːʒn/ n intrusione f

intuit|ion /ɪntjuˈɪʃn/ n intuito m. **~ive** /-ˈtjuːɪtɪv/ a intuitivo

inundate /ˈɪnəndeɪt/ vt fig inondare (with di)

invade /ɪnˈveɪd/ vt invadere. **~r** n invasore m

invalid[1] /ˈɪnvəlɪd/ n invalido, -a mf

invalid[2] /ɪnˈvælɪd/ a non valido. **~ate** vt invalidare

in'valuable a prezioso; (priceless) inestimabile

in'variabl|e a invariabile. **~y** adv invariabilmente

invasion /ɪnˈveɪʒn/ n invasione f

invective /ɪnˈvektɪv/ n invettiva f

invent /ɪnˈvent/ vt inventare. **~ion** /-enʃn/ n invenzione f. **~ive** /-tɪv/ a inventivo. **~or** n inventore, -trice mf

inventory /ˈɪnvəntrɪ/ n inventario m

inverse /ɪnˈvɜːs/ a inverso ●n inverso m

invert /ɪnˈvɜːt/ vt invertire; **in ~ed commas** tra virgolette

invest /ɪnˈvest/ vt investire ●vi fare investimenti; **~ in** (fam: buy) comprarsi

investigat|e /ɪnˈvestɪgeɪt/ vt investigare. **~ion** /-ˈgeɪʃn/ n investigazione f

invest|ment /ɪnˈvestmənt/ n investimento m. **~or** n investitore, -trice mf

inveterate /ɪnˈvetərət/ a inveterato

invidious /ɪnˈvɪdɪəs/ a ingiusto; (position) antipatico

invigilate /ɪnˈvɪdʒɪleɪt/ vi Sch sorvegliare lo svolgimento di un esame. **~or** n persona f che sorveglia lo svolgimento di un esame

invigorate /ɪnˈvɪgəreɪt/ vt rinvigorire

invigorating /ɪnˈvɪgəreɪtɪŋ/ a tonificante

invincible /ɪnˈvɪnsəbl/ a invincibile

inviolable /ɪn'vaɪələbl/ *a* inviolabile

invisible *a* invisibile

invitation /ɪnvɪ'teɪʃn/ *n* invito *m*

invit|e /ɪn'vaɪt/ *vt* invitare; (*attract*) attirare. **~ing** *a* invitante

invoice /'ɪnvɔɪs/ *n* fattura *f* ● *vt* ~ **sb** emettere una fattura a qcno

invoke /ɪn'vəʊk/ *vt* invocare

involuntary *a* involontario

involv|e /ɪn'vɒlv/ *vt* comportare; (*affect*, *include*) coinvolgere; (*entail*) implicare; **get ~d with sb** legarsi a qcno; (*romantically*) legarsi sentimentalmente a qcno. **~d** *a* complesso. **~ment** *n* coinvolgimento *m*

invulnerable *a* invulnerabile; (*position*) inattaccabile

inward /'ɪnwəd/ *a* interno; (*thoughts etc*) interiore; ~ **investment** *Comm* investimento *m* straniero. **~ly** *adv* interiormente. **~s** *adv* verso l'interno

iodine /'aɪədiːn/ *n* iodio *m*

iota /aɪ'əʊtə/ *n* briciolo *m*

IOU *n abbr* (**I owe you**) pagherò *m inv*

IQ *n abbr* (**intelligence quotient**) Q.I.

IRA *n abbr* (**Irish Republican Army**) I.R.A. *f*

Iran /ɪ'rɑːn/ *n* Iran *m*. **~ian** /ɪ'reɪnɪən/ *a* & *n* iraniano, -a *mf*

Iraq /ɪ'rɑːk/ *n* Iraq *m*. **~i** /ɪ'rɑːkɪ/ *a* & *n* iracheno, -a *mf*

irascible /ɪ'ræsɪbl/ *a* irascibile

irate /aɪ'reɪt/ *a* adirato

Ireland /'aɪələnd/ *n* Irlanda *f*

iris /'aɪrɪs/ *n Anat* iride *f*; *Bot* iris *f inv*

Irish /'aɪrɪʃ/ *a* irlandese ● *n* **the ~** *pl* gli irlandesi *mpl*. **~man** *n* irlandese *m*. **~woman** *n* irlandese *f*

iron /'aɪən/ *a* di ferro. **I~ Curtain** *n* cortina *f* di ferro ● *n* ferro *m*; (*appliance*) ferro *m* [da stiro] ● *vt/i* stirare. **iron out** *vt* eliminare stirando; *fig* appianare

ironic[al] /aɪ'rɒnɪk[l]/ *a* ironico

ironing /'aɪənɪŋ/ *n* stirare *m*;

(*articles*) roba *f* da stirare; **do the ~** stirare. **~-board** *n* asse *f* da stiro

ironmonger /-mʌŋgə(r)/ *n* **~'s** [**shop**] negozio *m* di ferramenta

irony /'aɪrənɪ/ *n* ironia *f*

irradiate /ɪ'reɪdɪeɪt/ *vt* irradiare

irrational /ɪ'ræʃənl/ *a* irrazionale

irreconcilable /ɪ'rekənsaɪləbl/ *a* irreconciliabile

irrefutable /ɪrɪ'fjuːtəbl/ *a* irrefutabile

irregular /ɪ'regjʊlə(r)/ *a* irregolare. **~ity** /-'lærətɪ/ *n* irregolarità *f inv*

irrelevant /ɪ'reləvənt/ *a* non pertinente

irreparable /ɪ'repərəbl/ *a* irreparabile. **~y** *adv* irreparabilmente

irreplaceable /ɪrɪ'pleɪsəbl/ *a* insostituibile

irrepressible /ɪrɪ'presəbl/ *a* irrefrenabile; (*person*) incontenibile

irresistible /ɪrɪ'zɪstəbl/ *a* irresistibile

irresolute /ɪ'rezəluːt/ *a* irrisoluto

irrespective /ɪrɪ'spektɪv/ *a* ~ **of** senza riguardo per

irresponsible /ɪrɪ'spɒnsɪbl/ *a* irresponsabile

irreverent /ɪ'revərənt/ *a* irreverente

irreversible /ɪrɪ'vɜːsəbl/ *a* irreversibile

irrevocable /ɪ'revəkəbl/ *a* irrevocabile. **~y** *adv* irrevocabilmente

irrigat|e /'ɪrɪgeɪt/ *vt* irrigare. **~ion** /-'geɪʃn/ *n* irrigazione *f*

irritability /ɪrɪtə'bɪlətɪ/ *n* irritabilità *f*

irritable /'ɪrɪtəbl/ *a* irritabile

irritant /'ɪrɪtənt/ *n* sostanza *f* irritante

irritat|e /'ɪrɪteɪt/ *vt* irritare. **~ing** *a* irritante. **~ion** /-'teɪʃn/ *n* irritazione *f*

is /ɪz/ *see* **be**

Islam /'ɪzlɑːm/ *n* Islam *m*. **~ic** /-'læmɪk/ *a* islamico

island /'aɪlənd/ *n* isola *f*; (*in road*)

isola *f* spartitraffico. **~er** *n* isolano, -a *mf*

isle /aɪl/ *n* isola *f*

isolat|e /ˈaɪsəleɪt/ *vt* isolare. **~ed** *a* isolato. **~ion** /-ˈleɪʃn/ *n* isolamento *m*

Israel /ˈɪzreɪl/ *n* Israele *m*. **~i** /ɪzˈreɪlɪ/ *a* & *n* israeliano, -a *mf*

issue /ˈɪʃuː/ *n* (*outcome*) risultato *m*; (*of magazine*) numero *m*; (*of stamps etc*) emissione *f*; (*offspring*) figli *mpl*; (*matter, question*) questione *f*; **at ~** in questione; **take ~ with sb** prendere posizione contro qcno ● *vt* distribuire (*supplies*); rilasciare (*passport*); emettere (*stamps, order*); pubblicare (*book*); **be ~d with sth** ricevere qcsa ● *vi* **~ from** uscire da

isthmus /ˈɪsməs/ *n* (*pl* **-muses**) istmo *m*

it /ɪt/ *pron* (*direct object*) lo *m*, la *f*; (*indirect object*) gli *m*, le *f*; **it's broken** è rotto/rotta; **will it be enough?** basterà?; **it's hot** fa caldo; **it's raining** piove; **it's me** sono io; **who is it?** chi è?; **it's two o'clock** sono le due; **I doubt it** ne dubito; **take it with you** prendilo con te; **give it a wipe** dagli una pulita

Italian /ɪˈtæljən/ *a* & *n* italiano, -a *mf*; (*language*) italiano *m*

italic /ɪˈtælɪk/ *a* italico. **~s** *npl* corsivo *msg*

Italy /ˈɪtəlɪ/ *n* Italia *f*

itch /ɪtʃ/ *n* prurito *m* ● *vi* avere prurito, prudere; **be ~ing to** *fam* avere una voglia matta di. **~y** *a* che prude; **my foot is ~y** ho prurito al piede

item /ˈaɪtəm/ *n* articolo *m*; (*on agenda, programme*) punto *m*; (*on invoice*) voce *f*; **~ [of news]** notizia *f*. **~ize** *vt* dettagliare (*bill*)

itinerant /aɪˈtɪnərənt/ *a* itinerante

itinerary /aɪˈtɪnərərɪ/ *n* itinerario *m*

its /ɪts/ *poss pron* suo *m*, sua *f*, suoi *mpl*, sue *fpl*. **~ mother/cage** sua madre/la sua gabbia

it's = **it is**, **it has**

itself /ɪtˈself/ *pron* (*reflexive*) si; (*emphatic*) essa stessa; **the baby looked at ~ in the mirror** il bambino si è guardato nello specchio; **by ~** da solo; **the machine in ~ is simple** la macchina di per sé è semplice

ITV *n abbr* (**Independent Television**) stazione *f* televisiva privata britannica

ivory /ˈaɪvərɪ/ *n* avorio *m*

ivy /ˈaɪvɪ/ *n* edera *f*

•••••••••••••••••••••••••••••••••••

Jj

•••••••••••••••••••••••••••••••••••

jab /dʒæb/ *n* colpo *m* secco; (*fam: injection*) puntura *f* ● *vt* (*pt/pp* **jabbed**) punzecchiare

jabber /ˈdʒæbə(r)/ *vi* borbottare

jack /dʒæk/ *n* *Auto* cric *m inv*; (*in cards*) fante *m*, jack *m inv* ● **jack up** *vt* *Auto* sollevare [con il cric]

jackdaw /ˈdʒækdɔː/ *n* taccola *f*

jacket /ˈdʒækɪt/ *n* giacca *f*; (*of book*) sopraccoperta *f*. **~ po'tato** *n* patata *f* cotta al forno con la buccia

jackpot *n* premio *m* (*di una lotteria*); **win the ~** vincere alla lotteria; **hit the ~** *fig* fare un colpo grosso

jade /dʒeɪd/ *n* giada *f* ● *attrib* di giada

jaded /ˈdʒeɪdɪd/ *a* spossato

jagged /ˈdʒægɪd/ *a* dentellato

jail /dʒeɪl/ = **gaol**

jalopy /dʒəˈlɒpɪ/ *n* *fam* vecchia carretta *f*

jam¹ /dʒæm/ *n* marmellata *f*

jam² *n* *Auto* ingorgo *m*; (*fam: difficulty*) guaio *m* ● *v* (*pt/pp* **jammed**) ● *vt* (*cram*) pigiare; disturbare (*broadcast*); inceppare (*mechanism, drawer etc*); **be ~med** (*roads:*) essere congestio-

nato ● *vi* ⟨*mechanism:*⟩ incepparsi; ⟨*window, drawer:*⟩ incastrarsi
Jamaica /dʒə'meɪkə/ *n* Giamaica *f*. **~n** *a* & *n* giamaicano, -a *mf*
jam-'packed *a fam* pieno zeppo
jangle /'dʒæŋgl/ *vt* far squillare ● *vi* squillare
janitor /'dʒænɪtə(r)/ *n* ⟨*caretaker*⟩ custode *m*; ⟨*in school*⟩ bidello, -a *mf*
January /'dʒænjʊərɪ/ *n* gennaio *m*
Japan /dʒə'pæn/ *n* Giappone *m*. **~ese** /dʒæpə'niːz/ *a* & *n* giapponese *mf*; ⟨*language*⟩ giapponese *m*
jar¹ /dʒɑː(r)/ *n* ⟨*glass*⟩ barattolo *m*
jar² *vi* ⟨*pt/pp* **jarred**⟩ ⟨*sound:*⟩ stridere
jargon /'dʒɑːgən/ *n* gergo *m*
jaundice /'dʒɔːndɪs/ *n* itterizia *f*. **~d** *a fig* inacidito
jaunt /dʒɔːnt/ *n* gita *f*
jaunty /'dʒɔːntɪ/ *a* (**-ier**, **-iest**) sbarazzino
javelin /'dʒævlɪn/ *n* giavellotto *m*
jaw /dʒɔː/ *n* mascella *f*; ⟨*bone*⟩ mandibola *f*
jay-walker /'dʒeɪwɔːkə(r)/ *n* pedone *m* distratto
jazz /dʒæz/ *n* jazz *m* ● **jazz up** *vt* ravvivare. **~y** *a* vistoso
jealous /'dʒeləs/ *a* geloso. **~y** *n* gelosia *f*
jeans /dʒiːnz/ *npl* ⟨*blue*⟩ jeans *mpl*
jeep /dʒiːp/ *n* jeep *f inv*
jeer /dʒɪə(r)/ *n* scherno *m* ● *vi* schernire; **~ at** prendersi gioco di ● *vt* ⟨*boo*⟩ fischiare
jell /dʒel/ *vi* concretarsi
jelly /'dʒelɪ/ *n* gelatina *f*. **~fish** *n* medusa *f*
jeopar|dize /'dʒepədaɪz/ *vt* mettere in pericolo. **~dy** /-dɪ/ *n* **in ~dy** in pericolo
jerk /dʒɜːk/ *n* scatto *m*, scossa *f* ● *vt* scattare ● *vi* sobbalzare; ⟨*limb, muscle:*⟩ muoversi a scatti. **~ily** *adv* a scatti. **~y** *a* traballante
jersey /'dʒɜːzɪ/ *n* maglia *f*; *Sport* maglietta *f*; ⟨*fabric*⟩ jersey *m*
jest /dʒest/ *n* scherzo *m*; **in ~** per scherzo ● *vi* scherzare

Jesus /'dʒiːzəs/ *n* Gesù *m*
jet¹ /dʒet/ *n* ⟨*stone*⟩ giaietto *m*
jet² *n* ⟨*of water*⟩ getto *m*; ⟨*nozzle*⟩ becco *m*; ⟨*plane*⟩ aviogetto *m*, jet *m inv*
jet: **~-'black** *a* nero ebano. **~lag** *n* scombussolamento *m* da fuso orario. **~-pro'pelled** *a* a reazione
jettison /'dʒetɪsn/ *vt* gettare a mare; *fig* abbandonare
jetty /'dʒetɪ/ *n* molo *m*
Jew /dʒuː/ *n* ebreo *m*
jewel /'dʒuːəl/ *n* gioiello *m*. **~ler** *n* gioielliere *m*; **~ler's** ⟨*shop*⟩ gioielleria *f*. **~lery** *n* gioielli *mpl*
Jew|ess /'dʒuːɪs/ *n* ebrea *f*. **~ish** *a* ebreo
jiffy /'dʒɪfɪ/ *n fam* **in a ~** in un batter d'occhio
jigsaw /'dʒɪgsɔː/ *n* ~ [**puzzle**] puzzle *m inv*
jilt /dʒɪlt/ *vt* piantare
jingle /'dʒɪŋgl/ *n* ⟨*rhyme*⟩ canzoncina *f* pubblicitaria ● *vi* tintinnare
jinx /dʒɪŋks/ *n* ⟨*person*⟩ iettatore, -trice *mf*; **it's got a ~ on it** è iellato
jitter|s /'dʒɪtəz/ *npl fam* **have the ~s** aver una gran fifa. **~y** *a fam* **in** preda alla fifa
job /dʒɒb/ *n* lavoro *m*; **this is going to be quite a ~** *fam* ⟨*questa*⟩ non sarà un'impresa facile; **it's a good ~ that...** meno male che.... **~ centre** *n* ufficio *m* statale di collocamento. **~less** *a* senza lavoro
jockey /'dʒɒkɪ/ *n* fantino *m*
jocular /'dʒɒkjʊlə(r)/ *a* scherzoso
jog /dʒɒg/ *n* colpetto *m*; **at a ~** in un balzo; *Sport* **go for a ~** andare a fare jogging ● *v* ⟨*pt/pp* **jogged**⟩ ● *vt* ⟨*hit*⟩ urtare; **~ sb's memory** farlo ritornare in mente a qcno ● *vi* *Sport* fare jogging. **~ging** *n* jogging *m*
john /dʒɒn/ *n* ⟨*Am fam: toilet*⟩ gabinetto *m*
join /dʒɔɪn/ *n* giuntura *f* ● *vt* raggiungere, unire; raggiungere ⟨*person*⟩; ⟨*become member of*⟩

iscriversi a; entrare in ⟨firm⟩ ● vi ⟨roads:⟩ congiungersi. **join in** vi partecipare. **join up** vi Mil arruolarsi ● vt unire

joiner /'dʒɔɪnə(r)/ n falegname m

joint /dʒɔɪnt/ a comune ● n articolazione f; (in wood, brickwork) giuntura f; Culin arrosto m; ⟨fam: bar⟩ bettola f; ⟨sl:drug⟩ spinello m. **~ly** adv unitamente

joist /dʒɔɪst/ n travetto m

jok|e /dʒəʊk/ n (trick) scherzo m; (funny story) barzelletta f ● vi scherzare. **~er** n burlone, -a mf; (in cards) jolly m inv. **~ing** n **~ing apart** scherzi a parte. **~ingly** adv per scherzo

jolly /'dʒɒlɪ/ a (-ier, -iest) allegro ● adv fam molto

jolt /dʒəʊlt/ n scossa f, sobbalzo m ● vt far sobbalzare ● vi sobbalzare

Jordan /'dʒɔ:dn/ n Giordania f; (river) Giordano f. **~ian** /-'deɪnɪən/ a & n giordano, -a m

jostle /'dʒɒsl/ vt spingere

jot /dʒɒt/ n nulla f ● **jot down** vt (pt/pp jotted) annotare. **~ter** n taccuino m

journal /'dʒɜ:nl/ n giornale m; (diary) diario m. **~ese** /-ə'li:z/ n gergo m giornalistico. **~ism** n giornalismo m. **~ist** n giornalista mf

journey /'dʒɜ:nɪ/ n viaggio m

jovial /'dʒəʊvɪəl/ a gioviale

joy /dʒɔɪ/ n gioia f. **~ful** a gioioso. **~ride** n fam giro m con una macchina rubata. **~stick** n Comput joystick m inv

jubil|ant /'dʒu:bɪlənt/ a giubilante. **~ation** /-'leɪʃn/ n giubilo m

jubilee /'dʒu:bɪli:/ n giubileo m

judder /'dʒʌdə(r)/ vi vibrare violentemente

judge /dʒʌdʒ/ n giudice m ● vt giudicare; (estimate) valutare; (consider) ritenere ● vi giudicare (by da). **~ment** n giudizio m; Jur sentenza f

judic|ial /dʒu:'dɪʃl/ a giudiziario. **~iary** /-ʃərɪ/ n magistratura f. **~ious** /-ʃəs/ a giudizioso

judo /'dʒu:dəʊ/ n judo m

jug /dʒʌg/ n brocca f; (small) bricco m

juggernaut /'dʒʌgənɔ:t/ n fam grosso autotreno m

juggle /'dʒʌgl/ vi fare giochi di destrezza. **~r** n giocoliere, -a mf

juice /dʒu:s/ n succo m

juicy /'dʒu:sɪ/ a (-ier, -iest) succoso; ⟨fam: story⟩ piccante

juke-box /'dʒu:k-/ n juke-box m inv

July /dʒʊ'laɪ/ n luglio m

jumble /'dʒʌmbl/ n accozzaglia f ● vt ~ [up] mischiare. **~ sale** n vendita f di beneficenza

jumbo /'dʒʌmbəʊ/ n **~ [jet]** jumbo jet m inv

jump /dʒʌmp/ n salto m; (in prices) balzo m; (in horse racing) ostacolo m ● vi saltare; (with fright) sussultare; ⟨prices:⟩ salire rapidamente; **~ to conclusions** saltare alle conclusioni ● vt saltare; **~ the gun** fig precipitarsi; **~ the queue** non rispettare la fila. **jump at** vt fig accettare con entusiasmo ⟨offer⟩. **jump up** vi rizzarsi in piedi

jumper /'dʒʌmpə(r)/ n (sweater) golf m inv

jumpy /'dʒʌmpɪ/ a nervoso

junction /'dʒʌŋkʃn/ n (of roads) incrocio m; (of motorway) uscita f; Rail nodo m ferroviario

juncture /'dʒʌŋktʃə(r)/ n **at this ~** a questo punto

June /dʒu:n/ n giugno m

jungle /'dʒʌŋgl/ n giungla f

junior /'dʒu:nɪə(r)/ a giovane; (in rank) subalterno; Sport junior inv ● n the **~s** Sch i più giovani. **~ school** n scuola f elementare

junk /dʒʌŋk/ n cianfrusaglie fpl. **~ food** n fam cibo m poco sano, porcherie fpl. **~ mail** posta f spazzatura

junkie /'dʒʌŋkɪ/ n sl tossico, -a mf

junk-shop n negozio m di rigattiere

jurisdiction /dʒʊərɪs'dɪkʃn/ n giurisdizione f

juror /'dʒʊərə(r)/ n giurato, -a mf

jury /'dʒʊərɪ/ n giuria f

just /dʒʌst/ a giusto ● adv (barely) appena; (simply) solo; (exactly) esattamente; **~ as tall** altrettanto alto; **~ as I was leaving** proprio quando stavo andando via; **I've ~ seen her** l'ho appena vista; **it's ~ as well** meno male; **~ at that moment** proprio in quel momento; **~ listen!** ascolta!; **I'm ~ going** sto andando proprio ora

justice /'dʒʌstɪs/ n giustizia f; **do ~ to** rendere giustizia a; **J~ of the Peace** giudice m conciliatore

justifiable /'dʒʌstɪfaɪəbl/ a giustificabile

justification /dʒʌstɪfɪ'keɪʃn/ n giustificazione f. **~fy** /'dʒʌstɪfaɪ/ vt (pt/pp **-ied**) giustificare

justly /'dʒʌstlɪ/ adv giustamente

jut /dʒʌt/ vi (pt/pp jutted) **~ out** sporgere

juvenile /'dʒuːvənaɪl/ a giovanile; (childish) infantile; (for the young) per i giovani ● n giovane mf. **~ delinquency** n delinquenza f giovanile

juxtapose /dʒʌkstə'pəʊz/ vt giustapporre

Kk

kangaroo /kæŋgə'ruː/ n canguro m

karate /kə'rɑːtɪ/ n karate m

kebab /kɪ'bæb/ n Culin spiedino m di carne

keel /kiːl/ n chiglia f ● **keel over** vi capovolgersi

keen /kiːn/ a (intense) acuto; (interest) vivo; (eager) entusiastico; (competition) feroce; (wind, knife) tagliente; **~ on** entusiasta di; **she's ~ on him** le piace molto; **be ~ to do sth** avere voglia di fare qcsa. **~ness** n entusiasmo m

keep /kiːp/ n (maintenance) mantenimento m; (of castle) maschio m; **for ~s** per sempre ● vt (pt/pp **kept**) ● vt tenere; (not throw away) conservare; (detain) trattenere; mantenere (family, promise); avere (shop); allevare (animals); rispettare (law, rules); **~ sth hot** tenere qcsa in caldo; **~ sb from doing sth** impedire a qcno di fare qcsa; **~ sb waiting** far aspettare qcno; **~ sth to oneself** tenere qcsa per sè; **~ sth from sb** tenere nascosto qcsa a qcno ● vi (remain) rimanere; (food:) conservarsi; **~ calm** rimanere calmo; **~ left/right** tenere la destra/la sinistra; **~ [on] doing sth** continuare a fare qcsa. **keep back** vt trattenere (person); **~ sth back from sb** tenere nascosto qcsa a qcno ● vi tenersi indietro. **keep in with** vt mantenersi in buoni rapporti con. **keep on** vi fam assillare (at sb qcno). **keep up** vi stare al passo ● vt (continue) continuare

keeper /'kiːpə(r)/ n custode mf. **~-fit** n ginnastica f. **~ing** n custodia f; **be in ~ing with** essere in armonia con. **~sake** n ricordo m

keg /keg/ n barilotto m

kennel /'kenl/ n canile m; **~s** pl (boarding) canile m; (breeding) allevamento m di cani

Kenya /'kenjə/ n Kenia m. **~n** a & n keniota mf

kept /kept/ see **keep**

kerb /kɜːb/ n bordo m del marciapiede

kernel /'kɜːnl/ n nocciolo m

kerosene /'kerəsiːn/ n Am cherosene m

ketchup /'ketʃʌp/ n ketchup m

kettle /'ketl/ n bollitore m; **put the ~ on** mettere l'acqua a bollire

key /kiː/ n also Mus chiave f; (of piano, typewriter) tasto m ● vt **~ [in]** digitare (character); **could you ~ this?** puoi battere questo? **key-** **~board** n Comput, Mus tastiera f. **~boarder** n tastierista mf.

~ed-up a (anxious) estremamente agitato; (ready to act) psicologicamente preparato. **~hole** n buco m della serratura. **~ring** n portachiavi m inv

khaki /'kɑːkɪ/ a cachi inv ● n cachi m

kick /kɪk/ n calcio m; (fam: thrill) piacere m; **for ~s** fam per spasso ● vt dar calci a; **~ the bucket** fam crepare ● vi (animal:) scalciare; (person:) dare calci. **kick off** vi Sport dare il calcio d'inizio; fam iniziare. **kick up** vt **~ up a row** fare una scenata

'kickback n (fam: percentage) tangente f

'kick-off n Sport calcio m d'inizio

kid /kɪd/ n capretto m; (fam: child) ragazzino, -a mf ● v (pt/pp **kidded**) ● vt prendere in giro ● vi fam scherzare

kidnap /'kɪdnæp/ vt (pt/pp **-napped**) rapire, sequestrare. **~per** n sequestratore, -trice mf, rapitore, -trice mf. **~ping** n rapimento m, sequestro m [di persona]

kidney /'kɪdnɪ/ n rene m; Culin rognone m. **~ machine** n rene m artificiale

kill /kɪl/ vt uccidere; fig metter fine a; ammazzare (time). **~er** n assassino, -a mf. **~ing** n uccisione f; (murder) omicidio m; **make a ~ing** fig fare un colpo grosso

'killjoy n guastafeste mf inv

kiln /kɪln/ n fornace f

kilo /'kiːləʊ/ n chilo m

kilo /'kɪləʊ/: **~byte** n kilobyte m inv. **~gram** n chilogrammo m. **~metre** /kɪ'lɒmɪtə(r)/ n chilometro m. **~watt** n chilowatt m inv

kilt /kɪlt/ n kilt m inv (gonnellino degli scozzesi)

kin /kɪn/ n congiunti mpl; **next of ~** parente m stretto; parenti mpl stretti

kind¹ /kaɪnd/ n genere m, specie f; (brand, type) tipo m; **~ of** fam alquanto; **two of a ~** due della stessa specie

kind² a gentile, buono; **~ to animals** amante degli animali; **~ regards** cordiali saluti

kindergarten /'kɪndəgɑːtn/ n asilo m infantile

kindle /'kɪndl/ vt accendere

kind|ly /'kaɪndlɪ/ a (-ier, -iest) benevolo ● adv gentilmente; (if you please) per favore. **~ness** n gentilezza f

kindred /'kɪndrɪd/ a **she's a ~ spirit** è la mia/sua/tua anima gemella

kinetic /kɪ'netɪk/ a cinetico

king /kɪŋ/ n re m inv. **~dom** n regno m

king: **~fisher** n martin m inv pescatore. **~-sized** a (cigarette) king-size inv, lungo; (bed) matrimoniale grande

kink /kɪŋk/ n nodo m. **~y** a fam bizzarro

kiosk /'kiːɒsk/ n chiosco m; Teleph cabina f telefonica

kip /kɪp/ n pisolino m; **have a ~** schiacciare un pisolino ● vi (pt/pp **kipped**) fam dormire

kipper /'kɪpə(r)/ n aringa f affumicata

kiss /kɪs/ n bacio m; **~ of life** respirazione f bocca a bocca ● vt baciare ● vi baciarsi

kit /kɪt/ n equipaggiamento m, kit m inv; (tools) attrezzi mpl; (construction ~) pezzi mpl da montare, kit m inv ● **kit out** vt (pt/pp **kitted**) equipaggiare. **~bag** n sacco m a spalla

kitchen /'kɪtʃɪn/ n cucina f ● attrib di cucina. **~ette** /kɪtʃɪ'net/ n cucinino m

kitchen: **~ garden** n orto m. **~ roll** or **towel** Scottex® m inv. **~'sink** n lavello m

kite /kaɪt/ n aquilone m

kitten /'kɪtn/ n gattino m

kitty /'kɪtɪ/ n (money) cassa f comune

kleptomaniac /kleptə'memiæk/ n cleptomane mf

knack /næk/ n tecnica f; **have the ~ for doing sth** avere la capacità di fare qcsa

knead /niːd/ vt impastare

knee /niː/ n ginocchio m. **~cap** n rotula f

kneel /niːl/ vi (pt/pp knelt) **~ [down]** inginocchiarsi; **be ~ing** essere inginocchiato

knelt /nelt/ see **kneel**

knew /njuː/ see **know**

knickers /'nɪkəz/ npl mutandine fpl

knick-knacks /'nɪknæks/ npl ninnoli mpl

knife /naɪf/ n (pl knives) coltello m ● vt fam accoltellare

knight /naɪt/ n cavaliere m; (in chess) cavallo m ● vt nominare cavaliere

knit /nɪt/ vt/i (pt/pp knitted) lavorare a maglia; **~ one, purl one** un diritto, un rovescio. **~ting** n lavorare m a maglia; (work) lavoro m a maglia. **~ting-needle** n ferro m da calza. **~wear** n maglieria f

knives /naɪvz/ see **knife**

knob /nɒb/ n pomello m; (of stick) pomo m; (of butter) noce f. **~bly** a nodoso; (bony) spigoloso

knock /nɒk/ n colpo m; **there was a ~ at the door** hanno bussato alla porta ● vt bussare a ⟨door⟩; (fam: criticize) denigrare; **~ a hole in sth** fare un buco in qcsa; **~ one's head** battere la testa (on contro) ● vi (at door) bussare. **knock about** vt malmenare ● vi fam girovagare. **knock down** vt far cadere; (with fist) stendere con un pugno; (in car) investire; (demolish) abbattere; (fam: reduce) ribassare ⟨price⟩. **knock off** vt (fam: steal) fregare; (fam: complete quickly) fare alla bell'e meglio ● vi (fam: cease work) staccare. **knock out** vt eliminare; (make unconscious) mettere K.O.; (fam: anaesthetize) addormenta-

re. **knock over** vt rovesciare; (in car) investire

knock: **~-down** a **~-down price** prezzo m stracciato. **~er** n battente m. **~-kneed** /-'niːd/ a con gambe storte. **~-out** n (in boxing) knock-out m inv

knot /nɒt/ n nodo m ● vt (pt/pp knotted) annodare

knotty /'nɒti/ a (-ier, -iest) fam spinoso

know /nəʊ/ v (pt knew, pp known) ● vt sapere; conoscere ⟨person, place⟩; (recognize) riconoscere; **get to ~ sb** conoscere qcno; **~ how to swim** sapere nuotare ● vi sapere; **did you ~ about this?** lo sapevi? ● n **in the ~** fam al corrente

know: **~-all** n fam sapientone, -a mf. **~-how** n abilità f. **~ing** a d'intesa. **~ingly** adv (intentionally) consapevolmente; ⟨smile etc⟩ con un'aria d'intesa

knowledge /'nɒlɪdʒ/ n conoscenza f. **~able** /-əbl/ a ben informato

known /nəʊn/ see **know** ● a noto

knuckle /'nʌkl/ n nocca f ● vt **knuckle down** vi darci sotto (to con). **knuckle under** vi sottomettersi

Koran /kə'rɑːn/ n Corano m

Korea /kə'riə/ n Corea f. **~n** a & n coreano, -a mf

kosher /'kəʊʃə(r)/ a kasher inv

kowtow /kaʊ'taʊ/ vi piegarsi

kudos /'kjuːdɒs/ n fam gloria f

lab /læb/ n fam laboratorio m

label /'leɪbl/ n etichetta f ● vt (pt/pp labelled) mettere un'etichetta a; fig etichettare ⟨person⟩

laboratory /lə'bɒrətrɪ/ n laboratorio m

laborious /lə'bɔːrɪəs/ a laborioso

labour /'leɪbə(r)/ n lavoro m; (workers) manodopera f; Med doglie fpl; **be in ~** avere le doglie; **L~** Pol partito m laburista ● attrib Pol laburista ● vi lavorare ● vt ~ **the point** fig ribadire il concetto. **~er** n manovale m

'labour-saving a che fa risparmiare lavoro e fatica

labyrinth /'læbərɪnθ/ n labirinto m

lace /leɪs/ n pizzo m; (of shoe) laccio m ● attrib di pizzo ● vt allacciare (shoes); correggere (drink)

lacerate /'læsəreɪt/ vt lacerare

lack /læk/ n mancanza f ● vt mancare di; **I ~ the time** mi manca il tempo ● vi **be ~ing** mancare; **be ~ing in sth** mancare di qcsa

lackadaisical /lækə'deɪzɪkl/ a senza entusiasmo

laconic /lə'kɒnɪk/ a laconico

lacquer /'lækə(r)/ n lacca f

lad /læd/ n ragazzo m

ladder /'lædə(r)/ n scala f; (in tights) sfilatura f

laden /'leɪdn/ a carico (with di)

ladle /'leɪdl/ n mestolo m ● vt ~ **[out]** versare (col mestolo)

lady /'leɪdɪ/ n signora f; (title) Lady; **ladies [room]** bagno m per donne

lady: **~bird** n, Am **~bug** n coccinella f. **~like** a signorile

lag[1] /læg/ vi (pt/pp lagged) ~ **behind** restare indietro

lag[2] vt (pt/pp lagged) isolare (pipes)

lager /'lɑːgə(r)/ n birra f chiara

lagoon /lə'guːn/ n laguna f

laid /leɪd/ see lay[3]

lain /leɪn/ see lie[2]

lair /leə(r)/ n tana f

lake /leɪk/ n lago m

lamb /læm/ n agnello m

lame /leɪm/ a zoppo; fig (argument) zoppicante; (excuse) traballante

lament /lə'ment/ n lamento m ● vt lamentare ● vi lamentarsi

lamentable /'læməntəbl/ a deplorevole

laminated /'læmɪneɪtɪd/ a laminato

lamp /læmp/ n lampada f; (in street) lampione m. **~post** n lampione m. **~shade** n paralume m

lance /lɑːns/ n fiocina f ● vt Med incidere. **~-'corporal** n appuntato m

land /lænd/ n terreno m; (country) paese m; (as opposed to sea) terra f; **plot of ~** pezzo m di terreno ● vt Naut sbarcare; (fam: obtain) assicurarsi; **be ~ed with sth** fam ritrovarsi fra capo e collo qcsa ● vi Aeron atterrare; (fall) cadere. **land up** vi fam finire

landing /'lændɪŋ/ n Naut sbarco m; Aeron atterraggio m; (top of stairs) pianerottolo m. **~-stage** n pontile m da sbarco. **~ strip** n pista f d'atterraggio di fortuna

land: **~lady** n proprietaria f; (of flat) padrona f di casa. **~-locked** a privo di sbocco sul mare. **~lord** n proprietario m; (of flat) padrone m di casa. **~mark** n punto m di riferimento; fig pietra f miliare. **~owner** n proprietario, -a mf terriero. **~scape** /-skeɪp/ n paesaggio m. **~slide** n frana f; Pol valanga f di voti

lane /leɪn/ n sentiero m; Auto, Sport corsia f

language /'læŋgwɪdʒ/ n lingua f; (speech, style) linguaggio m. **~ laboratory** n laboratorio m linguistico

languid /'læŋgwɪd/ a languido

languish /'læŋgwɪʃ/ vi languire

lank /læŋk/ a (hair) diritto

lanky /'læŋkɪ/ a (-ier, -iest) allampanato

lantern /'læntən/ n lanterna f

lap[1] /læp/ n grembo m

lap[2] n (of journey) tappa f; Sport giro m ● v (pt/pp lapped) ● vi (water:) ~ **against** lambire ● vt Sport doppiare

lap[3] vt (pt/pp lapped) ~ **up** bere avidamente; bersi completamente

⟨lies⟩; credere ciecamente a ⟨praise⟩

lapel /ləˈpel/ n bavero m

lapse /læps/ n sbaglio m; ⟨moral⟩ sbandamento m [morale]; ⟨of time⟩ intervallo m ● vi ⟨expire⟩ scadere; ⟨morally⟩ scivolare; ~ **into** cadere in

laptop /ˈlæptɒp/ n ~ [**computer**] computer m inv portabile, laptop m inv

larceny /ˈlɑːsənɪ/ n furto m

lard /lɑːd/ n strutto m

larder /ˈlɑːdə(r)/ n dispensa f

large /lɑːdʒ/ a grande; ⟨number, amount⟩ grande, grosso; **by and** ~ in complesso; **at** ~ in libertà; ⟨in general⟩ ampiamente. ~**ly** adv ampiamente; ~**ly because of** in gran parte a causa di

lark[1] /lɑːk/ n ⟨bird⟩ allodola f

lark[2] n ⟨joke⟩ burla f ● **lark about** vi giocherellare

larva /ˈlɑːvə/ n (pl **-vae** /-viː/) larva f

laryngitis /lærɪnˈdʒaɪtɪs/ n laringite f

larynx /ˈlærɪŋks/ n laringe f

lascivious /ləˈsɪvɪəs/ a lascivo

laser /ˈleɪzə(r)/ n laser m inv. ~ [**printer**] n stampante f laser

lash /læʃ/ n frustata f; ⟨eyelash⟩ ciglio m ● vt ⟨whip⟩ frustare; ⟨tie⟩ legare fermamente. **lash out** vi attaccare; ⟨spend⟩ sperperare (**on** in)

lashings /ˈlæʃɪŋz/ npl ~ **of** fam una marea di

lass /læs/ n ragazzina f

lasso /ləˈsuː/ n lazo m

last /lɑːst/ a ⟨final⟩ ultimo; ⟨recent⟩ scorso; ~ **year** l'anno scorso; ~ **night** ieri sera; **at** ~ alla fine; **at** ~**!** finalmente!; **that's the** ~ **straw** fam questa è l'ultima goccia ● n ultimo, -a mf; **the** ~ **but one** il penultimo ● adv per ultimo; ⟨last time⟩ l'ultima volta ● vi durare. ~**ing** a durevole. ~**ly** adv infine

late /leɪt/ a ⟨delayed⟩ in ritardo; ⟨at a late hour⟩ tardo; ⟨deceased⟩ de-

funto; **it's** ~ ⟨at night⟩ è tardi; **in** ~ **November** alla fine di Novembre ● adv tardi; **stay up** ~ stare alzati fino a tardi. ~**comer** n ritardatario, -a mf; ⟨to political party etc⟩ nuovo, -a arrivato, -a mf. ~**ly** adv recentemente. ~**ness** n ora f tarda; ⟨delay⟩ ritardo m

latent /ˈleɪtnt/ a latente

later /ˈleɪtə(r)/ a ⟨train⟩ che parte più tardi; ⟨edition⟩ più recente ● adv più tardi; ~ **on** più tardi, dopo

lateral /ˈlætərəl/ a laterale

latest /ˈleɪtɪst/ a ultimo, (most recent) più recente; **the** ~ [**news**] le ultime notizie ● n **six o'clock at the** ~ alle sei al più tardi

lathe /leɪð/ n tornio m

lather /ˈlɑːðə(r)/ n schiuma f ● vt insaponare ● vi far schiuma

Latin /ˈlætɪn/ a latino ● n latino m. ~ **America** America f Latina. ~ **American** a & n latino-americano, -a mf

latitude /ˈlætɪtjuːd/ n Geog latitudine f; fig libertà f d'azione

latter /ˈlætə(r)/ a ultimo; **the** ~ quest'ultimo. ~**ly** adv ultimamente

lattice /ˈlætɪs/ n traliccio m

Latvia /ˈlætvɪə/ n Lettonia f. ~**n** a & n lettone mf

laudable /ˈlɔːdəbl/ a lodevole

laugh /lɑːf/ n risata f ● vi ridere ⟨at/about di⟩; ~ **at sb** ⟨mock⟩ prendere in giro qcno. ~**able** /-əbl/ a ridicolo. ~**ing-stock** n zimbello m

laughter /ˈlɑːftə(r)/ n risata f

launch[1] /lɔːntʃ/ n ⟨boat⟩ varo m

launch[2] n lancio m; ⟨of ship⟩ varo m ● vt lanciare ⟨rocket, product⟩; varare ⟨ship⟩; sferrare ⟨attack⟩

launder /ˈlɔːndə(r)/ vt lavare e stirare; ~ **money** fig riciclare denaro sporco. ~**ette** /-ˈdret/ n lavanderia f automatica

laundry /ˈlɔːndrɪ/ n lavanderia f; ⟨clothes⟩ bucato m

laurel /'lɒrəl/ n lauro m; fig **rest on one's ~s** dormire sugli allori

lava /'lɑːvə/ n lava f

lavatory /'lævətrɪ/ n gabinetto m

lavender /'lævəndə(r)/ n lavanda f

lavish /'lævɪʃ/ a copioso; (wasteful) prodigo; **on a ~ scale** su vasta scala ● vt **~ sth on sb** ricoprire qcno di qcsa. **~ly** adv copiosamente

law /lɔː/ n legge f; **study ~** studiare giurisprudenza, studiare legge; **~ and order** ordine m pubblico

law: **~-abiding** a che rispetta la legge. **~court** n tribunale m. **~ful** a legittimo m. **~less** a senza legge. **~ school** n facoltà f di giurisprudenza

lawn /lɔːn/ n prato m [all'inglese]. **~-mower** n tosaerbe m inv

'law suit n causa f

lawyer /'lɔːjə(r)/ n avvocato m

lax /læks/ a negligente; (morals etc) lassista

laxative /'læksətɪv/ n lassativo m

laxity /'læksətɪ/ n lassismo m

lay[1] /leɪ/ a laico; fig profano

lay[2] see **lie**[2]

lay[3] vt (pt/pp **laid**) porre, mettere; apparecchiare (table) ● vi (hen:) fare le uova. **lay down** vt posare; stabilire (rules, conditions). **lay off** vt licenziare (workers) ● vi (fam: stop) **~ off!** smettila! **lay out** vt (display, set forth) esporre; (plan) pianificare (garden); (spend) sborsare; Typ impaginare

lay: **~about** n fannullone, -a mf. **~-by** n corsia f di sosta

layer /'leɪə(r)/ n strato m

lay: **~man** n profano m. **~out** n disposizione f, Typ impaginazione f, layout m inv

laze /leɪz/ vi **~ [about]** oziare

laziness /'leɪzɪnɪs/ n pigrizia f

lazy /'leɪzɪ/ a (-ier, -iest) pigro. **~-bones** n poltrone, -a mf

lb abbr (pound) libbra

lead[1] /led/ n piombo m; (of pencil) mina f

lead[2] /liːd/ n guida f; (leash)

giunzaglio m; (flex) filo m; (clue) indizio m; Theat parte f principale; (distance ahead) distanza f (over su); **in the ~** in testa ● v (pt/pp **led**) ● vt condurre; dirigere (expedition, party etc); (induce) indurre; **~ the way** mettersi in testa ● vi (be in front) condurre; (in race, competition) essere in testa; (at cards) giocare (per primo). **lead away** vt portar via. **lead to** vt portare a. **lead up to** vt preludere; **what's this ~ing up to?** dove porta questo?

leaded /'ledɪd/ a con piombo

leader /'liːdə(r)/ n capo m; (of orchestra) primo violino m; (in newspaper) articolo m di fondo. **~ship** n direzione f, leadership f inv; **show ~ship** mostrare capacità di comando

lead-free a senza piombo

leading /'liːdɪŋ/ a principale; **~ lady/man** attrice f/attore m principale; **~ question** domanda f tendenziosa

leaf /liːf/ n (pl **leaves**) foglia f; (of table) asse f ● **leaf through** vt sfogliare. **~let** n dépliant m inv; (advertising) dépliant m inv pubblicitario; (political) manifestino m

league /liːg/ n lega f; Sport campionato m; **be in ~ with** essere in combutta con

leak /liːk/ n (hole) fessura f; Naut falla f; (of gas & fig) fuga f ● vi colare; (ship:) fare acqua; (liquid, gas:) fuoriuscire ● vt **~ sth to sb** fig far trapelare qcsa a qcno. **~y** a che perde; Naut che fa acqua

lean[1] /liːn/ a magro

lean[2] v (pt/pp **leaned** or **leant** /lent/) ● vt appoggiare (against on contro/su) ● vi appoggiarsi (against/on contro/su); (not be straight) pendere; **be ~ing against** essere appoggiato contro; **~ on sb** (depend on) appoggiarsi a qcno; (fam: exert pressure on) stare alle calcagne di qcno. **lean**

back *vi* sporgersi indietro. **lean forward** *vi* piegarsi in avanti. **lean out** *vi* sporgersi. **lean over** *vi* piegarsi

leaning /'li:nɪŋ/ *a* pendente; **the L~** Tower of Pisa la torre pendente ● *n* tendenza *f*

leap /li:p/ *n* salto *m* ● *vi* (*pt/pp* **leapt** /lept/ *or* **leaped**) saltare; **he leapt at it** *fam* l'ha preso al volo. **~-frog** *n* cavallina *f*. **~ year** *n* anno *m* bisestile

learn /lɜ:n/ *v* (*pt/pp* **learnt** *or* **learned**) ● *vt* imparare; **~ to swim** imparare a nuotare; **I have ~ed that...** (*heard*) sono venuto a sapere che... ● *vi* imparare

learn|ed /'lɜ:nɪd/ *a* colto. **~er** *n* also *Auto* principiante *mf*. **~ing** *n* cultura *f*

lease /li:s/ *n* contratto *m* d'affitto; (*rental*) affitto *m* ● *vt* affittare

leash /li:ʃ/ *n* guinzaglio *m*

least /li:st/ *a* più piccolo; (*amount*) minore; **you've got ~ luggage** hai meno bagagli di tutti ● *n* the ~ il meno; **at ~** almeno; **not in the ~** niente affatto ● *adv* meno; **the ~ expensive wine** il vino meno caro

leather /'leðə(r)/ *n* pelle *f*; (*of soles*) cuoio ● *attrib* di pelle/cuoio. **~y** *a* (*meat, skin*) duro

leave /li:v/ *n* (*holiday*) congedo *m*; *Mil* licenza *f*; **on ~** in congedo/licenza ● *v* (*pt/pp* **left**) ● *vt* lasciare; uscire da (*house, office*); (*forget*) dimenticare; **there is nothing left** non è rimasto niente ● *vi* andare via; (*train, bus:*) partire. **leave behind** *vt* lasciare; (*forget*) dimenticare. **leave out** *vt* omettere; (*not put away*) lasciare fuori

leaves /li:vz/ *see* **leaf**

Leban|on /'lebənən/ *n* Libano *m*. **~ese** /-'ni:z/ *a* & *n* libanese *mf*

lectern /'lektз:n/ *n* leggio *m*

lecture /'lektʃə(r)/ *n* conferenza *f*; *Univ* lezione *f*; (*reproof*) ramanzi-

na *f* ● *vi* fare una conferenza (**on** su); *Univ* insegnare (**on sth** qcsa) ● *vt* ~ **sb** rimproverare qcno. **~r** *n* conferenziere, -a *mf*; *Univ* docente *mf* universitario, -a

led /led/ *see* **lead²**

ledge /ledʒ/ *n* cornice *f*; (*of window*) davanzale *m*

ledger /'ledʒə(r)/ *n* libro *m* mastro

leech /li:tʃ/ *n* sanguisuga *f*

leek /li:k/ *n* porro *m*

leer /lɪə(r)/ *n* sguardo *m* libidinoso ● *vi* ~ **[at]** guardare in modo libidinoso

leeway /'li:weɪ/ *n fig* libertà *f* di azione

left¹ /left/ *see* **leave**

left² /left/ *a* sinistro ● *adv* a sinistra ● *n* also *Pol* sinistra *f*; **on the ~** a sinistra;

left: **~-'handed** *a* mancino. **~-'luggage [office]** *n* deposito *m* bagagli. **~overs** *npl* rimasugli *mpl*. **~-'wing** *a Pol* di sinistra

leg /leg/ *n* gamba *f*; (*of animal*) zampa *f*; (*of journey*) tappa *f*; *Culin* (*of chicken*) coscia *f*; (*of lamb*) cosciotto *m*

legacy /'legəsɪ/ *n* lascito *m*

legal /'li:gl/ *a* legale; **take ~ action** intentare un'azione legale. **~ly** *adv* legalmente

legality /lɪ'gælətɪ/ *n* legalità *f*

legalize /'li:gəlaɪz/ *vt* legalizzare

legend /'ledʒənd/ *n* leggenda *f*. **~ary** *a* leggendario

legib|le /'ledʒəbl/ *a* leggibile. **~ly** *adv* in modo leggibile

legislat|e /'ledʒɪsleɪt/ *vi* legiferare. **~ion** /-'leɪʃn/ *n* legislazione *f*. **~ive** /'ledʒɪslətɪv/ *a* legislativo. **~ure** /-lertʃə(r)/ *n* legislatura *f*

legitima|te /lɪ'dʒɪtɪmət/ *a* legittimo; (*excuse*) valido

leisure /'leʒə(r)/ *n* tempo *m* libero; **at your ~** con comodo. **~ly** *a* senza fretta

lemon /'lemən/ *n* limone *m*. **~ade** /-'neɪd/ *n* limonata *f*

lend /lend/ *vt* (*pt/pp* **lent**) prestare;

~ **a hand** *fig* dare una mano. **~ing library** *n* biblioteca *f* per il prestito

length /leŋθ/ *n* lunghezza *f*; (*piece*) pezzo *m*; (*of wallpaper*) parte *f*; (*of visit*) durata *f*; **at** ~ a lungo; (*at last*) alla fine

length|en /'leŋθən/ *vt* allungare ●*vi* allungarsi. **~ways** *adv* per lungo

lengthy /'leŋθɪ/ *a* (**-ier, -iest**) lungo

lenien|ce /'liːnɪəns/ *n* indulgenza *f*. **~t** *a* indulgente

lens /lenz/ *n* lente *f*; *Phot* obiettivo *m*; (*of eye*) cristallino *m*

Lent /lent/ *n* Quaresima *f*

lent /lent/ *see* **lend**

lentil /'lentl/ *n Bot* lenticchia *f*

Leo /'liːəʊ/ *n Astr* Leone *m*

leopard /'lepəd/ *n* leopardo *m*

leotard /'liːətɑːd/ *n body m inv*

leprosy /'leprəsɪ/ *n* lebbra *f*

lesbian /'lezbɪən/ *a* lesbico ●*n* lesbica *f*

less /les/ *a* meno di; **~ and ~** sempre meno ●*adv* & *prep* meno ●*n* meno *m*

lessen /'lesn/ *vt/i* diminuire

lesser /'lesə(r)/ *a* minore

lesson /'lesn/ *n* lezione *f*

lest /lest/ *conj liter* per timore che

let /let/ *vt* (*pt/pp* **let**, *pres p* **letting**) lasciare, permettere; (*rent*) affittare; **~ alone** (*not to mention*) per non parlare di; **'to ~'** 'affittasi'; **~ us go** andiamo; **~ sb do sth** lasciare fare qcsa a qcno, permettere a qcno di fare qcsa; **~ me know** fammi sapere; **just ~ him try!** che ci provi solamente!; **~ oneself in for sth** *fam* impelagarsi in qcsa. **let down** *vt* sciogliersi (*hair*); abbassare (*blinds*); (*lengthen*) allungare; (*disappoint*) deludere; **don't ~ me down** conto su di te. **let in** *vt* far entrare. **let off** *vt* far partire; (*not punish*) perdonare; **~ sb off** doing sth abbonare qcsa a qcno. **let out** *vt* far uscire; (*make larger*) allargare; emettere

(*scream, groan*). **let through** *vt* far passare. **let up** *vi fam* diminuire

'let-down *n* delusione *f*

lethal /'liːθl/ *a* letale

letharg|ic /lɪ'θɑːdʒɪk/ *a* apatico. **~y** /'leθədʒɪ/ *n* apatia *f*

letter /'letə(r)/ *n* lettera *f*. **~-box** *n* buca *f* per le lettere. **~-head** *n* carta *f* intestata. **~ing** *n* caratteri *mpl*

lettuce /'letɪs/ *n* lattuga *f*

'let-up *n fam* pausa *f*

leukaemia /luːˈkiːmɪə/ *n* leucemia *f*

level /'levl/ *a* piano; (*in height, competition*) allo stesso livello; (*spoonful*) raso; **draw ~ with sb** affiancare qcno ●*n* livello *m*; **on the ~** *fam* giusto ●*vt* (*pt/pp* **levelled**) livellare; (*aim*) puntare (*at* su)

level: **~ 'crossing** *n* passaggio *m* a livello. **~-headed** *a* posato

lever /'liːvə(r)/ *n* leva *f* ●**lever up** *vt* sollevare (*con una leva*). **~age** /-rɪdʒ/ *n* azione *f* di una leva; *fig* influenza *f*

levy /'levɪ/ *vt* (*pt/pp* **levied**) imporre (*tax*)

lewd /ljuːd/ *a* osceno

liab|ility /laɪə'bɪlətɪ/ *n* responsabilità *f*; (*fam: burden*) peso *m*. **~ies** *pl* debiti *mpl*

liable /'laɪəbl/ *a* responsabile (*for* di); **be ~ to** (*rain, break etc*) rischiare di; (*tend to*) tendere a

liaise /lɪ'eɪz/ *vi fam* essere in contatto

liaison /lɪ'eɪzɒn/ *n* contatti *mpl*; *Mil* collegamento *m*; (*affair*) relazione *f*

liar /'laɪə(r)/ *n* bugiardo, -a *mf*

libel /'laɪbl/ *n* diffamazione *f* ●*vt* (*pt/pp* **libelled**) diffamare. **~lous** *a* diffamatorio

liberal /'lɪb(ə)rəl/ *a* (*tolerant*) di larghe vedute; (*generous*) generoso. **L~** *a Pol* liberale ●*n* liberale *mf*

liberat|e /'lɪbəreɪt/ *vt* liberare. **~ed** *a* (*woman*) emancipata. **~ion** /-'reɪʃn/ *n* liberazione *f*; (*of* *women*) emancipazione f. **~or** n liberatore, -trice mf

liberty /'lɪbətɪ/ n libertà f; **take the ~ of doing sth** prendersi la libertà di fare qcsa; **be at ~ to do sth** essere libero di fare qcsa

Libra /'li:brə/ n Astr Bilancia f

librarian /laɪ'breərɪən/ n bibliotecario, -a mf

library /'laɪbrərɪ/ n biblioteca f

Libya /'lɪbɪə/ n Libia f. **~n** a & n libico, -a mf

lice /laɪs/ see **louse**

licence /'laɪsns/ n licenza f; (for TV) canone m televisivo; (for driving) patente f; (freedom) sregolatezza f. **~-plate** n targa f

license /'laɪsns/ vt autorizzare; **be ~d** (car:) avere il bollo; (restaurant:) essere autorizzato alla vendita di alcolici

licentious /laɪ'senʃəs/ a licenzioso

lick /lɪk/ n leccata f; **a ~ of paint** una passata leggera di pittura ● vt leccare; (fam: defeat) battere; leccarsi (lips)

lid /lɪd/ n coperchio m; (of eye) palpebra f

lie[1] /laɪ/ n bugia f; **tell a ~** mentire ● vi (pt/pp **lied**, pres p **lying**) mentire

lie[2] vi (pt **lay**, pp **lain**, pres p **lying**) (person:) sdraiarsi; (object:) stare; (remain) rimanere. **leave sth lying about** or **around** lasciare qcsa in giro. **lie down** vi sdraiarsi

'lie: ~-down n **have a ~-down** fare un riposino. **~-in** n fam **have a ~-in** restare a letto fino a tardi

lieu /lju:/ n **in ~ of** in luogo di

lieutenant /lef'tenənt/ n tenente m

life /laɪf/ n (pl **lives**) vita f

life: ~belt n salvagente m. **~-boat** n lancia f di salvataggio; (on ship) scialuppa f di salvataggio. **~buoy** n salvagente m. **~-guard** n bagnino m. **~ insurance** n assicurazione f sulla vita. **~-jacket** n giubbotto m di salvataggio. **~less** a inanimato. **~like** a realistico. **~long** a

di tutta la vita. **~-size[d]** a in grandezza naturale. **~time** n vita f; **the chance of a ~time** un'occasione unica

lift /lɪft/ n ascensore m; Auto passaggio m ● vt sollevare; revocare (restrictions); (fam: steal) rubare ● vi (fog:) alzarsi. **lift up** vt sollevare

'lift-off n decollo m (di razzo)

ligament /'lɪgəmənt/ n Anat legamento m

light[1] /laɪt/ a (not dark) luminoso; **~ green** verde chiaro ● n luce f; (lamp) lampada f; **in the ~ of** fig alla luce di; **have you got a ~?** ha da accendere?; **come to ~** essere rivelato ● vt (pt/pp **lit** or **lighted**) accendere; (illuminate) illuminare. **light up** vi (face:) illuminarsi

light[2] a (not heavy) leggero ● adv **travel ~** viaggiare con poco bagaglio

'light-bulb n lampadina f

lighten[1] /'laɪtn/ vt illuminare

lighten[2] vt alleggerire (load)

lighter /'laɪtə(r)/ n accendino m

light: ~-fingered a svelto di mano. **~-headed** a sventato. **~-hearted** a spensierato. **~house** n faro m. **~ing** n illuminazione f. **~ly** adv leggermente; (accuse) con leggerezza; (without concern) senza dare importanza alla cosa; **get off ~ly** cavarsela a buon mercato. **~ness** n leggerezza f

lightning /'laɪtnɪŋ/ n lampo m, fulmine m. **~-conductor** n parafulmine m

light: ~weight a leggero ● n (in boxing) peso m leggero. **~ year** n anno m luce

like[1] /laɪk/ a simile ● prep come; **~ this/that** così; **what's he ~?** com'è? ● conj (fam: as) come; (Am: as if) come se

like[2] vt piacere, gradire; **I should/ would ~** vorrei, gradirei; **I ~ him** mi piace; **I ~ this car** mi piace questa macchina; **I ~ dancing** mi piace ballare; **I ~ that!** fam questa mi è piaciuta! ● n ~s and dislikes pl gusti mpl

like|able /'laikəbl/ a simpatico. ~**lihood** /-lihud/ n probabilità f. ~**ly** a (-ier, -iest) probabile ● adv probabilmente; **not** ~**ly!** fam neanche per sogno!

like-'minded a con gusti affini

liken /'laikən/ vt paragonare (**to** a)

like|ness /'laiknis/ n somiglianza f. '~**wise** adv lo stesso

liking /'laikiŋ/ n gusto m; **is it to your** ~? è di suo gusto?; **take a** ~ **to sb** prendere qcno in simpatia

lilac /'lailək/ n lillà m ● a color lillà

lily /'lili/ n giglio m. ~ **of the valley** n mughetto m

limb /lim/ n arto m

limber /'limbə(r)/ vi ~ **up** sciogliersi i muscoli

lime¹ /laim/ n (fruit) cedro m; (tree) tiglio m

lime² n calce f; '~**light** n be in the ~**light** essere molto in vista. '~**stone** n calcare m

limit /'limit/ n limite m; **that's the** ~! fam questo è troppo! ● vt limitare (**to** a). ~**ation** /-'teiʃn/ n limite m. ~**ed** a ristretto; ~**ed company** società f anonima

limousine /'liməzi:n/ n limousine f inv

limp¹ /limp/ n andatura f zoppicante; **have a** ~ zoppicare ● vi zoppicare

limp² a floscio

line¹ /lain/ n linea f; (length of rope, cord) filo m; (of writing) riga f; (of poem) verso m; (row) fila f; (wrinkle) ruga f; (of business) settore m; (Am: queue) coda f; **in** ~ **with** in conformità con ● vt segnare; fiancheggiare (street). **line up** vi allinearsi ● vt allineare

line² vt foderare (garment)

linear /'liniə(r)/ a lineare

lined¹ /laind/ a (face) rugoso; (paper) a righe

lined² a (garment) foderato

linen /'linin/ n lino m; (articles) biancheria f ● attrib di lino

liner /'lainə(r)/ n nave f di linea

linesman n Sport guardalinee m inv

linger /'liŋgə(r)/ vi indugiare

lingerie /'lõʒəri/ n biancheria f intima (da donna)

linguist /'liŋgwist/ n linguista mf

linguistic /liŋ'gwistik/ a linguistico. ~**s** n linguistica fsg

lining /'lainiŋ/ n (of garment) fodera f; (of brakes) guarnizione f

link /liŋk/ n (of chain) anello m; fig legame m ● vt collegare. **link up** vi unirsi (**with** a); TV collegarsi

lino /'lainəʊ/ n, **linoleum** /li'nəʊliəm/ n linoleum m

lint /lint/ n garza f

lion /'laiən/ n leone m. ~**ess** n leonessa f

lip /lip/ n labbro m (pl labbra f); (edge) bordo m

lip: ~**-read** vi leggere le labbra; ~**-reading** n lettura f delle labbra. ~**-service** n pay ~**-service** to approvare soltanto a parole. ~**-salve** n burro m [di] cacao. ~**stick** n rossetto m

liqueur /li'kjʊə(r)/ n liquore m

liquid /'likwid/ n liquido m ● a liquido

liquidate /'likwideit/ vt liquidare. ~**ion** /-'deiʃn/ n liquidazione f; Comm **go into** ~**ion** andare in liquidazione

liquidize /'likwidaiz/ vt rendere liquido. ~**r** n Culin frullatore m

liquor /'likə(r)/ n bevanda f alcoolica

liquorice /'likəris/ n liquirizia f

liquor store n Am negozio m di alcolici

lisp /lisp/ n pronuncia f con la lisca ● vi parlare con la lisca

list¹ /list/ n lista f ● vt elencare

list² vi (ship) inclinarsi

listen /'lisn/ vi ascoltare; ~ **to** ascoltare. ~**er** n ascoltatore, -trice mf

listings /'lɪstɪŋz/ *npl* TV programma *m*

listless /'lɪstlɪs/ *a* svogliato

lit /lɪt/ *see* **light**[1]

literacy /'lɪtərəsɪ/ *n* alfabetizzazione *f*

literal /'lɪtərəl/ *a* letterale. **~ly** *adv* letteralmente

literary /'lɪtərərɪ/ *a* letterario

literate /'lɪtərət/ *a* **be ~** saper leggere e scrivere

literature /'lɪtrətʃə(r)/ *n* letteratura *f*

Lithuania /lɪθjʊ'eɪnɪə/ *n* Lituania *f*. **~n** *a & n* lituano, -a *mf*

litigation /lɪtɪ'geɪʃn/ *n* causa *f* [giudiziaria]

litre /'li:tə(r)/ *n* litro *m*

litter /'lɪtə(r)/ *n* immondizie *fpl*; *Zool* figliata *f* ● *vt* **be ~ed with** essere ingombrato di. **~-bin** *n* bidone *m* della spazzatura

little /'lɪtl/ *a* piccolo; (*not much*) poco ● *adv & n* poco *m*; **a ~** un po'; **a ~ water** un po' d'acqua; **a ~ better** un po' meglio; **~ by ~** a poco a poco

liturgy /'lɪtədʒɪ/ *n* liturgia *f*

live[1] /laɪv/ *a* vivo; (*ammunition*) carico; **~ broadcast** trasmissione *f* in diretta; **be ~** *Electr* essere sotto tensione; **~ wire** *n* fig persona *f* dinamica ● *adv* (*broadcast*) in diretta

live[2] /lɪv/ *vi* vivere; (*reside*) abitare; **~ with** convivere con. **live down** *vt* far dimenticare. **live off** *vi* vivere alle spalle di. **live on** *vt* vivere di ● *vi* sopravvivere. **live up** *vt* **~ it up** far la bella vita. **live up to** *vt* essere all'altezza di

livelihood /'laɪvlɪhʊd/ *n* mezzi *mpl* di sostentamento. **~ness** *n* vivacità *f*

lively /'laɪvlɪ/ *a* (**-ier, -iest**) vivace

liven /'laɪvn/ *vt* **~ up** vivacizzare ● *vi* vivacizzarsi

liver /'lɪvə(r)/ *n* fegato *m*

lives /laɪvz/ *see* **life**

livestock /'laɪv-/ *n* bestiame *m*

livid /'lɪvɪd/ *a fam* livido

living /'lɪvɪŋ/ *a* vivo ● *n* **earn one's ~** guadagnarsi da vivere; **the ~** *pl* i vivi. **~-room** *n* soggiorno *m*

lizard /'lɪzəd/ *n* lucertola *f*

load /ləʊd/ *n* carico *m*; **~s of** *fam* un sacco di ● *vt* caricare. **~ed** *a* carico; (*fam: rich*) ricchissimo

loaf[1] /ləʊf/ *n* (*pl* **loaves**) pagnotta *f*

loaf[2] *vi* oziare

loan /ləʊn/ *n* prestito *m*; **on ~** in prestito ● *vt* prestare

loath /ləʊθ/ *a* **be ~ to do sth** essere restio a fare qcsa

loathe /ləʊð/ *vt* detestare. **~ing** *n* disgusto *m*. **~some** *a* disgustoso

loaves /ləʊvz/ *see* **loaf**

lobby /'lɒbɪ/ *n* atrio *m*; *Pol* gruppo *m* di pressione, lobby *m inv*

lobster /'lɒbstə(r)/ *n* aragosta *f*

local /'ləʊkl/ *a* locale; **I'm not ~** non sono del posto ● *n* abitante *mf* del luogo; (*fam: public house*) pub *m* locale. **~ au'thority** *n* autorità *f* locale. **~ call** *n Teleph* telefonata *f* urbana. **~ government** *n* autorità *f inv* locale

locality /ləʊ'kælətɪ/ *n* zona *f*

localized /'ləʊkəlaɪzd/ *a* localizzato

locally /'ləʊkəlɪ/ *adv* localmente; (*live, work*) nei paraggi

local network *n Comput* rete *f* locale

locat|e /ləʊ'keɪt/ *vt* situare; trovare ‹*person*›; **be ~ed** essere situato. **~ion** /-'keɪʃn/ *n* posizione *f*; **filmed on ~ion** girato in esterni

lock[1] /lɒk/ *n* (*hair*) ciocca *f*

lock[2] *n* (*on door*) serratura *f*; (*on canal*) chiusa *f* ● *vt* chiudere a chiave; bloccare ‹*wheels*› ● *vi* chiudersi. **lock in** *vt* chiudere dentro. **lock out** *vt* chiudere fuori. **lock up** *vt* (*in prison*) mettere dentro ● *vi* chiudere

locker /'lɒkə(r)/ *n* armadietto *m*

locket /'lɒkɪt/ *n* medaglione *m*

lock: ~-out *n* serrata *f*. **~smith** *n* fabbro *m*

locomotive /ləʊkə'məʊtɪv/ *n* locomotiva *f*

locum /'ləʊkəm/ n sostituto, -a mf

locust /'ləʊkəst/ n locusta f

lodge /lɒdʒ/ n (porter's) portineria f; (masonic) loggia f ● vt presentare ⟨claim, complaint⟩; (with bank, solicitor) depositare; be ~d essersi conficcato ● vi essere a pensione (with da); (become fixed) conficcarsi. ~r n inquilino, -a mf

lodgings /'lɒdʒɪŋz/ npl camere fpl in affitto

loft /lɒft/ n soffitta f

lofty /'lɒftɪ/ a (-ier, -iest) alto; (haughty) altezzoso

log /lɒg/ n ceppo m; Auto libretto m di circolazione; Naut giornale m di bordo ● vt (pt logged) registrare. **log on to** vt Comput connettersi a

logarithm /'lɒgərɪðm/ n logaritmo m

'log-book n Naut giornale m di bordo; Auto libretto m di circolazione

loggerheads /'lɒgə-/ npl be at ~ fam essere in totale disaccordo

logic /'lɒdʒɪk/ n logica f. ~al a logico. ~ally adv logicamente

logistics /lə'dʒɪstɪks/ npl logistica f

logo /'ləʊgəʊ/ n logo m inv

loin /lɔɪn/ n Culin lombata f

loiter /'lɔɪtə(r)/ vi gironzolare

lollipop /'lɒlɪpɒp/ n lecca-lecca m inv. ~y n lecca-lecca m; (fam: money) quattrini mpl

London /'lʌndən/ n Londra f ● attrib londinese, di Londra. ~er n londinese mf

lone /ləʊn/ a solitario. ~liness n solitudine f

lonely /'ləʊnlɪ/ a (-ier, -iest) solitario; (person) solo

lone|r /'ləʊnə(r)/ n persona f solitaria. ~some a solo

long¹ /lɒŋ/ a lungo; a ~ time molto tempo; a ~ way distante; in the ~ run a lungo andare; (in the end) alla fin fine ● adv a lungo, lungamente; how ~ is? quanto è lungo?; (in time) quanto dura?; all

day ~ tutto il giorno; **not** ~ **ago** non molto tempo fa; **before** ~ fra breve; **he's no** ~**er here** non è più qui; **as** or **so** ~ **as** finché; (provided that) purché; **so** ~! fam ciao!; **will you be** ~? [ti] ci vuole molto?

long² vi ~ **for** desiderare ardentemente

long-distance a a grande distanza; Sport di fondo; (call) interurbano

'longhand n **in** ~ in scrittura ordinaria

longing /'lɒŋɪŋ/ a desideroso ● n brama f. ~**ly** adv con desiderio

longitude /'lɒŋgɪtjuːd/ n Geog longitudine f

long: ~ **jump** n salto m in lungo. ~**-life 'milk** n latte m a lunga conservazione. ~**-lived** /-lɪvd/ a longevo. ~**-range** a Mil, Aeron a lunga portata; (forecast) a lungo termine. ~**-sighted** a presbite. ~**-sleeved** a a maniche lunghe. ~**-suffering** a infinitamente paziente. ~**-term** a a lunga scadenza. ~ **wave** n onde fpl lunghe. ~**-winded** /-'wɪndɪd/ a prolisso

loo /luː/ n fam gabinetto m

look /lʊk/ n occhiata f; (appearance) aspetto m; [good] ~**s** pl bellezza f; **have a** ~ dare un'occhiata a ● vi guardare; (seem) sembrare; ~ **here!** mi ascolti bene!; ~ **at** guardare; ~ **for** cercare; ~ **like** (resemble) assomigliare a. **look after** vt badare a. **look down** vi guardare in basso; ~ **down on sb** fig guardare dall'alto in basso qcno. **look forward to** vt essere impaziente di. **look in on** vt passare da. **look into** vt (examine) esaminare. **look on to** vt (room:) dare su. **look out** vi guardare fuori; (take care) fare attenzione; ~ **out for** cercare; ~ **out!** attento! **look round** vi girarsi; (in shop, town etc) dare un'occhiata. **look through** vt dare un'occhiata a (script, notes). **look up** vi guardare in alto; **~ up to sb** *fig* rispettare qcno ● *vt* cercare [nel dizionario] ⟨*word*⟩; ⟨*visit*⟩ andare a trovare

'**look-out** *n* guardia *f*; ⟨*prospect*⟩ prospettiva *f*; **be on the ~ for** tenere gli occhi aperti per

loom /luːm/ *vi* apparire; *fig* profilarsi

loony /'luːnɪ/ *a & n fam* matto, -a *mf*. **~ bin** *n* manicomio *m*

loop /luːp/ *n* cappio *m*; ⟨*on garment*⟩ passante *m*. **~hole** *n* ⟨*in the law*⟩ scappatoia *f*

loose /luːs/ *a* libero; ⟨*knot*⟩ allentato; ⟨*page*⟩ staccato; ⟨*clothes*⟩ largo; ⟨*morals*⟩ dissoluto; ⟨*inexact*⟩ vago; **be at a ~ end** non sapere cosa fare; **come ~** ⟨*knot:*⟩ sciogliersi; **set ~** liberare. **~ 'change** *n* spiccioli *mpl*. **~ly** *adv* scorrevolmente; ⟨*defined*⟩ vagamente

loosen /'luːsn/ *vt* sciogliere

loot /luːt/ *n* bottino *m* ● *vt/i* depredare. **~er** *n* predatore, -trice *mf*. **~ing** *n* saccheggio *m*

lop /lɒp/ **~ off** *vt* (*pt/pp* lopped) potare

lop'sided *a* sbilenco

lord /lɔːd/ *n* signore *m*; ⟨*title*⟩ Lord *m*; **House of L~s** Camera dei Lords; **the L~'s Prayer** il Padrenostro; **good L~!** Dio mio!

lore /lɔː(r)/ *n* tradizioni *fpl*

lorry /'lɒrɪ/ *n* camion *m inv*; **~ driver** camionista *mf*

lose /luːz/ *v* (*pt/pp* lost) ● *vt* perdere ● *vi* perdere; ⟨*clock:*⟩ essere indietro; **get lost** perdersi; **get lost!** *fam* va a quel paese! **~r** *n* perdente *mf*

loss /lɒs/ *n* perdita *f*; *Comm* **~es** perdite *fpl*; **be at a ~** essere perplesso; **be at a ~ for words** non trovare le parole

lost /lɒst/ *see* lose ● *a* perduto. **~ 'property office** *n* ufficio *m* oggetti smarriti

lot[1] /lɒt/ *n* (*at auction*) lotto *m*; **draw ~s** tirare a sorte

lot[2] *n* **the ~** il tutto; **a ~ of, ~s of**

molto/i; **the ~ of you** tutti voi; **it has changed a ~** è cambiato molto

lotion /'ləʊʃn/ *n* lozione *f*

lottery /'lɒtərɪ/ *n* lotteria *f*. **~ ticket** *n* biglietto *m* della lotteria

loud /laʊd/ *a* sonoro, alto; ⟨*colours*⟩ sgargiante ● *adv* forte; **out ~** ad alta voce. **~'hailer** *n* megafono *m*. **~ly** *adv* forte. **~'speaker** *n* altoparlante *m*

lounge /laʊndʒ/ *n* salotto *m*; ⟨*in hotel*⟩ salone *m* ● *vi* poltrire. **~ suit** *n* vestito *m* da uomo, completo *m* da uomo

louse /laʊs/ *n* (*pl* lice) pidocchio *m*

lousy /'laʊzɪ/ *a* (**-ier, -iest**) *fam* schifoso

lout /laʊt/ *n* zoticone *m*. **~ish** *a* rozzo

lovable /'lʌvəbl/ *a* adorabile

love /lʌv/ *n* amore *m*; *Tennis* zero *m*; **in ~** innamorato (**with** di) ● *vt* amare ⟨*person, country*⟩; **I ~ watching tennis** mi piace molto guardare il tennis. **~affair** *n* relazione *f* [sentimentale]. **~ letter** *n* lettera *f* d'amore

lovely /'lʌvlɪ/ *a* (**-ier, -iest**) bello; ⟨*in looks*⟩ bello, attraente; ⟨*in character*⟩ piacevole; ⟨*meal*⟩ delizioso; **have a ~ time** divertirsi molto

lover /'lʌvə(r)/ *n* amante *mf*

love: **~ song** *n* canzone *f* d'amore. **~ story** *n* storia *f* d'amore

loving /'lʌvɪŋ/ *a* affettuoso

low /ləʊ/ *a* basso; ⟨*depressed*⟩ giù *inv* ● *adv* basso; **feel ~** sentirsi giù ● *n* minimo *m*; *Meteorol* depressione *f*; **at an all-time ~** ⟨*prices etc*⟩ al livello minimo

low: **~brow** *a* di scarsa cultura. **~cut** *a* ⟨*dress*⟩ scollato

lower /'ləʊə(r)/ *a & adv see* low ● *vt* abbassare; **~ oneself** abbassarsi

low: **~'fat** *a* magro. **~grade** *a* di qualità inferiore. **~key** *fig* moderato. **~lands** /-ləndz/ *npl* pianure *fpl*. **~ 'tide** *n* bassa marea *f*

loyal /'lɔɪəl/ *a* leale. **~ty** *n* lealtà *f*

lozenge /ˈlɒzɪndʒ/ n losanga f; (tablet) pastiglia f

LP n abbr **long-playing record**

Ltd abbr (**Limited**) s.r.l.

lubricant /ˈluːbrɪkənt/ n lubrificante m

lubricat|e /ˈluːbrɪkeɪt/ vt lubrificare. **~ion** /-ˈkeɪʃn/ n lubrificazione f

lucid /ˈluːsɪd/ a (explanation) chiaro; (sane) lucido. **~ity** /-ˈsɪdətɪ/ n lucidità f; (of explanation) chiarezza f

luck /lʌk/ n fortuna f; **bad ~** sfortuna f; **good ~!** buona fortuna! **~ily** adv fortunatamente

lucky /ˈlʌkɪ/ a (**-ier, -iest**) fortunato; **be ~** essere fortunato; (thing:) portare fortuna. **~ 'charm** n portafortuna m inv

lucrative /ˈluːkrətɪv/ a lucrativo

ludicrous /ˈluːdɪkrəs/ a ridicolo. **~ly** adv (expensive, complex) eccessivamente

lug /lʌg/ vt (pt/pp **lugged**) fam trascinare

luggage /ˈlʌgɪdʒ/ n bagaglio m; **~-rack** n portabagagli m inv. **~ trolley** n carrello m portabagagli. **~-van** n bagagliaio m

lukewarm /ˈluːkˈwɔːm/ a tiepido; fig poco entusiasta

lull /lʌl/ n pausa f ● vt **~ to sleep** cullare

lullaby /ˈlʌləbaɪ/ n ninna nanna f

lumbago /lʌmˈbeɪgəʊ/ n lombaggine f

lumber /ˈlʌmbə(r)/ n cianfrusaglie fpl; (Am: timber) legname m ● vt fam **~ sb with sth** affibbiare qcsa a qcno. **~ jack** n tagliaboschi m inv

luminous /ˈluːmɪnəs/ a luminoso

lump[1] /lʌmp/ n (of sugar) zolletta f; (swelling) gonfiore m; (in breast) nodulo m; (in sauce) grumo m ● vt **~ together** ammucchiare

lump[2] vt **~ it** fam **you'll just have**

to ~ it che ti piaccia o no è così

lump sum n somma f globale

lumpy /ˈlʌmpɪ/ a (**-ier, -iest**) grumoso

lunacy /ˈluːnəsɪ/ n follia f

lunar /ˈluːnə(r)/ a lunare

lunatic /ˈluːnətɪk/ n pazzo, -a mf

lunch /lʌntʃ/ n pranzo m ● vi pranzare

luncheon /ˈlʌntʃn/ n (formal) pranzo m. **~ meat** n carne f in scatola. **~ voucher** n buono m pasto

lunch: ~-hour n intervallo m per il pranzo. **~-time** n ora f di pranzo

lung /lʌŋ/ n polmone m. **~ cancer** n cancro m al polmone

lunge /lʌndʒ/ vi lanciarsi [at su]

lurch[1] /lɜːtʃ/ n **leave in the ~** fam lasciare nei guai

lurch[2] vi barcollare

lure /lʊə(r)/ n esca f; fig lusinga f ● vt adescare

lurid /ˈlʊərɪd/ a (gaudy) sgargiante; (sensational) sensazionalistico

lurk /lɜːk/ vi appostarsi

luscious /ˈlʌʃəs/ a saporito; fig sexy inv

lush /lʌʃ/ a lussureggiante

lust /lʌst/ n lussuria f ● vi **~ after** desiderare [fortemente]. **~ful** a lussurioso

lusty /ˈlʌstɪ/ a (**-ier, -iest**) vigoroso

lute /luːt/ n liuto m

luxuriant /lʌgˈʒʊərɪənt/ a lussureggiante

luxurious /lʌgˈʒʊərɪəs/ a lussuoso

luxury /ˈlʌkʃərɪ/ n lusso m ● attrib di lusso

lying /ˈlaɪɪŋ/ see **lie**[1] & [2] ● n mentire m

lymph gland /ˈlɪmf/ n linfoghiandola f

lynch /lɪntʃ/ vt linciare

lynx /lɪŋks/ n lince f

lyric /ˈlɪrɪk/ a lirico. **~al** a lirico; (fam: enthusiastic) entusiasta. **~s** npl parole fpl

Mm

mac /mæk/ *n fam* impermeabile *m*

macabre /mə'kɑːbr/ *a* macabro

macaroni /mækə'rəʊnɪ/ *n* maccheroni *mpl*

mace[1] /meɪs/ *n* (*staff*) mazza *f*

mace[2] *n* (*spice*) macis *m f*

machinations /mækɪ'neɪʃnz/ *npl* macchinazioni *fpl*

machine /mə'ʃiːn/ *n* macchina *f* ● *vt* (*sew*) cucire a macchina; *Techn* lavorare a macchina. **~-gun** *n* mitragliatrice *f*

machinery /mə'ʃiːnərɪ/ *n* macchinario *m*

machinist /mə'ʃiːnɪst/ *n* macchinista *mf*; (*on sewing machine*) lavorante *mf* adetto alla macchina da cucire

machismo /mə'tʃɪzmʊ/ *n* machismo *m*

macho /'mætʃəʊ/ *a* macho *inv*

mackerel /'mæk(ə)l/ *n inv* sgombro *m*

mackintosh /'mækɪntʃ/ *n* impermeabile *m*

mad /mæd/ *a* (**madder, maddest**) pazzo, matto; (*fam: angry*) furioso (**at** con); **like** *~ fam* come un pazzo; **be** *~* **about sb/sth** (*fam: keen on*) andare matto per qcno/qcsa

madam /'mædəm/ *n* signora *f*

madden /'mædən/ *vt* (*make angry*) far diventare matto

made /meɪd/ *see* make; **~ to measure** [fatto] su misura

Madeira cake /mə'dɪərə/ *n* dolce *m* di pan di Spagna

mad|ly /'mædlɪ/ *adv fam* follemente; (*fam: love*) innamorato follemente. **~man** *n* pazzo *m*. **~ness** *n* pazzia *f*

madonna /mə'dɒnə/ *n* madonna *f*

magazine /mægə'ziːn/ *n* rivista *f*; *Mil, Phot* magazzino *m*

maggot /'mægət/ *n* verme *m*

Magi /'meɪdʒaɪ/ *npl* **the** *~* i Re *mpl* Magi

magic /'mædʒɪk/ *n* magia *f*; (*tricks*) giochi *mpl* di prestigio ● *a* magico; (*trick*) di prestigio. **~al** *a* magico

magician /mə'dʒɪʃn/ *n* mago, -a *mf*; (*entertainer*) prestigiatore, -trice *mf*

magistrate /'mædʒɪstreɪt/ *n* magistrato *m*

magnanim|ity /mægnə'nɪmətɪ/ *n* magnanimità *f*. **~ous** /-'nænɪməs/ *a* magnanimo

magnet /'mægnɪt/ *n* magnete *m*, calamita *f*. **~ic** /-'netɪk/ *a* magnetico. **~ism** *n* magnetismo *m*

magnification /mægnɪfɪ'keɪʃn/ *n* ingrandimento *m*

magnificen|ce /mæg'nɪfɪsəns/ *n* magnificenza *f*. **~t** *a* magnifico

magnify /'mægnɪfaɪ/ *vt* (*pt/pp* **-ied**) ingrandire; (*exaggerate*) ingigantire. **~ing glass** *n* lente *f* d'ingrandimento

magnitude /'mægnɪtjuːd/ *n* grandezza *f*; (*importance*) importanza *f*

magpie /'mægpaɪ/ *n* gazza *f*

mahogany /mə'hɒgənɪ/ *n* mogano *m* ● *attrib* di mogano

maid /meɪd/ *n* cameriera *f*; **old** *~ pej* zitella *f*

maiden /'meɪdn/ *n* (*liter*) fanciulla *f* ● *a* (*speech, voyage*) inaugurale. **~ 'aunt** *n* zia *f* zitella. **~ name** *n* nome *m* da ragazza

mail /meɪl/ *n* posta *f* ● *vt* impostare

mail: **~-bag** *n* sacco *m* postale. **~-box** *n Am* cassetta *f* delle lettere; (*e-mail*) casella *f* di posta elettronica. **~ing list** *n* elenco *m* d'indirizzi per un mailing. **~man** *n Am* postino *m*. **~ order** *n* vendita *f* per corrispondenza. **~-order firm** *n* ditta *f* di vendita per corrispondenza

mailshot /'meɪlʃɒt/ *n* mailing *m inv*

maim /meɪm/ *vt* menomare

main[1] /meɪn/ *n* (*water, gas, electricity*) conduttura *f* principale

main[2] *a* principale; **the ~ thing is**

to... la cosa essenziale è di... ● *n* in the ~ in complesso

main: ~**land** /-lənd/ *n* continente *m*. ~**ly** *adv* principalmente. ~**stay** *n fig* pilastro *m*. ~ **street** *n* via *f* principale

maintain /meɪn'teɪn/ *vt* mantenere; (*keep in repair*) curare la manutenzione di; (*claim*) sostenere

maintenance /'meɪntənəns/ *n* mantenimento *m*; (*care*) manutenzione *f*; (*allowance*) alimenti *mpl*

maisonette /meɪzə'net/ *n* appartamento *m* a due piani

majestic /mə'dʒestɪk/ *a* maestoso

majesty /'mædʒəstɪ/ *n* maestà *f*; His/Her M~ Sua Maestà

major /'meɪdʒə(r)/ *a* maggiore; ~ **road** strada *f* con diritto di precedenza ● *n Mil, Mus* maggiore *m* ● *vi Am* ~ in specializzarsi in

Majorca /mə'jɔːkə/ *n* Maiorca *f*

majority /mə'dʒɒrətɪ/ *n* maggioranza *f*; be in the ~ avere la maggioranza

make /meɪk/ *n* (*brand*) marca *f* ● *v* (*pt/pp* made) ● *vt* fare; (*earn*) guadagnare; rendere (*happy, clear*); prendere (*decision*); ~ **sb laugh** far ridere qcno; ~ **sb do sth** far fare qcsa a qcno; ~ **it** (*to party, top of hill etc*) farcela; **what time do you** ~ **it?** che ore fai? ● *vi* ~ **as if to** fare per. **make do** *vi* arrangiarsi. **make for** *vt* dirigersi verso. **make off** *vi* fuggire. **make out** *vt* (*distinguish*) distinguere; (*write out*) rilasciare (*cheque*); compilare (*list*); (*claim*) far credere. **make over** *vt* cedere. **make up** *vt* (*constitute*) comporre; (*complete*) completare; (*invent*) inventare; (*apply cosmetics to*) truccare; fare (*parcel*); ~ **up one's mind** decidersi; ~ **it up** (*after quarrel*) riconciliarsi ● *vi* (*after quarrel*) fare la pace; ~ **up for** compensare; ~ **up for lost time** recuperare il tempo perso

'**make-believe** *n* finzione *f*

maker /'meɪkə(r)/ *n* fabbricante *mf*; M~ Creatore *m*

make: ~ **shift** *a* di fortuna ● *n* espediente *m*. ~-**up** *n* trucco *m*; (*character*) natura *f*

making /'meɪkɪŋ/ *n* have the ~**s of** aver la stoffa di

maladjust|ed /mælə'dʒʌstɪd/ *a* disadattato

malaise /mə'leɪz/ *n fig* malessere *m*

malaria /mə'leərɪə/ *n* malaria *f*

Malaysia /mə'leɪzɪə/ *n* Malesia *f*

male /meɪl/ *a* maschile ● *n* maschio *m*. ~ **nurse** *n* infermiere *m*

malevolen|ce /mə'levələns/ *n* malevolenza *f*. ~**t** *a* malevolo

malfunction /mæl'fʌŋkʃn/ *n* funzionamento *m* imperfetto ● *vi* funzionare male

malice /'mælɪs/ *n* malignità *f*; **bear sb** ~ voler del male a qcno

malicious /mə'lɪʃəs/ *a* maligno

malign /mə'laɪn/ *vt* malignare su

malignan|cy /mə'lɪgnənsɪ/ *n* malignità *f*. ~**t** *a* maligno

malinger /mə'lɪŋɡə(r)/ *vi* fingersi malato. ~**er** *n* scansafatiche *mf inv*

malleable /'mælɪəbl/ *a* malleabile

mallet /'mælɪt/ *n* martello *m* di legno

malnutrition /mæl-/ *n* malnutrizione *f*

mal'practice *n* negligenza *f*

malt /mɔːlt/ *n* malto *m*

Malta /'mɔːltə/ *n* Malta *f*. ~**ese** /-iːz/ *a* & *n* maltese *mf*

mal'treat /mæl-/ *vt* maltrattare. ~**ment** *n* maltrattamento *m*

mammal /'mæml/ *n* mammifero *m*

mammoth /'mæməθ/ *a* mastodontico ● *n* mammut *m inv*

man /mæn/ *n* (*pl* **men**) uomo *m*; (*chess, draughts*) pedina *f* ● *vt* (*pt/pp* **manned**) equipaggiare; essere di servizio a (*counter, telephones*)

manage /'mænɪdʒ/ *vt* dirigere; gestire (*shop, affairs*); (*cope with*) farcela; ~ **to do sth** riuscire a fare qcsa ● *vi* riuscire; *(cope)* farcela (on con). **~able** /-əbl/ *a* ⟨*hair*⟩ docile; ⟨*size*⟩ maneggevole. **~ment** /-mənt/ *n* gestione *f*; **the ~ment** la direzione

manager /ˈmænɪdʒə(r)/ *n* direttore *m*; *(of shop, bar)* gestore *m*; *Sport* manager *m inv*. **~ess** /-ˈres/ *n* direttrice *f*. **~ial** /-ˈdʒɪərɪəl/ *a* **~ial staff** personale *m* direttivo

managing /ˈmænɪdʒɪŋ/ *a* **~ director** direttore, -trice *mf* generale

mandarin /ˈmændərɪn/ *n* [orange] mandarino *m*

mandate /ˈmændeɪt/ *n* mandato *m*. **~ory** /-dətrɪ/ *a* obbligatorio

mane /meɪn/ *n* criniera *f*

mangle /ˈmæŋɡl/ *vt* ⟨*damage*⟩ maciullare

mango /ˈmæŋɡəʊ/ *n* (*pl* **-es**) mango *m*

mangy /ˈmeɪndʒɪ/ *a* ⟨*dog*⟩ rognoso

man: **~handle** *vt* malmenare. **~hole** *n* botola *f*. **~hole cover** *n* tombino *m*. **~hood** *n* età *f* adulta; ⟨*quality*⟩ virilità *f*. **~hour** *n* ora *f* lavorativa. **~hunt** *n* caccia *f* all'uomo

mania /ˈmeɪnɪə/ *n* mania *f*. **~iac** /-ɪæk/ *n* maniaco, -a *mf*

manicure /ˈmænɪkjʊə(r)/ *n* manicure *f* ● *vt* fare la manicure a

manifest /ˈmænɪfest/ *a* manifesto ● *vt* **~ itself** manifestarsi. **~ly** *adv* palesemente

manifesto /mænɪˈfestəʊ/ *n* manifesto *m*

manifold /ˈmænɪfəʊld/ *a* molteplice

manipulate /məˈnɪpjʊleɪt/ *vt* manipolare. **~ion** /-ˈleɪʃn/ *n* manipolazione *f*

man'kind *n* genere *m* umano

manly /ˈmænlɪ/ *a* virile

'man-made *a* artificiale. **~ fibre** *n* fibra *f* sintetica

manner /ˈmænə(r)/ *n* maniera *f*; **in this ~** in questo modo; **have no ~s** avere dei pessimi modi;

good/bad ~s buone/cattive maniere *fpl*. **~ism** *n* affettazione *f*

manœuvre /məˈnuːvə(r)/ *n* manovra *f* ● *vt* fare manovra con ⟨*vehicle*⟩; manovrare ⟨*person*⟩

manor /ˈmænə(r)/ *n* maniero *m*

'manpower *n* manodopera *f*

mansion /ˈmænʃn/ *n* palazzo *m*

manslaughter *n* omicidio *m* colposo

mantelpiece /ˈmæntl-/ *n* mensola *f* di caminetto

manual /ˈmænjʊəl/ *a* manuale ● *n* manuale *m*

manufacture /mænjʊˈfæktʃə(r)/ *vt* fabbricare ● *n* manifattura *f*. **~r** *n* fabbricante *m*

manure /məˈnjʊə(r)/ *n* concime *m*

manuscript /ˈmænjʊskrɪpt/ *n* manoscritto *m*

many /ˈmenɪ/ *a & pron* molti; **there are as ~ boys as girls** ci sono tanti ragazzi quante ragazze; **as ~ as 500** ben 500; **as ~ as that** così tanti; **as ~** altrettanti; **very ~, a good/great ~** moltissimi; **~ a time** molte volte

map /mæp/ *n* carta *f* geografica; *(of town)* mappa *f* ● **map out** *vt* (*pt/pp* **mapped**) *fig* programmare

maple /ˈmeɪpl/ *n* acero *m*

mar /mɑː(r)/ *vt* (*pt/pp* **marred**) rovinare

marathon /ˈmærəθən/ *n* maratona *f*

marble /ˈmɑːbl/ *n* marmo *m*; *(for game)* pallina *f* ● *attrib* di marmo

March /mɑːtʃ/ *n* marzo *m*

march *n* marcia *f*; *(protest)* dimostrazione *f* ● *vi* marciare ● *vt* far marciare; **~ sb off** scortare qcno fuori

mare /meə(r)/ *n* giumenta *f*

margarine /mɑːdʒəˈriːn/ *n* margarina *f*

margin /ˈmɑːdʒɪn/ *n* margine *m*. **~al** *a* marginale. **~ally** *adv* marginalmente

marigold /ˈmærɪɡəʊld/ *n* calendula *f*

marijuana /mærʊˈwɑːnə/ n marijuana f

marina /məˈriːnə/ n porticciolo m

marinade /mærɪˈneɪd/ n marinata f ● vt marinare

marine /məˈriːn/ a marino ● n (sailor) soldato m di fanteria marina

marionette /mærɪəˈnet/ n marionetta f

marital /ˈmærɪtl/ a coniugale. ~ **status** stato m civile

maritime /ˈmærɪtaɪm/ a marittimo

mark¹ /mɑːk/ n (currency) marco m

mark² n (stain) macchia f; (sign, indication) segno m; Sch voto m ● vt segnare; (stain) macchiare; Sch correggere; Sport marcare; ~ **time** Mil segnare il passo; fig non far progressi; **~ my words** ricordati quello che dico. **mark out** vt delimitare; fig designare

marked /mɑːkt/ a marcato. ~ly /-kɪdlɪ/ adv notevolmente

marker /ˈmɑːkə(r)/ n (for highlighting) evidenziatore m; Sport marcatore m; (of exam) esaminatore, -trice mf

market /ˈmɑːkɪt/ n mercato m ● vt vendere al mercato; (launch) commercializzare; **on the** ~ sul mercato. **~ing** n marketing m. **re'search** n ricerca f di mercato

marksman /ˈmɑːksmən/ n tiratore m scelto

marmalade /ˈmɑːməleɪd/ n marmellata f d'arance

maroon /məˈruːn/ a marrone rossastro

marooned /məˈruːnd/ a abbandonato

marquee /mɑːˈkiː/ n tendone m

marquis /ˈmɑːkwɪs/ n marchese m

marriage /ˈmærɪdʒ/ n matrimonio m

married /ˈmærɪd/ a sposato; (life) coniugale

marrow /ˈmærəʊ/ n Anat midollo m; (vegetable) zucca f

marry /ˈmærɪ/ vt (pt/pp **married**) sposare; **get ~ied** sposarsi ● vi sposarsi

marsh /mɑːʃ/ n palude f

marshal /ˈmɑːʃl/ n (steward) cerimoniere m ● vt (pt/pp **marshalled**) fig organizzare (arguments)

marshy /ˈmɑːʃɪ/ a paludoso

marsupial /mɑːˈsuːpɪəl/ n marsupiale m

martial /ˈmɑːʃl/ a marziale

martyr /ˈmɑːtə(r)/ n martire mf ● vt martoriare. **~dom** /-dəm/ n martirio m. **~ed** a fam da martire

marvel /ˈmɑːvl/ n meraviglia f ● vi (pt/pp **marvelled**) meravigliarsi (at di). **~lous** /-vələs/ a meraviglioso

Marxis|m /ˈmɑːksɪzm/ n marxismo m. **~t** a & n marxista mf

marzipan /ˈmɑːzɪpæn/ n marzapane m

mascara /mæˈskɑːrə/ n mascara m inv

mascot /ˈmæskət/ n mascotte f inv

masculin|e /ˈmæskjʊlɪn/ a maschile ● n Gram maschile m. **~ity** /-ˈlɪnɪtɪ/ n mascolinità f

mash /mæʃ/ vt impastare. **~ed potatoes** npl purè m inv di patate

mask /mɑːsk/ n maschera f ● vt mascherare

masochis|m /ˈmæsəkɪzm/ n masochismo m. **~t** /-ɪst/ n masochista mf

Mason n massone m. **~ic** /məˈsɒnɪk/ a massonico

mason /ˈmeɪsn/ n muratore m

masonry /ˈmeɪsnrɪ/ n massoneria f

masquerade /mæskəˈreɪd/ n fig mascherata f ● vi ~ **as** (pose) farsi passare per

mass¹ /mæs/ n Relig messa f

mass² n massa f; **~es of** fam un sacco di ● vi ammassarsi

massacre /ˈmæsəkə(r)/ n massacro m ● vt massacrare

massage /ˈmæsɑːʒ/ n massaggio

m ● *vt* massaggiare; *fig* manipolare ⟨*statistics*⟩

masseu|r /mæˈsɜː(r)/ *n* massaggiatore *m*. **~se** /-ˈsɜːz/ *n* massaggiatrice *f*

massive /ˈmæsɪv/ *a* enorme

mass: ~ **media** *npl* mezzi *mpl* di comunicazione di massa, mass media *mpl*. **~-pro'duce** *vt* produrre in serie. **~-pro'duction** *n* produzione *f* in serie

mast /mɑːst/ *n Naut* albero *m*; ⟨*for radio*⟩ antenna *f*

master /ˈmɑːstə(r)/ *n* maestro *m*, padrone *m*; ⟨*teacher*⟩ professore *m*; ⟨*of ship*⟩ capitano *m*; **M~** ⟨*boy*⟩ signorino *m*

master: **~-key** *n* passe-partout *m inv*. **~ly** *a* magistrale. **~-mind** *n* cervello *m* ● *vt* ideare e dirigere. **~piece** *n* capolavoro *m*. **~-stroke** *n* colpo *m* da maestro. **~y** *n* ⟨*of subject*⟩ padronanza *f*

masturbat|e /ˈmæstəbeɪt/ *vi* masturbarsi. **~ion** /-ˈbeɪʃn/ *n* masturbazione *f*

mat /mæt/ *n* stuoia *f*; ⟨*on table*⟩ sottopiatto *m*

match¹ /mætʃ/ *n Sport* partita *f*; ⟨*equal*⟩ uguale *mf*; ⟨*marriage*⟩ matrimonio *m*; ⟨*person to marry*⟩ partito *m*; **be a good ~** ⟨*colours:*⟩ intonarsi bene; **be no ~ for** non essere dello stesso livello di ● *vt* ⟨*equal*⟩ uguagliare; ⟨*be like*⟩ andare bene con ● *vi* intonarsi

match² /mætʃ/ *n* fiammifero *m*. **~box** *n* scatola *f* di fiammiferi

matching /ˈmætʃɪŋ/ *a* intonato

mate¹ /meɪt/ *n* compagno, -a *mf*; ⟨*assistant*⟩ aiuto *m*; *Naut* secondo *m*; ⟨*fam: friend*⟩ amico, -a *mf* ● *vi* accoppiarsi ● *vt* accoppiare

mate² /meɪt/ *n* ⟨*in chess*⟩ scacco *m* matto

material /məˈtɪərɪəl/ *n* materiale *m*; ⟨*fabric*⟩ stoffa *f*; **raw ~s** materie *fpl* prime ● *a* materiale

material|ism /məˈtɪərɪəlɪzm/ *n* materialismo *m*. **~istic** /-ˈlɪstɪk/ *a* materialistico. **~ize** /-laɪz/ *vi* materializzarsi

maternal /məˈtɜːnl/ *a* materno

maternity /məˈtɜːnəti/ *n* maternità *f*. **~ clothes** *npl* abiti *mpl* premaman. **~ ward** *n* maternità *f inv*

matey /ˈmeɪti/ *a fam* amichevole

mathematic|al /mæθəˈmætɪkl/ *a* matematico. **~ian** /-məˈtɪʃn/ *n* matematico, -a *mf*

mathematics /mæθˈmætɪks/ *n* matematica *fsg*

maths /mæθs/ *n fam* matematica *fsg*

matinée /ˈmætɪneɪ/ *n Theat* matinée *f*

mating /ˈmeɪtɪŋ/ *n* accoppiamento *m*; **~ season** stagione *f* degli amori

matriculat|e /məˈtrɪkjʊleɪt/ *vi* immatricolarsi. **~ion** /-ˈleɪʃn/ *n* immatricolazione *f*

matrix /ˈmeɪtrɪks/ *n* ⟨*pl* **matrices** /-siːz/⟩ *n* matrice *f*

matted /ˈmætɪd/ *a* **~ hair** capelli *mpl* tutti appiccicati tra loro

matter /ˈmætə(r)/ *n* ⟨*affair*⟩ faccenda *f*; ⟨*question*⟩ questione *f*; ⟨*phys: substance*⟩ materia *f*; **as a ~ of fact** a dire la verità; **what is the ~?** che cosa c'è? ● *vi* importare; **~ to** essere importante per qcno; **it doesn't ~** non importa. **~-of-fact** *a* pratico

mattress /ˈmætrɪs/ *n* materasso *m*

matur|e /məˈtjʊə(r)/ *a* maturo; *Comm* in scadenza ● *vi* maturare ● *vt* far maturare. **~ity** *n* maturità *f*; *Fin* maturazione *f*

maul /mɔːl/ *vt* malmenare

Maundy /ˈmɔːndɪ/ *n* **~ Thursday** giovedì *m* santo

mauve /məʊv/ *a* malva

maxim /ˈmæksɪm/ *n* massima *f*

maximum /ˈmæksɪməm/ *a* massimo; **ten minutes ~** dieci minuti al massimo ● *n* ⟨*pl* **-ima**⟩ massimo *m*

May /meɪ/ *n* maggio *m*

may /meɪ/ *v aux* ⟨*solo al presente*⟩ potere; **~ I come in?** posso entrare?; **if I ~ say so** se mi posso permettere; **~ you both be very**

happy siate felici; **I ~ as well stay** potrei anche rimanere; **it ~ be true** potrebbe esser vero; **she ~ be old, but...** sarà anche vecchia, ma...

maybe /'meɪbi:/ adv forse, può darsi

'May Day n il primo maggio

mayonnaise /meɪə'neɪz/ n maionese f

mayor /'meə(r)/ n sindaco m. **~ess** n sindaco m; (wife of mayor) moglie f del sindaco

maze /meɪz/ n labirinto m

me /mi:/ pron (object) mi; (with preposition) me; **she called me** mi ha chiamato; **she called me, not you** ha chiamato me, non te; **give me the money** dammi i soldi; **give it to me** dammelo; **he gave it to me** me lo ha dato; **it's ~** sono io

meadow /'medəʊ/ n prato m

meagre /'mi:gə(r)/ a scarso

meal[1] /mi:l/ n pasto m

meal[2] n (grain) farina f

mealy-mouthed /mi:lɪ'maʊðd/ a ambiguo

mean[1] /mi:n/ a avaro; (unkind) meschino

mean[2] a medio ● n (average) media f; **Greenwich ~ time** ora f media di Greenwich

mean[3] vt (pt/pp meant) voler dire; (signify) significare; (intend) intendere; **I ~ it** lo dico seriamente; **~ well** avere buone intenzioni; **be meant for** ⟨present:⟩ essere destinato a; ⟨remark:⟩ essere riferito a

meander /mɪ'ændə(r)/ vi vagare

meaning /'mi:nɪŋ/ n significato m. **~ful** a significativo. **~less** a senza senso

means /mi:nz/ n mezzo m; **~ of transport** mezzo m di trasporto; **by ~ of** per mezzo di; **by all ~!** certamente!; **by no ~** niente affatto ● npl (resources) mezzi mpl

meant /ment/ see **mean**[3]

meantime n in the **~** nel frattempo ● adv intanto

'meanwhile adv intanto

measles /'mi:zlz/ n morbillo m

measly /'mi:zlɪ/ a fam misero

measurable /'meʒərəbl/ a misurabile

measure /'meʒə(r)/ n misura f ● vt/i misurare. **measure up to** vt fig essere all'altezza di. **~d** a misurato. **~ment** /-mənt/ n misura f

meat /mi:t/ n carne f. **~ ball** n Culin polpetta f di carne. **~ loaf** n polpettone m

mechanic /mɪ'kænɪk/ n meccanico m. **~ical** a meccanico; **~ical engineering** ingegneria f meccanica. **~ically** adv meccanicamente. **~ics** n meccanica f ● npl meccanismo msg

mechanism /'mekənɪzm/ n meccanismo m. **~ize** vt meccanizzare

medal /medl/ n medaglia f

medallion /mɪ'dælɪən/ n medaglione m

medallist /'medəlɪst/ n vincitore, -trice mf di una medaglia

meddle /medl/ vi immischiarsi (in di); (tinker) armeggiare (with con)

media /'mi:dɪə/ see **medium** ● npl the **~** i mass media

median /'mi:dɪən/ a **~ strip** Am banchina f spartitraffico

mediate /'mi:dɪeɪt/ vi fare da mediatore. **~ion** /-'eɪʃn/ n mediazione f. **~or** n mediatore, -trice mf

medical /'medɪkl/ a medico ● n visita f medica. **~ insurance** n assicurazione f sanitaria. **~ student** n studente, -essa mf di medicina

medicated /'medɪkeɪtɪd/ a medicato. **~ion** /-'keɪʃn/ n (drugs) medicinali mpl

medicinal /mɪ'dɪsɪnl/ a medicinale

medicine /'medsən/ n medicina f

medieval /medɪ'i:vl/ a medievale

mediocre /mi:dɪ'əʊkə(r)/ a mediocre. **~ity** /-'ɒkrɪt/ n mediocrità f

meditate /'medɪteɪt/ vi meditare (on su). **~ion** /-'teɪʃn/ n meditazione f

Mediterranean /medɪtə'reɪnɪən/ *n* **the ~ [Sea]** il [mare *m*] Mediterraneo *m* ● *a* mediterraneo

medium /'miːdɪəm/ *a* medio; *Culin* di media cottura ● *n* (*pl* **media**) mezzo *m*; (*pl* **-s**) (*person*) medium *mf inv*

medium: **~-sized** *a* di taglia media. **~ wave** *n* onde *fpl* medie

medley /'medlɪ/ *n* miscuglio *m*; *Mus* miscellanea *f*

meek /miːk/ *a* mite, mansueto. **~ly** *adv* docilmente

meet /miːt/ *v* (*pt/pp* **met**) ● *vt* incontrare; (*at station, airport*) andare incontro a; (*for first time*) far la conoscenza di; pagare (*bill*); soddisfare (*requirements*) ● *vi* incontrarsi; (*committee*) riunirsi; **~ with** incontrare (*problem*); incontrarsi con (*person*) ● *n* raduno *m* [*sportivo*]

meeting /'miːtɪŋ/ *n* riunione *f*, meeting *m inv*; (*large*) assemblea *f*; (*by chance*) incontro *m*

megabyte /'megəbaɪt/ *n* megabyte *m*

megalomania /megələ'meɪnɪə/ *n* megalomania *f*

megaphone /'megəfəʊn/ *n* megafono *m*

melancholy /'melənkəlɪ/ *a* malinconico ● *n* malinconia *f*

mellow /'meləʊ(r)/ *a* (*wine*) generoso; (*sound, colour*) caldo; (*person*) dolce ● *vi* (*person*) addolcirsi

melodic /mɪ'lɒdɪk/ *a* melodico

melodrama /'melə-/ *n* melodramma *m*. **~tic** /-drə'mætɪk/ *a* melodrammatico

melody /'melədɪ/ *n* melodia *f*

melon /'melən/ *n* melone *m*

melt /melt/ *vt* sciogliere ● *vi* sciogliersi. **melt down** *vt* fondere. **~ing-pot** *n fig* crogiuolo *m*

member /'membə(r)/ *n* membro *m*; **~ countries** paesi *mpl* membri; **M~ of Parliament** deputato, -a *mf*; **M~ of the European Parliament** eurodeputato, -a *mf*.

~ship *n* iscrizione *f*; (*members*) soci *mpl*

membrane /'membreɪn/ *n* membrana *f*

memo /'meməʊ/ *n* promemoria *m inv*

memoirs /'memwɑːz/ *n* ricordi *mpl*

memorable /'memərəbl/ *a* memorabile

memorandum /memə'rændəm/ *n* promemoria *m inv*

memorial /mɪ'mɔːrɪəl/ *n* monumento *m*. **~ service** *n* funzione *f* commemorativa

memorize /'meməraɪz/ *vt* memorizzare

memory /'memərɪ/ *n also Comput* memoria *f*; (*thing remembered*) ricordo *m*; **from ~** a memoria; **in ~ of** in ricordo di

men /men/ *see* **man**

menac|e /'menəs/ *n* minaccia *f*; (*nuisance*) piaga *f* ● *vt* minacciare. **~ing** *a* minaccioso

mend /mend/ *vt* riparare; (*darn*) rammendare ● *n* **on the ~** in via di guarigione

'menfolk *n* uomini *mpl*

menial /'miːnɪəl/ *a* umile

meningitis /menɪn'dʒaɪtɪs/ *n* meningite *f*

menopause /'menə-/ *n* menopausa *f*

menstruat|e /'menstrʊeɪt/ *vi* mestruare. **~ion** /-'eɪʃn/ *n* mestruazione *f*

mental /'mentl/ *a* mentale; (*fam: mad*) pazzo. **~ a'rithmetic** *n* calcolo *m* mentale. **~ i'llness** *n* malattia *f* mentale

mental|ity /men'tælətɪ/ *n* mentalità *f inv*. **~ly** *adv* mentalmente; **~ly ill** malato di mente

mention /'menʃn/ *n* menzione *f* ● *vt* menzionare; **don't ~ it** non c'è di che

menu /'menjuː/ *n* menu *m inv*

MEP *n abbr* **Member of the European Parliament**

mercenary /ˈmɜːsɪnərɪ/ a mercenario ● n mercenario m

merchandise /ˈmɜːtʃəndaɪz/ n merce f

merchant /ˈmɜːtʃənt/ n commerciante mf. ~ **bank** n banca f d'affari. ~ **navy** n marina f mercantile

merci|ful /ˈmɜːsɪfl/ a misericordioso. ~**fully** adv fam grazie a Dio. ~**less** a spietato

mercury /ˈmɜːkjʊrɪ/ n mercurio m

mercy /ˈmɜːsɪ/ n misericordia f; **be at sb's** ~ essere alla mercè di qcno, essere in balia di qcno

mere /mɪə(r)/ a solo. ~**ly** adv solamente

merest /ˈmɪərɪst/ a minimo

merge /mɜːdʒ/ vi fondersi

merger /ˈmɜːdʒə(r)/ n fusione f

meringue /məˈræŋ/ n meringa f

merit /ˈmerɪt/ n merito m; (advantage) qualità f inv ● vt meritare

mermaid /ˈmɜːmeɪd/ n sirena f

merri|ly /ˈmerɪlɪ/ adv allegramente. ~**ment** /-mənt/ n baldoria f

merry /ˈmerɪ/ a (-ier, -iest) allegro; ~ **Christmas!** Buon Natale! **merry**: ~**-go-round** n giostra f. ~**making** n festa f

mesh /meʃ/ n maglia f

mesmerize /ˈmezməraɪz/ vt ipnotizzare. ~**d** a fig ipnotizzato

mess /mes/ n disordine m, casino m fam; (trouble) guaio m; (something spilt) sporco m; Mil mensa f; **make a** ~ **of** (botch) fare un pasticcio di ● **mess about** vi perder tempo; ~ **about with** armeggiare con ● vt prendere in giro (person).

mess up vt mettere in disordine, incasinare fam; (botch) mandare all'aria

message /ˈmesɪdʒ/ n messaggio m

messenger /ˈmesɪndʒə(r)/ n messaggero m

Messiah /mɪˈsaɪə/ n Messia m

Messrs /ˈmesəz/ npl (on letter) ~ **Smith** Spett. ditta Smith

messy /ˈmesɪ/ a (-ier, -iest) disordinato; (in dress) sciatto

met /met/ see **meet**

metal /ˈmetl/ n metallo m ● a di metallo. ~**lic** /mɪˈtælɪk/ a metallico

metamorphosis /metəˈmɔːfəsɪs/ n (pl -**phoses** /-siːz/) metamorfosi f inv

metaphor /ˈmetəfə(r)/ n metafora f. ~**ical** /-ˈforɪkl/ a metaforico

meteor /ˈmiːtɪə(r)/ n meteora f. ~**ic** /-ˈɒrɪk/ a fig fulmineo

meteorological /miːtɪərəˈlɒdʒɪkl/ a meteorologico

meteorolog|ist /miːtɪəˈrɒlədʒɪst/ n meteorologo, -a mf. ~**y** n meteorologia f

meter[1] /ˈmiːtə(r)/ n contatore m

meter[2] n Am = **metre**

method /ˈmeθəd/ n metodo m

methodical /mɪˈθɒdɪkl/ a metodico. ~**ly** adv metodicamente

Methodist /ˈmeθədɪst/ n metodista mf

meths /meθs/ n fam alcol m denaturato

methylated /ˈmeθɪleɪtɪd/ a ~ **spirit[s]** alcol m denaturato

meticulous /mɪˈtɪkjʊləs/ a meticoloso. ~**ly** adv meticolosamente

metre /ˈmiːtə(r)/ n metro m

metric /ˈmetrɪk/ a metrico

metropolis /mɪˈtrɒpəlɪs/ n metropoli f inv

metropolitan /metrəˈpɒlɪtən/ a metropolitano

mew /mjuː/ n miao m ● vi miagolare

Mexican /ˈmeksɪkən/ a & n messicano, -a mf. '**Mexico** n Messico m

miaow /mɪˈaʊ/ n miao m ● vi miagolare

mice /maɪs/ see **mouse**

mickey /ˈmɪkɪ/ n **take the** ~ **out of** prendere in giro

microbe /ˈmaɪkrəʊb/ n microbo m

micro /ˈmaɪkrəʊ/: ~**chip** n microchip m. ~**computer** n microcomputer m. ~**film** n microfilm m. ~**phone** microfono m. ~**processor** n microprocesso-

re *m*. **~scope** *n* microscopio *m*.
~scopic /-'skɒpɪk/ *a* microscopico. **~wave** *n* microonda *f*; (*oven*) forno *m* a microonde

mid /mɪd/ *a* **~ May** metà maggio; **in ~ air** a mezz'aria

midday /mɪd'deɪ/ *n* mezzogiorno *m*

middle /'mɪdl/ *a* di centro; **the M~ Ages** il medioevo; **the ~ class[es]** la classe media; **the M~ East** il Medio Oriente ● *n* mezzo *m*; **in the ~ of** (*room, floor etc*) in mezzo a; **in the ~ of the night** nel pieno della notte, a notte piena

middle: **~-aged** *a* di mezza età. **~class** *a* borghese. **~man** *n* Comm intermediario *m*

middling /'mɪdlɪŋ/ *a* discreto

midge /mɪdʒ/ *n* moscerino *m*

midget /'mɪdʒɪt/ *n* nano, -a *mf*

Midlands /'mɪdləndz/ *npl* **the ~** l'Inghilterra *fsg* centrale

'midnight *n* mezzanotte *f*

midriff /'mɪdrɪf/ *n* diaframma *m*

midst /mɪdst/ *n* **in the ~ of** in mezzo a; **in our ~** fra di noi, in mezzo a noi

mid: **~summer** *n* mezza estate *f* **~way** *adv* a metà strada. **~wife** *n* ostetrica *f*. **~wifery** /-wɪfrɪ/ *n* ostetricia *f*. **~'winter** *n* pieno inverno *m*

might¹ /maɪt/ *v aux* I **~** potrei; **will you come? – I ~** vieni? – può darsi; **it ~ be true** potrebbe essere vero; **I ~ as well stay** potrei anche restare; **you ~ have drowned** avresti potuto affogare; **you ~ have said so!** avresti potuto dirlo!

might² *n* potere *m*

mighty /'maɪtɪ/ *a* (**-ier, -iest**) potente ● *adv* fam molto

migraine /'miːɡreɪn/ *n* emicrania *f*

migrant /'maɪɡrənt/ *a* migratore ● *n* (*bird*) migratore, -trice *mf*; (*person: for work*) emigrante *mf*

migrat|e /maɪ'ɡreɪt/ *vi* migrare. **~ion** /-'ɡreɪʃn/ *n* migrazione *f*

mike /maɪk/ *n* fam microfono *f*

Milan /mɪ'læn/ *n* Milano *f*

mild /maɪld/ *a* (*weather*) mite; (*person*) dolce; (*flavour*) delicato; (*illness*) leggero

mildew /'mɪldjuː/ *n* muffa *f*

mild|ly /'maɪldlɪ/ *adv* moderatamente; (*say*) dolcemente; **to put it ~ly** a dir poco, senza esagerazione. **~ness** *n* (*of person, words*) dolcezza *f*; (*of weather*) mitezza *f*

mile /maɪl/ *n* miglio *m* (= 1,6 km); **~s nicer** fam molto più bello

mile|age /-ɪdʒ/ *n* chilometraggio *m*. **~stone** *n* pietra *f* miliare

militant /'mɪlɪtənt/ *a* & *n* militante *mf*

military /'mɪlɪtrɪ/ *a* militare. **~ service** *n* servizio *m* militare

militate /'mɪlɪteɪt/ *vi* **~ against** opporsi a

militia /mɪ'lɪʃə/ *n* milizia *f*

milk /mɪlk/ *n* latte *m* ● *vt* mungere

milk: **~man** *n* lattaio *m*. **~ shake** *n* frappé *m inv*

milky /'mɪlkɪ/ *a* (**-ier, -iest**) latteo; (*tea etc*) con molto latte. **M~ Way** *n* Astr Via *f* Lattea

mill /mɪl/ *n* mulino *m*; (*factory*) fabbrica *f*; (*for coffee etc*) macinino *m* ● *vt* macinare (*grain*). **mill about, mill around** *vi* brulicare

millennium /mɪ'lenɪəm/ *n* millennio *m*

miller /'mɪlə(r)/ *n* mugnaio *m*

milli|gram /'mɪlɪ-/ *n* milligrammo *m*. **~metre** *n* millimetro *m*

million /'mɪljən/ *n* milione *m*; **a ~ pounds** un milione di sterline. **~aire** /-'neə(r)/ *n* miliardario, -a *mf*

'millstone *n* fig peso *m*

mime /maɪm/ *n* mimo *m* ● *vt* mimare

mimic /'mɪmɪk/ *n* imitatore, -trice *mf* ● *vt* (*pt/pp* **mimicked**) imitare. **~ry** *n* mimetismo *m*

mimosa /mɪ'məʊzə/ *n* mimosa *f*

mince /mɪns/ *n* carne *f* tritata ● *vt* Culin tritare; **not ~ one's words** parlare senza mezzi termini

mince: **~meat** *n* miscuglio *m* di frutta secca; **make ~meat of** fig demolire. **~'pie** *n* pasticcino *m* a base di frutta secca

mincer /'mɪnsə(r)/ *n* tritacarne *m inv*

mind /maɪnd/ *n* mente *f*; (sanity) ragione *f*; **to my** ~ a mio parere; **give sb a piece of one's** ~ dire chiaro e tondo a qcno quello che si pensa; **make up one's** ~ decidersi; **have sth in** ~ avere qcsa in mente; **bear sth in** ~ tenere presente qcsa; **have something on one's** ~ essere preoccupato; **have a good** ~ **to** avere una grande voglia di; **I have changed my** ~ ho cambiato idea; **in two** ~**s** sei indeciso; **are you out of your** ~? sei diventato matto? ● *vt* (look after) occuparsi di; **I don't** ~ **the noise** il rumore non mi dà fastidio; **I don't** ~ **what we do** non mi importa quello che facciamo; ~ **the step!** attenzione al gradino!; **I don't** ~ non mi importa; **never** ~! non importa!; **do you** ~ **if...?** ti dispiace se...? **mind out** *vi* ~ **out!** [fai] attenzione!

minder /'maɪndə(r)/ *n* (Br: bodyguard) gorilla *m inv*; (for child) baby-sitter *mf inv*

mind|ful *a* ~**ful of** attento a. ~**less** *a* noncurante

mine[1] /maɪn/ *poss pron* il mio *m*, la mia *f*, i miei *mpl*, le mie *fpl*; **a friend of** ~ un mio amico; **friends of** ~ dei miei amici; **that is** ~ questo è mio; (as opposed to yours) questo è il mio

mine[2] *n* miniera *f*; (explosive) mina *f* ● *vt* estrarre; *Mil* minare. ~ **detector** *n* rivelatore *m* di mine. ~**field** *n* campo *m* minato

miner /'maɪnə(r)/ *n* minatore *m*

mineral /'mɪnərəl/ *n* minerale *m* ● *a* minerale. ~ **water** *n* acqua *f* minerale

minesweeper /'maɪn-/ *n* dragamine *m inv*

mingle /'mɪŋgl/ *vi* ~ **with** mescolarsi a

mini /'mɪnɪ/ *n* (skirt) mini *f*

miniature /'mɪnɪtʃə(r)/ *a* in miniatura ● *n* miniatura *f*

mini|bus /'mɪnɪ-/ *n* minibus *m*, pulmino *m*. ~**cab** *n* taxi *m inv*

minim /'mɪnɪm/ *n* Mus minima *f*

minim|al /'mɪnɪml/ *a* minimo. ~**ize** *vt* minimizzare. ~**um** *n* (pl -ima) minimo *m* ● *a* minimo; **ten minutes** ~**um** minimo dieci minuti

mining /'maɪnɪŋ/ *n* estrazione *f* ● *a* estrattivo

miniskirt /'mɪnɪ-/ *n* minigonna *f*

minist|er /'mɪnɪstə(r)/ *n* ministro *m*; Relig pastore *m*. ~**erial** /-'stɪərɪəl/ *a* ministeriale

ministry /'mɪnɪstrɪ/ *n* Pol ministero *m*; **the** ~ Relig il ministero sacerdotale

mink /mɪŋk/ *n* visone *m*

minor /'maɪnə(r)/ *a* minore ● *n* minorenne *mf*

minority /maɪ'nɒrətɪ/ *n* minoranza *f*; (age) minore età *f*

minor road *n* strada *f* secondaria

mint[1] /mɪnt/ *n fam* patrimonio *m* ● *a* **in** ~ **condition** in condizione perfetta

mint[2] (herb) menta *f*

minus /'maɪnəs/ *prep* meno; (fam: without) senza ● *n* ~ [**sign**] meno *m*

minute[1] /'mɪnɪt/ *n* minuto *m*; **in a** ~ (shortly) in un minuto; ~**s** *pl* (of meeting) verbale *msg*

minute[2] /maɪ'nju:t/ *a* minuto; (precise) minuzioso

mirac|le /'mɪrəkl/ *n* miracolo *m*. ~**ulous** /-'rækjʊləs/ *a* miracoloso

mirage /'mɪrɑ:ʒ/ *n* miraggio *m*

mirror /'mɪrə(r)/ *n* specchio *m* ● *vt* rispecchiare

mirth /mɜ:θ/ *n* ilarità *f*

misad'venture /mɪs-/ *n* disavventura *f*

misanthropist /mɪ'zænθrəpɪst/ *n* misantropo, -a *mf*

misappre'hension *n* malinteso *m*; **be under a** ~ avere frainteso

misbe'have *vi* comportarsi male

miscalculate | mix

mis'calcu|late vt/i calcolare male. **~lation** n calcolo m sbagliato

'miscarriage n aborto m spontaneo; **~ of justice** errore m giudiziario. **mis'carry** vi abortire

miscellaneous /misə'leiniəs/ a assortito

mischief /'mistʃif/ n malefatta f; ⟨harm⟩ danno m

mischievous /'mistʃivəs/ a ⟨naughty⟩ birichino; ⟨malicious⟩ dannoso

miscon'ception n concetto m erroneo

mis'conduct n cattiva condotta f

misde'meanour n reato m

miser /'maizə(r)/ n avaro m

miserab|le /'mizrəbl/ a ⟨unhappy⟩ infelice; ⟨wretched⟩ miserabile; ⟨fig: weather⟩ deprimente. **~y** adv ⟨live, fail⟩ miseramente; ⟨say⟩ tristemente

miserly /'maizəli/ a avaro; ⟨amount⟩ ridicolo

misery /'mizəri/ n miseria f; ⟨fam: person⟩ piagnone, -a mf

mis'fire vi ⟨gun:⟩ far cilecca; ⟨plan etc:⟩ non riuscire

'misfit n disadattato, -a mf

mis'fortune n sfortuna f

mis'givings npl dubbi mpl

mis'guided a fuorviato

mishap /'mishæp/ n disavventura f

misin'terpret vt fraintendere

mis'judge vt giudicar male; ⟨estimate wrongly⟩ valutare male

mis'lay vt (pt/pp **-laid**) smarrire

mis'lead vt (pt/pp **-led**) fuorviare. **~ing** a fuorviante

mis'manage vt amministrare male. **~ment** n cattiva amministrazione f

misnomer /mis'nəumə(r)/ n termine m improprio

'misprint n errore m di stampa

mis'quote vt citare erroneamente

misrepre'sent vt rappresentare male

Miss n (pl **-es**) signorina f

miss /mis/ n colpo m mancato ● vt

⟨fail to hit or find⟩ mancare; perdere ⟨train, bus, class⟩; ⟨feel the loss of⟩ sentire la mancanza di; I **~ed that part** ⟨failed to notice⟩ mi è sfuggita quella parte ● vi **but he ~ed** ⟨failed to hit⟩ ma l'ha mancato. **miss out** vt saltare, omettere

misshapen /mis'ʃeipən/ a malformato

missile /'misail/ n missile m

missing /'misiŋ/ a mancante; ⟨person⟩ scomparso; Mil disperso; **be ~** essere introvabile

mission /'miʃn/ n missione f

missionary /'miʃənri/ n missionario, -a mf

mis'spell vt (pt/pp **-spelled**, **-spelt**) sbagliare l'ortografia di

mist /mist/ n ⟨fog⟩ foschia f ● **mist up** vi appannarsi, annebbiarsi

mistake /mi'steik/ n sbaglio m; **by ~** per sbaglio ● vt (pt mistook, pp mistaken) sbagliare ⟨road, house⟩; fraintendere ⟨meaning, words⟩; **~ for** prendere per

mistaken /mi'steikən/ a sbagliato; **be ~** sbagliarsi; **~ identity** errore m di persona. **~ly** adv erroneamente

mistletoe /'misltəu/ n vischio m

mistress /'mistris/ n padrona f; ⟨teacher⟩ maestra f; ⟨lover⟩ amante f

mis'trust n sfiducia f ● vt non aver fiducia in

misty /'misti/ a (-ier, -iest) nebbioso

misunder'stand vt (pt/pp **-stood**) fraintendere. **~ing** n malinteso m

misuse¹ /mis'ju:z/ vt usare male

misuse² /mis'ju:s/ n cattivo uso m

mite /mait/ n ⟨child⟩ piccino, -a mf

mitigat|e /'mitigeit/ vt attenuare. **~ing** a attenuante

mitten /'mitn/ n manopola f, muffola f

mix /miks/ n ⟨combination⟩ mescolanza f; Culin miscuglio m; ⟨ready-made⟩ preparato m ● vt mischiare ● vi mischiarsi; ⟨person:⟩ inserirsi; **~ with** ⟨associate with⟩ frequentare, un (*papers*); (*confuse, mistake for*) confondere

mixed /mɪkst/ *a* misto; **~ up** (*person*) confuso

mixer /ˈmɪksə(r)/ *n* Culin frullatore *m*, mixer *m inv*; **he's a good ~** è un tipo socievole

mixture /ˈmɪkstʃə(r)/ *n* mescolanza *f*; (*medicine*) sciroppo *m*; Culin miscela *f*

'mix-up *n* (*confusion*) confusione *f*; (*mistake*) pasticcio *m*

moan /məʊn/ *n* lamento *m* ● *vi* lamentarsi; (*complain*) lagnarsi

moat /məʊt/ *n* fossato *m*

mob /mɒb/ *n* folla *f*; (*rabble*) gentaglia *f*; (*fam: gang*) banda *f* ● *vt* (*pt/pp* mobbed) assalire

mobile /ˈməʊbaɪl/ *a* mobile ● *n* composizione *f* mobile. **~ 'home** *n* casa *f* roulotte. **~ [phone]** *n* [telefono *m*] cellulare *m*

mobility /məˈbɪlətɪ/ *n* mobilità *f*

mock /mɒk/ *a* finto ● *vt* canzonare. **~ery** *n* derisione *f*

'mock-up *n* modello *m* in scala

mode /məʊd/ *n* modo *m*; Comput modalità *f*

model /ˈmɒdl/ *n* modello *m*; [**fashion**] **~** indossatore, -trice *mf*, modello, -a *mf* ● *a* (*yacht, plane*) in miniatura; (*pupil, husband*) esemplare; modello *f* ● *v* (*pt/pp* modelled) ● *vt* indossare (*clothes*) ● *vi* fare il/la indossatore, -trice *mf*; (*for artist*) posare

modem /ˈməʊdem/ *n* modem *m inv*

moderate¹ /ˈmɒdəreɪt/ *vt* moderare ● *vi* moderarsi

moderate² /ˈmɒdərət/ *a* moderato ● *n* Pol moderato, -a *mf*. **~ly** *adv* (*drink, speak etc*) moderatamente; (*good, bad etc*) relativamente

moderation /mɒdəˈreɪʃn/ *n* moderazione *f*; **in ~** con moderazione

modern /ˈmɒdn/ *a* moderno. **~ize** *vt* modernizzare

modest /ˈmɒdɪst/ *a* modesto. **~y** *n* modestia *f*

modicum /ˈmɒdɪkəm/ *n* **a ~ of** po' di

modif|ication /mɒdɪfɪˈkeɪʃn/ *n* modificazione *f*. **~y** /ˈmɒdɪfaɪ/ *vt* (*pt/pp* **-fied**) modificare

module /ˈmɒdjuːl/ *n* modulo *m*

moist /mɔɪst/ *a* umido

moisten /ˈmɔɪsn/ *vt* inumidire

moistur|e /ˈmɔɪstʃə(r)/ *n* umidità *f*. **~izer** *n* [crema *f*] idratante *m*

molar /ˈməʊlə(r)/ *n* molare *m*

molasses /məˈlæsɪz/ *n* Am melassa *f*

mole¹ /məʊl/ *n* (*on face etc*) neo *m*

mole² *n* Zool talpa *f*

molecule /ˈmɒlɪkjuːl/ *n* molecola *f*

molest /məˈlest/ *vt* molestare

mollycoddle /ˈmɒlɪkɒdl/ *vt* tenere nella bambagia

molten /ˈməʊltən/ *a* fuso

mom /mɒm/ *n* Am fam mamma *f*

moment /ˈməʊmənt/ *n* momento *m*; **at the ~** in questo momento. **~arily** *adv* momentaneamente. **~ary** *a* momentaneo

momentous /məˈmentəs/ *a* molto importante

momentum /məˈmentəm/ *n* impeto *m*

monarch /ˈmɒnək/ *n* monarca *m*. **~y** *n* monarchia *f*

monast|ery /ˈmɒnəstrɪ/ *n* monastero *m*. **~ic** /məˈnæstɪk/ *a* monastico

Monday /ˈmʌndeɪ/ *n* lunedì *m inv*

monetary /ˈmʌnɪtrɪ/ *a* monetario

money /ˈmʌnɪ/ *n* denaro *m*. **~-box** *n* salvadanaio *m*. **~-lender** *n* usuraio *m*

mongrel /ˈmʌŋɡrəl/ *n* bastardo *m*

monitor /ˈmɒnɪtə(r)/ *n* Techn monitor *m inv* ● *vt* controllare

monk /mʌŋk/ *n* monaco *m*

monkey /ˈmʌŋkɪ/ *n* scimmia *f*. **~-nut** *n* nocciolina *f* americana. **~-wrench** *n* chiave *f* inglese a rullino

mono /ˈmɒnəʊ/ *n* mono *m*

monogram /ˈmɒnəɡræm/ *n* monogramma *m*

monologue /ˈmɒnəlɒg/ n monologo m

monopol|ize /məˈnɒpəlaɪz/ vt monopolizzare. **~y** n monopolio m

monosyllabic /ˌmɒnəsɪˈlæbɪk/ a monosillabico

monotone /ˈmɒnətəʊn/ n **speak in a ~** parlare con tono monotono

monoton|ous /məˈnɒtənəs/ a monotono. **~y** n monotonia f

monsoon /mɒnˈsuːn/ n monsone m

monster /ˈmɒnstə(r)/ n mostro m

monstrosity /mɒnˈstrɒsətɪ/ n mostruosità f

monstrous /ˈmɒnstrəs/ a mostruoso

month /mʌnθ/ n mese m. **~ly** a mensile ● adv mensilmente ● n (periodical) mensile m

monument /ˈmɒnjʊmənt/ n monumento m. **~al** /-ˈmentl/ a fig monumentale

moo /muː/ n muggito m ● vi (pt/pp **mooed**) muggire

mooch /muːtʃ/ vi **~ about** fam gironzolare (**the house** per casa)

mood /muːd/ n umore m; **be in a good/bad ~** essere di buon/cattivo umore; **be in the ~ for** essere in vena di

moody /ˈmuːdɪ/ a (-ier, -iest) (variable) lunatico; (bad-tempered) di malumore

moon /muːn/ n luna f. **over the ~** fam al settimo cielo

moon: **~light** n chiaro m di luna ● vi fam lavorare in nero. **~lit** a illuminato dalla luna

moor[1] /mʊə(r)/ n brughiera f

moor[2] vt Naut ormeggiare

moose /muːs/ n (pl **moose**) alce m

moot /muːt/ a **it's a ~ point** è un punto controverso

mop /mɒp/ n straccio m (per i pavimenti); **~ of hair** zazzera f ● vt (pt/pp **mopped**) lavare con lo straccio. **mop up** vt (dry) asciugare con lo straccio; (clean) pulire con lo straccio

mope /məʊp/ vi essere depresso

moped /ˈməʊped/ n ciclomotore m

moral /ˈmɒrəl/ a morale ● n morale f. **~ly** adv moralmente. **~s** pl moralità f

morale /məˈrɑːl/ n morale m

morality /məˈrælətɪ/ n moralità f

morbid /ˈmɔːbɪd/ a morboso

more /mɔː(r)/ a più; **a few ~ books** un po' più di libri; **some ~ tea?** ancora un po' di tè?; **there's no ~ bread** non c'è più pane; **there are no ~ apples** non ci sono più mele; **one ~ word and...** ancora una parola e... ● pron di più; **would you like some ~?** ne vuoi ancora?; **no ~, thank you** non ne voglio più, grazie ● adv più; **~ interesting** più interessante; **~ [and] quickly** [sempre] più veloce; **~ than** più di; **I don't love him any ~** no lo amo più; **once ~** ancora una volta; **~ or less** più o meno; **the ~ I see him, the ~ I like him** più lo vedo, più mi piace

moreover /mɔːrˈəʊvə(r)/ adv inoltre

morgue /mɔːg/ n obitorio m

moribund /ˈmɒrɪbʌnd/ a moribondo

morning /ˈmɔːnɪŋ/ n mattino m, mattina f; **in the ~** del mattino; (tomorrow) domani mattina

Morocc|o /məˈrɒkəʊ/ n Marocco m ● a **~an** a & n marocchino, -a mf

moron /ˈmɔːrɒn/ n fam deficiente mf

morose /məˈrəʊs/ a scontroso

morphine /ˈmɔːfiːn/ n morfina f

Morse /mɔːs/ n **~ [code]** [codice m] Morse m

morsel /ˈmɔːsl/ n (food) boccone m

mortal /ˈmɔːtl/ a & n mortale mf. **~ity** /mɔːˈtælətɪ/ n mortalità f. **~ly** adv (wounded, offended) a morte; (afraid) da morire

mortar /ˈmɔːtə(r)/ n mortaio m

mortgage /ˈmɔːgɪdʒ/ n mutuo m; (on property) ipoteca f ● vt ipotecare

mortuary /ˈmɔːtjʊərɪ/ n camera f mortuaria

mosaic /məʊˈzeɪɪk/ n mosaico m

Moscow /ˈmɒskəʊ/ n Mosca f

Moslem /ˈmɒzlɪm/ a & n musulmano, -a mf

mosque /mɒsk/ n moschea f

mosquito /mɒsˈkiːtəʊ/ n (pl -es) zanzara f

moss /mɒs/ n muschio m. ~y a muschioso

most /məʊst/ a (majority) la maggior parte di; **for the ~ part** per lo più ● adv più, maggiormente; (very) estremamente, molto; **the ~ interesting day** la giornata più interessante; **a ~ interesting day** una giornata estremamente interessante; **the ~ beautiful woman in the world** la donna più bella del mondo; ~ **unlikely** veramente improbabile ● pron ~ **of them** la maggior parte di loro; **at [the] ~** al massimo; **make the ~ of** sfruttare al massimo; ~ **of the time** la maggior parte del tempo. ~**ly** adv per lo più

MOT n revisione f obbligatoria di autoveicoli

motel /məʊˈtel/ n motel m inv

moth /mɒθ/ n falena f; (clothes-) ~ tarma f

moth: ~**ball** n pallina f di naftalina. ~**-eaten** a tarmato

mother /ˈmʌðə(r)/ n madre f; **M~'s Day** la festa della mamma ● vt fare da madre a

mother: ~**board** n Comput scheda f madre. ~**hood** n maternità f. ~**-in-law** n (pl ~**s-in-law**) suocera f. ~**ly** a materno. ~**-of-pearl** n madreperla f. ~**-to-be** n futura mamma f. ~ **tongue** n madrelingua f

mothproof /ˈmɒθ-/ a antitarmico

motif /məʊˈtiːf/ n motivo m

motion /ˈməʊʃn/ n moto m; (proposal) mozione f; (gesture) gesto m ● vt/i ~ [**to**] **sb to come in** fare segno a qcno di entrare. ~**less** a immobile. ~**lessly** adv senza alcun movimento

motivat|e /ˈməʊtɪveɪt/ vt motivare. ~**ion** /-ˈveɪʃn/ n motivazione f

motive /ˈməʊtɪv/ n movente m

motley /ˈmɒtlɪ/ a disparato

motor /ˈməʊtə(r)/ n motore m; (car) macchina f ● a a motore; Anat motore ● vi andare in macchina

Motorail /ˈməʊtəreɪl/ n treno m per trasporto auto

motor: ~ **bike** n fam moto f inv. ~ **boat** n motoscafo m. ~**cade** /-keɪd/ n Am corteo m di auto. ~ **car** n automobile f. ~ **cycle** n motocicletta f. ~**-cyclist** n motociclista mf. ~**ing** n automobilismo m. ~**ist** n automobilista mf. ~ **racing** n corse fpl automobilistiche. ~ **vehicle** n autoveicolo m. ~**way** n autostrada f

mottled /ˈmɒtld/ a chiazzato

motto /ˈmɒtəʊ/ n (pl -oes) motto m

mould[1] /məʊld/ n (fungus) muffa f

mould[2] n stampo m ● vt foggiare; fig formare. ~**ing** n Archit cornice f

mouldy /ˈməʊldɪ/ a ammuffito; (fam: worthless) ridicolo

moult /məʊlt/ vi (bird:) fare la muta; (animal:) perdere il pelo

mound /maʊnd/ n mucchio m; (hill) collinetta f

mount[1] /maʊnt/ n (horse) cavalcatura f; (of jewel, photo, picture) sta mf. ~**ing** n automobilismo m.

mount[2] /maʊnt/ n (horse) cavalcatura f; (of jewel, photo, picture) montatura f; (of horse) salire su (bicycle); incastonare (jewel); incorniciare (photo, picture) ● vi aumentare

mount up vi aumentare

mountain /ˈmaʊntɪn/ n montagna f. ~ **bike** n mountain bike f inv

mountaineer /maʊntɪˈnɪə(r)/ n alpinista mf. ~**ing** n alpinismo m

mountainous /ˈmaʊntɪnəs/ a montagnoso

mourn /mɔːn/ vt lamentare ● vi ~ **for** piangere la morte di. ~**er** n persona f che participa a un funerale. ~**ful** a triste. ~**ing** n in ~**ing** in lutto

mouse /maʊs/ n (pl mice) topo m;

Comput mouse *m inv.* **~trap** *n* trappola *f* [per topi]

mousse /muːs/ *n Culin* mousse *f inv*

moustache /məˈstɑːʃ/ *n* baffi *mpl*

mousy /ˈmaʊsɪ/ *a* ⟨colour⟩ grigio topo

mouth¹ /maʊð/ *vt* ~ sth dire qcsa silenziosamente muovendo solamente le labbra

mouth² /maʊθ/ *n* bocca *f*; ⟨of river⟩ foce *f*

mouth: **~ful** *n* boccone *m*. **~-organ** *n* armonica *f* (a bocca). **~piece** *n* imboccatura *f*; (fig: person) portavoce *m inv*. **~ watering** *a* che fa venire l'acquolina in bocca

movable /ˈmuːvəbl/ *a* mobile

move /muːv/ *n* mossa *f*; (moving house) trasloco *m*; **on the ~** in movimento; **get a ~ on** fam darsi una mossa ●*vt* muovere; (emotionally) commuovere; spostare ⟨car, furniture⟩; (transfer) trasferire; (propose) proporre ●*vi* muoversi; (move house) traslocare ●*vi* muoversi; (move house) traslocare. **move along** *vi* andare avanti ●*vt* muovere in avanti. **move away** *vi* allontanarsi; (move house) trasferirsi ●*vt* allontanare. **move forward** *vi* avanzare ●*vt* spostare avanti. **move in** *vi* (to a house) trasferirsi. **move off** *vi* ⟨vehicle:⟩ muoversi. **move out** *vi* (of house) andare via. **move over** *vi* spostarsi ●*vt* spostare. **move up** *vi* muoversi; (advance, increase) avanzare

movement /ˈmuːvmənt/ *n* movimento *m*

movie /ˈmuːvɪ/ *n* film *m inv*; **go to the ~s** andare al cinema

moving /ˈmuːvɪŋ/ *a* mobile; (touching) commovente

mow /məʊ/ *vt* (pt mowed, pp mown or mowed) tagliare ⟨lawn⟩. **mow down** *vt* (destroy) sterminare

mower /ˈməʊə(r)/ *n* tosaerbe *m inv*

MP *n abbr* Member of Parliament

Mr /ˈmɪstə(r)/ *n* (pl **Messrs**) Signor *m*

Mrs /ˈmɪsɪz/ *n* Signora *f*

Ms /mɪz/ *n* Signora *f* (modo *m* formale di rivolgersi ad una donna quando non si vuole connotarla come sposata o nubile)

much /mʌtʃ/ *a, adv & pron* molto; **~** as per quanto; **I love you just as ~ as before/him** ti amo quanto prima/lui; **as ~ as £5 million** ben cinque milioni di sterline; **as ~ as that** così tanto; **very ~** tantissimo, moltissimo; **~ the same** quasi uguale

muck /mʌk/ *n* (dirt) sporcizia *f*; (farming) letame *m*; (fam: filth) porcheria *f*. **muck about** *vi fam* perder tempo; **~ about with** trafficare con. **muck up** *vt fam* rovinare; (make dirty) sporcare

mucky /ˈmʌkɪ/ *a* (-ier, -iest) sudicio

mucus /ˈmjuːkəs/ *n* muco *m*

mud /mʌd/ *n* fango *m*

muddle /ˈmʌdl/ *n* disordine *m*; (mix-up) confusione *f* ●*vt* ~ **[up]** confondere ⟨dates⟩

muddy /ˈmʌdɪ/ *a* (-ier, -iest) ⟨path⟩ fangoso; ⟨shoes⟩ infangato

mudguard /ˈmʌdɡɑːd/ *n* parafango *m*

muesli /ˈmuːzlɪ/ *n* muesli *m inv*

muffle /ˈmʌfl/ *vt* smorzare ⟨sound⟩. **muffle** **[up]** *vt* (for warmth) imbaccucare

muffler /ˈmʌflə(r)/ *n* sciarpa *f*; Am Auto marmitta *f*

mug¹ /mʌɡ/ *n* tazza *f*; (for beer) boccale *m*; (fam: face) muso *m*; (fam: simpleton) pollo *m*

mug² *vt* (pt/pp mugged) aggredire e derubare. **~ger** *n* assalitore, -trice *mf*. **~ging** *n* aggressione *f* per furto

muggy /ˈmʌɡɪ/ *a* (-ier, -iest) afoso

mule /mjuːl/ *n* mulo *m*

mull /mʌl/ *vt* ~ **over** rimuginare su

mulled /mʌld/ *a* ~ **wine** vin brulé *m inv*

multi /ˈmʌltɪ/: **~coloured** *a* vario-

pinto. **~lingual** /-'lɪŋgwəl/ a
multilingue *inv.* **~media** n multimedia *mpl* ● a multimediale.
~'national a multinazionale ● n
multinazionale f

multiple /'mʌltɪpl/ a multiplo
multiplication /mʌltɪplɪ'keɪʃn/ n
moltiplicazione f
multiply /'mʌltɪplaɪ/ v (pt/pp -ied)
● vt moltiplicare (by per) ● vi
moltiplicarsi
multi-storey a ~ car park parcheggio m a più piani
mum[1] /mʌm/ a keep ~ fam non
aprire bocca
mum[2] n fam mamma f
mumble /'mʌmbl/ vt/i borbottare
mummy[1] /'mʌmɪ/ n fam mamma f
mummy[2] n Archaeol mummia f
mumps /mʌmps/ n orecchioni
mpl
munch /mʌntʃ/ vt/i sgranocchiare
mundane /mʌn'deɪn/ a (everyday)
banale
municipal /mju:'nɪsɪpl/ a municipale
mural /'mjʊərəl/ n dipinto m murale
murder /'mɜ:də(r)/ n assassinio m
● vt assassinare; (fam: ruin) massacrare. **~er** n assassino, -a mf.
~ous /-rəs/ a omicida
murky /'mɜ:kɪ/ a (-ier, -iest) oscuro
murmur /'mɜ:mə(r)/ n mormorio
m ● vt/i mormorare
muscle /'mʌsl/ n muscolo m
● **muscle in** n sl intromettersi
(on in)
muscular /'mʌskjʊlə(r)/ a muscolare; (strong) muscoloso
muse /mju:z/ vi meditare (on su)
museum /mju:'zɪəm/ n museo m
mushroom /'mʌʃrʊm/ n fungo m
● vi fig spuntare come funghi
music /'mju:zɪk/ n musica f;
(written) spartito m
musical /'mju:zɪkl/ a musicale; (person) dotato di senso musicale
● n commedia f musicale. **~ box** n

carillon m inv. **~ instrument** n
strumento m musicale
music: **~ box** n carillon m inv. **~
centre** n impianto m stereo; **'~-hall**
n teatro m di varietà
musician /mju:'zɪʃn/ n musicista
mf
Muslim /'mʊzlɪm/ a & n musulmano, -a mf
mussel /'mʌsl/ n cozza f
must /mʌst/ v aux (solo al presente)
dovere; **you ~ not be late** non
devi essere in ritardo; **she ~ have
finished by now** (probability)
deve aver finito ormai ● n a ~ fam
una cosa da non perdere
mustard /'mʌstəd/ n senape f
musty /'mʌstɪ/ a (-ier, -iest) stantio
mutation /mju:'teɪʃn/ n Biol mutazione f
mute /mju:t/ a muto
muted /'mju:tɪd/ a smorzato
mutilat|e /'mju:tɪleɪt/ vt mutilare.
~ion /-'leɪʃn/ n mutilazione f
mutin|ous /'mju:tɪnəs/ a ammutinato. **~y** n ammutinamento m
● vi (pt/pp -ied) ammutinarsi
mutter /'mʌtə(r)/ vt/i borbottare
mutton /'mʌtn/ n carne f di montone
mutual /'mju:tjʊəl/ a reciproco;
(fam: common) comune. **~ly** adv
reciprocamente
muzzle /'mʌzl/ n (of animal) muso
m; (of firearm) bocca f; (for dog)
museruola f ● vt fig mettere il bavaglio a
my /maɪ/ a il mio, la mia f, i miei
mpl, le mie fpl; **my mother/father**
mia madre/mio padre
myself /maɪ'self/ pron (reflexive)
mi; (emphatic) me stesso; (after
prep) me; **I've seen it ~** l'ho visto
io stesso; **by ~** da solo; **I thought
to ~** ho pensato tra me e me; **I'm
proud of ~** sono fiero di me
mysterious /mɪ'stɪərɪəs/ a misterioso. **~ly** adv misteriosamente
mystery /'mɪstərɪ/ n mistero m; **~
[story]** racconto m del mistero

mystic|[al] /ˈmɪstɪk[l]/ *a* mistico.
~cism /-sɪzm/ *n* misticismo *m*
mystified /ˈmɪstɪfaɪd/ *a* disorientato
mystify /ˈmɪstɪfaɪ/ *vt* (*pt/pp* **-ied**) disorientare
mystique /mɪˈstiːk/ *n* mistica *f*
myth /mɪθ/ *n* mito *m*. **~ical** *a* mitico
mythology /mɪˈθɒlədʒɪ/ *n* mitologia *f*

....

Nn

....

nab /næb/ *vt* (*pt/pp* **nabbed**) *fam* beccare
naff /næf/ *a* Br *fam* banale
nag[1] /næg/ *n* (*horse*) ronzino *m*
nag[2] (*pt/pp* **nagged**) *vt* assillare ● *vi* essere insistente ● *n* (*person*) brontolone, -a *mf*. **~ging** *a* (*pain*) persistente
nail /neɪl/ *n* chiodo *m*; (*of finger, toe*) unghia *f* ● **nail down** *vt* inchiodare; **~ sb down to a time/price** far fissare a qcno un'ora/un prezzo
nail: ~brush *n* spazzolino *m* da unghie. **~file** *n* limetta *f* da unghie. **~ polish** *n* smalto *m* [per unghie]. **~ scissors** *npl* forbicine *fpl* da unghie. **~ varnish** *n* smalto *m* [per unghie]
naïve /naɪˈiːv/ *a* ingenuo. **~ty** /-ətɪ/ *n* ingenuità *f*
naked /ˈneɪkɪd/ *a* nudo; **with the ~ eye** a occhio nudo
name /neɪm/ *n* nome *m*; **what's your ~?** come ti chiami?; **my ~ is Matthew** mi chiamo Matthew; **I know her by ~** la conosco di nome; **by the ~ of Bates** di nome Bates; **call sb ~s** *fam* insultare qcno ● *vt* (*to position*) nominare; chiamare (*baby*); (*identify*) citare; **be ~d after** essere chiamato col

nome di. **~less** *a* senza nome. **~ly** *adv* cioè
name: ~plate *n* targhetta *f*. **~sake** *n* omonimo, -a *mf*
nanny /ˈnænɪ/ *n* bambinaia *f*. **~goat** *n* capra *f*
nap /næp/ *n* pisolino *m*; **have a ~** fare un pisolino ● *vi* (*pt/pp* **napped**) **catch sb ~ping** cogliere qcno alla sprovvista
nape /neɪp/ *n* **~ [of the neck]** nuca *f*
napkin /ˈnæpkɪn/ *n* tovagliolo *m*
Naples /ˈneɪplz/ *n* Napoli *f*
nappy /ˈnæpɪ/ *n* pannolino *m*
narcotic /nɑːˈkɒtɪk/ *a & n* narcotico *m*
narrat|e /nəˈreɪt/ *vt* narrare. **~ion** /-eɪʃn/ *n* narrazione *f*
narrative /ˈnærətɪv/ *a* narrativo ● *n* narrazione *f*
narrator /nəˈreɪtə(r)/ *n* narratore, -trice *mf*
narrow /ˈnærəʊ/ *a* stretto; (*fig: views*) ristretto; (*margin, majority*) scarso ● *vi* restringersi. **~ly** *adv* **~ly escape death** evitare la morte per un pelo. **~-minded** *a* di idee ristrette
nasal /ˈneɪzl/ *a* nasale
nastily /ˈnɑːstɪlɪ/ *adv* (*spitefully*) con cattiveria
nasty /ˈnɑːstɪ/ *a* (**-ier, -iest**) (*smell, person, remark*) cattivo; (*injury, situation, weather*) brutto; **turn ~** (*person:*) diventare cattivo
nation /ˈneɪʃn/ *n* nazione *f*
national /ˈnæʃənl/ *a* nazionale ● *n* cittadino, -a *mf*
national: ~ 'anthem *n* inno *m* nazionale. **N~ 'Health Service** *n* Br servizio *m* sanitario. **N~ In'surance** *n* ≈ Previdenza *f* sociale
nationalism /ˈnæʃənəlɪzm/ *n* nazionalismo *m*
nationality /næʃəˈnælətɪ/ *n* nazionalità *f inv*
national|ization /næʃənəlaɪˈzeɪʃn/ *n* nazionalizzazione. **~ize** /ˈnæʃənəlaɪz/ *vt* nazionalizzare.

~ly /ˈnæʃənəlɪ/ *adv* a livello nazionale

'nation-wide /a su scala nazionale

native /ˈneɪtɪv/ a nativo; *(innate)* innato ●*n* nativo, -a *mf*; *(local inhabitant)* abitante *mf* del posto; *(outside Europe)* indigeno, -a *mf*; **she's a ~ of Venice** è originaria di Venezia

native: **~ 'land** *n* paese *m* nativo. **~ 'language** *n* lingua *f* madre

Nativity /nəˈtɪvɪtɪ/ *n* **the ~** la Natività *f*. **~ play** *n* rappresentazione *f* sulla nascita di Gesù

natter /ˈnætə(r)/ *vi fam* chiacchierare

natural /ˈnætʃrəl/ a naturale

natural: **~ 'gas** *n* metano *m*. **~ 'history** *n* storia *f* naturale

naturalist /ˈnætʃ(ə)rəlɪst/ *n* naturalista *mf*

natural|ization /nætʃ(ə)rəlaɪˈzeɪ-ʃn/ *n* naturalizzazione *f*. **~ize** /ˈnætʃ(ə)rəlaɪz/ *vt* naturalizzare

naturally /ˈnætʃ(ə)rəlɪ/ *adv* (*of course*) naturalmente; (*by nature*) per natura

nature /ˈneɪtʃə(r)/ *n* natura *f*; **by ~** per natura. **~ reserve** *n* riserva *f* naturale

naughtily /ˈnɔːtɪlɪ/ *adv* male

naughty /ˈnɔːtɪ/ a (**-ier, -iest**) monello, -a; (*slightly indecent*) spinto

nausea /ˈnɔːzɪə/ *n* nausea *f*

nause|ate /ˈnɔːzɪeɪt/ *vt* nauseare. **~ating** a nauseante. **~ous** /-ɪəs/ a **I feel ~ous** ho la nausea

nautical /ˈnɔːtɪkl/ a nautico. **~ mile** *n* miglio *m* marino

naval /ˈneɪvl/ a navale

nave /neɪv/ *n* navata *f* centrale

navel /ˈneɪvl/ *n* ombelico *m*

navigable /ˈnævɪgəbl/ a navigabile

navig|ate /ˈnævɪgeɪt/ *vi* navigare; *Auto* fare da navigatore ●*vt* navigare su (*river*). **~ion** /-ˈgeɪʃn/ *n* navigazione *f*. **~or** *n* navigatore *m*

navy /ˈneɪvɪ/ *n* marina *f* ● **[blue]** a blu marine *inv* ●*n* blu *m inv* marine

Neapolitan /nɪəˈpɒlɪtən/ a & *n* napoletano, -a *mf*

near /nɪə(r)/ a vicino; *(future)* prossimo; **the ~est bank** la banca più vicina ●*adv* vicino; **draw ~** avvicinarsi; **~ at hand** a portata di mano ● *prep* vicino a; **he was ~ to tears** aveva le lacrime agli occhi ● *vt* avvicinarsi a

near: **~'by** a *adv* vicino. **~ly** *adv* quasi; **it's not ~ly enough** non è per niente sufficiente. **~ness** *n* vicinanza *f*. **~ side** *n* Auto (*wheel*) (*left*) sinistro; (*right*) destro. **~-sighted** a Am miope

neat /niːt/ a (*tidy*) ordinato; (*clever*) efficace; (*undiluted*) liscio. **~ly** *adv* ordinatamente; (*cleverly*) efficacemente. **~ness** *n* (*tidiness*) ordine *m*

necessarily /nesəˈserɪlɪ/ *adv* necessariamente

necessary /ˈnesəsərɪ/ a necessario

necessit|ate /nɪˈsesɪteɪt/ *vt* rendere necessario. **~y** *n* necessità *f inv*

neck /nek/ *n* collo *m*; (*of dress*) colletto *m*; **~ and ~** testa a testa

necklace /ˈneklɪs/ *n* collana *f*

neck: **~line** *n* scollatura *f*. **~tie** *n* cravatta *f*

neé /neɪ/ a = **Brett** nata Brett

need /niːd/ *n* bisogno *m*; **be in ~ of** avere bisogno di; **if ~ be** se ce ne fosse bisogno; **there is a ~ for** c'è bisogno di; **there is no ~ for that** non ce n'è bisogno; **there is no ~ for you to go** non c'è bisogno che tu vada ● *vt* aver bisogno di; **I ~ to know** devo saperlo; **it ~s to be done** bisogna farlo ● *v aux* **you ~ not go** non c'è bisogno che tu vada; **~ I come?** devo [proprio] venire?

needle /ˈniːdl/ *n* ago *m*; (*for knitting*) uncinetto *m*; (*of record player*) puntina *f* ● *vt* (*fam: annoy*) punzecchiare

needless /ˈniːdlɪs/ a inutile

'needlework *n* cucito *m*

needy /'niːdɪ/ a (-ier, -iest) bisognoso

negation /nɪ'geɪʃn/ n negazione f

negative /'negtɪv/ a negativo ● n negazione f; *Phot* negativo m; **in the ~** *Gram* alla forma negativa

neglect /nɪ'glekt/ n trascuratezza f; **state of ~** stato m di abbandono ● vt trascurare; **he ~ed to write** non si è curato di scrivere. **~ed** a trascurato. **~ful** a negligente; **be ~ful of** trascurare

négligée /'neglɪʒeɪ/ n négligé m inv

negligen|ce /'neglɪdʒəns/ n negligenza f. **~t** a negligente

negligible /'neglɪdʒəbl/ a trascurabile

negotiable /nɪ'gəʊʃəbl/ a ⟨road⟩ transitabile; *Comm* negoziabile; **not ~** ⟨cheque⟩ non trasferibile

negotiat|e /nɪ'gəʊʃɪeɪt/ vt negoziare; *Auto* prendere ⟨bend⟩ ● vi negoziare. **~ion** /-'eɪʃn/ n negoziato m. **~or** n negoziatore, -trice mf

Negro /'niːgrəʊ/ a & n (pl **-es**) negro, -a mf

neigh /neɪ/ vi nitrire

neighbour /'neɪbə(r)/ n vicino, -a mf. **~hood** n vicinato m; **in the ~hood of** nei dintorni di; *fig* circa. **~ing** a vicino. **~ly** a amichevole

neither /'naɪðə(r)/ a & pron nessuno dei due, né l'uno né l'altro ● adv **~... nor** né... né ● conj nemmeno, neanche; **~ do/did I** nemmeno io

neon /'niːɒn/ n neon m. **~ light** n luce f al neon

nephew /'nevjuː/ n nipote m

nerve /nɜːv/ n nervo m; (fam: courage) coraggio m; (fam: impudence) faccia f tosta; **lose one's ~** perdersi d'animo. **~-racking** a logorante

nervous /'nɜːvəs/ a nervoso; **he makes me ~** mi mette in agitazione; **be a ~ wreck** avere i nervi a pezzi. **~ breakdown** n esaurimento m nervoso. **~ly** adv nervosamente. **~ness** n nervosismo m; (before important event) tensione f

nervy /'nɜːvɪ/ a (-ier, -iest) nervoso; (Am: impudent) sfacciato

nest /nest/ n nido m ● vi fare il nido. **~-egg** n gruzzolo m

nestle /'nesl/ vi accoccolarsi

net¹ /net/ n rete f ● vt (pt/pp **netted**) ⟨catch⟩ prendere ⟨con la rete⟩

net² a netto ● vt (pt/pp **netted**) incassare un utile netto di

netball n sport m inv femminile, simile a pallacanestro

Netherlands /'neðələndz/ npl **the ~** i Paesi mpl Bassi

netting /'netɪŋ/ n [wire] ~ reticolato m

nettle /'netl/ n ortica f

network n rete f

neuralgia /njʊə'rældʒə/ n nevralgia f

neurolog|ist /njʊə'rɒlədʒɪst/ n neurologo, -a mf

neur|osis /njʊə'rəʊsɪs/ n (pl **-oses** /-siːz/) nevrosi f inv. **~otic** /-'rɒtɪk/ a nevrotico

neuter /'njuːtə(r)/ a *Gram* neutro ● n *Gram* neutro m ● vt sterilizzare

neutral /'njuːtrəl/ a neutro; ⟨country, person⟩ neutrale ● n **in ~** *Auto* in folle. **~ity** /-'trælətɪ/ n neutralità f. **~ize** vt neutralizzare

never /'nevə(r)/ adv [non...] mai; (fam: expressing disbelief) ma va; **~ again** mai più; **well I ~!** che l'avrebbe detto!. **~-ending** a interminabile

nevertheless /nevəðə'les/ adv tuttavia

new /njuː/ a nuovo

new: **~-born** a neonato. **~comer** n nuovo, -a arrivato, -a mf. **~fangled** /-'fæŋgld/ a pej modernizzante. **~-laid** a fresco

newly adv (recently) di recente; **~-built** costruito di recente; **~-weds** npl sposini mpl

new: **~ moon** n luna f nuova. **~ness** n novità f

news /njuːz/ n notizie fpl; TV telegiornale m; Radio giornale m radio; **piece of ~** notizia f

news: **~agent** n giornalaio, -a •f. **~ bulletin** n notiziario m. **~caster** n giornalista mf televisivo, -a/radiofonico, -a. **~flash** n notizia f flash. **~letter** n bollettino m d'informazione. **~paper** n giornale m; (material) carta f di giornale. **~reader** n giornalista mf televisivo, -a/radiofonico, -a

new: **~ year** n (next year) anno nuovo; N~ Year's Day n Capodanno m. N~ Year's Eve n vigilia f di Capodanno. N~ Zealand /'ziːlənd/ n Nuova Zelanda f. N~ Zealander n neozelandese mf

next /nekst/ a prossimo; (adjoining) vicino; **who's ~?** a chi tocca?; **~ door** accanto; **~ to nothing** quasi niente; **the ~ day** il giorno dopo; **~ week** la settimana prossima; **the week after ~** fra due settimane •adv dopo; **when will you see him ~?** quando lo rivedi la prossima volta?; **~ to** accanto a •n seguente mf; **~ of kin** parente m prossimo

NHS n abbr **National Health Service**

nib /nɪb/ n pennino m

nibble /'nɪbl/ vt/i mordicchiare

nice /naɪs/ a (day, weather, holiday) bello; (person) gentile, simpatico; (food) buono; **it was ~ meeting you** è stato un piacere conoscerla. **~ly** adv gentilmente; (well) bene. **~ties** /'naɪsətɪz/ npl finezze fpl

niche /niːʃ/ n nicchia f

nick /nɪk/ n tacca f; (on chin etc) taglietto m; (fam: prison) galera f; (fam: police station) centrale f [di polizia]; **in the ~ of time** fam appena in tempo •vt intaccare; (fam: steal) fregare; (fam: arrest) beccare; **~ one's chin** farsi un taglietto nel mento

nickel /'nɪkl/ n nichel m; Am moneta f da cinque centesimi

'nickname n soprannome m •vt soprannominare

nicotine /'nɪkətiːn/ n nicotina f

niece /niːs/ n nipote f

Nigeria /naɪ'dʒɪərɪə/ n Nigeria f. **~n** a & n nigeriano, -a mf

niggling /'nɪglɪŋ/ a (detail) insignificante; (pain) fastidioso; (doubt) persistente

night /naɪt/ n notte f; (evening) sera f; **at ~** la notte, di notte; (in the evening) la sera, di sera; **Monday ~** lunedì notte/sera •a di notte

night: **~cap** n papalina f; (drink) bicchierino m bevuto prima di andare a letto. **~club** n locale m notturno, night[-club] m inv. **~dress** n camicia f da notte. **~fall** n crepuscolo m. **~gown**, fam **~ie** /'naɪtɪ/ n camicia f da notte

nightingale /'naɪtɪŋgeɪl/ n usignolo m

night: **~life** n vita f notturna. **~ly** a di notte, di sera •adv ogni notte, ogni sera. **~mare** n incubo m. **~school** scuola f serale. **~time** n at **~time** di notte, la notte. **~'watchman** n guardiano m notturno

nil /nɪl/ n nulla m; Sport zero m

nimble /'nɪmbl/ a agile. **~y** adv agilmente

nine /naɪn/ a nove inv •n nove m. **~teen** n diciannove inv •n diciannove. **~'teenth** a & n diciannovesimo, -a mf

ninetieth /'naɪntɪθ/ a & n novantesimo, -a mf

ninety /'naɪntɪ/ a novanta inv •n novanta m

ninth /naɪnθ/ a & n nono, -a mf

nip /nɪp/ n pizzicotto m; (bite) morso m •vt pizzicare; (bite) mordere; **~ in the bud** fig stroncare sul nascere •vi (fam: run) fare un salto

nipple /'nɪpl/ n capezzolo m; (Am: on bottle) tettarella f

nippy /'nɪpɪ/ a (-ier, -iest) fam (cold) pungente; (quick) svelto

nitrogen /'naɪtrədʒn/ n azoto m

nitwit /'nɪtwɪt/ n fam imbecille mf

no /nəʊ/ adv no ● n (pl noes) no m inv ● a nessuno; **I have no time** non ho tempo; **in no time** in un baleno; **'no parking'** 'sosta vietata'; **'no smoking'** 'vietato fumare'; **no one = nobody**

nobility /nəʊ'bɪlətɪ/ n nobiltà f

noble /'nəʊbl/ a nobile. **~man** n nobile m

nobody /'nəʊbədɪ/ pron nessuno; **he knows** ~ non conosce nessuno ● n he's a ~ non è nessuno

nocturnal /nɒk'tɜːnl/ a notturno

nod /nɒd/ n cenno m del capo ● v (pt/pp nodded) fare un cenno col capo; (in agreement) fare di sì col capo ● vt ~ one's head fare di sì col capo. **nod off** vi assopirsi

nodule /'nɒdjuːl/ n noduli m

noise /nɔɪz/ n rumore m; (loud) rumore m, chiasso m. **~less** a silenzioso. **~lessly** adv silenziosamente

noisy /'nɔɪzɪ/ a (-ier, -iest) rumoroso

nomad /'nəʊmæd/ n nomade mf. **~ic** /-'mædɪk/ a nomade

nominal /'nɒmɪnl/ a nominale

nominate /'nɒmɪnet/ vt proporre come candidato; (appoint) designare. **~ion** /-'neɪʃn/ n nomina f; (person nominated) candidato, -a mf

nominative /'nɒmɪnətɪv/ a & n Gram ~ [case] nominativo m

nominee /nɒmɪ'niː/ n persona f nominata

nonchalant /'nɒnʃələnt/ a disinvolto

non-com'missioned /nɒn-/ a ~ officer sottufficiale m

non-com'mittal /nɒn-/ a che non si sbilancia

nondescript /'nɒndɪskrɪpt/ a qualunque

none /nʌn/ pron (person) nessuno; (thing) niente; ~ of us nessuno di noi; ~ of this niente di questo; there's ~ left non ce n'è più ● adv she's ~ too pleased non è per niente soddisfatta; I'm ~ the wiser non so più di prima

nonentity /nɒ'nentətɪ/ n nullità f

non-event n delusione f

non-ex'istent a inesistente

non-'fiction n saggistica f

non-'iron a che non si stira

nonplussed /nɒn'plʌst/ a perplesso

nonsens|e /'nɒnsəns/ n sciocchezze fpl. **~ical** /-'sensɪkl/ a assurdo

non-'smoker n non fumatore, -trice mf; (compartment) scompartimento m non fumatori

non-'stick a antiaderente

non-'stop a ~ 'flight volo m diretto ● adv senza sosta; (fly) senza scalo

non-'violent a non violento

noodles /'nuːdlz/ npl taglierini mpl

nook /nʊk/ n cantuccio m

noon /nuːn/ n mezzogiorno m; at ~ a mezzogiorno

noose /nuːs/ n nodo m scorsoio

nor /nɔː(r)/ adv & conj né; ~ do I neppure io

Nordic /'nɔːdɪk/ a nordico

norm /nɔːm/ n norma f

normal /'nɔːml/ a normale. **~ity** /-'mælɪtɪ/ n normalità f. **~ly** adv (usually) normalmente

north /nɔːθ/ n nord m; to the ~ of a nord di ● a del nord, settentrionale ● adv a nord

north: N~ America f n America f del Nord. **~bound** a Auto in direzione nord. **~-east** a di nord-est, nordorientale ● n nord-est m ● adv a nord-est; (travel) verso nord-est

norther|ly /'nɔːðəlɪ/ a (direction) nord; (wind) del nord. **~n** a del nord, settentrionale. **N~n Ireland** n Irlanda f del Nord

north: N~ 'Pole n polo m nord. **N~ 'Sea** n Mare m del Nord. **~ward[s]** /-wəd[z]/ adv verso nord. **~-west** *a* di nord-ovest, nordoccidentale ● *n* nord-ovest *m* ● *adv* a nord-ovest; ⟨*travel*⟩ verso nord-ovest

Nor|way /'nɔ:wei/ *n* Norvegia *f*. **~wegian** /-'wi:dʒn/ *a* & *n* norvegese *mf*

nose /nəʊz/ *n* naso *m*

nose: **~bleed** *n* emorragia *f* nasale. **~dive** *n* *Aeron* picchiata *f*

nostalg|ia /nɒ'stældʒɪə/ *n* nostalgia *f*. **~ic** *a* nostalgico

nostril /'nɒstrɪl/ *n* narice *f*

nosy /'nəʊzɪ/ *a* (**-ier, -iest**) *fam* ficcanaso *inv*

not /nɒt/ *adv* non; **he is ~** Italian non è italiano; **I hope ~** spero di no; **~ all of us have been invited** non siamo stati tutti invitati; **if ~** se no; **~ at all** niente affatto; **~ a bit** per niente; **~ even** neanche; **~ yet** non ancora; **~ only... but also...** non solo... ma anche...

notabl|e /'nəʊtəbl/ *a* ⟨*remarkable*⟩ notevole. **~y** *adv* ⟨*in particular*⟩ in particolare

notary /'nəʊtərɪ/ *n* notaio *m*; **~ 'public** notaio *m*

notch /nɒtʃ/ *n* tacca *f* ● **notch up** *vt* ⟨*score*⟩ segnare

note /nəʊt/ *n* nota *f*; ⟨*short letter, banknote*⟩ biglietto *m*; ⟨*memo, written comment etc*⟩ appunto *m*; **of ~** ⟨*person*⟩ di spicco; ⟨*comments, event*⟩ degno di nota; **make a ~ of** prendere nota di; **take ~ of** ⟨*notice*⟩ prendere nota di ● *vt* ⟨*notice*⟩ notare; ⟨*write*⟩ annotare. **note down** *vt* annotare

'notebook *n* taccuino *m*; *Comput* notebook *m* *inv*

noted /'nəʊtɪd/ *a* noto, celebre (**for** per)

note: **~paper** *n* carta *f* da lettere. **~worthy** *a* degno di nota

nothing /'nʌθɪŋ/ *pron* niente, nulla ● *adv* niente affatto. **for ~** ⟨*free, in vain*⟩ per niente; ⟨*with no reason*⟩ senza motivo; **~ but** nient'altro che; **~ much** poco o nulla; **~ interesting** niente di interes-

sante; **it's ~ to ~ do with you** non ti riguarda

notice /'nəʊtɪs/ *n* ⟨*on board*⟩ avviso *m*; ⟨*review*⟩ recensione *f*; ⟨*termination of employment*⟩ licenziamento *m*; [**advance**] preavviso *m*; **two months ~** due mesi di preavviso; **at short ~** con breve preavviso; **until further ~** fino nuovo avviso; **give** [**in one's**] **~** ⟨*employee:*⟩ dare le dimissioni; **give an employee ~** dare il preavviso a un impiegato; **take no ~ of** non fare caso a; **take no ~!** non farci caso! ● *vt* notare. **~able** /-əbl/ *a* evidente. **~ably** *adv* sensibilmente. **~-board** *n* bacheca *f*

noti|fication /nəʊtɪfɪ'keɪʃn/ *n* notifica *f*. **~fy** /'nəʊtɪfaɪ/ *vt* (*pt/pp* **-ied**) notificare

notion /'nəʊʃn/ *n* idea *f*, nozione *f*; **~s** *pl* (*Am: haberdashery*) merceria *f*

notoriety /nəʊtə'raɪətɪ/ *n* notorietà *f*

notorious /nəʊ'tɔ:rɪəs/ *a* famigerato; **be ~ for** essere tristemente famoso per

notwith|standing *prep* malgrado ● *adv* ciononostante

nougat /'nu:ga:/ *n* torrone *m*

nought /nɔ:t/ *n* zero *m*

noun /naʊn/ *n* nome *m*, sostantivo *m*

nourish /'nʌrɪʃ/ *vt* nutrire. **~ing** *a* nutriente. **~ment** *n* nutrimento *m*

novel /'nɒvl/ *a* insolito ● *n* romanzo *m*. **~ist** *n* romanziere, -a *mf*. **~ty** *n* novità *f*; **~ties** *pl* ⟨*objects*⟩ oggettini *mpl*

November /nəʊ'vembə(r)/ *n* novembre *m*

novice /'nɒvɪs/ *n* novizio, -a *mf*

now /naʊ/ *adv* ora, adesso; **by ~** ormai; **just ~** proprio ora; **right ~** subito; **~ and again, ~ and then** ogni tanto; **~, ~!** su! ● *conj* **~** [**that**] ora che, adesso che

'nowadays *adv* oggigiorno

nowhere /'nəʊ-/ *adv* in nessun posto, da nessuna parte

noxious /'nɒkʃəs/ a nocivo
nozzle /'nɒzl/ n bocchetta f
nuance /'njuːɒ̃s/ n sfumatura f
nuclear /'njuːklɪə(r)/ a nucleare
nucleus /'njuːklɪəs/ n (pl **-lei**
/-lɪaɪ/) nucleo m
nude /njuːd/ a nudo ● n nudo m; **in
the ~** nudo
nudge /nʌdʒ/ n colpetto m di gomito ● vt dare un colpetto col gomito a
nudism /'njuːdɪzm/ n nudismo m
nud|ist /'njuːdɪst/ n nudista mf.
~ity n nudità f
nugget /'nʌgɪt/ n pepita f
nuisance /'njuːsns/ n seccatura f;
(person) piaga f; **what a ~!** che
seccatura!
null /nʌl/ a **~ and void** nullo
numb /nʌm/ a intorpidito; **~ with
cold** intirizzito dal freddo
number /'nʌmbə(r)/ n numero m;
a ~ of people un certo numero di
persone ● vt numerare; (include)
annoverare. **~-plate** n targa f
numeral /'njuːmərəl/ n numero m,
cifra f
numerate /'njuːmərət/ a **be ~** saper fare i calcoli
numerical /njuː'merɪkl/ a numerico; **in ~ order** in ordine numerico
numerous /'njuːmərəs/ a numero-
so
nun /nʌn/ n suora f
nurse /nɜːs/ n infermiere, -a mf;
children's ~ bambinaia f ● vt curare
nursery /'nɜːsəri/ n stanza f dei
bambini; (for plants) vivaio m;
[day] ~ asilo m. **~ rhyme** n filastrocca f. **~ school** n scuola f materna
nursing /'nɜːsɪŋ/ n professione f
d'infermiere. **~ home** n casa f di
cura per anziani
nurture /'nɜːtʃə(r)/ vt allevare; fig
coltivare
nut /nʌt/ n noce f; Techn dado m;
(fam: head) zucca f. **~s** npl frutta f
secca; **be ~s** fam essere svitato.

~crackers npl schiaccianoci m
inv. **~meg** n noce f moscata
nutrit|ion /njuː'trɪʃn/ n nutrizione
f. **~ious** /-ʃəs/ a nutriente
'nutshell n **in a ~** fig in parole povere
nuzzle /'nʌzl/ vt (horse, dog:) strofinare il muso contro
nylon /'naɪlɒn/ n nailon m; **~s** pl
calze fpl di nailon ● attrib di nailon

....

Oo

....

O /əʊ/ n Teleph zero m
oaf /əʊf/ n (pl **oafs**) zoticone, -a mf
oak /əʊk/ n quercia f ● attrib di
quercia
OAP n abbr (**old-age pensioner**)
pensionato, -a mf
oar /ɔː(r)/ n remo m. **~sman** n
vogatore m
oasis /əʊ'eɪsɪs/ n (pl **oases** /-siːz/)
oasi f inv
oath /əʊθ/ n giuramento m; (swear-
word) bestemmia f
oatmeal /'əʊt-/ n farina f d'avena
oats /əʊts/ npl avena fsg; Culin
[rolled] ~ fiocchi mpl di avena
obedien|ce /ə'biːdɪəns/ n ubbi-
dienza f. **~t** a ubbidiente
obes|e /ə'biːs/ a obeso. **~ity** n obe-
sità f
obey /ə'beɪ/ vt ubbidire a; osservare (instructions, rules) ● vi ubbidire
obituary /ə'bɪtjʊəri/ n necrolo-
gio m
object¹ /'ɒbdʒɪkt/ n oggetto m;
Gram complemento m oggetto;
money is no ~ i soldi non sono un
problema
object² /əb'dʒekt/ vi (be against)
opporsi (to a); **~ that...** obiettare
che...
objection /əb'dʒekʃn/ n obiezione
f; **have no ~** non avere niente in

contrario. **~able** /-əbl/ *a* discutibile; ⟨person⟩ sgradevole

objective /əb'dʒektɪv/ *a* oggettivo ● *n* obiettivo *m*. **~ely** *adv* obiettivamente. **~ity** /-'tɪvətɪ/ *n* oggettività *f*

obligation /ɒblɪ'ɡeɪʃn/ *n* obbligo *m*; **be under an ~** avere un obbligo; **without ~** senza impegno

obligatory /ə'blɪɡətrɪ/ *a* obbligatorio

oblig|e /ə'blaɪdʒ/ *vt* ⟨compel⟩ obbligare; **much ~ed** grazie mille. **~ing** *a* disponibile

oblique /ə'bliːk/ *a* obliquo; *fig* indiretto ● *n* ~ **[stroke]** barra *f*

obliterate /ə'blɪtəreɪt/ *vt* obliterare

oblivion /ə'blɪvɪən/ *n* oblio *m*

oblivious /ə'blɪvɪəs/ *a* **be ~** essere dimentico (**of**, **to** di)

oblong /'ɒblɒŋ/ *a* oblungo ● *n* rettangolo *m*

obnoxious /əb'nɒkʃəs/ *a* detestabile

oboe /'əʊbəʊ/ *n* oboe *m inv*

obscen|e /əb'siːn/ *a* osceno; ⟨profits, wealth⟩ vergognoso. **~ity** /-'senətɪ/ *n* oscenità *f inv*

obscur|e /əb'skjʊə(r)/ *a* oscuro ● *vt* oscurare; ⟨confuse⟩ mettere in ombra. **~ity** *n* oscurità *f*

obsequious /əb'siːkwɪəs/ *a* ossequioso

observa|nce /əb'zɜːvəns/ *n* ⟨of custom⟩ osservanza *f*. **~nt** *a* attento. **~tion** /ɒbzə'veɪʃn/ *n* osservazione *f*

observatory /əb'zɜːvətrɪ/ *n* osservatorio *m*

observe /əb'zɜːv/ *vt* osservare; ⟨notice⟩ notare; ⟨keep, celebrate⟩ celebrare. **~r** *n* osservatore, -trice *mf*

obsess /əb'ses/ *vt* **be ~ed by** essere fissato con. **~ion** /-eʃn/ *n* fissazione *f*. **~ive** /-ɪv/ *a* ossessivo

obsolete /'ɒbsəliːt/ *a* obsoleto; ⟨word⟩ desueto

obstacle /'ɒbstəkl/ *n* ostacolo *m*

obstetrician /ɒbstə'trɪʃn/ *n*

ostetrico, -a *mf*. **obstetrics** /əb'stetrɪks/ *n* ostetricia *f*

obstina|cy /'ɒbstɪnəsɪ/ *n* ostinazione *f*. **~te** /-nət/ *a* ostinato

obstreperous /əb'strepərəs/ *a* turbolento

obstruct /əb'strʌkt/ *vt* ostruire; ⟨hinder⟩ ostacolare. **~ion** /-ʌkʃn/ *n* ostruzione *f*; ⟨obstacle⟩ ostacolo *m*. **~ive** /-ɪv/ *a* **be ~ive** ⟨person:⟩ creare dei problemi

obtain /əb'teɪn/ *vt* ottenere. **~able** /-əbl/ *a* ottenibile

obtrusive /əb'truːsɪv/ *a* ⟨object⟩ stonato

obtuse /əb'tjuːs/ *a* ottuso

obvious /'ɒbvɪəs/ *a* ovvio. **~ly** *adv* ovviamente

occasion /ə'keɪʒn/ *n* occasione *f*; ⟨event⟩ evento *m*; **on ~** talvolta; **on the ~ of** in occasione di

occasional /ə'keɪʒənl/ *a* saltuario; **he has the ~ glass of wine** ogni tanto beve un bicchiere di vino. **~ly** *adv* ogni tanto

occult /ɒ'kʌlt/ *a* occulto

occupant /'ɒkjʊpənt/ *n* occupante *mf*; ⟨of vehicle⟩ persona *f* a bordo

occupation /ɒkjʊ'peɪʃn/ *n* occupazione *f*; ⟨job⟩ professione *f*. **~al** *a* professionale

occupier /'ɒkjʊpaɪə(r)/ *n* residente *mf*

occupy /'ɒkjʊpaɪ/ *vt* (*pt/pp* **occupied**) occupare; ⟨keep busy⟩ tenere occupato

occur /ə'kɜː(r)/ *vi* (*pt/pp* **occurred**) accadere; ⟨exist⟩ trovarsi; **it ~red to me that** mi è venuto in mente che. **~rence** /ə'kʌrəns/ *n* ⟨event⟩ fatto *m*

ocean /'əʊʃn/ *n* oceano *m*

o'clock /ə'klɒk/ *adv* **it's 7 ~** sono le sette; **at 7 ~** alle sette;

octave /'ɒktɪv/ *n Mus* ottava *f*

October /ɒk'təʊbə(r)/ *n* ottobre *m*

octopus /'ɒktəpəs/ *n* (*pl* **-puses**) polpo *m*

odd /ɒd/ *a* ⟨number⟩ dispari; ⟨not of set⟩ scompagnato; ⟨strange⟩ strano; **forty ~** quaranta e rotti;

~ **jobs** lavoretti *mpl*; **the ~ one out** l'eccezione; **at ~ moments** a tempo perso; **have the ~ glass of wine** avere un bicchiere di vino ogni tanto

odd|**ity** /'ɒdɪti/ *n* stranezza *f*. **~ly** *adv* stranamente; **~ly enough** stranamente. **~ment** *n* (*of fabric*) scampolo *m*

odds /ɒdz/ *npl* (*chances*) probabilità *fpl*; **at ~** in disaccordo; **~ and ends** cianfrusaglie *fpl*; **it makes no ~** non fa alcuna differenza

ode /aud/ *n* ode *f*

odour /'əʊdə(r)/ *n* odore *m*. **~less** *a* inodore

of /ɒv/, /əv/ *prep* di; **a cup of tea/coffee** una tazza di tè/caffè; **the hem of my skirt** l'orlo della mia gonna; **the summer of 1989** l'estate del 1989; **the two of us** noi due; **made of** di; **that's very kind of you** è molto gentile da parte tua; **a friend of mine** un mio amico; **a child of three** un bambino di tre anni; **the fourth of January** il quattro gennaio; **within a year of their divorce** a circa un anno dal loro divorzio; **half of it** la metà; **the whole of the room** tutta la stanza

off /ɒf/ *prep* da; (*distant from*) lontano da; **take £10 ~ the price** ridurre il prezzo di 10 sterline; **~ the coast** presso la costa; **a street ~ the main road** una traversa della via principale; (*near*) una strada vicino alla via principale; **get ~ the ladder** scendere dalla scala; **get off the bus** uscire dall'autobus; **leave the lid ~ the saucepan** lasciare la pentola senza il coperchio ●*adv* (*button, handle*) staccato; (*light, machine*) spento; (*brake*) tolto; (*tap*) chiuso; **'off'** (*on appliance*) 'off'; **2 kilometres ~** a due chilometri di distanza; **a long way ~** molto distante; (*time*) lontano; **~ and on** di tanto in tanto; **with his hat/coat ~** senza il cappello/cappot-

to; **with the light ~** a luce spenta; **20% ~** 20% di sconto; **be ~** (*leave*) andare via; *Sport* essere partito; (*food:*) essere andato a male; (*all gone*) essere finito; (*wedding, engagement:*) essere cancellato; **I'm ~ alcohol** ho smesso di bere; **be ~ one's food** non avere appetito; **she's ~ today** (*on holiday*) è in ferie oggi; (*ill*) è malata oggi; **I'm ~ home** vado a casa; **you'd be better ~ doing**… faresti meglio a fare…; **have a day ~** avere un giorno di vacanza; **drive/sail ~** andare via

offal /'ɒfl/ *n Culin* frattaglie *fpl*

'off-beat *a* insolito

'off-chance *n* possibilità *f* remota

off-'colour *a* (*not well*) giù di forma; (*joke, story*) sporco

offence /ə'fens/ *n* (*illegal act*) reato *m*; **give ~** offendere; **take ~** offendersi (**at** per)

offend /ə'fend/ *vt* offendere. **~er** *n Jur* colpevole *mf*

offensive /ə'fensɪv/ *a* offensivo ●*n* offensiva *f*

offer /'ɒfə(r)/ *n* offerta *f* ● *vt* offrire; opporre (*resistance*); **~ sb sth** offrire qcsa a qcno; **~ to do sth** offrirsi di fare qcsa. **~ing** *n* offerta *f*

off'hand *a* (*casual*) spiccio ●*adv* su due piedi

office /'ɒfɪs/ *n* ufficio *m*; (*post, job*) carica *f*. **~ hours** *pl* orario *m* d'ufficio

officer /'ɒfɪsə(r)/ *n* ufficiale *m*; (*police*) agente *m* [di polizia]

official /ə'fɪʃl/ *a* ufficiale ●*n* funzionario, -a *mf*; *Sport* dirigente *m*. **~ly** *adv* ufficialmente

officiate /ə'fɪʃɪeɪt/ *vi* officiare

'offing *n* **in the ~** in vista

'off-licence *n* negozio *m* per la vendita di alcolici

off-'load *vt* scaricare

'off-putting *a fam* scoraggiante

'offset *vt* (*pt/pp* **-set**, *pres p* **-setting**) controbilanciare

'offshoot *n* ramo *m*; *fig* diramazione *f*

'offshore a ⟨wind⟩ di terra; ⟨company, investment⟩ offshore. ● **rig** n piattaforma f petrolifera, offshore m inv

off'side a Sport [in] fuori gioco; ⟨wheel etc⟩ (left) sinistro; (right) destro

'offspring n prole m

off-'stage adv dietro le quinte

off-'white a bianco sporco

often /'ɒfn/ adv spesso; **how** ~ ogni quanto; **every so** ~ una volta ogni tanto

ogle /'əʊgl/ vt mangiarsi con gli occhi

oh /əʊ/ int oh!; ~ **dear** oh Dio!

oil /ɔɪl/ n olio m; ⟨petroleum⟩ petrolio m; ⟨for heating⟩ nafta f ● vt oliare

oil: ~**field** n giacimento m di petrolio. ~**painting** n pittura f a olio. ~ **refinery** n raffineria f di petrolio. ~ **rig** piattaforma f per trivellazione subacquea. ~**skins** npl vestiti mpl di tela cerata. ~**slick** n chiazza f di petrolio. ~**tanker** n petroliera f. ~ **well** n pozzo m petrolifero

oily /'ɔɪlɪ/ a (-ier, -iest) unto; fig untuoso

ointment /'ɔɪntmənt/ n pomata f

OK /əʊ'keɪ/ int & inter, o.k. ● **if that's OK with you** se ti va bene; **she's OK** (well) sta bene; **is the milk still OK?** il latte è ancora buono? ● adv (well) bene ● a ⟨anche okay⟩ (pt/pp **okayed**) dare l'o.k.

old /əʊld/ a vecchio; ⟨girlfriend⟩ ex; **how** ~ **is she?** quanti anni ha?; **she is ten years** ~ ha dieci anni

old: ~ **'age** n vecchiaia f. ~**age 'pensioner** n pensionato, -a mf. ~ **boy** n Sch ex-allievo m. ~**'fashioned** a antiquato. ~ **girl** ex-allieva f. ~ **'maid** n zitella f

olive /'ɒlɪv/ n ⟨fruit, colour⟩ oliva f; ⟨tree⟩ olivo m ● a d'oliva; ⟨colour⟩ olivastro. ~ **branch** n fig ramo-

scello m d'olivo. ~ **'oil** n olio m di oliva

Olympic /ə'lɪmpɪk/ a olimpico; ~**s, ~ Games** Olimpiadi fpl

omelette /'ɒmlɪt/ n omelette f inv

omen /'əʊmən/ n presagio m

ominous /'ɒmɪnəs/ a sinistro

omission /ə'mɪʃn/ n omissione f

omit /ə'mɪt/ vt (pt/pp **omitted**) omettere; ~ **to do sth** tralasciare di fare qcsa

omnipotent /ɒm'nɪpətənt/ a onnipotente

on /ɒn/ prep su; ⟨on horizontal surface⟩ su, sopra; **on Monday** lunedì; **on Mondays** di lunedì; **on the first of May** il primo di maggio; **on arriving** all'arrivo; **on one's finger** ⟨cut⟩ nel dito; ⟨ring⟩ al dito; **on foot** a piedi; **on the right/left** a destra/sinistra; **on the Rhine/Thames** sul Reno/Tamigi; **on the radio/television** alla radio/televisione; **on the bus/train** in autobus/treno; **go on the bus/train** andare in autobus/treno; **get on the bus/train** salire sull'autobus/sul treno; **on me** ⟨with me⟩ con me; **it's on me** fam tocca a me ● adv ⟨further on⟩ dopo; ⟨switched on⟩ acceso; ⟨brake⟩ inserito; ⟨in operation⟩ in funzione; 'on' ⟨on machine⟩ 'on'; **he had his hat/coat on** portava il cappello/cappotto; **without his hat/coat on** senza cappello/cappotto; **with/without the lid on** con/senza coperchio; **be on** ⟨film, programme, event⟩ esserci; **it's not on** fam non è giusto; **it's on at** fam tormentare ⟨to per⟩; **on and on** senza sosta; **on and off** a intervalli; **and so on** e così via; **go on** continuare; **drive on** spostarsi ⟨con la macchina⟩; **stick on** attaccare; **sew on** cucire ● a ⟨switched on⟩ acceso

once /wʌns/ adv una volta; ⟨formerly⟩ un tempo; ~ **upon a time there was** c'era una volta; **at** ~ subito; ⟨at the same time⟩ contemporaneamente; ~ **and for all** una volta per tutte ● conj [non] appena. **~over** n fam give sb/sth the **~-over** (look, check) dare un'occhiata veloce a qcno/qcsa

'oncoming a che si avvicina dalla direzione opposta

one /wʌn/ a uno, una; una; **not ~ person** nemmeno una persona ●n uno m ● pron uno; (impersonal) si; **~ another** l'un l'altro; **~ by ~** [a] uno a uno; **~ never knows** non si sa mai

one: **~-eyed** a con un occhio solo. **~-off** a unico. **~-parent 'family** n famiglia f con un solo genitore. **~self** pron (reflexive) si; (emphatic) sé, se stesso; **by ~self** da solo; **be proud of ~self** essere fieri di sé. **~-sided** a unilaterale. **~-way** a a senso unico; (ticket) di sola andata

onion /'ʌnjən/ n cipolla f

'onlooker n spettatore, -trice mf

only /'əʊnlɪ/ a solo; **~ child** figlio, -a mf unico, -a ● adv & conj solo, solamente; **~ just** appena

on/'off switch n pulsante m di accensione

'onset n (beginning) inizio m

onslaught /'ɒnslɔːt/ n attacco m

onus /'əʊnəs/ n **the ~ is on me** spetta a me la responsabilità (**to** di)

onward[**s**] /'ɒnwəd[z]/ adv in avanti; **from then ~** da allora [in poi]

ooze /uːz/ vi fluire

opal /'əʊpl/ n opale f

opaque /əʊ'peɪk/ a opaco

open /'əʊpən/ a aperto; (free to all) pubblico; (job) vacante; **in the ~-air** all'aperto ● n **in the ~** all'aperto; fig alla luce del sole ● vt aprire ● vi aprirsi; (shop:) aprire; (flower:) sbocciare. **open up** vt aprire ● vi aprirsi

open: **~-air 'swimming pool** n piscina f all'aperto. **~ day** n giorno m di apertura al pubblico

opener /'əʊpənə(r)/ n (for tins) apriscatole m inv; (for bottles) apribottiglie m inv

opening /'əʊpənɪŋ/ n apertura f; (beginning) inizio m; (job) posto m libero; **~ hours** npl orario m d'apertura

openly /'əʊpənlɪ/ adv apertamente

open: **~-minded** a aperto; (broadminded) di vedute larghe. **~-plan** a a pianta aperta. **~ 'sandwich** n tartina f. **~ secret** segreto m di Pulcinella. **~ ticket** biglietto m aperto. O**~ University** corsi mpl universitari per corrispondenza

opera /'ɒpərə/ n opera f

operable /'ɒpərəbl/ a operabile

opera: **~-glasses** npl binocolo msg da teatro. **~-house** n teatro m lirico. **~-singer** n cantante mf lirico, -a

operate /'ɒpəreɪt/ vt far funzionare (machine, lift); azionare (lever, brake); mandare avanti (business) ● vi Techn funzionare; (be in action) essere in funzione; Mil, fig operare; **~ on** Med operare

operatic /ɒpə'rætɪk/ a lirico, operistico

operation /ɒpə'reɪʃn/ n operazione f; Tech funzionamento m; **in ~** Techn in funzione; **come into ~** fig entrare in funzione; (law:) entrare in vigore; **have an ~** Med subire un'operazione. **~al** a operativo; (law etc) in vigore

operative /'ɒpərətɪv/ a operativo

operator /'ɒpəreɪtə(r)/ n (user) operatore, -trice mf; Teleph centralinista mf

operetta /ɒpə'retə/ n operetta f

opinion /ə'pɪnjən/ n opinione f; **in my ~** secondo me. **~ated** a dogmatico

opponent /ə'pəʊnənt/ n avversario, -a m

opportun|e /'ɒpətjuːn/ a opportuno. **~ist** /-'tjuːnɪst/ n opportunista mf. **~istic** a opportunistico

opportunity /ɒpə'tjuːnətɪ/ n opportunità f inv

oppos|e /ə'pəʊz/ vt opporsi a; **be ~ed to sth** essere contrario a qcsa; **as ~ed to** al contrario di.

~ing *a* avversario; *(opposite)* opposto
opposite /'ɒpəzɪt/ *a* opposto; *(house)* di fronte; *fig* controparte *f*; **the ~ sex** l'altro sesso ● *n* contrario *m* ● *adv* di fronte ● *prep* di fronte a
opposition /ɒpə'zɪʃn/ *n* opposizione *f*
oppress /ə'pres/ *vt* opprimere. **~ion** /-eʃn/ *n* oppressione *f*. **~ive** /-ɪv/ *a* oppressivo; *(heat)* opprimente. **~or** *n* oppressore *m*
opt /ɒpt/ *vi* **~ for** optare per; **~ out** dissociarsi **(of** da)
optical /'ɒptɪkl/ *a* ottico; **~ illusion** illusione *f* ottica
optician /ɒp'tɪʃn/ *n* ottico, -a *mf*
optimis|m /'ɒptɪmɪzm/ *n* ottimismo *m*. **~t** /-mɪst/ *n* ottimista *mf*. **~tic** /-'mɪstɪk/ *a* ottimistico
optimum /'ɒptɪməm/ *a* ottimale ● *n* (*pl* **-ima**) optimum *m*
option /'ɒpʃn/ *n* scelta *f*; *Comm* opzione *f*. **~al** *a* facoltativo; **~al extras** *pl* optional *m inv*
opulen|ce /'ɒpjʊləns/ *n* opulenza *f*. **~t** *a* opulento
or /ɔ:(r)/ *conj* o, oppure; *(after negative)* né; **or** [**else**] se no; **in a year or two** fra un anno o due
oracle /'ɒrəkl/ *n* oracolo *m*
oral /'ɔ:rəl/ *a* orale; *n fam* esame *m* orale. **~ly** *adv* oralmente
orange /'ɒrɪndʒ/ *n* arancia *f*; *(colour)* arancione *m* ● *a* arancione. **~ade** /-'dʒeɪd/ *n* aranciata *f*. **~ juice** *n* succo *m* d'arancia
orator /'ɒrətə(r)/ *n* oratore, -trice *mf*
oratorio /ɒrə'tɔ:rɪəʊ/ *n* oratorio *m*
oratory /'ɒrətərɪ/ *n* oratorio *m*
orbit /'ɔ:bɪt/ *n* orbita *f* ● *vt* orbitare. **~al** *a* **~al road** tangenziale *f*
orchard /'ɔ:tʃəd/ *n* frutteto *m*
orches|tra /'ɔ:kɪstrə/ *n* orchestra *f*. **~tral** /-'kestrəl/ *a* orchestrale. **~trate** *vt* orchestrare
orchid /'ɔ:kɪd/ *n* orchidea *f*

ordain /ɔ:'deɪn/ *vt* decretare; *Relig* ordinare
ordeal /ɔ:'di:l/ *n fig* terribile esperienza *f*
order /'ɔ:də(r)/ *n* ordine *m*; *Comm* ordinazione *f*; **out of ~** *(machine)* fuori servizio; **in ~ that** affinché; **in ~ to** per ● *vt* ordinare
orderly /'ɔ:dəlɪ/ *a* ordinato ● *n Mil* attendente *m*; *Med* inserviente *m*
ordinary /'ɔ:dɪnərɪ/ *a* ordinario
ordination /ɔ:dɪ'neɪʃn/ *n Relig* ordinazione *f*
ore /ɔ:(r)/ *n* minerale *m* grezzo
organ /'ɔ:gən/ *n Anat, Mus* organo *m*
organic /ɔ:'gænɪk/ *a* organico; *(without chemicals)* biologico. **~ally** *adv* organicamente. **~ally grown** coltivato biologicamente
organism /'ɔ:gənɪzm/ *n* organismo *m*
organist /'ɔ:gənɪst/ *n* organista *mf*
organization /ɔ:gənaɪ'zeɪʃn/ *n* organizzazione *f*
organize /'ɔ:gənaɪz/ *vt* organizzare. **~r** *n* organizzatore, -trice *mf*
orgasm /'ɔ:gæzm/ *n* orgasmo *m*
orgy /'ɔ:dʒɪ/ *n* orgia *f*
Orient /'ɔ:rɪənt/ *n* Oriente *m*. **o~al** /-'entl/ *a* orientale ● *n* orientale *mf*
orient|ate /'ɔ:rɪənteɪt/ *vt* **~ate oneself** orientarsi. **~ation** /-'teɪʃn/ *n* orientamento *m*
origin /'ɒrɪdʒɪn/ *n* origine *f*
original /ə'rɪdʒɪn(ə)l/ *a* originario; *(not copied, new)* originale ● *n* originale *m*; **in the ~** in versione originale. **~ity** /-'nælətɪ/ *n* originalità *f*. **~ly** *adv* originariamente
originat|e /ə'rɪdʒɪneɪt/ *vi* **~e in** avere origine in. **~or** *n* ideatore, -trice *mf*
ornament /'ɔ:nəmənt/ *n* ornamento *m*; *(on mantelpiece etc)* soprammobile *m*. **~al** /-'mentl/ *a* ornamentale. **~ation** /-'teɪʃn/ *n* decorazione *f*
ornate /ɔ:'neɪt/ *a* ornato
orphan /'ɔ:fn/ *n* orfano, -a *mf* ● *vt*

rendere orfano; **be ~ed** rimanere orfano. **~age** /-ɪdʒ/ *n* orfanotrofio *m*

orthodox /'ɔ:θədɒks/ *a* ortodosso

orthopaedic /ɔ:θə'pi:dɪk/ *a* ortopedico

oscillate /'ɒsɪleɪt/ *vi* oscillare

ostensibl|e /ɒsten'seɪbl/ *a* apparente. **~y** *adv* apparentemente

ostentat|ion /ɒsten'teɪʃn/ *n* ostentazione *f*. **~ious** /-ʃəs/ *a* ostentato

osteopath /'ɒstɪəpæθ/ *n* osteopata *mf*

ostracize /'ɒstrəsaɪz/ *vt* bandire

ostrich /'ɒstrɪtʃ/ *n* struzzo *m*

other /'ʌðə(r)/ *a, pron* & *n* altro, -a *mf*; **the ~ [one]** l'altro, -a *mf*; **the ~ two** gli altri due; **two ~s** altri due; **~ people** gli altri; **any ~ questions?** altre domande?; **every ~ day** (*alternate days*) a giorni alterni; **the ~ day** l'altro giorno; **the ~ evening** l'altra sera; **someone/something or ~** qualcuno/qualcosa ● *adv* **~ than him** tranne lui; **somehow or ~** in qualche modo; **somewhere or ~** da qualche parte

'otherwise *adv* altrimenti; (*differently*) diversamente

otter /'ɒtə(r)/ *n* lontra *f*

ouch /aʊtʃ/ *int* ahi!

ought /ɔ:t/ *v aux* **I/we ~ to stay** dovrei/dovremmo rimanere; **he ~ not to have done it** non avrebbe dovuto farlo; **that ~ to be enough** questo dovrebbe bastare

ounce /aʊns/ *n* oncia *f* (= 28, 35 g)

our /'aʊə(r)/ *a* il nostro *m*, la nostra *f*, i nostri *mpl*, le nostre *fpl*; **~ mother/father** nostra madre/nostro padre

ours /'aʊəz/ *poss pron* il nostro *m*, la nostra *f*, i nostri *mpl*, le nostre *fpl*; **a friend of ~** un nostro amico; **friends of ~** dei nostri amici; **that is ~** quello è il nostro; (*as opposed to yours*) quello è il nostro

ourselves /aʊə'selvz/ *pron* (*reflexive*) ci; (*emphatic*) noi, noi stessi; **we poured ~ a drink** ci siamo

versati da bere; **we heard it ~** l'abbiamo sentito noi stessi; **we are proud of ~** siamo fieri di noi; **by ~** da soli

out /aʊt/ *adv* fuori; (*not alight*) spento; **be ~** (*flower*): essere sbocciato; (*workers*): essere in sciopero; (*calculation*): essere sbagliato; *Sport* essere fuori; (*unconscious*) aver perso i sensi; (*fig: not feasible*) fuori questione; **the sun is ~** è uscito il sole; **~ and about** in piedi; **get ~!** *fam* fuori!; **you should get ~ more** dovresti uscire più spesso; **~ with it!** *fam* sputa il rospo!; ● *prep* **~** di fuori da; **~ of date** non aggiornato; (*passport*) scaduto; **~ of order** guasto; **~ of print/stock** esaurito; **be ~ of bed/the room** fuori dal letto/dalla stanza; **~ of breath** senza fiato; **~ of danger** fuori pericolo; **~ of work** disoccupato; **nine ~ of ten** nove su dieci; **be ~ of sugar/bread** rimanere senza zucchero/pane; **go ~ of the room** uscire dalla stanza

out'bid *vt* (*pt/pp* **-bid**, *pres p* **-bidding**) **~ sb** rilanciare l'offerta di qcno

'outboard *a* **~ motor** motore *m*

'outbreak *n* (*of war*) scoppio *m*; (*of disease*) insorgenza *f*

'outbuilding *n* costruzione *f* annessa

'outburst *n* esplosione *f*

'outcome *n* risultato *m*

'outcry *n* protesta *f*

out'dated *a* sorpassato

out'do *vt* (*pt* **-did**, *pp* **-done**) superare

'outdoor *a* (*life, sports*) all'aperto; **~ clothes** *pl* vestiti per uscire; **~ swimming pool** piscina *f* scoperta

out'doors *adv* all'aria aperta; **go ~** uscire [all'aria aperta]

'outer *a* esterno

'outfit *n* equipaggiamento *m*; (*clothes*) completo *m*; (*fam: organization*) organizzazione. **~ter** *n* **men's ~ter's** negozio *m* di abbigliamento maschile '**outgoing** *a* ⟨*president*⟩ uscente; ⟨*mail*⟩ in partenza; ⟨*sociable*⟩ estroverso. **~s** *npl* uscite *fpl*

out'**grow** *vi* (*pt* **-grew**, *pp* **-grown**) diventare troppo grande per

'**outhouse** *n* costruzione *f* annessa

'**outing** /'aυtιŋ/ *n* gita *f*

out'**landish** /aυt'lændιʃ/ *a* stravagante

'**outlaw** *n* fuorilegge *mf inv* ● *vt* dichiarare illegale

'**outlay** *n* spesa *f*

'**outlet** *n* sbocco *m*; *fig* sfogo *m*; *Comm* punto *m* [di] vendita

'**outline** *n* contorno *m*; ⟨*summary*⟩ sommario *m* ● *vt* tracciare il contorno di; ⟨*describe*⟩ descrivere

out'**live** *vt* sopravvivere a

'**outlook** *n* vista *f*; ⟨*future prospect*⟩ prospettiva *f*; ⟨*attitude*⟩ visione *f*

'**outlying** *a* **~ areas** *pl* zone *fpl* periferiche

out'**number** *vt* superare in numero

'**out-patient** *n* paziente *mf* esterno, -a; **~s' department** ambulatorio *m*

'**output** *n* produzione *f*

'**outrage** *n* oltraggio *m* ● *vt* oltraggiare. **~ous** /-'reιdʒəs/ *a* oltraggioso; ⟨*price*⟩ scandaloso

'**outright**[1] *a* completo; ⟨*refusal*⟩ netto

out'**right**[2] *adv* completamente; ⟨*at once*⟩ immediatamente; ⟨*frankly*⟩ francamente

'**outset** *n* inizio *m*; **from the ~** fin dall'inizio

'**outside**[1] *a* esterno ● *n* esterno *m*; **from the ~** dall'esterno; **at the ~** al massimo

out'**side**[2] *adv* all'esterno, fuori; ⟨*out of doors*⟩ fuori; **go ~** andare fuori ● *prep* fuori da; ⟨*in front of*⟩ davanti a

out'**sider** *n* estraneo, -a *mf*

'**outskirts** *npl* sobborghi *mpl*

out'**spoken** *a* schietto

out'**standing** *a* eccezionale; ⟨*landmark*⟩ prominente; ⟨*not settled*⟩ in sospeso

out'**stretched** *a* allungato

out'**strip** *vt* (*pt*/*pp* **-stripped**) superare

out'**vote** *vt* mettere in minoranza

'**outward** /-wəd/ *a* esterno; ⟨*journey*⟩ di andata ● *adv* verso l'esterno. **~ly** *adv* esternamente. **~s** *adv* verso l'esterno

out'**weigh** *vt* aver maggior peso di

out'**wit** *vt* (*pt*/*pp* **-witted**) battere in astuzia

oval /'əʊvl/ *a* ovale ● *n* ovale *m*

ovary /'əʊvərι/ *n* *Anat* ovaia *f*

ovation /əʊ'veιʃn/ *n* ovazione *f*

oven /'ʌvn/ *n* forno *m*. **~-ready** *a* pronto da mettere in forno

over /'əʊvə(r)/ *prep* sopra; ⟨*across*⟩ al di là di; ⟨*during*⟩ durante; ⟨*more than*⟩ più di; **~ the phone** al telefono; **~ the page** alla pagina seguente; **all ~ Italy** in tutta [l']Italia; ⟨*travel*⟩ per l'Italia ● *adv* **~ again** un'altra volta; **~ and ~** più volte; **~ and above** oltre a; **~ here/there** qui/là; **all ~** ⟨*everywhere*⟩ dappertutto; **it's all ~** è tutto finito; **I ache all ~** ho male dappertutto; **come/bring ~** venire/portare; **turn ~** girare

over- *pref* (*too much*) troppo

overall[1] /'əʊvərɔ:l/ *n* grembiule *m*; **~s** *pl* tuta *fsg* (da lavoro)

overall[2] /əʊvər'ɔ:l/ *a* complessivo; ⟨*general*⟩ generale ● *adv* complessivamente

over'**balance** *vi* perdere l'equilibrio

over'**bearing** *a* prepotente

'**overboard** *adv* *Naut* in mare

'**overcast** *a* coperto

over'**charge** *vt* **~ sb** far pagare più del dovuto a qcno ● *vi* far pagare più del dovuto

'**overcoat** *n* cappotto *m*

over'**come** *vt* (*pt* **-came**, *pp* **-come**) vincere; **be ~ by** essere sopraffatto da

over'**crowded** *a* sovraffollato

over'**do** *vt* (*pt* **-did**, *pp* **-done**) esagerare; ⟨*cook too long*⟩ stracuocere; **~ it** (*fam: do too much*) strafare

'overdose *n* overdose *f inv*

'overdraft *n* scoperto *m*; **have an ~** avere il conto scoperto

over'draw *vt* (*pt* -drew, *pp* -drawn) **~ one's account** andare allo scoperto; **be ~n by** (*account:*) essere [allo] scoperto di

over'due *a* in ritardo

over'estimate *vt* sopravvalutare

'overflow¹ *n* (*water*) acqua *f* che deborda; (*people*) pubblico *m* in eccesso; (*outlet*) scarico *m*

over'flow² *vi* debordare

over'grown *a* (*garden*) coperto di erbacce

'overhaul *n* revisione *f*

over'haul *vt* Techn revisionare

over'head¹ *adv* in alto

'overhead² *a* aereo; (*railway*) sopraelevato; (*lights*) da soffitto. **~s** *npl* spese *fpl* generali

over'hear *vt* (*pt/pp* -heard) sentire per caso (*conversation*)

over'heat *vi* Auto surriscaldarsi ● *vt* surriscaldare

over'joyed *a* felicissimo

'overland *a* & *adv* via terra; **~ route** via *f* terrestre

over'lap *v* (*pt/pp* -lapped) ● *vi* sovrapporsi ● *vt* sovrapporre

over'leaf *adv* sul retro

over'load *vt* sovraccaricare

over'look *vt* dominare; (*fail to see, ignore*) lasciarsi sfuggire

overly /'əʊvəlɪ/ *adv* eccessivamente

over'night¹ *adv* per la notte; **stay ~** fermarsi a dormire

'overnight² *a* notturno; **~ bag** piccola borsa *f* da viaggio; **~ stay** sosta *f* per la notte

'overpass *n* cavalcavia *m inv*

over'pay *vt* (*pt/pp* -paid) strapagare

over'populated *a* sovrappopolato

over'power *vt* sopraffare. **~ing** *a* insostenibile

over'priced *a* troppo caro

overpro'duce *vt* produrre in eccesso

over'rate *vt* sopravvalutare. **~d** *a* sopravvalutato

over'reach *vt* **~ oneself** puntare troppo in alto

overre'act *vi* avere una reazione eccessiva. **~ion** *n* reazione *f* eccessiva

over'rid|e *vt* (*pt* -rode, *pp* -ridden) passare sopra a. **~ing** *a* prevalente

over'rule *vt* annullare (*decision*)

over'run *vt* (*pt* -ran, *pp* -run, *pres p* -running) invadere; oltrepassare (*time*); **be ~ with** essere invaso da

over'seas¹ *adv* oltremare

'overseas² *a* d'oltremare

over'see *vt* (*pt* -saw, *pp* -seen) sorvegliare

over'shadow *vt* adombrare

over'shoot *vt* (*pt/pp* -shot) oltrepassare

'oversight *n* disattenzione *f*; **an ~** una svista

over'sleep *vi* (*pt/pp* -slept) svegliarsi troppo tardi

over'step *vt* (*pt/pp* -stepped) **~ the mark** oltrepassare ogni limite

overt /əʊ'vɜːt/ *a* palese

over'tak|e *vt/i* (*pt* -took, *pp* -taken) sorpassare. **~ing** *n* sorpasso *m*; **no ~ing** divieto di sorpasso

over'tax *vt fig* abusare di

'overthrow¹ *n* Pol rovesciamento *m*

over'throw² *vt* (*pt* -threw, *pp* -thrown) Pol rovesciare

'overtime *n* lavoro *m* straordinario ● *adv* **work ~** fare lo straordinario

over'tired *a* sovraffaticato

'overtone *n fig* sfumatura *f*

overture /'əʊvətjʊə/*n* Mus preludio *m*; **~s** *pl fig* approccio *msg*

over'turn *vt* ribaltare ● *vi* ribaltarsi

'overweight *a* sovrappeso

overwhelm /-'welm/ *vt* sommergere (**with** di); (*fig with emotion*) con-

fondere. **~ing** *a* travolgente;
〈*victory, majority*〉 schiacciante

over'work *n* lavoro *m* eccessivo
● *vt* far lavorare eccessivamente
● *vi* lavorare eccessivamente

ow|e /əʊ/ *vt also fig* dovere 〈[to] sb
a qcno〉; **~e sb sth** dovere qcsa a
qcno. **~ing a due** 〈*money:*〉 essere da pagare ● *prep* **~ing to** a
causa di

owl /aʊl/ *n* gufo *m*

own[1] /əʊn/ *a* proprio ● *pron* a **car
of my ~** una macchina per conto
mio; **on one's ~** da solo; **hold
one's ~ with** tener testa a; **get
one's ~ back** *fam* prendersi una
rivincita

own[2] *vt* possedere; ammettere; **I don't ~ it** non mi appar-
tiene. **own up** *vi* confessare 〈**to**
sth qcsa〉

owner /'əʊnə(r)/ *n* proprietario, -a
mf. **~ship** *n* proprietà *f*

ox /ɒks/ *n* (*pl* **oxen**) bue *m* (*pl* **buoi**)

oxide /'ɒksaɪd/ *n* ossido *m*

oxygen /'ɒksɪdʒən/ *n* ossigeno *m*;
~ mask maschera *f* a ossigeno

oyster /'ɔɪstə(r)/ *n* ostrica *f*

ozone /'əʊzəʊn/ *n* ozono *m*.
~·friendly *a* che non danneggia
l'ozono. **~ layer** *n* fascia *f* d'ozono

Pp

PA *abbr* (**per annum**) all'anno

pace /peɪs/ *n* passo *m*; 〈*speed*〉 ritmo *m*; **keep ~ with** camminare di
pari passo con ● *vi* **~ up and
down** camminare avanti e indietro. **~·maker** *n Med* pacemaker *m*;
〈*runner*〉 battistrada *m*

Pacific /pə'sɪfɪk/ *a* & *n* **the ~**
[**Ocean**] l'oceano *m* Pacifico, il Pacifico

pacifier /'pæsɪfaɪə(r)/ *n Am* ciuc-
cio *m*, succhiotto *m*

pacifist /'pæsɪfɪst/ *n* pacifista *mf*

pacify /'pæsɪfaɪ/ *vt* (*pt/pp* **-ied**)
placare 〈*person*〉; pacificare
〈*country*〉

pack /pæk/ *n* 〈*of cards*〉 mazzo *m*;
〈*of hounds*〉 muta *f*; 〈*of wolves,
thieves*〉 branco *m*; 〈*of cigarettes
etc*〉 pacchetto *m*; **a ~ of lies** un
mucchio di bugie ● *vt* impacchettare 〈*article*〉; fare 〈*suitcase*〉; mettere in valigia 〈*swimsuit etc*〉;
〈*press down*〉 comprimere; **~ed
[out]** 〈*crowded*〉 pieno zeppo ● *vi*
fare i bagagli; **send sb ~ing** *fam*
mandare qcno a stendere. **pack
up** *vt* impacchettare ● *vi*
〈*machine:*〉 piantare in asso

package /'pækɪdʒ/ *n* pacco *m* ● *vt*
impacchettare. **~ deal** offerta *f*
tutto compreso. **~ holiday** *n* vacanza *f* organizzata. **~ tour** viaggio *m* organizzato

packaging /'pækɪdʒɪŋ/ *n* confezio-
ne *f*

packed 'lunch *n* pranzo *m* al sacco

packet /'pækɪt/ *n* pacchetto *m*;
cost a ~ *fam* costare un sacco

packing /'pækɪŋ/ *n* imballaggio *m*

pact /pækt/ *n* patto *m*

pad[1] /pæd/ *n* imbottitura *f*; 〈*for
writing*〉 bloc-notes *m*, taccuino *m*;
〈*fam: home*〉 〈piccolo〉 appartamento *m* ● *vt* (*pt/pp* **padded**) imbottire. **pad out** *vt* gonfiare

pad[2] *vi* (*pt/pp* **padded**) camminare
con passo felpato

padded /'pædɪd/ *a* **~ bra** reggiseno *m* imbottito

padding /'pædɪŋ/ *n* imbottitura *f*;
〈*in written work*〉 fronzoli *mpl*

paddle[1] /'pæd(ə)l/ *n* pagaia *f* ● *vt*
〈*row*〉 spingere remando

paddle[2] *vi* 〈*wade*〉 sguazzare

paddock /'pædək/ *n* recinto *m*

padlock /'pædlɒk/ *n* lucchetto *m*
● *vt* chiudere con lucchetto

paediatrician /pi:dɪə'trɪʃn/ *n* pe-
diatra *mf*

paediatrics /pi:dɪ'ætrɪks/ *n* pedia-
tria *f*

page[1] /peɪdʒ/ *n* pagina *f*

page² /peɪʤ/ n (boy) paggetto m; (in hotel) fattorino m ● vt far chiamare (person)

pageant /ˈpæʤənt/ n parata f. **~ry** n cerimoniale m

pager /ˈpeɪʤə(r)/ n cercapersone m inv

paid /peɪd/ see **pay** ● a ~ **employment** lavoro m remunerato; **put** ~ **to** mettere un termine a

pail /peɪl/ n secchio m

pain /peɪn/ n dolore m; **be in ~** soffrire; **take ~s** darsi un gran d'affare; **~ in the neck** fam spina f nel fianco

pain: **~ful** a doloroso; (laborious) penoso.. **~-killer** n calmante m. **~less** a indolore

painstaking /ˈpeɪnzteɪkɪŋ/ a minuzioso

paint /peɪnt/ n pittura f; **~s** colori mpl ● vt/i pitturare; (artist:) dipingere. **~brush** n pennello m. **~er** n pittore, -trice mf; (decorator) imbianchino m. **~ing** n pittura f; (picture) dipinto m. **~work** n pittura f

pair /peə(r)/ n paio m; (of people) coppia f; **~ of trousers** paio m di pantaloni; **~ of scissors** paio m di forbici

pajamas /pəˈʤɑːməz/ npl Am pigiama msg

Pakistan /pɑːkɪˈstɑːn/ n Pakistan m. **~i** a pakistano ● n pakistano, -a mf

pal /pæl/ n fam amico, -a mf

palace /ˈpælɪs/ n palazzo m

palatable /ˈpælətəbl/ a gradevole (al gusto)

palate /ˈpælət/ n palato m

palatial /pəˈleɪʃl/ a sontuoso

palaver /pəˈlɑːvə(r)/ n (fam: fuss) storie fpl

pale /peɪl/ a pallido

Palestin|e /ˈpælɪstaɪn/ n Palestina f. **~ian** /pælɪˈstɪnɪən/ a palestinese ● n palestinese mf

palette /ˈpælɪt/ n tavolozza f

pallid /ˈpælɪd/ a pallido. **~or** n pallore m

palm /pɑːm/ n palmo m; (tree) palma f; **P~ 'Sunday** n Domenica f delle Palme ● **palm off** vt ~ **sth off on sb** rifilare qcsa a qcno

palpable /ˈpælpəbl/ a palpabile; (perceptible) tangibile

palpitat|e /ˈpælpɪteɪt/ vi palpitare. **~ions** /-ˈteɪʃnz/ npl palpitazioni fpl

paltry /ˈpɔːltrɪ/ a (-ier, -iest) insignificante

pamper /ˈpæmpə(r)/ vt viziare

pamphlet /ˈpæmflɪt/ n opuscolo m

pan /pæn/ n tegame m, pentola f; (for frying) padella f; (of scales) piatto m ● vt (pt/pp **panned**) (fam: criticize) stroncare

panache /pəˈnæʃ/ n stile m

pancake n crêpe f inv, frittella f

pancreas /ˈpæŋkrɪəs/ n pancreas m inv

panda /ˈpændə/ n panda m inv. **~ car** n macchina f della polizia

pandemonium /pændɪˈməʊnɪəm/ n pandemonio m

pander /ˈpændə(r)/ vi ~ **to sb** compiacere qcno

pane /peɪn/ n ~ **[of glass]** vetro m

panel /ˈpænl/ n pannello m; (group of people) giuria f; ~ **of experts** gruppo m di esperti. **~ling** n pannelli mpl

pang /pæŋ/ n ~**s of hunger** morsi mpl della fame; **~s of conscience** rimorsi mpl di coscienza

panic /ˈpænɪk/ n panico m ● vi (pt/pp **panicked**) lasciarsi prendere dal panico. **~-stricken** a in preda al panico

panorama /pænəˈrɑːmə/ n panorama m. **~ic** /-ˈræmɪk/ a panoramico

pansy /ˈpænzɪ/ n viola f del pensiero; (fam: effeminate man) finocchio m

pant /pænt/ vi ansimare

panther /ˈpænθə(r)/ n pantera f

panties /ˈpæntɪz/ npl mutandine fpl

pantomime /ˈpæntəmaɪm/ n pantomima f

pantry /'pæntrɪ/ n dispensa f

pants /pænts/ npl (underwear) mutande fpl; (woman's) mutandine fpl; (trousers) pantaloni mpl

'pantyhose n Am collant m inv

papal /'peɪpl/ a papale

paper /'peɪpə(r)/ n carta f; (wallpaper) carta f da parati; (newspaper) giornale m; (exam) esame m; (treatise) saggio m; ~s pl (documents) documenti mpl; (for identification) documento m [d'identità]; **on** ~ in teoria; **put down on** ~ mettere per iscritto ●attrib di carta ● vt tappezzare

paper: ~**back** n edizione f economica. ~**clip** n graffetta f. ~**knife** n tagliacarte m inv. ~**weight** n fermacarte m inv. ~**work** n lavoro m d'ufficio

par /pɑ:(r)/ n (in golf) par m inv; **on a** ~ **with** alla pari con; **feel below** ~ essere un po' giù di tono

parable /'pærəbl/ n parabola f

parachut|e /'pærəʃu:t/ n paracadute m ● vi lanciarsi col paracadute. ~**ist** n paracadutista f

parade /pə'reɪd/ n (military) parata f militare ● vi sfilare ● vt (show off) far sfoggio di

paradise /'pærədaɪs/ n paradiso m

paradox /'pærədɒks/ n paradosso m. ~**ical** /-'dɒksɪkl/ a paradossale. ~**ically** adv paradossalmente

paraffin /'pærəfɪn/ n paraffina f

paragon /'pærəgən/ n ~ **of virtue** modello m di virtù

paragraph /'pærəgrɑ:f/ n paragrafo m

parallel /'pærəlel/ a & adv parallelo. ~ **bars** npl parallele fpl. ~ **port** n Comput porta f parallela ● n Geog, fig parallelo m; (line) parallela f ● vt essere paragonabile a

paralyse /'pærəlaɪz/ vt also fig paralizzare

paralysis /pə'rælɪsɪs/ n (pl -ses) /-si:z/ paralisi f inv

parameter /pə'ræmɪtə(r)/ n parametro m

paramount /'pærəmaʊnt/ a supremo; **be** ~ essere essenziale

paranoia /pærə'nɔɪə/ n paranoia f

paranoid /'pærənɔɪd/ a paranoico

paraphernalia /pærəfə'neɪlɪə/ n armamentario m

paraphrase /'pærəfreɪz/ n parafrasi f ● vt parafrasare

paraplegic /pærə'pli:dʒɪk/ a paraplegico ● n paraplegico, -a mf

parasite /'pærəsaɪt/ n parassita mf

parasol /'pærəsɒl/ n parasole m

paratrooper /'pærətru:pə(r)/ n paracadutista m

parcel /'pɑ:sl/ n pacco m

parch /pɑ:tʃ/ vt disseccare; **be** ~**ed** (person:) morire dalla sete

pardon /'pɑ:dn/ n perdono m; Jur grazia f; ~? prego?; **I beg your** ~? fml chiedo scusa?; **I do beg your** ~ (sorry) chiedo scusa! ● vt perdonare; Jur graziare

pare /peə(r)/ vt (peel) pelare

parent /'peərənt/ n genitore, -trice mf; ~**s** pl i genitori mpl. ~**al** /pə'rentl/ a dei genitori

parenthesis /pə'renθəsɪs/ n (pl -ses) /-si:z/ parentesi f inv

Paris /'pærɪs/ n Parigi f

parish /'pærɪʃ/ n parrocchia f. ~**ioner** /pə'rɪʃənə(r)/ n parrocchiano, -a mf

Parisian /pə'rɪzɪən/ a & n parigino, -a mf

parity /'pærətɪ/ n parità f

park /pɑ:k/ n parco m ● vt/i Auto posteggiare, parcheggiare; ~ **oneself** fam installarsi

parka /'pɑ:kə/ n parka m inv

parking /'pɑ:kɪŋ/ n parcheggio m, posteggio m; **'no** ~' 'divieto di sosta'. ~**-lot** n Am posteggio m, parcheggio m. ~**-meter** n parchimetro m. ~ **space** n posteggio m, parcheggio m

parliament /'pɑ:ləmənt/ n parlamento m. ~**ary** /-'mentərɪ/ a parlamentare

parlour /'pɑ:lə(r)/ n salotto m

parochial /pəˈrəʊkɪəl/ *a* parrocchiale; *fig* ristretto

parody /ˈpærədɪ/ *n* parodia *f* ● *vt* (*pt/pp* -**ied**) parodiare

parole /pəˈrəʊl/ *n* **on** ~ in libertà condizionale● *vt* mettere in libertà condizionale

parquet /ˈpɑːkeɪ/ *n* ~ **floor** parquet *m*

parrot /ˈpærət/ *n* pappagallo *m*

parry /ˈpærɪ/ *vt* (*pt/pp* -**ied**) parare ⟨*blow*⟩; (*in fencing*) eludere

parsimonious /pɑːsɪˈməʊnɪəs/ *a* parsimonioso

parsley /ˈpɑːslɪ/ *n* prezzemolo *m*

parsnip /ˈpɑːsnɪp/ *n* pastinaca *f*

parson /ˈpɑːsn/ *n* pastore *m*

part /pɑːt/ *n* parte *f*; (*of machine*) pezzo *m*; **for my** ~ per quanto mi riguarda; **on the** ~ **of** da parte di; **take sb's** ~ prendere le parti di qcno; **take** ~ **in** prendere parte a ● *adv* in parte ● *vt* ~ **one's hair** farsi la riga ● *vi* ⟨*people:*⟩ separarsi; ~ **with** separarsi da

part-ex'change *n* take in ~ prendere indietro

partial /ˈpɑːʃl/ *a* parziale; **be** ~ **to** aver un debole per. ~**ly** *adv* parzialmente

particip|ant /pɑːˈtɪsɪpənt/ *n* partecipante *mf*. ~**ate** /-peɪt/ *vi* partecipare (**in** a). ~**ation** /-ˈpeɪʃn/ *n* partecipazione *f*

participle /ˈpɑːtɪsɪpl/ *n* participio *m*; **present/past** ~ participio presente/passato

particle /ˈpɑːtɪkl/ *n* Phys, Gram particella *f*

particular /pəˈtɪkjʊlə(r)/ *a* particolare; (*precise*) meticoloso; *pej* noioso; **in** ~ in particolare. ~**ly** *adv* particolarmente. ~**s** *npl* particolari *mpl*

parting /ˈpɑːtɪŋ/ *n* separazione *f*; (*in hair*) scriminatura *f* ● *attrib* di commiato

partisan /pɑːtɪˈzæn/ *n* partigiano, -a *mf*

partition /pɑːˈtɪʃn/ *n* (*wall*) parete *f* divisoria; *Pol* divisione *f* ● *vt* dividere (*in parti*). **partition off** *vt* separare

partly /ˈpɑːtlɪ/ *adv* in parte

partner /ˈpɑːtnə(r)/ *n* Comm socio, -a *mf*; (*sport, in relationship*) compagno, -a *mf*. ~**ship** *n* Comm società *f*

partridge /ˈpɑːtrɪdʒ/ *n* pernice *f*

part-'time *a & adv* part time; **be** or **work** ~ lavorare part time

party /ˈpɑːtɪ/ *n* ricevimento *m*, festa *f*; (*group*) gruppo *m*; *Pol* partito *m*; *Jur* parte *f* (*in causa*); **be a** ~ **to** essere parte attiva in

'party line[1] *n* Teleph duplex *m inv*

party 'line[2] *n* Pol linea *f* del partito

pass /pɑːs/ *n* lasciapassare *m inv*; (*in mountains*) passo *m*; Sport passaggio *m*; Sch ⟨*mark*⟩ sufficiente *m* [voto *m*]; **make a** ~ **at** fam fare delle avances a ● *vt* passare; (*overtake*) sorpassare; (*approve*) far passare; fare ⟨*remark*⟩; *Jur* pronunciare ⟨*sentence*⟩; ~ **the time** passare il tempo ● *vi* passare; (*in exam*) essere promosso. **pass away** *vi* mancare. **pass down** *vt* passare; *fig* trasmettere. **pass out** *vi* fam svenire. **pass round** *vt* far passare. **pass through** *vt* attraversare. **pass up** *vt* passare; (*fam: miss*) lasciarsi scappare

passable /ˈpɑːsəbl/ *a* ⟨*road*⟩ praticabile; (*satisfactory*) passabile

passage /ˈpæsɪdʒ/ *n* passaggio *m*; (*corridor*) corridoio *m*; (*voyage*) traversata *f*

passenger /ˈpæsɪndʒə(r)/ *n* passeggero, -a *mf*. ~ **seat** *n* posto *m* accanto al guidatore

passer-by /pɑːsəˈbaɪ/ *n* (*pl* ~**s-by**) passante *m*

'passing place *n* piazzola *f* di sosta per consentire il transito dei veicoli nei due sensi

passion /ˈpæʃn/ *n* passione *f*. ~**ate** /-ət/ *a* appassionato

passive /ˈpæsɪv/ *a* passivo ● *n* passivo *m*. ~**ness** *n* passività *f*

'pass-mark n Sch [voto m] sufficiente m

Passover /'pɑːsəʊvə(r)/ n Pasqua f ebraica

pass: ~**port** n passaporto m. ~**word** n parola f d'ordine

past /pɑːst/ a passato; (former) ex; **in the** ~ **few days** nei giorni scorsi; **that's all** ~ tutto questo è passato; **the** ~ **week** la settimana scorsa ● n passato m ● prep oltre; **at ten** ~ **two** alle due e dieci ● adv oltre; **go/come** ~ passare

pasta /'pæstə/ n pasta[sciutta] f

paste /peɪst/ n pasta f; (dough) impasto m; (adhesive) colla f ● vt incollare

pastel /'pæstl/ n pastello m ● attrib pastello

pasteurize /'pɑːstʃəraɪz/ vt pastorizzare

pastille /'pæstɪl/ n pastiglia f

pastime /'pɑːstaɪm/ n passatempo m

pastoral /'pɑːstərəl/ a pastorale

pastrami /pæ'strɑːmɪ/ n carne f di manzo affumicata

pastry /'peɪstrɪ/ n pasta f; ~**ies** pasticcini mpl

pasture /'pɑːstʃə(r)/ n pascolo m

pasty¹ /'pæstɪ/ n ≈ pasticcio m

pasty² /'peɪstɪ/ a smorto

pat /pæt/ n buffetto m; (of butter) pezzetto m ● adv **have sth off** ~ conoscere qcsa a menadito ● vt (pt/pp **patted**) dare un buffetto a; ~ **sb on the back** fig congratularsi con qcno

patch /pætʃ/ n toppa f; (spot) chiazza f; (period) periodo m; **not a** ~ **on** fam molto inferiore a ● vt mettere una toppa su. **patch up** vt riparare alla bell'e meglio; appianare (quarrel)

patchy /'pætʃɪ/ a incostante

pâté /'pæteɪ/ n pâté m inv

patent /'peɪtnt/ a palese ● n brevetto m ● vt brevettare. ~ **leather shoes** npl scarpe fpl di vernice. ~**ly** adv in modo palese

patern|al /pə'tɜːnl/ a paterno. ~**ity** n paternità f inv

path /pɑːθ/ n (pl ~**s** /pɑːðz/) sentiero m; (orbit) traiettoria m; fig strada f

pathetic /pə'θetɪk/ a patetico; (fam: very bad) penoso

pathological /pæθə'lodʒɪkl/ a patologico. ~**ist** /pə'θɒlədʒɪst/ n patologo, -a mf. ~**y** patologia f

pathos /'peɪθɒs/ n pathos m

patience /'peɪʃns/ n pazienza f; (game) solitario m

patient /'peɪʃnt/ a paziente ● n paziente mf. ~**ly** adv pazientemente

patio /'pætɪəʊ/ n terrazza f

patriot /'pætrɪət/ n patriota mf. ~**ic** /-'ɒtɪk/ a patriottico. ~**ism** n patriottismo m

patrol /pə'trəʊl/ n pattuglia f ● vt/i pattugliare. ~ **car** n autopattuglia f

patron /'peɪtrən/ n patrono m; (of charity) benefattore, -trice mf; (of the arts) mecenate mf; (customer) cliente mf

patroniz|e /'pætrənaɪz/ vt frequentare abitualmente; fig trattare con condiscendenza. ~**ing** a condiscendente. ~**ingly** adv con condiscendenza

patter¹ /'pætə(r)/ n picchiettio m ● vi picchiettare

patter² n (of salesman) chiacchiere fpl

pattern /'pætn/ n disegno m (stampato); (for knitting, sewing) modello m

paunch /pɔːntʃ/ n pancia f

pause /pɔːz/ n pausa f ● vi fare una pausa

pave /peɪv/ vt pavimentare; ~ **the way** preparare la strada (**for** a). ~**ment** n marciapiede m

pavilion /pə'vɪljən/ n padiglione m

paw /pɔː/ n zampa f ● vt fam mettere le zampe addosso a

pawn¹ /pɔːn/ n (in chess) pedone m; fig pedina f

pawn² vt impegnare ● n **in** ~ in pegno. ~**broker** n prestatore, -trice *mf* su pegno. **~shop** *n* monte *m* di pietà

pay /peɪ/ *n* paga *f*; **in the ~ of** al soldo di ● *v* (*pt/pp* **paid**) ● *vt* pagare; prestare ⟨*attention*⟩; fare ⟨*compliment*, *visit*⟩; **~ cash** pagare in contanti ● *vi* pagare; ⟨*be profitable*⟩ rendere; **it doesn't ~ to...** *fig* è fatica sprecata...; **~ for sth** pagare per qcsa. **pay back** *vt* ripagare. **pay in** *vt* versare. **pay off** *vt* saldare ⟨*debt*⟩ ● *vi fig* dare dei frutti. **pay up** *vi* pagare

payable /ˈpeɪəbl/ *a* pagabile; **make ~ to** intestare a

payee /peɪˈiː/ *n* beneficiario *m* (di una somma)

payment /ˈpeɪmənt/ *n* pagamento *m*

pay: **~ packet** *n* busta *f* paga. **~ phone** *n* telefono *m* pubblico

PC *n abbr* (**personal computer**) PC *m inv*

pea /piː/ *n* pisello *m*

peace /piːs/ *n* pace *f*; **~ of mind** tranquillità *f*

peace|able /ˈpiːsəbl/ *a* pacifico. **~ful** *a* calmo, sereno. **~fully** *adv* in pace. **~maker** *n* mediatore, -trice *mf*

peach /piːtʃ/ *n* pesca *f*; ⟨*tree*⟩ pesco *m*

peacock /ˈpiːkɒk/ *n* pavone *m*

peak /piːk/ *n* picco *m*; *fig* culmine *m*. **~ed 'cap** *n* berretto *m* a punta. **~ hours** *npl* ore *fpl* di punta

peaky /ˈpiːkɪ/ *a* malaticcio

peal /piːl/ *n* (*of bells*) scampanio *m*; **~s of laughter** fragore *m* di risate

'peanut *n* nocciolina *f* [americana]; **~s** *fam* miseria *f*

pear /peə(r)/ *n* pera *f*; ⟨*tree*⟩ pero *m*

pearl /pɜːl/ *n* perla *f*

peasant /ˈpezənt/ *n* contadino, -a *mf*

pebble /ˈpebl/ *n* ciottolo *m*

peck /pek/ *n* beccata *f*; ⟨*kiss*⟩ bacetto *m* ● *vt* beccare; ⟨*kiss*⟩ dare un bacetto a. **~ing order** *n* gerarchia *f*. **peck at** *vt* beccare

peckish /ˈpekɪʃ/ *a* **be ~** *fam* avere un languorino [allo stomaco]

peculiar /pɪˈkjuːlɪə(r)/ *a* strano; (*special*) particolare; **~ to** tipico di. **~ity** /-ˈærətɪ/ *n* stranezza *f*; (*feature*) particolarità *f inv*

pedal /ˈpedl/ *n* pedale *m* ● *vi* pedalare. **~ bin** *n* pattumiera *f* a pedale

pedantic /pɪˈdæntɪk/ *a* pedante

pedestal /ˈpedɪstl/ *n* piedistallo *m*

pedestrian /pɪˈdestrɪən/ *n* pedone *m* ● *a fig* scadente. **~ 'crossing** *n* passaggio *m* pedonale. **~ 'precinct** *n* zona *f* pedonale

pedicure /ˈpedɪkjʊə(r)/ *n* pedicure *f inv*

pedigree /ˈpedɪgriː/ *n* pedigree *m inv*; (*of person*) lignaggio *m* ● *attrib* ⟨*animal*⟩ di razza, con ● pedigree

pee /piː/ *vi* (*pt/pp* **peed**) *fam* fare [la] pipì

peek /piːk/ *vi fam* sbirciare

peel /piːl/ *n* buccia *f* ● *vt* sbucciare ● *vi* ⟨*nose etc.*⟩ spellarsi; ⟨*paint*⟩ staccarsi

peep /piːp/ *n* sbirciata *f* ● *vi* sbirciare

peer[1] /pɪə(r)/ *vi* **~ at** scrutare

peer[2] *n* nobile *m*; **his ~s** *pl* (*in rank*) i suoi pari *mpl*; (*in age*) i suoi coetanei *mpl*. **~age** *n* nobiltà *f*

peeved /piːvd/ *a fam* irritato

peg /peg/ *n* (*hook*) piolo *m*; (*for tent*) picchetto *m*; (*for clothes*) molletta *f*; **off the ~** *fam* prêt-à-porter

pejorative /pɪˈdʒɒrətɪv/ *a* peggiorativo

pelican /ˈpelɪkən/ *n* pellicano *m*

pellet /ˈpelɪt/ *n* pallottola *f*

pelt /pelt/ *vt* bombardare ● *vi* (*fam: run fast*) catapultarsi; **~ [down]** ⟨*rain:*⟩ venir giù a fiotti

pelvis /ˈpelvɪs/ *n Anat* bacino *m*

pen[1] /pen/ *n* (*for animals*) recinto *m*

pen[2] *n* penna *f*; (*ball-point*) penna *f* a sfera

penal /ˈpiːnl/ *a* penale. **~ize** *vt* penalizzare

penalty /ˈpenltɪ/ *n* sanzione *f*;

(*fine*) multa *f*; (*in football*) ~
[kick] [calcio *m* di] rigore *m*; ~
area *or* **box** area *f* di rigore
penance /'penəns/ *n* penitenza *f*
pence /pens/ *see* **penny**
pencil /'pensl/ *n* matita *f*.
~-sharpener *n* temperamatite *m*
inv
pendant /'pendənt/ *n* ciondolo *m*
pending /'pendɪŋ/ *a* in sospeso
● *prep* in attesa di
pendulum /'pendjʊləm/ *n* pendolo *m*
penetrat|e /'penɪtreɪt/ *vt/i* penetrare. **~ing** *a* acuto; (*sound, stare*)
penetrante. **~ion** /-'treɪʃn/ *n*
penetrazione *f*
'penfriend *n* amico, -a *mf* di penna
penguin /'peŋgwɪn/ *n* pinguino *m*
penicillin /penɪ'sɪlɪn/ *n* penicillina *f*
peninsula /pɪ'nɪnsjʊlə/ *n* penisola *f*
penis /'piːnɪs/ *n* pene *m*
peniten|ce /'penɪtəns/ *n* penitenza *f*. **~t** *a* penitente ● *n* penitente *mf*
penitentiary /penɪ'tenʃərɪ/ *n* Am penitenziario *m*
pen: **~knife** *n* temperino *m*.
~-name *n* pseudonimo *m*
pennant /'penənt/ *n* bandiera *f*
penniless /'penɪlɪs/ *a* senza un soldo
penny /'penɪ/ *n* (*pl* **pence**; *single coins* **pennies**) penny *m*; Am centesimo *m*; **spend a ~** *fam* andare in bagno
pension /'penʃn/ *n* pensione *f*. **~er** *n* pensionato, -a *mf*
pensive /'pensɪv/ *a* pensoso
Pentecost /'pentɪkɒst/ *n* Pentecoste *f*
pent-up /'pentʌp/ *a* represso
penultimate /pɪ'nʌltɪmət/ *a* penultimo
people /'piːpl/ *npl* persone *fpl*, gente *fsg*; (*citizens*) popolo *msg*; **a lot of ~** una marea di gente; **the ~** la gente; **English ~** gli inglesi; (*say*) si dice; **for four ~** per quattro ● *vt* popolare

pepper /'pepə(r)/ *n* pepe *m*; (*vegetable*) peperone *m* ● *vt* (*season*) pepare
pepper: **~corn** *n* grano *m* di pepe.
~ mill macinapepe *m inv*. **~mint** *n* menta *f* peperita; (*sweet*) caramella *f* alla menta. **~pot** *n* pepiera *f*
per /pɜː(r)/ *prep* per; **~ annum** all'anno; **~ cent** percento
perceive /pə'siːv/ *vt* percepire; (*interpret*) interpretare
percentage /pə'sentɪdʒ/ *n* percentuale *f*
percept|ible /pə'septəbl/ *a* percettibile; (*difference*) sensibile
percept|ion /pə'sepʃn/ *n* percezione *f*. **~ive** /-tɪv/ *a* perspicace
perch /pɜːtʃ/ *n* pertica *f* ● *vi* (*bird:*) appollaiarsi
percolator /'pɜːkəleɪtə(r)/ *n* caffettiera *f* a filtro
percussion /pə'kʌʃn/ *n* percussione *f*. **~ instrument** *n* strumento *m* a percussione
peremptory /pə'rempt(ə)rɪ/ *a* perentorio
perennial /pə'renɪəl/ *a* perenne ● *n* pianta *f* perenne
perfect[1] /'pɜːfɪkt/ *a* perfetto ● *n* Gram passato *m* prossimo
perfect[2] /pə'fekt/ *vt* perfezionare. **~ion** /-ekʃn/ *n* perfezione *f*; **to ~ion** alla perfezione. **~ionist** *n* perfezionista *mf*
perfectly /'pɜːfɪktlɪ/ *adv* perfettamente
perforat|e /'pɜːfəreɪt/ *vt* perforare.
~ed *a* perforato; (*ulcer*) perforante. **~ion** *n* perforazione *f*
perform /pə'fɔːm/ *vt* compiere, fare; eseguire (*operation, sonata*); recitare (*role*); mettere in scena (*play*) ● *vi* Theat recitare; Techn funzionare. **~ance** *n* esecuzione *f*; (*at theatre, cinema*) rappresentazione *f*; Techn rendimento *m*. **~er** *n* artista *mf*
perfume /'pɜːfjuːm/ *n* profumo *m*
perfunctory /pə'fʌŋktərɪ/ *a* superficiale
perhaps /pə'hæps/ *adv* forse

peril /'perɪl/ *n* pericolo *m*. **~ous**
/-əs/ *a* pericoloso

perimeter /pə'rɪmɪtə(r)/ *n* perime-
tro *m*

period /'pɪərɪəd/ *n* periodo *m*;
(*menstruation*) mestruazioni *fpl*;
Sch ora *f* di lezione; (*full stop*)
punto *m* fermo ● *attrib* (*costume*)
d'epoca; (*furniture*) in stile. **~ic**
/-'ɒdɪk/ *a* periodico. **~ical** /-'ɒdɪk/
n periodico *m*, rivista *f*

peripher|al /pə'rɪfərəl/ *a* periferi-
co. **~y** *n* periferia *f*

periscope /'perɪskəʊp/ *n* perisco-
pio *m*

perish /'perɪʃ/ *vi* (*rot*) deteriorarsi; (*die*) perire. **~able** /-əbl/ *a*
deteriorabile

perjur|e /'pɜːdʒə(r)/ *vt* **~e oneself**
spergiurare. **~y** *n* spergiuro *m*

perk /pɜːk/ *n fam* vantaggio *m*

perk up *vt* tirare su ● *vi* tirarsi su

perky /'pɜːkɪ/ *a* allegro

perm /pɜːm/ *n* permanente *f* ● *vt* **~**
sb's hair fare la permanente a
qno

permanent /'pɜːmənənt/ *a* permanente; (*job, address*) stabile. **~ly**
adv stabilmente

permeate /'pɜːmɪeɪt/ *vt* impregnare

permissible /pə'mɪsəbl/ *a* ammissibile

permission /pə'mɪʃn/ *n* permesso *m*

permissive /pə'mɪsɪv/ *a* permissi-
vo

permit[1] /pə'mɪt/ *vt* (*pt/pp* -mitted)
permettere; **~ sb to do sth** permettere a qcno di fare qcsa

permit[2] /'pɜːmɪt/ *n* autorizzazione *f*

perpendicular /pɜːpən'dɪkjʊlə(r)/
a perpendicolare ● *n* perpendicolare *f*

perpetual /pə'petjʊəl/ *a* perenne.
~ly *adv* perennemente

perpetuate /pə'petjʊeɪt/ *vt* perpe-
tuare

perplex /pə'pleks/ *vt* lasciare per-

plesso. **~ed** *a* perplesso. **~ity** *n*
perplessità *f inv*

persecut|e /'pɜːsɪkjuːt/ *vt* perse-
guitare. **~ion** /-'kjuːʃn/ *n* persecuzione *f*

perseverance /pɜːsɪ'vɪərəns/ *n*
perseveranza *f*

persevere /pɜːsɪ'vɪə(r)/ *vi* perseverare. **~ing** *a* assiduo

Persian /'pɜːʃn/ *a* persiano

persist /pə'sɪst/ *vi* persistere; **~ in**
doing sth persistere nel fare qcsa.
~ence *n* persistenza *f*. **~ent** *a*
persistente. **~ently** *adv* persisten-
temente

person /'pɜːsn/ *n* persona *f*; **in ~** di
persona

personal /'pɜːsənl/ *a* personale. **~**
hygiene *n* igiene *f* personale. **~ly**
adv personalmente. **~ organizer**
n Comput agenda *f* elettronica

personality /pɜːsə'nælətɪ/ *n* perso-
nalità *f inv*; (*on TV*) personaggio *m*

personnel /pɜːsə'nel/ *n* personale
m

perspective /pə'spektɪv/ *n* prospettiva *f*

persp|iration /pɜːspɪ'reɪʃn/ *n* su-
dore *m*. **~ire** /-'spaɪə(r)/ *vi* sudare

persua|de /pə'sweɪd/ *vt* persuade-
re. **~sion** /-eɪʒn/ *n* persuasione *f*;
(*belief*) convinzione *f*

persuasive /pə'sweɪsɪv/ *a* persuasivo. **~ly** *adv* in modo persuasivo

pertinent /'pɜːtɪnənt/ *a* pertinente
(**to** a)

perturb /pə'tɜːb/ *vt* perturbare

peruse /pə'ruːz/ *vt* leggere

perva|de /pə'veɪd/ *vt* pervadere.
~sive /-sɪv/ *a* pervasivo

perver|se /pə'vɜːs/ *a* irragionevo-
le. **~ion** /-ɜːʃn/ *n* perversione *f*

pervert /'pɜːvɜːt/ *n* pervertito, -a
mf

perverted /pə'vɜːtɪd/ *a* perverso

pessimis|m /'pesɪmɪzm/ *n* pessi-
mismo *m*. **~t** /-mɪst/ *n* pessimista
mf. **~tic** /-'mɪstɪk/ *a* pessimistico.
~tically *adv* in modo pessimistico

pest /pest/ n piaga f; (fam: person) peste f

pester /'pestə(r)/ vt molestare

pesticide /'pestisaid/ n pesticida m

pet /pet/ n animale m domestico; (favourite) cocco, -a mf ● a prediletto e v (pt/pp **petted**) ● vt coccolare ● vi (couple:) praticare il petting

petal /'petl/ n petalo m

peter /'pi:tə(r)/ vi ~ **out** finire

petite /pə'ti:t/ a minuto

petition /pə'tɪʃn/ n petizione f

pet 'name n vezzeggiativo m

petrify /'petrɪfaɪ/ vt (pt/pp **-ied**) pietrificare. **~ied** a (frightened) pietrificato

petrol /'petrəl/ n benzina f

petroleum /pɪ'trəʊlɪəm/ n petrolio m

petrol: **~-pump** n pompa f di benzina. **~ station** n stazione f di servizio. **~ tank** n serbatoio m della benzina

'pet shop n negozio m di animali [domestici]

petticoat /'petɪkəʊt/ n sottoveste f

petty /'petɪ/ a (**-ier, -iest**) insignificante; (mean) meschino. **~ 'cash** n cassa f per piccole spese

petulant /'petjʊlənt/ a petulante

pew /pju:/ n banco m (di chiesa)

pewter /'pju:tə(r)/ n peltro m

phallic /'fælɪk/ a fallico

phantom /'fæntəm/ n fantasma m

pharmaceutical /fɑ:mə'sju:tɪkl/ a farmaceutico

pharmacist /'fɑ:məsɪst/ n farmacista mf. **~y** n farmacia f

phase /feɪz/ n fase f ● vt phase in/out introdurre/eliminare gradualmente

Ph.D. n abbr (Doctor of Philosophy) ≈ dottorato m di ricerca

pheasant /'feznt/ n fagiano m

phenomenal /fɪ'nɒmɪnl/ a fenomenale; (incredible:) incredibile. **~ally** adv incredibilmente. **~on** n (pl **-na**) fenomeno m

philanderer /fɪ'lændərə(r)/ n donnaiolo m

philanthropic /fɪlən'θrɒpɪk/ a filantropico. **~ist** /fɪ'lænθrəpɪst/ n filantropo, -a mf

philately /fɪ'lætəlɪ/ n filatelia f. **~ist** n filatelico, -a mf

philharmonic /fɪlhɑ:'mɒnɪk/ n (orchestra) orchestra f filarmonica ● a filarmonico

Philippines /'fɪlɪpi:nz/ npl Filippine fpl

philistine /'fɪlɪstaɪn/ n filisteo, -a mf

philosopher /fɪ'lɒsəfə(r)/ n filosofo, -a mf. **~ical** /fɪlə'sɒfɪkl/ a filosofico. **~ically** adv con filosofia. **~y** n filosofia f

phlegm /flem/ n Med flemma f

phlegmatic /fleg'mætɪk/ a flemmatico

phobia /'fəʊbɪə/ n fobia f

phone /fəʊn/ n telefono m; **be on the ~** avere il telefono; (be phoning) essere al telefono ● vt telefonare a ● vi telefonare. **phone back** vt/i richiamare. **~ book** n guida f del telefono. **~ box** n cabina f telefonica. **~ card** n scheda f telefonica. **~ call** n telefonata f. **~-in** n trasmissione f con chiamate in diretta. **~ number** n numero m telefonico

phonetic /fə'netɪk/ a fonetico. **~s** n fonetica f s

phoney /'fəʊnɪ/ a (**-ier, -iest**) fasullo

phosphorus /'fɒsfərəs/ n fosforo m

photo /'fəʊtəʊ/ n foto f; **~ album** album m inv di fotografie. **~copier** n fotocopiatrice f. **~copy** n fotocopia f ● vt fotocopiare

photogenic /fəʊtəʊ'dʒenɪk/ a fotogenico

photograph /'fəʊtəgrɑ:f/ n fotografia f ● vt fotografare

photographer /fə'tɒgrəfə(r)/ n fotografo, -a mf. **~ic** /fəʊtə'græfɪk/ a fotografico. **~y** n fotografia f

phrase /freɪz/ n espressione f ● vt

esprimere. **~-book** n libro m di fraseologia

physical /'fɪzɪkl/ a fisico. **~ edu'cation** n educazione f fisica. **~ly** adv fisicamente

physician /fɪ'zɪʃn/ n medico m

physic|ist /'fɪzɪsɪst/ n fisico, -a mf. **~s** n fisica f

physiology /fɪzɪ'blədʒɪ/ n fisiologia f

physio'therap|ist /fɪzɪəʊ-/ n fisioterapista m. **~y** n fisioterapia f

physique /fɪ'ziːk/ n fisico m

pianist /'pɪənɪst/ n pianista mf

piano /pɪ'ænəʊ/ n piano m

pick[1] /pɪk/ n (tool) piccone m

pick[2] n scelta f; **take your ~** prendi quello che vuoi ● vt (select) scegliere; cogliere (flowers); scassinare (lock); borseggiare (pockets); **~ and choose** fare il difficile; **~ one's nose** mettersi le dita nel naso; **~ a quarrel** attaccar briga; **~ holes in** fam criticare; **~ at one's food** spilluzzicare. **pick on** vt (fam: nag) assillare; **he always ~s on me** ce l'ha con me. **pick out** vt (identify) individuare. **pick up** vt sollevare; (off the ground, information) raccogliere; prendere in braccio (baby); (learn) imparare; prendersi (illness); (buy) comprare; captare (signal); (collect) andare/venire a prendere; prendere (passengers, habit); ⟨police:⟩ arrestare (criminal); fam rimorchiare (girl); **~ oneself up** riprendersi ● vi (improve) recuperare; ⟨weather:⟩ rimettersi

'pickaxe n piccone m

picket /'pɪkɪt/ n picchettista mf ● vt picchettare. **~ line** n picchetto m

pickle /'pɪkl/ n **~s** pl sottaceti mpl; **in a ~** fig nei pasticci ● vt mettere sottaceto

pick: ~pocket n borsaiolo m. **~-up** n (truck) furgone m; (on record-player) pickup m inv

picnic /'pɪknɪk/ n picnic m ● vi (pt/pp **-nicked**) fare un picnic

picture /'pɪktʃə(r)/ n (painting) quadro m; (photo) fotografia f; (drawing) disegno m; (film) film m inv; **put sb in the ~** fig mettere qcno al corrente; **the ~s** il cinema ● vt (imagine) immaginare

picturesque /pɪktʃə'resk/ a pittoresco

pie /paɪ/ n torta f

piece /piːs/ n pezzo m; (in game) pedina f; **a ~ of bread/paper** un pezzo di pane/carta; **a ~ of news/advice** una notizia/un consiglio; **take to ~s** smontare. **~meal** adv un po' alla volta. **~-work** n lavoro m a cottimo **● piece together** vt montare; fig ricostruire

pier /pɪə(r)/ n molo m; (pillar) pilastro m

pierce /pɪəs/ vt perforare; **~e a hole in sth** fare un buco in qcsa. **~ing** a penetrante

pig /pɪg/ n maiale m

pigeon /'pɪdʒɪn/ n piccione m. **~-hole** n casella f

piggy /'pɪgɪ/ **~back** n **give sb a ~back** portare qcno sulle spalle. **~ bank** n salvadanaio m

pig'headed a fam cocciuto

pig: ~skin n pelle f di cinghiale. **~-tail** n (plait) treccina f

pile[1] /paɪl/ n (heap) pila f ● vt **~ sth on to sth** appilare qcsa su qcsa. **pile up** vt accatastare ● vi ammucchiarsi

piles /paɪlz/ npl emorroidi fpl

'pile-up n tamponamento m a catena

pilfering /'pɪlfərɪŋ/ n piccoli furti mpl

pilgrim /'pɪlgrɪm/ n pellegrino, -a mf. **~age** /-ɪdʒ/ n pellegrinaggio m

pill /pɪl/ n pillola f

pillage /'pɪlɪdʒ/ vt saccheggiare

pillar /'pɪlə(r)/ n pilastro m. **~-box** n buca f delle lettere

pillion /'pɪljən/ n sellino m posteriore; **ride ~** viaggiare dietro

pillory /'pɪlərɪ/ vt (pt/pp **-ied**) fig mettere alla berlina

pillow /'pɪləʊ/ n guanciale m.
~case n federa f

pilot /'paɪlət/ n pilota mf ● vt pilotare. **~-light** n fiamma f di sicurezza

pimp /pɪmp/ n protettore m

pimple /'pɪmpl/ n foruncolo m

pin /pɪn/ n spillo m; Electr spinotto m; Med chiodo m; **I have ~s and needles in my leg** fam mi formicola una gamba ● vt (pt/pp pinned) appuntare (**to/on** su); (sewing) fissare con gli spilli; (hold down) immobilizzare; **~ sb down to a date** ottenere un appuntamento da qcno; **~ sth on sb** fam addossare a qcno la colpa di qcsa. **pin up** vt appuntare; (on wall) affiggere

pinafore /'pɪnəfɔ:(r)/ n grembiule m. **~ dress** n scamiciato m

pincers /'pɪnsəz/ npl tenaglie fpl

pinch /pɪntʃ/ n pizzicotto m; (of salt) presa f; **at a ~** fam in caso di bisogno ● vt pizzicare; (fam: steal) fregare ● vi (shoe:) stringere

'pincushion n puntaspilli m inv

pine¹ /paɪn/ n (tree) pino m

pine² vi **she is pining for you** le manchi molto. **pine away** vi deperire

pineapple /paɪn-/ n ananas m inv

ping /pɪŋ/ n rumore m metallico

'ping-pong n ping-pong m

pink /pɪŋk/ a rosa m

pinnacle /'pɪnəkl/ n guglia f

PIN number n codice m segreto

pin: **~point** vt definire con precisione. **~stripe** a gessato

pint /paɪnt/ n pinta f (= 0,571, Am: 0,47 l); **a ~** fam una birra media

'pin-up n ragazza f da copertina, pin-up f inv

pioneer /paɪə'nɪə(r)/ n pioniere, -a mf ● vt essere un pioniere di

pious /'paɪəs/ a pio

pip /pɪp/ n (seed) seme m

pipe /paɪp/ n tubo m; (for smoking) pipa f; **the ~s** Mus la cornamusa ● vt far arrivare con tubature

(water, gas etc). **pipe down** vi fam abbassare la voce

pipe: **~-cleaner** n scovolino m. **~-dream** n illusione f. **~-line** n conduttura f; **in the ~-line** fam in cantiere

piper /'paɪpə(r)/ n suonatore m di cornamusa

piping /'paɪpɪŋ/ a **~ hot** bollente

pirate /'paɪrət/ n pirata m

Pisces /'paɪsi:z/ n Astr Pesci mpl

piss /pɪs/ vi sl pisciare

pistol /'pɪstl/ n pistola f

piston /'pɪstn/ n Techn pistone m

pit /pɪt/ n fossa f; (mine) miniera f; (for orchestra) orchestra f ● vt (pt/pp pitted) fig opporre (**against** a)

pitch¹ /pɪtʃ/ n (tone) tono m; (level) altezza f; (in sport) campo m; (fig: degree) grado m ● vt montare (tent). **pitch in** vi fam mettersi sotto

pitch² n **~-'black** a nero come la pece. **~-'dark** a buio pesto

'pitchfork n forca f

piteous /'pɪtɪəs/ a pietoso

'pitfall n fig trabocchetto m

pith /pɪθ/ n (of lemon, orange) interno m della buccia

pithy /'pɪθɪ/ a (-ier, -iest) fig conciso

piti|ful /'pɪtɪfl/ a pietoso. **~less** a spietato

pittance /'pɪtns/ n miseria f

pity /'pɪtɪ/ n pietà f; **[what a] ~!** (che peccato!); **take ~ on** avere compassione di ● vt aver pietà di

pivot /'pɪvət/ n perno m; fig fulcro m ● vi impernarsi (**on** su)

pizza /'pi:tsə/ n pizza f

placard /'plækɑ:d/ n cartellone m

placate /plə'keɪt/ vt placare

place /pleɪs/ n posto m; (fam: house) casa f; (in book) segno m; **feel out of ~** sentirsi fuori posto; **take ~** aver luogo; **all over the ~** dappertutto ● vt collocare; (remember) identificare; **~ an order** fare un'ordinazione; **be ~d** (in *race*) piazzarsi. **~-mat** *n* sottopiatto *m*

placid /ˈplæsɪd/ *a* placido

plagiar|ism /ˈpleɪdʒərɪzm/ *n* plagio *m*. **~ize** *vt* plagiare

plague /pleɪg/ *n* peste *f*

plaice /pleɪs/ *n inv* platessa *f*

plain /pleɪn/ *a* chiaro; (*simple*) semplice; (*not pretty*) scialbo; (*not patterned*) normale; ‹*chocolate*› fondente; **in ~ clothes** in borghese ● *adv* (*simply*) semplicemente ● *n* pianura *f*. **~ly** *adv* francamente; (*simply*) semplicemente; (*obviously*) chiaramente

plaintiff /ˈpleɪntɪf/ *n* Jur parte *f* lesa

plaintive /ˈpleɪntɪv/ *a* lamentoso

plait /plæt/ *n* treccia *f* ● *vt* intrecciare

plan /plæn/ *n* progetto *m*, piano *m* ● *vt* (*pt/pp* **planned**) progettare; (*intend*) prevedere

plane¹ /pleɪn/ *n* (*tree*) platano *m*

plane² *n* aeroplano *m*

plane³ *n* (*tool*) pialla *f* ● *vt* piallare

planet /ˈplænɪt/ *n* pianeta *m*

plank /plæŋk/ *n* asse *f*

planning /ˈplænɪŋ/ *n* pianificazione *f*. **~ permission** *n* licenza *f* edilizia

plant /plɑːnt/ *n* pianta *f*; (*machinery*) impianto *m*; (*factory*) stabilimento *m* ● *vt* piantare. **~ation** /plænˈteɪʃn/ *n* piantagione *f*

plaque /plɑːk/ *n* placca *f*

plasma /ˈplæzmə/ *n* plasma *m*

plaster /ˈplɑːstə(r)/ *n* intonaco *m*; Med gesso *m*; (*sticking ~*) cerotto *m*; **~ of Paris** gesso *m* ● *vt* intonacare (*wall*); (*cover*) ricoprire. **~ed** *a sl* sbronzo. **~er** *n* intonacatore *m*

plastic /ˈplæstɪk/ *n* plastica *f* ● *a* plastico

Plasticine® /ˈplæstɪsiːn/ *n* plastilina® *f*

plastic: ~ ˈsurgeon *n* chirurgo *m* plastico. **~ surgery** *n* chirurgia *f* plastica

plate /pleɪt/ *n* piatto *m*; (*flat sheet*)

placca *f*; (*gold and silverware*) argenteria *f*; (*in book*) tavola *f* [fuori testo] ● *vt* (*cover with metal*) placcare

plateau /ˈplætəʊ/ *n* (*pl* **~x** /-əʊz/) altopiano *m*

platform /ˈplætfɔːm/ *n* (*stage*) palco *m*; Rail marciapiede *m*; Pol piattaforma *f*. **~ 5** binario 5

platinum /ˈplætɪnəm/ *n* platino *m* ● *attrib* di platino

platitude /ˈplætɪtjuːd/ *n* luogo *m* comune

platonic /pləˈtɒnɪk/ *a* platonico

platoon /pləˈtuːn/ *n* Mil plotone *m*

platter /ˈplætə(r)/ *n* piatto *m* da portata

plausible /ˈplɔːzəbl/ *a* plausibile

play /pleɪ/ *n* gioco *m*; Theat, TV rappresentazione *f*; Radio sceneggiato *m* radiofonico; **~ on words** gioco *m* di parole ● *vt* giocare a; (*act*) recitare; suonare (*instrument*); giocare (*card*) ● *vi* giocare; Mus suonare; **~ safe** non prendere rischi. **play down** *vt* minimizzare. **play up** *vi fam* fare i capricci

play: ~boy *n* playboy *m inv*. **~er** *n* giocatore, -trice *mf*. **~ful** *a* scherzoso. **~ground** *n* Sch cortile *m* (*per la ricreazione*). **~group** *n* asilo *m*

playing: ~-card *n* carta *f* da gioco. **~-field** *n* campo *m* da gioco

play: ~mate *n* compagno, -a *mf* di gioco. **~-pen** *n* box *m inv*. **~thing** *n* giocattolo *m*. **~wright** /-raɪt/ *n* drammaturgo, -a *mf*

plc *n abbr* (**public limited company**) s.r.l.

plea /pliː/ *n* richiesta *f*; **make a ~ for** fare un appello a

plead /pliːd/ *vi* fare appello (**for a**); **~ guilty** dichiararsi colpevole; **~ with sb** implorare qcno

pleasant /ˈplez(ə)nt/ *a* piacevole. **~ly** *adv* piacevolmente; (*say, smile*) cordialmente

pleas|e /pliːz/ *adv* per favore; **~e do** prego ● *vt* far contento; **~e oneself** fare ciò che si vuole; **~e oneself** fare il proprio comodo;

~ yourself! come vuoi!; *pej* fai come ti pare!. **~ed** *a* lieto; **~ed with/about** contento di. **~ing** *a* gradevole

pleasurable /'pleʒərəbl/ *a* gradevole

pleasure /'pleʒə(r)/ *n* piacere *m*; **with ~** con piacere, volentieri

pleat /pli:t/ *n* piega *f* ● *vt* pieghettare. **~ed 'skirt** *n* gonna *f* a pieghe

pledge /pledʒ/ *n* pegno *m*; (*promise*) promessa *f* ● *vt* impegnarsi a; (*pawn*) impegnare

plentiful /'plentɪfl/ *a* abbondante

plenty /'plentɪ/ *n* abbondanza *f*; **~ of money** soldi *mpl*; **~ of people** molta gente; **I've got ~** ne ho in abbondanza

pliable /'plaɪəbl/ *a* flessibile

pliers /'plaɪəz/ *npl* pinze *fpl*

plight /plaɪt/ *n* condizione *f*

plimsolls /'plɪmsəlz/ *npl* scarpe *fpl* da ginnastica

plinth /plɪnθ/ *n* plinto *m*

plod /plɒd/ *vi* (*pt/pp* **plodded**) trascinarsi; (*work hard*) sgobbare

plonk /plɒŋk/ *n fam* vino *m* mediocre

plot /plɒt/ *n* complotto *m*; (*of novel*) trama *f*; **~ of land** appezzamento *m* [di terreno] ● *vt/i* complottare

plough /plaʊ/ *n* aratro *m* ● *vt/i* arare. **~man's [lunch]** piatto *m* di formaggi e sottaceti, servito con pane. **plough back** *vt Comm* reinvestire

ploy /plɔɪ/ *n fam* manovra *f*

pluck /plʌk/ *n* fegato *m* ● *vt* strappare; depilare (*eyebrows*); spennare (*bird*); cogliere (*flower*). **pluck up** *vt* **~ up courage** farsi coraggio

plucky /'plʌkɪ/ *a* (**-ier, -iest**) coraggioso

plug /plʌg/ *n* tappo *m*; *Electr* spina *f*; *Auto* candela *f*; (*fam: advertisement*) pubblicità *f inv* ● *vt* (*pt/pp* **plugged**) tappare; (*fam: advertise*) pubblicizzare con insistenza. **plug in** *vt Electr* inserire la spina di

plum /plʌm/ *n* prugna *f*; (*tree*) prugno *m*

plumage /'plu:mɪdʒ/ *n* piumaggio *m*

plumb /plʌm/ *a* verticale ● *adv* esattamente ● **plumb in** *vt* collegare

plumb|er /'plʌmə(r)/ *n* idraulico *m*. **~ing** *n* impianto *m* idraulico

'plumb-line *n* filo *m* a piombo

plume /plu:m/ *n* piuma *f*

plummet /'plʌmɪt/ *vi* precipitare

plump /plʌmp/ *a* paffuto ● **plump for** *vt* scegliere

plunge /plʌndʒ/ *n* tuffo *m*; **take the ~** *fam* buttarsi ● *vt* tuffare; *fig* sprofondare ● *vi* tuffarsi

plunging /'plʌndʒɪŋ/ *a* (*neckline*) profondo

plu'perfect /plu:-/ *n* trapassato *m* prossimo

plural /'plʊərəl/ *a* plurale ● *n* plurale *m*

plus /plʌs/ *prep* più ● *a* in più; **500 ~** più di 500 ● *n* più *m*; (*advantage*) extra *m inv*

plush /plʌʃ/ *a* lussuoso

plutonium /plu:'təʊnɪəm/ *n* plutonio *m*

ply /plaɪ/ *vt* (*pt/pp* **plied**) **~ sb with drink** continuare a offrire da bere a qcno. **~wood** *n* compensato *m*

PM *n abbr* Prime Minister

p.m. *abbr* (**post meridiem**) del pomeriggio

pneumatic /nju:'mætɪk/ *a* pneumatico. **~ 'drill** *n* martello *m* pneumatico

pneumonia /nju:'məʊnɪə/ *n* polmonite *f*

P.O. *abbr* Post Office

poach /pəʊtʃ/ *vt Culin* bollire; cacciare di frodo (*deer*); pescare di frodo (*salmon*). **~ed egg** uovo *m* in camicia. **~er** *n* bracconiere *m*

pocket /'pɒkɪt/ *n* tasca *f*; **be out of ~** rimetterci ● *vt* intascare. **~-book** *n* taccuino *m*; (*wallet*) portafoglio *m*. **~-money** *n* denaro *m* per le piccole spese

pod /pɒd/ n baccello m

podgy /'pɒdʒɪ/ a (**-ier, -iest**) grassoccio

poem /'pəʊɪm/ n poesia f

poet /'pəʊɪt/ n poeta m. **~ic** /-'etɪk/ a poetico

poetry /'pəʊɪtrɪ/ n poesia f

poignant /'pɔɪnjənt/ a emozionante

point /pɔɪnt/ n punto m. (sharp end) punta f; (meaning, purpose) senso m; Electr presa f [di corrente]; **~s** pl Rail scambio m; **~ of view** punto m di vista; **good/bad ~s** aspetti mpl positivi/negativi; **what is the ~?** a che scopo?; **the ~ is** il fatto è; **I don't see the ~** non vedo il senso; **up to a ~** fino a un certo punto; **be on the ~ of doing sth** essere sul punto di fare qcsa ● vt puntare (**at** verso) ● vi (with finger) puntare il dito; **~ at/to** (person:) mostrare col dito; (indicator:) indicare. **point out** vt far notare (fact); **~ sth out to sb** far notare qcsa a qcno

point-'blank a a bruciapelo

point|ed /'pɔɪntɪd/ a appuntito; (question) diretto. **~ers** npl (advice) consigli mpl. **~less** a inutile

poise /pɔɪz/ n padronanza f. **~d** a in equilibrio; **~d to** sul punto di

poison /'pɔɪzn/ n veleno m ● vt avvelenare. **~ous** a velenoso

poke /pəʊk/ n (piccola) spinta f ● vt spingere; (fire) attizzare; (put) ficcare; **~ fun at** prendere in giro. **poke about** vi frugare

poker¹ /'pəʊkə(r)/ n attizzatoio m

poker² /'pəʊkə(r)/ n (Cards) poker m

poky /'pəʊkɪ/ a (**-ier, -iest**) angusto

Poland /'pəʊlənd/ n Polonia f

polar /'pəʊlə(r)/ a polare. **~ 'bear** n orso m bianco. **~ize** vt polarizzare

Pole /pəʊl/ n polacco, -a mf

pole¹ n palo m

pole² n (Geog, Electr) polo m

'pole-star n stella f polare

'pole-vault n salto m con l'asta

police /pə'li:s/ npl polizia f ● vt pattugliare (area)

police: **~man** n poliziotto m. **~ state** n stato m militarista. **~ station** n commissariato m. **~woman** n donna f poliziotto

policy¹ /'pɒlɪsɪ/ n politica f

policy² n (insurance) polizza f

polio /'pəʊlɪəʊ/ n polio f

Polish /'pəʊlɪʃ/ a polacco ● n (language) polacco m

polish /'pɒlɪʃ/ n (shine) lucentezza f; (substance) lucido m; (for nails) smalto m; fig raffinatezza f ● vt lucidare; fig smussare. **polish off** vt fam finire in fretta; spazzolare (food)

polished /'pɒlɪʃt/ a (manner) raffinato; (performance) senza sbavature

polite /pə'laɪt/ a cortese. **~ly** adv cortesemente. **~ness** n cortesia f

politic /'pɒlɪtɪk/ a prudente

politic|al /pə'lɪtɪkl/ a politico. **~ally** adv dal punto di vista politico. **~ian** /pɒlɪ'tɪʃn/ n politico m

politics /'pɒlɪtɪks/ n politica f

poll /pəʊl/ n votazione f; (election) elezioni fpl; [opinion] **~** sondaggio m d'opinione; **go to the ~s** andare alle urne ● vt ottenere (votes)

pollen /'pɒlən/ n polline m

polling /'pəʊlɪŋ/: **~-booth** n cabina f elettorale. **~-station** n seggio m elettorale

'poll tax n imposta f locale sulle persone fisiche

pollutant /pə'lu:tənt/ n sostanza f inquinante

pollut|e /pə'lu:t/ vt inquinare. **~ion** /-u:ʃn/ n inquinamento m

polo /'pəʊləʊ/ n polo m. **~-neck** n collo m alto. **~ shirt** n dolcevita f

polyester /pɒlɪ'estə(r)/ n poliestere m

polystyrene® /pɒlɪ'staɪri:n/ n polistirolo m

polytechnic /pɒlɪ'teknɪk/ n politecnico m

polythene /'pɒlɪθi:n/ n politene m. **~ bag** n sacchetto m di plastica

polyun'saturated a polinsaturo

pomegranate /'pɒmɪgrænɪt/ n melagrana f

pomp /pɒmp/ n pompa f

pompon /'pɒmpɒn/ n pompon m

pompous /'pɒmpəs/ a pomposo

pond /pɒnd/ n stagno m

ponder /'pɒndə(r)/ vt/i ponderare

pong /pɒŋ/ n fam puzzo m

pontiff /'pɒntɪf/ n pontefice m

pony /'pəʊnɪ/ n pony m. **~tail** n coda f di cavallo. **~-trekking** n escursioni fpl col pony

poodle /'puːdl/ n barboncino m

pool¹ /puːl/ n (of water, blood) pozza f; [**swimming**] ~ piscina f

pool² n (common fund) cassa f comune; (in cards) piatto m; (game) biliardo m a buca. **~s** npl ≈ totocalcio msg ● vt mettere insieme

poor /pʊə(r)/ a povero; (not good) scadente; **in ~ health** in cattiva salute ● npl **the ~** i poveri. **~ly** a **be ~ly** non stare bene ● adv male

pop¹ /pɒp/ n botto m; (drink) bibita f gasata ● v (pt/pp **popped**) ● vt (burst) far scoppiare ● vi (burst) scoppiare.

pop in/out vi fam fare un salto/un salto fuori

pop² n fam musica f pop ● attrib pop

'popcorn n popcorn m inv

pope /pəʊp/ n papa m

poplar /'pɒplə(r)/ n pioppo m

poppy /'pɒpɪ/ n papavero m

popular /'pɒpjʊlə(r)/ a popolare; (belief) diffuso. **~ity** /-'lærətɪ/ n popolarità f inv

populat|e /'pɒpjʊleɪt/ vt popolare. **~ion** /-'leɪʃn/ n popolazione f

porcelain /'pɔːsəlɪn/ n porcellana f

porch /pɔːtʃ/ n portico m; Am veranda f

porcupine /'pɔːkjʊpaɪn/ n porcospino m

pore¹ /pɔː(r)/ n poro m

pore² vi **~ over** immergersi in

pork /pɔːk/ n carne f di maiale

porn /pɔːn/ n fam porno m. **~o** a fam porno inv

pornograph|ic /pɔːnə'græfɪk/ a

pornografico. **~y** /-'nɒgrəfɪ/ n pornografia f

porous /'pɔːrəs/ a poroso

porpoise /'pɔːpəs/ n focena f

porridge /'pɒrɪdʒ/ n farinata f di fiocchi d'avena

port¹ /pɔːt/ n porto m

port² n (Naut: side) babordo m

port³ n (wine) porto m

portable /'pɔːtəbl/ a portatile

porter /'pɔːtə(r)/ n portiere m; (for luggage) facchino m

portfolio /pɔːt'fəʊlɪəʊ/ n cartella f; Comm portafoglio m

'porthole n oblò m inv

portion /'pɔːʃn/ n parte f; (of food) porzione f

portly /'pɔːtlɪ/ a (-ier, -iest) corpulento

portrait /'pɔːtrɪt/ n ritratto m

portray /pɔː'treɪ/ vt ritrarre; (represent) descrivere; (actor:) impersonare. **~al** n ritratto m

Portugal /'pɔːtjʊgl/ n Portogallo m. **~uese** /-'giːz/ a portoghese ● n portoghese mf

pose /pəʊz/ n posa f ● vt porre (problem, question) ● vi (for painter) posare; **~ as** atteggiarsi a

posh /pɒʃ/ a fam lussuoso; (people) danaroso

position /pə'zɪʃn/ n posizione f; (job) posto m; (status) ceto m [sociale] ● vt posizionare

positive /'pɒzɪtɪv/ a positivo; (certain) sicuro; (progress) concreto ● n positivo m. **~ly** adv positivamente; (decidedly) decisamente

possess /pə'zes/ vt possedere. **~ion** /-'zeʃn/ n possesso m; **~ions** pl beni mpl

possess|ive /pə'zesɪv/ a possessivo. **~iveness** n carattere m possessivo. **~or** n possessore, -ditrice mf

possibility /pɒsə'bɪlətɪ/ n possibilità f inv

possib|le /'pɒsɪbl/ a possibile. **~ly** adv possibilmente; **I couldn't ~ly accept** non mi è possibile accettare; **he can't ~ly be right** non è possibile che abbia ragione; **could you ~ly...?** potrebbe per favore...?

post[1] /pəʊst/ n (pole) palo m ● vt affiggere ⟨notice⟩

post[2] n (place of duty) posto m ● vt appostare; (transfer) assegnare

post[3] n (mail) posta f; **by ~** per posta ● vt spedire; (put in letter-box) imbucare; (as opposed to fax) mandare per posta; **keep sb ~ed** tenere qcno al corrente

post- pref dopo

postage /ˈpəʊstɪdʒ/ n affrancatura f. **~ stamp** n francobollo m

postal /ˈpəʊstl/ a postale. **~ order** n vaglia m postale

post: **~-box** n cassetta f delle lettere. **~card** n cartolina f. **~code** n codice m postale. **~-date** vt postdatare

poster /ˈpəʊstə(r)/ n poster m inv; (advertising, election) cartellone m

posterior /pɒˈstɪərɪə(r)/ n fam posteriore m

posterity /pɒˈsterətɪ/ n posterità f

posthumous /ˈpɒstjʊməs/ a postumo. **~ly** adv dopo la morte

post: **~man** n postino m. **~mark** n timbro m postale

post-mortem /-ˈmɔːtəm/ n autopsia f

'post office n ufficio m postale

postpone /pəʊstˈpəʊn/ vt rimandare. **~ment** n rinvio m

posture /ˈpɒstʃə(r)/ n posizione f

post-'war a del dopoguerra

pot /pɒt/ n vaso m; (for tea) teiera f; (for coffee) caffettiera f; (for cooking) pentola f; **~s of money** fam un sacco di soldi; **go to ~** fam andare in malora

potassium /pəˈtæsɪəm/ n potassio m

potato /pəˈteɪtəʊ/ n (pl -es) patata f

poten|t /ˈpəʊtənt/ a potente. **~tate** n potentato m

potential /pəˈtenʃl/ a potenziale ● n potenziale m. **~ly** adv potenzialmente

pot: **~-hole** n cavità f inv; (in road) buca f. **~-holer** n speleologo, -a mf. **~-luck** n take **~-luck** affidarsi alla sorte. **~ 'plant** n pianta f da appartamento. **~-shot** n take a **~-shot** sparare a casaccio

potted /ˈpɒtɪd/ a conservato; (shortened) condensato. **~ 'plant** n pianta f da appartamento

potter[1] /ˈpɒtə(r)/ vi **~ about** gingillarsi

potter[2] n vasaio, -a mf. **~y** n lavorazione f della ceramica; (articles) ceramiche fpl; (place) laboratorio m di ceramiche

potty /ˈpɒtɪ/ a (-ier, -iest) fam matto ● n vasino m

pouch /paʊtʃ/ n marsupio m

pouffe /puːf/ n pouf m inv

poultry /ˈpəʊltrɪ/ n pollame m

pounce /paʊns/ vi balzare; **~ on** saltare su

pound[1] /paʊnd/ n libbra f (= 0,454 kg); (money) sterlina f

pound[2] vt battere ● vi ⟨heart:⟩ battere forte; (run heavily) correre pesantemente

pour /pɔː(r)/ vt versare ● vi riversarsi; (with rain) piovere a dirotto. **pour out** vi riversarsi fuori ● vt versare ⟨drink⟩; sfogare ⟨troubles⟩

pout /paʊt/ vi fare il broncio ● n broncio m

poverty /ˈpɒvətɪ/ n povertà f

powder /ˈpaʊdə(r)/ n polvere f; (cosmetic) cipria f ● vt polverizzare; (face) incipriare. **~y** a polveroso

power /ˈpaʊə(r)/ n potere m; Electr corrente f [elettrica]; Math potenza f. **~ cut** n interruzione f di corrente. **~ed** a **~ed by electricity** dotato di corrente [elettrica]. **~ful** a potente. **~less** a impotente. **~station** n centrale f elettrica

PR n abbr **public relations**

practicable /ˈpræktɪkəbl/ a praticabile

practical /ˈpræktɪkl/ a pratico. **~**

'**joke** n burla f. **~ly** adv praticamente

practice /'præktɪs/ n pratica f; (custom) usanza f; (habit) abitudine f; (exercise) esercizio m; Sport allenamento m; **in ~** (in reality) in pratica; **out of ~** fuori esercizio; **put into ~** mettere in pratica

practise /'præktɪs/ vt fare pratica in; (carry out) mettere in pratica; esercitare (profession) ● vi esercitarsi; (doctor:) praticare. **~d** a esperto

pragmatic /præg'mætɪk/ a pragmatico

praise /preɪz/ n lode f ● vt lodare. **~worthy** a lodevole

pram /præm/ n carrozzella f

prance /prɑːns/ vi saltellare

prank /præŋk/ n tiro m

prattle /'prætl/ vi parlottare

prawn /prɔːn/ n gambero m. **~ 'cocktail** n cocktail m inv di gamberetti

pray /preɪ/ vi pregare. **~er** /preə(r)/ n preghiera f

preach /priːtʃ/ vt/i predicare. **~er** n predicatore, -trice mf

preamble /priː'æmbl/ n preambolo m

pre-ar'range /priː-/ vt predisporre

precarious /prɪ'keərɪəs/ a precario. **~ly** adv in modo precario

precaution /prɪ'kɔːʃn/ n precauzione f; **as a ~** per precauzione. **~ary** a preventivo

precede /prɪ'siːd/ vt precedere

preceden|ce /'presɪdəns/ n precedenza f. **~t** n precedente m

preceding /prɪ'siːdɪŋ/ a precedente

precinct /'priːsɪŋkt/ n (traffic-free) zona f pedonale; (Am: district) circoscrizione f

precious /'preʃəs/ a prezioso; (style) ricercato ● adv fam **~ little** ben poco

precipice /'presɪpɪs/ n precipizio m

precipitate /prɪ'sɪpɪteɪt/ vt precipitare

précis /'preɪsiː/ n (pl précis /-siːz/) sunto m

precis|e /prɪ'saɪs/ a preciso. **~ely** adv precisamente. **~ion** /-'sɪʒn/ n precisione f

precursor /priː'kɜːsə(r)/ n precursore m

predator /'predətə(r)/ n predatore, -trice mf. **~y** a rapace

predecessor /'priːdɪsesə(r)/ n predecessore m

predicament /prɪ'dɪkəmənt/ n situazione f difficile

predicat|e /'predɪkət/ n Gram predicato m. **~ive** /prɪ'dɪkətɪv/ a predicativo

predict /prɪ'dɪkt/ vt predire. **~able** /-əbl/ a prevedibile. **~ion** /-'dɪkʃn/ n previsione f

pre'domin|ant /prɪ-/ a predominante. **~ate** vi predominare

pre-'eminent /priː-/ a preeminente

preen /priːn/ vt lisciarsi; **~ oneself** fig farsi bello

pre|fab /'priːfæb/ n fam casa f prefabbricata. **~'fabricated** a prefabbricato

preface /'prefɪs/ n prefazione f

prefect /'priːfekt/ n Sch studente, -tessa mf della scuola superiore con responsabilità disciplinari, ecc

prefer /prɪ'fɜː(r)/ vt (pt/pp preferred) preferire

prefera|ble /'prefərəbl/ a preferibile (to a). **~bly** adv preferibilmente

preferen|ce /'prefərəns/ n preferenza f. **~tial** /-'renʃl/ a preferenziale

prefix /'priːfɪks/ n prefisso m

pregnan|cy /'pregnənsɪ/ n gravidanza f. **~t** a incinta

prehi'storic /priː-/ a preistorico

prejudice /'predʒudɪs/ n pregiudizio m ● vt influenzare (against contro); (harm) danneggiare. **~d** a prevenuto

preliminary /prɪ'lɪmɪnərɪ/ a preliminare

prelude /'preljuːd/ n preludio m

pre-'marital *a* prematrimoniale

premature /'prematjʊə(r)/ *a* prematuro

pre'meditated /pri:-/ *a* premeditato

premier /'premɪə(r)/ *a* primario ● *n* Pol primo ministro *m*, premier *m inv*

première /'premɪeə(r)/ *n* prima *f*

premises /'premɪsɪz/ *npl* locali *mpl*; on the ~ sul posto

premium /'pri:mɪəm/ *n* premio *m*; be at a ~ essere una cosa rara

premonition /premə'nɪʃn/ *n* presentimento *m*

preoccupied /pri:'ɒkjʊpaɪd/ *a* preoccupato

prep /prep/ *n* Sch compiti *mpl*

preparation /prepə'reɪʃn/ *n* preparazione *f*. **~s** preparativi *mpl*

preparatory /prɪ'pærətrɪ/ *a* preparatorio ● *adv* ~ to prima di

prepare /prɪ'peə(r)/ *vt* preparare ● *vi* prepararsi (for per); **~d to** disposto a

pre'pay /pri:-/ *vt* (*pt/pp* -paid) pagare in anticipo

preposition /prepə'zɪʃn/ *n* preposizione *f*

prepossessing /pri:pə'zesɪŋ/ *a* attraente

preposterous /prɪ'pɒstərəs/ *a* assurdo

prerequisite /pri:'rekwɪzɪt/ *n* condizione *f* sine qua non

prescribe /prɪ'skraɪb/ *vt* prescrivere

prescription /prɪ'skrɪpʃn/ *n* Med ricetta *f*

presence /'prezns/ *n* presenza *f*; ~ **of mind** presenza *f* di spirito

present¹ /'preznt/ *a* presente ● *n* presente *m*; **at** ~ attualmente

present² *n* (*gift*) regalo *m*; **give sb sth as a** ~ regalare qcsa a qcno

present³ /prɪ'zent/ *vt* presentare; ~ **sb with an award** consegnare un premio a qcno. **~able** /-əbl/ *a* be **~able** essere presentabile

presentation /prezn'teɪʃn/ *n* presentazione *f*

presently /'prezntlɪ/ *adv* fra poco; (*Am:* now) attualmente

preservation /prezə'veɪʃn/ *n* conservazione *f*

preservative /prɪ'zɜ:vətɪv/ *n* conservante *m*

preserve /prɪ'zɜ:v/ *vt* preservare; (maintain, Culin) conservare ● *n* (in hunting & fig) riserva *f*; (jam) marmellata *f*

preside /prɪ'zaɪd/ *vi* presiedere (over a)

presidency /'prezɪdənsɪ/ *n* presidenza *f*

president /'prezɪdənt/ *n* presidente *m*. **~ial** /-'denʃl/ *a* presidenziale

press /pres/ *n* (machine) pressa *f*; (newspapers) stampa *f* ● *vt* premere; pressare (flower); (iron) stirare; (squeeze) stringere ● *vi* (urge) incalzare. **press for** vt fare pressione per; be **~ed for** essere a corto di. **press on** vi andare avanti

press: ~ **conference** *n* conferenza *f* stampa. ~ **cutting** *n* ritaglio *m* di giornale. **~ing** *a* urgente. **~-stud** *n* [bottone *m*] automatico *m*. **~-up** *n* flessione *f*

pressure /'preʃə(r)/ *n* pressione *f* ● *vt* = pressurize. **~-cooker** *n* pentola *f* a pressione. ~ **group** *n* gruppo *m* di pressione

pressurize /'preʃəraɪz/ *vt* far pressione su. **~d** *a* pressurizzato

prestige /pre'sti:ʒ/ *n* prestigio *m*. **~ious** /-'stɪdʒəs/ *a* prestigioso

presumably /prɪ'zju:məblɪ/ *adv* presumibilmente

presume /prɪ'zju:m/ *vt* presumere; ~ **to do sth** permettersi di fare qcsa

presumption /prɪ'zʌmpʃn/ *n* presunzione *f*; (boldness) impertinenza *f*. **~uous** /-'zʌmptjʊəs/ *a* impertinente

presup'pose /pri:-/ *vt* presupporre

pretence /prɪ'tens/ *n* finzione *f*; (pretext) pretesto *m*; **it's all** ~ è tutta una scena

pretend /pri'tend/ *vt* fingere; (*claim*) pretendere ● *vi* fare finta

pretentious /pri'tenʃəs/ *a* pretenzioso

pretext /'pri:tekst/ *n* pretesto *m*

pretty /'priti/ *a* (**-ier, -iest**) carino ● *adv* (*fam: fairly*) abbastanza

prevail /pri'veil/ *vi* prevalere; ~ **on sb to do sth** convincere qcno a fare qcsa. ~**ing** *a* prevalente

prevalen|ce /'prevələns/ *n* diffusione *f*. ~**t** *a* diffuso

prevent /pri'vent/ *vt* impedire; ~ **sb** [**from**] **doing sth** impedire a qcno di fare qcsa. ~**ion** /-enʃn/ *n* prevenzione *f*. ~**ive** /-iv/ *a* preventivo

preview /'pri:vju:/ *n* anteprima *f*

previous /'pri:viəs/ *a* precedente. ~**ly** *adv* precedentemente

pre-war /pri:-/ *a* anteguerra

prey /prei/ *n* preda *f*; **bird of** ~ uccello *m* rapace ● *vi* ~ **on** far preda di; ~ **on sb's mind** attanagliare qcno

price /prais/ *n* prezzo *m* ● *vt Comm* fissare il prezzo di. ~**less** *a* inestimabile; (*fam: amusing*) spassosissimo. ~**y** *a fam* caro

prick /prik/ *n* puntura *f* ● *vt* pungere. **prick up** *vt* ~ **up one's ears** rizzare le orecchie

prick|le /'prikl/ *n* spina *f*; (*sensation*) formicolio *m*. ~**y** *a* pungente; (*person*) irritabile

pride /praid/ *n* orgoglio *m* ● *vt* ~ **oneself** *vi* vantarsi di

priest /pri:st/ *n* prete *m*

prim /prim/ *a* (**primmer, primmest**) perbenino

primarily /'praimərili/ *adv* in primo luogo

primary /'praiməri/ *a* primario; (*chief*) principale. ~ **school** *n* scuola elementare

prime[1] /praim/ *a* principale, primo; (*first-rate*) eccellente ● *n* **be in one's** ~ essere nel fiore degli anni

prime[2] *vt* preparare (*surface, person*)

Prime Minister *n* Primo *m* Ministro

primeval /prai'mi:vl/ *a* primitivo

primitive /'primitiv/ *a* primitivo

primrose /'primrəuz/ *n* primula *f*

prince /prins/ *n* principe *m*

princess /prin'ses/ *n* principessa *f*

principal /'prinsəpl/ *a* principale ● *n Sch* preside *m*

principality /prinsi'pæləti/ *n* principato *m*

principally /'prinsəpli/ *adv* principalmente

principle /'prinsəpl/ *n* principio *m*; **in** ~ in teoria; **on** ~ per principio

print /print/ *n* (*mark, trace*) impronta *f*; *Phot* copia *f*; (*picture*) stampa *f*; **in** ~ (*printed out*) stampato; (*book*) in commercio; **out of** ~ esaurito ● *vt* stampare; (*write in capitals*) scrivere in stampatello. ~**ed matter** *n* stampe *fpl*

print|er /'printə(r)/ *n* stampante *f*; *Typ* tipografo, -a *mf*. ~**er port** *n* Comput porta *f* per la stampante. ~**ing** *n* tipografia *f*

printout *n* Comput stampa *f*

prior /'praiə(r)/ *a* precedente. ~ **to** *prep* prima di

priority /prai'ɒrəti/ *n* precedenza *f*; (*matter*) priorità *f inv*

prise /praiz/ *vt* ~ **open/up** forzare

prison /'priz(ə)n/ *n* prigione *f*. ~**er** *n* prigioniero, -a *mf*

privacy /'privəsi/ *n* privacy *f inv*

private /'praivət/ *a* privato; (*car, secretary, letter*) personale ● *n Mil* soldato *m* semplice; **in** ~ in privato. ~**ly** *adv* (*funded, educated etc*) privatamente; (*in secret*) in segreto; (*confidentially*) in privato; (*inwardly*) interiormente

privation /prai'veiʃn/ *n* privazione *f*; ~**s** *npl* stenti *mpl*

privatize /'praivətaiz/ *vt* privatizzare

privilege /'privəlidʒ/ *n* privilegio *m*. ~**d** *a* privilegiato

privy /'privi/ *a* **be** ~ **to** essere al corrente di

prize /praɪz/ n premio m ●a (*idiot etc*) perfetto ● vt apprezzare.
~-giving n premiazione f.
~-winner n vincitore, -trice mf.
~-winning a vincente

pro /prəʊ/ n (*fam: professional*) professionista mf; **the ~s and cons** il pro e il contro

probability /prɒbə'bɪlətɪ/ n probabilità f inv

probabl|e /'prɒbəbl/ a probabile.
~y adv probabilmente

probation /prə'beɪʃn/ n prova f; Jur libertà f vigilata. **~ary** a in prova; **~ary period** periodo m di prova

probe /prəʊb/ n sonda f; (*fig: investigation*) indagine f ● vt sondare; (*investigate*) esaminare a fondo

problem /'prɒbləm/ n problema m ●a difficile. **~atic** /-'mætɪk/ a problematico

procedure /prə'si:dʒə(r)/ n procedimento m

proceed /prə'si:d/ vi procedere ● vt ~ **to do sth** proseguire facendo qcsa

proceedings /prə'si:dɪŋz/ npl (*report*) atti mpl; Jur azione fsg legale

proceeds /'prəʊsi:dz/ npl ricavato msg

process /'prəʊses/ n processo m; (*procedure*) procedimento m; **in the ~** nel far ciò ● vt trattare; Admin occuparsi di; Phot sviluppare

procession /prə'seʃn/ n processione f

proclaim /prə'kleɪm/ vt proclamare

procure /prə'kjʊə(r)/ vt ottenere

prod /prɒd/ n colpetto m ● vt (*pt/pp* **prodded**) punzecchiare; fig incitare

prodigal /'prɒdɪgl/ a prodigo

prodigious /prə'dɪdʒəs/ a prodigioso

prodigy /'prɒdɪdʒɪ/ n [**infant**] ~ bambino m prodigio

produce¹ /'prɒdju:s/ n prodotti mpl; **~ of Italy** prodotto in Italia

produce² /prə'dju:s/ vt produrre; (*bring out*) tirar fuori; (*cause*) causare; (*fam: give birth to*) fare. **~r** n produttore m

product /'prɒdʌkt/ n prodotto m.
~ion /prə'dʌkʃn/ n produzione f; Theat spettacolo m

productive /prə'dʌktɪv/ a produttivo. **~ity** /-'tɪvɪtɪ/ n produttività f

profan|e /prə'feɪn/ a profano; (*blasphemous*) blasfemo. **~ity** /-'fænətɪ/ n (*oath*) bestemmia f

profession /prə'feʃn/ n professione f. **~al** a professionale; (*not amateur*) professionista; (*piece of work*) da professionista; (*man*) di professione ● n professionista mf.
~ally adv professionalmente

professor /prə'fesə(r)/ n professore m [universitario]

proficien|cy /prə'fɪʃnsɪ/ n competenza f. **~t** a **be ~t in** essere competente in

profile /'prəʊfaɪl/ n profilo m ● vi **~ from** trarre profitto da. **~able** /-əbl/ a proficuo. **~ably** adv in modo proficuo

profit /'prɒfɪt/ n profitto m ● vi **~ from** trarre profitto da. **~able** /-əbl/ a proficuo. **~ably** adv in modo proficuo

profound /prə'faʊnd/ a profondo.
~ly adv profondamente

profus|e /prə'fju:s/ a **~e apologies/flowers** una profusione di scuse/fiori. **~ion** /-ju:ʒn/ n profusione f; **in ~ion** in abbondanza

progeny /'prɒdʒənɪ/ n progenie f inv

prognosis /prɒg'nəʊsɪs/ n (*pl* **-oses**) prognosi f inv

program /'prəʊgræm/ n programma m ● vt (*pt/pp* **programmed**) programmare

programme /'prəʊgræm/ n Br programma m. **~r** n Comput programmatore, -trice mf

progress¹ /'prəʊgres/ n progresso m; **in ~** in corso; **make ~** fig fare progressi

progress² /prə'gres/ vi progredire; fig fare progressi

progressive /prə'gresɪv/ a progressivo; (reforming) progressista. **~ly** adv progressivamente

prohibit /prə'hɪbɪt/ vt proibire. **~ive** /-ɪv/ a proibitivo

project¹ /'prɒdʒekt/ n progetto m; Sch ricerca f

project² /prə'dʒekt/ vt proiettare (film, image) ● vi (jut out) sporgere

projectile /prə'dʒektaɪl/ n proiettile m

projector /prə'dʒektə(r)/ n proiettore m

prolific /prə'lɪfɪk/ a prolifico

prologue /'prəʊlɒg/ n prologo m

prolong /prə'lɒŋ/ vt prolungare

promenade /prɒmə'nɑ:d/ n lungomare m inv

prominent /'prɒmɪnənt/ a prominente; (conspicuous) di rilievo

promiscu|ity /prɒmɪ'skju:ətɪ/ n promiscuità f. **~ous** /prə'mɪskjʊəs/ a promiscuo

promis|e /'prɒmɪs/ n promessa f ● vt promettere; **~e sb that** promettere a qcno che; **I ~ed to** l'ho promesso. **~ing** a promettente

promot|e /prə'məʊt/ vt promuovere; **be ~ed** Sport essere promosso. **~ion** /-əʊʃn/ n promozione f

prompt /prɒmpt/ a immediato; (punctual) puntuale ● adv in punto ● vt incitare (**to** a); Theat suggerire a ● vi suggerire. **~er** n suggeritore, -trice mf. **~ly** adv puntualmente

Proms /prɒmz/ npl rassegna f di concerti estivi di musica classica presso l'Albert Hall a Londra

prone /prəʊn/ a **be ~ to do sth** essere incline a fare qcsa

prong /prɒŋ/ n dente m (di forchetta)

pronoun /'prəʊnaʊn/ n pronome m

pronounce /prə'naʊns/ vt pronunciare; (declare) dichiarare. **~d** a (noticeable) pronunciato

pronunciation /prənʌnsɪ'eɪʃn/ n pronuncia f

proof /pru:f/ n prova f; Typ bozza f, prova f ● a ~ **against** a prova di

prop¹ /prɒp/ n puntello m ● vt (pt/pp **propped**) ~ **open** tenere aperto; ~ **against** (lean) appoggiare a. **prop up** vt sostenere

prop² n Theat, fam accessorio m di scena

propaganda /prɒpə'gændə/ n propaganda f

propel /prə'pel/ vt (pt/pp **propelled**) spingere. **~ler** n elica f

proper /'prɒpə(r)/ a corretto; (suitable) adatto; (fam: real) vero [e proprio]. **~ly** adv correttamente. ~ '**name**, ~ '**noun** n nome m proprio

property /'prɒpətɪ/ n proprietà f inv. ~ **developer** n agente m immobiliare. ~ **market** n mercato m immobiliare

prophecy /'prɒfəsɪ/ n profezia f

prophesy /'prɒfɪsaɪ/ vt (pt/pp -**ied**) profetizzare

prophet /'prɒfɪt/ n profeta m. **~ic** /prə'fetɪk/ a profetico

proportion /prə'pɔ:ʃn/ n proporzione f; (share) parte f; **~s** pl (dimensions) proporzioni fpl. **~al** a proporzionale. **~ally** adv in proporzione

proposal /prə'pəʊzl/ n proposta f; (of marriage) proposta f di matrimonio

propose /prə'pəʊz/ vt proporre; (intend) proporsi ● vi fare una proposta di matrimonio

proposition /prɒpə'zɪʃn/ n proposta f; (fam: task) impresa f

proprietor /prə'praɪətə(r)/ n proprietario, -a mf

prosaic /prə'zeɪɪk/ a prosaico

prose /prəʊz/ n prosa f

prosecut|e /'prɒsɪkju:t/ vt intentare azione contro. **~ion** /-'kju:ʃn/ n azione f giudiziaria; **the ~ion** l'accusa f. **~or** n [**Public**] **P~or** il Pubblico Ministero m

prospect /'prɒspekt/ n (expectation) prospettiva f

prospect² /prə'spekt/ *vi* ~ **for** cercare

prospect|ive /prə'spektiv/ *a* (*future*) futuro; (*possible*) potenziale. ~**or** *n* cercatore *m*

prospectus /prə'spektəs/ *n* prospetto *m*

prosper /'prɒspə(r)/ *vi* prosperare; (*person*:) stare bene finanziariamente. ~**ity** /-'sperəti/ *n* prosperità *f*

prosperous /'prɒspərəs/ *a* prospero

prostitut|e /'prɒstitjuːt/ *n* prostituta *f*. ~**ion** /-'tjuːʃn/ *n* prostituzione *f*

prostrate /'prɒstreɪt/ *a* prostrato; ~ **with grief** *fig* prostrato dal dolore

protagonist /prəʊ'tægənɪst/ *n* protagonista *mf*

protect /prə'tekt/ *vt* proteggere (**from** da). ~**ion** /-ekʃn/ *n* protezione *f*. ~**ive** /-ɪv/ *a* protettivo. ~**or** *n* protettore, -trice *mf*

protégé /'prɒtɪʒeɪ/ *n* protetto *m*

protein /'prəʊtiːn/ *n* proteina *f*

protest¹ /'prəʊtest/ *n* protesta *f*

protest² /prə'test/ *vt/i* protestare

Protestant /'prɒtɪstənt/ *a* protestante ● *n* protestante *mf*

protester /prə'testə(r)/ *n* contestatore, -trice *mf*

protocol /'prəʊtəkɒl/ *n* protocollo *m*

prototype /'prəʊtə-/ *n* prototipo *m*

protract /prə'trækt/ *vt* protrarre

protrude /prə'truːd/ *vi* sporgere

proud /praʊd/ *a* fiero (**of** di). ~**ly** *adv* fieramente

prove /pruːv/ *vt* provare ● *vi* ~ **to be a lie** rivelarsi una bugia. ~**n** *a* dimostrato

proverb /'prɒvɜːb/ *n* proverbio *m*. ~**ial** /prə'vɜːbɪəl/ *a* proverbiale

provide /prə'vaɪd/ *vt* fornire; ~ **sb with sth** fornire qcsa a qcno ● *vi* ~ **for** (*law*:) prevedere

provided /prə'vaɪdɪd/ *conj* ~ [**that**] purché

providen|ce /'prɒvɪdəns/ *n* prov-

videnza *f*. ~**tial** /-'denʃl/ *a* provvidenziale

providing /prə'vaɪdɪŋ/ *conj* = provided

provinc|e /'prɒvɪns/ *n* provincia *f*; *fig* campo *m*. ~**ial** /prə'vɪnʃl/ *a* provinciale

provision /prə'vɪʒn/ *n* (*of food, water*) approvvigionamento *m* (**of** di); (*of law*) disposizione *f*; ~**s** *pl* provviste *fpl*. ~**al** *a* provvisorio

proviso /prə'vaɪzəʊ/ *n* condizione *f*

provocat|ion /prɒvə'keɪʃn/ *n* provocazione *f*. ~**ive** /prə'vɒkətɪv/ *a* provocatorio; (*sexually*) provocante. ~**ively** *adv* in modo provocatorio

provoke /prə'vəʊk/ *vt* provocare

prow /praʊ/ *n* prua *f*

prowess /'praʊɪs/ *n* abilità *f inv*

prowl /praʊl/ *vi* aggirarsi ● *n* **on the** ~ in cerca di preda. ~**er** *n* tipo *m* sospetto

proximity /prɒk'sɪmətɪ/ *n* prossimità *f*

proxy /'prɒksɪ/ *n* procura *f*; (*person*) persona *f* che agisce per procura

prude /pruːd/ *n* **be a** ~ essere eccessivamente pudico

pruden|ce /'pruːdəns/ *n* prudenza *f*. ~**t** *a* prudente; (*wise*) oculatezza *f*

prudish /'pruːdɪʃ/ *a* eccessivamente pudico

prune¹ /pruːn/ *n* prugna *f* secca

prune² *vt* potare

pry /praɪ/ *vi* (*pt/pp* **pried**) ficcare il naso

psalm /sɑːm/ *n* salmo *m*

pseudonym /'sjuːdənɪm/ *n* pseudonimo *m*

psychiatric /saɪkɪ'ætrɪk/ *a* psichiatrico

psychiatr|ist /saɪ'kaɪətrɪst/ *n* psichiatra *mf*. ~**y** *n* psichiatria *f*

psychic /'saɪkɪk/ *a* psichico; **I'm not** ~ non sono un indovino

psycho|analyse /saɪkəʊ-/ *vt* psicanalizzare. ~**a'nalysis** *n* psicanalisi f. ~'**analyst** n psicanalista mf

psychological /saɪkə'rɒdʒɪk!/ a psicologico

psycholog|ist /saɪ'kɒlədʒɪst/ n psicologo, -a mf. ~y n psicologia f

psychopath /'saɪkəpæθ/ n psicopatico, -a mf

P.T.O. abbr (**please turn over**) vedi retro

pub /pʌb/ n fam pub m inv

puberty /'pju:bətɪ/ n pubertà f

public /'pʌblɪk/ a pubblico ● n the ~ il pubblico; in ~ in pubblico. ~ly adv pubblicamente

publican /'pʌblɪkən/ n gestore, -trice mf/proprietario, -a mf di un pub

publication /pʌblɪ'keɪʃn/ n pubblicazione f

public: ~ con'**venience** n gabinetti mpl pubblici. ~ '**holiday** n festa f nazionale. ~ '**house** n pub m

publicity /pʌb'lɪsətɪ/ n pubblicità f

publicize /'pʌblɪsaɪz/ vt pubblicizzare

public: ~ '**library** n biblioteca f pubblica. ~ re'**lations** fpl. ~ '**school** n scuola f privata; Am scuola f pubblica. ~-'**spirited** a be ~-**spirited** essere dotato di senso civico. ~ '**transport** n mezzi mpl pubblici

publish /'pʌblɪʃ/ vt pubblicare. ~**er** n editore m; (firm) editore m, casa f editrice. ~**ing** n editoria f

pudding /'pʊdɪŋ/ n dolce m cotto al vapore; (course) dolce m

puddle /'pʌdl/ n pozzanghera f

pudgy /'pʌdʒɪ/ a (-ier, -iest) grassoccio

puff /pʌf/ n (of wind) soffio m; (of smoke) tirata f; (for powder) piumino m ● vt sbuffare. **puff at** vt tirare boccate da ⟨pipe⟩. **puff out** vt lasciare senza fiato ⟨person⟩; spegnere ⟨candle⟩. ~**ed** a (out of breath) senza fiato. ~ **pastry** n pasta f sfoglia

puffy /'pʌfɪ/ a gonfio

pull /pʊl/ n trazione f; (fig: attrac-

tion) attrazione f; (fam: influence) influenza f ● vt tirare; estrarre ⟨tooth⟩; stirarsi ⟨muscle⟩. ~ **faces** far boccace; ~ **oneself together** cercare di controllarsi; ~ **one's weight** mettercela tutta; ~ **sb's leg** fam prendere in giro qcno. **pull down** vt (demolish) demolire. **pull in** vi Auto accostare. **pull off** vt togliere; fam azzeccare. **pull out** vt tirar fuori ● vi Auto spostarsi; (of competition) ritirarsi. **pull through** vi (recover) farcela. **pull up** vt sradicare ⟨plant⟩; (reprimand) rimproverare ● vi Auto fermarsi

pulley /'pʊlɪ/ n Techn puleggia f

pullover /'pʊləʊvə(r)/ n pullover m

pulp /pʌlp/ n poltiglia f; (of fruit) polpa f; (for paper) pasta f

pulpit /'pʊlpɪt/ n pulpito m

pulsate /pʌl'seɪt/ vi pulsare

pulse /pʌls/ n polso m

pulses /'pʌlsɪz/ npl legumi mpl secchi

pulverize /'pʌlvəraɪz/ vt polverizzare

pumice /'pʌmɪs/ n pomice f

pummel /'pʌml/ vt (pt/pp **pummelled**) prendere a pugni

pump /pʌmp/ n pompa f ● vt pompare; fam cercare di estrorcere da. **pump up** vt (inflate) gonfiare

pumpkin /'pʌmpkɪn/ n zucca f

pun /pʌn/ n gioco m di parole

punch¹ /pʌntʃ/ n pugno m; (device) pinza f per forare ● vt dare un pugno a; forare ⟨ticket⟩; perforare ⟨hole⟩

punch² /pʌntʃ/ n (drink) ponce m inv

punch: ~ **line** n battuta f finale. ~-**up** n rissa f

punctual /'pʌŋktjʊəl/ a puntuale. ~**ity** /-'ælətɪ/ n puntualità f. ~**ly** adv puntualmente

punctuat|e /'pʌŋktʃʊeɪt/ vt punteggiare. ~**ion** /-'eɪʃn/ n punteggiatura f. ~**ion mark** n segno m di interpunzione

puncture /'pʌŋktʃə(r)/ n foro m; (tyre) foratura f ● vt forare

pungent /ˈpʌndʒənt/ *a* acre
punish /ˈpʌnɪʃ/ *vt* punire. **~able** /-əbl/ *a* punibile. **~ment** *n* punizione *f*
punitive /ˈpju:nɪtɪv/ *a* punitivo
punk /pʌŋk/ *n* punk *m inv*
punnet /ˈpʌnɪt/ *n* cestello *m* (*per frutta*)
punt /pʌnt/ *n* (*boat*) barchino *m*
punter /ˈpʌntə(r)/ *n* (*gambler*) scommettitore, -trice *mf*; (*client*) consumatore, -trice *mf*
puny /ˈpju:nɪ/ *a* (**-ier, -iest**) striminzito
pup /pʌp/ *n* = **puppy**
pupil /ˈpju:pl/ *n* alluno, -a *mf*; (*of eye*) pupilla *f*
puppet /ˈpʌpɪt/ *n* marionetta *f*; (*glove ~, fig*) burattino *m*
puppy /ˈpʌpɪ/ *n* cucciolo *m*
purchase /ˈpɜ:tʃəs/ *n* acquisto *m*; (*leverage*) presa *f* ● *vt* acquistare. **~r** *n* acquirente *mf*
pure /pjʊə(r)/ *a* puro. **~ly** *adv* puramente
purée /ˈpjʊəreɪ/ *n* purè *m*
purgatory /ˈpɜ:gətrɪ/ *n* purgatorio *m*
purge /pɜ:dʒ/ *Pol n* epurazione *f* ● *vt* epurare
puri|fication /pjʊərɪfɪˈkeɪʃn/ *n* purificazione *f*. **~fy** /ˈpjʊərɪfaɪ/ *vt* (*pt/pp* **-ied**) purificare
puritan /ˈpjʊərɪtən/ *n* puritano, -a *mf*. **~ical** *a* puritano
purity /ˈpjʊərɪtɪ/ *n* purità *f*
purple /ˈpɜ:pl/ *a* viola
purpose /ˈpɜ:pəs/ *n* scopo *m*; (*determination*) fermezza *f*; **on ~** apposta. **~-built** *a* costruito ad hoc. **~ful** *a* deciso. **~fully** *adv* con decisione. **~ly** *adv* apposta
purr /pɜ:(r)/ *vi* ‹*cat:*› fare le fusa
purse /pɜ:s/ *n* borsellino *m*; (*Am: handbag*) borsa *f* ● *vt* increspare ‹*lips*›
pursue /pəˈsju:/ *vt* inseguire; *fig* proseguire. **~r** /-ə(r)/ *n* inseguitore, -trice *mf*
pursuit /pəˈsju:t/ *n* inseguimento *m*; (*fig: of happiness*) ricerca *f*; (*pastime*) attività *f inv*; **in ~** all'inseguimento
pus /pʌs/ *n* pus *m*
push /pʊʃ/ *n* spinta *f*; (*fig: effort*) sforzo *m*; (*drive*) iniziativa *f*; **at a ~** in caso di bisogno; **get the ~** *fam* essere licenziato ● *vt* spingere; premere ‹*button*›; (*pressurize*) far pressione su; **be ~ed for time** *fam* non avere tempo ● *vi* spingere. **push aside** *vt* scostare. **push back** *vt* respingere. **push off** *vt* togliere ● *vi* (*fam: leave*) levarsi dai piedi. **push on** *vi* (*continue*) continuare. **push up** *vt* alzare ‹*price*›
push: ~-button *n* pulsante *m*. **~-chair** *n* passeggino *m*. **~-over** *n fam* bazzecola *f*. **~-up** *n* flessione *f*
pushy /ˈpʊʃɪ/ *a fam* troppo intraprendente
puss /pʊs/ *n*, **pussy** /ˈpʊsɪ/ *n* micio *m*
put /pʊt/ *vt* (*pt/pp* **put**, *pres p* **putting**) mettere; **~ the cost of sth at** valutare il costo di qcsa ● *vi* **~ to sea** salpare. **put aside** *vt* mettere da parte. **put away** *vt* mettere via. **put back** *vt* rimettere; mettere indietro ‹*clock*›. **put by** *vt* mettere da parte. **put down** *vt* mettere giù; (*suppress*) reprimere; (*kill*) sopprimere; (*write*) annotare; **~ one's foot down** *fam* essere fermo; *Auto* dare un'accelerata; **~ down to** (*attribute*) attribuire. **put forward** *vt* avanzare; mettere avanti ‹*clock*›. **put in** *vt* (*insert*) introdurre; (*submit*) presentare ● *vi* **~ in for** far domanda di. **put off** *vt* spegnere ‹*light*›; (*postpone*) rimandare; **~ sb off** tenere a bada qcno; (*deter*) smontare qcno; (*disconcert*) distrarre qcno; **~ sb off sth** (*disgust*) disgustare qcno di qcsa. **put on** *vt* mettersi ‹*clothes*›; mettere ‹*brake*›; *Culin* mettere su; accendere ‹*light*›; mettere in scena ‹*play*›; prendere ‹*accent*›; **~ on weight** mettere su qualche chilo. **put out** *vt* spegnere ‹*fire, light*›; tendere ‹*hand*›;

⟨hand⟩; ⟨inconvenience⟩ creare degli inconvenienti a. **put through** *vt* far passare; *Teleph* **I'll ~ you through to him** glielo passo. **put up** *vt* alzare; erigere ⟨building⟩; montare ⟨tent⟩; aprire ⟨umbrella⟩; affiggere ⟨notice⟩; aumentare ⟨price⟩; ospitare ⟨guest⟩; **~ sb up to sth** mettere qcsa in testa a qcno ● *vi* ⟨at hotel⟩ stare; **~ up with** sopportare ● **a stay ~!** rimani lì!

putty /'pʌtɪ/ *n* mastice *m*

put-up /'pʊtʌp/ **a ~ job** truffa *f*

puzzle /'pʌzl/ *n* enigma *m*; ⟨jigsaw⟩ puzzle *m inv* ● *vt* lasciare perplesso ● *vi* **~e over** scervellarsi su. **~ing** *a* inspiegabile

pygmy /'pɪgmɪ/ *n* pigmeo, -a *mf*

pyjamas /pə'dʒɑːməz/ *npl* pigiama *msg*

pylon /'paɪlən/ *n* pilone *m*

pyramid /'pɪrəmɪd/ *n* piramide *f*

python /'paɪθn/ *n* pitone *m*

....

Qq

quack¹ /kwæk/ *n* qua qua *m inv* ● *vi* fare qua qua

quack² *n* ⟨doctor⟩ ciarlatano *m*

quad /kwɒd/ *n* ⟨fam: court⟩ = **quadrangle**. **~s** *pl* = **quadruplets**

quadrangle /'kwɒdræŋgl/ *n* quadrangolo *m*; ⟨court⟩ cortile *m* quadrangolare

quadruped /'kwɒdrʊped/ *n* quadrupede *m*

quadruple /'kwɒdrʊpl/ *a* quadruplo ● *vt* quadruplicare ● *vi* quadruplicarsi. **~ts** /-plɪts/ *npl* quattro gemelli *mpl*

quagmire /'kwɒgmaɪə(r)/ *n* pantano *m*

quaint /kweɪnt/ *a* pittoresco; ⟨odd⟩ bizzarro

quake /kweɪk/ *n fam* terremoto *m* ● *vi* tremare

qualification /kwɒlɪfɪ'keɪʃn/ *n* qualifica *f*. **~ied** /-faɪd/ *a* qualificato; ⟨limited⟩ con riserva

qualify /'kwɒlɪfaɪ/ *v* ⟨*pt/pp* **-ied**⟩ ● *vt* ⟨course⟩ dare la qualifica a (**as** di); ⟨entitle⟩ autorizzare a; ⟨limit⟩ precisare ● *vi* ottenere la qualifica; *Sport* qualificarsi

quality /'kwɒlɪtɪ/ *n* qualità *f*

qualm /kwɑːm/ *n* scrupolo *m*

quandary /'kwɒndərɪ/ *n* dilemma *m*

quantity /'kwɒntɪtɪ/ *n* quantità *f inv*; **in ~** in grande quantità

quarantine /'kwɒrəntiːn/ *n* quarantena *f*

quarrel /'kwɒrəl/ *n* lite *f* ● *vi* ⟨*pt/pp* **quarrelled**⟩ litigare. **~some** *a* litigioso

quarry¹ /'kwɒrɪ/ *n* ⟨prey⟩ preda *f*

quarry² *n* cava *f*

quart /kwɔːt/ *n* 1.14 litro

quarter /'kwɔːtə(r)/ *n* quarto *m*; ⟨of year⟩ trimestre *m*; *Am* 25 centesimi *mpl*; **~s** *pl Mil* quartiere *msg*; **at [a] ~ to six** alle sei meno un quarto ● *vt* dividere in quattro. **~-'final** *n* quarto *m* di finale

quarterly /'kwɔːtəlɪ/ *a* trimestrale ● *adv* trimestralmente

quartet /kwɔː'tet/ *n* quartetto *m*

quartz /kwɔːts/ *n* quarzo *m*. **~ watch** *n* orologio *m* al quarzo

quash /kwɒʃ/ *vt* annullare; soffocare ⟨rebellion⟩

quaver /'kweɪvə(r)/ *vi* tremolare

quay /kiː/ *n* banchina *f*

queasy /'kwiːzɪ/ *a* **I feel ~** ho la nausea

queen /kwiːn/ *n* regina *f*. **~ mother** *n* regina *f* madre

queer /kwɪə(r)/ *a* strano; ⟨dubious⟩ sospetto; ⟨fam: homosexual⟩ finocchio ● *n fam* finocchio *m*

quell /kwel/ *vt* reprimere

quench /kwentʃ/ *vt* **~ one's thirst** dissetarsi

query /'kwɪərɪ/ *n* domanda *f*; ⟨question mark⟩ punto *m* interrogativo ● *vt* ⟨*pt/pp* **-ied**⟩ interrogare; ⟨doubt⟩ mettere in dubbio

quest /kwest/ n ricerca f (**for** di)

question /'kwestʃn/ n domanda f; (for discussion) questione f; **out of the ~** fuori discussione; **without ~** senza dubbio; **in ~** in questione ● vt interrogare; (doubt) mettere in dubbio. **~able** /-əbl/ a discutibile. **~ mark** n punto m interrogativo

questionnaire /kwestʃə'neə(r)/ n questionario m

queue /kju:/ n coda f, fila f ● vi ~ [up] mettersi in coda (**for** per)

quick /kwɪk/ a veloce; **be ~** sbrigati!; **have a ~ meal** fare uno spuntino ● adv in fretta ● n **be cut to the ~** fig essere punto sul vivo. **~ly** adv in fretta. **~-tempered** a collerico

quid /kwɪd/ n inv fam sterlina f

quiet /'kwaɪət/ a (calm) quieto; (silent) silenzioso; (voice, music) basso; **keep ~ about** fam non raccontare a nessuno ● n quiete f; **on the ~** di nascosto. **~ly** adv (peacefully) tranquillamente; (say) a bassa voce

quiet|en /'kwaɪətn/ vt calmare. **quieten down** vi calmarsi. **~ness** n quiete f

quilt /kwɪlt/ n piumino m. **~ed** a trapuntato

quins /kwɪnz/ npl fam = **quintuplets**

quintet /kwɪn'tet/ n quintetto m

quintuplets /'kwɪntjʊplɪts/ npl cinque gemelli mpl

quirk /kwɜ:k/ n stranezza f

quit /kwɪt/ v (pt/pp quitted, quit) ● vt lasciare; (give up) smettere (doing di fare) ● vi (fam: resign) andarsene; Comput uscire; **give sb notice to ~** (landlord:) dare a qcno il preavviso di sfratto

quite /kwaɪt/ a (fairly) abbastanza; (completely) completamente; (really) veramente; **~ [so]!** proprio così!; **~ a few** parecchi

quits /kwɪts/ a pari

quiver /'kwɪvə(r)/ vi tremare

quiz /kwɪz/ n (game) quiz m inv ● vt (pt/pp quizzed) interrogare

quota /'kwəʊtə/ n quota f

quotation /kwəʊ'teɪʃn/ n citazione f; (price) preventivo m; (of shares) quota f. **~ marks** npl virgolette fpl

quote /kwəʊt/ n fam = **quotation**; **in ~s** tra virgolette ● vt citare; quotare (price)

Rr

rabbi /'ræbaɪ/ n rabbino m; (title) rabbi

rabbit /'ræbɪt/ n coniglio m

rabble /'ræbl/ n **the ~** la plebaglia

rabies /'reɪbi:z/ n rabbia f

race[1] /reɪs/ n (people) razza f

race[2] n corsa f ● vi correre ● vt gareggiare con; fare correre (horse)

race: **~course** n ippodromo m. **~horse** n cavallo m da corsa. **~track** n pista m

racial /'reɪʃl/ a razziale. **~ism** n razzismo m

racing /'reɪsɪŋ/ n corse fpl; (horse-) corse fpl dei cavalli. **~ car** n macchina f da corsa. **~ driver** n corridore m automobilistico

racis|m /'reɪsɪzm/ n razzismo m. **~t** /-ɪst/ a razzista m

rack[1] /ræk/ n (for bikes) rastrelliera f; (for luggage) portabagagli m inv; (for plates) scolapiatti m inv ● vt ~ **one's brains** scervellarsi

rack[2] n **go to ~ and ruin** andare in rovina

racket[1] /'rækɪt/ n Sport racchetta f

racket[2] n (din) chiasso m; (swindle) truffa f; (crime) racket m inv, giro m

radar /'reɪdɑ:(r)/ n radar m inv

radian|ce /'reɪdɪəns/ n radiosità f inv. **~t** a raggiante

radiat|e /'reɪdɪeɪt/ vt irradiare ● vi

⟨*heat:*⟩ irradiarsi. **~ion** /-'eɪʃn/ n radiazione f

radiator /'reɪdɪeɪtə(r)/ n radiatore m

radical /'rædɪkl/ a radicale ● n radicale mf. **~ly** adv radicalmente

radio /'reɪdɪəʊ/ n radio f inv

radio|'active a radioattivo. **~'tivity** n radioattività f

radiograph|er /reɪdɪ'ɒgrəfə(r)/ n radiologo, -a mf. **~y** n radiografia f

radio'therapy n radioterapia f

radish /'rædɪʃ/ n ravanello m

radius /'reɪdɪəs/ n (pl -dii /-dɪaɪ/) raggio m

raffle /'ræfl/ n lotteria f

raft /rɑːft/ n zattera f

rafter /'rɑːftə(r)/ n trave f

rag /ræg/ n straccio m; (pej: newspaper) giornalaccio m; **in ~s** stracciato

rage /reɪdʒ/ n rabbia f; **all the ~** fam all'ultima moda ● vi infuriarsi; ⟨storm:⟩ infuriare; ⟨epidemic:⟩ imperversare

ragged /'rægɪd/ a logoro, ⟨edge⟩ frastagliato

raid /reɪd/ n (by thieves) rapina f, Mil incursione f, raid m inv; ⟨police⟩ irruzione f ● vt Mil fare un'incursione in; ⟨police, burglars:⟩ fare irruzione in. **~er** n (of bank) rapinatore, -trice mf

rail /reɪl/ n ringhiera f; ⟨hand~⟩ ringhiera f; Naut parapetto m; **by ~** per ferrovia

'railroad n Am = railway

railway n ferrovia f. **~man** n ferroviere m. **~ station** n stazione f ferroviaria

rain /reɪn/ n pioggia f ● vi piovere

rain: ~bow n arcobaleno m. **~coat** n impermeabile m. **~fall** n precipitazione f [atmosferica]

rainy /'reɪnɪ/ a (-ier, -iest) piovoso

raise /reɪz/ n Am aumento m ● vt alzare; levarsi ⟨hat⟩; allevare ⟨children, animals⟩; sollevare ⟨question⟩; ottenere ⟨money⟩

raisin /'reɪzn/ n uva f passa

rake /reɪk/ n rastrello m ● vt rastrellare. **rake up** vt raccogliere col rastrello; fam rivangare

rally /'rælɪ/ n raduno m; Auto rally m inv; Tennis scambio m ● vt (pt/pp -ied) radunare ● vi radunarsi; ⟨recover strength⟩ riprendersi

RAM /ræm/ n [memoria f] RAM f

ram /ræm/ n montone m; Astr Ariete m ● vt (pt/pp **rammed**) cozzare contro

ramble /'ræmbl/ n escursione f ● vi gironzolare; (in speech) divagare. **~er** n escursionista mf; ⟨rose⟩ rosa f rampicante. **~ing** a (in speech) sconnesso; ⟨club⟩ escursionistico

ramp /ræmp/ n rampa f; Aeron scaletta f mobile (di aerei)

rampage /'ræmpeɪdʒ/ n **be/go on the ~** scatenarsi ● vi **~ through the streets** scatenarsi per le strade

rampant /'ræmpənt/ a dilagante

rampart /'ræmpɑːt/ n bastione f

ramshackle /'ræmʃækl/ a sgangherato

ran /ræn/ see **run**

ranch /rɑːntʃ/ n ranch m

rancid /'rænsɪd/ a rancido

rancour /'ræŋkə(r)/ n rancore m

random /'rændəm/ a casuale; **~ sample** campione m a caso ● n **at ~** a casaccio

randy /'rændɪ/ a (-ier, -iest) fam eccitato

rang /ræŋ/ see **ring²**

range /reɪndʒ/ n serie f; Comm, Mus gamma f; ⟨of mountains⟩ catena f; ⟨distance⟩ raggio m; ⟨for shooting⟩ portata f; ⟨stove⟩ cucina f economica; **at a ~ of** a una distanza di ● vi estendersi; **~ from... to...** andare da... a.... **~r** n guardia f forestale

rank /ræŋk/ n ⟨row⟩ riga f; Mil grado m; ⟨social position⟩ rango m; **the ~ and file** la base f; **the ~s** Mil i soldati mpl semplici ● vt (*place*) annoverare (**among** tra) ● *vi* (*be placed*) collocarsi

rankle /'ræŋkl/ *vi* fig bruciare

ransack /'rænsæk/ *vt* rovistare; (*pillage*) saccheggiare

ransom /'rænsəm/ *n* riscatto *m*; **hold sb to ~** tenere qcno in ostaggio (*per il riscatto*)

rant /rænt/ *vi* ~ **[and rave]** inveire; **what's he ~ing on about?** cosa sta blaterando?

rap /ræp/ *n* colpo *m* [secco]; *Mus* rap *m* ● *v* (*pt/pp* **rapped**) ● *vt* dare colpetti a ● *vi* ~ **at** bussare a

rape /reɪp/ *n* (*sexual*) stupro *m* ● *vt* violentare, stuprare

rapid /'ræpɪd/ *a* rapido. **~ity** /rə'pɪdətɪ/ *n* rapidità *f*. **~ly** *adv* rapidamente

rapids /'ræpɪdz/ *npl* rapide *fsg*

rapist /'reɪpɪst/ *n* violentatore *m*

rapport /ræ'pɔː(r)/ *n* rapporto *m* di intesa

rapture /'ræptʃə(r)/ *n* estasi *f*. **~ous** /-rəs/ *a* entusiastico

rare¹ /reə(r)/ *a* raro. **~ly** *adv* raramente

rare² *a Culin* al sangue

rarefied /'reərɪfaɪd/ *a* rarefatto

rarity /'reərətɪ/ *n* rarità *f inv*

rascal /'rɑːskl/ *n* mascalzone *m*

rash¹ /ræʃ/ *n Med* eruzione *f*

rash² *a* avventato. **~ly** *adv* avventatamente

rasher /'ræʃə(r)/ *n* fetta *f* di pancetta

rasp /rɑːsp/ *n* (*noise*) stridio *m*. **~ing** *a* stridente

raspberry /'rɑːzbərɪ/ *n* lampone *m*

rat /ræt/ *n* topo *m*; (*fam: person*) carogna *f*; **smell a ~** *fam* sentire puzzo di bruciato

rate /reɪt/ *n* (*speed*) velocità *f*; (*of payment*) tariffa *f*; (*of exchange*) tasso *m*; **~s** *pl* (*taxes*) imposte *fpl* comunali sui beni immobili; **at any ~** in ogni caso; **at this ~** di questo passo ● *vt* stimare; **~ among** annoverare tra ● *vi* **~ as** essere considerato

rather /'rɑːðə(r)/ *adv* piuttosto; **~!** eccome!; **~ too...** un po' troppo...

ratification /rætɪfɪ'keɪʃn/ *n* ratifica *f*. **~fy** /'rætɪfaɪ/ *vt* (*pt/pp* **-ied**) ratificare

rating /'reɪtɪŋ/ *n* ~**s** *pl* Radio, TV indice *m* d'ascolto, audience *f inv*

ratio /'reɪʃɪəʊ/ *n* rapporto *m*

ration /'ræʃn/ *n* razione *f* ● *vt* razionare

rational /'ræʃənl/ *a* razionale. **~ize** *vt/i* razionalizzare

'rat race *n fam* corsa *f* al successo

rattle /'rætl/ *n* tintinnio *m*; (*toy*) sonaglio *m* ● *vi* tintinnare ● *vt* (*shake*) scuotere; *fam* innervosire. **rattle off** *vt fam* sciorinare

'rattlesnake *n* serpente *m* a sonagli

raucous /'rɔːkəs/ *a* rauco

rave /reɪv/ *vi* vaneggiare; **~ about** andare in estasi per

raven /'reɪvn/ *n* corvo *m* imperiale

ravenous /'rævənəs/ *a* (*person*) affamato

ravine /rə'viːn/ *n* gola *f*

raving /'reɪvɪŋ/ *a* **~ mad** *fam* matto da legare

ravishing /'rævɪʃɪŋ/ *a* incantevole

raw /rɔː/ *a* crudo; (*not processed*) grezzo; (*weather*) gelido; (*inexperienced*) inesperto; **get a ~ deal** *fam* farsi fregare. **~ ma'terials** *npl* materie *fpl* prime

ray /reɪ/ *n* raggio *m*; **~ of hope** barlume *m* di speranza

raze /reɪz/ *vt* **~ to the ground** radere al suolo

razor /'reɪzə(r)/ *n* rasoio *m*. **~-blade** *n* lametta *f* da barba

re /riː/ *prep* con riferimento a

reach /riːtʃ/ *n* portata *f*; **within ~ a** portata di mano; **out of ~ of** fuori dalla portata di; **within easy ~** facilmente raggiungibile ● *vt* arrivare a ⟨*place, decision*⟩; (*contact*) contattare; (*pass*) passare; **I can't ~ it** non ci arrivo ● *vi* arrivare (**to** a); **~ for** allungare la mano per prendere

re'act /rɪ-/ *vi* reagire

re'action /rɪ-/ n reazione f. **~ary** a reazionario, -a mf

reactor /rɪ'æktə(r)/ n reattore m

read /riːd/ vt (pt/pp **read** /red/) leggere; Univ studiare ● vi leggere; ⟨instrument:⟩ indicare. **read out** vt leggere ad alta voce

readable /'riːdəbl/ a piacevole a leggersi; ⟨legible⟩ leggibile

reader /'riːdə(r)/ n lettore, -trice mf; ⟨book⟩ antologia f

readily /'redɪlɪ/ adv volentieri; ⟨easily⟩ facilmente. **~ness** n disponibilità f inv; **in ~ness** pronto

reading /'riːdɪŋ/ n lettura f

rea'djust /riː-/ vt regolare di nuovo ● vi riabituarsi (**to** a)

ready /'redɪ/ a (**-ier, -iest**) pronto; ⟨quick⟩ veloce; **get ~** prepararsi

ready: **~'made** a confezionato. **~ 'money** n contanti mpl. **~-to-'wear** a prêt-à-porter

real /riːl/ a vero; ⟨increase⟩ reale ● adv Am fam veramente. **~ esta'te** n beni mpl immobili

realis|m /'rɪəlɪzm/ n realismo m. **~t** /-lɪst/ n realista mf. **~tic** /-'lɪstɪk/ a realistico

reality /rɪ'ælətɪ/ n realtà f inv

realization /rɪəlɑr'zeɪ∫n/ n realizzazione f

realize /'rɪəlaɪz/ vt realizzare

really /'rɪəlɪ/ adv davvero

realm /relm/ n regno m

realtor /'rɪəltə(r)/ n Am agente mf immobiliare

reap /riːp/ vt mietere

reap'pear /riː-/ vi riapparire

rear¹ /rɪə(r)/ a posteriore; Auto di dietro; **~ end** fam didietro m ● n **the ~** ⟨of building⟩ il retro m; ⟨of bus, plane⟩ la parte f posteriore; **from the ~** da dietro

rear² /rɪə(r)/ vt allevare ● vi **~ [up]** ⟨horse:⟩ impennarsi

'rear-light n luce f posteriore

re'arm /riː-/ vt riarmare ● vi riarmarsi

rear'range /riː-/ vt cambiare la disposizione di

rear-view 'mirror n Auto specchietto m retrovisore

reason /'riːzn/ n ragione f; **within ~** nei limiti del ragionevole ● vi ragionare; **~ with** cercare di far ragionare. **~able** /-əbl/ a ragionevole. **~ably** /-əblɪ/ adv ⟨in reasonable way, fairly⟩ ragionevolmente

reas'sur|ance /riː-/ n rassicurazione f. **~e** vt rassicurare; **~e sb of sth** rassicurare qcno su qcsa. **~ing** a rassicurante

rebate /'riːbeɪt/ n rimborso m; ⟨discount⟩ deduzione f

rebel¹ /'rebl/ n ribelle mf

rebel² /rɪ'bel/ vi (pt/pp **rebelled**) ribellarsi. **~lion** /-jən/ n ribellione f. **~lious** /-jəs/ a ribelle

re'bound¹ /rɪ-/ vi rimbalzare; fig ricadere

'rebound² /riː-/ n rimbalzo m

rebuff /rɪ'bʌf/ n rifiuto m

re'build /riː-/ vt (pt/pp **-built**) ricostruire

rebuke /rɪ'bjuːk/ vt rimproverare

rebuttal /rɪ'bʌtl/ n rifiuto m

re'call /rɪ-/ n richiamo m; **beyond ~** irrevocabile ● vt richiamare; riconoscere ⟨diplomat, parliament⟩; ⟨remember⟩ rievocare

recap /'riːkæp/ vt/i fam = **recapitulate** ● n ricapitolazione f

recapitulate /riːkə'pɪtjʊleɪt/ vt/i ricapitolare

re'capture /riː-/ vt riconquistare; ricatturare ⟨person, animal⟩

recede /rɪ'siːd/ vi allontanarsi. **~ing** a ⟨forehead, chin⟩ sfuggente; **have ~ing hair** essere stempiato

receipt /rɪ'siːt/ n ricevuta f; ⟨receiving⟩ ricezione f; **~s** pl Comm entrate fpl

receive /rɪ'siːv/ vt ricevere. **~r** n Teleph ricevitore m; Radio, TV apparecchio m ricevente; ⟨of stolen goods⟩ ricettatore, -trice mf

recent /'riːsnt/ a recente. **~ly** adv recentemente

receptacle /rɪ'septəkl/ n recipiente m

reception /rɪˈsepʃn/ n ricevimento m; (welcome) accoglienza f; Radio ricezione f; ~ **[desk]** (in hotel) reception f inv. ~**ist** n persona f alla reception

receptive /rɪˈseptɪv/ a ricettivo

recess /rɪˈses/ n rientranza f; (holiday) vacanza f; Am Sch intervallo m

recession /rɪˈseʃn/ n recessione f

re'charge /riː-/ vt ricaricare

recipe /ˈresəpɪ/ n ricetta f

recipient /rɪˈsɪpɪənt/ n (of letter) destinatario, -a mf; (of money) beneficiario, -a mf

reciprocal /rɪˈsɪprəkl/ a reciproco. ~**cate** /-keɪt/ vt ricambiare

recital /rɪˈsaɪtl/ n recital m inv

recite /rɪˈsaɪt/ vt recitare; (list) elencare

reckless /ˈreklɪs/ a (action, decision) sconsiderato; **be a** ~ **driver** guidare in modo pericoloso. ~**ly** adv in modo sconsiderato. ~**ness** n sconsideratezza f

reckon /ˈrekən/ vt calcolare; (consider) pensare. **reckon on/with** vt fare i conti con

re'claim /rɪ-/ vt reclamare; bonificare (land)

recline /rɪˈklaɪn/ vi sdraiarsi. ~**ing** a (seat) reclinabile

recluse /rɪˈkluːs/ n recluso, -a mf

recognition /rekəgˈnɪʃn/ n riconoscimento m; **beyond** ~ irriconoscibile

recognize /ˈrekəgnaɪz/ vt riconoscere

re'coil /rɪ-/ vi (in fear) indietreggiare

recollect /rekəˈlekt/ vt ricordare. ~**ion** /-ekʃn/ n ricordo m

recommend /rekəˈmend/ vt raccomandare. ~**ation** /-ˈdeɪʃn/ n raccomandazione f

recompense /ˈrekəmpens/ n ricompensa f

reconcile /ˈrekənsaɪl/ vt riconciliare; conciliare (facts); ~**cile oneself to** rassegnarsi a.

~ciliation /-sɪlɪˈeɪʃn/ n riconciliazione f

recon'dition /riː-/ vt ripristinare. ~**ed engine** n motore m che ha subito riparazioni

reconnaissance /rɪˈkɒnɪsns/ n Mil ricognizione f

reconnoitre /rekəˈnɔɪtə(r)/ vi (pres p -tring) fare una recognizione

recon'sider /riː-/ vt riconsiderare

recon'struct /riː-/ vt ricostruire. ~**ion** n ricostruzione f

record¹ /rɪˈkɔːd/ vt registrare; (make a note of) annotare

record² /ˈrekɔːd/ n (file) documentazione f; Mus disco m; Sport record m inv; ~**s** pl (files) registro msg; **keep a** ~ **of** tener nota di; **off the** ~ in via ufficiosa; **have a [criminal]** ~ avere la fedina penale sporca

recorder /rɪˈkɔːdə(r)/ n Mus flauto m dolce

recording /rɪˈkɔːdɪŋ/ n registrazione f

'record-player n giradischi m inv

recount /rɪˈkaʊnt/ vt raccontare

re-'count¹ /riː-/ vt ricontare

're-count² /ˈriː-/ n Pol nuovo conteggio m

recoup /rɪˈkuːp/ vt rifarsi di (losses)

recourse /rɪˈkɔːs/ n **have** ~ **to** ricorrere a

re-'cover /riː-/ vt rifoderare

recover /rɪˈkʌvə(r)/ vt/i recuperare. ~**y** n recupero m; (of health) guarigione m

recreation /rekrɪˈeɪʃn/ n ricreazione f. ~**al** a ricreativo

recrimination /rɪkrɪmɪˈneɪʃn/ n recriminazione f

recruit /rɪˈkruːt/ n Mil recluta f; **new** ~ (member) nuovo, -a adepto, -a mf; (worker) neoassunto, -a mf ● vt assumere (staff). ~**ment** n assunzione f

rectangle /ˈrektæŋgl/ n rettangolo m. ~**ular** /-ˈtæŋgjʊlə(r)/ a rettangolare

rectify /'rektɪfaɪ/ vt (pt/pp -ied) rettificare

recuperate /rɪ'ku:pəreɪt/ vi ristabilirsi

recur /rɪ'kɜ:(r)/ vi (pt/pp recurred) ricorrere; ‹illness:› ripresentarsi

recurrence /rɪ'kʌrəns/ n ricorrenza f; (of illness) ricomparsa f. **~t** a ricorrente

recycle /ri:'saɪkl/ vt riciclare

red /red/ a (redder, reddest) rosso ●n rosso m; **in the ~** (account) scoperto. **R~ Cross** n Croce f rossa

redden /'redn/ vt arrossare ●vi arrossire. **~ish** a rossastro

re'decorate /ri:-/ vt (paint) ridipingere; (wallpaper) ritappezzare

redeem /rɪ'di:m/ vt ~ing quality unico aspetto m positivo

redemption /rɪ'dempʃn/ n riscatto m

rede'ploy /ri:-/ vt ridistribuire

red: ~-haired a con i capelli rossi. **~-handed** a catch sb ~-handed cogliere qcno con le mani nel sacco. **~ 'herring** n diversione f. **~-hot** a rovente

red: ~ 'light n Auto semaforo m rosso

re'double /ri:-/ vt raddoppiare

redress /rɪ'dres/ n riparazione f ●vt ristabilire ‹balance›

red 'tape n fam burocrazia f

reduce /rɪ'dju:s/ vt ridurre; Culin far consumare. **~tion** /-'dʌkʃn/ n riduzione f

redundancy /rɪ'dʌndənsɪ/ n licenziamento m; (payment) cassa f integrazione. **~t** a superfluo; **be made ~t** essere licenziato

reed /ri:d/ n Bot canna f

reef /ri:f/ n scogliera f

reek /ri:k/ vi puzzare (of di)

reel /ri:l/ n bobina f ●vi (stagger) vacillare. **reel off** vt fig snocciolare

refectory /rɪ'fektərɪ/ n refettorio m; Univ mensa f universitaria

refer /rɪ'fɜ:(r)/ v (pt/pp referred) ●vt rinviare (matter) (to a); indirizzare (person) ●vi ~ **to** fare allusione a; (consult) rivolgersi a ‹book›

referee /refə'ri:/ n arbitro m; (for job) garante mf ●vt/i (pt/pp refereed) arbitrare

reference /'refərəns/ n riferimento m; (in book) nota f bibliografica; (for job) referenza f; Comm 'your ~' 'riferimento'; **with ~ to** con riferimento a; **make [a] ~ to** fare riferimento a. **~ book** n libro m di consultazione. **~ number** n numero m di riferimento

referendum /refə'rendəm/ n referendum m inv

re'fill¹ /ri:-/ vt riempire di nuovo; ricaricare ‹pen, lighter›

refill² /'ri:-/ n (for pen) ricambio m

refine /rɪ'faɪn/ vt raffinare. **~d** a raffinato. **~ment** n raffinatezza f; Techn raffinazione f. **~ry** /-ərɪ/ n raffineria f

reflect /rɪ'flekt/ vt riflettere; **be ~ed in** essere riflesso in ●vi (think) riflettere (on su); ~ **badly on sb** fig mettere in cattiva luce qcno. **~ion** /-ekʃn/ n riflessione f; (image) riflesso m; **on ~ion** dopo riflessione. **~ive** /-ɪv/ a riflessivo. **~or** n riflettore m

reflex /'ri:fleks/ n riflesso m ●attrib di riflesso

reflexive /rɪ'fleksɪv/ a riflessivo

reform /rɪ'fɔ:m/ n riforma f ●vt riformare ●vi correggersi. **R~ation** /refə'meɪʃn/ n Relig riforma f. **~er** n riformatore, -trice mf

refrain¹ /rɪ'freɪn/ n ritornello m

refrain² vi astenersi (from da)

refresh /rɪ'freʃ/ vt rinfrescare. **~ing** a rinfrescante. **~ments** npl rinfreschi mpl

refrigerate /rɪ'frɪdʒəreɪt/ vt conservare in frigo. **~or** n frigorifero m

re'fuel /riː-/ v (pt/pp -fuelled) ● vt rifornire (di carburante) ● vi fare rifornimento

refuge /'refjuːdʒ/ n rifugio m; **take ~** rifugiarsi

refugee /refjʊ'dʒiː-/ n rifugiato, -a mf

'refund[1] /'riː-/ n rimborso m

re'fund[2] /rɪ-/ vt rimborsare

refurbish /riː'fɜːbɪʃ/ vt rimettere a nuovo

refusal /rɪ'fjuːzl/ n rifiuto m

refuse[1] /rɪ'fjuːz/ vt/i rifiutare; **~ to do sth** rifiutare di fare qcsa

refuse[2] /'refjuːs/ n rifiuti mpl. **~ collection** n raccolta f dei rifiuti

refute /rɪ'fjuːt/ vt confutare

re'gain /rɪ-/ vt riconquistare

regal /'riːgl/ a regale

regalia /rɪ'geɪlɪə/ npl insegne fpl reali

regard /rɪ'gɑːd/ n (heed) riguardo m; (respect) considerazione f; **~s** pl saluti mpl; **send/give my ~s to your brother** salutami tuo fratello ● vt (consider) considerare (as come); **as ~s** riguardo a. **~less** adv senza badare a. **~less of** senza riguardo a

regatta /rɪ'gætə/ n regata f

regenerate /rɪ'dʒenəreɪt/ vt rigenerare ● vi rigenerarsi

regime /reɪ'ʒiːm/ n regime m

regiment /'redʒɪmənt/ n reggimento m. **~al** /-'mentl/ a reggimentale. **~ation** /-mən'teɪʃn/ n irregimentazione f

region /'riːdʒən/ n regione f; **in the ~ of** fig approssimativamente. **~al** a regionale

register /'redʒɪstə(r)/ n registro m ● vt registrare; mandare per raccomandata (letter); assicurare (luggage); immatricolare (vehicle); mostrare (feeling) ● vi (instrument:) funzionare; (student:) iscriversi (for a); **~ with** iscriversi nella lista di (doctor)

registrar /redʒɪ'strɑː(r)/ n ufficiale m di stato civile

registration /redʒɪ'streɪʃn/ n (of

vehicle) immatricolazione f; (of letter) raccomandazione f; (of luggage) assicurazione f; (for course) iscrizione f. **~ number** n Auto targa f

registry office /'redʒɪstrɪ-/ n anagrafe f

regret /rɪ'gret/ n rammarico m ● vt (pt/pp regretted) rimpiangere; **I ~ that** mi rincresce che. **~fully** adv con rammarico

regrettab|le /rɪ'gretəbl/ a spiacevole. **~ly** adv spiacevolmente; (before adjective) deplorevolmente

regular /'regjʊlə(r)/ a regolare; (usual) abituale ● n cliente mf abituale. **~ity** /-'lærətɪ/ n regolarità f. **~ly** adv regolarmente

regulat|e /'regjʊleɪt/ vt regolare. **~ion** /-'leɪʃn/ n (rule) regolamento m

rehabilitat|e /riːhə'bɪlɪteɪt/ vt riabilitare. **~ion** /-'teɪʃn/ n riabilitazione f

rehears|al /rɪ'hɜːsl/ n Theat prova f. **~e** vt/i provare

reign /reɪn/ n regno m ● vi regnare

reimburse /riːɪm'bɜːs/ vt **~ sb for sth** rimborsare qcsa a qcno

rein /reɪn/ n redine f

reincarnation /riːɪnkɑː'neɪʃn/ n reincarnazione f

reinforce /riːɪn'fɔːs/ vt rinforzare. **~d 'concrete** n cemento m armato. **~ment** n rinforzo m

reinstate /riːɪn'steɪt/ vt reintegrare

reiterate /riː'ɪtəreɪt/ vt reiterare

reject /rɪ'dʒekt/ vt rifiutare. **~ion** /-ekʃn/ n rifiuto m; Med rigetto m

rejoice /rɪ'dʒɔɪs/ vi liter rallegrarsi. **~ing** n gioia f

rejuvenate /rɪ'dʒuːvəneɪt/ vt ringiovanire

relapse /rɪ'læps/ n ricaduta f ● vi ricadere

relate /rɪ'leɪt/ vt (tell) riportare; (connect) collegare ● vi **~ to** riferirsi a; identificarsi con (person). **~d** a imparentato (to a); (ideas etc) affine

relation /rɪˈleɪʃn/ n rapporto m; (person) parente mf. **~ship** n rapporto m (blood tie) parentela f; (affair) relazione f

relative /ˈrelətɪv/ n parente mf ● a relativo. **~ly** adv relativamente

relax /rɪˈlæks/ vt rilassare; allentare (pace, grip) ● vi rilassarsi. **~ation** /-lækˈseɪʃn/ n rilassamento m, relax m inv; (recreation) svago m. **~ing** a rilassante

relay¹ /ˈriːleɪ/ vt (pt/pp -laid) ritrasmettere; Radio, TV trasmettere

relay² /ˈriːleɪ/ n Electr relais m inv; **work in ~s** fare i turni. **~ [race]** n [corsa f a] staffetta f

release /rɪˈliːs/ n rilascio m; (of film) distribuzione f ● vt liberare; lasciare (hand); togliere (brake); distribuire (film); rilasciare (information etc)

relegate /ˈrelɪɡeɪt/ vt relegare; be **~d** Sport essere retrocesso

relent /rɪˈlent/ vi cedere. **~less** a inflessibile; (unceasing) incessante. **~lessly** adv incessantemente

relevan|ce /ˈrelavns/ n pertinenza f. **~t** a pertinente (**to** a)

reliab|ility /rlaɪəˈbɪlətɪ/ n affidabilità f. **~le** /-ˈlaɪəbl/ a affidabile a. **~ly** adv in modo affidabile; be **~ly informed** sapere da fonte certa

relian|ce /rɪˈlaɪəns/ n fiducia f (**on** in). **~t** a fiducioso (**on** in)

relic /ˈrelɪk/ n Relig reliquia f. **~s** npl resti mpl

relief /rɪˈliːf/ n sollievo m; (assistance) soccorso m; (distraction) diversivo m; (replacement) cambio m; (in art) rilievo m; **in ~** in rilievo. **~ map** n carta f in rilievo. **~ train** n treno m supplementare

relieve /rɪˈliːv/ vt alleviare; (take over from) dare il cambio a; **~ of** liberare da (burden)

religion /rɪˈlɪdʒən/ n religione f

religious /rɪˈlɪdʒəs/ a religioso. **~ly** adv (conscientiously) scrupolosamente

relinquish /rɪˈlɪŋkwɪʃ/ vt abbandonare; **~ sth to sb** rinunciare a qcsa in favore di qcno

relish /ˈrelɪʃ/ n gusto m; Culin salsa f ● vt fig apprezzare

relo'cate /riː-/ vt trasferire

reluctan|ce /rɪˈlʌktəns/ n riluttanza f. **~t** a riluttante. **~tly** adv a malincuore

rely /rɪˈlaɪ/ vi (pt/pp -ied) **~ on** dipendere da; (trust) contare su

remain /rɪˈmeɪn/ vi restare. **~der** n resto m. **~ing** a restante. **~s** npl resti mpl; (dead body) spoglie fpl

remand /rɪˈmɑːnd/ n **on ~** in custodia cautelare ● vt **~ in custody** rinviare con detenzione provvisoria

remark /rɪˈmɑːk/ n osservazione f ● vt osservare. **~able** /-əbl/ a notevole. **~ably** adv notevolmente

remarry /riː-/ vi risposarsi

remedial /rɪˈmiːdɪəl/ a correttivo; Med curativo

remedy /ˈremədɪ/ n rimedio m (**for** contro) ● vt (pt/pp -ied) rimediare a

remember /rɪˈmembə(r)/ vt ricordare, ricordarsi; **~ to do sth** ricordarsi di fare qcsa; **~ me to him** salutamelo ● vi ricordarsi

remind /rɪˈmaɪnd/ vt **~ sb of sth** ricordare qcsa a qcno. **~er** n ricordo m; (memo) promemoria m; (letter) lettera f di sollecito

reminisce /remɪˈnɪs/ vi rievocare il passato. **~nces** /-ənsɪz/ npl reminiscenze fpl. **~nt** a be **~nt of** richiamare alla memoria

remiss /rɪˈmɪs/ a negligente

remission /rɪˈmɪʃn/ n remissione f; (of sentence) condono m

remit /rɪˈmɪt/ vt (pt/pp remitted) rimettere (money). **~tance** n rimessa f

remnant /ˈremnənt/ n resto m; (of material) scampolo m; (trace) traccia f

remonstrate /ˈremənstreɪt/ vi fare rimostranze; **~ with sb** fare rimostranze a qcno

remorse /rɪ'mɔːs/ *n* rimorso *m*.
~ful *a* pieno di rimorso. **~less** *a*
spietato. **~lessly** *adv* senza pietà

remote /rɪ'məʊt/ *a* remoto; *(slight)*
minimo. **~ access** *n* Comput accesso *m* remoto. **~ con'trol** *n* telecomando *m*. **~con'trolled** *a*
a telecomando. **~ly** *adv* lontanamente; **be not ~ly...** non essere
lontanamente...

re'movable /rɪ-/ *a* rimovibile

removal /rɪ'muːvl/ *n* rimozione *f*;
(from house) trasloco *m*. **~ van** *n*
camion *m* inv da trasloco

remove /rɪ'muːv/ *vt* togliere; togliersi *(clothes)*; eliminare *(stain,
doubts)*

remunerat|ion /rɪmjuːnə'reɪʃn/ *n*
rimunerazione *f*. **~ive** /-'mjuːn-
ərətɪv/ *a* rimunerativo

render /'rendə(r)/ *vt* rendere
(service)

rendering /'rendərɪŋ/ *n* Mus interpretazione *f*

renegade /'renɪgeɪd/ *n* rinnegato,
-a *mf*

renew /rɪ'njuː/ *vt* rinnovare
(contract). **~al** *n* rinnovo *m*

renounce /rɪ'naʊns/ *vt* rinunciare a

renovat|e /'renəveɪt/ *vt* rinnovare.
~ion /-'veɪʃn/ *n* rinnovo *m*

renown /rɪ'naʊn/ *n* fama *f*. **~ed** *a*
rinomato

rent /rent/ *n* affitto *m* ● *vt* affittare; **~ [out]** dare in affitto. **~al** *n* affitto *m*

renunciation /rɪnʌnsɪ'eɪʃn/ *n* rinuncia *f*

re'open /riː-/ *vt/i* riaprire

re'organize /riː-/ *vt* riorganizzare

rep /rep/ *n* Comm fam rappresentante *mf*; Theat ≈ teatro *m* stabile

repair /rɪ'peə(r)/ *n* riparazione *f*;
in good/bad ~ in cattive/buone
condizioni ● *vt* riparare

repatriat|e /riː'pætrɪeɪt/ *vt* rimpa-
triare. **~ion** /-'eɪʃn/ *n* rimpatrio *m*

re'pay /riː-/ *vt* *(pt/pp -paid)* ripagare. **~ment** *n* rimborso *m*

repeal /rɪ'piːl/ *n* abrogazione *f* ● *vt*
abrogare

repeat /rɪ'piːt/ *n* TV replica *f*
● *vt/i* ripetere; **~ oneself** ripeter-
si. **~ed** *a* ripetuto. **~edly** *adv*
ripetutamente

repel /rɪ'pel/ *vt* *(pt/pp* repelled*)* respingere; *fig* ripugnare. **~lent** *a*
ripulsivo

repent /rɪ'pent/ *vi* pentirsi. **~ance**
n pentimento *m*. **~ant** *a* pentito

repercussions /riːpə'kʌʃnz/ *npl*
ripercussioni *fpl*

repertoire /'repətwɑː(r)/ *n* reper-
torio *m*

repetit|ion /repɪ'tɪʃn/ *n* ripetizio-
ne *f*. **~ive** /rɪ'petɪtɪv/ *a* ripetitivo

re'place /rɪ-/ *vt* *(put back)* rimettere a posto; *(take the place of)* sostituire; **~ sth with sth** sostituire
qcsa con qcsa. **~ment** *n* sostitu-
zione *m*; *(person)* sostituto, -a *mf*.
~ment part *n* pezzo *m* di ricambio

'replay /riː-/ *n* Sport partita *f* ripe-
tuta; *[action]* **~** replay *m* inv

replenish /rɪ'plenɪʃ/ *vt* rifornire
(stocks); *(refill)* riempire di nuovo

replica /'replɪkə/ *n* copia *f*

reply /rɪ'plaɪ/ *n* risposta *f* **(to** *a)*
● *vt/i* *(pt/pp* replied*)* rispondere

report /rɪ'pɔːt/ *n* rapporto *m*; TV,
Radio servizio *m*; Journ cronaca *f*;
Sch pagella *f*; *(rumour)* diceria *f*
● *vt* riportare; **~ sb to the police**
denunciare qcno alla polizia ● *vi*
riportare; *(present oneself)* presentarsi **(to** *a)*. **~edly** *adv* secondo
quanto si dice. **~er** *n* cronista *mf*,
reporter *mf* inv

repose /rɪ'pəʊz/ *n* riposo *m*

repos'sess /riː-/ *vt* riprendere
possesso di

reprehensible /reprɪ'hensəbl/ *a*
riprovevole

represent /reprɪ'zent/ *vt* rappresentare

representative /reprɪ'zentətɪv/ *a*
rappresentativo ● *n* rappresentante *mf*

repress /rɪ'pres/ *vt* reprimere

~ion /-eʃn/ n repressione f. **~ive** /-ɪv/ a repressivo

reprieve /rɪ'priːv/ n commutazione f della pena capitale; (*postponement*) sospensione f della pena capitale; *fig* tregua f ● vt sospendere la sentenza a; *fig* risparmiare

reprimand /'reprɪmɑːnd/ n rimprovero m ● vt rimproverare

'reprint[1] /'riː-/ n ristampa f

re'print[2] /riː-/ vt ristampare

reprisal /rɪ'praɪzl/ n rappresaglia f; **in ~** for per rappresaglia contro

reproach /rɪ'prəʊtʃ/ n ammonimento m ● vt ammonire. **~ful** a rimprovevole. **~fully** adv con aria di rimprovero

repro'duc|e /riː-/ vt riprodurre ● vi riprodursi. **~tion** /-'dʌkʃn/ n riproduzione f. **~tive** /-dʌktɪv/ a riproduttivo

reprove /rɪ'pruːv/ vt rimproverare

reptile /'reptaɪl/ n rettile m

republic /rɪ'pʌblɪk/ n repubblica f. **~an** a repubblicano ● n repubblicano, -a mf

repudiate /rɪ'pjuːdɪeɪt/ vt ripudiare; (*view, suggestion*) respingere

repugnan|ce /rɪ'pʌgnəns/ n ripugnanza f. **~t** a ripugnante

repuls|ion /rɪ'pʌlʃn/ n repulsione f. **~ive** /-ɪv/ a ripugnante

reputable /'repjʊtəbl/ a affidabile

reputation /repjʊ'teɪʃn/ n reputazione f

repute /rɪ'pjuːt/ n reputazione f. **~d** /-ɪd/ a presunto; **he is ~d to be** si presume che sia. **~dly** adv presumibilmente

request /rɪ'kwest/ n richiesta f ● vt richiedere. **~ stop** n fermata f a richiesta

require /rɪ'kwaɪə(r)/ vt (*need*) necessitare di; (*demand*) esigere. **~d** a richiesto; **I am ~d to** si esige che io lo faccia. **~ment** n esigenza f; (*condition*) requisito m

requisite /'rekwɪzɪt/ a necessario ● n **toilet/travel ~s** pl articoli mpl da toilette/viaggio

re'sale /'riː-/ n rivendita f

rescue /'reskjuː/ n salvataggio m ● vt salvare. **~r** n salvatore, -trice mf

research /rɪ'sɜːtʃ/ n ricerca f ● vt fare ricerche su; *Journ* fare un'inchiesta su ● vi **~ into** fare ricerche su. **~er** n ricercatore, -trice mf

resem|blance /rɪ'zembləns/ n rassomiglianza f. **~ble** /-bl/ vt rassomigliare a

resent /rɪ'zent/ vt risentirsi per. **~ful** a pieno di risentimento. **~fully** adv con risentimento. **~ment** n risentimento m

reservation /rezə'veɪʃn/ n (*booking*) prenotazione f; (*doubt, enclosure*) riserva f

reserve /rɪ'zɜːv/ n riserva f; (*shyness*) riserbo m ● vt riservare; riservarsi (*right*). **~d** a riservato

reservoir /'rezəvwɑː(r)/ n bacino m idrico

re'shape /riː-/ vt ristrutturare

re'shuffle /riː-/ n *Pol* rimpasto m ● vt *Pol* rimpastare

reside /rɪ'zaɪd/ vi risiedere

residen|ce /'rezɪdəns/ n residenza f; (*stay*) soggiorno m. **~ permit** n permesso m di soggiorno

resident /'rezɪdənt/ a residente ● n residente mf. **~ial** /-'denʃl/ a residenziale

residue /'rezɪdjuː/ n residuo m

resign /rɪ'zaɪn/ vt dimettersi da; **~ oneself to** rassegnarsi a ● vi dare le dimissioni. **~ation** /rezɪg'neɪʃn/ n rassegnazione f; (*from job*) dimissioni fpl. **~ed** a rassegnato

resilient /rɪ'zɪlɪənt/ a elastico; *fig* con buone capacità di ripresa

resin /'rezɪn/ n resina f

resist /rɪ'zɪst/ vt resistere a ● vi resistere. **~ance** n resistenza f. **~ant** a resistente

resolut|e /'rezəluːt/ a risoluto. **~ely** adv con risolutezza. **~ion** /-'luːʃn/ n risolutezza f

resolve /rɪˈzɒlv/ vt ~ **to do** decidere di fare

resonan|ce /ˈrezənəns/ n risonanza f. ~**t** a risonante

resort /rɪˈzɔːt/ n (place) luogo m di villeggiatura; **as a last** ~ come ultima risorsa ● vi ~ **to** ricorrere a

resound /rɪˈzaʊnd/ vi risonare (**with** di). ~**ing** a (success) risonante

resource /rɪˈsɔːs/ n ~**s** pl risorse fpl. ~**ful** a pieno di risorse; (solution) ingegnoso. ~**fulness** n ingegnosità f inv

respect /rɪˈspekt/ n rispetto m; (aspect) aspetto m; **with** ~ **to** per quanto riguarda ● vt rispettare

respectability /rɪspektəˈbɪlətɪ/ n rispettabilità f inv

respect|able /rɪˈspektəbl/ a rispettabile. ~**ably** adv rispettabilmente. ~**ful** a rispettoso

respective /rɪˈspektɪv/ a rispettivo. ~**ly** adv rispettivamente

respiration /respɪˈreɪʃn/ n respirazione f

respite /ˈrespaɪt/ n respiro m

respond /rɪˈspɒnd/ vi rispondere; (react) reagire (**to** a); (patient:) rispondere (**to** a)

response /rɪˈspɒns/ n risposta f; (reaction) reazione f

responsibility /rɪspɒnsɪˈbɪlətɪ/ n responsabilità f inv

responsib|le /rɪˈspɒnsəbl/ a responsabile; (job) impegnativo

responsive /rɪˈspɒnsɪv/ a **be** ~ (audience etc:) reagire; (brakes:) essere sensibile

rest¹ /rest/ n riposo m; Mus pausa f; **have a** ~ riposarsi ● vt posare; (lean) appoggiare (**on** su); (place) appoggiare ● vi riposarsi; (elbows:) appoggiarsi; (hopes:) riposare

rest² n **the** ~ il resto m; (people) gli altri mpl ● vi **it** ~**s with you** sta a te

restaurant /ˈrestərɒnt/ n ristorante m. ~ **car** n vagone m ristorante

restful /ˈrestfl/ a riposante

restive /ˈrestɪv/ a irrequieto

restless /ˈrestlɪs/ a nervoso

restoration /restəˈreɪʃn/ n (of building) restauro m

restore /rɪˈstɔː(r)/ vt ristabilire; restaurare (building); (give back) restituire

restrain /rɪˈstreɪn/ vt trattenere; ~ **oneself** controllarsi. ~**ed** a controllato. ~**t** n restrizione f; (moderation) ritegno m

restrict /rɪˈstrɪkt/ vt limitare; ~ **to** limitarsi a. ~**ion** /-ɪkʃn/ n limite m; (restraint) restrizione f. ~**ive** /-ɪv/ a limitativo

'rest room n Am toilette f inv

result /rɪˈzʌlt/ n risultato m; **as a** ~ **a causa** (**of** di) ● vi ~ **from** risultare da; ~ **in** portare a

resume /rɪˈzjuːm/ vt/i riprendere

résumé /ˈrezjʊmeɪ/ n riassunto m; Am curriculum vitae m inv

resumption /rɪˈzʌmpʃn/ n ripresa f

resurgence /rɪˈsɜːdʒəns/ n rinascita f

resurrect /rezəˈrekt/ vt fig risuscitare. ~**ion** /-ekʃn/ n **the R**~**ion** Relig la Risurrezione

resuscitat|e /rɪˈsʌsɪteɪt/ vt rianimare. ~**ion** /-ˈteɪʃn/ n rianimazione f

retail /ˈriːteɪl/ n vendita f al minuto o al dettaglio ● a & adv al minuto ● vt vendere al minuto ● vi ~ **at** essere venduto al pubblico al prezzo di. ~**er** n dettagliante mf

retain /rɪˈteɪn/ vt conservare; (hold back) trattenere

retaliat|e /rɪˈtælɪeɪt/ vi vendicarsi. ~**ion** /-ˈeɪʃn/ n rappresaglia f; **in** ~**ion for** per rappresaglia contro

retarded /rɪˈtɑːdɪd/ a ritardato

retentive /rɪˈtentɪv/ a (memory) buono

rethink /riːˈθɪŋk/ vt (pt/pp **rethought**) ripensare

reticen|ce /ˈretɪsəns/ n reticenza f. ~**t** a reticente

retina /ˈretɪnə/ n retina f

retinue /ˈretɪnjuː/ n seguito m

retire /rɪˈtaɪə(r)/ vi andare in pensione; (withdraw) ritirarsi ● vt mandare in pensione (employee). ~d a in pensione. ~ment n pensione f; since my ~ment da quando sono andato in pensione

retiring /rɪˈtaɪərɪŋ/ a riservato

retort /rɪˈtɔːt/ n replica f ● vt ribattere

re'touch /riː-/ vt Phot ritoccare

re'trace /rɪ-/ vt ripercorrere; ~ one's steps ritornare sui propri passi

retract /rɪˈtrækt/ vt ritirare; ritrattare (statement, evidence) ● vi ritrarsi

re'train /riː-/ vt riqualificare ● vi riqualificarsi

retreat /rɪˈtriːt/ n ritirata f; (place) ritiro m ● vi ritirarsi; Mil battere in ritirata

re'trial /riː-/ n nuovo processo m

retribution /retrɪˈbjuːʃn/ n castigo m

retrieval /rɪˈtriːvl/ n recupero m

retrieve /rɪˈtriːv/ vt recuperare

retrograde /ˈretrəɡreɪd/ a retrogrado

retrospect /ˈretrəspekt/ n in ~ guardando indietro. ~ive /-ˈspektɪv/ a retrospettivo; (legislation) retroattivo ● n retrospettiva f

return /rɪˈtɜːn/ n ritorno m; (giving back) restituzione f; Comm profitto m; (ticket) biglietto m di andata e ritorno; by ~ [of post] a stretto giro di posta; in ~ in cambio (for di); many happy ~s! cento di questi giorni! ● vi ritornare ● vt (give back) restituire; ricambiare (affection, invitation); (put back) rimettere; (send back) mandare indietro; (elect) eleggere

return: ~ flight n volo m di andata e ritorno. ~ match n rivincita f. ~ ticket n biglietto m di andata e ritorno

reunion /riːˈjuːnjən/ n riunione f

reunite /riːjʊˈnaɪt/ vt riunire

re'usable /riː-/ a riutilizzabile. ~ vt riutilizzare

rev /rev/ n Auto, fam giro m (di motore) ● vi (pt/pp revved) ● vt [up] far andare su di giri ● vi andare su di giri

reveal /rɪˈviːl/ vt rivelare; (dress:) scoprire. ~ing a rivelatore; (dress) osé

revel /ˈrevl/ vi (pt/pp revelled) ~ in sth godere di qcsa

revelation /revəˈleɪʃn/ n rivelazione f

revelry /ˈrevlrɪ/ n baldoria f

revenge /rɪˈvendʒ/ n vendetta f; Sport rivincita f; take ~ vendicarsi ● vt vendicare

revenue /ˈrevənjuː/ n reddito m

reverberate /rɪˈvɜːbəreɪt/ vi riverberare

revere /rɪˈvɪə(r)/ vt riverire. ~nce /ˈrevərəns/ n riverenza f

Reverend /ˈrevərənd/ a reverendo

reverent /ˈrevərənt/ a riverente

reverse /rɪˈvɜːs/ a opposto; in ~ order in ordine inverso ● n contrario m; (back) rovescio m; Auto marcia m indietro ● vt invertire; ~ the car into the garage entrare in garage a marcia indietro; ~ the charges Teleph fare una telefonata a carico ● vi Auto fare marcia indietro

revert /rɪˈvɜːt/ vi ~ to tornare a

review /rɪˈvjuː/ n (survey) rassegna f; (re-examination) riconsiderazione f; Mil rivista f; (of book, play) recensione f ● vt riesaminare (situation); Mil passare in rivista; recensire (book, play). ~er n critico, -a mf

revile /rɪˈvaɪl/ vt ingiuriare

revise /rɪˈvaɪz/ vt rivedere; (for exam) ripassare. ~ion /-ˈvɪʒn/ n revisione f; (for exam) ripasso m

revival /rɪˈvaɪvl/ n ritorno m; (of patient) recupero m; (from coma) risveglio m

revive /rɪˈvaɪv/ vt resuscitare; rianimare (person) ● vi riprendersi; (person:) rianimarsi

revoke /rɪ'vəʊk/ vt revocare

revolt /rɪ'vəʊlt/ n rivolta f ● vi ribellarsi ● vt rivoltare. **~ing** a rivoltante

revolution /revə'lu:ʃn/ n rivoluzione f; Auto **~s** per minute giri mpl al minuto. **~ary** /-ərɪ/ a & n rivoluzionario, -a mf. **~ize** vt rivoluzionare

revolve /rɪ'vɒlv/ vi ruotare; **~ around** girare intorno

revolver /rɪ'vɒlvə(r)/ n rivoltella f, revolver m inv. **~ing** a ruotante

revue /rɪ'vju:/ n rivista f

revulsion /rɪ'vʌlʃn/ n ripulsione f

reward /rɪ'wɔ:d/ n ricompensa f ● vt ricompensare. **~ing** a gratificante

re'write /ri:-/ vt (pt rewrote, pp rewritten) riscrivere

rhapsody /'ræpsədɪ/ n rapsodia f

rhetoric /'retərɪk/ n retorica f. **~al** /rɪ'tɒrɪkl/ a retorico

rheuma|tic /ru'mætɪk/ a reumatico. **~tism** /'ru:mətɪzm/ n reumatismo m

Rhine /raɪn/ n Reno m

rhinoceros /raɪ'nɒsərəs/ n rinoceronte m

rhubarb /'ru:bɑ:b/ n rabarbaro m

rhyme /raɪm/ n rima f; (poem) filastrocca f ● vi rimare

rhythm /'rɪðm/ n ritmo m. **~ic[al]** a ritmico. **~ically** adv con ritmo

rib /rɪb/ n costola f

ribald /'rɪbld/ a spinto

ribbon /'rɪbən/ n nastro m; **in ~s** a brandelli

rice /raɪs/ n riso m

rich /rɪtʃ/ a ricco; (food) pesante ● n the **~** pl i ricchi mpl; **~es** pl ricchezze fpl. **~ly** adv riccamente; (deserve) largamente

rickety /'rɪkɪtɪ/ a malfermo

ricochet /'rɪkəʃeɪ/ n rimbalzare n rimbalzo m

rid /rɪd/ vt (pt/pp rid, pres p ridding) sbarazzare (of di); **get ~ of** sbarazzarsi di

riddance /'rɪdns/ n **good ~!** che liberazione!

ridden /'rɪdn/ see ride

riddle /'rɪdl/ n enigma m

riddled /'rɪdld/ a **~ with** crivellato di

ride /raɪd/ n (on horse) cavalcata f; (in vehicle) giro m; (journey) viaggio m; **take sb for a ~** fam prendere qcno in giro ● v (pt rode, pp ridden) ● vt montare (horse); andare su (bicycle) ● vi andare a cavallo; (jockey, showjumper:) cavalcare; (cyclist:) andare in bicicletta; (in vehicle) viaggiare. **~r** n cavallerizzo, -a mf; (in race) fantino m; (on bicycle) ciclista mf; (in document) postilla f

ridicule /'rɪdɪkju:l/ n ridicolo m ● vt mettere in ridicolo

ridiculous /rɪ'dɪkjʊləs/ a ridicolo

riding /'raɪdɪŋ/ n equitazione f ● attrib d'equitazione

rife /raɪf/ a **be ~** essere diffuso; **~ with** pieno di

riff-raff /'rɪfræf/ n marmaglia f

rifle /'raɪfl/ n fucile m; **~-range** tiro m al bersaglio ● vt [through] mettere a soqquadro

rift /rɪft/ n fessura f; fig frattura f

rig¹ /rɪg/ n equipaggiamento m; (at sea) piattaforma f per trivellazioni subacquee ● **rig out** vt (pt/pp rigged) equipaggiare. **rig up** vt allestire

rig² vt (pt/pp rigged) manovrare (election)

right /raɪt/ a giusto; (not left) destro; **be ~** (person:) aver ragione; (clock:) essere giusto; **put ~** mettere all'ora (clock); correggere (person); rimediare a (situation); **that's ~!** proprio così! ● adv (correctly) bene; (not left) a destra; (directly) proprio; (completely) completamente; **~ away** immediatamente ● n giusto m; (not left) destra f; (what is due) diritto m; **on/to the ~** a destra; **be in the ~** essere nel giusto; **know ~ from wrong** distinguere il bene dal male; **by ~s** secondo giustizia; **the R~** *Pol* la destra *f* ● *vt* raddrizzare; **~ a wrong** *fig* riparare a un torto. **~ angle** *n* angolo *m* retto

rightful /ˈraɪtfʊl/ *a* legittimo

right: **~-'handed** *a* che usa la mano destra. **~-hand 'man** *n fig* braccio *m* destro

rightly /ˈraɪtlɪ/ *adv* giustamente

right: **~ of way** *n* diritto *m* di transito; *(path)* passaggio *m*; *Auto* precedenza *f*. **~-'wing** *a Pol* di destra ● *n Sport* ala *f* destra

rigid /ˈrɪdʒɪd/ *a* rigido. **~ity** /-ˈdʒɪdətɪ/ *n* rigidità *f inv*

rigmarole /ˈrɪgmərəʊl/ *n* trafila *f*; *(story)* tiritera *f*

rigorous /ˈrɪgərəs/ *a* rigoroso

rile /raɪl/ *vt fam* irritare

rim /rɪm/ *n* bordo *m*; *(of wheel)* cerchione *m*

rind /raɪnd/ *n* *(on fruit)* scorza *f*; *(on cheese)* crosta *f*; *(on bacon)* cotenna *f*

ring[1] /rɪŋ/ *n* *(circle)* cerchio *m*; *(on finger)* anello *m*; *(boxing)* ring *m inv*; *(for circus)* pista *f*; **stand in a ~** essere in cerchio

ring[2] *n* suono *m*; **give sb a ~** *Teleph* dare un colpo di telefono a qcno ● *vt* (*pt* **rang,** *pp* **rung**) ● *vt* suonare; **~ [up]** *Teleph* telefonare a ● *vi* suonare; *Teleph* **~ [up]** telefonare. **ring back** *vt/i Teleph* richiamare. **ring off** *vi Teleph* riattaccare

ring: ~leader *n* capobanda *m*. **~ road** *n* circonvallazione *f*

rink /rɪŋk/ *n* pista *f* di pattinaggio

rinse /rɪns/ *n* risciacquo *m*; *(hair colour)* cachet *m inv* ● *vt* sciacquare

riot /ˈraɪət/ *n* rissa *f*; *(of colour)* accozzaglia *f*. **~s** *pl* disordini *mpl*; **run ~** impazzare ● *vi* creare disordini. **~er** *n* dimostrante *mf*. **~ous** /-əs/ *a* sfrenato

rip /rɪp/ *n* strappo *m* ● *vt* (*pt/pp* **ripped**) strappare; **~ open** aprire con uno strappo. **rip off** *vt fam* fregare

ripe /raɪp/ *a* maturo; *(cheese)* stagionato

ripen /ˈraɪpn/ *vi* maturare; *(cheese:)* stagionarsi ● *vt* far maturare; stagionare *(cheese)*

ripeness /ˈraɪpnɪs/ *n* maturità *f inv*

'rip-off *n fam* frode *f*

ripple /ˈrɪpl/ *n* increspatura *f*; *(sound)* mormorio *m* ●

rise /raɪz/ *n* levata *f*; *(fig: to fame, power)* ascesa *f*; *(increase)* aumento *m*; **give ~ to** dare adito a ● *vi* (*pt* **rose,** *pp* **risen**) alzarsi; *(sun:)* sorgere; *(dough:)* lievitare; *(prices, water level:)* aumentare; *(to power, position)* arrivare (**to** a). **~r** *n* **early ~r** *n* persona *f* mattiniera

rising /ˈraɪzɪŋ/ *a* *(sun)* levante; **~ generation** nuova generazione *f* ● *n* *(revolt)* sollevazione *f*

risk /rɪsk/ *n* rischio *m*; **at one's own ~** a proprio rischio e pericolo ● *vt* rischiare

risky /ˈrɪskɪ/ *a* (**-ier, -iest**) rischioso

risqué /ˈrɪskeɪ/ *a* spinto

rite /raɪt/ *n* rito *m*; **last ~s** estrema unzione *f*

ritual /ˈrɪtjʊəl/ *a* rituale ● *n* rituale *m*

rival /ˈraɪvl/ *a* rivale ● *n* rivale *mf*; **~s** *pl Comm* concorrenti *mpl* ● *vt* (*pt/pp* **rivalled**) rivaleggiare con. **~ry** *n* rivalità *f inv*; *Comm* concorrenza *f*

river /ˈrɪvə(r)/ *n* fiume *m*. **~-bed** *n* letto *m* del fiume

rivet /ˈrɪvɪt/ *n* rivetto *m* ● *vt* rivettare; **~ed by** *fig* inchiodato da

Riviera /rɪvɪˈeərə/ *n* **the Italian ~** la riviera ligure

road /rəʊd/ *n* strada *f*, via *f*; **be on the ~** viaggiare

road: ~-block *n* blocco *m* stradale. **~-hog** *n fam* pirata *m* della strada. **~-map** *n* carta *f* stradale. **~ safety** *n* sicurezza *f* sulle strade. **~ sense** *n* prudenza *f* (*per stra-*

da). ~**side** *n* bordo *m* della strada. ~**sign** cartello *m* stradale. ~**way** *n* carreggiata *f*, corsia *f*. ~**works** *npl* lavori *mpl* stradali. ~**worthy** *a* sicuro

roam /rəʊm/ *vi* girovagare

roar /rɔː(r)/ *n* ruggito *m*; ~**s of laughter** scroscio *msg* di risa ● *vi* ruggire; ⟨*lorry, thunder:*⟩ rombare; ~ **with laughter** ridere fragorosamente. ~**ing** *a* do a ~**ing trade** *fam* fare affari d'oro

roast /rəʊst/ *a* arrosto. ~ **pork** arrosto *m* di maiale ● *n* arrosto *m* ● *vt* arrostire ⟨*meat*⟩ ● *vi* arrostirsi

rob /rɒb/ *vt* (*pt/pp* **robbed**) derubare (**of** di); svaligiare ⟨*bank*⟩. ~**ber** *n* rapinatore *m*. ~**bery** *n* rapina *f*

robe /rəʊb/ *n* tunica *f*; (*Am:* *bathrobe*) accappatoio *m*

robin /ˈrɒbɪn/ *n* pettirosso *m*

robot /ˈrəʊbɒt/ *n* robot *m inv*

robust /rəʊˈbʌst/ *a* robusto

rock[1] /rɒk/ *n* roccia *f*; (*in sea*) scoglio *m*; (*sweet*) zucchero *m* candito. **on the ~s** ⟨*ship*⟩ incagliato; ⟨*marriage*⟩ finito; ⟨*drink*⟩ con ghiaccio

rock[2] *vt* cullare ⟨*baby*⟩; (*shake*) far traballare; (*shock*) scuotere ● *vi* dondolarsi

rock[3] *n Mus* rock *m inv*

rock-'bottom *a* bassissimo ● *n* livello *m* più basso

rockery /ˈrɒkərɪ/ *n* giardino *m* roccioso

rocket /ˈrɒkɪt/ *n* razzo *m* ● *vi* salire alle stelle

rocking /ˈrɒkɪŋ/: ~**-chair** *n* sedia *f* a dondolo. ~**-horse** *n* cavallo *m* a dondolo

rocky /ˈrɒkɪ/ *a* (**-ier, -iest**) roccioso; *fig* traballante

rod /rɒd/ *n* bacchetta *f*; (*for fishing*) canna *f*

rode /rəʊd/ *see* **ride**

rodent /ˈrəʊdnt/ *n* roditore *m*

roe /rəʊ/ *n* (*pl* **roe** *or* **roes**) ~**[-deer]** capriolo *m*

rogue /rəʊg/ *n* farabutto *m*

role /rəʊl/ *n* ruolo *m*

roll /rəʊl/ *n* rotolo *m*; (*bread*) panino *m*; (*list*) lista *f*; (*of ship, drum*) rullio *m* ● *vi* rotolare; **be ~ing in money** *fam* nuotare nell'oro ● *vt* spianare ⟨*lawn, pastry*⟩. **roll over** *vi* rigirarsi. **roll up** *vt* arrotolare; rimboccarsi ⟨*sleeves*⟩ ● *vi* *fam* arrivare

'roll-call *n* appello *m*

roller /ˈrəʊlə(r)/ *n* rullo *m*; (*for hair*) bigodino *m*. ~ **blind** *n* tapparella *f*. ~**-coaster** *n* montagne *fpl* russe. ~**-skate** *n* pattino *m* a rotelle

'rolling-pin *n* mattarello *m*

Roman /ˈrəʊmən/ *a* romano ● *n* romano, -a *mf*. ~ **Catholic** *a* cattolico ● *n* cattolico, -a *mf*

romance /rəʊˈmæns/ *n* (*love-affair*) storia *f* d'amore; (*book*) romanzo *m* rosa

Romania /rəʊˈmeɪnɪə/ *n* Romania *f*. ~**n** *a* rumeno ● *n* rumeno, -a *mf*

romantic /rəʊˈmæntɪk/ *a* romantico. ~**ally** *adv* romanticamente. ~**ism** /-tɪsɪzm/ *n* romanticismo *m*

Rome /rəʊm/ *n* Roma *f*

romp /rɒmp/ *n* gioco *m* rumoroso ● *vi* giocare rumorosamente. ~**ers** *npl* pagliaccetto *msg*

roof /ruːf/ *n* tetto *m*; (*of mouth*) palato *m* ● *vt* mettere un tetto su. ~**-rack** *n* portabagagli *m inv*. ~**-top** *n* tetto *m*

rook /rʊk/ *n* corvo *m*; (*in chess*) torre *f*

room /ruːm/ *n* stanza *f*; (*bedroom*) camera *f*; (*for functions*) sala *f*; (*space*) spazio *m*. ~**y** *a* spazioso; ⟨*clothes*⟩ ampio

roost /ruːst/ *vi* appollaiarsi

root[1] /ruːt/ *n* radice *f*; **take ~** mettere radici ● **root out** *vt fig* scovare

root[2] *vi* ~ **about** grufolare; ~ **for sb** *Am fam* fare il tifo per qcno

rope /rəʊp/ *n* corda *f*; **know the ~s** *fam* conoscere i trucchi del mestiere ● **rope in** *vt fam* coinvolgere

rosary /'rəʊzəri/ n rosario m

rose[1] /rəʊz/ n rosa f; (of watering-can) bocchetta f

rose[2] see **rise**

rosé /'rəʊzeɪ/ n [vino m] rosé m inv

rosemary /'rəʊzməri/ n rosmarino m

rosette /rəʊ'zet/ n coccarda f

roster /'rɒstə(r)/ n tabella f dei turni

rostrum /'rɒstrəm/ n podio m

rosy /'rəʊzi/ a (-ier, -iest) roseo

rot /rɒt/ n marciume m; (fam: nonsense) sciocchezze fpl ● vi (pt/pp rotted) marcire

rota /'rəʊtə/ n tabella f dei turni

rotary /'rəʊtəri/ a rotante

rotat|e /rəʊ'teɪt/ vt far ruotare; avvicendare (crops) ● vi ruotare. **~ion** /-eɪʃn/ n rotazione f; **in ~ion** a turno

rotten /'rɒtn/ a marcio; fam schifoso; (person) penoso

rotund /rəʊ'tʌnd/ a paffuto

rough /rʌf/ a (not smooth) ruvido; (ground) accidentato; (behaviour) rozzo; (sport) violento; (area) malfamato; (crossing, time) brutto; (estimate) approssimativo ● adv (play) grossolanamente; **sleep ~** dormire sotto i ponti ● vt **~ it** vivere senza comfort. **rough out** vt abbozzare

roughage /'rʌfɪdʒ/ n fibre fpl

rough 'draft n abbozzo m

rough|ly /'rʌfli/ adv rozzamente; (more or less) pressappoco. **~ness** n ruvidità f; (of behaviour) rozzezza f

rough paper n carta f da brutta

roulette /ru:'let/ n roulette f inv

round /raʊnd/ a rotondo ● n tondo m; (slice) fetta f; (of visits, drinks) giro m; (of competition) partita f; (boxing) ripresa f, round m inv; **do one's ~s** (doctor:) fare il giro delle visite ● prep intorno a; **open ~ the clock** aperto ventiquattr'ore ● adv **all ~** tutt'intorno; **ask sb ~** invitare qcno; **go/come ~ to** (a friend etc) andare da; **turn/look ~** girarsi; **~ about** (approximately) intorno a ● vt arrotondare; girare (corner). **round down** vt arrotondare (per difetto). **round off** vt (end) terminare. **round on** vt aggredire. **round up** vt radunare; arrotondare (prices)

roundabout /'raʊndəbaʊt/ a indiretto ● n giostra f; (for traffic) rotonda f

round: **~ 'trip** n viaggio m di andata e ritorno

rous|e /raʊz/ vt svegliare; risvegliare (suspicion, interest). **~ing** a di incoraggiamento

route /ru:t/ n itinerario m; Naut, Aeron rotta f; (of bus) percorso m

routine /ru:'ti:n/ a di routine ● n routine f inv; Theat numero m

rov|e /rəʊv/ vi girovagare. **~ing** a (reporter, ambassador) itinerante

row[1] /rəʊ/ n (line) fila f; **three years in a ~** tre anni di fila

row[2] vi (in boat) remare

row[3] /raʊ/ n (quarrel) litigata f; (noise) baccano m ● vi fam litigare

rowdy /'raʊdi/ a (-ier, -iest) chiassoso

rowing boat /'rəʊɪŋ-/ n barca f a remi

royal /'rɔɪəl/ a reale

royal|ty /'rɔɪəlti/ n appartenenza f alla famiglia reale; (persons) i membri mpl della famiglia reale. **~ies** npl (payments) diritti mpl d'autore

rpm abbr **revolutions per minute**

rub /rʌb/ n **give sth a ~** dare una sfregata a qcsa ● vt (pt/pp rubbed) sfregare. **rub in** vt **don't ~ it in** fam non rigirare il coltello nella piaga. **rub off** vt mandar via sfregando (stain); (from blackboard) cancellare ● vi andar via; **~ off on** essere trasmesso a. **rub out** vt cancellare

rubber /'rʌbə(r)/ n gomma f; (eraser) gomma f [da cancellare].

~ band *n* elastico *m.* **~y** *a* gommoso

rubbish /'rʌbɪʃ/ *n* immondizie *fpl;* *(fam: nonsense)* idiozie *fpl;* *(fam: junk)* robaccia *f* ● *vt fam* fare a pezzi. **~ bin** *n* pattumiera *f.* **~ dump** *n* discarica *f; (official)* discarica *f* comunale

rubble /'rʌbl/ *n* macerie *fpl*

ruby /'ru:bɪ/ *n* rubino *m* ● *attrib* di rubini; *(lips)* scarlatta

rucksack /'rʌksæk/ *n* zaino *m*

rudder /'rʌdə(r)/ *n* timone *m*

ruddy /'rʌdɪ/ *a* **(-ier, -iest)** rubicondo; *fam* maledetto

rude /ru:d/ *a* scortese; *(improper)* spinto. **~ly** *adv* scortesemente. **~ness** *n* scortesia *f*

rudiment /'ru:dɪmənt/ *n* **~s** *pl* rudimenti *mpl.* **~ary** /-'mentərɪ/ *a* rudimentale

rueful /'ru:fl/ *a* rassegnato

ruffian /'rʌfɪən/ *n* farabutto *m*

ruffle /'rʌfl/ *n* gala *f* ● *vt* scompigliare *(hair)*

rug /rʌg/ *n* tappeto *m; (blanket)* coperta *f*

rugby /'rʌgbɪ/ *n* ~ **[football]** rugby *m*

rugged /'rʌgɪd/ *a* *(coastline)* roccioso

ruin /'ru:ɪn/ *n* rovina *f;* **in ~s** in rovina ● *vt* rovinare. **~ous** /-əs/ *a* estremamente costoso

rule /ru:l/ *n* regola *f; (control)* ordinamento *m; (for measuring)* metro *m;* **~s** regolamento *msg;* **as a ~** generalmente ● *vt* governare; dominare *(colony, behaviour);* **~ that** stabilire che ● *vi* governare.
rule out *vt* escludere

ruled /ru:ld/ *a (paper)* a righe

ruler /'ru:lə(r)/ *n* capo *m* di Stato; *(sovereign)* sovrano, -a *mf; (measure)* righello *m,* regolo *m*

ruling /'ru:lɪŋ/ *a (class)* dirigente *(party)* di governo ● *n* decisione *f*

rum /rʌm/ *n* rum *m inv*

rumble /'rʌmbl/ *n* rombo *m; (of stomach)* brontolio *m* ● *vi* rombare; *(stomach:)* brontolare

rummage /'rʌmɪdʒ/ *vi* rovistare *(in/through in)*

rummy /'rʌmɪ/ *n* ramino *m*

rumour /'ru:mə(r)/ *n* diceria *f* ● *vt* **it is ~ed that** si dice che

rump /rʌmp/ *n* natiche *fpl.* **~ steak** *n* bistecca *f* di girello

rumpus /'rʌmpəs/ *n fam* baccano *m*

run /rʌn/ *n (on foot)* corsa *f; (distance to be covered)* tragitto *m; (outing)* giro *m; Theat* rappresentazioni *fpl; (in skiing)* pista *f; (Am: ladder)* smagliatura *f (in calze);* **at a ~** di corsa; **~ of bad luck** periodo *m* sfortunato; **on the ~** in fuga; **have the ~ of** avere a disposizione; **in the long ~** a lungo termine ● *vi (pt* **ran,** *pp* **run,** *pres p* **running)** ● *vi* correre; *(river:)* scorrere; *(nose, makeup:)* colare; *(bus:)* fare servizio; *(play:)* essere in cartellone; *(colours:)* sbiadire; *(in election)* presentarsi [come candidato] ● *vt (manage)* dirigere; tenere *(house); (drive)* dare un passaggio a; correre *(risk);* *Comput* lanciare; *Journ* pubblicare *(article); (pass)* far scorrere *(eyes, hand);* **~ a bath** far scorrere l'acqua per il bagno. **run across** *vi (meet, find)* imbattersi in. **run away** *vi* scappare [via]. **run down** *vi* scaricarsi; *(clock:)* scaricarsi; *(stocks:)* esaurirsi ● *vt Auto* investire; *(reduce)* esaurire; *(fam: criticize)* denigrare. **run in** *vi* entrare di corsa. **run into** *vi (meet)* imbattersi in; *(knock against)* urtare. **run off** *vi* andare via di corsa ● *vt* stampare *(copies).* **run out** *vi* uscire di corsa; *(supplies, money:)* esaurirsi; **~ out of** rimanere senza. **run over** *vi* correre; *(overflow)* traboccare ● *vt Auto* investire. **run through** *vi* scorrere. **run up** *vi* salire di corsa; *(towards)* arrivare di corsa ● *vt* accumulare *(debts, bill); (sew)* cucire

runaway *n* fuggitivo, -a *mf*

run-'down a ⟨area⟩ in abbandono; ⟨person⟩ esaurito ● n analisi f

rung[1] /rʌŋ/ n ⟨of ladder⟩ piolo m

rung[2] see **ring**[1]

runner /'rʌnə(r)/ n podista mf; ⟨in race⟩ corridore, -trice mf; ⟨on sledge⟩ pattino m. ~ **bean** n fagiolino m. ~**-up** n secondo, -a mf classificato, -a

running /'rʌnɪŋ/ a in corsa; ⟨water⟩ corrente; **four times ~** quattro volte di seguito ● n corsa f; ⟨management⟩ direzione f; **be in the ~** essere in lizza. ~ **'commentary** n cronaca f

runny /'rʌnɪ/ a semiliquido; ~ **nose** naso che cola

run: ~**-of-the-'mill** a ordinario. ~**-up** n Sport rincorsa f; **the ~-up to** il periodo precedente. ~**way** n pista f

rupture /'rʌptʃə(r)/ n rottura f; Med ernia f ● vt rompere; ~ **oneself** farsi venire l'ernia ● vi rompersi

rural /'rʊərəl/ a rurale

ruse /ruːz/ n astuzia f

rush[1] /rʌʃ/ n Bot giunco m

rush[2] n fretta f; **in a ~** di fretta ● vi precipitarsi ● vt far premura a; ~ **sb to hospital** trasportare qcno di corsa all'ospedale. ~**-hour** n ora f di punta

rusk /rʌsk/ n biscotto m

Russia /'rʌʃə/ n Russia f. ~**n** a & n russo, -a mf; ⟨language⟩ russo m

rust /rʌst/ n ruggine f ● vi arrugginirsi

rustic /'rʌstɪk/ a rustico

rustle /'rʌsl/ vi frusciare ● vt far frusciare; Am rubare ⟨cattle⟩. **rustle up** vt fam rimediare

'rustproof a a prova di ruggine

rusty /'rʌstɪ/ a (-ier, -iest) arrugginito

rut /rʌt/ n solco m; **in a ~** fam nella routine

ruthless /'ruːθlɪs/ a spietato. ~**ness** n spietatezza f

rye /raɪ/ n segale f

Ss

sabbath /'sæbəθ/ n domenica f; ⟨Jewish⟩ sabato m

sabbatical /sə'bætɪkl/ n Univ anno m sabbatico

sabot|age /'sæbətɑːʒ/ n sabotaggio m ● vt sabotare. ~**eur** /-'tɜː(r)/ n sabotatore, -trice mf

saccharin /'sækərɪn/ n saccarina f

sachet /'sæʃeɪ/ n bustina f; ⟨scented⟩ sacchetto m profumato

sack[1] /sæk/ vt ⟨plunder⟩ saccheggiare

sack[2] n sacco m; **get the ~** fam essere licenziato ● vt fam licenziare. ~**ing** n tela f per sacchi; ⟨fam: dismissal⟩ licenziamento m

sacrament /'sækrəmənt/ n sacramento m

sacred /'seɪkrɪd/ a sacro

sacrifice /'sækrɪfaɪs/ n sacrificio m ● vt sacrificare

sacrilege /'sækrɪlɪdʒ/ n sacrilegio m

sad /sæd/ a (sadder, saddest) triste. ~**den** vt rattristare

saddle /'sædl/ n sella f ● vt sellare; **I've been ~d with...** fig mi hanno affibbiato...

sadis|m /'seɪdɪzm/ n sadismo m. ~**t** /-dɪst/ n sadico, -a mf. ~**tic** /sə'dɪstɪk/ a sadico

sad|ly /'sædlɪ/ adv tristemente; ⟨unfortunately⟩ sfortunatamente. ~**ness** n tristezza f

safe /seɪf/ a sicuro; ⟨out of danger⟩ salvo; ⟨object⟩ al sicuro; ~ **and sound** sano e salvo ● n cassaforte f. ~**guard** n protezione f ● vt proteggere. ~**ly** adv in modo sicuro; ⟨arrive⟩ senza incidenti; ⟨assume⟩ con certezza

safety /'seɪftɪ/ n sicurezza f. ~**-belt** n cintura f di sicurezza. ~**-deposit box** n cassetta f di sicurezza. ~**-pin** n spilla f di sicurezza *o da balia.* **~-valve** *n* valvola *f* di sicurezza

sag /sæg/ *vi* (*pt/pp* sagged) abbassarsi

saga /'sɑ:gə/ *n* saga *f*

sage /seɪdʒ/ *n* (*herb*) salvia *f*

Sagittarius /sædʒɪ'teərɪəs/ *n* Sagittario *m*

said /sed/ *see* say

sail /seɪl/ *n* vela *f*; (*trip*) giro *m* in barca a vela ● *vi* navigare; *Sport* praticare la vela; (*leave*) salpare ● *vt* pilotare

'sailboard *n* tavola *f* del windsurf. **~ing** *n* windsurf *m inv*

sailing /'seɪlɪŋ/ *n* vela *f*. **~-boat** *n* barca *f* a vela. **~-ship** *n* veliero *m*

sailor /'seɪlə(r)/ *n* marinaio *m*

saint /seɪnt/ *n* santo, -a *mf*. **~ly** *a* da santo

sake /seɪk/ *n* for the ~ of (*person*) per il bene di; (*peace*) per amor di; **for the ~ of it** per il gusto di farlo

salad /'sæləd/ *n* insalata *f*. **~ bowl** *n* insalatiera *f*. **~ cream** *n* salsa *f* per condire l'insalata. **~-dressing** *n* condimento *m* per insalata

salary /'sælərɪ/ *n* stipendio *m*

sale /seɪl/ *n* vendita *f* (*at reduced prices*) svendita *f*; for/on ~ in vendita

sales|man /'seɪlzmən/ *n* venditore *m*; (*traveller*) rappresentante *m*. **~woman** *n* venditrice *f*

salient /'seɪlɪənt/ *a* saliente

saliva /sə'laɪvə/ *n* saliva *f*

sallow /'sæləʊ/ *a* giallastro

salmon /'sæmən/ *n* salmone *m*

saloon /sə'lu:n/ *n Auto* berlina *f*; (*Am: bar*) bar *m*

salt /sɔːlt/ *n* sale *m* ● *a* salato; (*fish, meat*) sotto sale ● *vt* salare; (*cure*) mettere sotto sale. **~-cellar** *n* saliera *f*. **~ 'water** *n* acqua *f* di mare. **~y** *a* salato

salutary /'sæljʊtərɪ/ *a* salutare

salute /sə'lu:t/ *Mil n* saluto *m* ● *vt* salutare ● *vi* fare il saluto

salvage /'sælvɪdʒ/ *n Naut* recupero *m* ● *vt* recuperare

salvation /sæl'veɪʃn/ *n* salvezza *f*. **S~ 'Army** *n* Esercito *m* della Salvezza

salvo /'sælvəʊ/ *n* salva *f*

same /seɪm/ *a* stesso (as di) ● *pron* **the ~** lo stesso; **be all the ~** essere tutti uguali ● *adv* **the ~** nello stesso modo; **all the ~** (*however*) lo stesso; **the ~ to you** altrettanto

sample /'sɑ:mpl/ *n* campione *m* ● *vt* testare

sanatorium /sænə'tɔ:rɪəm/ *n* casa *f* di cura

sanctimonious /sæŋktɪ'məʊnɪəs/ *a* moraleggiante

sanction /'sæŋkʃn/ *n* (*approval*) autorizzazione *f*; (*penalty*) sanzione *f* ● *vt* autorizzare

sanctity /'sæŋktɪtɪ/ *n* santità *f inv*

sanctuary /'sæŋktjʊərɪ/ *n Relig* santuario *m*; (*refuge*) asilo *m*; (*for wildlife*) riserva *f*

sand /sænd/ *n* sabbia *f* ● *vt* **~[down]** carteggiare

sandal /'sændl/ *n* sandalo *m*

sand: **~bank** *n* banco *m* di sabbia. **~paper** *n* carta *f* vetrata ● *vt* cartavetrare. **~-pit** *n* recinto *m* contenente sabbia dove giocano i bambini

sandwich /'sænwɪdʒ/ *n* tramezzino *m* ● *vt* **~ed between** schiacciato tra

sandy /'sændɪ/ *a* (**-ier**, **-iest**) (*beach, soil*) sabbioso; (*hair*) biondiccio

sane /seɪn/ *a* (*not mad*) sano di mente; (*sensible*) sensato

sang /sæŋ/ *see* sing

sanitary /'sænɪtərɪ/ *a* igienico; (*system*) sanitario. **~ napkin** *n Am*, **~ towel** *n* assorbente *m* igienico

sanitation /sænɪ'teɪʃn/ *n* impianti *mpl* igienici

sanity /'sænɪtɪ/ *n* sanità *f inv* di mente; (*common sense*) buon senso *m*

sank /sæŋk/ *see* sink

sapphire /'sæfaɪə(r)/ *n* zaffiro *m* ● *a* blu zaffiro

sarcas|m /'saːkæzm/ n sarcasmo m. **~tic** /-'kæstɪk/ a sarcastico
sardine /saː'diːn/ n sardina f
Sardinia /saː'dɪnɪə/ n Sardegna f. **~n** a & n sardo, -a mf
sardonic /saː'dɒnɪk/ a sardonico
sash /sæʃ/ n fascia f; (for dress) fusciacca f
sat /sæt/ see **sit**
satanic /sə'tænɪk/ a satanico
satchel /'sætʃl/ n cartella f
satellite /'sætəlaɪt/ n satellite m. **~ dish** n antenna f parabolica. **~ television** n televisione f via satellite
satin /'sætɪn/ n raso m ●attrib di raso
satire /'sætaɪə(r)/ n satira f
satirical /sə'tɪrɪkl/ a satirico
satir|ist /'sætɪrɪst/ n scrittore, -trice mf satirico, -a; (comedian) comico, -a mf satirico, -a. **~ize** vt satireggiare
satisfaction /sætɪs'fækʃn/ n soddisfazione f; **be to sb's ~** soddisfare qcno
satisfactor|y /sætɪs'fæktərɪ/ a soddisfacente. **~ily** adv in modo soddisfacente
satisf|y /'sætɪsfaɪ/ vt (pp/pp -fied) soddisfare; (convince) convincere; **be ~ied** essere soddisfatto. **~ying** a soddisfacente
satura|te /'sætʃəreɪt/ vt inzuppare (with di); Chem, fig saturare (with di). **~ed** a saturo
Saturday /'sætədeɪ/ n sabato m
sauce /sɔːs/ n salsa f; (cheek) impertinenza f. **~pan** n pentola f
saucer /'sɔːsə(r)/ n piattino m
saucy /'sɔːsɪ/ a (-ier, -iest) impertinente
Saudi Arabia /saʊdɪə'reɪbɪə/ n Arabia f Saudita
sauna /'sɔːnə/ n sauna f
saunter /'sɔːntə(r)/ vi andare a spasso
sausage /'sɒsɪdʒ/ n salsiccia f; (dried) salame m
savage /'sævɪdʒ/ a feroce; (tribe, custom) selvaggio ●n selvaggio,

-a mf ● vt fare a pezzi. **~ry** n ferocia f
save /seɪv/ n Sport parata f ● vt salvare (from da); (keep, collect) tenere; risparmiare (time, money); (avoid) evitare; Sport parare (goal); Comput salvare, memorizzare ● vi **~ [up]** risparmiare ● prep salvo
saver /'seɪvə(r)/ n risparmiatore, -trice mf
savings /'seɪvɪŋz/ npl (money) risparmi mpl. **~ account** n libretto m di risparmio. **~ bank** n cassa f di risparmio
saviour /'seɪvjə(r)/ n salvatore m
savour /'seɪvə(r)/ n sapore m ● vt assaporare. **~y** a salato; fig rispettabile
saw¹ /sɔː/ see **see¹**
saw² n sega f ● vt/i (pt sawed, pp sawn or sawed) segare. **~dust** n segatura f
saxophone /'sæksəfəʊn/ n sassofono m
say /seɪ/ n **have one's ~** dire la propria; **have a ~** avere voce in capitolo ● vt/i (pt/pp said) dire; **that is to ~** cioè; **that goes without ~ing** questo è ovvio; **when all is said and done** alla fine dei conti. **~ing** n proverbio m
scab /skæb/ n crosta f; pej crumiro m
scaffold /'skæfəld/ n patibolo m. **~ing** n impalcatura f
scald /skɔːld/ vt scottare; (milk) scaldare ●n scottatura f
scale¹ /skeɪl/ n (of fish) scaglia f
scale² n scala f; **on a grand ~** su vasta scale ● vt (climb) scalare. **scale down** vt diminuire
scales /skeɪlz/ npl (for weighing) bilancia fsg
scallop /'skɒləp/ n (shellfish) pettine m
scalp /skælp/ n cuoio m capelluto
scalpel /'skælpl/ n bisturi m inv
scam /skæm/ n fam fregatura f
scamper /'skæmpə(r)/ vi **~ away** sgattaiolare via

scampi /'skæmpɪ/ *npl* scampi *mpl*

scan /skæn/ *n Med* scanning *m inv*, scansioscintigrafia *f* ● *vt* (*pt/pp* **scanned**) scrutare; (*quickly*) dare una scorsa a; *Med* fare uno scanning di

scandal /'skændl/ *n* scandalo *m*; (*gossip*) pettegolezzi *mpl*. **~ize** /-d(ə)laɪz/ *vt* scandalizzare. **~ous** /-əs/ *a* scandaloso

Scandinavia /skændɪ'neɪvɪə/ *n* Scandinavia *f*. **~n** *a & n* scandinavo, -a *mf*

scanner /'skænə(r)/ *n Comput* scanner *m inv*

scant /skænt/ *a* scarso

scanty /'skæntɪ/ *a* (**-ier, -iest**) scarso; (*clothing*) succinto. **~ily** *adv* scarsamente; (*clothed*) succintamente

scapegoat /'skeɪp-/ *n* capro *m* espiatorio

scar /skɑ:(r)/ *n* cicatrice *f* ● *vt* (*pt/pp* **scarred**) lasciare una cicatrice a

scarce /skeəs/ *a* scarso; *fig* raro; **make oneself ~** *fam* svignarsela. **~ely** *adv* appena; **~ely anything** quasi niente. **~ity** *n* scarsezza *f*

scare /skeə(r)/ *n* spavento *m*; (*panic*) panico *m* ● *vt* spaventare; **be ~d** aver paura (**of** di)

'scarecrow *n* spaventapasseri *m inv*

scarf /skɑ:f/ *n* (*pl* **scarves**) sciarpa *f*; (*square*) foulard *m inv*

scarlet /'skɑ:lət/ *a* scarlatto. **~ 'fever** *n* scarlattina *f*

scary /'skeərɪ/ *a* **be ~** far paura

scathing /'skeɪðɪŋ/ *a* mordace

scatter /'skætə(r)/ *vt* spargere; (*disperse*) disperdere ● *vi* disperdersi. **~-brained** *a fam* scervellato. **~ed** *a* sparso

scatty /'skætɪ/ *a* (**-ier, -iest**) *fam* svitato

scavenge /'skævɪndʒ/ *vi* frugare nella spazzatura. **~r** *n* persona *f* che fruga nella spazzatura

scenario /sɪ'nɑ:rɪəʊ/ *n* scenario *m*

scene /si:n/ *n* scena *f*; (*quarrel*) scenata *f*; **behind the ~s** dietro le quinte

scenery /'si:nərɪ/ *n* scenario *m*

scenic /'si:nɪk/ *a* panoramico

scent /sent/ *n* odore *m*; (*trail*) scia *f*; (*perfume*) profumo *m*. **~ed** *a* profumato (**with** di)

sceptic|al /'skeptɪk(ə)l/ *a* scettico. **~ism** /-tɪsɪzm/ *n* scetticismo *m*

schedule /'ʃedju:l/ *n* piano *m*, programma *m*; (*of work*) programma *m*; (*timetable*) orario *m*; **behind ~** indietro; **on ~** nei tempi previsti; **according to ~** secondo i tempi previsti ● *vt* prevedere. **~d flight** *n* volo *m* di linea

scheme /ski:m/ *n* (*plan*) piano *m*; (*plot*) macchinazione *f* ● *vi pej* macchinare

schizophren|ia /skɪtsə'fri:nɪə/ *n* schizofrenia *f*. **~ic** /-'frenɪk/ *a* schizofrenico

scholar /'skɒlə(r)/ *n* studioso, -a *mf*. **~ly** *a* erudito. **~ship** *n* erudizione *f*; (*grant*) borsa *f* di studio

school /sku:l/ *n* scuola *f*; (*in university*) facoltà *f*; (*of fish*) branco *m*

school: **~boy** *n* scolaro *m*. **~girl** *n* scolara *f*. **~ing** *n* istruzione *f*. **~teacher** *n* insegnante *mf*

sciatica /saɪ'ætɪkə/ *n* sciatica *f*

scien|ce /saɪəns/ *n* scienza *f*; **~ce fiction** fantascienza *f*. **~tific** /-'tɪfɪk/ *a* scientifico. **~tist** *n* scienziato, -a *mf*

scintillating /'sɪntɪleɪtɪŋ/ *a* brillante

scissors /'sɪzəz/ *npl* forbici *fpl*

scoff[1] /skɒf/ *vi* **~ at** schernire

scoff[2] /skɒf/ *vt* divorare

scold /skəʊld/ *vt* sgridare. **~ing** *n* sgridata *f*

scone /skɒn/ *n* pasticcino *m* da tè

scoop /sku:p/ *n* paletta *f*; *Journ* scoop *m inv* ● *vt* **~ out** svuotare. **scoop up** *vt* tirar su

scoot /sku:t/ *vi fam* filare. **~er** *n* motoretta *f*

scope /skəʊp/ n portata f; (opportunity) opportunità f inv

scorch /skɔːtʃ/ vt bruciare. **~er** n fam giornata f torrida. **~ing** a caldissimo

score /skɔː(r)/ n punteggio m; (individual) punteggio m; Mus partitura f; (for film, play) musica f; **a ~ [of]** (twenty) una ventina [di]; **keep the ~** tenere il punteggio; **on that ~** a questo proposito ● vt segnare (goal); (cut) incidere ● vi far punti; (in football etc) segnare; (keep score) tenere il punteggio. **~r** n segnapunti m inv; (of goals) giocatore, -trice mf che segna

scorn /skɔːn/ n disprezzo m ● vt disprezzare. **~ful** a sprezzante

Scorpio /ˈskɔːpɪəʊ/ n Scorpione m

scorpion /ˈskɔːpɪən/ n scorpione m

Scot /skɒt/ n scozzese mf

Scotch /skɒtʃ/ a scozzese ● n (whisky) whisky m [scozzese]

scotch vt far cessare

scot-'free a **get off ~** cavarsela impunemente

Scot|land /ˈskɒtlənd/ n Scozia f. **~s, ~tish** a scozzese

scoundrel /ˈskaʊndrəl/ n mascalzone m

scour¹ /ˈskaʊə(r)/ vt (search) perlustrare

scour² vt (clean) strofinare

scourge /skɜːdʒ/ n flagello m

Scout n [Boy] **~** [boy]scout m inv

scout /skaʊt/ n Mil esploratore m ● vi **~ for** andare in cerca di

scowl /skaʊl/ n sguardo m torvo ● vi guardare [di] storto

Scrabble® /ˈskræbl/ n Scarabeo® m

scraggy /ˈskrægɪ/ a (-ier, -iest) pej scarno

scram /skræm/ vi fam levarsi dai piedi

scramble /ˈskræmbl/ n (climb) arrampicata f ● vi (clamber) arrampicarsi; **~ for** azzuffarsi per ● vt Teleph creare delle interferenze in; (eggs) strapazzare

scrap¹ /skræp/ n (fam: fight) litigio m

scrap² n pezzetto m; (metal) ferraglia f; **~s** pl (of food) avanzi mpl ● vt (pt/pp **scrapped**) buttare via

'scrap-book n album m inv

scrape /skreɪp/ vt raschiare; (damage) graffiare. **scrape through** vi passare per un pelo. **scrape together** vt racimolare

scraper /ˈskreɪpə(r)/ n raschietto m

scrappy /ˈskræpɪ/ a frammentario

'scrap-yard n deposito m di ferraglia; (for cars) cimitero m delle macchine

scratch /skrætʃ/ n graffio m; (to relieve itch) grattata f; **start from ~** partire da zero; **up to ~** (work) all'altezza ● vt graffiare; (to relieve itch) grattare ● vi grattarsi

scrawl /skrɔːl/ n scarabocchio m ● vt/i scarabocchiare

scrawny /ˈskrɔːnɪ/ a (-ier, -iest) pej magro

scream /skriːm/ n strillo m ● vt/i strillare

screech /skriːtʃ/ n stridore m ● vi stridere ● vt strillare

screen /skriːn/ n paravento m; Cinema, TV schermo m ● vt proteggere; (conceal) riparare; proiettare (film); (candidates) passare al setaccio; Med sottoporre a visita medica. **~ing** n Med visita f medica; (of film) proiezione f. **~play** n sceneggiatura f

screw /skruː/ n vite f ● vt avvitare. **screw up** vt (crumple) accartocciare; strizzare (eyes); storcere (face); (sl: bungle) mandare all'aria

'screwdriver n cacciavite m

screwy /ˈskruːɪ/ a (-ier, -iest) fam svitato

scribble /ˈskrɪbl/ n scarabocchio m ● vt/i scarabocchiare

545

script /skrɪpt/ n scrittura f (a mano); (of film) sceneggiatura f

'script-writer n sceneggiatore, -trice mf

scroll /skrəʊl/ n rotolo m (di pergamena); (decoration) voluta f

scrounge /skraʊndʒ/ vt/i scroccare. **~r** n scroccone, -a mf

scrub[1] /skrʌb/ n (land) boscaglia f

scrub[2] vt/i (pt/pp scrubbed) strofinare; (fam: cancel) cancellare ⟨plan⟩

scruff /skrʌf/ n **by the ~ of the neck** per la collottola

scruffy /'skrʌfɪ/ a (-ier, -iest) trasandato

scrum /skrʌm/ n (in rugby) mischia f

scruple /'skru:pl/ n scrupolo m

scrupulous /'skru:pjʊləs/ a scrupoloso

scrutin|ize /'skru:tɪnaɪz/ vt scrutinare. **~y** n (look) esame m minuzioso

scuffle /'skʌfl/ n tafferuglio m

sculpt /skʌlpt/ vt/i scolpire. **~or** /'skʌlptə(r)/ n scultore m. **~ure** /-tʃə(r)/ n scultura f

scum /skʌm/ n schiuma f; (people) feccia f

scurrilous /'skʌrɪləs/ a scurrile

scurry /'skʌrɪ/ vi (pt/pp -ied) affrettare il passo

scuttle /'skʌtl/ vi (hurry) **~ away** correre via

sea /si:/ n mare m; **at ~** in mare; fig confuso; **by ~** via mare. **~board** n costiera f. **~food** n frutti mpl di mare. **~gull** n gabbiano m

seal[1] /si:l/ n Zool foca f

seal[2] /si:l/ n sigillo m; Techn chiusura f ermetica ● vt sigillare; Techn chiudere ermeticamente. **seal off** vt bloccare ⟨area⟩

'sea-level n livello m del mare

seam /si:m/ n cucitura f; (of coal) strato m

'seaman n marinaio m

seamless /'si:mlɪs/ a senza cucitura

seamy /'si:mɪ/ a sordido; ⟨area⟩ malfamato

seance /'seɪɑ:ns/ n seduta f spiritica

sea: **~plane** n idrovolante m. **~port** n porto m di mare

search /sɜ:tʃ/ n ricerca f; (official) perquisizione f; **in ~ of** alla ricerca di ● vt frugare (for alla ricerca di); perlustrare ⟨area⟩; (officially) perquisire ● vi **~ for** cercare. **~ing** a penetrante

search: **~light** n riflettore m. **~party** n squadra f di ricerca

sea: **~sick** a **be/get ~** avere il mal di mare. **~side** n at/to the **~side** al mare. **~side resort** n stazione f balneare. **~side town** città f di mare

season /'si:zn/ n stagione f ● vt ⟨flavour⟩ condire. **~able** /-əbl/, **~al** a stagionale. **~ing** n condimento m

'season ticket n abbonamento m

seat /si:t/ n (chair) sedia f; (in car) sedile m; (place to sit) posto m [a sedere]; (bottom) didietro m; (of government) sede f; **take a ~** sedersi ● vt mettere a sedere; (have seats for) aver posti [a sedere] per; **remain ~ed** mantenere il proprio posto. **~-belt** n cintura f di sicurezza

sea: **~weed** n alga f marina. **~worthy** a in stato di navigare

secateurs /sekə'tɜ:z/ npl cesoie fpl

seclu|de /sɪ'klu:d/ vt appartato. **~sion** /-ʒn/ n isolamento m

second[1] /sɪ'kɒnd/ vt (transfer) distaccare

second[2] /'sekənd/ a secondo; **on ~ thoughts** ripensandoci meglio ● n secondo m; **~s** pl (goods) merce fsg di seconda scelta; **have ~s** (at meal) fare il bis; **John the S~** Giovanni Secondo ● adv (in race) al secondo posto ● vt assistere; appoggiare ⟨proposal⟩

secondary /'sekəndrɪ/ a secondario. **~ school** n ≈ scuola f media (inferiore e superiore)

second: **~-best** a secondo dopo il migliore; **be ~-best** pej essere un ripiego. **~ 'class** adv ‹travel, send› in seconda classe. **~-class** a di seconda classe

'second hand n (on clock) lancetta f dei secondi

second-'hand a & adv di seconda mano

secondly /'sekǝndlı/ adv in secondo luogo

second-'rate a di second'ordine

secrecy /'si:krǝsı/ n segretezza f; **in ~** in segreto

secret /'si:krıt/ a segreto ● n segreto m

secretarial /sekrǝ'teǝrıǝl/ a ‹work, staff› di segreteria

secretary /'sekrǝtǝrı/ n segretario, -a mf

secret|e /sı'kri:t/ vt secernere ‹poison›. **~ion** /-i:ʃn/ n secrezione f

secretive /'si:krǝtıv/ a riservato. **~ness** n riserbo m

secretly /'si:krıtlı/ adv segretamente

sect /sekt/ n setta f. **~arian** a settario

section /'sekʃn/ n sezione f

sector /'sektǝ(r)/ n settore m

secular /'sekjulǝ(r)/ a secolare; ‹education› laico

secure /sı'kjuǝ(r)/ a sicuro ● vt proteggere; chiudere bene ‹door›; rendere stabile ‹ladder›; ‹obtain› assicurarsi. **~ly** adv saldamente

securit|y /sı'kjuǝrǝtı/ n sicurezza f; (for loan) garanzia f. **~ies** npl titoli mpl

sedate¹ /sı'deıt/ a posato

sedate² vt somministrare sedativi a

sedation /sı'deıʃn/ n somministrazione f di sedativi; **be under ~** essere sotto l'effetto di sedativi

sedative /'sedǝtıv/ a sedativo ● n sedativo m

sedentary /'sedǝntǝrı/ a sedentario

sediment /'sedımǝnt/ n sedimento m

seduce /sı'dju:s/ vt sedurre

seduct|ion /sı'dʌkʃn/ n seduzione f. **~ive** /-tıv/ a seducente

see /si:/ v (pt saw, pp seen) ● vt vedere; (understand) capire; (escort) accompagnare; **go and ~** andare a vedere; (visit) andare a trovare; **~ you!** ci vediamo!; **~ you later!** a più tardi!; **~ing that** visto che ● vi vedere; (understand) capire; **~ that** (make sure) assicurarsi che; **~ about** occuparsi di. **see off** vt veder partire; (chase away) mandar via. **see through** vi vedere attraverso; fig non farsi ingannare da ● vt portare a buon fine. **see to** vi occuparsi di

seed /si:d/ n seme m; Tennis testa f di serie; **go to ~** fare seme; fig lasciarsi andare. **~ed player** n Tennis testa f di serie. **~ling** n pianticella f

seedy /'si:dı/ a (-ier, -iest) squallido

seek /si:k/ vt (pt/pp sought) cercare

seem /si:m/ vi sembrare. **~ingly** adv apparentemente

seen /si:n/ see **see¹**

seep /si:p/ vi filtrare

see-saw /'si:sɔ:/ n altalena f

seethe /si:ð/ vi **~ with anger** ribollire di rabbia

'see-through a trasparente

segment /'segmǝnt/ n segmento m; (of orange) spicchio m

segregat|e /'segrıgeıt/ vt segregare. **~ion** /-'geıʃn/ n segregazione f

seize /si:z/ vt afferrare; Jur confiscare. **seize up** vi Techn bloccarsi

seizure /'si:ʒǝ(r)/ n Jur confisca f; Med colpo m [apoplettico]

seldom /'seldǝm/ adv raramente

select /sı'lekt/ a scelto; (exclusive) esclusivo ● vt scegliere; selezionare ‹team›. **~ion** /-ekʃn/ n selezione f. **~ive** /-ıv/ a selettivo. **~or** n Sport selezionatore, -trice mf

self /self/ n io m

self: **~·ad'dressed** a con il proprio indirizzo. **~·ad'hesive** a autoadesivo. **~·as'surance** n sicurezza f di sé. **~·as'sured** a sicuro di sé. **~·'catering** a in appartamento attrezzato di cucina. **~·'centred** a egocentrico. **~·'confidence** n fiducia f in se stesso. **~·'confident** a sicuro di sé. **~·'conscious** a impacciato. **~·con'tained** a ⟨flat⟩ con ingresso indipendente. **~·con'trol** n autocontrollo m. **~·'defence** n autodifesa f. Jur legittima difesa f. **~·de'nial** n abnegazione f. **~·determi'nation** n autodeterminazione f. **~·em'ployed** a che lavora in proprio. **~·e'steem** n stima f di sé. **~·'evident** a ovvio. **~·'governing** a autonomo. **~·'help** n iniziativa f personale. **~·in'dulgent** a indulgente con se stesso. **~·'interest** n interesse m personale

self|ish /'selfɪʃ/ a egoista. **~ishness** n egoismo m. **~less** a disinteressato

self: **~·'made** a che si è fatto da sé. **~·'pity** n autocommiserazione f. **~·'portrait** n autoritratto m. **~·pos'sessed** a padrone di sé. **~·preser'vation** n istinto m di conservazione. **~·re'spect** n amor m proprio. **~·'righteous** a presuntuoso. **~·'sacrifice** n abnegazione f. **~·'satisfied** a compiaciuto di sé. **~·'service** n self-service m ● attrib self-service. **~·suf'ficient** a autosufficiente. **~·'willed** a ostinato

sell /sel/ v (pt/pp **sold**) ● vt vendere; **be sold out** essere esaurito ● vi vendersi. **sell off** vt liquidare

seller /'selə(r)/ n venditore, -trice mf

Sellotape® /'seləʊ-/ n nastro m adesivo, scotch® m

'sell-out n (fam: betrayal) tradimento m; **be a ~** ⟨concert:⟩ fare il tutto esaurito

selves /selvz/ pl of **self**

semblance /'sembləns/ n parvenza f

semen /'si:mən/ n Anat liquido m seminale

semester /sɪ'mestə(r)/ n Am semestre m

semi /'semɪ/: **~·breve** /'semɪbri:v/ n semibreve f. **~·circle** /'semɪs3:k(ə)l/ n semicerchio m. **~·circular** a semicircolare. **~·colon** n punto e virgola m. **~·de'tached** a gemella ● n casa f gemella. **~·'final** n semifinale f

seminar /'semɪna:(r)/ n seminario m. **~y** /-nərɪ/ n seminario m

semolina /semə'li:nə/ n semolino m

senat|e /'senət/ n senato m. **~or** n senatore m

send /send/ vt/i (pt/pp **sent**) mandare; **~ for** mandare a chiamare ⟨person⟩; far venire ⟨thing⟩. **~er** n mittente mf. **~·off** n commiato m

senile /'si:naɪl/ a arteriosclerotico; Med senile. **~ity** /sɪ'nɪlətɪ/ n senilismo m

senior /'si:nɪə(r)/ a più vecchio; (in rank) superiore ● n (in rank) superiore mf; (in sport) senior mf; **she's two years my ~** è più vecchia di me di due anni. **~ citizen** n anziano, -a mf

seniority /si:nɪ'ɒrətɪ/ n anzianità f inv di servizio

sensation /sen'seɪʃn/ n sensazione f. **~al** a sensazionale. **~ally** adv in modo sensazionale

sense /sens/ n senso m; (common ~) buon senso m; **in a ~** in un certo senso; **make ~** aver senso ● vt sentire. **~less** a insensato; (unconscious) privo di sensi

sensible /'sensəbl/ a sensato; (suitable) appropriato. **~y** adv in modo appropriato

sensitiv|e /'sensɪtɪv/ a sensibile; (touchy) suscettibile. **~ely** adv con sensibilità. **~ity** /-'tɪvɪtɪ/ n sensibilità f inv

sensory /'sensərɪ/ a sensoriale

sensual /ˈsensjʊəl/ a sensuale. **~ly** /-əlɪ/ adv sensualità f inv

sensuous /ˈsensjʊəs/ a voluttuoso

sent /sent/ see **send**

sentence /ˈsentəns/ n frase f; Jur sentenza f; (punishment) condanna f ● vt **to** condannare a

sentiment /ˈsentɪmənt/ n sentimento m; (opinion) opinione f; (sentimentality) sentimentalismo m. **~al** /-ˈmentl/ a sentimentale; pej sentimentalista. **~ality** /-ˈtælətɪ/ n sentimentalità f inv

sentry /ˈsentrɪ/ n sentinella f

separable /ˈsepərəbl/ a separabile

separate¹ /ˈsepərət/ a separato. **~ly** adv separatamente

separate² /ˈsepəreɪt/ vt separare ● vi separarsi. **~ion** /-ˈreɪʃn/ n separazione f

September /sepˈtembə(r)/ n settembre m

septic /ˈseptɪk/ a settico; **go ~** infettarsi. **~ tank** n fossa f biologica

sequel /ˈsiːkwəl/ n seguito m

sequence /ˈsiːkwəns/ n sequenza f

sequin /ˈsiːkwɪn/ n lustrino m, paillette f inv

serenade /serəˈneɪd/ n serenata f ● vt fare una serenata a

seren|e /sɪˈriːn/ a sereno. **~ity** /-ˈrenətɪ/ n serenità f inv

sergeant /ˈsɑːdʒənt/ n sergente m

serial /ˈsɪərɪəl/ n racconto m a puntate; TV sceneggiato m a puntate; Radio commedia f radiofonica. **~ize** vt pubblicare a puntate; Radio, TV trasmettere a puntate. **~ killer** n serial killer mf inv. **~ number** n numero m di serie. **~ port** n Comput porta f seriale

series /ˈsɪəriːz/ n serie f inv

serious /ˈsɪərɪəs/ a serio; (illness, error) grave. **~ly** adv seriamente; (ill) gravemente; **take ~ly** prendere sul serio. **~ness** n serietà f inv; (of situation) gravità f inv

sermon /ˈsɜːmən/ n predica f

serpent /ˈsɜːpənt/ n serpente m

serrated /seˈreɪtɪd/ a dentellato

serum /ˈsɪərəm/ n siero m

servant /ˈsɜːvənt/ n domestico, -a mf

serve /sɜːv/ n Tennis servizio m ● vt servire; scontare (sentence); **~ its purpose** servire al proprio scopo; **it ~s you right!** ben ti sta!; **~s two** per due persone ● vi prestare servizio; Tennis servire; **~ as** servire da

server /ˈsɜːvə(r)/ n Comput server m inv

service /ˈsɜːvɪs/ n servizio m; Relig funzione f; (maintenance) revisione f; **~s** pl forze fpl armate; (on motorway) area f di servizio; **in the ~s** sotto le armi; **of ~ to** utile a; **out of ~** (machine:) guasto ● vt Techn revisionare. **~able** /-əbl/ a utilizzabile; (hardwearing) resistente; (practical) pratico

service: ~ area n area f di servizio. **~ charge** n servizio m. **~man** n militare m. **~ provider** n fornitore, -trice mf di servizi. **~ station** n stazione f di servizio

serviette /sɜːvɪˈet/ n tovagliolo m

servile /ˈsɜːvaɪl/ a servile

session /ˈseʃn/ n seduta f; Jur sessione f; Univ anno m accademico

set /set/ n serie f, set m inv; (of crockery, cutlery) servizio m; TV, Radio apparecchio m; Math insieme m; Theat scenario m; Cinema, Tennis set m inv; (of people) circolo m; (of hair) messa f in piega ● a (ready) pronto; (rigid) fisso; (book) in programma; **be ~ on doing sth** essere risoluto a fare qcsa; **be ~ in one's ways** essere abitudinario ● v (pt/pp set, pres p setting) ● vt mettere, porre; mettere (alarm clock); assegnare (task, homework); fissare (date, limit); chiedere (questions); montare (gem); assestare (bone); apparecchiare (table); **~ fire to** dare fuoco a; **~ free** liberare ● vi (sun:) tramontare; (jelly, concrete:) solidificare; **~ about doing sth** mettersi a fare qcsa. **set back** vt mettere indietro; (hold up) ritardare; (fam: cost) costare a. **set off** vi partire ● vt avviare; mettere (alarm); fare esplodere (bomb). **set out** vi partire; ~ **out to do sth** proporsi di fare qcsa ● vt disporre; (state) esporre. **set to** vi mettersi all'opera. **set up** vt fondare (company); istituire (committee)

'set-back n passo m indietro

set 'meal n menù m fisso

settee /se'tiː/ n divano m

setting /'setɪŋ/ n scenario m; (position) posizione f; (of sun) tramonto m; (of jewel) montatura f

settle /'setl/ vt (decide) definire; risolvere (argument); fissare (date); calmare (nerves); saldare (bill) ● vi (to live) stabilirsi; (snow, dust, bird:) posarsi; (subside) assestarsi; (sediment:) depositarsi. **settle down** vi sistemarsi; (stop making noise) calmarsi. **settle for** vt accontentarsi di. **settle up** vi regolare i conti

settlement /'setlmənt/ n (agreement) accordo m; (of bill) saldo m; (colony) insediamento m

settler /'setlə(r)/ n colonizzatore, -trice mf

'set-to n fam zuffa f; (verbal) battibecco m

'set-up n situazione f

seven /'sevn/ a & n sette. ~**teen** a diciassette. ~**teenth** a diciassettesimo

seventh /'sevnθ/ a settimo

seventieth /'sevntɪɪθ/ a settantesimo

seventy /'sevntɪ/ a settanta

sever /'sevə(r)/ vt troncare (relations)

several /'sevrəl/ a & pron parecchi

severe /sɪ'vɪə(r)/ a severo; (pain) violento; (illness) grave; (winter) rigido. ~**ely** adv severamente; (ill) gravemente. ~**ity** /-'verɪtɪ/ n severità f inv; (of pain) violenza f; (of illness) gravità f; (of winter) rigore m

sew /səʊ/ vt/i (pt **sewed**, pp **sewn**

or **sewed**) cucire. **sew up** vt ricucire

sewage /'suːɪdʒ/ n acque fpl di scolo

sewer /'suːə(r)/ n fogna f

sewing /'səʊɪŋ/ n cucito m; (work) lavoro m di cucito. ~ **machine** n macchina f da cucire

sewn /səʊn/ see **sew**

sex /seks/ n sesso f; **have** ~ avere rapporti sessuali. ~**ist** a sessista. ~ **offender** n colpevole mf di delitti a sfondo sessuale

sexual /'seksjʊəl/ a sessuale. ~ **'intercourse** n rapporti mpl sessuali. ~**ity** /-'ælɪtɪ/ n sessualità f inv. ~**ly** adv sessualmente

sexy /'seksɪ/ a (-ier, -iest) sexy

shabb|y /'ʃæbɪ/ a (-ier, -iest) scialbo; (treatment) meschino. ~**iness** n trasandatezza f; (of treatment) meschinità f inv

shack /ʃæk/ n catapecchia f ● **shack up with** vt fam vivere con

shade /ʃeɪd/ n ombra f; (of colour) sfumatura f; (for lamp) paralume m; (Am: for window) tapparella f; **a** ~ **better** un tantino meglio ● vt riparare dalla luce; (draw lines on) ombreggiare. ~**s** npl fam occhiali mpl da sole

shadow /'ʃædəʊ/ n ombra f; **S-Cabinet** governo m ombra ● vt (follow) pedinare. ~**y** a ombroso

shady /'ʃeɪdɪ/ a (-ier, -iest) ombroso; (fam: disreputable) losco

shaft /ʃɑːft/ n Techn albero m; (of light) raggio m; (of lift, mine) pozzo m. ~**s** pl (of cart) stanghe fpl

shaggy /'ʃægɪ/ a (-ier, -iest) irsuto; (animal) dal pelo arruffato

shake /ʃeɪk/ n scrollata f ● v (pt **shook**, pp **shaken**) ● vt scuotere; agitare (bottle); far tremare (building); ~ **hands** with stringere la mano a ● vi tremare. **shake off** vt scrollarsi di dosso. ~**up** n Pol rimpasto m; Comm ristrutturazione f

shaky /'ʃeɪkɪ/ a (-ier, -iest) tremante; ⟨table etc⟩ traballante; ⟨unreliable⟩ vacillante

shall /ʃæl/ v aux I ~ go andrò; we ~ see vedremo; **what ~ I do?** cosa faccio?; **I'll come too, ~ I?** vengo anch'io, no?; **thou shalt not kill** liter non uccidere

shallow /ˈʃæləʊ/ a basso, poco profondo; ⟨dish⟩ poco profondo; fig superficiale

sham /ʃæm/ a falso ● n finzione f; ⟨person⟩ spaccone, -a mf ● vt ⟨pt/pp shammed⟩ simulare

shambles /ˈʃæmblz/ n baraonda fsg

shame /ʃeɪm/ n vergogna f; **it's a ~ that** è un peccato che; **what a ~!** che peccato! **~-faced** a vergognoso

shame|ful /ˈʃeɪmfl/ a vergognoso. **~less** a spudorato

shampoo /ʃæmˈpuː/ n shampoo m inv ● vt fare uno shampoo a

shandy /ˈʃændɪ/ n bevanda f a base di birra e gassosa

shan't /ʃɑːnt/ = **shall not**

shanty town /ˈʃæntɪtaʊn/ n bidonville f inv, baraccopoli f inv

shape /ʃeɪp/ n forma f; ⟨figure⟩ ombra f; **take ~** prendere forma; **get back in ~** ritornare in forma ● vt dare forma a ⟨into di⟩ ● vi ~ [up] mettere la testa a posto; **~ up nicely** mettersi bene. **~less** a informe

shapely /ˈʃeɪplɪ/ a (-ier, -iest) ben fatto

share /ʃeə(r)/ n porzione f; Comm azione f ● vt dividere; condividere ⟨views⟩ ● vi dividere. **~holder** n azionista mf

shark /ʃɑːk/ n squalo m, pescecane m; fig truffatore, -trice mf

sharp /ʃɑːp/ a ⟨knife etc⟩ tagliente; ⟨pencil⟩ appuntito; ⟨drop⟩ a picco; ⟨reprimand⟩ severo; ⟨outline⟩ marcato; ⟨alert⟩ acuto; ⟨unscrupulous⟩ senza scrupoli; **~ pain** fitta f ● adv in punto; Mus fuori tono; **look ~!** sbrigati! ● n Mus diesis m

inv. **~en** vt affilare ⟨knife⟩; appuntire ⟨pencil⟩

shatter /ˈʃætə(r)/ vt frantumare; fig mandare in frantumi; **~ed** ⟨fam: exhausted⟩ a pezzi ● vi frantumarsi

shav|e /ʃeɪv/ n rasatura f; **have a ~e** farsi la barba ● vt radere ● vi radersi. **~er** n rasoio m elettrico. **~ing-brush** n pennello m da barba; **~ing foam** n schiuma f da barba; **~ing soap** n sapone m da barba

shawl /ʃɔːl/ n scialle m

she /ʃiː/ pron lei

sheaf /ʃiːf/ n ⟨pl **sheaves**⟩ fascio m

shear /ʃɪə(r)/ vt ⟨pt **sheared**, pp **shorn** or **sheared**⟩ tosare

shears /ʃɪəz/ npl ⟨for hedge⟩ cesoie fpl

sheath /ʃiːθ/ n ⟨pl **~s** /ʃiːðz/⟩ guaina f

shed[1] /ʃed/ n baracca f; ⟨for cattle⟩ stalla f

shed[2] vt ⟨pt/pp **shed**, pres p **shedding**⟩ perdere; versare ⟨blood, tears⟩; **~ light on** far luce su

sheen /ʃiːn/ n lucentezza f

sheep /ʃiːp/ n inv pecora f. **~-dog** n cane m da pastore

sheepish /ˈʃiːpɪʃ/ a imbarazzato. **~ly** adv con aria imbarazzata

sheepskin /ˈʃiːpskɪn/ n [pelle f di] montone m

sheer /ʃɪə(r)/ a puro; ⟨steep⟩ a picco; ⟨transparent⟩ trasparente ● adv a picco

sheet /ʃiːt/ n lenzuolo m; ⟨of paper⟩ foglio m; ⟨of glass, metal⟩ lastra f

shelf /ʃelf/ n ⟨pl **shelves**⟩ ripiano m; ⟨set of shelves⟩ scaffale m

shell /ʃel/ n conchiglia f; ⟨of egg, snail, tortoise⟩ guscio m; ⟨of crab⟩ corazza f; ⟨of unfinished building⟩ ossatura f; Mil granata f ● vt sgusciare ⟨peas⟩; Mil bombardare. **shell out** vi fam sborsare

'shellfish n inv mollusco m; Culin frutti mpl di mare

shelter /ˈʃeltə(r)/ n rifugio m; ⟨air raid ~⟩ rifugio m antiaereo ● vt riparare (**from** da); *fig* mettere al riparo; (*give lodging to*) dare asilo a ● *vi* rifugiarsi. **~ed** *a* (*spot*) riparato; (*life*) blindato

shelve /ʃelv/ *vt* accantonare (*project*)

shelves /ʃelvz/ *see* shelf

shelving /ˈʃelvɪŋ/ *n* (*shelves*) ripiani *mpl*

shepherd /ˈʃepəd/ *n* pastore *m* ● *vt* guidare. **~'s pie** *n* pasticcio *m* di carne tritata e patate

sherry /ˈʃerɪ/ *n* sherry *m*

shield /ʃiːld/ *n* scudo *m*; (*for eyes*) maschera *f*; *Techn* schermo *m* ● *vt* proteggere (**from** da)

shift /ʃɪft/ *n* cambiamento *m*; (*in position*) spostamento *m*; (*at work*) turno *m* ● *vt* spostare; (*take away*) togliere; riversare (*blame*) ● *vi* spostarsi; (*wind*:) cambiare; (*fam*: *move quickly*) darsi una mossa

'shift work *n* turni *mpl*

shifty /ˈʃɪftɪ/ *a* (**-ier, -iest**) *pej* losco; (*eyes*) sfuggente

shilly-shally /ˈʃɪlɪʃælɪ/ *vi* titubare

shimmer /ˈʃɪmə(r)/ *n* luccichio *m* ● *vi* luccicare

shin /ʃɪn/ *n* stinco *m*

shine /ʃaɪn/ *n* lucentezza *f*; **give sth a ~** dare una lucidata a qcsa ● *v* (*pt/pp* **shone**) ● *vi* splendere; (*reflect light*) brillare; (*hair, shoes*:) essere lucido ● *vt* **~ a light on** puntare una luce su

shingle /ˈʃɪŋgl/ *n* (*pebbles*) ghiaia *f*

shingles /ˈʃɪŋglz/ *n Med* fuochi *mpl* di Sant'Antonio

shiny /ˈʃaɪnɪ/ *a* (**-ier, -iest**) lucido

ship /ʃɪp/ *n* nave *f* ● *vt* (*pt/pp* **shipped**) spedire; (*by sea*) spedire via mare

ship: **~ment** *n* spedizione *f*; (*consignment*) carico *m*. **~per** *n* spedizioniere *m*. **~ping** *n* trasporto *m*; (*traffic*) imbarcazioni *fpl*. **~shape** *a & adv* in perfetto ordine. **~wreck** *n* naufragio *m*. **~wrecked** *a* naufragato. **~yard** *n* cantiere *m* navale

shirk /ʃɜːk/ *vt* scansare. **~er** *n* scansafatiche *mf inv*

shirt /ʃɜːt/ *n* camicia *f*; **in ~-sleeves** in maniche di camicia

shit /ʃɪt/ *vulg n & int* merda *f* ● *vi* (*pt/pp* **shit**) cagare

shiver /ˈʃɪvə(r)/ *n* brivido *m* ● *vi* rabbrividire

shoal /ʃəʊl/ *n* (*of fish*) banco *m*

shock /ʃɒk/ *n* (*impact*) urto *m*; *Electr* scossa *f* [elettrica]; *fig* colpo *m*, shock *m inv*; *Med* shock *m inv*; **get a ~** *Electr* prendere la scossa ● *vt* scioccare. **~ing** *a* scioccante; (*fam*: *weather, handwriting etc*) tremendo

shod /ʃɒd/ *see* shoe

shoddy /ˈʃɒdɪ/ *a* (**-ier, -iest**) scadente

shoe /ʃuː/ *n* scarpa *f*; (*of horse*) ferro *m* ● *vt* (*pt/pp* **shod**, *pres p* **shoeing**) ferrare (*horse*)

shoe: **~horn** *n* calzante *m*. **~-lace** *n* laccio *m* da scarpa. **~maker** *n* calzolaio *m*. **~-shop** *n* calzoleria *f*. **~-string** *n* **on a ~-string** *fam* con una miseria

shone /ʃɒn/ *see* shine

shoo /ʃuː/ *vt* **~ away** cacciar via ● *int* sciò

shook /ʃʊk/ *see* shake

shoot /ʃuːt/ *n Bot* germoglio *m*; (*hunt*) battuta *f* di caccia ● *v* (*pt/pp* **shot**) ● *vt* sparare; girare (*film*) ● *vi* (*hunt*) andare a caccia. **shoot down** *vt* abbattere. **shoot out** *vi* (*rush*) precipitarsi fuori. **shoot up** *vi* (*grow*) crescere in fretta; (*prices*:) salire di colpo

'shooting-range *n* poligono *m* di tiro

shop /ʃɒp/ *n* negozio *m*; (*workshop*) officina *f*; **talk ~** *fam* parlare di lavoro ● *vi* (*pt/pp* **shopped**) far compere; **go ~ping** andare a fare compere. **shop around** *vi* confrontare i prezzi

shop: **~ assistant** *n* commesso, -a *mf*. **~keeper** *n* negoziante *mf*. **~-lifter** *n* taccheggiatore, -trice *mf.* **~-lifting** *n* taccheggio *m*; **~per** *n* compratore, -trice *mf*

shopping /'ʃɒpɪŋ/ *n* compere *fpl*; (*articles*) acquisti *mpl*; **do the ~** fare la spesa. **~ bag** *n* borsa *f* per la spesa. **~ centre** *n* centro *m* commerciale. **~ trolley** *n* carrello *m*

shop: **~-steward** *n* rappresentante *mf* sindacale. **~'window** *n* vetrina *f*

shore /ʃɔ:(r)/ *n* riva *f*

shorn /ʃɔ:n/ *see* **shear**

short /ʃɔ:t/ *a* corto; (*not lasting*) breve; (*person*) basso; (*curt*) brusco; **a ~ time ago** poco tempo fa; **be ~ of** essere a corto di; **be in ~ supply** essere scarso; *fig* essere raro; **Mick is ~ for Michael** Mick è il diminutivo di Michael ●*adv* bruscamente; **in ~** in breve; **~ of doing** a meno di fare; **go ~** essere privato (**of** di); **stop ~ of doing sth** non arrivare fino a fare qcsa; **cut ~** interrompere 〈*meeting, holiday*〉; **to cut a long story ~** per farla breve

shortage /'ʃɔ:tɪdʒ/ *n* scarsità *f inv*

short: **~bread** *n* biscotto *m* di pasta frolla. **~ circuit** *n* corto *m* circuito. **~coming** *n* difetto *m*. **'cut** *n* scorciatoia *f*

shorten /'ʃɔ:tn/ *vt* abbreviare; accorciare 〈*garment*〉

short: **~hand** *n* stenografia *f.* **~-handed** *a* a corto di personale. **~hand 'typist** *n* stenodattilografo, -a *mf.* **~ list** *n* lista *f* dei candidati selezionati per un lavoro. **~-lived** /-lɪvd/ *a* di breve durata

short|ly /'ʃɔ:tlɪ/ *adv* presto; **~ly before/after** poco prima/dopo. **~ness** *n* brevità *f inv*; (*of person*) bassa statura *f*

short-range *a* di breve portata

shorts /ʃɔ:ts/ *npl* calzoncini *mpl* corti

short: **~-'sighted** *a* miope. **~-'sleeved** *a* a maniche corte. **~-'staffed** *a* a corto di personale. **~ 'story** *n* racconto *m*, novella *f.*

~-'tempered *a* irascibile. **~-term** *a* a breve termine. **~ wave** *n* onde *fpl* corte

shot /ʃɒt/ *see* **shoot** ●*n* colpo *m*; (*person*) tiratore *m*; *Phot* foto *f*; (*injection*) puntura *f*; (*fam: attempt*) prova *f*; **like a ~** come un razzo. **~gun** *n* fucile *m* da caccia

should /ʃʊd/ *v aux* **I ~ go** dovrei andare; **I ~ have seen it** avrei dovuto vederlo; **I ~ like** mi piacerebbe; **this ~ be enough** questo dovrebbe bastare; **if he ~ come** se dovesse venire

shoulder /'ʃəʊldə(r)/ *n* spalla *f* ●*vt* mettersi in spalla; *fig* accollarsi. **~-bag** *n* borsa *f* a tracolla. **~-blade** *n* scapola *f.* **~-strap** *n* spallina *f*; (*of bag*) tracolla *f*

shout /ʃaʊt/ *n* grido *m* ●*vt/i* gridare. **shout at** *vi* alzar la voce con. **shout down** *vt* azzittire gridando

shouting /'ʃaʊtɪŋ/ *n* grida *fpl*

shove /ʃʌv/ *n* spintone *m* ●*vt* spingere; (*fam: put*) ficcare ●*vi* spingere. **shove off** *vi fam* togliersi di torno

shovel /'ʃʌvl/ *n* pala *f* ●*vt* (*pt/pp* **shovelled**) spalare

show /ʃəʊ/ *n* (*display*) manifestazione *f*; (*exhibition*) mostra *f*; (*ostentation*) ostentazione *f*; *Theat*, *TV* spettacolo *m*; (*programme*) programma *m*; **on ~** esposto ●*v* (*pt* **showed**, *pp* **shown**) ●*vt* mostrare; (*put on display*) esporre; proiettare 〈*film*〉 ●*vi* 〈*film:*〉 essere proiettato; **your slip is ~ing** ti si vede la sottoveste. **show in** *vt* fare accomodare. **show off** *vi fam* mettersi in mostra ●*vt* mettere in mostra. **show up** *vi* risaltare; (*fam: arrive*) farsi vedere ●*vt* (*fam: embarrass*) far fare una brutta figura a

'show-down *n* regolamento *m* dei conti

shower /'ʃaʊə(r)/ *n* doccia *f*; (*of rain*) acquazzone *m*; **have a ~** fare la doccia ● *vt* ~ **with** coprire di ● *vi* fare la doccia. ●**proof** *a* impermeabile. ~**y** *a* da acquazzoni

'show-jumping *n* concorso *m* ippico

shown /ʃəʊn/ *see* **show**

'show-off *n* esibizionista *mf*

showy /'ʃəʊɪ/ *a* appariscente

shrank /ʃræŋk/ *see* **shrink**

shred /ʃred/ *n* brandello *m*; *fig* briciolo *m* ● *vt* (*pt*/*pp* **shredded**) fare a brandelli; *Culin* tagliuzzare. ~**der** *n* distruttore *m* di documenti

shrewd /ʃruːd/ *a* accorto. ~**ness** *n* accortezza *f*

shriek /ʃriːk/ *n* strillo *m* ● *vt*/*i* strillare

shrift /ʃrɪft/ *n* **give sb short** ~ liquidare qcno rapidamente

shrill /ʃrɪl/ *a* penetrante

shrimp /ʃrɪmp/ *n* gamberetto *m*

shrine /ʃraɪn/ *n* (*place*) santuario *m*

shrink /ʃrɪŋk/ *vi* (*pt* **shrank**, *pp* **shrunk**) restringersi; (*draw back*) ritrarsi (**from** da)

shrivel /'ʃrɪvl/ *vi* (*pt*/*pp* **shrivelled**) raggrinzare

shroud /ʃraʊd/ *n* sudario *m*; *fig* manto *m*

Shrove /ʃrəʊv/ *n* ~ **'Tuesday** martedì *m* grasso

shrub /ʃrʌb/ *n* arbusto *m*

shrug /ʃrʌg/ *n* scrollata *f* di spalle ● *vt*/*i* (*pt*/*pp* **shrugged**) ~ [**one's shoulders**] scrollare le spalle

shrunk /ʃrʌŋk/ *see* **shrink**. ~**en** *a* rimpicciolito

shudder /'ʃʌdə(r)/ *n* fremito *m* ● *vi* fremere

shuffle /'ʃʌfl/ *vi* strascicare i piedi ● *vt* mescolare (*cards*)

shun /ʃʌn/ *vt* (*pt*/*pp* **shunned**) rifuggire

shunt /ʃʌnt/ *vt* smistare

shush /ʃʊʃ/ *int* zitto!

shut /ʃʌt/ *vt* (*pt*/*pp* **shut**, *pres p* **shutting**) ● *vt* chiudere ● *vi* chiudersi; (*shop:*) chiudere. **shut down** *vt*/*i* chiudere. **shut up** *vt*

chiudere; *fam* far tacere ● *vi fam* stare zitto; ~ **up!** stai zitto!

'shut-down *n* chiusura *f*

shutter /'ʃʌtə(r)/ *n* serranda *f*; *Phot* otturatore *m*

shuttle /'ʃʌtl/ *n* navetta *f* ● *vi* far la spola

shuttle: ~**cock** *n* volano *m*. ~ **service** *n* servizio *m* pendolare

shy /ʃaɪ/ *a* (*timid*) timido. ~**ness** *n* timidezza *f*

Siamese /saɪə'miːz/ *a* siamese

sibling /'sɪblɪŋ/ *n* (*brother*) fratello *m*; (*sister*) sorella *f*; ~**s** fratelli *mpl*

Sicil|y /'sɪsɪlɪ/ *n* Sicilia *f*. ~**ian** *a* & *n* siciliano, -a *mf*

sick /sɪk/ *a* ammalato; (*humour*) macabro; **be** ~ (*vomit*) vomitare; **be** ~ **of sth** *fam* essere stufo di qcsa; **feel** ~ aver la nausea

sicken /'sɪkn/ *vt* disgustare ● *vi* **be** ~**ing for something** covare qualche malanno. ~**ing** *a* disgustoso

sick|ly /'sɪklɪ/ *a* (-**ier**, -**iest**) malaticcio. ~**ness** *n* malattia *f*; (*vomiting*) vomitevole. ~**ness benefit** *n* indennità *f* di malattia

side /saɪd/ *n* lato *m*; (*of person, mountain*) fianco *m*; (*of road*) bordo *m*; **on the** ~ (*as sideline*) come attività secondaria; ~ **by** ~ fianco a fianco; **take** ~**s** immischiarsi; **take sb's** ~ prendere le parti di qcno; **be on the safe** ~ andare sul sicuro ● *attrib* laterale ● *vi* ~ **with** parteggiare per

side: ~**board** *n* credenza *f*. ~**burns** *npl* basette *fpl*. ~**-effect** *n* effetto *m* collaterale. ~**lights** *npl* luci *fpl* di posizione. ~**line** *n* attività *f inv* complementare. ~**-show** *n* attrazione *f*. ~**-step** *vt* schivare. ~**-track** *vt* sviare. ~**walk** *n Am* marciapiede *m*. ~**ways** *adv* obliquamente

siding /'saɪdɪŋ/ *n* binario *m* di raccordo

sidle /'saɪdl/ *vi* camminare furtivamente (**up to** verso)

siege /siːdʒ/ *n* assedio *m*

sieve /sɪv/ n setaccio m ● vt setacciare

sift /sɪft/ vt setacciare; ~ **[through]** fig passare al setaccio

sigh /saɪ/ n sospiro m ● vi sospirare

sight /saɪt/ n vista f; (on gun) mirino m; **the ~s** pl le cose da vedere; **at first ~** a prima vista; **be within/out of ~** essere in/non essere in vista; **lose ~ of** perdere di vista; **know by ~** conoscere di vista. **have bad ~** vederci male ● vt avvistare

'sightseeing n **go ~** andare a visitare posti

sign /saɪn/ n segno m; (notice) insegna f ● vt/i firmare. **sign on** vi (as unemployed) presentarsi all'ufficio di collocamento; Mil arruolarsi

signal /'sɪgnl/ n segnale m ● v (pt/pp **signalled**) ● vt segnalare ● vi fare segnali; ~ **to sb** far segno a qcno (**to** di). ~**-box** n cabina f di segnalazione

signature /'sɪgnətʃə(r)/ n firma f. ~ **tune** n sigla f [musicale]

signet-ring /'sɪgnɪt-/ n anello m con sigillo

significance /sɪg'nɪfɪkəns/ n significato m. ~**t** a significativo

signify /'sɪgnɪfaɪ/ vt (pt/pp **-ied**) indicare

sign-language n linguaggio m dei segni

signpost /'saɪn-/ n segnalazione f stradale

silence /'saɪləns/ n silenzio m ● vt far tacere. ~ **r** n (on gun) silenziatore m; Auto marmitta f

silent /'saɪlənt/ a silenzioso; (film) muto; **remain ~** rimanere in silenzio. ~**ly** adv silenziosamente

silhouette /sɪlu'et/ n sagoma f, silhouette f inv ● vt **be ~d** profilarsi

silicon /'sɪlɪkən/ n silicio m. ~ **chip** n piastrina f di silicio

silk /sɪlk/ n seta f ● attrib di seta. ~**worm** n baco m da seta

silky /'sɪlkɪ/ a (**-ier, -iest**) come la seta

sill /sɪl/ n davanzale m

silly /'sɪlɪ/ a (**-ier, -iest**) sciocco

silo /'saɪləʊ/ n silo m

silt /sɪlt/ n melma f

silver /'sɪlvə(r)/ a d'argento; (paper) argentato ● n argento m; (silverware) argenteria f

silver: ~**-plated** a placcato d'argento. ~**ware** n argenteria f. ~ **'wedding** n nozze fpl d'argento

similar /'sɪmɪlə(r)/ a simile. ~**ity** /-'lærətɪ/ n somiglianza f. ~**ly** adv in modo simile

simile /'sɪmɪlɪ/ n similitudine f

simmer /'sɪmə(r)/ vi bollire lentamente ● vt far bollire lentamente. **simmer down** vi calmarsi

simple /'sɪmpl/ a semplice; (person) sempliciotto. ~**-minded** a sempliciotto

simplicity /sɪm'plɪsətɪ/ n semplicità f inv

simpli|fication /sɪmplɪfɪ'keɪʃn/ n semplificazione f. ~**fy** /'sɪmplɪfaɪ/ vt (pt/pp **-ied**) semplificare

simply /'sɪmplɪ/ adv semplicemente

simulate /'sɪmjʊleɪt/ vt simulare. ~**ion** /-'leɪʃn/ n simulazione f

simultaneous /sɪml'teɪnɪəs/ a simultaneo

sin /sɪn/ n peccato m ● vi (pt/pp **sinned**) peccare

since /sɪns/ prep da ● adv da allora ● conj da quando; (because) siccome

sincere /sɪn'stə(r)/ a sincero. ~**ly** adv sinceramente; **Yours ~ly** distinti saluti

sincerity /sɪn'serətɪ/ n sincerità f inv

sinful /'sɪnfl/ a peccaminoso

sing /sɪŋ/ vt/i (pt **sang**, pp **sung**) cantare

singe /sɪndʒ/ vt (pres p **singeing**) bruciacchiare

singer /'sɪŋə(r)/ n cantante mf

single /'sɪŋgl/ a solo; (not double) semplice; (unmarried) celibe;

⟨*woman*⟩ nubile; ⟨*room*⟩ singolo; ⟨*bed*⟩ a una piazza ● *n* ⟨*ticket*⟩ biglietto *m* di sola andata; ⟨*record*⟩ singolo *m*; **~s** *pl* Tennis singolo *m* ● **single out** *vt* scegliere; ⟨*distinguish*⟩ distinguere

single: **~-breasted** *a* a un petto. **~-handed** *a* & *adv* da solo. **~-minded** *a* risoluto. **~ 'parent** *n* genitore *m* che alleva il figlio da solo

singly /'sɪŋglɪ/ *adv* singolarmente

singular /'sɪŋgjʊlə(r)/ *a* Gram singolare ● *n* singolare *m*. **~ly** *adv* singolarmente

sinister /'sɪnɪstə(r)/ *a* sinistro

sink /sɪŋk/ *n* lavandino *m* ● *v* (*pt* sank, *pp* sunk) ● *vi* affondare ● *vt* affondare ⟨*ship*⟩; scavare ⟨*shaft*⟩; investire ⟨*money*⟩. **sink in** *vi* penetrare; **it took a while to ~ in** ⟨*fam*: *be understood*⟩ c'è voluto un po' a capirlo

sinner /'sɪnə(r)/ *n* peccatore, -trice *mf*

sinus /'saɪnəs/ *n* seno *m* paranasale. **~itis** *n* sinusite *f*

sip /sɪp/ *n* sorso *m* ● *vt* (*pt/pp* sipped) sorseggiare

siphon /'saɪfn/ *n* (*bottle*) sifone *m* ● **siphon off** *vt* travasare (con sifone)

sir /sɜː(r)/ *n* signore *m*; **S~** ⟨*title*⟩ Sir *m*; **Dear S~s** Spettabile ditta

siren /'saɪrən/ *n* sirena *f*

sissy /'sɪsɪ/ *n* femminuccia *f*

sister /'sɪstə(r)/ *n* sorella *f*; ⟨*nurse*⟩ [infermiera *f*] caposala *f*. **~-in-law** *n* (*pl* **~s-in-law**) cognata *f*. **~ly** *a* da sorella

sit /sɪt/ *v* (*pt/pp* sat, *pres p* sitting) ● *vi* essere seduto; ⟨*sit down*⟩ sedersi; ⟨*committee*⟩ riunirsi ● *vt* sostenere ⟨*exam*⟩. **sit back** *vi* fig starsene con le mani in mano. **sit down** *vi* mettersi a sedere. **sit up** *vi* mettersi seduto; ⟨*not slouch*⟩ star seduto diritto; ⟨*stay up*⟩ stare alzato

site /saɪt/ *n* posto *m*; Archaeol sito

m; ⟨*building* ~⟩ cantiere *m* ● *vt* collocare

sit-in /'sɪtɪn/ *n* occupazione *f* ⟨*di fabbrica, ecc.*⟩

sitting /'sɪtɪŋ/ *n* seduta *f*; ⟨*for meals*⟩ turno *m*. **~-room** *n* salotto *m*

situat|e /'sɪtjʊeɪt/ *vt* situare. **~ed** *a* situato. **~ion** /-'eɪʃn/ *n* situazione *f*; ⟨*location*⟩ posizione *f*; ⟨*job*⟩ posto *m*

six /sɪks/ *a* sei. **~teen** *a* sedici. **~teenth** *a* sedicesimo

sixth /sɪksθ/ *a* sesto

sixtieth /'sɪkstɪɪθ/ *a* sessantesimo

sixty /'sɪkstɪ/ *a* sessanta

size /saɪz/ *n* dimensioni *fpl*; ⟨*of clothes*⟩ taglia *f*, misura *f*; ⟨*of shoes*⟩ numero *m*; **what ~ is the room?** che dimensioni ha la stanza? ● **size up** *vt* fam valutare

sizeable /'saɪzəbl/ *a* piuttosto grande

sizzle /'sɪzl/ *vi* sfrigolare

skate¹ /skeɪt/ *n inv* ⟨*fish*⟩ razza *f*

skate² *n* pattino *m* ● *vi* pattinare

skateboard /'skeɪtbɔːd/ *n* skateboard *m inv*

skater /'skeɪtə(r)/ *n* pattinatore, -trice *mf*

skating /'skeɪtɪŋ/ *n* pattinaggio *m*. **~-rink** *n* pista *f* di pattinaggio

skeleton /'skelɪtn/ *n* scheletro *m*. **~ 'key** *n* passe-partout *m inv*. **~ 'staff** *n* personale *m* ridotto

sketch /sketʃ/ *n* schizzo *m*; Theat sketch *m inv* ● *vt* fare uno schizzo di

sketch|y /'sketʃɪ/ *a* (**-ier, -iest**) abbozzato. **~ily** *adv* in modo abbozzato

skewer /'skjʊə(r)/ *n* spiedo *m*

ski /skiː/ *n* sci *m inv* ● *vi* (*pt/pp* skied, *pres p* skiing) sciare; **go ~ing** andare a sciare

skid /skɪd/ *n* slitta *f* ● *vi* (*pt/pp* skidded) slittare

skier /'skiːə(r)/ *n* sciatore, -trice *mf*

skiing /'skiːɪŋ/ *n* sci *m*

skilful /'skɪlfl/ *a* abile

'ski-lift *n* impianto *m* di risalita

skill /skɪl/ n abilità f inv. **~ed** a dotato; ⟨worker⟩ specializzato

skim /skɪm/ vt (pt/pp **skimmed**) schiumare; scremare ⟨milk⟩. **skim off** vt togliere. **skim through** vt scorrere

skimp /skɪmp/ vi **~ on** lesinare su

skimpy /'skɪmpɪ/ a (**-ier, -iest**) succinto

skin /skɪn/ n pelle f; ⟨on fruit⟩ buccia f ● vt (pt/pp **skinned**) spellare

skin: **~-deep** a superficiale. **~-diving** n nuoto m subacqueo

skinflint /'skɪnflɪnt/ n miserabile mf

skinny /'skɪnɪ/ a (**-ier, -iest**) molto magro

skip[1] /skɪp/ n ⟨container⟩ benna f

skip[2] n salto m ● v (pt/pp **skipped**) ● vi saltellare; ⟨with rope⟩ saltare la corda ● vt omettere

skipper /'skɪpə(r)/ n skipper m inv

skipping-rope /'skɪpɪŋrəʊp/ n corda f per saltare

skirmish /'skɜːmɪʃ/ n scaramuccia f

skirt /skɜːt/ n gonna f ● vt costeggiare

skit /skɪt/ n bozzetto m comico

skittle /'skɪtl/ n birillo m

skive /skaɪv/ vi fam fare lo scansafatiche

skulk /skʌlk/ vi aggirarsi furtivamente

skull /skʌl/ n cranio m

skunk /skʌŋk/ n moffetta f

sky /skaɪ/ n cielo m. **~light** n lucernario m. **~scraper** n grattacielo m

slab /slæb/ n lastra f; ⟨slice⟩ fetta f; ⟨of chocolate⟩ tavoletta f

slack /slæk/ a lento; ⟨person⟩ fiacco ● vi fare lo scansafatiche. **slack off** vi rilassarsi

slacken /'slækn/ vi allentare; **[off]** ⟨trade⟩: rallentare; ⟨speed, rain.⟩ diminuire ● vt allentare; diminuire ⟨speed⟩

slacks /slæks/ npl pantaloni mpl sportivi

slag /slæg/ n scorie fpl ● **slag off**

vt (pt/pp **slagged**) Br fam criticare

slain /sleɪn/ see **slay**

slam /slæm/ v (pt/pp **slammed**) ● vt sbattere; ⟨fam: criticize⟩ stroncare ● vi sbattere

slander /'slɑːndə(r)/ n diffamazione f ● vt diffamare. **~ous** /-rəs/ a diffamatorio

slang /slæŋ/ n gergo m. **~y** a gergale

slant /slɑːnt/ n pendenza f; ⟨point of view⟩ angolazione f; **on the ~** in pendenza ● vt pendere; fig distorcere ⟨report⟩ ● vi pendere

slap /slæp/ n schiaffo m ● vt (pt/pp **slapped**) schiaffeggiare; ⟨put⟩ schiaffare ● adv in pieno

slap: **~dash** a fam frettoloso. **~-up** a fam di prim'ordine

slash /slæʃ/ n taglio m ● vt tagliare; ridurre drasticamente ⟨prices⟩

slat /slæt/ n stecca f

slate /sleɪt/ n ardesia f ● vt fam fare a pezzi

slaughter /'slɔːtə(r)/ n macello m; ⟨of people⟩ massacro m ● vt macellare; massacrare ⟨people⟩. **~house** n macello m

Slav /slɑːv/ a slavo ● n slavo, -a mf

slave /sleɪv/ n schiavo, -a mf ● vi **~ [away]** lavorare come un negro. **~-driver** n schiavista mf

slav|ery /'sleɪvərɪ/ n schiavitù f inv. **~ish** a servile

Slavonic /slə'vɒnɪk/ a slavo

slay /sleɪ/ vt (pt **slew**, pp **slain**) ammazzare

sleazy /'sliːzɪ/ a (**-ier, -iest**) sordido

sledge /sledʒ/ n slitta f. **~-hammer** n martello m

sleek /sliːk/ a liscio, lucente; ⟨well-fed⟩ pasciuto

sleep /sliːp/ n sonno m; **go to ~** addormentarsi; **put to ~** far addormentare ● v (pt/pp **slept**) ● vi dormire ● vt **~s six** ha sei posti letto. **~er** n Rail treno m con vagoni letto; ⟨compartment⟩ vagone m letto; **be a light/heavy ~er** avere il sonno leggero/pesante

sleeping: **~-bag** *n* sacco *m* a pelo. **~-car** *n* vagone *m* letto. **~-pill** *n* sonnifero *m*

sleep: **~less** *a* insonne. **~lessness** *n* insonnia *f*. **~-walker** *n* sonnambulo, -a *mf*. **~-walking** *n* sonnambulismo *m*

sleepy /ˈsliːpɪ/ *a* (**-ier, -iest**) assonnato; **be ~** aver sonno

sleet /sliːt/ *n* nevischio *m* ● *vi* **it is ~ing** nevischia

sleeve /sliːv/ *n* manica *f*; (*for record*) copertina *f*. **~less** *a* senza maniche

sleigh /sleɪ/ *n* slitta *f*

sleight /slaɪt/ *n* **~ of hand** gioco *m* di prestigio

slender /ˈslendə(r)/ *a* snello; (*fingers, ankles*) affusolato; *fig* scarso; (*chance*) magro

slept /slept/ *see* **sleep**

sleuth /sluːθ/ *n* investigatore *m*, detective *m* *inv*

slew[1] /sluː/ *vi* girare

slew[2] *see* **slay**

slice /slaɪs/ *n* fetta *f* ● *vt* affettare; **~d bread** pane *m* a cassetta

slick /slɪk/ *a* liscio; (*cunning*) astuto ● *n* (*of oil*) chiazza *f* di petrolio

slide /slaɪd/ *n* scivolata *f*; (*in playground*) scivolo *m*; (*for hair*) fermaglio *m* (*per capelli*); *Phot* diapositiva *f* ● *vi* (*pt/pp* **slid**) ● *vi* scivolare ● *vt* far scivolare. **~-rule** *n* regolo *m* calcolatore. **~ing** *a* scorrevole; (*door, seat*) scorrevole; **~ing scale** scala *f* mobile

slight /slaɪt/ *a* leggero; (*importance*) poco; (*slender*) esile. **~est** *a* minimo; **not in the ~est** niente affatto ● *vt* offendere ● *n* offesa *f*. **~ly** *adv* leggermente

slim /slɪm/ *a* (**slimmer, slimmest**) snello; *fig* scarso; (*chance*) magro ● *vi* dimagrire

slim|**e** /slaɪm/ *n* melma *f*. **~y** *a* melmoso; *fig* viscido

sling /slɪŋ/ *n* *Med* benda *f* al collo ● *vt* (*pt/pp* **slung**) *fam* lanciare

slip /slɪp/ *n* scivolata *f*; (*mistake*) lieve errore *m*; (*petticoat*) sottoveste *f*; (*for pillow*) federa *f*; (*paper*) scontrino *m*; **give sb the ~** *fam* sbarazzarsi di qcno; **~ of the tongue** lapsus *m* *inv* ● *v* (*pt/pp* **slipped**) ● *vi* scivolare; (*go quickly*) sgattaiolare; (*decline*) retrocedere ● *vt* he **~ped it into his pocket** se l'è infilato in tasca; **~ sb's mind** sfuggire di mente ● *vi* **~ away** *vi* sgusciar via; (*time:*) sfuggire. **slip into** *vi* infilarsi (*clothes*). **slip up** *vi* *fam* sbagliare

slipped 'disc *n* *Med* ernia *f* del disco

slipper /ˈslɪpə(r)/ *n* pantofola *f*

slippery /ˈslɪpərɪ/ *a* scivoloso

slip-road *n* bretella *f*

slipshod /ˈslɪpʃɒd/ *a* trascurato

slip-up *n* *fam* sbaglio *m*

slit /slɪt/ *n* spacco *m*; (*tear*) strappo *m*; (*hole*) fessura *f* ● *vt* (*pt/pp* **slit**) tagliare

slither /ˈslɪðə(r)/ *vi* scivolare

sliver /ˈslɪvə(r)/ *n* scheggia *f*

slobber /ˈslɒbə(r)/ *vi* sbavare

slog /slɒg/ *n* [**hard**] **~** sgobbata *f* ● *vi* (*pt/pp* **slogged**) (*work*) sgobbare

slogan /ˈsləʊgən/ *n* slogan *m* *inv*

slop /slɒp/ *v* (*pt/pp* **slopped**) ● *vt* versare. **slop over** *vi* versarsi

slop|**e** /sləʊp/ *n* pendenza *f*; (*ski* ~) pista *f* ● *vi* essere inclinato, inclinarsi. **~ing** *a* in pendenza

sloppy /ˈslɒpɪ/ *a* (**-ier, -iest**) (*work*) trascurato; (*worker*) negligente; (*in dress*) sciatto; (*sentimental*) sdolcinato

slosh /slɒʃ/ *vi* *fam* (*person, feet:*) sguazzare; (*water:*) scrosciare ● *vt* (*fam: hit*) colpire

sloshed /slɒʃt/ *a* *fam* sbronzo

slot /slɒt/ *n* fessura *f*; (*time-*) spazio *m* ● *v* (*pt/pp* **slotted**) ● *vt* infilare. **slot in** *vi* incastrarsi

'slot-machine *n* distributore *m* automatico; (*for gambling*) slot-machine *f* *inv*

slouch /slaʊtʃ/ *vi* (*in chair*) stare scomposto

slovenly /'slʌvnlɪ/ *a* sciatto. **~iness** *n* sciatteria *f*

slow /sləʊ/ *a* lento; **be ~** (*clock:*) essere indietro; **in ~ motion** al rallentatore ● *adv* lentamente ● **slow down/up** *vt/i* rallentare

slow: **~coach** *n fam* tartaruga *f*. **~ly** *adv* lentamente. **~ness** *n* lentezza *f*

sludge /slʌdʒ/ *n* fanghiglia *f*

slug /slʌg/ *n* lumacone *m*; (*bullet*) pallottola *f*

sluggish /'slʌgɪʃ/ *a* lento

sluice /slu:s/ *n* chiusa *f*

slum /slʌm/ *n* (*house*) tugurio *m*; **~s** *pl* bassifondi *mpl*

slumber /'slʌmbə(r)/ *vi* dormire

slump /slʌmp/ *n* crollo *m*; (*economic*) depressione *f* ● *vi* crollare

slung /slʌŋ/ *see* **sling**

slur /slɜː(r)/ *n* (*discredit*) calunnia *f* ● *vt* (*pt/pp* **slurred**) biascicare

slurp /slɜːp/ *vt/i* bere rumorosamente

slush /slʌʃ/ *n* pantano *m* nevoso; *fig* sdolcinatezza *f*. **~ fund** *n* fondi *mpl* neri

slushy /'slʌʃɪ/ *a* fangoso; (*sentimental*) sdolcinato

slut /slʌt/ *n* sgualdrina *f*

sly /slaɪ/ *a* (**-er, -est**) scaltro ● *n* **on the ~** di nascosto

smack[1] /smæk/ *n* (*on face*) schiaffo *m*; (*on bottom*) sculaccione *m* ● *vt* (*on face*) schiaffeggiare; (*on bottom*) sculacciare; **~ one's lips** far schioccare le labbra ● *adv fam* in pieno

smack[2] *vi* **~ of** *fig* sapere di

small /smɔːl/ *a* piccolo; **be out/ work**/*etc* **until the ~ hours** fare le ore piccole ● **chop up ~** fare a pezzettini ● *n* **the ~ of the back** le reni *fpl*

small: **~ ads** *npl* annunci *mpl* [commerciali]. **~ 'change** *n* spiccioli *mpl*. **~-holding** *n* piccola te-

nuta *f*. **~pox** *n* vaiolo *m*. **~ talk** *n* chiacchiere *fpl*

smarmy /'smɑːmɪ/ *a* (**-ier, -iest**) *fam* untuoso

smart /smɑːt/ *a* elegante; (*clever*) intelligente; (*brisk*) svelto; **be ~** ● *vi* (*fam: cheeky*) fare il furbo ● *vi* (*hurt*) bruciare

smarten /'smɑːtn/ *vt* **~ oneself up** farsi bello

smash /smæʃ/ *n* fragore *m*; (*collision*) scontro *m*; *Tennis* schiacciata *f* ● *vt* spaccare; *Tennis* schiacciare ● *vi* spaccarsi; (*crash*) schiantarsi (**into** contro). **~ 'hit** *n* successo *m*. **~ing** *a fam* fantastico

smattering /'smætərɪŋ/ *n* infarinatura *f*

smear /smɪə(r)/ *n* macchia *f*; *Med* striscio *m* ● *vt* imbrattare; (*coat*) spalmare (**with** di); *fig* calunniare

smell /smel/ *n* odore *m*; (*sense*) odorato *m* ● *v* (*pt/pp* **smelt** *or* **smelled**) ● *vt* odorare; (*sniff*) annusare ● *vi* odorare (**of** di)

smelly /'smelɪ/ *a* (**-ier, -iest**) puzzolente

smelt[1] /smelt/ *see* **smell**

smelt[2] *vt* fondere

smile /smaɪl/ *n* sorriso *m* ● *vi* sorridere; **~ at** sorridere a (*sb*); sorridere di (*sth*)

smirk /smɜːk/ *n* sorriso *m* compiaciuto

smithereens /smɪðə'riːnz/ *npl* **to/in** *n* in mille pezzi

smitten /'smɪtn/ *a* **~ with** tutto preso da

smock /smɒk/ *n* grembiule *m*

smog /smɒg/ *n* smog *m inv*

smoke /sməʊk/ *n* fumo *m* ● *vt/i* fumare. **~less** *a* senza fumo; (*fuel*) che non fa fumo

smoker /'sməʊkə(r)/ *n* fumatore, -trice *mf*; *Rail* vagone *m* fumatori

smoke-screen *n* cortina *f* di fumo

smoking /'sməʊkɪŋ/ *n* fumo *m*; **'no ~'** 'vietato fumare'

smoky /'sməʊkɪ/ *a* (**-ier, -iest**) fumoso; (*taste*) di fumo

559   smooth | snow-plough

smooth /smuːð/ *a* liscio; ⟨*movement*⟩ scorrevole; ⟨*sea*⟩ calmo; ⟨*manners*⟩ mellifluo ●*vt* lisciare. **smooth out** *vt* lisciare. **~ly** *adv* in modo scorrevole

smother /ˈsmʌðə(r)/ *vt* soffocare

smoulder /ˈsmoʊldə(r)/ *vi* fumare; ⟨*with rage*⟩ consumarsi

smudge /smʌdʒ/ *n* macchia *f* ●*vt/i* imbrattare

smug /smʌg/ *a* (**smugger**, **smuggest**) compiaciuto. **~ly** *adv* con aria compiaciuta

smuggl|e /ˈsmʌgl/ *vt* contrabbandare. **~er** *n* contrabbandiere, *a mf.* **~ing** *n* contrabbando *m*

smut /smʌt/ *n* macchia *f* di fuliggine; *fig* sconcezza *f*

smutty /ˈsmʌtɪ/ *a* (**-ier, -iest**) fuligginoso; *fig* sconcio

snack /snæk/ *n* spuntino *m.* **~-bar** *n* snack bar *m inv*

snag /snæg/ *n* ⟨*problem*⟩ intoppo *m*

snail /sneɪl/ *n* lumaca *f*; **at a ~'s pace** a passo di lumaca

snake /sneɪk/ *n* serpente *m*

snap /snæp/ *n* colpo *m* secco; ⟨*photo*⟩ istantanea *f* ●*attrib* ⟨*decision*⟩ istantaneo ●*v* (*pt/pp* **snapped**) ●*vi* ⟨*break*⟩ spezzarsi; **~** *at* ⟨*dog:*⟩ cercare di azzannare; ⟨*person:*⟩ parlare seccamente ●*vt* ⟨*break*⟩ spezzare; ⟨*say*⟩ dire seccamente; *Phot* fare un'istantanea di. **snap up** *vt* afferrare

snappy /ˈsnæpɪ/ *a* (**-ier, -iest**) scorbutico; ⟨*smart*⟩ elegante; **make it ~!** sbrigati!

'snapshot *n* istantanea *f*

snare /sneə(r)/ *n* trappola *f*

snarl /snɑːl/ *n* ringhio *m* ●*vi* ringhiare

snatch /snætʃ/ *n* strappo *m*; ⟨*fragment*⟩ brano *m*; ⟨*theft*⟩ scippo *m*; **make a ~ at** cercare di afferrare qcsa ●*vt* strappare [di mano] (**from** *a*); ⟨*steal*⟩ scippare; rapire ⟨*child*⟩

sneak /sniːk/ *n fam* spia *mf* ●*vi* ⟨*fam: tell tales*⟩ fare la spia ●*vt* ⟨*take*⟩ rubare; **~ a look at** dare una sbirciata a. **sneak in/out** *vi* sgattaiolare dentro/fuori

sneakers /ˈsniːkəz/ *npl Am* scarpe *fpl* da ginnastica

sneaking /ˈsniːkɪŋ/ *a* furtivo; ⟨*suspicion*⟩ vago

sneaky /ˈsniːkɪ/ *a* sornione

sneer /snɪə(r)/ *n* ghigno *m* ●*vi* sogghignare; ⟨*mock*⟩ ridere di

sneeze /sniːz/ *n* starnuto *m* ●*vi* starnutire

snide /snaɪd/ *a fam* insinuante

sniff /snɪf/ *n* (*of* dog) annusata *f* ●*vi* tirare su col naso ●*vt* odorare ⟨*flower*⟩; sniffare ⟨*glue, cocaine*⟩; ⟨*dog:*⟩ annusare

snigger /ˈsnɪgə(r)/ *n* risatina *f* soffocata ●*vi* ridacchiare

snip /snɪp/ *n* taglio *m*; ⟨*fam: bargain*⟩ affare *m* ●*vt/i* (*pt/pp* **snipped**) ~ [at] tagliare

snipe /snaɪp/ *vi* **~ at** tirare su; *fig* sparare a zero su. **~r** *n* cecchino *m*

snippet /ˈsnɪpɪt/ *n* **~ of information/news** una breve notizia/informazione

snivel /ˈsnɪvl/ *vi* (*pt/pp* **snivelled**) piagnucolare. **~ling** *a* piagnucoloso

snob /snɒb/ *n* snob *mf.* **~bery** *n* snobismo *m.* **~bish** *a* da snob

snooker /ˈsnuːkə(r)/ *n* snooker *m*

snoop /snuːp/ *n* spia *f* ●*vi fam* curiosare

snooty /ˈsnuːtɪ/ *a fam* sdegnoso

snooze /snuːz/ *n* sonnellino *m* ●*vi* fare un sonnellino

snore /snɔː(r)/ *vi* russare

snorkel /ˈsnɔːkl/ *n* respiratore *m*

snort /snɔːt/ *n* sbuffo *m* ●*vi* sbuffare

snout /snaʊt/ *n* grugno *m*

snow /snəʊ/ *n* neve *f* ●*vi* nevicare; **~ed under** *with fig* sommerso di **snow: ~ball** *n* palla *f* di neve ●*vi* fare a palle di neve. **~-drift** *n* cumulo *m* di neve. **~-drop** *n* bucaneve *m.* **~fall** *n* nevicata *f.* **~flake** *n* fiocco *m* di neve. **~man** *n* pupazzo *m* di neve. **~-plough** *n* spazzaneve *m*. **~storm** *n* tormenta *f*. **~y** *a* nevoso

snub /snʌb/ *n* sgarbo *m* ● *vt* (*pt/pp* **snubbed**) snobbare

'snub-nosed *a* dal naso all'insù

snuff /snʌf/ *n* tabacco *m* da fiuto

snug /snʌg/ *a* (**snugger**, **snuggest**) comodo; (*tight*) aderente

snuggle /'snʌgl/ *vi* rannicchiarsi (**up to** accanto a)

so /səʊ/ *adv* così; **so far** finora; **so am I** anch'io; **so I see** così pare; **that is so** è così; **so much** così tanto; **so much the better** tanto meglio; **so it is** proprio così; **if so** se è così; **so as to** in modo da; **so long!** *fam* a presto! ● *pron* **I hope/ think/am afraid** *so* spero/penso/ temo di sì; **I told you so** te l'ho detto; **because I say so** perché te lo dico io; **I did so!** è vero!; **so saying/doing,...** così dicendo/facendo,...; **or so** circa; **very much so** sì, molto; **and so forth** or **on e** così via ● *conj* (*therefore*) perciò; (*in order that*) così; **so that** affinché; **so there!** ecco!; **so what!** e allora?; **so where have you been?** allora, dove sei stato?

soak /səʊk/ *vt* mettere a bagno ● *vi* stare a bagno; **~ into** (*liquid:*) penetrare. **soak up** *vt* assorbire

soaking /'səʊkɪŋ/ *n* ammollo *m* ● *a & adv* **~ [wet]** *fam* inzuppato

so-and-so /'səʊənsəʊ/ *n* Tal dei Tali *mf*; (*euphemism*) specie *f* di imbecille

soap /səʊp/ *n* sapone *m*. **~ opera** *n* telenovela *f*, soap opera *f inv*. **~ powder** *n* detersivo *m* in polvere

soapy /'səʊpɪ/ *a* (**-ier**, **-iest**) insaponato

soar /sɔː(r)/ *vi* elevarsi; (*prices:*) salire alle stelle

sob /sɒb/ *n* singhiozzo *m* ● *vi* (*pt/pp* **sobbed**) singhiozzare

sober /'səʊbə(r)/ *a* sobrio; (*serious*) serio ● **sober up** *vi* ritornare sobrio

'so-called *a* cosiddetto

soccer /'sɒkə(r)/ *n* calcio *m*

sociable /'səʊʃəbl/ *a* socievole

social /'səʊʃl/ *a* sociale; (*sociable*) socievole

socialis|m /'səʊʃəlɪzm/ *n* socialismo *m*. **~t** *-ɪst/ *a* socialista ● *n* socialista *mf*

socialize /'səʊʃəlaɪz/ *vi* socializzare

socially /'səʊʃəlɪ/ *adv* socialmente; **know sb** **~** frequentare qcno

social: **~ se'curity** *n* previdenza *f* sociale. **~ work** *n* assistenza *f* sociale. **~ worker** *n* assistente *mf* sociale

society /sə'saɪətɪ/ *n* società *f inv*

sociolog|ist /səʊsɪ'ɒlədʒɪst/ *n* sociologo *-a mf*. **~y** *n* sociologia *f*

sock¹ /sɒk/ *n* calzino *m*; (*kneelength*) calza *f*

sock² *n fam* pugno *m* ● *vt fam* dare un pugno a

socket /'sɒkɪt/ *n* (*wall plug*) presa *f* [di corrente]; (*for bulb*) portalampada *m inv*

soda /'səʊdə/ *n* soda *f*; *Am* gazzosa *f*. **~ water** *n* seltz *m inv*

sodden /'sɒdn/ *a* inzuppato

sodium /'səʊdɪəm/ *n* sodio *m*

sofa /'səʊfə/ *n* divano *m*. **~ bed** *n* divano *m* letto

soft /sɒft/ *a* morbido, soffice; (*voice*) sommesso; (*light, colour*) tenue; (*not strict*) indulgente; (*fam: silly*) stupido; **have a ~ spot for sb** avere un debole per qcno. **~ drink** *n* bibita *f* analcolica

soften /'sɒfn/ *vt* ammorbidire; *fig* attenuare ● *vi* ammorbidirsi

softly /'sɒftlɪ/ *adv* (*say*) sottovoce; (*treat*) con indulgenza; (*play music*) in sottofondo

soft: **~ toy** *n* pupazzo *m* di peluche. **~ware** *n* software *m*

soggy /'sɒgɪ/ *a* (**-ier**, **-iest**) zuppo

soil¹ /sɔɪl/ *n* suolo *m*

soil² *vt* sporcare

solar /'səʊlə(r)/ *a* solare

sold /səʊld/ *see* **sell**

solder /'səʊldə(r)/ *n* lega *f* da saldatura ● *vt* saldare

soldier /ˈsəʊldʒə(r)/ n soldato m
● **soldier on** vi perseverare

sole[1] /səʊl/ n (of foot) pianta f; (of shoe) suola f

sole[2] n (fish) sogliola f

sole[3] a unico, solo. **~ly** adv unicamente

solemn /ˈsɒləm/ a solenne. **~ity** /səˈlemnətɪ/ n solennità f

solicit /səˈlɪsɪt/ vt sollecitare ● vi ⟨prostitute:⟩ adescare

solicitor /səˈlɪsɪtə(r)/ n avvocato m

solid /ˈsɒlɪd/ a solido; ⟨oak, gold⟩ massiccio ● n (figure) solido m; **~s** pl (food) cibi mpl solidi

solidarity /sɒlɪˈdærətɪ/ n solidarietà f inv

solidify /səˈlɪdɪfaɪ/ vi (pt/pp -ied) solidificarsi

soliloquy /səˈlɪləkwɪ/ n soliloquio m

solitaire /sɒlɪˈteə(r)/ n solitario m

solitary /ˈsɒlɪtərɪ/ a solitario; ⟨sole⟩ solo. **~ con'finement** n cella f di isolamento

solitude /ˈsɒlɪtjuːd/ n solitudine f

solo /ˈsəʊləʊ/ n Mus assolo m ● a ⟨flight⟩ in solitario ● adv in solitario. **~ist** n solista mf

solstice /ˈsɒlstɪs/ n solstizio m

soluble /ˈsɒljʊbl/ a solubile

solution /səˈluːʃn/ n soluzione f

solve /sɒlv/ vt risolvere

solvent /ˈsɒlvənt/ a solvente ● n solvente m

sombre /ˈsɒmbə(r)/ a tetro; ⟨clothes⟩ scuro

some /sʌm/ a (a certain amount of) del; (a certain number of) qualche, alcuni; **~ day** un giorno o l'altro; **I need ~ money/books** ho bisogno di soldi/libri; **do ~ shopping** fare qualche acquisto ● pron (a certain amount) un po'; (a certain number) alcuni; **I want ~** ne voglio

some: ~body /-bədɪ/ pron & n qualcuno m. **~how** adv in qualche modo; **~how or other** in un modo o nell'altro. **~one** pron & n = **somebody**

somersault /ˈsʌməsɔːlt/ n capriola f; **turn a ~** fare una capriola

something pron qualcosa, qualcosa; **~ different** qualcosa di diverso; **~ like** un po' come; ⟨approximately⟩ qualcosa come; **see ~ of sb** vedere qcno un po'

some: ~time adv un giorno o l'altro; **~time last summer** durante l'estate scorsa. **~times** adv qualche volta. **~what** adv piuttosto. **~where** adv da qualche parte ● pron **~where to eat** un posto in cui mangiare

son /sʌn/ n figlio m

sonata /səˈnɑːtə/ n sonata f

song /sɒŋ/ n canzone f

sonic /ˈsɒnɪk/ a sonico. **~ 'boom** n bang m inv sonico

'son-in-law n (pl **~s-in-law**) genero m

sonnet /ˈsɒnɪt/ n sonetto m

soon /suːn/ adv presto; (in a short time) tra poco; **as ~ as** [non] appena; **as ~ as possible** il più presto possibile; **~er or later** prima o poi; **the ~er the better** prima è, meglio è; **no ~er had I arrived than...** ero appena arrivato quando...; **I would ~er go** preferirei andare; **~ after** subito dopo

soot /sʊt/ n fuliggine f

soothe /suːð/ vt calmare

sooty /ˈsʊtɪ/ a fuligginoso

sophisticated /səˈfɪstɪkeɪtɪd/ a sofisticato

soporific /sɒpəˈrɪfɪk/ a soporifero

sopping /ˈsɒpɪŋ/ a & adv **be ~ [wet]** essere bagnato fradicio

soppy /ˈsɒpɪ/ a (-ier, -iest) fam svenevole

soprano /səˈprɑːnəʊ/ n soprano m

sordid /ˈsɔːdɪd/ a sordido

sore /sɔː(r)/ a dolorante; ⟨Am: vexed⟩ arrabbiato; **it's ~** fa male; **have a ~ throat** avere mal di gola ● n piaga f. **~ly** adv ⟨tempted⟩ seriamente

sorrow /ˈsɒrəʊ/ n tristezza f. **~ful** a triste

sorry /ˈsɒrɪ/ a (-ier, -iest) ⟨sad⟩

spiacente; (*wretched*) pietoso; **you'll be ~!** te ne pentirai!; **I am ~** mi dispiace; **be** *or* **feel ~ for** provare compassione per; **~!** scusa!; (*more polite*) scusi!

sort /sɔːt/ *n* specie *f*; (*fam: person*) tipo *m*; **it's a ~ of fish** è un tipo di pesce; **be out of ~s** (*fam: unwell*) stare poco bene ● *vt* classificare. **sort out** *vt* selezionare (*papers*); *fig* risolvere (*problem*); occuparsi di (*person*)

'so-so *a & adv* così così

sought /sɔːt/ *see* **seek**

soul /səʊl/ *n* anima *f*

sound[1] /saʊnd/ *a* sano; (*sensible*) saggio; (*secure*) solido; (*thrashing*) clamoroso ● *adv* **~ asleep** profondamente addormentato

sound[2] *n* suono *m*; (*noise*) rumore *m*; **I don't like the ~ of it** *fam* non mi suona bene ● *vi* suonare; (*seem*) aver l'aria di ● *vt* (*pronounce*) pronunciare; *Med* auscultare (*chest*). **~ barrier** *n* muro *m* del suono. **~ card** *n* Comput scheda *f* sonora. **~less** *a* silenzioso. **sound out** *vt fig* sondare

soundly /'saʊndlɪ/ *adv* (*sleep*) profondamente; (*defeat*) clamorosamente

'sound: **~-proof** *a* impenetrabile al suono. **~-track** *n* colonna *f* sonora

soup /suːp/ *n* minestra *f*. **~ed-up** *a fam* (*engine*) truccato

soup: **~-plate** *n* piatto *m* fondo. **~-spoon** *n* cucchiaio *m* da minestra

sour /'saʊə(r)/ *a* agro; (*not fresh* &*fig*) acido

source /sɔːs/ *n* fonte *f*

south /saʊθ/ *n* sud *m*; **to the ~ of** a sud di ● *a* del sud, meridionale ● *adv* verso il sud

south: **S~ 'Africa** *n* Sudafrica *m*. **S~ A'merica** *n* America *f* del Sud. **S~ American** *a & n* sud-americano, -a *mf*. **~'east** *n* sud-est *m*

southerly /'sʌðəlɪ/ *a* del sud

southern /'sʌðən/ *a* del sud, meri-

dionale; **~ Italy** il Mezzogiorno *m*. **~er** *n* meridionale *mf*

South 'Pole *n* polo *m* Sud

'southward[s] /-wəd[z]/ *adv* verso sud

souvenir /suːvəˈnɪə(r)/ *n* ricordo *m*, souvenir *m inv*

sovereign /'sɒvrɪn/ *a* sovrano ● *n* sovrano, -a *mf*. **~ty** *n* sovranità *f inv*

Soviet /'səʊvɪət/ *a* sovietico; **~ Union** Unione *f* Sovietica

sow[1] /saʊ/ *n* scrofa *f*

sow[2] /səʊ/ *vt* (*pt* **sowed**, *pp* **sown** *or* **sowed**) seminare

soya /'sɔɪə/ *n* **~ bean** soia *f*

spa /spɑː/ *n* stazione *f* termale

space /speɪs/ *n* spazio *m* ● *a* (*research etc*) spaziale ● *vt* **~ [out]** distanziare

space: **~-ship** *n* astronave *f*. **~ shuttle** *n* navetta *f* spaziale

spacious /'speɪʃəs/ *a* spazioso

spade /speɪd/ *n* vanga *f*; (*for child*) paletta *f*; **~s** *pl* (*in cards*) picche *fpl*. **~work** *n* lavoro *m* preparatorio

Spain /speɪn/ *n* Spagna *f*

span[1] /spæn/ *n* spanna *f*; (*of arch*) luce *f*; (*of time*) arco *m*; (*of wings*) apertura *f* ● *vt* (*pt/pp* **spanned**) estendersi su

span[2] *see* **spick**

Span|**iard** /'spænjəd/ *n* spagnolo, -a *mf*. **~ish** *a* spagnolo ● *n* (*language*) spagnolo *m*; **the ~ish** *pl* gli spagnoli

spank /spæŋk/ *vt* sculacciare. **~ing** *n* sculacciata *f*

spanner /'spænə(r)/ *n* chiave *f* inglese

spar /spɑː(r)/ *vi* (*pt/pp* **sparred**) (*boxing*) allenarsi; (*argue*) litigare

spare /speə(r)/ *a* (*surplus*) in più; (*additional*) di riserva ● *n* (*part*) ricambio *m* ● *vt* risparmiare; (*do without*) fare a meno di; **can you ~ five minutes?** avresti cinque minuti?; **to ~** (*surplus*) in eccedenza. **~ part** *n* pezzo *m* di ricambio. **~ time** *n* tempo *m* libero. **~wheel** *n* ruota *f* di scorta

sparing /'speərɪŋ/ *a* parco (**with** di). **~ly** *adv* con parsimonia

spark /spɑːk/ *n* scintilla *f*. **~ing-plug** *n* *Auto* candela *f*

sparkl|e /'spɑːkl/ *n* scintillio *m* ● *vi* scintillare. **~ing** *a* frizzante; (*wine*) spumante

sparrow /'spærəʊ/ *n* passero *m*

sparse /spɑːs/ *a* rado. **~ly** *adv* scarsamente; **~ly populated** *a* bassa densità di popolazione

spartan /'spɑːtn/ *a* spartano

spasm /'spæzm/ *n* spasmo *m*. **~odic** /-'mɒdɪk/ *a* spasmodico

spastic /'spæstɪk/ *a* spastico ● *n* spastico, -a *mf*

spat /spæt/ *see* **spit¹**

spate /speɪt/ *n* (*series*) successione *f*; **be in full ~** essere in piena

spatial /'speɪʃl/ *a* spaziale

spatter /'spætə(r)/ *vt* schizzare

spatula /'spætjʊlə/ *n* spatola *f*

spawn /spɔːn/ *n* uova *fpl* (*di pesci, rane, ecc.*) ● *vi* deporre le uova ● *vt fig* generare

spay /speɪ/ *vt* sterilizzare

speak /spiːk/ *v* (*pt* **spoke**, *pp* **spoken**) ● *vi* parlare (**to** a); **~ing!** *Teleph* sono io! ● *vt* dire; **~ one's mind** dire quello che si pensa. **speak for** *vi* parlare a nome di. **speak up** *vi* parlare più forte; **~ up for oneself** parlare a favore di

speaker /'spiːkə(r)/ *n* parlante *mf*; (*in public*) oratore, -trice *mf*; (*of stereo*) cassa *f*

spear /spɪə(r)/ *n* lancia *f*

spec /spek/ *n* **on ~** *fam* senza certezza

special /'speʃl/ *a* speciale. **~ist** *n* specialista *mf*. **~ity** /-ʃɪ'ælətɪ/ *n* specialità *f inv*

specialize /'speʃəlaɪz/ *vi* specializzarsi. **~ly** *adv* specialmente; (*particularly*) particolarmente

species /'spiːʃiːz/ *n* specie *f inv*

specific /spə'sɪfɪk/ *a* specifico. **~ally** *adv* in modo specifico

specifications /spesɪfɪ'keɪʃnz/ *npl* descrizione *f*

specify /'spesɪfaɪ/ *vt* (*pt/pp* **-ied**) specificare

specimen /'spesɪmən/ *n* campione *m*

speck /spek/ *n* macchiolina *f*; (*particle*) granello *m*

speckled /'spekld/ *a* picchiettato

specs /speks/ *npl fam* occhiali *mpl*

spectacle /'spektəkl/ *n* (*show*) spettacolo *m*. **~s** *npl* occhiali *mpl*

spectacular /spek'tækjʊlə(r)/ *a* spettacolare

spectator /spek'teɪtə(r)/ *n* spettatore, -trice *mf*

spectre /'spektə(r)/ *n* spettro *m*

spectrum /'spektrəm/ *n* (*pl* **-tra**) spettro *m*; *fig* gamma *f*

speculat|e /'spekjʊleɪt/ *vi* speculare. **~ion** /-'leɪʃn/ *n* speculazione *f*. **~ive** /-ɪv/ *a* speculativo. **~or** *n* speculatore, -trice *mf*

sped /sped/ *see* **speed**

speech /spiːtʃ/ *n* linguaggio *m*; (*address*) discorso *m*. **~less** *a* senza parole

speed /spiːd/ *n* velocità *f inv*; (*gear*) marcia *f*; **at ~** a tutta velocità ● *vi* (*pt/pp* **sped**) andare veloce; (*pt/pp* **speeded**) (*go too fast*) andare a velocità eccessiva. **speed up** (*pt/pp* **speeded up**) *vt/i* accelerare

speed: **~boat** *n* motoscafo *m*. **~ing** *n* eccesso *m* di velocità. **~ limit** *n* limite *m* di velocità

speedometer /spiː'dɒmɪtə(r)/ *n* tachimetro *m*

speedy /'spiːdɪ/ *a* (**-ier, -iest**) rapido. **~ily** *adv* rapidamente

spell¹ /spel/ *n* (*turn*) turno *m*; (*of weather*) periodo *m*

spell² *v* (*pt/pp* **spelled, spelt**) ● *vt* **how do you ~...?** come si scrive...?; **could you ~ that for me?** me lo può compitare?; **~ disaster** essere disastroso ● *vi* **he can't ~** fa molti errori d'ortografia

spell³ *n* (*magic*) incantesimo *m*. **~bound** *a* affascinato

spelling /'spelɪŋ/ n ortografia f
spelt /spelt/ see **spell²**
spend /spend/ vt/i (pt/pp **spent**) spendere; passare ⟨time⟩
spent /spent/ see **spend**
sperm /spɜːm/ n spermatozoo m; ⟨semen⟩ sperma m
spew /spjuː/ vt/i vomitare
spher|e /sfɪə(r)/ n sfera f. **~ical** /'sferɪkl/ a sferico
spice /spaɪs/ n spezia f; fig pepe m
spick /spɪk/ a **~ and span** lindo
spicy /'spaɪsɪ/ a piccante
spider /'spaɪdə(r)/ n ragno m
spik|e /spaɪk/ n punta f; Bot, Zool spina f; ⟨on shoe⟩ chiodo m. **~y** a ⟨plant⟩ pungente
spill /spɪl/ v (pt/pp **spilt** or **spilled**) ●vt versare ⟨blood⟩ ●vi ro- sciarsi
spin /spɪn/ v (pt/pp **spun**, pres p **spinning**) ●vt far girare; filare ⟨wool⟩; centrifugare ⟨washing⟩ ●vi girare; ⟨washing machine:⟩ centrifugare ●n rotazione f; ⟨short drive⟩ giretto m. **spin out** vt far durare
spinach /'spɪnɪdʒ/ n spinaci mpl
spinal /'spaɪnl/ a spinale. **~ cord** n midollo m spinale
spindle /'spɪndl/ n fuso m. **~y** a af- fusolato
spin-'drier n centrifuga f
spine /spaɪn/ n spina f dorsale; ⟨of book⟩ dorso m; Bot, Zool spina f. **~less** a fig smidollato
spinning /'spɪnɪŋ/ n filatura f. **~-wheel** n filatoio m
'**spin-off** n ricaduta f
spiral /'spaɪrəl/ a a spirale ●n spi- rale f ●vi (pt/pp **spiralled**) forma- re una spirale. **~ 'staircase** n sca- la f a chiocciola
spire /spaɪə(r)/ n guglia f
spirit /'spɪrɪt/ n spirito m; ⟨cour- age⟩ ardore m; **~s** pl ⟨alcohol⟩ liquori mpl; **in good ~s** di buon umore; **in low ~s** abbattuto
spirited /'spɪrɪtɪd/ a vivace; ⟨courageous⟩ pieno d'ardore
spirit: ~-level n livella f a bolla

d'aria. **~ stove** n fornellino m [da campeggio]
spiritual /'spɪrɪtjʊəl/ a spirituale ●n retica m. **~ism** /-ɪzm/ n spi- ritismo m. **~ist** /-ɪst/ n spiritista mf
spit¹ /spɪt/ n ⟨for roasting⟩ spie- do m
spit² n sputo m ●vt/i (pt/pp **spat**, pres p **spitting**) sputare; ⟨cat:⟩ sof- fiare; ⟨fat:⟩ sfrigolare; **it's ~ting [with rain]** pioviggina; **the ~ting image of** il ritratto spiccicato di
spite /spaɪt/ n dispetto m; **in ~ of** malgrado ●vt far dispetto a. **~ful** a indispettito
spittle /'spɪtl/ n saliva f
splash /splæʃ/ n schizzo m; ⟨of colour⟩ macchia f; ⟨fam: drop⟩ goc- cio m ●vt schizzare; **~ sb with sth** schizzare qcno di qcsa ●vi schizzare. **splash about** vi schiz- zarsi. **splash down** vi ⟨space- craft:⟩ ammarare
spleen /spliːn/ n Anat milza f
splendid /'splendɪd/ a splendido
splendour /'splendə(r)/ n splendo- re m
splint /splɪnt/ n Med stecca f
splinter /'splɪntə(r)/ n scheggia f ●vi scheggiarsi
split /splɪt/ n fessura f; ⟨quarrel⟩ rottura f; ⟨division⟩ scissione f; ⟨tear⟩ strappo m ●v (pt/pp **split**, pres p **splitting**) ●vt spaccare; ⟨share, divide⟩ dividere; ⟨tear⟩ strappare ●vi spaccarsi; ⟨tear⟩ strapparsi; ⟨divide⟩ dividersi; **~ on sb** fam denunciare qcno ●a a **~ second** una frazione f di secon- do. **split up** vt dividersi ●vi ⟨couple:⟩ separarsi
splutter /'splʌtə(r)/ vi farfugliare
spoil /spɔɪl/ n **~s** pl bottino msg ●v (pt/pp **spoilt** or **spoiled**) ●vt rovinare; viziare ⟨person⟩ ●vi an- dare a male. **~sport** n guastafeste mf fnv
spoke¹ /spəʊk/ n raggio m
spoke², spoken /'spəʊkn/ see **speak**

'spokesman n portavoce m inv

sponge /spʌndʒ/ n spugna f ●vt pulire (con la spugna) ●vi **~ on** scroccare da. **~-cake** n pan m di Spagna

spong|er /spʌndʒə(r)/ n scroccone, -a mf. **~y** a spugnoso

sponsor /spɒnsə(r)/ n garante m; Radio, TV sponsor m inv; (godparent) padrino m, madrina f; (for membership) socio, -a mf garante ●vt sponsorizzare. **~ship** n sponsorizzazione f

spontaneous /spɒn'teɪnɪəs/ a spontaneo

spoof /spuːf/ n fam parodia f

spooky /'spuːkɪ/ a (-ier, -iest) fam sinistro

spool /spuːl/ n bobina f

spoon /spuːn/ n cucchiaio m ●vt mettere col cucchiaio. **~-feed** vt (pt/pp -fed) fig imboccare. **~ful** n cucchiaiata f

sporadic /spə'rædɪk/ a sporadico

sport /spɔːt/ n sport m inv ●vt sfoggiare. **~ing** a sportivo; **~ing chance** possibilità f

sports: **~car** n automobile f sportiva. **~ coat** n, **~ jacket** n giacca f sportiva. **~man** n sportivo m. **~woman** n sportiva f

sporty /'spɔːtɪ/ a (-ier, -iest) sportivo

spot /spɒt/ n macchia f; (pimple) brufolo m; (place) posto m; (in pattern) pois m inv; (of rain) goccia f; (of water) goccio m; **~s** pl (rash) sfogo msg; **a ~ of** fam un po' di; **a ~ of bother** qualche problema; **on the ~** sul luogo; (immediately) immediatamente; **in a [tight] ~** fam in difficoltà ●vt (pt/pp **spotted**) macchiare; (fam: notice) individuare

spot: **~ 'check** n (without warning) controllo m a sorpresa; **do a ~ check on sth** dare una controllata a qcsa. **~less** a immacolato. **~light** n riflettore m

spotted /'spɒtɪd/ a (material) a pois

spotty /'spɒtɪ/ a (-ier, -iest) (pimply) brufoloso

spouse /spaʊz/ n consorte mf

spout /spaʊt/ n becco m ●vi zampillare (from da)

sprain /spreɪn/ n slogatura f ●vt slogare

sprang /spræŋ/ see **spring²**

sprawl /sprɔːl/ vi (in chair) stravaccarsi; (city etc.) estendersi; **go ~ing** (fall) cadere disteso

spray /spreɪ/ n spruzzo m; (preparation) spray m inv; (container) spruzzatore m inv ●vt spruzzare. **~-gun** n pistola f a spruzzo

spread /spred/ n estensione f; (of disease) diffusione f; (paste) crema f; (fam: feast) banchetto m ●v (pt/pp **spread**) ●vt spargere; spalmare (butter, jam); stendere (cloth, arms); diffondere (news, disease); dilazionare (payments) ●vi **~ sth with** spalmare qcsa di ●vi spargersi; (butter:) spalmarsi; (disease:) diffondersi. **~sheet** n Comput foglio m elettronico. **spread out** vt sparpagliare ●vi sparpagliarsi

spree /spriː/ n fam **go on a ~** far baldoria; **go on a shopping ~** fare spese folli

sprig /sprɪg/ n rametto m

sprightly /'spraɪtlɪ/ a (-ier, -iest) vivace

spring¹ /sprɪŋ/ n primavera f ●attrib primaverile

spring² n (jump) balzo m; (water) sorgente f; (device) molla f; (elasticity) elasticità f ●v (pt **sprang**, pp **sprung**) ●vi balzare; (arise) provenire (from da) ●vt he **just sprang it on me** me l'ha detto a cose fatte compiuto. **spring up** balzare; fig spuntare

spring: **~board** n trampolino m. **~-cleaning** n pulizie fpl di Pasqua. **~time** n primavera f

sprinkle /'sprɪŋkl/ vt spruzzare (liquid); spargere (flour, cocoa); **~ sth with** spruzzare qcsa di (liquid); cospargere qcsa di 〈flour, cocoa〉. **~er** n sprinkler m inv; 〈for lawn〉 irrigatore m. **~ing** n 〈of liquid〉 spruzzata f; 〈of pepper, salt〉 pizzico m; 〈of flour, sugar〉 spolverizzata f; 〈of knowledge〉 infarinata f; 〈of people〉 pugno m

sprint /sprɪnt/ n sprint m inv ●vi fare uno sprint; Sport sprintare. **~er** n sprinter mf inv

sprout /spraʊt/ n germoglio m; [**Brussels**] **~s** pl cavolini mpl di Bruxelles ●vi germogliare

spruce /spruːs/ a elegante ●n abete m

sprung /sprʌŋ/ see **spring²** ●a molleggiato

spud /spʌd/ n fam patata f

spun /spʌn/ see **spin**

spur /spɜː(r)/ n sperone m; 〈stimulus〉 stimolo m; 〈road〉 svincolo m; **on the ~ of the moment** su due piedi ●vt (pt/pp **spurred**) **~ [on]** fig spronare [a]

spurious /ˈspjʊərɪəs/ a falso

spurn /spɜːn/ vt sdegnare

spurt /spɜːt/ n getto m; Sport scatto m; **put on a ~** fare uno scatto ●vi sprizzare; 〈increase speed〉 scattare

spy /spaɪ/ n spia f ●v (pt/pp **spied**) ●vi spiare m ●vt 〈fam: see〉 spiare. **spy on** vi spiare

spying /ˈspaɪɪŋ/ n spionaggio m

squabble /ˈskwɒbl/ n bisticcio m ●vi bisticciare

squad /skwɒd/ n squadra f; Sport squadra

squadron /ˈskwɒdrən/ n Mil squadrone m; Aeron, Naut squadriglia f

squalid /ˈskwɒlɪd/ a squallido

squalor /ˈskwɒlə(r)/ n squallore m

squander /ˈskwɒndə(r)/ vt sprecare

square /skweə(r)/ a quadrato; 〈meal〉 sostanzioso; 〈fam: old-fashioned〉 vecchio stampo; **all ~** fam pari ●n quadrato m; 〈in city〉 piazza f; 〈on chessboard〉 riquadro m ●vt 〈settle〉 far quadrare; Math

elevare al quadrato ●vi 〈agree〉 armonizzare

squash /skwɒʃ/ n 〈drink〉 spremuta f; 〈sport〉 squash m; 〈vegetable〉 zucca f ●vt schiacciare; soffocare 〈rebellion〉

squat /skwɒt/ a tarchiato ●n fam edificio m occupato abusivamente ●vi (pt/pp **squatted**) accovacciarsi; **~** in occupare abusivamente. **~ter** n occupante mf abusivo, -a

squawk /skwɔːk/ n gracchio m ●vi gracchiare

squeak /skwiːk/ n squittio m; 〈of hinge, brakes〉 scricchiolio m ●vi squittire; 〈hinge, brakes〉 scricchiolare

squeal /skwiːl/ n strillo m; 〈of brakes〉 cigolio m ●vi strillare; sl spifferare

squeamish /ˈskwiːmɪʃ/ a dallo stomaco delicato

squeeze /skwiːz/ n stretta f; 〈crush〉 pigia pigia m inv ●vt premere; 〈to get juice〉 spremere; stringere 〈hand〉; 〈force〉 spingere a forza; 〈fam: extort〉 estorcere 〈out of da〉. **squeeze in/out** vi sgusciare dentro/fuori. **squeeze up** vi stringersi

squelch /skweltʃ/ vi sguazzare

squid /skwɪd/ n calamaro m

squiggle /ˈskwɪgl/ n scarabocchio m

squint /skwɪnt/ n strabismo m ●vi essere strabico

squire /ˈskwaɪə(r)/ n signorotto m di campagna

squirm /skwɜːm/ vi contorcersi; 〈feel embarrassed〉 sentirsi imbarazzato

squirrel /ˈskwɪrəl/ n scoiattolo m

squirt /skwɜːt/ n spruzzo m; 〈fam: person〉 presuntuoso m ●vt/i spruzzare

St abbr 〈Saint〉 S; abbr **Street**

stab /stæb/ n pugnalata f, coltellata f; 〈sensation〉 fitta f; 〈fam: attempt〉 tentativo m ●vt (pt/pp **stabbed**) pugnalare, accoltellare

stability /stə'bɪlətɪ/ n stabilità f inv

stabilize /'steɪbɪlaɪz/ vt stabilizzare ● vi stabilizzarsi

stable¹ /'steɪbl/ a stabile

stable² n stalla f; (establishment) scuderia f

stack /stæk/ n catasta f; (of chimney) comignolo m; (chimney) ciminiera f; (fam: large quantity) montagna f ● vt accatastare

stadium /'steɪdɪəm/ n stadio m

staff /stɑ:f/ n (stick) bastone m; (employees) personale m; (teachers) corpo m insegnante; Mil Stato m Maggiore ● vt fornire di personale. **~-room** n Sch sala f insegnanti

stag /stæg/ n cervo m

stage /steɪdʒ/ n palcoscenico m; (profession) teatro m; (in journey) tappa f; (in process) stadio m; **go on the ~** darsi al teatro; **by or in ~s** a tappe ● vt mettere in scena; (arrange) organizzare

stage: **~ door** n ingresso m degli artisti. **~ fright** n panico m da scena. **~ manager** n direttore, -trice mf di scena

stagger /'stægə(r)/ vi barcollare ● vt stupire; scaglionare (holidays etc); **I was ~ed** sono rimasto sbalordito ● n vacillamento m. **~ing** a sbalorditivo

stagnant /'stægnənt/ a stagnante

stagnate /stæg'neɪt/ vi fig [ri]stagnare. **~ion** /-'neɪʃn/ n fig inattività f

stag party n addio m al celibato

staid /steɪd/ a posato

stain /steɪn/ n macchia f; (for wood) mordente m ● vt macchiare; (wood) dare il mordente a; **~ed glass** vetro m colorato; **~ed glass window** vetrata f colorata. **~less** a senza macchia; (steel) inossidabile. **~ remover** n smacchiatore m

stair /steə(r)/ n gradino m; **~s** pl scale fpl. **~case** n scale fpl

stake /steɪk/ n palo m; (wager) po-

sta f; Comm partecipazione f; **at ~** in gioco ● vt puntellare; (wager) scommettere

stale /steɪl/ a stantio; (air) viziato; (uninteresting) trito [e ritrito]. **~mate** n (in chess) stallo m; (deadlock) situazione f di stallo

stalk¹ /stɔ:k/ n gambo m

stalk² vt inseguire ● vi camminare impettito

stall /stɔ:l/ n box m inv; **~s** pl Theat platea f; (in market) bancarella f ● vi (engine:) spegnersi; fig temporeggiare ● vt far spegnere (engine); tenere a bada (person)

stallion /'stæljən/ n stallone m

stalwart /'stɔ:lwət/ a fedele

stamina /'stæmɪnə/ n [capacità f inv di] resistenza f

stammer /'stæmə(r)/ n balbettio m ● vt/i balbettare

stamp /stæmp/ n (postage ~) francobollo m; (instrument) timbro m, fig impronta f ● vt affrancare (letter); timbrare (bill); battere (feet). **stamp out** vt spegnere; fig soffocare

stampede /stæm'pi:d/ n fuga f precipitosa; fam fuggi-fuggi m ● vi fuggire precipitosamente

stance /stɑ:ns/ n posizione f

stand /stænd/ n (for bikes) rastrelliera f; (at exhibition) stand m inv; (in market) bancarella f; (in stadium) gradinata f inv; fig posizione f ● v (pt/pp **stood**) ● vi stare in piedi; (rise) alzarsi [in piedi]; (be) trovarsi; (be candidate) essere candidato (for a); (stay valid) rimanere valido; **~ still** non muoversi; **I don't know where I ~** non so qual'è la mia posizione; **~ firm** fig tener duro; **~ together** essere solidali; **~ to lose/gain** rischiare di perdere/vincere; **~ to reason** essere logico ● vt (withstand) resistere a; (endure) sopportare; (place) mettere; **~ a chance** avere una possibilità; **~ one's ground** tener duro; **~ the test of time** superare la prova del tempo; **~ sb a**

beer offrire una birra a qcno.
stand by vi stare a guardare; (be ready) essere pronto ● vt (support) appoggiare. **stand down** vi (retire) ritirarsi. **stand for** vt (mean) significare; (tolerate) tollerare. **stand in for** vt sostituire. **stand out** vi spiccare. **stand up** vi alzarsi [in piedi]. **stand up for** vt prendere le difese di; ~ **up for oneself** farsi valere. **stand up to** vt affrontare

standard /'stændəd/ a standard; **be ~ practice** essere pratica corrente ● n standard m inv; Techn norma f; (level) livello m; (quality) qualità f inv; (flag) stendardo m; **~s** pl (morals) valori mpl; **~ of living** tenore m di vita. **~ize** vt standardizzare

'**standard lamp** n lampada f a stelo

'**stand-by** n riserva f; **on** ~ (at airport) in lista d'attesa

'**stand-in** n controfigura f

standing /'stændɪŋ/ a (erect) in piedi; (permanent) permanente ● n posizione f; (duration) durata f. ~ **'order** n addebitamento m diretto. ~-**room** n posti mpl in piedi

stand-: ~-**offish** /stænd'ɒfɪʃ/ a sostante. ~**point** n punto m di vista. ~**still** n come to a ~**still** fermarsi; **at a ~still** in un periodo di stasi

stank /stæŋk/ see **stink**

staple[1] /'sterpl/ n (product) prodotto m principale

staple[2] n graffa f ● vt pinzare. ~**r** n pinzatrice f, cucitrice f

star /stɑː(r)/ n (also: (asterisk) asterisco m; Theat, Cinema, Sport divo, -a mf, stella f ● vi (pt/pp **starred**) essere l'interprete principale

starboard /'stɑːbəd/ n tribordo m

starch /stɑːtʃ/ n amido m ● vt inamidare. ~**y** a ricco di amido; fig compito

stare /steə(r)/ n sguardo m fisso ● vi **it's rude to** ~ è da maleducati

fissare la gente; ~ **at** fissare; ~ **into space** guardare nel vuoto

'**starfish** n stella f di mare

stark /stɑːk/ a austero; (contrast) forte ● adv completamente; ~ **naked** completamente nudo

starling /'stɑːlɪŋ/ n storno m

'**starlit** a stellato

starry /'stɑːrɪ/ a stellato

start /stɑːt/ n inizio m; (departure) partenza f; (jump) sobbalzo m; **from the** ~ [fin] dall'inizio; **for a** ~ tanto per cominciare; **give sb a** ~ Sport dare un vantaggio a qcno ● vi [in]cominciare; (set out) avviarsi; (engine, car:) partire; (jump) trasalire; **to** ~ **with,...** tanto per cominciare,... ● vt [in]cominciare; (cause) dare inizio a; (found) mettere su; mettere in moto (car); mettere in giro (rumour). ~**er** n Culin primo m (piatto m); (in race: giving signal) starter m inv; (participant) concorrente mf; Auto motorino m d'avviamento. ~**ing-point** n punto m di partenza

startle /'stɑːtl/ vt far trasalire; (news:) sconvolgere

starvation /stɑː'veɪʃn/ n fame f

starve /stɑːv/ vi morire di fame ● vt far morire di fame

stash /stæʃ/ vt fam ~ **[away]** nascondere

state /steɪt/ n stato m; (grand style) pompa f; ~ **of play** punteggio m; **be in a** ~ (person:) essere agitato; **lie in** ~ essere esposto ● attrib di Stato; Sch pubblico; (with ceremony) di gala ● vt dichiarare; (specify) precisare. ~**less** a apolide

stately /'steɪtlɪ/ a (-ier, -iest) maestoso. ~'**home** n dimora f signorile

statement /'steɪtmənt/ n dichiarazione f; Jur deposizione f; (in banking) estratto m conto; (account) rapporto m

'**statesman** n statista mf

static /'stætɪk/ a statico

station /'steɪʃn/ n stazione f; (police) commissariato m ● vt appostare (guard); **be ~ed** in Germania essere di stanza in Germania. **~ary** /-ərɪ/ a immobile

stationer /'steɪʃənə(r)/ n ~'s [shop] cartoleria f. **~y** n cartoleria f

'**station-wagon** n Am familiare f

statistic|al /stə'tɪstɪkl/ a statistico. **~s** n & pl statistica f

statue /'stætʃuː/ n statua f

stature /'stætʃə(r)/ n statura f

status /'steɪtəs/ n condizione f; (high rank) alto rango m. **~ symbol** n status symbol m inv

statut|e /'stætjuːt/ n statuto m. **~ory** a statutario

staunch /stɔːntʃ/ a fedele. **~ly** adv fedelmente

stave /steɪv/ vt **~ off** tenere lontano

stay /steɪ/ n soggiorno m ● vi restare, rimanere; (reside) alloggiare; **~ the night** passare la notte; **~ put** non muoversi ● vt **~ the course** resistere fino alla fine. **stay away** vi stare lontano. **stay behind** vi non andare con gli altri. **stay in** vi (at home) stare in casa; Sch restare a scuola dopo le lezioni. **stay up** vi stare su; (person:) stare alzato

stead /sted/ n **in his ~** in sua vece; **stand sb in good ~** tornare utile a qcno. **~fast** a fedele; (refusal) fermo

steadily /'stedɪlɪ/ adv (continually) continuamente

steady /'stedɪ/ a (-ier, -iest) saldo, fermo; (breathing) regolare; (job, boyfriend) fisso; (dependable) serio

steak /steɪk/ n (for stew) spezzatino m; (for grilling, frying) bistecca f

steal /stiːl/ v (pt **stole**, pp **stolen**) ● vt rubare (from da). **steal in/out** vi entrare/uscire furtivamente

stealth /stelθ/ n **by ~** di nascosto. **~y** a furtivo

steam /stiːm/ n vapore m; **under one's own ~** fam da solo ● vt Culin cucinare a vapore ● vi fumare. **steam up** vi appannarsi

'**steam-engine** n locomotiva f

steamer /'stiːmə(r)/ n piroscafo m; (saucepan) pentola f a vapore

'**steamroller** n rullo m compressore

steamy /'stiːmɪ/ a appannato

steel /stiːl/ n acciaio m ● vt **~ oneself** temprarsi

steep¹ /stiːp/ vt (soak) lasciare a bagno

steep² a ripido; (fam: price) esorbitante. **~ly** adv ripidamente

steeple /'stiːpl/ n campanile m. **~chase** n corsa f ippica a ostacoli

steer /stɪə(r)/ vt/i guidare; **~ clear of** stare alla larga da. **~ing** n Auto sterzo m. **~ing-wheel** n volante m

stem¹ /stem/ n stelo m; (of glass) gambo m; (of word) radice f ● vi (pt/pp **stemmed**) **~ from** derivare da

stem² vt (pt/pp **stemmed**) contenere

stench /stentʃ/ n fetore m

step /step/ n passo m; (stair) gradino m; **~s** pl (ladder) scala f portatile; **in ~** al passo; **be out of ~** non stare al passo; **~ by ~** un passo alla volta ● vi (pt/pp **stepped**) **~ into** entrare in; **~ out of** uscire da; **~ out of line** sgarrare. **step down** vi fig dimettersi. **step forward** vi farsi avanti. **step in** vi fig intervenire. **step up** vt (increase) aumentare

step: **~brother** n fratellastro m. **~child** n figliastro, -a mf. **~daughter** n figliastra f. **~father** n patrigno m. **~ladder** n scala f portatile. **~mother** n matrigna f

'**stepping-stone** n pietra f per guadare; fig trampolino m

step: **~sister** n sorellastra f. **~son** n figliastro m

stereo /'sterɪəʊ/ n stereo m; in

in stereofonia. **~phonic** /-'fɒnɪk/ a stereofonico

stereotype /'sterɪətaɪp/ n stereotipo m. **~d** a stereotipato

steril|e /'steraɪl/ a sterile. **~ity** /stə'rɪlətɪ/ n sterilità f inv

steriliz|ation /sterəlaɪ'zeɪʃn/ n sterilizzazione f. **~e** /'ster-/ vt sterilizzare

sterling /'stɜːlɪŋ/ a fig apprezzabile; **~ silver** argento m pregiato ●n sterlina f

stern[1] /stɜːn/ a severo

stern[2] n (of boat) poppa f

stethoscope /'steθəskəʊp/ n stetoscopio m

stew /stjuː/ n stufato m; **in a ~** fam agitato ●vt/i cuocere in umido; **~ed fruit** frutta f cotta

steward /'stjuːəd/ n (at meeting) organizzatore, -trice mf; (on ship, aicraft) steward m inv. **~ess** f inv hostess f inv

stick[1] /stɪk/ n bastone m; (of celery, rhubarb) gambo m; Sport mazza f

stick[2] v (pt/pp stuck) ●vt (stab) [con]ficcare; (glue) attaccare; (fam: put) mettere; (fam: endure) sopportare ●vi (adhere) attaccarsi (to a); (jam) bloccarsi; **~ to** attenersi a ⟨facts⟩; mantenere ⟨story⟩; perseverare in ⟨task⟩; **~ at it** tener duro; **~ at nothing** fam non fermarsi di fronte a niente; **be stuck** ⟨vehicle, person:⟩ essere bloccato; ⟨drawer:⟩ essere incastrato; **be stuck with sth** fam farsi incastrare con qcsa. **stick out** vi (project) sporgere; (fam: catch the eye) risaltare ●vt fam fare ⟨tongue⟩. **stick up for** vt fam difendere

sticker /'stɪkə(r)/ n autoadesivo m

'sticking plaster n cerotto m

stick-in-the-mud n retrogrado m

stickler /'stɪklə(r)/ n **be a ~ for** tenere molto a

sticky /'stɪkɪ/ a (-ier, -iest) appiccicoso; ⟨adhesive⟩ adesivo; ⟨fig: difficult⟩ difficile

stiff /stɪf/ a rigido; ⟨brush, task⟩

duro; ⟨person⟩ controllato; ⟨drink⟩ forte; ⟨penalty⟩ severo; ⟨price⟩ alto; **bored ~** fam annoiato a morte. **~ neck** torcicollo m. **~en** vt irrigidire ●vi irrigidirsi. **~ness** n rigidità f inv

stifl|e /'staɪfl/ vt soffocare. **~ing** a soffocante

stigma /'stɪgmə/ n marchio m

stiletto /strʲ'letəʊ/ n stiletto m; **~ heels** tacchi mpl a spillo; **~s** ⟨shoes⟩ scarpe fpl coi tacchi a spillo

still[1] /stɪl/ n distilleria f

still[2] a fermo; ⟨drink⟩ non gasato; **keep/stand ~** stare fermo ●n quiete f; ⟨photo⟩ posa f ●adv ancora; ⟨nevertheless⟩ nondimeno, comunque; **I'm ~ not sure** non sono ancora sicuro

'stillborn a nato morto

still 'life n natura f morta

stilted /'stɪltɪd/ a artificioso

stilts /stɪlts/ npl trampoli mpl

stimulant /'stɪmjʊlənt/ n eccitante m

stimulat|e /'stɪmjʊleɪt/ vt stimolare. **~ion** /-'leɪʃn/ n stimolo m

stimulus /'stɪmjʊləs/ n (pl -li /-laɪ/) stimolo m

sting /stɪŋ/ n puntura f; ⟨from nettle, jellyfish⟩ sostanza f irritante; ⟨organ⟩ pungiglione m ●v (pt/pp stung) ●vt pungere; ⟨jellyfish:⟩ pizzicare ●vi ⟨insect:⟩ pungere. **~ing nettle** n ortica f

stingy /'stɪndʒɪ/ a (-ier, -iest) tirchio

stink /stɪŋk/ n puzza f ●vi (pt stank, pp stunk) puzzare

stint /stɪnt/ n lavoro m; **do one's ~** fare la propria parte ●vi **~ on** lesinare su

stipulat|e /'stɪpjʊleɪt/ vt porre come condizione. **~ion** /-'leɪʃn/ n condizione f

stir /stɜː(r)/ n mescolata f; ⟨commotion⟩ trambusto m ●v (pt/pp stirred) ●vt muovere; ⟨mix⟩ mescolare ●vi muoversi

stirrup /'stɪrəp/ n staffa f

stitch /stɪtʃ/ n punto m; (in knitting) maglia f; (pain) fitta f; **have sb in ~es** fam far ridere qcno a crepapelle ● vt cucire

stock /stɒk/ n (for use or selling) scorta f, stock m inv; (livestock) bestiame m; (lineage) stirpe f; Fin titoli mpl; Culin brodo m; **in ~** disponibile; **out of ~** esaurito; **take ~** fig fare il punto ● a (product, size) standard; (fig: reply) consueto ● vt (shop): vendere; approvvigionare (shelves). **stock up** vi far scorta (with di)

stock: **~broker** n agente m di cambio. **~ cube** n dado m [da brodo]. **S~ Exchange** n Borsa f Valori

stocking /stɒkɪŋ/ n calza f

stockist /stɒkɪst/ n rivenditore m

stock: **~market** n mercato m azionario. **~pile** vt fare scorta di ● n riserva f. **~'still** a immobile. **~taking** n Comm inventario m

stocky /stɒkɪ/ a (-ier, -iest) tarchiato

stodgy /stɒdʒɪ/ a indigesto

stoic /stəʊɪk/ n stoico, -a m f. **~al** a stoico. **~ism** /-ɪsɪzm/ stoicismo m

stoke /stəʊk/ vt alimentare

stole[1] /stəʊl/ n stola f

stole[2], **stolen** /stəʊln/ see **steal**

stolid /stɒlɪd/ a apatico

stomach /stʌmək/ n pancia f; Anat stomaco m ● vt fam reggere. **~ache** n mal m di pancia

stone /stəʊn/ n pietra f; (in fruit) nocciolo m; Med calcolo m; (weight) 6.348 kg ● a di pietra; (wall, Age) della pietra ● vt snocciolare (fruit). **~cold** a gelido. **~'deaf** a fam sordo come una campana

stony /stəʊnɪ/ a pietroso; (glare) glaciale

stood /stʊd/ see **stand**

stool /stuːl/ n sgabello m

stoop /stuːp/ n curvatura f ● vi stare curvo; (bend down) chinarsi; fig abbassarsi

stop /stɒp/ n (break) sosta f; (for bus, train) fermata f; Gram punto m; **come to a ~** fermarsi; **put a ~**

to sth mettere fine a qcsa ● v (pt/pp **stopped**) ● vt fermare; arrestare (machine); (prevent) impedire; **~ sb doing sth** impedire a qcno di fare qcsa; **~ doing sth** smettere di fare qcsa; **~ that!** smettila! ● vi fermarsi; (rain:) smettere ● int fermo!. **stop off** vi fare una sosta. **stop up** vt otturare (sink); tappare (hole). **stop with** vi (fam: stay with) fermarsi da

stop: **~gap** n palliativo m; (person) tappabuchi m inv. **~over** n sosta f; Aeron scalo m

stoppage /stɒpɪdʒ/ n ostruzione f; (strike) interruzione f; (deduction) trattenuta fpl

stopper /stɒpə(r)/ n tappo m

stop: **~press** n ultimissime fpl. **~watch** n cronometro m

storage /stɔːrɪdʒ/ n deposito m; (in warehouse) immagazzinaggio m; Comput memoria f

store /stɔː(r)/ n (stock) riserva f; (shop) grande magazzino m; (depot) deposito m; **in ~** in deposito; **what the future has in ~ for me** cosa mi riserva il futuro; **set great ~ by** tenere in gran conto ● vt tenere; (in warehouse, Comput) immagazzinare. **~room** n magazzino m

storey /stɔːrɪ/ n piano m

stork /stɔːk/ n cicogna f

storm /stɔːm/ n temporale m; (with thunder) tempesta f ● vt prendere d'assalto. **~y** a tempestoso

story /stɔːrɪ/ n storia f; (in newspaper) articolo m

stout /staʊt/ a (shoes) resistente; (fat) robusto; (defence) strenuo

stove /stəʊv/ n stufa f; (for cooking) cucina f [economica]

stow /stəʊ/ vt mettere via. **~away** n passeggero, -a m f clandestino, -a

straddle /strædl/ vt stare a cavalcioni su; (standing) essere a cavallo su

straggle /strægl/ vi crescere disordinatamente; (dawdle) rimanere indietro. **~er** *n* persona *f* che rimane indietro. **~y** *a* in disordine

straight /streɪt/ *a* diritto, dritto; ⟨answer, question, person⟩ diretto; ⟨tidy⟩ in ordine; ⟨drink, hair⟩ liscio ● *adv* diritto, dritto; ⟨directly⟩ direttamente; **~ away** immediatamente; **~ on** *or* **ahead** diritto; **~ out** *fig* apertamente; **go ~** *fam* rigare diritto; **put sth ~** mettere qcsa in ordine; **sit/stand up ~** stare diritto

straighten /'streɪtn/ *vt* raddrizzare ● *vi* raddrizzarsi; **~ up** ⟨person⟩ mettersi diritto. **~ out** *vt fig* chiarire ⟨situation⟩

straight'forward *a* franco; ⟨simple⟩ semplice

strain¹ /streɪn/ *n* ⟨streak⟩ vena *f*; *Bot* varietà *f inv*; ⟨of virus⟩ forma *f*

strain² *n* tensione *f*; ⟨injury⟩ stiramento *m*; **~s** *pl* ⟨of music⟩ note *fpl* ● *vt* tirare; sforzare ⟨eyes, voice⟩; stirarsi ⟨muscle⟩; *Culin* scolare ● *vi* sforzarsi. **~ed** *a* ⟨relations⟩ teso. **~er** *n* colino *m*

strait /streɪt/ *n* stretto *m*; **in dire ~s** in serie difficoltà. **~jacket** *n* camicia *f* di forza. **~-laced** *a* puritano

strand¹ /strænd/ *n* ⟨of thread⟩ gugliata *f*; ⟨of beads⟩ filo *m*; ⟨of hair⟩ capello *m*

strand² *vt* **be ~ed** rimanere bloccato

strange /streɪndʒ/ *a* strano; ⟨not known⟩ sconosciuto; ⟨unaccustomed⟩ estraneo. **~ly** *adv* stranamente; **~ly enough** curiosamente. **~r** *n* estraneo, -a *mf*

strangle /'stræŋgl/ *vt* strangolare; *fig* reprimere

strangulation /stræŋgjʊ'leɪʃn/ *n* strangolamento *m*

strap /stræp/ *n* cinghia *f* ⟨to grasp in vehicle⟩ maniglia *f*; ⟨of watch⟩ cinturino *m*; ⟨shoulder -⟩ bretella *f*, spallina *f* ● *vt* ⟨pt/pp **strapped**⟩ legare; **~ in** *or* **down** assicurare

strapping /'stræpɪŋ/ *a* robusto

strata /'strɑːtə/ *npl see* **stratum**

stratagem /'strætədʒəm/ *n* stratagemma *m*

strategic /strə'tiːdʒɪk/ *a* strategico

strategy /'strætədʒɪ/ *n* strategia *f*

stratum /'strɑːtəm/ *n* ⟨pl **strata**⟩ strato *m*

straw /strɔː/ *n* paglia *f*; ⟨single piece⟩ fuscello *m*; ⟨for drinking⟩ cannuccia *f*; **the last ~** l'ultima goccia

strawberry /'strɔːbərɪ/ *n* fragola *f*

stray /streɪ/ *a* ⟨animal⟩ randagio ● *n* randagio *m* ● *vi* andarsene per conto proprio; ⟨deviate⟩ deviare ⟨from⟩ da

streak /striːk/ *n* striatura *f*; ⟨fig: trait⟩ vena *f* ● *vi* sfrecciare. **~y** *a* striato; ⟨bacon⟩ grasso

stream /striːm/ *n* ruscello *m*; ⟨current⟩ corrente *f*; ⟨of blood, people⟩ flusso *m*; *Sch* classe *f* ● *vi* scorrere. **stream in/out** *vi* entrare/uscire a fiotti

streamer /'striːmə(r)/ *n* ⟨paper⟩ stella *f* filante; ⟨flag⟩ pennone *m*

'streamline *vt* rendere aerodinamico; ⟨simplify⟩ snellire. **~d** *a* aerodinamico

street /striːt/ *n* strada *f*. **~car** *n* *Am* tram *m inv*. **~lamp** *n* lampione *m*

strength /streŋθ/ *n* forza *f*; ⟨of wall, bridge etc⟩ solidità *f inv*; **~s** punti *mpl* forti; **on the ~ of** grazie a. **~en** *vt* rinforzare

strenuous /'strenjʊəs/ *a* faticoso; ⟨attempt, denial⟩ energico

stress /stres/ *n* ⟨emphasis⟩ insistenza *f*; *Gram* accento *m* tonico; ⟨mental⟩ stress *m inv*; *Mech* spinta *f* ● *vt* ⟨emphasize⟩ insistere su; *Gram* mettere l'accento [tonico] su. **~ed** *a* ⟨mentally⟩ stressato. **~ful** *a* stressante

stretch /stretʃ/ *n* stiramento *m*; ⟨period⟩ periodo *m* di tempo; ⟨of road⟩ estensione *f*; ⟨elasticity⟩ elasticità *f inv*; **at a ~** di fila; **have a ~** stirarsi ● *vt* tirare; allargare ⟨shoes, arms etc⟩; ⟨person:⟩ allungare ● *vi* (*become wider*) allargarsi; (*extend*) estendersi; (*person:*) stirarsi. **~er** *n* barella *f*

strew /stru:/ *vt* (*pp* **strewn** *o* **strewed**) sparpagliare

stricken /'strɪkn/ *a* prostrato; **~ with** affetto da (*illness*)

strict /strɪkt/ *a* severo; (*precise*) preciso. **~ly** *adv* severamente; **~ly speaking** in senso stretto

stride /straɪd/ *n* [lungo] passo *m*; **take sth in one's ~** accettare qcsa con facilità ● *vi* (*pt* **strode**, *pp* **stridden**) andare a gran passi

strident /'straɪdnt/ *a* stridente; (*colour*) vistoso

strife /straɪf/ *n* conflitto *m*

strike /straɪk/ *n* sciopero *m*; *Mil* attacco *m*; **on ~** in sciopero ● *v* (*pt/pp* **struck**) ● *vt* colpire; accendere (*match*); trovare (*oil, gold*); (*delete*) depennare; (*occur to*) venire in mente a; *Mil* attaccare ● *vi* (*lightning*:) cadere; (*clock*:) suonare; *Mil* attaccare; (*workers*:) scioperare. **~ lucky** azzeccarla. **strike off, strike out** *vt* eliminare. **strike up** *vt* fare (*friendship*); attaccare (*conversation*). **~-breaker** *n* persona *f* che non aderisce a uno sciopero

striker /'straɪkə(r)/ *n* scioperante *mf*

striking /'straɪkɪŋ/ *a* impressionante; (*attractive*) affascinante

string /strɪŋ/ *n* spago *m*; (*of musical instrument, racket*) corda *f*; (*of pearls*) filo *m*; (*of lies*) serie *f*; **the ~s** *Mus* gli archi; **pull ~s** *fam* usare le proprie conoscenze ● *vt* (*pt/pp* **strung**) (*thread*) infilare (*beads*). **~ed** *a* (*instrument*) a corda

stringent /'strɪndʒnt/ *a* rigido

strip /strɪp/ *n* striscia *f* ● *v* (*pt/pp* **stripped**) ● *vt* spogliare; togliere le lenzuola da (*bed*); scrostare (*wood, furniture*); smontare (*machine*); (*deprive*) privare (**of** di) ● *vi* (*undress*) spogliarsi. **~ car-**

toon *n* striscia *f*. **~ club** *n* locale *m* di strip-tease

stripe /straɪp/ *n* striscia *f*; *Mil* gallone *m*. **~d** *a* a strisce

'striplight *n* tubo *m* al neon

stripper /'strɪpə(r)/ *n* spogliarellista *mf*; (*solvent*) sverniciatore *m*

strip-'tease *n* spogliarello *m*, strip-tease *m inv*

strive /straɪv/ *vi* (*pt* **strove**, *pp* **striven**) sforzarsi (**to** di); **~ for** sforzarsi di ottenere

strode /strəʊd/ *see* **stride**

stroke[1] /strəʊk/ *n* colpo *m*; (*of pen*) tratto *m*; (*in swimming*) bracciata *f*; *Med* ictus *m inv*; **~ of luck** colpo *m* di fortuna; **put sb off his ~** far perdere il filo a qcno

stroke[2] *vt* accarezzare

stroll /strəʊl/ *n* passeggiata *f* ● *vi* passeggiare. **~er** *n* (*Am*: *push-chair*) passeggino *m*

strong /strɒŋ/ *a* (**-er** /-gə/, **-est** /-gɪst/) forte; (*argument*) valido

strong: **~-box** *n* cassaforte *f*. **~-hold** *n* roccaforte *f*. **~ly** *adv* fortemente. **~-'minded** *a* risoluto. **~-room** *n* camera *f* blindata

stroppy /'strɒpɪ/ *a* scorbutico

strove /strəʊv/ *see* **strive**

struck /strʌk/ *see* **strike**

structural /'strʌktʃərəl/ *a* strutturale. **~ly** *adv* strutturalmente

structure /'strʌktʃə(r)/ *n* struttura *f*

struggle /'strʌgl/ *n* lotta *f*; **with a ~** a lottare con ● *vi* lottare; **~ for breath** respirare con fatica; **~ to do sth** fare fatica a fare qcsa; **~ to one's feet** alzarsi con fatica

strum /strʌm/ *vt/i* (*pt/pp* **strummed**) strimpellare

strung /strʌŋ/ *see* **string**

strut[1] /strʌt/ *n* (*component*) puntello *m*

strut[2] *vi* (*pt/pp* **strutted**) camminare impettito

stub /stʌb/ *n* mozzicone *m*; (*counterfoil*) matrice *f* ● *vt* (*pt/pp* **stubbed**) **~ one's toe** sbattere il dito del piede (**on** contro). **stub out** *vt* spegnere *⟨cigarette⟩*

stubble /'stʌbl/ *n* barba *f* ispida. **~ly** *a* ispido

stubborn /'stʌbən/ *a* testardo; *⟨refusal⟩* ostinato

stubby /'stʌbɪ/ *a* (-ier, -iest) tozzo

stucco /'stʌkəʊ/ *n* stucco *m*

stuck /stʌk/ *see* **stick**? **~-'up** *a fam* snob

stud[1] /stʌd/ *n* (**on** boot) tacchetto *m*; (**on** jacket) borchia *f*; (**for** ear) orecchino *m* [a bottone]

stud[2] *n* (**of** horses) scuderia *f*

student /'stju:dənt/ *n* studente *m*, studentessa *f*; *⟨school child⟩* scolaro, -a *mf*. **~ nurse** *n* studente, studentessa infermiere, -a

studied /'stʌdɪd/ *a* intenzionale; *⟨politeness⟩* studiato

studio /'stju:dɪəʊ/ *n* studio *m*

studious /'stju:dɪəs/ *a* studioso; *⟨attention⟩* studiato

study /'stʌdɪ/ *n* studio *m* ● *vt/i* (*pt/pp* **studied**) studiare

stuff /stʌf/ *n* materiale *m*; (fam: things) roba *f* ● *vt* riempire; (with padding) imbottire; *Culin* farcire; **~ sth into a drawer/one's pocket** ficcare qcsa alla rinfusa in un cassetto/in tasca. **~ing** *n* (padding) imbottitura *f*; *Culin* ripieno *m*

stuffy /'stʌfɪ/ *a* (-ier, -iest) che sa di chiuso; *⟨old-fashioned⟩* antiquato

stumble /'stʌmbl/ *vi* inciampare; **~e across** *or* **on** imbattersi in. **~ing-block** *n* ostacolo *m*

stump /stʌmp/ *n* ceppo *m*; (**of** limb) moncone *m*. **~ed** *a fam* perplesso ● **stump up** *vt/i fam* sganciare

stun /stʌn/ *vt* (*pt/pp* **stunned**) stordire; *⟨astonish⟩* sbalordire

stung /stʌŋ/ *see* **sting**

stunk /stʌŋk/ *see* **stink**

stunning /'stʌnɪŋ/ *a fam* favoloso; *⟨blow, victory⟩* sbalorditivo

stunt[1] /stʌnt/ *n fam* trovata *f* pubblicitaria

stunt[2] *vt* arrestare lo sviluppo di. **~ed** *a* stentato

stupendous /stju:'pendəs/ *a* stupendo. **~ly** *adv* stupendamente

stupid /'stju:pɪd/ *a* stupido. **~ity** /-'pɪdətɪ/ *n* stupidità *f*. **~ly** *adv* stupidamente

stupor /'stju:pə(r)/ *n* torpore *m*

sturdy /'stɜ:dɪ/ *a* (-ier, -iest) robusto; *⟨furniture⟩* solido

stutter /'stʌtə(r)/ *n* balbuzie *f* ● *vt/i* balbettare

sty, stye /staɪ/ *n* (*pl* **styes**) *Med* orzaiolo *m*

style /staɪl/ *n* stile *m*; *⟨fashion⟩* moda *f*; (sort) tipo *m*; (hair~) pettinatura *f*; **in ~** in grande stile

stylish /'staɪlɪʃ/ *a* elegante. **~ly** *adv* con eleganza

stylist /'staɪlɪst/ *n* stilista *mf*; (hair~) parrucchiere, -a *mf*. **~ic** /-'lɪstɪk/ *a* stilistico

stylized /'staɪlaɪzd/ *a* stilizzato

stylus /'staɪləs/ *n* (**on** record player) puntina *f*

suave /swɑ:v/ *a* dai modi garbati

sub'conscious /sʌb-/ *a* subcosciente ● *n* subcosciente *m*. **~ly** *adv* in modo inconscio

subcon'tract *vt* subappaltare (**to** a). **~or** *n* subappaltatore *m*

'subdivide *vt* suddividere. **~sion** *n* suddivisione *f*

subdue /səb'dju:/ *vt* sottomettere; *⟨make quieter⟩* attenuare. **~d** *a* *⟨light⟩* attenuato; *⟨person, voice⟩* pacato

subhuman /sʌb'hju:mən/ *a* disumano

subject[1] /'sʌbdʒɪkt/ *a* **~ to** soggetto a; *⟨depending on⟩* subordinato a; **~ to availability** nei limiti della disponibilità ● *n* soggetto *m*; (**of** ruler) suddito, -a *mf*; *Sch* materia *f*

subject[2] /səb'dʒekt/ *vt* *⟨to attack, abuse⟩* sottoporre; assoggettare *⟨country⟩*

subjective /səb'dʒektɪv/ *a* soggettivo. **~ly** *adv* soggettivamente

subjugate /'sʌbdʒʊgeɪt/ *vt* soggiogare

subjunctive /səb'dʒʌŋktɪv/ *a & n* congiuntivo *m*

sub'let *vt* (*pt/pp* -let) subaffittare

sublime /sə'blaɪm/ *a* sublime. ~**ly** *adv* sublimemente

subliminal /sʌb'lɪmɪnl/ *a* subliminale

sub-ma'chine-gun *n* mitraglietta *f*

subma'rine *n* sommergibile *m*

submerge /səb'mɜːdʒ/ *vt* immergere; **be** ~**d** essere sommerso ● *vi* immergersi

submiss|ion /səb'mɪʃn/ *n* sottomissione *f*. ~**ive** /-sɪv/ *a* sottomesso

submit /səb'mɪt/ *v* (*pt/pp* -mitted, *pres p* -mitting) ● *vt* sottoporre ● *vi* sottomettersi

subordinate /sə'bɔːdɪnət/ *a* subordinato (**to** a)

subscribe /səb'skraɪb/ *vi* contribuire; ~ **to** abbonarsi a (*newspaper*); sottoscrivere (*fund*); *fig* aderire a. ~**r** *n* abbonato, -a *mf*

subscription /səb'skrɪpʃn/ *n* (**to** *club*) sottoscrizione *f*; (*to newspaper*) abbonamento *m*

subsequent /'sʌbsɪkwənt/ *a* susseguente. ~**ly** *adv* in seguito

subservient /səb'sɜːvɪənt/ *a* subordinato; (*servile*) servile. ~**ly** *adv* servilmente

subside /səb'saɪd/ *vi* sprofondare; (*ground:*) avvallarsi; (*storm:*) placarsi

subsidiary /səb'sɪdɪərɪ/ *a* secondario ● *n* **[company]** filiale *f*

subsid|ize /'sʌbsɪdaɪz/ *vt* sovvenzionare. ~**y** *n* sovvenzione *f*

subsist /səb'sɪst/ *vi* vivere (**on** di). ~**ence** *n* sussistenza *f*

substance /'sʌbstəns/ *n* sostanza *f*

sub'standard *a* di qualità inferiore

substantial /səb'stænʃl/ *a* solido; (*meal*) sostanzioso; (*considerable*) notevole. ~**ly** *adv* notevolmente; (*essentially*) sostanzialmente

substantiate /səb'stænʃɪeɪt/ *vt* comprovare

substitut|e /'sʌbstɪtjuːt/ *n* sostituto ● *vt* ~**e A for B** sostituire B con A ● *vi* ~ **for sb** sostituire qcno. ~**ion** /-'tjuːʃn/ *n* sostituzione *f*

subterranean /sʌbtə'reɪnɪən/ *a* sotterraneo

'subtitle *n* sottotitolo *m*

subt|le /'sʌtl/ *a* sottile; (*taste, perfume*) delicato. ~**tlety** *n* sottigliezza *f*. ~**tly** *adv* sottilmente

subtract /səb'trækt/ *vt* sottrarre. ~**ion** /-ækʃn/ *n* sottrazione *f*

suburb /'sʌbɜːb/ *n* sobborgo *m*; **in the** ~**s** in periferia. ~**an** /sə'bɜːbən/ *a* suburbano. ~**ia** /sə'bɜːbɪə/ *n* i sobborghi *mpl*

subversive /səb'vɜːsɪv/ *a* sovversivo

'subway *n* sottopassaggio *m*; (*Am: railway*) metropolitana *f*

succeed /sək'siːd/ *vi* riuscire; (*follow*) succedere a; ~ **in doing** riuscire a fare ● *vt* succedere a (*king*). ~**ing** *a* successivo

success /sək'ses/ *n* successo *m*; **be a** ~ (*in life*) aver successo. ~**ful** *a* di successo; (*businessman, artist etc*) di successo. ~**fully** *adv* con successo

succession /sək'seʃn/ *n* successione *f*; **in** ~ di seguito

successive /sək'sesɪv/ *a* successivo. ~**ly** *adv* successivamente

successor /sək'sesə(r)/ *n* successore *m*

succinct /sək'sɪŋkt/ *a* succinto

succulent /'sʌkjʊlənt/ *a* succulento

succumb /sə'kʌm/ *vi* soccombere (**to** a)

such /sʌtʃ/ *a* tale; ~ **a** book un libro di questo genere; ~ **a thing** una cosa di questo genere; ~ **a long time ago** talmente tanto tempo fa; **there is no** ~ **thing** non esiste una cosa così; **there is no** ~ **person** non esiste una persona così ● *pron* **as** ~ come tale; ~ **as** chi; **and** ~ e simili; **as it is** così com'è. ~**like** *pron fam* di tal genere

suck /ʃʌk/ *n* succhiare. **suck up** *vt* assorbire. **suck up to** *vt fam* fare il lecchino con

sucker /ʃʌkə(r)/ *n Bot* pollone *m*; (*fam: person*) credulone, -a *mf*

suction /ˈsʌkʃn/ *n* aspirazione *f*

sudden /ˈsʌdn/ *a* improvviso ● **n all of a ~** all'improvviso. ~**ly** *adv* improvvisamente

sue /su:/ *vt* (*pres p* **suing**) fare causa a (**for** per) ● *vi* fare causa

suede /sweɪd/ *n* pelle *f* scamosciata

suet /ˈsu:ɪt/ *n* grasso *m* di rognone

suffer /ˈsʌfə(r)/ *vi* soffrire (**from** per) ● *vt* soffrire; subire (*loss etc*); (*tolerate*) subire. ~**ing** *n* sofferenza *f*

suffice /səˈfaɪs/ *vi* bastare

sufficient /səˈfɪʃnt/ *a* sufficiente. ~**ly** *adv* sufficientemente

suffix /ˈsʌfɪks/ *n* suffisso *m*

suffocat|e /ˈsʌfəkeɪt/ *vt/i* soffocare. ~**ion** /-ˈkeɪʃn/ *n* soffocamento *m*

sugar /ˈʃʊgə(r)/ *n* zucchero *m* ● *vt* zuccherare. ~ **basin**, ~**bowl** *n* zuccheriera *f*. ~**y** *a* zuccheroso; *fig* sdolcinato

suggest /səˈdʒest/ *vt* suggerire; (*indicate, insinuate*) fare pensare a. ~**ion** /-estʃən/ *n* suggerimento *m*; (*trace*) traccia *f*. ~**ive** /-ɪv/ *a* allusivo. ~**ively** *adv* in modo allusivo

suicidal /su:ɪˈsaɪdl/ *a* suicida

suicide /ˈsu:ɪsaɪd/ *n* suicidio *m*; (*person*) suicida *mf*; **commit** ~ suicidarsi

suit /su:t/ *n* vestito *m*; (*woman's*) tailleur *m inv*; (*in cards*) seme *m*; *Jur* causa *f*; **follow** ~ *fig* fare lo stesso ● *vt* andar bene a; (*adapt*) adattare (**to** a); (*be convenient for*) andare bene per; **be** ~**ed to** or **for** essere adatto a; ~ **yourself!** fa' come vuoi!

suitab|le /ˈsu:təbl/ *a* adatto. ~**y** *adv* convenientemente

'suitcase *n* valigia *f*

suite /swi:t/ *n* suite *f inv*; (*of furniture*) divano *m* e poltrone *fpl* assortiti

sulk /sʌlk/ *vi* fare il broncio. ~**y** *a* imbronciato

sullen /ˈsʌlən/ *a* svogliato

sulphur /ˈsʌlfə(r)/ *n* zolfo *m*. ~**ic** /-ˈfjʊːrɪk/ *a* ~**ic acid** *n* acido *m* solforico

sultana /sʌlˈtɑːnə/ *n* uva *f* sultanina

sultry /ˈsʌltrɪ/ *a* (**-ier, -iest**) (*weather*) afoso; *fig* sensuale

sum /sʌm/ *n* somma *f*; *Sch* addizione *f* ● **sum up** (*pt/pp* **summed**) *vi* riassumere ● *vt* valutare

summar|ize /ˈsʌməraɪz/ *vt* riassumere. ~**y** *n* sommario *m* ● *a* sommario; (*dismissal*) sbrigativo

summer /ˈsʌmə(r)/ *n* estate *f*. ~**house** *n* padiglione *m*. ~**time** *n* (*season*) estate *f*

summery /ˈsʌmərɪ/ *a* estivo

summit /ˈsʌmɪt/ *n* cima *f*. ~ **conference** *n* vertice *m*

summon /ˈsʌmən/ *vt* convocare; *Jur* citare. **summon up** *vt* raccogliere (*strength*); rievocare (*memory*)

summons /ˈsʌmənz/ *n Jur* citazione *f* ● *vt* citare in giudizio

sump /sʌmp/ *n Auto* coppa *f* dell'olio

sumptuous /ˈsʌmptjʊəs/ *a* sontuoso. ~**ly** *adv* sontuosamente

sun /sʌn/ *n* sole *m* ● *vt* (*pt/pp* **sunned**) ~ **oneself** prendere il sole

sun: ~**bathe** *vi* prendere il sole. ~**bed** *n* lettino *m* solare. ~**burn** *n* scottatura *f* (*solare*). ~**burnt** *a* scottato (*dal sole*)

sundae /ˈsʌndeɪ/ *n* gelato *m* guarnito

Sunday /ˈsʌndeɪ/ *n* domenica *f*

'sundial *n* meridiana *f*

sundry /ˈsʌndrɪ/ *a* svariati; **all and ~** tutti quanti

'sunflower *n* girasole *m*

sung /sʌŋ/ *see* **sing**

'sun-glasses *npl* occhiali *mpl* da sole

sunk /sʌŋk/ *see* sink

sunken /'sʌŋkn/ *a* incavato

'sunlight *n* luce *f* del] sole *m*

sunny /'sʌnɪ/ *a* (**-ier**, **-iest**) assolato

sun: ~**rise** *n* alba *f.* ~**roof** *n* Auto tettuccio *m* apribile. ~**set** *n* tramonto *m.* ~**shade** *n* parasole *m.* ~**shine** *n* [luce *f* del] sole *m.* ~**stroke** *n* insolazione *f.* ~**tan** *n* abbronzatura *f.* ~**tanned** *a* abbronzato. ~**tan oil** *n* olio *m* solare

super /'suːpə(r)/ *a fam* fantastico

superb /suː'pɜːb/ *a* splendido

supercilious /suːpə'sɪlɪəs/ *a* altezzoso

superficial /suːpə'fɪʃl/ *a* superficiale. ~**ly** *adv* superficialmente

superfluous /suː'pɜːfluəs/ *a* superfluo

super'human *a* sovrumano

superintendent /suːpərɪn'tendənt/ *n* (*of police*) commissario *m* di polizia

superior /suː'pɪərɪə(r)/ *a* superiore ● *n* superiore, -a *mf.* ~**ity** /-'ɒrətɪ/ *n* superiorità *f*

superlative /suː'pɜːlətɪv/ *a* eccellente ● *n* superlativo *m*

'superman *n* superuomo *m*

'supermarket *n* supermercato *m*

'supermodel *n* top model *f inv*

super'natural *a* soprannaturale

'superpower *n* superpotenza *f*

supersede /suːpə'siːd/ *vt* rimpiazzare

super'sonic *a* supersonico

superstiti|on /suːpə'stɪʃn/ *n* superstizione *f.* ~**ous** /-'stɪʃəs/ *a* superstizioso

supervis|e /'suːpəvaɪz/ *vt* supervisionare. ~**ion** /-'vɪʒn/ *n* supervisione *f.* ~**or** *n* supervisore *m*

supper /'sʌpə(r)/ *n* cena *f*

supple /'sʌpl/ *a* slogato

supplement /'sʌplɪmənt/ *n* supplemento *m* ● *vt* integrare. ~**ary** /-'mentərɪ/ *a* supplementare

supplier /sə'plaɪə(r)/ *n* fornitore, -trice *mf*

supply /sə'plaɪ/ *n* fornitura *f;* (*in economics*) offerta *f;* **supplies** *pl* Mil approvvigionamenti *mpl* ● *vt* (*pt/pp* **-ied**) fornire; ~ **sb with sth** fornire qcsa a qcno

support /sə'pɔːt/ *n* sostegno *m;* (*base*) supporto *m;* (*keep*) sostentamento *m* ● *vt* sostenere; mantenere (*family*); (*give money to*) mantenere finanziariamente; Sport fare il tifo per. ~**er** *n* sostenitore, -trice *mf;* Sport tifoso, -a *mf.* ~**ive** /-ɪv/ *a* incoraggiante

suppose /sə'pəuz/ *vt* (*presume*) supporre; (*imagine*) pensare; **be ~d to** dover fare; **not be ~d to** *fam* non avere il permesso di; **I ~ so** suppongo di sì. ~**dly** /-ɪdlɪ/ *adv* presumibilmente

suppress /sə'pres/ *vt* sopprimere. ~**ion** /-eʃn/ *n* soppressione *f*

supremacy /suː'preməsɪ/ *n* supremazia *f*

supreme /suː'priːm/ *a* supremo

surcharge /'sɜːtʃɑːdʒ/ *n* supplemento *m*

sure /ʃuə(r)/ *a* sicuro, certo; **make ~** accertarsi; **be ~ to do it** mi raccomando di farlo ● *adv* Am *fam* certamente; ~ **enough** infatti. ~**ly** *adv* certamente; (*Am: gladly*) volentieri

surety /'ʃuərətɪ/ *n* garanzia *f;* **stand ~ for** garantire

surf /sɜːf/ *n* schiuma *f* ● *vt* Comput ~ **the Net** surfare in Internet

surface /'sɜːfɪs/ *n* superficie *f;* **on the ~** *fig* in apparenza ● *vi* (*emerge*) emergere. ~ **mail** *n* **by ~ mail** per posta ordinaria

'surfboard *n* tavola *f* da surf

surfing /'sɜːfɪŋ/ *n* surf *m inv*

surge /sɜːdʒ/ *n* (*of sea*) ondata *f;* (*of interest*) aumento *m;* (*in demand*) impennata *f;* (*of anger, pity*) impeto *m* ● *vi* riversarsi; ~ **forward** buttarsi in avanti

surgeon /'sɜːdʒən/ *n* chirurgo *m*

surgery /'sɜːdʒərɪ/ *n* chirurgia *f;* (*place, consulting room*) ambulatorio *m;* (*hours*) ore *fpl* di visita;

have ~ subire un'intervento [chirurgico]

surgical /'sɜːdʒɪkl/ a chirurgico

surly /'sɜːlɪ/ a (-ier, -iest) scontroso

surmise /sə'maɪz/ vt supporre

surmount /sə'maʊnt/ vt sormontare

surname /'sɜːneɪm/ n cognome m

surpass /sə'pɑːs/ vt superare

surplus /'sɜːpləs/ a d'avanzo ● n sovrappiù m

surprise /sə'praɪz/ n sorpresa f ● vt sorprendere; be ~ed essere sorpreso (at da). ~ing a sorprendente. ~ingly adv sorprendentemente

surrender /sə'rendə(r)/ n resa f ● vi arrendersi ● vt cedere

surreptitious /sʌrəp'tɪʃəs/ a & adv di nascosto

surrogate /'sʌrəgət/ n surrogato m. ~ 'mother n madre f surrogata

surround /sə'raʊnd/ vt circondare. ~ing a circostante. ~ings npl dintorni mpl

surveillance /sə'veɪləns/ n sorveglianza f

survey¹ /'sɜːveɪ/ n sguardo m; (poll) sondaggio m; (investigation) indagine f; (of land) rilevamento m; (of house) perizia f

survey² /sə'veɪ/ vt esaminare; fare un rilevamento di (land); fare una perizia di (building). ~or n perito m; (of land) topografo, -a m

survival /sə'vaɪvl/ n sopravvivenza f; (relic) resto m

survive /sə'vaɪv/ vt sopravvivere a ● vi sopravvivere. ~or n superstite mf; be a ~or fam riuscire sempre a cavarsela

susceptible /sə'septəbl/ a influenzabile; ~ to sensibile a

suspect¹ /sə'spekt/ vt sospettare; (assume) supporre

suspect² /'sʌspekt/ a & n sospetto, -a mf

suspend /sə'spend/ vt appendere; (stop, from duty) sospendere. ~er belt n reggicalze m inv. ~ders npl

giarretiere fpl; (Am: braces) bretelle mpl

suspense /sə'spens/ n tensione f; (in book etc) suspense f

suspension /sə'spenʃn/ n Auto sospensione f. ~ bridge n ponte m sospeso

suspicion /sə'spɪʃn/ n sospetto m; (trace) pizzico m; under ~on sospettato. ~ous /-ʃəs/ a sospettoso; (arousing suspicion) sospetto. ~ously adv sospettosamente; (arousing suspicion) in modo sospetto

sustain /sə'steɪn/ vt sostenere; mantenere (life); subire (injury)

sustenance /'sʌstɪnəns/ n nutrimento m

swab /swɒb/ n Med tampone m

swagger /'swægə(r)/ vi pavoneggiarsi

swallow¹ /'swɒləʊ/ vt/i inghiottire. **swallow up** vt divorare; (earth, crowd:) inghiottire

swallow² /'swɒləʊ/ n (bird) rondine f

swam /swæm/ see swim

swamp /swɒmp/ n palude f ● vt fig sommergere. ~y a paludoso

swan /swɒn/ n cigno m

swap /swɒp/ n fam scambio m ● vt (pt/pp swapped) fam scambiare (for con) ● vi fare cambio

swarm /swɔːm/ n sciame m ● vi sciamare; be ~ing with brulicare di

swarthy /'swɔːðɪ/ a (-ier, -iest) di carnagione scura

swastika /'swɒstɪkə/ n svastica f

swat /swɒt/ vt (pt/pp swatted) schiacciare

sway /sweɪ/ n fig influenza f ● vi oscillare; (person:) ondeggiare ● vt (influence) influenzare

swear /sweə(r)/ v (pt swore, pp sworn) ● vi giurare ● vi giurare; (curse) dire parolacce; ~ at sb imprecare contro qcno; ~ by fam credere ciecamente in. ~-word n parolaccia f

sweat /swet/ n sudore m ● vi sudare

sweater /'swetə(r)/ n golf m inv
sweaty /'swetɪ/ a sudato
swede /swiːd/ n rapa f svedese
Swed|e n svedese mf. **~en** n Svezia f. **~ish** a svedese
sweep /swiːp/ n scopata f, spazzata f; (curve) curva f; (movement) movimento m ampio; **make a clean ~** fig fare piazza pulita ● v (pt/pp swept) ● vt scopare, spazzare; (wind:) spazzare ● vi (go swiftly) andare rapidamente; (wind:) soffiare. **sweep away** vt fig spazzare via. **sweep up** vt spazzare
sweeping /'swiːpɪŋ/ a (gesture) ampio; (statement) generico; (changes) radicale
sweet /swiːt/ a dolce; **have a ~ tooth** essere goloso ● n caramella f; (dessert) dolce m. **~ corn** n mais m
sweeten /'swiːtn/ vt addolcire. **~er** n dolcificante m
sweet: **~heart** n innamorato, -a mf; **hi, ~heart** ciao, tesoro. **~ness** n dolcezza f. **~'pea** n pisello m odoroso. **~shop** n negozio m di dolciumi
swell /swel/ n (of swelled, pp swollen or swelled) ● vi gonfiarsi; (increase) aumentare ● vt gonfiare; (increase) far salire. **~ing** n gonfiore m
swelter /'sweltə(r)/ vi soffocare [dal caldo]
swept /swept/ see **sweep**
swerve /swɜːv/ vi deviare bruscamente
swift /swɪft/ a rapido. **~ly** adv rapidamente
swlg /swɪg/ n fam sorso m ● vt (pt/pp swigged) fam scolarsi
swill /swɪl/ n (for pigs) brodaglia f ● vt (~ out) risciacquare
swim /swɪm/ n **have a ~** fare una nuotata ● vi (pt swam, pp swum) ● vi nuotare; (room:) girare; **my head is ~ming** mi gira la testa ● vt percorrere a nuoto. **~mer** n nuotatore, -trice mf
swimming /'swɪmɪŋ/ n nuoto m.

~baths npl piscina fsg. **~ costume** n costume m da bagno. **~pool** n piscina f. **~ trunks** npl calzoncini mpl da bagno
'swim-suit n costume m da bagno
swindle /'swɪndl/ n truffa f ● vt truffare. **~r** n truffatore, -trice mf
swine /swaɪn/ n fam porco m
swing /swɪŋ/ n oscillazione f; (shift) cambiamento m; (seat) altalena f; Mus swing m; **in full ~** in piena attività ● v (pt/pp swung) ● vi oscillare; (on swing, sway) dondolare; (dangle) penzolare; (turn) girare ● vt oscillare; far deviare (vote). **~'door** n porta f a vento
swingeing /'swɪndʒɪŋ/ a (increase) drastico
swipe /swaɪp/ n fam botta f ● vt fam colpire; (steal) rubare; far passare nella macchinetta (credit card)
swirl /swɜːl/ n (of smoke, dust) turbine m ● vi (water:) fare mulinello
swish /swɪʃ/ a fam chic ● vi schioccare
Swiss /swɪs/ a & n svizzero, -a mf; **the ~** pl gli svizzeri. **~ 'roll** n rotolo m di pan di Spagna ripieno di marmellata
switch /swɪtʃ/ n interruttore m; (change) mutamento m ● vt cambiare; (exchange) scambiare ● vi cambiare; **~ to** passare a. **switch off** vt spegnere. **switch on** vt accendere
switch: **~back** n montagne fpl russe. **~board** n centralino m
Switzerland /'swɪtsələnd/ n Svizzera f
swivel /'swɪvl/ v (pt/pp swivelled) ● vt girare ● vi girarsi
swollen /'swəʊlən/ see **swell** ● a gonfio. **~-headed** a presuntuoso
swoop /swuːp/ n (by police) incursione f ● vi (~ **down**) (bird:) piombare; fig fare un'incursione
sword /sɔːd/ n spada f

swore /swɔː(r)/ *see* **swear**
sworn /swɔːn/ *see* **swear**
swot /swɒt/ *n fam* sgobbone, -a *f* ● *vt* (*pt/pp* **swotted**) *fam* sgobbare
swum /swʌm/ *see* **swim**
swung /swʌŋ/ *see* **swing**
syllable /ˈsɪləbl/ *n* sillaba *f*
syllabus /ˈsɪləbəs/ *n* programma *m* [dei corsi]
symbol /ˈsɪmbl/ *n* simbolo *m* (**of** di). ~**ic** /-ˈbɒlɪk/ *a* simbolico. ~**ism** /-ɪzm/ *n* simbolismo *m*. ~**ize** *vt* simboleggiare
symmetric|al /sɪˈmetrɪkl/ *a* simmetrico. ~**y** /ˈsɪmətrɪ/ *n* simmetria *f*
sympathetic /sɪmpəˈθetɪk/ *a* (*understanding*) comprensivo; (*showing pity*) compassionevole. ~**ally** *adv* con comprensione/compassione
sympathize /ˈsɪmpəθaɪz/ *vi* capire; (*in grief*) solidarizzare. ~ **with sb** capire qcno/solidarizzare con qcno. ~**r** *n Pol* simpatizzante *mf*
sympathy /ˈsɪmpəθɪ/ *n* comprensione *f*; (*pity*) compassione *f*; (*condolences*) condoglianze *fpl*; **in ~ with** (*strike*) per solidarietà con
symphony /ˈsɪmfənɪ/ *n* sinfonia *f*
symptom /ˈsɪmptəm/ *n* sintomo *m*. ~**atic** /-ˈmætɪk/ *a* sintomatico (**of** di)
synagogue /ˈsɪnəgɒg/ *n* sinagoga *f*
synchronize /ˈsɪŋkrənaɪz/ *vt* sincronizzare
syndicate /ˈsɪndɪkət/ *n* gruppo *m*
syndrome /ˈsɪndrəʊm/ *n* sindrome *f*
synonym /ˈsɪnənɪm/ *n* sinonimo *m*. ~**ous** /-ˈnɒnɪməs/ *a* sinonimo
synopsis /sɪˈnɒpsɪs/ *n* (*pl* -**opses** /-siːz/) (*of opera, ballet*) trama *f*; (*of book*) riassunto *m*
syntax /ˈsɪntæks/ *n* sintassi *f inv*
synthesize /ˈsɪnθəsaɪz/ *vt* sintetizzare. ~**r** *n Mus* sintetizzatore *m*
synthetic /sɪnˈθetɪk/ *a* sintetico ● *n* fibra *f* sintetica
Syria /ˈsɪrɪə/ *n* Siria *f*. ~**n** *a* & *n* siriano, -a *mf*

syringe /sɪˈrɪndʒ/ *n* siringa *f*
syrup /ˈsɪrəp/ *n* sciroppo *m*; *Br* tipo *m* di melassa
system /ˈsɪstəm/ *n* sistema *m*. ~**atic** /-ˈmætɪk/ *a* sistematico

Tt

tab /tæb/ *n* linguetta *f*; (*with name*) etichetta *f*; **keep ~s on** fam sorvegliare; **pick up the ~** *fam* pagare il conto
tabby /ˈtæbɪ/ *n* gatto *m* tigrato
table /ˈteɪbl/ *n* tavolo *m*; (*list*) tavola *f*; **at [the] ~** a tavola; **~ of contents** tavola *f* delle materie ● *vt* proporre. ~**cloth** *n* tovaglia *f*. ~**spoon** *n* cucchiaio *m* da tavola. ~**spoon[ful]** *n* cucchiaiata *f*
tablet /ˈtæblɪt/ *n* pastiglia *f*; (*slab*) lastra *f*. ~ **of soap** saponetta *f*
table tennis *n* tennis *m* da tavolo; (*everyday level*) ping pong *m*
tabloid /ˈtæblɔɪd/ *n* [giornale *m* formato] tabloid *m inv*; *pej* giornale *m* scandalistico
taboo /təˈbuː/ *a* tabù *inv* ● *n* tabù *m inv*
tacit /ˈtæsɪt/ *a* tacito
taciturn /ˈtæsɪtɜːn/ *a* taciturno
tack /tæk/ *n* (*nail*) chiodino *m*; (*stitch*) imbastitura *f*; *Naut* virata *f*; *fig* linea *f* di condotta ● *vt* inchiodare; (*sew*) imbastire ● *vi Naut* virare
tackle /ˈtækl/ *n* (*equipment*) attrezzatura *f*; (*football etc*) contrasto *m*, tackle *m inv* ● *vt* affrontare
tacky /ˈtækɪ/ *a* (*paint*) non ancora asciutto; (*glue*) appiccicoso; *fig* pacchiano
tact /tækt/ *n* tatto *m*. ~**ful** *a* pieno di tatto; (*remark*) delicato. ~**fully** *adv* con tatto
tactic|al /ˈtæktɪkl/ *a* tattico. ~**s** *npl* tattica *fsg*
tactless /ˈtæktlɪs/ *a* privo di tatto.

~ly *adv* senza tatto. **~ness** *n* mancanza *f* di tatto; *(of remark)* indelicatezza *f*

tadpole /'tædpəʊl/ *n* girino *m*

tag[1] /tæg/ *n* (label) etichetta *f* ● *vt* (pt/pp **tagged**) attaccare l'etichetta a. **tag along** *vi* seguire passo passo

tag[2] *n* (game) acchiapparello *m*

tail /teɪl/ *n* coda *f*; **~s** *pl* (tailcoat) frac *m inv* ● *vt* (fam: follow) pedinare. **tail off** *vi* diminuire

tail: **~back** *n* coda *f*. **~-end** *n* parte *f* finale; *(of train)* coda *f*. **~ light** *n* fanalino *m* di coda

tailor /'teɪlə(r)/ *n* sarto *m*. **~-made** *a* fatto su misura

'**tail wind** *n* vento *m* di coda

taint /teɪnt/ *vt* contaminare

take /teɪk/ *n Cinema* ripresa *f* ● *vt* (pt **took**, pp **taken**) *vt* prendere; (to a place) portare *(person, object)*; (contain) contenere *(passengers etc)*; (endure) sopportare; (require) occorrere; (teach) insegnare; (study) studiare *(subject)*; fare *(exam, holiday, photograph, walk, bath)*; sentire *(pulse)*; misurare *(sb's temperature)*; **~ sb prisoner** fare prigioniero qcno; **be ~n ill** ammalarsi. **~ sth calmly** prendere con calma qcsa ● *vi* *(plant)*: attecchire. **take after** *vt* assomigliare a. **take away** *vt* (with one) portare via; (remove) togliere; (subtract) sottrarre; '**to ~ away**' 'da asporto'. **take back** *vt* riprendere; ritirare *(statement)*; (return) riportare [indietro]. **take down** *vt* portare giù; (remove) tirare giù; (write down) prendere nota di. **take in** *vt* (bring indoors) portare dentro; (to one's home) ospitare; (understand) capire; (deceive) ingannare; riprendere *(garment)*; (include) includere. **take off** *vt* togliersi *(clothes)*; (deduct) togliere; (mimic) imitare; **~ time off** prendere delle vacanze; **~ oneself off** andarsene ● *vi Aeron* decollare. **take on** *vt* farsi

carico di; assumere *(employee)*; (as opponent) prendersela con. **take out** *vt* portare fuori; togliere *(word, stain)*; (withdraw) ritirare *(money, books)*; **~ out a subscription to sth** abbonarsi a qcsa; **~ it out on sb** *fam* prendersela con qcno. **take over** *vt* assumere il controllo di *(firm)* ● *vi* **~ over from sb** sostituire qcno; (permanently) succedere a qcno. **take to** *vt* (as a habit) darsi a; **I took to her** (liked) mi è piaciuta. **take up** *vt* portare su; accettare *(offer)*; intraprendere *(profession)*; dedicarsi a *(hobby)*; prendere *(time)*; occupare *(space)*; tirare su *(floorboards)*; accorciare *(dress)*; **~ sth up with sb** discutere qcsa con qcno ● *vi* **~ up with sb** legarsi a qcno

take: **~-away** *n* (meal) piatto *m* da asporto; (restaurant) ristorante *m* che prepara piatti da asporto. **~-off** *n Aeron* decollo *m*. **~-over** *n* rilevamento *m*. **~-over bid** offerta *f* di assorbimento

takings /'teɪkɪŋz/ *npl* incassi *mpl*

talcum /'tælkəm/ *n* ~ [**powder**] talco *m*

tale /teɪl/ *n* storia *f*; *pej* fandonia *f*

talent /'tælənt/ *n* talento *m*. **~ed** *a* [ricco] di talento

talk /tɔːk/ *n* conversazione *f*; (lecture) conferenza *f*; (gossip) chiacchere *fpl*; **make small ~** parlare del più e del meno ● *vi* parlare ● *vt* parlare di *(politics etc)*; **~ sb into sth** convincere qcno di qcsa. **talk over** *vt* discutere

talkative /'tɔːkətɪv/ *a* loquace

'**talking-to** *n* sgridata *f*

talk show *n* talk show *m inv*

tall /tɔːl/ *a* alto. **~boy** *n* cassettone *m*. **~ order** *n* impresa *f* difficile. **~ story** *n* frottola *f*

tally /'tælɪ/ *n* conteggio *m*; **keep a ~ of** tenere il conto di ● *vi* coincidere

tambourine /tæmbə'riːn/ *n* tamburello *m*

tame /teɪm/ a ⟨animal⟩ domestico; ⟨dull⟩ insulso ● vt domare. **~ly** adv docilmente ● n domatore, -trice mf

tamper /'tæmpə(r)/ vi **~ with** manomettere

tampon /'tæmpɒn/ n tampone m

tan /tæn/ a marrone rossiccio ● n marrone m rossiccio; ⟨from sun⟩ abbronzatura f ● v (pt/pp **tanned**) ● vt conciare ⟨hide⟩ ● vi abbronzarsi

tang /tæŋ/ n sapore m forte; ⟨smell⟩ odore m penetrante

tangent /'tændʒənt/ n tangente f

tangible /'tændʒɪbl/ a tangibile

tangle /'tæŋgl/ n groviglio m; ⟨in hair⟩ nodo m ● vt **~[up]** aggrovigliare ● vi aggrovigliarsi

tango /'tæŋgəʊ/ n tango m inv

tank /tæŋk/ n contenitore m; ⟨for petrol⟩ serbatoio m; ⟨fish ~⟩ acquario m; Mil carro m armato

tankard /'tæŋkəd/ n boccale m

tanker /'tæŋkə(r)/ n nave f cisterna; ⟨lorry⟩ autobotte f

tanned /tænd/ a abbronzato

tantaliz|e /'tæntəlaɪz/ vt tormentare. **~ing** a allettante; ⟨smell⟩ stuzzicante

tantamount /'tæntəmaʊnt/ a **~ to** equivalente a

tantrum /'tæntrəm/ n scoppio m d'ira

tap /tæp/ n rubinetto m; ⟨knock⟩ colpo m; **on ~** a disposizione ● v (pt/pp **tapped**) ● vt dare un colpetto a; sfruttare ⟨resources⟩; mettere sotto controllo ⟨telephone⟩ ● vi picchiettare. **~-dance** n tip tap m ● vi ballare il tip tap

tape /teɪp/ n nastro m; ⟨recording⟩ cassetta f ● vt legare con nastro; ⟨record⟩ registrare

'tape: **~ backup drive** n Comput unità f di backup a nastro. **~-deck** n piastra f m. **~-measure** n metro m [a nastro]

taper /'teɪpə(r)/ n candela f sottile ● **taper off** vi assottigliarsi

'tape: **~ recorder** n registratore m. **~ recording** n registrazione f

tapestry /'tæpɪstrɪ/ n arazzo m

'tap water n acqua f del rubinetto

tar /tɑ:(r)/ n catrame m ● vt (pt/pp **tarred**) incatramare

tardy /'tɑ:dɪ/ a (-ier, -iest) tardivo

target /'tɑ:gɪt/ n bersaglio m; fig obiettivo m

tariff /'tærɪf/ n ⟨price⟩ tariffa f; ⟨duty⟩ dazio m

Tarmac® /'tɑ:mæk/ n macadam m al catrame. **tarmac** n Aeron pista f di decollo

tarnish /'tɑ:nɪʃ/ vi ossidarsi ● vt ossidare; fig macchiare

tarpaulin /tɑ:'pɔ:lɪn/ n telone m impermeabile

tart¹ /tɑ:t/ a aspro; fig acido

tart² n crostata f; ⟨individual⟩ crostatina f; ⟨sl: prostitute⟩ donnaccia f ● **tart up** vt fam **~ oneself up** agghindarsi

tartan /'tɑ:tn/ n tessuto m scozzese, tartan m inv ● attrib di tessuto scozzese

tartar /'tɑ:tə(r)/ n ⟨on teeth⟩ tartaro m

tartar 'sauce /tɑ:tə-/ n salsa f tartara

task /tɑ:sk/ n compito m; **take sb to ~** riprendere qcno. **~ force** n Pol commissione f; Mil task-force f inv

tassel /'tæsl/ n nappa f

taste /teɪst/ n gusto m; ⟨sample⟩ assaggio m; **get a ~ of sth** fig assaporare il gusto di qcsa ● vt sentire il sapore di; ⟨sample⟩ assaggiare ● vi sapere ⟨of di⟩; **it ~s lovely** è ottimo. **~ful** a di [buon] gusto. **~fully** adv con gusto. **~less** a senza gusto. **~lessly** adv con cattivo gusto

tasty /'teɪstɪ/ a (-ier, -iest) saporito

tat /tæt/ see **tit²**

tatter|ed /'tætəd/ a cencioso; ⟨pages⟩ stracciato. **~s** npl **in ~s** a brandelli

tattoo¹ /tæ'tu:/ n tatuaggio m ● vt tatuare

tattoo² n Mil parata f militare

tatty /'tætɪ/ a (**-ier, -iest**) ⟨clothes, person⟩ trasandato; ⟨book⟩ malandato

taught /tɔːt/ see **teach**

taunt /tɔːnt/ n scherno m ● vt schernire

Taurus /'tɔːrəs/ n Toro m

taut /tɔːt/ a teso

tawdry /'tɔːdrɪ/ a (**-ier, -iest**) pacchiano

tax /tæks/ n tassa f; (on income) imposte fpl; before ~ (price) tasse escluse; ⟨salary⟩ lordo ● vt tassare; fig mettere alla prova; ~ **with** accusare di. **~able** /-əbl/ a tassabile. **~ation** /-'seɪʃn/ n tasse fpl. ~ **evasion** n evasione f fiscale. **~-free** a esentasse. **~ haven** n paradiso m fiscale

taxi /'tæksɪ/ n taxi m inv ● vi (pt/pp **taxied**, pres p **taxiing**) ⟨aircraft:⟩ rullare. ~ **driver** n tassista mf. ~ **rank** n posteggio m per taxi

'taxpayer n contribuente mf

tea /tiː/ n tè m inv. **~-bag** n bustina f di tè. **~-break** n intervallo m per il tè

teach /tiːtʃ/ vt/i (pt/pp **taught**) insegnare; ~ **sb sth** insegnare qcsa a qcno. **~er** n insegnante mf; (primary) maestro, -a mf. **~ing** n insegnamento m

tea: ~-cloth n (for drying) asciugapiatti m inv. **~-cup** n tazza f da tè

teak /tiːk/ n tek m

'tea-leaves npl tè m inv sfuso; (when infused) fondi mpl di tè

team /tiːm/ n squadra f, fig équipe f inv ● **team up** vi unirsi

'team-work n lavoro m di squadra, fig lavoro m d'équipe

teapot n teiera f

tear¹ /teə(r)/ n strappo m ● v (pt **tore**, pp **torn**) ● vt strappare ● vi strapparsi; ⟨material:⟩ strapparsi; (run) precipitarsi. **tear apart** vt (fig: criticize) fare a pezzi; (separate) dividere. **tear away** vt ~

oneself away andare via; ~ **oneself away from** staccarsi da ⟨television⟩. **tear open** vt aprire strappando. **tear up** vt strappare; rompere ⟨agreement⟩

tear² /tɪə(r)/ n lacrima f. **~ful** a ⟨person⟩ in lacrime; ⟨farewell⟩ lacrimevole. **~fully** adv in lacrime. **~gas** n gas m lacrimogeno

tease /tiːz/ vt prendere in giro ⟨person⟩; tormentare ⟨animal⟩

tea: ~-set n servizio m da tè. **~-shop** n sala f da tè. **~-spoon** n cucchiaino m [da tè]. **~spoon[ful]** n cucchiaino m

teat /tiːt/ n capezzolo m; (on bottle) tettarella f

'tea-towel n strofinaccio m [per i piatti]

technical /'teknɪkl/ a tecnico. **~ity** /-'kælətɪ/ n tecnicismo m; Jur cavillo m giuridico. **~ly** adv tecnicamente; (strictly) strettamente

technician /tek'nɪʃn/ n tecnico, -a mf

technique /tek'niːk/ n tecnica f

technological /teknə'lɒdʒɪkl/ a tecnologico

technology /tek'nɒlədʒɪ/ n tecnologia f

teddy /'tedɪ/ n ~ [**bear**] orsacchiotto m

tedious /'tiːdɪəs/ a noioso

tedium /'tiːdɪəm/ n tedio m

tee /tiː/ n (in golf) tee m inv

teem /tiːm/ vi (rain) piovere a dirotto; **be ~ing with** (full of) pullulare di

teenage /'tiːneɪdʒ/ a per ragazzi; ~ **boy/girl** adolescente mf. **~r** n adolescente mf

teens /tiːnz/ npl **the** ~ l'adolescenza fsg; **be in one's** ~ essere adolescente

teeny /'tiːnɪ/ a (**-ier, -iest**) piccolissimo

teeter /'tiːtə(r)/ vi barcollare

teeth /tiːθ/ see **tooth**

teethe /tiːð/ vi mettere i [primi] denti. **~ing troubles** npl fig difficoltà fpl iniziali

teetotal /tiː'təʊtl/ a astemio. **~ler** n astemio, -a mf

telecommunications /telɪkəmjuːnɪ'keɪʃnz/ npl telecomunicazioni fpl

telegram /'telɪgræm/ n telegramma m

telegraph /'telɪgrɑːf/ n telegrafo m. **~ic** /-'græfɪk/ a telegrafico. **~ pole** n palo m del telegrafo

telepathy /tɪ'lepəθɪ/ n telepatia f

telephone /'telɪfəʊn/ n telefono m; **be on the ~** (be telephoning) essere al telefono ● vi telefonare a ● vi telefonare

telephone: ~ book n elenco m telefonico. **~ booth** n, **~ box** n cabina f telefonica. **~ directory** n elenco m telefonico. **~ number** n numero m di telefono

telephonist /tɪ'lefənɪst/ n telefonista mf

telephoto /'telɪ-/ a **~ lens** teleobiettivo m

telescop|e /'telɪskəʊp/ n telescopio m. **~ic** /-'skɒpɪk/ a telescopico

televise /'telɪvaɪz/ vt trasmettere per televisione

television /'telɪvɪʒn/ n televisione f; **watch ~** guardare la televisione. **~ set** n televisore m

telex /'teleks/ n telex m inv

tell /tel/ vt (pt/pp told) dire; raccontare (story); (distinguish) distinguere (from da); **~ sb sth** dire qcsa a qcno; **~ the time** dire l'ora; **I couldn't ~ why...** non sapevo perché... ● vi (produce an effect) avere effetto; **time will ~** il tempo ce lo dirà; **his age is beginning to ~** l'età comincia a farsi sentire [per lui]; **you mustn't ~** non devi dire niente. **tell off** vt sgridare

teller /'telə(r)/ n (in bank) cassiere, -a mf

telling /'telɪŋ/ a significativo; (argument) efficace

telly /'telɪ/ n fam tv f inv

temerity /tɪ'merətɪ/ n audacia f

temp /temp/ n fam impiegato, -a mf temporaneo, -a

temper /'tempə(r)/ n (disposition) carattere m; (mood) umore m; (anger) collera f; **lose one's ~** arrabbiarsi; **be in a ~** essere arrabbiato; **keep one's ~** mantenere la calma

temperament /'temprəmənt/ n temperamento m. **~al** /-'mentl/ a (moody) capriccioso

temperate /'tempərət/ a (climate) temperato

temperature /'temprətʃə(r)/ n temperatura f; **have a ~** avere la febbre

tempest /'tempɪst/ n tempesta f. **~uous** /-'pestjʊəs/ a tempestoso

temple¹ /'templ/ n tempio m

temple² n Anat tempia f

tempo /'tempəʊ/ n ritmo m; Mus tempo m

temporar|y /'tempərərɪ/ a temporaneo; (measure, building) provvisorio. **~ily** adv temporaneamente; (introduced, erected) provvisoriamente

tempt /tempt/ vt tentare; sfidare (fate); **~ sb to** indurre qcno a; **be ~ed** essere tentato (to di); **I am ~ed by the offer** l'offerta mi tenta. **~ation** /-'teɪʃn/ n tentazione f. **~ing** a allettante; (food, drink) invitante

ten /ten/ a dieci

tenable /'tenəbl/ a fig sostenibile

tenaci|ous /tɪ'neɪʃəs/ a tenace. **~ty** /-'næsətɪ/ n tenacia f

tenant /'tenənt/ n inquilino, -a mf; Comm locatario, -a mf

tend¹ /tend/ vt (look after) prendersi cura di

tend² vi **~ to do sth** tendere a far qcsa

tendency /'tendənsɪ/ n tendenza f

tender¹ /'tendə(r)/ n Comm offerta f; **be legal ~** avere corso legale ● vt offrire; presentare (resignation)

tender² a tenero; (painful) dolorante. **~ly** adv teneramente. **~ness** n tenerezza f; (painfulness) dolore m

tendon /'tendən/ n tendine m

tenement /'tenəmənt/ n casamento m

tenner /'tenə(r)/ n fam biglietto m da dieci sterline

tennis /'tenɪs/ n tennis m. **~-court** n campo m da tennis. **~ player** n tennista m/f

tenor /'tenə(r)/ n tenore m

tense[1] /tens/ n Gram tempo m

tense[2] a teso ● vt tendere (muscle). **tense up** vi tendersi

tension /'tenʃn/ n tensione f

tent /tent/ n tenda f

tentacle /'tentəkl/ n tentacolo m

tentative /'tentətɪv/ a provvisorio; ⟨smile, gesture⟩ esitante. **~ly** adv timidamente; ⟨accept⟩ provvisoriamente

tenterhooks /'tentəhʊks/ npl **be on ~** essere sulle spine

tenth /tenθ/ a decimo ● n decimo, -a m/f

tenuous /'tenjʊəs/ a fig debole

tepid /'tepɪd/ a tiepido

term /tɜːm/ n periodo m; Sch Univ trimestre m; ⟨expression⟩ termine m; **~s** pl ⟨conditions⟩ condizioni fpl; **~ of office** carica f; **in the short/long ~** a breve/lungo termine; **be on good/bad ~s** essere in buoni/cattivi rapporti; **come to ~s with** accettare ⟨past, fact⟩; **easy ~s** facilità f di pagamento

terminal /'tɜːmɪn(ə)l/ a finale; Med terminale ● n Aeron terminal m inv; Rail stazione f di testa; ⟨of bus⟩ capolinea m; ⟨on battery⟩ morsetto m; Comput terminale m. **~ly** adv **~ly ill** essere in fase terminale

terminate /'tɜːmɪneɪt/ vt terminare; rescindere ⟨contract⟩; interrompere ⟨pregnancy⟩ ● vi terminare; **~ in** finire in. **~ion** /-'neɪʃn/ n termine m; Med interruzione f di gravidanza

terminology /tɜːmɪ'nɒlədʒɪ/ n terminologia f

terminus /'tɜːmɪnəs/ n (pl **-ni**

/-naɪ/) ⟨for bus⟩ capolinea m; ⟨for train⟩ stazione f di testa

terrace /'terəs/ n terrazza f; ⟨houses⟩ fila f di case a schiera; **the ~s** Sport le gradinate. **~d house** n casa f a schiera

terrain /te'reɪn/ n terreno m

terrible /'terəbl/ a terribile. **~y** adv terribilmente

terrier /'terɪə(r)/ n terrier m inv

terrific /tə'rɪfɪk/ a fam ⟨excellent⟩ fantastico; ⟨huge⟩ enorme. **~ally** adv fam terribilmente

terrify /'terɪfaɪ/ vt ⟨pt/pp -ied⟩ atterrire; **be ~fied** essere terrorizzato. **~fying** a terrificante

territorial /terɪ'tɔːrɪəl/ a territoriale

territory /'terɪtərɪ/ n territorio m

terror /'terə(r)/ n terrore m. **~ism** /-ɪzm/ n terrorismo m. **~ist** /-ɪst/ n terrorista mf. **~ize** vt terrorizzare

terse /tɜːs/ a conciso

test /test/ n esame m; ⟨in laboratory⟩ esperimento m; ⟨of friendship, machine⟩ prova m; ⟨of intelligence, aptitude⟩ test m inv; **put to the ~** mettere alla prova ● vt esaminare; provare ⟨machine⟩

testament /'testəmənt/ n testamento m; **Old/New T~** Antico/Nuovo Testamento m

testicle /'testɪkl/ n testicolo m

testify /'testɪfaɪ/ vt/i ⟨pt/pp -ied⟩ testimoniare

testimonial /testɪ'məʊnɪəl/ n lettera f di referenze

testimony /'testɪmənɪ/ n testimonianza f

'test: ~ match n partita f internazionale. **~-tube** n provetta f. **~-tube 'baby** n fam bambino, -a m/f in provetta

tetanus /'tetənəs/ n tetano m

tether /'teðə(r)/ n **be at the end of one's ~** non poterne più

text /tekst/ n testo m. **~book** n manuale m

textile /'tekstaɪl/ a tessile ● n stoffa f

texture /'tekstʃə(r)/ n ⟨of skin⟩ grana f; (of food) consistenza f; **of a smooth ~** (to the touch) soffice al tatto

Thai /taɪ/ a & n tailandese mf. **~land** n Tailandia f

Thames /temz/ n Tamigi m

than /ðən/, accentato /ðæn/ conj che; (with numbers, names) di; **older ~ me** più vecchio di me

thank /θæŋk/ vt ringraziare; **~ you** [**very much**] grazie [mille]. **~ful** a grato. **~fully** adv con gratitudine; (happily) fortunatamente. **~less** a ingrato

thanks /θæŋks/ npl ringraziamenti mpl; **~!** fam grazie!; **~ to** grazie a

that /ðæt/ a & pron (pl **those**) quel, quei pl; (before s + consonant, gn, ps and z) quello, quegli pl; (before vowel) quell' mf, quegli mpl, (before vowel) quell' mf, quegli mpl, (before fpl; **~ one** quello; **I don't like those** quelli non mi piacciono; **~ is** cioè: **is ~ you?** sei tu?; **who is ~?** chi è?; **what did you do after ~?** cosa hai fatto dopo?; **like ~** in questo modo, così; **a man like ~** un uomo così; **~ is why** ecco perché; **~'s it!** (you've understood) ecco!; (I've finished) ecco fatto!; (I've had enough) basta così! (there's nothing more) tutto qui!; **~'s ~!** (with job) ecco fatto!; (in relationship) è tutto finito!; **and ~'s ~!** punto e basta! **all ~ I know** tutto quello che so ● adv così; **it wasn't ~ good** non era poi così buono ● rel pron che; **the man ~ I spoke to** l'uomo con cui ho parlato; **the day ~ I saw him** il giorno in cui l'ho visto; **all ~ I know** tutto quello che so ● conj che; **I think ~...** penso che...

thatch /θætʃ/ n tetto m di paglia. **~ed** a coperto di paglia

thaw /θɔː/ n disgelo m ● vt fare scongelare (food) ● vi (food:) scongelarsi; it's **~ing** sta sgelando

the /ðə/, di fronte a una vocale /ðiː/ def art il, la f; i mpl, le fpl; (before s + consonant, gn, ps and z) lo, gli

mpl; (before vowel) l' mf, gli mpl, le fpl; **at ~ cinema/station** al cinema/alla stazione; **from ~ cinema/ station** dal cinema/dalla stazione ● adv **~ more ~ better** più ce n'è meglio è; (with reference to pl) più ce ne sono, meglio è; **all ~ better** tanto meglio

theatre /ˈθɪətə(r)/ n teatro m; Med sala f operatoria

theatrical /θɪˈætrɪkl/ a teatrale; (showy) melodrammatico

theft /θeft/ n furto m

their /ðeə(r)/ a il loro m, la loro f, i loro mpl, le loro fpl; **~ mother/ father** la loro madre/il loro padre

theirs /ðeəz/ poss pron il loro m, la loro f, i loro mpl, le loro fpl; **a friend of ~** un loro amico; **friends of ~** dei loro amici; **those are ~** quelli sono loro; (as opposed to ours) quelli sono i loro

them /ðem/ pron (direct object) li m, le f; (indirect object) gli, loro fml; (after prep: with people) loro; (after preposition: with things) essi; **we haven't seen ~** non li/le abbiamo visti/viste; **give ~ the money** dai loro or dagli i soldi; **give it to ~** dagliello; **I've spoken to ~** ho parlato con loro; **it's ~** sono loro

theme /θiːm/ n tema m. **~ song** n motivo m conduttore

them'selves pron (reflexive) si; (emphatic) se stessi; **they poured ~ a drink** si sono versati da bere; **they said so ~** lo hanno detto loro stessi; **they kept it to ~** se lo sono tenuti per sé; **by ~** da soli

then /ðen/ adv allora; (next) poi; **by ~** (in the past) ormai; (in the future) per allora; **since ~** sin da allora; **before ~** prima di allora; **from ~ on** da allora in poi; **now and ~** ogni tanto; **there and ~** all'istante ● a di allora

theolog'ian /θɪəˈləʊdʒɪən/ n teologo, -a mf. **~y** /ˈɒlədʒɪ/ n teologia f

theorem /ˈθɪərəm/ n teorema m

theoretical /θɪəˈretɪkl/ a teorico

theory /'θɪərɪ/ n teoria f; **in ~** in teoria

therapeutic /θerə'pjuːtɪk/ a terapeutico

therapist /'θerəpɪst/ n terapista mf. **~y** n terapia f

there /ðeə(r)/ adv là, lì; **down/up ~** laggiù/lassù; **~ is/are** c'è/ci sono; **~ he/she is** eccolo/eccola ● int **~, ~!** su, su!

there: **~abouts** adv [or] **~abouts** (roughly) all'incirca. **~'after** adv dopo di che. **~by** adv in tal modo. **~fore** /-fɔː(r)/ adv perciò

thermal /'θɜːm(ə)l/ a termale; **~ 'underwear** n biancheria f che mantiene la temperatura corporea

thermometer /θə'mɒmɪtə(r)/ n termometro m

Thermos® /'θɜːməs/ n **~ [flask]** termos m inv

thermostat /'θɜːməstæt/ n termostato m

thesaurus /θɪ'sɔːrəs/ n dizionario m dei sinonimi

these /ðiːz/ see this

thesis /'θiːsɪs/ n (pl **-ses** /-siːz/) tesi f inv

they /ðeɪ/ pron loro; **~ are tired** sono stanchi; **we're going, but ~ are not** noi andiamo, ma loro no; **~ say** (generalizing) si dice; **~ are building a new road** stanno costruendo una nuova strada

thick /θɪk/ a spesso; (forest) fitto; (liquid) denso; (hair) folto; (fam: stupid) ottuso; (fam: close) molto unito; **be 5 mm ~** essere 5 mm di spessore ● adv densamente ● n **in the ~ of** nel mezzo di. **~en** vt ispessire (sauce) ● vi ispessirsi; (fog:) infittirsi. **~ly** adv densamente; (cut) a fette spesse. **~ness** n spessore m

thick: **~set** a tozzo. **~'skinned** a fam insensibile

thief /θiːf/ n (pl **thieves**) ladro, -a mf

thieving /'θiːvɪŋ/ a ladro ● n furti mpl

thigh /θaɪ/ n coscia f

thimble /'θɪmbl/ n ditale m

thin /θɪn/ a (thinner, thinnest) sottile; (shoes, sweater) leggero; (liquid) liquido; (person) magro; (fig: excuse, plot) inconsistente ● adv **= thinly** ● v (pt/pp **thinned**) ● vt diluire (liquid) ● vi diradarsi. **thin out** vi diradarsi. **~ly** adv scarsamente; (disguised) leggermente; (cut) a fette sottili

thing /θɪŋ/ n cosa f; **~s** pl (belongings) roba fsg; **for one ~** in primo luogo; **the right ~** la cosa giusta; **just the ~!** proprio quel che ci vuole!; **how are ~s?** come vanno le cose?; **the latest ~** fam l'ultima cosa; **the best ~ would be la cosa migliore sarebbe; poor ~!** poveretto!

think /θɪŋk/ vt/i (pt/pp **thought**) pensare; (believe) credere; **I ~ so** credo di sì; **what do you ~?** (what is your opinion?) cosa ne pensi?; **~ of/about** pensare a; **what do you ~ of it?** cosa ne pensi di questo?. **think over** vt riflettere su. **think up** vt escogitare

third /θɜːd/ a & n terzo, -a. **~ly** adv terzo. **~rate** a scadente

thirst /θɜːst/ n sete f. **~ily** adv con sete. **~y** a assetato; **be ~y** aver sete

thirteen /θɜː'tiːn/ a tredici. **~th** a tredicesimo

thirtieth /'θɜːtɪɪθ/ a trentesimo

thirty /'θɜːtɪ/ a trenta

this /ðɪs/ a (pl **these**) questo; **~ man/woman** quest'uomo/questa donna; **these men/women** questi uomini/queste donne; **~ one** questo; **~ morning/evening** stamattina/stasera ● pron (pl **these**) questo; **we talked about ~ and that** abbiamo parlato del più e del meno; **like ~** così; **~ is Peter** questo è Peter; Teleph sono Peter; **who is ~?** chi è?; Teleph chi parla? ● adv così; **~ big** così grande

thistle /'θɪsl/ n cardo m

thorn /θɔːn/ n spina f. **~y** a spinoso

thorough /ˈθʌrə/ a completo; ⟨knowledge⟩ profondo; ⟨clean, search, training⟩ a fondo; ⟨person⟩ scrupoloso

thorough: **~bred** n purosangue m inv. **~fare** n via f principale; '**no ~fare**' 'strada non transitabile '

thorough|ly /ˈθʌrəlɪ/ adv ⟨clean, search, know sth⟩ a fondo; ⟨extremely⟩ estremamente. **~ness** n completezza f

those /ðəʊz/ see **that**

though /ðəʊ/ conj sebbene; **as ~** come se ● adv fam tuttavia

thought /θɔ:t/ see **think** ● n pensiero m; ⟨idea⟩ idea f. **~ful** a pensieroso; ⟨considerate⟩ premuroso. **~fully** adv pensierosamente; ⟨considerately⟩ premurosamente. **~less** a ⟨inconsiderate⟩ considerato. **~lessly** adv con noncuranza

thousand /ˈθaʊznd/ a one/a ~ mille m inv ● n mille m inv; **~s of** migliaia fpl di. **~th** a millesimo ● n millesimo, -a mf

thrash /θræʃ/ vt picchiare; ⟨defeat⟩ sconfiggere. **thrash out** vt mettere a punto

thread /θred/ n filo m; ⟨of screw⟩ filetto m ● vt infilare ⟨beads⟩; **one's way through** farsi strada fra. **~bare** a logoro

threat /θret/ n minaccia f

threaten /ˈθretn/ vt minacciare ⟨to do sth⟩ ● vi fig incalzare. **~ing** a minaccioso; ⟨sky, atmosphere⟩ sinistro

three /θri:/ a tre. **~fold** a & adv triplo. **~some** /-səm/ n trio m

thresh /θreʃ/ vt trebbiare

threshold /ˈθreʃəʊld/ n soglia f

threw /θru:/ see **throw**

thrift /θrɪft/ n economia f. **~y** a parsimonioso

thrill /θrɪl/ n emozione f; ⟨of fear⟩ brivido m ● vt entusiasmare; **be ~ed with** essere entusiasta di. **~er** n ⟨book⟩ [romanzo m] giallo m; ⟨film⟩ [film m] giallo m. **~ing** a eccitante

thrive /θraɪv/ vi ⟨pt thrived or

throve, pp thrived or thriven /ˈθrɪvn/⟩ ⟨business:⟩ prosperare; ⟨child, plant:⟩ crescere bene; **I ~ on pressure** mi piace essere sotto tensione

throat /θrəʊt/ n gola f; **sore ~** mal m di gola

throb /θrɒb/ n pulsazione f; ⟨of heart⟩ battito m ● vi ⟨pt/pp throbbed⟩ ⟨vibrate⟩ pulsare; ⟨heart:⟩ battere

throes /θrəʊz/ npl **in the ~ of** fig alle prese con

thrombosis /θrɒmˈbəʊsɪs/ n trombosi f

throne /θrəʊn/ n trono m

throng /θrɒŋ/ n calca f

throttle /ˈθrɒtl/ n ⟨on motorbike⟩ manopola f di accelerazione ● vt strozzare

through /θru:/ prep attraverso; ⟨during⟩ durante; ⟨by means of⟩ tramite; ⟨thanks to⟩ grazie a; **Saturday ~ Tuesday** Am da sabato a martedì incluso ● adv attraverso; **~ and ~** fino in fondo; **wet ~** completamente bagnato; **read sth ~** dare una lettura a qcsa; **let ~** lasciar passare ⟨sb⟩ ● a ⟨train⟩ diretto; **be ~** ⟨finished⟩ aver finito; Teleph avere la comunicazione

throughout /θru:ˈaʊt/ prep per tutto ● adv completamente; ⟨time⟩ per tutto il tempo

throw /θrəʊ/ n tiro m ● vt ⟨pt threw, pp thrown⟩ lanciare; ⟨throw away⟩ gettare; azionare ⟨switch⟩; disarcionare ⟨rider⟩; ⟨fam: disconcert⟩ disorientare; fam dare ⟨party⟩. **throw away** vt gettare via. **throw out** vt gettare via; rigettare ⟨plan⟩; buttare fuori ⟨person⟩. **throw up** vt alzare ● vi ⟨vomit⟩ vomitare

'throw-away a ⟨remark⟩ buttato lì; ⟨paper cup⟩ usa e getta inv

thrush /θrʌʃ/ n tordo m

thrust /θrʌst/ n spinta f ● vt ⟨pt/pp thrust⟩ ⟨push⟩ spingere; ⟨insert⟩ conficcare; **~ [up]on** imporre a

thud /θʌd/ n tonfo m

thug /θʌg/ n delinquente m

thumb /θʌm/ n pollice m; as a rule of ~ come regola generale; under sb's ~ succube di qcno ● vt ~ a lift fare l'autostop. ~-index n indice m a rubrica. ~-tack n Am puntina f da disegno

thump /θʌmp/ n colpo m; (noise) tonfo m ● vt battere su ⟨table, door⟩; battere ⟨fist⟩; colpire ⟨person⟩ ● vi battere (on su); ⟨heart:⟩ battere forte. thump about vi camminare pesantemente

thunder /ˈθʌndə(r)/ n tuono m; (loud noise) rimbombo m ● vi tuonare; (make loud noise) rimbombare. ~clap n rombo m di tuono. ~storm n temporale m. ~y a temporalesco

Thursday /ˈθɜːzdeɪ/ n giovedì m inv

thus /ðʌs/ adv così

thwart /θwɔːt/ vt ostacolare

thyme /taɪm/ n timo m

Tiber /ˈtaɪbə(r)/ n Tevere m

tick /tɪk/ n (sound) ticchettio m; (mark) segno m; (fam: instant) attimo m ● vi ticchettare. tick off vt spuntare; (fam sgridare. tick over vi ⟨engine:⟩ andare al minimo

ticket /ˈtɪkɪt/ n biglietto m; (for item deposited, library) tagliando m; (label) cartellino m; (fine) multa f. ~-collector n controllore m. ~-office n biglietteria f

tick|le /ˈtɪkl/ n solletico m ● vt fare il solletico a; (amuse) divertire ● vi fare prurito. ~lish /ˈtɪklɪʃ/ a che soffre il solletico

tidal /ˈtaɪdl/ a ⟨river, harbour⟩ di marea. ~ wave n onda f di marea

tiddly-winks /ˈtɪdlɪwɪŋks/ n gioco m delle pulci

tide /taɪd/ n marea f; (of events) corso m; the ~ is in/out c'è alta/bassa marea ● tide over vt ~ sb over aiutare qcno a andare avanti

tidily /ˈtaɪdɪlɪ/ adv in modo ordinato

tidiness /ˈtaɪdɪnɪs/ n ordine m

tidy /ˈtaɪdɪ/ a (-ier, -iest) ordinato; (fam: amount) bello ● vt (pt/pp -ied) ~ [up] ordinare; ~ oneself up mettersi in ordine

tie /taɪ/ n cravatta f; (cord) legaccio m; (fig: bond) legame m; (restriction) impedimento m; Sport pareggio m ● v (pres p tying) ● vt legare; fare ⟨knot⟩; be ~d (in competition) essere in parità ● vi pareggiare. tie in with vi corrispondere a. tie up vt legare; vincolare ⟨capital⟩; be ~d up (busy) essere occupato

tier /tɪə(r)/ n fila f; (of cake) piano m; (in stadium) gradinata f

tiff /tɪf/ n battibecco m

tiger /ˈtaɪgə(r)/ n tigre f

tight /taɪt/ a stretto; (taut) teso; (fam: drunk) sbronzo; (fam: mean) spilorcio; ~ corner (fam) brutta situazione f ● adv strettamente; ⟨hold⟩ forte; ⟨closed⟩ bene

tighten /ˈtaɪtn/ vt stringere; avvitare ⟨screw⟩; intensificare ⟨control⟩ ● vi stringersi

tight: ~-fisted a tirchio. ~-fitting a aderente. ~ly adv strettamente; ⟨hold⟩ forte; ⟨closed⟩ bene. ~rope n fune f (da funamboli)

tights /taɪts/ npl collant m inv

tile /taɪl/ n mattonella f; (on roof) tegola f ● vt rivestire di mattonelle ⟨wall⟩

till[1] /tɪl/ prep & conj = until

till[2] /tɪl/ n cassa f

tiller /ˈtɪlə(r)/ n barra f del timone

tilt /tɪlt/ n inclinazione f; at full ~ a tutta velocità ● vt inclinare ● vi inclinarsi

timber /ˈtɪmbə(r)/ n legname m

time /taɪm/ n tempo m; (occasion) volta f; (by clock) ora f; two ~s four due volte quattro; at any ~ in qualsiasi momento; this ~ questa volta; at ~s, from ~ to ~ ogni tanto; ~ and again cento volte; two at a ~ due alla volta; on ~ in orario; in ~ in tempo; (eventually) col tempo; in no ~ at all velocemente; in a year's ~ fra un'anno;

behind ~ in ritardo; **behind the ~s** antiquato; **for the ~ being** per il momento; **what is the ~?** che ora è?; **by the ~ we arrive** quando arriviamo; **did you have a nice ~?** ti sei divertito?; **have a good ~!** divertiti! ● *vt* scegliere il momento per; cronometrare (*race*); **be well ~d** essere ben calcolato
time: ~ **bomb** *n* bomba *f* a orologeria. **~lag** *n* intervallo *m* di tempo. **~less** *a* eterno. **~ly** *a* opportuno. **~-switch** *n* interruttore *m* a tempo. **~-table** *n* orario *m*
timid /'tɪmɪd/ *a* (*shy*) timido; (*fearful*) timoroso
timing /'taɪmɪŋ/ *n* Sport, Techn cronometraggio *m*; **the ~ of the election** il momento scelto per le elezioni
tin /tɪn/ *n* stagno *m*; (*container*) barattolo *m* ● *vt* (*pt/pp* **tinned**) inscatolare. **~ foil** *n* [carta *f*] stagnola *f*
tinge /tɪndʒ/ *n* sfumatura *f* ● *vt* **~d with** *fig* misto a
tingle /'tɪŋgl/ *vi* pizzicare
tinker /'tɪŋkə(r)/ *vi* armeggiare
tinkle /'tɪŋkl/ *n* tintinnio *m*; (*fam: phone call*) colpo *m* di telefono ● *vi* tintinnare
tinned /tɪnd/ *a* in scatola
tin opener *n* apriscatole *m inv*
tinsel /'tɪnsl/ *n* filo *m* d'argento
tint /tɪnt/ *n* tinta *f* ● *vt* tingersi ⟨*hair*⟩
tiny /'taɪnɪ/ *a* (**-ier, -iest**) minuscolo
tip¹ /tɪp/ *n* punta *f*
tip² *n* (*money*) mancia *f*; (*advice*) consiglio *m*; (*for rubbish*) discarica *f* ● *v* (*pt/pp* **tipped**) ● *vt* (*tilt*) inclinare; (*overturn*) capovolgere; (*pour*) versare; (*reward*) dare una mancia ● *vi* inclinarsi; (*overturn*) capovolgersi. **tip off** *vt* ~ **sb off** (*inform*) fare una soffiata a qcno. **tip out** *vt* rovesciare. **tip over** *vt* capovolgere ● *vi* capovolgersi
'tip-off *n* soffiata *f*

tipped /tɪpt/ *a* ⟨*cigarette*⟩ col filtro
tipsy /'tɪpsɪ/ *a fam* brillo
tiptoe /'tɪptəʊ/ *n* **on ~** in punta di piedi
tiptop /tɪp'tɒp/ *a fam* in condizioni perfette
tire /'taɪə(r)/ *vt* stancare ● *vi* stancarsi. **~d** *a* stanco; **~d of** stanco di; **~d out** stanco morto. **~less** *a* instancabile. **~some** /-səm/ *a* fastidioso
tiring /'taɪərɪŋ/ *a* stancante
tissue /'tɪʃuː/ *n* tessuto *m*; (*handkerchief*) fazzolettino *m* di carta. **~-paper** *n* carta *f* velina
tit¹ /tɪt/ *n* ⟨*bird*⟩ cincia *f*
tit² *n* **~ for tat** pan per focaccia
title /'taɪtl/ *n* titolo *m*. **~-deed** *n* atto *m* di proprietà. **~-role** *n* ruolo *m* principale
tittle-tattle /'tɪtltætl/ *n* pettegolezzi *mpl*
to /tuː/, *atono* /tə/ *prep* a; (*to countries*) in; (*towards*) verso; (*up to, until*) fino a; **I'm going to John's/the butcher's** vado da John/dal macellaio; **come/go to sb** venire/andare da qcno; **to Italy/Switzerland** in Italia/Svizzera; **I've never been to Rome** non sono mai stato a Roma; **go to the market** andare al mercato; **to the toilet/my room** in bagno/camera mia; **to an exhibition** a una mostra; **to university** all'università; **twenty/quarter to eight** le otto meno venti/un quarto; **5 to 6 kilos** da 5 a 6 chili; **to the end** alla fine; **to this day** fino a oggi; **to the best of my recollection** per quanto mi possa ricordare; **give/say sth to sb** dare/dire qcsa a qcno; **give it to me** dammelo; **there's nothing to it** è una cosa da niente ● *verbal constructions* **to go** andare; **learn to swim** imparare a nuotare; **I want to/have to go** voglio/devo andare; **it's easy to forget** è facile da dimenticare; **too ill/tired to go** troppo malato/stanco per andare; **you have to** devi; **I

don't want to non voglio; **live to be** 90 vivere fino a 90 anni; **he was the last to arrive** è stato l'ultimo ad arrivare; **to be honest,...** per essere sincero,... ● adv **pull to** chiudere; **to and fro** avanti e indietro

toad /təʊd/ n rospo m. **~stool** n fungo m velenoso

toast /təʊst/ n pane m tostato; (drink) brindisi m ● vt tostare (bread); (drink a ~ to) brindare a . **~er** n tostapane m inv

tobacco /tə'bækəʊ/ n tabacco m. **~nist's** [shop] n tabaccheria f

toboggan /tə'bɒgən/ n toboga m ● vi andare in toboga

today /tə'deɪ/ n & adv oggi m; **a week ~** una settimana a oggi; **~'s paper** il giornale di oggi

toddler /'tɒdlə(r)/ n bambino, -a mf ai primi passi

to-do /tə'du:/ n fam baccano m

toe /təʊ/ n dito m del piede; (of footwear) punta f; **big ~** alluce m ● vt ~ **the line** rigar diritto. **~nail** n unghia f del piede

toffee /'tɒfɪ/ n caramella f al mou

together /tə'geðə(r)/ adv insieme; (at the same time) allo stesso tempo; **~ with** insieme a

toilet /'tɔɪlɪt/ n (lavatory) gabinetto m. **~ paper** n carta f igienica

toiletries /'tɔɪlɪtrɪz/ npl articoli mpl da toilette

toilet: **~ roll** n rotolo m di carta igienica. **~ water** n acqua f di colonia

token /'təʊkən/ n segno m; (counter) gettone m; (voucher) buono m ● attrib simbolico

told /təʊld/ see **tell** ● a **all ~** in tutto

tolerable /'tɒl(ə)rəbl/ a tollerabile; (not bad) discreto. **~y** adv discretamente

toleranｌce /'tɒl(ə)r(ə)ns/ n tolleranza f. **~t** a tollerante. **~tly** adv con tolleranza

tolerate /'tɒləreɪt/ vt tollerare

toll[1] /təʊl/ n pedaggio m; **death ~** numero m di morti

toll[2] vi suonare a morto

tom /tɒm/ n (cat) gatto m maschio

tomato /tə'mɑ:təʊ/ n (pl -es) pomodoro m. **~ ketchup** n ketchup m. **~ purée** n concentrato m di pomodoro

tomb /tu:m/ n tomba f

tomboy /'tɒmbɔɪ/ n maschiaccio m

tombstone /'tu:mstəʊn/ n pietra f tombale

tom-cat n gatto m maschio

tomfoolery /tɒm'fu:lərɪ/ n stupidaggini fpl

tomorrow /tə'mɒrəʊ/ n & adv domani m; **~ morning** domani mattina; **the day after ~** dopodomani; **see you ~**! a domani!

ton /tʌn/ n tonnellata f (= 1,016 kg.); **~s of** fam un sacco di

tone /təʊn/ n tono m; (colour) tonalità f inv **tone down** vt attenuare. **tone up** vt tonificare (muscles)

toner /'təʊnə(r)/ n toner m

tongs /tɒŋz/ npl pinze fpl

tongue /tʌŋ/ n lingua f; **~ in cheek** fam: say) ironicamente. **~-twister** n scioglilingua m inv

tonic /'tɒnɪk/ n tonico m; (for hair) lozione f per i capelli; fig toccasana m inv; **~ [water]** acqua f tonica

tonight /tə'naɪt/ adv stanotte; (evening) stasera ● n questa notte f; (evening) questa sera f

tonne /tʌn/ n tonnellata f metrica

tonsil /'tɒnsl/ n Anat tonsilla f. **~litis** /-sə'laɪtɪs/ n tonsillite f

too /tu:/ adv troppo; (also) anche; **~ many** troppi; **~ much** troppo; **~ little** troppo poco

took /tʊk/ see **take**

tool /tu:l/ n attrezzo m

toot /tu:t/ n suono m di clacson ● vi Auto clacsonare

tooth /tu:θ/ n (pl teeth) dente m

tooth: **~ache** n mal m di denti. **~brush** n spazzolino m da denti. **~less** a sdentato. **~paste** n dentifricio m. **~pick** n stuzzicadenti m inv

top¹ /tɒp/ n (toy) trottola f

top² n cima f; Sch giorno, -a mf; (upper part or half) parte f superiore; (of page, list, street) inizio m; (upper surface) superficie f; (lid) coperchio m; (of bottle) tappo m; (garment) maglia f; (blouse) camicia f; Auto marcia f più alta; **at the ~** fig al vertice; **at the ~ of one's voice** a squarciagola; **on ~/ on ~ of** sopra; **on ~ of that** (besides) per di più; **from ~ to bottom** da cima a fondo ●**a** in alto; (official, floor of building) superiore; (pupil, musician etc) migliore; (speed) massimo ●**vt** (pt/pp topped) essere in testa a (list); (exceed) sorpassare; **~ped with ice-cream** ricoperto di gelato. **top up** vt riempire

top: **~'floor** n ultimo piano m. **~ hat** n cilindro m. **~heavy** a con la parte superiore sovraccarica

topic /ˈtɒpɪk/ n soggetto m; (of conversation) argomento m. **~al** a d'attualità

top: **~less** a & adv topless. **~most** a più alto

topple /ˈtɒpl/ vt rovesciare ●**vi** rovesciarsi. **topple off** vi cadere

top-'secret a segretissimo, top secret inv

topsy-turvy /tɒpsɪˈtɜːvɪ/ a & adv sottosopra

torch /tɔːtʃ/ n torcia f (elettrica); (flaming) fiaccola f

tore /tɔː(r)/ see **tear¹**

torment¹ /ˈtɔːment/ n tormento m

torment² /tɔːˈment/ vt tormentare

torn /tɔːn/ see **tear¹** ●**a** bucato m

tornado /tɔːˈneɪdəʊ/ n (pl -es) tornado m inv

torpedo /tɔːˈpiːdəʊ/ n (pl -es) siluro m ●**vt** silurare

torrent /ˈtɒrənt/ n torrente m. **~ial** /təˈrenʃl/ a (rain) torrenziale

torso /ˈtɔːsəʊ/ n torso m; (in art) busto m

tortoise /ˈtɔːtəs/ n tartaruga f

tortuous /ˈtɔːtʃʊəs/ a tortuoso

torture /ˈtɔːtʃə(r)/ n tortura f ●**vt** torturare

Tory /ˈtɔːrɪ/ a & n fam conservatore, -trice mf

toss /tɒs/ vt gettare; (into the air) lanciare in aria; (shake) scrollare; (horse:) disarcionare; mescolare (salad); rivoltare facendo saltare in aria (pancake); **~ a coin** fare testa o croce ●**vi** **~ and turn** (in bed) rigirarsi; **let's ~ for it** facciamo testa o croce

tot¹ /tɒt/ n bimbetto, -a mf; (fam: of liquor) goccio m

tot² vt (pt/pp totted) **~ up** fam fare la somma di

total /ˈtəʊtl/ a totale ●**n** totale m ●**vt** (pt/pp totalled) ammontare a; (add up) sommare

totalitarian /təʊtælɪˈteərɪən/ a totalitario

totally /ˈtəʊtəlɪ/ adv totalmente

totter /ˈtɒtə(r)/ vi barcollare; (government:) vacillare

touch /tʌtʃ/ n tocco m; (sense) tatto m; (contact) contatto m; (trace) traccia f; (of irony, humour) tocco m; **get/be in ~** mettersi/essere in contatto ●**vt** toccare; (lightly) sfiorare; (equal) eguagliare; (fig: move) commuovere ●**vi** toccarsi. **touch down** vi Aeron atterrare. **touch on** vt fig accennare a. **touch up** vt ritoccare (painting)

touch|ing /ˈtʌtʃɪŋ/ a commovente. **~y** a permaloso; (subject) delicato

tough /tʌf/ a duro; (severe, harsh) severo; (durable) resistente; (resilient) forte

toughen /ˈtʌfn/ vt rinforzare. **toughen up** vt rendere più forte (person)

tour /tʊə(r)/ n giro m; (of building, town) visita f; Theat, Sport tournée f inv; (of duty) servizio m ●**vt** visitare ●**vi** fare un giro turistico; Theat essere in tournée

tourism /ˈtʊərɪzm/ n turismo m. **~t** /-rɪst/ n turista mf ●**attrib** turistico. **~t office** n ufficio m turistico

tournament /'tʊənəmənt/ n torneo m

'tour operator n tour operator mf inv, operatore, -trice mf turistico

tousle /'taʊzl/ vt spettinare

tout /taʊt/ n (ticket ~) bagarino m; (horse-racing) informatore m ● vi ~ **for** sollecitare

tow /taʊ/ n rimorchio m; 'on ~' a rimorchio'; in ~ fam al seguito ● vt rimorchiare. **tow away** vt portare via col carro attrezzi

toward[s] /tə'wɔːd(z)/ prep verso (with respect to) nei riguardi di

towel /taʊəl/ n asciugamano m. ~ling n spugna f

tower /taʊə(r)/ n torre f ● vi ~ **above** dominare. ~ **block** n palazzone m. ~ing a torreggiante; (rage) violento

town /taʊn/ n città f inv. ~ **hall** n municipio m

tow: ~**path** n strada f alzaia. ~**rope** n cavo m da rimorchio

toxic /'tɒksɪk/ a tossico

toxin /'tɒksɪn/ n tossina f

toy /tɔɪ/ n giocattolo m. ~**shop** n negozio m di giocattoli. **toy with** vt giocherellare con

trace /treɪs/ n traccia f ● vt seguire le tracce di; (find) rintracciare; (draw) tracciare; (with tracing-paper) ricalcare

track /træk/ n traccia f; (path, Sport) pista f; Rail binario m. **keep ~ of** tenere d'occhio ● vt seguire le tracce di. **track down** vt scovare

track: ~**ball** n Comput trackball f inv. ~**suit** n tuta f da ginnastica

tractor /'træktə(r)/ n trattore m

trade /treɪd/ n commercio m; (line of business) settore m; (craft) mestiere m; **by** ~ di mestiere ● vi commerciare; ~ **sth for sth** scambiare qcsa per qcsa ● vt commerciare. **trade in** vt (give in part exchange) dare in pagamento parziale

'trade mark n marchio m di fabbrica

trader /'treɪdə(r)/ n commerciante mf

trade: ~**sman** n (joiner etc) operaio m. ~ **union** n sindacato m. ~ **unionist** n sindacalista mf

tradition /trə'dɪʃn/ n tradizione f. ~**al** a tradizionale. ~**ally** adv tradizionalmente

traffic /'træfɪk/ n traffico m ● vi (pt/pp trafficked) trafficare

traffic: ~ **circle** n Am isola f rotatoria. ~ **jam** n ingorgo m. ~ **lights** npl semaforo msg. ~ **warden** n vigile m [urbano]; (woman) vigilessa f

tragedy /'trædʒədɪ/ n tragedia f

tragic /'trædʒɪk/ a tragico. ~**ally** adv tragicamente

trail /treɪl/ n traccia f; (path) sentiero m ● vi strisciare; (plant:) arrampicarsi; ~ **[behind]** rimanere indietro; (in competition) essere in svantaggio ● vt trascinare

trailer /'treɪlə(r)/ n Auto rimorchio m; (Am: caravan) roulotte f inv; (film) presentazione f (di un film)

train /treɪn/ n treno m; ~ **of thought** n fil dei pensieri ● vt formare professionalmente; Sport allenare; (aim) puntare; educare (child); addestrare (animal, soldier) ● vi fare il tirocinio; Sport allenarsi. ~**ed** (animal) addestrato (**to do** a fare)

trainee /treɪ'niː/ n apprendista mf

train|er /'treɪnə(r)/ n Sport allenatore, -trice mf; (in circus) domatore, -trice mf; (of dog, racehorse) addestratore, -trice mf; ~**ers** pl scarpe fpl da ginnastica. ~**ing** n tirocinio m; Sport allenamento m; (of animal, soldier) addestramento m

traipse /treɪps/ vi ~ **around** fam andare in giro

trait /treɪt/ n caratteristica f

traitor /'treɪtə(r)/ n traditore, -trice mf

tram /træm/ *n* tram *m inv*. **~-lines** *npl* rotaie *fpl* del tram

tramp /træmp/ *n* (*hike*) camminata *f*; (*vagrant*) barbone, -a *mf*; (*of feet*) calpestio *m* ● *vi* camminare con passo pesante; (*hike*) percorrere a piedi

trample /'træmpl/ *vt/i* ● **[on]** calpestare

trampoline /'træmpəli:n/ *n* trampolino *m*

trance /trɑ:ns/ *n* trance *f inv*

tranquil /'træŋkwil/ *a* tranquillo. **~lity** /-'kwiləti/ *n* tranquillità *f*

tranquillizer /'træŋkwilaizə(r)/ *n* tranquillante *m*

transact /træn'zækt/ *vt* trattare. **~ion** /-ækʃn/ *n* transazione *f*

transatlantic /trænzət'læntik/ *a* transatlantico

transcend /træn'send/ *vt* trascendere

transfer¹ /'trænsfɜ:(r)/ *n* trasferimento *m*; *Sport* cessione *f*; (*design*) decalcomania *f*

transfer² /træns'fɜ:(r)/ *v* (*pt/pp* **transferred**) ● *vt* trasferire; *Sport* cedere ● *vi* trasferirsi; (*when travelling*) cambiare. **~able** /-əbl/ *a* trasferibile

transform /træns'fɔ:m/ *vt* trasformare. **~ation** /-fə'meiʃn/ *n* trasformazione *f*. **~er** *n* trasformatore *m*

transfusion /træns'fju:ʒn/ *n* trasfusione *f*

transient /'trænziənt/ *a* passeggero

transistor /træn'zistə(r)/ *n* transistor *m inv*; (*radio*) radiolina *f* a transistor

transit /'trænzit/ *n* transito *m*; **in ~** (*goods*) in transito

transition /træn'ziʃn/ *n* transizione *f*. **~al** *a* di transizione

transitive /'trænzitiv/ *a* transitivo

transitory /'trænzitəri/ *a* transitorio

translat|e /trænz'leit/ *vt* tradurre. **~ion** /-'leiʃn/ *n* traduzione *f*. **~or** *n* traduttore, -trice *mf*

transmission /trænz'miʃn/ *n* trasmissione *f*

transmit /trænz'mit/ *vt* (*pt/pp* **transmitted**) trasmettere. **~ter** *n* trasmettitore *m*

transparen|cy /træn'spærənsi/ *n* *Phot* diapositiva *f*. **~t** *a* trasparente

transpire /træn'spaiə(r)/ *vi* emergere; (*fam: happen*) accadere

transplant¹ /'trænsplɑ:nt/ *n* trapianto *m*

transplant² /træns'plɑ:nt/ *vt* trapiantare

transport¹ /'trænspɔ:t/ *n* trasporto *m*

transport² /træn'spɔ:t/ *vt* trasportare. **~ation** /-'teiʃn/ *n* trasporto *m*

transvestite /trænz'vestait/ *n* travestito, -a *mf*

trap /træp/ *n* trappola *f*; (*fam: mouth*) boccaccia *f* ● *vt* (*pt/pp* **trapped**) intrappolare; schiacciare (*finger in door*). **~'door** *n* botola *f*

trapeze /trə'pi:z/ *n* trapezio *m*

trash /træʃ/ *n* robaccia *f*; (*rubbish*) spazzatura *f*; (*nonsense*) schiocchezze *fpl*. **~can** *n* *Am* secchio *m* della spazzatura. **~y** *a* scadente

trauma /'trɔ:mə/ *n* trauma *m*. **~tic** /-'mætik/ *a* traumatico. **~tize** /-taiz/ *vt* traumatizzare

travel /'trævl/ *n* viaggi *mpl* ● *v* (*pt/pp* **travelled**) ● *vi* viaggiare; (*to work*) andare ● *vt* percorrere (*distance*). **~ agency** *n* agenzia *f* di viaggi. **~ agent** *n* agente *mf* di viaggio

traveller /'trævələ(r)/ *n* viaggiatore, -trice *mf*; *Comm* commesso *m* viaggiatore; **~s** *pl* (*gypsies*) zingari *mpl*. **~'s cheque** *n* traveller's cheque *m inv*

trawler /'trɔ:lə(r)/ *n* peschereccio *m*

tray /trei/ *n* vassoio *m*; (*for baking*) teglia *f*; (*for documents*) vaschetta *f* sparticarta; (*of printer, photocopier*) vassoio *m*

treacher|ous /'tretʃərəs/ *a* traditore; *(weather, currents)* pericoloso. **~y** *n* tradimento *m*

treacle /'triːkl/ *n* melassa *f*

tread /tred/ *n* andatura *f*; *(step)* gradino *m*; *(of tyre)* battistrada *m* inv ● *v* *(pt* trod, *pp* trodden) ● *vi* *(walk)* camminare. **tread on** *vt* calpestare *(grass)*; pestare *(foot)*

treason /'triːzn/ *n* tradimento *m*

treasure /'treʒə(r)/ *n* tesoro *m* ● *vt* tenere in gran conto. **~r** *n* tesoriere, -a *f*

treasury /'treʒəri/ *n* the T~ il Ministero del Tesoro

treat /triːt/ *n* piacere *m*; *(present)* regalo *m*; **give sb a ~** fare una sorpresa a qcno ● *vt* trattare; *Med* curare; **~ sb to sth** offrire qcsa a qcno

treatise /'triːtɪz/ *n* trattato *m*

treatment /'triːtmənt/ *n* trattamento *m*; *Med* cura *f*

treaty /'triːtɪ/ *n* trattato *m*

treble /'trebl/ *a* triplo ● *n* *Mus* *(voice)* voce *f* bianca ● *vt* triplicare ● *vi* triplicarsi. **~ clef** *n* chiave *f* di violino

tree /triː/ *n* albero *m*

trek /trek/ *n* scarpinata *f*; *(as holiday)* trekking *m* inv ● *vi* *(pt/pp* trekked) farsi una scarpinata; *(on holiday)* fare trekking

tremble /'trembl/ *vi* tremare

tremendous /trɪ'mendəs/ *a* *(huge)* enorme; *(fam: excellent)* formidabile. **~ly** *adv* *(very)* straordinariamente; *(a lot)* enormemente

tremor /'tremə(r)/ *n* tremito *m*; [**earth**] **~** scossa *f* [sismica]

trench /trentʃ/ *n* fosso *m*; *Mil* trincea *f*. **~ coat** *n* trench *m* inv

trend /trend/ *n* tendenza *f*; *(fashion)* moda *f*. **~y** *a* (-**ier**, -**iest**) *fam* di o alla moda

trepidation /trepɪ'deɪʃn/ *n* trepidazione *f*

trespass /'trespəs/ *vi* ~ **on** introdursi abusivamente in; *fig* abusare di. **~er** *n* intruso, -a *f*

trial /'traɪəl/ *n* *Jur* processo *m*;

(test, ordeal) prova *f*; **on ~** in prova; *Jur* in giudizio; **by ~ and error** per tentativi

triang|le /'traɪæŋgl/ *n* triangolo *m*. **~ular** /-'æŋgjʊlə(r)/ *a* triangolare

tribe /traɪb/ *n* tribù *f* inv

tribulation /trɪbjʊ'leɪʃn/ *n* tribolazione *f*

tribunal /traɪ'bjuːnl/ *n* tribunale *m*

tributary /'trɪbjʊtərɪ/ *n* affluente *m*

tribute /'trɪbjuːt/ *n* tributo *m*; **pay ~** rendere omaggio

trice /traɪs/ *n* **in a ~** in un attimo

trick /trɪk/ *n* trucco *m*; *(joke)* scherzo *m*; *(in cards)* presa *f*; **do the ~** *fam* funzionare; **play a ~** on fare uno scherzo a ● *vt* imbrogliare

trickle /'trɪkl/ *vi* colare

trick|ster /'trɪkstə(r)/ *n* imbroglione, -a *mf*. **~y** *a* (-**ier**, -**iest**) *a* *(operation)* complesso; *(situation)* delicato

tricycle /'traɪsɪkl/ *n* triciclo *m*

tried /traɪd/ *see* **try**

trifl|e /'traɪfl/ *n* inezia *f*; *Culin* zuppa *f* inglese. **~ing** *a* insignificante

trigger /'trɪgə(r)/ *n* grilletto *m* ● *vt* **~** [**off**] scatenare

trigonometry /trɪgə'nɒmɪtrɪ/ *n* trigonometria *f*

trim /trɪm/ *a* (**trimmer**, **trimmest**) curato; *(figure)* snello ● *n* *(of hair, hedge)* spuntata *f*; *(decoration)* rifinitura *f*; **in good ~** in buono stato; *(person)* in forma ● *vt* *(pt/pp* trimmed) spuntare *(hair etc)*; *(decorate)* ornare; *Naut* orientare. **~ming** *n* bordo *m*; **~mings** *pl* *(decorations)* guarnizioni *fpl*; **with all the ~mings** *Culin* guarnito

trinket /'trɪŋkɪt/ *n* ninnolo *m*

trio /'triːəʊ/ *n* trio *m*

trip /trɪp/ *n* *(excursion)* gita *f*; *(journey)* viaggio *m*; *(stumble)* passo *m* falso ● *v* *(pt/pp* tripped) ● *vt* far inciampare ● *vi* inciampare (**on/over** in). **trip up** *vt* far inciampare

tripe /traɪp/ *n* trippa *f*; *(sl: nonsense)* fesserie *fpl*

triple /'trɪpl/ a triplo ● vt triplicare ● vi triplicarsi

triplets /'trɪplɪts/ npl tre gemelli mpl

triplicate /'trɪplɪkət/ n **in** ~ in triplice copia

tripod /'traɪpɒd/ n treppiede m inv

tripper /'trɪpə(r)/ n gitante mf

trite /traɪt/ a banale

triumph /'traɪʌmf/ n trionfo m ● vi trionfare (**over** su). **~ant** /-'ʌmf(ə)nt/ a trionfante. **~antly** adv (exclaim) con tono trionfante

trivial /'trɪvɪəl/ a insignificante. **~ity** /-'ælɪtɪ/ n banalità f inv

trod, trodden /trɒd, 'trɒdn/ see **tread**

trolley /'trɒlɪ/ n carrello m; (Am: tram) tram m inv. **~ bus** n filobus m inv

trombone /trɒm'bəʊn/ n trombone m

troop /truːp/ n gruppo m; **~s** pl truppe fpl ● vi **~ in/out** entrare/ uscire in gruppo

trophy /'trəʊfɪ/ n trofeo m

tropic /'trɒpɪk/ n tropico m; **~s** pl tropici mpl. **~al** a tropicale

trot /trɒt/ n trotto m ● vi (pt/pp trotted) trottare

trouble /'trʌbl/ n guaio m; (difficulties) problemi mpl; (inconvenience, Med) disturbo m; (conflict) conflitto m; **be in** ~ essere nei guai; (swimmer, climber:) essere in difficoltà; **get into** ~ finire nei guai; **get sb into** ~ mettere qcno nei guai; **take the** ~ **to do sth** darsi la pena di far qcsa ● vt (worry) preoccupare; (inconvenience) disturbare; (conscience, old wound:) tormentare ● vi don't ~! non ti disturbare!. **~maker** n be a ~-**maker** seminare zizzania. **~some** /-səm/ a fastidioso

trough /trɒf/ n trogolo m; (atmospheric) depressione f

trounce /traʊns/ vt (in competition) schiacciare

troupe /truːp/ n troupe f inv

trousers /'traʊzəz/ npl pantaloni mpl

trout /traʊt/ n inv trota f

trowel /'traʊəl/ n (for gardening) paletta f; (for builder) cazzuola f

truant /'truːənt/ n **play** ~ marinare la scuola

truce /truːs/ n tregua f

truck /trʌk/ n (lorry) camion m inv

trudge /trʌdʒ/ n camminata f faticosa ● vi arrancare

true /truː/ a vero; **come** ~ avverarsi

truffle /'trʌfl/ n tartufo m

truism /'truːɪzm/ n truismo m

truly /'truːlɪ/ adv veramente; **Yours** ~ distinti saluti

trump /trʌmp/ n (in cards) atout m inv

trumpet /'trʌmpɪt/ n tromba f. **~er** n trombettista mf

truncheon /'trʌntʃn/ n manganello m

trunk /trʌŋk/ n (of tree, body) tronco m; (of elephant) proboscide f; (for travelling, storage) baule m; (Am: of car) bagagliaio m; **~s** pl calzoncini mpl da bagno

truss /trʌs/ n Med cinto m erniario

trust /trʌst/ n fiducia f; (group of companies) trust m inv; (organization) associazione f; **on** ~ sulla parola ● vt fidarsi di; (hope) augurarsi ● vi **~ in** credere in; **~ to** affidarsi a. **~ed** a fidato

trustee /trʌsˈtiː/ n amministratore, -trice mf fiduciario, a

trust|ful /'trʌstfl/ a fiducioso. **~ing** a fiducioso. **~worthy** a fidato

truth /truːθ/ n (pl **-s** /truːðz/) verità f inv. **~ful** a veritiero. **~fully** adv sinceramente

try /traɪ/ n tentativo m, prova f; (in rugby) meta f ● v (pt/pp **tried**) ● vt provare; (be a strain on) mettere a dura prova; Jur processare (person); discutere (case). **~ to do sth** provare a fare qcsa ● vi provare. **try on** vt provarsi (garment). **try out** vt provare

trying /'traɪɪŋ/ a duro; ⟨person⟩ irritante

T-shirt /'tiː-/ n maglietta f

tub /tʌb/ n tinozza f; ⟨carton⟩ vaschetta f; ⟨bath⟩ vasca f da bagno

tuba /'tjuːbə/ n Mus tuba f

tubby /'tʌbɪ/ a (-ier, -iest) tozzo

tube /tjuːb/ n tubo m; ⟨of toothpaste⟩ tubetto m; Rail metro f

tuber /'tjuːbə(r)/ n tubero m

tuberculosis /tjuːbɜːkjʊ'ləʊsɪs/ n tubercolosi f

tubular /'tjuːbjʊlə(r)/ a tubolare

tuck /tʌk/ n piega f ● vt ⟨put⟩ infilare. **tuck in** vt rimboccare; ~ **sb in** rimboccare le coperte a qcno ● vi ⟨fam: eat⟩ mangiare con appetito. **tuck up** vt rimboccarsi ⟨sleeves⟩; ⟨in bed⟩ rimboccare le coperte a

Tuesday /'tjuːzdeɪ/ n martedì m inv

tuft /tʌft/ n ciuffo m

tug /tʌɡ/ n strattone m; Naut rimorchiatore m ● v (pt/pp **tugged**) ● vt tirare ● vi dare uno strattone. ~ **of war** n tiro m alla fune

tuition /tjuː'ɪʃn/ n lezioni fpl

tulip /'tjuːlɪp/ n tulipano m

tumble /'tʌmbl/ n ruzzolone m ● vi ruzzolare. **~down** a cadente. **~-drier** n asciugabiancheria f

tumbler /'tʌmblə(r)/ n bicchiere m ⟨senza stelo⟩

tummy /'tʌmɪ/ n fam pancia f

tumour /'tjuːmə(r)/ n tumore m

tumult /'tjuːmʌlt/ n tumulto m. **~uous** /-'mʌltjʊəs/ a tumultuoso

tuna /'tjuːnə/ n tonno m

tune /tjuːn/ n motivo m; **out of/in** ~ ⟨instrument⟩ scordato/accordato; ⟨person⟩ stonato/intonato; **to the** ~ **of** fam per la modesta somma di ● vt accordare ⟨instrument⟩; sintonizzare ⟨radio, TV⟩; mettere a punto ⟨engine⟩. **tune in** vt sintonizzare ● vi sintonizzarsi ⟨to su⟩. **tune up** vi ⟨orchestra⟩ accordare gli strumenti

tuneful /'tjuːnfl/ a melodioso

tuner /'tjuːnə(r)/ n accordatore

-trice mf; Radio, TV sintonizzatore m

tunic /'tjuːnɪk/ n tunica f; Mil giacca f; Sch ≈ grembiule m

Tunisia /tjuː'nɪzɪə/ n Tunisia f. **~n** a & n tunisino, -a mf

tunnel /'tʌnl/ n tunnel m inv ● vi (pt/pp **tunnelled**) scavare un tunnel

turban /'tɜːbən/ n turbante m

turbine /'tɜːbaɪn/ n turbina f

turbulen|ce /'tɜːbjʊləns/ n turbolenza f. **~t** a turbolento

turf /tɜːf/ n erba f; ⟨segment⟩ zolla f erbosa ● **turf out** vt fam buttar fuori

Turin /tjuː'rɪn/ n Torino f

Turk /tɜːk/ n turco, -a mf

turkey /'tɜːkɪ/ n tacchino m

Turk|ey n Turchia f. **~ish** a turco

turmoil /'tɜːmɔɪl/ n tumulto m

turn /tɜːn/ n ⟨rotation, short walk⟩ giro m; ⟨in road⟩ curva f; ⟨development⟩ svolta f; Theat numero m; ⟨fam: attack⟩ crisi f inv; **a ~ for the better/worse** un miglioramento/peggioramento; **do sb a good ~** rendere un servizio a qcno; **take ~s** fare a turno; **in ~** a turno; **out of ~** ⟨speak⟩ a sproposito; **it's your ~** tocca a te ● vt girare; voltare ⟨back, eyes⟩; dirigere ⟨gun, attention⟩ ● vi girare; ⟨person⟩ girarsi; ⟨leaves⟩ ingiallire; ⟨become⟩ diventare; **~ right/left** girare a destra/sinistra; **~ sour** inacidirsi; **~ to sb** girarsi verso qcno; fig rivolgersi a qcno. **turn against** vi diventare ostile a ● vt mettere contro. **turn away** vt mandare via ⟨people⟩; girare dall'altra parte ⟨head⟩ ● vi girarsi dall'altra parte. **turn down** vt piegare ⟨collar⟩; abbassare ⟨heat, gas, sound⟩; respingere ⟨person, proposal⟩. **turn in** vt ripiegare in dentro ⟨edges⟩; consegnare ⟨lost object⟩ ● vi ⟨fam: go to bed⟩ andare a letto; **~ into the drive** entrare nel viale. **turn off** vt spegnere; chiudere ⟨tap, water⟩ ● vi ⟨car:

girare. **turn on** vt accendere; aprire ⟨tap, water⟩; ⟨fam: attract⟩ eccitare ● vi ⟨attack⟩ attaccare. **turn
out** vt ⟨expel⟩ mandar via; spegnere ⟨light, gas⟩; ⟨produce⟩ produrre; ⟨empty⟩ svuotare ⟨room,
cupboard⟩ ● vi ⟨transpire⟩ risultare; ~ **out well/badly** ⟨cake, dress:⟩
riuscire bene/male; ⟨situation:⟩
andare bene/male. **turn over** vt girare ● vi girarsi; **please ~ over**
vedi retro. **turn round** vt girarsi;
⟨car:⟩ girare. **turn up** vt tirare su
⟨collar⟩; alzare ⟨heat, gas, sound,
radio⟩ ● vi farsi vedere

turning /'tɜːnɪŋ/ n svolta f. ~**-point**
n svolta f decisiva

turnip /'tɜːnɪp/ n rapa f

turn: ~**-out** n ⟨of people⟩ affluenza
f. ~**over** n Comm giro m d'affari;
⟨of staff⟩ ricambio m. ~**pike** n Am
autostrada f. ~**stile** n cancelletto
m girevole. ~**table** n piattaforma f
girevole; ⟨on record-player⟩ piatto
m ⟨di giradischi⟩. ~**-up** n ⟨of
trousers⟩ risvolto m

turpentine /'tɜːpəntaɪn/ n tremen-
tina f

turquoise /'tɜːkwɔɪz/ a ⟨colour⟩
turchese ● n turchese m

turret /'tʌrɪt/ n torretta f

turtle /'tɜːtl/ n tartaruga f acqua-
tica

tusk /tʌsk/ n zanna f

tussle /'tʌsl/ n zuffa f ● vi azzuffarsi

tutor /'tjuːtə(r)/ n insegnante m
privato, -a; ⟨Univ insegnante mf
universitario, -a che segue indivi-
dualmente un ristretto numero di
studenti. ~**ial** /-'tɔːrɪəl/ n discussione f col tutor

tuxedo /tʌk'siːdəʊ/ n Am smoking
m inv

TV n abbr ⟨television⟩ tv f inv, tivù
f inv

twaddle /'twɒdl/ n scemenze fpl

twang /twæŋ/ n ⟨in voice⟩ suono m
nasale ● vt far vibrare

tweed /twiːd/ n tweed m inv

tweezers /'twiːzəz/ npl pinzette fpl

twelfth /twelfθ/ a dodicesimo

twelve /twelv/ a dodici

twentieth /'twentɪɪθ/ a ventesimo

twenty /'twentɪ/ a venti

twerp /twɜːp/ n fam stupido, -a mf

twice /twaɪs/ adv due volte

twiddle /'twɪdl/ vt giocherellare
con; ~ **with** fig girarsi i
pollici

twig[1] /twɪg/ n ramoscello m

twig[2] vt/i ⟨pt/pp **twigged**⟩ fam in-
tuire

twilight /'twaɪ-/ n crepuscolo m

twin /twɪn/ n gemello, -a mf
● attrib gemello. ~ **beds** npl letti
mpl gemelli

twine /twaɪn/ n spago m ● vi in-
trecciarsi; ⟨plant:⟩ attorcigliarsi
● vt intrecciare

twinge /twɪndʒ/ n fitta f; ~ **of
conscience** rimorso m di coscienza

twinkle /'twɪŋkl/ n scintillio m
● vi scintillare

twin 'town n città f inv gemellata

twirl /twɜːl/ vt far roteare ● vi volteggiare ● vi piroetta f

twist /twɪst/ n torsione f; ⟨curve⟩
curva f; ⟨in rope⟩ attorcigliata f;
⟨in book, plot⟩ colpo m di scena
● vt attorcigliare ⟨rope⟩; torcere
⟨metal⟩; girare ⟨knob, cap⟩;
⟨distort⟩ distorcere; ~ **one's ankle**
storcersi la caviglia ● vi attorcigliarsi; ⟨road:⟩ essere pieno di
curve

twit /twɪt/ n fam cretino, -a mf

twitch /twɪtʃ/ n tic m inv; ⟨jerk⟩
strattone m ● vi contrarsi

twitter /'twɪtə(r)/ n cinguettio m
● vi cinguettare; ⟨person:⟩ cian-
ciare

two /tuː/ a due

two: ~**-faced** a falso. ~**-piece** a
⟨swimsuit⟩ due pezzi m inv; ⟨suit⟩
completo m. ~**some** /-səm/ n coppia f. ~**-way** a ⟨traffic⟩ a doppio
senso di marcia

tycoon /taɪ'kuːn/ n magnate m

tying /'taɪɪŋ/ see **tie**

type /taɪp/ n tipo m; ⟨printing⟩ carattere *m* [tipografico] ● *vt* scrivere a macchina ● *vi* scrivere a macchina. **~writer** *n* macchina *f* da scrivere. **~written** *a* dattiloscritto

typhoid /'taɪfɔɪd/ *n* febbre *f* tifoidea

typical /'tɪpɪkl/ *a* tipico. **~ly** *adv* tipicamente; *(as usual)* come al solito

typify /'tɪpɪfaɪ/ *vt* (*pt/pp* -**ied**) essere tipico di

typing /'taɪpɪŋ/ *n* dattilografia *f*

typist /'taɪpɪst/ *n* dattilografo, -a *mf*

typography /taɪ'pɒgrəfɪ/ *n* tipografia *f*

tyrannical /tɪ'rænɪkl/ *a* tirannico

tyranny /'tɪrənɪ/ *n* tirannia *f*

tyrant /'taɪrənt/ *n* tiranno, -a *mf*

tyre /'taɪə(r)/ *n* gomma *f*, pneumatico *m*

....

Uu

....

ubiquitous /juː'bɪkwɪtəs/ *a* onnipresente

udder /'ʌdə(r)/ *n* mammella *f* (*di vacca, capra etc*)

ugl|iness /'ʌglɪnɪs/ *n* bruttezza *f*. **~y** *a* (-**ier**, -**iest**) brutto

UK *n abbr* **United Kingdom**

ulcer /'ʌlsə(r)/ *n* ulcera *f*

ulterior /ʌl'tɪərɪə(r)/ *a* **~ motive** secondo fine *m*

ultimate /'ʌltɪmət/ *a* definitivo; *(final)* finale; *(fundamental)* fondamentale. **~ly** *adv* alla fine

ultimatum /ʌltɪ'meɪtəm/ *n* ultimatum *m inv*

ultrasound /'ʌltrə-/ *n Med* ecografia *f*

ultra'violet *a* ultravioletto

umbilical /ʌm'bɪlɪkl/ *a* **~ cord** cordone *m* ombelicale

umbrella /ʌm'brelə/ *n* ombrello *m*

umpire /'ʌmpaɪə(r)/ *n* arbitro *m* ● *vt/i* arbitrare

umpteen /ʌmp'tiːn/ *a fam* innumerevole. **~th** *a fam* ennesimo. **for the ~th time** per l'ennesima volta

UN *n abbr* (**United Nations**) ONU *f*

un'able /ʌn-/ *a* **be ~ to do sth** non potere fare qcsa; *(not know how)* non sapere fare qcsa

una'bridged *a* integrale

unac'companied *a* non accompagnato; *(luggage)* incustodito

unac'countabl|e *a* inspiegabile. **~y** *adv* inspiegabilmente

unac'customed *a* insolito; **be ~ to** non essere abituato a

una'dulterated *a* *(water)* puro; *(wine)* non sofisticato; *fig* assoluto

un'aided *a* senza aiuto

unanimity /juːnə'nɪmətɪ/ *n* unanimità *f*

unanimous /juː'nænɪməs/ *a* unanime. **~ly** *adv* all'unanimità

un'armed *a* disarmato; **~ combat** *n* lotta *f* senza armi

unas'suming *a* senza pretese

unat'tached *a* staccato; *(person)* senza legami

unat'tended *a* incustodito

un'authorized *a* non autorizzato

una'voidable *a* inevitabile

una'ware *a* **be ~ of sth** non rendersi conto di qcsa. **~s** /-eəz/ *adv* **catch sb ~s** prendere qcno alla sprovvista

un'balanced *a* non equilibrato; *(mentally)* squilibrato

un'bearabl|e *a* insopportabile. **~y** *adv* insopportabilmente

unbeat|able /ʌn'biːtəbl/ *a* imbattibile. **~en** *a* imbattuto

unbe'known /ʌnbɪ'nəʊn/ *a fam* **~ to me** a mia insaputa

unbe'lievable *a* incredibile

un'bend *vi* (*pt/pp* -**bent**) *(relax)* distendersi

un'biased *a* obiettivo

un'block *vt* sbloccare

un'bolt *vt* togliere il chiavistello di

un'breakable *a* infrangibile

un'bridled /ʌn'braɪdld/ *a* sfrenato

un'burden *vt* **~ oneself** *fig* sfogarsi (**to** con)

un'button vt sbottonare

uncalled-for /ʌn'kɔːldfɔː(r)/ a fuori luogo

un'canny a sorprendente; ⟨silence, feeling⟩ inquietante

un'ceasing a incessante

uncere'monious a ⟨abrupt⟩ brusco. **~ly** adv senza tante cerimonie

un'certain a incerto; ⟨weather⟩ instabile; **in no ~ terms** senza mezzi termini. **~ty** n incertezza f

un'changed a invariato

un'charitable a duro

uncle /'ʌŋkl/ n zio m

un'comfortable a scomodo; imbarazzante ⟨silence, situation⟩; **feel ~e** fig sentirsi a disagio. **~y** adv ⟨sit⟩ scomodamente; ⟨causing alarm etc⟩ spaventosamente

un'common a insolito

un'compromising a intransigente

uncon'ditional a incondizionato. **~ly** adv incondizionatamente

un'conscious a privo di sensi; ⟨unaware⟩ inconsapevole; **be ~ of sth** non rendersi conto di qcsa. **~ly** adv inconsapevolmente

uncon'ventional a poco convenzionale

unco'operative a poco cooperativo

un'cork vt sturare

uncouth /ʌn'kuːθ/ a zotico

un'cover vt scoprire; portare alla luce ⟨buried object⟩

unde'cided a indeciso; ⟨not settled⟩ incerto

undeniable /ʌndɪ'naɪəbl/ a innegabile. **~y** adv innegabilmente

under /'ʌndə(r)/ prep sotto; ⟨less than⟩ al di sotto di; **~ there** lì sotto; **~ repair/construction** in riparazione/costruzione; **~ way** fig in corso ● adv ⟨~ water⟩ sott'acqua; ⟨unconscious⟩ sotto anestesia

'undercarriage n Aeron carrello m

'underclothes npl biancheria fsg intima

'undercover a clandestino

'undercurrent n corrente f sottomarina; fig sottofondo m

under'cut vt ⟨pt/pp -cut⟩ Comm vendere a minor prezzo di

'underdog n perdente m

under'done a ⟨meat⟩ al sangue

under'estimate vt sottovalutare

under'fed a denutrito

under'foot adv sotto i piedi; **trample ~** calpestare

under'go vt ⟨pt -went, pp -gone⟩ subire ⟨operation, treatment⟩; **~ repair** essere in riparazione

under'graduate n studente, -tessa mf universitario, a

under'ground¹ adv sotterra

'underground² a sotterraneo; ⟨secret⟩ clandestino ● n ⟨railway⟩ metropolitana f. **~ car park** n parcheggio m sotterraneo

'undergrowth n sottobosco m

'underhand a subdolo

'underlay n strato m di gomma o feltro posto sotto la moquette

under'lie vt ⟨pt -lay, pp -lain, pres p -lying⟩ fig essere alla base di

under'line vt sottolineare

underling /'ʌndəlɪŋ/ n pej subalterno, -a mf

under'lying a fig fondamentale

under'mine vt fig minare

underneath /ʌndə'niːθ/ prep sotto; **~ it** sotto ● adv sotto

under'paid a mal pagato

'underpants npl mutande fpl

'underpass n sottopassaggio m

under'privileged a non abbiente

under'rate vt sottovalutare

'underseal n Auto antiruggine m inv

'undershirt n Am maglia f della pelle

under'staffed /-'stɑːft/ a a corto di personale

under'stand vt ⟨pt/pp -stood⟩ capire; **I ~ that...** ⟨have heard⟩ mi risulta che... ● vi capire. **~able** /-əbl/ a comprensibile. **~ably** /-əblɪ/ adv comprensibilmente

under'standing a comprensivo

●*n* comprensione *f*; (*agreement*) accordo *m*; **on the ~ that** a condizione che

'understatement *n* understatement *m inv*

'understudy *n* Theat sostituto, -a *mf*

under'take *vt* (*pt* -took, *pp* -taken) intraprendere; **~ to do sth** impegnarsi a fare qcsa

'undertaker *n* impresario *m* di pompe funebri; **[firm of] ~s** *n* impresa *f* di pompe funebri

under'taking *n* impresa *f*; (*promise*) promessa *f*

'undertone *n fig* sottofondo *m*; **in an ~** sottovoce

under'value *vt* sottovalutare

'underwater[1] *a* subacqueo

under'water[2] *adv* sott'acqua

'underwear *n* biancheria *f* intima

under'weight *a* sotto peso

'underworld *n* (*criminals*) malavita *f*

'underwriter *n* assicuratore *m*

unde'sirable *a* indesiderato; (*person*) poco raccomandabile

undies /'ʌndɪz/ *npl fam* biancheria *fsg* intima (*da donna*)

un'dignified *a* non dignitoso

un'do *vt* (*pt* -did, *pp* -done) disfare; slacciare (*dress, shoes*), sbottonare (*shirt*); *fig*, Comput annullare

un'done *a* (*shirt, button*) sbottonato; (*shoes, dress*) slacciato; (*not accomplished*) non fatto; **leave ~** (*job*) tralasciare

un'doubted *a* indubbio. **~ly** *adv* senza dubbio

un'dress *vt* spogliare; **get ~ed** spogliarsi ● *vi* spogliarsi

un'due *a* eccessivo

undulating /'ʌndjuleɪtɪŋ/ *a* ondulato; (*country*) collinoso

un'duly *adv* eccessivamente

un'dying *a* eterno

un'earth *vt* dissotterrare; *fig* scovare; scoprire (*secret*). **~ly** *a* soprannaturale; **at an ~ly hour** *fam* a un'ora impossibile

un'easi|e *n* disagio *m*. **~y** *a* a disagio; (*person*) inquieto; (*feeling*) inquietante; (*truce*) precario

un'eatable *a* immangiabile

uneco'nomic *a* poco remunerativo

uneco'nomical *a* poco economico

unem'ployed *a* disoccupato ● *npl* **the ~** i disoccupati

unem'ployment *n* disoccupazione *f*. **~ benefit** *n* sussidio *m* di disoccupazione

un'ending *a* senza fine

un'equal *a* disuguale; (*struggle*) impari; **be ~ to a task** non essere all'altezza di un compito

unequivocal /ʌnɪ'kwɪvəkl/ *a* inequivocabile; (*person*) esplicito

unerring /ʌn'ɜːrɪŋ/ *a* infallibile

un'ethical *a* immorale

un'even *a* irregolare; (*distribution*) ineguale; (*number*) dispari

unex'pected *a* inaspettato. **~ly** *adv* inaspettatamente

un'failing *a* infallibile

un'fair *a* ingiusto. **~ly** *adv* ingiustamente. **~ness** *n* ingiustizia *f*

un'faithful *a* infedele

unfa'miliar *a* sconosciuto; **be ~ with** non conoscere

un'fasten *vt* slacciare; (*detach*) staccare

un'favourable *a* sfavorevole; (*impression*) negativo

un'feeling *a* insensibile

un'finished *a* da finire; (*business*) in sospeso

un'fit *a* inadatto; (*morally*) indegno; Sport fuori forma; **~ for work** non in grado di lavorare

unflinching /ʌn'flɪntʃɪŋ/ *a* risoluto

un'fold *vt* spiegare; (*spread out*) aprire; *fig* rivelare ● *vi* (*view:*) spiegarsi

unfore'seen *a* imprevisto

unforgettable /ʌnfə'getəbl/ *a* indimenticabile

unforgivable /ʌnfə'gɪvəbl/ *a* imperdonabile

un'fortunate *a* sfortunato; (*regret-*

table) spiacevole; (*remark, choice*)
infelice. **~ly** *adv* purtroppo
un'founded *a* infondato
unfurl /ʌn'fɜ:l/ *vt* spiegare
un'furnished *a* non ammobiliato
ungainly /ʌn'geɪnlɪ/ *a* sgraziato
un'godly /ʌn'gɒdlɪ/ *a* empio; **~**
hour *fam* ora *f* impossibile
un'grateful *a* ingrato. **~ly** *adv* senza riconoscenza
un'happily *adv* infelicemente;
(*unfortunately*) purtroppo. **~ness**
n infelicità *f*
un'happy *a* infelice; (*not content*)
insoddisfatto (**with** di)
un'harmed *a* incolume
un'healthy *a* poco sano; (*insanitary*) malsano
un'hook *vt* sganciare
un'hurt *a* illeso
unhy'gienic *a* non igienico
unification /ju:nɪfɪ'keɪʃn/ *n* unificazione *f*
uniform /'ju:nɪfɔ:m/ *a* uniforme
● *n* uniforme *f*. **~ly** *adv* uniformemente
unify /'ju:nɪfaɪ/ *vt* (*pt/pp* **-ied**) unificare
uni'lateral /ju:nɪ-/ *a* unilaterale
uni'maginable *a* inimmaginabile
unim'portant *a* irrilevante
unin'habited *a* disabitato
unin'tentional *a* involontario. **~ly**
adv involontariamente
union /'ju:nɪən/ *n* unione *f*; (*trade*
~) sindacato *m*. **U~ Jack** *n* bandiera *f* del Regno Unito
unique /ju:'ni:k/ *a* unico. **~ly** *adv*
unicamente
unison /'ju:nɪsn/ *n* **in ~** all'unisono
unit /'ju:nɪt/ *n* unità *f inv*; (*department*) reparto *m*; (*of furniture*)
elemento *m*
unite /ju:'naɪt/ *vt* unire ● *vi* unirsi
united /ju:'naɪtɪd/ *a* unito. **U~**
'Kingdom *n* Regno *m* Unito. **U~**
'Nations *n* [Organizzazione *f* delle] Nazioni Unite *fpl*. **U~ States**
[of America] *n* Stati *mpl* Uniti
[d'America]

unity /'ju:nɪtɪ/ *n* unità *f*;
(*agreement*) accordo *m*
universal /ju:nɪ'vɜ:sl/ *a* universale. **~ly** *adv* universalmente
universe /'ju:nɪvɜ:s/ *n* universo *m*
university /ju:nɪ'vɜ:sətɪ/ *n* università *f* ● *attrib* universitario
un'just *a* ingiusto
unkempt /ʌn'kempt/ *a* trasandato;
(*hair*) arruffato
un'kind *a* scortese. **~ly** *adv* in
modo scortese. **~ness** *n* mancanza *f* di gentilezza
un'known *a* sconosciuto
un'lawful *a* illecito, illegale
un'leaded /ʌn'ledɪd/ *a* senza piombo
un'leash *vt fig* scatenare
unless /ʌn'les/ *conj* a meno che; **~**
I am mistaken se non mi sbaglio
un'like *a* (*not the same*) diversi
● *prep* diverso da; **that's ~ him**
non è da lui; **~ me, he...** diversamente da me, lui...
un'likely *a* improbabile
un'limited *a* illimitato
un'load *vt* scaricare
un'lock *vt* aprire (*con chiave*)
un'lucky *a* sfortunato; **it's ~ to...**
porta sfortuna...
un'manned *a* senza equipaggio
un'married *a* non sposato. **~**
'mother *n* ragazza *f* madre
un'mask *vt fig* smascherare
unmistakable /ʌnmɪ'steɪkəbl/ *a*
inconfondibile. **~y** *adv* chiaramente
un'mitigated *a* assoluto
un'natural *a* innaturale; *pej* anormale. **~ly** *adv* in modo innaturale;
pej in modo anormale
un'necessary *a* inutile. **~ily** *adv*
inutilmente
un'noticed *a* inosservato
unob'tainable *a* (*product*) introvabile; (*phone number*) non ottenibile
unob'trusive *a* discreto. **~ly** *adv*
in modo discreto
unof'ficial *a* non ufficiale. **~ly** *adv*
ufficiosamente

un'pack *vi* disfare le valigie ● *vt* svuotare 〈*parcel*〉; spacchettare 〈*books*〉; ~ **one's case** disfare la valigia

un'paid *a* da pagare; 〈*work*〉 non retribuito

un'palatable *a* sgradevole

un'paralleled *a* senza pari

un'pick *vt* disfare

un'pleasant *a* sgradevole; 〈*person*〉 maleducato. **~ly** *adv* sgradevolmente; 〈*behave*〉 maleducatamente. **~ness** *n* (*bad feeling*) tensioni *fpl*

un'plug *vt* (*pt/pp* **-plugged**) staccare

un'popular *a* impopolare

un'precedented *a* senza precedenti

unpre'dictable *a* imprevedibile

unpre'meditated *a* involontario

unpre'pared *a* impreparato

unpre'tentious *a* senza pretese

un'principled *a* senza principi; 〈*behaviour*〉 scorretto

unpro'fessional *a* non professionale; **it's ~** è una mancanza di professionalità

un'profitable *a* non redditizio

un'qualified *a* non qualificato; (*fig: absolute*) assoluto

un'questionable *a* incontestabile

un'quote *vi* chiudere le virgolette

unravel /ʌnˈrævl/ *vt* (*pt/pp* **-ravelled**) districare; (*in knitting*) disfare

un'real *a* irreale; *fam* inverosimile

un'reasonable *a* irragionevole

unre'lated *a* 〈*fact*〉 senza rapporto (**to** con); 〈*person*〉 non imparentato (**to** con)

unre'liable *a* inattendibile; 〈*person*〉 inaffidabile, che non dà affidamento

unre'quited /ʌnrɪˈkwaɪtɪd/ *a* non corrisposto

unre'servedly /ʌnrɪˈzɜːvɪdlɪ/ *adv* senza riserve; 〈*frankly*〉 francamente

un'rest *n* fermenti *mpl*

un'rivalled *a* ineguagliato

un'roll *vt* srotolare ● *vi* srotolarsi

unruly /ʌnˈruːlɪ/ *a* indisciplinato

un'safe *a* pericoloso

un'said *a* inespresso

un'salted *a* non salato

unsatis'factory *a* poco soddisfacente

un'savoury *a* equivoco

un'scathed /ʌnˈskeɪðd/ *a* illeso

un'screw *vt* svitare

un'scrupulous *a* senza scrupoli

un'seemly *a* indecoroso

un'selfish *a* disinteressato

un'settled *a* in agitazione; 〈*weather*〉 variabile; 〈*bill*〉 non saldato

unshakeable /ʌnˈʃeɪkəbl/ *a* categorico

unshaven /ʌnˈʃeɪvn/ *a* non rasato

unsightly /ʌnˈsaɪtlɪ/ *a* brutto

un'skilled *a* non specializzato. **~ worker** *n* manovale *m*

un'sociable *a* scontroso

unso'phisticated *a* semplice

un'sound *a* 〈*building, reasoning*〉 poco solido; 〈*advice*〉 poco sensato; **of ~ mind** malato di mente

un'speakable /ʌnˈspiːkəbl/ *a* indicibile

un'stable *a* instabile; (*mentally*) squilibrato

un'steady *a* malsicuro

un'stuck *a* **come ~** staccarsi; 〈*fam: project*〉 andare a monte

unsuc'cessful *a* fallimentare; **be ~** (*in attempt*) non aver successo. **~ly** *adv* senza successo

un'suitable *a* (*inappropriate*) inadatto; (*inconvenient*) inopportuno

unsus'pecting *a* fiducioso

unthinkable /ʌnˈθɪŋkəbl/ *a* impensabile

un'tidiness *n* disordine *m*

un'tidy *a* disordinato

un'tie *vt* slegare

until /ənˈtɪl/ *prep* fino a; **not ~** non prima di; ~ **the evening** fino alla sera; ~ **his arrival** fino al suo arrivo ● *conj* finché, fino a quando; **not ~ you've seen it** non prima che tu l'abbia visto

untimely /ʌnˈtaɪmlɪ/ *a* inopportuno; ⟨*premature*⟩ prematuro

un'tiring *a* instancabile

un'told *a* ⟨*wealth*⟩ incalcolabile; ⟨*suffering*⟩ indescrivibile; ⟨*story*⟩ inedito

unto'ward *a* **if nothing ~ happens** se non capita un imprevisto

un'true *a* falso; **that's ~** non è vero

unused[1] /ʌnˈjuːzd/ *a* non ⟨ancora⟩ usato

unused[2] /ʌnˈjuːst/ *a* **be ~ to** non essere abituato a

un'usual *a* insolito. **~ly** *adv* insolitamente

un'veil *vt* scoprire

un'wanted *a* indesiderato

un'warranted *a* ingiustificato

un'welcome *a* sgradito

un'well *a* indisposto

unwieldy /ʌnˈwiːldɪ/ *a* ingombrante

un'willing *a* riluttante. **~ly** *adv* malvolentieri

un'wind *v* (*pt/pp* **unwound**) ● *vt* svolgere, srotolare ● *vi* svolgersi, srotolarsi; ⟨*fam: relax*⟩ rilassarsi

un'wise *a* imprudente

un'witting /ʌnˈwɪtɪŋ/ *a* involontario; ⟨*victim*⟩ inconsapevole. **~ly** *adv* involontariamente

un'worthy *a* non degno

un'wrap *vt* (*pt/pp* **-wrapped**) scartare ⟨*present, parcel*⟩

un'written *a* tacito

up /ʌp/ *adv* su; ⟨*not in bed*⟩ alzato; ⟨*road*⟩ smantellato; ⟨*theatre curtain, blinds*⟩ alzato; ⟨*shelves, tent*⟩ montato; ⟨*notice*⟩ affisso; ⟨*building*⟩ costruito; **prices are up** i prezzi sono aumentati; **be up for sale** essere in vendita; **up here** quassù/lassù; **time's up** tempo scaduto; **what's up?** *fam* cosa è successo?; **up to** (*as far as*) fino a; **be up to** essere all'altezza di ⟨*task*⟩; **what's he up to?** *fam* cosa sta facendo?; ⟨*plotting*⟩ cosa sta combinando?; **I'm up to page 100** sono arrivato a pagina 100; **feel up to it** sentirsela; **be one up on sb** *fam* essere in vantaggio su qcno; **go up** salire; **lift up** alzare; **up against** *fig* alle prese con ● *prep* su; **the cat ran/is up the tree** il gatto è salito di corsa/è sull'albero; **further up this road** più avanti su questa strada; **row up the river** risalire il fiume; **go up the stairs** salire su per le scale; **be up the pub** *fam* essere al pub; **be up on** or *in* sth essere bene informato su qcsa ● *n* **ups and downs** *npl* alti *mpl* e bassi

'upbringing *n* educazione *f*

up'date[1] *vt* aggiornare

'update[2] *n* aggiornamento *m*

up'grade *vt* promuovere ⟨*person*⟩; modernizzare ⟨*equipment*⟩

upgradeable /ʌpˈɡreɪdəbl/ *a* Comput upgradabile

upheaval /ʌpˈhiːvl/ *n* scompiglio *m*

up'hill *a* in salita; *fig* arduo ● *adv* in salita

up'hold *vt* (*pt/pp* **upheld**) sostenere ⟨*principle*⟩; confermare ⟨*verdict*⟩

upholster /ʌpˈhəʊlstə(r)/ *vt* tappezzare. **~er** *n* tappezziere, -a *mf*. **~y** *n* tappezzeria *f*

'upkeep *n* mantenimento *m*

up-'market *a* di qualità

upon /əˈpɒn/ *prep* su; **~ arriving home** una volta arrivato a casa

upper /ˈʌpə(r)/ *a* superiore ● *n* (*of shoe*) tomaia *f*

upper: ~ circle *n* seconda galleria *f*. **~ class** *n* alta borghesia *f*. **~ hand** *n* **have the ~ hand** avere il sopravvento. **~most** *a* più alto; **that's ~most in my mind** è la mia preoccupazione principale

'upright *a* dritto; ⟨*piano*⟩ verticale; ⟨*honest*⟩ retto ● *n* montante *m*

'uprising *n* rivolta *f*

'uproar *n* tumulto *m*; **be in an ~** essere in trambusto

up'root *vt* sradicare

up'set[1] *vt* (*pt/pp* **upset**, *pres p* **upsetting**) rovesciare; sconvolgere ⟨*plan*⟩; ⟨*distress*⟩ turbare; **get ~ about sth** prendersela per qcsa; **be very ~** essere sconvolto; **have an ~ stomach** avere l'intestino disturbato

'**upset²** *n* scombussolamento *m*

'**upshot** *n* risultato *m*

upside 'down *adv* sottosopra; **turn ~ ~** capovolgere

up'**stairs¹** *adv* [al piano] di sopra

'**upstairs²** *a* del piano superiore

'**upstart** *n* arrivato, -a *mf*

up'**stream** *adv* controcorrente

'**upsurge** *n* (*in sales*) aumento *m* improvviso; ⟨*of enthusiasm, crime*⟩ ondata *f*

'**uptake** *n* **be slow on the ~** essere lento nel capire; **be quick on the ~** capire le cose al volo

up'**tight** *a* teso

up-to-'**date** *a* moderno; ⟨*news*⟩ ultimo; ⟨*records*⟩ aggiornato

'**upturn** *n* ripresa *f*

'**upward** /'ʌpwəd/ *a* verso l'alto, in su; **~ slope** salita *f* ● *adv* **~[s]** verso l'alto; **~s of** oltre

uranium /jʊ'reɪnɪəm/ *n* uranio *m*

urban /'ɜːbən/ *a* urbano

urge /ɜːdʒ/ *n* forte desiderio *m* ● *vt* esortare (**to** a). **urge on** *vt* spronare

urgen|cy /'ɜːdʒənsɪ/ *n* urgenza *f*. **~t** *a* urgente

urinate /'jʊərɪneɪt/ *vi* urinare

urine /'jʊərɪn/ *n* urina *f*

urn /ɜːn/ *n* urna *f*; ⟨*for tea*⟩ contenitore *m* munito di cannella che si trova nei self-service, mense, ecc

us /ʌs/ *pron* ci; ⟨*after prep*⟩ noi; **they know us** ci conoscono; **give us the money** dateci i soldi; **give it to us** datecelo; **they showed it to us** ce l'hanno fatto vedere; **they meant us, not you** intendevano noi, non voi; **it's us** siamo noi; **she hates us** ci odia

US[A] *n[pl] abbr* (**United States**

[**of America**] U.S.A. *mpl*

usable /'juːzəbl/ *a* usabile

usage /'juːsɪdʒ/ *n* uso *m*

use¹ /juːs/ *n* uso *m*; **be of ~** essere utile; **be of no ~** essere inutile; **make ~ of** usare; ⟨*exploit*⟩ sfruttare; **it is no ~** è inutile; **what's the ~?** a che scopo?

use² /juːz/ *vt* usare. **use up** *vt* consumare

used¹ /juːzd/ *a* usato

used² /juːst/ *pr* **be ~ to sth** essere abituato a qcsa; **get ~ to** abituarsi a; **he ~ to live here** viveva qui

useful /'juːsfl/ *a* utile. **~ness** *n* utilità *f*

useless /'juːslɪs/ *a* inutile; ⟨*fam: person*⟩ incapace

user /'juːzə(r)/ *n* utente *mf*. **~-'friendly** *a* facile da usare

usher /'ʌʃə(r)/ *n* *Theat* maschera *f*; *Jur* usciere *m*; ⟨*at wedding*⟩ persona *f* che accompagna gli invitati a un matrimonio ai loro posti in chiesa ● *vt* **usher in** *vt* fare entrare

usherette /ʌʃə'ret/ *n* maschera *f*

usual /'juːʒʊəl/ *a* usuale; **as ~** come al solito. **~ly** *adv* di solito

usurp /jʊ'zɜːp/ *vt* usurpare

utensil /juː'tensl/ *n* utensile *m*

uterus /'juːtərəs/ *n* utero *m*

utilitarian /jʊtɪlɪ'teərɪən/ *a* funzionale

utility /juː'tɪlətɪ/ *n* servizio *m*. **~ room** *n* stanza *f* in casa privata per il lavaggio, la stiratura dei panni, ecc

utilize /'juːtɪlaɪz/ *vt* utilizzare

utmost /'ʌtməʊst/ *a* estremo ● *n* **one's ~** tutto il possibile

utter¹ /'ʌtə(r)/ *a* totale. **~ly** *adv* completamente

utter² *vt* emettere ⟨*sigh, sound*⟩; proferire ⟨*word*⟩. **~ance** /-əns/ *n* dichiarazione *f*

U-turn /'juː-/ *n* *Auto* inversione *f* a U; *fig* marcia *f* in dietro

Vv

vacan|cy /'veɪk(ə)nsɪ/ n ⟨job⟩ posto m vacante; ⟨room⟩ stanza f disponibile. **~t** a libero; ⟨position⟩ vacante; ⟨look⟩ assente

vacate /və'keɪt/ vt lasciare libero

vacation /və'keɪʃn/ n Univ & Am vacanza f

vaccinat|e /'væksɪmeɪt/ vt vaccinare. **~ion** /-'neɪʃn/ n vaccinazione f

vaccine /'væksi:n/ n vaccino m

vacuum /'vækjʊəm/ n vuoto m ● vt passare l'aspirapolvere in su. **~ cleaner** n aspirapolvere m inv. **~ flask** n thermos® m inv. **~-packed** a confezionato sotto-vuoto

vagabond /'vægəbɒnd/ n vagabondo, -a mf

vagina /və'dʒaɪnə/ n Anat vagina f

vagrant /'veɪgrənt/ n vagabondo, -a mf

vague /veɪg/ a vago; ⟨outline⟩ impreciso; ⟨absent-minded⟩ distratto; **I'm still ~ about it** non ho ancora le idee chiare in proposito. **~ly** adv vagamente

vain /veɪn/ a vanitoso; ⟨hope, attempt⟩ vano; **in ~** invano. **~ly** adv vanamente

valentine /'vælentaɪn/ n ⟨card⟩ biglietto m di San Valentino

valiant /'væliənt/ a valoroso

valid /'vælɪd/ a valido. **~ate** vt ⟨confirm⟩ convalidare. **~ity** /-'lɪdətɪ/ n validità f

valley /'vælɪ/ n valle f

valour /'vælə(r)/ n valore m

valuable /'væljʊəbl/ a di valore; fig prezioso. **~s** npl oggetti mpl di valore

valuation /vælju'eɪʃn/ n valutazione f

value /'vælju:/ n valore m; ⟨usefulness⟩ utilità f ● vt valutare; ⟨cher-

ish⟩ apprezzare. **~ 'added tax** n imposta f sul valore aggiunto

valve /vælv/ n valvola f

vampire /'væmpaɪə(r)/ n vampiro m

van /væn/ n furgone m

vandal /'vændl/ n vandalo, -a mf. **~ism** /-ɪzm/ n vandalismo m. **~ize** vt vandalizzare

vanilla /və'nɪlə/ n vaniglia f

vanish /'vænɪʃ/ vi svanire

vanity /'vænətɪ/ n vanità f. **~ bag** or **case** n beauty-case m inv

vantage-point /'vɑ:ntɪdʒ-/ n punto m d'osservazione; fig punto m di vista

vapour /'veɪpə(r)/ n vapore m

variable /'veərɪəbl/ a variabile; ⟨adjustable⟩ regolabile

variance /'veərɪəns/ n **be at ~** essere in disaccordo

variant /'veərɪənt/ n variante f

variation /veərɪ'eɪʃn/ n variazione f

varicose /'værɪkəʊs/ a **~ veins** vene fpl varicose

varied /'veərɪd/ a vario; ⟨diet⟩ diversificato; ⟨life⟩ movimentato

variety /və'raɪətɪ/ n varietà f inv

various /'veərɪəs/ a vario

varnish /'vɑːnɪʃ/ n vernice f; ⟨for nails⟩ smalto m ● vt verniciare; **~ one's nails** mettersi lo smalto

vary /'veərɪ/ vt/i ⟨pt/pp -ied⟩ variare. **~ing** a variabile; ⟨different⟩ diverso

vase /vɑːz/ n vaso m

vast /vɑːst/ a vasto; ⟨difference, amusement⟩ enorme. **~ly** adv ⟨superior⟩ di gran lunga; ⟨different, amused⟩ enormemente

VAT /vi:eɪ'tiː, væt/ n abbr **(value added tax)** I.V.A. f

vat /væt/ n tino m

vault¹ /vɔːlt/ n ⟨roof⟩ volta f; ⟨in bank⟩ caveau m inv; ⟨tomb⟩ cripta f

vault² /vɔːlt/ n salto m ● vt/i **~ [over]** saltare

VDU n abbr **(visual display unit)** VDU m

veal /viːl/ n carne f di vitello
● *attrib* di vitello

veer /vɪə(r)/ vi cambiare direzione; *Naut, Auto* virare

vegetable /ˈvedʒtəbl/ n (*food*) verdura f; (*when growing*) ortaggio m
● *attrib* (*oil, fat*) vegetale

vegetarian /vedʒɪˈteərɪən/ a & n vegetariano, -a mf

vegetat|e /ˈvedʒɪteɪt/ vi vegetare.
~ion /-ˈteɪʃn/ n vegetazione f

vehemen|ce /ˈviːəmens/ n veemenza f. **~t** a veemente. **~tly** adv
con veemenza

vehicle /ˈviːɪkl/ n veicolo m; (*fig: medium*) mezzo m

veil /veɪl/ n velo m ● vt velare

vein /veɪn/ n vena f; (*mood*) umore m; (*manner*) tenore m. **~ed** a
venato

Velcro® /ˈvelkrəʊ/ n ~ **fastening** chiusura f con velcro®

velocity /vɪˈlɒsətɪ/ n velocità f

velvet /ˈvelvɪt/ n velluto m. **~y** a
vellutato

vendetta /venˈdetə/ n vendetta f

vending-machine /ˈvendɪŋ-/ n distributore m automatico

veneer /vəˈnɪə(r)/ n impiallacciatura f; *fig* vernice f. **~ed** a
impiallacciato

venereal /vɪˈnɪərɪəl/ a ~ **disease**
malattia f venerea

Venetian /vəˈniːʃn/ a & n veneziano, -a mf. **v~ blind** n persiana f
alla veneziana

vengeance /ˈvendʒəns/ n vendetta f; **with a ~** *fam* a più non posso

Venice /ˈvenɪs/ n Venezia f

venison /ˈvenɪsn/ n *Culin* carne f
di cervo

venom /ˈvenəm/ n veleno m. **~ous**
/-əs/ a velenoso

vent[1] /vent/ n presa f d'aria; **give
to** *fig* dar libero sfogo a ● vt fig
sfogare (*anger*)

vent[2] n (*in jacket*) spacco m

ventilat|e /ˈventɪleɪt/ vt ventilare.
~ion /-ˈleɪʃn/ n ventilazione f;
(*installation*) sistema m di ventilazione. **~or** n ventilatore m

ventriloquist /venˈtrɪləkwɪst/ n
ventriloquo, -a mf

venture /ˈventʃə(r)/ n impresa f
● vt azzardare ● vi avventurarsi

venue /ˈvenjuː/ n luogo m (*di convegno, concerto, ecc.*)

veranda /vəˈrændə/ n veranda f

verb /vɜːb/ n verbo m. **~al** a verbale

verbatim /vɜːˈbeɪtɪm/ a & adv letterale ● adv parola per parola

verbose /vɜːˈbəʊs/ a prolisso

verdict /ˈvɜːdɪkt/ n verdetto m;
(*opinion*) parere m

verge /vɜːdʒ/ n orlo m; **be on the ~
of doing sth** essere sul punto di
fare qcsa ● vi *fig* rasentare

verger /ˈvɜːdʒə(r)/ n sagrestano m

verify /ˈverɪfaɪ/ vt (pt/pp -**ied**) verificare; (*confirm*) confermare

vermin /ˈvɜːmɪn/ n animali mpl nocivi

vermouth /ˈvɜːməθ/ n vermut m

vernacular /vəˈnækjʊlə(r)/ n vernacolo m

versatil|e /ˈvɜːsətaɪl/ a versatile.
~ity /-ˈtɪlətɪ/ n versatilità f

verse /vɜːs/ n verso m; (*of Bible*)
versetto m; (*poetry*) versi mpl

versed /vɜːst/ a ~ **in** versato in

version /ˈvɜːʃn/ n versione f

versus /ˈvɜːsəs/ prep contro

vertebra /ˈvɜːtɪbrə/ n (pl -**brae**
/-briː/) *Anat* vertebra f

vertical /ˈvɜːtɪkl/ a & n verticale m

vertigo /ˈvɜːtɪgəʊ/ n *Med* vertigine f

verve /vɜːv/ n verve f

very /ˈverɪ/ adv molto; **~ much**
molto; **~ little** pochissimo; **~
many** moltissimi; **~ few** pochissimi; **~ probably** molto probabilmente; **~ well** benissimo; **at the ~
most** tutt'al più; **at the ~ latest** al
più tardi ● a the **~ first** il primissimo; **the ~ thing** proprio ciò che
ci vuole; **at the ~ end/beginning**
proprio alla fine/all'inizio; **that ~
day** proprio quel giorno; **the ~**

thought la sola idea; **only a ~ little** solo un pochino

vessel /'vesl/ n nave f

vest /vest/ n maglia f della pelle; (Am: waistcoat) gilè m inv. **~ed interest** n interesse m personale

vestige /'vestɪdʒ/ n (of past) vestigio m

vestment /'vestmənt/ n Relig paramento m

vestry /'vestrɪ/ n sagrestia f

vet /vet/ n veterinario, -a mf ● vt (pt/pp **vetted**) controllare minuziosamente

veteran /'vetərən/ n veterano, -a mf

veterinary /'vetərɪnərɪ/ a veterinario. **~ surgeon** n medico m veterinario

veto /'vi:təʊ/ n (pl **-es**) veto m ● vt proibire

vex /veks/ vt irritare. **~ation** /-'seɪʃn/ n irritazione f. **~ed** a irritato; **~ed question** questione f controversa

VHF n abbr (**very high frequency**) VHF

via /'vaɪə/ prep via; (by means of) attraverso

viable /'vaɪəbl/ a (life form, relationship, company) in grado di sopravvivere; (proposition) attuabile

viaduct /'vaɪədʌkt/ n viadotto m

vibrate /vaɪ'breɪt/ vi vibrare. **~ion** /-'breɪʃn/ n vibrazione f

vicar /'vɪkə(r)/ n parroco m (protestante). **~age** /-rɪdʒ/ n casa f parrocchiale

vicarious /vɪ'keərɪəs/ a indiretto

vice¹ /vaɪs/ n vizio m

vice² n Techn morsa f

vice 'chairman n vicepresidente mf

vice 'president n vicepresidente mf

vice versa /vaɪsɪ'vɜːsə/ adv viceversa

vicinity /vɪ'sɪnətɪ/ n vicinanza f; **in the ~ of** nelle vicinanze di

vicious /'vɪʃəs/ a cattivo; (attack)

brutale; (animal) pericoloso. **~ 'circle** n circolo m vizioso. **~ly** adv (attack) brutalmente

victim /'vɪktɪm/ n vittima f. **~ize** vt fare delle rappresaglie contro

victor /'vɪktə(r)/ n vincitore m

victorious /vɪk'tɔːrɪəs/ a vittorioso. **~y** /'vɪktərɪ/ n vittoria f

video /'vɪdɪəʊ/ n video m; (cassette) videocassetta f; (recorder) videoregistratore m ● attrib video ● vt registrare

video: **~ card** n Comput scheda f video. **~ cas'sette** n videocassetta f. **~conference** n videoconferenza f. **~ game** n videogioco m. **~ recorder** n videoregistratore m. **~tape** n videocassetta f

vie /vaɪ/ vi (pres p **vying**) rivaleggiare

view /vju:/ n vista f; (photographed, painted) veduta f; (opinion) visione f; **look at the ~** guardare il panorama; **in my ~** secondo me; **in ~ of** in considerazione di; **on ~** esposto; **with a ~ to** con l'intenzione di ● vt visitare (house); (consider) considerare ● vi TV guardare. **~er** n TV telespettatore, -trice mf; Phot visore m

view: **~finder** n Phot mirino m. **~point** n punto m di vista

vigil /'vɪdʒɪl/ n veglia f

vigilance /'vɪdʒɪləns/ n vigilanza f. **~t** a vigile

vigorous /'vɪgərəs/ a vigoroso

vigour /'vɪgə(r)/ n vigore m

vile /vaɪl/ a disgustoso; (weather) orribile; (temper, mood) pessimo

villa /'vɪlə/ n (for holidays) casa f di villeggiatura

village /'vɪlɪdʒ/ n paese m. **~r** n paesano, -a mf

villain /'vɪlən/ n furfante m; (in story) cattivo m

vindicate /'vɪndɪkeɪt/ vt (from guilt) discolpare; **you are ~d** ti sei dimostrato nel giusto

vindictive /vɪn'dɪktɪv/ a vendicativo

vine /vaɪn/ n vite f

vinegar /ˈvɪnɪgə(r)/ n aceto m

vineyard /ˈvɪnjɑːd/ n vigneto m

vintage /ˈvɪntɪdʒ/ a (wine) d'annata ● n (year) annata f

viola /vɪˈəʊlə/ n Mus viola f

violat|e /ˈvaɪəleɪt/ vt violare. **~ion** /-ˈleɪʃn/ n violazione f

violen|ce /ˈvaɪələns/ n violenza f. **~t** a violento

violet /ˈvaɪələt/ a violetto ● n (flower) violetta f; (colour) violetto m

violin /vaɪəˈlɪn/ n violino m. **~ist** n violinista mf

VIP n abbr (**very important person**) vip mf

virgin /ˈvɜːdʒɪn/ a vergine ● n vergine f. **~ity** /-ˈdʒɪnətɪ/ n verginità f

Virgo /ˈvɜːgəʊ/ n Vergine f

viril|e /ˈvɪraɪl/ a virile. **~ity** /-ˈrɪlətɪ/ n virilità f

virtual /ˈvɜːtjʊəl/ a effettivo. **~ reality** n realtà f virtuale. **~ly** adv praticamente

virtue /ˈvɜːtjuː/ n virtù f inv; (advantage) vantaggio m; **by** or **in ~ of** a causa di

virtuoso /vɜːtʊˈəʊzəʊ/ n (pl **-si** /-ziː/) virtuoso m

virtuous /ˈvɜːtjʊəs/ a virtuoso

virulent /ˈvɪrʊlənt/ a virulento

virus /ˈvaɪərəs/ n virus m inv

visa /ˈviːzə/ n visto m

vis-à-vis /viːzɑːˈviː/ prep rispetto a

viscount /ˈvaɪkaʊnt/ n visconte m

viscous /ˈvɪskəs/ a vischioso

visibility /vɪzəˈbɪlətɪ/ n visibilità f

visib|le /ˈvɪzəbl/ a visibile. **~ly** adv visibilmente

vision /ˈvɪʒn/ n visione f; (sight) vista f

visit /ˈvɪzɪt/ n visita f ● vt andare a trovare (person); andare da (doctor etc); visitare (town, building). **~ing hours** npl orario m delle visite. **~or** n ospite mf; (of town, museum) visitatore, -trice mf; (in hotel) cliente mf

visor /ˈvaɪzə(r)/ n visiera f; Auto parasole m

vista /ˈvɪstə/ n (view) panorama m

visual /ˈvɪzjʊəl/ a visivo. **~ aids** npl supporto m visivo. **~ dis|play unit** n visualizzatore m. **~ly** adv visualmente; **~ly handicapped** non vedente

visualize /ˈvɪzjʊəlaɪz/ vt visualizzare

vital /ˈvaɪtl/ a vitale. **~ity** /vaɪˈtælətɪ/ n vitalità f. **~ly** /ˈvaɪtəlɪ/ adv estremamente

vitamin /ˈvɪtəmɪn/ n vitamina f

vivaci|ous /vɪˈveɪʃəs/ a vivace. **~ty** /-ˈvæsətɪ/ n vivacità f

vivid /ˈvɪvɪd/ a vivido. **~ly** adv in modo vivido

vocabulary /vəˈkæbjʊlərɪ/ n vocabolario m; (list) glossario m

vocal /ˈvəʊkl/ a vocale; (vociferous) eloquente. **~ cords** npl corde fpl vocali

vocalist /ˈvəʊkəlɪst/ n vocalista mf

vocation /vəˈkeɪʃn/ n vocazione f. **~al** a di orientamento professionale

vociferous /vəˈsɪfərəs/ a vociante

vodka /ˈvɒdkə/ n vodka f inv

vogue /vəʊg/ n moda f; **in ~** in voga

voice /vɔɪs/ n voce f ● vt esprimere. **~mail** n posta f elettronica vocale

void /vɔɪd/ a (not valid) nullo; **~ of** privo di ● n vuoto m

volatile /ˈvɒlətaɪl/ a volatile; (person) volubile

volcanic /vɒlˈkænɪk/ a vulcanico

volcano /vɒlˈkeɪnəʊ/ n vulcano m

volition /vəˈlɪʃn/ n of **his own ~** di sua spontanea volontà

volley /ˈvɒlɪ/ n (of gunfire) raffica f; Tennis volée f inv

volt /vəʊlt/ n volt m inv. **~age** /-ɪdʒ/ n Electr voltaggio m

volub|le /ˈvɒljʊbl/ a loquace

volume /ˈvɒljuːm/ n volume m; (of work, traffic) quantità f inv. **~ control** n volume m

voluntar|y /ˈvɒləntərɪ/ a volontario. **~y work** n volontariato m. **~ily** adv volontariamente

volunteer /vɒlən'tɪə(r)/ n volontario, -a *mf* ● *vt* offrire volontariamente *(information)* ● *vi* offrirsi volontario; *Mil* arruolarsi come volontario

voluptuous /və'lʌptjʊəs/ a voluttuoso

vomit /'vɒmɪt/ n vomito m ● *vt/i* vomitare

voracious /və'reɪʃəs/ a vorace

vot|e /vəʊt/ n voto m; *(ballot)* votazione f; *(right)* diritto m di voto; **take a ~e on** votare su ● *vi* votare ● *vt* **~e sb president** eleggere qcno presidente. **~er** n elettore, -trice *mf*. **~ing** n votazione f

vouch /vaʊtʃ/ *vi* **~ for** garantire per. **~er** n buono m

vow /vaʊ/ n voto m ● *vt* giurare

vowel /'vaʊəl/ n vocale f

voyage /'vɔɪɪdʒ/ n viaggio m [marittimo]; *(in space)* viaggio m [nello spazio]

vulgar /'vʌlgə(r)/ a volgare. **~ity** /-'gærətɪ/ n volgarità f inv

vulnerable /'vʌlnərəbl/ a vulnerabile

vulture /'vʌltʃə(r)/ n avvoltoio m

vying /'vaɪɪŋ/ *see* **vie**

·······················

Ww

·······················

wad /wɒd/ n batuffolo m; *(bundle)* rotolo m. **~ding** n ovatta f

waddle /'wɒdl/ *vi* camminare ondeggiando

wade /weɪd/ *vi* guadare; **~ through** *fam* procedere faticosamente in *(book)*

wafer /'weɪfə(r)/ n cialda f, wafer m inv; *Relig* ostia f

waffle¹ /'wɒfl/ *vi fam* blaterare

waffle² n *Culin* cialda f

waft /wɒft/ *vt* trasportare ● *vi* diffondersi

wag /wæg/ v *(pt/pp wagged)* ● *vt* agitare ● *vi* agitarsi

wage¹ /weɪdʒ/ *vt* dichiarare *(war)*; lanciare *(campaign)*

wage² n & **~s** pl salario msg. **~ packet** n busta f paga

waggle /'wægl/ *vt* dimenare ● *vi* dimenarsi

wagon /'wægən/ n carro m; *Rail* vagone m merci

wail /weɪl/ n piagnucolio m; *(of wind)* lamento m; *(of baby)* vagito m ● *vi* piagnucolare; *(wind:)* lamentarsi; *(baby:)* vagire

waist /weɪst/ n vita f. **~coat** /'weɪskəʊt/ n gilè m inv; *(of man's suit)* panciotto m. **~line** n vita f

wait /weɪt/ n attesa f; **lie in ~ for** appostarsi per sorprendere ● *vi* aspettare; **~ for** aspettare ● *vt* **~ one's turn** aspettare il proprio turno. **wait on** *vt* servire

waiter /'weɪtə(r)/ n cameriere m

waiting: **~-list** n lista f d'attesa. **~-room** n sala f d'aspetto

waitress /'weɪtrɪs/ n cameriera f

waive /weɪv/ *vt* rinunciare a *(claim)*; non tener conto di *(rule)*

wake¹ /weɪk/ n veglia f funebre ● *v (pt woke, pp woken)* **~ [up]** ● *vt* svegliare ● *vi* svegliarsi

wake² n *Naut* scia f; **in the ~ of** *fig* nella scia di

waken /'weɪkn/ *vt* svegliare ● *vi* svegliarsi

Wales /weɪlz/ n Galles m

walk /wɔːk/ n passeggiata f; *(gait)* andatura f; *(path)* sentiero m; **go for a ~** andare a fare una passeggiata ● *vi* camminare; *(as opposed to drive etc)* andare a piedi; *(ramble)* passeggiare ● *vt* portare a spasso *(dog)*; percorrere *(streets)*. **walk out** *vi* *(husband, employee:)* andarsene; *(workers:)* scioperare. **walk out on** *vt* lasciare

walker /'wɔːkə(r)/ n camminatore, -trice *mf*; *(rambler)* escursionista *mf*

walking /'wɔːkɪŋ/ n camminare m; *(rambling)* fare delle escursioni. **~-stick** n bastone m da passeggio

'**Walkman**® n Walkman® m inv

walk: **~-out** n sciopero m. **~-over** n fig vittoria f facile

wall /wɔːl/ n muro m; **go to the ~** fam andare a rotoli; **drive sb up the ~** fam far diventare matto qcno ● **wall up** vt murare

wallet /ˈwɒlɪt/ n portafoglio m

wallop /ˈwɒləp/ n fam colpo m ● vt (pt/pp **walloped**) fam colpire

wallow /ˈwɒləʊ/ vi sguazzare; (in self-pity, grief) crogiolarsi

'**wallpaper** n tappezzeria f ● vt tappezzare

walnut /ˈwɔːlnʌt/ n noce f

waltz /wɔːlts/ n valzer m inv ● vi ballare il valzer

wan /wɒn/ a esangue

wand /wɒnd/ n (magic ~) bacchetta f (magica)

wander /ˈwɒndə(r)/ vi girovagare; (fig: digress) divagare. **wander about** vi andare a spasso

wane /weɪn/ n be on the ~ essere in fase calante ● vi calare

wangle /ˈwæŋgl/ vt fam rimediare (invitation, holiday)

want /wɒnt/ n (for want) bisogno m; (lack) mancanza f ● vt volere; (need) aver bisogno di; ~ to do sth volere fare qcsa; ~ sb to do sth voler che qcno faccia qcsa; we ~ to stay vogliamo rimanere; **I ~ you to go** voglio che tu vada; **it ~s painting** ha bisogno d'essere dipinto; **you ~ to learn to swim** bisogna che impari a nuotare ● vi **~ for** mancare di. **~ed** a ricercato. **~ing** a be **~ing** in mancare di

wanton /ˈwɒntən/ a (cruelty, neglect) gratuito; (morally) debosciato

war /wɔː(r)/ n guerra f; fig lotta f (on contro); **at ~** in guerra

ward /wɔːd/ n (in hospital) reparto m; (child) minore m sotto tutela ● **ward off** vt evitare; parare (blow)

warden /ˈwɔːdn/ n guardiano, -a mf

warder /ˈwɔːdə(r)/ n guardia f carceraria

wardrobe /ˈwɔːdrəʊb/ n guardaroba m

warehouse /ˈweəhaʊs/ n magazzino m

war: **~fare** n guerra f. **~head** n testata f

warily /ˈweərɪlɪ/ adv cautamente

warlike /ˈwɔːlaɪk/ a bellicoso

warm /wɔːm/ a caldo; (welcome) caloroso; **be ~** (person:) aver caldo; **it is ~** (weather) fa caldo ● vt scaldare. **warm up** vt scaldare ● vi scaldarsi; fig animarsi. **~-hearted** a espansivo. **~ly** adv (greet) calorosamente; (dress) in modo pesante

warmth /wɔːmθ/ n calore m

warn /wɔːn/ vt avvertire. **~ing** n avvertimento m; (advance notice) preavviso m

warp /wɔːp/ vt deformare; fig distorcere ● vi deformarsi

'**war-path** n on the ~ sul sentiero di guerra

warped /wɔːpt/ a fig contorto; (sexuality) deviato; (view) distorto

warrant /ˈwɒrənt/ n (for arrest, search) mandato m ● vt (justify) giustificare; (guarantee) garantire

warranty /ˈwɒrəntɪ/ n garanzia f

warring /ˈwɔːrɪŋ/ a in guerra

warrior /ˈwɒrɪə(r)/ n guerriero, -a mf

'**warship** n nave f da guerra

wart /wɔːt/ n porro m

'**wartime** n tempo m di guerra

wary /ˈweərɪ/ a (-ier, -iest) (careful) cauto; (suspicious) diffidente

was /wɒz/ see **be**

wash /wɒʃ/ n lavata f; (clothes) bucato m; (in washing machine) lavaggio m; **have a ~** darsi una lavata ● vt lavare; (sea:) bagnare; ~ **one's hands** lavarsi le mani ● vi lavarsi. **wash out** vt sciacquare (soap); sciacquarsi (mouth). **wash up** vt lavare ● vi lavare i piatti; Am lavarsi

washable /ˈwɒʃəbl/ a lavabile

wash: ~-**basin** n lavandino m. ~-**cloth** n Am ≈ guanto m da bagno

washed 'out a (faded) scolorito; (tired) spossato

washer /ˈwɒʃə(r)/ n Techn guarnizione f; (machine) lavatrice f

washing /ˈwɒʃɪŋ/ n bucato m. ~-**machine** n lavatrice f. ~-**powder** n detersivo m. ~-**up** n do the ~**up** lavare i piatti. ~-**up liquid** n detersivo m per i piatti

wash: ~-**out** n disastro m. ~-**room** n bagno m

wasp /wɒsp/ n vespa f

wastage /ˈweɪstɪdʒ/ n perdita f

waste /weɪst/ n spreco m; (rubbish) rifiuto m; ~ **of time** perdita f di tempo ● a (product) di scarto; (land) desolato; **lay** ~ devastare ● vt sprecare. **waste away** vi deperire

waste: ~-**di'sposal unit** n eliminatore m di rifiuti. ~-**ful** a dispendioso. ~ '**paper** n carta f straccia. ~-'**paper basket** n cestino m per la carta [straccia]

watch /wɒtʃ/ n guardia f; (period of duty) turno m di guardia; (timepiece) orologio m; **be on the** ~ **stare all'erta** ● vt guardare (film, match, television); (be careful of, look after) stare attento a ● vi guardare. **watch out** vi (be careful) stare attento. **watch out for** vt (look for) fare attenzione all'arrivo di (person)

watch: ~-**dog** n cane m da guardia. ~-**ful** a attento. ~-**maker** n orologiaio, -a m/f. ~-**man** n guardiano m. ~-**strap** n cinturino m dell'orologio. ~-**word** n motto m

water /ˈwɔːtə(r)/ n acqua f ● vt annaffiare (garden, plant); (dilute) annacquare ● vi (eyes:) lacrimare; **my mouth was** ~**ing** avevo l'acquolina in bocca. **water down** vt diluire; fig attenuare

water: ~-**colour** n acquerello m. ~**cress** n crescione m. ~-**fall** n cascata f

'**watering-can** n annaffiatoio m

water: ~-**lily** n ninfea f. ~ **logged** a inzuppato. ~-**main** n conduttura f dell'acqua. ~ **polo** n pallanuoto f. ~-**power** n energia f idraulica. ~-**proof** a impermeabile. ~-**shed** n spartiacque m inv; fig svolta f. ~-**skiing** n sci m nautico. ~-**tight** a stagno; fig irrefutabile. ~-**way** n canale m navigabile

watery /ˈwɔːtəri/ a acquoso; (eyes) lacrimoso

watt /wɒt/ n watt m inv

wave /weɪv/ n onda f; (gesture) cenno m; fig ondata f ● vt agitare; ~ **one's hand** agitare la mano ● vi far segno; (flag:) sventolare. ~**length** n lunghezza f d'onda

waver /ˈweɪvə(r)/ vi vacillare; (hesitate) esitare

wavy /ˈweɪvi/ a ondulato

wax[1] /wæks/ vi (moon:) crescere; (fig: become) diventare

wax[2] n cera f; (in ear) cerume m ● vt dare la cera a. ~**works** n museo m delle cere

way /weɪ/ n percorso m; (direction) direzione f; (manner, method) modo m; ~**s** pl (customs) abitudini fpl; **be in the** ~ essere in mezzo; **on the** ~ **to Rome** andando a Roma; **I'll do it on the** ~ lo faccio mentre vado; **it's on my** ~ è sul mio percorso; **a long** ~ **off** lontano; **this** ~ da questa parte; (like this) così; **by the** ~ a proposito; **by** ~ **of** come; (via) via; **either** ~ (whatever we do) in un modo o nell'altro; **in some** ~**s** sotto certi aspetti; **in a** ~ in un certo senso; **in a bad** ~ (person) molto grave; **out of the** ~ fuori mano; **under** ~ in corso; **lead the** ~ far strada; fig aprire la strada; **make** ~ far posto (**for** a); **give** ~ Auto dare la precedenza; **go out of one's** ~ fig accomodarsi (**to** per); **get one's [own]** ~ averla vinta ● adv ~ **behind** molto indietro. ~ '**in** n entrata f

way'lay vt (pt/pp -laid) aspettare al varco (person)

way 'out n uscita f; fig via f d'uscita

way-'out a fam eccentrico

wayward /'weɪwəd/ a capriccioso

WC n abbr WC; **the WC** il gabinetto m

we /wiː/ pron noi; **we're the last** siamo gli ultimi; **they're going, but we're not** loro vanno, ma noi no

weak /wiːk/ a debole; ‹liquid› leggero. **~en** vt indebolire ● vi indebolirsi. **~ling** n smidollato, -a mf. **~ness** n debolezza f; ‹liking› debole m

wealth /welθ/ n ricchezza f; fig gran quantità f. **~y** a ‹-ier, -iest› ricco

wean /wiːn/ vt svezzare

weapon /'wepən/ n arma f

wear /weə(r)/ n ‹clothing› abbigliamento m; **for everyday** ~ da portare tutti i giorni; ~ [and tear] usura f ● v (pt wore, pp worn) ● vt portare; ‹damage› consumare; ~ **a hole in sth** logorare qcsa fino a fare un buco; **what shall I** ~? cosa mi metto? ● vi consumarsi; ‹last› durare. **wear off** vi scomparire; ‹effect:› finire. **wear out** vi consumare [fino in fondo]; ‹exhaust› estenuare ● vi estenuarsi

wearable /'weərəbl/ a portabile

weary /'wɪərɪ/ a ‹-ier, -iest› sfinito ● v (pt/pp wearied) ● vt sfinire ● vi ~y of stancarsi di. **~ily** adv stancamente

weasel /'wiːzl/ n donnola f

weather /'weðə(r)/ n tempo m; **in this** ~ con questo tempo; **under the** ~ fam giù di corda ● vt sopravvivere a ‹storm›

weather: **~-beaten** a ‹face› segnato dalle intemperie. **~-cock** n gallo m segnavento. ~ **forecast** n previsioni fpl del tempo

weave¹ /wiːv/ vi (pt/pp weaved) ‹move› zigzagare

weave² n tessuto m ● vt (pt wove, pp woven) tessere; intrecciare ‹flowers etc›; intrecciare le fila di ‹story etc›. **~r** n tessitore, -trice mf

web /web/ n rete f; (of spider) ragnatela f. **~bed feet** npl piedi mpl palmati. **W~ page** n Comput pagina f web. **W~ site** n Comput sito m web

wed /wed/ vt (pt/pp wedded) sposare ● vi sposarsi. **~ding** n matrimonio m

wedding: ~ **cake** n torta f nuziale. ~ **day** n giorno m del matrimonio. ~ **dress** n vestito m da sposa. **~-ring** n fede f

wedge /wedʒ/ n zeppa f; (for splitting wood) cuneo m; (of cheese) fetta f ● vt (fix) fissare

wedlock /'wedlɒk/ n **born out of** ~ nato fuori dal matrimonio

Wednesday /'wenzdeɪ/ n mercoledì m inv

wee¹ /wiː/ a fam piccolo

wee² vi fam fare la pipì

weed /wiːd/ n erbaccia f; (fam: person) mollusco m ● vt estirpare le erbacce da. **weed out** vt fig eliminare

'weed-killer n erbicida m

weedy /'wiːdɪ/ a fam mingherlino

week /wiːk/ n settimana f. **~day** n giorno m feriale. **~end** n fine settimana m

weekly /'wiːklɪ/ a settimanale ● n settimanale m ● adv settimanalmente

weep /wiːp/ vi (pt/pp wept) piangere

weigh /weɪ/ vt/i pesare; ~ **anchor** levare l'ancora. **weigh down** vt fig piegare. **weigh up** vt fig soppesare; valutare ‹person›

weight /weɪt/ n peso m; **put on/lose** ~ ingrassare/dimagrire. **~ing** n ‹allowance› indennità f inv

weight: **~lessness** n assenza f di gravità. **~-lifting** n sollevamento m pesi

weighty /'weɪtɪ/ a ‹-ier, -iest› pesante; (important) di un certo peso

weir /wɪə(r)/ n chiusa f

weird /wɪəd/ a misterioso; (bizarre) bizzarro

welcome /'welkəm/ *a* benvenuto; **you're ~!** prego!; **you're ~ to have it/to come** prendilo/vieni pure ● *n* accoglienza *f* ● *vt* accogliere; *(appreciate)* gradire

weld /weld/ *vt* saldare. **~er** *n* saldatore *m*

welfare /'welfeə(r)/ *n* benessere *m*; *(aid)* assistenza *f*. **W~ State** *n* Stato *m* assistenziale

well[1] /wel/ *n* pozzo *m*; *(of staircase)* tromba *f*

well[2] *adv* (**better**, **best**) bene; **as ~** anche; **as ~ as** *(in addition)* oltre a; **~ done!** bravo!; **very ~** benissimo ● *a* **he is not ~** non sta bene; **get ~ soon!** guarisci presto! ● *int* beh!; **~ I never!** ma va!

well: **~-behaved** *a* educato. **~-being** *n* benessere *m*. **~-bred** *a* beneducato. **~-heeled** *a fam* danaroso

wellingtons /'welɪŋtənz/ *npl* stivali *mpl* di gomma

well: **~-known** *a* famoso. **~-meaning** *a* con buone intenzioni. **~-meant** *a* con le migliori intenzioni. **~-off** *a* benestante. **~-read** *a* colto. **~-to-do** *a* ricco

Welsh /welʃ/ *a & n* gallese; the ~ *pl* i gallesi. **~man** *n* gallese *m*. **~ rabbit** *n* toast *m inv* al formaggio

went /went/ *see* **go**

wept /wept/ *see* **weep**

were /wɜː(r)/ *see* **be**

west /west/ *n* ovest *m*; **to the ~ of** a ovest di; the **W~** l'Occidente *m* ● *a* occidentale ● *adv* verso occidente; **go ~** *fam* andare in malora. **~erly** *a* verso ovest; occidentale *(wind)*. **~ern** *a* occidentale ● *n* western *m inv*

West: **~ 'Germany** *n* Germania *f* Occidentale. **~ 'Indian** *a & n* antillese *mf*. **~ 'Indies** /'ɪndɪz/ *npl* Antille *fpl*

'westward[s] /[-wəd[z]/ *adv* verso ovest

wet /wet/ *a* (**wetter**, **wettest**) bagnato; fresco *(paint)*; *(rainy)* piovoso; *(fam: person)* smidollato;

get ~ bagnarsi ● *vt* *(pt/pp* **wet**, **wetted**) bagnare. **~ 'blanket** *n* guastafeste *mf inv*

whack /wæk/ *n fam* colpo *m* ● *vt fam* dare un colpo a. **~ed** *a fam* stanco morto. **~ing** *a* *(fam: huge)* enorme

whale /weɪl/ *n* balena *f*; **have a ~ of a time** *fam* divertirsi un sacco

wham /wæm/ *int* bum

wharf /wɔːf/ *n* banchina *f*

what /wɒt/ *pron* che, [che] cosa; **~ for?** perché?; **~ is that for?** a che cosa serve?; **~ is it?** *(what do you want)* cosa c'è?; **~ is it like?** com'è?; **~ is your name?** come ti chiami?; **~ is the weather like?** com'è il tempo?; **~ is the film about?** di cosa parla il film?; **~ is he talking about?** di cosa sta parlando?; **he asked me ~ she had said** mi ha chiesto cosa ho detto; **~ about going to the cinema?** e se andassimo al cinema?; **~ about the children?** *(what will they do)* e i bambini?; **~ if it rains?** e se piove? ● *a* quale, che; **take ~ books you want** prendi tutti i libri che vuoi; **~ kind of a** che tipo di; **at ~ time?** a che ora? ● *adv* che; **a lovely day!** che bella giornata! ● *int* **~!** [che] cosa!; **~?** [che] cosa?

what'ever *a* qualunque ● *pron* qualsiasi cosa; **~ is it?** cos'è?; **he does** qualsiasi cosa faccia; **~ happens** qualunque cosa succeda; **nothing ~** proprio niente

whatso'ever *a & pron* = **whatever**

wheat /wiːt/ *n* grano *m*, frumento *m*

wheedle /'wiːd(ə)l/ *vt* **~ sth out of sb** ottenere qcsa da qualcuno con le lusinghe

wheel /wiːl/ *n* ruota *f*; *(steering ~)* volante *m*; **at the ~** al volante ● *vi (push)* spingere ● *vi (circle)* ruotare; **~ [round]** ruotare

wheel: **~barrow** *n* carriola *f*. **~chair** *n* sedia *f* a rotelle. **~clamp** *n* ceppo *m* bloccaruote

wheeze /wiːz/ *vi* ansimare

when /wen/ adv & conj quando; **the day ~** il giorno in cui; **~ swimming/reading** nuotando/leggendo

when'ever adv & conj in qualsiasi momento; (every time that) ogni volta che; **~ did it happen?** quando è successo?

where /weə(r)/ adv & conj dove; **the street ~** I live la via in cui abito; **~ do you come from?** da dove vieni?

whereabouts¹ /'weərə'baʊts/ adv dove

'whereabouts² nobody knows his ~ nessuno sa dove si trova

where'as conj dal momento che; (in contrast) mentre

where'by adv attraverso il quale

whereu'pon adv dopo di che

wher'ever adv & conj dovunque; **~ is he?** dov'è mai?; **~ possible** dovunque sia possibile

whet /wet/ vt (pt/pp whetted) aguzzare ⟨appetite⟩

whether /'weðə(r)/ conj se; **~ you like it or not** che ti piaccia o no

which /wɪtʃ/ a & pron quale; **~ one?** quale?; **~ one of you?** chi di voi?; **~ way?** (direction) in che direzione? ● rel pron (object) che; **he does frequently** cosa che fa spesso; **after ~** dopo di che; **on/in ~** su/in cui

which'ever a & pron qualunque; **~ it is** qualunque sia; **~ one of you** chiunque tra voi

whiff /wɪf/ n zaffata f; **have a ~ of** sth odorare qcsa

while /waɪl/ n a long ~ un bel po'; **a little ~** un po' ● conj mentre; (as long as) finché; (although) sebbene ● **while away** vt passare ⟨time⟩

whilst /waɪlst/ conj see while

whim /wɪm/ n capriccio m

whimper /'wɪmpə(r)/ vi piagnucolare; ⟨dog:⟩ guaire

whimsical /'wɪmzɪkl/ a capriccioso; ⟨story⟩ fantasioso

whine /waɪn/ n lamento m; (of dog)

guaito m ● vi lamentarsi; ⟨dog:⟩ guaire

whip /wɪp/ n frusta f; (pol: person) parlamentare mf incaricato, -a di assicurarsi della presenza dei membri del suo partito alle votazioni ● vt (pt/pp whipped) frustare; Culin sbattere; (snatch) afferrare; (fam: steal) fregare. **whip up** vt (incite) stimolare; fam improvvisare ⟨meal⟩. **~ped 'cream** n panna f montata

whirl /wɜːl/ n (movement) rotazione f; **my mind's in a ~** ho le idee confuse ● vi girare rapidamente ● vt far girare rapidamente. **~pool** n vortice m. **~wind** n turbine m

whirr /wɜː(r)/ vi ronzare

whisk /wɪsk/ n Culin frullino m ● vt Culin frullare. **whisk away** vt portare via

whisker /'wɪskə(r)/ n **~s** (of cat) baffi mpl; (on man's cheek) basette fpl; **by a ~** per un pelo

whisky /'wɪskɪ/ n whisky m inv

whisper /'wɪspə(r)/ n sussurro m; (rumour) diceria f ● vt/i sussurrare

whistle /'wɪsl/ n fischio m; (instrument) fischietto m ● vt fischiettare ● vi fischiettare; ⟨referee:⟩ fischiare

white /waɪt/ a bianco; **go ~** (pale) sbiancare ● n bianco m; (of egg) albume m; (person) bianco, -a mf

white: ~ 'coffee n caffè m inv macchiato. **~-'collar worker** n colletto m bianco

'Whitehall n strada f di Londra, sede degli uffici del governo britannico; fig amministrazione f britannica

white 'lie n bugia f pietosa

whiten /'waɪtn/ vt imbiancare ● vi sbiancare

whiteness /'waɪtnɪs/ n bianchezza f

'whitewash n intonaco m; fig copertura f ● vt dare una mano d'intonaco a; fig coprire

Whitsun /'wɪtsn/ n Pentecoste f

whittle /'wɪtl/ vt **~ down** ridurre

whiz[z] /wɪz/ vi (pt/pp whizzed) sibilare. **~-kid** n fam giovane m prodigio

who /hu:/ inter pron chi • rel pron che; **the children, ~ were all tired,...** i bambini, che erano tutti stanchi,...

who'ever pron chiunque; **~ he is** chiunque sia; **~ can that be?** chi può mai essere?

whole /həʊl/ a tutto; (not broken) intatto; **the ~ truth** tutta la verità; **the ~ world** il mondo intero; **the ~ lot** (everything) tutto; (pl) tutti; **the ~ lot of you** tutti voi • n tutto m; **as a ~** nell'insieme; **on the ~** tutto considerato; **the ~ of Italy** tutta l'Italia

whole: **~food** n cibo m macrobiotico. **~-hearted** a di tutto cuore. **~meal** a integrale

'wholesale a & adv all'ingrosso; fig in massa. **~r** n grossista mf

wholesome /'həʊlsəm/ a sano

wholly /'həʊlɪ/ adv completamente

whom /hu:m/ rel pron che; **the man ~ I saw** l'uomo che ho visto; **to/with ~** a/con cui • inter pron chi; **to ~ did you speak?** con chi hai parlato?

whooping cough /'hu:pɪŋ/ n pertosse f

whopping /'wɒpɪŋ/ a fam enorme

whore /hɔ:(r)/ n puttana f vulg

whose /hu:z/ rel pron il cui; **people ~ name begins with D** le persone i cui nomi cominciano con la D • inter pron di chi; **~ is that?** di chi è quello? • a **~ car did you use?** di chi è la macchina che hai usato?

why /waɪ/ adv (inter) perché; **the reason ~** la ragione per cui; **that's ~** per questo • int diamine

wick /wɪk/ n stoppino m

wicked /'wɪkɪd/ a cattivo; (mischievous) malizioso

wicker /'wɪkə(r)/ n vimini mpl • attrib di vimini

wide /waɪd/ a largo; (experience, knowledge) vasto; (difference) profondo; (far from target) lontano; **10 cm ~** largo 10 cm; **how ~ is it?** quanto è largo? • adv (off target) lontano dal bersaglio; **~ awake** del tutto sveglio; **~ open** spalancato; **far and ~** in lungo e in largo. **~ly** adv largamente; (known, accepted) generalmente; (different) profondamente

widen /'waɪdn/ vt allargare • vi allargarsi

'widespread a diffuso

widow /'wɪdəʊ/ n vedova f. **~ed** a vedovo. **~er** n vedovo m

width /wɪdθ/ n larghezza f; (of material) altezza f

wield /wi:ld/ vt maneggiare; esercitare (power)

wife /waɪf/ n (pl wives) moglie f

wig /wɪg/ n parrucca f

wiggle /'wɪgl/ vi dimenarsi • vt dimenare

wild /waɪld/ a selvaggio; (animal, flower) selvatico; (furious) furibondo; (applause) fragoroso; (idea) folle; (with joy) pazzo; (guess) azzardato; **be ~ about** (keen on) andare pazzo per • adv **run** ~ crescere senza controllo • n **in the ~** allo stato naturale; **the ~s** pl le zone fpl sperdute

wilderness /'wɪldənɪs/ n deserto m; (fig: garden) giungla f

'wildfire n **spread like ~** allargarsi a macchia d'olio

wild: **~-'goose chase** n ricerca f inutile. **~life** n animali mpl selvatici

wilful /'wɪlfl/ a intenzionale; (person, refusal) ostinato. **~ly** adv intenzionalmente; (refuse) ostinatamente

will[1] /wɪl/ v aux **he ~ arrive tomorrow** arriverà domani; **I won't tell him** non glielo dirò; **you ~ be back soon, won't you?** tornerai presto, no?; **he ~ be there, won't he?** sarà là, no?; **she ~ be there by now** sarà là ormai; **~**

you go? (*do you intend to go*) pensi di andare?; **~ you go to the baker's and buy...?** puoi andare dal panettiere a comprare...?; **~ you be quiet!** vuoi stare calmo?; **~ you have some wine?** vuoi del vino?; **the engine won't start** la macchina non parte

will[2] *n* volontà *f inv*; (*document*) testamento *m*

willing /'wɪlɪŋ/ *a* disposto; (*eager*) volonteroso. **~ly** *adv* volentieri. **~ness** *n* buona volontà *f*

willow /'wɪləʊ/ *n* salice *m*

'will-power *n* forza *f* di volontà

willy-'nilly *adv* (*at random*) a casaccio; (*wanting to or not*) volente o nolente

wilt /wɪlt/ *vi* appassire

wily /'waɪlɪ/ *a* (**-ier, -iest**) astuto

wimp /wɪmp/ *n* rammollito, -a *mf*

win /wɪn/ *n* vittoria *f*; **have a ~** riportare una vittoria ●*v* (*pt/pp won*; *pres p winning*) ●*vt* vincere; conquistare (*fame*) ●*vi* vincere. **win over** *vt* convincere

wince /wɪns/ *vi* contrarre il viso

winch /wɪntʃ/ *n* argano *m*

wind[1] /wɪnd/ *n* vento *m*; (*breath*) fiato *m*; (*fam: flatulence*) aria *f*; **get/have the ~ up** *fam* aver fifa; **get ~ of** aver sentore di; **in the ~** nell'aria ●*vt* **~ sb** lasciare qcno senza fiato

wind[2] /waɪnd/ *v* (*pt/pp wound*) ●*vt* (*wrap*) avvolgere; (*move by turning*) far girare; (*clock*) caricare ●*vi* (*road:*) serpeggiare. **wind up** *vt* caricare (*clock*); concludere (*proceedings*); *fam* prendere in giro (*sb*)

wind /wɪnd/: **~fall** *n* fig fortuna *f* inaspettata

winding /'waɪndɪŋ/ *a* tortuoso

wind: **~ instrument** *n* strumento *m* a fiato. **~mill** *n* mulino *m* a vento

window /'wɪndəʊ/ *n* finestra *f*; (*of car*) finestrino *m*; (*of shop*) vetrina *f*

window: **~-box** *n* cassetta *f* per

i fiori. **~-cleaner** *n* (*person*) lavavetri *mf inv*. **~-dresser** *n* vetrinista *mf*. **~-dressing** *n* vetrinistica *f*; fig fumo *m* negli occhi. **~-pane** *n* vetro *m*. **~-shopping** *n*: **go ~-shopping** andare in giro a vedere le vetrine. **~-sill** *n* davanzale *m*

'windscreen *n*, *Am* **'windshield** *n* parabrezza *m inv*. **~ washer** *n* getto *m* d'acqua. **~-wiper** *n* tergicristallo *m*

wind: **~ surfing** *n* windsurf *m inv*. **~-swept** *a* esposto al vento; (*person*) scompigliato

windy /'wɪndɪ/ *a* (**-ier, -iest**) ventoso

wine /waɪn/ *n* vino *m*

wine: **~-bar** *n* enoteca *f*. **~glass** *n* bicchiere *m* da vino. **~-list** *n* carta *f* dei vini

winery /'waɪnərɪ/ *n Am* vigneto *m*

'wine-tasting *n* degustazione *f* di vini

wing /wɪŋ/ *n* ala *f*; *Auto* parafango *m*; **~s** *pl Theat* quinte *fpl*. **~er** *n Sport* ala *f*

wink /wɪŋk/ *n* strizzata *f* d'occhio; **not sleep a ~** non chiudere occhio ●*vi* strizzare l'occhio; (*light:*) lampeggiare

winner /'wɪnə(r)/ *n* vincitore, -trice *mf*

winning /'wɪnɪŋ/ *a* vincente; (*smile*) accattivante. **~-post** *n* linea *f* d'arrivo. **~s** *npl* vincite *fpl*

winter /'wɪntə(r)/ *n* inverno *m*. **~ry** *a* invernale

wipe /waɪp/ *n* passata *f*; (*to dry*) asciugata *f* ●*vt* strofinare; (*dry*) asciugare. **wipe off** *vt* asciugare; (*erase*) cancellare. **wipe out** *vt* annientare; eliminare (*village*); estinguere (*debt*). **wipe up** *vt* asciugare (*dishes*)

wire /waɪə(r)/ *n* fil *m* di ferro; (*electrical*) filo *m* elettrico

wireless /'waɪəlɪs/ *n* radio *f*

wire 'netting *n* rete *f* metallica

wiring /'waɪərɪŋ/ *n* impianto *m* elettrico

wiry /'waɪərɪ/ *a* (-ier, -iest) ⟨person⟩ dal fisico asciutto; ⟨hair⟩ ispido

wisdom /'wɪzdəm/ *n* saggezza *f*; ⟨of action⟩ sensatezza *f*. ~ **tooth** *n* dente *m* del giudizio

wise /waɪz/ *a* saggio; ⟨prudent⟩ sensato. ~**ly** *adv* saggiamente; ⟨act⟩ sensatamente

wish /wɪʃ/ *n* desiderio *m*; **make a** ~ esprimere un desiderio; **with best** ~**es** con i migliori auguri ● *vt* desiderare; ~ **sb well** fare tanti auguri a qcno; **I** ~ **you every success** ti auguro buona fortuna; **I** ~ **you could stay** vorrei che tu potessi rimanere ● *vi* ~ **for sth** desiderare qcsa. ~**ful** *a* ~**ful thinking** illusione *f*

wishy-washy /'wɪʃɪwɒʃɪ/ *a* ⟨colour⟩ spento; ⟨personality⟩ insignificante

wisp /wɪsp/ *n* ⟨of hair⟩ ciocca *f*; ⟨of smoke⟩ filo *m*; ⟨of grass⟩ ciuffo *m*

wistful /'wɪstfl/ *a* malinconico

wit /wɪt/ *n* spirito *m*; ⟨person⟩ persona *f* di spirito; **be at one's** ~**s' end** non saper che pesci pigliare

witch /wɪtʃ/ *n* strega *f*. ~**craft** *n* magia *f*. ~**-hunt** *n* caccia *f* alle streghe

with /wɪð/ *prep* con; ⟨fear, cold, jealousy etc⟩ di; **I'm not** ~ **you** fam non ti seguo; **can I leave it** ~ **you?** puoi occuparten tu?; ~ **no regrets/money** senza rimpianti/soldi; **be** ~ **it** fam essere al passo coi tempi; ⟨alert⟩ essere concentrato

withdraw *v* (*pt* -drew, *pp* -drawn) ● *vt* ritirare; prelevare ⟨money⟩ ● *vi* ritirarsi. ~**al** *n* ritiro *m*; ⟨from money⟩ prelevamento *m*; ⟨from drugs⟩ crisi *f inv* di astinenza; *Psych* chiusura *f* in se stessi. ~**al symptoms** *npl* sintomi *mpl* da crisi di astinenza

withdrawn *see* withdraw ● *a* ⟨person⟩ chiuso in se stesso

wither /'wɪðə(r)/ *vi* ⟨flower:⟩ appassire

withhold *vt* (*pt/pp* -held) rifiutare ⟨consent⟩ (from a); nascondere ⟨information⟩ (from a); trattenere ⟨smile⟩

within *prep* in; ⟨before the end of⟩ entro; ~ **the law** legale ● *adv* all'interno

without *prep* senza; ~ **stopping** senza fermarsi

withstand *vt* (*pt/pp* -stood) resistere a

witness /'wɪtnɪs/ *n* testimone *mf* ● *vt* autenticare ⟨signature⟩; essere testimone di ⟨accident⟩. ~**-box** *n*, *Am* ~**-stand** *n* banco *m* dei testimoni

witticism /'wɪtɪsɪzm/ *n* spiritosaggine *f*

wittingly /'wɪtɪŋlɪ/ *adv* consapevolmente

witty /'wɪtɪ/ *a* (-ier, -iest) spiritoso

wives /waɪvz/ *see* **wife**

wizard /'wɪzəd/ *n* mago *m*. ~**ry** *n* stregoneria *f*

wobble /'wɒbl/ *vi* traballare. ~**ly** *a* traballante

wodge /wɒdʒ/ *n* fam mucchio *m*

woe /wəʊ/ *n* afflizione *f*

woke, woken /wəʊk, 'wəʊkn/ *see* **wake**[1]

wolf /wʊlf/ *n* (*pl* **wolves** /wʊlvz/) lupo *m*; ⟨fam: womanizer⟩ donnaiolo *m* ● *vt* ~ [**down**] divorare. ~ **whistle** *n* fischio *m* ● *vi* ~**-whistle at sb** fischiare dietro a qcno

woman /'wʊmən/ *n* (*pl* **women**) donna *f*. ~**izer** *n* donnaiolo *m*. ~**ly** *a* femmineo

womb /wu:m/ *n* utero *m*

women /'wɪmɪn/ *see* **woman**. **W**~'**s Libber** /'lɪbə(r)/ *n* femminista *f*. **W**~'**s Liberation** *n* movimento *m* femminista

won /wʌn/ *see* **win**

wonder /'wʌndə(r)/ *n* meraviglia *f*; ⟨surprise⟩ stupore *m*; **no** ~! non c'è da stupirsi!; **it's a** ~ **that...** è incredibile che... ● *vi* restare in ammirazione; ⟨be surprised⟩ essere sorpreso; **I** ~ è quello che mi chiedo; **I** ~ **whether she is ill** mi chiedo se è malata?. **~ful** a meraviglioso. **~fully** adv meravigliosamente

won't /wəʊnt/ = will not

woo /wuː/ vt corteggiare; fig cercare di accattivarsi ⟨voters⟩

wood /wʊd/ n legno m; ⟨for burning⟩ legna f; ⟨forest⟩ bosco m; **out of the ~** fig fuori pericolo; **touch ~!** tocca ferro!

wood: **~ed** /-ɪd/ a boscoso. **~en** a di legno; fig legnoso. **~ wind** n strumenti mpl a fiato. **~work** n ⟨wooden parts⟩ parti fpl in legno; ⟨craft⟩ falegnameria f. **~worm** n tarlo m. **~y** a legnoso; ⟨hill⟩ boscoso

wool /wʊl/ n lana f ● attrib di lana. **~len** a di lana. **~lens** npl capi mpl di lana

woolly /ˈwʊlɪ/ a (**-ier, -iest**) ⟨sweater⟩ di lana; fig confuso

word /wɜːd/ n parola f; ⟨news⟩ notizia f; **by ~ of mouth** a viva voce; **have a ~ with** dire due parole a; **have ~s** bisticciare; **in other ~s** in altre parole. **~ing** n parole fpl. **~ processor** n programma m di videoscrittura, word processor m inv

wore /wɔː(r)/ see **wear**

work /wɜːk/ n lavoro m; ⟨of art⟩ opera f. **~s** pl ⟨factory⟩ fabbrica fsg; ⟨mechanism⟩ meccanismo msg; **at ~** al lavoro; **out of ~** disoccupato ● vi lavorare; ⟨machine, ruse⟩ funzionare; ⟨study⟩ studiare ● vt far funzionare ⟨machine⟩; far lavorare ⟨employee⟩; far studiare ⟨student⟩. **work off** vt sfogare ⟨anger⟩; lavorare per estinguere ⟨debt⟩; fare sport per smaltire ⟨weight⟩. **work out** vt elaborare ⟨plan⟩; risolvere ⟨problem⟩; calcolare ⟨bill⟩; **I ~ed out how he did it** ho capito come l'ha fatto ● vi evolvere. **work up** vt **I've ~ed up an appetite** mi è venuto appetito; **don't get ~ed up** ⟨anxious⟩ non farti prendere dal panico; ⟨angry⟩ non arrabbiarti

workable /ˈwɜːkəbl/ a ⟨feasible⟩ fattibile

workaholic /wɜːkəˈhɒlɪk/ n stacanovista mf

worker /ˈwɜːkə(r)/ n lavoratore, -trice mf; ⟨manual⟩ operaio, -a mf

working /ˈwɜːkɪŋ/ a ⟨clothes etc⟩ da lavoro; ⟨day⟩ feriale; **in ~ order** funzionante. **~ class** n classe f operaia. **~-class** a operaio

work: **~man** n operaio m. **~manship** n lavorazione f. **~-out** n allenamento m. **~shop** n officina f; ⟨discussion⟩ dibattito m

world /wɜːld/ n mondo m; **a ~ of difference** una differenza abissale; **out of this ~** favoloso; **think the ~ of sb** andare matto per qcno. **~ly** a materiale; ⟨person⟩ materialista. **~-wide** a mondiale ● adv mondialmente

worm /wɜːm/ n verme m ● vt **~ one's way into sb's confidence** conquistarsi la fiducia di qcno in modo subdolo. **~-eaten** a tarlato

worn /wɔːn/ see **wear** ● a sciupato. **~-out** a consumato; ⟨person⟩ sfinito

worried /ˈwʌrɪd/ a preoccupato

worry /ˈwʌrɪ/ n preoccupazione f ● v (pt/pp **worried**) ● vt preoccupare; ⟨bother⟩ disturbare ● vi occuparsi. **~ing** a preoccupante

worse /wɜːs/ a peggiore ● adv peggio ● n peggio m

worsen /ˈwɜːsn/ vt/i peggiorare

worship /ˈwɜːʃɪp/ n culto m; ⟨service⟩ funzione f; **Your/His W~** ⟨to judge⟩ signor giudice/il giudice ● v (pt/pp **-shipped**) ● vt venerare ● vi andare a messa

worst /wɜːst/ a peggiore ● adv peggio [di tutti] ● n the **~** il peggio; **get the ~ of it** avere la peggio; **if the ~ comes to the ~** nella peggiore delle ipotesi

worth /wɜːθ/ n valore m; **£10 ~ of petrol** 10 sterline di benzina ● a **be ~** valere; **be ~ it** fig valerne la pena; **it's ~ trying** vale la pena di provare; **it's ~ my while** mi con-

viene. **~less** a senza valore.
~while a che vale la pena; ⟨cause⟩
lodevole

worthy /'wɜːðɪ/ a degno; ⟨cause,
motive⟩ lodevole

would /wʊd/ v aux **I ~ do it** lo farei; **~ you go?** andresti?; **~ you
mind if I opened the window?** ti
dispiace se apro la finestra?; **he ~
come if he could** verrebbe se potesse; **he said he ~n't** ha detto di
no; **~ you like a drink?** vuoi qualcosa da bere?; **what ~ you like to
drink?** cosa prendi da bere?; **you
~n't, ~ you?** non lo faresti, vero?

wound¹ /wuːnd/ n ferita f ● vt ferire

wound² /waʊnd/ see **wind²**

wove, woven /wəʊv, 'wəʊvn/ see
weave

wrangle /'ræŋgl/ n litigio m ● vi litigare

wrap /ræp/ n ⟨shawl⟩ scialle m ● vt
(pt/pp **wrapped**) **~ [up]** avvolgere; ⟨present⟩ incartare; **be ~ped
up** in fig essere completamente
preso da ● vi **~ up** warmly coprirsi bene. **~per** n ⟨for sweet⟩ carta f
[di caramella]. **~ping** n materiale
m da imballaggio. **~ping paper** n
carta f da pacchi; ⟨for gift⟩ carta f
da regalo

wrath /rɒθ/ n ira f

wreak /riːk/ vt **~ havoc with sth**
scombussolare qcsa

wreath /riːθ/ n (pl **~s** /-ðz/) corona f

wreck /rek/ n ⟨of ship⟩ relitto m;
⟨of car⟩ carcassa f; ⟨person⟩ rotta me m ● vt far naufragare; demolire ⟨car⟩. **~age** /-ɪdʒ/ n rottami
mpl; fig brandelli mpl

wrench /rentʃ/ n ⟨injury⟩ slogatura f; ⟨tool⟩ chiave f inglese; ⟨pull⟩
strattone m ● vt ⟨pull⟩ strappare;
slogarsi ⟨wrist, ankle etc⟩

wrest /rest/ vt strappare ⟨from a⟩

wrestle /'resl/ vi lottare corpo
a corpo; fig lottare. **~er** n lottatore, -trice mf. **~ing** n lotta f libera;
⟨all-in⟩ catch m

wretch /retʃ/ n disgraziato, -a mf.
~ed /-ɪd/ a odioso; ⟨weather⟩ orribile; **feel ~** ⟨unhappy⟩ essere
triste; ⟨ill⟩ sentirsi malissimo

wriggle /'rɪgl/ n contorsione f ● vi
contorcersi; ⟨move forward⟩ strisciare; **~ out of sth** fam sottrarsi
a qcsa

wring /rɪŋ/ vt (pt/pp **wrung**) torcere ⟨sb's neck⟩; strizzare ⟨clothes⟩;
~ one's hands torcersi le mani;
~ing wet inzuppato

wrinkle /'rɪŋkl/ n grinza f; ⟨on
skin⟩ ruga f ● vt/i raggrinzire. **~d**
a ⟨skin, face⟩ rugoso; ⟨clothes⟩
raggrinzito

wrist /rɪst/ n polso m. **~-watch** n
orologio m da polso

writ /rɪt/ n Jur mandato m

write /raɪt/ vt/i (pt **wrote**, pp
written, pres p **writing**) scrivere.
write down vt annotare. **write off**
vt cancellare ⟨debt⟩; distruggere
⟨car⟩

'write-off n ⟨car⟩ rottame m

writer /'raɪtə(r)/ n autore, -trice
mf; **she's a ~** è una scrittrice

'write-up n ⟨review⟩ recensione f

writhe /raɪð/ vi contorcersi

writing /'raɪtɪŋ/ n ⟨occupation⟩
scrivere m; ⟨words⟩ scritte fpl;
⟨handwriting⟩ scrittura f; **in ~** per
iscritto. **~-paper** n carta f da lettera

written /'rɪtn/ see **write**

wrong /rɒŋ/ a sbagliato; **be ~**
⟨person:⟩ sbagliare; **what's ~?**
cosa c'è che non va? ● adv ⟨spelt⟩
in modo sbagliato; **go ~** ⟨person:⟩
sbagliare; ⟨machine:⟩ funzionare
male; ⟨plan:⟩ andar male ● n ingiustizia f; **in the ~** dalla parte del
torto; **know right from ~** distinguere il bene dal male ● vt fare
torto a. **~ful** a ingiusto. **~ly** adv in
modo sbagliato; ⟨accuse, imagine⟩
a torto; ⟨informed⟩ male

wrote /rəʊt/ see **write**

wrought iron /rɔːt-/ n ferro m battuto ● attrib di ferro battuto

wrung /rʌŋ/ see **wring**

wry /raɪ/ a (-er, -est) ⟨humour, smile⟩ beffardo

Xx

Xmas /'krɪsməs/ n fam Natale m

X-ray n ⟨picture⟩ radiografia f; **have an ~** farsi fare una radiografia ● vt passare ai raggi X

Yy

yacht /jɒt/ n yacht m inv; ⟨for racing⟩ barca f a vela. **~ing** n vela f

Yank n fam americano, -a mf

yank /jæŋk/ vt fam tirare

yap /jæp/ vi (pt/pp yapped) ⟨dog:⟩ guaire

yard[1] /jɑːd/ n cortile m; ⟨for storage⟩ deposito m

yard[2] n iarda f (= 91,44 cm). **~stick** n fig pietra f dil paragone

yarn /jɑːn/ n filo m; ⟨fam: tale⟩ storia f

yawn /jɔːn/ n sbadiglio m ● vi sbadigliare. **~ing** a **~ing gap** sbadiglio m

year /jɪə(r)/ n anno m; ⟨of wine⟩ annata f; **for ~s** fam da secoli. **~-book** n annuario m. **~ly** a annuale ● adv annualmente

yearn /jɜːn/ vi struggersi. **~ing** n desiderio m struggente

yeast /jiːst/ n lievito m

yell /jel/ n urlo m ● vi urlare

yellow /'jeləʊ/ a & n giallo m

yelp /jelp/ n ⟨of dog⟩ guaito m ● vi ⟨dog:⟩ guaire

yen /jen/ n forte desiderio m (**for** di)

yes /jes/ adv sì ● n sì m inv

yesterday /'jestədeɪ/ a & adv ieri

m inv; **~'s paper** il giornale di ieri; **the day before ~** l'altroieri

yet /jet/ adv ancora; **as ~** fino ad ora; **not ~** non ancora; **the best ~** il migliore finora ● conj eppure

yew /juː/ n tasso m ⟨albero⟩

yield /jiːld/ n resa f; ⟨profit⟩ reddito m ● vt produrre; fruttare ⟨profit⟩ ● vi cedere; Am Auto dare la precedenza

yodel /'jəʊdl/ vi (pt/pp yodelled) cantare jodel

yoga /'jəʊgə/ n yoga m

yoghurt /'jɒgət/ n yogurt m inv

yoke /jəʊk/ n giogo m; ⟨of garment⟩ carré m inv

yokel /'jəʊkl/ n zotico, -a mf

yolk /jəʊk/ n tuorlo m

you /juː/ pron ⟨subject⟩ tu, voi pl; ⟨formal⟩ lei, voi pl; ⟨direct/indirect object⟩ ti, vi pl; ⟨formal: direct object⟩ la; ⟨formal: indirect object⟩ le; ⟨after prep⟩ te, voi pl; ⟨formal: after prep⟩ lei; **~ are very kind** ⟨sg⟩ sei molto gentile; ⟨formal⟩ è molto gentile; ⟨pl & formal pl⟩ siete molto gentili; **~ can stay, but he has to go** ⟨sg⟩ tu puoi rimanere, ma lui deve andarsene; ⟨pl⟩ voi potete rimanere, ma lui deve andarsene; **all of ~** tutti voi; **I'll give ~ the money** ⟨sg⟩ ti darò i soldi; ⟨pl⟩ vi darò i soldi; **I'll give it to ~** ⟨sg⟩ te|⟨pl⟩ ve lo darò; **it was ~!** ⟨sg⟩ eri tu!; ⟨pl⟩ eravate voi!; **~ have to be careful** ⟨one⟩ si deve fare attenzione

young /jʌŋ/ a giovane ● npl ⟨animals⟩ piccoli mpl; **the ~** ⟨people⟩ i giovani mpl. **~ lady** n signorina f. **~ man** n giovanotto. **~ster** n ragazzo, -a mf; ⟨child⟩ bambino, -a mf

your /jɔː(r)/ a il tuo m, la tua f, i tuoi mpl, le tue fpl; ⟨formal⟩ il suo m, la sua f, i suoi mpl, le sue fpl; ⟨pl & formal pl⟩ il vostro m, la vostra f, i vostri mpl, le vostre fpl; **~ mother/father** tua madre/tuo pa-

dre; (formal) sua madre/suo padre; (pl & formal pl) vostra
madre/vostro padre

yours /jɔːz/ poss pron il tuo m, la
tua f; i tuoi mpl, le tue fpl;
(formal) il suo m, la sua f; i suoi
mpl, le sue fpl; (pl & formal pl) il
vostro m, la vostra f, i vostri mpl,
le vostre fpl; **a friend of ~** un
tuo/suo/vostro amico; **friends of
~** dei tuoi/vostri/suoi amici; **that
is ~** quello è tuo/vostro/suo; (as
opposed to mine) quello è il tuo/il
vostro/il suo

your'self pron (reflexive) ti; (formal) si; (emphatic) te stesso; (formal) sé, se stesso; **do pour ~ a
drink** versati da bere; (formal) si
versi da bere; **you said so ~** lo
hai detto tu stesso; (formal) lo ha
detto lei stesso; **you can be proud
of ~** puoi essere fiero di te/di sé;
by ~ da solo

your'selves pron (reflexive) vi;
(emphatic) voi stessi; **do pour ~ a
drink** versatevi da bere; **you said
so ~** lo avete detto voi stessi; **you
can be proud of ~** potete essere
fieri di voi; **by ~** da soli

youth /juːθ/ n (pl youths /-ðːz/) gioventù f inv; (boy) giovanetto m;
the ~ (young people) i giovani
mpl. **~ful** a giovanile. **~ hostel** n
ostello m [della gioventù]

Yugoslav /'juːgəslɑːv/ a & n jugo-
slavo, -a m f

Yugoslavia /-'slɑːvɪə/ n Jugosla-
via f

....

Zz

....

zany /'zeɪnɪ/ a (-ier, -iest) demen-
ziale

zeal /ziːl/ n zelo m

zealous /'zeləs/ a zelante. **~ly** adv
con zelo

zebra /'zebrə/ n zebra f. **~'**

crossing n passaggio m pedonale,
zebre fpl

zero /'zɪərəʊ/ n zero m

zest /zest/ n gusto m

zigzag /'zɪgzæg/ n zigzag m inv ● vi
(pt/pp **-zagged**) zigzagare

zilch /zɪltʃ/ n fam zero m assoluto

zinc /zɪŋk/ n zinco m

zip /zɪp/ n ~ [fastener] cerniera f
[lampo] ● vt (pt/pp **zipped**) ~ [up]
chiudere con la cerniera [lampo]

'Zip code n Am codice m postale

zipper /'zɪpə(r)/ n Am cerniera f
[lampo]

zodiac /'zəʊdɪæk/ n zodiaco m

zombie /'zɒmbɪ/ n fam zombi mf
inv

zone /zəʊn/ n zona f

zoo /zuː/ n zoo m inv

zoologist /zəʊ'ɒlədʒɪst/ n zoologo,
-a mf. **~y** zoologia f

zoom /zuːm/ vi sfrecciare. **~ lens**
n zoom m inv

ITALIAN VERB TABLES

REGULAR VERBS:

1. in **-are** (*eg* **compr|are**)

   Present ~o, ~i, ~a, ~iamo, ~ate, ~ano
   Imperfect ~avo, ~avi, ~ava, ~avamo, ~avate, ~avano
   Past historic ~ai, ~asti, ~ò, ~ammo, ~aste, ~arono
   Future ~erò, ~erai, ~erà, ~eremo, ~erete, ~eranno
   Present subjunctive ~i, ~i, ~i, ~iamo, ~iate, ~ino
   Past subjunctive ~assi, ~assi, ~asse, ~assimo, ~aste, ~assero
   Present participle ~ando
   Past participle ~ato
   Imperative ~a (*fml* ~i), ~iamo, ~ate
   Conditional ~erei, ~eresti, ~erebbe, ~eremmo, ~ereste,
   ~erebbero

2. in **-ere** (*eg* **vend|ere**)

   Pres ~o, ~i, ~e, ~iamo, ~ete, ~ono
   Impf ~evo, ~evi, ~eva, ~evamo, ~evate, ~evano
   Past hist ~ei *or* ~etti, ~esti, ~è *or* ~ette, ~emmo, ~este, ~erono
   or ~ettero
   Fut ~erò, ~erai, ~erà, ~eremo, ~erete, ~eranno
   Pres sub ~a, ~a, ~a, ~iamo, ~iate, ~ano
   Past sub ~essi, ~essi, ~esse, ~essimo, ~este, ~essero
   Pres part ~endo
   Past part ~uto
   Imp ~i (*fml* ~a), ~iamo, ~ete
   Cond ~erei, ~eresti, ~erebbe, ~eremmo, ~ereste, ~erebbero

3. in **-ire** (*eg* **dorm|ire**)

   Pres ~o, ~i, ~e, ~iamo, ~ite, ~ono
   Impf ~ivo, ~ivi, ~iva, ~ivamo, ~ivate, ~ivano
   Past hist ~ii, ~isti, ~ì, ~immo, ~iste, ~irono
   Fut ~irò, ~irai, ~irà, ~iremo, ~irete, ~iranno
   Pres sub ~a, ~a, ~a, ~iamo, ~iate, ~ano
   Past sub ~issi, ~issi, ~isse, ~issimo, ~iste, ~issero
   Pres part ~endo
   Past part ~ito
   Imp ~i (*fml* ~a), ~iamo, ~ite
   Cond ~irei, ~iresti, ~irebbe, ~iremmo, ~ireste, ~irebbero

Notes

- Many verbs in the third conjugation take *isc* between the stem and the ending in the first, second, and third person singular and in the third person plural of the present, the present subjunctive, and the imperative: fin|ire **Pres** ~isco, ~isci, ~isce, ~iscono. **Pres sub** ~isca, ~iscano **Imp** ~isci.

- The three forms of the imperative are the same as the corresponding forms of the present for the second and third conjugation. In the first conjugation the forms are also the same except for the second person singular: present *compri*, imperative *compra*. The negative form of the second person singular is formed by putting *non* before the infinitive for all conjugations: *non comprare*. In polite forms the third person of the present subjunctive is used instead for all conjugations: *compri*.

IRREGULAR VERBS:

Certain forms of all irregular verbs are regular (except for *essere*). These are: the second person plural of the present, the past subjunctive, and the present participle. All forms not listed below are regular and can be derived from the parts given. Only those irregular verbs considered to be the most useful are shown in the tables.

accadere	*as* **cadere**
accendere	• **Past hist** accesi, accendesti • **Past part** acceso
affliggere	• **Past hist** afflissi, affliggesti • **Past part** afflitto
ammettere	*as* **mettere**
andare	• **Pres** vado, vai, va, andiamo, andate, vanno • **Fut** andrò *etc* • **Pres sub** vada, vadano • **Imp** va', vada, vadano
apparire	• **Pres** appaio *or* apparisco, appari *or* apparisci, appare *or* apparisce, appaiono *or* appariscono • **Past hist** apparvi *or* apparsi, apparisti, apparve *or* appari *or* apparse, apparvero *or* apparirono *or* apparsero • **Pres sub** appaia *or* apparisca
aprire	• **Pres** apro • **Past hist** aprii, apristi • **Pres sub** apra • **Past part** aperto

avere
• **Pres** ho, hai, ha, abbiamo, hanno • **Past hist** ebbi, avesti, ebbe, avemmo, aveste, ebbero • **Fut** avrò *etc* • **Pres sub** abbia *etc* • **Imp** abbi, abbia, abbiamo, abbiano

bere
• **Pres** bevo *etc* • **Impf** bevevo *etc* • **Past hist** bevvi *or* bevetti, bevesti • **Fut** berrò *etc* • **Pres sub** beva *etc* • **Past sub** bevessi *etc* • **Pres part** bevendo • **Cond** berrei *etc*

cadere
• **Past hist** caddi, cadesti • **Fut** cadrò *etc*

chiedere
• **Past hist** chiesi, chiedesti • **Pres sub** chieda *etc* • **Past part** chiesto *etc*

chiudere
• **Past hist** chiusi, chiudesti • **Past part** chiuso

cogliere
• **Pres** colgo, colgono • **Past hist** colsi, cogliesti • **Pres sub** colga • **Past part** colto

correre
• **Past hist** corsi, corresti • **Past part** corso

crescere
• **Past hist** crebbi • **Past part** cresciuto

cuocere
• **Pres** cuocio, cuociamo, cuociono • **Past hist** cossi, cocesti • **Past part** cotto

dare
• **Pres** do, dai, dà, diamo, danno • **Past hist** diedi *or* detti, desti • **Fut** darò *etc* • **Pres sub** dia *etc* • **Past sub** dessi *etc* • **Imp** da' (*fml* dia)

dire
• **Pres** dico, dici, dice, diciamo, dicono • **Impf** dicevo *etc* • **Past hist** dissi, dicesti • **Fut** dirò *etc* • **Pres sub** dica, diciamo, diciate, dicano • **Past sub** dicessi *etc* • **Pres part** dicendo • **Past part** detto • **Imp** di' (*fml* dica)

dovere
• **Pres** devo *or* debbo, devi, deve, dobbiamo, devono *or* debbono • **Fut** dovrò *etc* • **Pres sub** deva *or* debba, dobbiamo, dobbiate, devano *or* debbano • **Cond** dovrei *etc*

essere
• **Pres** sono, sei, è, siamo, siete, sono • **Impf** ero, eri, era, eravamo, eravate, erano • **Past hist** fui, fosti, fu, fummo, foste, furono • **Fut** sarò *etc* • **Pres sub** sia *etc* • **Past sub** fossi, fossi, fosse, fossimo, foste, fossero • **Past part** stato • **Imp** sii (*fml* sia), siate • **Cond** sarei *etc*

fare
• **Pres** faccio, fai, fa, facciamo, fanno • **Impf** facevo *etc* • **Past hist** feci, facesti • **Fut** farò *etc* • **Pres sub** faccia *etc* • **Past sub** facessi *etc* • **Pres part** facendo • **Past part** fatto • **Imp** fa' (*fml* faccia) • **Cond** farei *etc*

fingere	• **Past hist** finsi, fingesti, finsero • **Past part** finto
giungere	• **Past hist** giunsi, giungesti, giunsero • **Past part** giunto
leggere	• **Past hist** lessi, leggesti • **Past part** letto
mettere	• **Past hist** misi, mettesti • **Past part** messo
morire	• **Pres** muoio, muori, muore, muoiono • **Fut** morirò or morrò etc • **Pres sub** muoia • **Past part** morto
muovere	• **Past hist** mossi, movesti • **Past part** mosso
nascere	• **Past hist** nacqui, nascesti • **Past part** nato
offrire	• **Past hist** offersi or offrii, offristi • **Pres sub** offra • **Past part** offerto
parere	• **Pres** paio, pari, pare, pariamo, paiono • **Past hist** parvi or parsi, paresti • **Fut** parrò etc • **Pres sub** paia, paiamo or pariamo, pariate, paiano • **Past part** parso
piacere	• **Pres** piaccio, piaci, piace, piacciamo, piacciono • **Past hist** piacqui, piacesti, piacque, piacemmo, piaceste, piacquero • **Pres sub** piaccia etc • **Past part** piaciuto
porre	• **Pres** pongo, poni, pone, poniamo, ponete, pongono • **Impf** ponevo etc • **Past hist** posi, ponesti • **Fut** porrò etc • **Pres sub** ponga, poniamo, poniate, pongano • **Past sub** ponessi etc
potere	• **Pres** posso, puoi, può, possiamo, possono • **Fut** potrò etc • **Pres sub** possa, possiamo, possiate, possano • **Cond** potrei etc
prendere	• **Past hist** presi, prendesti • **Past part** preso
ridere	• **Past hist** risi, ridesti • **Past part** riso
rimanere	• **Pres** rimango, rimani, rimane, rimaniamo, rimangono • **Past hist** rimasi, rimanesti • **Fut** rimarrò etc • **Pres sub** rimanga • **Past part** rimasto • **Cond** rimarrei
salire	• **Pres** salgo, sali, sale, saliamo, salgono • **Pres sub** salga, saliate, salgano
sapere	• **Pres** so, sai, sa, sappiamo, sanno • **Past hist** seppi, sapesti • **Fut** saprò etc • **Pres sub** sappia etc • **Imp** sappi (fml sappia), sappiate • **Cond** saprei etc

scegliere • **Pres** scelgo, scegli, sceglie, scegliamo, scelgono • **Past hist** scelsi, scegliesti *etc* • **Past part** scelto

scrivere • **Past hist** scrissi, scrivesti *etc* • **Past part** scritto

sedere • **Pres** siedo *or* seggo, siedi, siede, siedono • **Pres sub** sieda *or* segga

spegnere • **Pres** spengo, spengono • **Past hist** spensi, spegnesti • **Past part** spento

stare • **Pres** sto, stai, sta, stiamo, stanno • **Past hist** stetti, stesti • **Fut** starò *etc* • **Pres sub** stia *etc* • **Past sub** stessi *etc* • **Past part** stato • **Imp** sta' (*fml* stia)

tacere • **Pres** taccio, tacciono • **Past hist** tacqui, tacque, tacquero • **Pres sub** taccia

tendere • **Past hist** tesi • **Past part** teso

tenere • **Pres** tengo, tieni, tiene, tengono • **Past hist** tenni, tenesti • **Fut** terrò *etc* • **Pres sub** tenga

togliere • **Pres** tolgo, tolgono • **Past hist** tolsi, tolse, tolsero • **Pres sub** tolga, tolgano • **Past part** tolto • *Imp fml* tolga

trarre • **Pres** traggo, trai, trae, traiamo, traete, traggono • **Past hist** trassi, traesti • **Fut** trarrò *etc* • **Pres sub** tragga • **Past sub** traessi *etc* • **Past part** tratto

uscire • **Pres** esco, esci, esce, escono • **Pres sub** esca • **Imp** esci (*fml* esca)

valere • **Pres** valgo, valgono • **Past hist** valsi, valesti • **Fut** varrò *etc* • **Pres sub** valga, valgano • **Past part** valso • **Cond** varrei *etc*

vedere • **Past hist** vidi, vedesti • **Fut** vedrò *etc* • **Past part** visto *or* veduto • **Cond** vedrei *etc*

venire • **Pres** vengo, vieni, viene, vengono • **Past hist** venni, venisti • **Fut** verrò *etc*

vivere • **Past hist** vissi, vivesti • **Fut** vivrò *etc* • **Past part** vissuto • **Cond** vivrei *etc*

volere • **Pres** voglio, vuoi, vuole, vogliamo, volete, vogliono • **Past hist** volli, volesti • **Fut** vorrò *etc* • **Pres sub** voglia *etc* • **Imp** vogliate • **Cond** vorrei *etc*

ENGLISH IRREGULAR VERBS

Infinitive	Past Tense	Past Participle	Infinitive	Past Tense	Past Participle
Infinito	*Passato*	*Participio passato*	*Infinito*	*Passato*	*Participio passato*
arise	arose	arisen	cling	clung	clung
awake	awoke	awoken	come	came	come
be	was	been	cost	cost,	cost,
bear	bore	borne		costed (*vt*)	costed
beat	beat	beaten	creep	crept	crept
become	became	become	cut	cut	cut
begin	began	begun	deal	dealt	dealt
behold	beheld	beheld	dig	dug	dug
bend	bent	bent	do	did	done
beseech	beseeched	beseeched	draw	drew	drawn
	besought	besought	dream	dreamt,	dreamt,
bet	bet,	bet,		dreamed	dreamed
	betted	betted	drink	drank	drunk
bid	bade,	bidden,	drive	drove	driven
	bid	bid	dwell	dwelt	dwelt
bind	bound	bound	eat	ate	eaten
bite	bit	bitten	fall	fell	fallen
bleed	bled	bled	feed	fed	fed
blow	blew	blown	feel	felt	felt
break	broke	broken	fight	fought	fought
breed	bred	bred	find	found	found
bring	brought	brought	flee	fled	fled
build	built	built	fling	flung	flung
burn	burnt,	burnt,	fly	flew	flown
	burned	burned	forbid	forbade	forbidden
burst	burst	burst	forget	forgot	forgotten
bust	busted,	busted,	forgive	forgave	forgiven
	bust	bust	forsake	forsook	forsaken
buy	bought	bought	freeze	froze	frozen
cast	cast	cast	get	got	got,
catch	caught	caught			gotten *Am*
choose	chose	chosen	give	gave	given

Infinitive Infinito	Past Tense Passato	Past Participle Participio passato	Infinitive Infinito	Past Tense Passato	Past Participle Participio passato
go	went	gone	mow	mowed	mown, mowed
grind	ground	ground			
grow	grew	grown	overhang	overhung	overhung
hang	hung, hanged (vt)	hung, hanged	pay	paid	paid
			put	put	put
have	had	had	quit	quitted, quit	quitted, quit
hear	heard	heard			
hew	hewed	hewed, hewn	read	read /red/	read /red/
			rid	rid	rid
hide	hid	hidden	ride	rode	ridden
hit	hit	hit	ring	rang	rung
hold	held	held	rise	rose	risen
hurt	hurt	hurt	run	ran	run
keep	kept	kept	saw	sawed	sawn, sawed
kneel	knelt	knelt			
know	knew	known	say	said	said
lay	laid	laid	see	saw	seen
lead	led	led	seek	sought	sought
lean	leaned, leant	leaned, leant	sell	sold	sold
			send	sent	sent
leap	leapt, leaped	leapt, leaped	set	set	set
			sew	sewed	sewn, sewed
learn	learnt, learned	learnt, learned			
leave	left	left	shake	shook	shaken
lend	lent	lent	shear	sheared	shorn, sheared
let	let	let			
lie	lay	lain	shed	shed	shed
light	lit, lighted	lit, lighted	shine	shone	shone
			shit	shit	shit
			shoe	shod	shod
lose	lost	lost	shoot	shot	shot
make	made	made	show	showed	shown
mean	meant	meant	shrink	shrank	shrunk
meet	met	met	shut	shut	shut

Infinitive	Past Tense	Past Participle	Infinitive	Past Tense	Past Participle
Infinito	*Passato*	*Participio passato*	*Infinito*	*Passato*	*Participio passato*
sing	sang	sung	**stride**	strode	stridden
sink	sank	sunk	**strike**	struck	struck
sit	sat	sat	**string**	strung	strung
slay	slew	slain	**strive**	strove	striven
sleep	slept	slept	**swear**	swore	sworn
slide	slid	slid	**sweep**	swept	swept
sling	slung	slung	**swell**	swelled	swollen, swelled
slit	slit	slit			
smell	smelt, smelled	smelt, smelled	**swim**	swam	swum
			swing	swung	swung
sow	sowed	sown, sowed	**take**	took	taken
			teach	taught	taught
speak	spoke	spoken	**tear**	tore	torn
speed	sped, speeded	sped, speeded	**tell**	told	told
			think	thought	thought
spell	spelled, spelt	spelled, spelt	**thrive**	thrived, throve	thrived, thriven
spend	spent	spent	**throw**	threw	thrown
spill	spilt, spilled	spilt, spilled	**thrust**	thrust	thrust
			tread	trod	trodden
spin	spun	spun	**understand**	understood	understood
spit	spat	spat			
split	split	split	**undo**	undid	undone
spoil	spoilt, spoiled	spoilt, spoiled	**wake**	woke	woken
			wear	wore	worn
spread	spread	spread	**weave**	wove	woven
spring	sprang	sprung	**weep**	wept	wept
stand	stood	stood	**wet**	wet, wetted	wet, wetted
steal	stole	stolen			
stick	stuck	stuck	**win**	won	won
sting	stung	stung	**wind**	wound	wound
stink	stank	stunk	**wring**	wrung	wrung
strew	strewed	strewn, strewed	**write**	wrote	written